W9-CHW-298

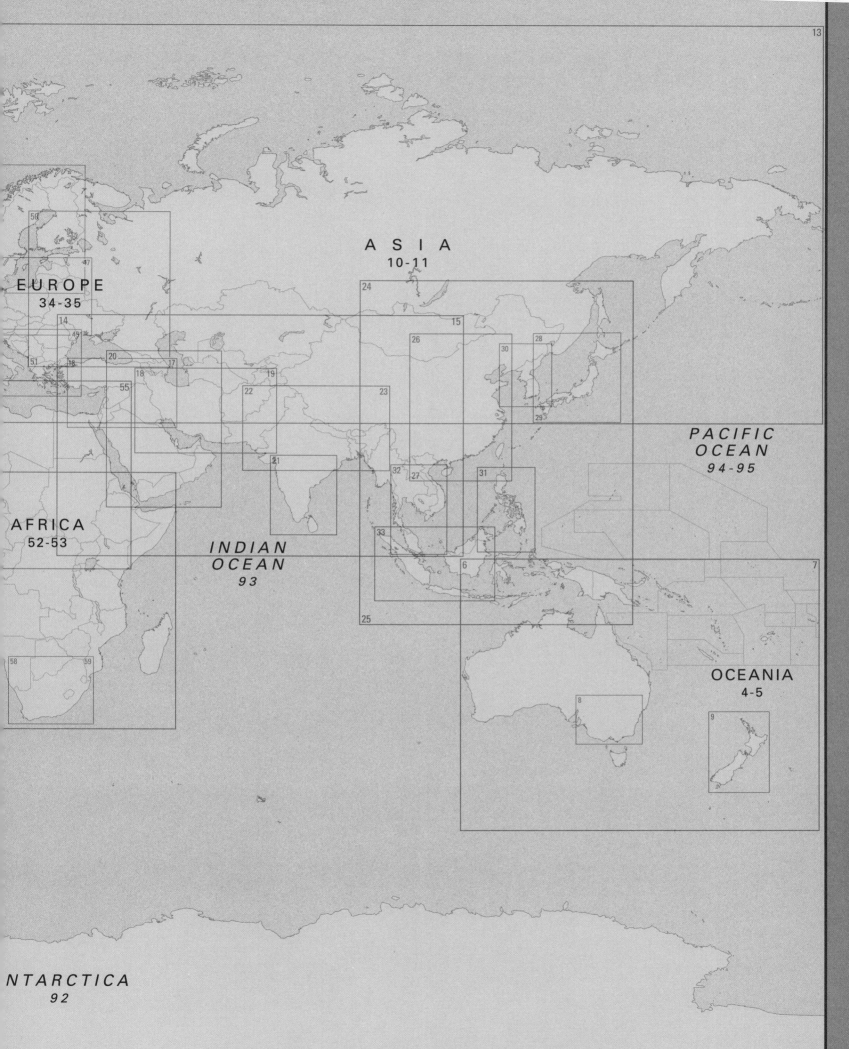

13

ASIA
10-11

EUROPE
34-35

50

47

14

49

51

18

20

17

18

55

24

15

26

30

28

19

22

23

29

PACIFIC
OCEAN
94-95

AFRICA
52-53

21

32

27

31

INDIAN
OCEAN
93

33

6

7

25

OCEANIA
4-5

58

59

8

9

NTARCTICA
92

THE TIMES

ATLAS OF THE WORLD

NEW REFERENCE EDITION

TIMES BOOKS

WORLD INFORMATION

THE TIMES ATLAS OF THE WORLD
NEW REFERENCE EDITION

TIMES BOOKS, London
77–85 Fulham Palace Road,
London W6 8JB

First published 1997

Copyright © Times Books 1997
Maps © Bartholomew 1997

Printed in Italy by Rotolito Lombarda

British Library Cataloguing in Publication Data. A catalogue record for this book is available from the British Library.

ISBN 0 7230 0996 1

KH 9296 Imp 001

The maps in this product are also available for purchase in digital format, from Bartholomew Data Sales, Telephone +44 (0) 181 307 4065, Fax +44 (0) 181 307 4813

All rights reserved. No part of this publication may be reproduced, stored in a retrieval system, or transmitted, in any form or by any means, electronic, mechanical, photocopying, recording or otherwise without the prior written permission of the publisher and copyright owners.

The contents of this edition of the Times Atlas of the World New Reference Edition are believed correct at the time of printing. Nevertheless the publisher can accept no responsibility for errors or omissions, changes in the detail given or for any expense or loss thereby caused.

COUNTRY-FINDER

© Bartholomew

IN THIS GUIDE to States and Territories all independent states and major territories appear. The states and territories are arranged in alphabetical order using the same English-language conventional name form as is used on the maps. The name of the capital city is given in either its local form or in English-language form, whichever is more commonly used and understood. This reflects the names on the maps where alternative forms are also shown in brackets.

The statistics used for the area and population, and as the basis for languages and religions, are from the latest available sources. The information for the internal divisions in federal states may be for a less recent date than that for the entire country, but are the latest available.

The order of the different languages and religions reflects their relative importance within the country; generally all languages and religions with over one or two per cent speakers or adherents are mentioned.

For independent states membership of the following international organizations is shown by the abbreviations below. Territories are not shown as having separate membership of these international organizations.

ASEAN   Association of Southeast Asian Nations

CARICOM Caribbean Community

CIS   Commonwealth of Independent States

COMM.   Commonwealth

EU   European Union

NAFTA   North American Free Trade Area

OAU   Organization of African Unity

OECD   Organization for Economic Cooperation and Development

OPEC   Organization of Petroleum Exporting Countries

SADC   Southern African Development Community

UN   United Nations

AFGHANISTAN
Status : REPUBLIC
Area : 652,225 sq km (251,825 sq mls)
Population : 20,141,000
Capital : KĀBUL
Language : DARI, PUSHTU, UZBEK, TURKMEN
Religion : SUNNI MUSLIM, SHI'A MUSLIM
Currency : AFGHANI
Organizations : UN

MAP PAGE: 19

ALANDLOCKED COUNTRY in central Asia, Afghanistan borders Pakistan, Iran, Turkmenistan, Uzbekistan, Tajikistan and China. Its central highlands are bounded by the Hindu Kush to the north and desert to the south and west. Most farming is on the plains round Kabul, the most populated area, and in the far northeast. The climate is dry, with extreme temperatures. Civil war has disrupted the rural-based economy. Exports include dried fruit, nuts, carpets, wool, hides and cotton.

ALBANIA
Status : REPUBLIC
Area : 28,748 sq km (11,100 sq mls)
Population : 3,645,000
Capital : TIRANA
Language : ALBANIAN (GHEG, TOSK DIALECTS), GREEK
Religion : SUNNI MUSLIM, GREEK ORTHODOX, R.CATHOLIC
Currency : LEK
Organizations : UN

MAP PAGE: 49

ALBANIA LIES IN the western Balkans of south Europe, on the Adriatic Sea. It is mountainous, with coastal plains which support half the population. The economy is based mainly on agriculture and mining, chiefly chromite. The fall of communism brought reform and foreign aid for the ailing economy.

ALGERIA
Status : REPUBLIC
Area : 2,381,741 sq km (919,595 sq mls)
Population : 28,548,000
Capital : ALGIERS
Language : ARABIC, FRENCH, BERBER
Religion : SUNNI MUSLIM, R.CATHOLIC
Currency : DINAR
Organizations : OAU, OPEC, UN

MAP PAGE: 54-55

ALGERIA IS ON the Mediterranean coast of North Africa. The second largest country in Africa, it extends southwards from the coast into the Sahara Desert. Over 85 per cent of the land area is a dry sandstone plateau, cut by valleys and rocky mountains, including the Hoggar Massif in the southeast. Though hot, arid and largely uninhabited, the region contains oil and gas reserves. To the north lie the Atlas Mountains, enclosing the grassland of the Chott Plateau. The mountains separate the arid south from the narrow coastal plain which has a Mediterranean climate and is well suited to agriculture. Most people live on the plain and on the fertile northern slopes of the Atlas. Hydrocarbons have been the mainstay of the economy. Though reserves are dwindling, oil, natural gas and related products still account for over 90 per cent of export earnings. Other industries produce building materials, food products, iron, steel and vehicles. Agriculture employs a quarter of the workforce, producing mainly food crops. Political unrest including Islamic militancy in the early 1990s weakened the economy.

AMERICAN SAMOA
Status : US TERRITORY
Area : 197 sq km (76 sq mls)
Population : 56,000
Capital : PAGO PAGO
Language : SAMOAN, ENGLISH
Religion : PROTESTANT, R.CATHOLIC
Currency : US DOLLAR

MAP PAGE: 5

LYING IN THE South Pacific Ocean, American Samoa consists of five islands and two coral atolls. The main island is Tutuila.

ANDORRA
Status : PRINCIPALITY
Area : 465 sq km (180 sq mls)
Population : 68,000
Capital : ANDORRA LA VELLA
Language : CATALAN, SPANISH, FRENCH
Religion : R.CATHOLIC
Currency : FRENCH FRANC, SPANISH PESETA
Organizations : UN

MAP PAGE: 45

ALANDLOCKED STATE in southwest Europe, Andorra nestles in the Pyrenees between France and Spain. It consists of deep valleys and gorges, surrounded by mountains. Winter lasts six months, with heavy snowfalls; spring and summer are warm. One-third of the population lives in the capital. Tourism (about 12 million visitors a year), trade and banking are the main activities. Livestock, tobacco and timber are also important. Exports include clothing, mineral water, cattle, electrical equipment, and paper and paper products.

ANGOLA
Status : REPUBLIC
Area : 1,246,700 sq km (481,354 sq mls)
Population : 11,072,000
Capital : LUANDA
Language : PORTUGUESE, MANY LOCAL LANGUAGES
Religion : R.CATHOLIC, PROTESTANT, TRAD.BELIEFS
Currency : KWANZA
Organizations : OAU, SADC, UN

MAP PAGE: 56-57

ANGOLA LIES ON the Atlantic coast of southern central Africa. Its northern province, Cabinda, is separated from the rest of the country by part of Zaire. Much of Angola is high plateau, with a fertile coastal plain where most people live. The climate is equatorial in the north but desert in the south. Over half the workforce are farmers, growing cassava, maize, bananas, coffee, cotton and sisal. Angola is rich in minerals. Oil and diamonds account for 90 per cent of exports. Civil war has slowed economic development.

ANGUILLA
Status : UK TERRITORY
Area : 155 sq km (60 sq mls)
Population : 8,000
Capital : THE VALLEY
Language : ENGLISH

Religion : PROTESTANT, R.CATHOLIC
Currency : E. CARIB. DOLLAR

MAP PAGE: 83

ANGUILLA LIES AT the northern end of the Leeward Islands in the Caribbean Sea. Tourism and fishing are the basis of the economy.

ANTIGUA AND BARBUDA
Status : MONARCHY
Area : 442 sq km (171 sq mls)
Population : 66,000
Capital : ST JOHN'S
Language : ENGLISH, CREOLE
Religion : PROTESTANT, R.CATHOLIC
Currency : E. CARIB. DOLLAR
Organizations : CARICOM, COMM., UN

MAP PAGE: 83

THE STATE COMPRISES Antigua, Barbuda and Redonda, three of the Leeward Islands in the eastern Caribbean. Antigua, the largest and most populous, is mainly hilly scrubland, with many beaches and a warm, dry climate. The economy relies heavily on tourism.

ARGENTINA
Status : REPUBLIC
Area : 2,766,889 sq km (1,068,302 sq mls)
Population : 34,768,000
Capital : BUENOS AIRES
Language : SPANISH, ITALIAN, AMERINDIAN LANGUAGES
Religion : R.CATHOLIC, PROTESTANT, JEWISH
Currency : PESO
Organizations : UN

MAP PAGE: 88

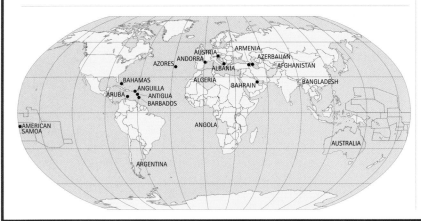

ARGENTINA OCCUPIES ALMOST the whole of the southern part of South America, from Bolivia to Cape Horn and from the Andes to the Atlantic Ocean. The second largest South American state has four geographical regions: the subtropical forests and swampland of the Chaco in the north; the temperate fertile plains or Pampas in the centre, which support most of the farming and the bulk of the population; the wooded foothills and valleys of the Andes in the west; and the cold, semi-arid plateaux of Patagonia, south of the Colorado river. Farming was the making of Argentina and still plays an important part in terms of export earnings. Beef, mutton and wool are the main produce but grains, sugarcane, soybeans, oilseeds and cotton are also important. Industry now makes the biggest contribution to the economy. Oil and gas are being produced and some mineral resources, chiefly iron ore, are being exploited. Manufacturing has expanded to include not only food processing but also textiles, motor vehicles, steel products, iron and steel, industrial chemicals and machinery.

ARMENIA
Status : REPUBLIC
Area : 29,800 sq km (11,506 sq mls)
Population : 3,599,000
Capital : YEREVAN
Language : ARMENIAN, AZERI, RUSSIAN
Religion : ARMENIAN ORTHODOX, R.CATHOLIC, SHI'A MUSLIM
Currency : DRAM
Organizations : CIS, UN

MAP PAGE: 17

A LANDLOCKED STATE in southwest Asia, Armenia is in southwest Transcaucasia and borders Georgia, Azerbaijan, Iran and Turkey. It is mountainous, with a central plateau-basin, and dry, with warm summers and cold winters. One-third of the population lives in Yerevan. War over Nagorno-Karabakh, the majority-Armenian enclave in Azerbaijan, has crippled the economy. Manufacturing and mining were the main activities. Agriculture was also important, producing mostly grapes (for brandy), vegetables, wheat and tobacco.

ARUBA

Status : NETHERLANDS TERRITORY
Area : 193 sq km (75 sq mls)
Population : 70,000
Capital : ORANJESTAD
Language : DUTCH, PAPIAMENTO, ENGLISH
Religion : R.CATHOLIC, PROTESTANT
Currency : FLORIN

MAP PAGE: 83

T HE MOST SOUTHWESTERLY of the islands in the Lesser Antilles, Aruba lies just off the coast of Venezuela. Tourism and offshore finance are the most important activities.

AUSTRALIA

Status : FEDERATION
Area : 7,682,300 sq km (2,966,153 sq mls)
Population : 18,054,000
Capital : CANBERRA
Language : ENGLISH, ITALIAN, GREEK, ABORIGINAL LANGUAGES
Religion : PROTESTANT, R.CATHOLIC, ORTHODOX, ABORIGINAL
Currency : DOLLAR
Organizations : COMM., OECD, UN

MAP PAGE: 6-7

A USTRALIA, THE WORLD'S sixth largest country, occupies the smallest, flattest and driest continent. The western half of the continent is mostly arid plateaux, ridges and vast deserts. The central-eastern area comprises lowlands of river systems draining into Lake Eyre, while to the east is the Great Dividing Range, a belt of ridges and plateaux running from Queensland to Tasmania. Climatically more than two-thirds of the country is arid or semi-arid. The north is tropical monsoon: the south is subtropical in the west, temperate in the east. A majority of Australia's highly urbanized population lives in cities along on the east, southeast and southwest coasts. Australia is richly endowed with natural resources. It has vast mineral deposits and various sources of energy. Over 50 per cent of the land is suitable for livestock rearing, though only 6 per cent can be used for crop growing. Forests cover 18 per cent of the land and fishing grounds off the coasts are teeming with marine life. Agriculture was the main sector of the economy, but its contribution to national income has fallen in recent years, as other sectors have grown. Sheep-rearing is still the main activity and Australia is the world's leading wool producer. It is also a major beef exporter and wheat grower. Wool, wheat, meat (beef and mutton), sugar and dairy products account for a third of export earnings. Minerals have overtaken agricultural produce as an export earner. As well as being among the world's leading producers of iron ore, bauxite, nickel and uranium, Australia also exploits lead, gold, silver, zinc and copper ores, tungsten and gems. Its is a major producer of coal; petroleum and natural gas are also being exploited. Manufacturing and processing has shifted from being based on agricultural produce (chiefly food processing and textiles) to being based on mineral production. The main products are: iron and steel, construction materials, petrochemicals, motor vehicles, electrical goods. Along with manufacturing, trade and services are the key growth sectors of the economy. Tourism is a major foreign exchange earner, with 1.5 million visitors a year.

AUSTRALIAN CAPITAL TERRITORY
Status: FEDERAL TERRITORY
Area: 2,400 sq km (927 sq mls)
Population: 299,000
Capital: CANBERRA

NEW SOUTH WALES
Status: STATE
Area: 801,600 sq km (309,499 sq mls)
Population: 6,009,000
Capital: SYDNEY

NORTHERN TERRITORY
Status: TERRITORY
Area: 1,346,200 sq km (519,771 sq mls)
Population: 168,000
Capital: DARWIN

QUEENSLAND
Status: STATE
Area: 1,727,200 sq km (666,876 sq mls)
Population: 3,113,000
Capital: BRISBANE

SOUTH AUSTRALIA
Status: STATE
Area: 984,000 sq km (379,925 sq mls)
Population: 1,462,000
Capital: ADELAIDE

TASMANIA
Status: STATE
Area: 67,800 sq km (26,178 sq mls)
Population: 472,000
Capital: HOBART

VICTORIA
Status: STATE
Area: 227,600 sq km (87,877 sq mls)
Population: 4,462,000
Capital: MELBOURNE

WESTERN AUSTRALIA
Status: STATE
Area: 2,525,000 sq km (974,908 sq mls)
Population: 1,678,000
Capital: PERTH

AUSTRIA

Status : REPUBLIC
Area : 83,855 sq km (32,377 sq mls)
Population : 8,053,000
Capital : VIENNA
Language : GERMAN, SERBO-CROAT, TURKISH
Religion : R.CATHOLIC, PROTESTANT
Currency : SCHILLING
Organizations : EU, OECD, UN

MAP PAGE: 46

A LANDLOCKED STATE in central Europe, Austria borders the Czech Republic, Italy, Slovenia, Hungary, Germany, Switzerland and Liechtenstein. Two-thirds of the country, from the Swiss border to eastern Austria, lies within the Alps, with the low mountains of the Bohemian Massif to the north. The only lowlands are in the east. The Vienna Basin and Danube river valley in the northeast contain almost all the agricultural land and most of the population. Austria also has a large forested area, minerals, chiefly iron ore, and fast-flowing rivers for hydroelectric power. The climate varies according to altitude, but in general summers are warm and winters cold with heavy snowfalls. Industry is the mainstay of the economy. Manufactures include machinery, iron and steel, electrical goods, chemicals, food products, vehicles, and paper products. Agricultural output covers 90 per cent of food needs. Crops include cereals, fruit (chiefly grapes) and vegetables as well as silage, sugar beet and rapeseed. Dairy and timber products are exported. With 15 million visitors a year, tourism is a major industry.

AZERBAIJAN

Status : REPUBLIC
Area : 86,600 sq km (33,436 sq mls)
Population : 7,499,000
Capital : BAKU
Language : AZERI, ARMENIAN, RUSSIAN, LEZGIAN
Religion : SHI'A MUSLIM, SUNNI MUSLIM, RUSSIAN AND ARMENIAN
Currency : MANAT
Organizations : CIS, UN

MAP PAGE: 17

A ZERBAIJAN IS IN east Transcaucasia, southwest Asia, on the Caspian Sea. Its region of Nakhichevan is separated from the rest of the country by part of Armenia. It has mountains in the northeast and west, valleys in the centre and a coastal plain. The climate is continental. It is rich in energy and mineral resources. Oil production onshore and offshore is the main industry and the basis of heavy industries. Agriculture is still important, with cotton and tobacco the main cash crops. War with Armenia has reduced output.

AZORES

Status : PORTUGUESE TERRITORY
Area : 2,247 sq km (868 sq mls)
Population : 237,800
Capital : PONTA DELGADA
Language : PORTUGUESE
Religion : R.CATHOLIC, PROTESTANT
Currency : PORT. ESCUDO

MAP PAGE: 34

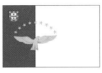

A GROUP OF islands in the Atlantic Ocean around 1500 kilometres (1000 miles) west of Portugal.

THE BAHAMAS

Status : MONARCHY
Area : 13,939 sq km (5,382 sq mls)
Population : 278,000
Capital : NASSAU
Language : ENGLISH, CREOLE, FRENCH CREOLE
Religion : PROTESTANT, R.CATHOLIC
Currency : DOLLAR
Organizations : CARICOM, COMM., UN

MAP PAGE: 83

T HE BAHAMAS IS an archipelago of about 700 islands and 2,400 cays in the northern Caribbean between the Florida coast of the USA and Haiti. Twenty-two islands are inhabited, and two thirds of the population live on the main island of New Providence. The climate is warm for much of the year, with heavy rainfall in the summer. Tourism is the islands' main industry. Banking, insurance and ship registration are also major foreign exchange earners. Exports include oil transhipments, chemicals, pharmaceuticals, crayfish and rum.

BAHRAIN

Status : MONARCHY
Area : 691 sq km (267 sq mls)
Population : 586,000
Capital : AL MANĀMAH
Language : ARABIC, ENGLISH
Religion : SHI'A MUSLIM, SUNNI MUSLIM, CHRISTIAN
Currency : DINAR
Organizations : UN

MAP PAGE: 18

B AHRAIN'S 33 ARID islands lie in a bay in The Gulf, southwest Asia, off the coasts of Saudi Arabia and Qatar. Bahrain Island, the largest, has irrigated areas in the north where most people live. Oil is the main sector of the economy. Banking is also strong.

BANGLADESH

Status : REPUBLIC
Area : 143,998 sq km (55,598 sq mls)
Population : 120,433,000
Capital : DHAKA
Language : BENGALI, BIHARI, HINDI, ENGLISH, LOCAL LANGUAGES
Religion : SUNNI MUSLIM, HINDU, BUDDHIST, CHRISTIAN
Currency : TAKA
Organizations : COMM., UN

MAP PAGE: 23

T HE SOUTH ASIAN state of Bangladesh is in the northeast of the Indian subcontinent, on the Bay of Bengal. It consists almost entirely of the low-lying alluvial plains and deltas of the Ganges and Brahmaputra rivers. The southwest is swampy, with mangrove forests in the delta area. The north, northeast and southeast have low forested hills. With a cultivable area of 70 per cent and few other natural resources, Bangladesh has a strong agricultural base, engaging two-thirds of the workforce. Food crops include rice, wheat, fruit and pulses; cash crops include jute, sugar cane, oilseeds, spices and tea. The main industries produce fertilizers, iron and steel, paper and glass as well as agricultural, marine and timber products. Exports include garments, raw and manufactured jute, fish and prawns, leather and tea. Bangladesh faces problems of overpopulation, low world commodity prices and the vagaries of climate. Floods and cyclones during the summer monsoon season often destroy crops. As a result, the country relies on foreign aid and remittances from its workers abroad.

BARBADOS

Status : MONARCHY
Area : 430 sq km (166 sq mls)
Population : 264,000
Capital : BRIDGETOWN
Language : ENGLISH, CREOLE (BAJAN)
Religion : PROTESTANT, R.CATHOLIC
Currency : DOLLAR
Organizations : UN, COMM., CARICOM

MAP PAGE: 83

T HE MOST EASTERLY of the Caribbean islands, Barbados is small and densely populated, with a fairly flat terrain, white-sand beaches and a tropical climate. The economy is based on tourism, financial services, light industries and sugar production.

© Bartholomew

BELARUS

Status: REPUBLIC
Area: 207,600 sq km (80,155 sq mls)
Population: 10,141,000
Capital: MINSK
Language: BELORUSSIAN, RUSSIAN, UKRAINIAN
Religion: BELORUSSIAN ORTHODOX, R.CATHOLIC
Currency: ROUBLE
Organizations: CIS, UN

MAP PAGE: 47

BELARUS IS A landlocked state in east Europe, bounded by Lithuania, Latvia, Russia, Ukraine and Poland. Belarus consists of low hills and forested plains, with many lakes, rivers and, in the south, extensive marshes. It has a continental climate. Agriculture contributes a third of national income, with beef cattle and grains as the major products. Manufacturing produces a range of items, from machinery and crude steel to computers and watches. Output has fallen since the ending of cheap Soviet energy supplies and raw materials.

BELGIUM

Status: MONARCHY
Area: 30,520 sq km (11,784 sq mls)
Population: 10,113,000
Capital: BRUSSELS
Language: DUTCH (FLEMISH), FRENCH, GERMAN (ALL OFFICIAL), ITALIAN
Religion: R.CATHOLIC, PROTESTANT
Currency: FRANC
Organizations: EU, OECD, UN

MAP PAGE: 42

BELGIUM LIES ON the North Sea coast of west Europe. Beyond low sand dunes and a narrow belt of reclaimed land are fertile plains which extend to the Sambre-Meuse river valley from where the land rises to the forested Ardennes plateau in the southeast. Belgium has mild winters and cool summers. It is densely populated and has a highly urbanized population. The economy is based on trade, industry and services. With few mineral resources, Belgium imports raw materials for processing and manufacture, and exports semi-finished and finished goods. Metal working, machine building, food processing and brewing, chemical production, iron and steel, and textiles are the major industries. External trade is equivalent to over 70 per cent of national income. Exports include cars, machinery, chemicals, foodstuffs and animals, iron and steel, diamonds, textiles and petroleum products. The agricultural sector is small, but provides for most food needs and a tenth of exports. A large services sector reflects Belgium's position as the home base for over 800 international institutions.

BELIZE

Status: MONARCHY
Area: 22,965 sq km (8,867 sq mls)
Population: 217,000
Capital: BELMOPAN
Language: ENGLISH, CREOLE, SPANISH, MAYAN
Religion: R.CATHOLIC, PROTESTANT, HINDU
Currency: DOLLAR
Organizations: CARICOM, COMM., UN

MAP PAGE: 82

BELIZE IS ON the Caribbean coast of central America and includes cays and a large barrier reef offshore. Belize's coastal areas are flat and swampy; the north and west are hilly, and the southwest contains the Maya mountain range. Jungle covers about half of the country. The climate is tropical, but tempered by sea breezes. A third of the population lives in the capital. The economy is based primarily on agriculture, forestry and fishing. Exports include sugar, clothing, citrus concentrates, bananas and lobsters.

BENIN

Status: REPUBLIC
Area: 112,620 sq km (43,483 sq mls)
Population: 5,561,000
Capital: PORTO-NOVO
Language: FRENCH, FON, YORUBA, ADJA, LOCAL LANGUAGES
Religion: TRAD.BELIEFS, R.CATHOLIC, SUNNI MUSLIM
Currency: CFA FRANC
Organizations: OAU, UN

MAP PAGE: 54

BENIN IS IN west Africa, on the Gulf of Guinea. The Atakora range lies in the northwest; the Niger plains in the northeast. To the south are plateaux, then a fertile plain and finally an area of lagoons and sandy coast. The climate is tropical in the north, but equatorial in the south. The economy is based mainly on agriculture and transit trade. Agricultural products, chiefly cotton, coffee, cocoa beans and oil palms, account for two thirds of export earnings. Oil, produced offshore, is also a major export.

BERMUDA

Status: UK TERRITORY
Area: 54 sq km (21 sq mls)
Population: 63,000
Capital: HAMILTON
Language: ENGLISH
Religion: PROTESTANT, R.CATHOLIC
Currency: DOLLAR

MAP PAGE: 83

IN THE ATLANTIC Ocean to the east of the USA, Bermuda is a group of small islands. The climate is warm and humid. The economy is based on tourism, insurance and shipping.

BHUTAN

Status: MONARCHY
Area: 46,620 sq km (18,000 sq mls)
Population: 1,638,000
Capital: THIMPHU
Language: DZONGKHA, NEPALI, ASSAMESE, ENGLISH
Religion: BUDDHIST, HINDU
Currency: NGULTRUM, INDIAN RUPEE
Organizations: UN

MAP PAGE: 23

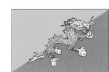

BHUTAN NESTLES IN the eastern Himalayas of south Asia, between China and India. It is mountainous in the north, with fertile valleys in the centre, where most people live, and forested lowlands in the south. The climate ranges between permanently cold in the far north and subtropical in the south. Most of the working population is involved in livestock raising and subsistence farming, though fruit and cardamon are exported. Electricity, minerals, timber and cement are the main exports. Bhutan relies heavily on aid.

BOLIVIA

Status: REPUBLIC
Area: 1,098,581 sq km (424,164 sq mls)
Population: 7,414,000
Capital: LA PAZ
Language: SPANISH, QUECHUA, AYMARA
Religion: R.CATHOLIC, PROTESTANT, BAHA'I
Currency: BOLIVIANO
Organizations: UN

MAP PAGE: 86-87

A LANDLOCKED STATE in central South America, Bolivia borders Brazil, Paraguay, Argentina, Chile and Peru. Most Bolivians live in the high plateau within the Andes ranges. The lowlands range between dense Amazon forest in the northeast and semi-arid grasslands in the southeast. Bolivia is rich in minerals, and sales (chiefly zinc, tin, silver and gold) generate half of export income. Natural gas and timber are also exported. Subsistence farming predominates, though sugar, soya beans and, unofficially, coca are exported.

BOSNIA-HERZEGOVINA

Status: REPUBLIC
Area: 51,130 sq km (19,741 sq mls)
Population: 4,484,000
Capital: SARAJEVO
Language: SERBO-CROAT
Religion: SUNNI MUSLIM, SERBIAN ORTHODOX, R.CATHOLIC, PROTESTANT
Currency: DINAR
Organizations: UN

MAP PAGE: 48-49

BOSNIA-HERZEGOVINA LIES IN the western Balkans of south Europe, on the Adriatic Sea. It is mountainous, with ridges crossing the country northwest-southeast. The main low-

lands are around the Sava valley in the north. Summers are warm, but winters can be very cold. Civil war has ruined the economy, which was based on agriculture, sheep rearing and forestry. All production has ceased, the currency is worthless and only the black economy operates. Much of the population relies on UN relief.

BOTSWANA

Status: REPUBLIC
Area: 581,370 sq km (224,468 sq mls)
Population: 1,456,000
Capital: GABORONE
Language: ENGLISH (OFFICIAL), SETSWANA, SHONA, LOCAL LANGUAGES
Religion: TRAD.BELIEFS, PROTESTANT, R.CATHOLIC
Currency: PULA
Organizations: COMM., OAU, SADC, UN

MAP PAGE: 57

BOTSWANA, A LANDLOCKED state in south Africa, borders South Africa, Namibia, Zambia and Zimbabwe. Over half of the country lies within the upland Kalahari desert, with swamps to the north and salt-pans to the northeast. Most people live near the eastern border. The climate is subtropical, but drought-prone. The economy was founded upon cattle rearing, and beef is an important export, but now it is based on mining and industry. Diamonds account for 80 per cent of export earnings. Copper-nickel matte is also exported.

BRAZIL

Status: REPUBLIC
Area: 8,511,965 sq km (3,286,488 sq mls)
Population: 155,822,000
Capital: BRASÍLIA
Language: PORTUGUESE, GERMAN, JAPANESE, ITALIAN, AMERINDIAN LANGUAGES
Religion: R.CATHOLIC, SPIRITIST, PROTESTANT
Currency: REAL
Organizations: UN

MAP PAGE: 86-88

BRAZIL, IN EASTERN South America, covers almost half of the continent - making it the world's fifth largest country - and borders ten countries and the Atlantic Ocean. The northwest contains the vast Amazon Basin, backed by the Guiana Highlands. The centre west is largely a vast plateau of savannah and rock escarpments. The northeast is mostly semi-arid plateaux, while the east and south contain the rugged mountains and fertile valleys of the Brazilian Highlands and narrow, fertile coastal plains. The Amazon basin is hot, humid and wet; the rest of Brazil is cooler and drier, with seasonal variations. The northeast is drought-prone. Most Brazilians live in urban areas along the coast and on the central plateau, chiefly São Paulo, Rio de Janeiro and Salvador. Brazil is well endowed with minerals and energy resources. Over 50 per cent of the land is forested and 7 per cent is cultivated. Agriculture employs a quarter of the workforce. Brazil is the world's largest producer of coffee and a leading producer of sugar, cocoa, soya beans and beef. Timber production and fish catches are also important. Brazil is a major producer of iron, bauxite and manganese ores, zinc, copper, tin, gold and diamonds as well as oil and coal. Manufacturing contributes a quarter of national income. Industrial products include food, machinery, iron and steel, textiles, cars, pharmaceuticals, chemicals, refined oil, metal products and paper products. The main exports are machinery, metallic ores, cars, metal products, coffee beans, soya products, electrical and electronic goods, and

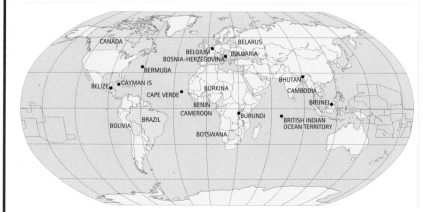

orange juice. Despite its natural wealth and one of the largest economies in the world, Brazil has a large external debt and growing poverty gap.

BRITISH INDIAN OCEAN TERRITORY
Status: UK TERRITORY
Area: 60 sq km (23 sq mls)
Population: 3,100

MAP PAGE: 10

THE TERRITORY CONSISTS of the Chagos Archipelago in the middle of the Indian Ocean. The islands are uninhabited apart from the joint British-US military base on Diego Garcia.

BRUNEI
Status: MONARCHY
Area: 5,765 sq km (2,226 sq mls)
Population: 285,000
Capital: BANDAR SERI BEGAWAN
Language: MALAY, ENGLISH, CHINESE
Religion: SUNNI MUSLIM, BUDDHIST, CHRISTIAN
Currency: DOLLAR (RINGGIT)
Organizations: ASEAN, COMM., UN

MAP PAGE: 33

THE SOUTHEAST ASIAN state of Brunei lies on the northwest coast of the island of Borneo, on the South China Sea. Its two enclaves are surrounded inland by Malaysia. The western part is hilly with a narrow coastal plain which supports some crops and most of the population. The eastern part is mountainous and more forested. Tropical rainforest covers over two thirds of Brunei. The economy is dominated by the oil and gas industries.

BULGARIA
Status: REPUBLIC
Area: 110,994 sq km (42,855 sq mls)
Population: 8,402,000
Capital: SOFIA
Language: BULGARIAN, TURKISH, ROMANY, MACEDONIAN
Religion: BULGARIAN ORTHODOX, SUNNI MUSLIM
Currency: LEV
Organizations: UN

MAP PAGE: 49

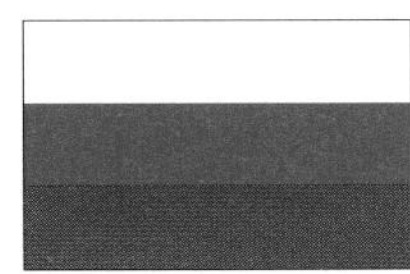

BULGARIA, IN SOUTH Europe, borders Romania, Yugoslavia, Macedonia, Greece, Turkey and the Black Sea. The Balkan Mountains separate the Danube plains in the north from the Rhodope massif and the lowlands in the south. The climate is subject to regional variation. The economy is based on agriculture and manufacturing, chiefly machinery, consumer goods, chemicals and metals. Disruption of Soviet-dominated trade has reduced output.

BURKINA
Status: REPUBLIC
Area: 274,200 sq km (105,869 sq mls)
Population: 10,200,000
Capital: OUAGADOUGOU
Language: FRENCH, MORE (MOSSI), FULANI, LOCAL LANGUAGES
Religion: TRAD.BELIEFS, SUNNI MUSLIM, R.CATHOLIC
Currency: CFA FRANC
Organizations: OAU, UN

MAP PAGE: 54

BURKINA, A LANDLOCKED country in west Africa, borders Mali, Niger, Benin, Togo, Ghana and Côte d'Ivoire. The north of Burkina lies in the Sahara and is arid. The south is mainly semi-arid savannah. Rainfall is erratic and droughts are common. Settlements centre on the country's rivers. Livestock rearing and farming are the main activities. Cotton, livestock, groundnuts and some minerals are exported. Burkina relies heavily on aid.

BURUNDI
Status: REPUBLIC
Area: 27,835 sq km (10,747 sq mls)
Population: 5,982,000
Capital: BUJUMBURA
Language: KIRUNDI (HUTU, TUTSI), FRENCH
Religion: R.CATHOLIC, TRAD.BELIEFS, PROTESTANT, SUNNI MUSLIM
Currency: FRANC
Organizations: OAU, UN

MAP PAGE: 56

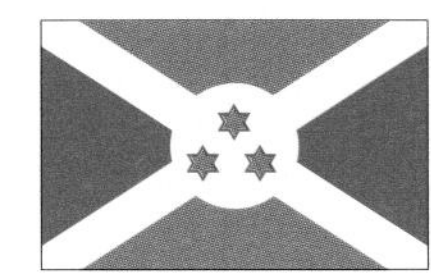

THE DENSELY POPULATED east African state of Burundi borders Rwanda, Zaire, Tanzania and Lake Tanganyika. It is hilly with high plateaux and a tropical climate. Burundi depends upon subsistence farming, coffee exports and foreign aid.

CAMBODIA
Status: MONARCHY
Area: 181,000 sq km (69,884 sq mls)
Population: 9,836,000
Capital: PHNUM PENH
Language: KHMER, VIETNAMESE
Religion: BUDDHIST, R.CATHOLIC, SUNNI MUSLIM
Currency: RIEL
Organizations: UN

MAP PAGE: 32

CAMBODIA LIES IN southeast Asia, on the Gulf of Thailand. It consists of the Mekong river basin, with the Tonle Sap (Great Lake) at its centre. To the north, northeast and east are plateaux and to the southwest are mountains. The climate is tropical monsoon, with forests covering half the land. Most people live on the plains and are engaged in farming (chiefly rice growing), fishing and forestry. Devastated by civil war, Cambodia is dependent on aid.

CAMEROON
Status: REPUBLIC
Area: 475,442 sq km (183,569 sq mls)
Population: 13,277,000
Capital: YAOUNDÉ
Language: FRENCH, ENGLISH, FANG, BAMILEKE, MANY LOCAL LANGUAGES
Religion: TRAD.BELIEFS, R.CATHOLIC, SUNNI MUSLIM, PROTESTANT
Currency: CFA FRANC
Organizations: OAU, UN, COMM.

MAP PAGE: 54-55

CAMEROON IS IN west Africa, on the Gulf of Guinea. The coastal plains, southern and central plateaux are covered with tropical forest. The northern lowlands are semi-arid savannah, and the western highlands, around Mount Cameroon, support a range of crops. A majority of Cameroonians are farmers. Cocoa, coffee and cotton are the main cash crops, though crude oil, sawn wood and logs account for over half of export earnings.

CANADA
Status: FEDERATION
Area: 9,970,610 sq km (3,849,674 sq mls)
Population: 29,606,000
Capital: OTTAWA
Language: ENGLISH, FRENCH, AMERINDIAN LANGUAGES, INUKTITUT (ESKIMO)
Religion: R.CATHOLIC, PROTESTANT, GREEK ORTHODOX, JEWISH
Currency: DOLLAR
Organizations: COMM., NAFTA, OECD, UN

MAP PAGE: 62-63

THE WORLD'S SECOND largest country, Canada covers the northern two-fifths of North America and has coastlines on the Atlantic, Arctic and Pacific Oceans. On the west coast, the Cordilleran region contains coastal mountains, interior plateaux and the Rocky Mountains. To the east lie the fertile prairies. Further east, covering about half the total land area, is the Canadian, or Laurentian, Shield, fairly flat U-shaped lowlands around the Hudson Bay extending to Labrador. The Shield is bordered to the south by the fertile Great Lakes-St Lawrence lowlands. In the far north climatic conditions are polar. In general, however, Canada has a continental climate. Winters are long and cold with heavy snowfalls, while summers are hot with light to moderate rainfall. Most Canadians live in the south, chiefly in the southeast, in the urban areas of the Great Lakes-St Lawrence basin, principally Toronto and Montreal. Canada is well endowed with minerals, energy resources, forests and rich coastal waters. Only 5 per cent of land is classified as arable, but that is still a large area. Canada is among the world's leading exporter of wheat. Other major agricultural exports are apples, beef cattle, potatoes, oilseeds and feed grain. Canada is also a leading exporter of wood from its vast coniferous forests, and fish and seafood from its rich Atlantic and Pacific fishing grounds. It is a top producer of iron ore, uranium, nickel, copper, zinc and other minerals, as well as crude oil and natural gas. Its abundant raw materials are the basis of for manufacturing industries. The principal ones are car manufacture, food processing, chemical production, lumber, woodpulp and paper making, oil refining, iron and steel, and metal refining, Canada is an important trading nation. External trade is equivalent to about 30 per cent of national income. Exports include cars, crude materials, minerals fuels (chiefly oil and gas), food (chiefly wheat), newsprint, lumber, wood pulp, industrial machinery and aluminium. Canada has an important banking and insurance sector.

ALBERTA
Status: PROVINCE
Area: 661,190 sq km (255,287 sq mls)
Population: 2,672,000
Capital: EDMONTON

BRITISH COLUMBIA
Status: PROVINCE
Area: 947,800 sq km (365,948 sq mls)
Population: 3,570,000
Capital: VICTORIA

MANITOBA
Status: PROVINCE
Area: 649,950 sq km (250,947 sq mls)
Population: 1,117,000
Capital: WINNIPEG

NEW BRUNSWICK
Status: PROVINCE
Area: 73,440 sq km (28,355 sq mls)
Population: 751,000
Capital: FREDERICTON

NEWFOUNDLAND
Status: PROVINCE
Area: 405,720 sq km (156,649 sq mls)
Population: 581,000
Capital: ST JOHN'S

NORTHWEST TERRITORIES
Status: TERRITORY
Area: 3,426,320 sq km (1,322,910 sq mls)
Population: 63,000
Capital: YELLOWKNIFE

NOVA SCOTIA
Status: PROVINCE
Area: 55,490 sq km (21,425 sq mls)
Population: 925,000
Capital: HALIFAX

ONTARIO
Status: PROVINCE
Area: 1,068,580 sq km (412,581 sq mls)
Population: 10,795,000
Capital: TORONTO

PRINCE EDWARD ISLAND
Status: PROVINCE
Area: 5,660 sq km (2,158 sq mls)
Population: 132,000
Capital: CHARLOTTETOWN

QUEBEC
Status: PROVINCE
Area: 1,540,680 sq km (594,860 sq mls)
Population: 7,226,000
Capital: QUÉBEC

SASKATCHEWAN
Status: PROVINCE
Area: 652,330 sq km (251,866 sq mls)
Population: 1,002,000
Capital: REGINA

YUKON TERRITORY
Status: TERRITORY
Area: 483,450 sq km (186,661 sq mls)
Population: 33,000
Capital: WHITEHORSE

CAPE VERDE
Status: REPUBLIC
Area: 4,033 sq km (1,557 sq mls)
Population: 392,000
Capital: PRAIA
Language: PORTUGUESE, PORTUGUESE CREOLE
Religion: R.CATHOLIC, PROTESTANT, TRAD.BELIEFS
Currency: ESCUDO
Organizations: OAU, UN

MAP PAGE: 54

CAPE VERDE COMPRISES ten semi-arid volcanic islands and five islets off the coast of west Africa. The economy is based on fishing and subsistence farming, but relies on workers' remittances and foreign aid.

CAYMAN ISLANDS
Status: UK TERRITORY
Area: 259 sq km (100 sq mls)
Population: 31,000
Capital: GEORGE TOWN
Language: ENGLISH
Religion: PROTESTANT, R.CATHOLIC
Currency: DOLLAR

MAP PAGE: 83

IN THE CARIBBEAN, northwest of Jamaica, there are three main islands: Grand Cayman, Little Cayman and Cayman Brac. They form one of the world's major offshore financial centres, though tourism is also important.

© Bartholomew

8

CENTRAL AFRICAN REPUBLIC
Status: REPUBLIC
Area: 622,436 sq km (240,324 sq mls)
Population: 3,315,000
Capital: BANGUI
Language: FRENCH, SANGO, BANDA, BAYA, LOCAL LANGUAGES
Religion: PROTESTANT, R.CATHOLIC, TRAD. BELIEFS, SUNNI MUSLIM
Currency: CFA FRANC
Organizations: OAU, UN

MAP PAGE: 56

THE LANDLOCKED CENTRAL African Republic borders Chad, Sudan, Zaire, Congo and Cameroon. Most of the country is savannah plateaux, drained by the Ubangi and Chari river systems, with mountains to the north and west. The climate is hot with high rainfall. Most of the population live in the south and west, and a majority of the workforce is involved in subsistence farming. Some cotton, coffee, tobacco and timber are exported. However, diamonds and some gold account for more than half of export earnings.

CHAD
Status: REPUBLIC
Area: 1,284,000 sq km (495,755 sq mls)
Population: 6,361,000
Capital: NDJAMENA
Language: ARABIC, FRENCH, MANY LOCAL LANGUAGES
Religion: SUNNI MUSLIM, TRAD.BELIEFS, R.CATHOLIC
Currency: CFA FRANC
Organizations: OAU, UN

MAP PAGE: 55

CHAD IS A landlocked state of central Africa, bordered by Libya, Sudan, Central African Republic, Niger, Nigeria and Cameroon. It consists of plateaux, the Tibesti massif in the north and Lake Chad basin in the west. Climatic conditions range between desert in the north and tropical forest in the southwest. Most people live in the south and near Lake Chad. Farming and cattle herding are the main activities, cattle and raw cotton the chief exports. Impoverished by civil war and drought, Chad relies upon foreign aid.

CHILE
Status: REPUBLIC
Area: 756,945 sq km (292,258 sq mls)
Population: 14,210,000
Capital: SANTIAGO
Language: SPANISH, AMERINDIAN LANGUAGES
Religion: R.CATHOLIC, PROTESTANT
Currency: PESO
Organizations: UN

MAP PAGE: 88

CHILE HUGS THE Pacific coast of the southern half of South America. Between the High Andes in the east and the lower coastal ranges is a central valley, with a mild climate, where most Chileans live. To the north is arid desert, to the south is cold, wet forested grassland. Chile is a leading exporter of copper, and is rich in other minerals and nitrates. Agriculture, forestry and fishing are important activities. Timber products, chemicals products and other manufactures account for a third of exports.

CHINA
Status: REPUBLIC
Area: 9,560,900 sq km (3,691,484 sq mls)
Population: 1,221,462,000
Capital: BEIJING
Language: CHINESE (MANDARIN OFFICIAL), MANY REGIONAL LANGUAGES
Religion: CONFUCIAN, TAOIST, BUDDHIST, SUNNI MUSLIM, R.CATHOLIC
Currency: YUAN
Organizations: UN

MAP PAGE: 15, 24-25

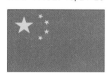

CHINA, THE WORLD'S third largest country, occupies almost the whole of east Asia, borders fourteen states and has coastlines on the Yellow, East China and South China seas. It has an amazing variety of landscapes. The southwest contains the high Tibetan plateau, flanked by the Himalayas and Kunlun mountains. The northwest is mountainous with arid basins and extends from the Tien Shan and Altai ranges and vast Taklimakan desert in the west to the Mongolian plateau and Gobi desert in the centre-east. Eastern China is predominantly lowland and is divided broadly into the basins of the Huang He (Yellow River) in the north, Chang Jiang (Yangtze) in the centre and Xi Jiang (Pearl River) in the southeast. The main exceptions are the Manchurian uplands, loess plateau, Qin Ling range, southeast mountains and the Yunnan plateau in the far south. Climatic conditions and vegetation are as diverse as the topography. Northern China has an extreme continental climate, much of the country experiences temperate conditions, while the southwest enjoys a moist, warm subtropical climate. More than 70 per cent of China's huge population live in rural areas, chiefly in the northern part of the eastern lowlands and along the coast. Agriculture and livestock rearing involves two thirds of the working population. China is the world's largest producer of rice, wheat, soya beans and sugar and is self-sufficient in cereals, fish and livestock. Cotton, soya bean and oilseeds are the major cash crops. China is rich in coal, oil, natural gas and many minerals, chiefly iron ore, wolfram (tungsten ore), tin and phosphates. Industrial and agricultural production were given a boost by the economic reforms of the 1980s which introduced a degree of private enterprise. Industry also benefited from the setting up of joint ventures and the inflow of foreign investment. The major industries produce iron and steel, machinery, textiles, processed foods, chemicals and building materials. China's chief exports are textiles and clothing, petroleum and products, machinery and transport equipment, agricultural products, metal products, iron and steel.

ANHUI (ANHWEI)
Status: PROVINCE
Area: 139,000 sq km (53,668 sq miles)
Population: 58,340,000
Capital: HEFEI

BEIJING (PEKING)
Status: MUNICIPALITY
Area: 16,800 sq km (6,487 sq miles)
Population: 11,020,000
Capital: BEIJING

FUJIAN (FUKIEN)
Status: PROVINCE
Area: 121,400 sq km (46,873 sq miles)
Population: 31,160,000
Capital: FUZHOU

GANSU (KANSU)
Status: PROVINCE
Area: 453,700 sq km (175,175 sq miles)
Population: 23,140,000
Capital: LANZHOU

GUANGDONG (KWANGTUNG)
Status: PROVINCE
Area: 178,000 sq km (68,726 sq miles)
Population: 65,250,000
Capital: GUANGZHOU

GUANGXI ZHUANG (KWANGSI CHUANG)
Status: AUTONOMOUS REGION
Area: 236,000 sq km (91,120 sq miles)
Population: 43,800,000
Capital: NANNING

GUIZHOU (KWEICHOW)
Status: PROVINCE
Area: 176,000 sq km (67,954 sq miles)
Population: 33,610,000
Capital: GUIYANG

HAINAN
Status: PROVINCE
Area: 34,000 sq km (13,127 sq miles)
Population: 6,860,000
Capital: HAIKOU

HEBEI (HOPEI)
Status: PROVINCE
Area: 187,700 sq km (72,471 sq miles)
Population: 62,750,000
Capital: SHIJIAZHUANG

HEILONGJIANG (HEILUNGKIANG)
Status: PROVINCE
Area: 454,600 sq km (175,522 sq miles)
Population: 36,080,000
Capital: HARBIN

HENAN (HONAN)
Status: PROVINCE
Area: 167,000 sq km (64,479 sq miles)
Population: 88,620,000
Capital: ZHENGZHOU

HONG KONG
Status: SPECIAL ADMINISTRATIVE REGION
Area: 1,075 sq km (415 sq mls)
Population: 6,190,000
Capital: HONG KONG
Language: CHINESE (CANTONESE, MANDARIN), ENGLISH
Religion: BUDDHIST, TAOIST, PROTESTANT
Currency: DOLLAR

HUBEI (HUPEI)
Status: PROVINCE
Area: 185,900 sq km (71,776 sq miles)
Population: 55,800,000
Capital: WUHAN

HUNAN
Status: PROVINCE
Area: 210,000 sq km (81,081 sq miles)
Population: 62,670,000
Capital: CHANGSHA

JIANGSU (KIANGSU)
Status: PROVINCE
Area: 102,600 sq km (39,614 sq miles)
Population: 69,110,000
Capital: NANJING

JIANGXI (KIANGSI)
Status: PROVINCE
Area: 166,900 sq km (64,440 sq miles)
Population: 39,130,000
Capital: NANCHANG

JILIN (KIRIN)
Status: PROVINCE
Area: 187,000 sq km (72,201 sq miles)
Population: 25,320,000
Capital: CHANGCHUN

LIAONING
Status: PROVINCE
Area: 147,400 sq km (56,911 sq miles)
Population: 40,160,000
Capital: SHENYANG

NEI MONGOL (INNER MONGOLIA)
Status: AUTONOMOUS REGION
Area: 1,183,000 sq km (456,759 sq miles)
Population: 22,070,000
Capital: HOHHOT

NINGXIA HUI (NINGHSIA HUI)
Status: AUTONOMOUS REGION
Area: 66,400 sq km (25,637 sq miles)
Population: 4,870,000
Capital: YINCHUAN

QINGHAI (TSINGHAI)
Status: PROVINCE
Area: 721,000 sq km (278,380 sq miles)
Population: 4,610,000
Capital: XINING

SHAANXI (SHENSI)
Status: PROVINCE
Area: 205,600 sq km (79,383 sq miles)
Population: 34,050,000
Capital: XI'AN

SHANDONG (SHANTUNG)
Status: PROVINCE
Area: 153,300 sq km (59,189 sq miles)
Population: 86,100,000
Capital: JINAN

SHANGHAI
Status: MUNICIPALITY
Area: 6,300 sq km (2,432 sq miles)
Population: 13,450,000
Capital: SHANGHAI

SHANXI (SHANSI)
Status: PROVINCE
Area: 156,300 sq km (60,348 sq miles)
Population: 29,790,000
Capital: TAIYUAN

SICHUAN (SZECHWAN)
Status: PROVINCE
Area: 569,000 sq km (219,692 sq miles)
Population: 109,980,000
Capital: CHENGDU

TIANJIN (TIENTSIN)
Status: MUNICIPALITY
Area: 11,300 sq km (4,363 sq miles)
Population: 9,200,000
Capital: TIANJIN

XIZANG (TIBET)
Status: AUTONOMOUS REGION
Area: 1,228,400 sq km (474,288 sq miles)
Population: 2,280,000
Capital: LHASA

8

XINJIANG UYGUR (SINKIANG UIGHUR)
Status: AUTONOMOUS REGION
Area: 1,600,000 sq km (617,763 sq miles)
Population: 15,810,000
Capital: ÜRÜMQI

YUNNAN
Status: PROVINCE
Area: 394,000 sq km (152,124 sq miles)
Population: 38,320,000
Capital: KUNMING

ZHEJIANG (CHEKIANG)
Status: PROVINCE
Area: 101,800 sq km (39,305 sq miles)
Population: 42,360,000
Capital: HANGZHOU

CHRISTMAS ISLAND
Status: AUSTRALIAN TERRITORY
Area: 135 sq km (52 sq mls)
Population: 2,000
Capital: THE SETTLEMENT
Language: ENGLISH
Religion: BUDDHIST, SUNNI MUSLIM, PROTESTANT, R.CATHOLIC
Currency: AUSTR. DOLLAR

MAP PAGE: 25

COCOS ISLANDS
Status: AUSTRALIAN TERRITORY
Area: 14 sq km (5 sq mls)
Population: 1,000
Capital: HOME ISLAND
Language: ENGLISH
Religion: SUNNI MUSLIM, CHRISTIAN
Currency: AUSTR. DOLLAR

MAP PAGE: 25

THE COCOS ISLANDS are two separate coral atolls in the east of the Indian Ocean between Sri Lanka and Australia. Most of the population live on West Island and Home Island.

COLOMBIA
Status: REPUBLIC
Area: 1,141,748 sq km (440,831 sq mls)
Population: 35,099,000
Capital: BOGOTÁ
Language: SPANISH, AMERINDIAN LANGUAGES
Religion: R.CATHOLIC, PROTESTANT
Currency: PESO
Organizations: UN

MAP PAGE: 86

A STATE IN northwest South America, Colombia has coastlines on the Pacific Ocean and the Caribbean Sea. Behind coastal plains lie three ranges of the Andes, separated by high valleys and plateaus where most Colombians live. To the southeast are the prairies and then the jungle of the Amazon. Colombia has a tropical climate, though temperatures vary with altitude. Only 5 per cent of land can be cultivated, but a range of crops are grown. Coffee (Colombia is the world's second largest producer), sugar, bananas, cotton and flowers are exported. Petroleum and its products are the main export. Coal, nickel, gold, silver, platinum and emeralds (Colombia is the world's largest producer) are mined. Industry involves mainly processing minerals and agricultural produce. In spite of government efforts to stop the drugs trade, coca growing and cocaine smuggling are rife.

COMOROS
Status: REPUBLIC
Area: 1,862 sq km (719 sq mls)
Population: 653,000
Capital: MORONI
Language: COMORIAN, FRENCH, ARABIC
Religion: SUNNI MUSLIM, R.CATHOLIC
Currency: FRANC
Organizations: OAU, UN

MAP PAGE: 57

THE STATE COMPRISES three volcanic islands Grande Comore, Anjouan and Mohéil and some coral atolls in the Indian Ocean, off the east African coast. The tropical islands are mountainous, with poor soil. Subsistence farming predominates, but vanilla, cloves and ylang-ylang (an essential oil) are exported.

CONGO
Status: REPUBLIC
Area: 342,000 sq km (132,047 sq mls)
Population: 2,590,000
Capital: BRAZZAVILLE
Language: FRENCH (OFFICIAL), KONGO, MONOKUTUBA, LOCAL LANGUAGES
Religion: R.CATHOLIC, PROTESTANT, TRAD. BELIEFS, SUNNI MUSLIM
Currency: CFA FRANC
Organizations: OAU, UN

MAP PAGE: 56

CONGO, IN CENTRAL Africa, is for the most part forest or savannah-covered plateaux drained by the Ubangi-Congo river systems. Sand dunes and lagoons line the short Atlantic coast. The climate is hot and tropical. Most Congolese live in the southern third of the country. Oil is the main source of export revenue. Diamonds, lead, zinc and gold are also mined. Hardwoods are the second biggest export earner. Half of the workforce are farmers, growing food crops and cash crops including sugar, coffee, cocoa and oil palms.

CONGO (ZAIRE)
Status: REPUBLIC
Area: 2,345,410 sq km (905,568 sq mls)
Population: 43,901,000
Capital: KINSHASA
Language: FRENCH, LINGALA, SWAHILI, KONGO, MANY LOCAL LANGUAGES
Religion: R.CATHOLIC, PROTESTANT, SUNNI MUSLIM, TRAD. BELIEFS
Currency: ZAÏRE
Organizations: OAU, UN

MAP PAGE: 56-57

THE CENTRAL AFRICAN state of Congo consists of the basin of the Congo river flanked by plateaux, with high mountain ranges to the north and east and a short Atlantic coastline to the west. The climate is tropical with rainforest close to the Equator and savannah to the north and south. Congo has fertile land that grows a range of food crops and cash crops, chiefly coffee. It has vast mineral resources, copper and diamonds being the most important. However economic mismanagement and political turmoil have ruined the economy.

COOK ISLANDS
Status: NEW ZEALAND TERRITORY
Area: 293 sq km (113 sq mls)
Population: 19,000
Capital: AVARUA
Language: ENGLISH, MAORI
Religion: PROTESTANT, R.CATHOLIC
Currency: DOLLAR

MAP PAGE: 5

COSTA RICA
Status: REPUBLIC
Area: 51,100 sq km (19,730 sq mls)
Population: 3,333,000
Capital: SAN JOSÉ
Language: SPANISH
Religion: R.CATHOLIC, PROTESTANT
Currency: COLÓN
Organizations: UN

MAP PAGE: 83

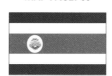

COSTA RICA HAS coastlines on the Caribbean Sea and Pacific Ocean. From the tropical coastal plains the land rises to mountains and a temperate central plateau where most people live. Farming is the main activity and exports include bananas, coffee, sugar, flowers and beef. There is some mining and a strong manufacturing sector, producing a range of goods from clothing (the main export) and electrical components to food products and cement.

CÔTE D'IVOIRE
Status: REPUBLIC
Area: 322,463 sq km (124,504 sq mls)
Population: 14,230,000
Capital: YAMOUSSOUKRO
Language: FRENCH (OFFICIAL), AKAN, KRU, GUR, LOCAL LANGUAGES
Religion: TRAD.BELIEFS, SUNNI MUSLIM, R.CATHOLIC
Currency: CFA FRANC
Organizations: OAU, UN

MAP PAGE: 54

CÔTE D'IVOIRE (IVORY Coast) is in west Africa, on the Gulf of Guinea. In the north are plateaux and savannah, in the south are low undulating plains and rainforest, with sandbars and lagoons on the coast. Temperatures are warm, and rainfall is heavier in the south. Most of the workforce is engaged in farming. Côte d'Ivoire is a major producer of cocoa and coffee, and agricultural products (including cotton and timber) are the main export. Gold and diamonds are mined and some oil is produced offshore.

CROATIA
Status: REPUBLIC
Area: 56,538 sq km (21,829 sq mls)
Population: 4,495,000
Capital: ZAGREB
Language: SERBO-CROAT
Religion: R.CATHOLIC, ORTHODOX, SUNNI MUSLIM
Currency: KUNA
Organizations: UN

MAP PAGE: 48-49

THE SOUTH EUROPEAN state of Croatia has a long coastline on the Adriatic Sea and many offshore islands. Coastal areas have a Mediterranean climate, inland is colder and wetter. Croatia was strong agriculturally and industrially, but secessionist and ethnic conflict, the loss of markets and the loss of tourist revenue have caused economic difficulties.

CUBA
Status: REPUBLIC
Area: 110,860 sq km (42,803 sq mls)
Population: 11,041,000
Capital: HAVANA
Language: SPANISH
Religion: R.CATHOLIC, PROTESTANT
Currency: PESO
Organizations: UN

MAP PAGE: 83

CUBA COMPRISES THE island of Cuba, the largest island in the Caribbean, and many islets and cays. A fifth of Cubans live in and around Havana. Sugar, with molasses and rum, account for two thirds of export earnings. Severe recession followed the disruption of traditional trade with east Europe and the ending of Russian subsidies.

CYPRUS
Status: REPUBLIC
Area: 9,251 sq km (3,572 sq mls)
Population: 742,000
Capital: NICOSIA
Language: GREEK, TURKISH, ENGLISH
Religion: GREEK (CYPRIOT) ORTHODOX, SUNNI MUSLIM
Currency: POUND
Organizations: COMM., UN

MAP PAGE: 16

THE MEDITERRANEAN ISLAND of Cyprus has hot summers and mild winters. The economy of the Greek south is based mainly on specialist agriculture and tourism, though shipping and offshore banking are also major sources of income. The Turkish north depends upon agriculture, tourism and aid from Turkey.

CZECH REPUBLIC
Status: REPUBLIC
Area: 78,864 sq km (30,450 sq mls)
Population: 10,331,000
Capital: PRAGUE
Language: CZECH, MORAVIAN, SLOVAK
Religion: R.CATHOLIC, PROTESTANT
Currency: KORUNA
Organizations: UN, OECD

MAP PAGE: 46-47

THE LANDLOCKED CZECH Republic in central Europe consists of rolling countryside, wooded hills and fertile valleys. The climate is temperate, but summers are warm and winters fairly cold. The country has substantial reserves of coal and lignite, timber and some minerals, chiefly iron ore, graphite, garnets and silver. It is highly industrialized and major manufactures include industrial machinery, consumer goods, cars, iron and steel, chemicals and glass. Since separation from Slovakia in January 1993, trade between the two countries has declined, exacerbating the difficulties the economy was already experiencing from the introduction of a free-market economy. There is, however, a growing tourist industry.

© Bartholomew

DENMARK
Status: MONARCHY
Area: 43,075 sq km (16,631 sq mls)
Population: 5,228,000
Capital: COPENHAGEN
Language: DANISH
Religion: PROTESTANT, R.CATHOLIC
Currency: KRONE
Organizations: EU, OECD, UN

MAP PAGE: 37

THE KINGDOM OF Denmark in north Europe occupies the Jutland Peninsula and nearly 500 islands in and between the North and Baltic seas. The country is low-lying, with a mixture of fertile and sandy soils, and long, indented coastlines. The climate is cool and temperate, with rainfall throughout the year. A fifth of the population lives in Greater Copenhagen on the largest of the islands, Zealand. Denmark's main natural resource is its agricultural potential; two thirds of the total area is fertile farmland or pasture. Agriculture, forestry and fishing are all important sectors of the economy. The chief agricultural products are cheese and other dairy products, beef and bacon, much of which is exported. Some oil and natural gas is produced from fields in the North Sea. Manufacturing, largely based on imported raw materials, now accounts for over half of exports. The main industries are iron and metal working, food processing and brewing, chemicals and engineering. Exports include machinery, food, chemicals, furniture, fuels and energy, and transport equipment.

DJIBOUTI
Status: REPUBLIC
Area: 23,200 sq km (8,958 sq mls)
Population: 577,000
Capital: DJIBOUTI
Language: SOMALI, FRENCH, ARABIC, ISSA, AFAR
Religion: SUNNI MUSLIM, R.CATHOLIC
Currency: FRANC
Organizations: OAU, UN

MAP PAGE: 56

DJIBOUTI LIES IN northeast Africa, on the Gulf of Aden. It consists mostly of low-lying desert, with some areas below sea level and a mountainous area to the north. Temperatures are high and rainfall is low. Most people live in the coastal strip. There is some camel, sheep and goat herding, and cattle, hides and skins are the main exports. With few natural resources, the economy is based on services and trade. The deep-water port and the railway line to Addis Ababa account for about two thirds of national income.

DOMINICA
Status: REPUBLIC
Area: 750 sq km (290 sq mls)
Population: 71,000
Capital: ROSEAU
Language: ENGLISH, FRENCH CREOLE
Religion: R.CATHOLIC, PROTESTANT
Currency: E. CARIB. DOLLAR, POUND STERLING, FRENCH FRANC
Organizations: CARICOM, COMM., UN

MAP PAGE: 83

DOMINICA IS THE most northerly of the Windward Islands in the eastern Caribbean. It is mountainous and forested, with a coastline of steep cliffs, and features geysers and hot springs. The climate is tropical and rainfall abundant. A quarter of Dominicans live in the capital. The economy is based on agriculture, with bananas (the major export), coconuts and citrus fruits the most important crops. There is some forestry, fishing and mining. Manufactured exports include soap, coconut oil, rum and bottled water. Tourism is growing.

DOMINICAN REPUBLIC
Status: REPUBLIC
Area: 48,442 sq km (18,704 sq mls)
Population: 7,915,000
Capital: SANTO DOMINGO
Language: SPANISH, FRENCH CREOLE
Religion: R.CATHOLIC, PROTESTANT
Currency: PESO
Organizations: UN

MAP PAGE: 83

THE STATE OCCUPIES the eastern two thirds of the Caribbean island of Hispaniola. It has a series of mountain ranges, including the highest peaks in the region, fertile valleys and a large coastal plain in the east. The climate is hot tropical, with heavy rainfall. A third of the population lives in the capital. Sugar, coffee and cocoa are the main cash crops. Bauxite, nickel (the main export), gold and silver are mined, and there is some light industry. Tourism is the main foreign exchange earner.

ECUADOR
Status: REPUBLIC
Area: 272,045 sq km (105,037 sq mls)
Population: 11,460,000
Capital: QUITO
Language: SPANISH, QUECHUA, AMERINDIAN LANGUAGES
Religion: R.CATHOLIC, PROTESTANT
Currency: SUCRE
Organizations: UN

MAP PAGE: 86

ECUADOR IS IN northwest South America, on the Pacific coast. It consists of a broad coastal plain, the high ranges of the Andes and the forested upper Amazon basin to the east. The climate is tropical, moderated by altitude. Most people live on the coast or in the mountain valleys. Ecuador is one of the continent's leading oil producers. Mineral reserves include gold, silver, zinc and copper. Most of the workforce depends on agriculture. Ecuador is the world's leading producer of bananas. Shrimps, coffee and cocoa are also exported.

EGYPT
Status: REPUBLIC
Area: 1,000,250 sq km (386,199 sq mls)
Population: 59,226,000
Capital: CAIRO
Language: ARABIC, FRENCH
Religion: SUNNI MUSLIM, COPTIC CHRISTIAN
Currency: POUND
Organizations: OAU, UN

MAP PAGE: 55

EGYPT, ON THE eastern Mediterranean coast of North Africa, is low-lying, with areas below sea level in the west, and in the Qattara depression, and mountain ranges along the Red Sea coast and in the Sinai peninsula. It is a land of desert and semi-desert, except for the Nile valley, where 99 per cent of Egyptians live, about half of them in towns. The summers are hot, the winters mild and rainfall is negligible. Less than 4 per cent of land (chiefly around the Nile floodplain and delta) is cultivated, but farming employs half the workforce and contributes a sixth of exports. Cotton is the main cash crop. Rice, fruit and vegetables are exported, but Egypt imports over half its food needs. It has major reserves of oil and natural gas, phosphates, iron ore, manganese and nitrates. Oil and its products account for half of export earnings. Manufactures include cement, fertilizers, textiles, electrical goods, cars and processed foods. Workers' remittances, Suez canal tolls and tourist receipts are major sources of income, though attacks on tourists by Islamic militants has reduced the latter.

EL SALVADOR
Status: REPUBLIC
Area: 21,041 sq km (8,124 sq mls)
Population: 5,768,000
Capital: SAN SALVADOR
Language: SPANISH
Religion: R.CATHOLIC, PROTESTANT
Currency: COLÓN
Organizations: UN

MAP PAGE: 82

A DENSELY POPULATED state on the Pacific coast of central American, El Salvador has a coastal plain and volcanic mountain ranges that enclose a plateau where most people live. The coast is hot, with heavy summer rainfall, the highlands are cooler. Coffee (the chief export), sugar and cotton are main cash crops. Shrimps are also exported. Manufactures include processed foods, cosmetics, pharmaceuticals, textiles and clothing.

EQUATORIAL GUINEA
Status: REPUBLIC
Area: 28,051 sq km (10,831 sq mls)
Population: 400,000
Capital: MALABO
Language: SPANISH, FANG
Religion: R.CATHOLIC, TRAD.BELIEFS
Currency: CFA FRANC
Organizations: OAU, UN

MAP PAGE: 54

THE STATE CONSISTS of Rio Muni, an enclave on the Atlantic coast of central Africa, and the islands of Bioco, Annobón and Corisco group. Most people live on the coastal plain and upland plateau of the mainland; the capital is on the fertile volcanic island of Bioco. The climate is hot, humid and wet. Cocoa and timber are the main exports, but the economy depends heavily upon foreign aid.

ERITREA
Status: REPUBLIC
Area: 117,400 sq km (45,328 sq mls)
Population: 3,531,000
Capital: ASMARA
Language: TIGRINYA, ARABIC, TIGRE, ENGLISH
Religion: SUNNI MUSLIM, COPTIC CHRISTIAN
Currency: ETHIOPIAN BIRR
Organizations: OAU, UN

MAP PAGE: 56

ERITREA, ON THE Red Sea coast of northeast Africa, consists of high plateau in the north and a coastal plain that widens to the south. The coast is hot, inland is cooler. Rainfall is unreliable. The agricultural-based economy has suffered from 30 years of war and occasional poor rains. Coffee and cotton were the main cash crops, though food crops were important to reduce food aid.

ESTONIA
Status: REPUBLIC
Area: 45,200 sq km (17,452 sq mls)
Population: 1,530,000
Capital: TALLINN
Language: ESTONIAN, RUSSIAN
Religion: PROTESTANT, RUSSIAN ORTHODOX
Currency: KROON
Organizations: UN

MAP PAGE: 37

ESTONIA IS IN north Europe, on the Gulf of Finland and Baltic Sea. The land, one third of which is forested, is generally low-lying, with many lakes. The climate is temperate. About one third of Estonians live in Tallinn. Forests and oil-shale deposits are the main natural resources. Agriculture is limited to livestock and dairy farming. Industries include timber, furniture production, shipbuilding, leather, fur and food processing.

ETHIOPIA
Status: REPUBLIC
Area: 1,133,880 sq km (437,794 sq mls)
Population: 56,677,000
Capital: ADDIS ABABA
Language: AMHARIC, OROMO, LOCAL LANGUAGES
Religion: ETHIOPIAN ORTHODOX, SUNNI MUSLIM, TRAD.BELIEFS
Currency: BIRR
Organizations: OAU, UN

MAP PAGE: 56

ETHIOPIA, IN NORTHEAST Africa, borders Eritrea, Djibouti, Somalia, Kenya and Sudan. The western half is a mountainous region traversed by the Great Rift Valley. To the east is mostly arid plateaux. The highlands are warm with summer rainfall, though droughts occur; the east is hot and dry. Most people live in the

centre-north. Secessionist wars have hampered economic development. Subsistence farming is the main activity, though droughts have led to famine. Coffee is the main export and there is some light industry.

FALKLAND ISLANDS
Status: UK TERRITORY
Area: 12,170 sq km (4,699 sq mls)
Population: 2,000
Capital: STANLEY
Language: ENGLISH
Religion: PROTESTANT, R.CATHOLIC
Currency: POUND

MAP PAGE: 88

LYING IN THE southwest Atlantic Ocean, northeast of Cape Horn, the Falklands consists of two main islands, West Falkland and East Falkland, where most of the population live, and many smaller islands. The economy is based on sheep farming and the sale of fishing licences, though oil has been discovered off-shore.

FAROE ISLANDS
Status: DANISH TERRITORY
Area: 1,399 sq km (540 sq mls)
Population: 47,000
Capital: TÓRSHAVN
Language: DANISH, FAEROESE
Religion: PROTESTANT
Currency: DANISH KRONE

MAP PAGE: 36

A SELF GOVERNING territory, the Faeroes lie in the north Atlantic Ocean between the UK and Iceland. The islands benefit from the Gulf Stream which has a moderating effect on the climate. The economy is based on deep-sea fishing and sheep farming.

FIJI
Status: REPUBLIC
Area: 18,330 sq km (7,077 sq mls)
Population: 784,000
Capital: SUVA
Language: ENGLISH, FIJIAN, HINDI
Religion: PROTESTANT, HINDU, R.CATHOLIC, SUNNI MUSLIM
Currency: DOLLAR
Organizations: UN

MAP PAGE: 7

FIJI COMPRISES TWO main islands, of volcanic origin and mountainous, and over 300 smaller islands in the South Pacific Ocean. The climate is tropical and the economy is based on agriculture (chiefly sugar, the main export), fishing, forestry, gold mining and tourism.

FINLAND
Status: REPUBLIC
Area: 338,145 sq km (130,559 sq mls)
Population: 5,108,000
Capital: HELSINKI
Language: FINNISH, SWEDISH
Religion: PROTESTANT, FINNISH (GREEK) ORTHODOX
Currency: MARKKA
Organizations: EU, OECD, UN

MAP PAGE: 36-37

FINLAND IS IN north Europe, on the Gulf of Bothnia and the Gulf of Finland. It is low-lying apart from mountainous areas in the northwest. Forests cover 70 per cent of the land area, lakes and tundra over 20 per cent. Only 8 per cent is cultivated. Summers are short and warm, and winters are long and severe, particularly in the north. Most people live in the southern third of the country, along the coast or near the many lakes. Timber is the main resource and products of the forest-based industries account for a third of exports. Finland has a large fishing industry and its agricultural sector produces enough cereals and dairy products to cover domestic needs. It has some mineral deposits, chiefly zinc, copper, nickel, gold and silver. Finland is a highly industrialised country, though it must import most of the raw materials. Apart from the timber and related industries, it has important metal working, shipbuilding and engineering industries. Other industries produce chemicals, pharmaceuticals, plastics, rubber, textiles, electronic equipment, glass and ceramics.

F.Y.R.O.M. (MACEDONIA)
Status: REPUBLIC
Area: 25,713 sq km (9,928 sq mls)
Population: 2,163,000
Capital: SKOPJE
Language: MACEDONIAN, ALBANIAN, SERBO-CROAT, TURKISH, ROMANY
Religion: MACEDONIAN ORTHODOX, SUNNI MUSLIM, R.CATHOLIC
Currency: DENAR
Organizations: UN

MAP PAGE: 49

FYROM, FORMERLY THE Yugoslav republic of Macedonia, is a landlocked state of south Europe, bordered by Yugoslavia, Bulgaria, Greece and Albania. Lying within the south Balkans, it is a rugged country, traversed north-south by the Vardar valley. It has fine, hot summers, but very cold winters. The economy is based on industry, mining and, to a lesser degree, agriculture. But conflict with Greece and UN sanctions against Yugoslavia have reduced trade, caused economic difficulties and discouraged investment.

FRANCE
Status: REPUBLIC
Area: 543,965 sq km (210,026 sq mls)
Population: 58,143,000
Capital: PARIS
Language: FRENCH, FRENCH DIALECTS, ARABIC, GERMAN (ALSATIAN), BRETON
Religion: R.CATHOLIC, PROTESTANT, SUNNI MUSLIM
Currency: FRANC
Organizations: EU, OECD, UN

MAP PAGE: 44

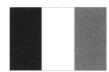

FRANCE LIES IN southwest Europe, with coastlines on the North Sea, Atlantic Ocean and Mediterranean Sea; it includes the Mediterranean island of Corsica. Northern and western regions consist mostly of flat or rolling countryside, and include the major lowlands of the Paris basin, the Loire valley and the Aquitaine basin, drained by the Seine, Loire and Garonne river systems respectively. The centre-south is dominated by the Massif Central. Eastwards, beyond the fourth major lowland area of the Rhône-Saône valley, are the Alps and the Jura mountains. In the southwest, the Pyrenees form a natural border with Spain. The climate of northern parts is temperate and wet, but in the centre and east it is continental, with warmer summers and milder winters. Along the south coast a Mediterranean climate prevails, with hot, dry summers and mild winters with some rainfall. Some 75 per cent of the population live in towns, but Greater Paris is the only major conurbation, with a sixth of the French population. Rich soil, a large cultivable area and contrasts in temperature and relief have given France a strong and varied agricultural base. It is a major producer of both fresh and processed food and the world's second largest exporter of agricultural products, after the USA. Major exports include cereals (chiefly wheat), dairy products, wines and sugar. France has relatively few mineral resources, though iron ore, potash salts, zinc and uranium are mined. It has coal reserves, some oil and natural gas, but it relies mainly for its energy needs on nuclear and hydroelectric power and imported fuels. France is the world's fourth largest industrial power after the USA, Japan and Germany. Heavy industries include iron, steel and aluminium production and oil refining. Other major industries are food processing, motor vehicles, aerospace, chemicals and pharmaceuticals, telecommunications, computers and armaments as well as luxury goods, fashion and perfumes. The main exports are machinery, agricultural products, cars and other transport equipment. France has a strong services sector and tourism is a major source of revenue and employment.

FRENCH GUIANA
Status: FRENCH TERRITORY
Area: 90,000 sq km (34,749 sq mls)
Population: 147,000
Capital: CAYENNE
Language: FRENCH, FRENCH CREOLE
Religion: R.CATHOLIC, PROTESTANT
Currency: FRENCH FRANC

MAP PAGE: 87

FRENCH GUIANA, ON the northeast coast of South America, is densely forested and is mountainous in the south. The climate is tropical with high rainfall. Most people live in the coastal strip and most workers are involved in subsistence farming, though sugar is exported. Livestock rearing and fishing are also important. Timber and mineral resources are largely unexploited and industry is limited. French Guiana depends upon French aid.

FRENCH POLYNESIA
Status: FRENCH TERRITORY
Area: 3,265 sq km (1,261 sq mls)
Population: 220,000
Capital: PAPEETE
Language: FRENCH, POLYNESIAN LANGUAGES
Religion: PROTESTANT, R.CATHOLIC, MORMON
Currency: PACIFIC FRANC

MAP PAGE: 5

EXTENDING OVER A vast area of the southeast Pacific Ocean, French Polynesia comprises more than 130 islands and coral atolls. The main island groups are the Marquesas, the Tuamotu Archipelago and the Society Islands. The capital, Papeete, is on Tahiti in the Society Islands. The climate is subtropical and the economy is based on tourism.

FRENCH SOUTHERN AND ANTARCTIC LANDS
Status: FRENCH TERRITORY
Area: 7,781 sq km (3,004 sq mls)

MAP PAGE: 3

THIS TERRITORY INCLUDES Crozet Island, Kerguelen, Amsterdam Island and St Paul Island. All are uninhabited apart from scientific research staff. In accordance with the Antarctic Treaty, French territorial claims in Antarctica have been suspended.

GABON
Status: REPUBLIC
Area: 267,667 sq km (103,347 sq mls)
Population: 1,320,000
Capital: LIBREVILLE
Language: FRENCH, FANG, LOCAL LANGUAGES
Religion: R.CATHOLIC, PROTESTANT, TRAD.BELIEFS
Currency: CFA FRANC
Organizations: OAU, UN

MAP PAGE: 56

GABON, ON THE Atlantic coast of central Africa consists of low plateaus, with a coastal plain lined by lagoons and mangrove swamps. The climate is tropical and rainforests cover 75 per cent of the land. Half of the population lives in towns, chiefly Libreville and Port Gentil. The economy is heavily dependent on mineral resources, mainly oil but also manganese and uranium. Timber, chiefly okoumé, is exported. Agriculture is mainly at subsistence level, but oil palms, bananas, sugarcane and rubber are grown.

THE GAMBIA
Status: REPUBLIC
Area: 11,295 sq km (4,361 sq mls)
Population: 1,118,000
Capital: BANJUL
Language: ENGLISH (OFFICIAL), MALINKE, FULANI, WOLOF
Religion: SUNNI MUSLIM, PROTESTANT
Currency: DALASI
Organizations: COMM., OAU, UN

MAP PAGE: 54

THE GAMBIA, ON the coast of west Africa, occupies a strip of land along the lower Gambia River. Sandy beaches are backed by mangrove swamps, beyond which is savannah. The climate is tropical, with rainfall in the summer. Over 70 per cent of Gambians are farmers, growing chiefly groundnuts (the main export) but also seed cotton, oil palms and food crops. Livestock rearing and fishing are important, while manufacturing is limited. Re-exports, mainly from Senegal, and tourism are major sources of income.

GAZA
Status: AUTONOMOUS REGION
Area: 363 sq km (140 sq mls)
Population: 756,000
Capital: GAZA
Language: ARABIC
Religion: SUNNI MUSLIM, SHI'A MUSLIM
Currency: ISRAELI SHEKEL

MAP PAGE: 16

GAZA IS A narrow strip of land on the southeast corner of the Mediterranean Sea, between Egypt and Israel. The territory has limited autonomy from Israel. The economy is based on agriculture and remittances from work in Israel.

© Bartholomew

GEORGIA

Status: REPUBLIC
Area: 69,700 sq km (26,911 sq mls)
Population: 5,457,000
Capital: T'BILISI
Language: GEORGIAN, RUSSIAN, ARMENIAN, AZERI, OSSETIAN, ABKHAZ
Religion: GEORGIAN ORTHODOX, RUSSIAN ORTHODOX, SHI'A MUSLIM
Currency: LARI
Organizations: CIS, UN

MAP PAGE: 51

GEORGIA IS IN northwest Transcaucasia, southwest Asia, on the Black Sea. Mountain ranges in the north and south flank the Kura and Rioni valleys. The climate is generally mild, but subtropical along the coast. Agriculture is important, with tea, grapes, citrus fruits and tobacco the major crops. Mineral resources include manganese, coal and oil, and the main industries are iron and steel, oil refining and machine building. However, economic activity has been seriously affected by separatist wars and political unrest.

GERMANY

Status: REPUBLIC
Area: 357,868 sq km (138,174 sq mls)
Population: 81,642,000
Capital: BERLIN
Language: GERMAN, TURKISH
Religion: PROTESTANT, R.CATHOLIC, SUNNI MUSLIM
Currency: MARK
Organizations: EU, OECD, UN

MAP PAGE: 46

THE WEST EUROPEAN state of Germany borders nine countries and has coastlines on the North and Baltic seas. It includes the southern part of the Jutland peninsula and Frisian islands. Behind the indented coastline and covering about one third of the country is the north German plain, a region of fertile farmland and sandy heaths drained by the country's major rivers. The central highlands are a belt of forested hills and plateaux which stretches from the Eifel region in the west to the Erzgebirge (Ore mountains) along the border with the Czech Republic. Farther south the land rises to the Swabian and Jura mountains, with the high rugged and forested Black Forest in the southwest and the Bavarian plateau and Alps to the southeast. The climate is temperate, with continental conditions in eastern areas where winters are colder. Rainfall is evenly spread throughout the year. Divided in 1945 after defeat in the second world war, Germany was reunified in 1990, barely a year after the collapse of communism in eastern Europe. It had been thought that west Germany, the world's third largest industrial economy and second largest exporter, would easily absorb east Germany, less than half the size and with a quarter of the population. But the initial cost of unification was high. The overhaul of east German industry led to 30 per cent unemployment there, while the high level of investment and the rising social security bill led to tax increases in the west. In addition unification coincided with recession in the west German economy and rising unemployment, which created social tensions. However, by 1994 there were signs that the economy was pulling out of the recession. Germany lacks minerals and other industrial raw materials, with the exception of lignite and potash. It has a small agricultural base, though a few products (chiefly wines and beers) enjoy an international reputation. It is predominantly an industrial economy, dominated by the mechanical and engineering, iron and steel, chemical, pharmaceutical, motor, textile and high-tech industries. It also has a large service sector, with tourism, banking and finance being important.

BADEN-WÜRTTEMBERG

Status: STATE
Area: 35,751 sq km (13,804 sq miles)
Population: 10,344,009
Capital: STUTTGART

BAYERN (BAVARIA)

Status: STATE
Area: 70,554 sq km (27,241 sq miles)
Population: 12,014,674
Capital: MÜNCHEN

BERLIN

Status: STATE
Area: 889 sq km (343 sq miles)
Population: 3,467,322
Capital: BERLIN

BRANDENBURG

Status: STATE
Area: 29,056 sq km (11,219 sq miles)
Population: 2,545,511
Capital: POTSDAM

BREMEN

Status: STATE
Area: 404 sq km (156 sq miles)
Population: 678,731
Capital: BREMEN

HAMBURG

Status: STATE
Area: 755 sq km (292 sq miles)
Population: 1,708,528
Capital: HAMBURG

HESSEN (HESSE)

Status: STATE
Area: 21,114 sq km (8,152 sq miles)
Population: 6,016,251
Capital: WIESBADEN

MECKLENBURG-VORPOMMERN (MECKLENBURG-WEST POMERANIA)

Status: STATE
Area: 23,559 sq km (9,096 sq miles)
Population: 1,829,587
Capital: SCHWERIN

NIEDERSACHSEN (LOWER SAXONY)

Status: STATE
Area: 47,351 sq km (18,282 sq miles)
Population: 7,795,149
Capital: HANNOVER

NORDRHEIN-WESTFALEN (NORTH RHINE-WESTPHALIA)

Status: STATE
Area: 34,070 sq km (13,155 sq miles)
Population: 17,908,473
Capital: DÜSSELDORF

RHEINLAND-PFALZ (RHINELAND-PALATINATE)

Status: STATE
Area: 19,849 sq km (7,664 sq miles)
Population: 3,983,282
Capital: MAINZ

SAARLAND

Status: STATE
Area: 2,570 sq km (992 sq miles)
Population: 1,083,119
Capital: SAARBRÜCKEN

SACHSEN (SAXONY)

Status: STATE
Area: 18,341 sq km (7,081 sq miles)
Population: 4,557,210
Capital: DRESDEN

SACHSEN-ANHALT (SAXONY-ANHALT)

Status: STATE
Area: 20,607 sq km (7,956 sq miles)
Population: 2,731,463
Capital: MAGDEBURG

SCHLESWIG-HOLSTEIN

Status: STATE
Area: 15,731 sq km (6,074 sq miles)
Population: 2,730,595
Capital: KIEL

THÜRINGEN (THURINGIA)

Status: STATE
Area: 16,251 sq km (6,275 sq miles)
Population: 2,496,685
Capital: ERFURT

GHANA

Status: REPUBLIC
Area: 238,537 sq km (92,100 sq mls)
Population: 17,453,000
Capital: ACCRA
Language: ENGLISH (OFFICIAL), HAUSA, AKAN, LOCAL LANGUAGES
Religion: PROTESTANT, R.CATHOLIC, SUNNI MUSLIM, TRAD. BELIEFS
Currency: CEDI
Organizations: COMM., OAU, UN

MAP PAGE: 54

A WEST AFRICAN STATE on the Gulf of Guinea, Ghana is a land of plains and low plateaux covered with savannah and, in the west, rainforest. In the east is the Volta basin. The climate is tropical, with high rainfall in the south, where most people live. Ghana is a major producer of cocoa. Timber is also an important commodity. Bauxite, gold, diamonds and manganese ore are mined, and there are a number of industries around Tema.

GIBRALTAR

Status: UK TERRITORY
Area: 6.5 sq km (2.5 sq mls)
Population: 28,000
Capital: GIBRALTAR
Language: ENGLISH, SPANISH
Religion: R.CATHOLIC, PROTESTANT, SUNNI MUSLIM
Currency: POUND

MAP PAGE: 45

GIBRALTAR LIES ON the south coast of Spain at the western entrance to the Mediterranean Sea. The economy depends on tourism, offshore banking and entrepôt trade.

GREECE

Status: REPUBLIC
Area: 131,957 sq km (50,949 sq mls)
Population: 10,458,000
Capital: ATHENS
Language: GREEK, MACEDONIAN
Religion: GREEK ORTHODOX, SUNNI MUSLIM
Currency: DRACHMA
Organizations: EU, OECD, UN

MAP PAGE: 49

GREECE OCCUPIES THE southern part of the Balkan Peninsula of south Europe and many islands in the Ionian, Aegean and Mediterranean Seas. The islands make up over one fifth of its area. Mountains and hills cover much of the country. The most important lowlands are the plains of Thessaly in the centre-east and Salonica in the northeast. Summers are hot and dry. Winters are mild and wet, colder in the north with heavy snowfalls in the mountains. One third of Greeks live in the Athens area. Agriculture involves one quarter of the workforce and exports include citrus fruits, raisins, wine, olives and olive oil. A variety of ores and minerals are mined and a wide range of manufactures are produced including food and tobacco products, textiles, clothing, chemical products and metal products. Tourism is an important industry and there is a large services sector. Tourism, shipping and remittances from Greeks abroad are major foreign exchange earners. The war in former Yugoslavia and UN embargo on trade to Serbia have lost Greece an important market and regular trade route.

GREENLAND

Status: DANISH TERRITORY
Area: 2,175,600 sq km (840,004 sq mls)
Population: 58,000
Capital: NUUK
Language: GREENLANDIC, DANISH
Religion: PROTESTANT
Currency: DANISH KRONE

MAP PAGE: 63

SITUATED TO THE northeast of North America between the Atlantic and Arctic Oceans, Greenland is the largest island in the world. It has a polar climate and over 80 per cent of the land area is permanent ice-cap. The economy is based on fishing and fish processing.

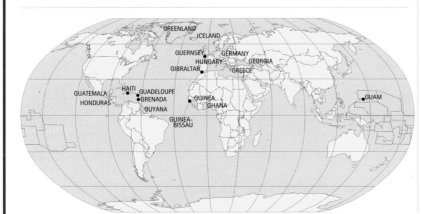

GRENADA

Status: MONARCHY
Area: 378 sq km (146 sq mls)
Population: 92,000
Capital: ST GEORGE'S
Language: ENGLISH, CREOLE
Religion: R.CATHOLIC, PROTESTANT
Currency: E. CARIB. DOLLAR
Organizations: CARICOM, COMM., UN

MAP PAGE: 83

THE CARIBBEAN STATE comprises Grenada, the most southerly of the Windward Islands, and the southern Grenadines. Grenada has wooded hills, beaches in the southwest, a warm climate and good rainfall. Agriculture is the main activity, with bananas, nutmeg and cocoa the main exports. Tourism and manufacturing are important. Grenada relies on grant aid.

GUADELOUPE

Status: FRENCH TERRITORY
Area: 1,780 sq km (687 sq mls)
Population: 428,000
Capital: BASSE TERRE
Language: FRENCH, FRENCH CREOLE
Religion: R.CATHOLIC, HINDU
Currency: FRENCH FRANC

MAP PAGE: 83

GUADELOUPE, IN THE Caribbean's Leeward group, consists of two main islands, Basse Terre and Grande Terre, connected by a bridge, and a few outer islands. The climate is tropical, but moderated by trade winds. Bananas, sugar and rum, tourism and French aid are the main sources of foreign exchange.

GUAM

Status: US TERRITORY
Area: 541 sq km (209 sq mls)
Population: 149,000
Capital: AGANA
Language: CHAMORRO, ENGLISH, TAGALOG
Religion: R.CATHOLIC
Currency: US DOLLAR

MAP PAGE: 25

LYING AT THE south end of the North Mariana Islands in the Western Pacific Ocean, Guam has a humid tropical climate. The island has a large US military base and the economy relies on that and tourism which is beginning to develop.

GUATEMALA

Status: REPUBLIC
Area: 108,890 sq km (42,043 sq mls)
Population: 10,621,000
Capital: GUATEMALA
Language: SPANISH, MAYAN LANGUAGES
Religion: R.CATHOLIC, PROTESTANT
Currency: QUETZAL
Organizations: UN

MAP PAGE: 82

THE MOST POPULOUS country in Central America after Mexico, Guatemala has a long Pacific and a short Caribbean coastline. Northern areas are lowland tropical forests. To the south lie mountain ranges with some active volcanoes, then the Pacific coastal plain. The climate is hot tropical in the lowlands, cooler in the highlands, where most people live. Farming is the main activity, coffee, sugar and bananas are the main exports. There is some mining and manufacturing (chiefly clothing and textiles). Tourism is important. Guerrilla activity is rife in certain areas.

GUERNSEY

Status: UK TERRITORY
Area: 78 sq km (30 sq mls)
Population: 64,000
Capital: ST PETER PORT
Language: ENGLISH, FRENCH
Religion: PROTESTANT, R.CATHOLIC
Currency: POUND

MAP PAGE: 44

ONE OF THE Channel Islands lying off the west coast of the Cherbourg peninsula in northern France.

GUINEA

Status: REPUBLIC
Area: 245,857 sq km (94,926 sq mls)
Population: 6,700,000
Capital: CONAKRY
Language: FRENCH, FULANI, MALINKE, LOCAL LANGUAGES
Religion: SUNNI MUSLIM, TRAD.BELIEFS, R.CATHOLIC
Currency: FRANC
Organizations: OAU, UN

MAP PAGE: 54

GUINEA IS IN west Africa, on the Atlantic Ocean. The coastal plains are lined with mangrove swamps. Inland are the Fouta Djallon mountains and plateaux. To the east are savannah plains drained by the upper Niger river system, while to the southeast are mountains. The climate is tropical, with high coastal rainfall. Agriculture is the main activity, with coffee, bananas and pineapples the chief cash crops. Bauxite, alumina, iron ore, gold and diamonds are the main exports, but Guinea relies upon foreign aid.

GUINEA-BISSAU

Status: REPUBLIC
Area: 36,125 sq km (13,948 sq mls)
Population: 1,073,000
Capital: BISSAU
Language: PORTUGUESE, PORTUGUESE CREOLE, LOCAL LANGUAGES
Religion: TRAD.BELIEFS, SUNNI MUSLIM, R.CATHOLIC
Currency: CFA FRANC
Organizations: OAU, UN

MAP PAGE: 54

GUINEA-BISSAU, ON THE Atlantic coast of west Africa, includes the Bijagos Archipelago. The mainland coast is swampy and contains many estuaries. Inland are forested plains and to the east are savannah plateaux. The climate is tropical. The economy is based mainly on subsistence farming. There is some fishing, but little industry. Forestry and mineral resources are largely unexploited. The main exports are cashews, groundnuts, oil palms and their products. Donors largely suspended support in 1991 because of payment arrears.

GUYANA

Status: REPUBLIC
Area: 214,969 sq km (83,000 sq mls)
Population: 835,000
Capital: GEORGETOWN
Language: ENGLISH, CREOLE, HINDI, AMERINDIAN LANGUAGES
Religion: PROTESTANT, HINDU, R.CATHOLIC, SUNNI MUSLIM
Currency: DOLLAR
Organizations: CARICOM, COMM., UN

MAP PAGE: 86-87

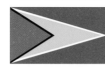

GUYANA, ON THE northeast coast of South America, consists of the densely forested highlands in the west, and the savannah uplands of the southwest. A lowland coastal belt supports crops and most of the population. The generally hot, humid and wet conditions are modified along the coast by sea breezes. The economy is based on agriculture, mining, forestry and fishing. Sugar, bauxite, gold and rice are the main exports. Other exports are shrimps and timber.

HAITI

Status: REPUBLIC
Area: 27,750 sq km (10,714 sq mls)
Population: 7,180,000
Capital: PORT-AU-PRINCE
Language: FRENCH, FRENCH CREOLE
Religion: R.CATHOLIC, PROTESTANT, VOODOO
Currency: GOURDE
Organizations: UN

MAP PAGE: 83

HAITI, OCCUPYING THE western third of the Caribbean island of Hispaniola, is a mountainous state, with small coastal plains and a central valley. The climate is tropical, hottest in coastal areas. Haiti has few natural resources, is overpopulated and relies on exports of local manufactures and coffee, and remittances from workers abroad. Political unrest and UN sanctions from 1991 to 1994 hit the economy badly.

HONDURAS

Status: REPUBLIC
Area: 112,088 sq km (43,277 sq mls)
Population: 5,953,000
Capital: TEGUCIGALPA
Language: SPANISH, AMERINDIAN LANGUAGES
Religion: R.CATHOLIC, PROTESTANT
Currency: LEMPIRA
Organizations: UN

MAP PAGE: 82-83

HONDURAS, IN CENTRAL America, is a mountainous and forested country with lowland areas along its long Caribbean and short Pacific coasts. Coastal areas are hot and humid with heavy summer rainfall, inland is cooler and drier. Most people live in the central valleys. Coffee and bananas are the main exports, along with shrimps, lead, zinc and timber. Industry involves mainly agricultural processing. Honduras depends on foreign aid.

HUNGARY

Status: REPUBLIC
Area: 93,030 sq km (35,919 sq mls)
Population: 10,225,000
Capital: BUDAPEST
Language: HUNGARIAN, ROMANY, GERMAN, SLOVAK
Religion: R.CATHOLIC, PROTESTANT
Currency: FORINT
Organizations: UN, OECD

MAP PAGE: 46-49

A LANDLOCKED COUNTRY in central Europe, Hungary borders Austria, Slovakia, Ukraine, Romania, Yugoslavia, Croatia and Slovenia. The Danube river flows north-south through central Hungary. To the east lies a great plain, flanked by highlands in the north. To the west low mountains and Lake Balaton separate a small plain and southern uplands. The climate is continental, with warm summers and cold winters. Rainfall is fairly evenly distributed thoughout the year. Half the population lives in urban areas, and one fifth lives in Budapest. Hungary has a predominantly industrial economy. The main industries produce metals, machinery, transport equipment (chiefly buses), textiles, chemicals and food products. Some minerals and energy reources are exploited, chiefly bauxite, coal and natural gas. Farming remains important, though output has fallen. Fruit, vegetables, cigarettes and wine are the main agricultural exports. Tourism is an important foreign exchange earner. Progress towards creating a market economy has been proved slow.

ICELAND

Status: REPUBLIC
Area: 102,820 sq km (39,699 sq mls)
Population: 269,000
Capital: REYKJAVIK
Language: ICELANDIC
Religion: PROTESTANT, R.CATHOLIC
Currency: KRÓNA
Organizations: OECD, UN

MAP PAGE: 36

THE NORTHWEST EUROPEAN island of Iceland lies in the Atlantic Ocean, near the Arctic Circle. It consists mainly of a plateau of basalt lava flows. Some of its 200 volcanoes are active, and there are geysers and hot springs, but one tenth of the country is covered by ice caps. Only coastal lowlands can be cultivated and settled, and over half the population lives in the Reykjavik area. The climate is fairly mild, moderated by the North Atlantic Drift and southwesterly winds. The mainstay of the economy is fishing and fish processing, which account for 80 per cent of exports. Agriculture involves mainly sheep and dairy farming. Iceland is self-sufficient in meat and dairy products, and exports wool and sheepskins. Diatomite is the only mineral resource but hydro-electric and geothermal energy resources are considerable. The main industries produce aluminium, ferro-silicon, electrical equipment, books, fertilizers, textiles and clothing. Tourism is growing in importance.

© Bartholomew

INDIA

Status: REPUBLIC
Area: 3,287,263 sq km (1,269,219 sq mls)
Population: 935,744,000
Capital: NEW DELHI
Language: HINDI, ENGLISH (OFFICIAL), MANY REGIONAL LANGUAGES
Religion: HINDU, SUNNI MUSLIM, SIKH, CHRISTIAN, BUDDHIST, JAIN
Currency: RUPEE
Organizations: COMM., UN

MAP PAGE: 14-15

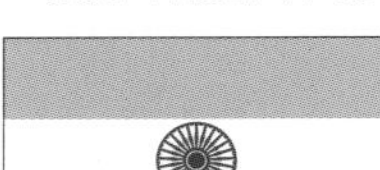

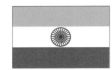

MOST OF THE South Asian state of India occupies a peninsula that juts out into the Indian Ocean between the Arabian Sea and Bay of Bengal. The heart of the peninsula is the Deccan plateau, bordered on either side by ranges of hills, the Western Ghats and the lower Eastern Ghats, which fall away to narrow coastal plains. To the north is a broad plain, drained by the Indus, Ganges and Brahmaputra rivers and their tributaries. The plain is intensively farmed and is the most populous region. In the west is the Thar Desert. The Himalayas form India's northern border, together with parts of the Karakoram and Hindu Kush ranges in the northwest. The climate shows marked seasonal variation: the hot season from March to June; the monsoon season from June to October; and the cold season from November to February. Rainfall ranges between heavy in the northeast Assam region and negligible in the Thar Desert, while temperatures range from very cold in the Himayalas to tropical heat over much of the south. India is among the ten largest economies in the world. It has achieved a high degree of self-sufficiency and its involvement in world trade is relatively small, though growing. Agriculture, forestry and fishing account for one third of national output and two thirds of employment. Much of the farming is on a subsistence basis and involves mainly rice and wheat growing. India is a major world producer of tea, sugar, jute, cotton and tobacco. Livestock is raised mainly for dairy products and hides. India has substantial reserves of coal, oil and natural gas and many minerals including iron, manganese and copper ores, bauxite, diamonds and gold. The manufacturing sector is large and diverse. The main manufactures are chemicals and chemical products, textiles, iron and steel, food products, electrical goods and transport equipment. The main exports are diamonds, clothing, chemicals and chemical products, textiles, leather and leather goods, iron ore, fish products, electronic goods and tea. However, with a huge population - the second largest in the world - India receives foreign aid to support its balance of payments.

INDONESIA

Status: REPUBLIC
Area: 1,919,445 sq km (741,102 sq mls)
Population: 194,564,000
Capital: JAKARTA
Language: INDONESIAN (OFFICIAL), MANY LOCAL LANGUAGES
Religion: SUNNI MUSLIM, PROTESTANT, R.CATHOLIC, HINDU, BUDDHIST
Currency: RUPIAH
Organizations: ASEAN, OPEC, UN

MAP PAGE: 25

INDONESIA, THE LARGEST and most populous country in southeast Asia, consists of 13,677 islands extending along the Equator between the Pacific and Indian oceans. Sumatra, Java, Sulawesi, Kalimantan (two thirds of Borneo) and Irian Jaya (western New Guinea) make up 90 per cent of the land area. Most of Indonesia is mountainous and covered with rainforest or mangrove swamps, and there are over 300 volcanoes, some still active. Two thirds of the population live in the lowland areas of Java and Madura. In general the climate is tropical monsoon. Indonesia is rich in energy resources, minerals, forests and fertile soil. It is among the world's top producers of rice, palm oil, tea, coffee, rubber and tobacco. It is the world's leading exporter of natural gas and a major exporter of oil and timber. In recent years manufacturing output has risen. A range of goods are produced including textiles, clothing, cement, fertilizer and vehicles. Tourism has also increased. However, given its huge population, Indonesia remains a relatively poor country.

IRAN

Status: REPUBLIC
Area: 1,648,000 sq km (636,296 sq mls)
Population: 67,283,000
Capital: TEHRĀN
Language: FARSI (PERSIAN), AZERI, KURDISH, REGIONAL LANGUAGES
Religion: SHI'A MUSLIM, SUNNI MUSLIM, BAHA'I, CHRISTIAN, ZOROASTRIAN
Currency: RIAL
Organizations: OPEC, UN

MAP PAGE: 18-19

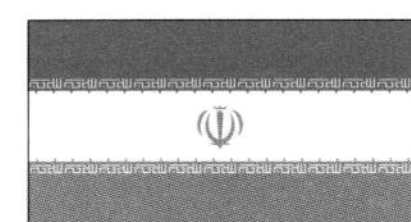

IRAN IS IN southwest Asia, on The Gulf, the Gulf of Oman and Caspian Sea. Eastern Iran is high plateaux country, with large salt pans and a vast sand desert. In the west the Zagros Mountains form a series of ridges, while to the north lie the Elburz Mountains. Most farming and settlement is on the narrow plain along the Caspian Sea and the foothills of the north and west. The climate is one of extremes, with hot summers and very cold winters. Most of the light rainfall is in the winter months. Agriculture involves one quarter of the workforce. Wheat is the main crop but fruit (chiefly dates) and pistachio nuts are grown for export. Fishing in the Caspian Sea is important and caviar is exported. Petroleum (the main export) and natural gas are Iran's leading natural resources. There are also reserves of coal, iron ore, copper ore and other minerals. Manufactures include carpets, clothing, food products, construction materials, chemicals, vehicles, leather goods and metal products. The 1979 revolution and 1980-88 war with Iraq slowed economic development.

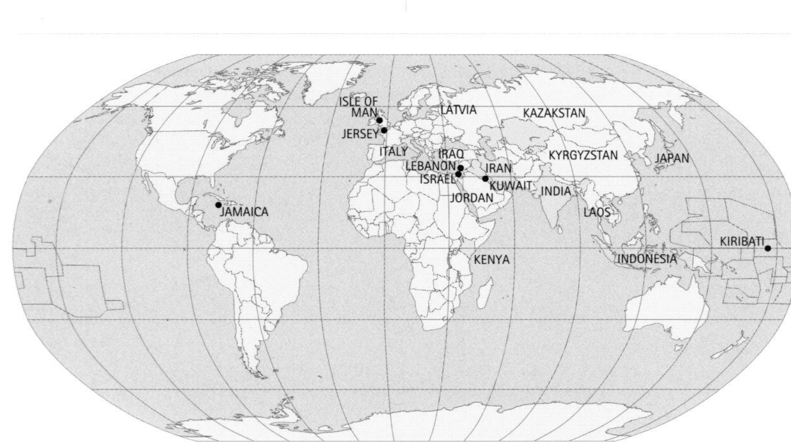

IRAQ

Status: REPUBLIC
Area: 438,317 sq km (169,235 sq mls)
Population: 20,449,000
Capital: BAGHDĀD
Language: ARABIC, KURDISH, TURKMEN
Religion: SHI'A MUSLIM, SUNNI MUSLIM, R.CATHOLIC
Currency: DINAR
Organizations: OPEC, UN

MAP PAGE: 17

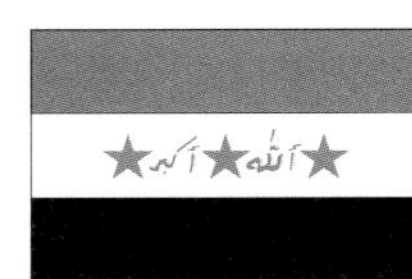

IRAQ, WHICH LIES on the northwest shores of The Gulf in southwest Asia, has at its heart the lowland valley of the Tigris and Euphrates rivers. In the southeast where the two rivers join are marshes and the Shatt al Arab waterway. Northern Iraq is hilly, rising to the Zagros Mountains, while western Iraq is desert. Summers are hot and dry, while winters are mild with light though unreliable rainfall. The Tigris-Euphrates valley contains most of the arable land and population, including one in five who live in Baghdad. One third of the workforce is involved in agriculture, with dates, cotton, wool, hides and skins exported in normal times. However, the 1980-88 war with Iran, defeat in the 1991 Gulf war and international sanctions have ruined the economy and caused considerable hardship. Petroleum and natural gas sales, which had accounted for 98 per cent of export earnings, were severely restricted. Much of the infrastructure was dam aged and industrial output - which had included petroleum products, cement, steel, textiles, bitumen and pharmaceuticals - was reduced.

ISLE OF MAN

Status: UK TERRITORY
Area: 572 sq km (221 sq mls)
Population: 72 ,000
Capital: DOUGLAS
Language: ENGLISH
Religion: PROTESTANT, R.CATHOLIC
Currency: POUND

MAP PAGE: 38

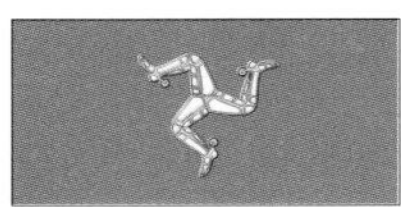

ISRAEL

Status: REPUBLIC
Area: 20,770 sq km (8,019 sq mls)
Population: 5,545,000
Capital: JERUSALEM
Language: HEBREW, ARABIC, YIDDISH, ENGLISH, RUSSIAN
Religion: JEWISH, SUNNI MUSLIM, CHRISTIAN, DRUZE
Currency: SHEKEL
Organizations: UN

MAP PAGE: 16

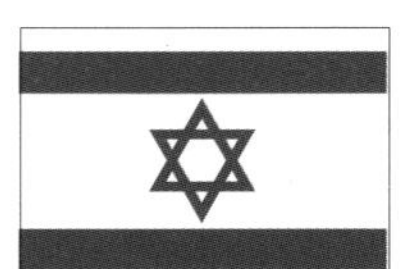

ISRAEL LIES ON the Mediterranean coast of southwest Asia. Beyond the coastal plain of Sharon are the hills and valleys of Judea and Samaria with the Galilee highlands to the north. In the east is the rift valley, which extends from Lake Tiberias to the Gulf of Aqaba and contains the Jordan river and Dead Sea. In the south is the Negev, a triangular semi-desert plateau. Most people live on the coastal plain or in northern and central areas. Much of Israel has warm summers and mild winters, during which most rain falls. Southern Israel is hot and dry. Agricultural production was boosted by the inclusion of the West Bank of the Jordan in 1967. Citrus fruit, vegetables and flowers are exported. Mineral resources are few but potash, bromine and some oil and gas are produced. Manufacturing makes the largest contribution to the economy. Israel produces finished diamonds, textiles, clothing and food products as well as chemical and metal products, military and transport equipment, electrical and electronic goods. Tourism and foreign aid are important to the economy.

ITALY

Status: REPUBLIC
Area: 301,245 sq km (116,311 sq mls)
Population: 57,187,000
Capital: ROME
Language: ITALIAN, ITALIAN DIALECTS
Religion: R.CATHOLIC
Currency: LIRA
Organizations: EU, OECD, UN

MAP PAGE: 48

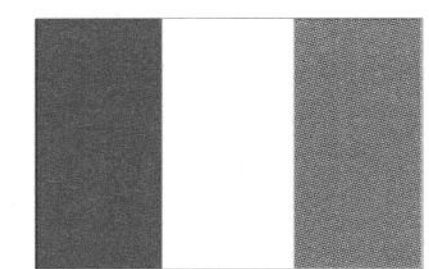

MOST OF THE south European state of Italy occupies a peninsula that juts out into the Mediterranean Sea. It includes the main islands of Sicily and Sardinia and about 70 smaller islands in the surrounding seas. Italy is mountainous and dominated by two high ranges: the Alps, which form its northern border; and the Apennines, which run almost the full length of the peninsula. Many of Italy's mountains are of volcanic origin and its two active volcanoes are Vesuvius near Naples and Etna on Sicily. The main lowland area is the Po river valley in the northeast, which is the main agricultural and industrial area and is the most populous region. Italy has a Mediterranean climate with warm, dry summers and mild winters. Sicily and Sardinia are warmer and drier than the mainland. Northern Italy experiences colder, wetter winters, with heavy snow in the Alps. Italy's natural resources are limited. Only about 20 per cent of the land is suitable for cultivation. Some oil, natural gas and coal are produced, but most fuels and minerals used by industry must be imported. Italy has a fairly diversified economy. Agriculture flourishes, with cereals, wine, fruit (including olives) and vegetables the main crops. Italy is the world's largest wine producer. Cheese is also an important product. However, Italy is a net food importer. The north is the centre of Italian industry, especially around Turin, Milan and Genoa, while the south is largely agricultural with production based on smaller, less mechanized farms. Thus average income in the north is much higher than that in the south. Another feature of the Italian economy is the size of the state sector, which is much larger than that of other European Union countries. Italy's leading manufactures include industrial and office equipment, domestic appliances, cars, textiles, clothing, leather goods, chemicals and metal products and its famous brand names include Olivetti, Fiat and Benetton. Italy has a strong service sector. With over 25 million visitors a year, tourism is a major employer and accounts for 5 per cent of national income. Finance and banking are also important.

JAMAICA

Status: MONARCHY
Area: 10,991 sq km (4,244 sq mls)
Population: 2,530,000
Capital: KINGSTON
Language: ENGLISH, CREOLE
Religion: PROTESTANT, R.CATHOLIC, RASTAFARIAN
Currency: DOLLAR
Organizations: CARICOM, COMM., UN

MAP PAGE: 83

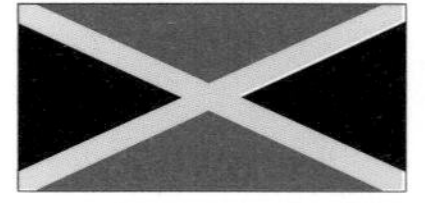

JAMAICA, THE THIRD largest Caribbean island, has beaches and densely populated coastal plains traversed by hills and plateaux rising to the forested Blue Mountains in the east. The climate is tropical, cooler and wetter on high ground. The economy is based on tourism, agriculture, mining and light manufacturing. Bauxite, alumina, sugar and bananas are the main exports. Jamaica depends on foreign aid.

JAPAN

Status: MONARCHY
Area: 377,727 sq km (145,841 sq mls)
Population: 125,197,000
Capital: TŌKYŌ
Language: JAPANESE
Religion: SHINTOIST, BUDDHIST, CHRISTIAN
Currency: YEN
Organizations: OECD, UN

MAP PAGE: 28-29

JAPAN, WHICH LIES in the Pacific Ocean off the coast of east Asia, consists of four main islands - Hokkaido, Honshu, Shikoku and Kyushu - which extend northeast-southwest over 1,600 km (995 miles). It includes more than 3,000 smaller volcanic islands in the surrounding Sea of Japan, East China Sea and Pacific Ocean. The central island of Honshu occupies 60 per cent of the total land area and contains 80 per cent of the population, mostly in the east-central Kanto plain which includes Tokyo, Kawasaki and Yokohama. Behind the long and deeply indented coastline, nearly three quarters of Japan is mountainous and heavily forested. The most rugged range crosses Honshu and includes the country's highest point, Mount Fuji, which reaches a height of 3,776 m (12,388 ft). Japan has over 60 active volcanoes, and is subject to frequent major earthquakes, monsoons, typhoons and tidal waves. The climate is generally temperate maritime, with warm summers and mild winters, except in western Hokkaido and northwest Honshu, where the winters are very cold with heavy snow. Rain falls mainly in June and July, and typhoons sometimes occur in September. Japan has few natural resources. It has a limited land area of which only 14 per cent is suitable for cultivation, and production of its few industrial raw materials (chiefly coal, oil, natural gas and copper) is insufficient for its industry. Most raw materials must be imported, including about 90 per cent of energy requirements. Yet, in a fairly short space of time, Japan has become the world's second largest industrial economy. Its economic success is based on manufacturing, which employs one third of the workforce and accounts for one third of national output. Japan has a range of heavy and light industries centred mainly round the major ports of Yokohama, Osaka and Tokyo. It is the world's largest manufacturer of cars, motorcycles and merchant ships, and a major producer of steel, textiles, chemicals and cement. It is a leading producer of many consumer durables, such as washing machines, and electronic equipment, chiefly office equipment and computers. Recent years have seen the spread of Japanese business overseas, with many industrial plants sited in the European Union and the USA. Japan has a strong service sector, banking and finance are particularly important and Tokyo is one of the world's major stock exchanges. Owing to intensive agricultural production, Japan is 70 per cent self-sufficient in food. The main food crops are rice, barley, fruit, wheat and soya beans. Livestock raising (chiefly cattle, pigs and chickens) and fishing are also important. Japan has one of the largest fishing fleets in the world. In spite of its forestry resources, Japan has to import timber as well as food.

JERSEY

Status: UK TERRITORY
Area: 116 sq km (45 sq mls)
Population: 87,000
Capital: ST HELIER
Language: ENGLISH, FRENCH
Religion: PROTESTANT, R.CATHOLIC
Currency: POUND

MAP PAGE: 44

ONE OF THE Channel Islands lying off the west coast of the Cherbourg peninsula in northern France.

JORDAN

Status: MONARCHY
Area: 89,206 sq km (34,443 sq mls)
Population: 5,439,000
Capital: 'AMMĀN
Language: ARABIC
Religion: SUNNI MUSLIM, CHRISTIAN, SHI'A MUSLIM
Currency: DINAR
Organizations: UN

MAP PAGE: 16-17

JORDAN, IN SOUTHWEST Asia, has a short coastline on the Gulf of Aqaba. Much of Jordan is rocky desert plateaux. In the west, behind a belt of hills, the land falls below sea level to the Dead Sea and Jordan river. Much of Jordan is hot and dry, the west is cooler and wetter and most people live in the northwest. Phosphates, potash, fertilizers, pharmaceuticals, fruit and vegetables are the main exports. Jordan relies upon tourism, workers' remittances and foreign aid, all of which were affected by the 1991 Gulf crisis.

KAZAKSTAN

Status: REPUBLIC
Area: 2,717,300 sq km (1,049,155 sq mls)
Population: 16,590,000
Capital: ALMATY
Language: KAZAKH, RUSSIAN, GERMAN, UKRAINIAN, UZBEK, TATAR
Religion: SUNNI MUSLIM, RUSSIAN ORTHODOX, PROTESTANT
Currency: TANGA
Organizations: CIS, UN

MAP PAGE: 12

STRETCHING ACROSS CENTRAL Asia, Kazakstan covers a vast area of steppe land and semi-desert. The land is flat in the west rising to mountains in the southeast. The climate is continental and mainly dry. Agriculture and livestock rearing are the main activities, with cotton and tobacco the main cash crops. Kazakstan is very rich in minerals, such as oil, natural gas, coal, iron ore, chromium, gold, lead and zinc. Mining, metallurgy, machine building and food processing are major industries.

KENYA

Status: REPUBLIC
Area: 582,646 sq km (224,961 sq mls)
Population: 30,522,000
Capital: NAIROBI
Language: SWAHILI (OFFICIAL), ENGLISH, MANY LOCAL LANGUAGES
Religion: R.CATHOLIC, PROTESTANT, TRAD.BELIEFS
Currency: SHILLING
Organizations: COMM., OAU, UN

MAP PAGE: 56

KENYA IS IN east Africa, on the Indian Ocean. Beyond the coastal plains the land rises to plateaux interrupted by volcanic mountains. The Rift Valley runs northwest of Nairobi to Lake Turkana. Most people live in central Kenya. Conditions are tropical on the coast, semi-desert in the north and savannah in the south. Agricultural products, chiefly tea and coffee, provide half export earnings. Light industry is important. Tourism is the main foreign exchange earner; oil refining and re-exports for landlocked neighbours are others.

KIRIBATI

Status: REPUBLIC
Area: 717 sq km (277 sq mls)
Population: 79,000
Capital: BAIRIKI
Language: I-KIRIBATI (GILBERTESE), ENGLISH
Religion: R.CATHOLIC, PROTESTANT, BAHA'I, MORMON
Currency: AUSTR. DOLLAR
Organizations: COMM.

MAP PAGE: 7

KIRIBATI COMPRISES 32 coral islands in the Gilbert, Phoenix and Line groups and the volcanic island of Banaba, which straddle the Equator in the Pacific Ocean. Most people live on the Gilbert islands, and the capital, Bairiki, is on Tarawa, one of the Gilbert Islands. The climate is hot, wetter in the north. Kiribati depends on subsistence farming and fishing. Copra and fish exports and licences for foreign fishing fleets are the main foreign exchange earners.

KUWAIT

Status: MONARCHY
Area: 17,818 sq km (6,880 sq mls)
Population: 1,691,000
Capital: KUWAIT
Language: ARABIC
Religion: SUNNI MUSLIM, SHI'A MUSLIM, OTHER MUSLIM, CHRISTIAN, HINDU
Currency: DINAR
Organizations: OPEC, UN

MAP PAGE: 17

KUWAIT LIES ON the northwest shores of The Gulf in southwest Asia. It is mainly low-lying desert, with irrigated areas along the Bay of Kuwait where most people live. Summers are hot and dry, winters are cool with some rainfall. The oil industry, which accounts for 80 per cent of exports, has largely recovered from the damage caused by Iraq in 1991. Income is also derived from extensive overseas investments.

KYRGYZSTAN

Status: REPUBLIC
Area: 198,500 sq km (76,641 sq mls)
Population: 4,668,000
Capital: BISHKEK
Language: KIRGHIZ, RUSSIAN, UZBEK
Religion: SUNNI MUSLIM, RUSSIAN ORTHODOX
Currency: SOM
Organizations: CIS, UN

MAP PAGE: 14-15

A LANDLOCKED CENTRAL Asian state, Kyrgyzstan is rugged and mountainous, lying in the western Tien Shan range. Most people live in the valleys of the north and west. Summers are hot and winters cold. Agriculture (chiefly livestock farming) is the main activity. Coal, gold, antimony and mercury are produced. Manufactures include machinery, metals and food products. Disruption of Russian-dominated trade has caused economic problems.

LAOS

Status: REPUBLIC
Area: 236,800 sq km (91,429 sq mls)
Population: 4,882,000
Capital: VIENTIANE
Language: LAO, LOCAL LANGUAGES
Religion: BUDDHIST, TRAD.BELIEFS, R.CATHOLIC, SUNNI MUSLIM
Currency: KIP
Organizations: UN

MAP PAGE: 25

A LANDLOCKED COUNTRY in southeast Asia, Laos borders Vietnam, Cambodia, Thailand, Myanmar and China. Forested mountains and plateaux predominate. The climate is tropical monsoon. Most people live in the Mekong valley and the low plateau in the south, and grow food crops, chiefly rice. Electricity, timber, coffee and tin are exported. Foreign aid and investment and the opium trade are important.

LATVIA

Status: REPUBLIC
Area: 63,700 sq km (24,595 sq mls)
Population: 2,515,000
Capital: RĪGA
Language: LATVIAN, RUSSIAN
Religion: PROTESTANT, R.CATHOLIC, RUSSIAN ORTHODOX
Currency: LAT
Organizations: UN

MAP PAGE: 37

LATVIA IS IN north Europe, on the Baltic Sea and Gulf of Riga. The land is flat near the coast but hilly with woods and lakes inland. Latvia has a modified continental climate. One third of the people live in Riga. Crop and livestock farming are important. Industry is varied but specialist products include telephones, diesel trains, buses and paper. Latvia has few natural resources. Economic priorities are creating a market economy and reducing economic dependence on Russia.

LEBANON

Status: REPUBLIC
Area: 10,452 sq km (4,036 sq mls)
Population: 3,009,000
Capital: BEIRUT
Language: ARABIC, FRENCH, ARMENIAN
Religion: SHI'A, SUNNI AND OTHER MUSLIM, PROTESTANT, R.CATHOLIC
Currency: POUND
Organizations: UN

MAP PAGE: 16

LEBANON LIES ON the Mediterranean coast of southwest Asia. Beyond the coastal strip, where most people live, are two parallel mountain ranges, separated by the Bekaa Valley. In general the climate is Mediterranean. Civil war crippled the traditional sectors of banking, commerce and tourism, but some fruit production and light industry survived. Reconstruction is under way.

© Bartholomew

LESOTHO
Status: MONARCHY
Area: 30,355 sq km (11,720 sq mls)
Population: 2,050,000
Capital: MASERU
Language: SESOTHO, ENGLISH, ZULU
Religion: R.CATHOLIC, PROTESTANT, TRAD.BELIEFS
Currency: LOTI
Organizations: COMM., OAU, SADC, UN

MAP PAGE: 59

LESOTHO IS A landlocked state surrounded by the Republic of South Africa. It is a mountainous country lying within the Drakensberg range. Most people live in the western lowlands and southern Orange and Caledon river valleys. In general Lesotho has hot moist summers and cool, dry winters, with lower temperatures in the mountains. Subsistence farming and herding are the main activities. Exports include livestock, vegetables, wool and mohair. The economy depends heavily on South Africa for transport links and employment.

LIBERIA
Status: REPUBLIC
Area: 111,369 sq km (43,000 sq mls)
Population: 2,760,000
Capital: MONROVIA
Language: ENGLISH, CREOLE, MANY LOCAL LANGUAGES
Religion: TRAD. BELIEFS, SUNNI MUSLIM, PROTESTANT, R.CATHOLIC
Currency: DOLLAR
Organizations: OAU, UN

MAP PAGE: 54

LIBERIA IS ON the Atlantic coast of west Africa. Beyond the coastal belt of sandy beaches and mangrove swamps the land rises to a forested plateau, with highlands along the Guinea border. A quarter of the population lives along the coast. The climate is hot with heavy rainfall. The 1989-93 civil war ruined the economy. Before the war exports included iron ore, diamonds and gold along with rubber, timber and coffee. Ship registration was a major foreign exchange earner. Liberia now relies on foreign aid.

LIBYA
Status: REPUBLIC
Area: 1,759,540 sq km (679,362 sq mls)
Population: 5,407,000
Capital: TRIPOLI
Language: ARABIC, BERBER
Religion: SUNNI MUSLIM, R.CATHOLIC
Currency: DINAR
Organizations: OAU, OPEC, UN

MAP PAGE: 54-55

LIBYA LIES ON the Mediterranean coast of north Africa. The desert plains and hills of

the Sahara dominate the landscape and the climate is hot and dry. Most people live in cities near the coast, where the climate is cooler with moderate rainfall. Farming and herding, chiefly in the northwest, are important but the main industry is oil, which accounts for about 95 per cent of export earnings. There is some heavy industry. In 1993 the UN imposed economic sanctions because of alleged sponsorship of terrorism.

LIECHTENSTEIN
Status: MONARCHY
Area: 160 sq km (62 sq mls)
Population: 31,000
Capital: VADUZ
Language: GERMAN
Religion: R.CATHOLIC, PROTESTANT
Currency: SWISS FRANC
Organizations: UN

MAP PAGE: 46

A LANDLOCKED STATE between Switzerland and Austria in central Europe, Liechtenstein occupies the floodplains of the upper Rhine valley and part of the Austrian Alps. It has a temperate climate with cool winters. Dairy farming is important, but manufacturing is dominant. Major products include precision instruments, dentistry equipment, pharmaceuticals, ceramics and textiles. There is also some metal working. Finance, chiefly banking, is very important. Tourism and postal stamps provide additional revenue.

LITHUANIA
Status: REPUBLIC
Area: 65,200 sq km (25,174 sq mls)
Population: 3,715,000
Capital: VILNIUS
Language: LITHUANIAN, RUSSIAN, POLISH
Religion: R.CATHOLIC, PROTESTANT, RUSSIAN ORTHODOX
Currency: LITAS
Organizations: UN

MAP PAGE: 37

LITHUANIA IS IN north Europe, on the eastern shores of the Baltic Sea. It is mainly lowland with many lakes, small rivers and marshes. The climate is generally temperate. About 15 per cent of people live in Vilnius. Agriculture, fishing and forestry are important, but manufacturing dominates the economy. The main products are processed foods, light industrial goods, machinery and metalworking equipment. Progress towards a market economy is slow. The economy remains heavily dependent on Russia.

LUXEMBOURG
Status: MONARCHY
Area: 2,586 sq km (998 sq mls)
Population: 410,000
Capital: LUXEMBOURG
Language: LETZEBURGISH, GERMAN, FRENCH, PORTUGUESE
Religion: R.CATHOLIC, PROTESTANT
Currency: FRANC
Organizations: EU, OECD, UN

MAP PAGE: 42

LUXEMBOURG, A LANDLOCKED country in west Europe, borders Belgium, France and Germany. The hills and forests of the Ardennes dominate the north, with rolling pasture to the south, where the main towns, farms and industries are found. Summers are warm and winters mild, though colder in the north. The iron and steel industry is still important, but light industries (including textiles, chemicals and food products) are growing. Luxembourg is a major banking centre and the home base of key European Union institutions.

MACAU
Status: PORTUGUESE TERRITORY
Area: 17 sq km (7 sq mls)
Population: 418,000
Capital: MACAU
Language: CANTONESE, PORTUGUESE
Religion: BUDDHIST, R.CATHOLIC, PROTESTANT
Currency: PATACA

MAP PAGE: 27

AN ENCLAVE ON the south coast of China, Macau consists of an area of the mainland and the two islands of Taipa and Coloane. The territory is scheduled to revert to China in 1999.

MADAGASCAR
Status: REPUBLIC
Area: 587,041 sq km (226,658 sq mls)
Population: 14,763,000
Capital: ANTANANARIVO
Language: MALAGASY, FRENCH
Religion: TRAD.BELIEFS, R.CATHOLIC, PROTESTANT, SUNNI MUSLIM
Currency: FRANC
Organizations: OAU, UN

MAP PAGE: 57

MADAGASCAR AND ADJACENT islets lie off the east coast of south Africa. The world's fourth largest island is in the main a high plateau with a coastal strip to the east and scrubby plain to the west. The climate is tropical with heavy rainfall in the north and east. Most people live on the plateau. Exports include coffee, vanilla, cloves, sugar and shrimps. The main industries are agricultural processing, textile manufacturing, oil refining and mining (chiefly chromite). Tourism and foreign aid are important.

MADEIRA
Status: PORTUGUESE TERRITORY
Area: 794 sq km (307 sq mls)
Population: 253,000
Capital: FUNCHAL
Language: PORTUGUESE
Religion: R.CATHOLIC, PROTESTANT
Currency: PORT. ESCUDO

MAP PAGE: 54

AN ISLAND GROUP in the Atlantic Ocean to the southwest of Portugal. Tourism is important to the economy.

MALAWI
Status: REPUBLIC
Area: 118,484 sq km (45,747 sq mls)
Population: 9,788,000
Capital: LILONGWE
Language: CHICHEWA, ENGLISH, LOMWE
Religion: PROTESTANT, R.CATHOLIC, TRAD. BELIEFS, SUNNI MUSLIM
Currency: KWACHA
Organizations: COMM., OAU, SADC, UN

MAP PAGE: 57

LANDLOCKED MALAWI IN central Africa is a narrow hilly country at the southern end of the East African Rift Valley. One fifth of the country is covered by Lake Malawi, which lies above sea level. Most people live in the southern regions. The climate is mainly subtropical with varying rainfall. The economy is predominantly agricultural. Tobacco, tea and sugar are the main exports. Manufacturing involves mainly chemicals, textiles and agricultural products. Malawi relies heavily on foreign aid.

MALAYSIA
Status: FEDERATION
Area: 332,665 sq km (128,442 sq mls)
Population: 20,140,000
Capital: KUALA LUMPUR
Language: MALAY, ENGLISH, CHINESE, TAMIL, LOCAL LANGUAGES
Religion: SUNNI MUSLIM, BUDDHIST, HINDU, CHRISTIAN, TRAD. BELIEFS
Currency: DOLLAR (RINGGIT)
Organizations: ASEAN, COMM., UN

MAP PAGE: 33

THE FEDERATION OF Malaysia, in southeast Asia, comprises two regions, separated by the South China Sea. Peninsular Malaysia occupies the southern Malay peninsula, which has a chain of mountains dividing the eastern coastal strip from the wider plains to the west. To the east, the states of Sabah and Sarawak in the north of the island of Borneo are mainly rainforest-covered hills and mountains with mangrove swamps along the coast. Both regions have a tropical climate with heavy rainfall. About 80 per cent of the population lives in Peninsular Malaysia, mainly on the coasts. The country is rich in natural resources. It is the world's largest producer of tin, palm oil, pepper and tropical hardwoods, and a major producer of natural rubber, coconut and cocoa. It also has vast reserves of minerals and fuels. However high economic growth in recent years has come from manufacturing which now provides most exports and involves mainly processing industries, electronics assembly and engineering (chiefly car production). With over 7 million visitors a year, tourism is also a major industry.

PENINSULAR MALAYSIA
Status: DIVISION
Area: 131,585 sq km (50,805 sq mls)
Population: 14,942,697
Capital: KUALA LUMPUR

SABAH
Status: STATE
Area: 76,115 sq km (29,388 sq mls)
Population: 1,583,726
Capital: KOTA KINABALU

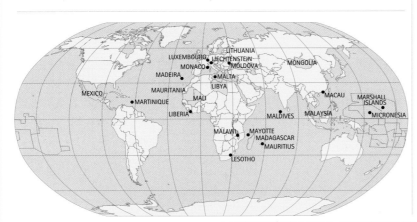

SARAWAK

Status: STATE
Area: 124,965 sq km (48,249 sq mls)
Population: 1,708,737
Capital: KUCHING

MALDIVES

Status: REPUBLIC
Area: 298 sq km (115 sq mls)
Population: 254,000
Capital: MALE
Language: DIVEHI (MALDIVIAN)
Religion: SUNNI MUSLIM
Currency: RUFIYAA
Organizations: COMM., UN

MAP PAGE: 15

THE MALDIVE ARCHIPELAGO comprises 1,190 coral atolls (202 of which are inhabited), in the Indian Ocean, southwest of India. The climate is hot, humid and monsoonal. The islands depend mainly on fishing and fish processing, light manufacturing (chiefly clothing) and tourism.

MALI

Status: REPUBLIC
Area: 1,240,140 sq km (478,821 sq mls)
Population: 10,795,000
Capital: BAMAKO
Language: FRENCH, BAMBARA, MANY LOCAL LANGUAGES
Religion: SUNNI MUSLIM, TRAD.BELIEFS, R.CATHOLIC
Currency: CFA FRANC
Organizations: OAU, UN

MAP PAGE: 54

A LANDLOCKED STATE in west Africa, Mali is low-lying, rising to mountains in the northeast. Northern regions lie within the Sahara desert. To the south, around the Niger river, are marshes and savannah grassland. Rainfall is unreliable. Most people live along the Niger and Senegal rivers. Exports include cotton and groundnuts. Some gold is produced. Mali relies heavily on foreign aid.

MALTA

Status: REPUBLIC
Area: 316 sq km (122 sq mls)
Population: 371,000
Capital: VALLETTA
Language: MALTESE, ENGLISH
Religion: R.CATHOLIC
Currency: LIRA
Organizations: COMM., UN

MAP PAGE: 48

THE ISLANDS OF Malta and Gozo lie in the Mediterranean Sea, off the coast of south Italy. Malta, the main island, has low hills and an indented coastline. Two thirds of the population lives in the Valletta area. The islands have hot, dry summers and mild winters. The main industries are tourism, ship building and repair, and export manufacturing (chiefly clothing). Vegetables, flowers, wine and tobacco are also exported.

MARSHALL ISLANDS

Status: REPUBLIC
Area: 181 sq km (70 sq mls)
Population: 56,000
Capital: DALAP-ULIGA-DARRIT

Language: MARSHALLESE, ENGLISH
Religion: PROTESTANT, R.CATHOLIC
Currency: US DOLLAR
Organizations: UN

MAP PAGE: 4

THE MARSHALL ISLANDS consist of over 1,000 atolls, islands and islets, within two chains, in the North Pacific Ocean. The main atolls are Majuro (home to half the population), Kwajalein, Jaluit, Enewetak and Bikini. The climate is tropical with heavy autumn rainfall. The islands depend on farming, fishing, tourism, financial services, and US aid and rent for a missile base.

MARTINIQUE

Status: FRENCH TERRITORY
Area: 1,079 sq km (417 sq mls)
Population: 379,000
Capital: FORT-DE-FRANCE
Language: FRENCH, FRENCH CREOLE
Religion: R.CATHOLIC, PROTESTANT, HINDU, TRAD.BELIEFS
Currency: FRENCH FRANC

MAP PAGE: 83

MARTINIQUE, ONE OF the Caribbean's Windward Islands, has volcanic peaks in the north, a populous central plain, and hills and beaches in the south. The tropical island depends on fruit growing (chiefly bananas), oil refining, rum distilling, tourism and French aid.

MAURITANIA

Status: REPUBLIC
Area: 1,030,700 sq km (397,955 sq mls)
Population: 2,284,000
Capital: NOUAKCHOTT
Language: ARABIC, FRENCH, LOCAL LANGUAGES
Religion: SUNNI MUSLIM
Currency: OUGUIYA
Organizations: OAU, UN

MAP PAGE: 54

MAURITANIA IS ON the Atlantic coast of northwest Africa and lies almost entirely within the Sahara desert. Oases and a fertile strip along the Senegal river to the south are the only areas suitable for cultivation. The climate is generally hot and dry. A quarter of Mauritanians live in Nouakchott. Livestock rearing and subsistence farming are important. The economy is heavily dependent on iron ore mining and fishing, which together account for 90 per cent of export earnings, and foreign aid.

MAURITIUS

Status: REPUBLIC
Area: 2,040 sq km (788 sq mls)
Population: 1,122,000
Capital: PORT LOUIS
Language: ENGLISH, FRENCH CREOLE, HINDI, INDIAN LANGUAGES
Religion: HINDU, R.CATHOLIC, SUNNI MUSLIM, PROTESTANT
Currency: RUPEE
Organizations: COMM., OAU, UN, SADC

MAP PAGE: 53

THE STATE COMPRISES Mauritius, Rodrigues and some 20 small islands in the Indian Ocean, east of Madagascar. The main island of Mauritius is volcanic in origin and has a coral coast rising to a central plateau. Most people live on the west side of the island. The climate is warm and humid. Mauritius depends mainly on sugar production, light manufacturing (chiefly clothing) and tourism.

MAYOTTE

Status: FRENCH TERRITORY
Area: 373 sq km (144 sq mls)
Population: 110,000
Capital: DZAOUDZI
Language: MAHORIAN (SWAHILI), FRENCH
Religion: SUNNI MUSLIM, R.CATHOLIC
Currency: FRENCH FRANC

MAP PAGE: 57

LYING IN THE Indian Ocean off the east coast of Central Africa, Mayotte is part of the Comoros Archipelago, but remains a French Territory.

MEXICO

Status: REPUBLIC
Area: 1,972,545 sq km (761,604 sq mls)
Population: 90,487,000
Capital: MÉXICO
Language: SPANISH, MANY AMERINDIAN LANGUAGES
Religion: R.CATHOLIC, PROTESTANT
Currency: PESO
Organizations: NAFTA, OECD, UN

MAP PAGE: 82

THE LARGEST COUNTRY in central America, Mexico extends southwards from the USA to Guatemala and Belize, and from the Pacific Ocean to the Gulf of Mexico. The greater part of the country is high plateaux flanked by the western and eastern Sierra Madre mountain ranges. The principal lowland is the Yucatán peninsula in the southeast. The climate varies with latitude and altitude: hot and humid in the lowlands, warm in the plateaux and cool with cold winters in the mountains. The north is arid, while the far south has heavy rainfall. Mexico City is one of the world's largest conurbations and the centre of trade and industry. Agriculture involves a quarter of the workforce and exports include coffee, fruit and vegetables. Shrimps are also exported and timber production is important for allied industries. Mexico is rich in minerals, including copper, zinc, lead and sulphur, and is the world's leading producer of silver. It is one of the world's largest producers of oil, from vast oil and gas resources in the Gulf of Mexico. The oil and petrochemical industries are still the mainstay, but a variety of manufactures are now produced including iron and steel, motor vehicles, textiles and electronic goods. Tourism is growing in importance.

FEDERATED STATES OF MICRONESIA

Status: REPUBLIC
Area: 701 sq km (271 sq mls)
Population: 105,000
Capital: PALIKIR
Language: ENGLISH, TRUKESE, POHNPEIAN, LOCAL LANGUAGES
Religion: PROTESTANT, R.CATHOLIC
Currency: US DOLLAR
Organizations: UN

MAP PAGE: 4

MICRONESIA COMPRISES 607 atolls and islands in the Carolines group in the North Pacific Ocean. A third of the population lives on Pohnpei. The climate is tropical with heavy

rainfall. Fishing and subsistence farming are the main activities. Copra and fish are the main exports. Income also derives from tourism and the licensing of foreign fishing fleets. The islands depend on US aid.

MOLDOVA

Status: REPUBLIC
Area: 33,700 sq km (13,012 sq mls)
Population: 4,432,000
Capital: CHIŞINĂU
Language: ROMANIAN, RUSSIAN, UKRAINIAN, GAGAUZ
Religion: MOLDOVAN ORTHODOX, RUSSIAN ORTHODOX
Currency: LEU
Organizations: CIS, UN

MAP PAGE: 47

MOLDOVA IS IN east Europe, sandwiched between Romania and Ukraine. It consists of hilly steppe land, drained by the Prut and Dnestr rivers; the latter provides access to the Black Sea through Ukrainian territory. Moldova has long hot summers and mild winters. The economy is mainly agricultural, with tobacco, wine and fruit the chief products. Food processing and textiles are the main industries. Ethnic tension, which erupted into civil war in 1992, has slowed economic reform.

MONACO

Status: MONARCHY
Area: 2 sq km (0.8 sq ml)
Population: 32,000
Capital: MONACO
Language: FRENCH, MONEGASQUE, ITALIAN
Religion: R.CATHOLIC
Currency: FRENCH FRANC
Organizations: UN

MAP PAGE: 44

THE PRINCIPALITY, IN south Europe, occupies a rocky peninsula and a strip of land on France's Mediterranean coast. It depends on service industries (chiefly tourism, banking and finance) and light industry.

MONGOLIA

Status: REPUBLIC
Area: 1,565,000 sq km (604,250 sq mls)
Population: 2,410,000
Capital: ULAANBAATAR
Language: KHALKA (MONGOLIAN), KAZAKH, LOCAL LANGUAGES
Religion: BUDDHIST, SUNNI MUSLIM, TRAD.BELIEFS
Currency: TUGRIK
Organizations: UN

MAP PAGE: 24

MONGOLIA IS A landlocked country in east Asia between Russia and China. Much of it is high steppe land, with mountains and lakes in the west and north. In the south is the Gobi desert. Mongolia has long, cold winters and short, mild summers. A quarter of the population lives in the capital. Mongolia is rich in minerals and fuels. Copper accounts for half export earnings. Livestock breeding and agricultural processing are important. The demise of the Soviet Union caused economic problems and Mongolia depends on foreign aid.

© Bartholomew

MONTSERRAT
Status: UK TERRITORY
Area: 100 sq km (39 sq mls)
Population: 11,000
Capital: PLYMOUTH
Language: ENGLISH
Religion: PROTESTANT, R.CATHOLIC
Currency: E. CARIB. DOLLAR
Organizations: CARICOM

MAP PAGE: 83

MOROCCO
Status: MONARCHY
Area: 446,550 sq km (172,414 sq mls)
Population: 27,111,000
Capital: RABAT
Language: ARABIC, BERBER, FRENCH,
SPANISH
Religion: SUNNI MUSLIM, R.CATHOLIC
Currency: DIRHAM
Organizations: UN

MAP PAGE: 54

LYING IN THE northwest corner of Africa, Morocco has both Atlantic and Mediterranean coasts. The Atlas ranges separate the arid south and disputed Western Sahara from the fertile regions of the west and north, which have a milder climate. Most Moroccans live on the Atlantic coastal plain. The economy is based mainly on agriculture, phosphate mining and tourism. Manufacturing (chiefly textiles and clothing) and fishing are important.

MOZAMBIQUE
Status: REPUBLIC
Area: 799,380 sq km (308,642 sq mls)
Population: 17,423,000
Capital: MAPUTO
Language: PORTUGUESE, MAKUA,
TSONGA, MANY LOCAL LANGUAGES
Religion: TRAD.BELIEFS, R.CATHOLIC,
SUNNI MUSLIM
Currency: METICAL
Organizations: OAU, SADC, UN, COMM.

MAP PAGE: 57

MOZAMBIQUE LIES ON the east coast of southern Africa. The land is mainly a savannah plateau drained by the Zambezi and other rivers, with highlands to the north. Most people live on the coast or in the river valleys. In general the climate is tropical with winter rainfall, but droughts occur. Reconstruction began in 1992 after 16 years of civil war. The economy is based on agriculture and trade. Exports include shrimps, cashews, cotton and sugar, but Mozambique relies heavily on aid.

MYANMAR
Status: REPUBLIC
Area: 676,577 sq km (261,228 sq mls)
Population: 46,527,000
Capital: YANGON
Language: BURMESE, SHAN, KAREN,
LOCAL LANGUAGES
Religion: BUDDHIST, SUNNI MUSLIM,
PROTESTANT, R.CATHOLIC
Currency: KYAT
Organizations: UN

MAP PAGE: 24-25

MYANMAR IS IN southeast Asia, on the Bay of Bengal and Andaman Sea. Most people live in the valley and delta of the Irrawaddy river, which is flanked on three sides by mountains and high plateaux. The climate is hot and monsoonal, and rainforest covers much of the land. Most people depend on agriculture. Exports include teak and rice. Myanmar is rich in oil and gemstones. Political unrest has affected economic development.

NAMIBIA
Status: REPUBLIC
Area: 824,292 sq km (318,261 sq mls)
Population: 1,540,000
Capital: WINDHOEK
Language: ENGLISH, AFRIKAANS,
GERMAN, OVAMBO
Religion: PROTESTANT, R.CATHOLIC
Currency: DOLLAR
Organizations: COMM., OAU, SADC, UN

MAP PAGE: 57

NAMIBIA LIES ON the Atlantic coast of southern Africa. Mountain ranges separate the coastal Namib Desert from the interior plateau, bordered to the south and east by the Kalahari desert. Namibia is hot and dry, but some summer rain falls in the north which supports crops, herds and most of the population. The economy is based mainly on agriculture and diamond and uranium mining. Fishing is increasingly important.

NAURU
Status: REPUBLIC
Area: 21 sq km (8 sq mls)
Population: 11,000
Capital: YAREN
Language: NAURUAN, GILBERTESE,
ENGLISH
Religion: PROTESTANT, R.CATHOLIC
Currency: AUSTR. DOLLAR
Organizations: COMM.

MAP PAGE: 7

NAURU IS A coral island in the South Pacific Ocean, with a fertile coastal strip, a barren central plateau and a tropical climate. The economy is based on phosphate mining, but reserves are near exhaustion.

NEPAL
Status: MONARCHY
Area: 147,181 sq km (56,827 sq mls)
Population: 21,918,000
Capital: KATHMANDU
Language: NEPALI, MAITHILI,
BHOJPURI, ENGLISH,
MANY LOCAL LANGUAGES
Religion: HINDU, BUDDHIST,
SUNNI MUSLIM
Currency: RUPEE
Organizations: UN

MAP PAGE: 22-23

THE SOUTH ASIAN country of Nepal lies in the southern Himalayas between India and China. High mountains (including Everest) dominate northern Nepal. Most people live in the temperate central valleys and subtropical southern plains. The economy is based largely on agriculture and forestry. Manufacturing (chiefly textiles) and tourism are important. Nepal relies upon foreign aid.

NETHERLANDS
Status: MONARCHY
Area: 41,526 sq km (16,033 sq mls)
Population: 15,451,000
Capital: AMSTERDAM/THE HAGUE
Language: DUTCH, FRISIAN, TURKISH
Religion: R.CATHOLIC, PROTESTANT,
SUNNI MUSLIM
Currency: GUILDER
Organizations: EU, OECD, UN

MAP PAGE: 42

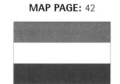

THE NETHERLANDS LIES on the North Sea coast of west Europe. Apart from hills in the far southeast, the land is flat and low-lying, much of it below sea level. The coastal region contains the delta of five rivers and polders (reclaimed land), protected by sand dunes, dikes and canals. The climate is temperate, with cool summers and mild winters. Rainfall is spread evenly throughout the year. The Netherlands is a densely populated country, with the majority of people living in the western Amsterdam-Rotterdam-The Hague area. Horticulture and dairy farming are important activities, with exports of eggs, butter and cheese. The Netherlands is Europe's leading producer and exporter of natural gas from reserves in the North Sea, but otherwise lacks raw materials. The economy is based mainly on international trade and manufacturing industry. Industrial sites are centred mainly around the port of Rotterdam. The chief industries produce food products, chemicals, machinery, electric and electronic goods and transport equipment. Financial services and tourism are important.

NETHERLANDS ANTILLES
Status: NETHERLANDS TERRITORY
Area: 800 sq km (309 sq mls)
Population: 205,000
Capital: WILLEMSTAD
Language: DUTCH, PAPIAMENTO
Religion: R.CATHOLIC, PROTESTANT
Currency: GUILDER

MAP PAGE: 83

THE TERRITORY COMPRISES two separate island groups: Curacao and Bonaire off the northern coast of South America, and Saba, Sint Eustatius and the southern part of Sint Maarten in the northern Lesser Antilles.

NEW CALEDONIA
Status: FRENCH TERRITORY
Area: 19,058 sq km (7,358 sq mls)
Population: 186,000
Capital: NOUMÉA
Language: FRENCH,
LOCAL LANGUAGES
Religion: R.CATHOLIC, PROTESTANT,
SUNNI MUSLIM
Currency: PACIFIC FRANC

MAP PAGE: 7

AN ISLAND GROUP, lying in the southwest Pacific, with a sub-tropical climate. The economy is based on nickel mining, tourism and agriculture.

NEW ZEALAND
Status: MONARCHY
Area: 270,534 sq km (104,454 sq mls)
Population: 3,542,000
Capital: WELLINGTON
Language: ENGLISH, MAORI
Religion: PROTESTANT, R.CATHOLIC
Currency: DOLLAR
Organizations: COMM., OECD, UN

MAP PAGE: 9

NEW ZEALAND, IN Australasia, comprises two main islands separated by the narrow Cook Strait, and a number of smaller islands. North Island, where three quarters of the population lives, has mountain ranges, broad fertile valleys and a volcanic central plateau with hot springs and two active volcanoes. South Island is also mountainous, the Southern Alps running its entire length. The only major lowland area is the Canterbury Plains in the east. The climate is generally temperate, though South Island has cooler winters with upland snow. Rainfall is distributed throughout the year. Farming is the mainstay of the economy. New Zealand is one of the world's leading producers of meat (beef, lamb and mutton), wool and dairy products. Specialist foods, such as kiwi fruit, and fish are also important. Coal, oil and natural gas are produced, but hydroelectric and geothermal power provide much of the country's energy needs. Other industries produce timber, wood pulp, iron, aluminium, machinery and chemicals. Tourism is the largest foreign exchange earner.

NICARAGUA
Status: REPUBLIC
Area: 130,000 sq km (50,193 sq mls)
Population: 4,539,000
Capital: MANAGUA
Language: SPANISH,
AMERINDIAN LANGUAGES
Religion: R.CATHOLIC, PROTESTANT
Currency: CÓRDOBA
Organizations: UN

MAP PAGE: 82-83

NICARAGUA LIES AT the heart of Central America, with both Pacific and Caribbean coasts. Mountain ranges separate the east, which is largely jungle, from the more developed western regions, which include Lake Nicaragua and some active volcanoes. The highest land is in the north. The climate is tropical. The economy is largely agricultural.

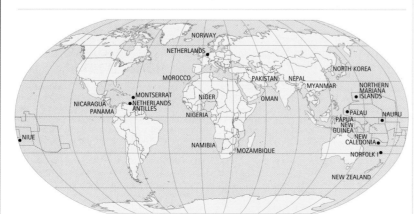

Traditional exports include cotton, coffee, bananas and gold. The aid-dependent economy has suffered from civil war (1978-89) and US sanctions.

NIGER

Status: REPUBLIC
Area: 1,267,000 sq km (489,191 sq mls)
Population: 9,151,000
Capital: NIAMEY
Language: FRENCH (OFFICIAL), HAUSA, FULANI, LOCAL LANGUAGES
Religion: SUNNI MUSLIM, TRAD.BELIEFS
Currency: CFA FRANC
Organizations: OAU, UN

MAP PAGE: 54-55

A LANDLOCKED STATE of west Africa, Niger lies mostly within the Sahara desert, but with savannah land in the south and Niger valley. The Air massif dominates central regions. Much of the country is hot and dry. The south has some summer rainfall, though droughts occur. The economy depends on subsistence farming and herding, uranium exports and foreign aid.

NIGERIA

Status: REPUBLIC
Area: 923,768 sq km (356,669 sq mls)
Population: 111,721,000
Capital: ABUJA
Language: ENGLISH, CREOLE, HAUSA, YORUBA, IBO, FULANI
Religion: SUNNI MUSLIM, PROTESTANT, R.CATHOLIC, TRAD. BELIEFS
Currency: NAIRA
Organizations: COMM., OAU, OPEC, UN

MAP PAGE: 54-55

N IGERIA IS IN west Africa, on the Gulf of Guinea, and is the most populous country in the African continent. The Niger delta dominates coastal areas, fringed with sandy beaches, mangrove swamps and lagoons. Inland is a belt of rainforest that gives way to woodland or savannah on high plateaux. The far north is the semi-desert edge of the Sahara. The climate is tropical with heavy summer rainfall in the south but low rainfall in the north. Most people live in the coastal lowlands or in western Nigeria. About half the workforce is involved in agriculture, mainly growing subsistence crops, and Nigeria is virtually self-sufficient in food. Cocoa and rubber are the only significant export crops. The economy is heavily dependent on vast oil resources in the Niger delta and shallow offshore waters, which account for about 90 per cent of export earnings. Nigeria also has natural gas reserves and some mineral deposits, but these are as yet largely undeveloped. Industry involves mainly oil refining, chemicals (chiefly fertilizer), agricultural processing, textiles, steel manufacture and vehicle assembly. Economic mismanagement in the oil boom of the 1970s and political instability have left Nigeria with a heavy debt, poverty and rising unemployment.

NIUE

Status: NEW ZEALAND TERRITORY
Area: 258 sq km (100 sq mls)
Population: 2,000
Capital: ALOFI
Language: ENGLISH, POLYNESIAN (NIUEAN)
Religion: PROTESTANT, R.CATHOLIC
Currency: NZ DOLLAR

MAP PAGE: 7

NORFOLK ISLAND

Status: AUSTRALIAN TERRITORY
Area: 35 sq km (14 sq mls)
Population: 2,000
Capital: KINGSTON
Language: ENGLISH
Religion: PROTESTANT, R.CATHOLIC
Currency: AUSTR. DOLLAR

MAP PAGE: 7

NORTH KOREA

Status: REPUBLIC
Area: 120,538 sq km (46,540 sq mls)
Population: 23,917,000
Capital: P'YŎNGYANG
Language: KOREAN
Religion: TRAD.BELIEFS, CHONDOIST, BUDDHIST, CONFUCIAN, TAOIST
Currency: WON
Organizations: UN

MAP PAGE: 30

O CCUPYING THE NORTHERN half of the Korean peninsula in east Asia, North Korea is a rugged and mountainous country. The principal lowlands and the main agricultural areas are the Pyongyang and Chaeryong plains in the southwest. More than half the population lives in urban areas, mainly on the coastal plains, which are wider along the Yellow Sea to the west than the Sea of Japan to the east. North Korea has a continental climate, with cold, dry winters and hot, wet summers. About half the workforce is involved in agriculture, mainly growing food crops on cooperative farms. A variety of minerals and ores, chiefly iron ore, are mined and are the basis of the country's heavy industry. Exports include minerals (chiefly lead, magnesite and zinc) and metal products (chiefly iron and steel). North Korea depends heavily on aid, but has suffered since support from Russia and China was ended in in 1991 and 1993 respectively. Agricultural, mining and manufacturing output have fallen. Living standards are much lower than in South Korea from which it was separated in 1945.

NORTHERN MARIANA ISLANDS

Status: US TERRITORY
Area: 477 sq km (184 sq mls)
Population: 47,000
Capital: SAIPAN
Language: ENGLISH, CHAMORRO, TAGALOG, LOCAL LANGUAGES
Religion: R.CATHOLIC, PROTESTANT
Currency: US DOLLAR

MAP PAGE: 24-25

A CHAIN OF islands in the Western Pacific Ocean, tourism is increasingly important to the economy.

NORWAY

Status: MONARCHY
Area: 323,878 sq km (125,050 sq mls)
Population: 4,360,000
Capital: OSLO
Language: NORWEGIAN
Religion: PROTESTANT, R.CATHOLIC
Currency: KRONE
Organizations: OECD, UN

MAP PAGE: 36-37

A COUNTRY OF NORTH Europe, Norway stretches along the north and west coasts of Scandinavia, from the Arctic Ocean to the North Sea. Its extensive coastline is indented

with fjords and fringed with many islands. Inland, the terrain is mountainous, with coniferous forests and lakes in the south. The only major lowland areas are along the southern North Sea and Skagerrak coasts, where most people live. The climate on the west coast is modified by the North Atlantic Drift. Inland, summers are warmer but winters are colder. Norway has vast petroleum and natural gas resources in the North Sea. It is west Europe's leading producer of oil and gas, which account for over 40 per cent of export earnings. Related industries include engineering (such as oil and gas platforms) and petrochemicals. More traditional industries process local raw materials: fish, timber and minerals. Agriculture is limited, but fishing and fish farming are important. Norway is the world's leading exporter of salmon. Merchant shipping and tourism are major sources of foreign exchange.

OMAN

Status: MONARCHY
Area: 309,500 sq km (119,499 sq mls)
Population: 2,163,000
Capital: MUSCAT
Language: ARABIC, BALUCHI, FARSI, SWAHILI, INDIAN LANGUAGES
Religion: IBADHI MUSLIM, SUNNI MUSLIM
Currency: RIAL
Organizations: UN

MAP PAGE: 20

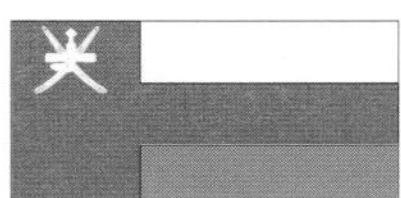

T HE SULTANATE OF southwest Asia occupies the southeast coast of Arabia and an enclave north of the United Arab Emirates. Oman is a desert land, with mountains in the north and south. The climate is hot and mainly dry. Most people live on the coastal strip on the Gulf of Oman. The majority depends on farming and fishing, but the oil and gas industries dominate the economy. Copper is mined.

PAKISTAN

Status: REPUBLIC
Area: 803,940 sq km (310,403 sq mls)
Population: 129,808,000
Capital: ISLAMABAD
Language: URDU (OFFICIAL), PUNJABI, SINDHI, PUSHTU, ENGLISH
Religion: SUNNI MUSLIM, SHI'A MUSLIM, CHRISTIAN, HINDU
Currency: RUPEE
Organizations: COMM., UN

MAP PAGE: 14-15

P AKISTAN IS IN the northwest part of the Indian subcontinent in south Asia, on the Arabian Sea. Eastern and southern Pakistan are dominated by the great basin drained by the Indus river system. It is the main agricultural area and contains most of the population. To the north the land rises to the mountains of the Karakoram and part of the Hindu Kush and Himalayas. The west is semi-desert plateaux and mountain ranges. The climate ranges between dry desert and polar ice cap. However, temperatures are generally warm and rainfall is monsoonal. Agriculture is the main sector of the economy, employing about half the workforce and accounting for over two thirds of export earnings. Cultivation is based on extensive irrigation schemes. Pakistan is one of the world's leading producers of cotton and an important exporter of rice. However, much of the country's food needs must be imported. Pakistan produces natural gas and has a variery of mineral deposits including coal and gold,

but they are little developed. The main industries are textiles and clothing manufacture and food processing, with fabrics and readymade clothing the leading exports. Pakistan also produces leather goods, fertilizers, chemicals, paper and precision instruments. The country depends heavily upon foreign aid and remittances from Pakistanis working abroad.

PALAU

Status: REPUBLIC
Area: 497 sq km (192 sq mls)
Population: 17,000
Capital: KOROR
Language: PALAUAN, ENGLISH
Religion: R.CATHOLIC, PROTESTANT, TRAD.BELIEFS
Currency: US DOLLAR
Organizations: UN

MAP PAGE: 25

P ALAU COMPRISES OVER 300 islands in the western Carolines group of the North Pacific Ocean. Two thirds of the people live on Koror. The climate is tropical. Palau depends on farming, fishing, tourism and US aid.

PANAMA

Status: REPUBLIC
Area: 77,082 sq km (29,762 sq mls)
Population: 2,631,000
Capital: PANAMÁ
Language: SPANISH, ENGLISH CREOLE, AMERINDIAN LANGUAGES
Religion: R.CATHOLIC, PROTESTANT, SUNNI MUSLIM, BAHA'I
Currency: BALBOA
Organizations: UN

MAP PAGE: 83

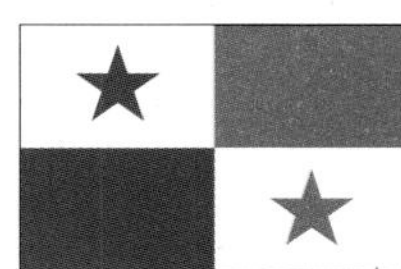

P ANAMA IS THE most southerly state in Central America and has Pacific and Caribbean coasts. It is hilly, with mountains in the west and jungle near the Colombian border. The climate is tropical. Most people live on the drier Pacific side. The economy is based mainly on services related to the canal, shipping, banking and tourism. Exports include bananas, shrimps, sugar and petroleum products.

PAPUA NEW GUINEA

Status: MONARCHY
Area: 462,840 sq km (178,704 sq mls)
Population: 4,074,000
Capital: PORT MORESBY
Language: ENGLISH, TOK PISIN (PIDGIN), LOCAL LANGUAGES
Religion: PROTESTANT, R.CATHOLIC, TRAD.BELIEFS
Currency: KINA
Organizations: COMM., UN

MAP PAGE: 6

P APUA NEW GUINEA, in Australasia, occupies the eastern half of New Guinea and includes many island groups. Papua New Guinea has a forested and mountainous interior, bordered by swampy plains, and a tropical monsoon climate. Most of the workforce are farmers. Timber, copra, coffee and cocoa are important, but exports are dominated by minerals, chiefly copper and gold. The country depends on foreign aid.

© Bartholomew

PARAGUAY

Status: REPUBLIC
Area: 406,752 sq km (157,048 sq mls)
Population: 4,828,000
Capital: ASUNCIÓN
Language: SPANISH, GUARANÍ
Religion: R.CATHOLIC, PROTESTANT
Currency: GUARANÍ
Organizations: UN

MAP PAGE: 88

PARAGUAY IS A landlocked country in central South America, bordering Bolivia, Brazil and Argentina. The river Paraguay separates a sparsely populated western zone of marsh and flat alluvial plains from a more developed, hilly and forested region to the east. The climate is subtropical. The mainstay of the economy is agriculture and agricultural processing. Exports include cotton, soya bean and edible oil products, timber and meat. The largest hydro-electric dam in the world is at Itaipú on the river Paraná.

PERU

Status: REPUBLIC
Area: 1,285,216 sq km (496,225 sq mls)
Population: 23,560,000
Capital: LIMA
Language: SPANISH, QUECHUA, AYMARA
Religion: R.CATHOLIC, PROTESTANT
Currency: SOL
Organizations: UN

MAP PAGE: 86

PERU LIES ON the Pacific coast of South America. Most people live on the coastal strip and the slopes of the high Andes. East of the Andes is high plateau country and the Amazon rainforest. The coast is temperate with low rainfall, while the east is hot, humid and wet. Agriculture involves one third of the workforce. Sugar, cotton, coffee and, illegally, coca are the main cash crops. Fishmeal and timber are also important, but copper, zinc, lead, gold, silver, petroleum and its products are the main exports.

PHILIPPINES

Status: REPUBLIC
Area: 300,000 sq km (115,831 sq mls)
Population: 70,267,000
Capital: MANILA
Language: ENGLISH, FILIPINO (TAGALOG), CEBUANO
Religion: R.CATHOLIC, AGLIPAYAN, SUNNI MUSLIM, PROTESTANT
Currency: PESO
Organizations: ASEAN, UN

MAP PAGE: 31

THE PHILIPPINES, IN southeast Asia, consists of 7,100 islands and atolls lying between the South China Sea and the Pacific

Ocean. The islands of Luzon and Mindanao occupy two thirds of the land area. They and nine other fairly large islands are mountainous and forested. There are ten active volcanoes and earthquakes are common. Most people live in the intermontane plains on the larger islands or on the coastal strips. The climate is hot and humid with heavy monsoonal rainfall. Coconuts, sugar, pineapples and bananas are the main agricultural exports. Fish and timber are also important. The Philippines produces copper, gold, silver, chromium and nickel as well as oil, though geothermal power is also used. The main industries process raw materials and produce electrical and electronic equipment and components, footwear and clothing, textiles and furniture. Tourism is being encouraged. Foreign aid and remittances from workers abroad are important to the economy, which faces problems of high population growth rate and high unemployment.

PITCAIRN ISLANDS

Status: UK TERRITORY
Area: 45 sq km (17 sq mls)
Population: 71
Capital: ADAMSTOWN
Language: ENGLISH
Religion: PROTESTANT
Currency: DOLLAR

MAP PAGE: 5

AN ISLAND GROUP in the southeast Pacific Ocean consisting of Pitcairn Island and three uninhabited islands. It was originally settled by mutineers from HMS Bounty.

POLAND

Status: REPUBLIC
Area: 312,683 sq km (120,728 sq mls)
Population: 38,588,000
Capital: WARSAW
Language: POLISH, GERMAN
Religion: R.CATHOLIC, POLISH ORTHODOX
Currency: ZŁOTY
Organizations: UN, OECD

MAP PAGE: 46-47

POLAND LIES ON the Baltic coast of central Europe. The Oder and Vistula deltas dominate the coast, fringed with sand dunes. Inland much of Poland is low-lying (part of the North European plain), with woods and lakes. In the south the land rises to the Sudeten and western Carpathian mountains which form the borders with the Czech Republic and Slovakia respectively. The climate is continental, with warm summers and cold winters. Conditions are milder in the west and on the coast. A third of the workforce is involved in agriculture, forestry and fishing. Agricultural exports include livestock products and sugar. The

economy is heavily industrialized, with mining and manufacturing accounting for 40 per cent of national income. Poland is one of the world's major producers of coal. It also produces copper, zinc, lead, nickel, sulphur and natural gas. The main industries are ship building, car manufacture, metal and chemical production. The transition to a market economy has resulted in 15 per cent unemployment and economic hardship.

PORTUGAL

Status: REPUBLIC
Area: 88,940 sq km (34,340 sq mls)
Population: 10,797,000
Capital: LISBON
Language: PORTUGUESE
Religion: R.CATHOLIC, PROTESTANT
Currency: ESCUDO
Organizations: EU, OECD, UN

MAP PAGE: 45

PORTUGAL LIES IN the western part of the Iberian peninsula in southwest Europe, has an Atlantic coastline and is flanked by Spain to the north and east. North of the river Tagus are mostly highlands with forests of pine and cork. South of the river is undulating lowland. The climate in the north is cool and moist, influenced by the Atlantic Ocean. The south is warmer, with dry, mild winters. Most Portuguese live near the coast, with one third of the total population in Lisbon and Oporto. Agriculture, fishing and forestry involve 12 per cent of the workfork. Wines, tomatoes, citrus fruit, cork (Portugal is the world's largest producer) and sardines are important exports. Mining and manufacturing are the main sectors of the economy. Portugal produces pyrite, kaolin, zinc, tungsten and other minerals. Export manufactures include textiles, clothing and footwear, electrical machinery and transport equipment, cork and wood products, and chemicals. Service industries, chiefly tourism and banking, are important to the economy as are remittances from workers abroad.

PUERTO RICO

Status: US TERRITORY
Area: 9,104 sq km (3,515 sq mls)
Population: 3,674,000
Capital: SAN JUAN
Language: SPANISH, ENGLISH
Religion: R.CATHOLIC, PROTESTANT
Currency: US DOLLAR

MAP PAGE: 83

THE CARIBBEAN ISLAND of Puerto Rico has a forested, hilly interior, coastal plains and a tropical climate. Half the population lives in the San Juan area. The economy is based on export manufacturing (chiefly chemicals and electronics), tourism and agriculture.

QATAR

Status: MONARCHY
Area: 11,437 sq km (4,416 sq mls)
Population: 551,000
Capital: DOHA
Language: ARABIC, INDIAN LANGUAGES
Religion: SUNNI MUSLIM, CHRISTIAN, HINDU
Currency: RIYAL
Organizations: OPEC, UN

MAP PAGE: 18

THE EMIRATE OCCUPIES a peninsula that extends northwards from east-central Arabia into The Gulf in southwest Asia. The

peninsula is flat and barren with sand dunes and salt pans. The climate is hot and mainly dry. Most people live in the Doha area. The economy is heavily dependent on petroleum, natural gas and the oil-refining industry. Income also comes from overseas investment.

REPUBLIC OF IRELAND

Status: REPUBLIC
Area: 70,282 sq km (27,136 sq mls)
Population: 3,582,000
Capital: DUBLIN
Language: ENGLISH, IRISH
Religion: R.CATHOLIC, PROTESTANT
Currency: PUNT
Organizations: EU, OECD, UN

MAP PAGE: 41

A STATE IN northwest Europe, the Irish republic occupies some 80 per cent of the island of Ireland in the Atlantic Ocean. It is a lowland country of wide valleys, lakes and peat bogs, with isolated mountain ranges around the coast. The west coast is rugged and indented with many bays. The climate is mild due to the North Atlantic Drift and rainfall is plentiful, though highest in the west. Nearly 60 per cent of people live in urban areas, Dublin and Cork being the main cities. Agriculture, the traditional mainstay, involves mainly the production of livestock, meat and dairy products, which account for about 20 percent of exports. Manufactured goods form the bulk of exports. The main industries are electronics, pharmaceuticals and engineering as well as food processing, brewing and textiles. Natural resources include petroleum, natural gas, peat, lead and zinc. Services industries are expanding, with tourism a major foreign exchange earner. The economy could benefit from peace in Northern Ireland, which is part of the United Kingdom.

RÉUNION

Status: FRENCH TERRITORY
Area: 2,551 sq km (985 sq mls)
Population: 653,000
Capital: ST-DENIS
Language: FRENCH, FRENCH CREOLE
Religion: R.CATHOLIC
Currency: FRENCH FRANC

MAP PAGE: 53

THE INDIAN OCEAN island of Réunion is mountainous, with coastal lowlands and a warm climate. It depends heavily on sugar, tourism and French aid. Some uninhabited islets to the east are administered from Réunion.

ROMANIA

Status: REPUBLIC
Area: 237,500 sq km (91,699 sq mls)
Population: 22,680,000
Capital: BUCHAREST
Language: ROMANIAN, HUNGARIAN
Religion: ROMANIAN ORTHODOX, R.CATHOLIC, PROTESTANT
Currency: LEU
Organizations: UN

MAP PAGE: 47. 49

ROMANIA LIES ON the Black Sea coast of east Europe. Mountains separate the Transylvanian plateau from the populous plains of the east and south and the Danube delta. The climate is continental. Romania is rich in fuels and metallic ores. Mining and manufacturing (chiefly metallurgy and machine building) predominate but agriculture is

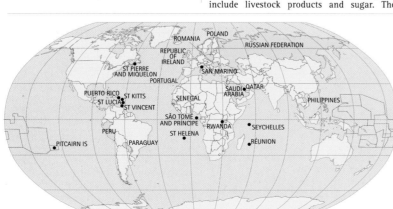

important. Pre-1989 mismanagement and economic reforms of the 1990s have caused hardship.

RUSSIAN FEDERATION
Status: REPUBLIC
Area: 17,075,400 sq km (6,592,849 sq mls)
Population: 148,141,000
Capital: MOSCOW
Language: RUSSIAN, TATAR, UKRAINIAN, LOCAL LANGUAGES
Religion: RUSSIAN ORTHODOX, SUNNI MUSLIM, OTHER CHRISTIAN, JEWISH
Currency: ROUBLE
Organizations: CIS, UN

MAP PAGE: 12-13

RUSSIA OCCUPIES MUCH of east Europe and all of north Asia, and is the world's largest state, nearly twice the size of the USA. It borders thirteen countries to the west and south and has long coastlines on the Arctic and Pacific oceans to the north and east. European Russia, which lies west of the Ural mountains, is part of the North European plain. To the south the land rises to uplands and the Caucasus Mountains on the border with Georgia and Azerbaijan. East of the Urals lies the flat Siberian plain. Much of central Siberia is plateaux. In the south is Lake Baikal, the world's deepest lake, and the Altai and Sayan ranges on the border with Azerbaijan and Mongolia. Eastern Siberia is rugged and mountainous with active volcanoes, notably in the Kamchatka peninsula. Russia's major rivers are the Volga in the west and the Ob, Yenisey, Lena and Amur in Siberia. The climate and vegetation range between Arctic tundra in the north and semi-arid steppe towards the Black and Caspian Sea coasts in the south. In general, the climate is continental with extreme temperatures. The majority of the population (the sixth largest in the world), industry and agriculture are concentrated in European Russia, but there has been increased migration to Siberia to exploit its vast natural resources. The economy is heavily dependent on exploitation of its raw materials and heavy industry. Russia has a wealth of mineral resources, though they are often difficult to exploit because of the climate. It is one of the world's leading producers of petroleum, natural gas and coal as well as iron and manganese ores, platinum, potash, asbestos and many precious and rare metals. Mining provides important exports and is the basis of heavy industry. Russia is a major producer of steel and machinery such as tractors, motor vehicles and generators, as well as chemicals and textiles. Other light industries are less important to the economy. Forests cover about 40 per cent of the land area and supply an important timber, paper and pulp industry. About 8 per cent of land is suitable for cultivation. However farming is generally inefficient and much of food needs, especially grains, must be imported. Fishing is important and Russia operates a large fleet throughout the world. Economic reforms begun in the late 1980s to liberalize the economy met with mixed success, largely because of political unrest. The transition to a free market economy, which was speeded up in the 1990s has been painful, with rising unemployment.

RWANDA
Status: REPUBLIC
Area: 26,338 sq km (10,169 sq mls)
Population: 7,952,000
Capital: KIGALI
Language: KINYARWANDA, FRENCH, ENGLISH
Religion: R.CATHOLIC, TRAD.BELIEFS, PROTESTANT, SUNNI MUSLIM
Currency: FRANC
Organizations: OAU, UN

MAP PAGE: 56

A DENSELY POPULATED and landlocked state in east Africa, Rwanda consists mainly of mountains and plateaux to the east of the Rift Valley. The climate is warm with a summer dry season. Rwanda depends upon subsistence farming, coffee and tea exports, light industry and foreign aid, but the 1990-93 civil war and ethnic conflict have devastated the country.

ST HELENA
Status: UK TERRITORY
Area: 411 sq km (159 sq mls)
Population: 7,000
Capital: JAMESTOWN
Language: ENGLISH
Religion: PROTESTANT, R.CATHOLIC
Currency: POUND STERLING

MAP PAGE: 53

ST HELENA AND its dependencies, Ascension and Tristan da Cunha are isolated island groups lying in the south Atlantic Ocean. Ascension is over 1000 kilometres (620 miles) northwest of St Helena and Tristan da Cunha over 2000 kilometres (1240 miles) to the south.

ST KITTS-NEVIS
Status: MONARCHY
Area: 261 sq km (101 sq mls)
Population: 42,000
Capital: BASSETERRE
Language: ENGLISH, CREOLE
Religion: PROTESTANT, R.CATHOLIC
Currency: E. CARIB. DOLLAR
Organizations: CARICOM, COMM., UN

MAP PAGE: 83

ST KITTS-NEVIS are in the Leeward group in the Caribbean Sea. Both volcanic islands are mountainous and forested with sandy beaches and a warm, wet climate. Some 75 per cent of the population lives on St Kitts. Agriculture is the main activity, with sugar, molasses and sea island cotton the main products. Tourism and manufacturing (chiefly garments and electronic components) are important.

ST LUCIA
Status: MONARCHY
Area: 616 sq km (238 sq mls)
Population: 145,000
Capital: CASTRIES
Language: ENGLISH, FRENCH CREOLE
Religion: R.CATHOLIC, PROTESTANT
Currency: E. CARIB. DOLLAR
Organizations: CARICOM, COMM., UN

MAP PAGE: 83

ST LUCIA, PART OF the Windward group in the Caribbean Sea, is a volcanic island with forested mountains, hot springs, sandy beaches and a wet tropical climate. Agriculture is the main activity, with bananas accounting for over half export earnings. Tourism, agricultural processing and manufacturing (chiefly garments, cardboard boxes and electronic components) are increasingly important.

ST PIERRE AND MIQUELON
Status: FRENCH TERRITORY
Area: 242 sq km (93 sq mls)
Population: 6,000
Capital: ST-PIERRE
Language: FRENCH

Religion: R.CATHOLIC
Currency: FRENCH FRANC

MAP PAGE: 67

A GROUP OF islands off the south coast of Newfoundland in eastern Canada.

ST VINCENT AND THE GRENADINES
Status: MONARCHY
Area: 389 sq km (150 sq mls)
Population: 111,000
Capital: KINGSTOWN
Language: ENGLISH, CREOLE
Religion: PROTESTANT, R.CATHOLIC
Currency: E. CARIB. DOLLAR
Organizations: CARICOM, COMM., UN

MAP PAGE: 83

ST VINCENT, WHOSE TERRITORY includes 32 islets and cays in the Grenadines, is in the Windward Islands group in the Caribbean Sea. St Vincent is forested and mountainous, with an active volcano, Mount Soufrière. The climate is tropical and wet. The economy is based mainly on agriculture and tourism. Bananas account for about half export earnings. Arrowroot is also important.

SAN MARINO
Status: REPUBLIC
Area: 61 sq km (24 sq mls)
Population: 25,000
Capital: SAN MARINO
Language: ITALIAN
Religion: R.CATHOLIC
Currency: ITALIAN LIRA
Organizations: UN

MAP PAGE: 48

LANDLOCKED SAN MARINO lies on the slopes of Mt Titano in northeast Italy. It has a mild climate. A third of the people live in the capital. There is some agriculture and light industry, but most income comes from tourism and postage stamp sales.

SÃO TOMÉ AND PRÍNCIPE
Status: REPUBLIC
Area: 964 sq km (372 sq mls)
Population: 127,000
Capital: SÃO TOMÉ
Language: PORTUGUESE, PORTUGUESE CREOLE
Religion: R.CATHOLIC, PROTESTANT
Currency: DOBRA
Organizations: OAU, UN

MAP PAGE: 54

THE TWO MAIN islands and adjacent islets lie off the coast of west Africa in the Gulf of Guinea. São Tomé is the larger island and supports over 90 per cent of the population. Both São Tomé and Principe are mountainous and tree-covered, and have a hot and humid climate. The economy is heavily dependent on cocoa, which accounts for over 90 per cent of export earnings.

SAUDI ARABIA
Status: MONARCHY
Area: 2,200,000 sq km (849,425 sq mls)
Population: 17,880,000
Capital: RIYADH
Language: ARABIC
Religion: SUNNI MUSLIM, SHI'A MUSLIM
Currency: RIYAL
Organizations: OPEC, UN

MAP PAGE: 20

SAUDI ARABIA OCCUPIES most of the Arabian peninsula in southwest Asia. The terrain is desert or semi-desert plateaux, which rise to mountains running parallel to the Red Sea in the west and slope down to plains in the southeast and along The Gulf in the east. Most people live in urban areas, one third in the cities of Riyadh, Jiddah and Mecca. Summers are hot, winters are warm and rainfall is low. Saudi Arabia has the world's largest reserves of oil and gas, located in the northeast, both onshore and in The Gulf. Crude oil and refined products account for over 90 per cent of export earnings. Other industries and irrigated agriculture are being encouraged, but most food and raw materials are imported. Saudi Arabia has important banking and commercial interests. Each year 2 million pilgrims visit Islam's holiest cities, Mecca and Medina, in the west.

SENEGAL
Status: REPUBLIC
Area: 196,720 sq km (75,954 sq mls)
Population: 8,347,000
Capital: DAKAR
Language: FRENCH (OFFICIAL), WOLOF, FULANI, LOCAL LANGUAGES
Religion: SUNNI MUSLIM, R.CATHOLIC, TRAD.BELIEFS
Currency: CFA FRANC
Organizations: OAU, UN

MAP PAGE: 54

SENEGAL LIES ON the Atlantic coast of west Africa. The north is arid semi-desert, while the south is mainly fertile savannah bushland. The climate is tropical with summer rains, though droughts occur. One fifth of the population lives in Dakar. Groundnuts, phosphates and fish are the main resources. There is some oil refining and Dakar is a major port. Senegal relies heavily on aid.

SEYCHELLES
Status: REPUBLIC
Area: 455 sq km (176 sq mls)
Population: 75,000
Capital: VICTORIA
Language: SEYCHELLOIS (SESELWA, FRENCH CREOLE), ENGLISH
Religion: R.CATHOLIC, PROTESTANT
Currency: RUPEE
Organizations: COMM., OAU, UN

MAP PAGE: 53

THE SEYCHELLES COMPRISES an archipelago of 115 granitic and coral islands in the western Indian Ocean. The main island, Mahé, contains about 90 per cent of the population. The climate is hot and humid with heavy rainfall. The economy is based mainly on tourism, transit trade, and light manufacturing, with fishing and agriculture (chiefly copra, cinnamon and tea) also important.

© Bartholomew

SIERRA LEONE

Status: REPUBLIC
Area: 71,740 sq km (27,699 sq mls)
Population: 4,509,000
Capital: FREETOWN
Language: ENGLISH, CREOLE, MENDE, TEMNE, LOCAL LANGUAGES
Religion: TRAD. BELIEFS, SUNNI MUSLIM, PROTESTANT, R.CATHOLIC
Currency: LEONE
Organizations: COMM., OAU, UN

MAP PAGE: 54

SIERRA LEONE LIES on the Atlantic coast of west Africa. Its coast is heavily indented and lined with mangrove swamps. Inland is a forested area rising to savannah plateaux, with the mountains to the northeast. The climate is tropical and rainfall is heavy. Most of the workforce is involved in subsistence farming. Cocoa and coffee are the main cash crops, but rutile (titanium ore), bauxite and diamonds are the main exports. Civil war and economic decline have caused serious difficulties.

SINGAPORE

Status: REPUBLIC
Area: 639 sq km (247 sq mls)
Population: 2,987,000
Capital: SINGAPORE
Language: CHINESE, ENGLISH, MALAY, TAMIL
Religion: BUDDHIST, TAOIST, SUNNI MUSLIM, CHRISTIAN, HINDU
Currency: DOLLAR
Organizations: ASEAN, COMM., UN

MAP PAGE: 32

THE STATE COMPRISES the main island of Singapore and 57 other islands, lying off the southern tip of the Malay Peninsula in southeast Asia. A causeway links Singapore to the mainland across the Johor Strait. Singapore is generally low-lying and includes land reclaimed from swamps. It is hot and humid, with heavy rainfall throughout the year. There are fish farms and vegetable gardens in the north and east of the island, but most food needs must be imported. Singapore also lacks mineral and energy resources. Manufacturing industries and services are the main sectors of the economy. Their rapid development has fuelled the nation's impressive economic growth over the last three decades to become the richest of Asia's four 'little dragons'. The main industries include electronics, oil refining, chemicals, pharmaceuticals, ship building and repair, iron and steel, food processing and textiles. Singapore is a major financial centre. Its port is one of the world's largest and busiest and acts as an entrepot for neighbouring states. Tourism is also important.

SLOVAKIA

Status: REPUBLIC
Area: 49,035 sq km (18,933 sq mls)
Population: 5,364,000
Capital: BRATISLAVA
Language: SLOVAK, HUNGARIAN, CZECH
Religion: R.CATHOLIC, PROTESTANT, ORTHODOX
Currency: KORUNA
Organizations: UN

MAP PAGE: 46-47

A LANDLOCKED COUNTRY in central Europe, Slovakia borders the Czech Republic, Poland, Ukraine, Hungary and Austria. Slovakia is mountainous along the border with Poland in the north, but low-lying along the plains of the Danube in the southwest. The climate is continental. Slovakia is the smaller, less populous and less developed part of former Czechoslovakia. With few natural resources, uncompetitive heavy industry and loss of federal subsidies, the economy has suffered economic difficulties.

SLOVENIA

Status: REPUBLIC
Area: 20,251 sq km (7,819 sq mls)
Population: 1,984,000
Capital: LJUBLJANA
Language: SLOVENE, SERBO-CROAT
Religion: R.CATHOLIC, PROTESTANT
Currency: TÓLAR
Organizations: UN

MAP PAGE: 48

SLOVENIA LIES IN the northwest Balkans of south Europe and has a short coastline on the Adriatic Sea. It is mountainous and hilly, with lowlands on the coast and in the Sava and Drava river valleys. The climate is generally continental, but Mediterranean nearer the coast. Dairy farming, mercury mining, light manufacturing and tourism are the main activities. Conflict in the other former Yugoslav states, which has affected tourism and international trade, has caused serious economic problems.

SOLOMON ISLANDS

Status: MONARCHY
Area: 28,370 sq km (10,954 sq mls)
Population: 378,000
Capital: HONIARA
Language: ENGLISH, SOLOMON ISLANDS PIDGIN, MANY LOCAL LANGUAGES
Religion: PROTESTANT, R.CATHOLIC
Currency: DOLLAR
Organizations: COMM., UN

MAP PAGE: 7

THE STATE CONSISTS of the southern Solomon, Santa Cruz and Shortland islands in Australasia. The six main islands are volcanic, mountainous and forested, though Guadalcanal, the most populous, has a large area of flat land. The climate is generally hot and humid. Subsistence farming and fishing predominate. Exports include fish, timber, copra and palm oil. The islands depend on foreign aid.

SOMALIA

Status: REPUBLIC
Area: 637,657 sq km (246,201 sq mls)
Population: 9,250,000
Capital: MOGADISHU
Language: SOMALI, ARABIC (OFFICIAL)
Religion: SUNNI MUSLIM
Currency: SHILLING
Organizations: OAU, UN

MAP PAGE: 56

SOMALIA IS IN the Horn of northeast Africa, on the Gulf of Aden and Indian Ocean. It consists of a dry scrubby plateau, rising to highlands in the north. The climate is hot and dry, but coastal areas and the Jubba and Shebele river valleys support crops and the bulk of the population. Subsistence farming and herding are the main activities. Exports include livestock and bananas. Drought and war have ruined the economy.

SOUTH AFRICA

Status: REPUBLIC
Area: 1,219,080 sq km (470,689 sq mls)
Population: 41,244,000
Capital: PRETORIA/CAPE TOWN
Language: AFRIKAANS, ENGLISH, NINE LOCAL LANGUAGES (ALL OFFICIAL)
Religion: PROTESTANT, R.CATHOLIC, SUNNI MUSLIM, HINDU
Currency: RAND
Organizations: COMM., OAU, SADC, UN

MAP PAGE: 58-59

SOUTH AFRICA OCCUPIES most of the southern part of Africa. It borders five states, surrounds Lesotho and has a long coastline on the Atlantic and Indian oceans. Much of the land is a vast plateau, covered with grassland or bush and drained by the Orange and Limpopo river systems. A fertile coastal plain rises to mountain ridges in the south and east, including Table Mountain near Cape Town and the Drakensberg range in the east. Gauteng is the most populous province, with Johannesburg and Pretoria its main cities. South Africa has warm summers and mild winters. Most of the country has rainfall in summer, but the coast around Cape Town has winter rains. South Africa is the largest and most developed economy in Africa, though wealth is unevenly distributed. Agriculture provides one third of exports, including fruit, wine, wool and maize. South Africa is rich in minerals. It is the world's leading producer of gold, which accounts for one third of export earnings. Coal, diamonds, platinum, uranium, chromite and other minerals are also mined. The main industries process minerals and agricultural produce, and manufacture chemical products, motor vehicles, electrical equipment and textiles. Financial services are also important.

SOUTH KOREA

Status: REPUBLIC
Area: 99,274 sq km (38,330 sq mls)
Population: 44,851,000
Capital: SEOUL
Language: KOREAN
Religion: BUDDHIST, PROTESTANT, R.CATHOLIC, CONFUCIAN, TRADITIONAL
Currency: WON
Organizations: UN, OECD

MAP PAGE: 30

THE STATE CONSISTS of the southern half of the Korean Peninsula in east Asia and many islands lying off the western and southern coasts in the Yellow Sea. The terrain is mountainous, though less rugged than that of North Korea. Population density is high and most people live on the western coastal plains and in the Han basin in the northwest and Naktong basin in the southeast. South Korea has a continental climate, with hot, wet summers and dry, cold winters. Arable land is limited by the mountainous terrain, but because of intensive farming South Korea is nearly self-sufficient in food. Sericulture is important as is fishing, which contributes to exports. South Korea has few mineral resources, except for coal and tungsten. It is one of Asia's four 'little dragons' (Hong Kong, Singapore and Taiwan being the others), which have achieved high economic growth based mainly on export manufacturing. In South Korea industry is dominated by a few giant conglomerates, such as Hyundai and Samsung. The main manufactures are cars, electronic and electrical goods, ships, steel, chemicals, and toys as well as textiles, clothing, footwear and food products. Banking and other financial services are increasingly important.

SPAIN

Status: MONARCHY
Area: 504,782 sq km (194,897 sq mls)
Population: 39,210,000
Capital: MADRID
Language: SPANISH, CATALAN, GALICIAN, BASQUE
Religion: R.CATHOLIC
Currency: PESETA
Organizations: EU, OECD, UN

MAP PAGE: 45

SPAIN OCCUPIES THE greater part of the Iberian peninsula in southwest Europe, with coastlines on the Atlantic Ocean (Bay of Biscay and Gulf of Cadiz) and Mediterranean Sea. It includes the Balearic and Canary island groups in the Mediterranean and Atlantic, and two enclaves in north Africa. Much of the mainland is a high plateau, the Meseta, drained by the Duero, Tagus and Guadiana rivers. The plateau is interrupted by a low mountain range and bounded to the east and north also by mountains, including the Pyrenees which form the border with France and Andorra. The main lowland areas are the Ebro basin in the northeast, the eastern coastal plains and the Guadalquivir basin in the southwest. Three quarters of the population lives in urban areas, chiefly Madrid and Barcelona, which alone contain one quarter of the population. The plateau experiences hot summers and cold winters. Conditions are cooler and wetter to the north, though warmer and drier to the south. Agriculture involves about 10 per cent of the workforce and fruit, vegetables and wine are exported. Fishing is an important industry and Spain has a large fishing fleet. Mineral resources include iron, lead, copper and mercury. Some oil is produced, but Spain has to import most energy needs. The economy is based mainly on manufacturing and services. Manufacturing industries account for one third of national income and are based mainly around Madrid and Barcelona. The principal products are machinery and transport equip-

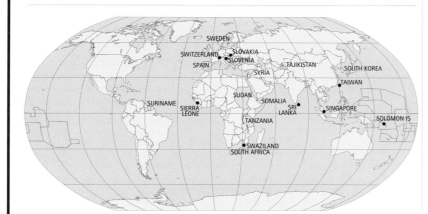

ment. Spain is a leading manufacturer of motor vehicles (SEAT). Other manufactures are agricultural products, chemicals, steel and other metals, paper products, wood and cork products, clothing and footwear, and textiles. With some 50 million visitors a year, tourism is a major industry, accounting for 10 per cent of national income and employing about the same percentage of the workforce. Banking and commerce are also important.

SRI LANKA

Status: REPUBLIC
Area: 65,610 sq km (25,332 sq mls)
Population: 18,354,000
Capital: COLOMBO
Language: SINHALESE, TAMIL, ENGLISH
Religion: BUDDHIST, HINDU,
SUNNI MUSLIM, R.CATHOLIC
Currency: RUPEE
Organizations: COMM., UN

MAP PAGE: 21

SRI LANKA LIES in the Indian Ocean off the southeast coast of India in south Asia. It has rolling coastal plains with mountains in the centre-south. The climate is hot and monsoonal and most people live on the west coast. Manufactures (chiefly textiles and clothing), tea, rubber, copra and gems are exported. The economy relies on aid and workers' remittances. Tourism has been damaged by separatist activities.

SUDAN

Status: REPUBLIC
Area: 2,505,813 sq km (967,500 sq mls)
Population: 28,098,000
Capital: KHARTOUM
Language: ARABIC, DINKA, NUBIAN,
BEJA, NUER, LOCAL LANGUAGES
Religion: SUNNI MUSLIM, TRAD.
BELIEFS, R.CATHOLIC, PROTESTANT
Currency: DINAR
Organizations: OAU, UN

MAP PAGE: 55

AFRICA'S LARGEST COUNTRY, Sudan is in northeast Africa, on the Red Sea. It lies within the Upper Nile basin, much of which is arid plain but with swamps to the south. Mountains lie to the northeast and south. The climate is hot and arid with light summer rainfall, though droughts occur. Most people live along the Nile and are farmers and herders. Cotton, gum arabic, livestock and other agricultural products are exported. In southern Sudan civil war has ruined the economy.

SURINAME

Status: REPUBLIC
Area: 163,820 sq km (63,251 sq mls)
Population: 423,000
Capital: PARAMARIBO
Language: DUTCH, SURINAMESE
(SRANAN TONGO), ENGLISH, HINDI,
JAVANESE
Religion: HINDU, R.CATHOLIC,
PROTESTANT, SUNNI MUSLIM
Currency: GUILDER
Organizations: CARICOM, UN

MAP PAGE: 87

SURINAME, ON THE Atlantic coast of northern South America, consists of a swampy coastal plain (where most people live), central plateaux and the Guiana Highlands. The climate is tropical and rainforest covers much of the land. Bauxite mining is the main industry.

Alumina and aluminium are the chief exports, with shrimps, rice, bananas and timber. Suriname depends on Dutch aid.

SWAZILAND

Status: MONARCHY
Area: 17,364 sq km (6,704 sq mls)
Population: 908,000
Capital: MBABANE
Language: SWAZI (SISWATI), ENGLISH
Religion: PROTESTANT, R.CATHOLIC,
TRAD.BELIEFS
Currency: EMALANGENI
Organizations: COMM., OAU, SADC, UN

MAP PAGE: 59

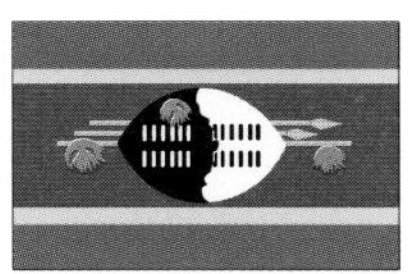

LANDLOCKED SWAZILAND IN southern Africa lies between Mozambique and South Africa. Savannah plateaux descend from mountains in the west towards hill country in the east. The climate is subtropical, temperate in the mountains. Subsistence farming predominates. Asbestos, coal and diamonds are mined. Exports include sugar, fruit and wood pulp. Tourism and workers' remittances are important.

SWEDEN

Status: MONARCHY
Area: 449,964 sq km (173,732 sq mls)
Population: 8,831,000
Capital: STOCKHOLM
Language: SWEDISH
Religion: PROTESTANT, R.CATHOLIC
Currency: KRONA
Organizations: EU, OECD, UN

MAP PAGE: 36-37

SWEDEN, THE LARGEST and most populous of the Scandinavian countries, occupies the eastern part of the peninsula in north Europe and borders the North and Baltic Seas and Gulf of Bothnia. Forested mountains cover the northern half of the country, part of which lies within the Arctic Circle. Southwards is a lowland lake region, where most of the population lives. Farther south is an upland region, and then a fertile plain at the tip of the peninsula. Sweden has warm summers and cold winters, though the latter are longer and more severe in the north and milder in the far south. Sweden's natural resources include coniferous forests, mineral deposits and water resources. There is little agriculture, though some dairy products, meat, cereals and vegetables are produced in the south. The forests supply timber for export and for the important pulp, paper and furniture industries. Sweden is one of the world's leading producers of iron ore. Copper, zinc, lead, uranium and other metallic ores are also mined. Mineral industries, chiefly iron and steel, are the basis for the production of a range of products, but chiefly machinery and transport equipment of which cars and trucks (Volvo and Saab) are the most important export. Sweden also manufactures chemicals, electrical goods (Electrolux) and telecommunications equipment (Ericsson). Like their Scandinavian neighbours, Swedes enjoy a high standard of living.

SWITZERLAND

Status: FEDERATION
Area: 41,293 sq km (15,943 sq mls)
Population: 7,040,000
Capital: BERN
Language: GERMAN, FRENCH, ITALIAN,
ROMANSCH
Religion: R.CATHOLIC, PROTESTANT
Currency: FRANC
Organizations: OECD

MAP PAGE: 46

SWITZERLAND IS A landlocked country of southwest Europe that is surrounded by France, Germany, Austria, Liechtenstein and Italy. It is also Europe's most mountainous country. The southern half of the nation lies within the Alps, while the northwest is dominated by the Jura mountains. The rest of the land is a high plateau, which contains the bulk of the population and economic activity. The climate varies greatly, depending on altitude and relief, but in general summers are mild and winters are cold with heavy snowfalls. Switzerland has one of the highest standards of living in the world. Yet it has few mineral resources and, owing to its mountainous terrain, agriculture is based mainly on dairy and stock farming. Most food and industrial raw materials have to be imported. Manufacturing makes the largest contribution to the economy and though varied is specialist in certain products. Engineering is the most important industry, producing precision instruments such as scientific and optical instruments, watches and clocks, and heavy machinery such as turbines and generators. Other industries produce chemicals, pharmaceuticals, metal products, textiles, clothing and food products (cheese and chocolate). Banking and other financial services are very important and Zurich is one of the world's leading banking cities. Tourism and international organisations based in Switzerland are also major foreign currency earners.

SYRIA

Status: REPUBLIC
Area: 185,180 sq km (71,498 sq mls)
Population: 14,186,000
Capital: DAMASCUS
Language: ARABIC, KURDISH,
ARMENIAN
Religion: SUNNI MUSLIM,
OTHER MUSLIM, CHRISTIAN
Currency: POUND
Organizations: UN

MAP PAGE: 16-17

SYRIA IS IN southwest Asia, on the Mediterranean Sea. Behind the coastal plain lies a range of hills and then a plateau cut by the Euphrates river. Mountains flank the borders with Lebanon and Israel, east of which is desert. The climate is Mediterranean in coastal regions, hotter and drier inland. Most Syrians live on the coast or in the river valleys. Cotton, cereals and fruit are important, but the main exports are petroleum and its products, textiles and chemicals. Syria receives support from Gulf states.

TAIWAN

Status: REPUBLIC
Area: 36,179 sq km (13,969 sq mls)
Population: 21,211,000
Capital: T'AI-PEI
Language: CHINESE (MANDARIN
OFFICIAL, FUKIEN, HAKKA),
LOCAL LANGUAGES
Religion: BUDDHIST, TAOIST,
CONFUCIAN, CHRISTIAN
Currency: DOLLAR

MAP PAGE: 27

THE EAST ASIAN state consists of the island of Taiwan, separated from mainland China by the Taiwan Strait, and several much smaller islands. Much of Taiwan itself is mountainous and forested. Densely populated coastal plains in the west contain the bulk of the population and most economic activity. Taiwan has a tropical monsoon climate, with warm, wet summers and mild winters. Agriculture is highly productive. Taiwan is virtually self-sufficient in food and exports some products. Coal, oil and natural gas are produced and a few minerals are mined but none of them are of great significance to the economy. Taiwan depends heavily on imports of raw materials and exports of manufactured goods. The latter is equivalent to 50 per cent of national income. The country's main manufactures are electrical and electronic goods, including television sets, watches, personal computers and calculators. Other products include clothing, footwear (chiefly track shoes), textiles and toys. In contrast to mainland China, Taiwan has enjoyed considerable prosperity.

TAJIKISTAN

Status: REPUBLIC
Area: 143,100 sq km (55,251 sq mls)
Population: 5,836,000
Capital: DUSHANBE
Language: TAJIK, UZBEK, RUSSIAN
Religion: SUNNI MUSLIM
Currency: ROUBLE
Organizations: CIS, UN

MAP PAGE: 14-15

LANDLOCKED TAJIKISTAN IN central Asia is a mountainous country, occupying the western Tien Shan and part of the Pamir ranges. In less mountainous western areas summers are warm though winters are cold. Most activity is in the Fergana basin. Agriculture is the main sector of the economy, chiefly cotton growing and cattle breeding. Mineral and fuel deposits include lead, zinc, uranium and oil. Textiles and clothing are the main manufactures. Civil war has damaged the economy, which depends heavily on Russian support.

TANZANIA

Status: REPUBLIC
Area: 945,087 sq km (364,900 sq mls)
Population: 30,337,000
Capital: DODOMA
Language: SWAHILI, ENGLISH,
NYAMWEZI, MANY LOCAL
LANGUAGES
Religion: R.CATHOLIC, SUNNI MUSLIM,
TRAD. BELIEFS, PROTESTANT
Currency: SHILLING
Organizations: COMM., OAU, SADC, UN

MAP PAGE: 56-57

TANZANIA LIES ON the coast of east Africa and includes Zanzibar in the Indian Ocean. Most of the mainland is a savannah plateau lying east of the great Rift Valley. In the north are Mount Kilimanjaro and the Serangeti National Park. The climate is tropical and most people live on the narrow coastal plain or in the north. The economy is mainly agricultural. Coffee, cotton and sisal are the main exports, with cloves from Zanzibar. Agricultural processing and diamond mining are the main industries, though tourism is growing. Tanzania depends heavily on aid.

© Bartholomew

THAILAND
Status: MONARCHY
Area: 513,115 sq km (198,115 sq mls)
Population: 59,401,000
Capital: BANGKOK
Language: THAI, LAO, CHINESE, MALAY, MON-KHMER LANGUAGES
Religion: BUDDHIST, SUNNI MUSLIM
Currency: BAHT
Organizations: ASEAN, UN

MAP PAGE: 32

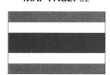

A COUNTRY IN southeast Asia, Thailand borders Myanmar, Laos, Cambodia and Malaysia and has coastlines on the Gulf of Thailand and Andaman Sea. Central Thailand is dominated by the Chao Phraya river basin, which contains Bangkok, the only major urban centre, and most economic activity. To the east is a dry plateau drained by tributaries of the Mekong river, while to the north, west and south, extending halfway down the Malay peninsula, are forested hills and mountains. Many small islands line the coast. The climate is hot, humid and monsoonal. About half the workforce is involved in agriculture. Thailand is the world's leading exporter of rice and rubber, and a major exporter of maize and tapioca. Fish and fish processing are important. Thailand produces natural gas, some oil and lignite, metallic ores (chiefly tin and tungsten) and gemstones. Manufacturing is the largest contributor to national income, with electronics, textiles, clothing and footwear, and food processing the main industries. With over 5 million visitors a year, tourism is the major source of foreign exchange.

TOGO
Status: REPUBLIC
Area: 56,785 sq km (21,925 sq mls)
Population: 4,138,000
Capital: LOMÉ
Language: FRENCH, EWE, KABRE, MANY LOCAL LANGUAGES
Religion: TRAD. BELIEFS, R.CATHOLIC, SUNNI MUSLIM, PROTESTANT
Currency: CFA FRANC
Organizations: OAU, UN

MAP PAGE: 54

T OGO IS A long narrow country in west Africa with a short coastline on the Gulf of Guinea. The interior consists of plateaux rising to mountainous areas. The climate is tropical, drier inland. Agriculture is the mainstay of the economy. Cotton, coffee and cocoa are exported, but phosphates are the main exports. Oil refining and food processing are the main industries. Lomé is an entrepôt trade centre.

TOKELAU
Status: NEW ZEALAND TERRITORY
Area: 10 sq km (4 sq mls)
Population: 2,000
Language: ENGLISH, TOKELAUAN

Religion: PROTESTANT, R.CATHOLIC
Currency: NZ DOLLAR

MAP PAGE: 7

TONGA
Status: MONARCHY
Area: 748 sq km (289 sq mls)
Population: 98,000
Capital: NUKU'ALOFA
Language: TONGAN, ENGLISH
Religion: PROTESTANT, R.CATHOLIC, MORMON
Currency: PA'ANGA
Organizations: COMM.

MAP PAGE: 7

T ONGA COMPRISES SOME 170 islands in the South Pacific Ocean, northeast of New Zealand. The three main groups are Tongatapu (where 60 per cent of Tongans live), Ha'apai and Vava'u. The climate is warm with good rainfall and the economy relies heavily on agriculture. Exports include coconut products, root crops, bananas and vanilla. Fishing, tourism and light industry are increasingly important.

TRINIDAD AND TOBAGO
Status: REPUBLIC
Area: 5,130 sq km (1,981 sq mls)
Population: 1,306,000
Capital: PORT OF SPAIN
Language: ENGLISH, CREOLE, HINDI
Religion: R.CATHOLIC, HINDU, PROTESTANT, SUNNI MUSLIM
Currency: DOLLAR
Organizations: CARICOM, COMM., UN

MAP PAGE: 83

T RINIDAD, THE MOST southerly Caribbean island, lies off the Venezuelan coast. It is hilly in the north, with a populous central plain. Tobago, to the northeast, is smaller, more mountainous and less developed. The climate is tropical. Oil and petrochemicals dominate the economy. Asphalt is also important. Sugar, fruit, cocoa and coffee are produced. Tourism is important on Tobago.

TUNISIA
Status: REPUBLIC
Area: 164,150 sq km (63,379 sq mls)
Population: 8,896,000
Capital: TUNIS
Language: ARABIC, FRENCH
Religion: SUNNI MUSLIM
Currency: DINAR
Organizations: OAU, UN

MAP PAGE: 54-55

T UNISIA IS ON the Mediterranean coast of north Africa. The north is mountainous with valleys and coastal plains, where most people live. Beyond a central area of salt pans are Saharan plains. The north has a Mediterranean climate, the south is hot and arid. Oil and phosphates are the main resources. Olive oil, citrus fruit and textiles are also exported. Tourism is important.

TURKEY
Status: REPUBLIC
Area: 779,452 sq km (300,948 sq mls)
Population: 61,644,000
Capital: ANKARA
Language: TURKISH, KURDISH
Religion: SUNNI MUSLIM, SHI'A MUSLIM
Currency: LIRA
Organizations: OECD, UN

MAP PAGE: 16-17

T URKEY OCCUPIES THE Asia Minor peninsula of southwest Asia and has coastlines on the Black, Mediterranean and Aegean seas. It includes eastern Thrace, which is in south Europe and separated from the rest of the country by the Bosporus, Sea of Marmara and Dardanelles. The Asian mainland consists of the semi-arid Anatolian plateau, flanked to the north, south and east by mountains. Over 40 per cent of Turks live in central Anatolia and the Marmara and Aegean coastal plains. The coast has a Mediterranean climate, but inland conditions are more extreme with hot, dry summers and cold, snowy winters. Agriculture involves about half the workforce and exports include cotton, tobacco, fruit, nuts and livestock. Turkey is one of the world's major producers of chrome. Coal and lignite, petroleum, iron ore and boron are also exploited. Apart from food products, the main manufactures are textiles (the chief export), iron and steel, vehicles and chemicals. With over 7 million visitors a year, tourism is a major industry. Remittances by workers aboard are also important.

TURKMENISTAN
Status: REPUBLIC
Area: 488,100 sq km (188,456 sq mls)
Population: 4,099,000
Capital: ASHGABAT
Language: TURKMEN, RUSSIAN
Religion: SUNNI MUSLIM
Currency: MANAT
Organizations: CIS, UN

MAP PAGE: 14

T URKMENISTAN, IN CENTRAL Asia, lies mainly within the desert plains of the Kara Kum. Most people live on the fringes: the foothills of the Kopet Dag in the south, Amudarya valley in the north and Caspian Sea plains in the west. The climate is dry with extreme temperatures. The economy is based mainly on irrigated agriculture, chiefly cotton growing. Turkmenistan is rich in oil, natural gas (the main export) and minerals.

TURKS AND CAICOS ISLANDS
Status: UK TERRITORY
Area: 430 sq km (166 sq mls)
Population: 14,000
Capital: GRAND TURK
Language: ENGLISH
Religion: PROTESTANT
Currency: US DOLLAR

MAP PAGE: 83

T HE STATE CONSISTS of 40 or so low-lying islands and cays in the northern Caribbean. Only eight islands are inhabited, two fifths of people living on Grand Turk and Salt Cay. The climate is tropical. The islands depend on fishing, tourism and offshore banking.

TUVALU
Status: MONARCHY
Area: 25 sq km (10 sq mls)
Population: 10,000
Capital: FONGAFALE
Language: TUVALUAN, ENGLISH (OFFICIAL)
Religion: PROTESTANT
Currency: DOLLAR
Organizations: COMM.

MAP PAGE: 7

T UVALU COMPRISES NINE coral atolls in the South Pacific Ocean. One third of the population lives on Funafuti and most people depend on subsistence farming and fishing. The islands export copra, stamps and clothing, but rely heavily on UK aid.

UGANDA
Status: REPUBLIC
Area: 241,038 sq km (93,065 sq mls)
Population: 19,848,000
Capital: KAMPALA
Language: ENGLISH, SWAHILI (OFFICIAL), LUGANDA, MANY LOCAL LANGUAGES
Religion: R.CATHOLIC, PROTESTANT, SUNNI MUSLIM, TRAD. BELIEFS
Currency: SHILLING
Organizations: COMM., OAU, UN

MAP PAGE: 56

A LANDLOCKED COUNTRY in east Africa, Uganda consists of a savannah plateau with mountains and lakes. It includes part of Lake Victoria from which the Nile flows northwards to Sudan. The climate is warm and wet. Most people live in the southern half of the country. Agriculture dominates the economy. Coffee is the main export, with some cotton and tea. Uganda relies heavily on aid.

UKRAINE
Status: REPUBLIC
Area: 603,700 sq km (233,090 sq mls)
Population: 51,639,000
Capital: KIEV
Language: UKRAINIAN, RUSSIAN, REGIONAL LANGUAGES
Religion: UKRAINIAN ORTHODOX, R.CATHOLIC
Currency: HRYVNIA
Organizations: CIS, UN

MAP PAGE: 51

U KRAINE LIES ON the Black Sea coast of east Europe. Much of the land is steppe, generally flat and treeless, but with rich black soil and drained by the river Dnieper. Along the border with Belarus are forested, marshy plains. The only uplands are the Carpathian mountains in the west and smaller ranges on the Crimean peninsula. Summers are warm and winters are

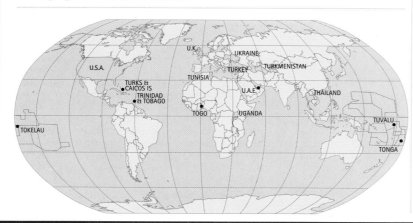

cold, with milder conditions in the Crimea. About a quarter of the population lives in the mainly industrial provinces of Donetsk, Kiev and Dnepropetrovsk. The Ukraine is rich in natural resources: fertile soil, substantial mineral deposits and forests. Agriculture, livestock raising and viticulture are important, but mining and manufacturing predominate, contributing over 40 per cent of national income. Coal mining, iron and steel production, engineering and chemicals are the main industries. Output has fallen and few state enterprises have been privatized since Ukraine became independent in 1991.

UNITED ARAB EMIRATES
(UAE)
Status: FEDERATION
Area: 77,700 sq km (30,000 sq mls)
Population: 2,314,000
Capital: ABU DHABI
Language: ARABIC (OFFICIAL), ENGLISH, HINDI, URDU, FARSI
Religion: SUNNI MUSLIM, SHI'A MUSLIM, CHRISTIAN
Currency: DIRHAM
Organizations: OPEC, UN

MAP PAGE: 20

THE UAE IS in east-central Arabia, southwest Asia. Six emirates lie on The Gulf while the seventh, Fujairah, fronts the Gulf of Oman. Most of the land is flat desert with sand dunes and salt pans. The only hilly area is in the northeast. Three emirates - Abu Dhabi, Dubai and Sharjah - contain 85 per cent of the population. Summers are hot and winters are mild with occasional rainfall in coastal areas. Fruit and vegetables are grown in oases and irrigated areas. The state's wealth is based on hydrocarbons, mainly within Abu Dhabi, but with smaller supplies in Dubai, Sharjah and Ras al Khaimah. Dubai is a thriving entrepot trade centre.

ABU DHABI
Status: EMIRATE
Area: 64,750 sq km (25,000 sq miles)
Population: 800,000

AJMAN
Status: EMIRATE
Area: 260 sq km (100 sq miles)
Population: 76,000

DUBAI
Status: EMIRATE
Area: 3,900 sq km (1,506 sq miles)
Population: 500,000

FUJAIRAH
Status: EMIRATE
Area: 1,170 sq km (452 sq miles)
Population: 63,000

RAS AL KHAIMAH
Status: EMIRATE
Area: 1,690 sq km (653 sq miles)
Population: 130,000

SHARJAH
Status: EMIRATE
Area: 2,600 sq km (1,004 sq miles)
Population: 314,000

UMM AL QAIWAIN
Status: EMIRATE
Area: 780 sq km (301 sq miles)
Population: 27,000

UNITED KINGDOM
(UK)
Status: MONARCHY
Area: 244,082 sq km (94,241 sq mls)
Population: 58,258,000
Capital: LONDON
Language: ENGLISH, SOUTH INDIAN LANGUAGES, CHINESE, WELSH, GAELIC
Religion: PROTESTANT, R.CATHOLIC, MUSLIM, SIKH, HINDU, JEWISH
Currency: POUND
Organizations: COMM., EU, OECD, UN

MAP PAGE: 34

A COUNTRY OF northwest Europe, the United Kingdom occupies the island of Great Britain, part of Ireland and many small adjacent islands in the Atlantic Ocean. Great Britain comprises the countries of England, Scotland and Wales. England covers over half the land area and supports over four-fifths of the population, chiefly in the southeast region. The landscape is flat or rolling with some uplands, notably the Cheviot Hills on the Scottish border, the Pennines in the centre-north and the Cumbrian mountains in the northwest. Scotland consists of southern uplands, central lowlands, highlands (which include the UK's highest peak) and islands. Wales is a land of mountains and river valleys. Northern Ireland contains uplands, plains and the UK's largest lake, Lough Neagh. The climate is mild, wet and variable. The UK has few mineral deposits, but has important energy resources. Over 40 per cent of land is suitable for grazing, over 25 per cent is cultivated, and 10 per cent is forested. Agriculture involves mainly sheep and cattle raising and dairy farming, with crop and fruit growing in the east and southeast. Productivity is high, but about one third of food needs must be imported. Both forestry and fishing are also important. The UK produces petroleum and natural gas from reserves in the North Sea and is self-sufficient in energy in net terms. It also has reserves of coal, though the coal industry has contracted in recent years. Manufacturing accounts for over 20 per cent of national income and relies heavily on imported raw materials. Major manufactures are food and drinks, motor vehicles and parts, aerospace equipment, machinery, electronic and electrical equipment, and chemicals and chemical products. However, the economy is dominated by service industries, including banking, insurance, finance, business services, retail and catering. London is one of the world's major banking, financial and insurance capitals. Tourism is a major industry, with over 18 million visitors a year. International trade is also important, equivalent to a third of national income and the UK has a large merchant fleet.

ENGLAND
Status: CONSTITUENT COUNTRY
Area: 130,423 sq km (50,357 sq miles)
Population: 48,532,700
Capital: LONDON

NORTHERN IRELAND
Status: CONSTITUENT REGION
Area: 14,121 sq km (5,452 sq miles)
Population: 1,631,800
Capital: BELFAST

SCOTLAND
Status: CONSTITUENT COUNTRY
Area: 78,772 sq km (30,414 sq miles)
Population: 5,120,200
Capital: EDINBURGH

WALES
Status: PRINCIPALITY
Area: 20,766 sq km (8,018 sq miles)
Population: 2,906,500
Capital: CARDIFF

UNITED STATES OF AMERICA
(USA)
Status: REPUBLIC
Area: 9,809,386 sq km (3,787,425 sq mls)
Population: 263,034,000
Capital: WASHINGTON D.C.
Language: ENGLISH, SPANISH, AMERINDIAN LANGUAGES
Religion: PROTESTANT, R.CATHOLIC, SUNNI MUSLIM, JEWISH, MORMON
Currency: DOLLAR
Organizations: NAFTA, OECD, UN

MAP PAGE: 70-71

THE USA COMPRISES 48 contiguous states in North America, bounded by Canada and Mexico, and the states of Alaska, to the northwest of Canada, and Hawaii, in the Pacific Ocean. The populous eastern states consist of the Atlantic coastal plain (which includes the Florida peninsula and the Gulf of Mexico coast) and the Appalachian mountains. The central states form a vast interior plain drained by the Mississippi-Missouri river system. To the west lie the Rocky Mountains, separated from the Pacific coastal ranges by the intermontane plateaux. The coastal ranges, which are prone to earthquakes, extend northwards into Alaska. Hawaii is a group of some 20 volcanic islands. Climatic conditions range between arctic in Alaska to desert in the intermontane plateaux. Most of the USA is temperate, though the interior has continental conditions. The USA has abundant natural resources. It has major reserves minerals and energy resources. About 20 per cent of the land can be used for crops, over 25 per cent is suitable for livestock rearing and over 30 per cent is forested. The USA has the largest economy in the world, which is based mainly on manufacturing and services. Though agriculture accounts for only about 2 per cent national income, productivity is high and the USA is a net exporter of food, chiefly grains and fruit. Major industrial crops include cotton, tobacco and sugarbeet. Livestock rearing, forestry and fishing are also important. Mining is well developed. The USA produces iron ore, bauxite, copper, lead, zinc, phosphate and many other minerals. It is a major producer of coal, petroleum and natural gas, though being the world's biggest energy user it must import significant quanities of petroleum and its products. Manufacturing is well diversified. The main products are: iron, steel and aluminium metals and products, machinery, transport equipment (chiefly motor vehicles and aircraft), electrical and electronic goods, food products, chemicals, textiles and clothing. Tourism is a major foreign currency earner. Other important service industries are banking and finance, and Wall Street in New York is a major stock exchange.

ALABAMA
Status: STATE
Area: 135,775 sq km (52,423 sq miles)
Population: 4,273,084
Capital: MONTGOMERY

ALASKA
Status: STATE
Area: 1,700,130 sq km (656,424 sq miles)
Population: 607,007
Capital: JUNEAU

ARIZONA
Status: STATE
Area: 295,274 sq km (114,006 sq miles)
Population: 4,428,068
Capital: PHOENIX

ARKANSAS
Status: STATE
Area: 137,741 sq km (53,182 sq miles)
Population: 2,509,793
Capital: LITTLE ROCK

CALIFORNIA
Status: STATE
Area: 423,999 sq km (163,707 sq miles)
Population: 31,878,234
Capital: SACRAMENTO

COLORADO
Status: STATE
Area: 269,618 sq km (104,100 sq miles)
Population: 3,822,676
Capital: DENVER

CONNECTICUT
Status: STATE
Area: 14,359 sq km (5,544 sq miles)
Population: 3,274,238
Capital: HARTFORD

DISTRICT OF COLUMBIA
Status: FEDERAL DISTRICT
Area: 176 sq km (68 sq miles)
Population: 543,213
Capital: WASHINGTON

DELAWARE
Status: STATE
Area: 6,446 sq km (2,489 sq miles)
Population: 724,842
Capital: DOVER

FLORIDA
Status: STATE
Area: 170,312 sq km (65,758 sq miles)
Population: 14,399,985
Capital: TALLAHASSEE

GEORGIA
Status: STATE
Area: 153,951 sq km (59,441 sq miles)
Population: 7,353,225
Capital: ATLANTA

HAWAII
Status: STATE
Area: 28,314 sq km (10,932 sq miles)
Population: 1,183,723
Capital: HONOLULU

IDAHO
Status: STATE
Area: 216,456 sq km (83,574 sq miles)
Population: 1,189,251
Capital: BOISE

ILLINOIS
Status: STATE
Area: 150,007 sq km (57,918 sq miles)
Population: 11,846,544
Capital: SPRINGFIELD

INDIANA
Status: STATE
Area: 94,327 sq km (36,420 sq miles)
Population: 5,840,528
Capital: INDIANAPOLIS

IOWA
Status: STATE
Area: 145,754 sq km (56,276 sq miles)
Population: 2,851,792
Capital: DES MOINES

KANSAS
Status: STATE
Area: 213,109 sq km (82,282 sq miles)
Population: 2,572,150
Capital: TOPEKA

KENTUCKY
Status: STATE
Area: 104,664 sq km (40,411 sq miles)
Population: 3,883,723
Capital: FRANKFORT

LOUISIANA
Status: STATE
Area: 134,273 sq km (51,843 sq miles)
Population: 4,350,579
Capital: BATON ROUGE

© Bartholomew

USA
continued

MAINE
Status: STATE
Area: 91,652 sq km (35,387 sq miles)
Population: 1,243,316
Capital: AUGUSTA

MARYLAND
Status: STATE
Area: 32,134 sq km (12,407 sq miles)
Population: 5,071,604
Capital: ANNAPOLIS

MASSACHUSETTS
Status: STATE
Area: 27,337 sq km (10,555 sq miles)
Population: 6,092,352
Capital: BOSTON

MICHIGAN
Status: STATE
Area: 250,737 sq km (96,810 sq miles)
Population: 9,594,350
Capital: LANSING

MINNESOTA
Status: STATE
Area: 225,181 sq km (86,943 sq miles)
Population: 4,657,758
Capital: ST PAUL

MISSISSIPPI
Status: STATE
Area: 125,443 sq km (48,434 sq miles)
Population: 2,716,115
Capital: JACKSON

MISSOURI
Status: STATE
Area: 180,545 sq km (69,709 sq miles)
Population: 5,358,692
Capital: JEFFERSON CITY

MONTANA
Status: STATE
Area: 380,847 sq km (147,046 sq miles)
Population: 879,372
Capital: HELENA

NEBRASKA
Status: STATE
Area: 200,356 sq km (77,358 sq miles)
Population: 1,652,093
Capital: LINCOLN

NEVADA
Status: STATE
Area: 286,367 sq km (110,567 sq miles)
Population: 1,603,163
Capital: CARSON CITY

NEW HAMPSHIRE
Status: STATE
Area: 24,219 sq km (9,351 sq miles)
Population: 1,162,481
Capital: CONCORD

NEW JERSEY
Status: STATE
Area: 22,590 sq km (8,722 sq miles)
Population: 7,987,933
Capital: TRENTON

NEW MEXICO
Status: STATE
Area: 314,937 sq km (121,598 sq miles)
Population: 1,713,407
Capital: SANTA FE

NEW YORK
Status: STATE
Area: 141,090 sq km (54,475 sq miles)
Population: 18,184,774
Capital: ALBANY

NORTH CAROLINA
Status: STATE
Area: 139,396 sq km (53,821 sq miles)
Population: 7,322,870
Capital: RALEIGH

NORTH DAKOTA
Status: STATE
Area: 183,123 sq km (70,704 sq miles)
Population: 643,539
Capital: BISMARCK

OHIO
Status: STATE
Area: 116,104 sq km (44,828 sq miles)
Population: 11,172,782
Capital: COLUMBUS

OKLAHOMA
Status: STATE
Area: 181,048 sq km (69,903 sq miles)
Population: 3,300,902
Capital: OKLAHOMA CITY

OREGON
Status: STATE
Area: 254,819 sq km (98,386 sq miles)
Population: 3,203,735
Capital: SALEM

PENNSYLVANIA
Status: STATE
Area: 119,290 sq km (46,058 sq miles)
Population: 12,056,112
Capital: HARRISBURG

RHODE ISLAND
Status: STATE
Area: 4,002 sq km (1,545 sq miles)
Population: 990,225
Capital: PROVIDENCE

SOUTH CAROLINA
Status: STATE
Area: 82,898 sq km (32,007 sq miles)
Population: 3,698,746
Capital: COLUMBIA

SOUTH DAKOTA
Status: STATE
Area: 199,742 sq km (77,121 sq miles)
Population: 732,405
Capital: PIERRE

TENNESSEE
Status: STATE
Area: 109,158 sq km (42,146 sq miles)
Population: 5,319,654
Capital: NASHVILLE

TEXAS
Status: STATE
Area: 695,673 sq km (268,601 sq miles)
Population: 19,128,261
Capital: AUSTIN

UTAH
Status: STATE
Area: 219,900 sq km (84,904 sq miles)
Population: 2,000,494
Capital: SALT LAKE CITY

VERMONT
Status: STATE
Area: 24,903 sq km (9,615 sq miles)
Population: 588,654
Capital: MONTPELIER

VIRGINIA
Status: STATE
Area: 110,771 sq km (42,769 sq miles)
Population: 6,675,451
Capital: RICHMOND

WASHINGTON
Status: STATE
Area: 184,674 sq km (71,303 sq miles)
Population: 5,532,939
Capital: OLYMPIA

WEST VIRGINIA
Status: STATE
Area: 62,758 sq km (24,231 sq miles)
Population: 1,825,754
Capital: CHARLESTON

WISCONSIN
Status: STATE
Area: 169,652 sq km (65,503 sq miles)
Population: 5,159,795
Capital: MADISON

WYOMING
Status: STATE
Area: 253,347 sq km (97,818 sq miles)
Population: 481,400
Capital: CHEYENNE

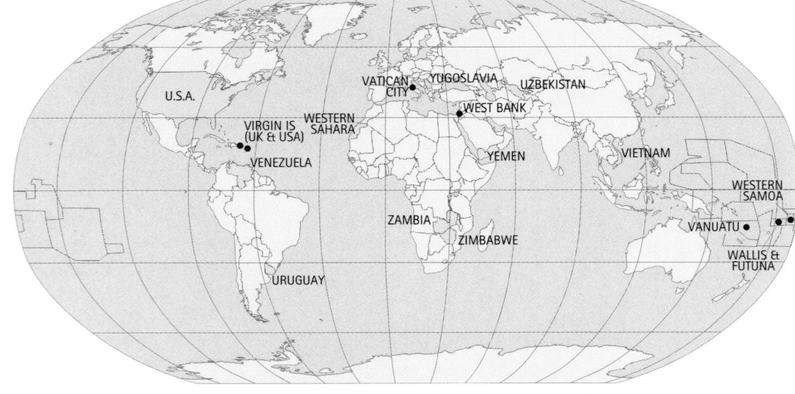

URUGUAY
Status: REPUBLIC
Area: 176,215 sq km (68,037 sq mls)
Population: 3,186,000
Capital: MONTEVIDEO
Language: SPANISH
Religion: R.CATHOLIC, PROTESTANT, JEWISH
Currency: PESO
Organizations: UN

MAP PAGE: 91

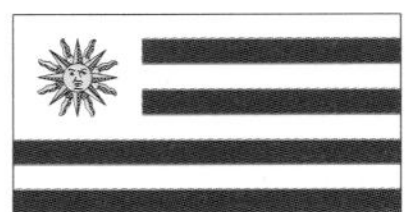

URUGUAY, ON THE Atlantic coast of central South America, is a low-lying land of prairies. The coast and the River Plate estuary in the south are fringed with lagoons and sand dunes. Almost half the population lives in Montevideo. Uruguay has warm summers and mild winters. The economy was founded on cattle and sheep ranching, and meat, wool and hides are major exports. The main industries produce food, textiles, petroleum products, chemicals and transport equipment. Offshore banking and tourism are important.

UZBEKISTAN
Status: REPUBLIC
Area: 447,400 sq km (172,742 sq mls)
Population: 22,843,000
Capital: TASHKENT
Language: UZBEK, RUSSIAN, TAJIK, KAZAKH
Religion: SUNNI MUSLIM, RUSSIAN ORTHODOX
Currency: SOM
Organizations: CIS, UN

MAP PAGE: 14

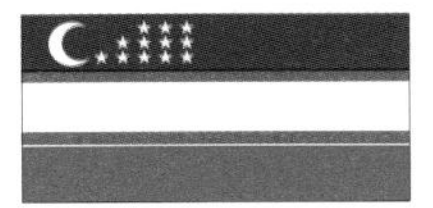

A REPUBLIC OF central Asia, Uzbekistan borders the Aral Sea and five countries. It consists mainly of the flat desert of the Kyzyl Kum, which rises eastwards towards the mountains of the western Pamirs. Most settlement is in the Fergana basin. The climate is dry and arid. The economy is based mainly on irrigated agriculture, chiefly cotton production. Industry specializes in fertilizers and machinery for cotton harvesting and textile manufacture. Uzbekistan is rich in minerals and has the largest gold mine in the world.

VANUATU
Status: REPUBLIC
Area: 12,190 sq km (4,707 sq mls)
Population: 169,000
Capital: PORT VILA
Language: ENGLISH, BISLAMA (ENGLISH CREOLE), FRENCH (ALL OFFICIAL)
Religion: PROTESTANT, R.CATHOLIC, TRAD.BELIEFS
Currency: VATU
Organizations: COMM., UN

MAP PAGE: 7

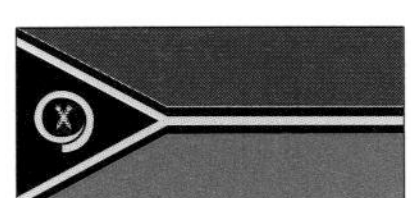

VANUATU OCCUPIES AN archipelago of some 80 islands in Oceania. Many of the islands are mountainous, of volcanic origin and densely forested. The climate is tropical with heavy rainfall. Half the population lives on the main islands of Efate, Santo and Tafea, and the majority of people live by farming. Copra, beef, seashells, cocoa and timber are the main exports. Tourism is growing and foreign aid is important.

VATICAN CITY
Status: ECCLESIASTICAL STATE
Area: 0.4 sq km (0.2 sq ml)
Population: 1,000
Language: ITALIAN
Religion: R.CATHOLIC
Currency: ITALIAN LIRA

MAP PAGE: 48

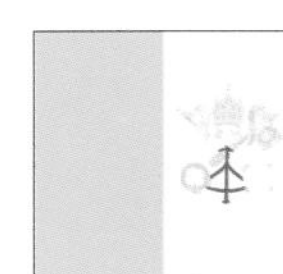

THE WORLD'S SMALLEST sovereign state, the Vatican City occupies a hill to the west of the river Tiber in the Italian capital, Rome. It is the headquarters of the Roman Catholic church and income comes from investments, voluntary contributions and tourism.

VENEZUELA
Status: REPUBLIC
Area: 912,050 sq km (352,144 sq mls)
Population: 21,644,000
Capital: CARACAS
Language: SPANISH, AMERINDIAN LANGUAGES
Religion: R.CATHOLIC, PROTESTANT
Currency: BOLÍVAR
Organizations: OPEC, UN

MAP PAGE: 89

VENEZUELA IS IN northern South America, on the Caribbean Sea. Its coast is much indented, with the oil-rich area of Lake Maracaibo at the western end and the swampy Orinoco delta in the east. Mountain ranges run parallel to the coast then turn southwestwards to form the northern extension of the Andes chain. Central Venezuela is lowland grasslands drained by the Orinoco river system, while to the south are the Guiana Highlands which contain the Angel Falls, the world's highest waterfall. About 85 per cent of the population lives in towns, mostly in the coastal mountain areas. The climate is tropical, with summer rainfall. Temperatures are lower in the mountains. Venezuela is an important oil producer, and sales account for about 75 per cent of export earnings. Bauxite, iron ore and gold are also mined and manufactures include aluminium, iron and steel, textiles, timber and wood products, and petrochemicals. Farming is important, particularly cattle ranching and dairy farming. Coffee, cotton, maize, rice and sugarcane are major crops.

VIETNAM
Status: REPUBLIC
Area: 329,565 sq km (127,246 sq mls)
Population: 74,545,000
Capital: HA NÔI
Language: VIETNAMESE, THAI, KHMER, CHINESE, MANY LOCAL LANGUAGES
Religion: BUDDHIST, TAOIST, R.CATHOLIC, CAO DAI, HOA HAO
Currency: DONG
Organizations: UN, ASEAN

MAP PAGE: 24-25

VIETNAM EXTENDS ALONG the east coast of the Indochina peninsula in southeast Asia, with the South China Sea to the east and south. The Red River (Song-koi) delta lowlands in the north are separated from the huge Mekong delta in the south by narrow coastal plains backed by the generally rough mountainous and forested terrain of the Annam highlands. Most people live in the river deltas. The climate is tropical, with summer monsoon rains. Over three quarters of the workforce is involved in agriculture, forestry and fishing. Rice growing is the main activity, and Vietnam is the world's third largest rice exporter, after the USA and Thailand. Coffee, tea and rubber are the main cash crops. The north is fairly rich in minerals including some oil, coal, iron ore, manganese, apatite and gold. The food processing and textile industries are important, but the steel, oil and gas and car industries are growing rapidly. The 1992 economic reform programme, inflow of foreign investment and the 1994 lifting of the US trade embargo are boosting an economy which suffered from decades of war and strife.

VIRGIN ISLANDS (UK)
Status: UK TERRITORY
Area: 153 sq km (59 sq mls)
Population: 19,000
Capital: ROAD TOWN
Language: ENGLISH
Religion: PROTESTANT, R.CATHOLIC
Currency: US DOLLAR

MAP PAGE: 83

THE CARIBBEAN TERRITORY comprises four main islands and some 36 islets at the eastern end of the Virgin Islands group. Apart from the flat coral atoll of Anegada, the islands are volcanic in origin and hilly. The climate is subtropical and tourism is the main industry.

VIRGIN ISLANDS (USA)
Status: US TERRITORY
Area: 352 sq km (136 sq mls)
Population: 105,000
Capital: CHARLOTTE AMALIE
Language: ENGLISH, SPANISH
Religion: PROTESTANT, R.CATHOLIC
Currency: US DOLLAR

MAP PAGE: 83

THE TERRITORY CONSISTS of three main islands and some 50 islets in the Caribbean's western Virgin Islands. The islands are mostly hilly and of volcanic origin and the climate is subtropical. The economy is based on tourism, with some manufacturing on St Croix.

WALLIS AND FUTUNA
Status: FRENCH TERRITORY
Area: 274 sq km (106 sq mls)
Population: 14,000
Capital: MATA-UTU
Language: FRENCH, POLYNESIAN (WALLISIAN, FUTUNIAN)
Religion: R.CATHOLIC
Currency: PACIFIC FRANC

MAP PAGE: 7

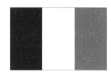

THE SOUTH PACIFIC territory comprises the volcanic islands of the Wallis archipelago and Hoorn Islands. The climate is tropical. The islands depend upon subsistence farming, the sale of licences to foreign fishing fleets, workers' remittances and French aid.

WEST BANK
Status: TERRITORY
Area: 5,860 sq km (2,263 sq mls)
Population: 1,219,000
Language: ARABIC, HEBREW
Religion: SUNNI MUSLIM, JEWISH, SHI'A MUSLIM, CHRISTIAN

MAP PAGE: 16

THE TERRITORY CONSISTS of the west bank of the river Jordan and parts of Judea and Samaria in southwest Asia. The land was annexed by Israel in 1967, but the Jericho area was granted self-government under an agreement between Israel and the PLO in 1993.

WESTERN SAHARA
Status: TERRITORY
Area: 266,000 sq km (102,703 sq mls)
Population: 283,000
Capital: LAÂYOUNE
Language: ARABIC
Religion: SUNNI MUSLIM
Currency: MOROCCAN DIRHAM

MAP PAGE: 54

SITUATED ON THE northwest coast of Africa, the territory of Western Sahara is controlled by Morocco.

WESTERN SAMOA
Status: MONARCHY
Area: 2,831 sq km (1,093 sq mls)
Population: 171,000
Capital: APIA
Language: SAMOAN, ENGLISH
Religion: PROTESTANT, R.CATHOLIC, MORMON
Currency: TALA
Organizations: COMM., UN

MAP PAGE: 7

WESTERN SAMOA CONSISTS of two main mountainous and forested islands and seven small islands in the South Pacific Ocean. Seventy per cent of people live on Upolu. The climate is tropical. The economy is based on agriculture, with some fishing and light manufacturing. Traditional exports are coconut products, timber, taro, cocoa and fruit, but cyclones in recent years devastated the coconut palms. Tourism is increasing, but the islands depend upon workers' remittances and foreign aid.

YEMEN
Status: REPUBLIC
Area: 527,968 sq km (203,850 sq mls)
Population: 14,501,000
Capital: ŞAN'Ā
Language: ARABIC
Religion: SUNNI MUSLIM, SHI'A MUSLIM
Currency: DINAR, RIAL
Organizations: UN

MAP PAGE: 20

YEMEN OCCUPIES THE southwestern Arabian Peninsula, on the Red Sea and Gulf of Aden. Beyond the Red Sea coastal plain the land rises to a mountain range then descends to desert plateaux. Much of Yemen is hot and arid, but rainfall in the west supports crops and most settlement. Farming and fishing are the main activities, with cotton the main cash crop. Oil production is increasingly important. Remittances from workers abroad are the main foreign exchange earner.

YUGOSLAVIA
Status: REPUBLIC
Area: 102,173 sq km (39,449 sq mls)
Population: 10,544,000
Capital: BELGRADE
Language: SERBO-CROAT, ALBANIAN, HUNGARIAN
Religion: SERBIAN ORTHODOX, MONTENEGRIN ORTHODOX, SUNNI MUSLIM
Currency: DINAR
Organizations: UN

MAP PAGE: 49

THE SOUTH EUROPEAN state comprises only two of the former Yugoslav republics: the large and populous but landlocked Serbia and the much smaller Montenegro on the Adriatic Sea. The landscape is for the most part rugged, mountainous and forested. Northern Serbia (including the formerly autonomous province of Vojvodina) is low-lying, drained by the Danube river system. The climate is Mediterranean on the coast, continental inland. War and economic sanctions have ruined Serbia's economy and damaged that of Montenegro.

ZAIRE
see CONGO page 9

MAP PAGE: 124-125

ZAMBIA
Status: REPUBLIC
Area: 752,614 sq km (290,586 sq mls)
Population: 9,373,000
Capital: LUSAKA
Language: ENGLISH, BEMBA, NYANJA, TONGA, MANY LOCAL LANGUAGES
Religion: PROTESTANT, R.CATHOLIC, TRAD. BELIEFS, SUNNI MUSLIM
Currency: KWACHA
Organizations: COMM., OAU, SADC, UN

MAP PAGE: 57

A LANDLOCKED STATE in central Africa, Zambia borders seven countries. It is dominated by high savannah plateaux and flanked by the Zambezi river in the south. Most people live in the central Copperbelt. The climate is tropical with a rainy season from November to May. Agriculture, which involves 70 per cent of the workforce, is mainly at subsistence level. Copper is still the mainstay of the economy, though reserves are declining. Lead, zinc, cobalt and tobacco are also exported. Manufacturing and tourism are important.

ZIMBABWE
Status: REPUBLIC
Area: 390,759 sq km (150,873 sq mls)
Population: 11,526,000
Capital: HARARE
Language: ENGLISH (OFFICIAL), SHONA, NDEBELE
Religion: PROTESTANT, R.CATHOLIC, TRAD.BELIEFS
Currency: DOLLAR
Organizations: COMM., OAU, SADC, UN

MAP PAGE: 57

ZIMBABWE, A LANDLOCKED state in southern central Africa, consists of high plateaux flanked by the Zambezi river valley and Lake Kariba in the north and the Limpopo in the south. Climatic conditions are temperate because of altitude. Most people live in central Zimbabwe. Tobacco, cotton, sugar, tea, coffee and beef are produced for export as are a variety of minerals including gold, nickel, asbestos and copper. Manufacturing provides a wide range of goods. Tourism is a major foreign exchange earner.

© Bartholomew

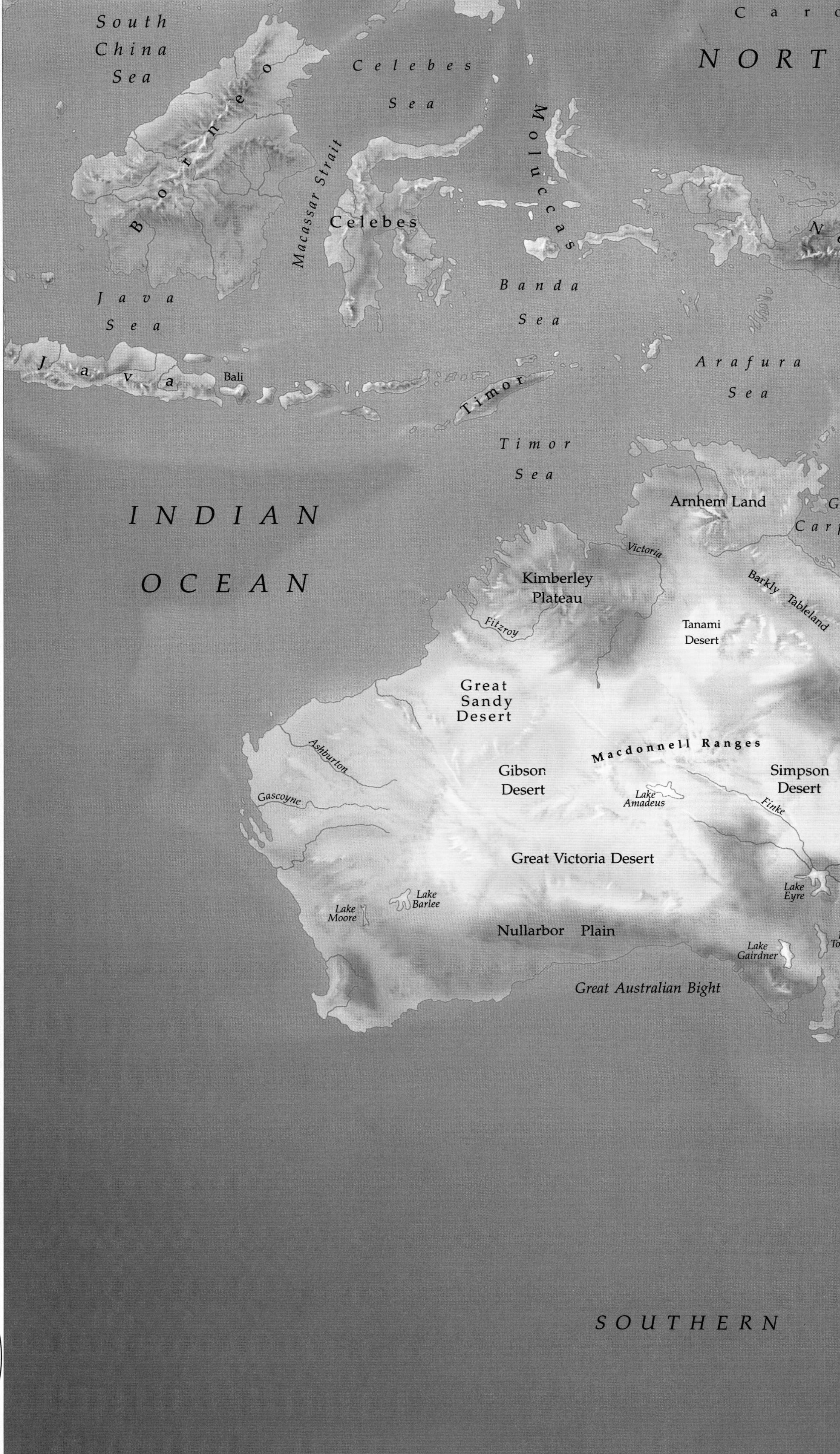

GEOGRAPHICAL STATISTICS

MOUNTAINS

m		ft
4,509	MT WILHELM	14,793
4,073	MT VICTORIA	13,364
4,000	MT HAGEN	13,124
3,754	MT COOK	12,316
2,230	MT KOSCIUSKO	7,316

INLAND WATERS

sq km		sq miles
0–8,900	LAKE EYRE	0–3,435
0–5,780	LAKE TORRENS	0–2,230
0–4,770	LAKE GAIRDNER	0–1,840
0–2,410	LAKE FROME	0–930

ISLANDS

sq km		sq miles
808,510	NEW GUINEA	312,085
757,050	BORNEO	292,220
189,040	CELEBES (Sulawesi)	72,970
150,460	SOUTH ISLAND	58,080
134,045	JAVA	51,740
114,690	NORTH ISLAND	44,270
68,330	TASMANIA	26,375
36,500	NEW BRITAIN	14,090
33,915	TIMOR	13,090

RIVERS

km		miles
3,750	MURRAY–DARLING	2,330
1,480	LACHLAN	920
840	FLINDERS	520
820	GASCOYNE	510
650	VICTORIA	400

DRAINAGE BASINS

sq km		sq miles
910,000	MURRAY–DARLING	351,000
108,000	FLINDERS	42,000
85,000	LACHLAN	33,000
80,000	GASCOYNE	31,000
78,000	VICTORIA	30,000

MAXIMUM WATER DEPTHS

m		ft
9,175	CORAL SEA	30,102
7,440	BANDA SEA	24,409
6,220	CELEBES SEA	20,410
5,514	SOUTH CHINA SEA	18,091
4,570	TASMAN SEA	14,993
3,310	TIMOR SEA	10,860

SEE MAPS pages 4–9, 33

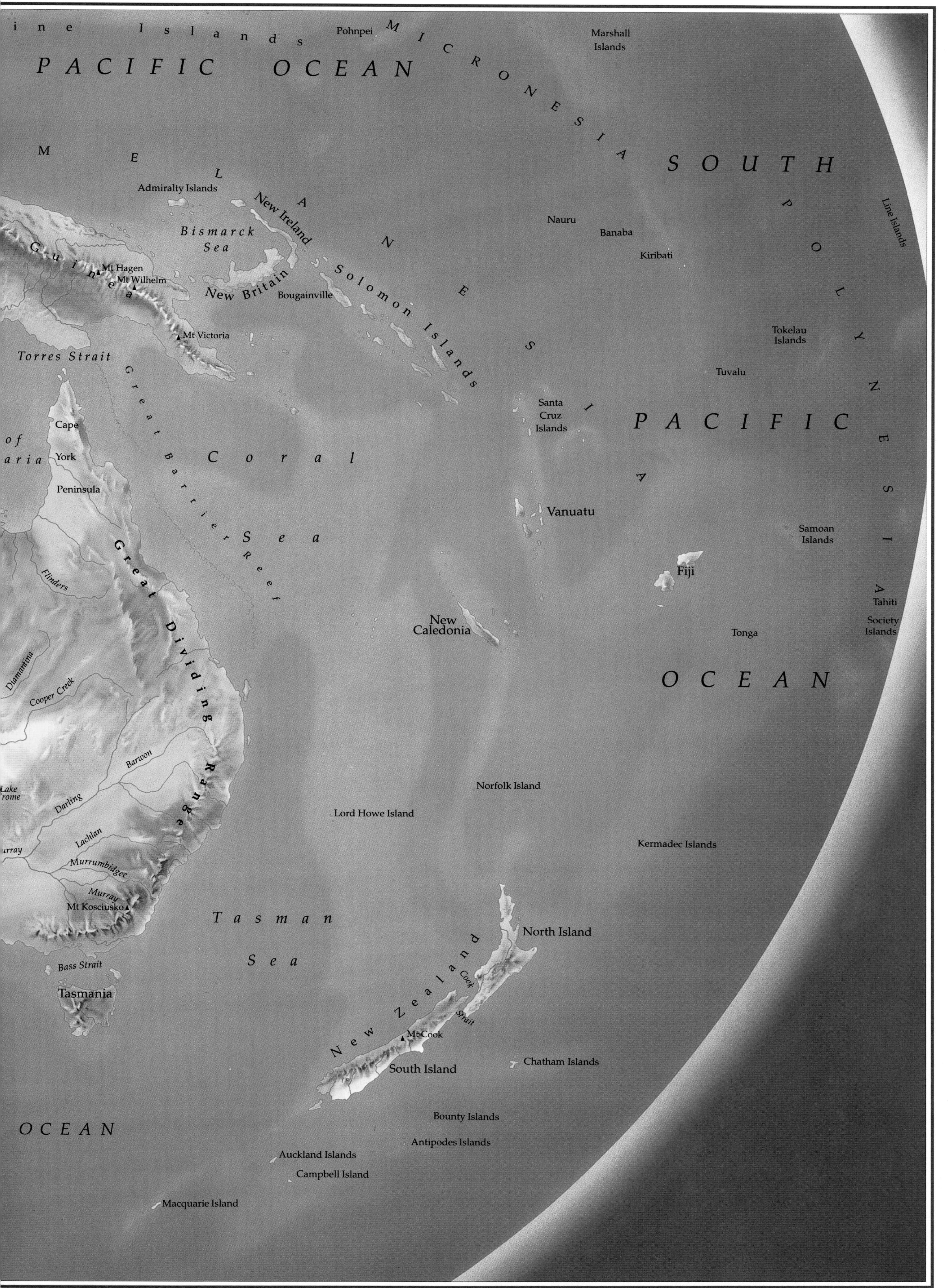

ine Islands

Pohnpei

Marshall
Islands

PACIFIC OCEAN

MICRONESIA

SOUTH

M

E

L

A

Admiralty Islands

Nauru

Banaba

Kiribati

Line Islands

New Ireland

Bismarck
Sea

N

E

S

I

POLYNESIA

Mt Hagen
Mt Wilhelm

New Britain

Bougainville

Solomon Islands

A

Tokelau
Islands

Guinea

Mt Victoria

Tuvalu

Torres Strait

Santa
Cruz
Islands

PACIFIC

Great Barrier Reef

Cape

York

Peninsula

Coral

Sea

Vanuatu

A

Samoan
Islands

of
aria

Fiji

Flinders

New
Caledonia

Tahiti

Society
Islands

Great Dividing Range

Tonga

OCEAN

Diamantina

Cooper Creek

Barwon

Lake
rome

Darling

Norfolk Island

Lord Howe Island

Lachlan

Kermadec Islands

urray

Murrumbidgee

Murray

Mt Kosciusko

Tasman

Sea

North Island

Cook

Bass Strait

Tasmania

New Zealand

Strait

Mt Cook

Chatham Islands

South Island

OCEAN

Bounty Islands

Antipodes Islands

Auckland Islands

Campbell Island

Macquarie Island

©Bartholomew

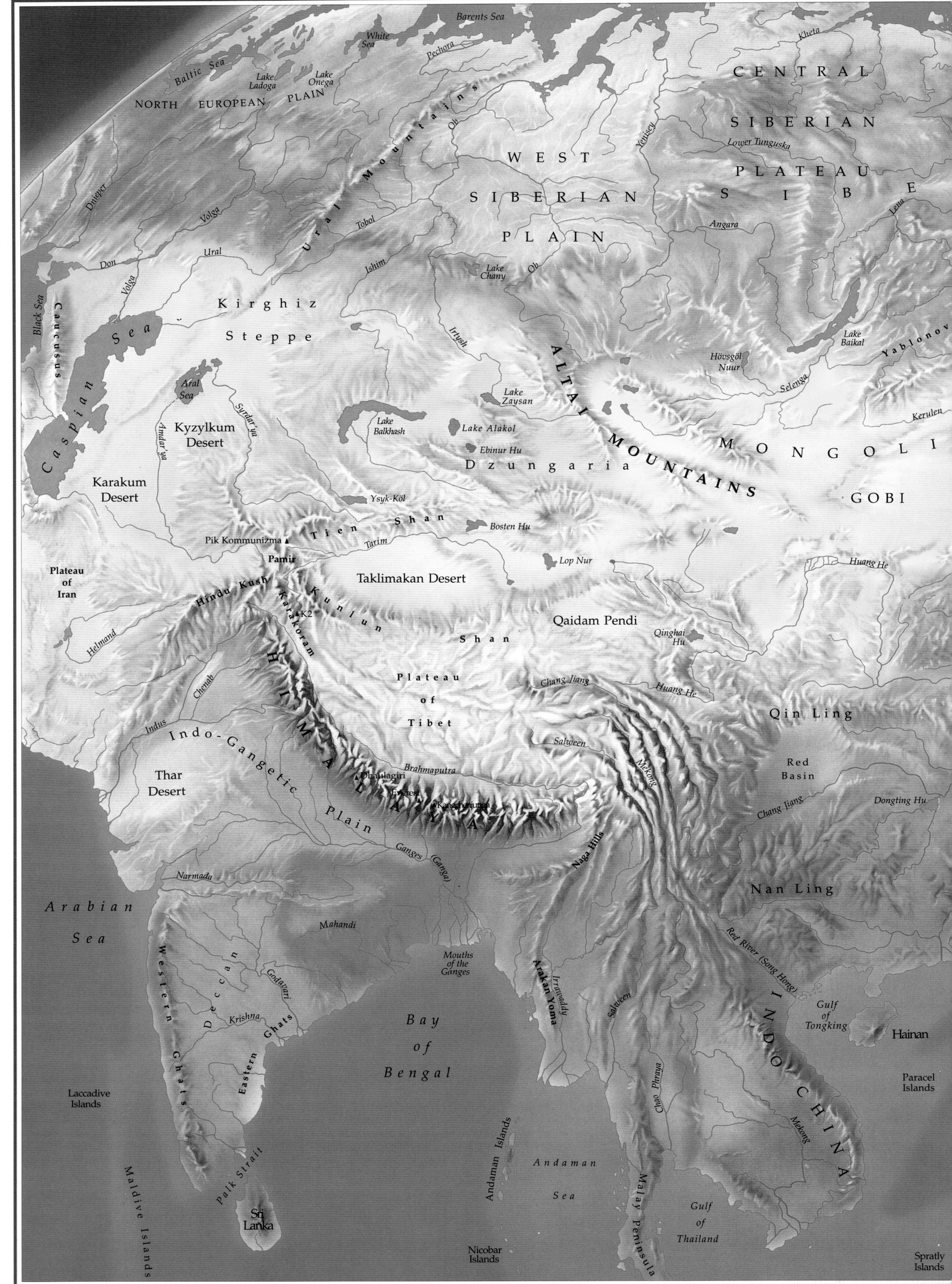

Barents Sea

White Sea

Baltic Sea

Lake Ladoga

Lake Onega

NORTH EUROPEAN PLAIN

Dnieper

Volga

Ural Mountains

Tobol

Ob

Kheta

CENTRAL SIBERIAN PLATEAU

Lower Tunguska

WEST SIBERIAN PLAIN

SIBE

Yenisey

Volga

Don

Ural

Ishim

Ob

Angara

Lena

Black Sea

Caucasus

Caspian Sea

Aral Sea

KIRGHIZ Steppe

Irtysh

Lake Chany

Lake Zaysan

ALTAI MOUNTAINS

Hövsgöl Nuur

Lake Baikal

Yablonov

Selenga

Kerulen

Kyzylkum Desert

Syrdar'ya

Lake Balkhash

Lake Alakol

Ebinur Hu

DZungaria

MONGOLI

Karakum Desert

Amdar'ya

Ysyk-Köl

Bosten Hu

GOBI

Plateau of Iran

Pik Kommunizma

Pamir

Tien Shan

Tarim

Taklimakan Desert

Lop Nur

Huang He

Hindu Kush

Karakoram

K2

Kunlun

Shan

Qaidam Pendi

Qinghai Hu

Helmand

HIMALAYA

Plateau of Tibet

Chang Jiang

Huang He

Qin Ling

Indus

Chenab

Dhaulagiri

Everest

Kangchenjunga

Brahmaputra

Salween

Mekong

Red Basin

Chang Jiang

Dongting Hu

Thar Desert

Indo-Gangetic Plain

Ganges (Ganga)

Naga Hills

Nan Ling

Narmada

Red River (Song Hong)

Arabian Sea

Mahandi

Western Ghats

Deccan

Godavari

Eastern Ghats

Krishna

Mouths of the Ganges

Bay of Bengal

Arakan Yoma

Irrawaddy

Salween

INDO CHINA

Gulf of Tongking

Hainan

Laccadive Islands

Chao Phraya

Mekong

Paracel Islands

Palk Strait

Sri Lanka

Andaman Islands

Andaman Sea

Malay Peninsula

Gulf of Thailand

Maldive Islands

Nicobar Islands

Spratly Islands

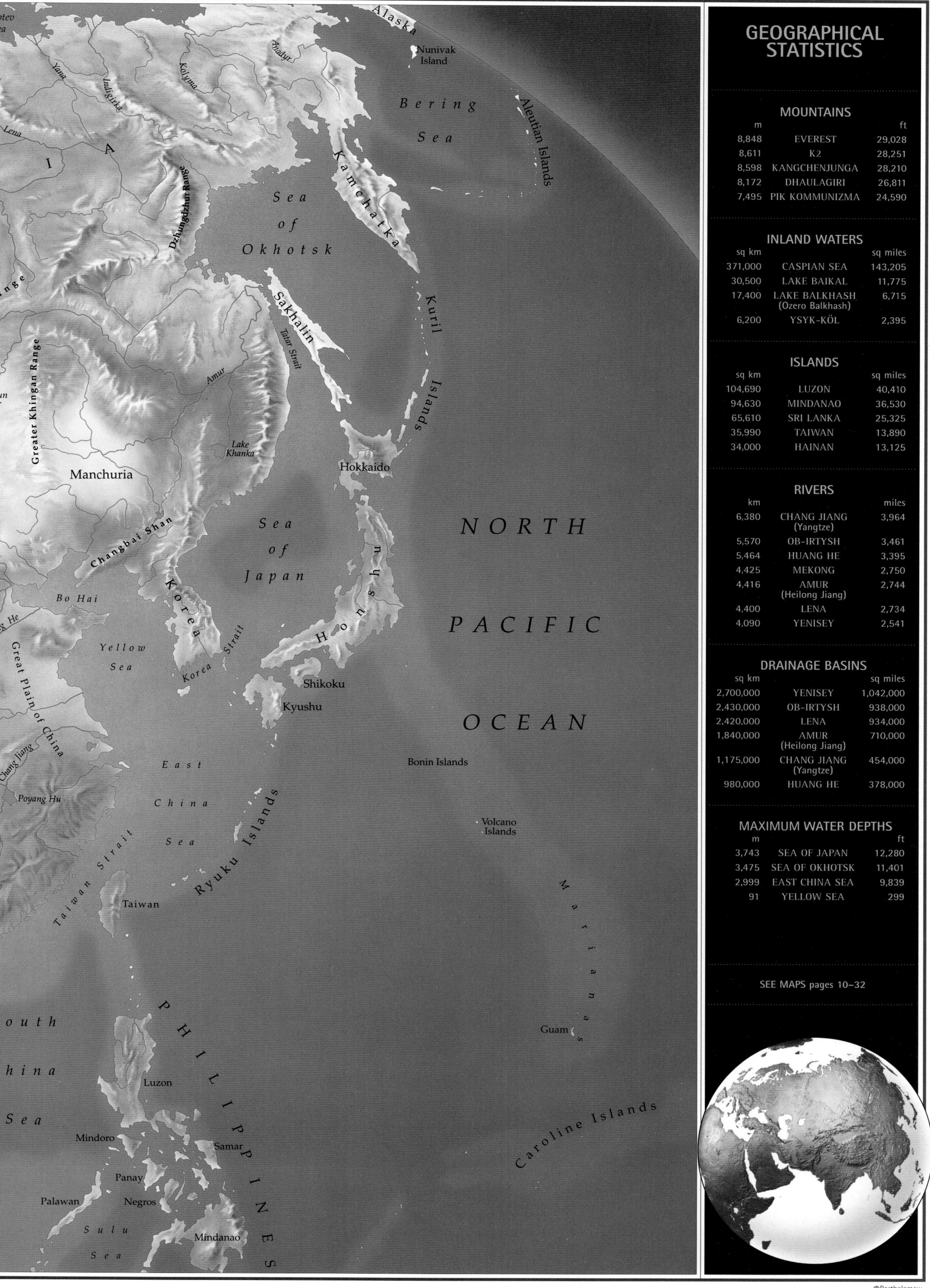

GEOGRAPHICAL STATISTICS

MOUNTAINS

m		ft
8,848	EVEREST	29,028
8,611	K2	28,251
8,598	KANGCHENJUNGA	28,210
8,172	DHAULAGIRI	26,811
7,495	PIK KOMMUNIZMA	24,590

INLAND WATERS

sq km		sq miles
371,000	CASPIAN SEA	143,205
30,500	LAKE BAIKAL	11,775
17,400	LAKE BALKHASH (Ozero Balkhash)	6,715
6,200	YSYK-KÖL	2,395

ISLANDS

sq km		sq miles
104,690	LUZON	40,410
94,630	MINDANAO	36,530
65,610	SRI LANKA	25,325
35,990	TAIWAN	13,890
34,000	HAINAN	13,125

RIVERS

km		miles
6,380	CHANG JIANG (Yangtze)	3,964
5,570	OB-IRTYSH	3,461
5,464	HUANG HE	3,395
4,425	MEKONG	2,750
4,416	AMUR (Heilong Jiang)	2,744
4,400	LENA	2,734
4,090	YENISEY	2,541

DRAINAGE BASINS

sq km		sq miles
2,700,000	YENISEY	1,042,000
2,430,000	OB-IRTYSH	938,000
2,420,000	LENA	934,000
1,840,000	AMUR (Heilong Jiang)	710,000
1,175,000	CHANG JIANG (Yangtze)	454,000
980,000	HUANG HE	378,000

MAXIMUM WATER DEPTHS

m		ft
3,743	SEA OF JAPAN	12,280
3,475	SEA OF OKHOTSK	11,401
2,999	EAST CHINA SEA	9,839
91	YELLOW SEA	299

SEE MAPS pages 10–32

©Bartholomew

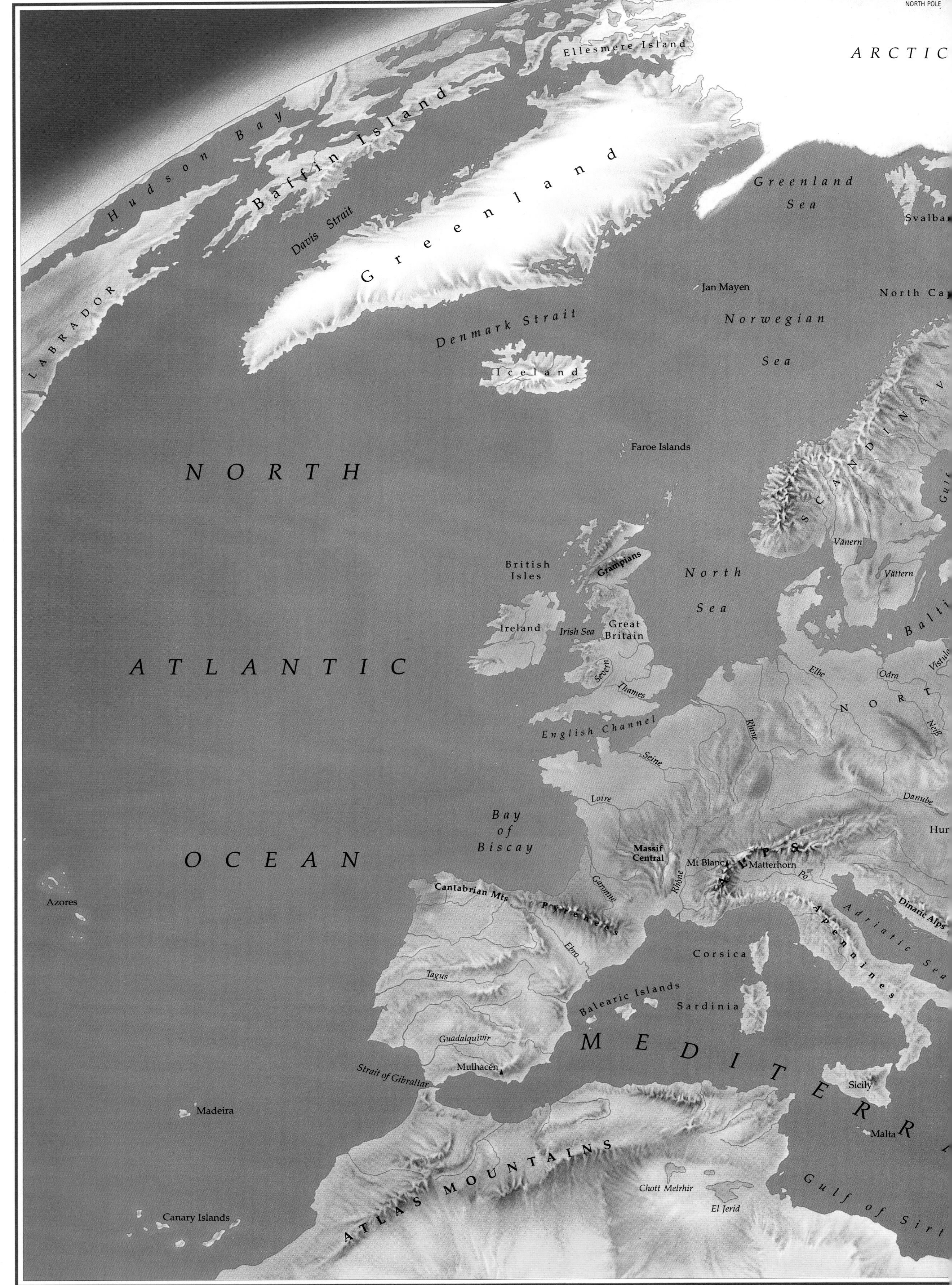

NORTH POLE

A R C T I C

Ellesmere Island

G r e e n l a n d
Sea

Svalba

Hudson Bay

Baffin Island

Davis Strait

G r e e n l a n d

Jan Mayen

North Ca

N o r w e g i a n

Denmark Strait

S e a

Iceland

LABRADOR

Faroe Islands

N O R T H

S C A N D I N A V

Gul

Vänern

British
Isles

Grampians

N o r t h

Vättern

A T L A N T I C

Ireland

Irish Sea

Great
Britain

S e a

B a l t i

Elbe

Odra

Vistul

Severn

N

Neß

Thames

O

R

English Channel

Seine

Rhine

O C E A N

B a y
o f
B i s c a y

Loire

Danube

Hur

**Massif
Central**

Rhône

Mt Blanc

Matterhorn

A L P S

Po

A d r i a t i c

Azores

Cantabrian Mts

Garonne

P y r e n e e s

A p e n n i n e s

S e a

Dinaric Alps

Ebro

Corsica

Tagus

Balearic Islands

Sardinia

Guadalquivir

M E D I T E R R

Strait of Gibraltar

Mulhacén ▲

Madeira

Sicily

Malta

A T L A S   M O U N T A I N S

Chott Melrhir

Gulf of Sirt

Canary Islands

El Jerid

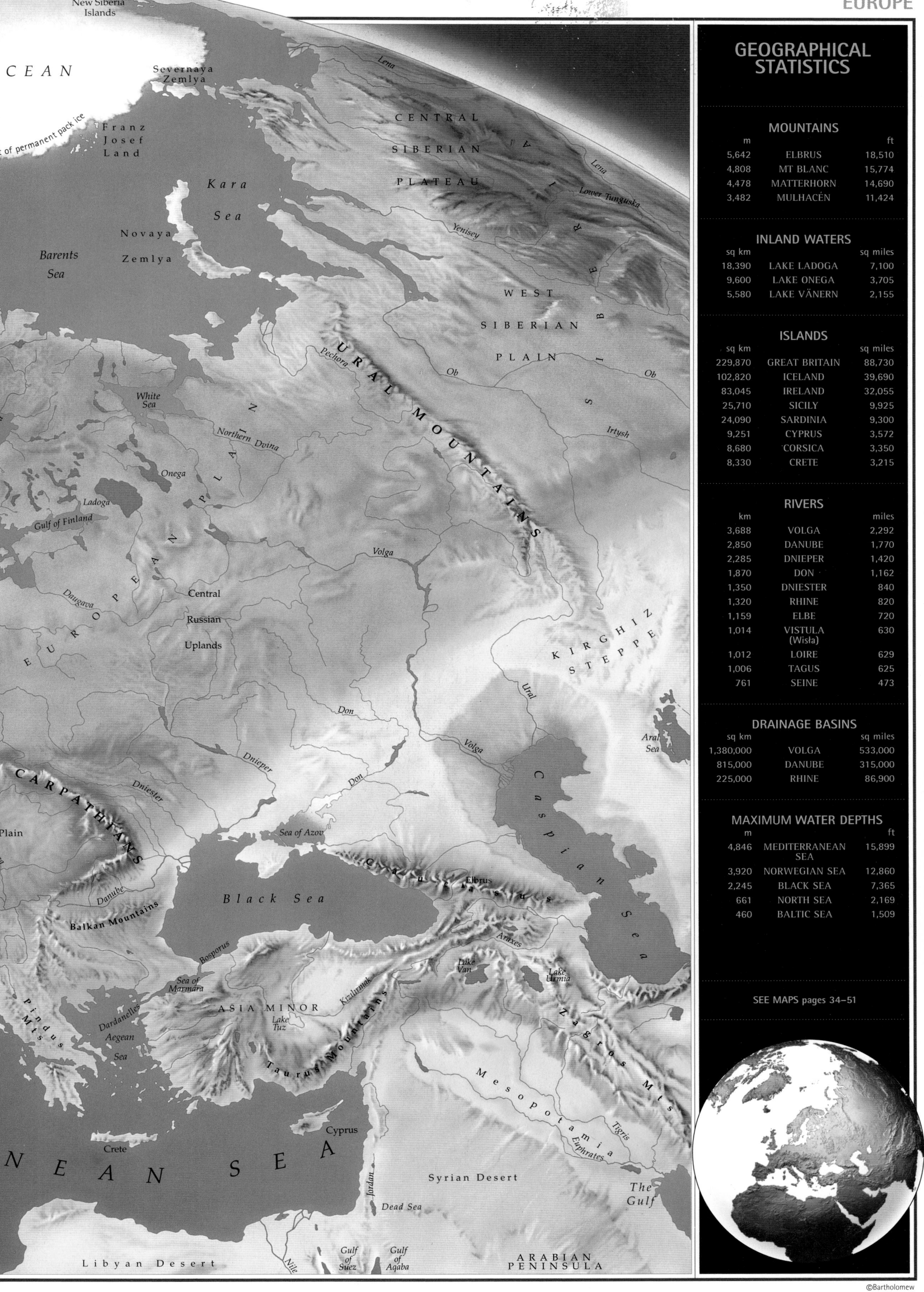

GEOGRAPHICAL STATISTICS

MOUNTAINS

m		ft
5,642	ELBRUS	18,510
4,808	MT BLANC	15,774
4,478	MATTERHORN	14,690
3,482	MULHACÉN	11,424

INLAND WATERS

sq km		sq miles
18,390	LAKE LADOGA	7,100
9,600	LAKE ONEGA	3,705
5,580	LAKE VÄNERN	2,155

ISLANDS

sq km		sq miles
229,870	GREAT BRITAIN	88,730
102,820	ICELAND	39,690
83,045	IRELAND	32,055
25,710	SICILY	9,925
24,090	SARDINIA	9,300
9,251	CYPRUS	3,572
8,680	CORSICA	3,350
8,330	CRETE	3,215

RIVERS

km		miles
3,688	VOLGA	2,292
2,850	DANUBE	1,770
2,285	DNIEPER	1,420
1,870	DON	1,162
1,350	DNIESTER	840
1,320	RHINE	820
1,159	ELBE	720
1,014	VISTULA (Wisła)	630
1,012	LOIRE	629
1,006	TAGUS	625
761	SEINE	473

DRAINAGE BASINS

sq km		sq miles
1,380,000	VOLGA	533,000
815,000	DANUBE	315,000
225,000	RHINE	86,900

MAXIMUM WATER DEPTHS

m		ft
4,846	MEDITERRANEAN SEA	15,899
3,920	NORWEGIAN SEA	12,860
2,245	BLACK SEA	7,365
661	NORTH SEA	2,169
460	BALTIC SEA	1,509

SEE MAPS pages 34–51

©Bartholomew

Azores

Iberian
Peninsula

Strait of Gibraltar

Malta

Crete

Mediterranean

Gulf of Sirte

Chott
Melrhir

El Jerid

Madeira

ATLAS MOUNTAINS

Canary Islands

S A H A R A

Libyan

Hoggar

Tibesti

Jebel
Marra

Lac Faguibine

Niger

S A H E L

Lake Chad

Cape Verde
Islands

Sénégal

Gambia

Lake
Volta

Benue

Ubangi

Uele

Grain Coast

Ivory Coast

Gold Coast

Bight of
Benin

Mouths
of the Niger

Mt Cameroun

Sanaga

Congo (Zaïre)

Gulf of Guinea

Bioco

Príncipe

São Tomé

Lac
Mai-Ndome

St Paul Rocks

Annobón

Congo

Kasai

Lake
Upemba

Ascension

Cuango

SOUTH AMERICA

S O U T H

Bié
Plateau

St Helena

A T L A N T I C

Cunene

Okavango

Etosha Pan

Namib Desert

Makgadikgadi
Pan

Lake
Ngami

K A L A H A R I

O C E A N

D e s e r t

Orange

Great
Karoo

Cape of Good Hope

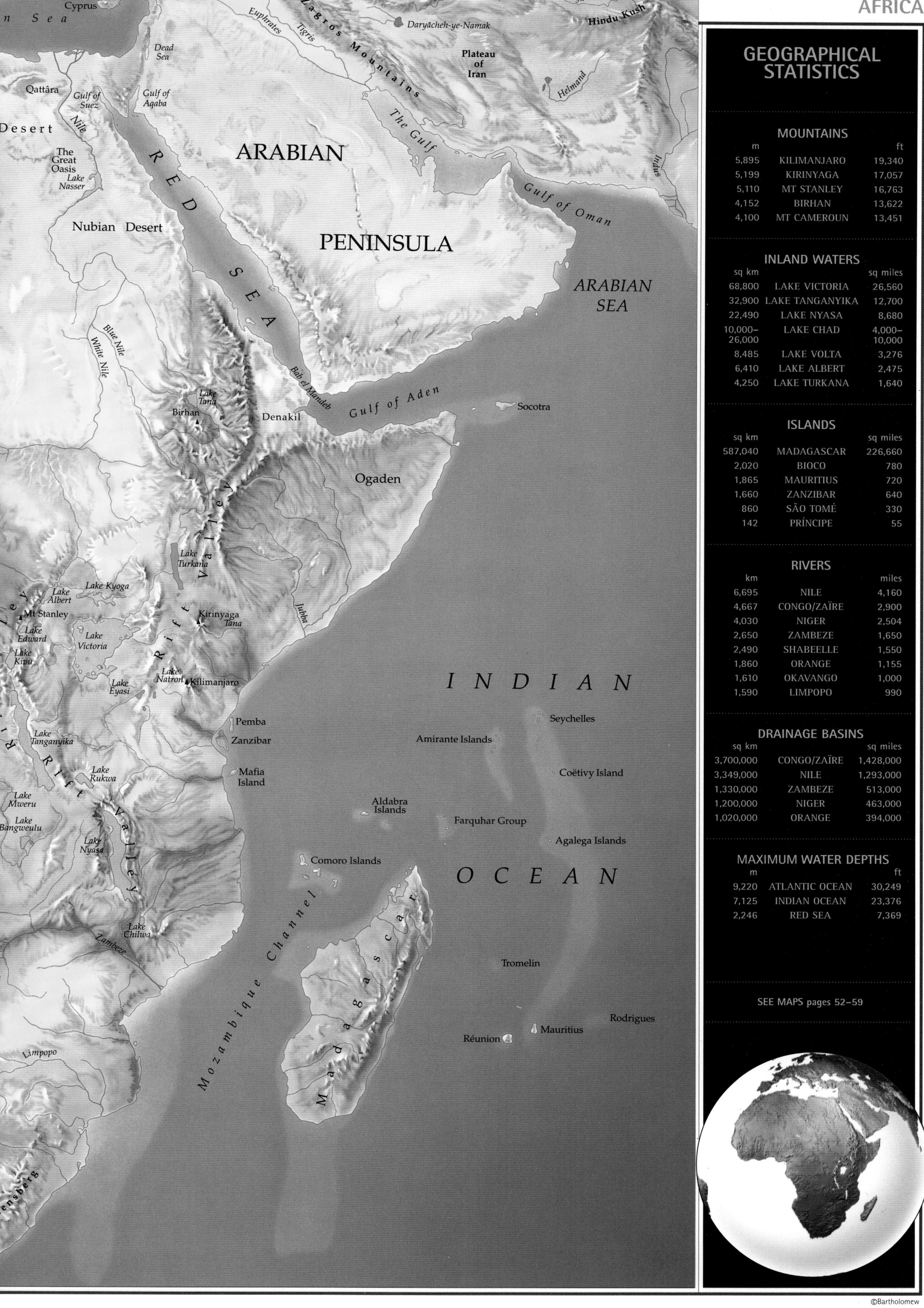

Cyprus
n Sea
Euphrates
Tigris
Zagros Mountains
Amudar'ya
Daryācheh-ye-Namak
Hindu Kush
Dead Sea
Plateau of Iran
Qattâra
Gulf of Suez
Gulf of Aqaba
Helmand
Desert
Nile
The Great Oasis
Lake Nasser
ARABIAN
Nubian Desert
R E D   S E A
Gulf of Oman
PENINSULA
ARABIAN SEA
Blue Nile
White Nile
Lake Tana
Birhan
Denakil
Bab el Mandeb
Gulf of Aden
Socotra
Ogaden
Rift Valley
Lake Turkana
Lake Kyoga
Lake Albert
Mt Stanley
Lake Edward
Lake Kivu
Lake Victoria
Kirinyaga
Tana
Jubba
Lake Eyasi
Lake Natron
Kilimanjaro
Rift Valley
Pemba
Zanzibar
INDIAN
Lake Tanganyika
Seychelles
Amirante Islands
Mafia Island
Coëtivy Island
Lake Rukwa
Aldabra Islands
Lake Mweru
Farquhar Group
Lake Bangweulu
Lake Nyasa
Agalega Islands
Comoro Islands
OCEAN
Lake Chilwa
Zambeze
Mozambique Channel
Madagascar
Tromelin
Limpopo
Rodrigues
Réunion
Mauritius
kensberg

GEOGRAPHICAL STATISTICS

MOUNTAINS

m		ft
5,895	KILIMANJARO	19,340
5,199	KIRINYAGA	17,057
5,110	MT STANLEY	16,763
4,152	BIRHAN	13,622
4,100	MT CAMEROUN	13,451

INLAND WATERS

sq km		sq miles
68,800	LAKE VICTORIA	26,560
32,900	LAKE TANGANYIKA	12,700
22,490	LAKE NYASA	8,680
10,000–26,000	LAKE CHAD	4,000–10,000
8,485	LAKE VOLTA	3,276
6,410	LAKE ALBERT	2,475
4,250	LAKE TURKANA	1,640

ISLANDS

sq km		sq miles
587,040	MADAGASCAR	226,660
2,020	BIOCO	780
1,865	MAURITIUS	720
1,660	ZANZIBAR	640
860	SÃO TOMÉ	330
142	PRÍNCIPE	55

RIVERS

km		miles
6,695	NILE	4,160
4,667	CONGO/ZAÏRE	2,900
4,030	NIGER	2,504
2,650	ZAMBEZE	1,650
2,490	SHABEELLE	1,550
1,860	ORANGE	1,155
1,610	OKAVANGO	1,000
1,590	LIMPOPO	990

DRAINAGE BASINS

sq km		sq miles
3,700,000	CONGO/ZAÏRE	1,428,000
3,349,000	NILE	1,293,000
1,330,000	ZAMBEZE	513,000
1,200,000	NIGER	463,000
1,020,000	ORANGE	394,000

MAXIMUM WATER DEPTHS

m		ft
9,220	ATLANTIC OCEAN	30,249
7,125	INDIAN OCEAN	23,376
2,246	RED SEA	7,369

SEE MAPS pages 52–59

©Bartholomew

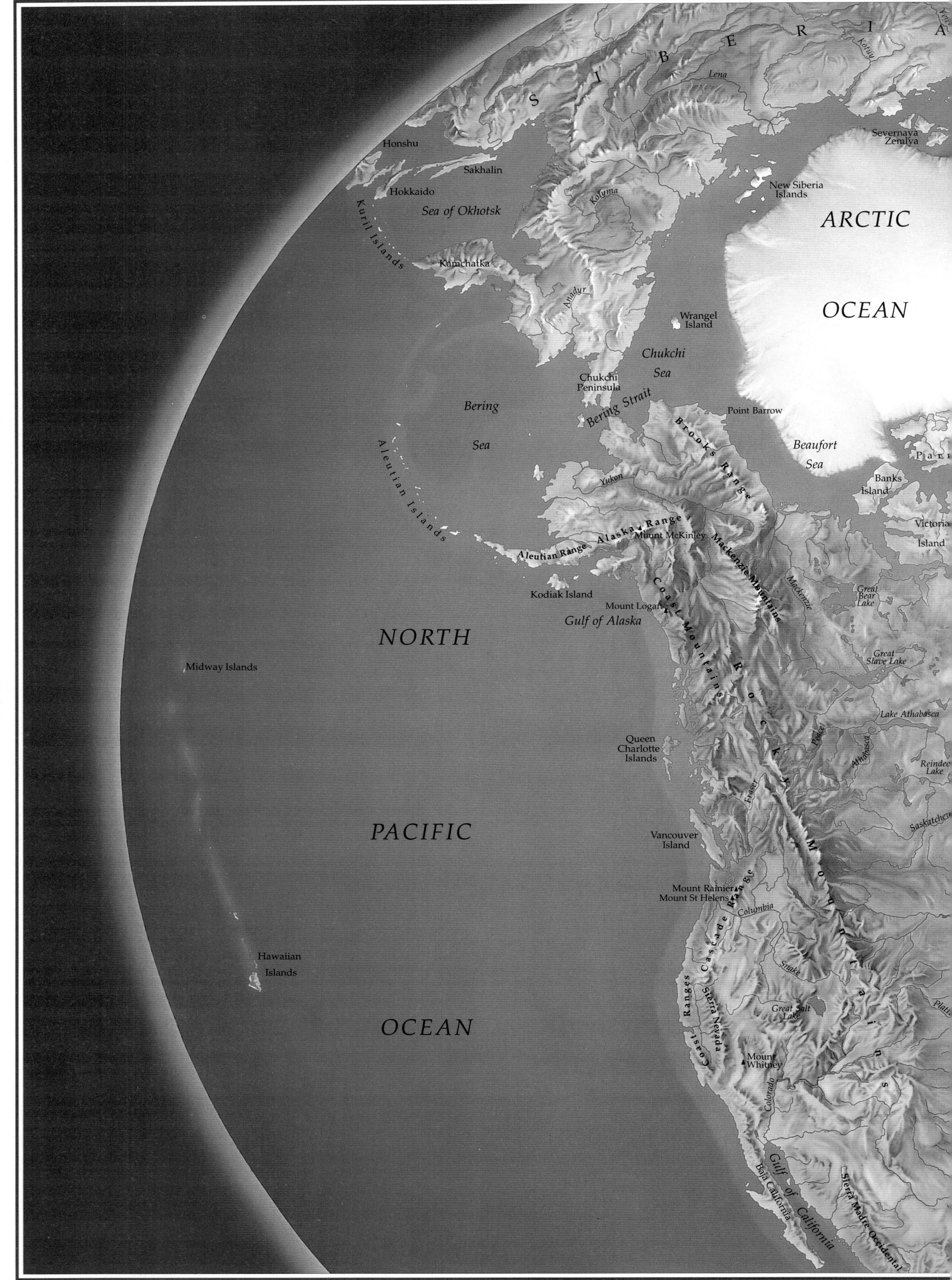

S I B E R I A

Lena

Kolyma

Severnaya
Zemlya

Honshu

Sakhalin

New Siberia
Islands

ARCTIC

Hokkaido

Sea of Okhotsk

OCEAN

Kuril Islands

Kamchatka

Wrangel
Island

*Chukchi
Sea*

Bering

Chukchi
Peninsula

Point Barrow

*Beaufort
Sea*

Sea

Bering Strait

Brooks Range

Pa

Banks
Island

Anadyr

Yukon

Aleutian Islands

Mackenzie Mountains

Victoria
Island

Aleutian Range

Alaska Range

Mount McKinley

Mackenzie

Kodiak Island

Mount Logan

*Great
Bear
Lake*

Coast Mountains

Gulf of Alaska

NORTH

R o c k y

*Great
Slave
Lake*

Midway Islands

Lake Athabasca

Peace

PACIFIC

Queen
Charlotte
Islands

Athabasca

*Reindeer
Lake*

Fraser

Saskatchewa

Vancouver
Island

Mount Rainier

Mount St Helens

M o u n t a i n s

Cascade Range

Columbia

OCEAN

Snake

Hawaiian
Islands

Ranges

Sierra Nevada

*Great Salt
Lake*

Platt

Coast

Mount
Whitney

Colorado

*Gulf
of
California*

Baja California

Sierra Madre Occidental

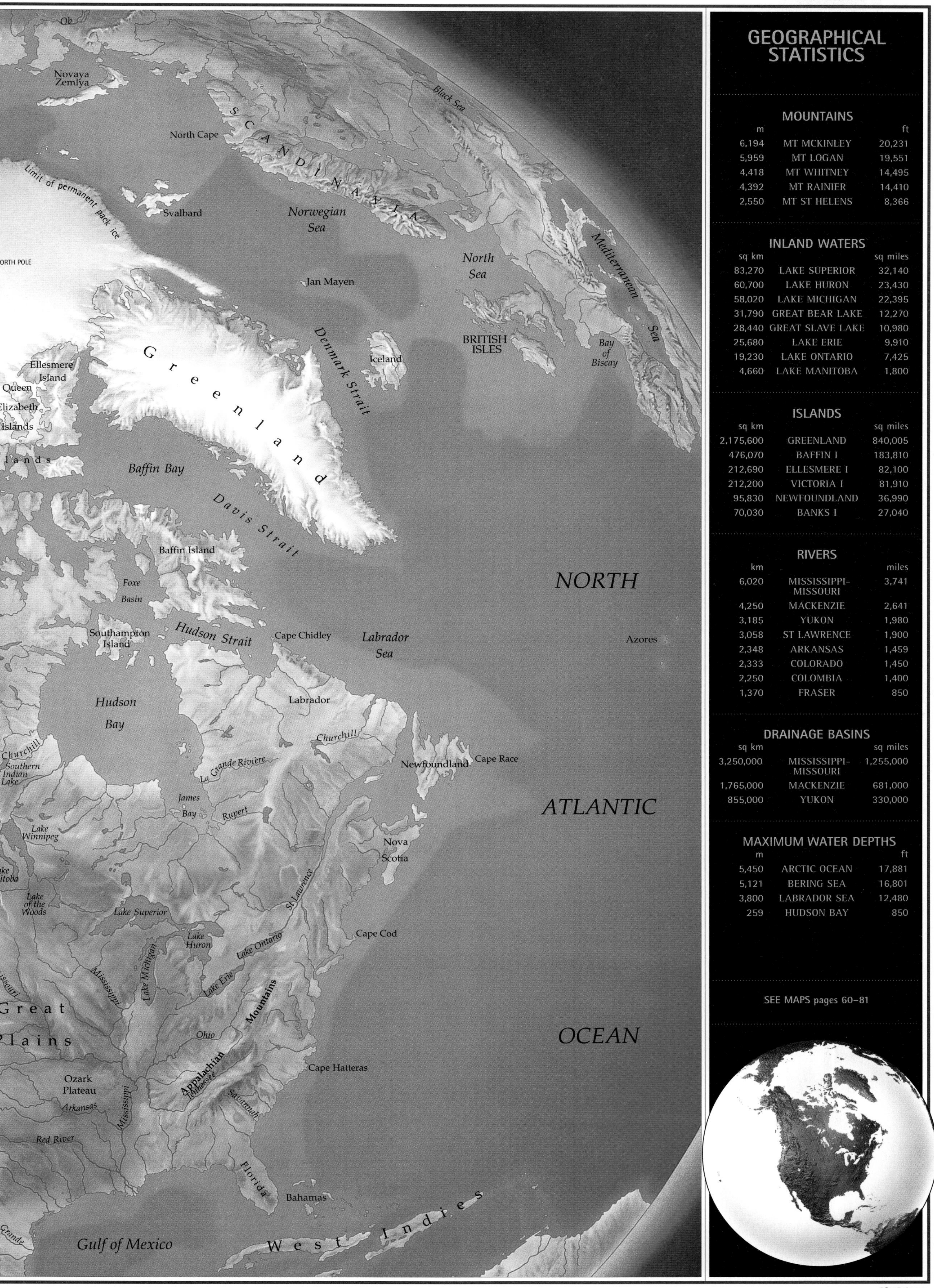

GEOGRAPHICAL STATISTICS

MOUNTAINS

m		ft
6,194	MT MCKINLEY	20,231
5,959	MT LOGAN	19,551
4,418	MT WHITNEY	14,495
4,392	MT RAINIER	14,410
2,550	MT ST HELENS	8,366

INLAND WATERS

sq km		sq miles
83,270	LAKE SUPERIOR	32,140
60,700	LAKE HURON	23,430
58,020	LAKE MICHIGAN	22,395
31,790	GREAT BEAR LAKE	12,270
28,440	GREAT SLAVE LAKE	10,980
25,680	LAKE ERIE	9,910
19,230	LAKE ONTARIO	7,425
4,660	LAKE MANITOBA	1,800

ISLANDS

sq km		sq miles
2,175,600	GREENLAND	840,005
476,070	BAFFIN I	183,810
212,690	ELLESMERE I	82,100
212,200	VICTORIA I	81,910
95,830	NEWFOUNDLAND	36,990
70,030	BANKS I	27,040

RIVERS

km		miles
6,020	MISSISSIPPI-MISSOURI	3,741
4,250	MACKENZIE	2,641
3,185	YUKON	1,980
3,058	ST LAWRENCE	1,900
2,348	ARKANSAS	1,459
2,333	COLORADO	1,450
2,250	COLOMBIA	1,400
1,370	FRASER	850

DRAINAGE BASINS

sq km		sq miles
3,250,000	MISSISSIPPI-MISSOURI	1,255,000
1,765,000	MACKENZIE	681,000
855,000	YUKON	330,000

MAXIMUM WATER DEPTHS

m		ft
5,450	ARCTIC OCEAN	17,881
5,121	BERING SEA	16,801
3,800	LABRADOR SEA	12,480
259	HUDSON BAY	850

SEE MAPS pages 60–81

©Bartholomew

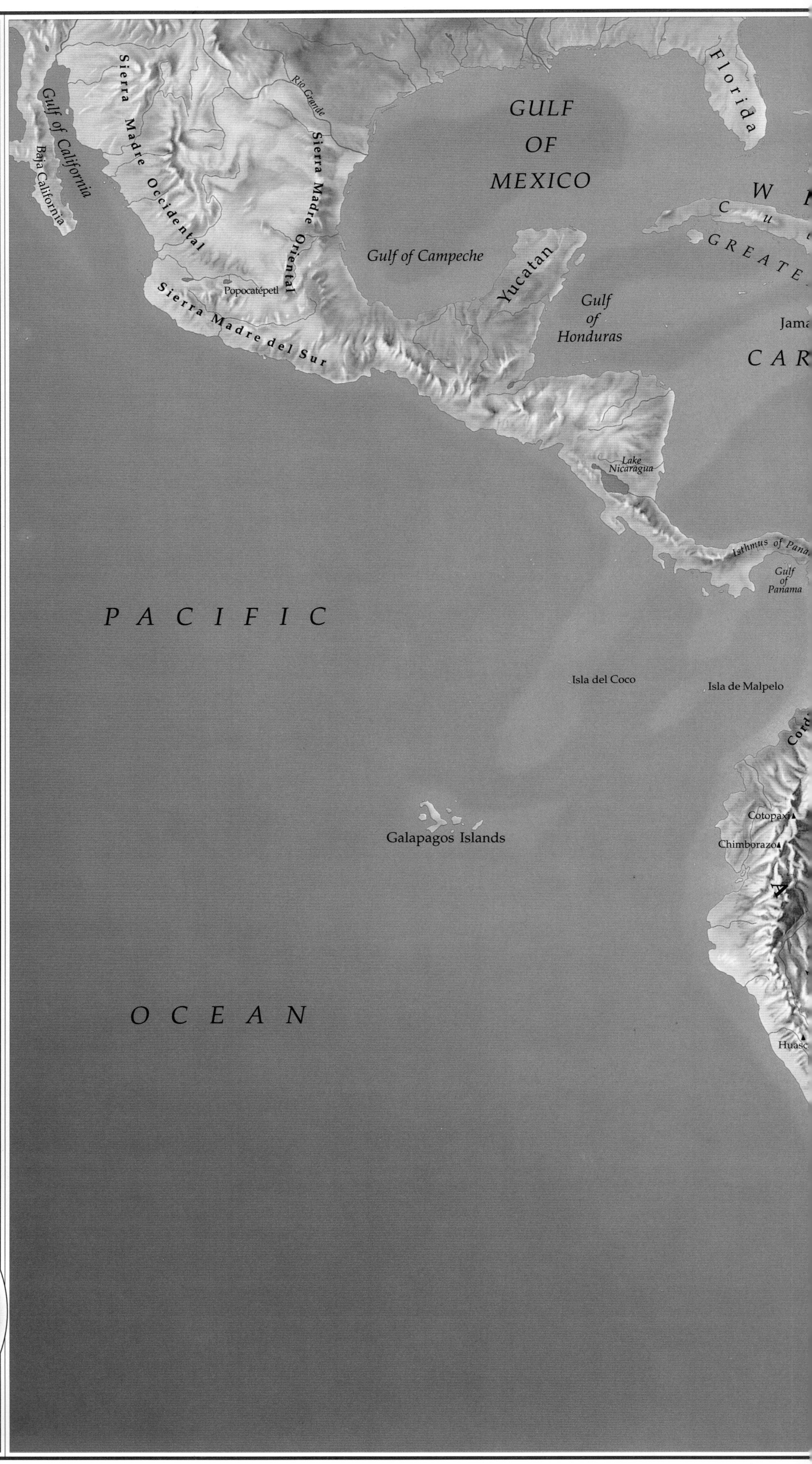

GEOGRAPHICAL STATISTICS

38

MOUNTAINS

m		ft
6,768	HUASCARAN	22,205
6,388	ANCOHUMA	20,958
6,310	CHIMBORAZO	20,702
5,896	COTOPAXI	19,344
5,452	POPOCATÉPETL	17,887
2,810	RORAIMA	9,219

INLAND WATERS

sq km		sq miles
8,340	LAKE TITICACA	3,220
8,270	LAKE NICARAGUA	3,190
1,340	LAKE POOPO	520

ISLANDS

sq km		sq miles
114,525	CUBA	44,205
78,460	HISPANIOLA	30,285
10,990	JAMAICA	4,245
8,895	PUERTO RICO	3,435

RIVERS

km		miles
6,516	AMAZON	4,049
3,200	MADEIRA	1,990
3,000	PURUS	1,860
2,900	SÃO FRANCISCO	1,800
2,870	RIO GRANDE	1,785
2,500	ORINOCO	1,555
2,200	ARAGUAIA	1,370
2,100	XINGU	1,300
2,000	NEGRO	1,240
1,700	PARNAÍBA	1,060
1,609	MARAÑON	1,000
1,550	MAGDALENA	963
1,350	CAUCA	840

DRAINAGE BASINS

sq km		sq miles
7,050,000	AMAZON	2,721,000
1,000,000	NEGRO	386,000
945,000	ORINOCO	365,000
623,000	SÃO FRANCISCO	241,000
260,000	MAGDALENA	100,000

MAXIMUM WATER DEPTHS

m		ft
11,022	PACIFIC OCEAN	36,161
7,100	CARIBBEAN SEA	23,294
4,377	GULF OF MEXICO	14,360

SEE MAPS pages 82–87, 89–90

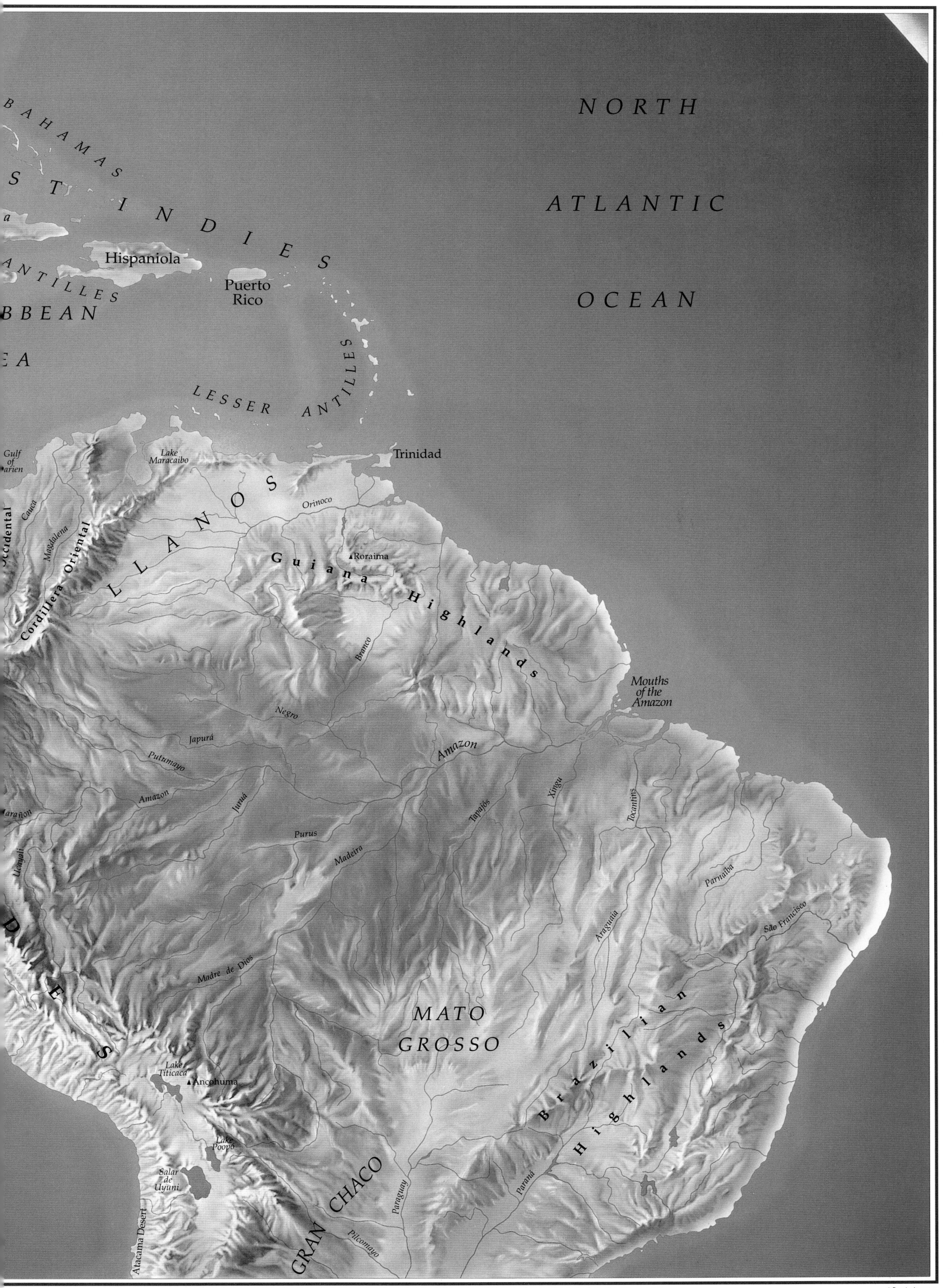

NORTH

ATLANTIC

OCEAN

BAHAMAS

WEST INDIES

Hispaniola

ANTILLES

Puerto
Rico

CARIBBEAN

SEA

LESSER ANTILLES

Gulf
of
Darien

Lake
Maracaibo

Trinidad

Cauca

Magdalena

Cordillera Oriental

L L A N O S

Orinoco

Guiana

▲Roraima

Highlands

Branco

Mouths
of the
Amazon

Negro

Japurá

Putumayo

Amazon

Amazon

Juruá

Tapajós

Xingu

Tocantins

Purus

Madeira

Marañón

Ucayali

Madre de Dios

Parnaíba

Araguaia

São Francisco

MATO
GROSSO

Lake
Titicaca

▲Ancohuma

ANDES

Brazilian

Highlands

Lake
Poopó

GRAN CHACO

Paraguay

Paraná

Salar
de
Uyuni

Atacama Desert

Pilcomayo

©Bartholomew

GEOGRAPHICAL STATISTICS

MOUNTAINS

m		ft
6,960	ACONCAGUA	22,834
6,908	OJOS DEL SALADO	22,664
4,897	VINSON MASSIF	16,066
4,528	MT KIRKPATRICK	14,856
4,181	MT SIDLEY	13,718
3,794	MT EREBUS	12,447

ISLANDS

sq km		sq miles
47,000	TIERRA DEL FUEGO	18,140
12,175	FALKLAND IS	4,700
3,760	SOUTH GEORGIA	1,450

RIVERS

km		miles
4,500	PARANÁ	2,800
2,600	PARAGUAY	1,615
2,200	URUGUAY	1,370
1,500	SALADO	930
1,100	PILCOMAYO	680
810	CHUBUT	500

DRAINAGE BASINS

sq km		sq miles
3,100,000	PARANÁ	1,197,000
1,100,000	PARAGUAY	425,000
800,000	SALADO	309,000
307,000	URUGUAY	119,000

ANTARCTICA

The continental area is 13,340,000 sq km (5,149,000 sq miles).

Ice sheet permanently covers 98% of this, of which 87% lies on continental rock, whilst 11% is floating ice shelves.

The total volume of ice is 30,000,000 cu km (7,000,000 cu miles) with the greatest thickness being 4,700 m (15,420 ft) in east Antarctica.

SEE MAPS pages 88, 91–92

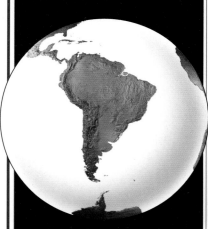

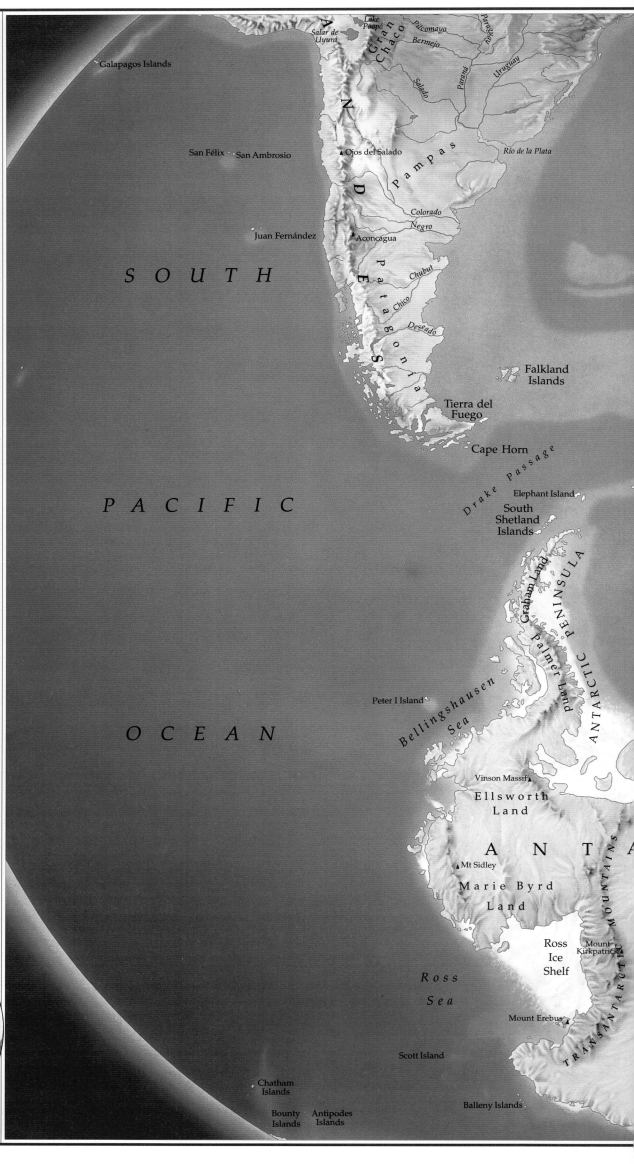

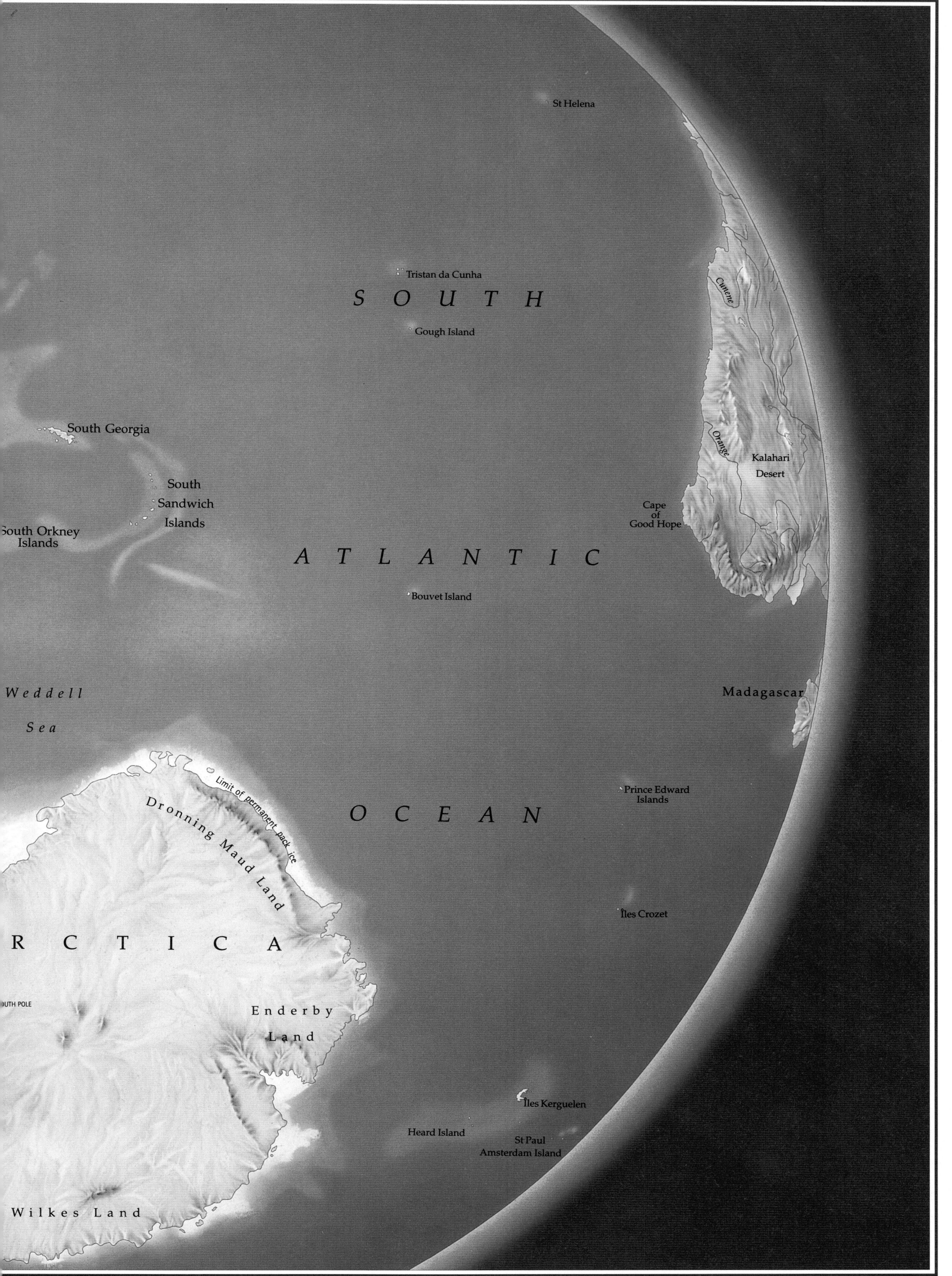

St Helena

Tristan da Cunha

S O U T H

Gough Island

Cunene

Orange

Kalahari
Desert

South Georgia

South
Sandwich
Islands

Cape
of
Good Hope

South Orkney
Islands

A T L A N T I C

Bouvet Island

Madagascar

Weddell

Sea

Prince Edward
Islands

O C E A N

Limit of permanent pack ice

Dronning Maud Land

RCTICA

Enderby

Land

Îles Crozet

OUTH POLE

Îles Kerguelen

Heard Island

St Paul
Amsterdam Island

Wilkes Land

©Bartholomew

42

WORLD EXTREMES

Highest Mountain
8,848 m — Everest; Asia — 29,028 ft

Largest Inland Water Area
371,000 sq km — Caspian Sea; Asia — 143,205 sq mls

Largest Island
2,175,600 sq km — Greenland; North America — 839,780 sq mls

Longest River
6,695 km — Nile; Africa — 4,160 mls

Largest Drainage Basin
7,050,000 sq km — Amazon; South America — 2,721,000 sq mls

Deepest Water
11,022 m Marianas Trench; Pacific Ocean 36,161 ft

Iceland
102,820
39,690

Great Britain
229,870
88,730

Ireland
83,045
32,055

Greenland
2,175,600
839,780

EUROPE
9,909,000
3,826,000

Sardinia
24,090
9,300

L.Onega
9,600
3,705

Sicily
25,710
9,925

L.Ladoga
18,390
7,100

Great Slave Lake
28,440
10,980

Great Bear Lake
31,790
12,270

L.Superior
83,270
32,140

Baffin I.
476,070
183,810

The Great Lakes

L.Huron
60,700
23,430

L.Ontario
19,230
7,425

L.Michigan
58,020
22,395

Newfoundland
95,830
36,990

L.Erie
25,680
9,910

Cuba
114,525
44,205

NORTH AMERICA
25,680,000
9,529,000

Hispaniola
78,460
30,285

SOUTH AMERICA
17,815,000
6,879,000

L.Titicaca
8,340
3,220

ANTARCTICA
13,340,000
5,149,000

AFRICA
30,344,000
11,716,000

Tierra del Fuego
47,000
18,140

Arctic Ocean
14,056,000
5,426,000

Baltic Sea
422,000
163,000

North Sea
575,000
222,000

Black Sea
461,000
178,000

L.Victoria
68,800
26,560

Hudson Bay
1,233,300
476,000

Gulf of Mexico
1,544,000
596,000

Mediterranean Sea
2,505,000
967,000

ATLANTIC OCEAN
82,217,000
31,736,000

Caribbean Sea
1,943,000
750,000

L.Tanganyika
32,900
12,700

L.Nyasa
22,490
8,680

Madagascar
587,040
226,660

ATLANTIC OCEAN

Commonly divided into North Atlantic (36,000,000 sq km) and South Atlantic (26,000,000 sq km). The greatest breadth in the North is 7,200 km (Morocco to Florida) and in the South is 9,600 km (Guinea to Brazil). The average depth is 3,600 m; the greatest depths are the Puerto Rico Trench (9,220 m), South Sandwich Trench (8,325 m), and the Romanche Gap (7,728 m).

Tropic of Cancer

Equator

Tropic of Capricorn

KEY

Continents and Oceans

Land area ▪ = 1,000,000 sq km
386,000 sq mls

Water area ▪ = 1,000,000 sq km
386,000 sq mls

Islands and Inland Waters

Land area ▪ = 10,000 sq km
3,860 sq mls

Inland water area ▪ = 1,000 sq km
386 sq mls

Sakhalin
76,400
29,490

Hokkaidō
78,460
30,285

L.Baikal
30,500
11,775

Honshū
230,455
88,955

Caspian Sea (salt)
371,000
143,205

Ozero Balkhash
17,400
6,715

Kyūshū
42,010
16,215

Shikoku
18,780
7,250

Taiwan
35,990
13,890

Ysyk-Köl
6,200
2,395

Luzon
104,690
40,410

ASIA
45,036,000
17,389,000

Borneo
757,050
292,220

Sri Lanka
65,610
25,325

Mindanao
94,630
36,530

Sulawesi
189,040
72,970

Java
134,045
51,740

Sumatera
524,100
202,300

PACIFIC OCEAN

Covers nearly 40% of the world's total sea area, and is the largest of the oceans. The greatest breadth (E/W) is 16,000 km and the greatest length (N/S) is 11,000 km. The average depth is 4,200 m-this makes it the deepest world ocean. Generally the west is deeper than the east and the north is deeper than the south. The greatest depths occur near island groups and include the Marianas Trench (11,022 m), Tonga Trench (10,882 m), Philippine Trench (10,497 m), and Kermadec Trench (10,047 m).

New Guinea
808,510
312,085

Sea of Okhotsk
1,528,000
590,000

Red Sea
438,000
169,000

L.Eyre (salt)
0-8,900
0-3,435

Sea of Japan
1,008,000
389,000

Bering Sea
2,269,000
876,000

Yellow Sea
404,000
156,000

INDIAN OCEAN
73,481,000
28,364,000

AUSTRALASIA
8,923,000
3,444,000

East China Sea
1,248,000
482,000

L.Torrens (salt)
0-5,780
0-2,230

South China Sea
2,318,000
895,000

PACIFIC OCEAN
165,384,000
63,838,000

North Island
114,690
44,270

Tasmania
68,330
26,375

South Island
150,460
58,080

INDIAN OCEAN

Mainly confined to the southern hemisphere, the greatest breadth (Tasmania to Cape Agulhas) is 9,600 km. The average depth is 4,000 m; the greatest depth is the Java Trench (7,125 m).

© Bartholomew

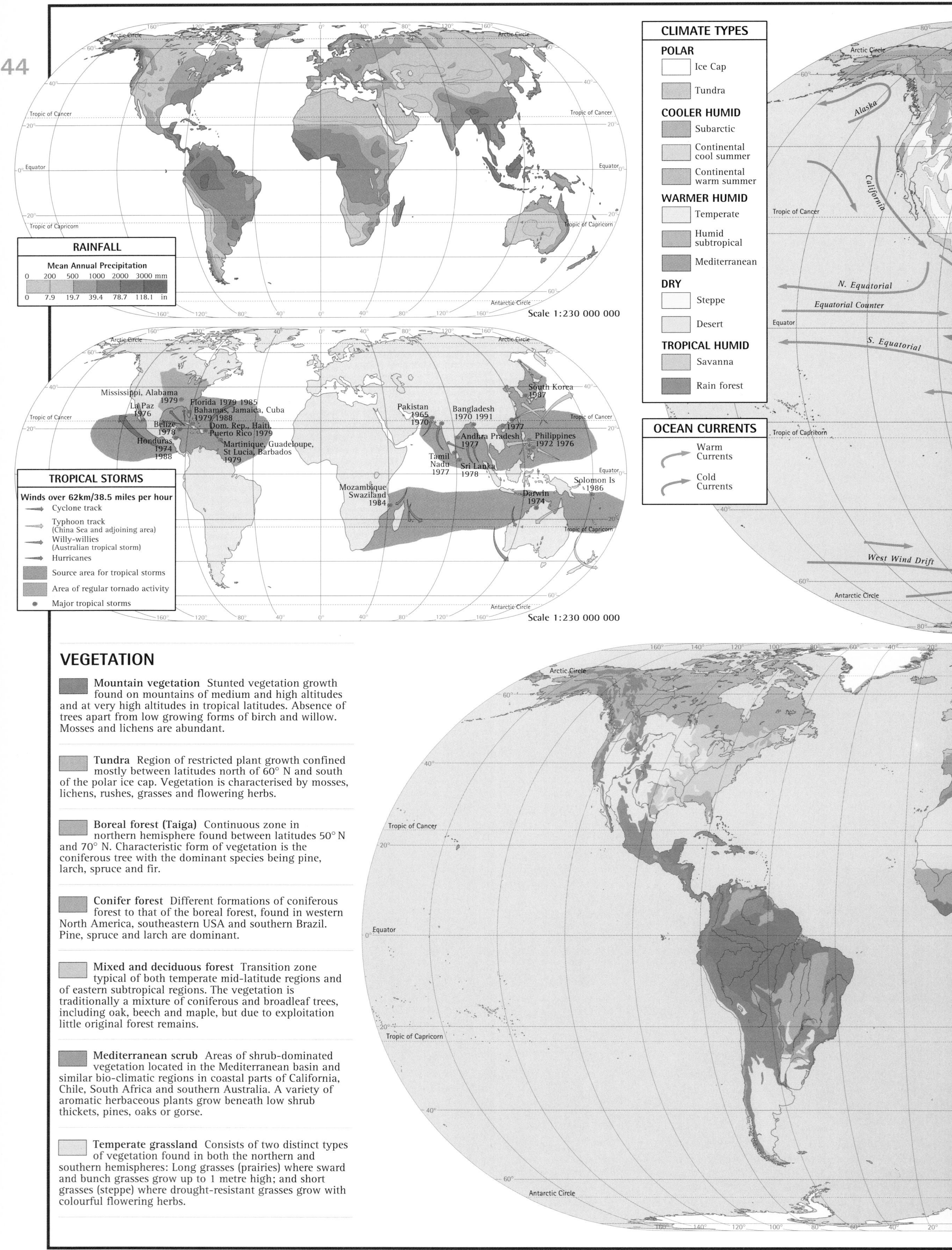

RAINFALL

Mean Annual Precipitation

0	200	500	1000	2000	3000 mm
0	7.9	19.7	39.4	78.7	118.1 in

Scale 1:230 000 000

CLIMATE TYPES

POLAR
- Ice Cap
- Tundra

COOLER HUMID
- Subarctic
- Continental cool summer
- Continental warm summer

WARMER HUMID
- Temperate
- Humid subtropical
- Mediterranean

DRY
- Steppe
- Desert

TROPICAL HUMID
- Savanna
- Rain forest

OCEAN CURRENTS

→ Warm Currents

→ Cold Currents

Alaska
California
N. Equatorial
Equatorial Counter
S. Equatorial
West Wind Drift

TROPICAL STORMS

Winds over 62km/38.5 miles per hour

→ Cyclone track
→ Typhoon track (China Sea and adjoining area)
→ Willy-willies (Australian tropical storm)
→ Hurricanes
- Source area for tropical storms
- Area of regular tornado activity
• Major tropical storms

Mississippi, Alabama 1979
La Paz 1976
Belize 1978
Honduras 1974 1988
Florida 1979 1985
Bahamas, Jamaica, Cuba 1979 1988
Dom. Rep., Haiti, Puerto Rico 1979
Martinique, Guadeloupe, St Lucia, Barbados 1979
Pakistan 1965 1970
Bangladesh 1970 1991
1977
Andhra Pradesh 1977
South Korea 1987
Philippines 1972 1976
Tamil Nadu 1977
Sri Lanka 1978
Mozambique Swaziland 1984
Darwin 1974
Solomon Is 1986

Scale 1:230 000 000

VEGETATION

Mountain vegetation Stunted vegetation growth found on mountains of medium and high altitudes and at very high altitudes in tropical latitudes. Absence of trees apart from low growing forms of birch and willow. Mosses and lichens are abundant.

Tundra Region of restricted plant growth confined mostly between latitudes north of 60° N and south of the polar ice cap. Vegetation is characterised by mosses, lichens, rushes, grasses and flowering herbs.

Boreal forest (Taiga) Continuous zone in northern hemisphere found between latitudes 50° N and 70° N. Characteristic form of vegetation is the coniferous tree with the dominant species being pine, larch, spruce and fir.

Conifer forest Different formations of coniferous forest to that of the boreal forest, found in western North America, southeastern USA and southern Brazil. Pine, spruce and larch are dominant.

Mixed and deciduous forest Transition zone typical of both temperate mid-latitude regions and of eastern subtropical regions. The vegetation is traditionally a mixture of coniferous and broadleaf trees, including oak, beech and maple, but due to exploitation little original forest remains.

Mediterranean scrub Areas of shrub-dominated vegetation located in the Mediterranean basin and similar bio-climatic regions in coastal parts of California, Chile, South Africa and southern Australia. A variety of aromatic herbaceous plants grow beneath low shrub thickets, pines, oaks or gorse.

Temperate grassland Consists of two distinct types of vegetation found in both the northern and southern hemispheres: Long grasses (prairies) where sward and bunch grasses grow up to 1 metre high; and short grasses (steppe) where drought-resistant grasses grow with colourful flowering herbs.

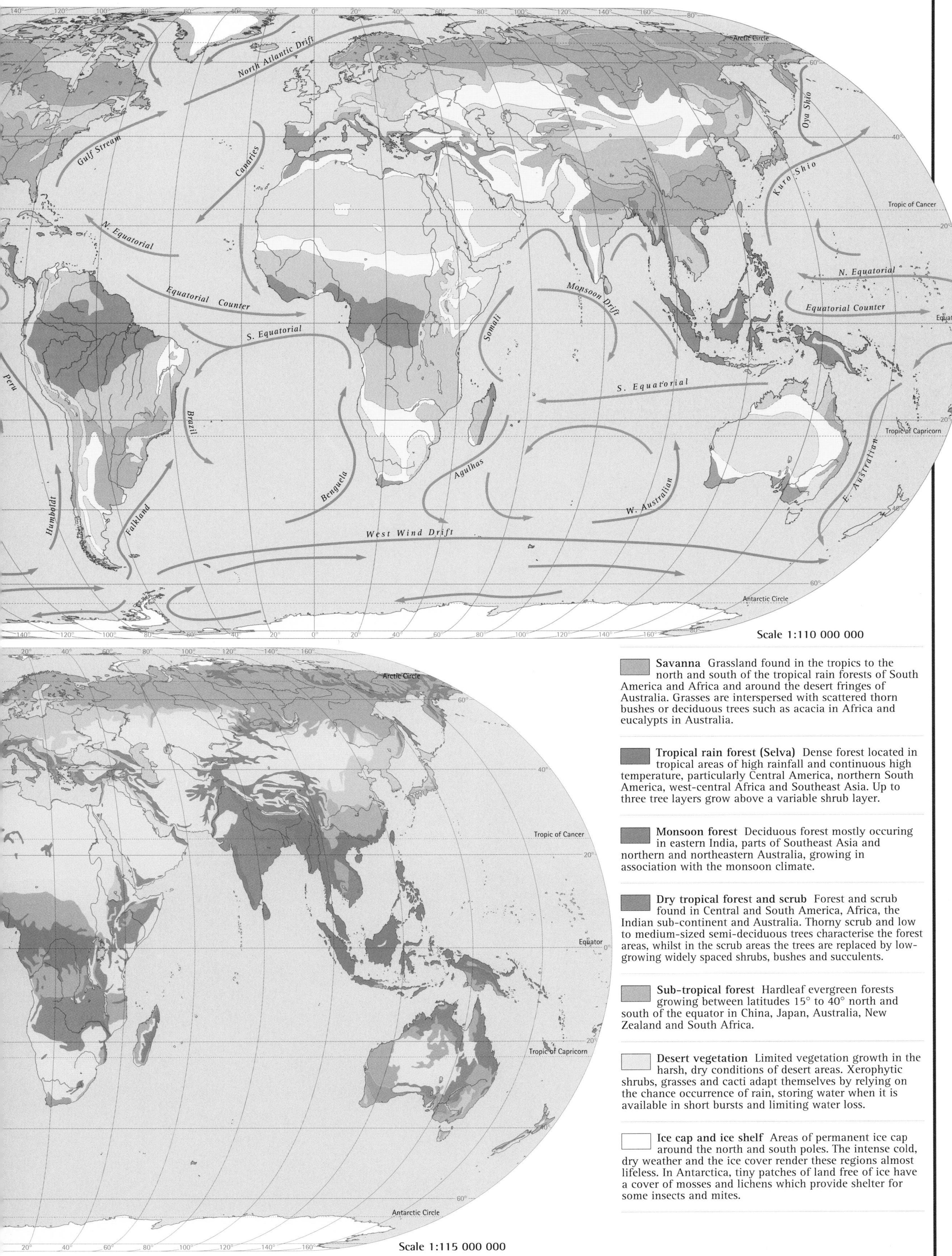

Scale 1:110 000 000

Scale 1:115 000 000

Savanna Grassland found in the tropics to the north and south of the tropical rain forests of South America and Africa and around the desert fringes of Australia. Grasses are interspersed with scattered thorn bushes or deciduous trees such as acacia in Africa and eucalypts in Australia.

Tropical rain forest (Selva) Dense forest located in tropical areas of high rainfall and continuous high temperature, particularly Central America, northern South America, west-central Africa and Southeast Asia. Up to three tree layers grow above a variable shrub layer.

Monsoon forest Deciduous forest mostly occuring in eastern India, parts of Southeast Asia and northern and northeastern Australia, growing in association with the monsoon climate.

Dry tropical forest and scrub Forest and scrub found in Central and South America, Africa, the Indian sub-continent and Australia. Thorny scrub and low to medium-sized semi-deciduous trees characterise the forest areas, whilst in the scrub areas the trees are replaced by low-growing widely spaced shrubs, bushes and succulents.

Sub-tropical forest Hardleaf evergreen forests growing between latitudes 15° to 40° north and south of the equator in China, Japan, Australia, New Zealand and South Africa.

Desert vegetation Limited vegetation growth in the harsh, dry conditions of desert areas. Xerophytic shrubs, grasses and cacti adapt themselves by relying on the chance occurrence of rain, storing water when it is available in short bursts and limiting water loss.

Ice cap and ice shelf Areas of permanent ice cap around the north and south poles. The intense cold, dry weather and the ice cover render these regions almost lifeless. In Antarctica, tiny patches of land free of ice have a cover of mosses and lichens which provide shelter for some insects and mites.

© Bartholomew

URBAN AGGLOMERATIONS

The populations given below are for selected urban agglomerations. These are defined as adjacent areas of settlement inhabited at urban levels of residential density, without regard to administrative boundaries.

Oceania
3,590,000 Sydney *Australia*
3,094,000 Melbourne *Australia*
1,450,000 Brisbane *Australia*
1,220,000 Perth *Australia*
1,039,000 Adelaide *Australia*
　945,000 Auckland *New Zealand*

Asia
26,836,000 Tōkyō *Japan**
15,093,000 Bombay *India*
15,082,000 Shanghai *China*
12,362,000 Beijing *China*
11,673,000 Calcutta *India*
11,641,000 Seoul *S. Korea*
11,500,000 Jakarta *Indonesia*
10,687,000 Tianjin *China*
10,601,000 Ōsaka-Kōbe *Japan*
9,882,000 Delhi *India*
9,863,000 Karachi *Pakistan*
9,280,000 Manila-Quezon City
　　　　　 Philippines
7,832,000 Dhaka *Bangladesh*
6,830,000 Tehrän *Iran*
6,566,000 Bangkok *Thailand*
5,906,000 Madras *India*
5,574,000 Hong Kong *China*
5,343,000 Hyderabad *India*
5,310,000 Shenyang *China*
5,085,000 Lahore *Pakistan*
4,749,000 Bangalore *India*
4,478,000 Baghdād *Iraq*
4,399,000 Wuhan *China*
4,082,000 Pusan *S. Korea*
4,056,000 Guangzhou *China*
3,851,000 Yangon *Myanmar*
3,688,000 Ahmadabad *India*
3,555,000 Hô Chi Minh *Vietnam*
3,525,000 Chongqing *China*
3,417,000 T'ai-pei *Taiwan*
3,401,000 Chengdu *China*
3,303,000 Harbin *China*
3,283,000 Xi'an *China*
3,196,000 Nagoya *Japan*
3,132,000 Dalian *China*
3,019,000 Jinan *China*
2,977,000 Bandung *Indonesia*
2,965,000 Nanjing *China*
2,940,000 Pune *India*
2,848,000 Singapore *Singapore*
2,826,000 Ankara *Turkey*
2,742,000 Surabaya *Indonesia*
2,704,000 Kita-Kyūshū *Japan*
2,576,000 Riyadh *Saudi Arabia*
2,523,000 Changchun *China*
2,502,000 Taiyuan *China*
2,470,000 P'yŏngyang *N. Korea*
2,432,000 Taegu *S. Korea*
2,356,000 Kanpur *India*
2,288,000 Tashkent *Uzbekistan*
2,222,000 Medan *Indonesia*
2,052,000 Damascus *Syria*
2,034,000 Kābul *Afghanistan*
2,031,000 İzmir *Turkey*
2,029,000 Lucknow *India*
2,011,000 Mashhad *Iran*
1,999,000 Zhengzhou *China*
1,942,000 Kunming *China*
1,921,000 Tel Aviv-Yafo *Israel*
1,875,000 Faisalabad *Pakistan*
1,855,000 Aleppo *Syria*
1,853,000 Baku *Azerbaijan*
1,792,000 Guiyang *China*
1,726,000 Kao-hsiung *Taiwan*
1,676,000 Peshawar *Pakistan*
1,643,000 Ürümqi *China*
1,581,000 Hangzhou *China*
1,563,000 Beirut *Lebanon*
1,498,000 Nanning *China*
1,469,000 Novosibirsk *Rus.Fed.*
1,353,000 T'bilisi *Georgia*
1,305,000 Yerevan *Armenia*
1,262,000 Almaty *Kazakstan*
1,247,000 Ha Nôi *Vietnam*
1,238,000 Kuala Lumpur *Malaysia*
1,187,000 'Ammān *Jordan*

Europe
9,469,000 Paris *France*
9,233,000 Moscow *Rus.Fed.*
7,817,000 İstanbul *Turkey*
7,335,000 London *U.K.*
6,481,000 Essen *Germany*
5,111,000 St Petersburg *Rus.Fed.*
4,251,000 Milan *Italy*
4,072,000 Madrid *Spain*
3,693,000 Athens *Greece*
3,606,000 Frankfurt am Main
　　　　　 Germany
3,552,000 Katowice *Poland*
3,317,000 Berlin *Germany*
3,012,000 Naples *Italy*
2,984,000 Cologne *Germany*
2,931,000 Rome *Italy*
2,819,000 Barcelona *Spain*
2,809,000 Kiev *Ukraine*
2,625,000 Hamburg *Germany*
2,316,000 Warsaw *Poland*

2,302,000 Birmingham *U.K.*
2,277,000 Manchester *U.K.*
2,090,000 Bucharest *Romania*
2,060,000 Vienna *Austria*
2,017,000 Budapest *Hungary*
1,863,000 Lisbon *Portugal*
1,766,000 Minsk *Belarus*
1,680,000 Kharkiv *Ukraine*
1,545,000 Stockholm *Sweden*
1,454,000 Nizhniy Novgorod
　　　　　 Rus.Fed.
1,413,000 Yekaterinburg *Rus.Fed.*
1,405,000 Belgrade *Yugoslavia*
1,384,000 Sofia *Bulgaria*
1,326,000 Copenhagen *Denmark*
1,311,000 Lyons *France*
1,230,000 Dnipropetrovs'k *Ukraine*
1,225,000 Prague *Czech Rep.*
1,109,000 Amsterdam *Netherlands*

Africa
10,287,000 Lagos *Nigeria*
9,656,000 Cairo *Egypt*
4,214,000 Kinshasa *Congo (Zaire)*
3,702,000 Algiers *Algeria*
3,577,000 Alexandria *Egypt*
3,289,000 Casablanca *Morocco*
3,272,000 Tripoli *Libya*
2,797,000 Abidjan *Côte d'Ivoire*
2,671,000 Cape Town *S. Africa*
2,429,000 Khartoum *Sudan*
2,227,000 Maputo *Mozambique*
2,209,000 Addis Ababa
　　　　　 Ethiopia
2,207,000 Luanda *Angola*
2,079,000 Nairobi *Kenya*
2,037,000 Tunis *Tunisia*
1,986,000 Dakar *Senegal*
1,849,000 Johannesburg
　　　　　 S. Africa
1,734,000 Dar es Salaam
　　　　　 Tanzania
1,687,000 Accra *Ghana*
1,578,000 Rabat *Morocco*
1,322,000 Douala *Cameroon*
1,044,000 Harare *Zimbabwe*

North America
16,329,000 New York *U.S.A.*
15,643,000 México *Mexico*
12,410,000 Los Angeles *U.S.A.*
6,846,000 Chicago *U.S.A.*
4,483,000 Toronto *Canada*
4,304,000 Philadelphia *U.S.A.*
4,111,000 Washington D.C. *U.S.A.*
3,866,000 San Francisco *U.S.A.*
3,725,000 Detroit *U.S.A.*
3,612,000 Dallas *U.S.A.*
3,447,000 Miami-Fort Lauderdale
　　　　　 U.S.A.
3,320,000 Montréal *Canada*
3,166,000 Houston *U.S.A.*
3,165,000 Guadalajara *Mexico*
2,842,000 Boston *U.S.A.*
2,806,000 Monterrey *Mexico*
2,716,000 San Diego *U.S.A.*
2,580,000 Santo Domingo
　　　　　 Dominican Republic
2,464,000 Atlanta *U.S.A.*
2,353,000 Phoenix *U.S.A.*
2,241,000 Havana *Cuba*
2,239,000 Minneapolis *U.S.A.*
2,009,000 St Louis *U.S.A.*
1,969,000 Baltimore *U.S.A.*
1,939,000 Seattle *U.S.A.*
1,905,000 Tampa *U.S.A.*
1,823,000 Vancouver *Canada*
1,692,000 Cleveland *U.S.A.*
1,692,000 Pittsburg *U.S.A.*
1,682,000 Norfolk *U.S.A.*
1,611,000 Denver *U.S.A.*
1,266,000 Port-au-Prince *Haiti*
1,101,000 San Juan *Puerto Rico*
　946,000 Guatemala *Guatemala*

South America
16,417,000 São Paulo *Brazil*
10,990,000 Buenos Aires
　　　　　 Argentina
9,888,000 Rio de Janeiro *Brazil*
7,452,000 Lima *Peru*
5,614,000 Bogotá *Colombia*
5,065,000 Santiago *Chile*
3,899,000 Belo Horizonte *Brazil*
3,349,000 Porto Alegre *Brazil*
3,168,000 Recife *Brazil*
2,959,000 Caracas *Venezuela*
2,819,000 Salvador *Brazil*
2,660,000 Fortaleza *Brazil*
1,778,000 Brasília *Brazil*
1,769,000 Cali *Colombia*
1,717,000 Guayaquil *Ecuador*
1,607,000 Campinas *Brazil*
1,600,000 Maracaibo *Venezuela*
1,326,000 Montevideo *Uruguay*
1,294,000 Córdoba *Argentina*
1,246,000 La Paz *Bolivia*
1,244,000 Quito *Ecuador*

*includes Yokohama, Kawasaki, Chiba, and other adjacent towns and cities.

Source: United Nations. World urbanization prospects: the 1994 revision: estimates and projections of urban and rural populations and of urban agglomerations.

46

Eckert IV Projection

POPULATION DENSITY
Persons per sq km
0　2　10　40　100

URBAN POPULATION
No data　Percentage Urban
0　15　30　44.8　59　74　89　100
World average=44.8%

Scale 1:180 000 000

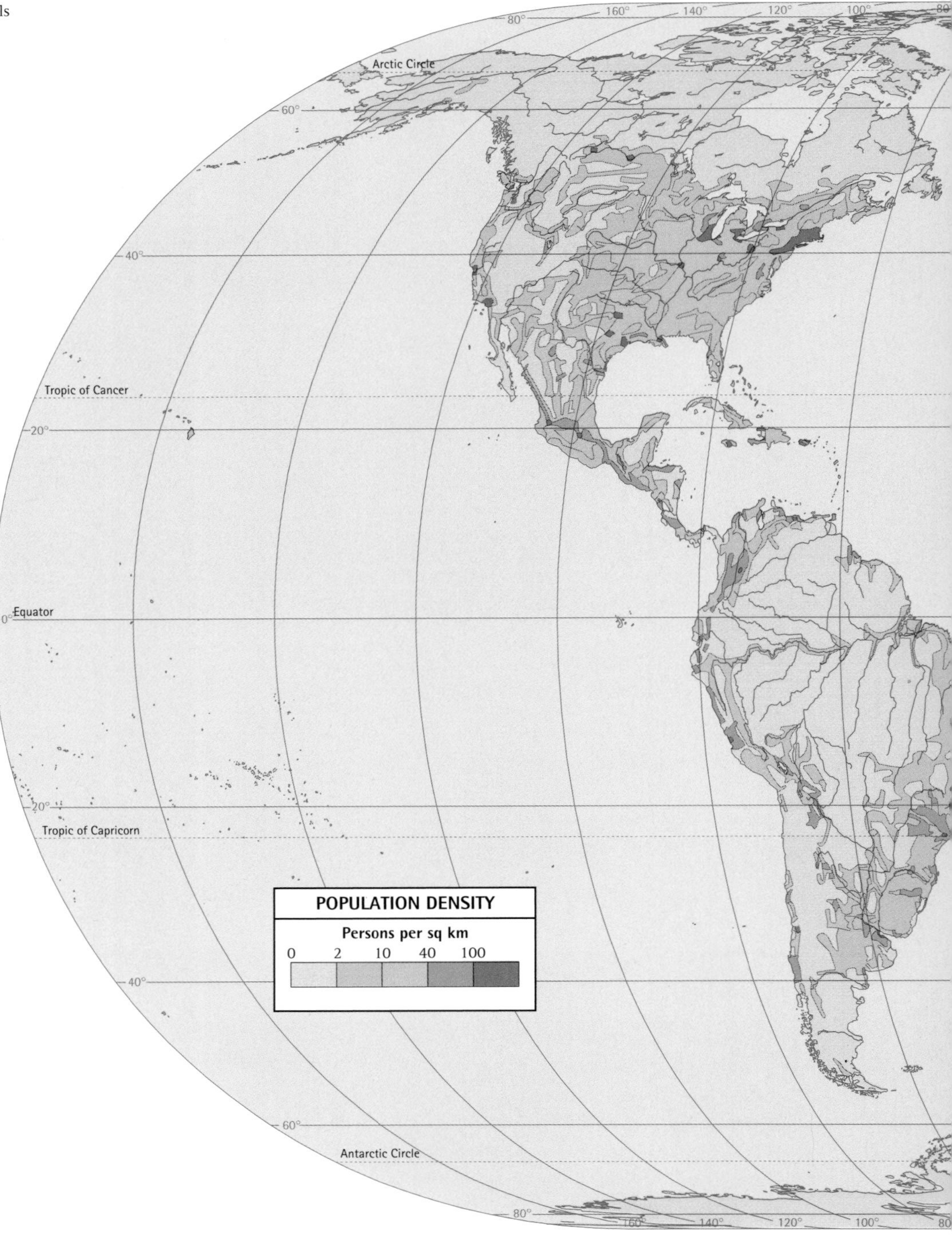

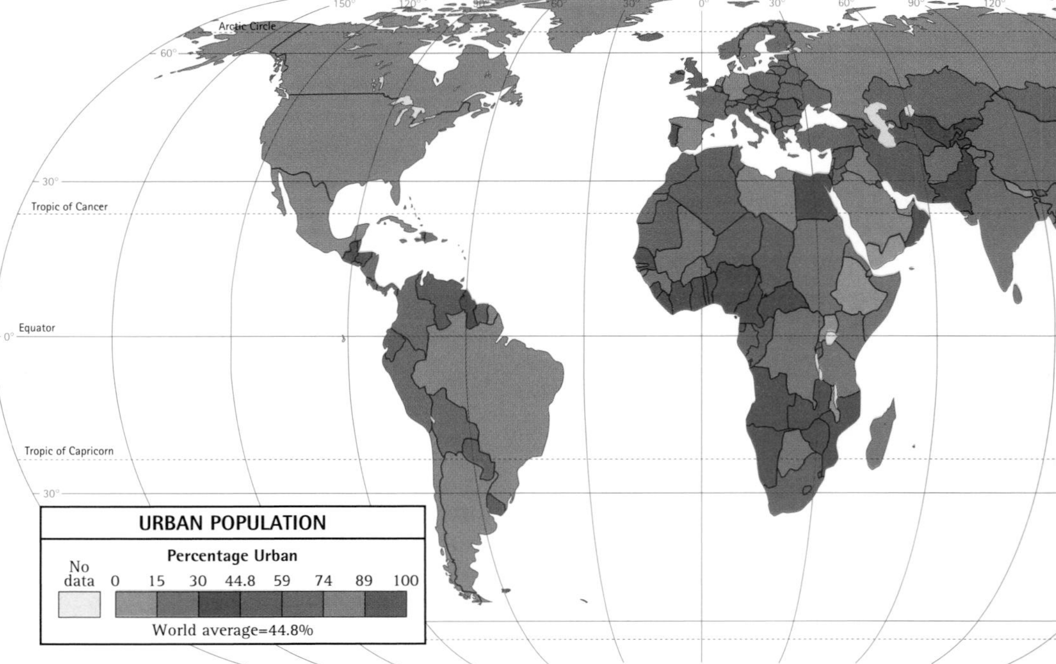

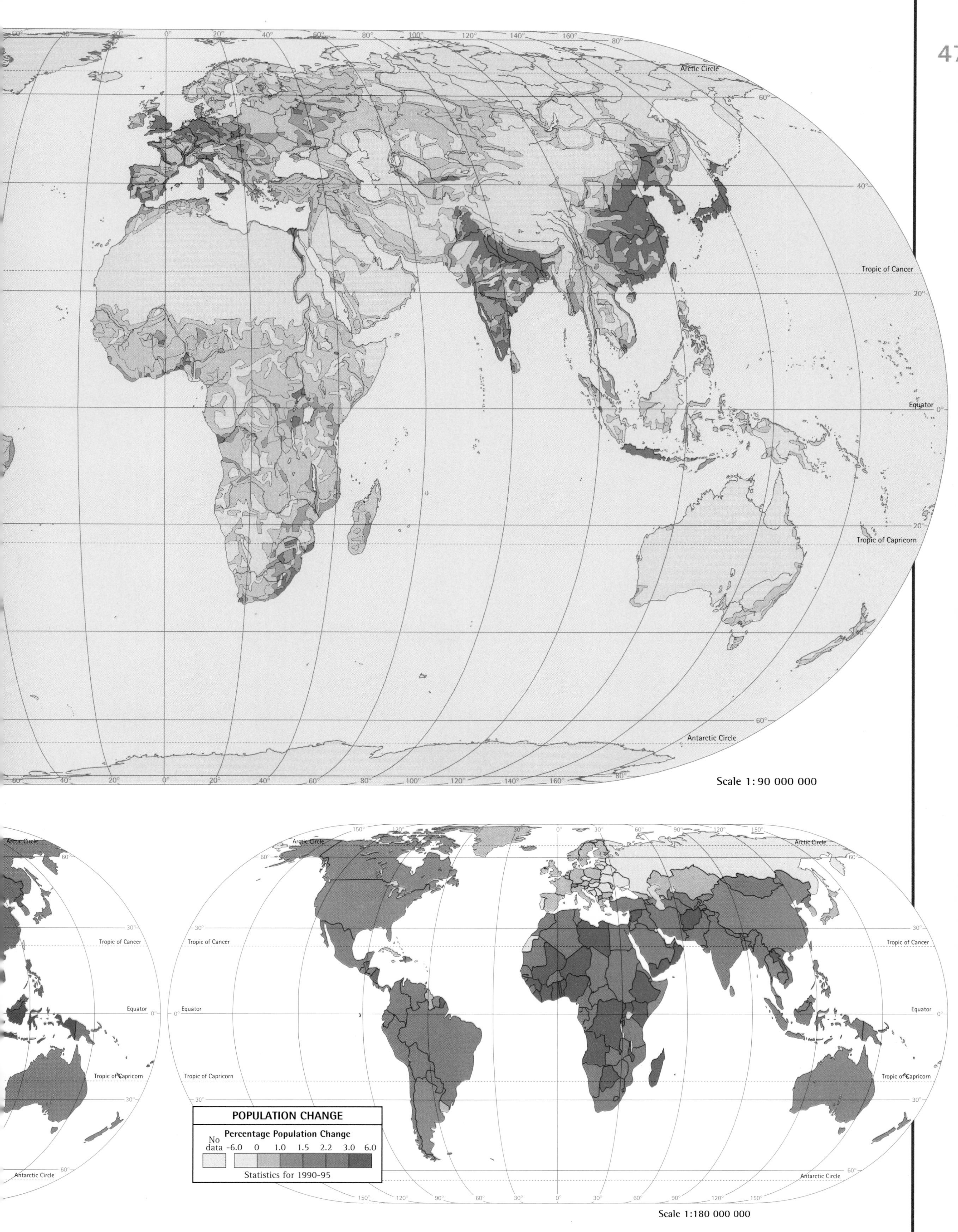

Scale 1: 90 000 000

POPULATION CHANGE

Percentage Population Change

| No data | -6.0 | 0 | 1.0 | 1.5 | 2.2 | 3.0 | 6.0 |

Statistics for 1990-95

Scale 1:180 000 000

© Bartholomew

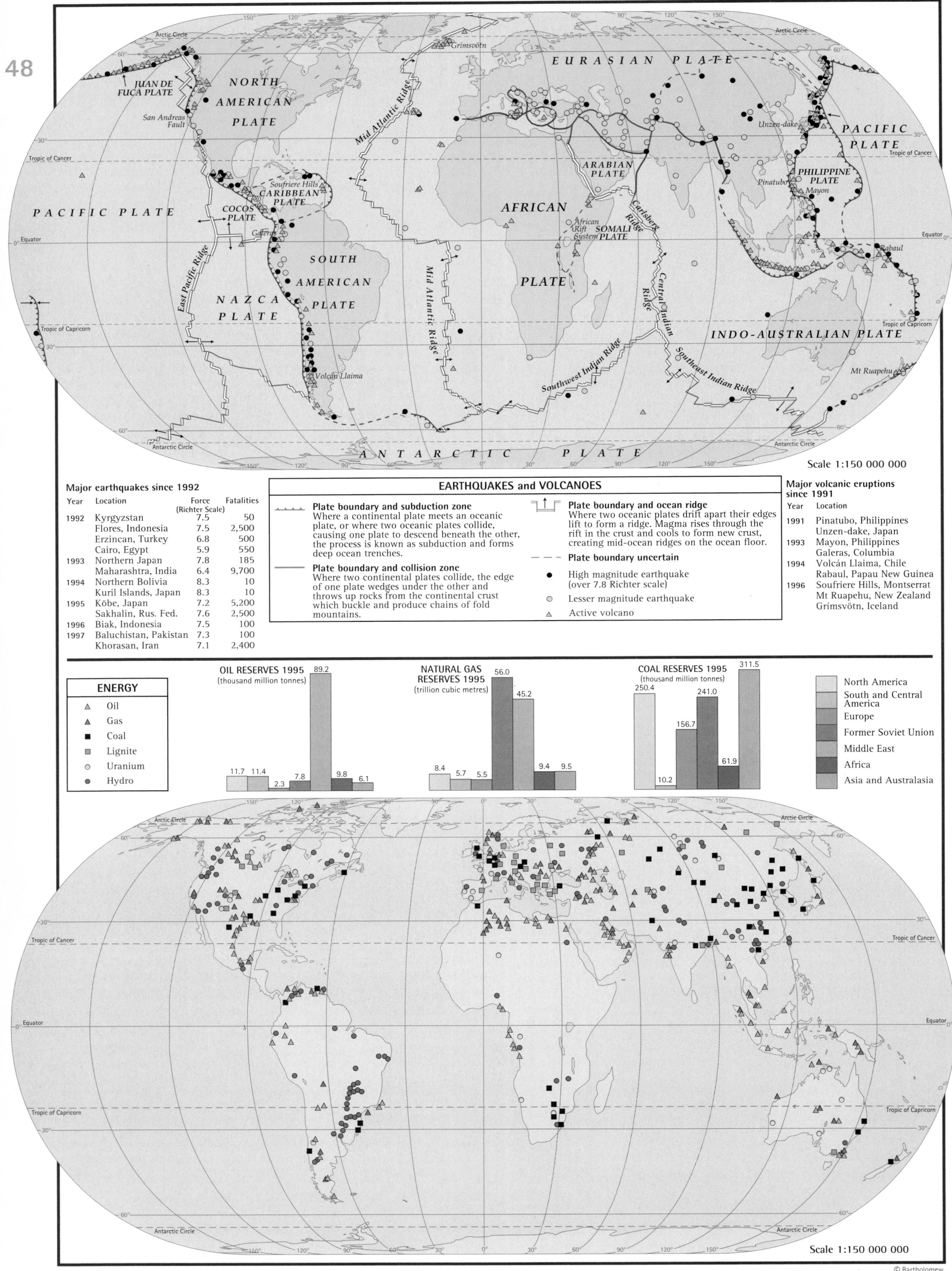

JUAN DE FUCA PLATE

NORTH AMERICAN PLATE

San Andreas Fault

Grimsvötn

EURASIAN PLATE

PACIFIC PLATE

Unzen-dake

PHILIPPINE PLATE

Mayon

Pinatubo

Arctic Circle

Tropic of Cancer

Soufriere Hills

CARIBBEAN PLATE

COCOS PLATE

Galeras

Mid Atlantic Ridge

ARABIAN PLATE

AFRICAN PLATE

African Rift System

SOMALI PLATE

Carlsberg Ridge

PACIFIC PLATE

NAZCA PLATE

SOUTH AMERICAN PLATE

Mid Atlantic Ridge

Central Indian Ridge

INDO-AUSTRALIAN PLATE

Rabaul

Equator

Volcán Llaima

Tropic of Capricorn

Southwest Indian Ridge

Southeast Indian Ridge

Mt Ruapehu

ANTARCTIC PLATE

Antarctic Circle

Scale 1:150 000 000

Major earthquakes since 1992

Year	Location	Force (Richter Scale)	Fatalities
1992	Kyrgyzstan	7.5	50
	Flores, Indonesia	7.5	2,500
	Erzincan, Turkey	6.8	500
	Cairo, Egypt	5.9	550
1993	Northern Japan	7.8	185
	Maharashtra, India	6.4	9,700
1994	Northern Bolivia	8.3	10
	Kuril Islands, Japan	8.3	10
1995	Köbe, Japan	7.2	5,200
	Sakhalin, Rus. Fed.	7.6	2,500
1996	Biak, Indonesia	7.5	100
1997	Baluchistan, Pakistan	7.3	100
	Khorasan, Iran	7.1	2,400

EARTHQUAKES and VOLCANOES

⊥⊤⊥ Plate boundary and subduction zone
Where a continental plate meets an oceanic plate, or where two oceanic plates collide, causing one plate to descend beneath the other, the process is known as subduction and forms deep ocean trenches.

— Plate boundary and collision zone
Where two continental plates collide, the edge of one plate wedges under the other and throws up rocks from the continental crust which buckle and produce chains of fold mountains.

Plate boundary and ocean ridge
Where two oceanic plates drift apart their edges lift to form a ridge. Magma rises through the rift in the crust and cools to form new crust, creating mid-ocean ridges on the ocean floor.

- - - Plate boundary uncertain

● High magnitude earthquake (over 7.8 Richter scale)

○ Lesser magnitude earthquake

△ Active volcano

Major volcanic eruptions since 1991

Year	Location
1991	Pinatubo, Philippines
	Unzen-dake, Japan
1993	Mayon, Philippines
	Galeras, Columbia
1994	Volcán Llaima, Chile
	Rabaul, Papau New Guinea
1996	Soufriere Hills, Montserrat
	Mt Ruapehu, New Zealand
	Grimsvötn, Iceland

ENERGY

△ Oil

△ Gas

■ Coal

▣ Lignite

○ Uranium

● Hydro

OIL RESERVES 1995 (thousand million tonnes)

11.7 11.4 2.3 7.8 89.2 9.8 6.1

NATURAL GAS RESERVES 1995 (trillion cubic metres)

8.4 5.7 5.5 56.0 45.2 9.4 9.5

COAL RESERVES 1995 (thousand million tonnes)

250.4 10.2 156.7 241.0 61.9 311.5

Legend:
- North America
- South and Central America
- Europe
- Former Soviet Union
- Middle East
- Africa
- Asia and Australasia

Scale 1:150 000 000

© Bartholomew

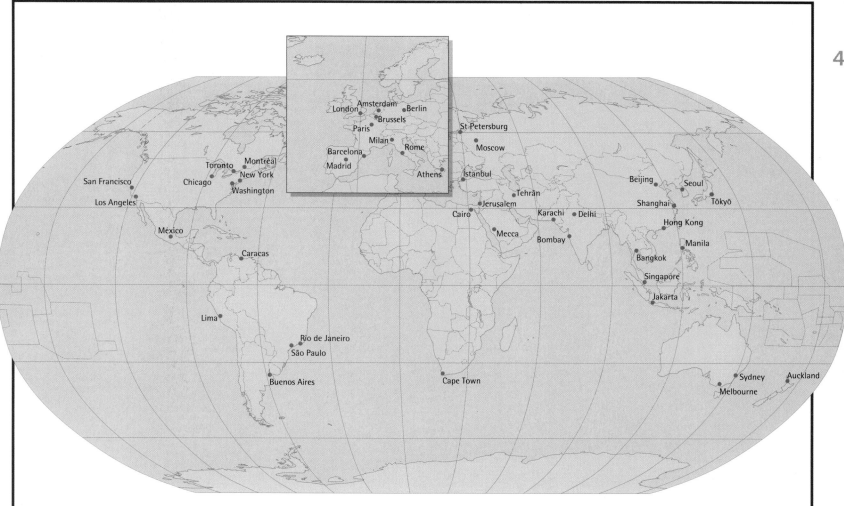

Contents

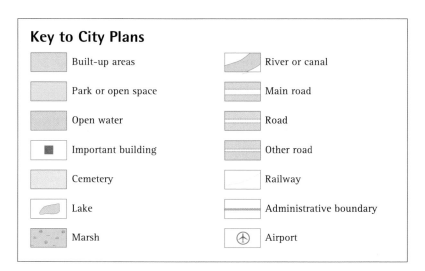

Key to City Plans

Built-up areas		River or canal	
Park or open space		Main road	
Open water		Road	
Important building		Other road	
Cemetery		Railway	
Lake		Administrative boundary	
Marsh		Airport	

© Bartholomew

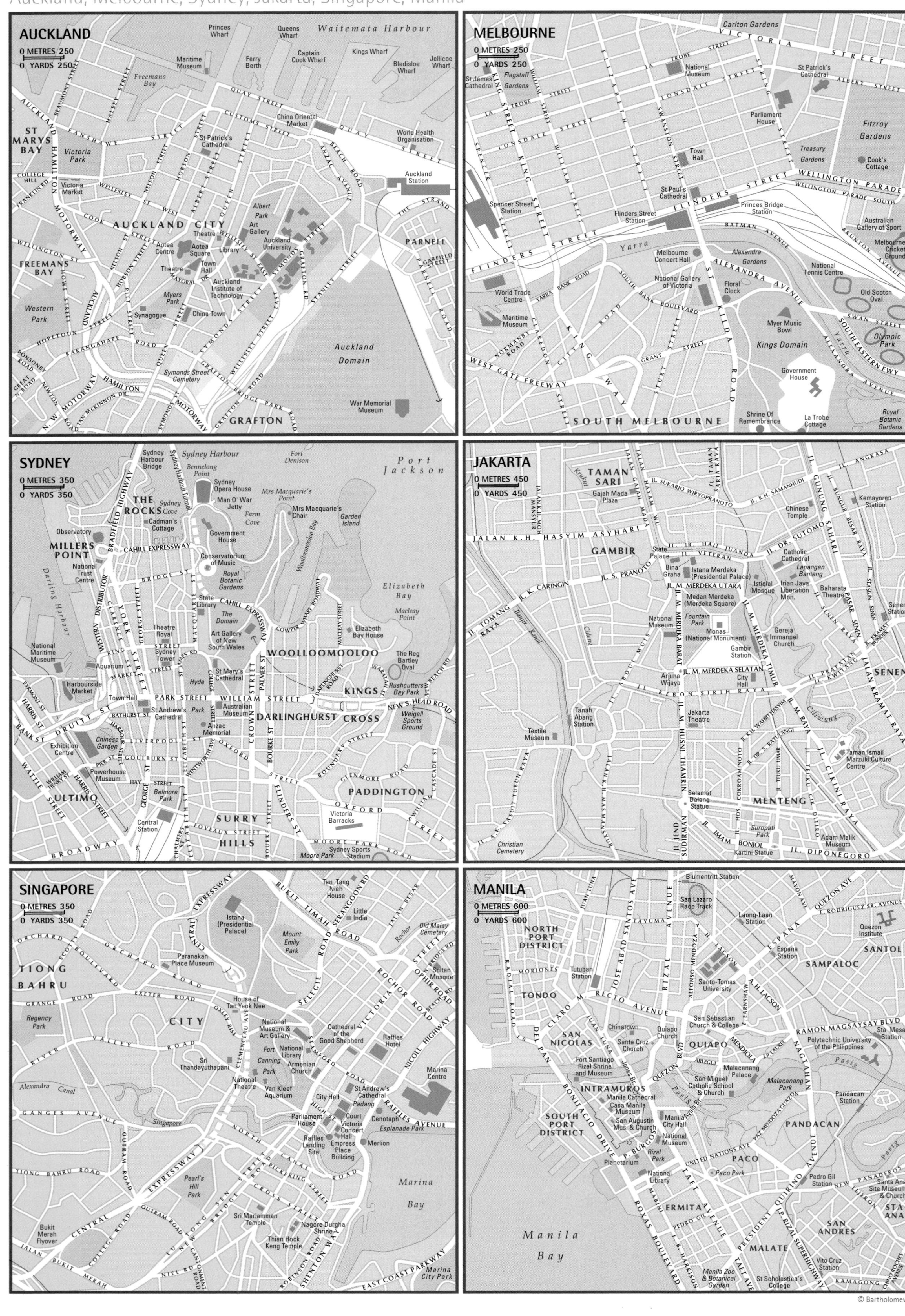
AUCKLAND
Waitemata Harbour
AUCKLAND CITY
Auckland Domain
FREEMANS BAY
PARNELL
GRAFTON
ST MARYS BAY
MELBOURNE
Fitzroy Gardens
Kings Domain
SOUTH MELBOURNE
Yarra
SYDNEY
Sydney Harbour
Port Jackson
THE ROCKS
MILLERS POINT
WOOLLOOMOOLOO
DARLINGHURST
KINGS CROSS
PADDINGTON
SURRY HILLS
ULTIMO
Darling Harbour
JAKARTA
TAMAN SARI
GAMBIR
SENEN
MENTENG
SINGAPORE
TIONG BAHRU
CITY
Marina Bay
MANILA
NORTH PORT DISTRICT
TONDO
SAN NICOLAS
QUIAPO
SAMPALOC
SANTOL
INTRAMUROS
SOUTH PORT DISTRICT
PACO
PANDACAN
ERMITA
MALATE
SAN ANDRES
STA ANA
Manila Bay
© Bartholomew

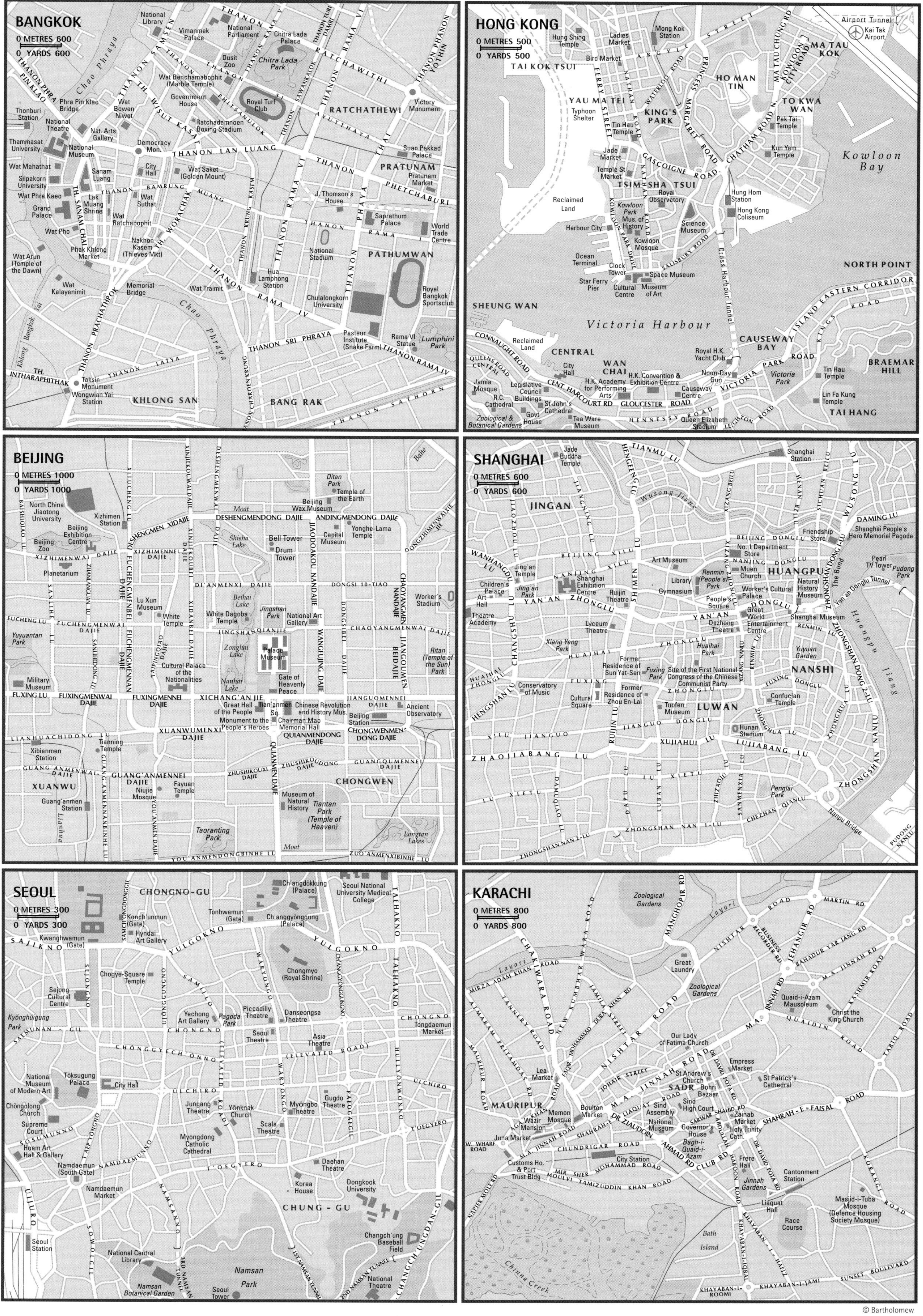

BANGKOK

0 METRES 600
0 YARDS 600

National Library
Vimanmek Palace
National Parliament
Chitra Lada Palace
Chitra Lada Park
Dusit Zoo
Wat Benchamabophit (Marble Temple)
Government House
Wat Bowen Niwet
Ratchadamnoen Boxing Stadium
Royal Turf Club
Victory Monument
Suan Pakkad Palace
RATCHATHEWI
PRATUNAM
Pratunam Market
PHETCHABURI
J. Thomson's House
Saprathum Palace
World Trade Centre
PATHUMWAN
National Stadium
Chulalongkorn University
Royal Bangkok Sportsclub
Lumphini Park
Pasteur Institute (Snake Farm)
Rama VI Statue
BANG RAK
KHLONG SAN
THANON SATHORN

Phra Pin Klao Bridge
Thonburi Station
National Theatre
Nat. Arts Gallery
Thammasat University
National Museum
Wat Mahathat
Silpakorn University
Wat Phra Kaeo
Grand Palace
Wat Pho
Wat Arum (Temple of the Dawn)
Wat Kalayanimit
TH. INTHARAPHITHAK
Democracy Mon.
City Hall
Sanam Luang
Th. Muang Shrine
Wat Ratchabophit
Nakhon Kasem (Thieves Mkt)
Phak Khlong Market
Memorial Bridge
Wat Traimit
Hua Lamphong Station
National Stadium
Taksin Monument
Wongwian Yai Station
National Parliament

HONG KONG

0 METRES 500
0 YARDS 500

Airport Tunnel
Kai Tak Airport
Hung Shing Temple
Ladies Market
Mong Kok Station
MA TAU KOK
Bird Market
TAI KOK TSUI
YAU MA TEI
Typhoon Shelter
KING'S PARK
Tin Hau Temple
Temple St Market
HO MAN TIN
TO KWA WAN
Pak Tai Temple
Jade Market
Kun Yam Temple
Kowloon Bay
TSIM SHA TSUI
Royal Observatory
Reclaimed Land
Kowloon Park Mus. of History
Hung Hom Station
Hong Kong Coliseum
Harbour City
Kowloon Mosque
Science Museum
NORTH POINT
Ocean Terminal
Clock Tower
Space Museum
Star Ferry Pier
Cultural Centre
Museum of Art
SHEUNG WAN
Victoria Harbour
ISLAND EASTERN CORRIDOR
CONNAUGHT ROAD
Reclaimed Land
CENTRAL
QUEENS ROAD CENTRAL
WAN CHAI
H.K. Convention & Exhibition Centre
CAUSEWAY BAY
VICTORIA PARK ROAD
BRAEMAR HILL
City Hall
CENT. HARCOUR
H.K. Academy for Performing Arts
Causeway Centre
Victoria Park
Tin Hau Temple
Jamia Mosque
Legislative Council Buildings
GLOUCESTER ROAD
Noon-Day Gun
Royal H.K. Yacht Club
TAI HANG
Lin Fa Kung Temple
R.C. Cathedral
St John's Cathedral
Govt House
Tea Ware House
Zoological & Botanical Gardens
HENNESSY
Queen Elizabeth Stadium

BEIJING

0 METRES 1000
0 YARDS 1000

North China Jiaotong University
Baihe
Ditan Park
Temple of the Earth
Xizhimen Station
Beijing Wax Museum
Beijing Exhibition Centre
DESHENGMENDONG DAJIE
ANDINGMENDONG DAJIE
Shisha Lake
Bell Tower
Drum Tower
Yonghe-Lama Temple
Capital Museum
Planetarium
DONGSI 10-TIAO
Lu Xun Museum
DI'ANMENXI DAJIE
CHAOYANGMEN NANDAJIE
Bethai Lake
Jingshan Park
White Dagoba Temple
National Art Gallery
Yuyuantan Park
JINGSHANQIANJIE
Zonghai Lake
Palace Museum
DONGSIBEI DAJIE
Ritan (Temple of the Sun) Park
Military Museum
Cultural Palace of the Nationalities
Nanhai Lake
JIANGUOMENNEI DAJIE
FUXING LU
FUXINGMENWAI DAJIE
FUXINGMENNEI DAJIE
XICHANG'AN JIE
Great Hall of the People
Tian'anmen Sq.
Chinese Revolution and History Mus.
Beijing Station
Ancient Observatory
Monument to the People's Heroes
Chairman Mao Memorial Hall
CHONGWENMEN DONG DAJIE
Xibianmen Station
XUANWUMENXI DAJIE
QIANMENDONG DAJIE
Tianning Temple
CHONGWEN
XUANWU
GUANG'ANMENWAI DAJIE
GUANG'ANMENNEI DAJIE
Niujie Mosque
ZHUSHIKOUXI DAJIE
ZHUSHIKOUDONG DAJIE
GUANGQUMENNEI DAJIE
Fayuan Temple
Guang'anmen Station
Lianhua
Museum of Natural History
Taoranting Park
Tiantan Park (Temple of Heaven)
Moat
Longtan Lakes
YOU ANMENDONGBINHE LU
ZUO ANMENXIBINHE LU

SHANGHAI

0 METRES 600
0 YARDS 600

Jade Buddha Temple
TIANMU LU
Shanghai Station
HENGFENG LU
JINGAN
DAMING LU
Wusong Jiang
No. 1 Department Store
Friendship Store
Shanghai People's Hero Memorial Pagoda
Art Museum
BEIJING DONGLU
NANJING DONGLU
HUANGPU
Pearl TV Tower
Jing'an Temple
NANJING XILU
Muen Church
Pudong Park
Children's Palace Art Hall
Shanghai Exhibition Centre
Library
Renmin (People's) Park
Natural History Museum
YAN'AN ZHONGLU
Gymnasium
Worker's Cultural Palace
The Bund
Theatre Academy
Lyceum Theatre
People's Square
Great World Entertainment Centre
Shanghai Museum
Yan an Donglu Tunnel
Xiang Yeng Park
Dazhong Theatre
RENMIN
HUAIHAI ZHONGLU
Huaihai Park
Former Residence of Sun Yat-Sen
Fuxing Site of the First National Congress of the Chinese Communist Party
NANSHI
Conservatory of Music
Former Residence of Zhou En-Lai
Cultural Square
Tuofen Museum
LUWAN
Yuyuan Garden
Confucian Temple
HENGSHAN LU
RUIJIN LU
ZHONGSHAN DONG 2-LU
XILU JIANGUO
JIANGUO
FUXING
Hunan Stadium
XUJIAHUI
ZHAOJIABANG LU
LUJIABANG LU
Pengtai Park
LU XIETU
ZHONGSHAN NAN-LU
TUBAN LU
ZHIZAOJU
SANMENXIA
Nanpu Bridge
CHEZHAN QIANLU
PUDONG NANLU
ZHONGSHAN NAN 2-LU

SEOUL

0 METRES 300
0 YARDS 300

CHONGNO-GU
Ch'angdokkung (Palace)
Seoul National University Medical College
Tonhwamun (Gate)
Konch'unmun (Gate)
Ch'anggyonggung (Palace)
Hyundai Art Gallery
YULGOKNO
TAEHAKNO
Kwanghwamun (Gate)
YULGOKNO
SAJIKNO
Chongmyo (Royal Shrine)
Sejong Cultural Centre
Chogye-Square Temple
Yechong Art Gallery
Piccadilly Theatre
Danseongsa Theatre
Kyonghuigung Park
Pagoda Park
Asia Theatre
CHONGNO
Seoul Theatre
Tongdaemun Market
National Museum of Modern Art
Toksugung Palace
City Hall
CHONGGYECHONNO (ELEVATED) ROAD
(ELEVATED ROAD)
Chongdong Church
Supreme Court
ULCHIRO
Jungang Theatre
Yonknak Church
Myongdong Theatre
Scala Theatre
Gugdo Theatre
Dongkook University
Hoam Art Hall & Gallery
Namdaemun (South Gate)
Namdaemun Market
Korea House
Myongdong Catholic Cathedral
Daehan Theatre
CHUNG-GU
Changch'ung Baseball Field
Seoul Station
National Central Library
Namsan Park
Namsan Botanical Garden
Seoul Tower
National Theatre

KARACHI

0 METRES 800
0 YARDS 800

Zoological Gardens
MANGHOPIR RD
Lavari
MARTIN RD
NISHTAR ROAD
Great Laundry
Quaid-i-Azam Mausoleum
Zoological Gardens
Christ the King Church
Our Lady of Fatima Church
Empress Market
Lea Market
St Andrew's Church
St Patrick's Cathedral
MAURIPUR
M.A. JINNAH ROAD
SADR
Bohri Bazaar
NISHTAR ROAD
Memon Mosque
Sind High Court
National Museum
Zainab Market
Holy Trinity Cath.
Governor's House
SHAHRAH-E-FAISAL
Wazir Mansion
Boulton Market
W. WHARF ROAD
Juna Market
Bagh-i-Quaid-i-Azam
Customs Ho. & Port Trust Bldg
City Station
Frere Hall
NAPIER MOLE
City Station
CHUNDRIGAR ROAD
Jinnah Gardens
Cantonment Station
Masjid-i-Tuba Mosque (Defence Housing Society Mosque)
Liaquat Hall
Race Course
Bath Island
China Creek
KHAYABAN-I-ROOMI
KHAYABAN-I-IAMI
SUNSET BOULEVARD

© Bartholomew

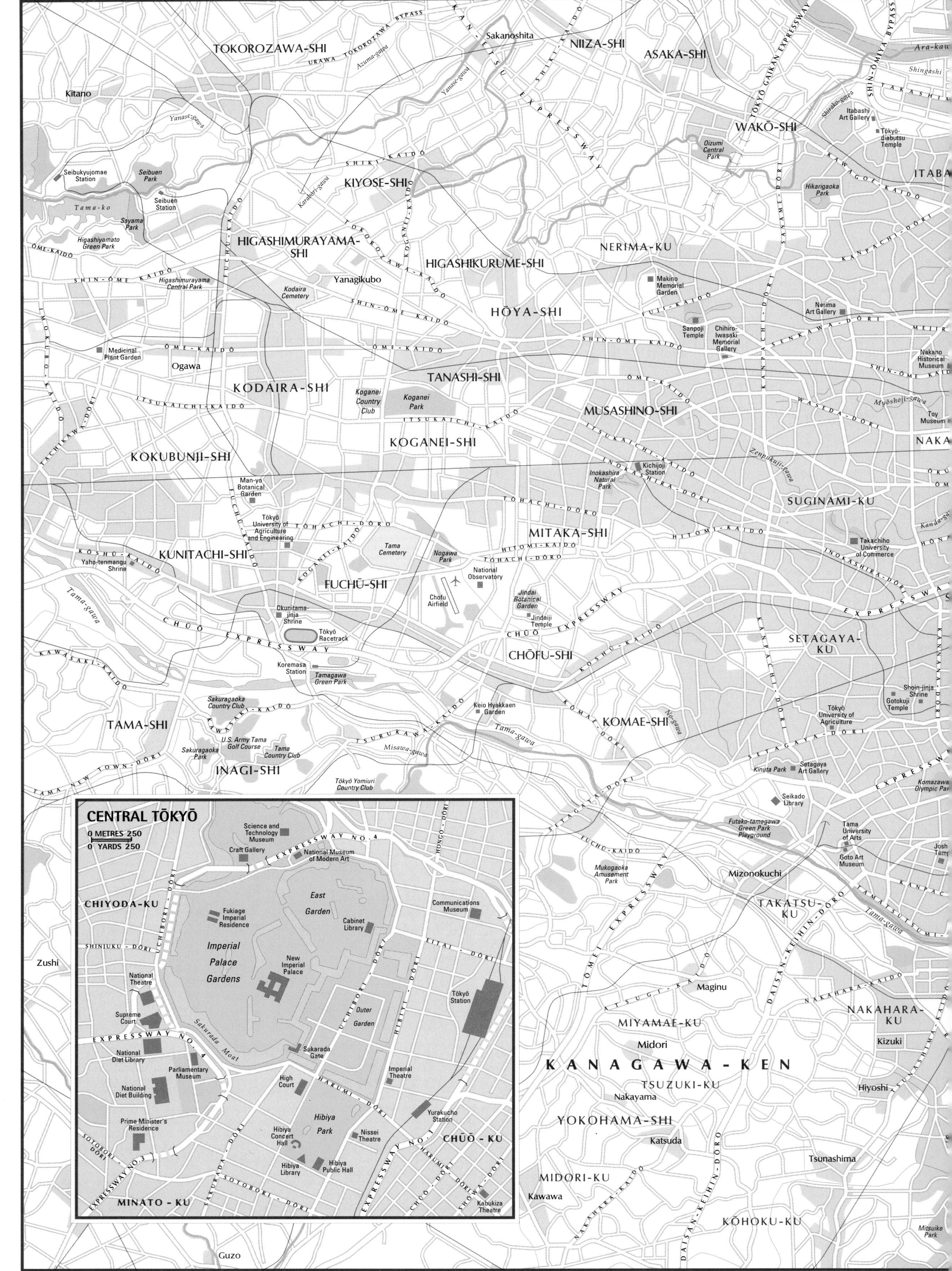
TOKOROZAWA-SHI
NIIZA-SHI
ASAKA-SHI
WAKŌ-SHI
ITABA
Kitano
Sakanoshita
Seibukyujomae Station
Seibuen Park
Seibuen Station
Tama-ko
Sayama Park
Higashiyamato Green Park
KIYOSE-SHI
HIGASHIMURAYAMA-SHI
HIGASHIKURUME-SHI
NERIMA-KU
Yanagikubo
Kodaira Cemetery
Higashimurayama Central Park
HŌYA-SHI
Makino Memorial Garden
Sanpoji Temple
Chihiro-Iwasaki Memorial Gallery
Nerima Art Gallery
Itabashi Art Gallery
Tōkyō-diabutsu Temple
Oizumi Central Park
Hikarigaoka Park
Medicinal Plant Garden
Ogawa
KODAIRA-SHI
TANASHI-SHI
Koganei Country Club
Koganei Park
MUSASHINO-SHI
Nakano Historical Museum
Toy Museum
KOGANEI-SHI
KOKUBUNJI-SHI
Kichijoji Station
Inokashira Natural Park
SUGINAMI-KU
NAKA
Man-yo Botanical Garden
Tōkyō University of Agriculture and Engineering
Tama Cemetery
Nogawa Park
MITAKA-SHI
Takachiho University of Commerce
KUNITACHI-SHI
Yaho-tenmangu Shrine
FUCHŪ-SHI
National Observatory
Chofu Airfield
Jindai Botanical Garden
Jindaiji Temple
Okunitama-jinja Shrine
Tōkyō Racetrack
CHŌFU-SHI
SETAGAYA-KU
Koremasa Station
Tamagawa Green Park
Keio Hyakkaen Garden
Shoin-jinja Shrine
Gotokuji Temple
Tōkyō University of Agriculture
KOMAE-SHI
Sakuragaoka Country Club
TAMA-SHI
U.S. Army Tama Golf Course
Tama Country Club
Sakuragaoka Park
INAGI-SHI
Tōkyō Yomiuri Country Club
Kinuta Park
Setagaya Art Gallery
Komazawa Olympic Par
Seikado Library
Futako-tamagawa Green Park Playground
Tama University of Arts
Goto Art Museum
Mukogaoka Amusement Park
Mizonokuchi
TAKATSU-KU
Zushi
Maginu
NAKAHARA-KU
MIYAMAE-KU
Midori
Kizuki
KANAGAWA-KEN
TSUZUKI-KU
Hiyoshi
Nakayama
YOKOHAMA-SHI
Katsuda
Tsunashima
MIDORI-KU
Kawawa
KŌHOKU-KU
Mitsuike Park
Guzo
Tama-gawa
KAN-ETSU EXPRESSWAY
TŌKYŌ GAIKAN EXPRESSWAY
CHŪŌ EXPRESSWAY
TŌMEI EXPRESSWAY
ŌME-KAIDŌ
SHIN-ŌME KAIDŌ
ITSUKAICHI-KAIDŌ
KŌSHŪ-KAIDŌ
TŌHACHI-DŌRO
FUCHŪ-KAIDŌ
KAWASAKI-KAIDŌ
TSURUKAWA-KAIDŌ
SETAGAYA-DŌRI
KANPACHI-DŌRI
SASAME-DŌRI
DAISAN-KEIHIN-DŌRO
CENTRAL TŌKYŌ
0 METRES 250
0 YARDS 250
Science and Technology Museum
Craft Gallery
National Museum of Modern Art
CHIYODA-KU
East Garden
Communications Museum
Fukiage Imperial Residence
Cabinet Library
Imperial Palace Gardens
New Imperial Palace
National Theatre
Supreme Court
Tōkyō Station
Outer Garden
Sakurada Moat
National Diet Library
Sukarada Gate
Parliamentary Museum
Imperial Theatre
National Diet Building
High Court
Hibiya Park
Yurakucho Station
Prime Minister's Residence
Hibiya Concert Hall
Nissei Theatre
CHŪŌ - KU
Hibiya Library
Hibiya Public Hall
MINATO - KU
Kabukiza Theatre

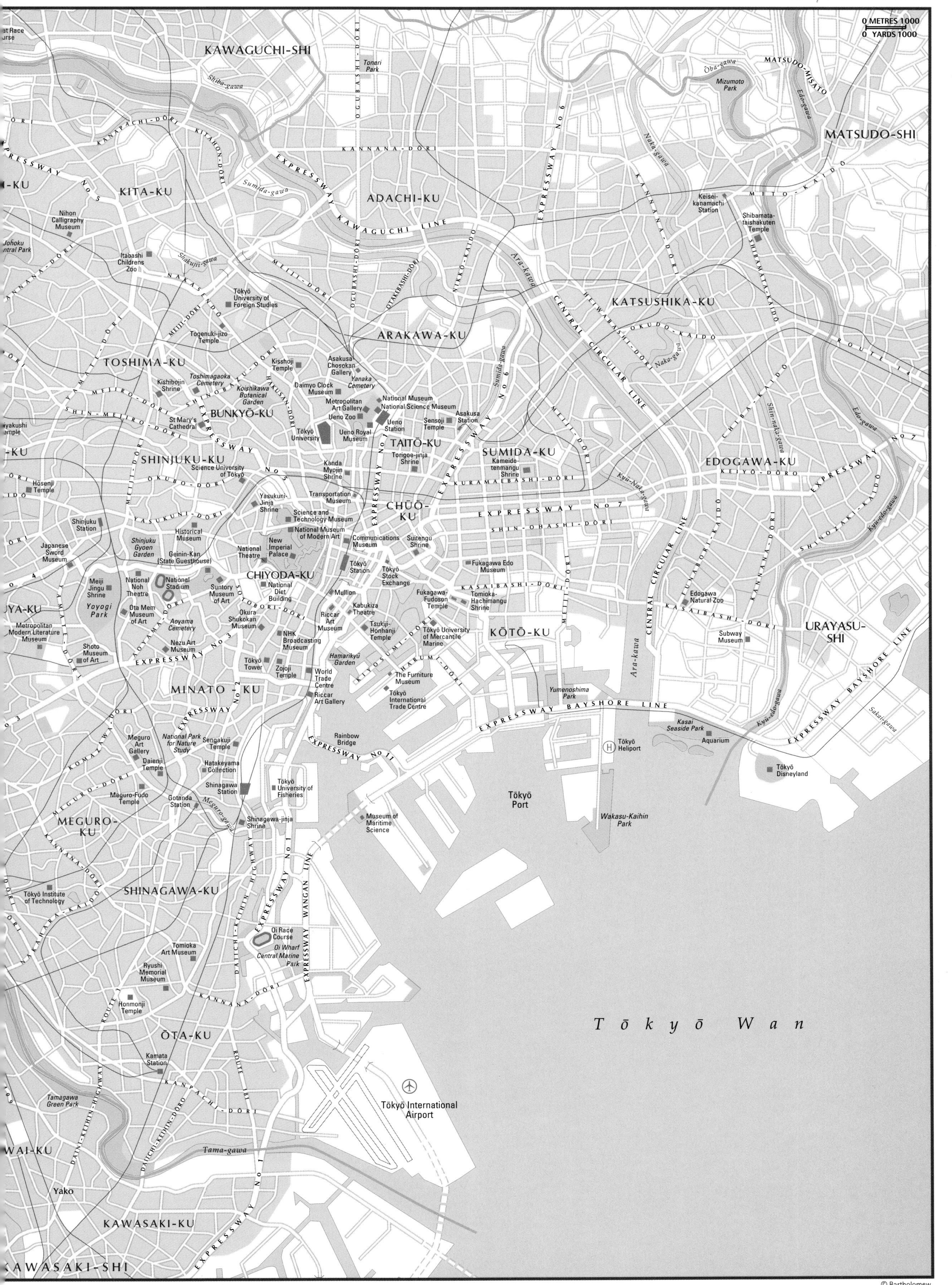

0 METRES 1000
0 YARDS 1000

KAWAGUCHI-SHI

Toneri Park

Shiba-gawa

Ōba-gawa

Mizumoto Park

MATSUDO-MISATO

at Race urse

KANPACHI-DORI

EXPRESSWAY No 5

KITAHON-DORI

KITA-KU

OGUBASHI-DORI

KANNANA-DORI

Sumida-gawa

ADACHI-KU

EXPRESSWAY KAWAGUCHI LINE

NIKKO-KAIDO

Arakawa

EXPRESSWAY No 6

KANNAN-DORI

Naka-gawa

HEIWABASHI-DORI

CENTRAL CIRCULAR LINE

OKUDO-KAIDO

Naka-gawa

MATSUDO-SHI

Keisei-kanamachi Station

MITO-KAIDO

SHIBAMATA-KAIDO

Shibamata-taishakuten Temple

-KU

Nihon Calligraphy Museum

Jōhoku Central Park

Itabashi Childrens Zoo

MEIJI-DORI

Shinkujii-gawa

NAKASENDO

TŌKYŌ University of Foreign Studies

Togenuki-iizo Temple

ARAKAWA-KU

OGUBASHI-DORI

OJIKABASHI-DORI

KATSUSHIKA-KU

EDOGAWA-KU

KEIYŌ-DŌRO

Edo-gawa

ROUTE 14

MEIJI-DORI

TOSHIMA-KU

SHIN-MEIRO-DORI

MEIRO-DORI

Kishibojin Shrine

Toshimagaoka Cemetery

SHINOBANZ-DORI

HAKUSAN-DORI

Kisshoji Temple

Daimyo Clock Museum

Asakusa Chosokan Gallery

Yanaka Cemetery

National Museum

Sumida-gawa

SUMIDA-KU

MEIJI-DORI

Shin-naka-gawa

CHIBA-KAIDO

EXPRESSWAY No 7

akayakushi emple

-KU

Hōseni Temple

St Mary's Cathedral

Koishikawa Botanical Garden

BUNKYŌ-KU

Metropolitan Art Gallery

Ueno Zoo

National Science Museum

Sensoji Temple

Asakusa Station

Kameido-tenmangu Shrine

Kyū-Naka-gawa

EXPRESSWAY No 7

SHINJUKU-KU

Science University of Tōkyō

OKUBO-DORI

TŌkyō University

Ueno Royal Museum

Ueno Station

TAITŌ-KU

Torigoe-jinja Shrine

KURAMAEBASHI-DORI

Kanda Myojin Shrine

CHUO-KU

SHIN-OHASHI-DORI

Shinjuku Station

YASUKUNI-DORI

Yasukuni-Jinja Shrine

Transportation Museum

Science and Technology Museum

National Museum of Modern Art

Communications Museum

Suitengu Shrine

Fukagawa Edo Museum

KASAIBASHI-DORI

Edogawa Natural Zoo

URAYASU-SHI

EXPRESSWAY BAYSHORE LINE

Japanese Sword Museum

Historical Museum

Shinjuku Gyoen Garden

Geinin-Kan (State Guesthouse)

National Theatre

New Imperial Palace

TŌkyō Station

TŌkyō Stock Exchange

Fukagawa-Fudoson Temple

Tomioka-Hachimangu Shrine

CENTRAL CIRCULAR LINE

Ara-kawa

Subway Museum

Meiji Jingu Shrine

National Noh Theatre

Ota Mem Museum of Art

National Stadium

National Museum of Art

Suntory Museum of Art

Okura Shukokan Museum

Aoyama Cemetery

Nezu Art Museum

CHIYODA-KU

National Diet Building

Mullion

Riccar Art Museum

Kabukiza Theatre

Tsukiji-Honhanji Temple

TŌkyō University of Mercantile Marine

KŌTŌ-KU

Yumenoshima Park

Kasai Seaside Park

Aquarium

Kyū-edo-gawa

EXPRESSWAY BAYSHORE LINE

Sakai-gawa

Yoyogi Park

Metropolitan Modern Literature Museum

Shoto Museum of Art

KOMAZAWA-DORI

NHK Broadcasting Museum

TŌkyō Tower

Zojoji Temple

Hamarikyū Garden

World Trade Centre

Riccar Art Gallery

KIYOSUMI-DORI

HARUMI-DORI

The Furniture Museum

TŌkyō International Trade Centre

TŌkyō Heliport

TŌkyō Disneyland

UYA-KU

EXPRESSWAY No 3

MINATO-KU

EXPRESSWAY

National Park for Nature Study

Sengakuji Temple

Hatakeyama Collection

Rainbow Bridge

EXPRESSWAY No 11

TŌkyō Port

Wakasu-Kaihin Park

Meguro Art Gallery

Daieni Temple

Shinagawa Station

TŌkyō University of Fisheries

Museum of Maritime Science

MEGURO-KU

Meguro-Fudo Temple

Gotanda Station

Meguro-gawa

Shinagawa-jinja Shrine

EXPRESSWAY No 1

TŌkyō Institute of Technology

SHINAGAWA-KU

DAIICHI-KEIHIN HIGHWAY

EXPRESSWAY WANGAN LINE

NAKAHARA-KAIDO

KANNANA-DORI

Tomioka Art Museum

Ryushi Memorial Museum

 Honmonji Temple

Oi Race Course

Oi Wharf Central Marine Park

Tōkyō Wan

ROUTE 1

ŌTA-KU

Kamata Station

KANPACHI-DORI

Tamagawa Green Park

DAINI-KEIHIN HIGHWAY

Tama-gawa

⊕ TŌkyō International Airport

KAWASAKI-KU

Yako

WAI-KU

KAWASAKI-SHI

© Bartholomew

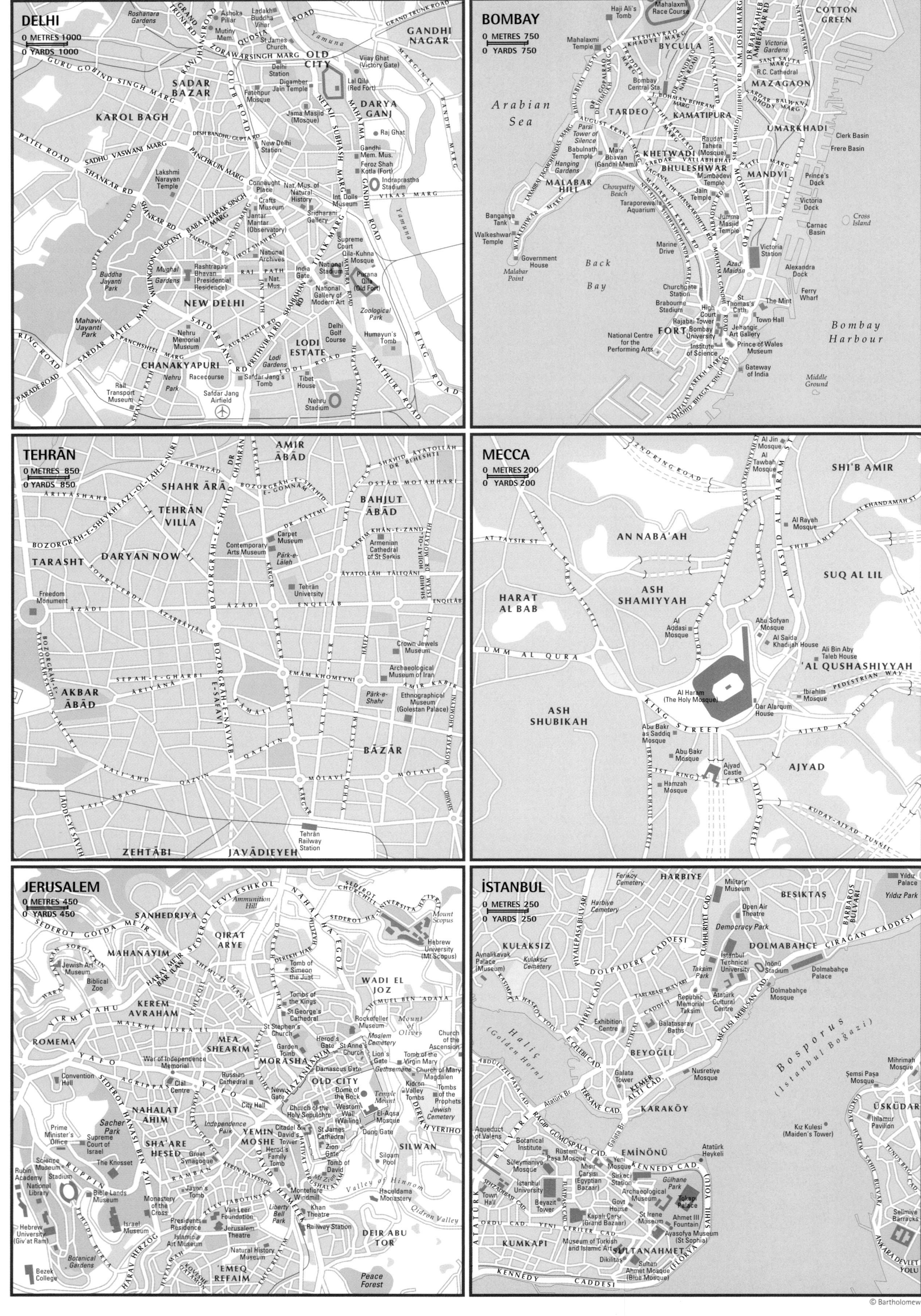

Delhi, Bombay, Tehrān, Mecca, Jerusalem, İstanbul

54

DELHI

0 METRES 1000
0 YARDS 1000

Roshanara Gardens, Ashoka Pillar, Ladakh Buddha Vihar, GANDHI NAGAR, Mutiny Mem., St James Church, OLD CITY, Vijay Ghat (Victory Gate), Delhi Station, Digamber Jain Temple, Lal Qila (Red Fort), SADAR BAZAR, Fatehpur Mosque, Jama Masjid (Mosque), DARYA GANJ, KAROL BAGH, Raj Ghat, Lakshmi Narayan Temple, New Delhi Station, Gandhi Mem., Feroz Shah Kotla (Fort), Indraprastha Stadium, Connaught Place, Crafts Museum, Jantar Mantar (Observatory), Nat. Mus. of Natural History, Int. Dolls Museum, Sridharani Gallery, Buddha Jayanti Park, Mughal Gardens, Rashtrapati Bhavan (Presidential Residence), National Archives, Supreme Court, Qila-Kuhna Mosque, India Gate, National Stadium, Nat. Mus., NEW DELHI, National Gallery of Modern Art, Purana Qila (Old Fort), Zoological Park, Mahavir Jayanti Park, Nehru Memorial Museum, Delhi Golf Course, Humayun's Tomb, CHANAKYAPURI, LODI ESTATE, Lodi Gardens, Tibet House, Nehru Park, Racecourse, Safdar Jang's Tomb, Rail Transport Museum, Safdar Jang Airfield, Nehru Stadium

BOMBAY

0 METRES 750
0 YARDS 750

Haji Ali's Tomb, Mahalaxmi Race Course, COTTON GREEN, Mahalaxmi Temple, BYCULLA, Victoria Gardens, R.C. Cathedral, Bombay Central Sta., MAZAGAON, TARDEO, Parsi Tower of Silence, KHETWADI (Mosque), UMARKHADI, Clerk Basin, Frere Basin, Arabian Sea, Raudat Tahera (Mosque), Mani Bhavan (Gandhi Mem.), Hanging Gardens, MANDVI, Prince's Dock, Victoria Dock, MALABAR HILL, Chowpatty Beach, Taraporewalla Aquarium, BHULESHWAR, Mumbadevi Temple, Jain Temple, Jumma Masjid Temple, Carnac Basin, Bangana Tank, Walkeshwar Temple, Marine Drive, Cross Island, Victoria Station, Alexandra Dock, Malabar Point, Back Bay, Government House, Azad Maidan, Ferry Wharf, Churchgate Station, Brabourne Stadium, High Court, The Mint, St Thomas's Cath., Town Hall, Bombay Harbour, Rajabai Tower, FORT, Bombay University, National Centre for the Performing Arts, Jehangir Art Gallery, Prince of Wales Museum, Institute of Science, Middle Ground, Gateway of India

TEHRĀN

0 METRES 850
0 YARDS 850

AMIR ĀBĀD, SHAHR ĀRĀ, TEHRĀN VILLA, BAHJUT ĀBĀD, Carpet Museum, TARASHT, DARYAN NOW, Contemporary Arts Museum, Pārk-e-Lāleh, Armenian Cathedral of St Sarkis, Freedom Monument, Tehrān University, AKBAR ĀBĀD, Crown Jewels Museum, Archaeological Museum of Iran, EMĀM KHOMEYNI, Pārk-e-Shahr, Ethnographical Museum (Golestan Palace), BĀZĀR, ZEHTĀBI, JAVĀDIEYEH, Tehrān Railway Station

MECCA

0 METRES 200
0 YARDS 200

2ND RING ROAD, Al Jin Mosque, Al Tawbah Mosque, SHI'B AMIR, AN NABA'AH, SUQ AL LIL, Al Rayah Mosque, HARAT AL BAB, ASH SHAMIYYAH, Abu Sofyan Mosque, Al Addasi Mosque, Al Saida Khadijah House, Ali Bin Aby Taleb House, 'AL QUSHASHIYYAH, UMM AL QURA, Al Haram (The Holy Mosque), Dar Alarqum House, Ibrahim Mosque, ASH SHUBIKAH, KING STREET, Abu Bakr as Saddiq Mosque, Abu Bakr Mosque, Ajyad Castle, Hamzah Mosque, AJYAD, KUDAY-AJYAD TUNNEL

JERUSALEM

0 METRES 450
0 YARDS 450

SANHEDRIYA, Ammunition Hill, Mount Scopus, QIRAT ARYE, MAHANAYIM, Hebrew University (Mt Scopus), Jewish Art Museum, Biblical Zoo, Tomb of Simeon the Just, WADI EL JOZ, KEREM AVRAHAM, Tombs of the Kings, Rockefeller Museum, ROMEMA, St George's Cathedral, St Stephen's Church, Mount of Olives, Church of the Ascension, MEA SHEARIM, Herod's Gate, Moslem Cemetery, St Anne's Church, Lion's Gate, Tomb of the Virgin Mary, Church of Mary Magdalen, War of Independence Memorial, MORASHA, Garden Tomb, Gethsemane, Convention Hall, Russian Cathedral, Damascus Gate, Kidron Valley, Tombs of the Prophets, Prime Minister's Office, Cial Centre, New Gate, OLD CITY, Dome of the Rock, Temple Mount, SILWAN, NAHALAT AHIM, City Hall, Church of the Holy Sepulchre, Western Wall (Wailing), Jewish Cemetery, SHA'ARE HESED, Independence Park, YEMIN MOSHE, Citadel & David's Tower, El-Aqsa Mosque, Siloam Pool, Sacher Park, Supreme Court of Israel, The Knesset, Great Synagogue, St James Cathedral, Zion Gate, Tomb of David, Science Museum, Rubin Academy, Bible Lands Museum, Monastery of the Cross, Presidents Residence, Van Leer Foundation, Jason's Tomb, Liberty Bell Park, Khan Theatre, Montefiore Windmill, National Library, Hebrew University (Giv'at Ram), Israel Museum, Islamic Art Museum, Jerusalem Theatre, Natural History Museum, 'EMEQ REFAIM, Railway Station, Haceldama Monastery, Valley of Hinnom, DEIR ABU TOR, Bezek College, Botanical Gardens, Peace Forest

İSTANBUL

0 METRES 250
0 YARDS 250

Feriköy Cemetery, HARBIYE, Military Museum, Yıldız Palace, BEŞIKTAŞ, Yıldız Park, KULAKSIZ, Harbiye Cemetery, Open Air Theatre, Democracy Park, İstanbul Technical University, DOLMABAHÇE, Aynalıkavak Palace (Museum), Kulaksız Cemetery, Taksim Park, İnönü Stadium, Dolmabahçe Palace, Taksim, Republic Memorial Taksim, Atatürk Cultural Centre, Dolmabahçe Mosque, Galatasaray Baths, Exhibition Centre, BEYOĞLU, Galata Tower, Nusretiye Mosque, Haliç (Golden Horn), KEMER, Mihrimah Mosque, Bosporus (İstanbul Boğazı), Şemsi Paşa Mosque, KARAKÖY, Aqueduct of Valens, Galata Br., ÜSKÜDAR, Botanical Institute, Süleymaniye Mosque, Rüstem Paşa Mosque, Yeni Mosque, Mısır Çarşısı (Egyptian Bazaar), Sirkeci Station, Gülhane Park, Kız Kulesi (Maiden's Tower), İstanbul University, Govt House, Archaeological Museum, Topkapı Palace, Beyazit Tower, Kapalı Çarşı (Grand Bazaar), St Irene Museum, Ahmet III Fountain, İhlamur Pavilion, EMINÖNÜ, KUMKAPI, Museum of Turkish and Islamic Art, Ayasofya Museum (St Sophia), Selimiye Barracks, Dikilitaş, Sultan Ahmet Mosque (Blue Mosque), SULTANAHMET, ANKARA DEVLET YOLU

© Bartholomew

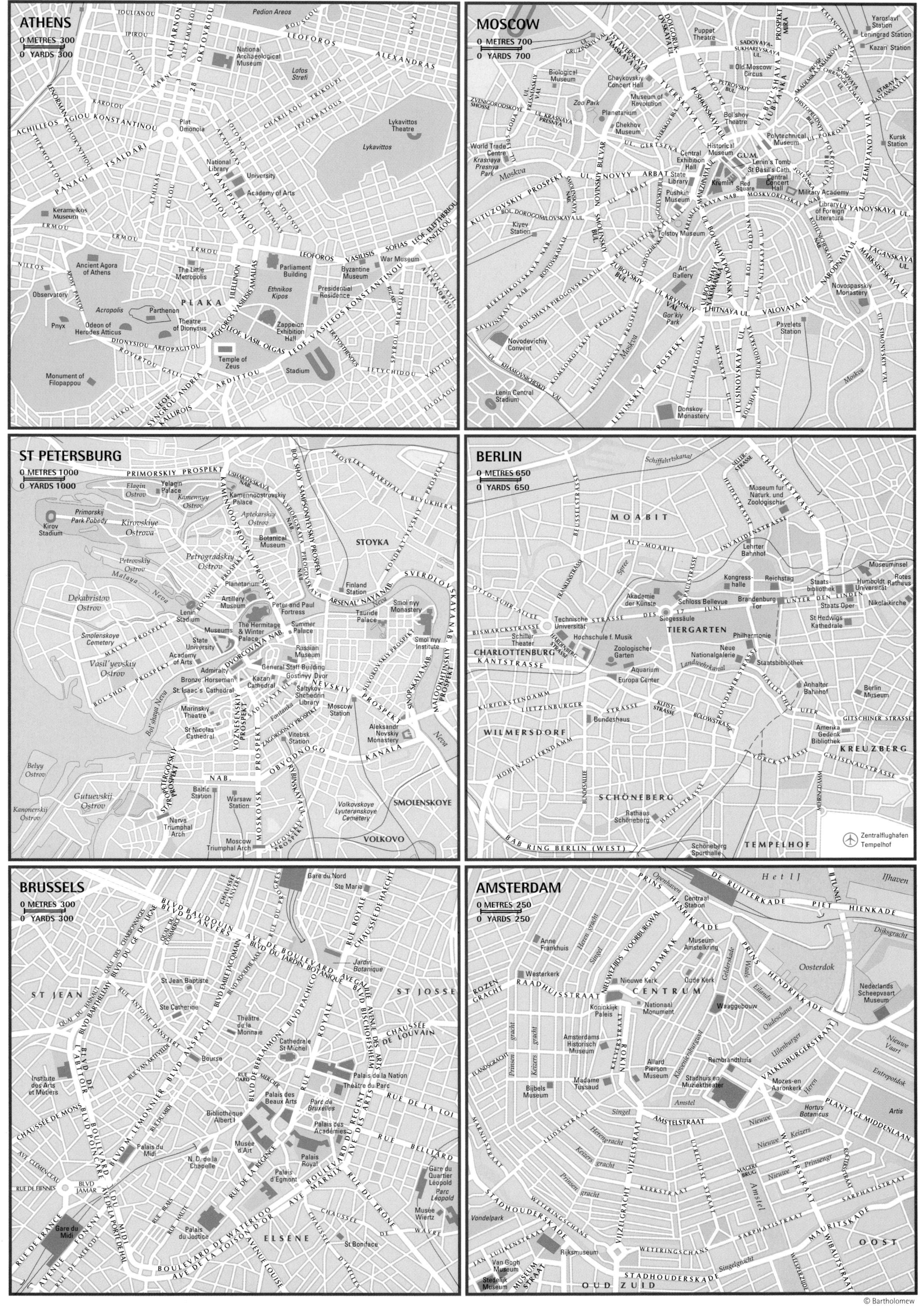

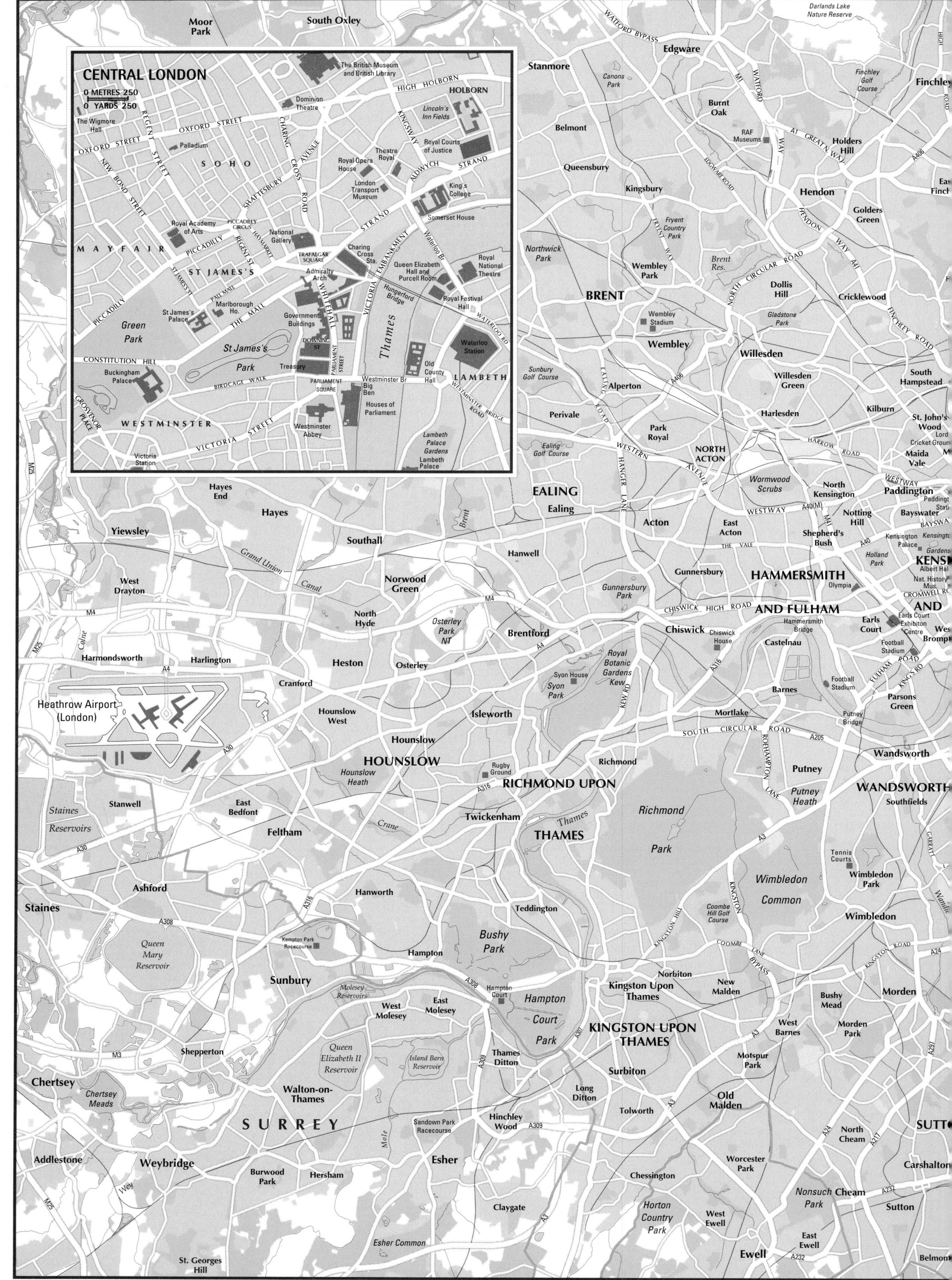
CENTRAL LONDON
0 METRES 250
0 YARDS 250
Moor Park
South Oxley
Stanmore
Edgware
Belmont
Queensbury
Kingsbury
Burnt Oak
Holders Hill
Hendon
Golders Green
Finchley
BRENT
Wembley Park
Wembley
Willesden
Dollis Hill
Cricklewood
Alperton
Perivale
Harlesden
Kilburn
South Hampstead
Park Royal
NORTH ACTON
Maida Vale
Paddington
EALING
Ealing
Acton
East Acton
North Kensington
Notting Hill
Bayswater
Shepherd's Bush
HAMMERSMITH AND FULHAM
Hayes End
Hayes
Yiewsley
Southall
Hanwell
West Drayton
Norwood Green
North Hyde
Osterley Park NT
Brentford
Gunnersbury
Chiswick
Castelnau
Earls Court
Harmondsworth
Harlington
Heston
Osterley
Cranford
Heathrow Airport (London)
Hounslow West
Isleworth
Hounslow
HOUNSLOW
Hounslow Heath
Barnes
Mortlake
Parsons Green
Richmond
Putney
Wandsworth
WANDSWORTH
RICHMOND UPON THAMES
Twickenham
Richmond Park
Stanwell
East Bedfont
Feltham
Staines Reservoirs
Ashford
Staines
Hanworth
Teddington
Bushy Park
Wimbledon Common
Wimbledon
Queen Mary Reservoir
Hampton
Sunbury
Kingston Upon Thames
New Malden
Morden
West Molesey
East Molesey
Hampton Court Park
KINGSTON UPON THAMES
West Barnes
Shepperton
Thames Ditton
Surbiton
Motspur Park
Chertsey
Walton-on-Thames
Long Ditton
Old Malden
Tolworth
SURREY
Hinchley Wood
North Cheam
Addlestone
Weybridge
Burwood Park
Hersham
Esher
Chessington
Worcester Park
Carshalton
Cheam
Sutton
Claygate
Horton Country Park
West Ewell
East Ewell
Ewell
St. Georges Hill

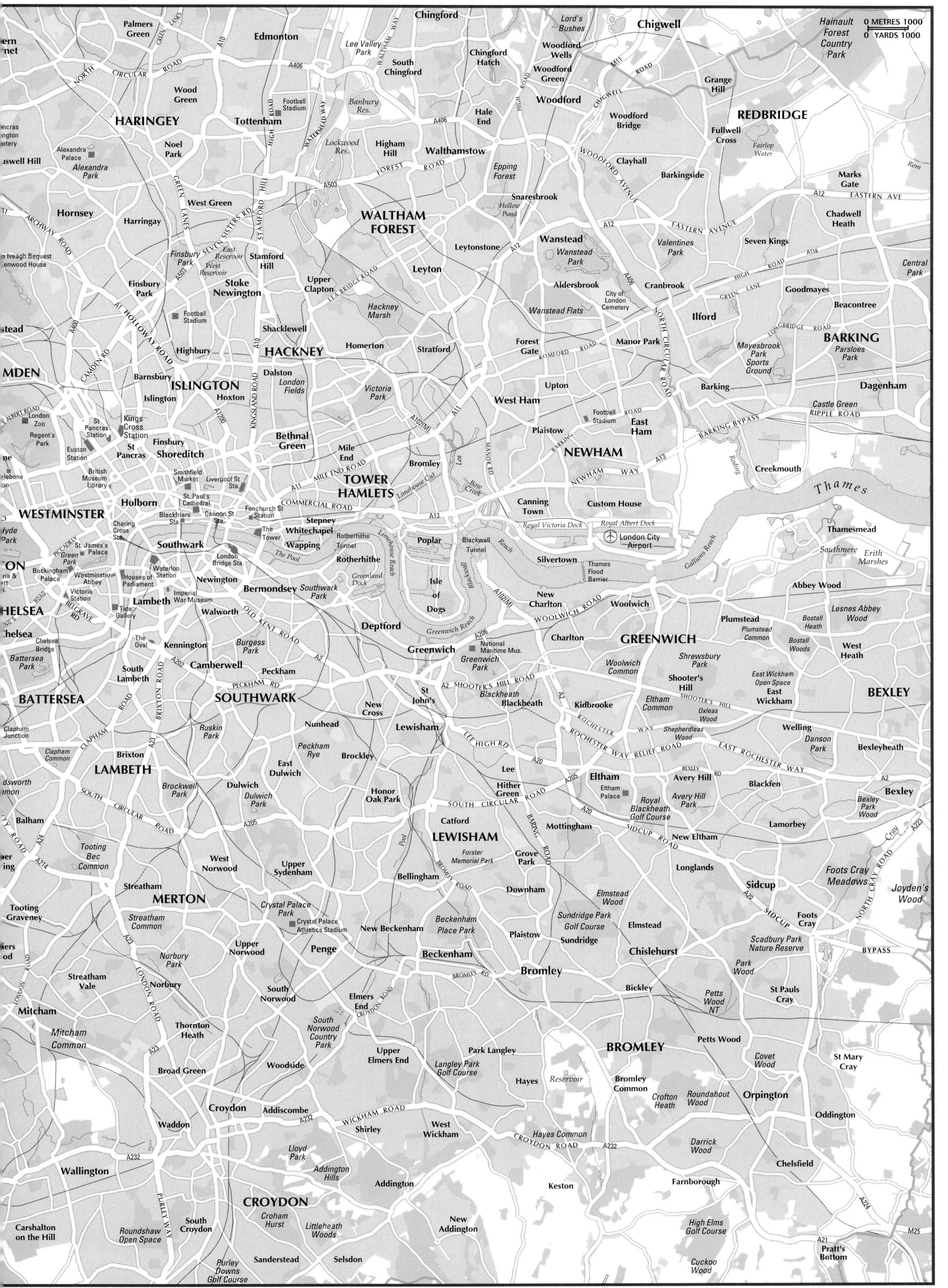

0 METRES 1000
0 YARDS 1000

Palmers Green
Edmonton
Chingford
Lord's Bushes
Chigwell
Hainault Forest Country Park

Woodford Wells
Woodford Green

Wood Green
Noel Park
South Chingford
Chingford Hatch
Woodford
Grange Hill

HARINGEY
Tottenham
Lee Valley Park
Banbury Res.
Hale End
Woodford Bridge
Clayhall
Fullwell Cross
Fairlop Water

Football Stadium
Higham Hill
Walthamstow
Woodford Avenue
Barkingside
REDBRIDGE
Marks Gate

Alexandra Palace
Alexandra Park
Lockwood Res.
Epping Forest
EASTERN AVE
Chadwell Heath

Hornsey
Harringay
West Green
Stamford Hill
Snaresbrook
Hollow Pond
Valentines Park
Seven Kings
Goodmayes

Iveagh Bequest Kenwood House
Finsbury Park
East Reservoir
West Reservoir
Stoke Newington
Wanstead
Wanstead Park
Cranbrook
Ilford
Beacontree

Finsbury Park
Shacklewell
Leytonstone
Leyton
Aldersbrook
Wanstead Flats
City of London Cemetery

Camden
Barnsbury
Highbury
Football Stadium
Upper Clapton
HACKNEY
Homerton
Hackney Marsh
Stratford
Forest Gate
Manor Park
BARKING
Parsloes Park

ISLINGTON
Islington
Hoxton
Dalston
London Fields
Shacklewell
Victoria Park
West Ham
Upton
Barking
Dagenham

London Zoo
Regent's Park
St Pancras Station
Kings Cross Station
Finsbury Sq
Shoreditch
Bethnal Green
Mile End
Bromley
Plaistow
East Ham
NEWHAM
Castle Green

Euston Station
British Museum Library
Smithfield Market
Liverpool St Sta.
TOWER HAMLETS
Mile End Road
Lea
Football Stadium

Holborn
St. Paul's Cathedral
Stepney
Whitechapel
Wapping
Bow Creek
Canning Town
Custom House
Creekmouth

WESTMINSTER
Charing Cross Sta.
Blackfriars Sta.
Cannon St Sta.
Fenchurch Station
COMMERCIAL ROAD
Rotherhithe Tunnel
Poplar
Blackwall Tunnel
Royal Victoria Dock
Royal Albert Dock
London City Airport
Thamesmead

Green Park
St James's Palace
The Tower
Rotherhithe
Isle of Dogs
Silvertown
Thames Flood Barrier
Southmere
Erith Marshes

Buckingham Palace
Westminster Abbey
Houses of Parliament
Southwark
London Bridge Sta.
The Pool
Greenland Dock
New Charlton
Woolwich
Abbey Wood

CHELSEA
Victoria Station
Lambeth
Tate Gallery
Newington
Bermondsey
Southwark Park
Deptford
Charlton
WOOLWICH ROAD
Plumstead
Lesnes Abbey Wood

Chelsea
Battersea Park
Chelsea Bridge
The Oval
Kennington
Walworth
OLD KENT ROAD
Greenwich Reach
Greenwich
National Maritime Mus.
GREENWICH
Plumstead Common
Bostall Heath
West Heath

BATTERSEA
South Lambeth
Camberwell
Burgess Park
Peckham
Greenwich Park
Woolwich Common
Shrewsbury Park
Bostall Woods
BEXLEY

Clapham Junction
Brixton
SOUTHWARK
PECKHAM RD
Nunhead
New Cross
St John's
Blackheath
Blackheath
Kidbrooke
Shooter's Hill
East Wickham Open Space
East Wickham
Welling

Clapham Common
LAMBETH
Ruskin Park
Peckham Rye
Brockley
Lewisham
Lee High Rd
Lee
Eltham Common
Oxleas Wood
Welling
Danson Park
Bexleyheath

Balham
Brockwell Park
Dulwich
Dulwich Park
East Dulwich
Honor Oak Park
Hither Green
Eltham
Eltham Palace
Avery Hill
Avery Hill Park
Blackfen
Bexley
Bexley Park Wood

Tooting Bec Common
Streatham
West Norwood
Catford
Mottingham
Royal Blackheath Golf Course
New Eltham
Lamorbey

MERTON
Streatham Common
Upper Sydenham
LEWISHAM
Grove Park
Longlands
Sidcup
Foots Cray Meadows
Joyden's Wood

Tooting Graveney
Crystal Palace Park
Bellingham
Downham
Elmstead Wood
New Eltham
Foots Cray
SIDCUP ROAD

Streatham Vale
Norbury Park
Upper Norwood
Crystal Palace Athletics Stadium
New Beckenham
Beckenham Place Park
Plaistow
Sundridge Park Golf Course
Elmstead
Sundridge
Scadbury Park Nature Reserve
Park Wood

Mitcham
Norbury
Penge
Beckenham
Chislehurst

Streatham Vale
South Norwood
Elmers End
Bromley
Bickley
Petts Wood NT
St Pauls Cray

Mitcham Common
Thornton Heath
Woodside
South Norwood Country Park
Upper Elmers End
Langley Park Golf Course
Park Langley
BROMLEY
Petts Wood
Covet Wood
St Mary Cray

Broad Green
Hayes
Reservoir
Bromley Common
Crofton Heath
Roundabout Wood
Orpington
Oddington

Croydon
Addiscombe
Shirley
West Wickham
Hayes Common
Darrick Wood
Chelsfield

Waddon
Lloyd Park
Addington Hills
CROYDON ROAD
Farnborough

CROYDON
Croham Hurst
Littleheath Woods
New Addington
Keston
High Elms Golf Course
Cuckoo Wood
M25

Wallington
Addington
Pratt's Bottom

Carshalton on the Hill
Roundshaw Open Space
Purley Downs Golf Course
Sanderstead
Selsdon
South Croydon

© Bartholomew

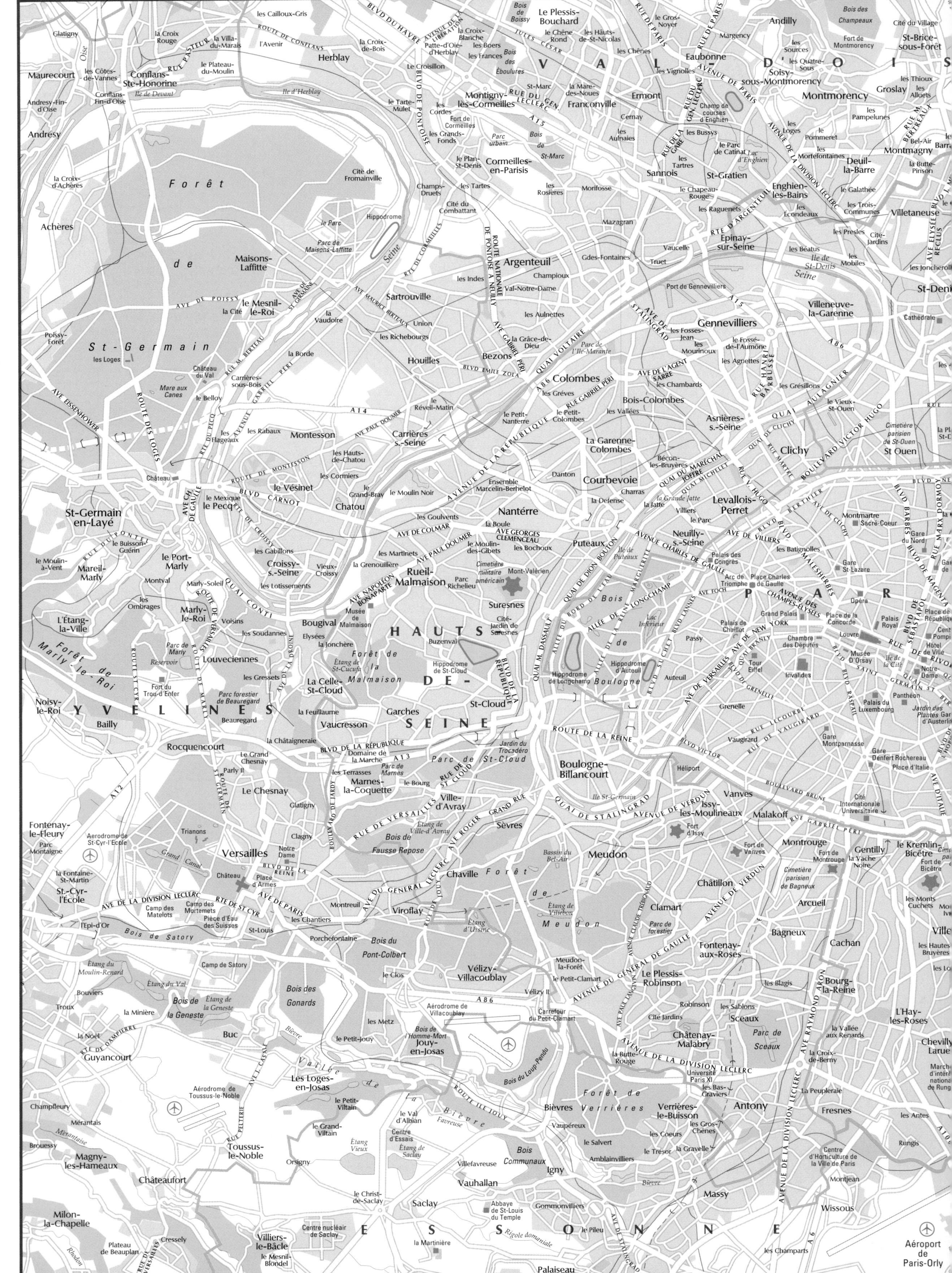
V A L - D ' O I S E
Y V E L I N E S
H A U T S - D E - S E I N E
E S S O N N E
P A R
Forêt de St-Germain
Forêt de Marly-le-Roi
Forêt de la Malmaison
Forêt de Meudon
Forêt de Verrières
Bois de Boulogne
Parc de St-Cloud
Seine
Maurecourt
Conflans-Ste-Honorine
Andrésy
Achères
Herblay
Montigny-lès-Cormeilles
Franconville
Ermont
Eaubonne
Soisy-sous-Montmorency
Montmorency
Andilly
Groslay
St-Brice-sous-Forêt
Le Plessis-Bouchard
Cormeilles-en-Parisis
Sannois
St-Gratien
Enghien-les-Bains
Deuil-la-Barre
Montmagny
Villetaneuse
Epinay-sur-Seine
Argenteuil
Maisons-Laffitte
Sartrouville
le Mesnil-le-Roi
Houilles
Bezons
Colombes
Gennevilliers
Villeneuve-la-Garenne
St-Denis
Bois-Colombes
Asnières-s.-Seine
Clichy
St Ouen
La Garenne-Colombes
Courbevoie
Levallois-Perret
Neuilly-s.-Seine
Carrières-s.-Seine
Montesson
le Vésinet
Chatou
le Pecq
St-Germain-en-Laye
Nanterre
Puteaux
Croissy-s.-Seine
Rueil-Malmaison
Suresnes
le Port-Marly
Mareil-Marly
Marly-le-Roi
L'Étang-la-Ville
Louveciennes
Bougival
La Celle-St-Cloud
Garches
Vaucresson
St-Cloud
Noisy-le-Roi
Bailly
Rocquencourt
Le Chesnay
Marnes-la-Coquette
Ville-d'Avray
Sèvres
Boulogne-Billancourt
Issy-les-Moulineaux
Vanves
Malakoff
Montrouge
Gentilly
le Kremlin-Bicêtre
Versailles
Chaville
Viroflay
Meudon
Clamart
Châtillon
Bagneux
Arcueil
Cachan
Fontenay-aux-Roses
Le Plessis-Robinson
Bourg-la-Reine
Sceaux
L'Hay-les-Roses
Châtenay-Malabry
Antony
Fresnes
Vélizy-Villacoublay
Fontenay-le-Fleury
St-Cyr-l'École
Guyancourt
Buc
Jouy-en-Josas
Les Loges-en-Josas
Toussus-le-Noble
Magny-les-Hameaux
Châteaufort
Milon-la-Chapelle
Villiers-le-Bâcle
Saclay
Vauhallan
Igny
Bièvres
Verrières-le-Buisson
Massy
Palaiseau
Wissous
Rungis
Aéroport de Paris-Orly
Aérodrome de Villacoublay
Aérodrome de Toussus-le-Noble
Aerodrome de St-Cyr-l'École
Hippodrome de Longchamp
Hippodrome d'Auteuil
Hippodrome de St-Cloud
Tour Eiffel
Arc de Triomphe
Place Charles de Gaulle
Sacré-Cœur
Invalides
Louvre
Opéra
Gare St-Lazare
Gare du Nord
Gare Montparnasse
Palais du Luxembourg
Cité Internationale Universitaire
Université Paris XI
A13
A14
A15
A86
A12
A6

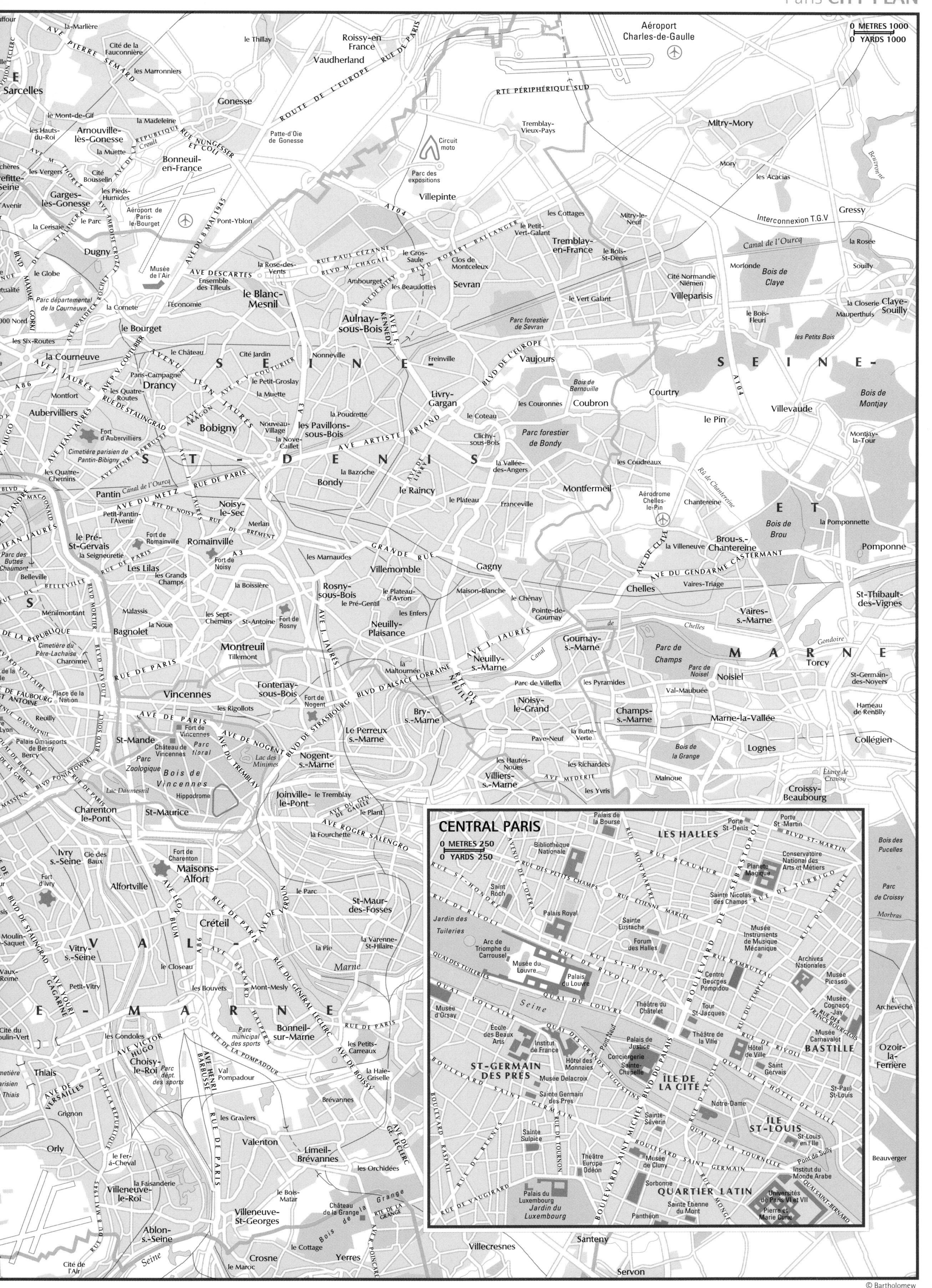

ROME

0 METRES 400
0 YARDS 400

MILAN

0 METRES 250
0 YARDS 250

MADRID

0 METRES 250
0 YARDS 250

BARCELONA

0 METRES 450
0 YARDS 450

CAIRO

0 METRES 450
0 YARDS 450

CAPE TOWN

0 METRES 250
0 YARDS 250

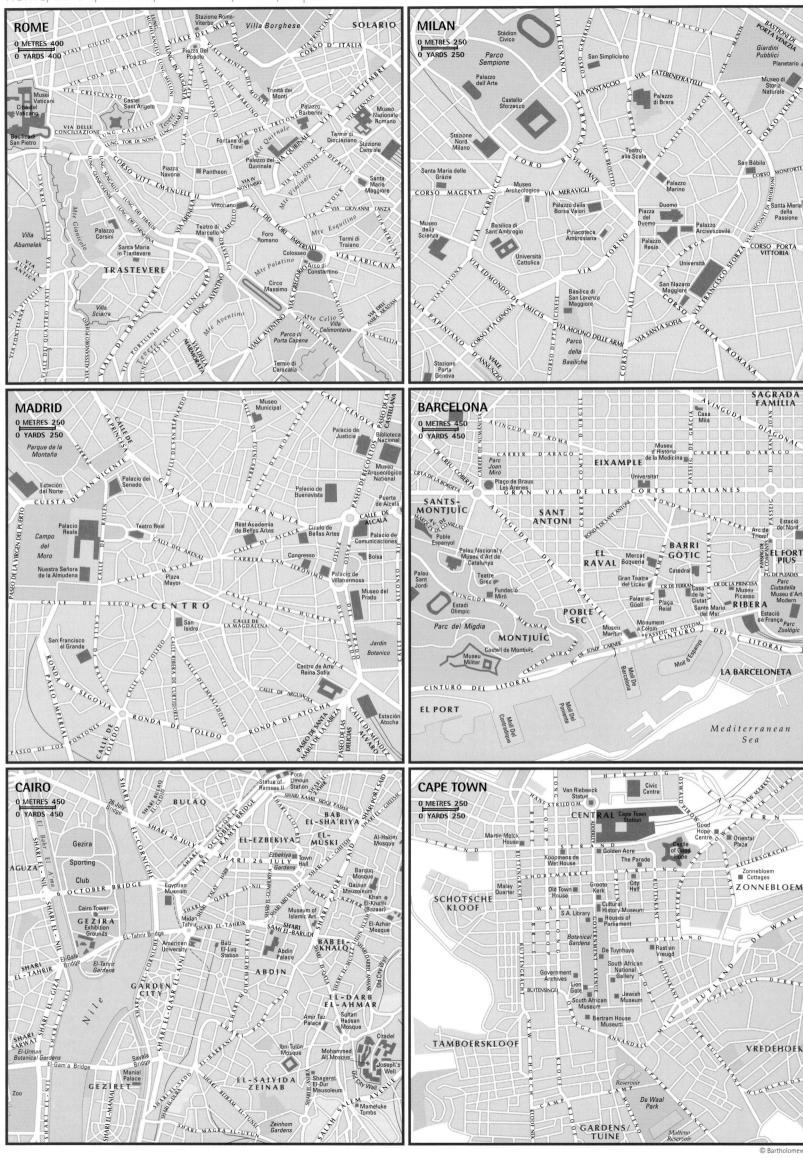

© Bartholomew

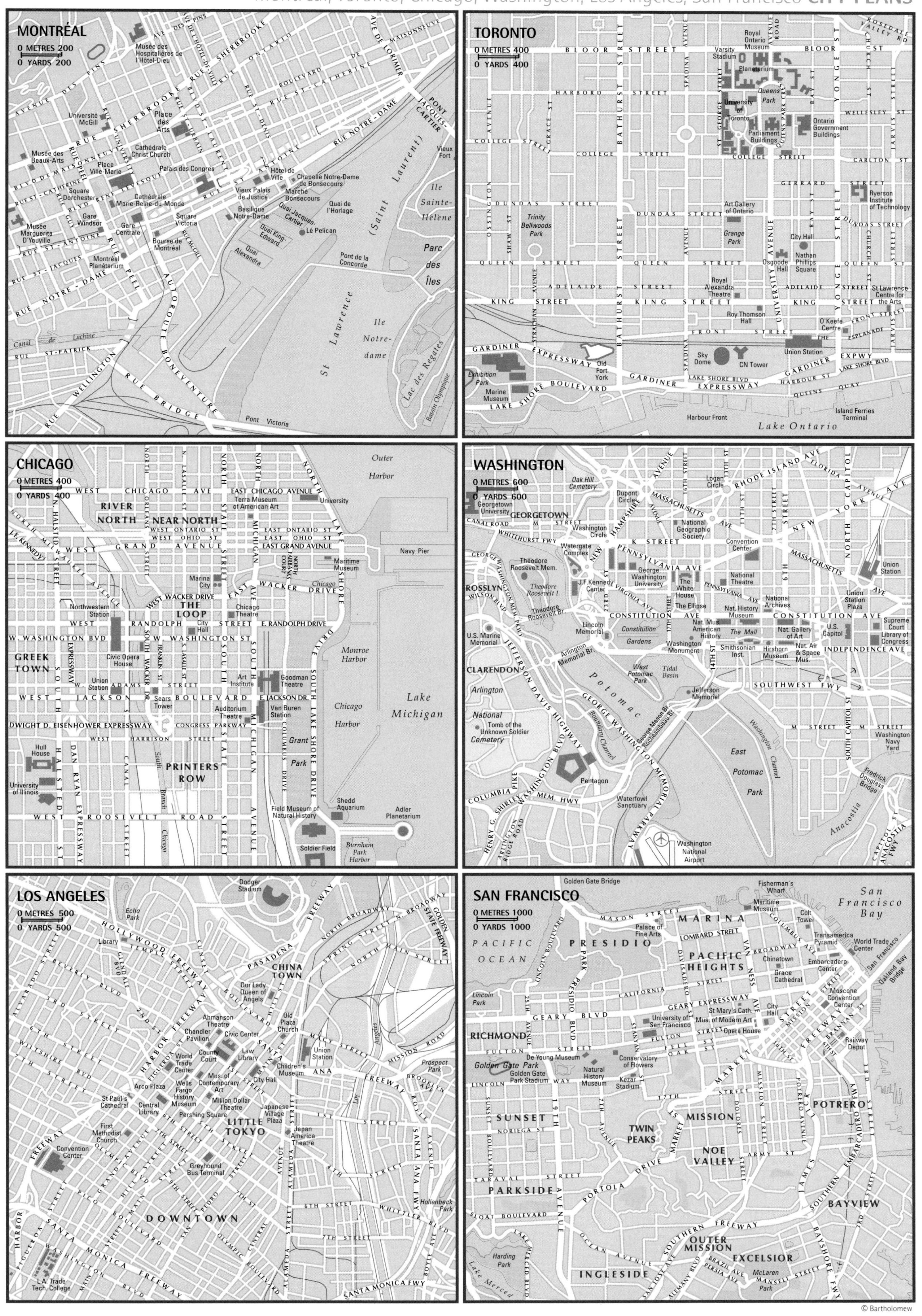

MONTRÉAL

0 METRES 200
0 YARDS 200

AVENUE DES PINS
BOULEVARD ST-JOSEPH
RUE ST-HUBERT
RUE ST-DENIS
RUE SHERBROOKE
RUE SHERBROOKE
AVE DE MAISONNEUVE
Musée des Hospitalières de l'Hôtel-Dieu
Université McGill
Place des Arts
RUE ONTARIO
AVE DE LORIMER
PONT JACQUES CARTIER
Cathédrale Christ Church
Musée des Beaux-Arts
RUE ST-CATHERINE
Vieux Fort
RUE ST-LAURENT
RUE NOTRE-DAME
Hôtel de Ville
Chapelle Notre-Dame de Bonsecours
Vieux Palais de Justice
Marché Bonsecours
Quai de l'Horloge
Cathédrale Marie-Reine-du-Monde
Basilique Notre-Dame
Quai Jacques-Cartier
Ile Sainte-Hélène
Palais des Congrès
Square Dorchester
Square Victoria
Musée Marguerite D'Youville
Place Ville-Marie
Gare Windsor
Gare Centrale
Bourse de Montréal
Quai King-Edward
Le Pelican
Parc des Iles
Montréal Planétarium
Quai Alexandra
Pont de la Concorde
RUE NOTRE-DAME
RUE ST-JACQUES
RUE WELLINGTON
AUTOROUTE BONEVENTURE
St Lawrence
Canal de Lachine
RUE ST-PATRICK
PONT BRIDGE
Pont Victoria
Bassin Olympique
Ile Notre-dame
Lac des Regates
RUE PEEL
RUE GUY
BLVD DE MAISONNEUVE O UEST
RUE UNIVERSITY
RUE METCALFE
RUE MANSFIELD

TORONTO

0 METRES 400
0 YARDS 400

BLOOR STREET
Royal Ontario Museum
ROSEDALE VALLEY ROAD
Varsity Stadium
Planetarium
BLOOR
HARBORD STREET
University of Toronto
Queen's Park
COLLEGE STREET
Parliament Buildings
Ontario Government Buildings
WELLESLEY ST
COLLEGE STREET
CARLTON ST
GERRARD STREET
Ryerson Institute of Technology
Art Gallery of Ontario
DUNDAS STREET
DUNDAS STREET
Trinity Bellwoods Park
Grange Park
City Hall
QUEEN STREET
Osgoode Hall
Nathan Phillips Square
QUEEN STREET
ADELAIDE STREET
Royal Alexandra Theatre
ADELAIDE STREET
St Lawrence Centre for the Arts
KING STREET
KING STREET
Roy Thomson Hall
KING STREET
O'Keefe Centre
FRONT STREET
ESPLANADE
GARDINER EXPRESSWAY
Old Fort York
Sky Dome
CN Tower
Union Station
GARDINER EXPWY
LAKE SHORE BLVD
Exhibition Park
Marine Museum
LAKE SHORE BOULEVARD
GARDINER EXPRESSWAY
LAKE SHORE BLVD
HARBOUR ST
QUEENS QUAY
Harbour Front
Island Ferries Terminal
Lake Ontario
BATHURST STREET
STRACHAN AVE
SPADINA AVENUE
BAY STREET
UNIVERSITY AVENUE
YONGE STREET
CHURCH STREET
JARVIS STREET

CHICAGO

0 METRES 400
0 YARDS 400

WEST CHICAGO AVE
EAST CHICAGO AVENUE
Outer Harbor
RIVER NORTH
NEAR NORTH
University
Terra Museum of American Art
WEST ONTARIO ST
EAST ONTARIO ST
WEST OHIO ST.
EAST OHIO ST
WEST GRAND AVENUE
EAST GRAND AVENUE
Maritime Museum
Marina City
Navy Pier
WACKER DRIVE
Chicago River
WEST WACKER DRIVE
THE LOOP
Chicago Theatre
Northwestern Station
RANDOLPH STREET
City Hall
E. RANDOLPH DRIVE
WEST WASHINGTON BLVD
W. WASHINGTON ST
GREEK TOWN
Civic Opera House
Union Station
ADAMS STREET
WEST JACKSON STREET
E. JACKSON DR.
Monroe Harbor
Art Institute
Goodman Theatre
Van Buren Station
Auditorium Theatre
Sears Tower
DWIGHT D. EISENHOWER EXPRESSWAY
CONGRESS PARKWAY
Chicago Harbor
Lake Michigan
WEST HARRISON STREET
PRINTERS ROW
Grant Park
Hull House
University of Illinois
WEST ROOSEVELT ROAD
Field Museum of Natural History
Shedd Aquarium
Adler Planetarium
Soldier Field
Burnham Park Harbor
JF KENNEDY EXPRESSWAY
WEST MILWAUKEE AVE
NORTH HALSTED STREET
NORTH DESPLAINES ST
NORTH CLINTON ST
NORTH CANAL ST
NORTH WACKER DR.
NORTH FRANKLIN ST
NORTH LA SALLE ST.
NORTH WELLS STREET
NORTH STATE STREET
NORTH MICHIGAN AVENUE
NORTH LAKE SHORE DRIVE
SOUTH WACKER DR.
SOUTH FRANKLIN ST
SOUTH LA SALLE ST
SOUTH STATE STREET
COLUMBUS DRIVE
SOUTH LAKE SHORE DRIVE
SOUTH MICHIGAN AVENUE
DAN RYAN EXPRESSWAY
South Branch Chicago

WASHINGTON

0 METRES 600
0 YARDS 600

Oak Hill Cemetery
Logan Circle
FLORIDA AVE
Dupont Circle
RHODE ISLAND AVE
Georgetown University
GEORGETOWN
Washington Circle
MASSACHUSETTS AVE
National Geographic Society
NEW YORK AVE
Convention Center
Union Station
CANAL ROAD
WHITEHURST FWY
Watergate Complex
K STREET
MASSACHUSETTS AVE
Theodore Roosevelt Mem.
PENNSYLVANIA AVE
George Washington University
National Theatre
Union Station Plaza
ROSSLYN
J.F. Kennedy Center
The White House
PENNSYLVANIA AVE
National Archives
Theodore Roosevelt I.
The Ellipse
Nat. Portrait Gallery
Supreme Court
WILSON BLVD
Theodore Roosevelt Br.
Lincoln Memorial
CONSTITUTION AVE
Nat. Mus. American History
CONSTITUTION AVE
U.S. Capitol
Library of Congress
U.S. Marine Memorial
Constitution Gardens
Washington Monument
Smithsonian Inst.
Nat. Gallery of Art
INDEPENDENCE AVE
CLARENDON
Arlington Memorial Br.
The Mall
Hirshhorn Museum
Nat. Air & Space Mus.
Arlington
West Potomac Park
Tidal Basin
SOUTHWEST FWY
National
Jefferson Memorial
Tomb of the Unknown Soldier
Cemetery
POTOMAC
East Potomac Park
Washington Navy Yard
COLUMBIA PIKE
SHIRLEY HIGHWAY
GEORGE WASHINGTON MEMORIAL PARKWAY
Pentagon
Boundary Channel
Washington Channel
SOUTH CAPITOL ST
M STREET
M STREET
Waterfowl Sanctuary
Fredrick Douglass Bridge
HENRY G. SHIRLEY MEM. HWY
ARLINGTON RIDGE ROAD
Washington National Airport
Anacostia
SUITLAND PKWY
CAPITOL ST
George Mason Br.
Rochambeau Br.
JEFFERSON DAVIS HIGHWAY
16TH STREET

LOS ANGELES

0 METRES 500
0 YARDS 500

Dodger Stadium
Echo Park
PASADENA FREEWAY
STATE FREEWAY
GOLDEN FREEWAY
NORTH BROADWAY
NORTH SPRING STREET
N BROADWAY
N. MAIN STREET
HOLLYWOOD FREEWAY
Library
SUNSET BOULEVARD
CHINA TOWN
BEVERLY BLVD
TEMPLE STREET
Our Lady Queen of Angels
Old Plaza Church
GLENDALE BLVD
HARBOR FREEWAY
Ahmanson Theatre
Chandler Pavilion
Civic Center
Union Station
MISSION ROAD
ALVARADO STREET
2ND STREET
World Trade Center
Law Library
City Hall
SANTA ANA FREEWAY
WILSHIRE BOULEVARD
Arco Plaza
Wells Fargo History Museum
Mus. of Contemporary Art
Children's Museum
Japanese Village Plaza
St Paul's Cathedral
Central Library
FIGUEROA STREET
Million Dollar Theatre
Pershing Square
LITTLE TOKYO
Japan America Theatre
First Methodist Church
GRAND AVENUE
HILL STREET
BROADWAY
SPRING STREET
MAIN STREET
LOS ANGELES STREET
SAN PEDRO STREET
Convention Center
OLYMPIC BOULEVARD
PICO BOULEVARD
SANTA MONICA BOULEVARD
Greyhound Bus Terminal
ALAMEDA STREET
CENTRAL AVENUE
3RD STREET
4TH STREET
6TH STREET
7TH STREET
Hollenbeck Park
WHITTIER FWY
SANTA ANA FWY
DOWNTOWN
HARBOR FREEWAY
SANTA MONICA FWY
WASHINGTON BOULEVARD
L.A. Trade Tech. College

SAN FRANCISCO

0 METRES 1000
0 YARDS 1000

Golden Gate Bridge
Fisherman's Wharf
Maritime Museum
San Francisco Bay
MASON STREET
MARINA
Colt Tower
Palace of Fine Arts
LOMBARD STREET
PRESIDIO
PACIFIC OCEAN
Transamerica Pyramid
World Trade Center
COLUMBUS AVE
PACIFIC HEIGHTS
Chinatown
BROADWAY
Embarcadero Center
Lincoln Park
Grace Cathedral
VAN NESS AVE
DIVISADERO ST
Oakland Bay Bridge
CALIFORNIA STREET
GEARY EXPRESSWAY
St Mary's Cath.
Moscone Convention Center
RICHMOND
GEARY BLVD
University of San Francisco
Mus. of Modern Art
City Hall
Opera House
FULTON STREET
FULTON STREET
OAK STREET
De Young Museum
Golden Gate Park
MARKET STREET
Railway Depot
Golden Gate Park
Conservatory of Flowers
Kezar Stadium
LINCOLN WAY
Golden Gate Park Stadium
Natural History Museum
POTRERO
SUNSET
17TH ST
19TH AVENUE
TWIN PEAKS
MISSION
NOE VALLEY
PARKSIDE
NORIEGA ST
PORTOLA DRIVE
DOLORES ST
BAYVIEW
TARAVAL STREET
SLOAT BOULEVARD
OUTER MISSION
Harding Park
Lake Merced
OCEAN AVENUE
INGLESIDE
EXCELSIOR
McLaren Park
MISSION ST
ALEMANY BLVD
BAYSHORE BLVD
SOUTHERN FREEWAY
SOUTHERN FREEWAY
ARMY STREET
BRAZIL AVE
PERSIA AVE
SAN JOSE AVE
BAYSHORE FWY
EMBARCADERO FWY
CESAR CHAVEZ
JAMES LICK FREEWAY
BRANNAN ST

© Bartholomew

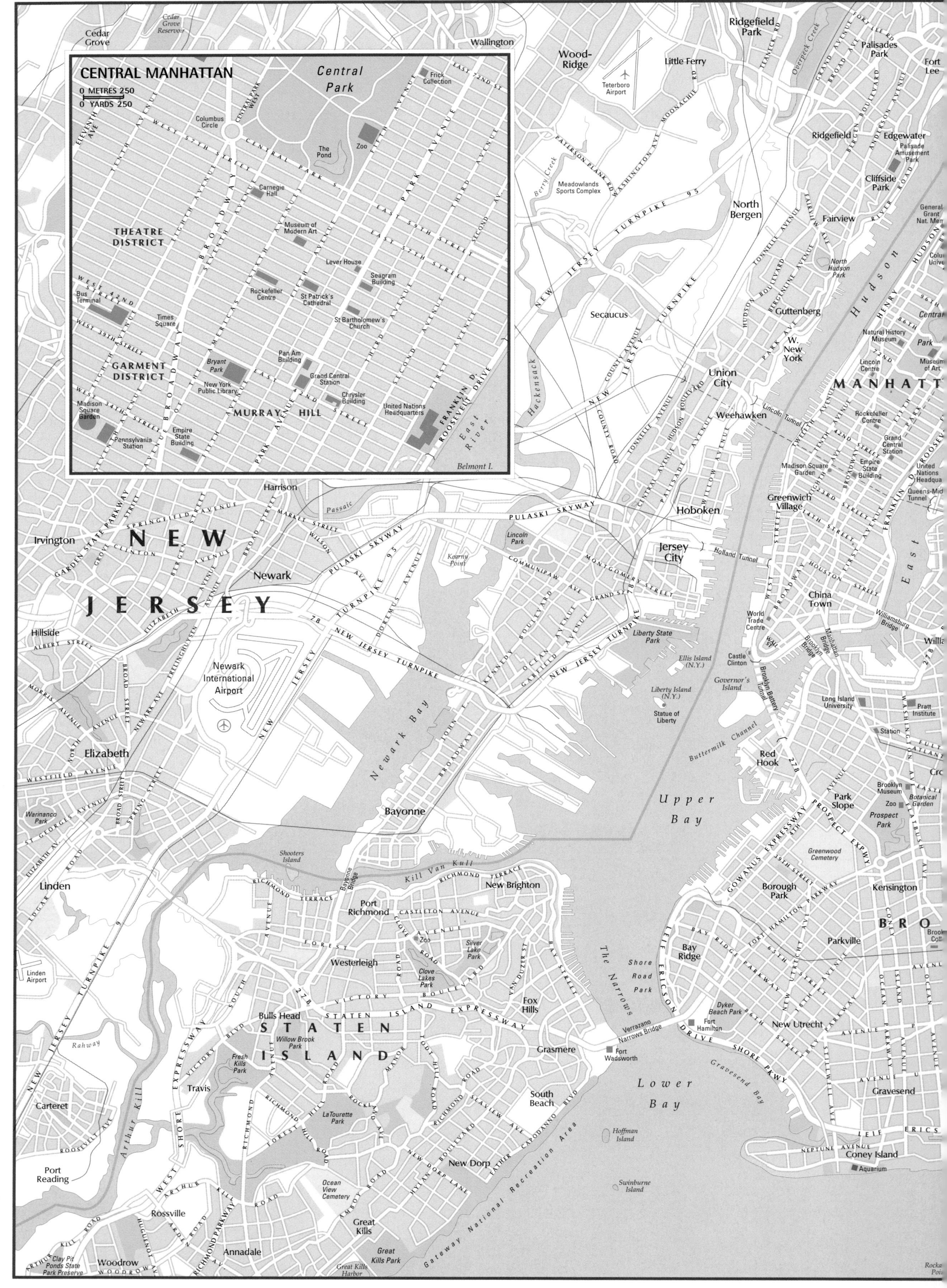
CENTRAL MANHATTAN
0 METRES 250
0 YARDS 250
Central Park
Frick Collection
Columbus Circle
The Pond
Zoo
Carnegie Hall
Museum of Modern Art
THEATRE DISTRICT
Lever House
Seagram Building
Rockefeller Centre
St Patrick's Cathedral
Bus Terminal
Times Square
St Bartholomew's Church
Pan Am Building
GARMENT DISTRICT
Bryant Park
Grand Central Station
New York Public Library
Chrysler Building
United Nations Headquarters
Madison Square Garden
Pennsylvania Station
Empire State Building
MURRAY HILL
East River
Belmont I.
ELEVENTH AVE
TENTH AVENUE
WEST 57TH STREET
CENTRAL PARK WEST
CENTRAL PARK S.
FIFTH AVENUE
PARK AVENUE
THIRD AVENUE
SECOND AV.
EAST 72ND ST
EAST 59TH STREET
EAST 52ND STREET
BROADWAY
EIGHTH AVENUE
SEVENTH AVENUE
SIXTH AVENUE
WEST 42ND STREET
WEST 39TH STREET
WEST 34TH STREET
EAST 42ND STREET
FRANKLIN D. ROOSEVELT DRIVE
FIRST AVENUE
Cedar Grove
Cedar Grove Reservoir
Wallington
Wood-Ridge
Little Ferry
Teterboro Airport
Ridgefield Park
Palisades Park
Fort Lee
Ridgefield
Edgewater
Palisade Amusement Park
Cliffside Park
Meadowlands Sports Complex
Berry Creek
North Bergen
Fairview
General Grant Nat. Mem
North Hudson Park
Secaucus
Guttenberg
W. New York
Union City
Weehawken
Lincoln Tunnel
Hackensack
Hudson
Natural History Museum
Lincoln Centre
Museum of Art
MANHATT
Harrison
Passaic
Hoboken
PULASKI SKYWAY
NEW JERSEY TURNPIKE
Irvington
NEW JERSEY
Newark
Lincoln Park
Kearny Point
Jersey City
Holland Tunnel
Greenwich Village
China Town
Hillside
Newark International Airport
Liberty State Park
Ellis Island (N.Y.)
Castle Clinton
World Trade Centre
Williamsburg Bridge
Manhattan Bridge
Brooklyn Bridge
Brooklyn Battery Tunnel
Governor's Island
Liberty Island (N.Y.)
Statue of Liberty
Long Island University
Pratt Institute
Elizabeth
Newark Bay
Buttermilk Channel
Red Hook
Warinanco Park
Bayonne
Upper Bay
Park Slope
Brooklyn Museum
Botanical Garden
Prospect Park
Shooters Island
Kill Van Kull
Bayonne Bridge
Greenwood Cemetery
Linden
New Brighton
Port Richmond
Borough Park
Kensington
Zoo
Silver Lake Park
Westerleigh
Clove Lakes Park
Linden Airport
The Narrows
Shore Road Park
Bay Ridge
Parkville
Fox Hills
Bulls Head
STATEN ISLAND
Willow Brook Park
Fresh Kills Park
Dyker Beach Park
Fort Hamilton
New Utrecht
Verrazano Narrows Bridge
Grasmere
Fort Wadsworth
Rahway
Travis
Lower Bay
Gravesend Bay
Gravesend
South Beach
Carteret
Arthur Kill
LaTourette Park
Hoffman Island
Coney Island
Aquarium
Port Reading
New Dorp
Ocean View Cemetery
Swinburne Island
Gateway National Recreation Area
Rossville
Great Kills
Annadale
Great Kills Park
Great Kills Harbor
Woodrow
Clay Pit Ponds State Park Preserve

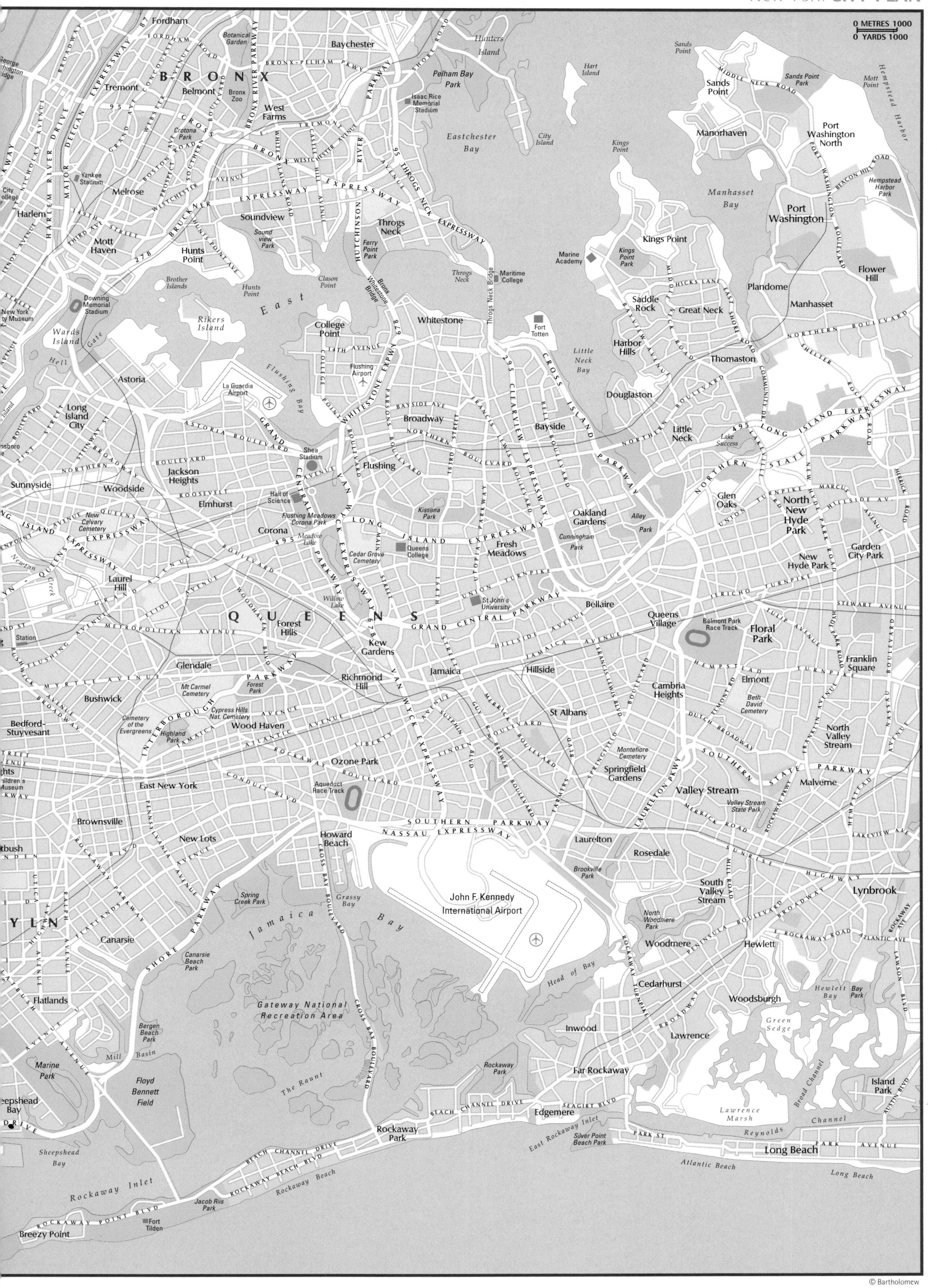

© Bartholomew

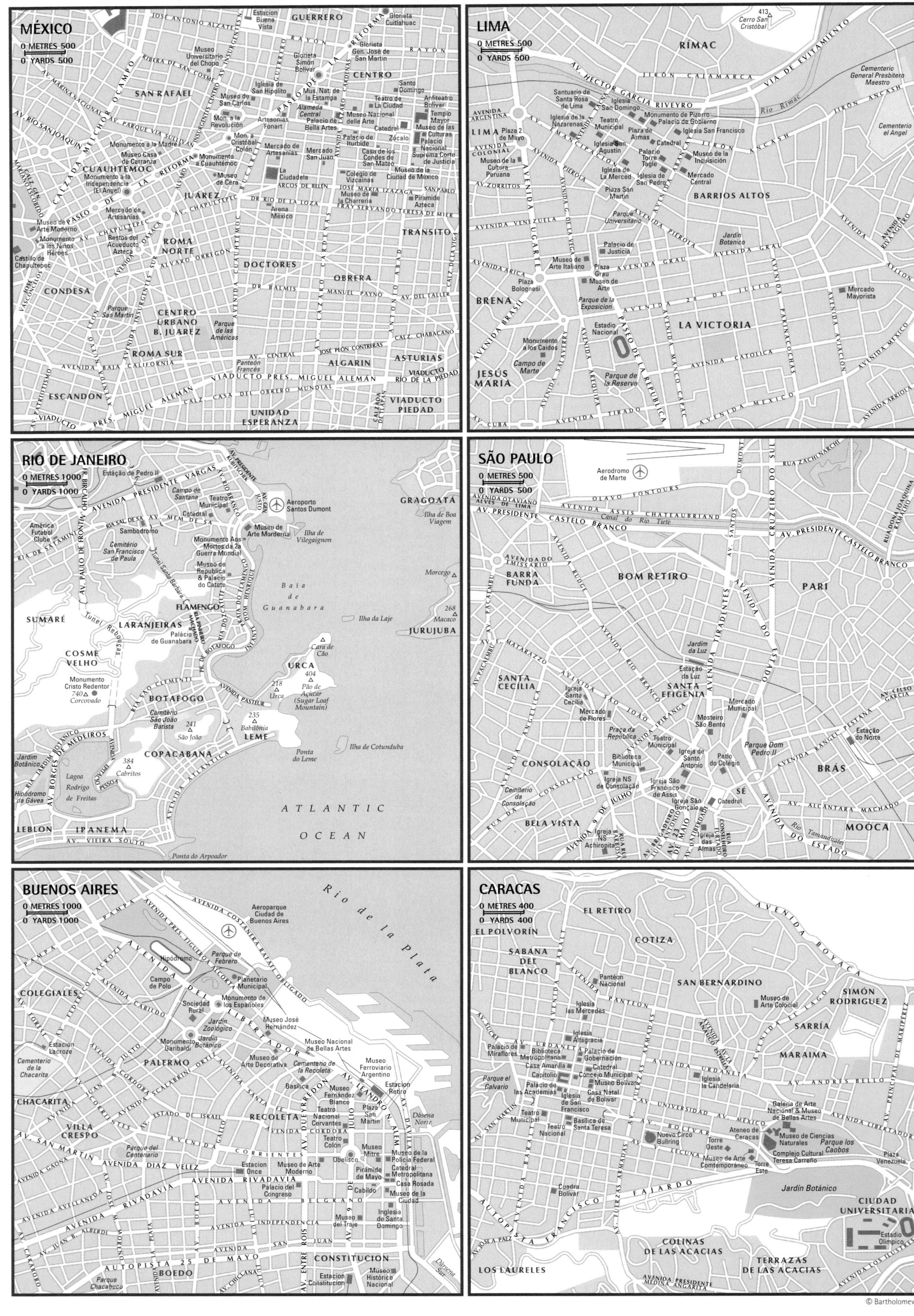

© Bartholomew

RELIEF

Contour intervals used in layer colouring

Metres	Feet
6000	19686
5000	16404
4000	13124
3000	9843
2000	6562
1000	3281
500	1640
200	656
SEA	LEVEL
200	656
2000	6562
4000	13124
6000	19686

Additional bathymetric contour layers are shown at scales greater than 1:2 million. These are labelled on an individual basis.

213
△ Summit
height in metres

PHYSICAL FEATURES

Freshwater lake

Seasonal freshwater lake

Saltwater lake *or* Lagoon

Seasonal saltwater lake

Dry salt lake *or* Saltpan

Marsh

River

Waterfall

Dam *or* Barrage

Seasonal river *or* Wadi

Canal

Flood dyke

Reef

Volcano

Lava field

Sandy desert

Rocky desert

Oasis

Escarpment

Mountain pass
height in metres
923

Ice cap *or* Glacier

COMMUNICATIONS

Motorway

Motorway
under construction

Motorway tunnel

Motorways are classified separately at scales greater than 1:5 million. At smaller scales motorways are classified with main roads.

Main road

Main road
under construction

Main road tunnel

Other road

Other road
under construction

Other road tunnel

Track

Main railway

Main railway
under construction

Main railway tunnel

Other railway

Other railway
under construction

Other railway tunnel

Main airport

Other airport

BOUNDARIES

International

International
disputed

Ceasefire line

Main administrative (U.K.)

Main administrative

Main administrative
through water

OTHER FEATURES

National park

Reserve

Ancient wall

Historic *or* Tourist site

Urban area

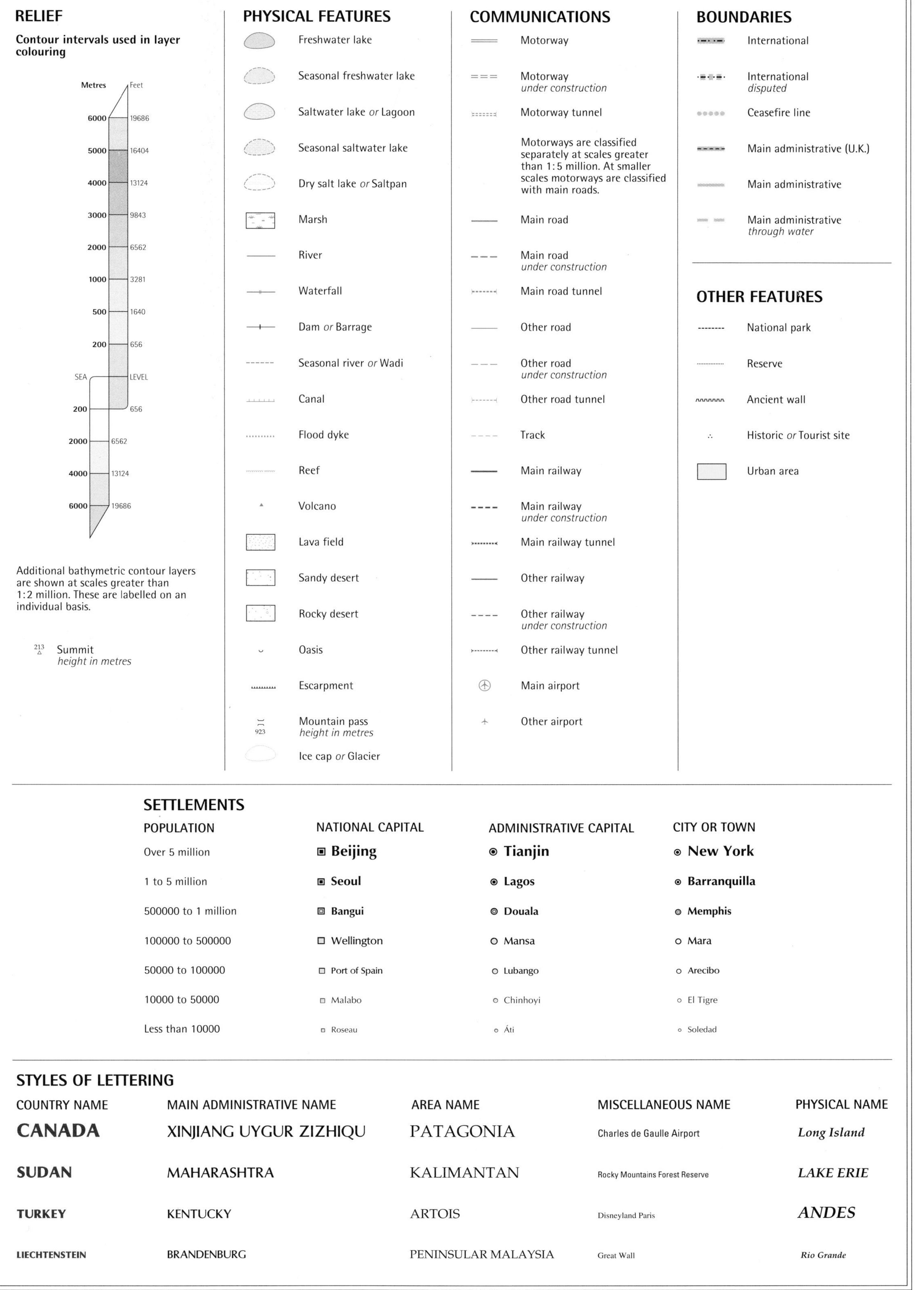

SETTLEMENTS

POPULATION	NATIONAL CAPITAL	ADMINISTRATIVE CAPITAL	CITY OR TOWN
Over 5 million	▣ **Beijing**	◉ **Tianjin**	◉ **New York**
1 to 5 million	▣ **Seoul**	◉ **Lagos**	◉ **Barranquilla**
500000 to 1 million	▣ **Bangui**	◎ **Douala**	◎ **Memphis**
100000 to 500000	▢ Wellington	○ Mansa	○ Mara
50000 to 100000	▢ Port of Spain	○ Lubango	○ Arecibo
10000 to 50000	▫ Malabo	○ Chinhoyi	○ El Tigre
Less than 10000	▫ Roseau	○ Áti	○ Soledad

STYLES OF LETTERING

COUNTRY NAME	MAIN ADMINISTRATIVE NAME	AREA NAME	MISCELLANEOUS NAME	PHYSICAL NAME
CANADA	XINJIANG UYGUR ZIZHIQU	PATAGONIA	Charles de Gaulle Airport	*Long Island*
SUDAN	MAHARASHTRA	KALIMANTAN	Rocky Mountains Forest Reserve	*LAKE ERIE*
TURKEY	KENTUCKY	ARTOIS	Disneyland Paris	*ANDES*
LIECHTENSTEIN	BRANDENBURG	PENINSULAR MALAYSIA	Great Wall	*Rio Grande*

© Bartholomew

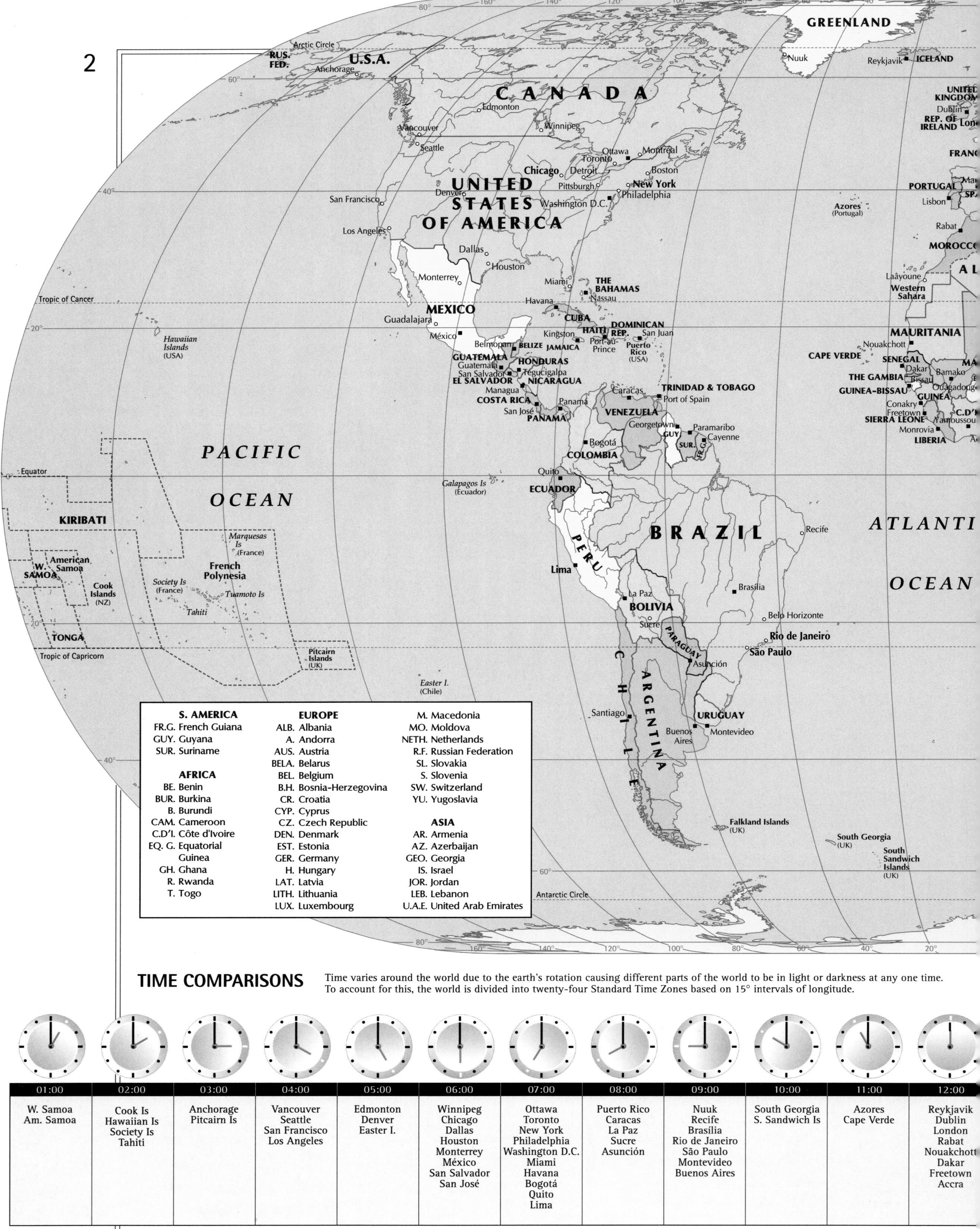

2

GREENLAND

Nuuk · Reykjavik · ICELAND

RUS. FED. · Anchorage · U.S.A.

Arctic Circle

C A N A D A

Edmonton

Vancouver · Winnipeg

Seattle · Ottawa · Montréal

Toronto · Boston

Chicago · Detroit

Pittsburgh · New York

San Francisco · Denver · Philadelphia

UNITED STATES OF AMERICA

Washington D.C.

Los Angeles

UNITED KINGDOM
Dublin · Lon
REP. OF IRELAND
FRANC

Azores (Portugal)

PORTUGAL
Lisbon · SP.

Dallas

Houston

Monterrey

Rabat

MOROCCO

Tropic of Cancer

Guadalajara

México

Miami

THE BAHAMAS

Nassau

Havana · CUBA

Laâyoune · A L

Western Sahara

MEXICO

DOMINICAN
HAITI · REP.
Port-au-
Prince · San Juan
Puerto Rico (USA)

MAURITANIA

Nouakchott

Belmopan · BELIZE · Kingston · JAMAICA

GUATEMALA
Guatemala · HONDURAS

San Salvador · Tegucigalpa

EL SALVADOR · NICARAGUA

CAPE VERDE

Dakar · SENEGAL · MA

THE GAMBIA · Bamako

GUINEA-BISSAU · Bissau · Ouadadoug

Managua

COSTA RICA

San José · PANAMA

Caracas

Panama

TRINIDAD & TOBAGO

Port of Spain

GUINEA

Conakry · C.D'I
Freetown · Yamoussou

SIERRA LEONE

Monrovia · A

LIBERIA

VENEZUELA

Bogotá

COLOMBIA

Georgetown · Paramaribo

GUY · Cayenne

SUR. · FR.G.

PACIFIC

OCEAN

Quito

ECUADOR

Galapagos Is (Ecuador)

B R A Z I L

Recife

ATLANTI

OCEAN

KIRIBATI

Marquesas Is (France)

PERU

Lima

American Samoa

W. SAMOA

French Polynesia

Society Is (France)

Tahiti

Tuamoto Is

Cook Islands (NZ)

La Paz

BOLIVIA

Sucre

Brasília

Belo Horizonte

Rio de Janeiro

PARAGUAY

São Paulo

Asunción

TONGA

Tropic of Capricorn

Pitcairn Islands (UK)

Easter I. (Chile)

Santiago

C H I L E

A R G E N T I N A

Buenos Aires

URUGUAY

Montevideo

Falkland Islands (UK)

South Georgia (UK)

South Sandwich Islands (UK)

S. AMERICA	EUROPE	
FR.G. French Guiana	ALB. Albania	M. Macedonia
GUY. Guyana	A. Andorra	MO. Moldova
SUR. Suriname	AUS. Austria	NETH. Netherlands
	BELA. Belarus	R.F. Russian Federation
AFRICA	BEL. Belgium	SL. Slovakia
BE. Benin	B.H. Bosnia-Herzegovina	S. Slovenia
BUR. Burkina	CR. Croatia	SW. Switzerland
B. Burundi	CYP. Cyprus	YU. Yugoslavia
CAM. Cameroon	CZ. Czech Republic	
C.D'I. Côte d'Ivoire	DEN. Denmark	**ASIA**
EQ. G. Equatorial	EST. Estonia	AR. Armenia
Guinea	GER. Germany	AZ. Azerbaijan
GH. Ghana	H. Hungary	GEO. Georgia
R. Rwanda	LAT. Latvia	IS. Israel
T. Togo	LITH. Lithuania	JOR. Jordan
	LUX. Luxembourg	LEB. Lebanon
		U.A.E. United Arab Emirates

Antarctic Circle

Eckert IV Projection

TIME COMPARISONS

Time varies around the world due to the earth's rotation causing different parts of the world to be in light or darkness at any one time. To account for this, the world is divided into twenty-four Standard Time Zones based on 15° intervals of longitude.

01:00	02:00	03:00	04:00	05:00	06:00	07:00	08:00	09:00	10:00	11:00	12:00
W. Samoa Am. Samoa	Cook Is Hawaiian Is Society Is Tahiti	Anchorage Pitcairn Is	Vancouver Seattle San Francisco Los Angeles	Edmonton Denver Easter I.	Winnipeg Chicago Dallas Houston Monterrey México San Salvador San José	Ottawa Toronto New York Philadelphia Washington D.C. Miami Havana Bogotá Quito Lima	Puerto Rico Caracas La Paz Sucre Asunción	Nuuk Recife Brasília Rio de Janeiro São Paulo Montevideo Buenos Aires	South Georgia S. Sandwich Is	Azores Cape Verde	Reykjavik Dublin London Rabat Nouakchott Dakar Freetown Accra

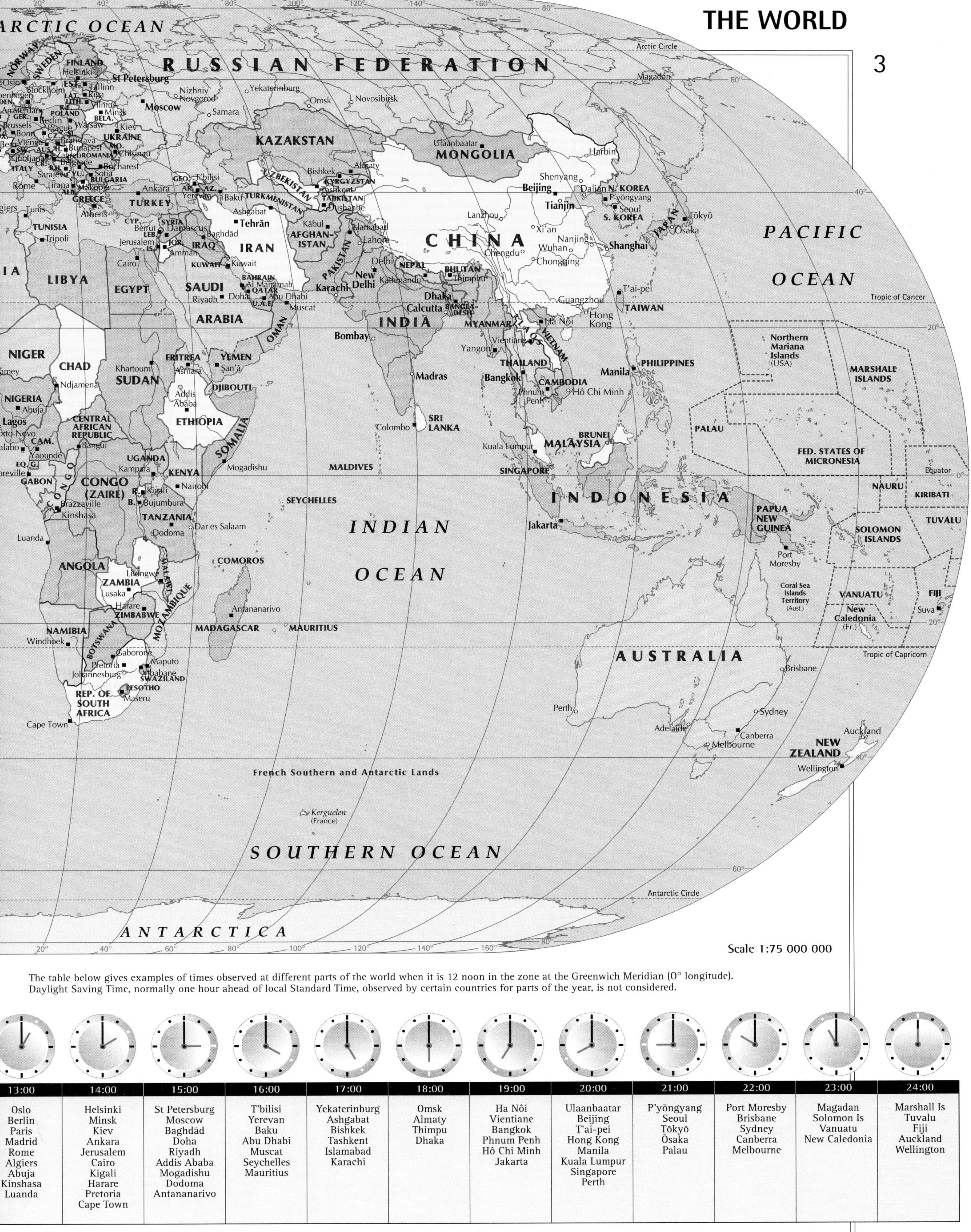

THE WORLD

3

ARCTIC OCEAN

Arctic Circle

RUSSIAN FEDERATION

NORWAY
SWEDEN
FINLAND
Helsinki
St Petersburg
Nizhniy
Novgorod
Yekaterinburg
Omsk
Novosibirsk
Magadan

Oslo
EST.
Riga
Moscow
Samara

Stockholm
LAT.
penhagen
DEN.
LITH.
Minsk
BELA.
Amsterdam
POLAND
Warsaw
Kiev
UKRAINE
MO.
Brussels
Berlin
Prague
GER.
Bonn
Vienna
Budapest
Bucharest
HUNG.
Chisinau
Bern
Ljubljana
CR.
Zagreb
Belgrade
BULGARIA
Sofia
Ankara
T'bilisi
GEO.
AZ.
Baku
Bishkek
Almaty
KAZAKSTAN
ULAANBAATAR
MONGOLIA
Harbin
giers
Tunis
Tirana
YU.
GREECE
Athens
TURKEY
ARM.
Yerevan
UZBEKISTAN
KYRGYZSTAN
TAJIKISTAN
Dushanbe
Shenyang
Dalian
N. KOREA
P'yŏngyang
S. KOREA
Seoul
JAPAN
Tōkyō
Osaka
Sarajevo
ITALY
TUNISIA
Tripoli
Athens
SYRIA
Damascus
Beirut
LEB.
Baghdād
IRAQ
IRAN
Tehrān
TURKMENISTAN
Ashgabat
AFGHAN-ISTAN
Kābul
Islamabad
Lahore
Lanzhou
Xi'an
Beijing
Tianjin
CHINA
Shanghai
Jerusalem
IS.
Amman
JOR.
KUWAIT
Kuwait
Delhi
Nanjing
Wuhan
Chengdu
Chongqing

PACIFIC

OCEAN

Cairo
SAUDI
Riyadh
BAHRAIN
Al Manamah
QATAR
Doha
Abu Dhabi
U.A.E.
Muscat
New Delhi
NEPAL
Kathmandu
BHUTAN
Thimphu
Dhaka
BANGLA-DESH
Guangzhou
Hong Kong
T'ai-pei
TAIWAN

LIBYA
EGYPT
ARABIA
OMAN
Karachi
PAKISTAN
INDIA
Calcutta
MYANMAR
Ha Nội
VIETNAM

Tropic of Cancer

IA
NIGER
CHAD
SUDAN
Khartoum
ERITREA
Asmara
YEMEN
Şan'ā
DJIBOUTI
Bombay
Madras
Yangon
Vientiane
THAILAND
Bangkok
CAMBODIA
Phnum Penh
Hồ Chi Minh
Manila
PHILIPPINES
Northern Mariana Islands (USA)
MARSHALL ISLANDS

amey
NIGERIA
Abuja
Lagos
CENTRAL AFRICAN REPUBLIC
Bangui
ETHIOPIA
Addis Ababa
SOMALIA
Colombo
SRI LANKA
BRUNEI
MALAYSIA
Kuala Lumpur
PALAU
FED. STATES OF MICRONESIA
NAURU
KIRIBATI

orto-Novo
CAM.
Yaoundé
alabo
EQ. G.
oreville
GABON
CONGO (ZAIRE)
UGANDA
Kampala
KENYA
Nairobi
Kigali
R.
B.
Bujumbura
MALDIVES
SINGAPORE
INDONESIA
Equator

Luanda
Brazzaville
Kinshasa
TANZANIA
Dodoma
Dar es Salaam
SEYCHELLES
Jakarta
PAPUA NEW GUINEA
SOLOMON ISLANDS
TUVALU

ANGOLA
Lilongwe
ZAMBIA
Lusaka
INDIAN
OCEAN
COMOROS
Port Moresby
Coral Sea Islands Territory (Aust.)
VANUATU
FIJI
Suva

NAMIBIA
Windhoek
ZIMBABWE
Harare
MALAWI
MOZAMBIQUE
Antananarivo
MADAGASCAR
MAURITIUS
New Caledonia (Fr.)

BOTSWANA
Gaborone
Pretoria
Johannesburg
Maputo
Mbabane
SWAZILAND
Tropic of Capricorn

AUSTRALIA
Brisbane

REP. OF SOUTH AFRICA
LESOTHO
Maseru
Perth
Sydney
Auckland
Canberra

Cape Town
Adelaide
Melbourne
NEW ZEALAND
Wellington

French Southern and Antarctic Lands

Kerguelen (France)

SOUTHERN OCEAN

Antarctic Circle

ANTARCTICA

Scale 1:75 000 000

The table below gives examples of times observed at different parts of the world when it is 12 noon in the zone at the Greenwich Meridian (0° longitude). Daylight Saving Time, normally one hour ahead of local Standard Time, observed by certain countries for parts of the year, is not considered.

13:00	14:00	15:00	16:00	17:00	18:00	19:00	20:00	21:00	22:00	23:00	24:00
Oslo	Helsinki	St Petersburg	T'bilisi	Yekaterinburg	Omsk	Ha Nôi	Ulaanbaatar	P'yŏngyang	Port Moresby	Magadan	Marshall Is
Berlin	Minsk	Moscow	Yerevan	Ashgabat	Almaty	Vientiane	Beijing	Seoul	Brisbane	Solomon Is	Tuvalu
Paris	Kiev	Baghdād	Baku	Bishkek	Thimpu	Bangkok	T'ai-pei	Tōkyō	Sydney	Vanuatu	Fiji
Madrid	Ankara	Doha	Abu Dhabi	Tashkent	Dhaka	Phnum Penh	Hong Kong	Ōsaka	Canberra	New Caledonia	Auckland
Rome	Jerusalem	Riyadh	Muscat	Islamabad		Hồ Chi Minh	Manila	Palau	Melbourne		Wellington
Algiers	Cairo	Addis Ababa	Seychelles	Karachi		Jakarta	Kuala Lumpur				
Abuja	Kigali	Mogadishu	Mauritius				Singapore				
Kinshasa	Harare	Dodoma					Perth				
Luanda	Pretoria	Antananarivo									
	Cape Town										

© Bartholomew

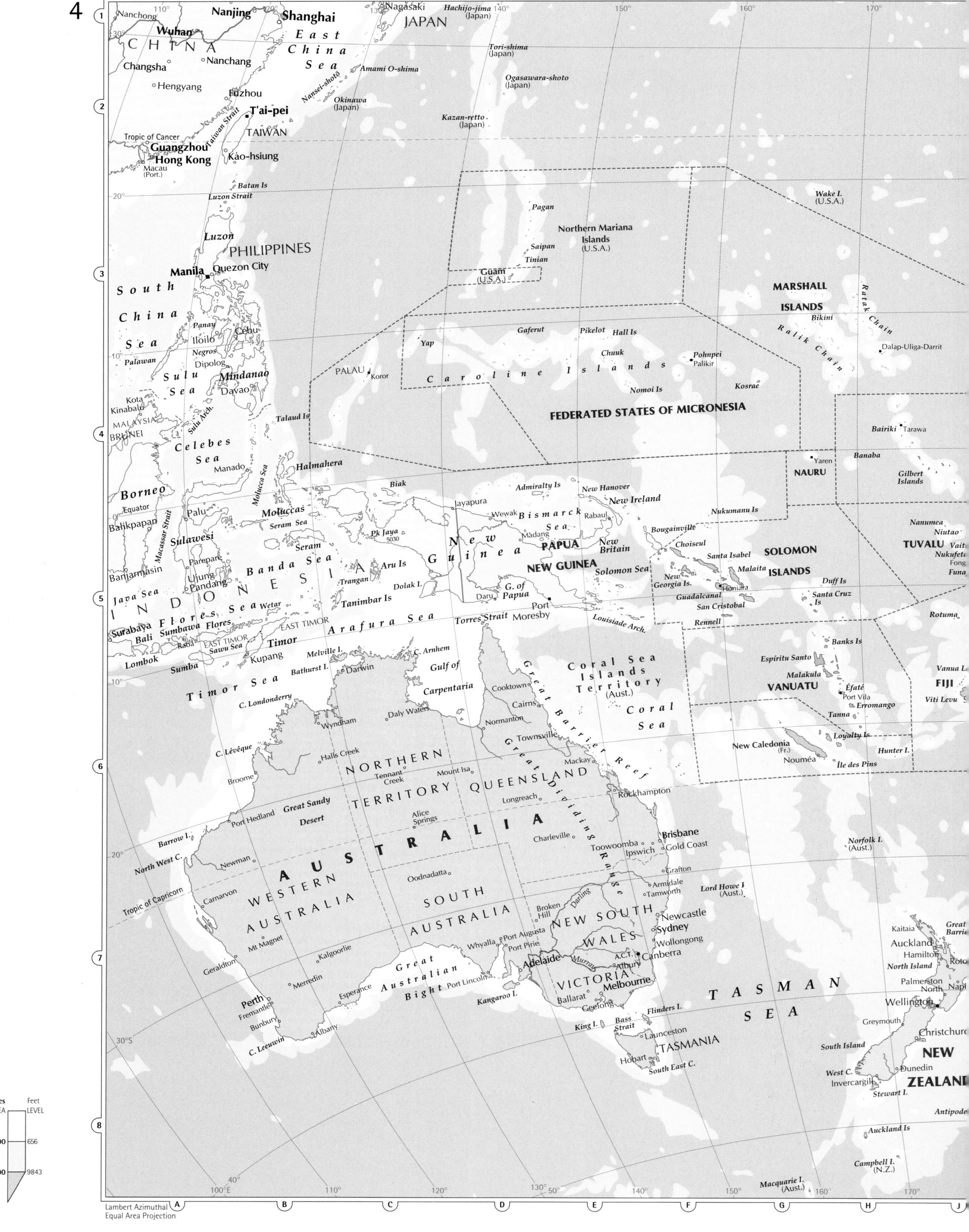

4

CHINA
Nanchong
110°
Nanjing
Wuhan
30°
Changsha
Nanchang
Hengyang
Fuzhou
Tropic of Cancer
Guangzhou
Hong Kong
Macau
(Port.)

Shanghai
*East
China
Sea*
Nagasaki
JAPAN
Hachijo-jima
(Japan)
140°
Tori-shima
(Japan)
Amami O-shima
Ogasawara-shoto
(Japan)
Okinawa
(Japan)
Nansei-shotō
150°
160°
170°
Kazan-retto
(Japan)
Wake I.
(U.S.A.)
20°
Batan Is
Luzon Strait
T'ai-pei
TAIWAN
Kao-hsiung
Taiwan Strait
Pagan

Luzon
PHILIPPINES
Northern Mariana
Islands
(U.S.A.)
Saipan
Tinian
MARSHALL
ISLANDS
Bikini
Ratak Chain

Manila
Quezon City
South
China
Sea
Panay
Iloilo
Cebu
Negros
Palawan
Dipolog
Sulu
Davao
Mindanao
Sea
Kota
Kinabalu
MALAYSIA
BRUNEI

Guam
(U.S.A.)
Yap
PALAU
Koror
Gaferut
Pikelot
Hall Is
Chuuk
Caroline Islands
Nomoi Is
Pohnpei
Palikir
Kosrae
Ralik Chain
Dalap-Uliga-Darrit
10°

FEDERATED STATES OF MICRONESIA

Bairiki Tarawa
Banaba
Gilbert
Islands

Celebes
Sea
Talaud Is
Manado
Molucca Sea
Halmahera
Moluccas
Seram Sea
Seram
Biak
Jayapura
Wewak
Admiralty Is
New Hanover
New Ireland
Bismarck
Sea
Rabaul
Nukumanu
NAURU
Yaren
NAURU
4°
Borneo
Equator
Palu
Balikpapan
Macassar Strait
Sulawesi
Parepare
Banjarmasin
Ujung
Pandang
Banda Sea
INDONESIA
Pk Jaya
5030
Aru Is
Trangan
Dolak I.
New Guinea
Madang
PAPUA
NEW GUINEA
New
Britain
Bougainville
Choiseul
Santa Isabel
New
Georgia Is.
Guadalcanal
Honiara
San Cristobal
Rennell
Malaita
SOLOMON
ISLANDS
Solomon Sea
Duff Is
Santa Cruz
Is
Rotuma
Nanumea
Niutao
TUVALU *Vait*
Nukufeta
Fong
Funa

Java Sea
Surabaya
Bali
Lombok
Flores Sea
Sumbawa
Raba
Sawu Sea
Sumba
Kupang
EAST TIMOR
Wetar
Flores
Timor
EAST TIMOR
Tanimbar Is
Arafura Sea
Melville I.
Bathurst I.
Darwin
Timor Sea
C. Londonderry
Torres Strait
Moresby
Daru
G. of
Papua
Port
Moresby
Louisiade Arch.
Banks Is
5°
10°
Melville I.
C. Arnhem
Gulf of
Carpentaria
Coral Sea
Islands
Territory
(Aust.)
Coral
Sea
Espiritu Santo
Malakula
VANUATU
Éfaté
Port Vila
Erromango
Tanna
Vanua Le
FIJI
Viti Levu

Vanua L

C. Lévêque
Halls Creek
NORTHERN
Tennant
Creek
Mount Isa
Daly Waters
Normanton
Cooktown
Cairns
Townsville
Great Barrier Reef
Mackay
Great Dividing Range
New Caledonia
(Fr.)
Nouméa
Île des Pins
Loyalty Is
Hunter I.
6°

Broome
Port Hedland
Great Sandy
Desert
TERRITORY
Alice
Springs
QUEENSLAND
Longreach
Rockhampton
Norfolk I.
(Aust.)
Barrow I.
Newman
20°
North West C.
Tropic of Capricorn
Carnarvon
WESTERN
AUSTRALIA
Mt Magnet
AUSTRALIA
Oodnadatta
SOUTH
AUSTRALIA
Charleville
Toowoomba
Brisbane
Ipswich
Gold Coast
Grafton
Armidale
Tamworth
Lord Howe I
(Aust.)
Kaitaia
Great
Barrie
Auckland
Hamilton
North Island
Ro
Geraldton
Kalgoorlie
Merredin
Great
Australian
Bight
Whyalla
Port Augusta
Broken
Hill
Port Pirie
Port Lincoln
Whyalla
Darling
NEW SOUTH
WALES
Murray
A.C.T.
Canberra
Newcastle
Sydney
Wollongong
Palmerston
North
Napi
Wellington
7°
30°S
Perth
Fremantle
Bunbury
C. Leeuwin
Albany
Esperance
Kangaroo I.
Adelaide
VICTORIA
Ballarat
Albury
Melbourne
Geelong
King I.
Bass
Strait
Flinders I.
Launceston
TASMANIA
Hobart
South East C.
TASMAN
SEA
Greymouth
West C.
South Island
Christchur
Dunedin
Invercargill
NEW
ZEALAND
Stewart I.

40°
100° E
110°
120°
130°
50°
140°
150°
160°
170°
Macquarie I.
(Aust.)
Antipode
8°
Auckland Is
Campbell I.
(N.Z.)

Metres | Feet
SEA | LEVEL

200 | 656
3000 | 9843

Lambert Azimuthal
Equal Area Projection

A   B   C   D   E   F   G   H   J

5

NORTH PACIFIC OCEAN

MEXICO

Gulf of California

Baja California

Guadalupe (Mex.)

Kure Atoll

Midway Is

Laysan I.

Gardner Pinnacles

Necker I.

Hawaiian Islands

Kauai

Oahu

Honolulu

Maui

U.S.A.

Hilo

Hawaii

Tropic of Cancer

I. Clarión (Mex.)

Johnston I. (U.S.A.)

Palmyra I. (U.S.A.)

Teraina

Tabuaeran

Line Islands

Kiritimati

Howland I. (U.S.A.)

Baker I. (U.S.A.)

Jarvis I. (U.S.A.)

Phoenix Islands

Kanton I.

Rawaki

McKean I.

Nikumaroro

Orona

Manra

Malden I.

Starbuck I.

KIRIBATI

Equator

Tokelau (N.Z.)

Atafu

Nukunono

kulaelae

Rakahanga

Tongareva

Danger Is

Manihiki

Swains I.

American Samoa

Nassau

(New Zealand)

Vostok I.

Caroline I.

Nuku Hiva

Marquesas Islands

Hiva Oa

Flint I.

Suvorov I.

Îles Wallis

WESTERN

lis & Futuna

Savaii

Apia

Upolu

Manua Is

Îles de Horn

SAMOA

Tutuila

Îles du Roi Georges

Îles de Désappointement

Motu One

Rangiroa

Tuamotu Archipelago

French

Palmerston I.

Society Islands

Aitutaki

Cook Is (N.Z.)

Hervey Is

Tahiti

Méhétia

Hao

Vava'u Group

Niue (N.Z.)

Héréhérétué

Rarotonga

Îles Duc de Gloucester

Polynesia

TONGA

Nuku'alofa

Tongatapu Group

Mangaia

Tubuai Islands

Mururoa

Groupe Actéon

Îles Gambier

Pitcairn Islands (U.K.)

Raoul

Rapa

Marotiri

Henderson I. (U.K.)

Kermadec Is (N.Z.)

Pitcairn I.

Ducie I.

Tropic of Capricorn

SOUTH PACIFIC OCEAN

I. Sala y Gómez (Chile)

Easter I. (Chile)

Chatham Is (N.Z.)

nty Is

Km 2000
Miles 1250

1750

1000

1500

1250

750

1000

750

500

500

250

250

0

0

1:35M

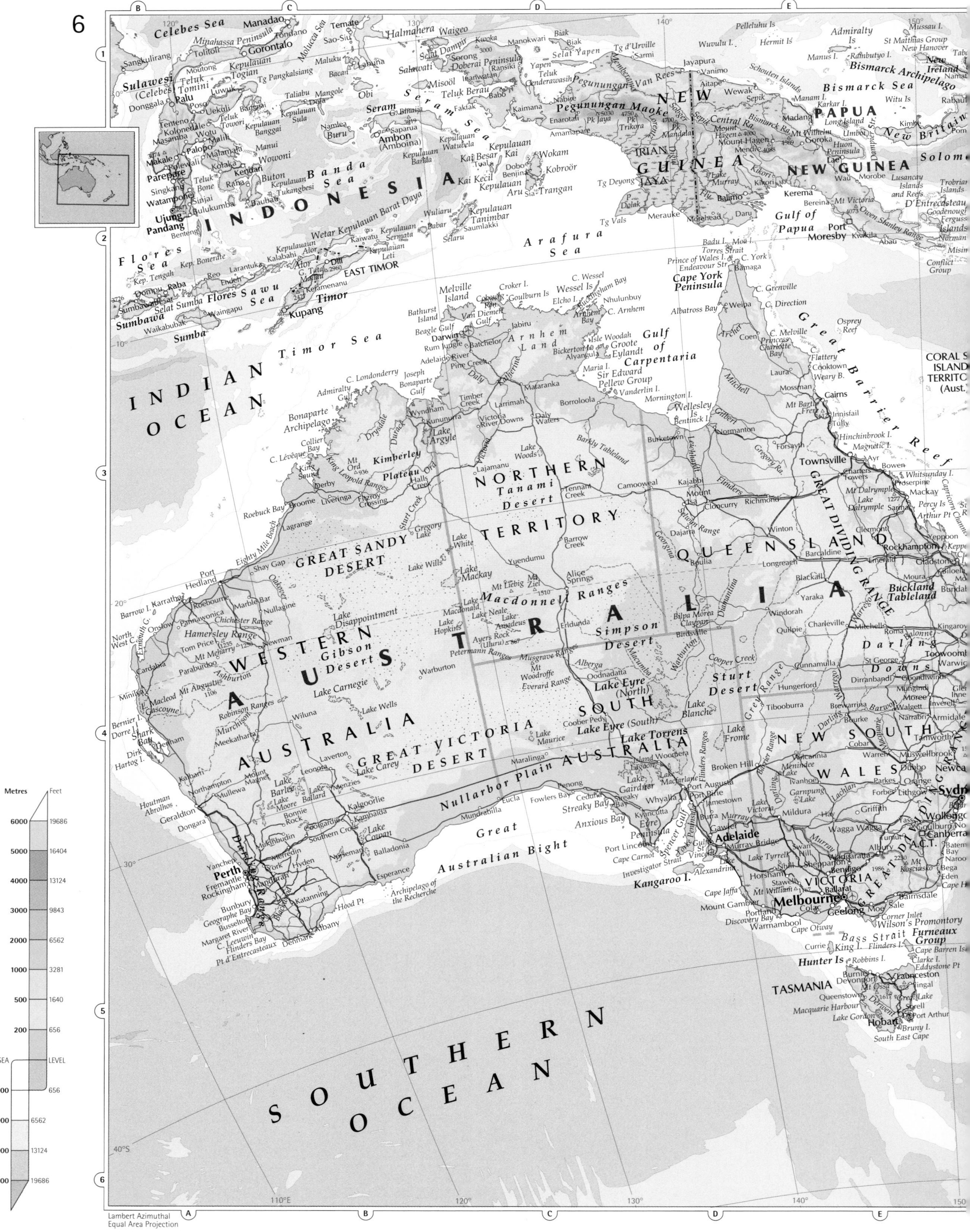

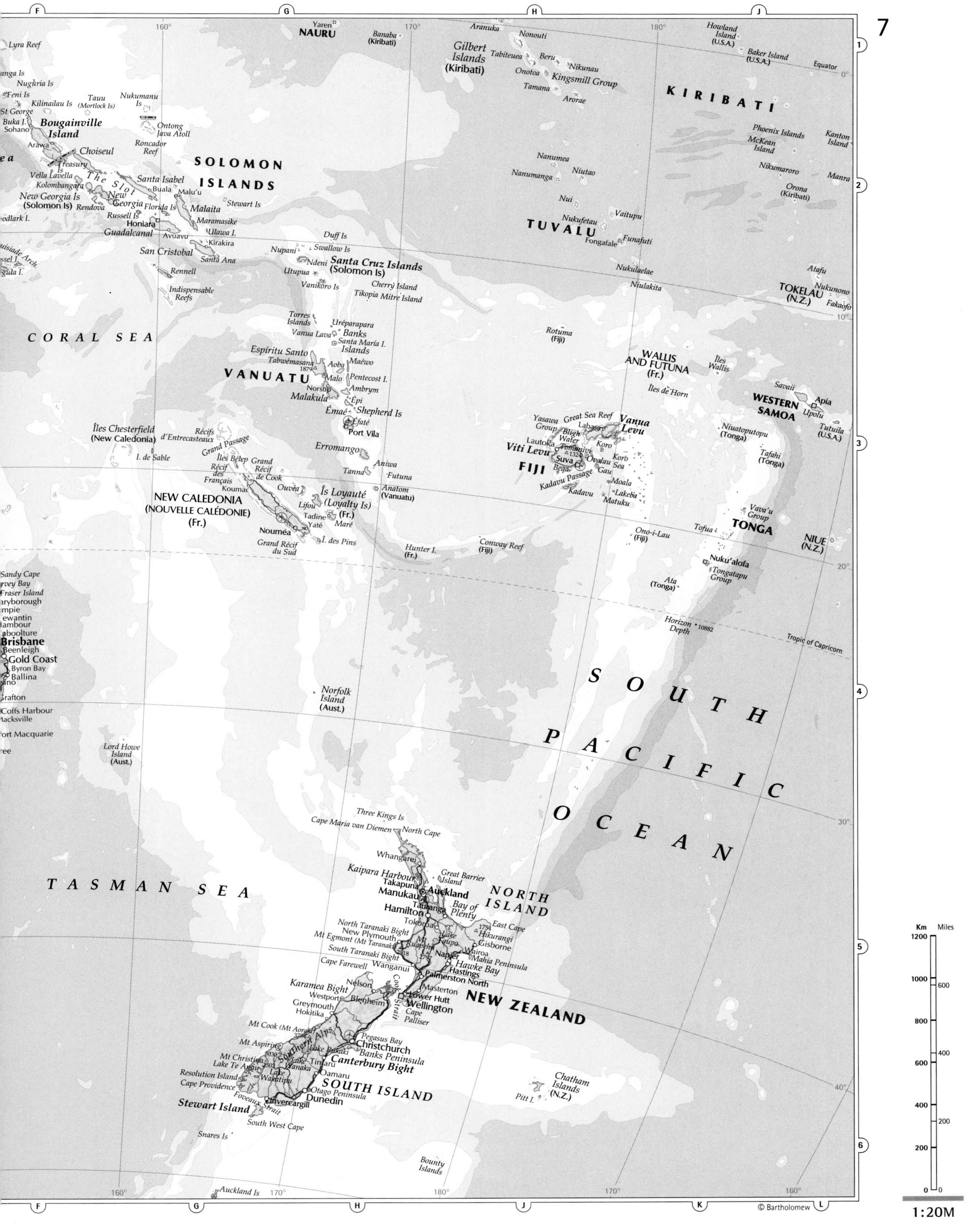

NAURU
Yaren
Banaba (Kiribati)
Aranuka
Nonouti
Howland Island (U.S.A.)
Baker Island (U.S.A.)
Equator

Gilbert Islands (Kiribati)
Tabiteuea
Beru
Nikunau
Onotoa
Kingsmill Group
Tamana
Arorae

KIRIBATI
Phoenix Islands
McKean Island
Kanton Island
Nikumaroro
Orona (Kiribati)
Manra

Lyra Reef
Nuguria Is
Feni Is
Kilinailau Is
Tauu (Mortlock Is)
Nukumanu Is
St George
Buka I.
Sohano
Arawa
Bougainville Island
Choiseul
Treasury
Vella Lavella
Kolombangara
Santa Isabel
Buala
Malu'u
Malaita
New Georgia Is (Solomon Is)
Rendova
Russell Is
Florida Is
Maramasike
Honiara
Guadalcanal
Avuavu
Ulawa I.
Kirakira
San Cristobal

SOLOMON ISLANDS

Stewart Is

Nanumea
Niutao
Nanumanga
Nui

Nukufetau
Vaitupu

TUVALU
Fongafale
Funafuti

Nukulaelae
Niulakita

Atafu
Nukunono

TOKELAU (N.Z.)
Fakaofo

Nupani
Swallow Is
Duff Is
Ndeni
Santa Cruz Islands (Solomon Is)
Utupua
Cherry Island
Vanikoro Is
Tikopia
Mitre Island

Rotuma (Fiji)

Rennell
Indispensable Reefs

CORAL SEA

Torres Islands
Uréparapara
Vanua Lava
Banks Islands
Santa María I.
Espíritu Santo
Tabwémasana 1879△
Aoba
Maéwo
Malo
Pentecost I.
VANUATU
Norsup
Ambrym
Malakula
Épi
Émaé
Shepherd Is
Éfaté
Port Vila
Erromango
Aniwa
Tanna
Futuna
Anatom (Vanuatu)

Yasawa Group
Great Sea Reef
Labasa
Vanua Levu
Bligh Water
Lautoka
Koro
Viti Levu 1322△
Ovalau
Koro Sea
Suva
Bega
Gau
Moala
Kadavu Passage
Kadavu
Matuku
Lakeba

FIJI

Niulakita

WALLIS AND FUTUNA (Fr.)
Îles Wallis
Îles de Horn

Savaii
WESTERN SAMOA
Upolu
Apia
Tutuila (U.S.A.)

Niuatoputapu (Tonga)
Tafahi (Tonga)

Vava'u Group
Tofua
TONGA
Ono-i-Lau (Fiji)
Ata (Tonga)
Nuku'alofa
Tongatapu Group

NIUE (N.Z.)

Nuku'alofa
Tongatapu Group

Îles Chesterfield (New Caledonia)
Récifs d'Entrecasteaux
Grand Passage
Îles Bélep
Grand Récif de Cook
Récif des Français
I. de Sable
Koumac
Ouvéa
Îs Loyauté (Loyalty Is) (Fr.)
Lifou
Tadine
Yaté
Maré

NEW CALEDONIA (NOUVELLE CALÉDONIE) (Fr.)
Nouméa
Grand Récif du Sud
I. des Pins

Hunter I. (Fr.)
Conway Reef (Fiji)

Horizon Depth △10882
Tropic of Capricorn

Sandy Cape
rcey Bay
Fraser Island
aryborough
mpie
ewantin
ambour
aboolture
Brisbane
Beenleigh
Gold Coast
Byron Bay
ino
Ballina
rafton
Coffs Harbour
tacksville
ort Macquarie
ree

Lord Howe Island (Aust.)

Norfolk Island (Aust.)

**S O U T H
P A C I F I C
O C E A N**

T A S M A N   S E A

Three Kings Is
Cape Maria van Diemen
North Cape
Whangarei
Kaipara Harbour
Great Barrier Island
Takapuna
Auckland
Manukau
Tauranga
Bay of Plenty
Hamilton
Tokoroa
East Cape
Hikurangi
NORTH ISLAND
North Taranaki Bight
New Plymouth
Mt Taranaki
Lake Taupo
Gisborne
Mt Egmont (Mt Taranaki)
Wairoa
Mahia Peninsula
South Taranaki Bight
Napier
Hawke Bay
Cape Farewell
Wanganui
Hastings
Palmerston North
Karamea Bight
Nelson
Masterton
Westport
Blenheim
Cook Strait
Lower Hutt
Greymouth
Wellington
Hokitika
Cape Palliser

NEW ZEALAND

Mt Cook (Mt Aoraki)
Southern Alps
Pegasus Bay
Mt Aspiring
Christchurch
Banks Peninsula
Mt Christina
Lake Pukaki
Canterbury Bight
Lake Tekapo
Lake Te Anau
Lake Wanaka
Timaru
Resolution Island
Lake Wakatipu
Oamaru
Cape Providence
Otago Peninsula
SOUTH ISLAND
Foveaux Strait
Invercargill
Stewart Island
Dunedin
South West Cape

Chatham Islands (N.Z.)
Pitt I.

Snares Is
Auckland Is
Bounty Islands

© Bartholomew

Km Miles
1200
1000 600
800
600 400
400 200
200
0

1:20M

8

TASMAN SEA

SOUTHERN OCEAN

NEW SOUTH WALES

VICTORIA

SOUTH AUSTRALIA

AUSTRALIAN CAPITAL TERRITORY

GIPPSLAND

Riverina

Gourock Range

New England Ra.

Liverpool Plains

Liverpool Ra.

Warrumbungle Ra.

Blue Mts.

Snowy Mts.

Barrier Range

Flinders Ranges

Mt Lofty Ra.

Grampians

Sydney

Melbourne

Canberra

Adelaide

Newcastle

Wollongong

Geelong

Broken Hill

Dubbo

Tamworth

Armidale

Port Jackson

Botany Bay

Wilson's Promontory

Wilson's Promontory Nat. Park

Cape Otway

Cape Howe

Kangaroo I.

Yorke Pen.

Gulf St Vincent

Spencer Gulf

Lake Torrens

Lake Alexandrina

Murray

Darling

Lachlan

Murrumbidgee

Kosciusko Nat. Park

Mt Kosciusko 2228

Metres / Feet

Metres	Feet
6000	19686
5000	16404
4000	13124
3000	9843
2000	6562
1000	3281
500	1640
200	656
SEA	LEVEL
200	656
2000	6562
4000	13124
6000	19686

Km / Miles

Km	Miles
300	
250	150
200	
150	100
100	50
50	
0	0

1:5M

Lambert Azimuthal Equal Area Projection

© Bartholomew

TASMAN SEA

SOUTH PACIFIC OCEAN

NORTH ISLAND

SOUTH ISLAND

Three Kings Is
Cape Reinga   North Cape
Cape Maria van Diemen
Te Paki
Parengarenga Harbour
Rangaunu Bay   C. Karikari
Doubtless Bay
Awanui   Kaeo   Bay of Islands   Cape Brett
Kaitaia   Kerikeri   Russell
Ahipara Bay   Ahipara   Kawakawa   Towai
Tauroa Pt   Poor Knights Is
Broadwood
Hokianga Harbour   Tabeke   Whangarei
Pakotai
Donnellys Crossing   Bream Bay
Dargaville   Mokohinau Is
Maumaturoto   Little Barrier   Port Fitzroy
Tangaehe   Wellsford   Leigh   Great Barrier Island
North Head   Warkworth   Colville   Coromandel Peninsula   Whitianga
East Coast Bays   Kawau I.   Colville Chan.
Takapuna   Waiheke I.   Mercury Islands
Kaipara Harbour   Orewa   Coromandel
Auckland   Kohukohunu   The Aldermen Is
Manukau   Papatoetoe
Manukau Harbour   Papakura   Thames   837   Whangamata
Pukekohe   Waitakaruru   Mayor I.
Waiuku   Paeroa   Bay of Plenty
Port Waikato   Waihi   Matakana I.   Cape Runaway
Te Aroha   Tauranga   White I.   Waikawa Pt   Hicks Bay   Te Araroa
Glen Afton   Huntly   Katikati   Mt Te Puke   East Cape
Ngaruawahia   Waitoa   Whakatane   Hikurangi 1754   Ruatoria
Hamilton   Waiharoa   Rotorua   Opotiki   Tokomaru Bay
Kawhia Harbour   Cambridge   Murupara   Matawai   Mawhai Pt   Tolaga Bay
Kawhia   Te Awamutu   Mt Tarawera 1111   Gisborne
Otorohanga   1213   Urewera Nat. Park   Poverty Bay
Awakino   Te Kuiti   Tokoroa   Waitahanui   1369   Nuhaka   Table Cape
Mokau   Mangakino   Lake Taupo   Mahia Pen.   Portland I.
Aria   Piopio   Mt Ngauruhoe   Mohaka   Bay View
Okahukura   Hauhungaroa 1078   Wairakei   Taupo   **Napier**   **Hawke Bay**
New Plymouth   Whangamomona   **Hastings**   C. Kidnappers
Waitara   Egmont Nat. Park   Mt Ruapehu 2797   Havelock North
Cape Egmont   Mt Egmont (Mt Taranaki) 2518   Tongariro Nat. Park   Kaimanawa Mts   Waipawa   Waimarama
Egmont Nat. Park   Stratford   Raetihi   Ohakune   Waipukurau
Opunake   Taihape   Onganga   Takapau   Porangahau
Hawera   Kokatahi   Waiouru   Kimbolton   Dannevirke   Cape Turnagain
South Taranaki Bight   Patea   Mangaweka   Woodville   Wanstead
Wanganui   Turakina   Marton   Feilding   Pahiatua
Rongotea   Palmerston North   803   Castlepoint
Foxton   Levin   Pongaroa
Cape Farewell   Farewell Spit   Cape Stephens   Otaki   Eketahuna
Collingwood   Cape   Kapiti I.   Mitre   Castlepoint
Kahurangi Pt   Golden Bay   Separation Pt   Paraparaumu   Upper Hutt   Masterton
Takaka   D'Urville I.   Porirua   Featherston   Te Wharau
Abel Tasman Nat. Park   French Pass   **Wellington**   Flat Point
Upper Takaka   Tasman Bay   Picton   Lower Hutt   564
Mts   Riwaka   Nelson   Mt Ross 983
Karamea   Richmond   Canvastown   Cloudy B.   Cape Palliser
Mts   Wakefield   Tuamarina   Palliser Bay
Karamea Bight   Hope Saddle   Blenheim
Waimangaroa   Owen River   Richmond Ra.   Renwick   Seddon   Clifford B.
Cape Foulwind   Westport   Rotoiti   Natratt   Cape Campbell
Charleston   Inangahua Junction   Mt Travers 2338   St Arnaud Range
Buller   2131   Pinnacle   Tapuaenuku 2885
Reefton   Mt   Inland Kaikoura Range
1832   Lewis Pass   Clarence   Mayakau 2610
Runanga   Springs Junction   Hanmer Springs   Kaikoura
Greymouth   Maruia   Rotherham   Oaro   Kaikoura Peninsula
Hokitika   Mt Ajax 1832   Culverden   Parnassus
Kowhitirangi   L. Brunner   L. Sumner   Cheviot
Ross   Kanieri   Mt Crosbie 1987   Waiau   Waipara
Abut Head   Otira   Arthur's Pass   Waikari
Hari Hari   Arthur's Pass Nat. Park   Rangiora   Pegasus Bay
Franz Josef Glacier   Mt Arrowsmith 2795   Oxford   Kaiapoi   Belfast
Fox Glacier   Mt Elie 2621   Sheffield   **Christchurch**
Mt Cook   Aoraki 3754   Te Piraia   Rolleston   Sumner
Westland Nat. Park   Mt Beaumont   Banks Peninsula
Mt Cook Nat. Park   Mayfield   Akaroa
Haast   Paringa   Mt Ward   Southbridge   Lake Ellesmere   Akaroa Harb.
Jackson Head   Cook   Rangitata R.   Canterbury Plains
Cascade Pt   Mt Aspiring Nat. Park   Lake Tekapo   Ashburton
Mt Aspiring 3027   Lake Pukaki   Geraldine
Awarua Pt   Mt Alta 2347   Pukaki   Temuka   Canterbury Bight
Milford Sd   L. Ohau   Timaru   SOUTH ISLAND
Milford Sound   Hawea   Mt Hutt 688   Pareora
George Sd   Wanaka   Benmore   Waimate
Caswell Sd   Mt Piso 2087   Panorama   Kurow   Studholme Junction
Fiordland National Park   1879   Kingston   Otematata   Glenavy
Secretary I.   L. Te Anau   Cromwell   St Mary's Pk 2195   C. Wanbrow
Doubtful Sd   Queenstown   Alexandra   Naseby   Oamaru
Breaksea Sd   Manapouri   2028   1695   Hyde   Palmerston
Resolution I.   Mossburn   Roxburgh   Dunback   Moeraki Pt
Dusky Sd   Te Anau   Balfour   Middlemarch   Shag Pt
Mt Ward   Lumsden   Waikouaiti
Cape Providence   Carolne Pt   Winton   Gore   Mosgiel   **Dunedin**
Chalky In.   Gore   Mataura   Milton   Brighton
Puysegur Pt   Tuatapere   Otautau   Balclutha   Otago Peninsula
Te Waewae Bay   Orepuki   Mataura South   Kaitangata
Riverton   **Invercargill**   Nugget Pt
Foveaux Strait   Bluff   Waipapa Pt   Chaslands Mistake
Solander I.   Ruapuke I.   Long Pt
Codfish I.   Halfmoon Bay   Long Pt
Mason B.   Stewart Island   Shelter Pt
Muttonbird Is   South West Cape

Southern Alps

Cook Strait

South Taranaki Bight
North Taranaki Bight

Km / Miles scale

Metres	Feet
6000	19686
5000	16404
4000	13124
3000	9843
2000	6562
1000	3281
500	1640
200	656
SEA LEVEL	LEVEL
200	656
2000	6562
4000	13124
6000	19686

Km	Miles
300	
250	150
200	100
150	
100	50
50	
0	0

© Bartholomew

Conic Equidistant Projection

1:5M

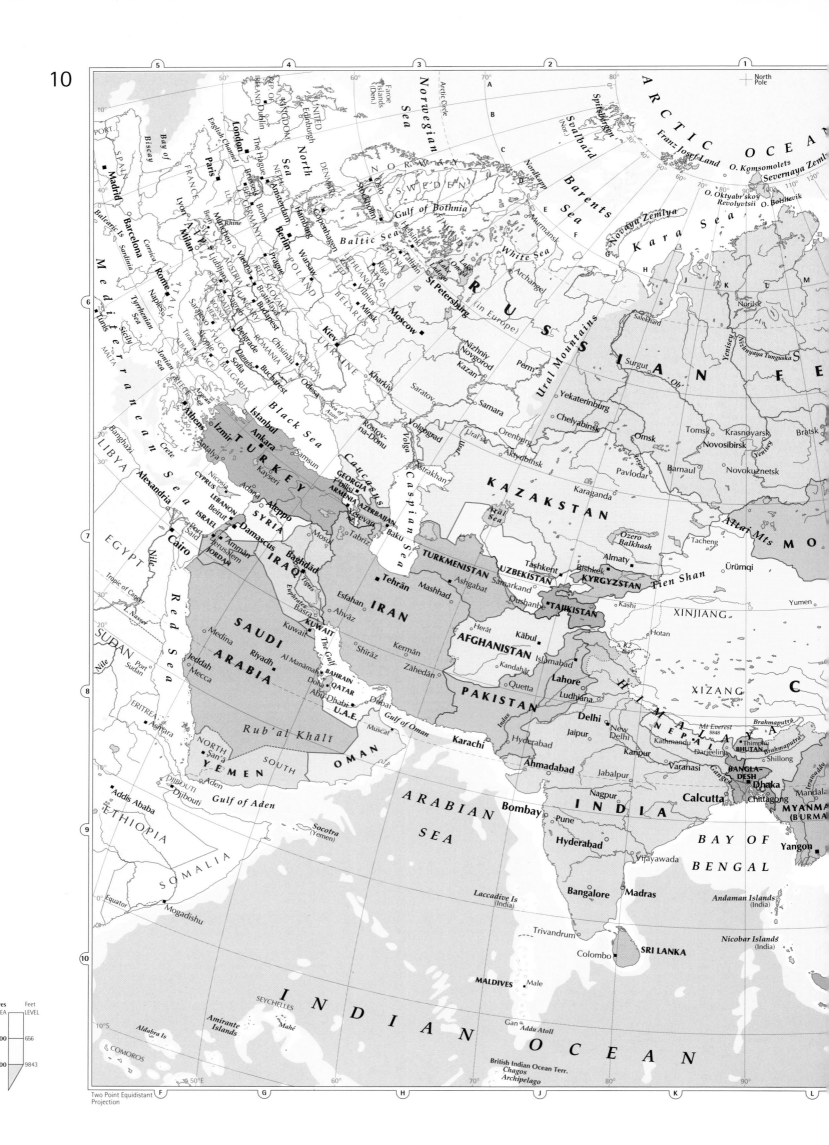

10

North
Pole

ARCTIC OCEAN

Svalbard
(Nor.)
Spitsbergen
Franz Josef Land
O. Komsomolets
Severnaya Zemlya
O. Oktyabr'skoy Revolyutsii O. Bolshevik
Novaya Zemlya
Kara Sea
Barents Sea
Murmansk
Archangel
White Sea

PORT
SPAIN
Madrid
Bay of Biscay
Balearic Is
Barcelona
Corsica
Sardinia
Tyrrhenian Sea
Sicily
Tunis
MALTA
Mediterranean Sea

IRELAND
Dublin
UNITED KINGDOM
London
Edinburgh
English Channel
The Hague
NETH.
Amsterdam
Brussels
BELG.
Paris
FRANCE
Lyon
Rhine
Bern
SWITZ.
Milan
Turin
Genoa
ITALY
Rome
Naples
Faroe Islands
(Den.)
Arctic Circle
Norwegian Sea
N O R W A Y
S W E D E N
Oslo
Stockholm
Nordkapp
DENMARK
Copenhagen
Hamburg
Berlin
GERMANY
Munich
Prague
CZECH REP.
Vienna
AUSTRIA
Ljubljana
Zagreb
SLOVENIA
BOSNIA
Sarajevo
Zagreb
CROATIA
HUNGARY
Budapest
Bratislava
SLOVAKIA
POLAND
Warsaw
Gulf of Bothnia
Baltic Sea
FINLAND
Helsinki
Tallinn
ESTONIA
Lake Ladoga
Lake Onega
St Petersburg
Riga
LATVIA
LITHUANIA
Vilnius
BELARUS
Minsk
Moscow
R U S S I A N
(in Europe)
Nizhniy Novgorod
Perm
Ural Mountains
Salekhard
Yenisey
Nizhnyaya Tunguska
Surgut
Ob'
Norilsk
F E
Danube
ROMANIA
Belgrade
YUGO.
Skopje
MACE.
ALBANIA
Tirana
Sofia
BULGARIA
Bucharest
Chisinau
MOLDOVA
Odesa
UKRAINE
Kiev
Kharkiv
Rostov-na-Donu
Sea of Azov
Don
Volgograd
Volga
Saratov
Samara
Kazan
Astrakhan'
Orenburg
Ural'sk
Aktyubinsk
Yekaterinburg
Chelyabinsk
Omsk
Pavlodar
Irtysh
Barnaul
Novosibirsk
Tomsk
Krasnoyarsk
Bratsk
Yenisey
Novokuznetsk
M O
Altai Mts

Greece
GREECE
Athens
Ionian Sea
Crete
Aegean Sea
Izmir
Antalya
TURKEY
Ankara
Istanbul
Black Sea
Samsun
Adana
Kayseri
CYPRUS
Nicosia
LEBANON
Beirut
SYRIA
Aleppo
Damascus
ISRAEL
Jerusalem
Amman
JORDAN
Caucasus
GEORGIA
Tbilisi
ARMENIA
Yerevan
AZERBAIJAN
Baku
Tabriz
Mosul
Caspian Sea
KAZAKSTAN
Karaganda
Aral Sea
Ozero Balkhash
Tacheng
Almaty
Bishkek
KYRGYZSTAN
Tashkent
Samarkand
UZBEKISTAN
Dushanbe
TAJIKISTAN
TURKMENISTAN
Ashgabat
Tien Shan
Kashi
Hotan
XINJIANG
Ürümqi
Yumen

LIBYA
Banghāzī
Alexandria
EGYPT
Cairo
Nile
Tropic of Cancer
Port Said
Red Sea
SUDAN
Port Sudan
L. Nasser
Nile
ERITREA
Asmara
ETHIOPIA
Addis Ababa
DJIBOUTI
Djibouti
Gulf of Aden
Aden
NORTH YEMEN
San'ā
SOUTH YEMEN
SOMALIA
Mogadishu
Equator
10°S

Baghdad
IRAQ
Euphrates
Basra
Tigris
KUWAIT
Kuwait
Tehrān
Esfahan
Ahvāz
IRAN
Kermān
Shīrāz
Zāhedān
Mashhad
Herāt
AFGHANISTAN
Kābul
Kandahār
Quetta
Islamabad
PAKISTAN
Lahore
Ludhiana
K2
Indus
Karachi
Hyderabad
Ahmadabad
Bombay
Pune
Hyderabad
INDIA
Nagpur
Jabalpur
Jaipur
Delhi
New Delhi
Kanpur
Varanasi
Ganges
Mt Everest
8848
NEPAL
Kathmandu
Darjeeling
Thimphu
BHUTAN
Brahmaputra
HIMALAYA
XIZANG
C
H I M A L A Y A
Shillong
BANGLA-DESH
Dhaka
Chittagong
Ganges
Brahmaputra
Irrawaddy
Mandalay
MYANMA
(BURMA)
Yangon
Calcutta
BAY OF BENGAL
Bangalore
Madras
Vijayawada
Andaman Islands
(India)
Nicobar Islands
(India)
Trivandrum
Colombo
SRI LANKA
Laccadive Is
(India)
MALDIVES
Male
Gan
Addu Atoll
British Indian Ocean Terr.
Chagos Archipelago

SAUDI ARABIA
Medina
Mecca
Jeddah
Riyadh
BAHRAIN
Al Manāmah
QATAR
Doha
Abū Dhabi
U.A.E.
Dubai
The Gulf
Gulf of Oman
OMAN
Muscat
Rub'al Khālī
ARABIAN SEA

SEYCHELLES
Amirante Islands
Mahé
Aldabra Is
COMOROS
INDIAN OCEAN

Metres
SEA
200
3000

Feet
LEVEL
656
9843

Two Point Equidistant
Projection

50°E
60°
70°
80°
90°

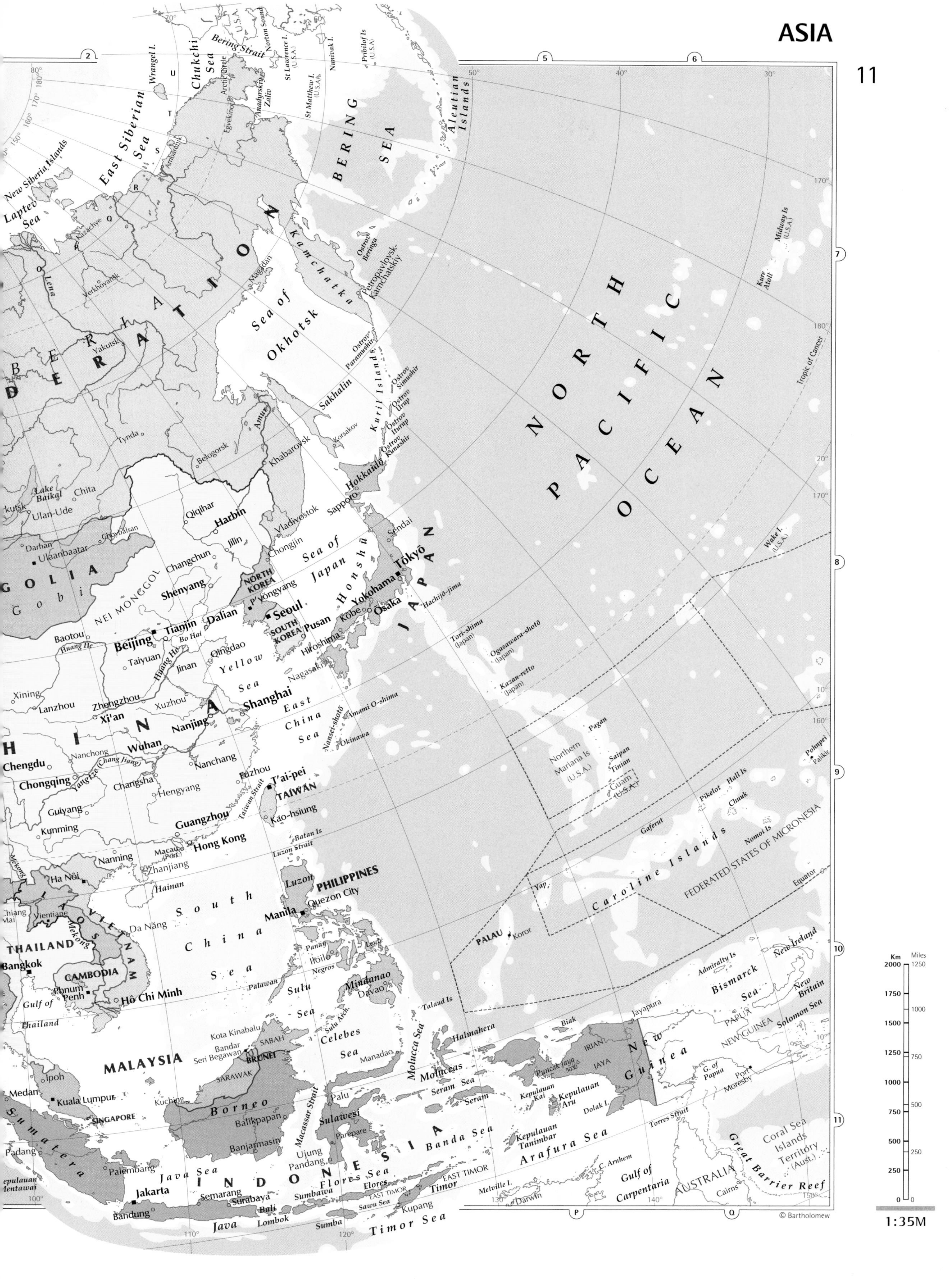

NORTH PACIFIC OCEAN

BERING SEA

Sea of Okhotsk

East Siberian Sea

Chukchi Sea

Bering Strait

Laptev Sea

New Siberian Islands

Wrangel I.

Arctic Circle

St Lawrence I. (U.S.A.)

St Matthew I. (U.S.A.)

Pribilof Is (U.S.A.)

Nunivak I.

Norton Sound

Aleutian Islands

Midway Is (U.S.A.)

Tropic of Cancer

Wake I. (U.S.A.)

Kerr Atoll

R U S S I A N   F E D E R A T I O N

Lena

Yakutsk

Verkhoyansk

Tynda

Magadan

Belogorsk

Khabarovsk

Kamchatka

Petropavlovsk-Kamchatskiy

Ostrov Beringa

Ostrov Paramushir

Kuril Islands

Sakhalin

Korsakov

Ostrov Simushir

Ostrov Urup

Ostrov Iturup

Ostrov Kunashir

Lake Baikal

Chita

Ulan-Ude

kutsk

Darhan

Ulaanbaatar

M O N G O L I A

Gobi

Choybalsan

Qiqihar

Harbin

Jilin

Changchun

Shenyang

Vladivostok

Chongjin

Sea of Japan

Hokkaido

Sapporo

Sendai

NEI MONGGOL

Baotou

Huang He

Beijing

Tianjin

Dalian

NORTH KOREA

Pyongyang

Seoul

SOUTH KOREA

Pusan

Honshū

Tōkyō

Yokohama

Kobe

Ōsaka

J A P A N

Hachijō-jima

Taiyuan

Huang He

Bo Hai

Qingdao

Jinan

Hiroshima

Nagasaki

Xining

Lanzhou

Zhengzhou

Xuzhou

Yellow Sea

Nansei-shotō

Tori-shima (Japan)

Ogasawara-shotō (Japan)

Xi'an

Nanjing

Shanghai

East China Sea

Amami O-shima

Kazan-retto (Japan)

C H I N A

Chengdu

Nanchong

Wuhan

Nanchang

Okinawa

Pagan

Chongqing

Chang Jiang

Changsha

Hengyang

Fuzhou

Fuzhou

T'ai-pei

TAIWAN

Kao-hsiung

Northern Mariana Is (U.S.A.)

Saipan

Tinian

Guam (U.S.A.)

Yangtze

Guiyang

Guangzhou

Batan Is

Luzon Strait

Pikelot

Hall Is

Chuuk

Kunming

Nanning

Macau (Port.)

Hong Kong

Taiwan Strait

Gaferut

Nomot Is

Zhanjiang

Hainan

Ha Nôi

South China Sea

Luzon

PHILIPPINES

Quezon City

Yap

Caroline Islands

FEDERATED STATES OF MICRONESIA

Pohnpei

Palikir

Equator

Chiang Mai

V I E T N A M

L A O S

Vientiane

Da Nang

Manila

PALAU

Koror

THAILAND

Bangkok

Mekong

CAMBODIA

Phnom Penh

Hô Chi Minh

Panay

Iloilo

Leyte

Negros

Palawan

Mindanao

Davao

Gulf of Thailand

Sulu Sea

Sulu Arch.

Talaud Is

Admiralty Is

Bismarck Sea

New Ireland

New Britain

Medan

Ipoh

Kuala Lumpur

SINGAPORE

M A L A Y S I A

Kota Kinabalu

SABAH

Bandar Seri Begawan

BRUNEI

SARAWAK

Kuching

Borneo

Celebes Sea

Manadao

Molucca Sea

Moluccas

Seram Sea

Seram

Halmahera

Biak

Jayapura

PAPUA NEW GUINEA

Solomon Sea

IRIAN JAYA

Puncak Jaya 5030

New Guinea

G. of Papua

Port Moresby

Sumatera

Padang

Kepulauan Mentawai

Palembang

Balikpapan

Banjarmasin

Ujung Pandang

Sulawesi

Parepare

Palu

Macassar Strait

I N D O N E S I A

Kepulauan Kai

Kepulauan Aru

Dolak I.

Torres Strait

AUSTRALIA

Cairns

Great Barrier Reef

Coral Sea Islands Territory (Aust.)

Jakarta

Bandung

Semarang

Surabaya

Java

Java Sea

Bali

Lombok

Sumbawa

Sumba

Flores

Flores Sea

Elores

EAST TIMOR

Kupang

Timor

Sawu Sea

Banda Sea

Timor Sea

Arafura Sea

C. Arnhem

Gulf of Carpentaria

Melville I.

Darwin

1:35M

© Bartholomew

Km	Miles
2000	1250
1750	1000
1500	750
1250	
1000	500
750	
500	250
250	
0	0

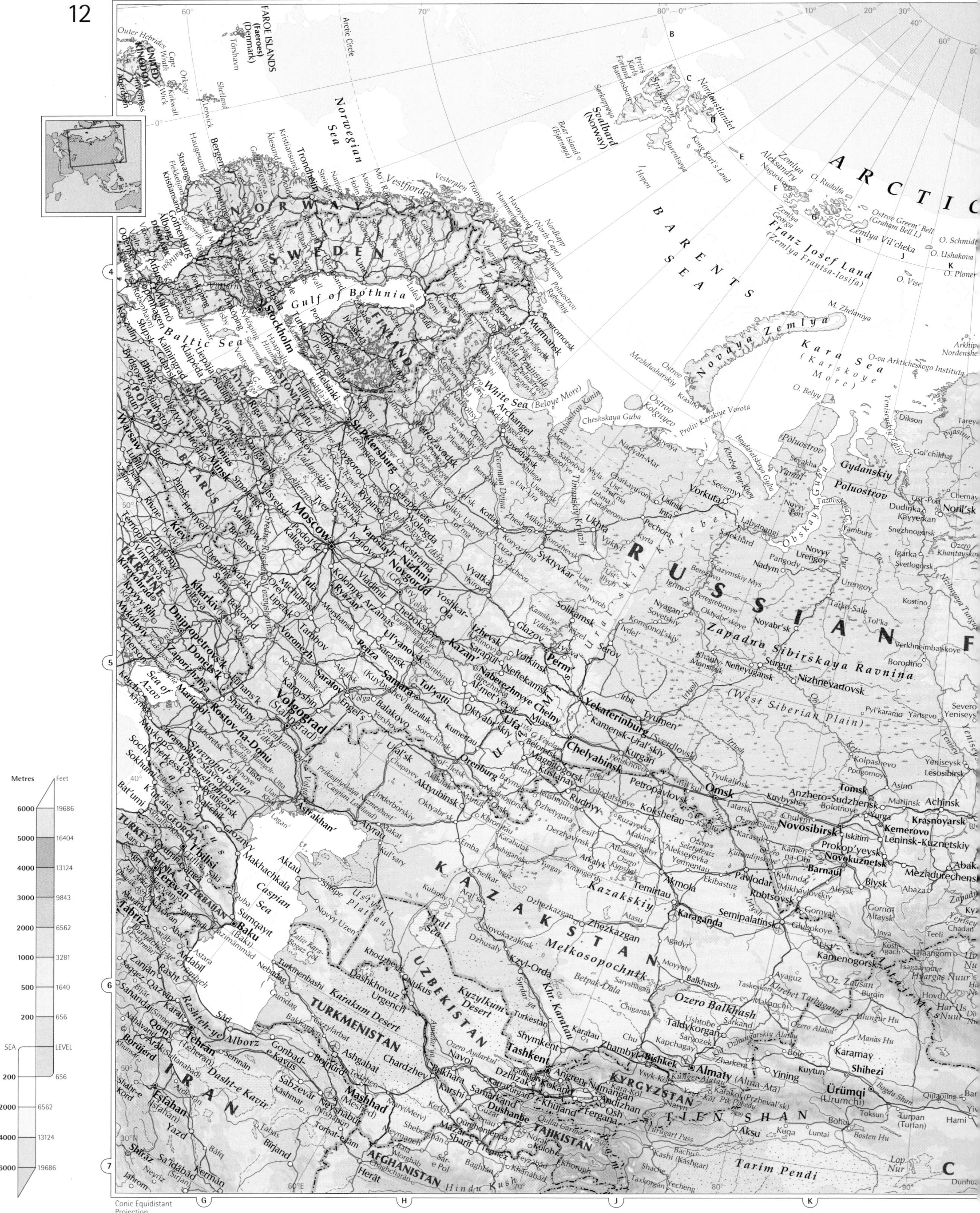

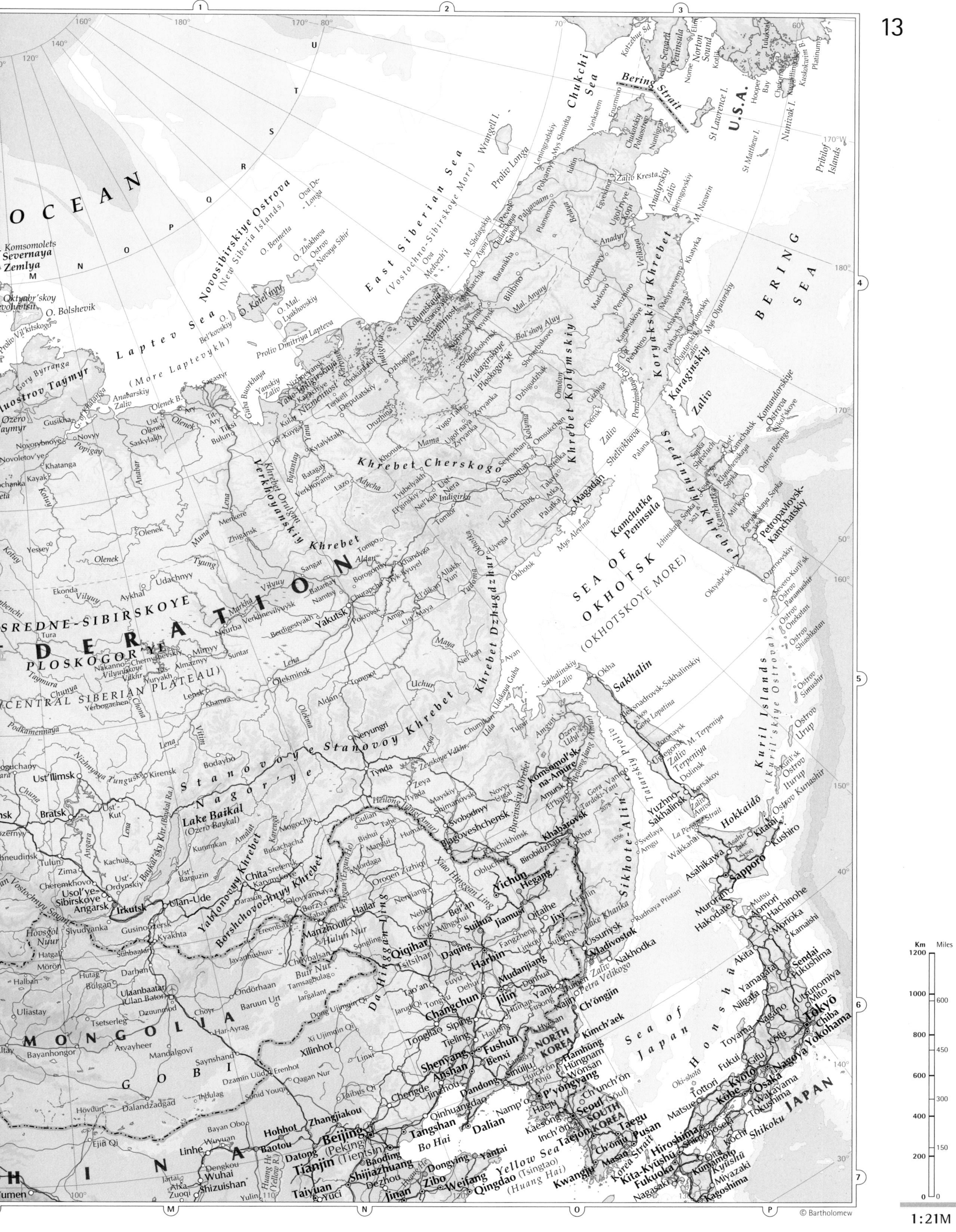

© Bartholomew

1:21M

OCEAN

O. Komsomolets
Severnaya Zemlya

O. Oktyabr'skoy revolyutsii
O. Bolshevik

Proliv Vil'kitskogo

Gory Byrranga
Poluostrov Taymyr

Ozero Taymyr

Novorybnoye
Novoletov'ye

Khatanga

Kayak

Yessey

Ekonda

Tura

SREDNE-SIBIRSKOYE
PLOSKOGOR'YE

(CENTRAL SIBERIAN PLATEAU)

Podkamennaya

Baykit

Bratsk
Ust'-Ilimsk

Zima
Tulun

Cheremkhovo
Usol'ye-Sibirskoye
Angarsk
Irkutsk

Slyudyanka

Ulan-Ude

Hövsgöl Nuur

Hatgal

Möron
Hutag

Halban
Bulgan

Uliastay

MONGOLIA

Tsetserleg

Altay
Bayanhongor

Arvayheer

Laptev Sea
(More Laptevykh)

Novosibirskiye Ostrova
(New Siberia Islands)

O. Kotel'nyy

East Siberian Sea
(Vostochno-Sibirskoye More)

Wrangell I.

Proliv Longa

Chukchi Sea

Bering Strait

U.S.A.

St Lawrence I.

St Matthew I.

Pribilof Islands

BERING SEA

Anadyr

Koryakskiy Khrebet

Karaginskiy Zaliv

Ostrova Komandorskiye

Petropavlovsk-Kamchatskiy

Kamchatka Peninsula

Sredinnyy Khrebet

Magadan

SEA OF OKHOTSK
(OKHOTSKOYE MORE)

Okhotsk

Khrebet Cherskogo

Verkhoyanskiy Khrebet

Yakutsk

FEDERATION

Khrebet Dzhugdzhur

Sakhalin

Kuril Islands
(Kuril'skiye Ostrova)

Ostrov Urup

Ostrov Iturup

Ostrov Kunashir

Yuzhno-Sakhalinsk

Komsomol'sk-na-Amure

Amursk

Khabarovsk

Sikhote-Alin

Hokkaidō

Asahikawa
Sapporo
Hakodate

Neryungri

Tynda

Stanovoy Khrebet

Stanovoye Nagor'ye

Lake Baikal
(Ozero Baykal)

Chita

Yablonovyy Khrebet

Borshchovochnyy Khrebet

Da Hinggan Ling

Hulun Nur

Buir Nur

Ulaanbaatar
Ulan Bator

GOBI

Hohhot
Baotou

Beijing (Peking)

Datong
Tianjin (Tientsin)

Shijiazhuang

Taiyuan

Wuhai
Shizuishan

Yumen

Bei'an

Qiqihar (Tsitsihar)

Daqing

Harbin

Suihua

Jiamusi

Hegang

Yichun

Mudanjiang

Jilin

Changchun

Tongliao

Tieling

Shenyang
Fushun
Benxi
Anshan

NORTH KOREA

P'yŏngyang

Namp'o

Vladivostok
Nakhodka
Ussuriysk

Sea of Japan

SOUTH KOREA

Seoul (Sŏul)
Inch'ŏn
Suwŏn
Taejŏn

Taegu
Pusan

Kwangju

Korea Strait

HONSHŪ

Sendai
Fukushima
Niigata
Yamagata
Akita

Utsunomiya
Mito
Tōkyō
Chiba
Yokohama

Nagoya
Gifu
Fukui
Toyama

Kyōto
Ōsaka
Kōbe

Hiroshima

Fukuoka
KYŪSHŪ
Nagasaki
Kumamoto
Miyazaki
Kagoshima

JAPAN

SHIKOKU

CHINA

Yellow Sea
(Huang Hai)

Qingdao (Tsingtao)
Weifang
Zibo
Jinan

Dalian

Bo Hai

Tangshan

Yantai

Dongying

Km	Miles
1200	
1000	600
800	450
600	300
400	
200	150
0	0

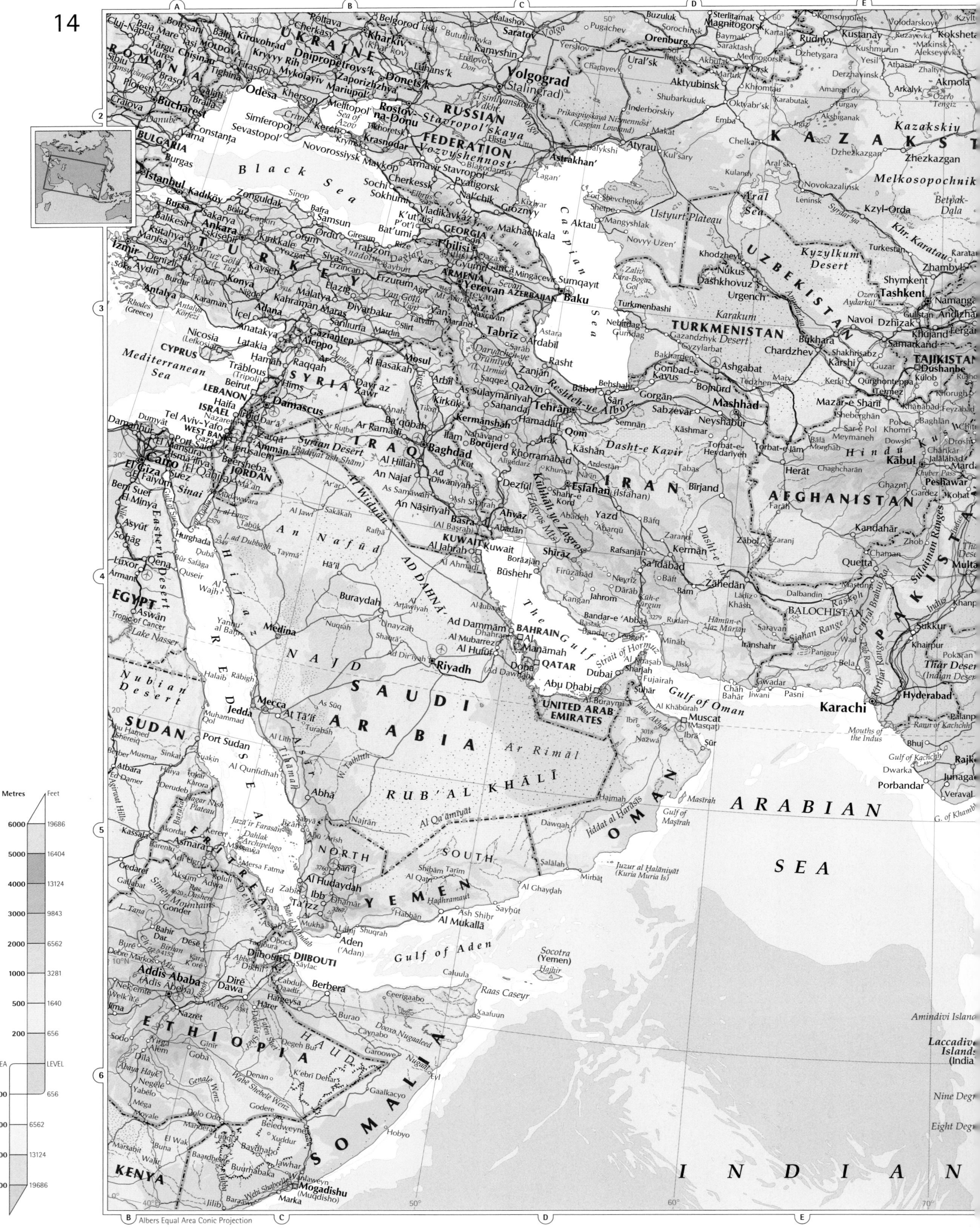

Albers Equal Area Conic Projection

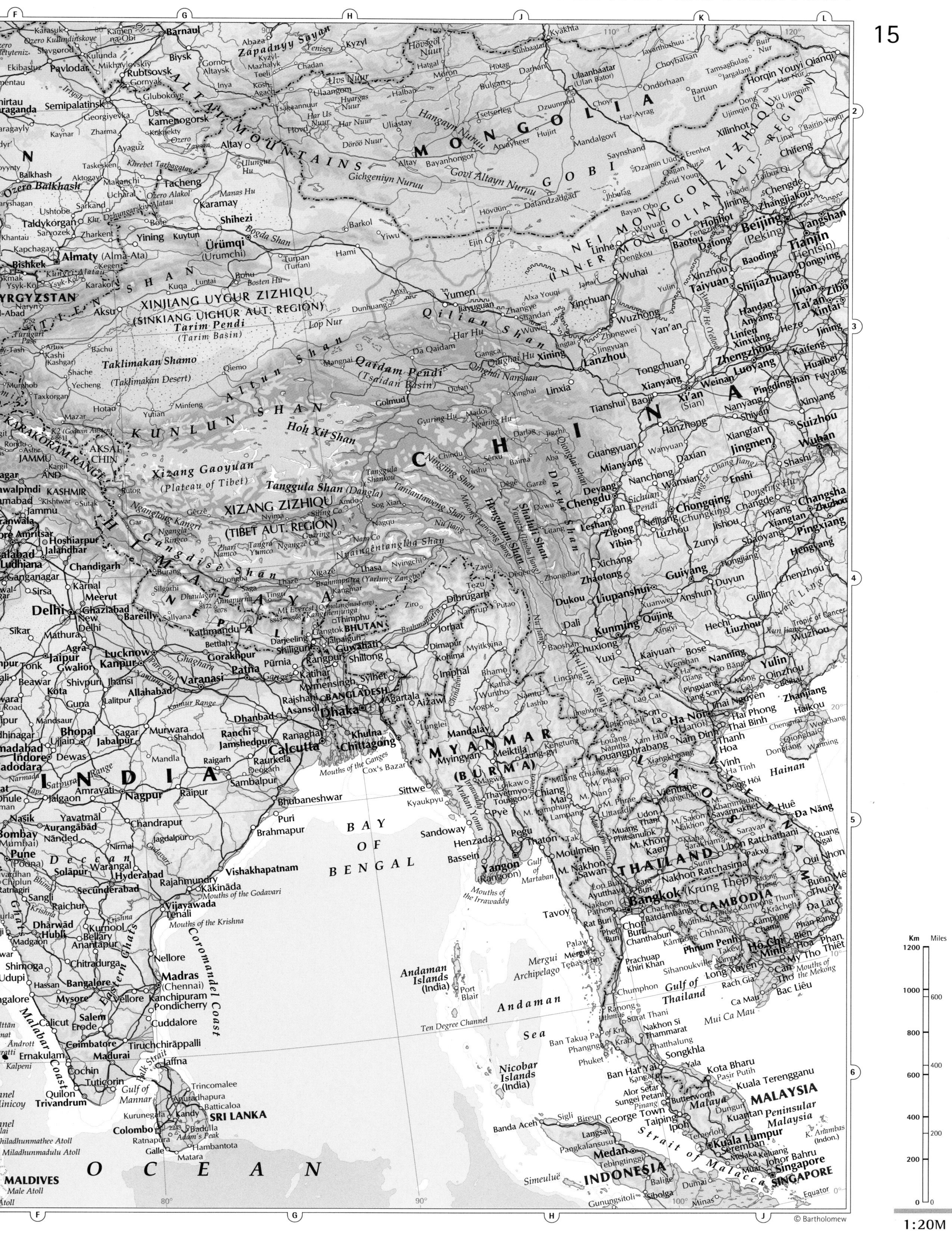

© Bartholomew

1:20M

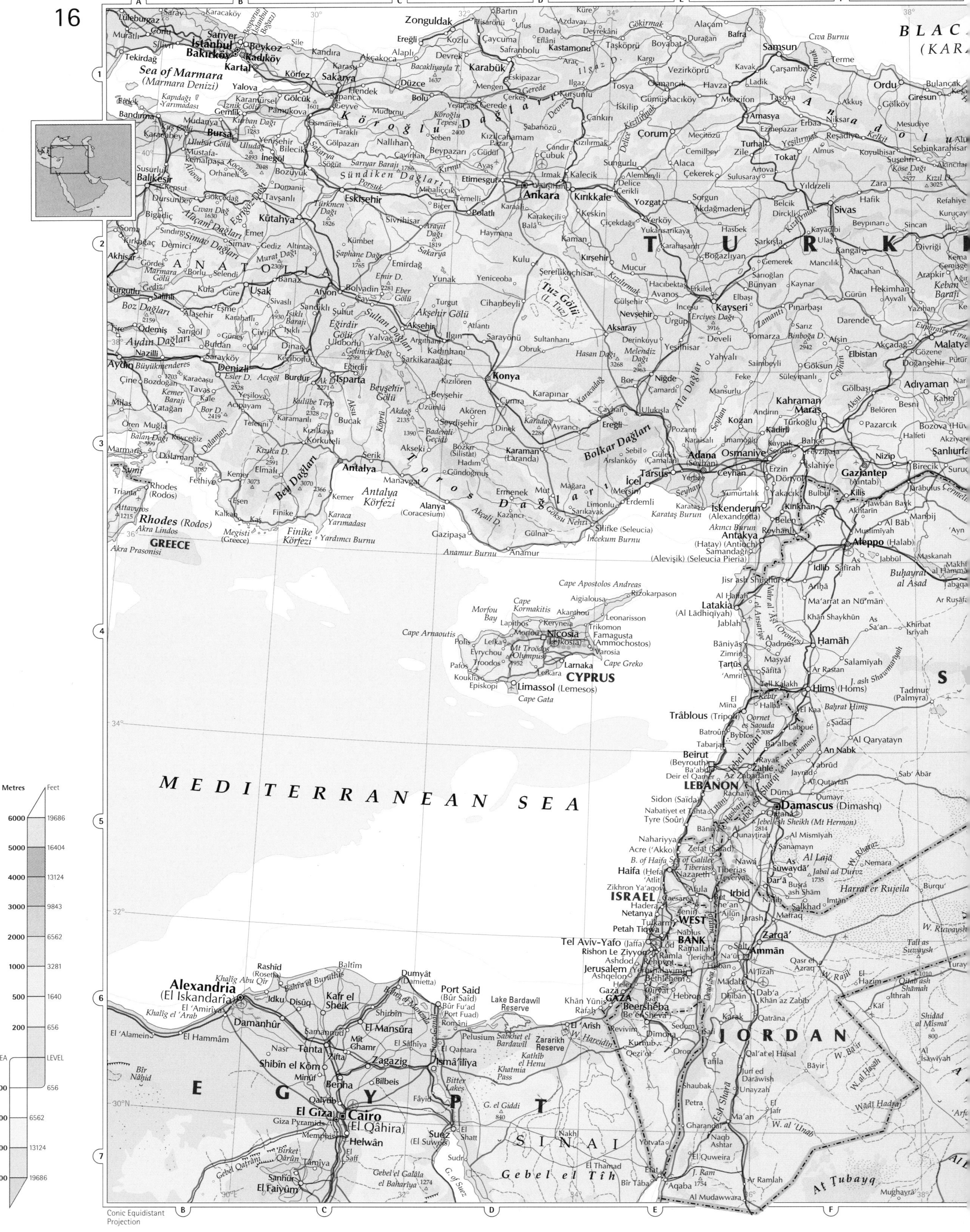

BLACK SEA
TURKEY
ANATOLIA
Sea of Marmara (Marmara Denizi)
İstanbul
Ankara
Konya
Adana
Antalya
Kayseri
Sivas
Samsun
Rhodes (Rodos)
GREECE
CYPRUS
Nicosia (Lefkosia)
Limassol (Lemesos)
MEDITERRANEAN SEA
LEBANON
Beirut (Beyrouth)
SYRIA
Aleppo (Halab)
Hims (Homs)
Hamāh
Damascus (Dimashq)
ISRAEL
Tel Aviv-Yafo (Jaffa)
Jerusalem
WEST BANK
GAZA
JORDAN
Ammān
EGYPT
Alexandria (El Iskandarîya)
Port Said (Bûr Saʻîd)
El Gîza
Cairo (El Qâhira)
Suez (El Suweis)
SINAI
Metres
Feet
6000
19686
5000
16404
4000
13124
3000
9843
2000
6562
1000
3281
500
1640
200
656
SEA
LEVEL
Conic Equidistant Projection

BLACK SEA (KARADENİZ)

GEORGIA

ARMENIA

AZERBAIJAN

AZER.

CASPIAN SEA

TURKEY

IRAN

KHAMSEH

MESOPOTAMIA

IRAQ

SYRIA

SAUDI ARABIA

Syrian Desert

KUWAIT

Tabrīz

Yerevan (Erevan)

Baku (Bakı)

Mosul (Al Mawşil)

Kirkūk

As Sulaymānīyah

Baghdad

Kādhimain

Karbalā'

An Najaf

An Nāşirīyah

Basra

Ābādān

Ahvāz

Kermānshāh

Hamadān

Zanjan

Sanandaj (Sinneh)

Khorramābād

Borūjerd

Dezfūl

Masjed Soleymān

Erzurum

Diyarbakır

Al Qāmishlī

Al Hasakah

Dayr az Zawr (Deir-ez-Zor)

Ar Ramādī

Ad Dīwānīyah

Al 'Amārah

Kuwait (Al Kuwayt)

Scale 1:5M

Km 300 250 200 150 100 50 0   Miles 150 100 50 0

© Bartholomew

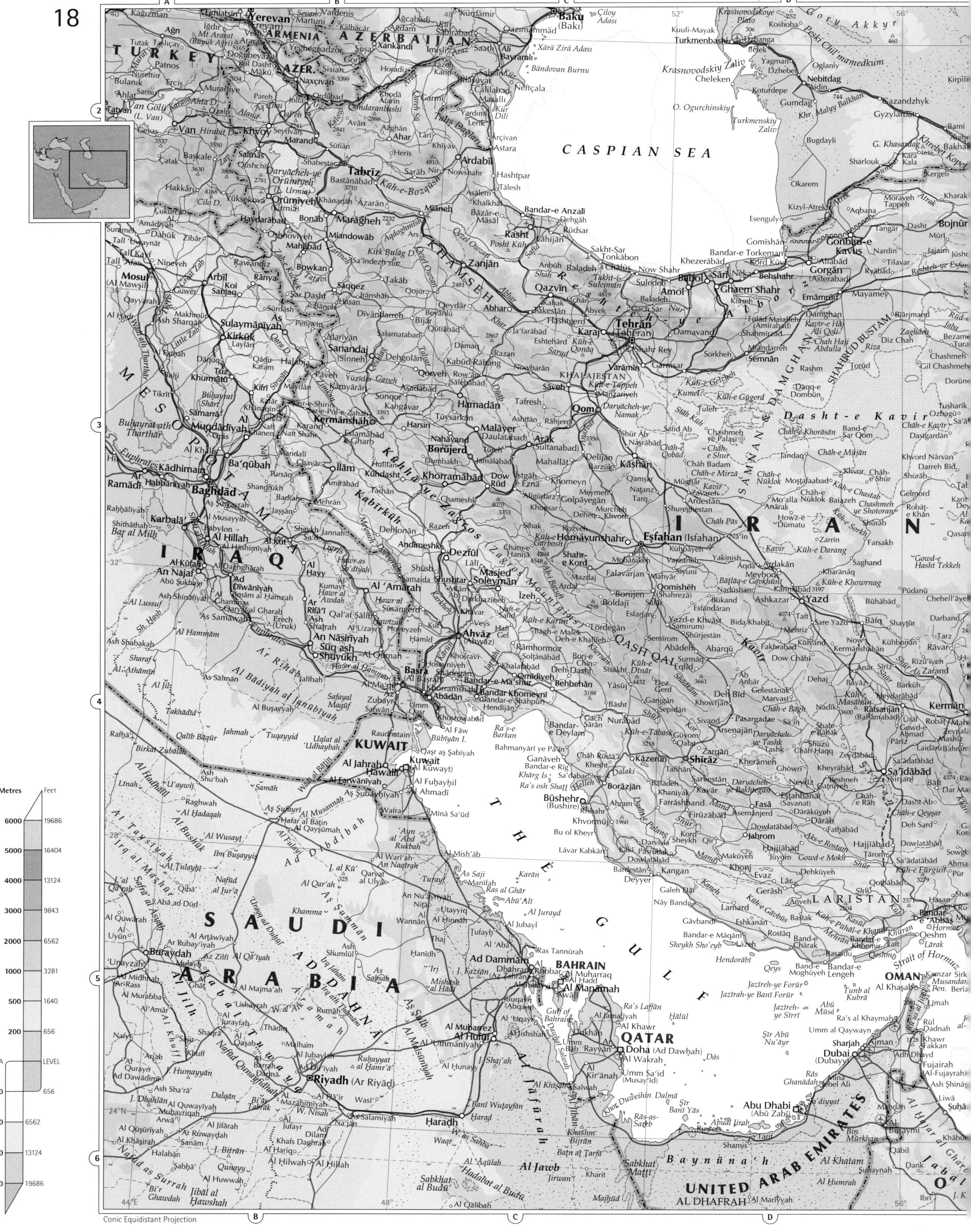

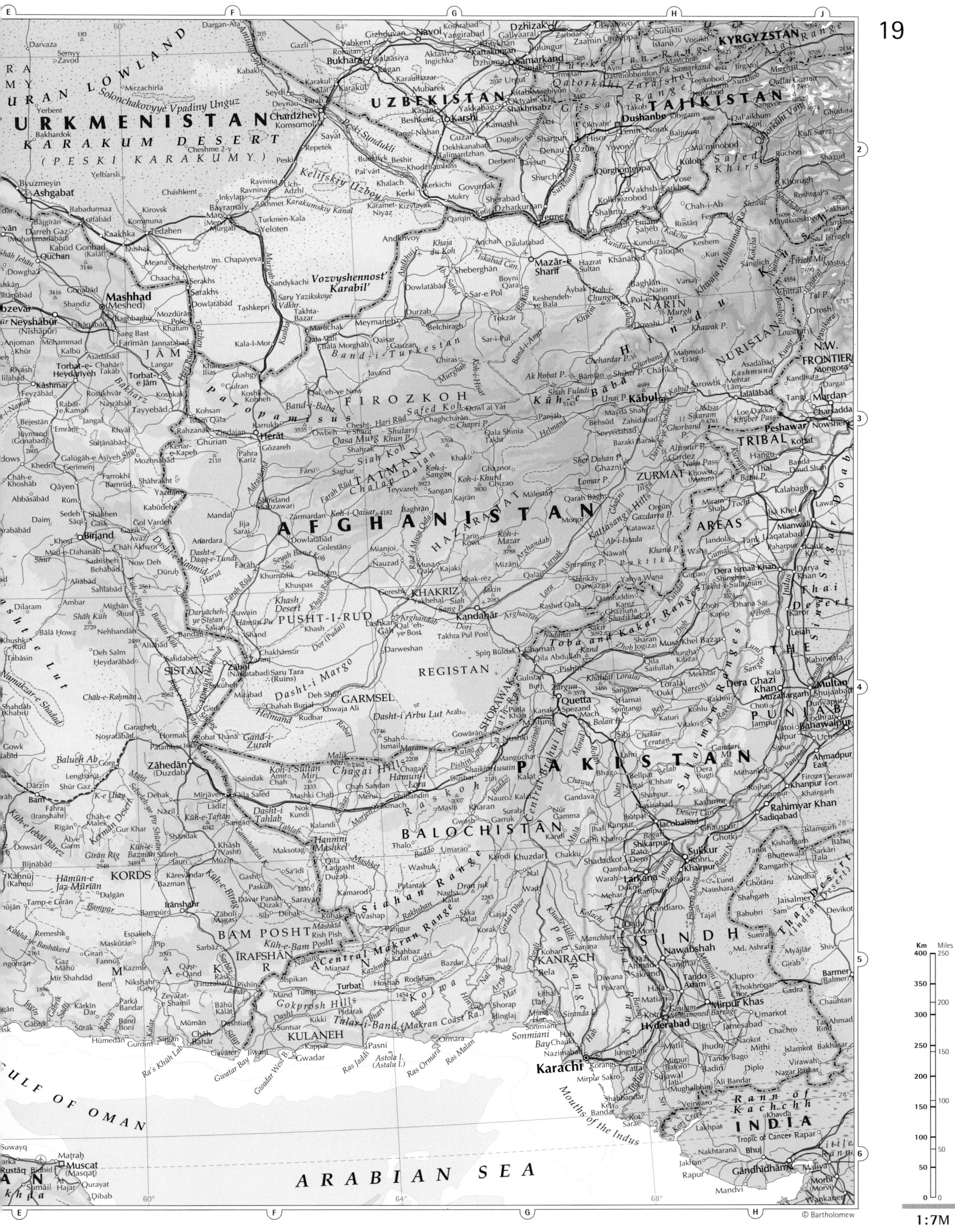

© Bartholomew

1:7M

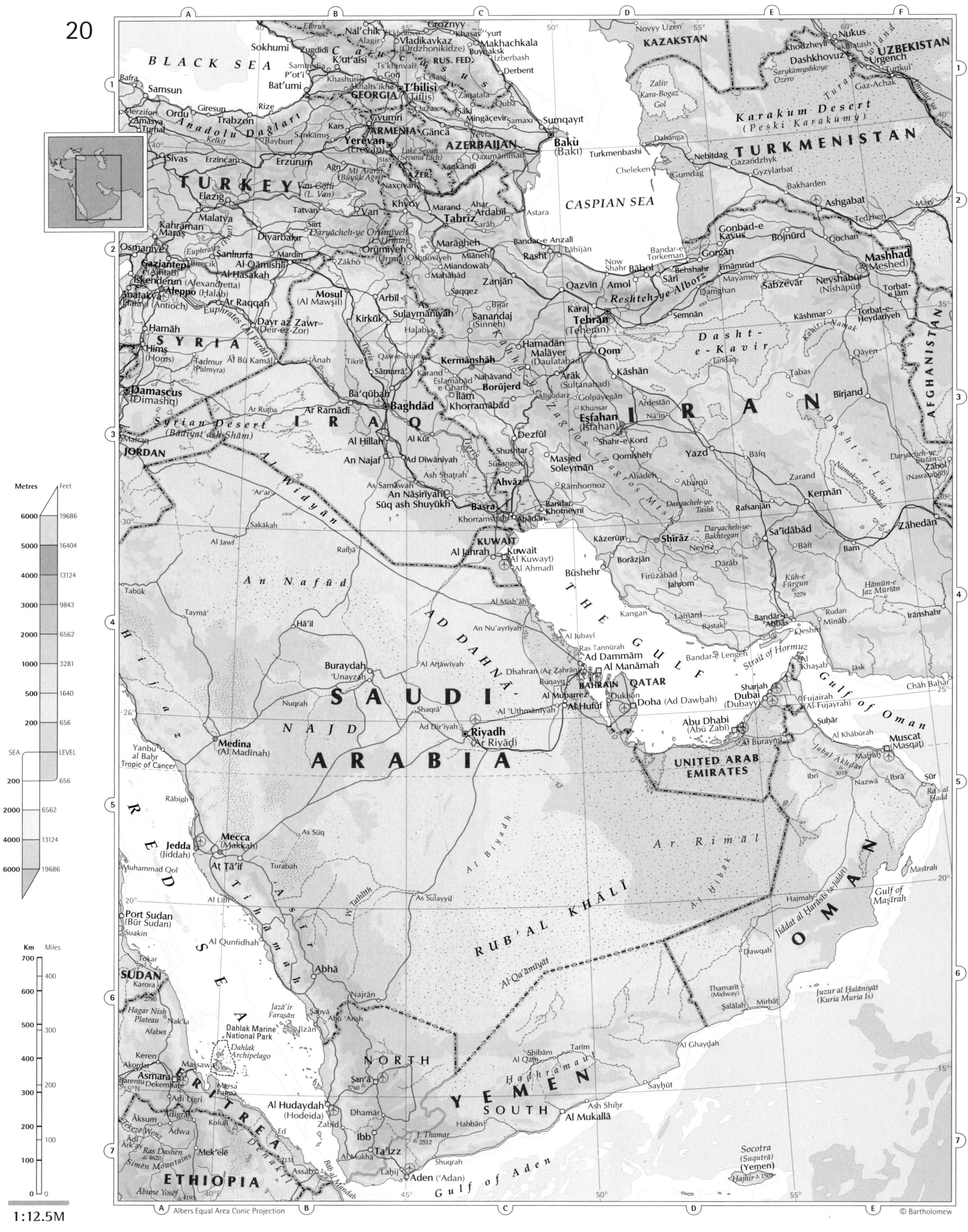

1:12.5M

Albers Equal Area Conic Projection

© Bartholomew

Metres / Feet

Metres	Feet
6000	19686
5000	16404
4000	13124
3000	9843
2000	6562
1000	3281
500	1640
200	656
SEA	LEVEL
200	656
2000	6562
4000	13124
6000	19686

Km / Miles

Km	Miles
700	400
600	
500	300
400	200
300	
200	100
100	
0	0

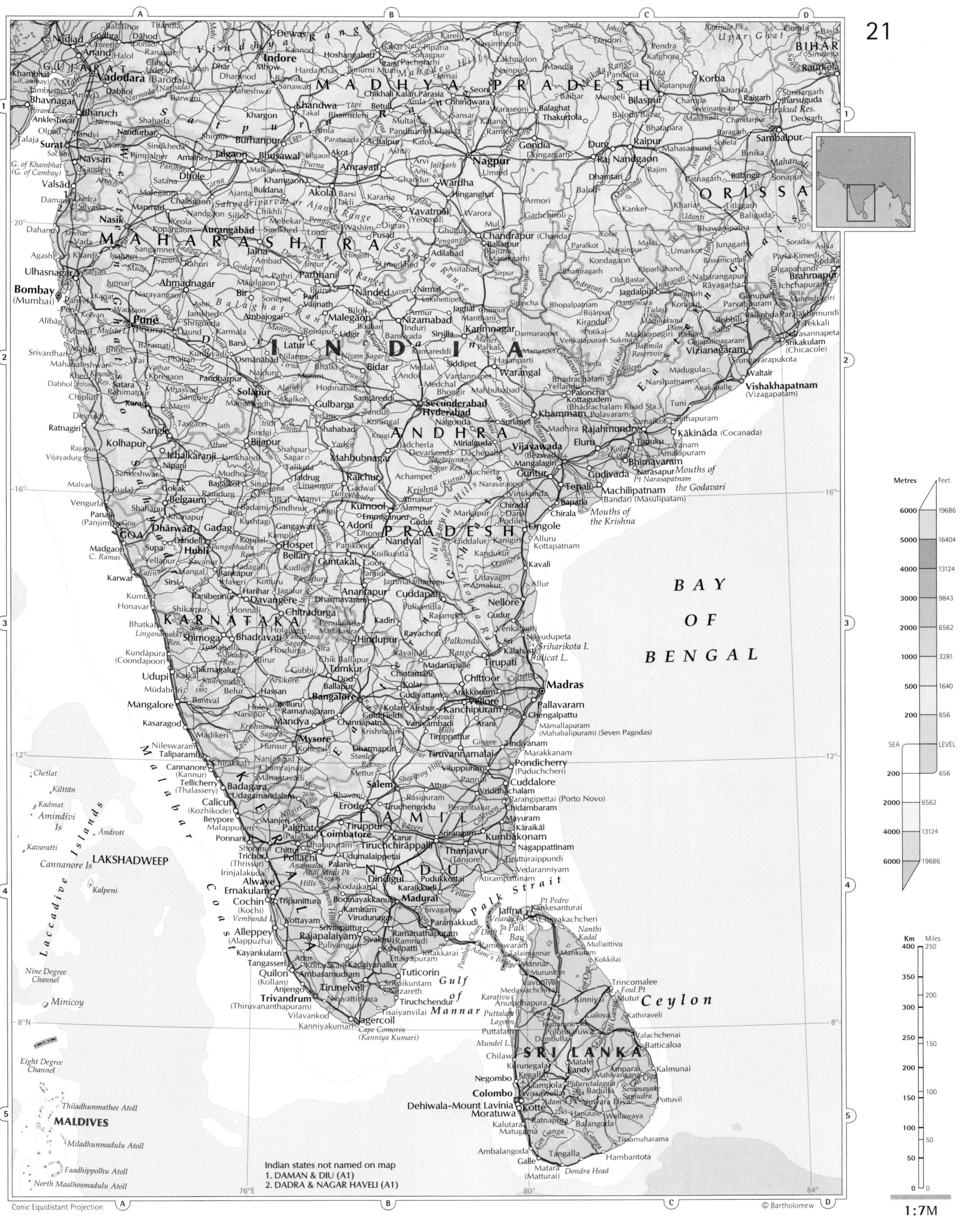

BAY
OF
BENGAL

LAKSHADWEEP

MALDIVES

Ceylon

SRI LANKA

Indian states not named on map
1. DAMAN & DIU (A1)
2. DADRA & NAGAR HAVELI (A1)

Conic Equidistant Projection

© Bartholomew

1:7M

Metres	Feet
6000	19686
5000	16404
4000	13124
3000	9843
2000	6562
1000	3281
500	1640
200	656
SEA	LEVEL
200	656
2000	6562
4000	13124
6000	19686

Km	Miles
400	250
350	200
300	
250	150
200	100
150	
100	50
50	
0	0

Metres | Feet

6000 — 19686
5000 — 16404
4000 — 13124
3000 — 9843
2000 — 6562
1000 — 3281
500 — 1640
200 — 656
SEA — LEVEL
200 — 656
2000 — 6562
4000 — 13124
6000 — 19686

Indian states not named on map
1. DAMAN & DIU (C5)
2. DADRA & NAGAR HAVELI (C5)

Conic Equidistant Projection

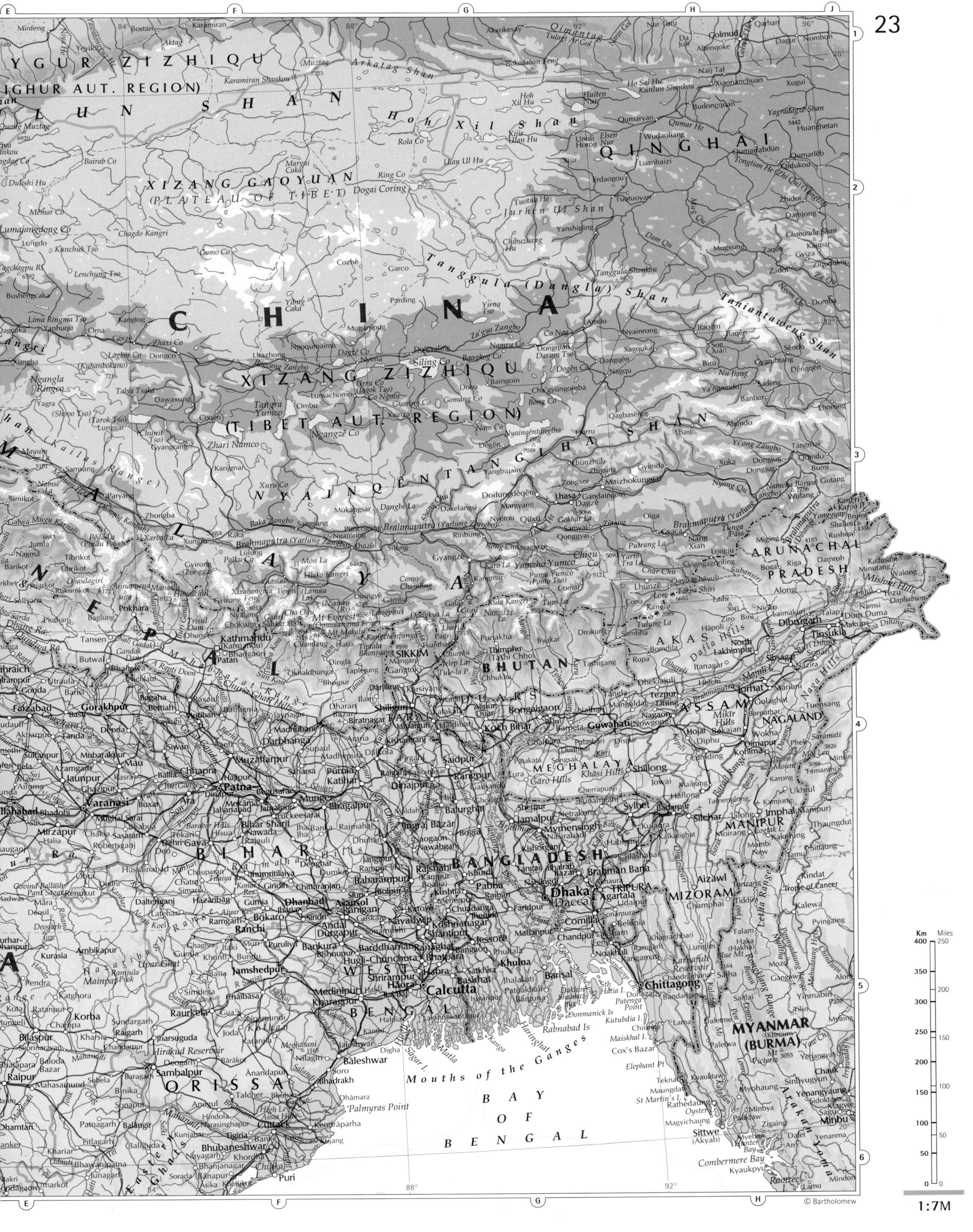
CHINA
XIZANG ZIZHIQU
(TIBET AUT. REGION)
XIZANG GAOYUAN
(PLATEAU OF TIBET)
QINGHAI
Hoh Xil Shan
Arkatag Shan
Tanggula (Dangla) Shan
Taniantaweng Shan
NYAINQÊNTANGLHA SHAN
Jurhen Ul Shan
HIMALAYA
NEPAL
BHUTAN
SIKKIM
BANGLADESH
ARUNACHAL PRADESH
ASSAM
NAGALAND
MEGHALAYA
MANIPUR
MIZORAM
TRIPURA
BIHAR
WEST BENGAL
ORISSA
MYANMAR (BURMA)
BAY OF BENGAL
Mouths of the Ganges
Brahmaputra (Yarlung Zangbo)
Lhasa
Kathmandu
Thimphu
Dhaka (Dacca)
Calcutta
Patna
Varanasi
Allahabad
Guwahati
Shillong
Chittagong
Imphal
Dibrugarh
Jamshedpur
Ranchi
Cuttack
Bhubaneshwar
Puri
Golmud
Mt Everest (Qomolangma Feng)
Kangchenjunga
Lhotse
Makalu
Km
Miles
1:7M
© Bartholomew

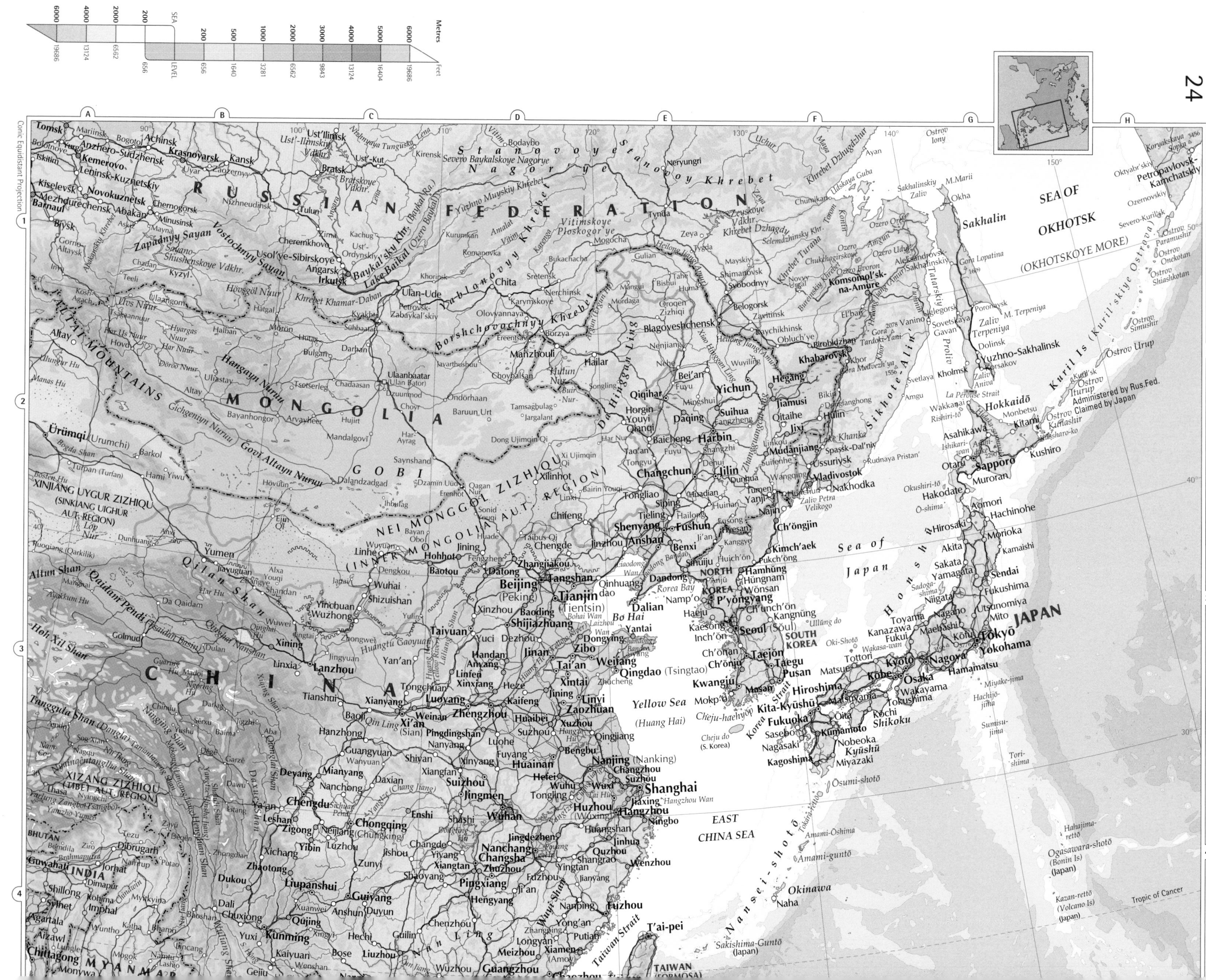

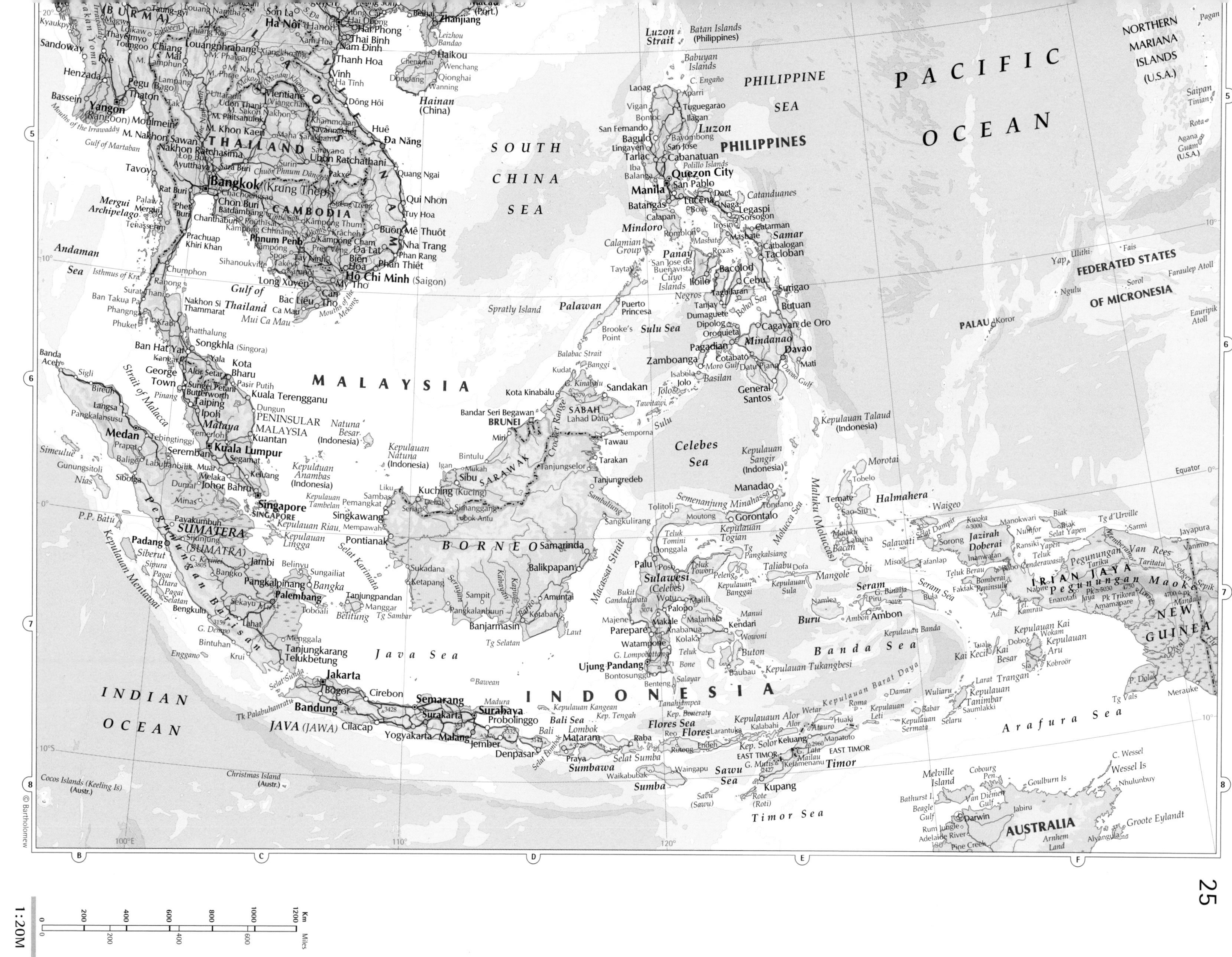

PACIFIC OCEAN

PHILIPPINE SEA

SOUTH CHINA SEA

INDONESIA

AUSTRALIA

NORTHERN MARIANA ISLANDS (U.S.A.)

FEDERATED STATES OF MICRONESIA

PALAU

PHILIPPINES

Quezon City
Manila

MALAYSIA

PENINSULAR MALAYSIA

Kuala Lumpur

SINGAPORE
Singapore

SUMATERA (SUMATRA)

JAVA (JAWA)

Jakarta
Bandung

Surabaya
Semarang
Surakarta

BORNEO

SABAH

SARAWAK

BRUNEI
Bandar Seri Begawan

KALIMANTAN

Celebes Sea

Sulu Sea

Sulawesi (Celebes)

Banda Sea

Flores Sea

Timor Sea

Java Sea

Arafura Sea

NEW GUINEA

IRIAN JAYA

INDIAN OCEAN

BURMA (MYANMAR)

THAILAND

Bangkok (Krung Thep)

CAMBODIA

Phnum Pénh

LAOS

VIETNAM

Ho Chi Minh (Saigon)

Hainan (China)

Luzon

Mindanao

Palawan

Mindoro

Samar

Panay

Medan

Padang

Palembang

Maluku (Moluccas)

Halmahera

Strait of Malacca

Gulf of Thailand

Andaman Sea

Da Nang

Ha Nôi

Km	Miles
1200	
1000	600
800	
	400
600	
400	200
200	
0	0

© Bartholomew

1:20M

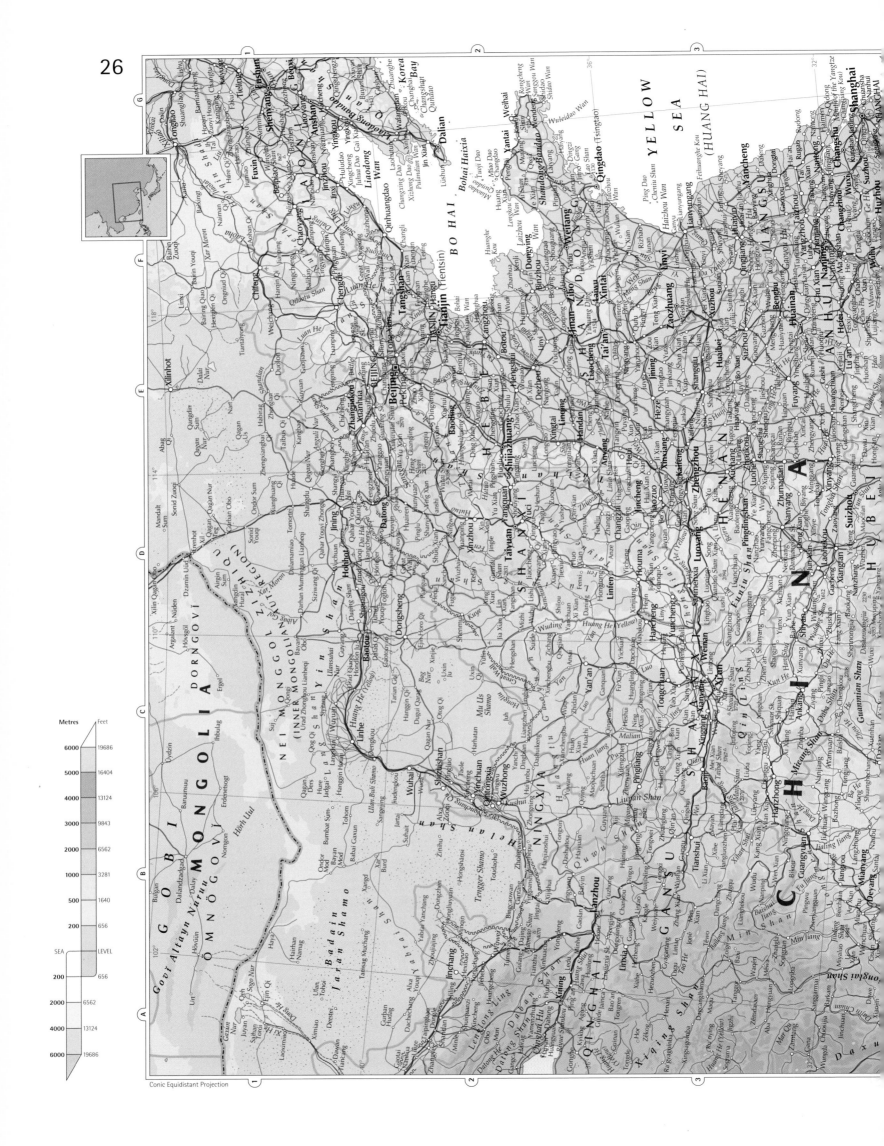
CHINA
MONGOLIA
GOBI
Govĭ Altayn Nuruu
DORNGOVĬ
ÖMNÖGOVĬ
NEI MONGGOL ZIZHIQU
(INNER MONGOLIAN AUT. REGION)
YELLOW SEA
(HUANG HAI)
BO HAI
Bohai Haixia
Liaodong Wan
Korea Bay
Liaodong Bandao
Shandong Bandao
LIAONING
HEBEI
SHANXI
SHANDONG
HENAN
JIANGSU
ANHUI
HUBEI
SHAANXI
NINGXIA
GANSU
QINGHAI
TIANJIN
BEIJING
SHANGHAI
Beijing (Peking)
Tianjin (Tientsin)
Qingdao (Tsingtao)
Shenyang
Dalian
Shijiazhuang
Taiyuan
Zhengzhou
Xi'an
Lanzhou
Xining
Yinchuan
Hohhot
Baotou
Jinan
Nanjing
Hefei
Shanghai
Huang He (Yellow)
Yin Shan
Qin Ling
Helan Shan
Liupan Shan
Badain Jaran Shamo
Tengger Shamo
Mu Us Shamo
Funiu Shan
Micang Shan
Daba Shan
Guanmian Shan
Qinghai Hu
Metres
Feet
6000
19686
5000
16404
4000
13124
3000
9843
2000
6562
1000
3281
500
1640
200
656
SEA
LEVEL
200
656
2000
6562
4000
13124
6000
19686
Conic Equidistant Projection

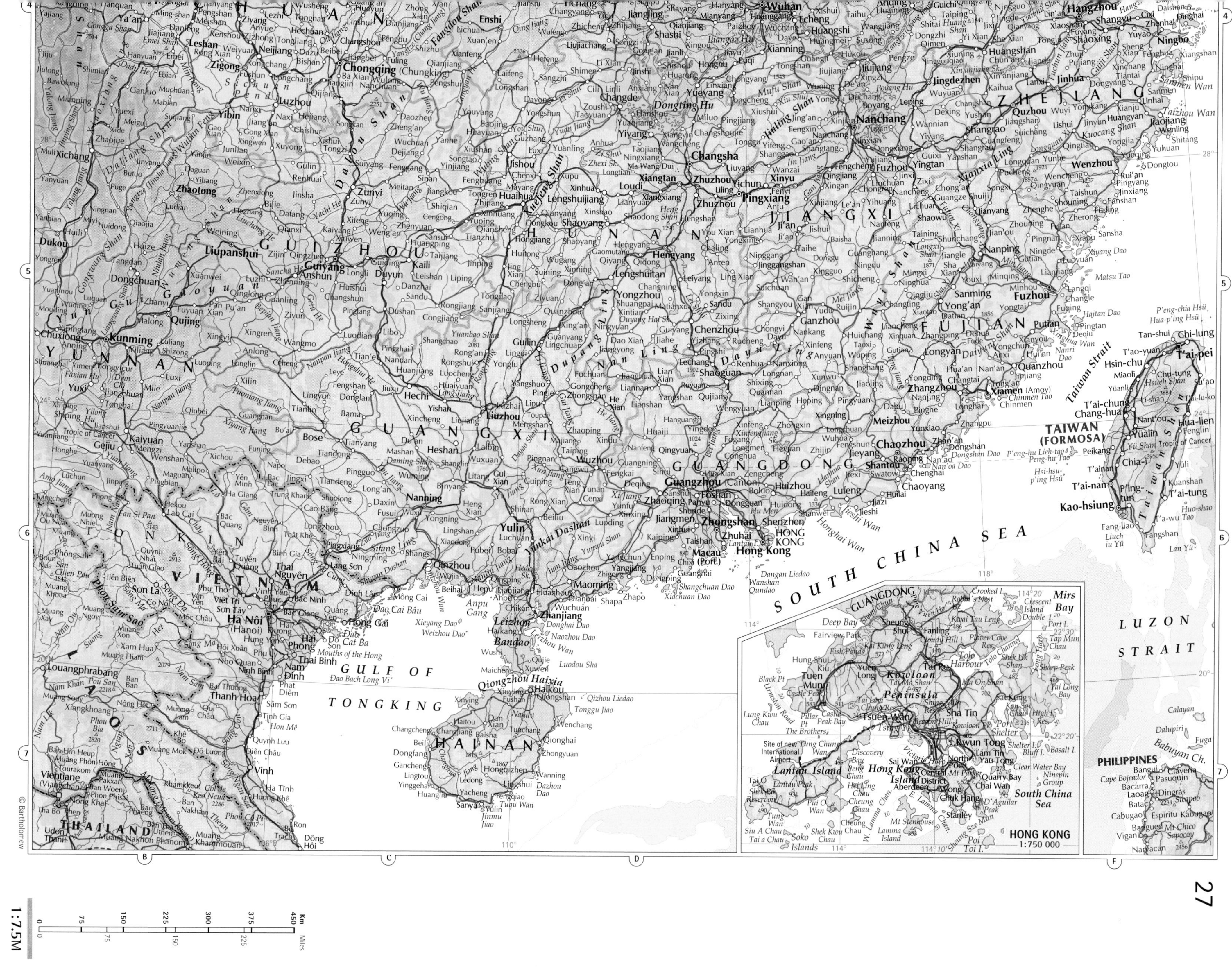

© Bartholomew

1:7.5M

HONG KONG
1:750 000

Km   Miles
450
      225
375
300   150
225
      75
150
75
0   0

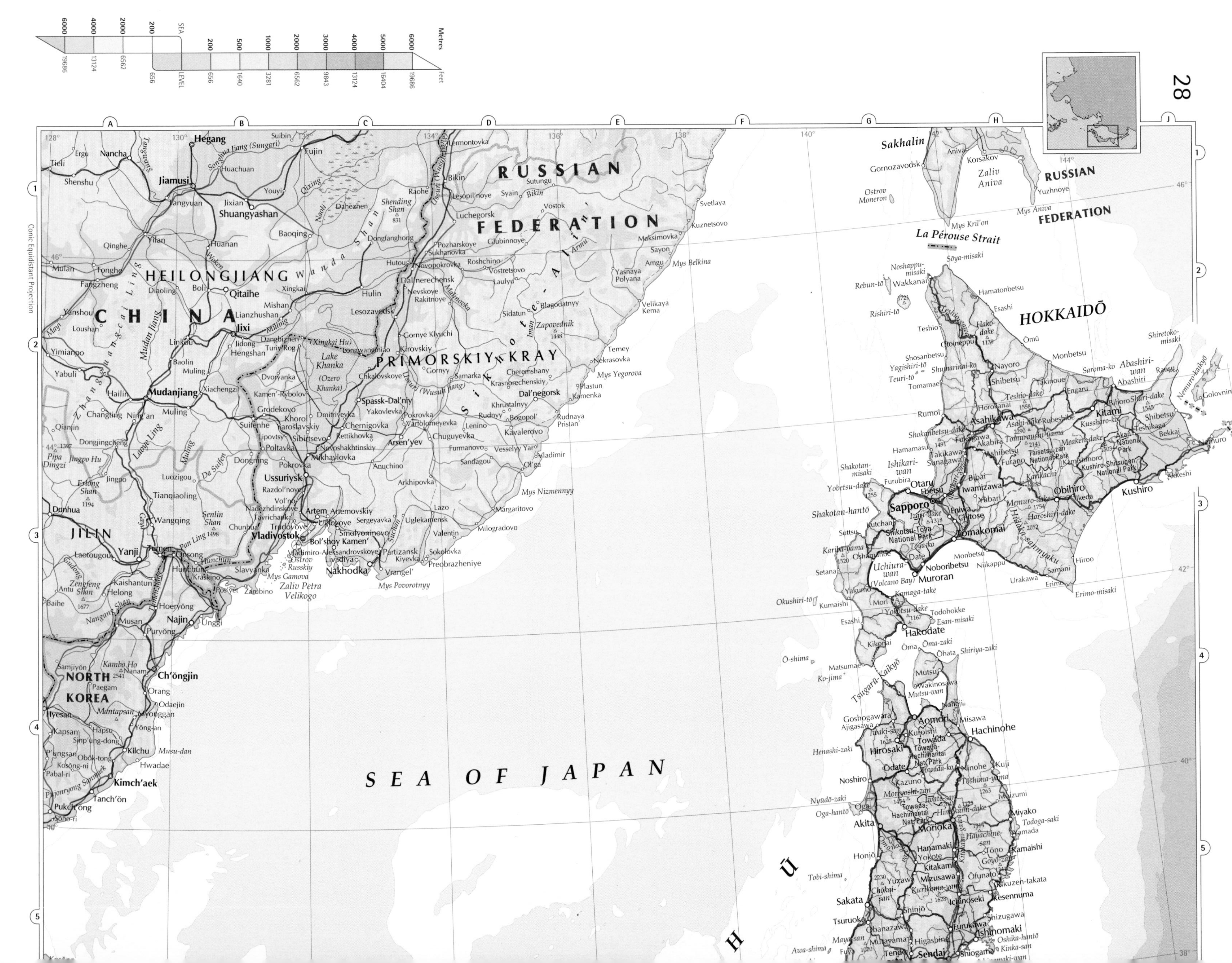

RUSSIAN FEDERATION

Sakhalin

HOKKAIDŌ

La Pérouse Strait

Sapporo

Hakodate

SEA OF JAPAN

RUSSIAN FEDERATION

PRIMORSKIY KRAY

Vladivostok

Nakhodka

HEILONGJIANG

CHINA

JILIN

NORTH KOREA

Metres / Feet

Metres	Feet
6000	19686
5000	16404
4000	13124
3000	9843
2000	6562
1000	3281
500	1640
200	656
SEA	LEVEL
200	656
2000	6562
4000	13124
6000	19686

Conic Equidistant Projection

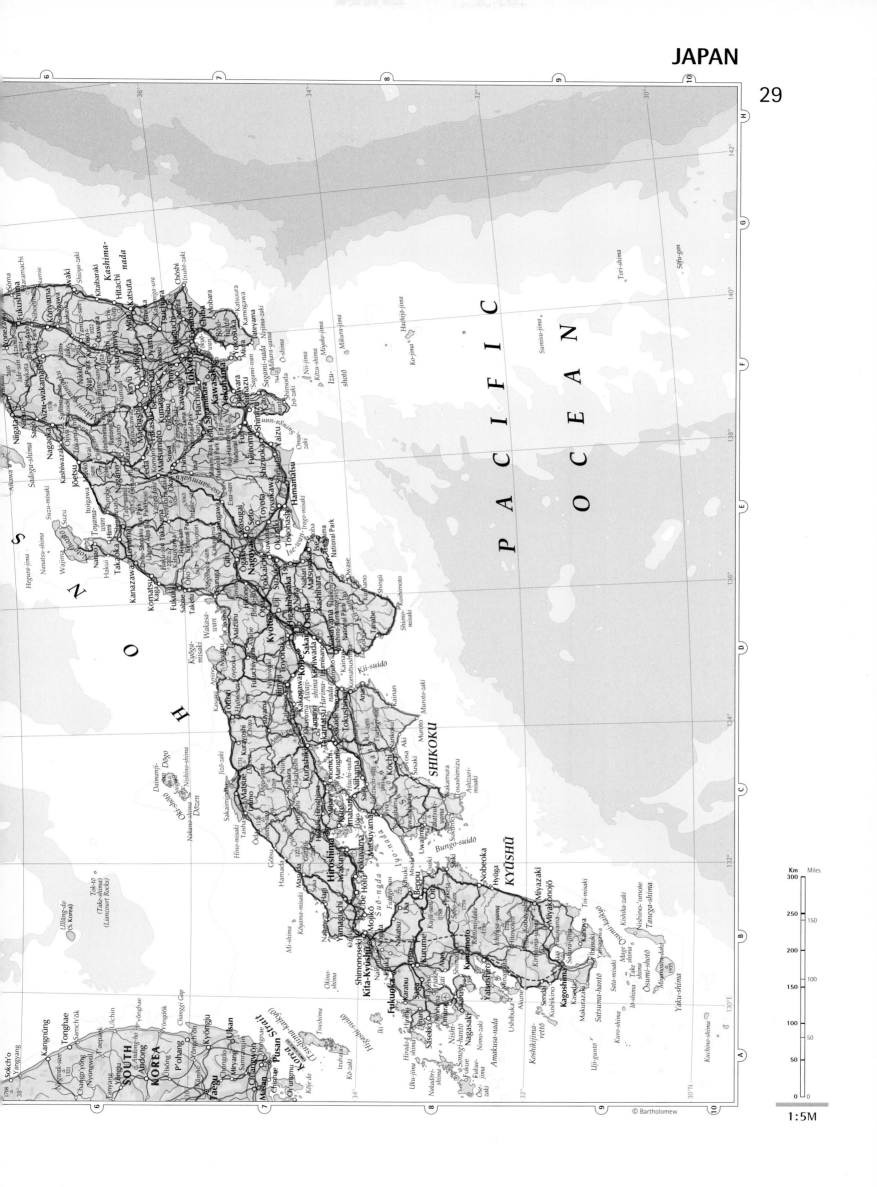

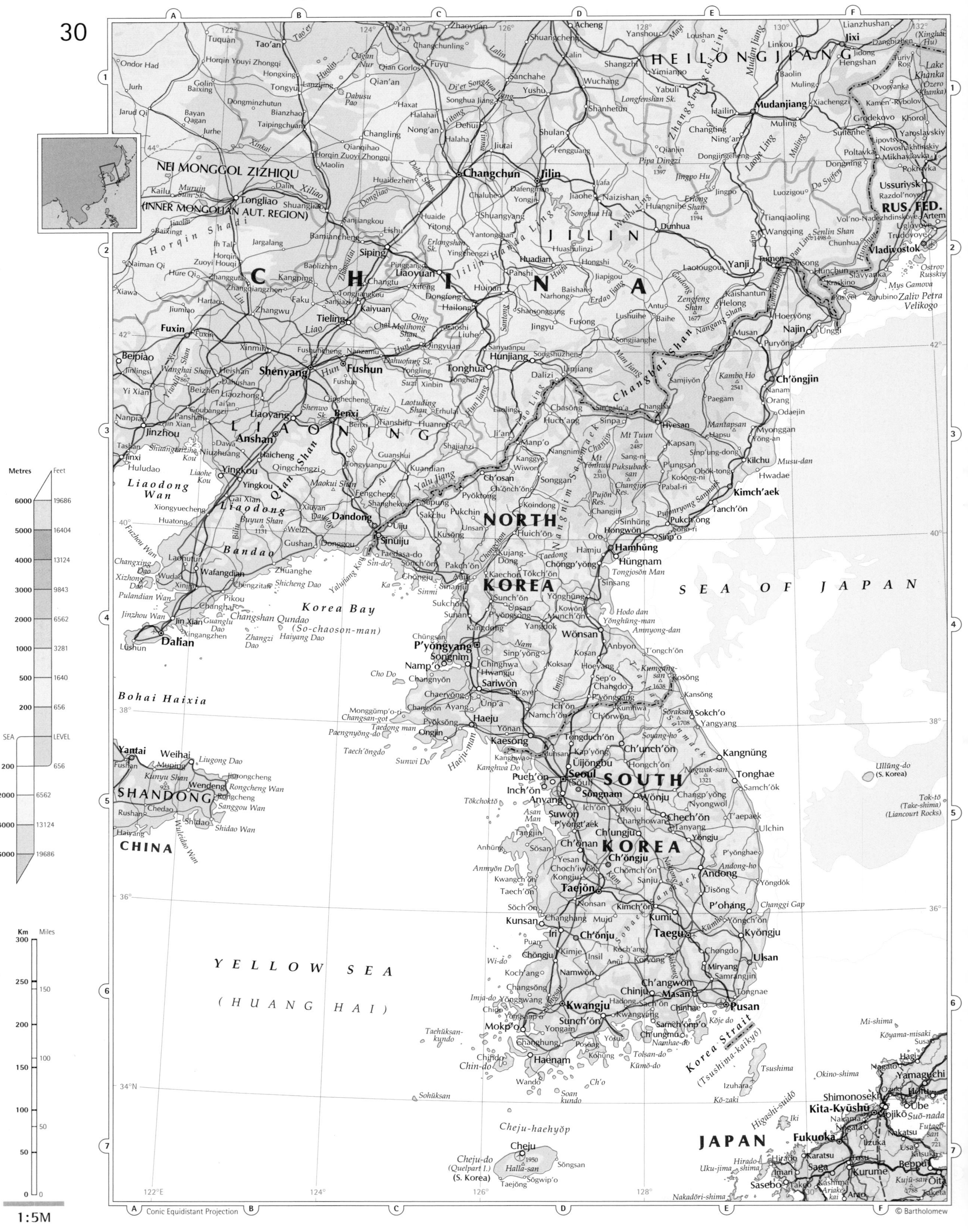

Conic Equidistant Projection

© Bartholomew

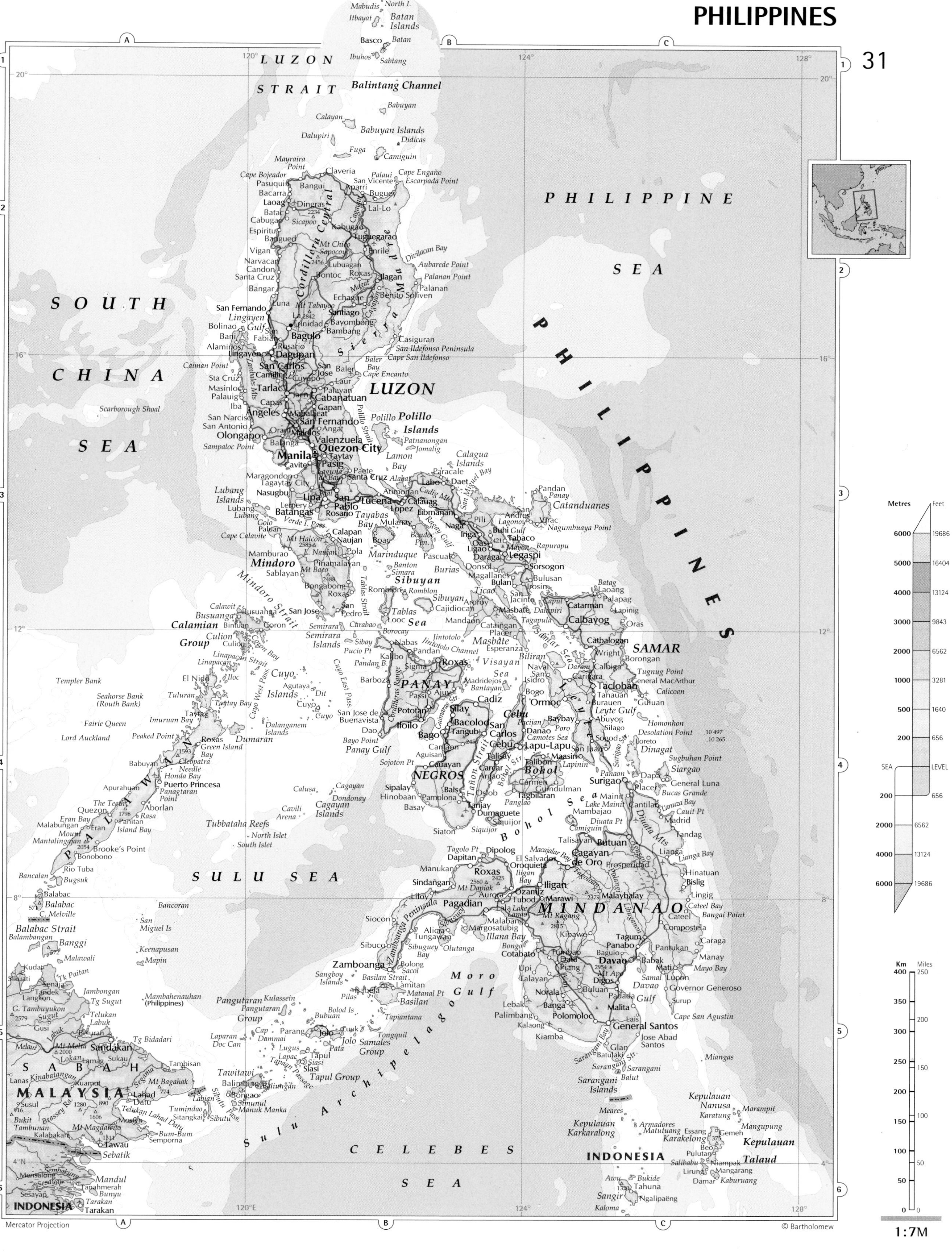

LUZON STRAIT

Balintang Channel

North I.
Mabudis
Itbayat   Batan
Basco   Batan
Ibuhos   Sabtang
Batan Islands

PHILIPPINE

SEA

Babuyan

Calayan   Babuyan Islands
Dalupiri   Didicas
Fuga   Camiguin

Mayraira Point
Cape Bojeador   Claveria   Palaui   Cape Engaño
Pasuquin   Bangui   Aparri   San Vicente   Escarpada Point
Bacarra   Laoag   Dingras   Buguey
Batac   Sicapoo   Lal-lo
Espiritu   2234   Kabugao   Tuguegarao
Cabugao   Bagued   Enrile   Divilacan Bay
Vigan   Bontoc   Roxas   Ilagan   Aubarede Point
Narvacan   2456   Lubuagan   Palanan Point
Candon   Echague   Palanan
Santa Cruz   Bangar   Santiago   Benito Soliven

San Fernando   Tuao   Mt Tabayo
Bolinao   Luna   Trinidad   Bayombong
Bani   Fabian   Bambang
Alaminos   Rosario   Casiguran
Lingayen   Dagupan   San Ildefonso Peninsula
Caiman Point   San Carlos   San   Baler   Cape San Ildefonso
Sta Cruz   Camiling   Jose   Baler Bay
Masinloc   Cuyapo   Laur   Cape Encanto
Palauig   Tarlac   Jaen   Cabanatuan   Polillo
Iba   Capas   Gapan   Polillo
San Narciso   Angeles   Mabalacat   Angat   Islands
San Antonio   San Fernando   Patnanongan   Jomalig
Olongapo   Orani   Valenzuela   Lamon Bay   Calagua
Sampaloc Point   Balanga   Quezon City   Paete   Islands
Maragondon   Manila   Taytay   Santa Cruz   Paracale
Cavite   Pasig   Alabat   Pandan
Tagaytay City   Laguna Bay   Daet   Panay
Nasugbu   Lipa   San   Lucena   Calauag   Labo   Catanduanes
Lubang   Lemery   Pablo   Lopez   Libmanan   Virac
Islands   Batangas   Rosario   Tayabas   Pili   Andres   Nagumbuaya Point
Lubang   Golo   Bay   Mulanay   Naga   Iriga   San
Lubang   Verde I. Pass   Bondoc   Lagonoy   Buhi Gulf
Paluan   Cape Calavite   Pan.   Pasacao   Oas   Rapurapu
Mamburao   Mt Halcon   Calapan   Boac   Ligao   Mayon   Tabaco
2585   Naujan   Marinduque   Daraga   2421   Legaspi
Mindoro   Pola   Simara   Donsol   Sorsogon
Sablayan   L. Naujan   Banton   Burias   Magallanes
Mt Baco   Pinamalayan   Sibuyan   Bulan   Irosin
2488   Bongabong   Romblon   Ticao   San
Mindoro Strait   Roxas   Sibuyan   Masbate   Jacinto   Batag
San   Tablas   Aroroy   Capul   Laoang   Palapag
Calawit   Busuanga   Pedro   Looc   Sea   Cataingan   Tagapula   Catarman   Oras
Culion   Binluan   Coron   Curabao   Mandaon   Lapinig
Calamian   Semirara   Cajidiocan   Masbate   Esperanza   Calbayog
Group   Culion   Islands   Borocay   Nabas   Jintotolo   Biliran   Catbalogan
Linapacan   Cuyo West Pass   Semirara   Sibay   Jintotolo Channel   Naval   San   Wright   SAMAR
El Nido   Islands   Pucio Pt   Pandan   Daram   Tagubilaran   Borongan
Agutaya   Dit   Kalibo   Pandan B.   Sigma   Calbiga   Tugnug Point
Tuluran   Cuyo   Sigma   Madridejos   Bogo   General MacArthur
Taytay   Cuyo   Roxas   Bantayan   Calicoan
Imuruan Bay   East Pass   PANAY   Passi   Tahauan   Guiuan
Tagtay Bay   Cuyo   Ajuy   Carcar   Leyte   Buraen   Tacloban
Templer Bank   Islands   Cadiz   Leyte Gulf   Abuyog
Seahorse Bank   Dalanganem   San Jose de   Pototan   Silay   Cebu   Baybay   Homonhon
(Routh Bank)   Islands   Buenavista   Iloilo   Bacolod   San   Danao   Poro   Homonhon
Fairie Queen   Bayo Point   Bago   Carlos   Cebu   Camotes Sea   Sogod   .10 497
Peaked Point   Dumaran   Panay Gulf   Dao   Tangub   Lapu-Lapu   Sogod St.   Desolation Point   .10 265
Lord Auckland   Roxas   Sojoton Pt   Talisay   Maasin   Doreto
Green Island   Cauayan   NEGROS   Argao   Panaon   Sugbuhan Point
Cleopatra   Honda Bay   Aguinsan   Bohol   Lapinin   Dinagat
Needle   Apurahuan   Sipalay   Bais   Talibon   Siargao
Puerto Princesa   1798   Hinobaan   Pamplona   Tagbilaran   Dapa   General Luna
Panagtaran Pt   Calusa   Pamplona   Guindulman   Maasin   Bucas Grande
Quezon   Aborlan   Dondonay   Basay   Tanjay   Cantilan   Place
Eran Bay   Island Bay   Cagayan   Dumaguete   Bohol   Mainit   Madrid
Eran   Panitan   Islands   Cavili   Siaton   Siquijor   Sea   Lake Mainit   Tandag
Malabungan   Cagayan   Arena   Camiguin   Diuata Pt   Cauit Pt
Mantalingajan   Tubbataha Reefs   Talisayan   Butuan   Diuata Mts
Mount   Brooke's Point   North Islet   Tagolo Pt   Dipolog   Macajalar Bay   Prosperidad   Lianga   Lianga Bay
2054   Bonobono   South Islet   Dapitan   El Salvador   Cagayan de Oro   Hinatuan
Bancalan   Rio Tuba   SULU SEA   Manukan   Iligan   Oroquieta   Bislig
Bugsuk   Sindangan   Iligan   Ozamiz   Malaybalay   Lingig
Balabac   Aurora   Tubod   Marawi   2379   Cateel Bay
57   C. Melville   Siocon   2560   Mt Dapiak   Lake Lanao   Mt Ragang   Bangai Point
Balabac   Liloy   2425   Marbel   2815   Compostela
Balabac Strait   Pagadian   MINDANAO   Caraga
Balambangan   Banggi   Zamboanga Peninsula   Kibawe   Tagum   Manay
Bunyu   Malawali   Bisuco   Malabang   Bongo   Panabo   Pantukan
Kudat   Malawali   Margosatubig   Illana Bay   Cotabato   Davao   Babak   Mati   Mayo Bay
Mapin   Alicia   Upi   Piang   2954   Samal   Lupon   Governor Generoso
Keenapusan   Tungawan   Kidapawan   Davao   Diges   Gulf   Surup
Banggi   San Miguel Is   Zamboanga   Norala   Banga   Padada   Cape San Agustin
Pangutaran   Kulassein   Bolong   Lebak   Palimbang   Polomoloc   Malita
Pangutaran   Sacol   Lamitan   Moro   Kalaong   Malita   Lais
Mambahenauhan   Group   Isabela   Basilan   Gulf   General Santos
(Philippines)   Sangboy   Basilan Strait   Mt Matanal Pt   Kiamba   Batulaki Gr   Jose Abad
Laparan   Islands   Pilas   Tapiantana   Saranggani Bay   Santos
Doc Can   Bubuan   Bold Is   Glan   Miangas
Cap.   Parang   Jolo   Tongquil   Samales   Saranggani   Balut   Saranggani
Dammai   Lugus   Pata   Group   Islands   Saranggani   Sarangani Islands
Tapul   Siasi   Meares   Armadores
Tapul Group   Siasi   Kepulauan   Matutuang Essang   Gemeh
Tawitawi   Balimbing   Bulongan   Karkaralong   Karakelong   Marampit
Sitangkai   Simunul   Manuk Manka   Kepulauan   Beo   Karatung
Sibutu   Nanusa   Mangupung
Kudat   Kalabakan   Langkon   Bagahak   Talaud   Lirung   Mangarang

SOUTH CHINA SEA

Scarborough Shoal

Lingayen Gulf

LUZON

South China Sea

Lubang Islands

Sibuyan Sea

Visayan Sea

Tablas Strait

Tañon Strait

Bohol Sea

Moro Gulf

SULU SEA

Sulu Archipelago

SABAH

MALAYSIA

Sandakan
Labuk
Lahad Datu
Semporna
Tawau
Sebatik
Tarakan

INDONESIA

CELEBES SEA

INDONESIA

PALAWAN

PHILIPPINE SEA

PHILIPPINES

© Bartholomew

Mercator Projection

1:7M

Metres	Feet
6000	19686
5000	16404
4000	13124
3000	9843
2000	6562
1000	3281
500	1640
200	656
SEA	LEVEL
200	656
2000	6562
4000	13124
6000	19686

Km	Miles
400	250
350	200
300	
250	150
200	100
150	
100	50
50	
0	0

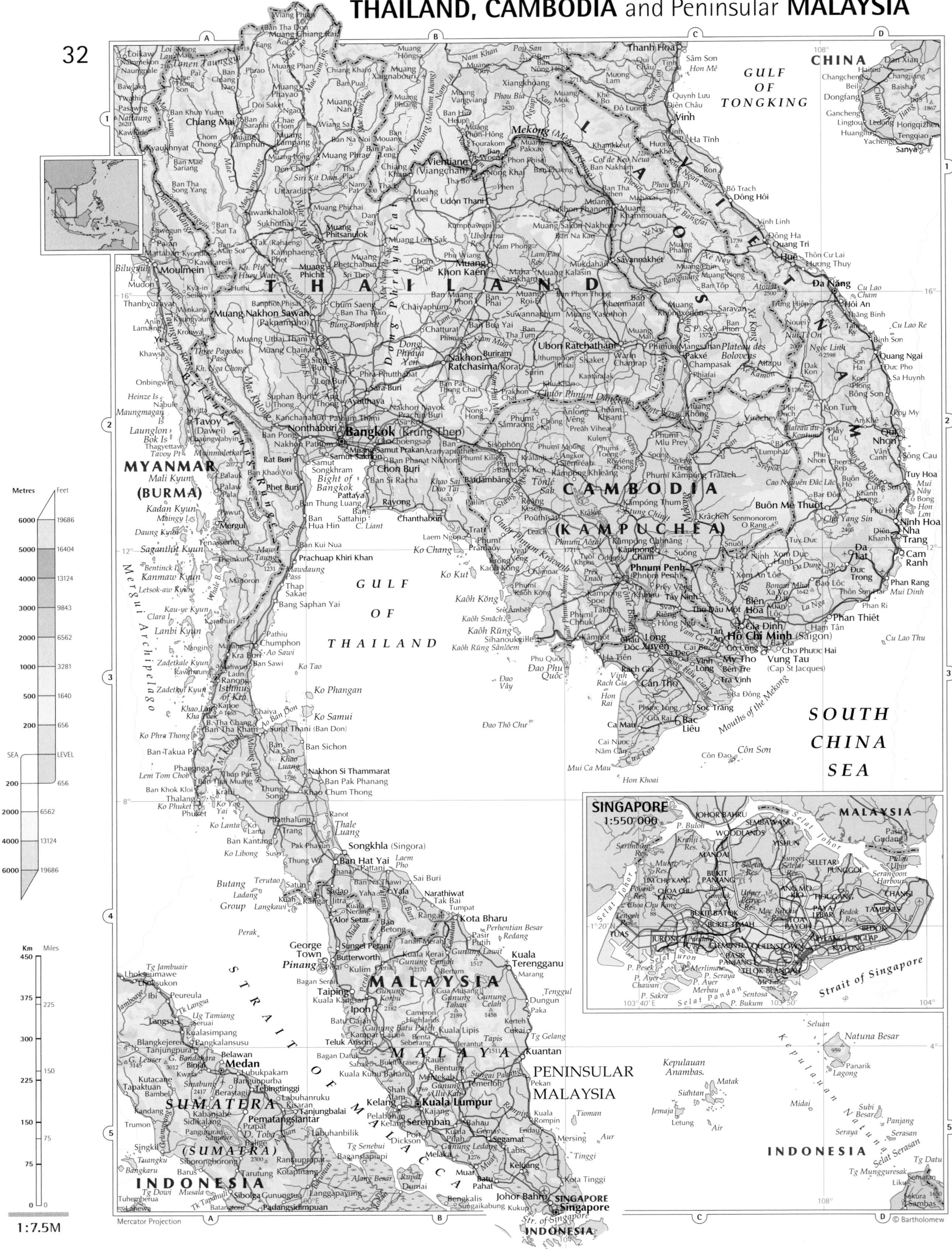

32

1:7.5M

Mercator Projection

© Bartholomew

West INDONESIA

Seas and Oceans
Celebes Sea
South China Sea
Andaman Sea
Java Sea
Bali Sea
Indian Ocean
Strait of Malacca
Macassar Strait
Balabac Strait
Selat Karimata

Countries / Regions
THAILAND
MALAYSIA
PENINSULAR MALAYSIA
SINGAPORE
BRUNEI
INDONESIA
SABAH
SARAWAK
BORNEO
KALIMANTAN
SUMATERA
PEGUNUNGAN BARISAN
Java (Jawa)

Selected place names

Sabah / Sarawak / Borneo (Kalimantan)
Sandakan, Tawau, Sebatik, Tarakan, Kota Kinabalu, Labuan (Victoria), Bandar Seri Begawan, Miri, Seria, Lutong, Bintulu, Sibu, Kuching, Pemangkat, Singkawang, Mempawah, Pontianak, Ketapang, Sukadana, Pangkalanbuun, Sampit, Palangkaraya, Banjarmasin, Martapura, Amuntai, Samarinda, Balikpapan, Longiram, Tanjungredeb, Tanjungselor, Sangkulirang

Sulawesi (Celebes)
Donggala, Parepare, Ujung Pandang, Bontosunggu, Majene, Mamuju, Polewali, Kotabaru

Sumatera
Banda Aceh, Sigli, Bireun, Langsa, Lhokseumawe, Medan, Pematangsiantar, Prapat, Sibolga, Padangsidimpuan, Rantauprapat, Labuhanbilik, Bukittinggi, Payakumbuh, Padang, Padangpanjang, Pekanbaru, Dumai, Jambi, Muarabungo, Sungaipenuh, Bengkulu, Manna, Bintuhan, Lubuklinggau, Lahat, Tebingtinggi, Baturaja, Kotabumi, Metro, Tanjungkarang Telukbetung, Palembang, Pangkalpinang, Pangkalbalam, Mentok, Belinyu, Tanjungpandan, Manggar, Tanjungpinang, Tanjungbalai

Peninsular Malaysia / Thailand / Singapore
Songkhla (Singora), Hat Yai, Pattani, Narathiwat, Kota Bharu, Yala, Alor Setar, Sungei Petani, George Town, Pinang, Butterworth, Taiping, Ipoh, Teluk Anson, Kuala Lumpur, Klang, Seremban, Melaka, Muar, Batu Pahat, Kluang, Segamat, Kuala Lipis, Kuantan, Kuala Terengganu, Dungun, Cukai, Mersing, Johor Bahru, Singapore

Java (Jawa)
Jakarta, Serang, Bogor, Sukabumi, Cianjur, Bandung, Tasikmalaya, Garut, Ciamis, Cirebon, Tegal, Pekalongan, Pemalang, Purwakarta, Karawang, Semarang, Salatiga, Kudus, Pati, Rembang, Tuban, Bojonegoro, Madiun, Kediri, Surakarta, Yogyakarta, Kebumen, Cilacap, Purwokerto, Magelang, Surabaya, Malang, Pasuruan, Probolinggo, Jember, Lumajang, Banyuwangi, Tulungagung, Pacitan

Bali / Lombok / Sumbawa
Denpasar, Singaraja, Mataram, Raba, Dompu, Sumbawa, Taliwang

Map scale / legend

Metres / Feet
6000 — 19686
5000 — 16404
4000 — 13124
3000 — 9843
2000 — 6562
1000 — 3281
500 — 1640
200 — 656
SEA LEVEL
200 — 656
2000 — 6562
4000 — 13124
6000 — 19686

Km / Miles
600 /
500 / 300
400 /
300 / 200
200 / 100
100 /
0 / 0

Mercator Projection

© Bartholomew

1:10M

Map Labels

Ocean and Sea Names:
Labrador Sea · Denmark Strait · Greenland Sea · Norwegian Sea · North Sea · ATLANTIC OCEAN · Bay of Biscay · English Channel · Irish Sea · Skagerrak · Kattegat · Adriatic Sea · MEDITERRANEAN

Greenland:
Greenland (Den.) · Kong Christian IX Land · Kong Frederick VI Kys · Arctic Circle · Prins Christian Sund · Scoresby Sund

Iceland:
ICELAND · Reykjavík · Keflavík · Vatnajökull · Húnaflói

Islands:
Jan Mayen (Nor.) · Svalbard (Nor.) · Shannon I. · Faroe Islands (Den.) · Shetland · Orkney · Outer Hebrides · Channel Is. (U.K.)

Azores:
Azores (Port.) · São Jorge · Terceira · Pico · São Miguel · Santa Maria

Madeira / Canary Islands:
Madeira (Port.) · Funchal · Canary Islands (Spain) · La Palma · Tenerife · Santa Cruz · Gran Canaria · Las Palmas · Fuerteventura · Lanzarote

United Kingdom & Ireland:
UNITED KINGDOM · SCOTLAND · ENGLAND · WALES · N. IRELAND · REP. OF IRELAND · London · Birmingham · Manchester · Leeds · Liverpool · Cardiff · Glasgow · Edinburgh · Belfast · Dublin · Cork

Norway / Sweden / Denmark:
NORWAY · SWEDEN · DENMARK · Oslo · Bergen · Voss · Trondheim · Stavanger · Kristiansand · Drammen · Lillehammer · Copenhagen · Malmö · Gothenburg · Ålborg · Odense · Esbjerg · Bornholm · Vänern · Vättern · Uppsala

Germany / Low Countries:
GERMANY · NETHERLANDS · BELGIUM · LUXEMBOURG · Berlin · Hamburg · Hannover · Bonn · Cologne · Essen · Frankfurt · Leipzig · Stuttgart · München · Koblenz · Amsterdam · Rotterdam · The Hague · Brussels · Lille · Poznań · Wrocław · Prague · CZECH REP. · Brno · Elbe · Rhine · Danube

France:
FRANCE · Paris · Orléans · Tours · Dijon · Strasbourg · Reims · Bordeaux · Toulouse · Nîmes · Marseille · Nice · Lyon · La Rochelle · Seine · Loire · Rhône

Switzerland / Austria:
SWITZERLAND · AUSTRIA · LIECHTENSTEIN · Bern · Geneva · Lausanne · Zürich · Salzburg · Vienna · Bratislava · Mt. Blanc 4808

Spain / Portugal / Andorra:
SPAIN · PORTUGAL · ANDORRA · Andorra la Vella · Madrid · Barcelona · Zaragoza · Bilbao · Ourense · Oporto · Lisbon · Toledo · Seville · Granada · Málaga · Cádiz · Valencia · Alicante · Cartagena · Pyrenees · Tagus · Douro · Cabo Fisterra · Cabo de São Vicente · Gibraltar (U.K.) · Str. of Gibraltar

Balearic Islands:
Balearic Islands · Mallorca · Menorca · Ibiza · Palma de Mallorca

Italy:
ITALY · Rome · Milan · Turin · Genoa · Venice · Bologna · Florence · Livorno · Pisa · Naples · MONACO · SAN MARINO · VATICAN CITY · Corsica · Sardinia · Sicily · Palermo · Syracuse · MALTA · Valletta

Slovenia / Croatia / Bosnia:
SLOVENIA · CROATIA · BOSNIA-HERZEGOVINA · Ljubljana · Zagreb · Split · Sarajevo

North Africa:
MOROCCO · ALGERIA · TUNISIA · Casablanca · Rabat · Fès · Marrakech · Tangier · Oran · Algiers · Annaba · Tunis · Tripoli · Béchar

Grid labels: B · C · D · E · F · 2 · 3 · 4 · 5 · 6
Latitude/Longitude: 60° · 40° · 70° · 30° · 10° · 0° · 50° · 40° · 30° · 20° · 30°N · 10°W

Metres SEA LEVEL · Feet LEVEL · 200 · 656 · 3000 · 9843

Chamberlin Trimetric Projection

EUROPE

35

BARENTS SEA
Kara Sea
White Sea
FINLAND
RUSSIAN FEDERATION (in Asia)
Ural Mountains
Moscow
Kiev
UKRAINE
KAZAKSTAN
Aral Sea
UZBEKISTAN
TURKMENISTAN
Caspian Sea
Black Sea
TURKEY
GREECE
Athens
ROMANIA
Bucharest
BULGARIA
Sofia
Istanbul
Ankara
SYRIA
IRAQ
Baghdad
IRAN
Tehrān
The Gulf

1:18M

© Bartholomew

36

BARENTS SEA

MURMANSKAYA OBLAST

RUSSIAN FEDERATION

RESP. KARELIYA

FINLAND

LAPPLAND

VÄINHÖL

Bottenviken (Perämeri)

NORRLAND

NORWEGIAN SEA

ICELAND
at the same scale

FAROE ISLANDS (Denmark)
at the same scale

Metres	Feet
6000	19686
5000	16404
4000	13124
3000	9843
2000	6562
1000	3281
500	1640
200	656
SEA	LEVEL
200	656
2000	6562
4000	13124
6000	19686

Conic Equidistant Projection

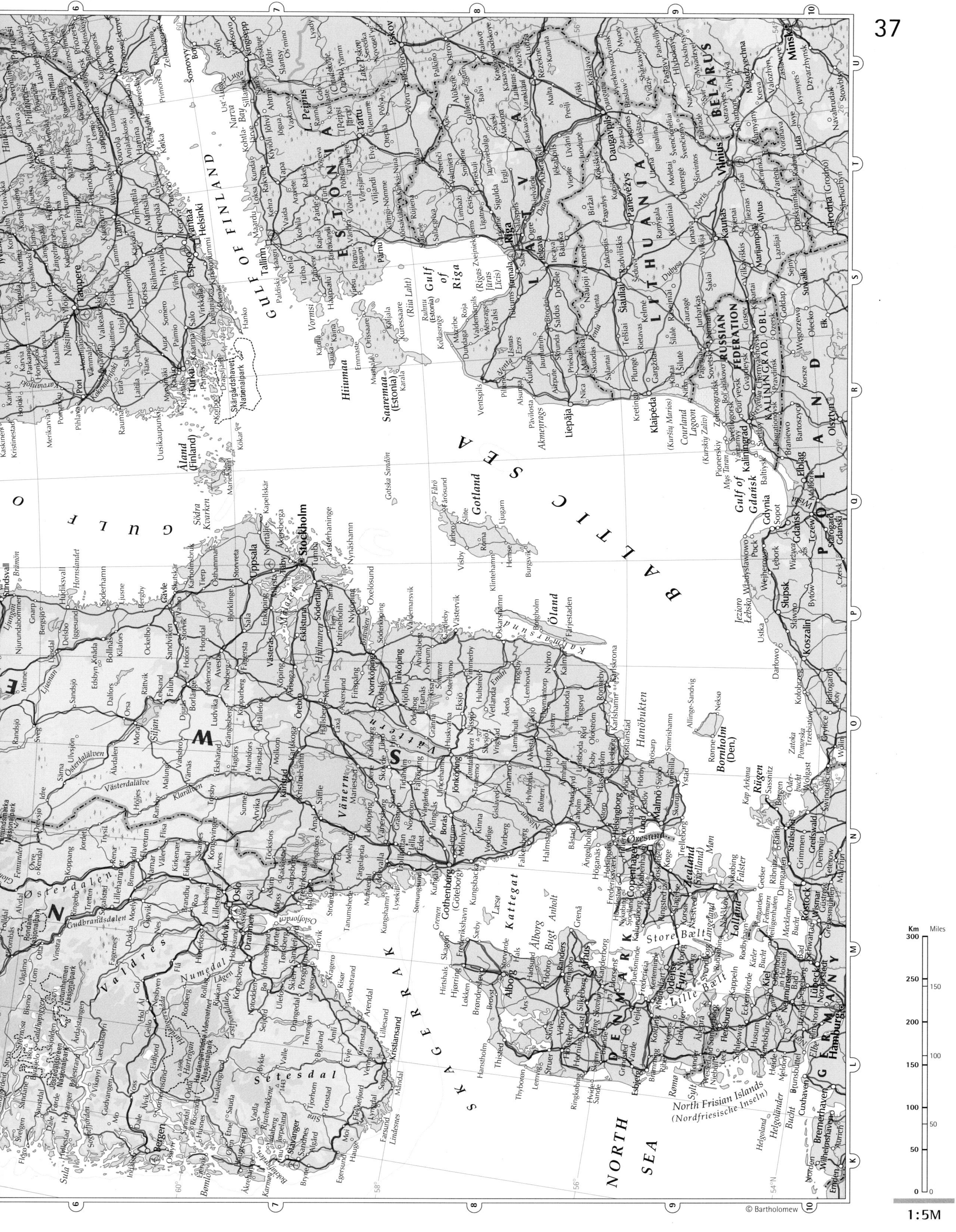

1:5M

© Bartholomew

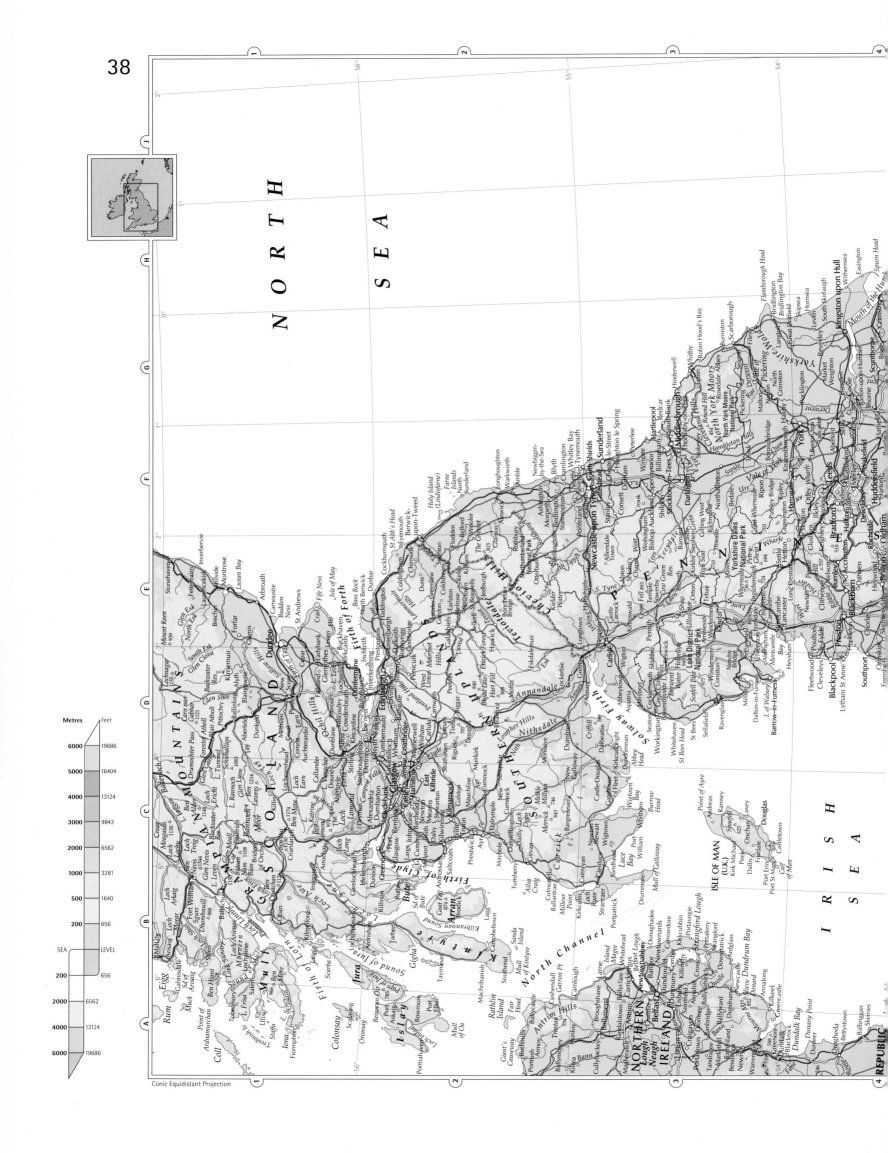

38

NORTH SEA

IRISH SEA

Metres / Feet

Metres	Feet
6000	19686
5000	16404
4000	13124
3000	9843
2000	6562
1000	3281
500	1640
200	656
SEA	LEVEL
200	656
2000	6562
4000	13124
6000	19686

Conic Equidistant Projection

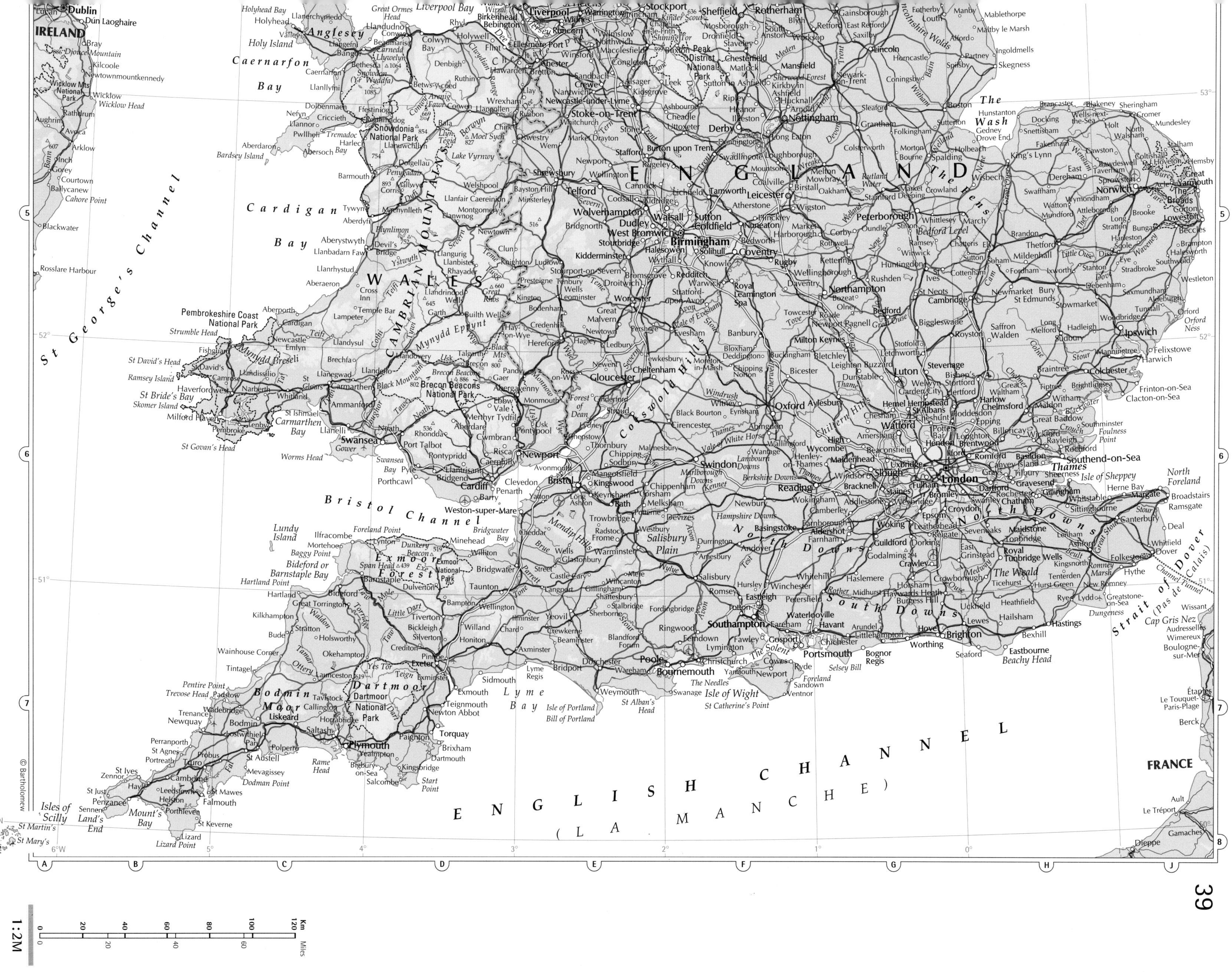

FRANCE

IRELAND

Km Miles
120
100   60
80
60   40
40
20
0   0

1:2M

© Bartholomew

ATLANTIC OCEAN

NORTH SEA

SCOTLAND

ENGLAND

NORTHERN IRELAND

Regions / Mountains
- Outer Hebrides
- Lewis
- Harris
- North Uist
- South Uist
- Benbecula
- Barra
- Skye
- Cuillin Hills
- Grampian Mountains
- Monadhliath Mountains
- Cairngorm Mountains
- Southern Uplands
- Cheviot Hills
- Argyll
- Kintyre
- Mull
- Islay
- Jura
- Arran
- Rannoch Moor
- Black Isle
- Inishowen
- Sperrin Mts

Firths & Seas
- The Minch
- Little Minch
- Inner Sound
- Moray Firth
- Pentland Firth
- Firth of Lorn
- Sound of Mull
- Sound of Jura
- Firth of Clyde
- Firth of Forth
- Firth of Tay
- Solway Firth
- North Channel
- Dornoch Firth
- Cromarty Firth

Islands
- Orkney Is
- Shetland
- Fair Isle
- Mainland
- Hoy
- Westray
- Sanday
- Stronsay
- Eday
- Rousay
- Unst
- Yell
- Fetlar
- Whalsay
- Bressay
- Foula
- Rona
- Flannan Isles
- Scarp
- Taransay
- Scalpay
- Raasay
- Rum
- Eigg
- Muck
- Canna
- Coll
- Tiree
- Mull
- Iona
- Colonsay
- Oronsay
- Gigha
- Bute
- Cumbrae
- Ailsa Craig
- Bass Rock
- Holy Island (Lindisfarne)
- Isle of May
- Rathlin Island
- Sanda Island
- Isle of Noss

Mountains / Heights
- Ben Nevis 1344
- Ben Macdui
- Ben Lawers 1214
- Ben More
- Ben Hope 927
- Ben Loyal 764
- Ben Klibreck 961
- Ben Wyvis
- Foinaven 915
- Clisham 799
- The Storr 719
- Cairn Gorm 1245
- Ben Alder
- Schiehallion
- Goat Fell 874
- Merrick 843
- The Cheviot 815
- Broad Law 840
- Hart Fell 808
- Meikle Millyea 746
- Mount Keen 939

Cities & Towns
- Aberdeen
- Edinburgh
- Glasgow
- Dundee
- Inverness
- Fort William
- Oban
- Perth
- Stirling
- Ayr
- Dumfries
- Stranraer
- Kilmarnock
- Paisley
- Greenock
- Motherwell
- Hamilton
- East Kilbride
- Falkirk
- Livingston
- Dunfermline
- Kirkcaldy
- St Andrews
- Montrose
- Arbroath
- Brechin
- Forfar
- Peterhead
- Fraserburgh
- Elgin
- Nairn
- Wick
- Thurso
- John o' Groats
- Ullapool
- Stornoway
- Portree
- Mallaig
- Campbeltown
- Lerwick
- Kirkwall
- Stromness
- Carlisle
- Newcastle upon Tyne
- Berwick-upon-Tweed
- Londonderry
- Belfast
- Ballymena
- Larne

Lochs
- Loch Ness
- Loch Lomond
- Loch Awe
- Loch Fyne
- Loch Long
- Loch Shin
- Loch Maree
- Loch Tay
- Loch Rannoch
- Loch Ericht
- Loch Katrine
- Loch Lochy
- Loch Linnhe
- Loch Shiel
- Loch Morar
- Loch Arkaig
- Loch Leven
- Lough Neagh
- Lough Foyle

Other features
- Cape Wrath
- Dunnet Head
- Duncansby Head
- Mull of Kintyre
- Mull of Galloway
- Butt of Lewis
- Rattray Head
- Kinnaird Head
- Sumburgh Head
- Herma Ness
- Malin Head
- Giant's Causeway
- Lake District National Park
- Northumberland National Park

Scale / Legend
Metres / Feet
- 6000 / 19686
- 5000 / 16404
- 4000 / 13124
- 3000 / 9843
- 2000 / 6562
- 1000 / 3281
- 500 / 1640
- 200 / 656
- SEA LEVEL
- 200 / 656
- 2000 / 6562
- 4000 / 13124
- 6000 / 19686

Km / Miles
- 120 /
- 100 / 60
- 80 /
- 60 / 40
- 40 /
- 20 /
- 0 / 0

SHETLAND at the same scale

1:2M

Conic Equidistant Projection

© Bartholomew

IRELAND

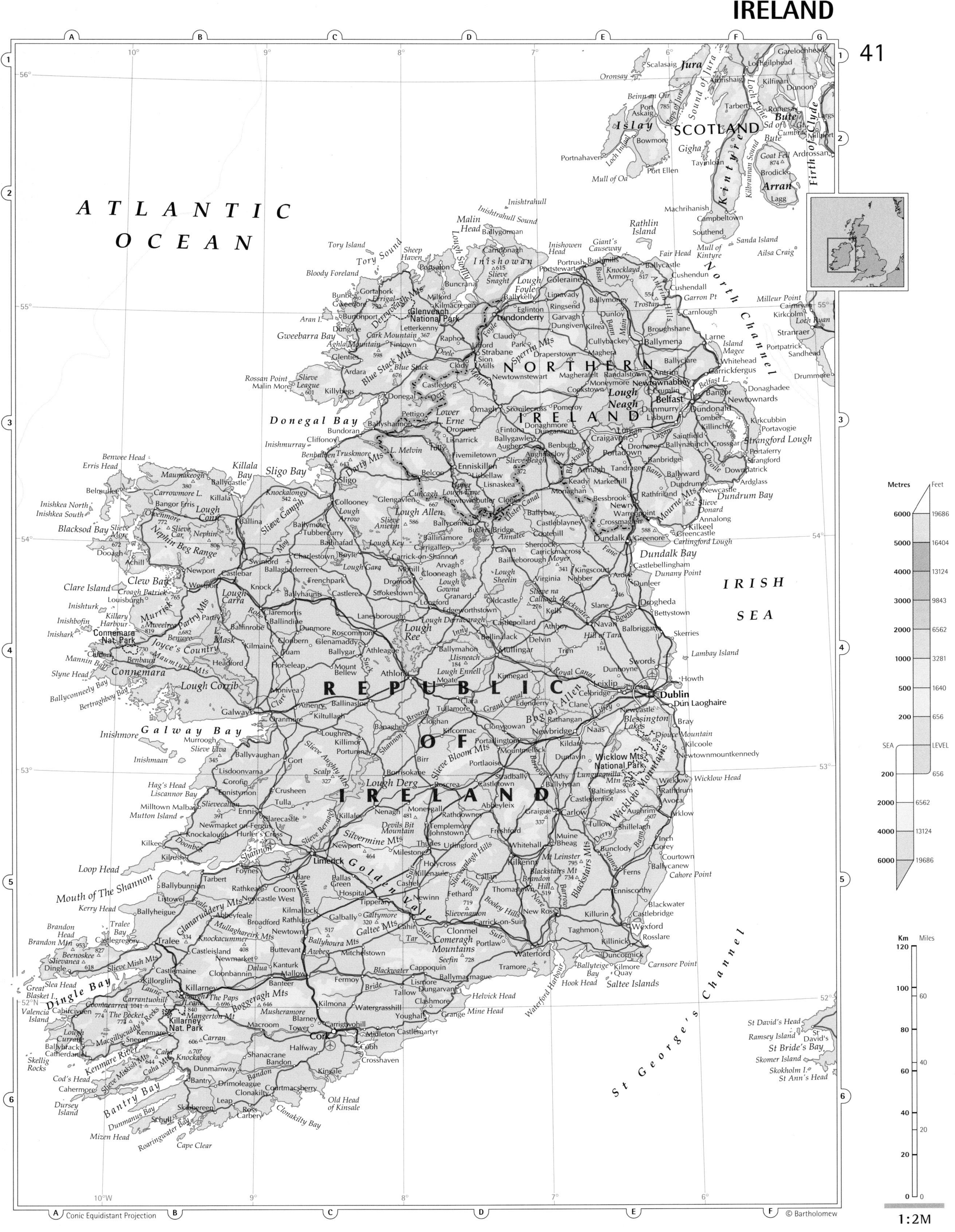
ATLANTIC OCEAN
IRISH SEA
North Channel
St George's Channel
SCOTLAND
NORTHERN IRELAND
REPUBLIC OF IRELAND
Jura
Islay
Kintyre
Arran
Bute
Firth of Clyde
Sound of Jura
Loch Fyne
Kilbrannan Sound
Oronsay
Scalasaig
Lochgilphead
Garelochhead
Ardrishaig
Kilfinan
Dunoon
Tarbert
Rothesay
Beinn an Oir
Port Askaig
Bowmore
Portnahaven
Loch Indaal
Port Ellen
Mull of Oa
Gigha
Tayinloan
Goat Fell
Brodick
Ardrossan
Millport
Cumbrae
Lagg
Machrihanish
Campbeltown
Southend
Mull of Kintyre
Sanda Island
Ailsa Craig
Milleur Point
Cairnryan
Kirkcolm
Loch Ryan
Stranraer
Portpatrick
Sandhead
Drummore
Inishtrahull
Inishtrahull Sound
Malin Head
Ballygorman
Rathlin Island
Giant's Causeway
Inishowen Head
Fair Head
Tory Island
Tory Sound
Sheep Haven
Bloody Foreland
Lough Swilly
Inishowen
Slieve Snaght
Carndonagh
Buncrana
Lough Foyle
Portrush
Portstewart
Bushmills
Ballycastle
Knocklayd
Armoy
Cushendun
Cushendall
Garron Pt
Coleraine
Limavady
Ballykelly
Eglinton
Londonderry
Ringsend
Garvagh
Dungiven
Kilrea
Ballymoney
Dunloy
Trostan
Antrim Hills
Carnlough
Broughshane
Ballymena
Larne
Island Magee
Whitehead
Carrickfergus
Belfast L.
Bangor
Donaghadee
Newtownards
Newtownabbey
Belfast
Dundonald
Comber
Killinchy
Kirkcubbin
Portavogie
Strangford Lough
Portaferry
Strangford
Downpatrick
Ardglass
Dundrum Bay
Newcastle
Slieve Donard
Annalong
Kilkeel
Greencastle
Carlingford Lough
Bunbeg
Gweedore
Gortahork
Errigal
Derryveagh Mts
Glenveagh National Park
Milford
Kilmacrenan
Burtonport
Aran I.
Dungloe
Letterkenny
Cark Mountain
Gweebarra Bay
Aghla Mountain
Fintown
Glenties
Raphoe
Lifford
Strabane
Sion Mills
Claudy
Park
Sperrin Mts
Draperstown
Maghera
Cullybackey
Ballyclare
Randalstown
Antrim
Magherafelt
Moneymore
Cookstown
Lough Neagh
Crumlin
Dunmurry
Lisburn
Newtownstewart
Blue Stack Mts
Blue Stack
Ardara
Killybegs
Rossan Point
Malin More
Slieve League
Donegal
Donegal Bay
Ballyshannon
Bundoran
Castlederg
Pettigo
Lower Lough Erne
Omagh
Dromore
Sixmilecross
Pomeroy
Donaghmore
Dungannon
Lisnarrick
Fintona
Ballygawley
Augher
Aughnacloy
Portadown
Lurgan
Craigavon
Saintfield
Ballynahinch
Crossgar
Dromore
Banbridge
Tandragee
Armagh
Markethill
Keady
Ballyward
Dundrum
Rathfriland
Mourne Mts
Bessbrook
Newry
Warrenpoint
Crossmaglen
Inishmurray
Cliffoney
Benbulben
Truskmore
Dartry Mts
L. Melvin
Tully
Fivemiletown
Enniskillen
Lisbellaw
Lisnaskea
Slieve Beagh
Belcoo
Cuilcagh
Upper Lough Erne
Newtownbutler
Clones
Ulster Canal
Monaghan
Ballybay
Castleblayney
Cootehill
Dundalk
Greenore
Dundalk Bay
Benwee Head
Erris Head
Killala Bay
Maumakeogh
Ballycastle
Belmullet
Carrowmore L.
Killala
Inishkea North
Inishkea South
Bangor Erris
Lough Conn
Ballina
Sligo Bay
Sligo
Knockalongy
Slieve Gamph
Collooney
Lough Arrow
Glengavlen
Lough Allen
Slieve Anierin
Ballyconnell
Butlers Bridge
Annalee
Blacksod Bay
Slieve More
Nephin
Nephin Beg Range
Dooagh
Achill
Ballymote
Tubbercurry
Ballinafad
Lough Key
Carrigallen
Ballinamore
Cavan
Shercock
Carrickmacross
Bailieborough
Moyer
Kingscourt
Nobber
Ardee
Castlebellingham
Dunany Point
Dunleer
Drogheda
Bettystown
Clare Island
Clew Bay
Croagh Patrick
Louisburgh
Newport
Castlebar
Westport
Swinford
Charlestown
Boyle
Carrick-on-Shannon
Arvagh
Ballaghaderreen
Lough Gara
Mohill
Cloonagh
Lough Gowna
Granard
Lough Sheelin
Virginia
Oldcastle
Slieve na Calliagh
Kells
Slane
Navan
Athboy
Inishturk
Killary Harbour
Murrisk
Partry Mts
Lough Carra
Knock
Ballyhaunis
Frenchpark
Castlerea
Dromod
Strokestown
Longford
Edgeworthstown
Lough Derravaragh
Castlepollard
Inishbofin
Inishark
Connemara Nat. Park
Mweelrea
Benwee
Joyce's Country
Maumturk Mts
Lough Mask
Ballinrobe
Claremorris
Ballindine
Dunmore
Roscommon
Lanesborough
Lough Ree
Ballinalack
Delvin
Trim
Hill of Tara
Balbriggan
Skerries
Lambay Island
Swords
Howth
Dublin
Dún Laoghaire
Mannin Bay
Clifden
Benbaun
Slyne Head
Connemara
Ballyconneely Bay
Bertraghboy Bay
Headford
Lough Corrib
Kilmaine
Clonberne
Tuam
Glenamaddy
Ballygar
Athleague
Horseleap
Mount Bellew
Athlone
Ballymahon
Uisneach
Lough Ennell
Moate
Mullingar
Kinnegad
Royal Canal
Dunboyne
Leixlip
Lucan
Celbridge
Monivea
Clare
Athenry
Ballinasloe
Kiltullagh
Galway
Oranmore
Galway Bay
Inishmore
Inishmaan
Murroogh
Slieve Elva
Ballyvaughan
Gort
Loughrea
Killimor
Portumna
Slieve Aughty Mts
Scalp
Banagher
Shannon
Brosna
Cloghan
Birr
Clara
Tullamore
Grand Canal
Edenderry
Bog of Allen
Rathangan
Kilcormac
Clonygowan
Portarlington
Mountmellick
Newbridge
Naas
Kildare
Liffey
Newcastle
Blessington Lakes
Bray
Djouce Mountain
Kilcoole
Newtownmountkennedy
Wicklow Mts National Park
Lugnaquilla Mtn
Wicklow Mountains
Wicklow
Wicklow Head
Rathdrum
Avoca
Arklow
Aughrim
Shillelagh
Inch
Gorey
Courtown
Ballycanew
Cahore Point
Lisdoonvarna
Hag's Head
Liscannor Bay
Corofin
Ennistymon
Crusheen
Tulla
Milltown Malbay
Mutton Island
Slievecallan
Ennis
Clarecastle
Newmarket on Fergus
Hurler's Cross
Knockalough
Kilkee
Doonbeg
Kilrush
Lough Derg
Borrisokane
Roscrea
Slieve Bloom Mts
Portlaoise
Stradbally
Castletown
Athy
Ballylynan
Baltinglass
Castledermot
Killaloe
Nenagh
Monegall
Rathdowney
Abbeyleix
Devils Bit Mountain
Templemore
Johnstown
Silvermine Mts
Slieve Bernagh
Newport
Thurles
Urlingford
Freshford
Kilkenny
Graigue
Carlow
Tullow
Muine Bheag
Whitehall
Mt Leinster
Blackstairs Mt
Blackstairs Mts
Bunclody
Ferns
Enniscorthy
Limerick
Golden Vale
Loop Head
Mouth of The Shannon
Kerry Head
Tarbert
Foynes
Adare
Ballybunnion
Listowel
Rathkeale
Croom
Pallas Green
Hospital
Cashel
Killenaule
Holycross
Tipperary
Newcastle West
Abbeyfeale
Kilmallock
Rathluirc
Galbally
Galtymore
Galtee Mts
Cahir
Tar
Newinn
Fethard
Callan
Thomastown
Brandon Hill
New Ross
Barrow
Nore
Booley Hills
Slievenamon
Clonmel
Carrick-on-Suir
Suir
Waterford
Tramore
Waterford Harbour
Ballyhoura Mts
Mitchelstown
Comeragh Mountains
Seefin
Portlaw
Killurin
Wexford
Rosslare
Taghmon
Killinick
Duncormick
Kilmore Quay
Ballyteige Bay
Hook Head
Saltee Islands
Carnsore Point
Brandon Head
Brandon Mtn
Tralee Bay
Castlegregory
Tralee
Ballyheigue
Glanaruddery Mts
Mullaghareirk Mts
Knockacummer
Broadford
Newtown
Buttevant
Castleisland
Newmarket
Kanturk
Mallow
Awbeg
Fermoy
Blackwater
Cappoquin
Ballymacmague
Lismore
Dungarvan
Clashmore
Helvick Head
Mine Head
Youghal
Beenoskee
Slievanea
Dingle
Slieve Mish Mts
Castlemaine
Cloonbannin
Dalua
Banteer
Dingle Bay
Great Blasket I.
Slea Head
Killorglin
Laune
Killarney
The Paps
Boggeragh Mts
Musheramore
Kilmona
Watergrasshill
Carrigtwohill
Midleton
Castlemartyr
Cobh
Cork
Crosshaven
Valencia Island
Cahirciveen
Coomacarrea
Carrantuohill
Leane
Killarney Nat. Park
Mangerton Mt
Macroom
Blarney
Tower
The Pocket
Lough Currane
Macgillycuddy's Reeks
Kenmare
Sneem
Ballybrack
Catherdaniel
Skellig Rocks
Kenmare River
Slieve Miskish Mts
Caha Mts
Carran
Knockaboy
Shanacrane
Bandon
Halfway
Kinsale
Old Head of Kinsale
Cod's Head
Cahermore
Dursey Island
Bantry Bay
Bantry
Dunmanway
Drimoleague
Clonakilty
Courtmacsberry
Clonakilty Bay
Leap
Ross Carbery
Skibbereen
Schull
Dunmanus Bay
Roaringwater Bay
Mizen Head
Cape Clear
St David's Head
Ramsey Island
St David's
St Bride's Bay
Skomer Island
Skokholm I.
St Ann's Head
Metres
Feet
6000
5000
4000
3000
2000
1000
500
200
SEA
LEVEL
19686
16404
13124
9843
6562
3281
1640
656
Km
Miles
Conic Equidistant Projection
© Bartholomew

1:2M

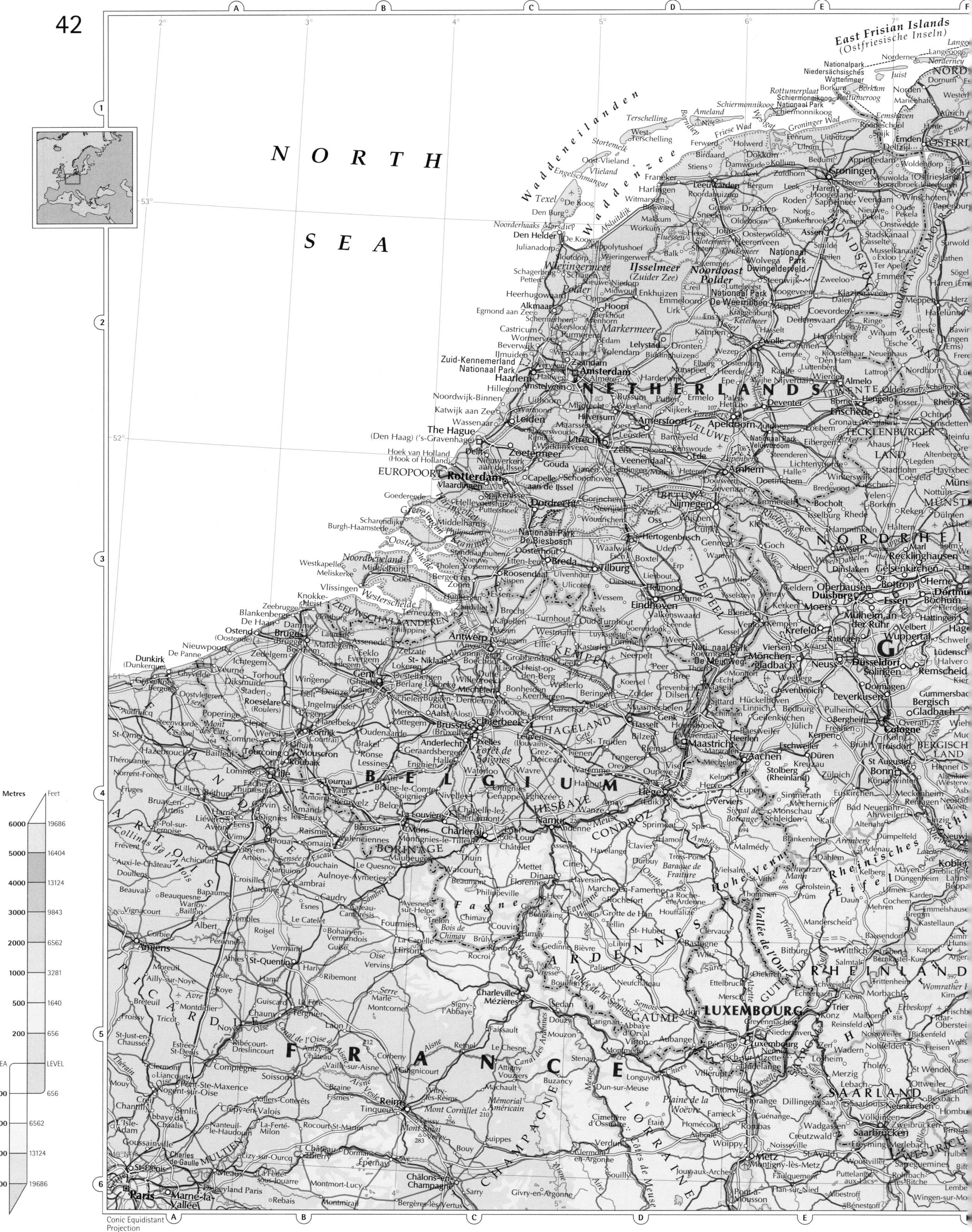

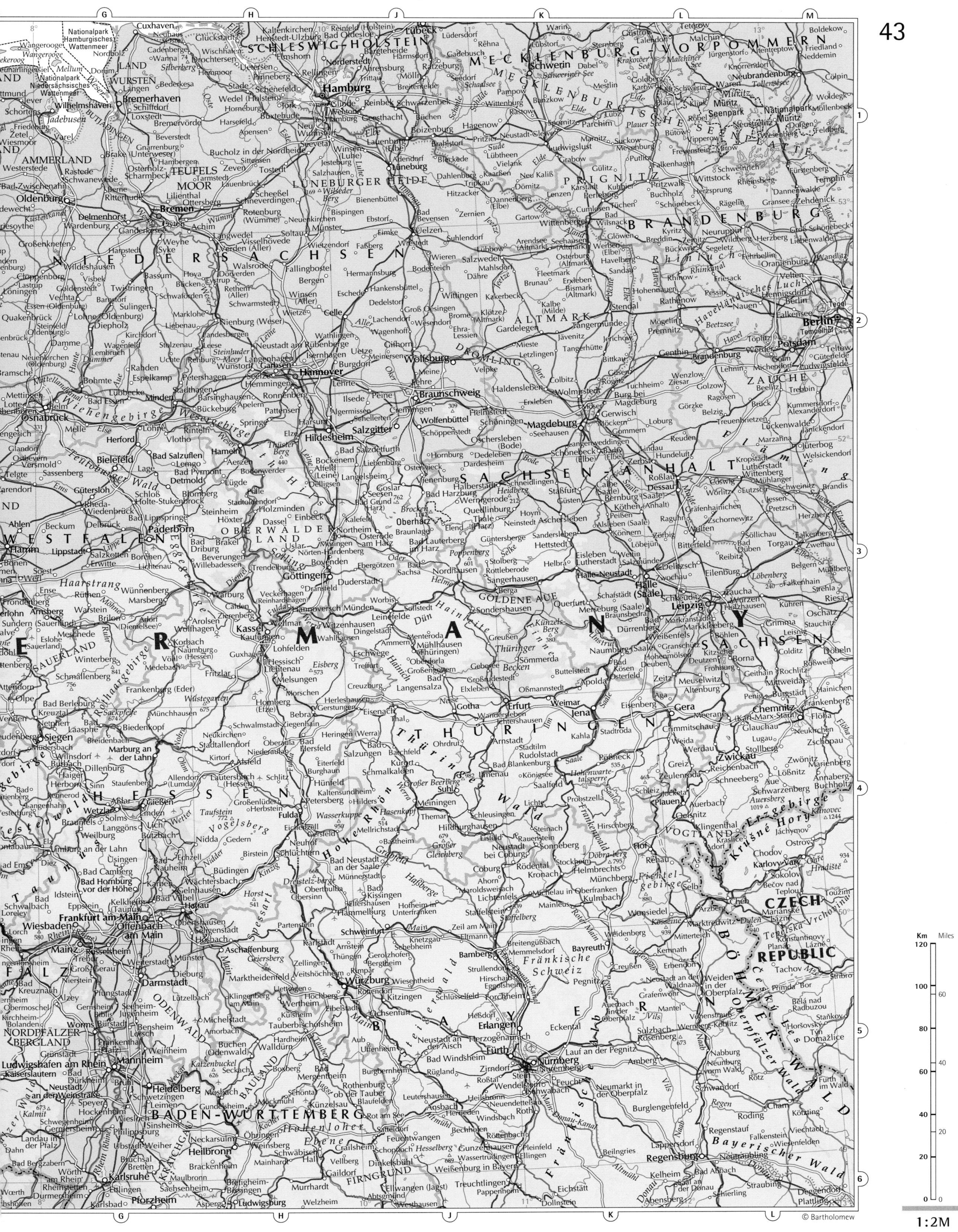

SCHLESWIG-HOLSTEIN
MECKLENBURG-VORPOMMERN
NIEDERSACHSEN
BRANDENBURG
SACHSEN-ANHALT
WESTFALEN
HESSEN
THÜRINGEN
SACHSEN
BAYERN
BADEN-WÜRTTEMBERG
GERMANY
CZECH REPUBLIC
LÜNEBURGER HEIDE
ALTMARK
TEUFELS MOOR
Hamburg
Bremen
Bremerhaven
Hannover
Braunschweig
Magdeburg
Berlin
Potsdam
Schwerin
Lübeck
Leipzig
Halle (Saale)
Dessau
Erfurt
Kassel
Göttingen
Hildesheim
Osnabrück
Bielefeld
Oldenburg
Wolfsburg
Chemnitz
Zwickau
Gera
Jena
Weimar
Gotha
Fulda
Frankfurt am Main
Wiesbaden
Mainz
Darmstadt
Würzburg
Bamberg
Bayreuth
Nürnberg
Fürth
Erlangen
Regensburg
Heidelberg
Mannheim
Ludwigshafen am Rhein
Karlsruhe
Heilbronn
Pforzheim
Ludwigsburg
Siegen
Marburg an der Lahn
Paderborn
Hamm
Celle
Lüneburg
Uelzen
Salzgitter
Plauen
Karlovy Vary
Cheb
Fränkische Schweiz
Thüringer Wald
Erzgebirge
Böhmer Wald
Bayerischer Wald
Km
Miles
© Bartholomew
1:2M

1:5M

Conic Equidistant Projection

© Bartholomew

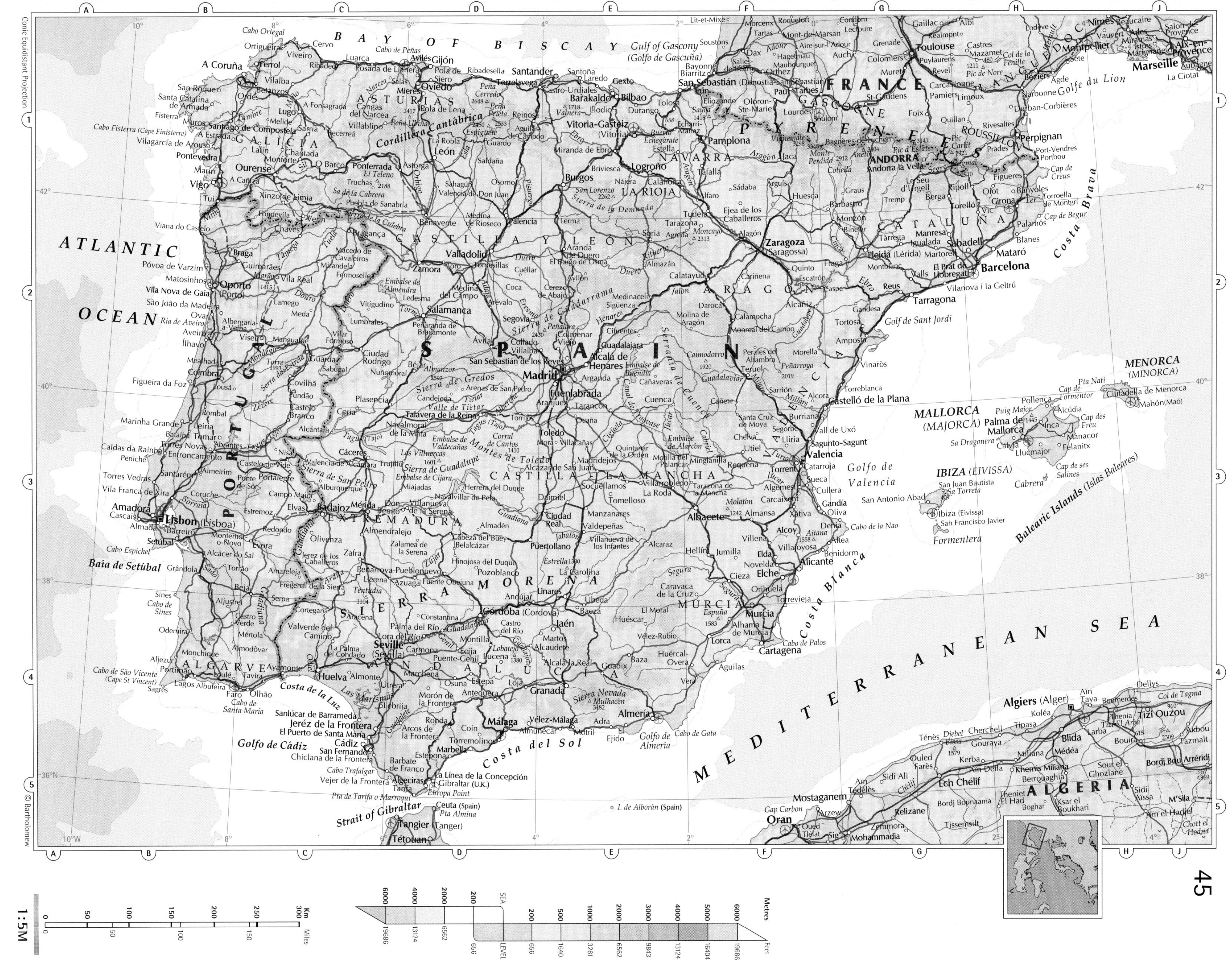

Conic Equidistant Projection

© Bartholomew

1:5M

Metres	Feet
6000	19686
5000	16404
4000	13124
3000	9843
2000	6562
1000	3281
500	1640
200	656
SEA	LEVEL
200	656
2000	6562
4000	13124
6000	19686

Km	Miles
300	
250	150
200	
	100
150	
100	50
50	
0	0

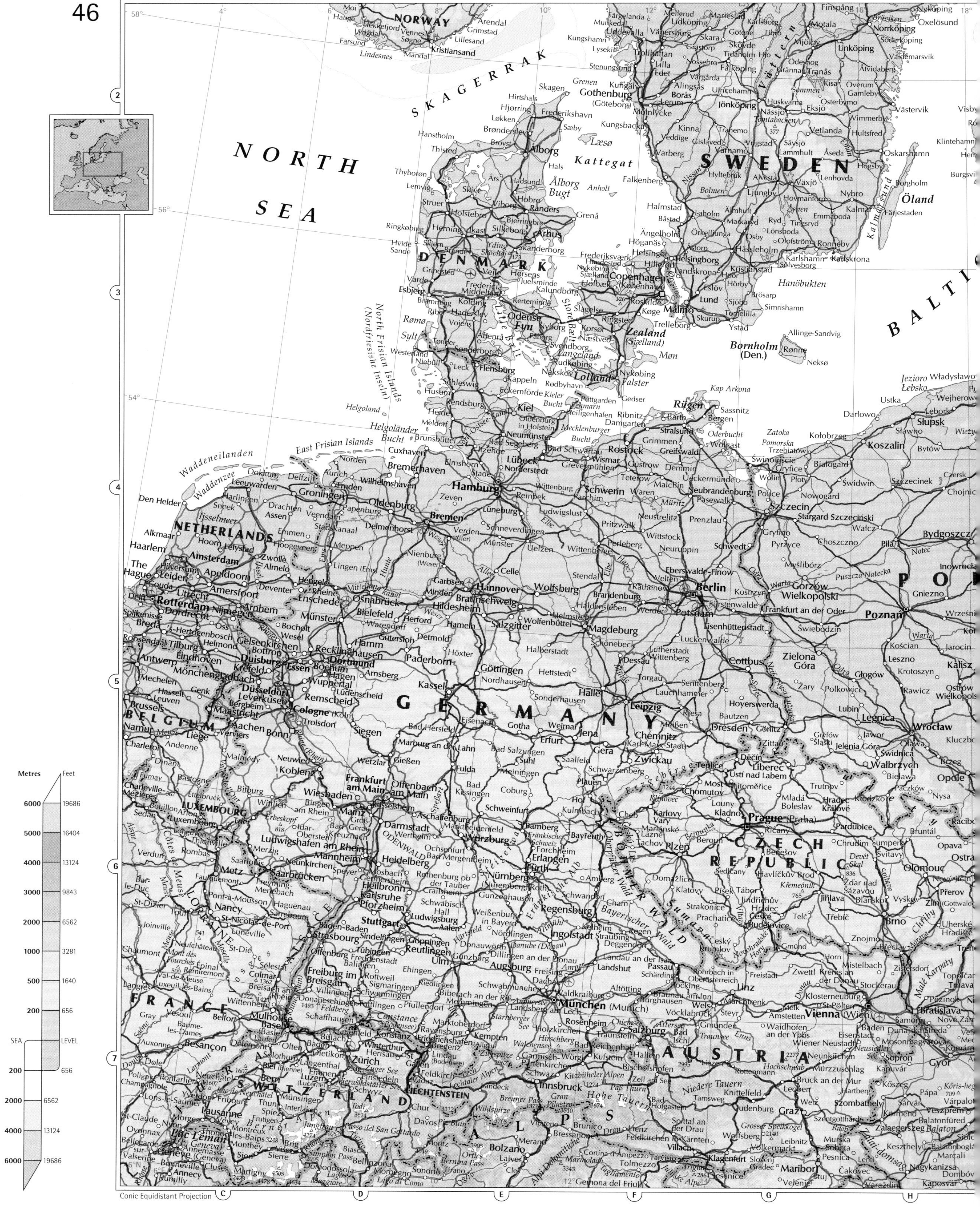
NORTH SEA
SKAGERRAK
Kattegat
BALTI
NORWAY
SWEDEN
DENMARK
NETHERLANDS
BELGIUM
LUXEMBOURG
GERMANY
FRANCE
SWITZERLAND
LIECHTENSTEIN
AUSTRIA
CZECH REPUBLIC
POL
ALPS
Öland
Bornholm (Den.)
Rügen
Zealand (Sjælland)
Fyn
Lolland
Falster
Møn
North Frisian Islands (Nordfriesishe Inseln)
East Frisian Islands
Waddeneilanden
Waddenzee
Helgoland
Hanöbukten
Kristiansand
Gothenburg (Göteborg)
Copenhagen (København)
Malmö
Hamburg
Bremen
Berlin
Hannover
Amsterdam
Rotterdam
The Hague
Brussels
Cologne (Köln)
Düsseldorf
Frankfurt am Main
Stuttgart
München (Munich)
Leipzig
Dresden
Prague (Praha)
Vienna (Wien)
Bratislava
Zürich
Bern
Genève (Geneva)
Lac Léman
Innsbruck
Salzburg
Szczecin
Poznań
Wrocław
Metres
Feet
6000
5000
4000
3000
2000
1000
500
200
SEA
LEVEL
19686
16404
13124
9843
6562
3281
1640
656
Conic Equidistant Projection

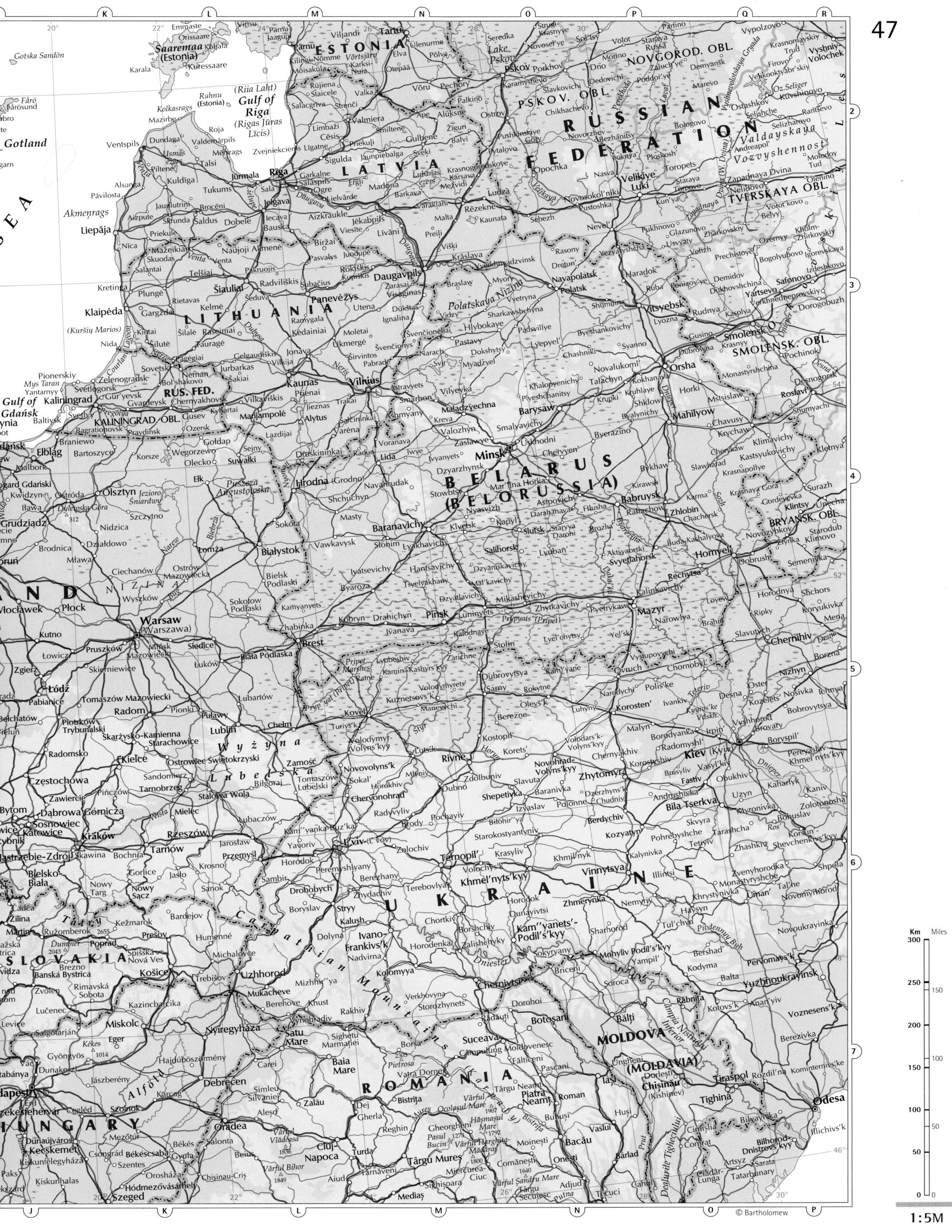

Km Miles
300
250
200
150
100
50
0

1:5M

© Bartholomew

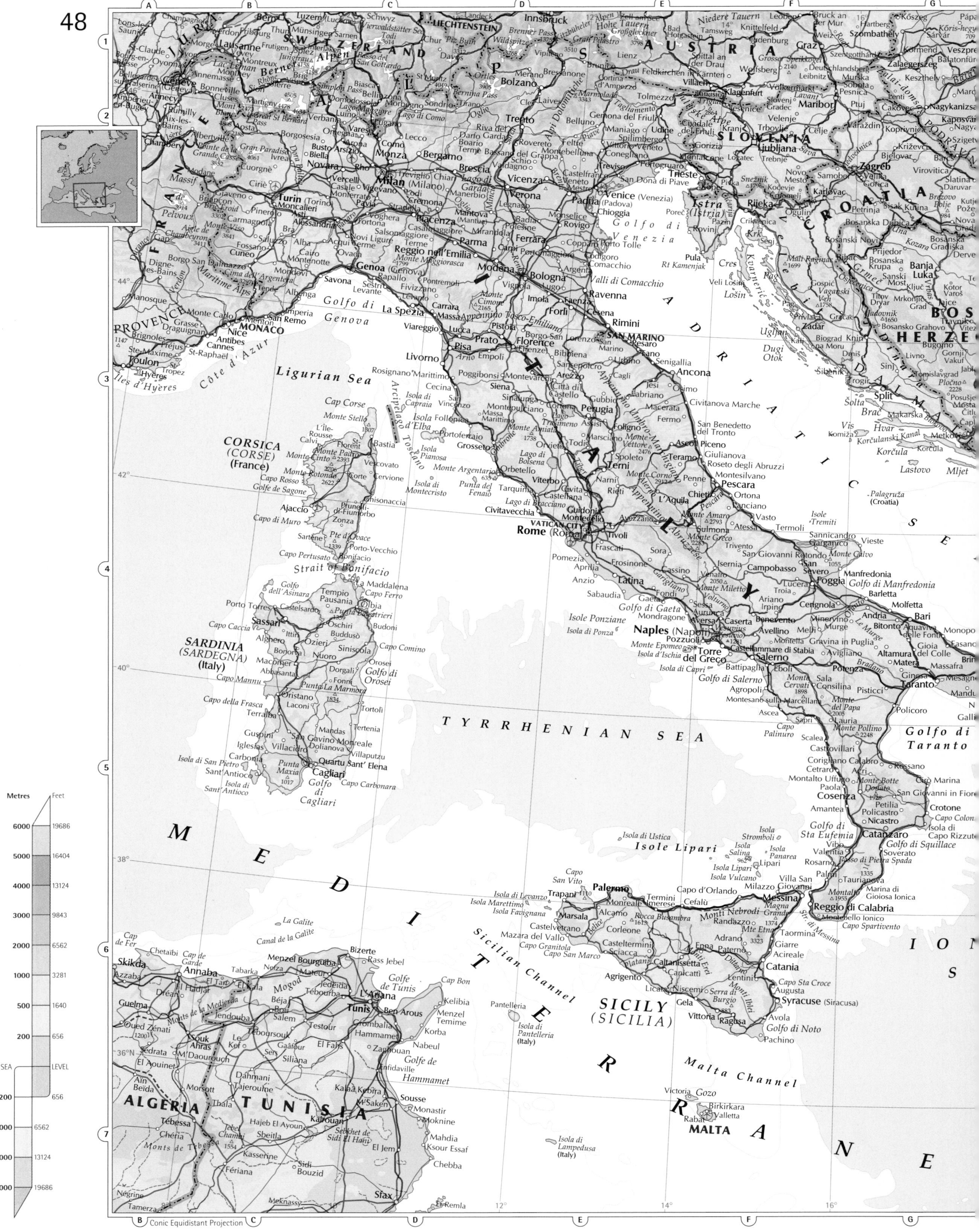
A
B
C
D
E
F
G
1
2
3
4
5
6
7
SWITZERLAND
LIECHTENSTEIN
AUSTRIA
SLOVENIA
CROATIA
FRANCE
ITALY
MONACO
SAN MARINO
VATICAN CITY
ALGERIA
TUNISIA
MALTA
CORSICA
(CORSE)
(France)
SARDINIA
(SARDEGNA)
(Italy)
SICILY
(SICILIA)
Alps
PROVENCE
Côte d'Azur
Ligurian Sea
Golfo di Genova
Golfo di Venezia
ADRIATIC SEA
TYRRHENIAN SEA
MEDITERRANEAN
Sicilian Channel
Malta Channel
Strait of Bonifacio
Golfo di Taranto
Isole Lipari
Isole Ponziane
Innsbruck
Bern
Lausanne
Genève
Luzern
Bolzano
Trento
Milan (Milano)
Turin (Torino)
Monza
Bergamo
Brescia
Verona
Vicenza
Padua (Padova)
Venice (Venezia)
Trieste
Ljubljana
Zagreb
Rijeka
Graz
Maribor
Klagenfurt
Genoa (Genova)
Parma
Modena
Bologna
Ferrara
Ravenna
Rimini
La Spezia
Livorno
Pisa
Prato
Florence (Firenze)
Siena
Perugia
Ancona
Pescara
Split
Zadar
Rome (Roma)
Latina
Naples (Napoli)
Salerno
Foggia
Bari
Taranto
Cosenza
Catanzaro
Reggio di Calabria
Messina
Palermo
Catania
Syracuse (Siracusa)
Cagliari
Sassari
Ajaccio
Bastia
Nice
Toulon
Cannes
Tunis
Bizerte
Annaba
Sousse
Sfax
Valletta
Gozo
Pantelleria
Isola di Lampedusa
(Italy)
Metres
Feet
6000
5000
4000
3000
2000
1000
500
200
SEA
LEVEL
19686
16404
13124
9843
6562
3281
1640
656
Conic Equidistant Projection
12°
14°
16°
36°N
38°
40°
42°
44°

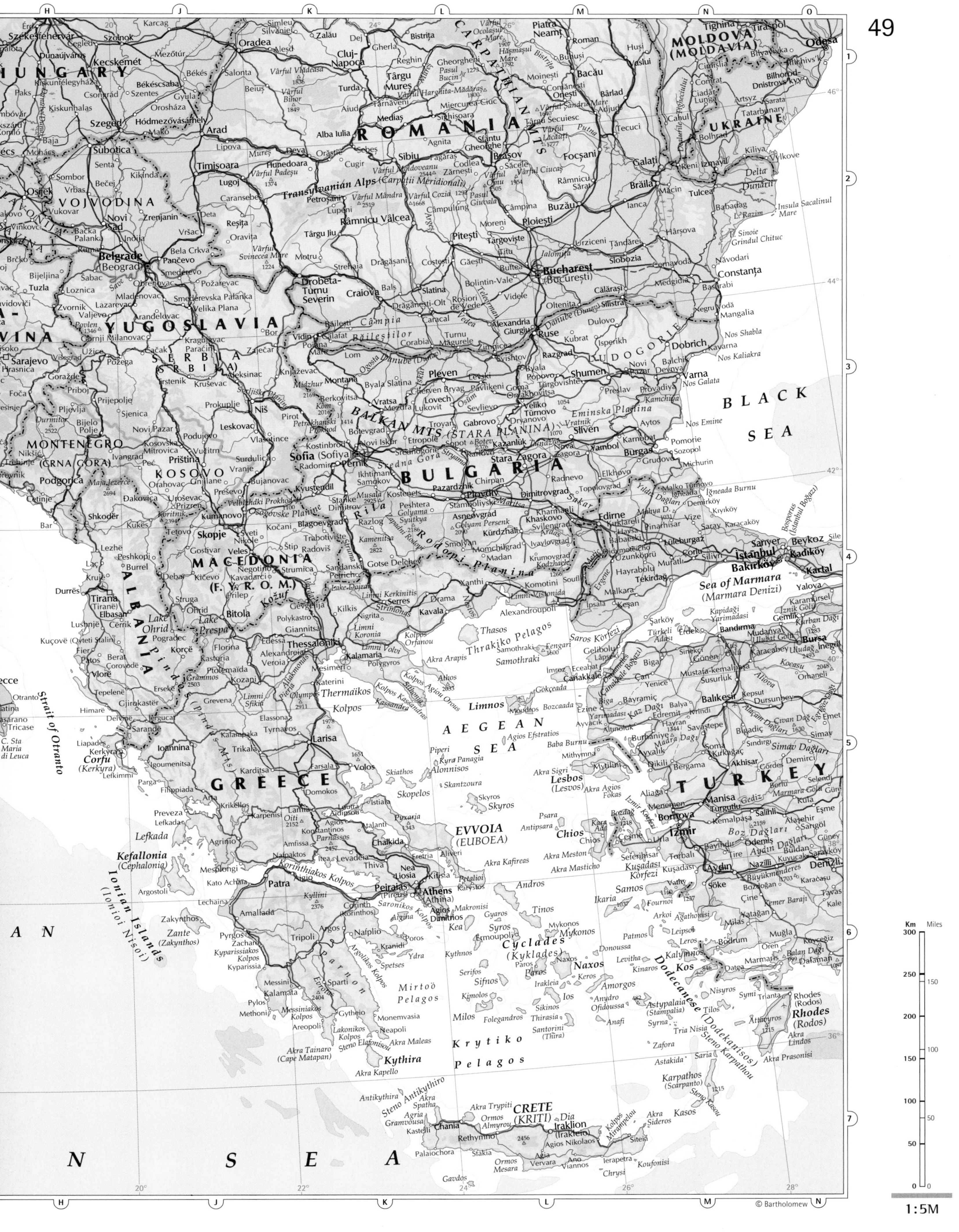

© Bartholomew

1:5M

Km 300
Miles

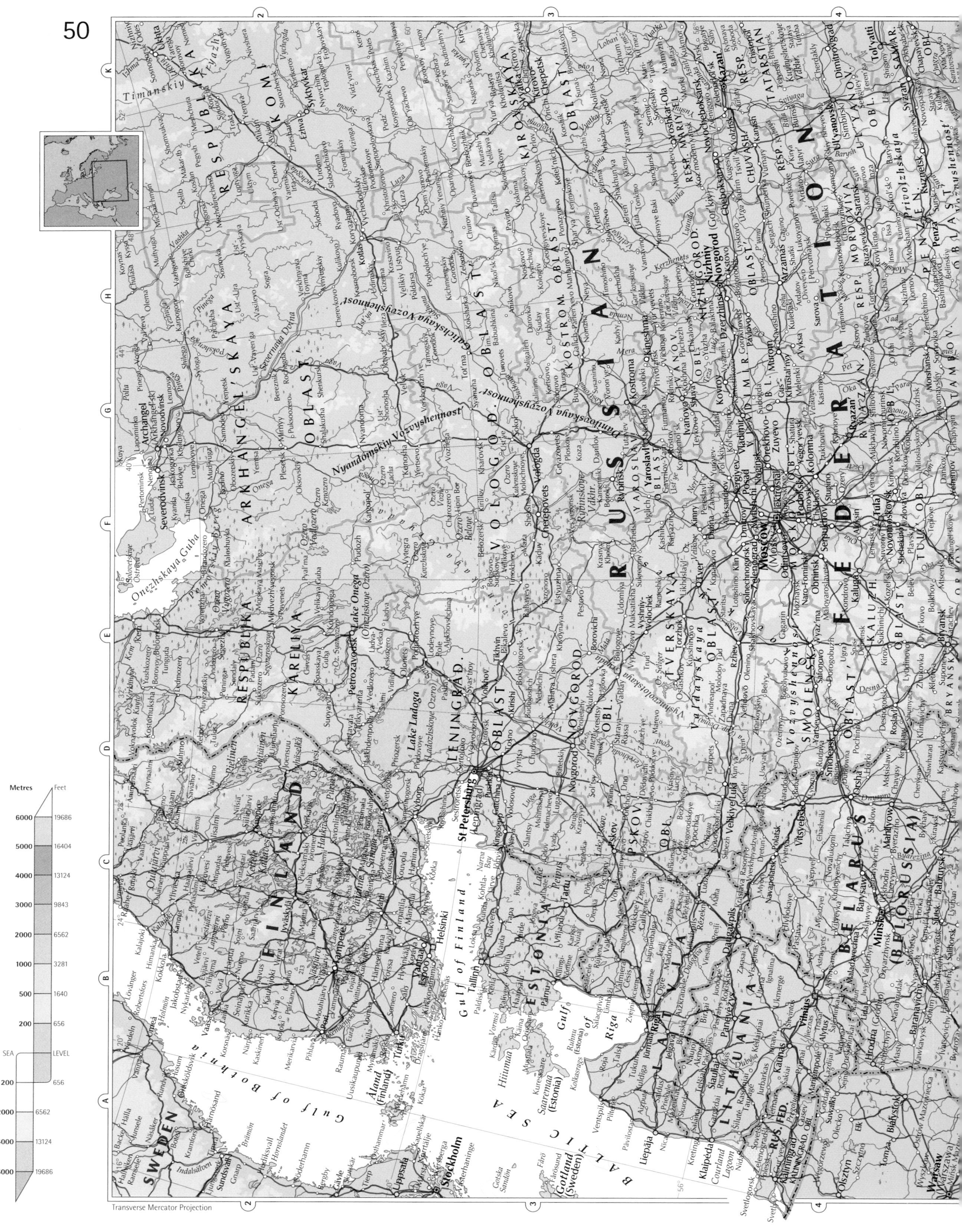

Metres | Feet

Metres	Feet
6000	19686
5000	16404
4000	13124
3000	9843
2000	6562
1000	3281
500	1640
200	656
SEA	LEVEL
200	656
2000	6562
4000	13124
6000	19686

Transverse Mercator Projection

Major labels

KAZAKSTAN

SARATOVSKAYA OBLAST'

VOLGOGRAD. OBLAST'

A S T R A K H A N.

KALMYKIYA Chernyye Zemli

RESPUBLIKA

VORONEZH OBLAST'

BELGOROD OBL.

KURSK OBLAST'

ROSTOV. OBL.

STAVROPOL' KRAY

KRASNODAR. KRAY.

DAGESTAN

CHECHEN. RESPUBLIKA

GEORGIA

AZERBAIJAN

ARMENIA

U K R A I N E

MOLDOVA (MOLDAVA)

ROMANIA

BULGARIA

GREECE

T U R K E Y

CASPIAN SEA (KASPIYSKOYE MORE)

Sea of Azov

Gulf of Taganrog

BLACK SEA (KARA DENIZ)

CHERNOYE MORE)

Crimea

Caucasus

Yergeni

Carpathian Mountains

Transylvanian Alps

Divisions of Rus. Fed. not named on map
1. RESP. ADYGEYA (G6)
2. RESP. SEVERNAYA OSETIYA (H7)
3. INGUSHSKAYA RESP. (H7)

KARACHAYEVO-CHERKESS. RESP.

KABARDINO-BALKAR. RESP.

Yerevan (Erevan)

Tbilisi

Bat'umi

Sokhumi

Astrakhan

Volgograd (Stalingrad)

Saratov

Voronezh

Kharkiv (Khar'kov)

Rostov-na-Donu

Stavropol'

Krasnodar

Maykop

Groznyy

Vladikavkaz

Makhachkala

Kaspiysk

Kiev (Kyiv)

Odesa

Dnipropetrovs'k

Zaporizhzhya

Donets'k

Mariupol'

Luhans'k

Chişinău

Bucharest

Sevastopol'

Simferopol'

Yalta

Bursa

Samsun

Trabzon

Zonguldak

© Bartholomew

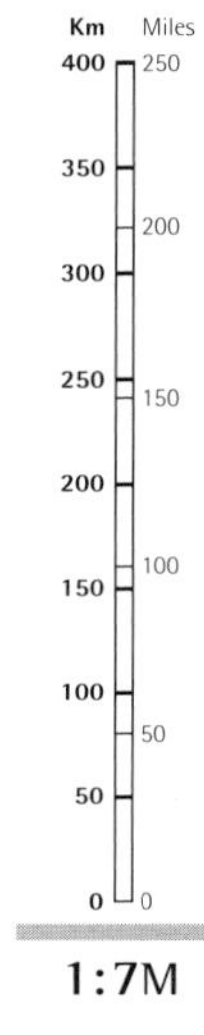

Km Miles
400   250
350   200
300
250   150
200   100
150
100   50
50
0   0

1:7M

52

Metres SEA LEVEL
Feet LEVEL
200 — 656
3000 — 9843

Oblated Stereographic Projection

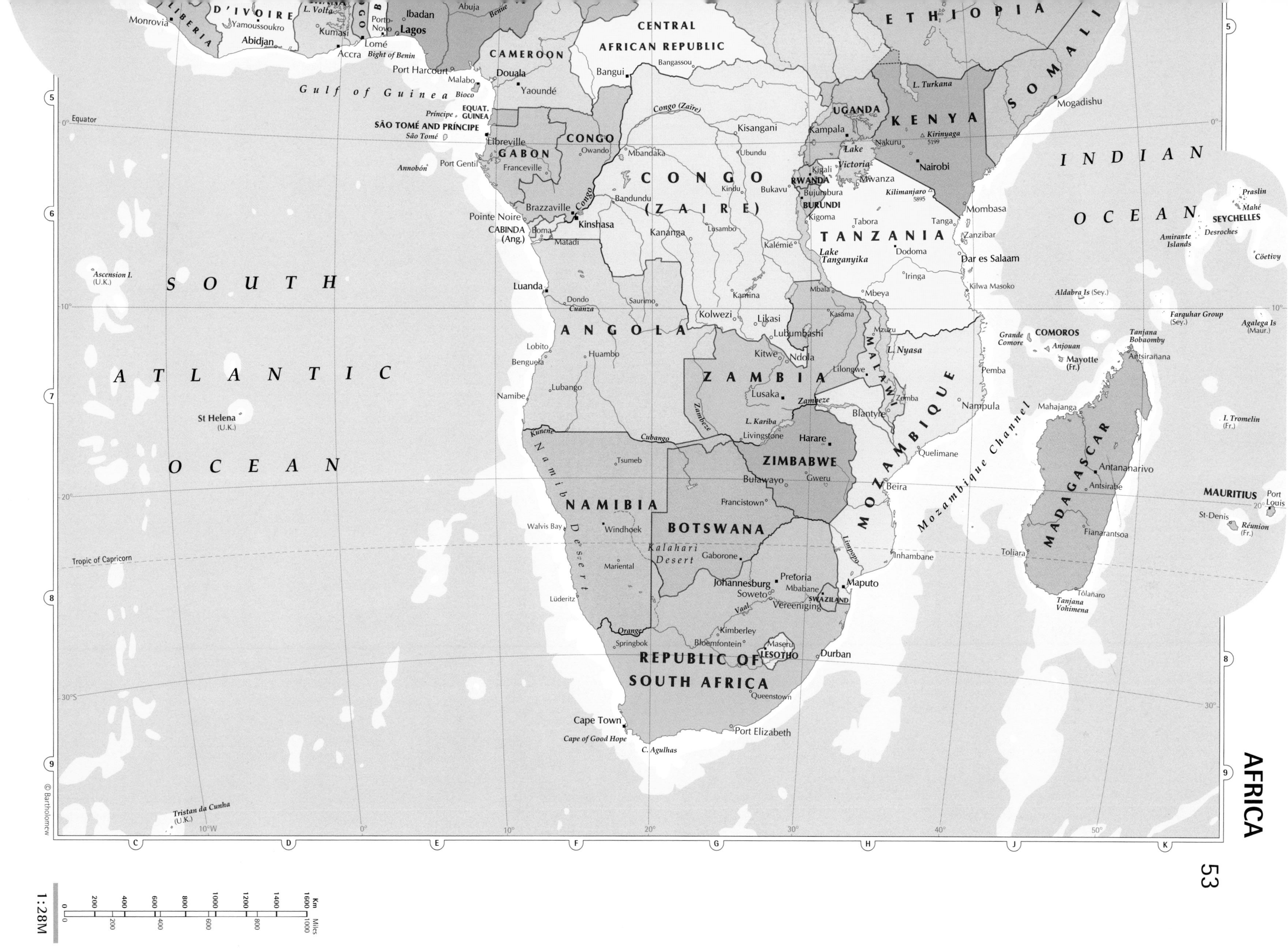

1:28M

© Bartholomew

Km   Miles
1600 1000

1400   800

1200

1000   600

800   400

600

400   200

200

0   0

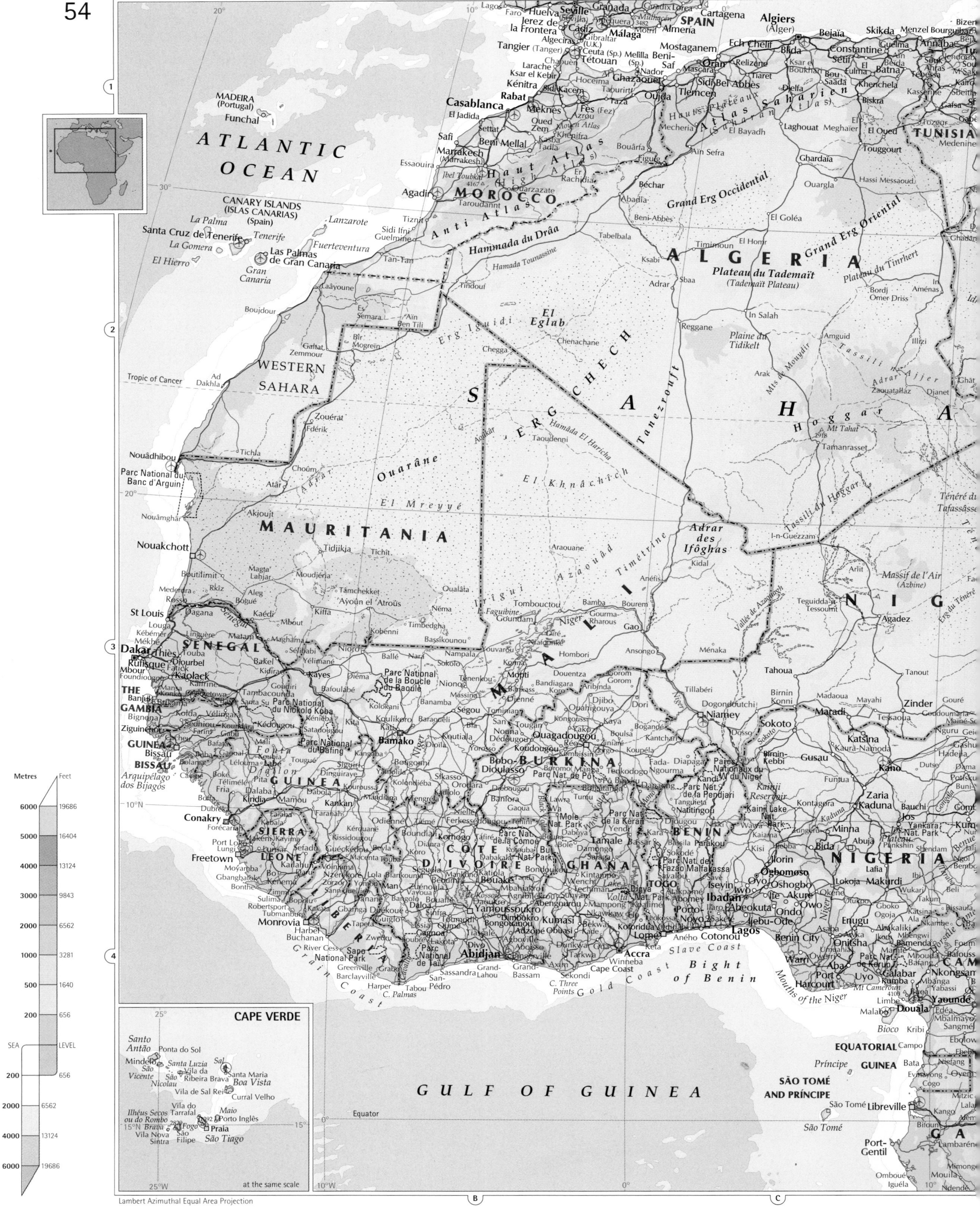

ATLANTIC

OCEAN

MADEIRA
(Portugal)
Funchal

CANARY ISLANDS
(ISLAS CANARIAS)
(Spain)
La Palma   Lanzarote
Santa Cruz de Tenerife   Tenerife
La Gomera   Fuerteventura
El Hierro   Las Palmas
de Gran Canaria
Gran
Canaria

SPAIN

Lagos Faro Huelva Seville Granada Guadix Lorca Cartagena Algiers
Jerez de   (Sevilla)   Antequera   Murcia   Almería   (Alger)
la Frontera Cádiz Gibraltar Málaga Motril
Tangier (Tanger) Ceuta (Sp.) Melilla Beni-
Algeciras (U.K.)   (Sp.) Nador Saf
Larache   Tétouan Oujda
Ksar el Kebir Hoceima Taourirt
Rabat Kénitra Sidi Kacem Fès (Fez) Taza
Casablanca Meknès
El Jadida Oued Moyen Atlas
Settat Zem Kasba Bouârfa Figuig
Safi Beni Mellal Tadla
Marrakech Haut Atlas
(Marrakesh) High Atlas
Essaouira Ibel Toubkal Ouarzazate
4167 Anti Atlas Er Rachidia
Agadir Taroudannt
MOROCCO

MOSTAGANEM Oran Relizane Ech Cheliff Blida Constantine
Mascara Tiaret Bou Saada Sétif
Sidi Bel Abbès Djelfa Batna
Tlemcen Hauts Plateaux Laghouat Meghaïer El Oued
Mecheria El Bayadh Ghardaïa Ouargla
Aïn Sefra Hassi Messaoud
Béchar Abadla Grand Erg Occidental El Goléa

TUNISIA

ALGERIA

Tiznit Hammada du Drâa Figuig Timimoun In Salah Bordj
Sidi Ifni Tan-Tan Hamada Tounassine Adrar Sbaa Plateau du Tademaït Omer Driss
Guelmime Ksabi Reggane (Tademaït Plateau) Plateau du Tinrhert

Laâyoune Tindouf Chenachane Plaine du Amguid
Boujdour El Eglab Tidikelt Arak Mts à Moydir

WESTERN Es Aïn Chegga ERG CHECH Hoggar Tassili n'Ajjer
SAHARA Semara Ben Tili S A H A R A Zaouatallaz Djanet
Tropic of Cancer Galtat Mt Tahat
Ad Zemmour Bir Aoukâr 2918
Dakhla Mogrein Hamâda El Haricha Tamanrasset
Er Taoudenni
Fdérik El Khnâchîch

Nouâdhibou Tichla Zouérat Araouane In-Guezzam Ténéré du
Parc National du Choûm Adrar Ouarâne Kidal Tafassâsse
Banc d'Arguin Atâr El Mreyyé Adrar Arlit
Nouâmghar Akjoujt des Timétrine Massif de l'Air
Tidjikja Tichît Araouane Ifôghas (Azbine)
Nouakchott Néma Tombouctou Menaka NIGER
Boutilimit Moudjéria Oualâta Timbedgha Bamba Agadez
Magta' Tâmchekket Faguibine Niger Rharous Gao
Mederdra Lahjar 'Ayoun el 'Atroûs Goundam Ansongo Teguidda-n- Tessoumt
Rkiz Kiffa Néma Dîré Tessoumt Tahoua Tanout
St Louis Aleg Kaédi Kobénni Nampala Tillabéri Birnin Mâdaoua Mayahi Zinder
Louga Bogué Mbout Bassikounou Konni Tessaoua
Kébémèr Maghama Maghama MAURITANIA Douentza Dogondoutchi Maradi
Dakar Linguère Matam Bandiagara Niamey Sokoto Katsina
Thiès Touba Sélibabi Nara Nioro Mopti Dosso Dogondoutchi Gusau
Rufisque Diourbel Bakel Yélimané Diéma Ségou Koro Gummi
Mbour Kaolack Kiffa Balé Sokolo San Tougan Kaya Birnin- Zaria
Foundiougne SENEGAL Kidira Diara Niono Djenné Ouahigouya Dori Kebbi Kaduna
THE Kaffrine Goudiri Nioro Banamba Koutiala Bobo Tenkodogo Gaoua Kandi NIGERIA
GAMBIA Tambacounda Santa Su Kita Kati Dédougou Bénin Kano Jos
Banjul Parc National Kolokani BURKINA Fada- Diapaga Kainji Funtua
GUINEA du Niokolo Koba Bamako Bobo- Ngourma Parc Lake Kontagora Bauchi
BISSAU Vélingara Bafoulabé Séguéla Dioulasso Parc Nat de Pô Nat'l Nat de W Minna
Ziguinchor Koundara Kédougou Siguiri Koulikoro Banfora Koupéla du Niger Abuja
BISSAU Labé Satadougou Kangaba Baraouéli Parc Nat. Natitingou Kaiama Zaria Kaduna
Bignona Gabú Fouta Dabola Kankan Sikasso Orodara Tumu Lawra Kara de la Pendjari Kainji Gusau
GUINEA Kolda Mali Kindia Kouroussa Kérouané Odienné Korhogo Bole BENIN Reservoir Katsina
Télimélé Boké Pita Dinguiraye Mandiana Tombougou Bouna Gaoua Parc Nat Parakou Kontagora
Arquipélago Fria Télimélé Dabola Faranah Odienné Ferkessédougou Parc Nat. du Kandi Bida Oshogbo Minna
dos Bijagós Dalaba Labé Kissidougou Sefadou de la Comoé Bobo de la Kéran Sokodé Ilorin Lokoja Makurdi
Boffa Mamou Kabala Béyla Beoumi Man Bouna Yendi Bassar Natitingou Ife Oyo Akure Wukari
Conakry Dubréka Télimélé Nzérékoré Voinjama Bondoukou Tamale Parakou Iseyin Abeokuta Enugu Ogbomoso
SIERRA Forécariah Makeni Kenema Gbarnga Yamoussoukro Mampong Atakpamé Ilorin Ibadan Onitsha
Port Loko LEONE Kailahun Danané Bouaké Wenchi Sokodé Abomey Porto- Lagos Benin City Calabar
Lungi Bo Zorzor Man Dabakala Techiman Kpalimé Novo Lafia Warri
Freetown Moyamba Sulima Daloa Touba Bouaflé Kumasi Koforidua Lomé Cotonou Port Aba Calabar
Gbangbama Bopolu Zwedru Gagnoa Divo Abengourou Obuasi Keta Aného Harcourt Uyo Bamenda
Bonthe Harbel River Cess Sassandra Divo CÔTE Dimbokro GHANA Accra Slave Coast Mt Cameroun Mbengwi
LIBERIA Robertsport Buchanan Greenville D'IVOIRE Grand- Cape Coast Bight 4100 Limbe Douala
Tubmanburg Kakata Zwedru Lahou Sekondi of Benin Ekonga Foumban
Monrovia National Park Sapo Grand- C. Three Port EQUATORIAL Bioco Yaoundé
Harper National Park Bassam Points Gold Coast Mouths of the Niger Harcourt Bata GUINEA Campo Edéa
C. Palmas Barclayville Tabou San- Bioco Kribi Mbalmayo Sangmelima
Grain Coast Pédro GULF OF GUINEA Príncipe GUINEA Ebolowa
Parc Grabo Grand- SÃO TOMÉ Evinayong Oyem
National de Taï Lahou Equator AND PRÍNCIPE Bitam Oyem
São Tomé Libreville Mitzic
Santo Ponta do Sol Port- GABON Kango
Antão Mindelo Santa Luzia Sal Gentil Ombové Iguéla
São Santa Maria São Tomé Mimongé
Vicente Nicolau Boa Vista Lambaréné Ndjolé
Ilhéus Secos São Vila de Sal Rei Fougamou
ou do Rombo Tarrafal Curral Velho Moabi
Brava Fogo Maio Ndendé
Vila Nova São Porto Inglês
Sintra Filipe Praia
São Tiago

CAPE VERDE

Metres Feet
6000 19686
5000 16404
4000 13124
3000 9843
2000 6562
1000 3281
500 1640
200 656
SEA LEVEL
200 656
2000 6562
4000 13124
6000 19686

at the same scale

Lambert Azimuthal Equal Area Projection

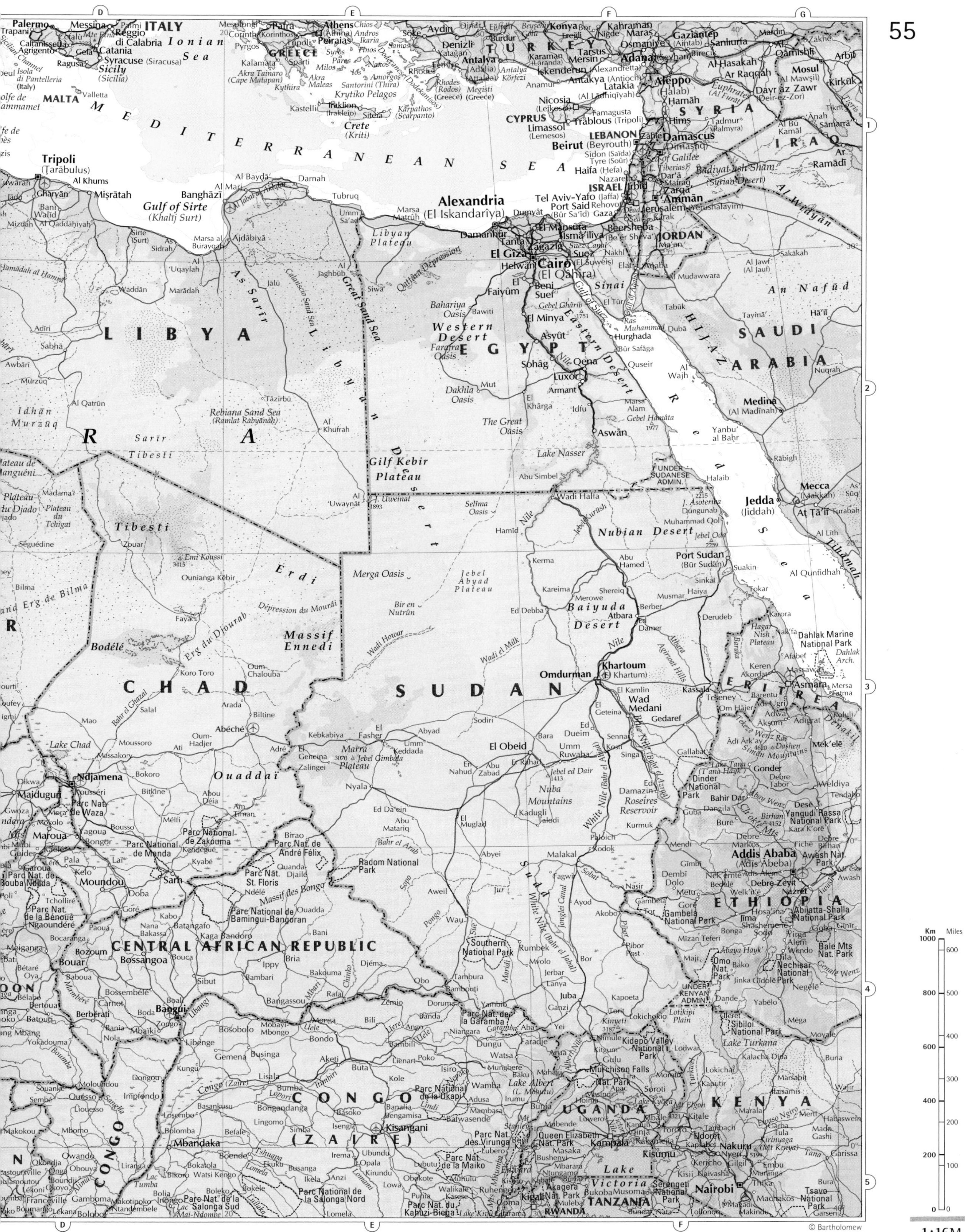

1:16M

© Bartholomew

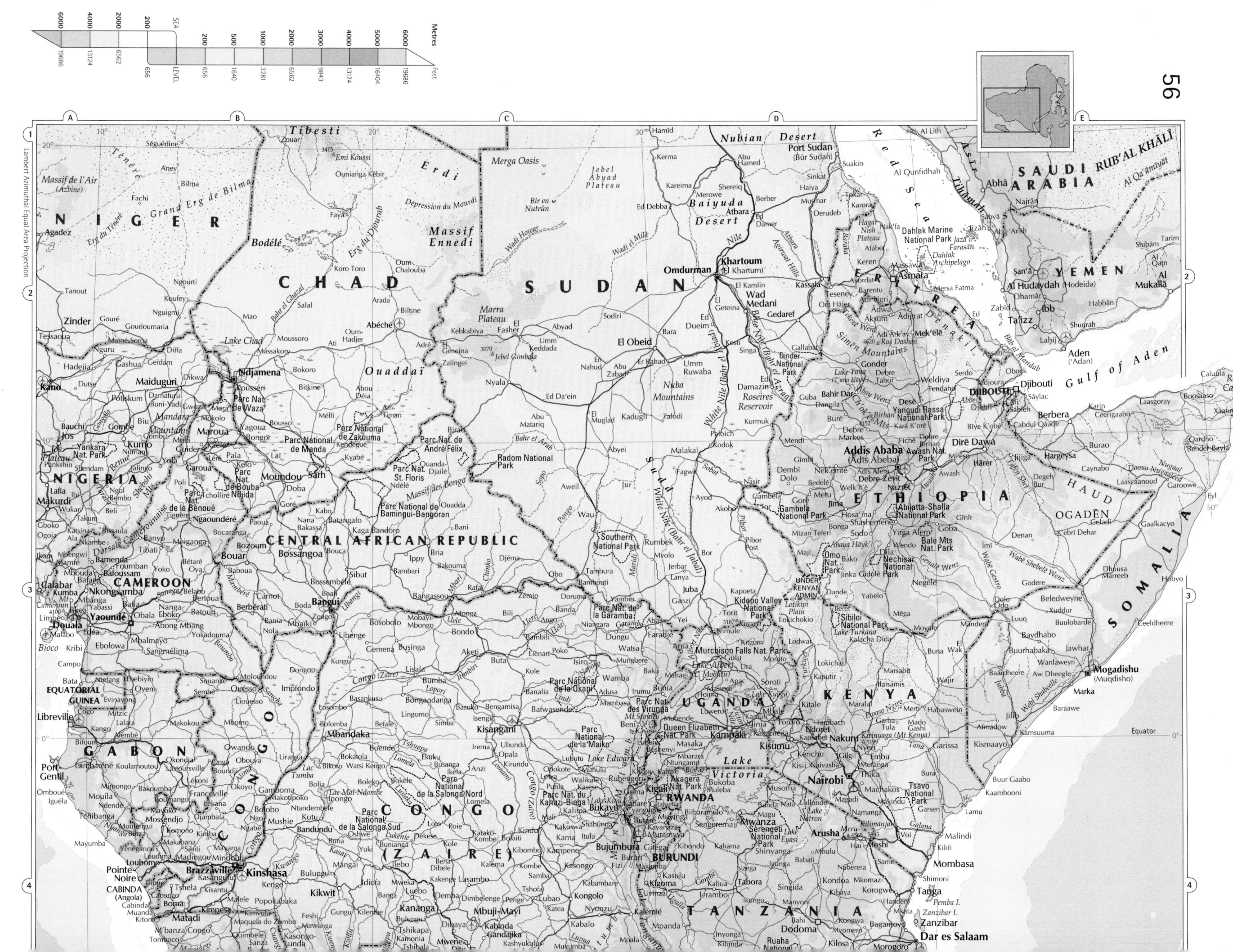
NIGER
CHAD
SUDAN
NIGERIA
CAMEROON
CENTRAL AFRICAN REPUBLIC
ERITREA
ETHIOPIA
SOMALIA
KENYA
UGANDA
TANZANIA
RWANDA
BURUNDI
CONGO (ZAIRE)
CONGO
GABON
EQUATORIAL GUINEA
DJIBOUTI
YEMEN
SAUDI ARABIA
RUB'AL KHĀLĪ
Red Sea
Gulf of Aden
Nubian Desert
Baiyuda Desert
Tibesti
Erdi
Massif Ennedi
Grand Erg de Bilma
Marra Plateau
Ouaddai
Nuba Mountains
Sudd
Simēn Mountains
HAUD
OGADĒN
Lake Chad
Lake Victoria
Khartoum (El Khartum)
Omdurman
Port Sudan (Būr Sudān)
El Obeid
Wad Medani
Asmara
Addis Ababa (Adis Abeba)
Dirē Dawa
Djibouti
Aden ('Adan)
Mogadishu (Muqdisho)
Nairobi
Mombasa
Kampala
Kigali
Bujumbura
Dodoma
Dar es Salaam
Zanzibar
Ndjamena
Abéché
Maiduguri
Kano
Zinder
Agadez
Yaoundé
Douala
Bangui
Libreville
Kisangani
Mbandaka
Kinshasa
Brazzaville
Pointe-Noire
White Nile (Bahr el Abiad)
Blue Nile (Bahr el Azraq)
White Nile (Bahr el Jabal)
Congo (Zaïre)
Equator
Lambert Azimuthal Equal Area Projection
Metres
Feet
6000
19686
5000
16404
4000
13124
3000
9843
2000
6562
1000
3281
500
1640
200
656
SEA
LEVEL
200
656
2000
6562
4000
13124
6000
19686

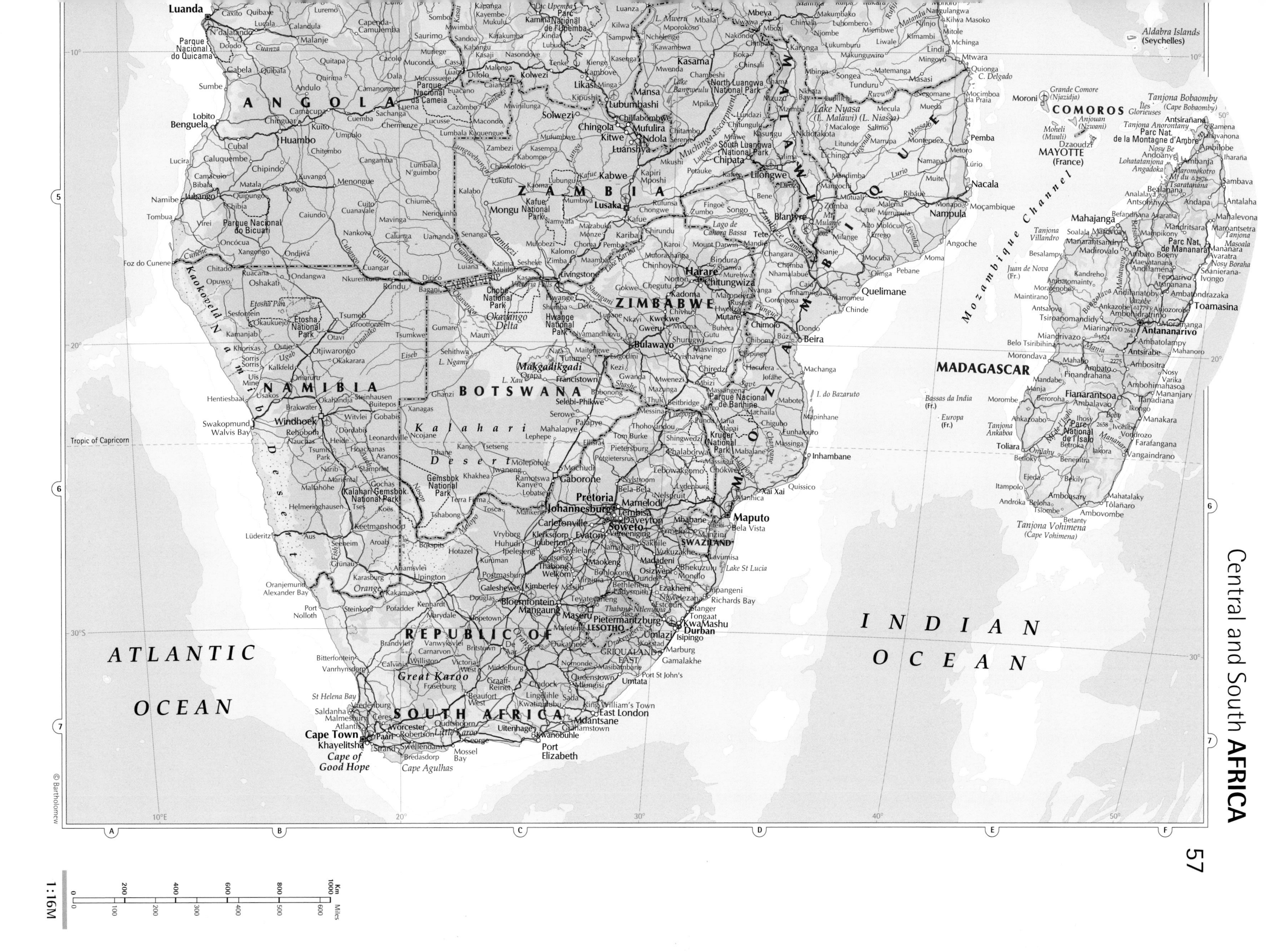
ANGOLA
ZAMBIA
MALAWI
MOZAMBIQUE
ZIMBABWE
BOTSWANA
NAMIBIA
REPUBLIC OF SOUTH AFRICA
LESOTHO
SWAZILAND
MADAGASCAR
COMOROS
MAYOTTE (France)
Mozambique Channel
INDIAN OCEAN
ATLANTIC OCEAN
Kalahari Desert
Namib Desert
Luanda
Lusaka
Harare
Lilongwe
Maputo
Pretoria
Johannesburg
Cape Town
Durban
Windhoek
Gaborone
Antananarivo
Bulawayo
Beira
Port Elizabeth
East London
Tropic of Capricorn
Cape of Good Hope
Km
Miles
1:16M
© Bartholomew

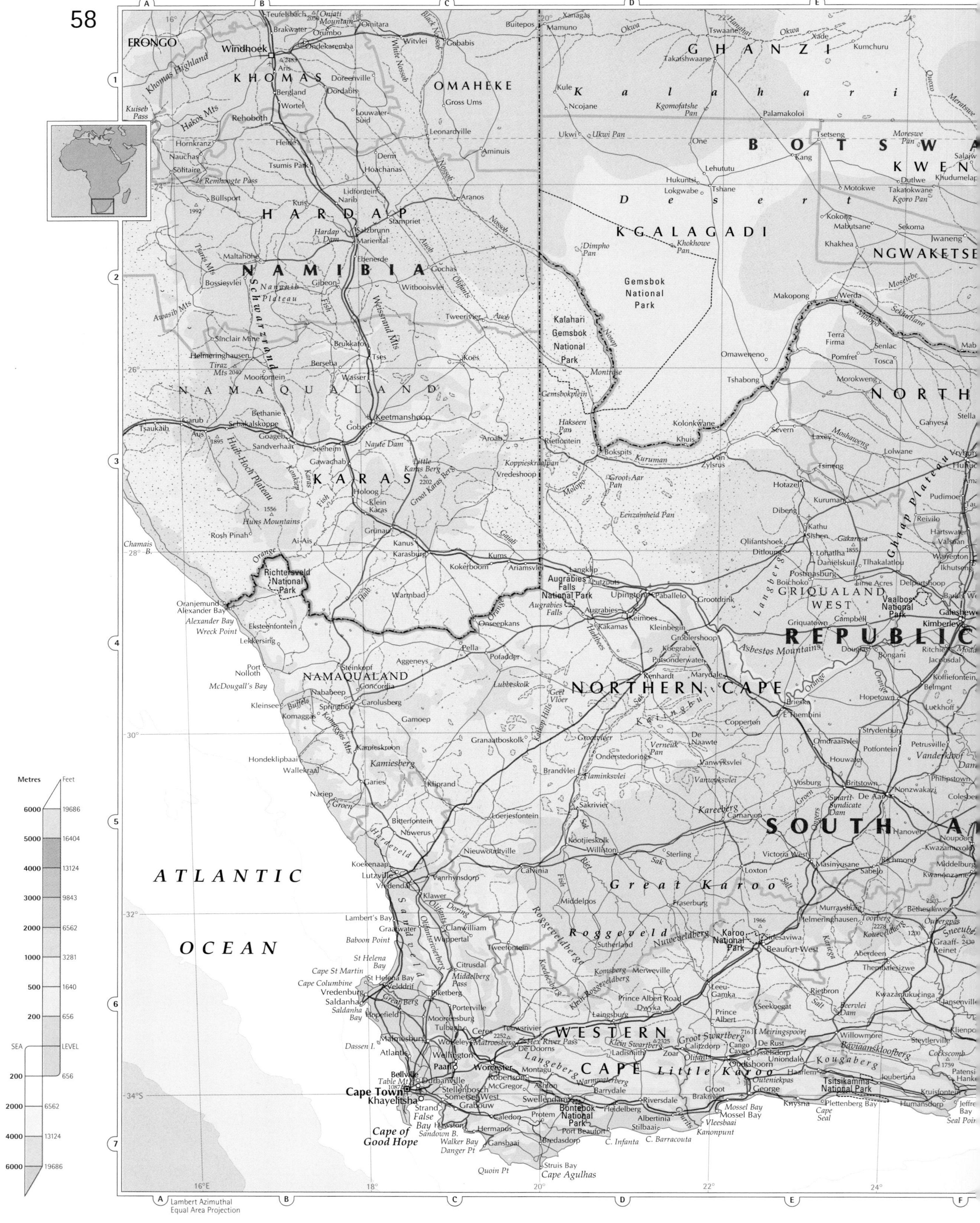
ERONGO
Windhoek
KHOMAS
OMAHEKE
Khomas Highland
Kuiseb Pass
Hakos Mts
Rehoboth
Gobabis
Witvlei
Buitepos
Mamuno
Okwa
GHANZI
Kalahari Desert
BOTSWANA
KWENENG
KGALAGADI
NGWAKETSE
Gemsbok National Park
Kalahari Gemsbok National Park
Nossob
Molopo
HARDAP
Hardap Dam
Mariental
NAMIBIA
Schwarzrand
Naukluft Plateau
Maltahöhe
Gibeon
Weissrand Mts
Tiraz Mts
NAMAQUALAND
Bethanie
Keetmanshoop
Aus
Lüderitz
Huib-Hoch Plateau
KARAS
Great Karas Berg
Huns Mountains
Rosh Pinah
Ai-Ais
Karasburg
Orange
Richtersveld National Park
Oranjemund
Alexander Bay
Port Nolloth
Augrabies Falls National Park
Upington
Kuruman
NORTHERN CAPE
Springbok
NAMAQUALAND
Kamiesberg
Asbestos Mountains
GRIQUALAND WEST
Vaalbos National Park
Kimberley
REPUBLIC
SOUTH AFRICA
Ghaap Plateau
Calvinia
Great Karoo
Roggeveld
Nuweveldberg
Karoo National Park
Beaufort West
ATLANTIC OCEAN
Lambert's Bay
St Helena Bay
Cape Columbine
Saldanha Bay
Dassen I.
Malmesbury
Paarl
Worcester
Stellenbosch
Table Mt
Cape Town
Khayelitsha
False Bay
Cape of Good Hope
Walker Bay
Danger Pt
WESTERN CAPE
Langeberg
Little Karoo
Bontebok National Park
Swellendam
Oudtshoorn
George
Mossel Bay
Knysna
Plettenberg Bay
Tsitsikamma National Park
Cape Agulhas
Struis Bay
C. Infanta
C. Barracouta
Metres
Feet
SEA LEVEL
6000
5000
4000
3000
2000
1000
500
200
19686
16404
13124
9843
6562
3281
1640
656
Lambert Azimuthal Equal Area Projection

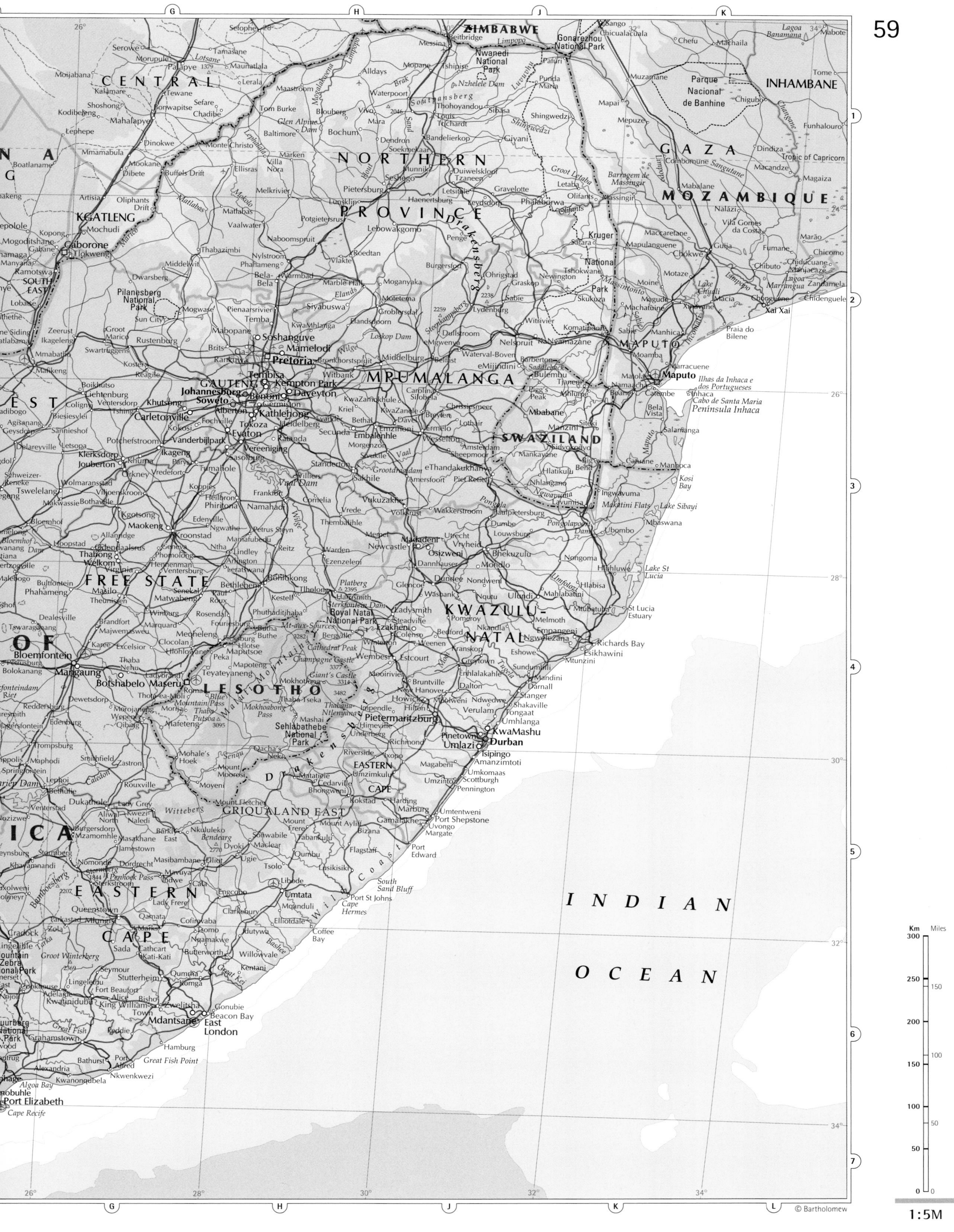

© Bartholomew

1:5M

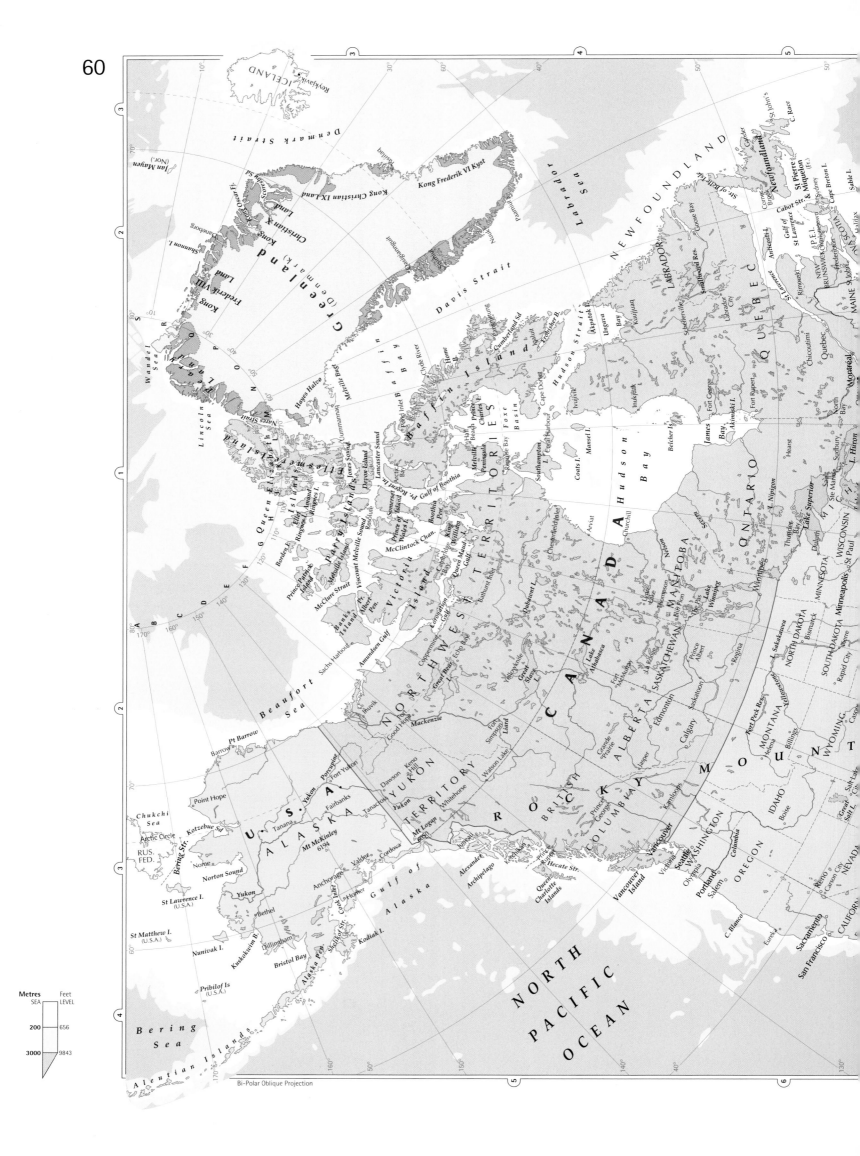

60

Metres | Feet
SEA | LEVEL
200 | 656
3000 | 9843

Bi-Polar Oblique Projection

ICELAND
Reykjavík

Jan Mayen
(Nor.)

Denmark Strait

Kong Frederik VI Kyst

Kong Christian IX Land

Kong Christian X Land

Scoresby Sd
Kaiser Fr
Oscar Fj

Shannon I.
Danneborg

Frederik VIII Land

Kong Frederik VIII Land

Wandel Sea

G R E E N L A N D
(Denmark)

Peary Land

Lincoln Sea

Hayes Halvø

Nares Strait

Labrador
Sea

Davis Strait

NEWFOUNDLAND

St John's
Gander
C. Race

St Pierre & Miquelon (Fr.)
Newfoundland
Corner Brook
Cabot Str. & Sydney
Cape Breton I.
Gulf of St Lawrence
Anticosti I.
P.E.I.
Charlottetown
NOVA SCOTIA
Halifax
Sable I.
NEW BRUNSWICK
Fredericton
MAINE
Saint John

Str of Belle Isle

Q U E B E C

Labrador City
Schefferville
Smallwood Res.

LABRADOR

Goose Bay

Ungava Bay

Kuujjuaq

Baffin
Bay

Clyde River
Home
Pond Inlet
Frobisher B.
Iqaluit
Cumberland Sd
Cape Dyer
Hall Beach
Prince Charles I.

Melville Peninsula
Foxe Basin
Foxe Channel
Southampton I.
Coats I.
Mansel I.
Repulse Bay
Cape Dorset

Hudson Strait

Akpatok
Ivujivik

Belcher Is

Inukjuak

H u d s o n   B a y

James Bay
Fort George
Fort Rupert
Akimiski I.

Chicoutimi
Québec
Montréal

O N T A R I O

Hearst

Chesterfieldinlet
Arviat
Churchill

Nelson
Thompson

Lake Winnipeg
The Pas
L. Winnipeg
Lake Winnipegosis

M A N I T O B A

Thunder Bay
Sudbury
Ste Marie
L. Huron
Sault

Duluth
Lake Superior

WISCONSIN
Minneapolis
St Paul
MINNESOTA

Winnipeg

N O R T H W E S T   T E R R I T O R I E S

Baffin Island

Lancaster Sound
Devon Island
Arctic Bay
Jones Sound
Ellesmere Island

QUEEN ELIZABETH ISLANDS

Axel Heiberg Island
Amund Ringnes I.
Ellef Ringnes I.

PARRY ISLANDS

Bathurst Island
Melville Island
Prince Patrick Island
Borden I.

Viscount Melville Sound

McClure Strait
Banks Island
Sachs Harbour

Pr. Albert Pen.

Amundsen Gulf

Beaufort Sea

Prince of Wales Island
Somerset Island
Boothia Pen.
Gulf of Boothia
Pr. Regent Inl.
Resolute

King William I.
McClintock Chan.

Victoria Island

Queen Maud Gulf
Cambridge Bay
Coppermine
Coronation Gulf

Great Bear Lake
Echo Bay
Good Hope
Mackenzie
Fort Good Hope

Inuvik

Great Slave Lake
Yellowknife

Fort Simpson
Fort Liard

Dubawnt Lake

Baker Lake

Reindeer Lake

Lake Athabasca
Stony Rapids
Fort McMurray

S A S K A T C H E W A N

Prince Albert
Saskatoon
Regina

NORTH DAKOTA
Bismarck
SOUTH DAKOTA
Rapid City
Pierre

C A N A D A

A L B E R T A

Grande Prairie
Edmonton
Jasper
Calgary

MONTANA
Helena
Billings
Fort Peck Res.

R O C K Y   M O U N T

WYOMING
Casper

Saskatchewan

Y U K O N   T E R R I T O R Y

Dawson
Keno Hill
Whitehorse
Watson Lake
Mt Logan 5951

Porcupine
Fort Yukon
Yukon
Tanacross
Yukon

B R I T I S H   C O L U M B I A

Prince George
Kamloops

Vancouver

Vancouver Island
Victoria

Queen Charlotte Islands
Prince Rupert
Hecate Str.

Juneau
Alexander Archipelago

WASHINGTON
Seattle
Olympia

IDAHO
Boise

OREGON
Portland
Salem

NEVADA
Reno
Carson City

Great Salt Lake

Columbia

U . S . A .

A L A S K A

Fairbanks
Tanana
Mt McKinley 6194
Anchorage
Valdez
Cordova
Cook Inlet
Homer
Kodiak I.
Kenai

Gulf of Alaska

Point Hope

Kotzebue Sd
Nome
Norton Sound
Bethel
Yukon

St Lawrence I. (U.S.A.)

Chukchi Sea
Arctic Circle
RUS. FED.
Bering Str.
Pt Barrow
Barrow

St Matthew I. (U.S.A.)
Nunivak I.

Kuskokwim B.
Dillingham
Bristol Bay
Alaska Pen.
Shelikof Str.

Pribilof Is (U.S.A.)

Bering Sea

Aleutian Islands

N O R T H
P A C I F I C
O C E A N

Sacramento
San Francisco
CALIFORNIA
C. Blanco
Eureka

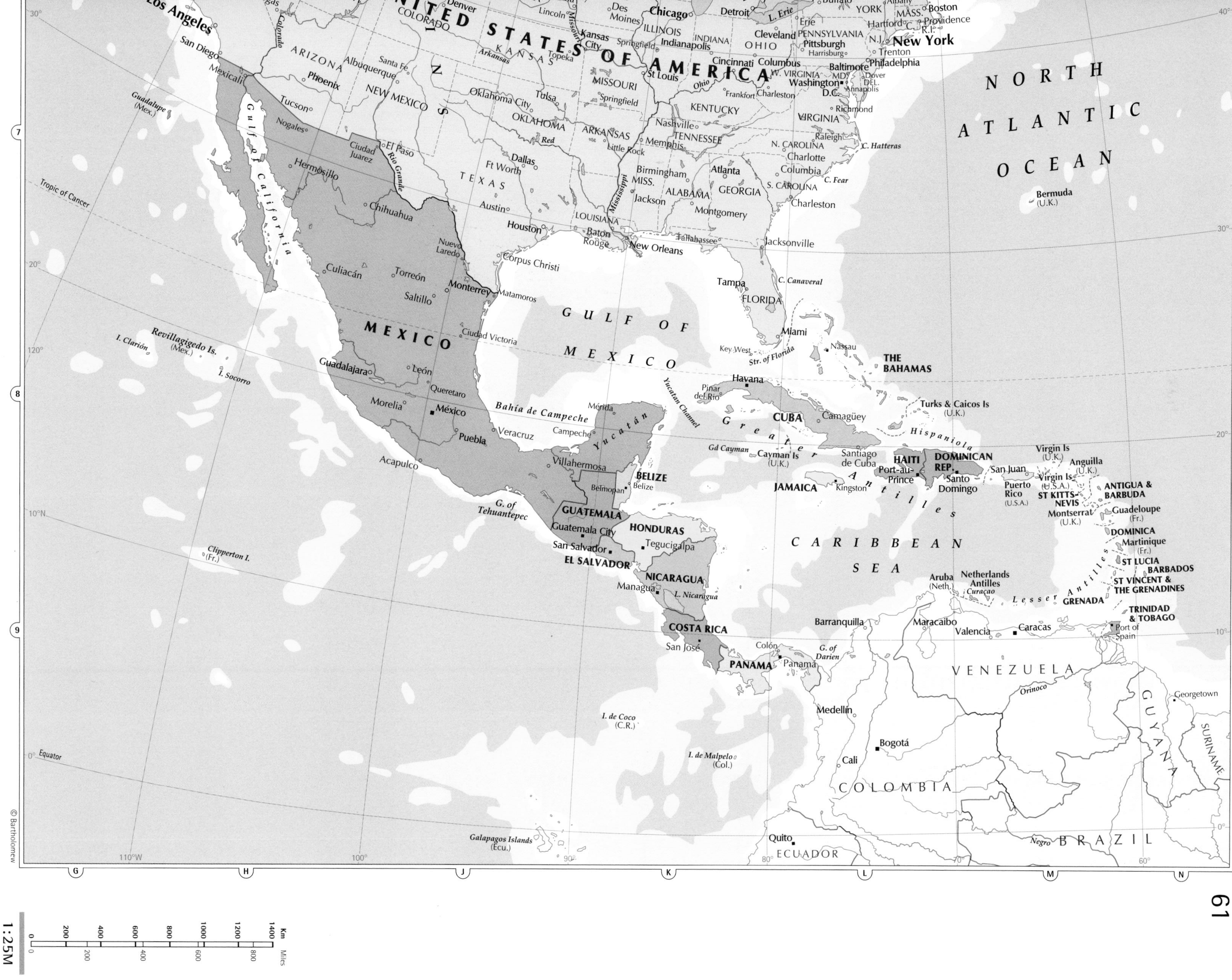

NORTH

ATLANTIC

OCEAN

GUYANA

SURINAME

Georgetown

BRAZIL

Negro

VENEZUELA

COLOMBIA

Caracas

Orinoco

Maracaibo

Valencia

Barranquilla

G. of
Darién

Medellín

Bogotá

Cali

ECUADOR

Quito

Galapagos Islands
(Ecu.)

Equator

ANTIGUA &
BARBUDA

Guadeloupe
(Fr.)

DOMINICA

Martinique
(Fr.)

ST LUCIA

BARBADOS

ST VINCENT &
THE GRENADINES

TRINIDAD
& TOBAGO

GRENADA

Port of
Spain

Anguilla
(U.K.)

Virgin Is
(U.K.)

Virgin Is.
(U.S.A.)

ST KITTS &
NEVIS

Montserrat
(U.K.)

Lesser Antilles

Netherlands
Antilles

Aruba
(Neth.)

Curaçao

Bermuda
(U.K.)

San Juan

Puerto
Rico
(U.S.A.)

Hispaniola

HAITI

DOMINICAN
REP.

Port-au-
Prince

Santo
Domingo

Turks & Caicos Is
(U.K.)

THE
BAHAMAS

Nassau

CUBA

Camagüey

Santiago
de Cuba

Greater Antilles

Kingston

JAMAICA

Cayman Is
(U.K.)

Gd Cayman

Havana

Pinar
del Río

Yucatan Channel

CARIBBEAN

SEA

Colón

PANAMA

Panamá

I. de Malpelo
(Col.)

I. de Coco
(C.R.)

COSTA RICA

San José

NICARAGUA

L. Nicaragua

Managua

HONDURAS

Tegucigalpa

EL SALVADOR

San Salvador

GUATEMALA

Guatemala City

BELIZE

Belize

Belmopan

Yucatan

Mérida

Campeche

Villahermosa

G. of
Tehuantepec

Veracruz

Bahía de Campeche

MEXICO

Puebla

México

Querétaro

León

Morelia

Guadalajara

Acapulco

Ciudad Victoria

Monterrey

Matamoros

Nuevo
Laredo

Saltillo

Torreón

Chihuahua

Ciudad
Juárez

El Paso

Rio Grande

Culiacán

Hermosillo

Gulf of California

Mexicali

Nogales

Tucson

Phoenix

ARIZONA

Colorado

San Diego

Los Angeles

Guadalupe
(Mex.)

Revillagigedo Is.
(Mex.)

I. Clarión

I. Socorro

Clipperton I.
(Fr.)

Tropic of Cancer

UNITED STATES OF AMERICA

PLAINS

NEW MEXICO

Albuquerque

Santa Fe

COLORADO

Denver

Lincoln

Topeka

KANSAS

Tulsa

OKLAHOMA

Oklahoma
City

Ft Worth

Dallas

Austin

TEXAS

San Antonio

Corpus Christi

Houston

Baton
Rouge

LOUISIANA

New Orleans

Mississippi

Red

Arkansas

Little Rock

ARKANSAS

MISSOURI

St Louis

Springfield

Des
Moines

Kansas
City

Missouri

ILLINOIS

Chicago

Springfield

INDIANA

Indianapolis

OHIO

Columbus

Cincinnati

Cleveland

L. Erie

Detroit

Buffalo

KENTUCKY

Frankfort

Nashville

TENNESSEE

Memphis

MISS.

Jackson

ALABAMA

Birmingham

Montgomery

GEORGIA

Atlanta

FLORIDA

Tallahassee

Tampa

Miami

Key West

Str. of Florida

C. Canaveral

Jacksonville

S. CAROLINA

Columbia

Charleston

N. CAROLINA

Raleigh

Charlotte

C. Fear

C. Hatteras

VIRGINIA

Richmond

W. VIRGINIA

D.C.

Washington

Annapolis

MD.

DEL.
Dover

Baltimore

Philadelphia

Harrisburg

PENNSYLVANIA

Pittsburgh

NEW YORK

Albany

New York

Trenton

N.J.

Hartford

CONN. R.I.
Providence

MASS.
Boston

Gulf of
Mexico

© Bartholomew

Km	Miles
1400	
1200	800
1000	600
800	
600	400
400	200
200	
0	0

1:25M

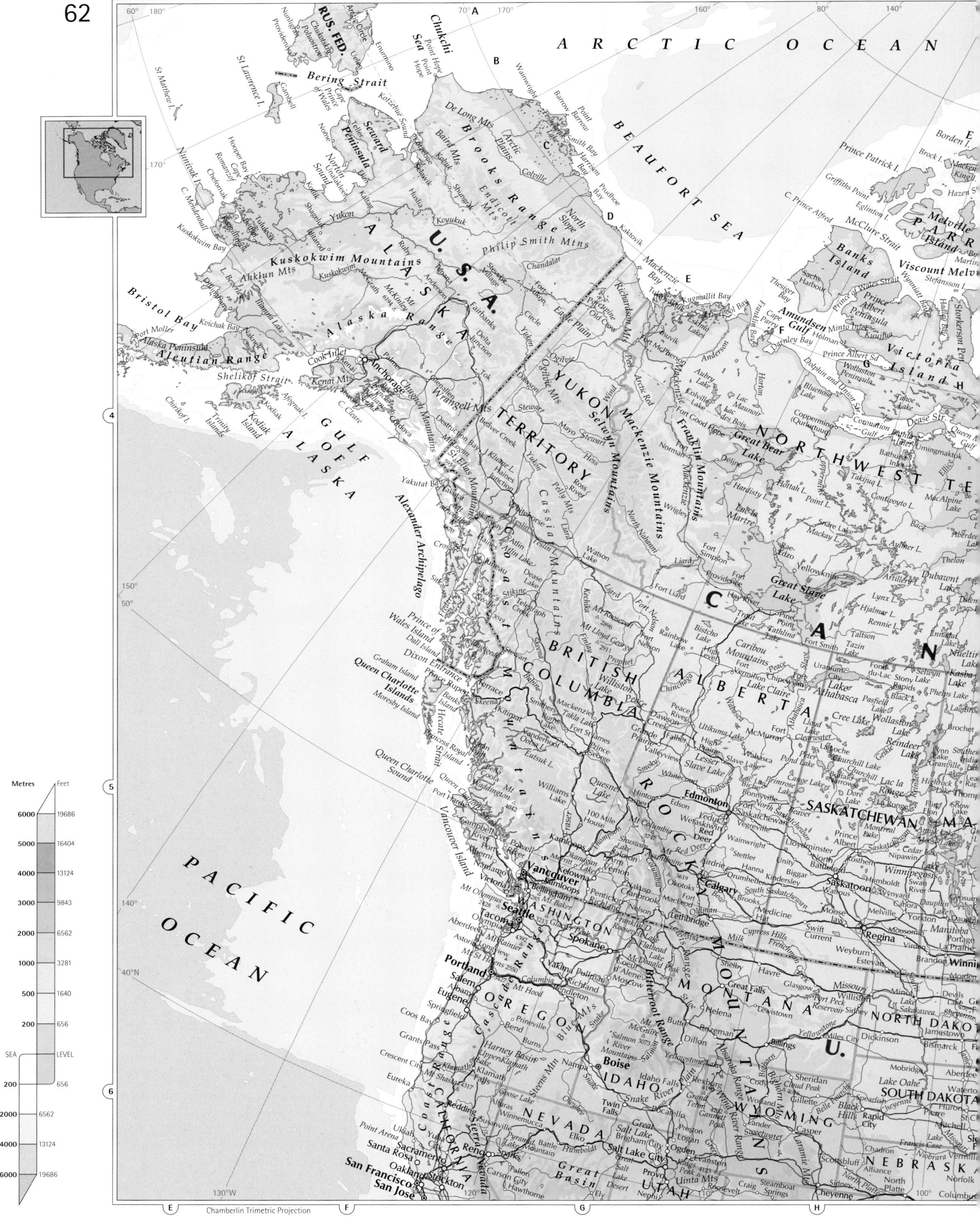
ARCTIC OCEAN
BEAUFORT SEA
Chukchi Sea
Bering Strait
RUS. FED.
U.S.A.
ALASKA
YUKON TERRITORY
NORTHWEST TE
BRITISH COLUMBIA
ALBERTA
SASKATCHEWAN
CAN
GULF OF ALASKA
PACIFIC OCEAN
Brooks Range
Kuskokwim Mountains
Alaska Range
Aleutian Range
Alaska Peninsula
Bristol Bay
Seward Peninsula
Norton Sound
Kodiak Island
Cook Inlet
Anchorage
Fairbanks
Wrangell Mts
Chugach Mountains
St Elias Mountains
Alexander Archipelago
Mackenzie Mountains
Selwyn Mountains
Ogilvie Mts
Richardson Mts
Franklin Mountains
Cassiar Mountains
Coast Mountains
Rocky Mountains
Great Bear Lake
Great Slave Lake
Lake Athabasca
Banks Island
Victoria Island
Melville Island
Prince Patrick I.
Amundsen Gulf
Viscount Melville
Queen Charlotte Islands
Queen Charlotte Sound
Vancouver Island
Prince of Wales Island
Dixon Entrance
Edmonton
Calgary
Regina
Saskatoon
Vancouver
Victoria
Seattle
Tacoma
Spokane
Portland
Salem
Eugene
Boise
Helena
Billings
Salt Lake City
Reno
Sacramento
San Francisco
San Jose
Oakland
Stockton
Cheyenne
WASHINGTON
OREGON
IDAHO
MONTANA
WYOMING
NEVADA
UTAH
CALIFORNIA
NORTH DAKO
SOUTH DAKOTA
NEBRASK
U.
Bitterroot Range
Great Basin
Blue Mts
Cascade Range
Sierra Nevada
Metres
Feet
6000 19686
5000 16404
4000 13124
3000 9843
2000 6562
1000 3281
500 1640
200 656
SEA LEVEL
200 656
2000 6562
4000 13124
6000 19686
Chamberlin Trimetric Projection

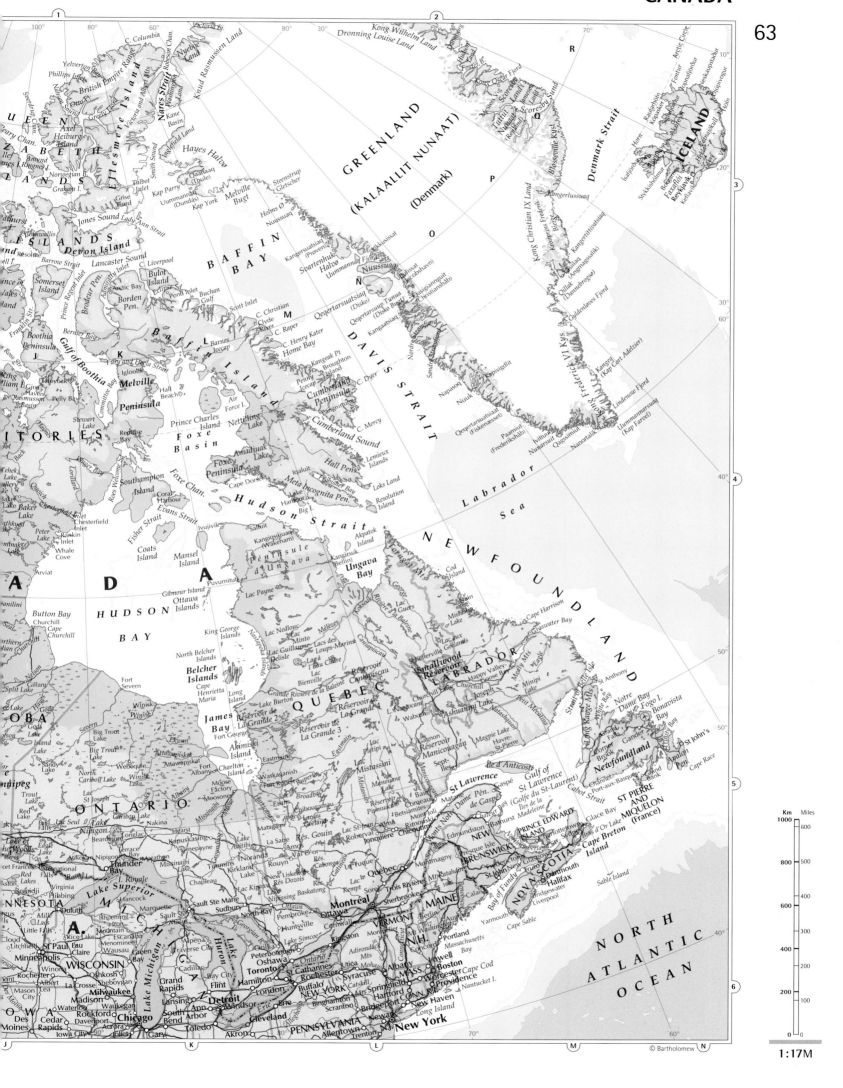

GREENLAND
(KALAALLIT NUNAAT)
(Denmark)

ICELAND

BAFFIN
BAY

DAVIS
STRAIT

Labrador
Sea

NEWFOUNDLAND

HUDSON
BAY

James
Bay

LABRADOR

QUEBEC

ONTARIO

Lake Superior

Lake Michigan

Lake Huron

Lake Erie

Lake Ontario

NEW
BRUNSWICK

PRINCE EDWARD
ISLAND

NOVA
SCOTIA

Cape Breton
Island

ST PIERRE
AND
MIQUELON
(France)

Gulf of
St Lawrence
(Golfe du St-Laurent)

MAINE

VERMONT

N.H.

MASS.

CONN.

R.I.

NEW
YORK

PENNSYLVANIA

WISCONSIN

MICHIGAN

Montréal

Ottawa

Toronto

Detroit

Chicago

Minneapolis

New York

Boston

NORTH
ATLANTIC
OCEAN

© Bartholomew

Km	Miles
1000	600
800	500
600	400
	300
400	200
200	100
0	0

1:17M

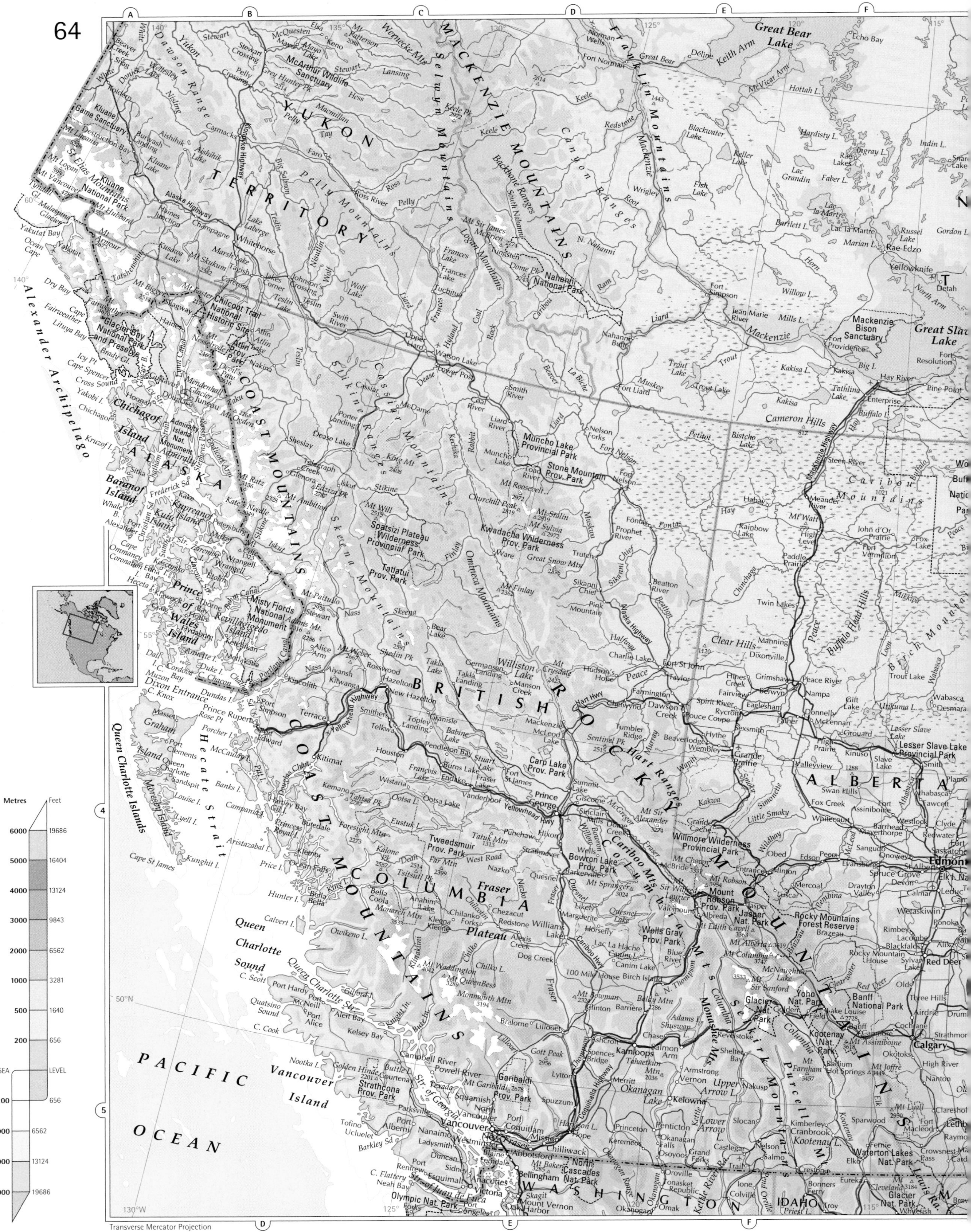

HUDSON
BAY
MANITOBA
SASKATCHEWAN
ONTARIO
NORTH DAKOTA
MINNESOTA
U. S. A.
Southampton Island
Thelon Game Sanctuary
Lake Athabasca
Lake Winnipeg
Lake Winnipegosis
Lake Manitoba
Reindeer Lake
Wollaston Lake
Southern Indian Lake
Cree Lake
Kasba Lake
Dubawnt Lake
Nueltin Lake
Baker Lake
Chesterfield Inlet
Rankin Inlet
Whale Cove
Arviat
Churchill
Cape Churchill
Thompson
Flin Flon
The Pas
Saskatoon
Regina
Moose Jaw
Prince Albert
North Battleford
Lloydminster
Swift Current
Yorkton
Brandon
Winnipeg
Portage la Prairie
Kenora
Dryden
Fort Frances
Grand Forks
Minot
Williston
Fort Chipewyan
Uranium City
La Ronge
Lac La Ronge Provincial Park
Meadow Lake Provincial Park
Prince Albert National Park
Narrow Hills Provincial Park
Clearwater River Provincial Park
Grass River Prov. Park
Paint Lake Provincial Recr. Park
Porcupine Prov. Forest
Greenwater Provincial Park
Riding Mountain Nat. Park
Whiteshell Prov. Park
Opasquia Provincial Park
Grasslands Nat. Park
Cypress Hills
Lake of the Woods
Voyageurs Nat. Park
Km
Miles
1:7M
© Bartholomew

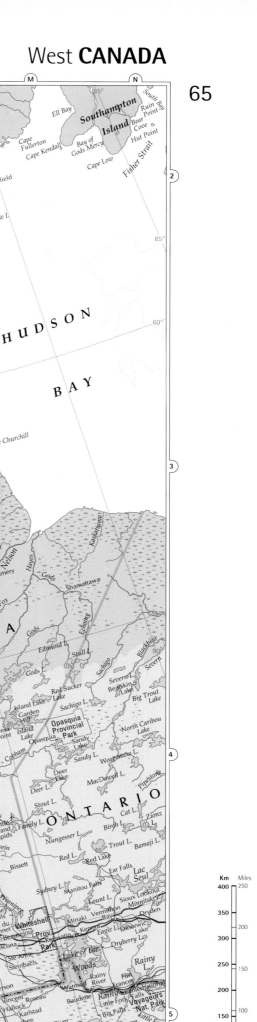

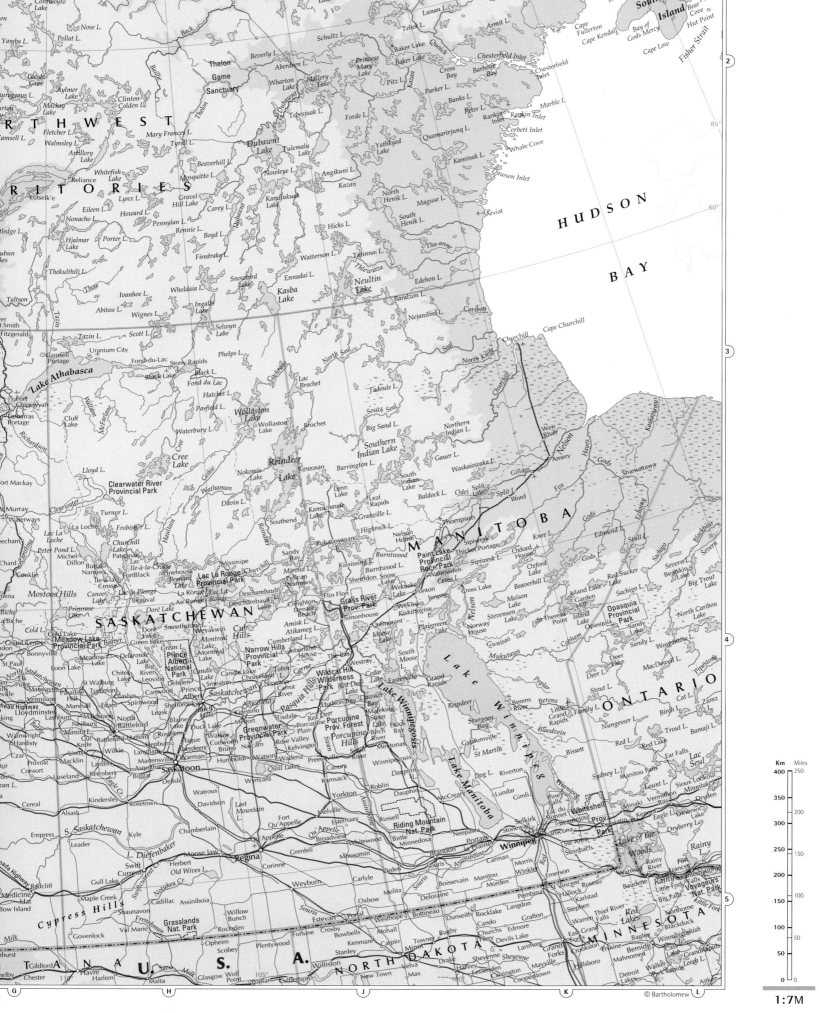

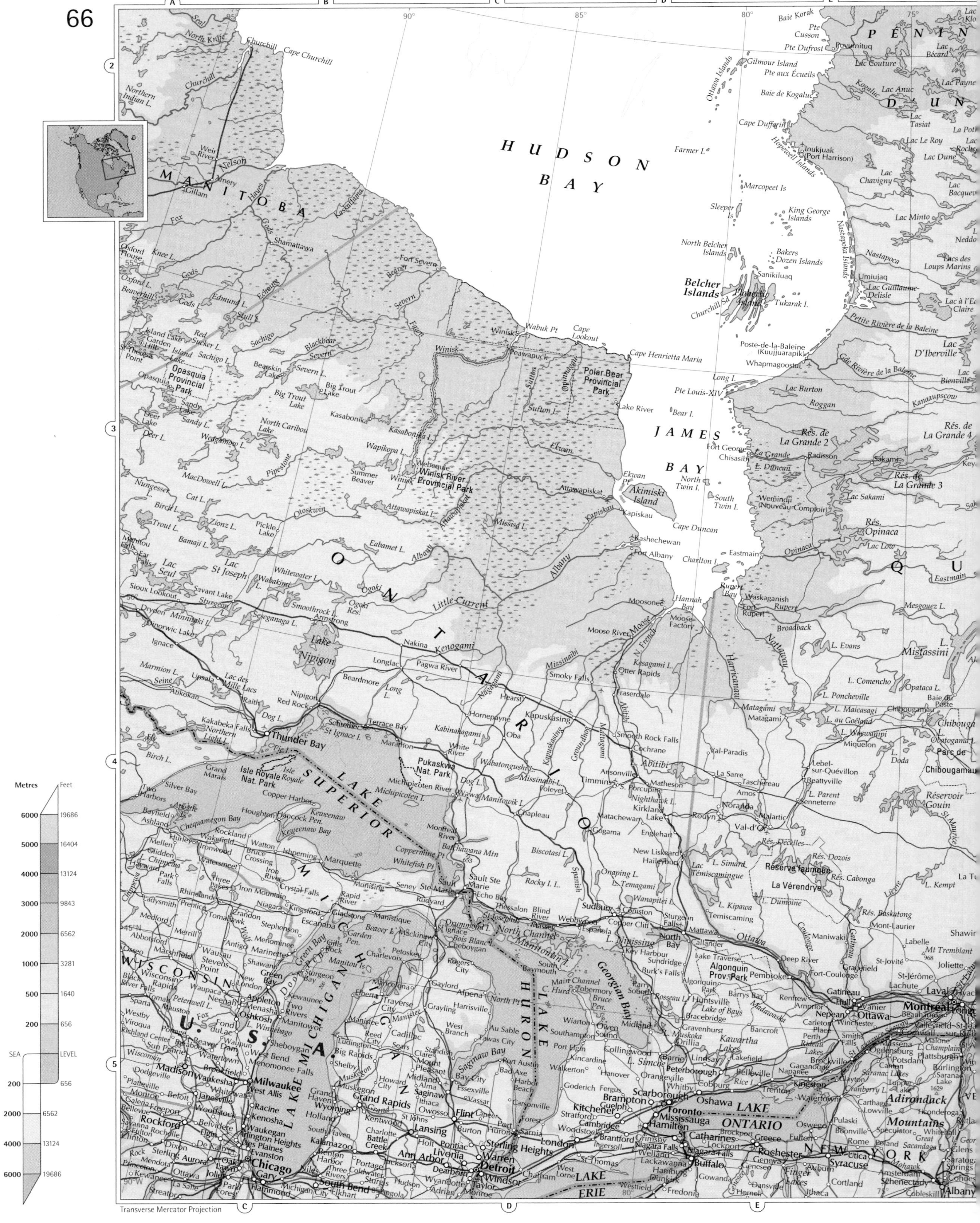

Transverse Mercator Projection

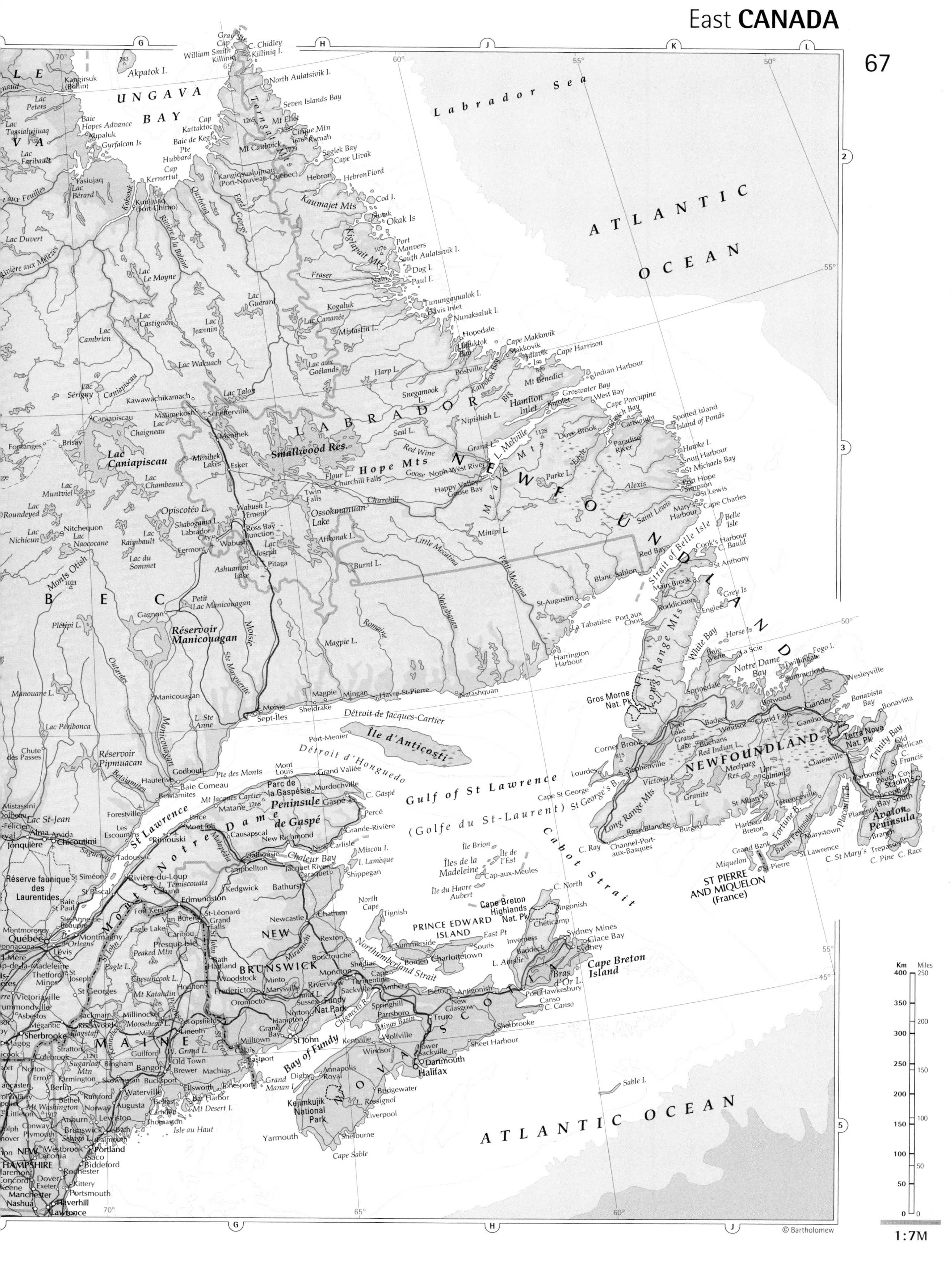

ATLANTIC OCEAN

Labrador Sea

UNGAVA BAY

LABRADOR

NEWFOUNDLAND

QUÉBEC

Gulf of St Lawrence
(Golfe du St-Laurent)

Île d'Anticosti

Détroit de Jacques-Cartier

Cabot Strait

ST PIERRE
AND MIQUELON
(France)

Avalon
Peninsula

PRINCE EDWARD
ISLAND

Cape Breton
Island

NEW
BRUNSWICK

NOVA SCOTIA

MAINE

NEW
HAMPSHIRE

Bay of Fundy

ATLANTIC OCEAN

Peninsule
de Gaspé

Réservoir
Manicouagan

Smallwood Res.

Lac
Caniapiscau

Gros Morne
Nat. Pk

Terra Nova
Nat. Pk

Cape Breton
Highlands
Nat. Pk

Fundy
Nat. Park

Kejimkujik
National Park

© Bartholomew

Km	Miles
400	250
350	200
300	150
250	
200	100
150	
100	50
50	
0	0

1:7M

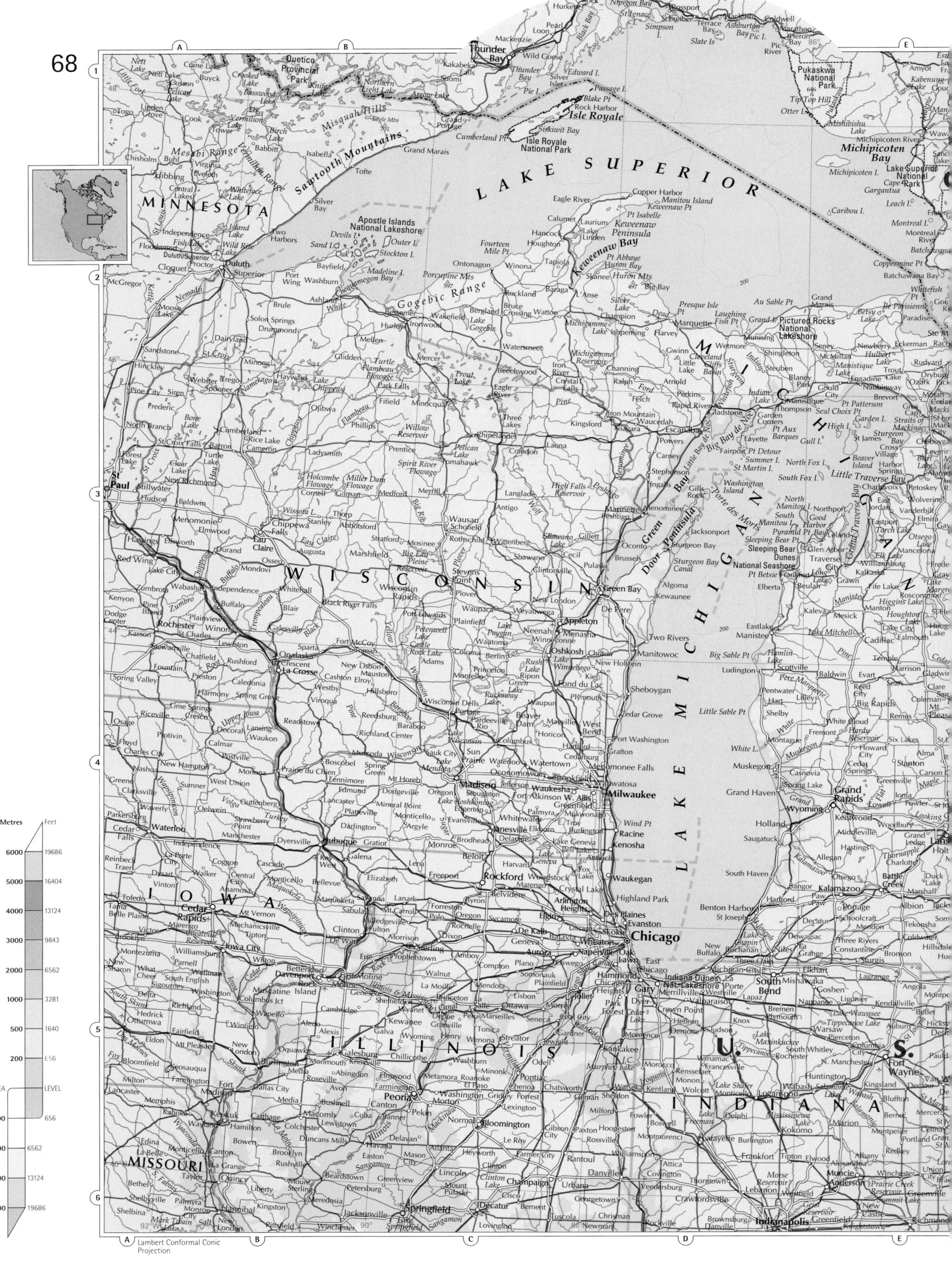

MINNESOTA

LAKE SUPERIOR

Isle Royale
Isle Royale
National Park

Apostle Islands
National Lakeshore

Keweenaw
Peninsula

Gogebic Range

Pictured Rocks
National
Lakeshore

MICHIGAN

WISCONSIN

Green Bay

LAKE MICHIGAN

Milwaukee

IOWA

Chicago

South
Bend

U. S.

ILLINOIS

Fort
Wayne

INDIANA

MISSOURI

Indianapolis

Metres   Feet
6000   19686
5000   16404
4000   13124
3000   9843
2000   6562
1000   3281
500   1640
200   656
SEA   LEVEL
200   656
2000   6562
4000   13124
6000   19686

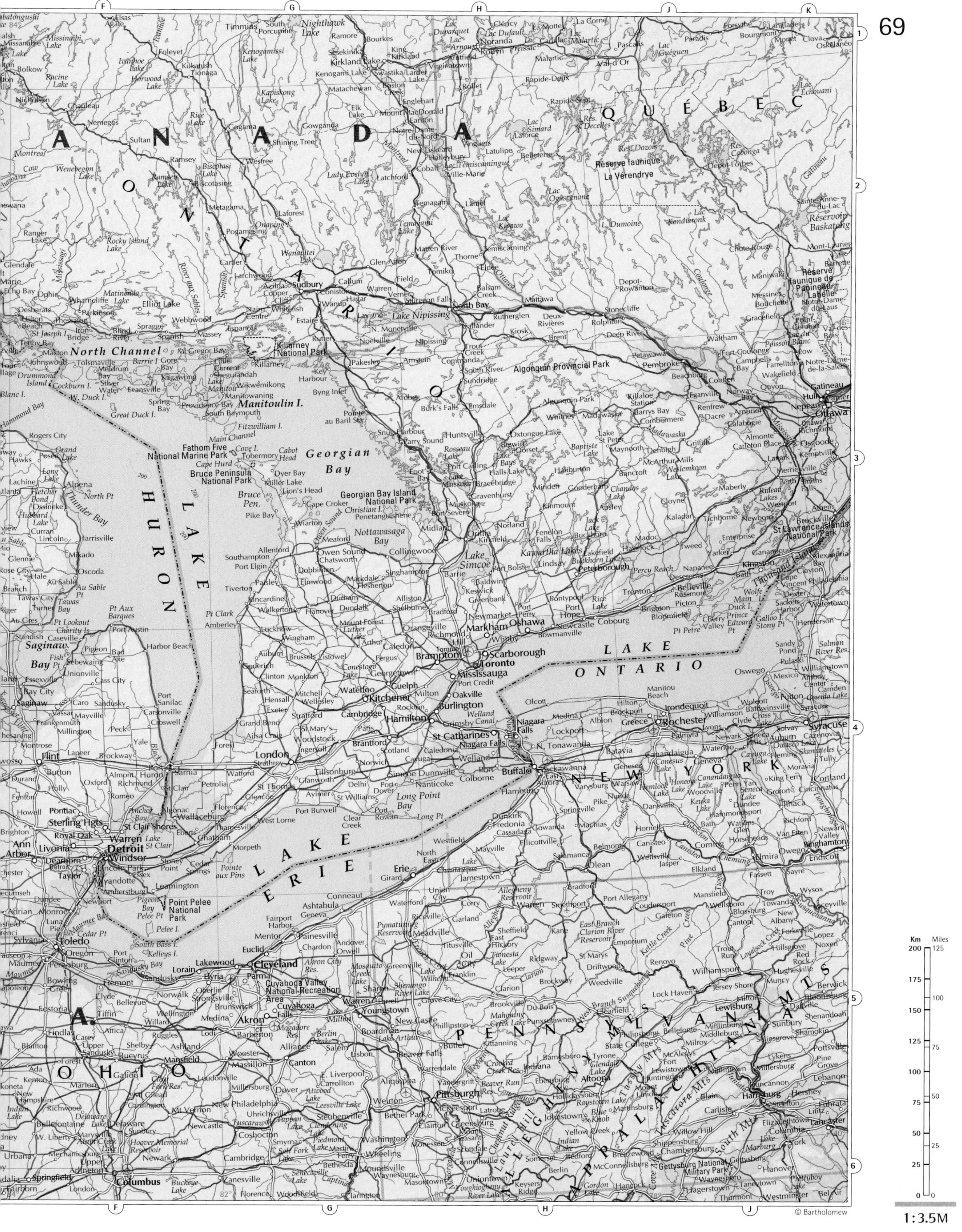
CANADA
ONTARIO
QUÉBEC
U.S.A.
OHIO
PENNSYLVANIA
NEW YORK
LAKE HURON
LAKE ONTARIO
LAKE ERIE
Georgian Bay
North Channel
Manitoulin I.
Lake Simcoe
Lake Nipissing
Algonquin Provincial Park
Réserve faunique La Vérendrye
Saginaw Bay
ALLEGHENY MTS
APPALACHIAN MTS
Km
Miles
© Bartholomew

1:3.5M

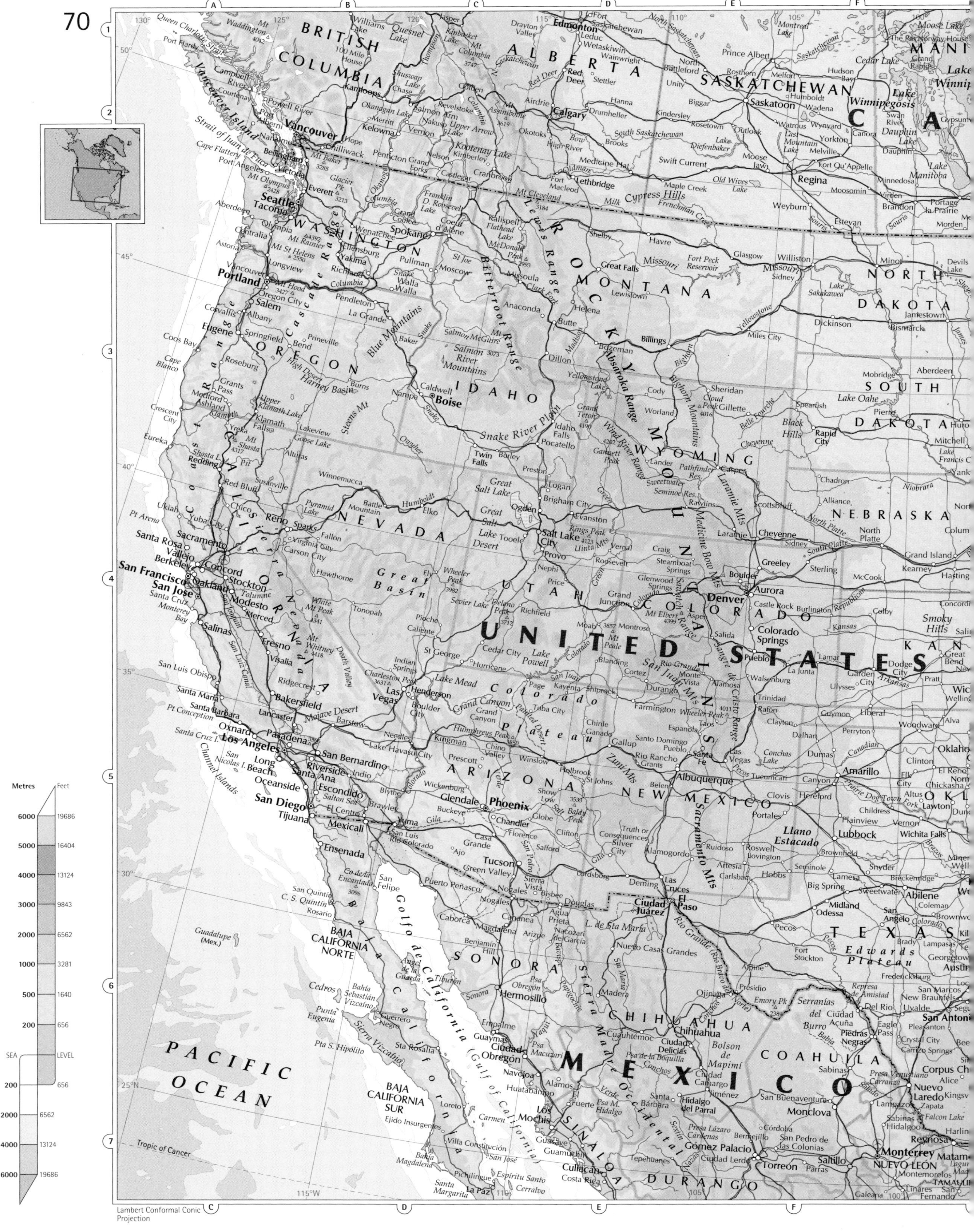

BRITISH COLUMBIA
ALBERTA
SASKATCHEWAN
MANI
CA
WASHINGTON
OREGON
IDAHO
MONTANA
NORTH DAKOTA
SOUTH DAKOTA
WYOMING
NEBRASKA
NEVADA
UTAH
COLORADO
CALIFORNIA
ARIZONA
NEW MEXICO
TEXAS
KAN
OKL
UNITED STATES
MEXICO
SONORA
CHIHUAHUA
COAHUILA
SINALOA
DURANGO
NUEVO LEÓN
BAJA CALIFORNIA NORTE
BAJA CALIFORNIA SUR
PACIFIC OCEAN
Golfo de California (Gulf of California)
Baja California
Sierra Madre Occidental
ROCKY MOUNTAINS
Cascade Range
Coast Ranges
Sierra Nevada
Great Basin
Colorado Plateau
Snake River Plain
Bitterroot Range
Lewis Range
Blue Mountains
Salmon River Mountains
Absaroka Range
Bighorn Mountains
Wind River Range
Medicine Bow Mts
Laramie Mts
Uinta Mts
San Juan Mts
Sangre de Cristo Range
Sacramento Mts
Zuni Mts
Llano Estacado
Edwards Plateau
Great Salt Lake
Great Salt Lake Desert
Mojave Desert
Painted Desert
Death Valley
Vancouver Island
Strait of Juan de Fuca
Queen Charlotte Strait
Channel Islands
Tropic of Cancer
Edmonton
Calgary
Saskatoon
Regina
Vancouver
Victoria
Seattle
Tacoma
Spokane
Portland
Salem
Eugene
Boise
Salt Lake City
Reno
Sacramento
San Francisco
Oakland
San Jose
Fresno
Bakersfield
Los Angeles
Long Beach
San Diego
Tijuana
Mexicali
Las Vegas
Phoenix
Tucson
Albuquerque
Santa Fe
Denver
Aurora
Colorado Springs
Pueblo
Cheyenne
Billings
Great Falls
El Paso
Ciudad Juárez
Chihuahua
Hermosillo
Monterrey
Torreón
Saltillo
Culiacán
Amarillo
Lubbock
Abilene
San Antonio
Corpus Christi
Nuevo Laredo
Mt Rainier 4392
Mt St Helens 2550
Mt Hood 3427
Mt Shasta 4317
Mt Whitney 4418
Mt Elbert 4399
Grand Teton 4196
Lambert Conformal Conic Projection
Metres
Feet
6000
5000
4000
3000
2000
1000
500
200
SEA
LEVEL
19686
16404
13124
9843
6562
3281
1640
656

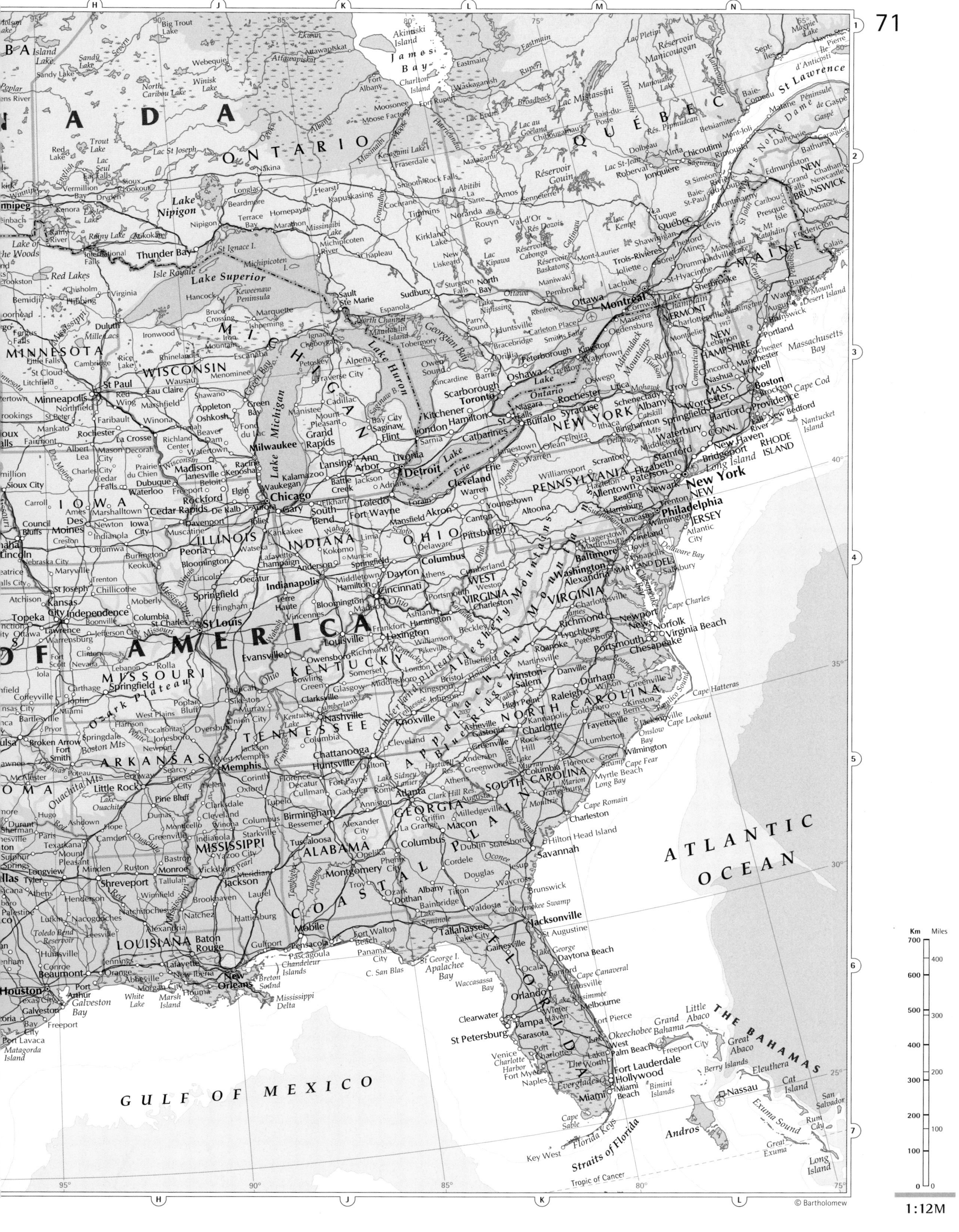

CANADA
ONTARIO
QUÉBEC
NEW BRUNSWICK
James Bay
Lake Superior
Lake Michigan
Lake Huron
Lake Ontario
Lake Erie
Georgian Bay
Lake Nipigon
St Lawrence
MINNESOTA
WISCONSIN
MICHIGAN
IOWA
ILLINOIS
INDIANA
OHIO
PENNSYLVANIA
NEW YORK
VERMONT
NEW HAMPSHIRE
MAINE
MASS.
CONN.
RHODE ISLAND
NEW JERSEY
MARYLAND
DEL.
WEST VIRGINIA
VIRGINIA
KENTUCKY
MISSOURI
ARKANSAS
TENNESSEE
NORTH CAROLINA
SOUTH CAROLINA
GEORGIA
ALABAMA
MISSISSIPPI
LOUISIANA
FLORIDA
OF AMERICA
Appalachian Mountains
Allegheny Mountains
Blue Ridge
Cumberland Plateau
Ozark Plateau
Adirondack Mountains
COASTAL PLAIN
Ottawa
Montréal
Québec
Toronto
Detroit
Chicago
Milwaukee
Minneapolis
St Paul
St Louis
Indianapolis
Columbus
Cleveland
Pittsburgh
Philadelphia
New York
Boston
Baltimore
Washington
Richmond
Nashville
Memphis
Atlanta
Charlotte
Jacksonville
Orlando
Tampa
Miami
New Orleans
Houston
Nassau
Cape Cod
Cape Hatteras
Cape Canaveral
Florida Keys
Straits of Florida
Tropic of Cancer
Key West
THE BAHAMAS
Andros
Great Abaco
Grand Bahama
Eleuthera
Cat Island
Long Island
ATLANTIC OCEAN
GULF OF MEXICO
95°
90°
85°
80°
75°
40°
35°
30°
25°
H
J
K
L
M
N
1
2
3
4
5
6
7
Km
Miles
700
600
500
400
300
200
100
0
400
300
200
100
0
1:12M
© Bartholomew

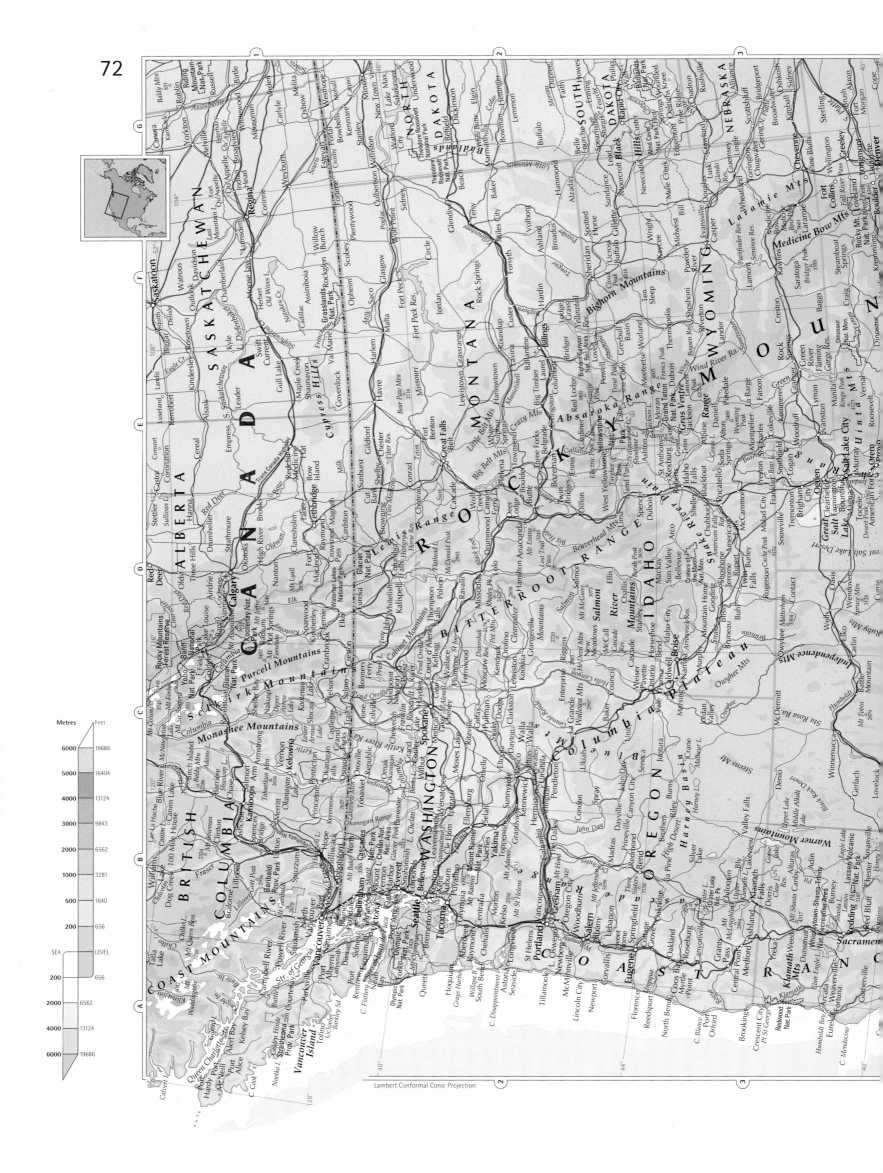
Metres
Feet
6000 19686
5000 16404
4000 13124
3000 9843
2000 6562
1000 3281
500 1640
200 656
SEA LEVEL
200 656
2000 6562
4000 13124
6000 19686
Lambert Conformal Conic Projection
CANADA
BRITISH COLUMBIA
ALBERTA
SASKATCHEWAN
NORTH DAKOTA
SOUTH DAKOTA
NEBRASKA
MONTANA
WYOMING
IDAHO
WASHINGTON
OREGON
COAST MOUNTAINS
BITTERROOT RANGE
Columbia Plateau
Blue Mts
Harney Basin
Cypress Hills
Vancouver Island
Vancouver
Seattle
Portland
Spokane
Calgary
Regina
Saskatoon
Boise
Salt Lake City
Denver

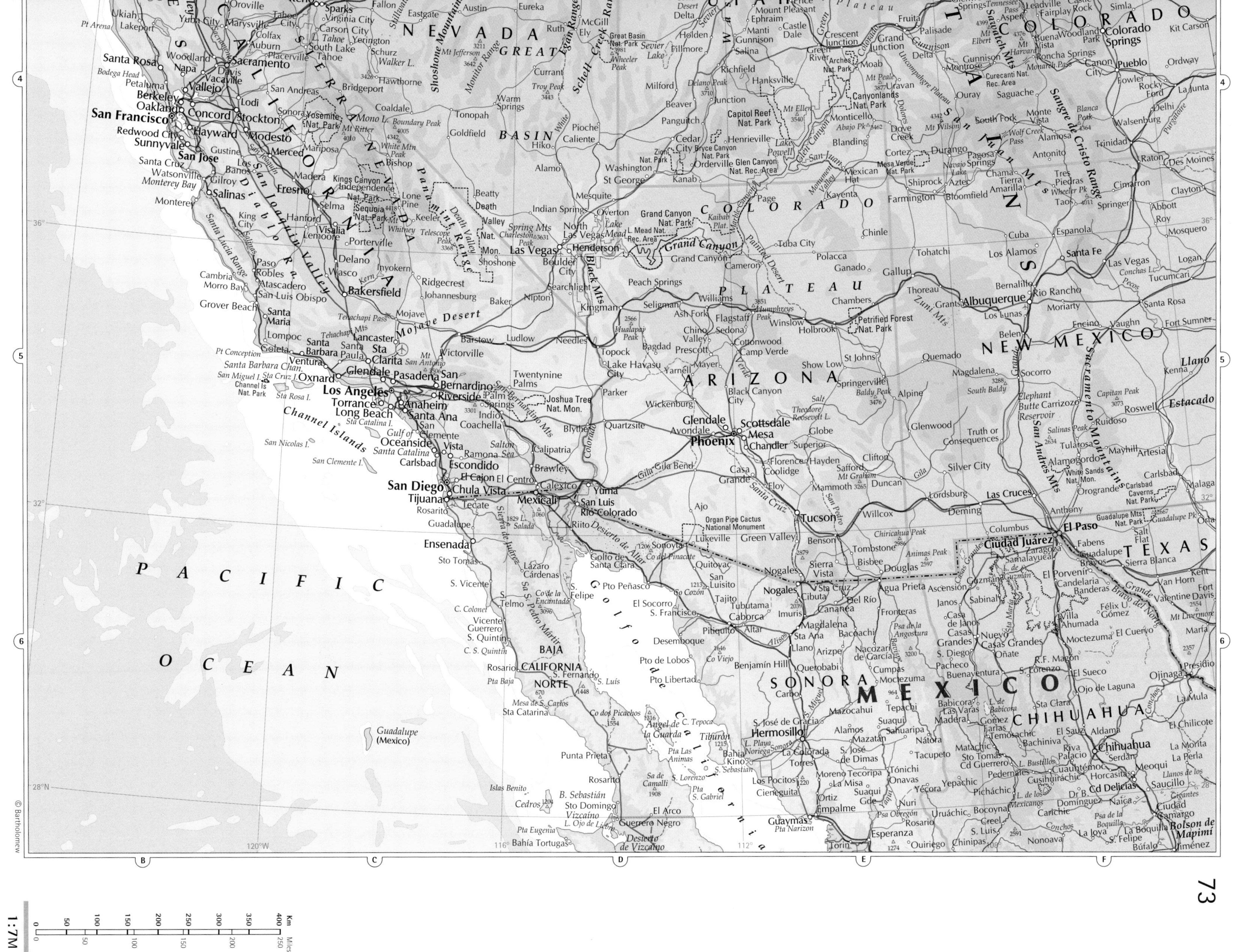

Km   Miles
400 — 250

350 — 200

300 —
      — 150
250 —

200 — 100

150 —
      — 50
100 —

50 —

0 — 0

© Bartholomew

1:7M

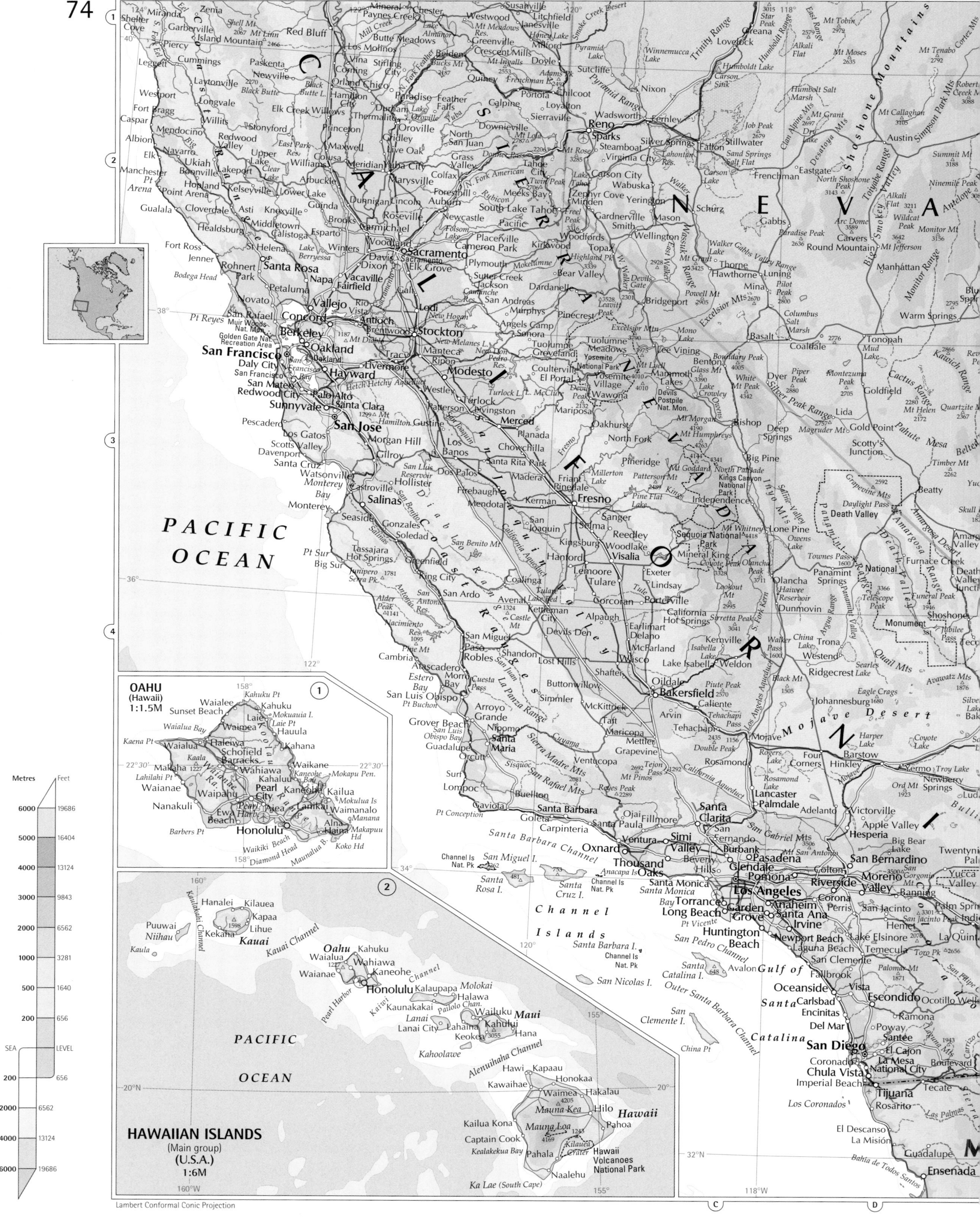

CALIFORNIA
NEVADA
SIERRA NEVADA
PACIFIC OCEAN
Channel Islands
Mojave Desert
Death Valley
OAHU
(Hawaii)
1:1.5M
HAWAIIAN ISLANDS
(Main group)
(U.S.A.)
1:6M
PACIFIC OCEAN
Metres
Feet
SEA
LEVEL
Lambert Conformal Conic Projection

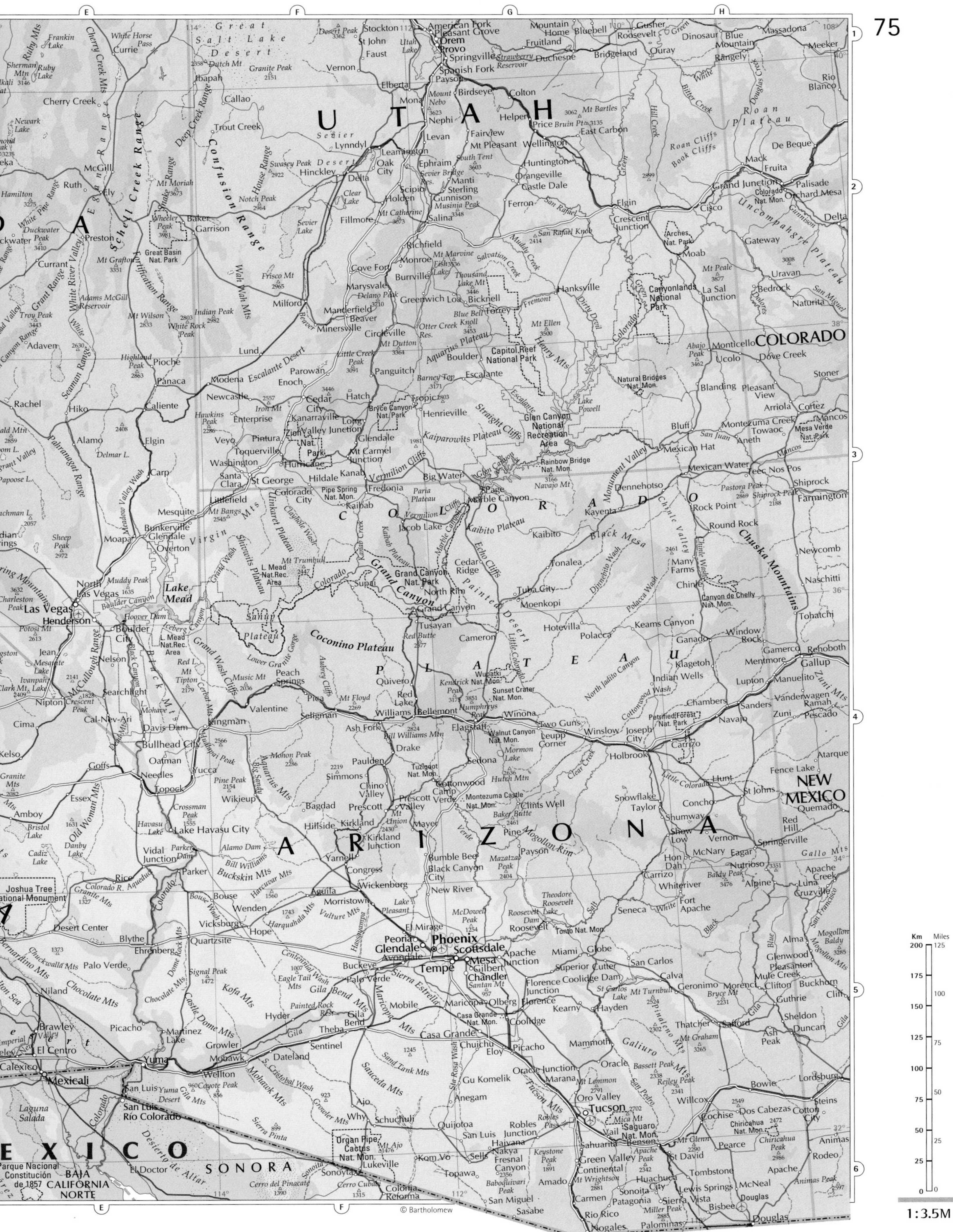

© Bartholomew

1:3.5M

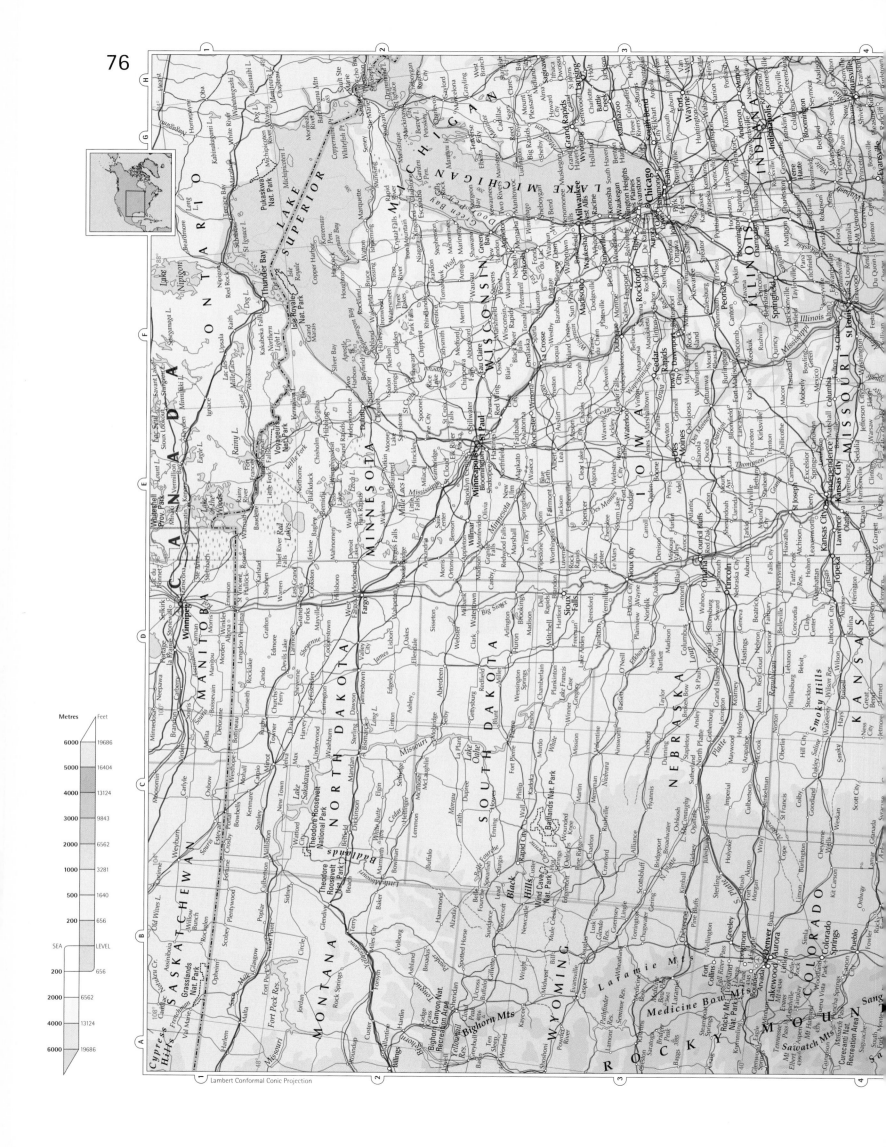
Metres
Feet
6000
19686
5000
16404
4000
13124
3000
9843
2000
6562
1000
3281
500
1640
200
656
SEA
LEVEL
200
656
2000
6562
4000
13124
6000
19686
Lambert Conformal Conic Projection
C A N A D A
O N T A R I O
MANITOBA
SASKATCHEWAN
LAKE SUPERIOR
LAKE MICHIGAN
MICHIGAN
WISCONSIN
MINNESOTA
NORTH DAKOTA
SOUTH DAKOTA
IOWA
ILLINOIS
INDIANA
MISSOURI
NEBRASKA
KANSAS
MONTANA
WYOMING
COLORADO
ROCKY MOUNTAINS
Winnipeg
Thunder Bay
Duluth
Minneapolis
St Paul
Milwaukee
Chicago
Madison
Des Moines
Omaha
Lincoln
Kansas City
St Louis
Indianapolis
Fargo
Bismarck
Sioux Falls
Denver
Billings
Cheyenne
Black Hills
Bighorn Mts
Smoky Hills
Laramie Mts
Medicine Bow Mts

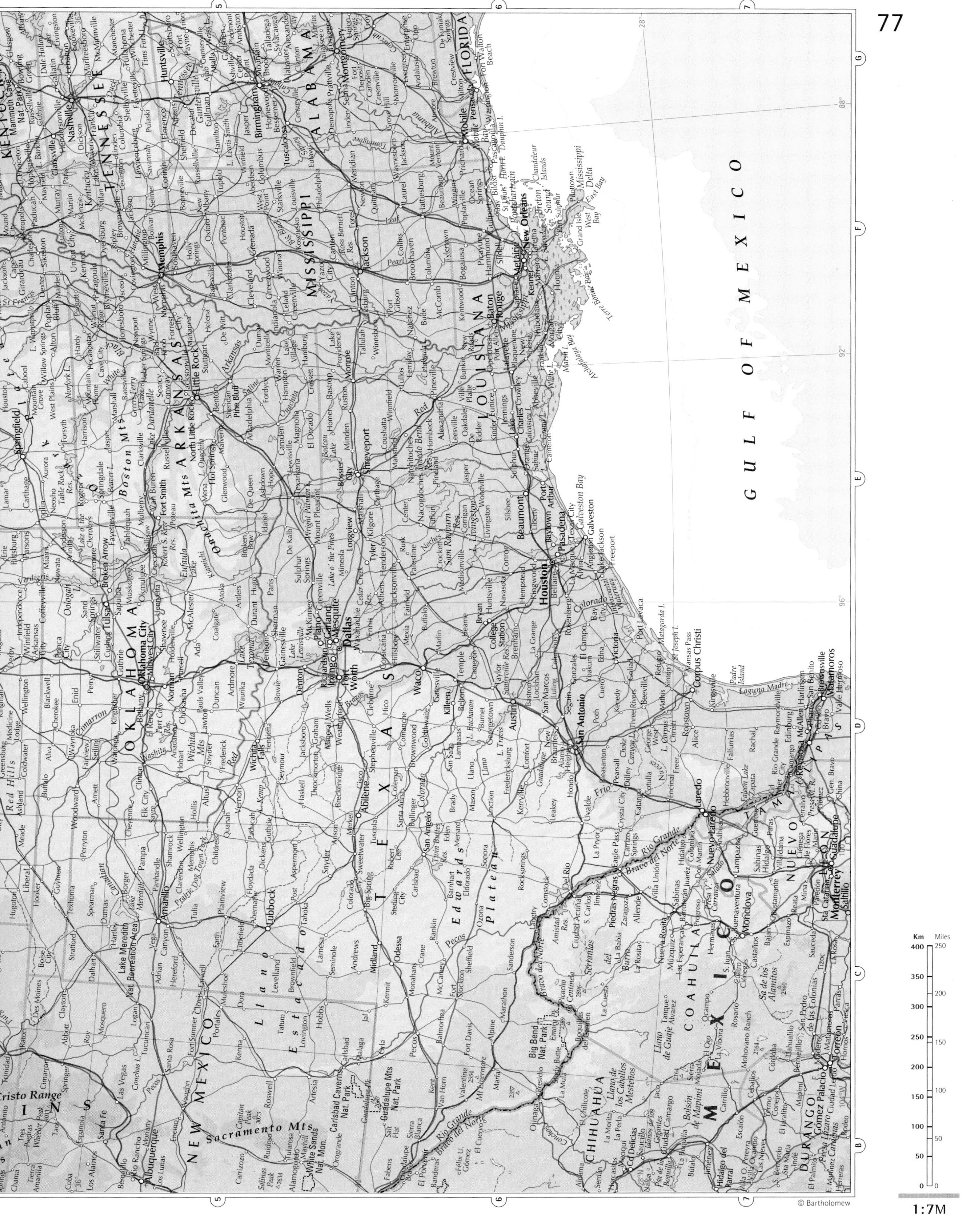

1:7M

© Bartholomew

Km   Miles
400   250

350

300   200

250   150

200

150   100

100

50   50

0   0

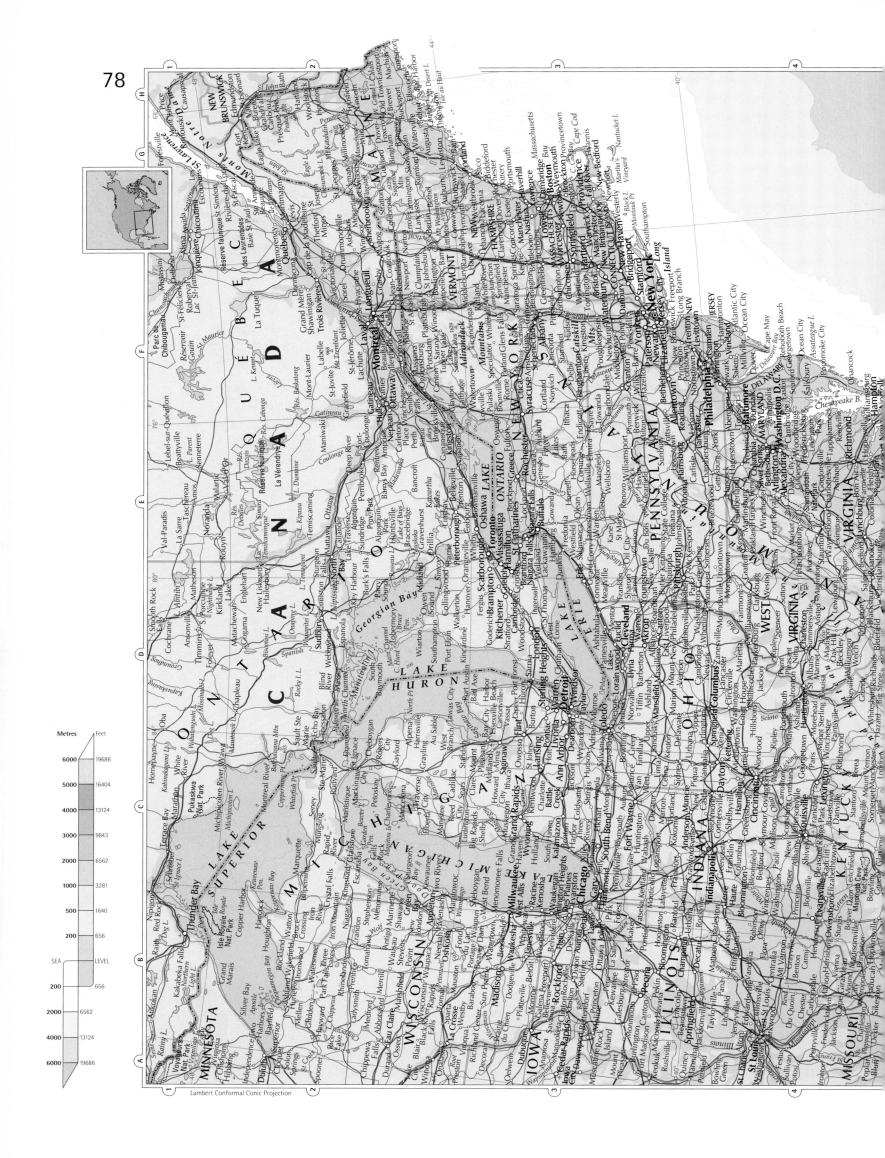
Metres
Feet
6000 19686
5000 16404
4000 13124
3000 9843
2000 6562
1000 3281
500 1640
200 656
SEA LEVEL
200 656
2000 6562
4000 13124
6000 19686
Lambert Conformal Conic Projection
C A N A D A
O N T A R I O
Q U É B E C
NEW BRUNSWICK
M A I N E
VERMONT
NEW HAMPSHIRE
MASSACHUSETTS
CONNECTICUT
NEW YORK
PENNSYLVANIA
NEW JERSEY
MARYLAND
DELAWARE
WEST VIRGINIA
VIRGINIA
KENTUCKY
OHIO
INDIANA
ILLINOIS
MICHIGAN
WISCONSIN
MINNESOTA
IOWA
MISSOURI
LAKE SUPERIOR
LAKE MICHIGAN
LAKE HURON
LAKE ERIE
LAKE ONTARIO
Georgian Bay
Chesapeake B.
Long Island
Thunder Bay
Sault Ste Marie
Sudbury
North Bay
Toronto
Hamilton
Ottawa
Montréal
Québec
Trois Rivières
Chicago
Milwaukee
Detroit
Cleveland
Toledo
Columbus
Cincinnati
Indianapolis
Louisville
St Louis
Pittsburgh
Buffalo
Rochester
Syracuse
Albany
Boston
Providence
New York
Philadelphia
Baltimore
Washington D.C.
Richmond
Portland

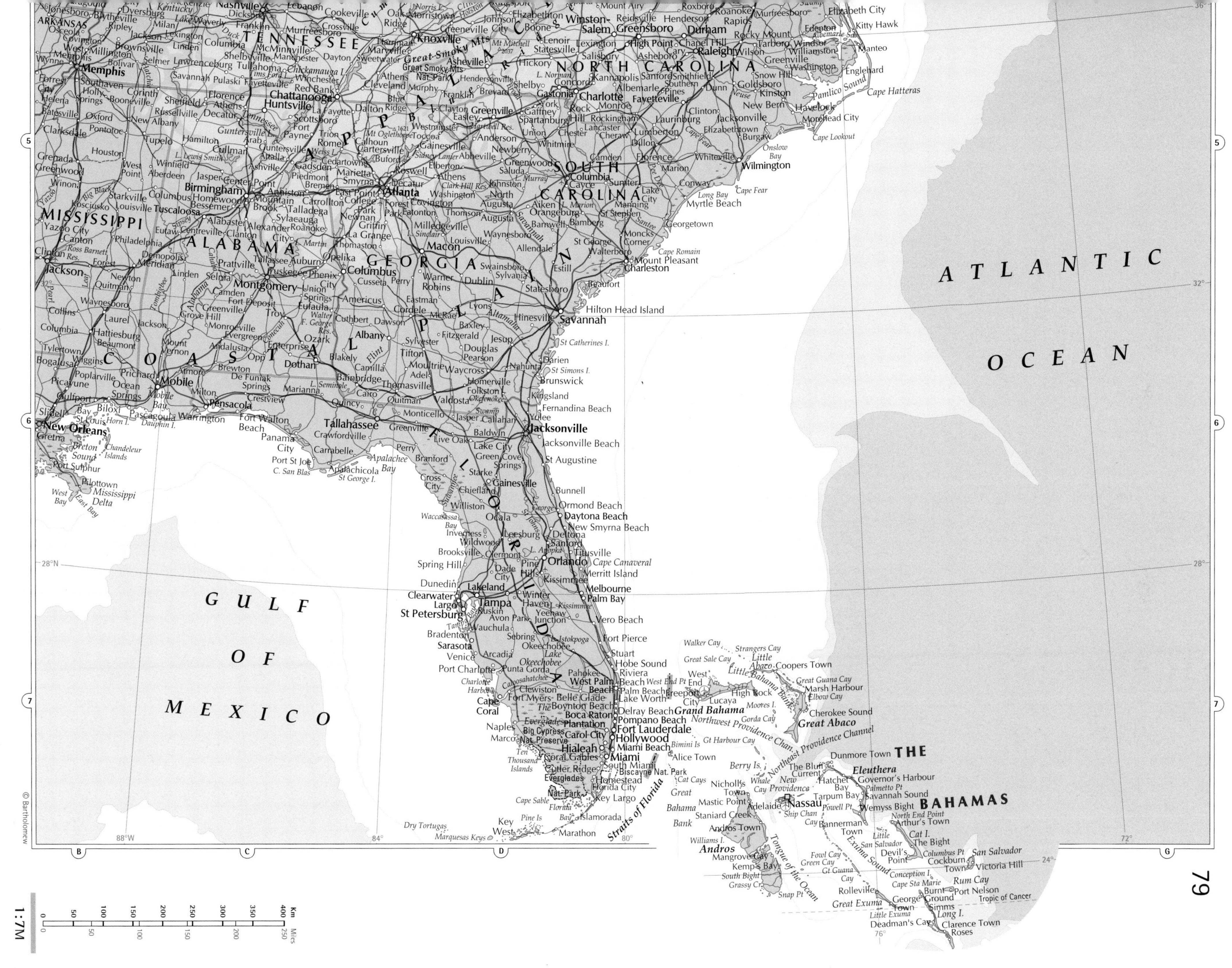

ATLANTIC

OCEAN

GULF

OF

MEXICO

BAHAMAS

THE

TENNESSEE

NORTH CAROLINA

SOUTH CAROLINA

GEORGIA

ALABAMA

MISSISSIPPI

FLORIDA

COASTAL PLAIN

APPALACHIAN

Straits of Florida

Tongue of the Ocean

Km   Miles
400 — 250
350 —
      — 200
300 —
      — 150
250 —
200 —
      — 100
150 —
100 —
      — 50
50 —
0 — 0

© Bartholomew

1:7M

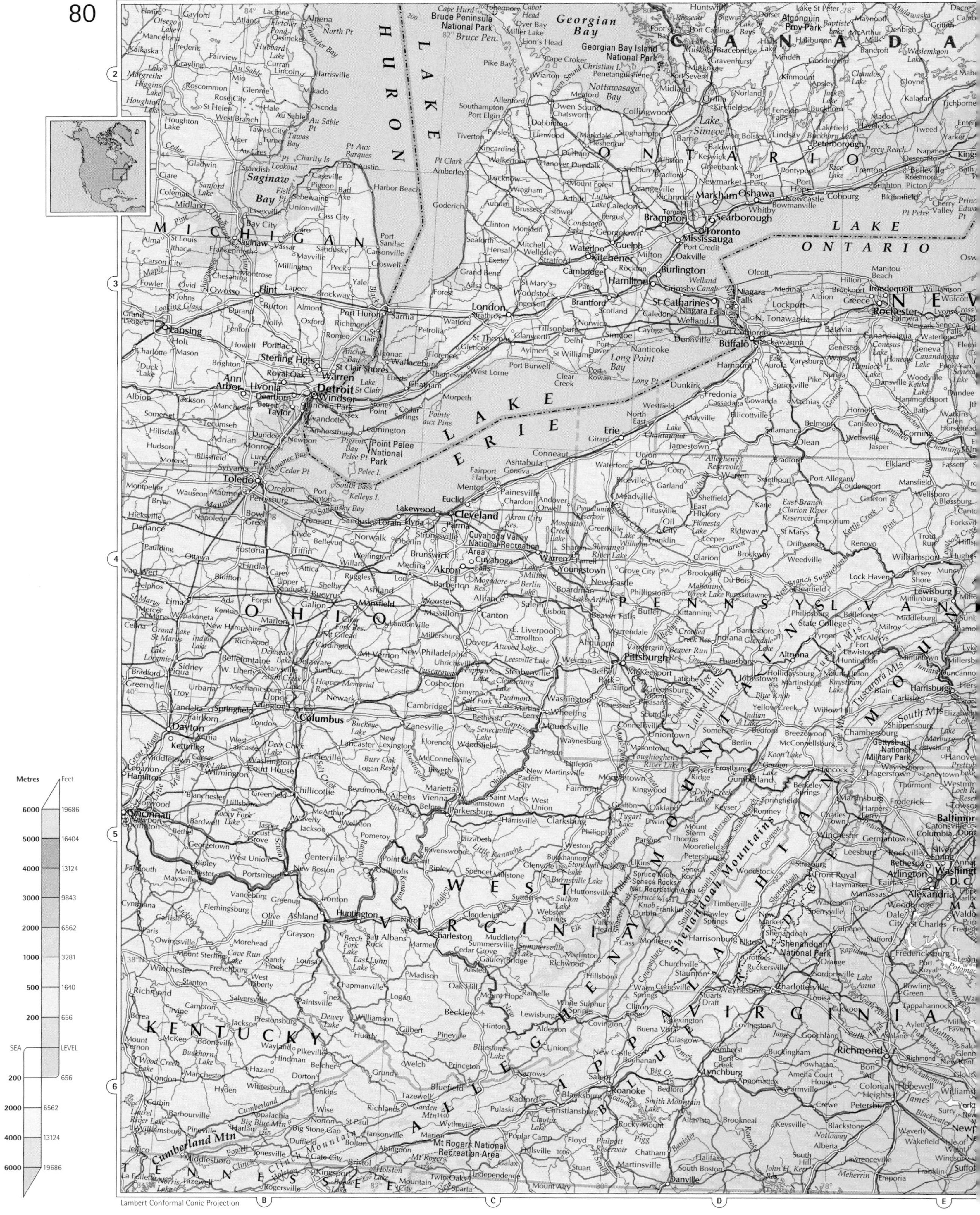

A
B
C
D
E
2
3
4
5
6
LAKE HURON
Georgian Bay
CANADA
ONTARIO
Nottawasaga Bay
Lake Simcoe
LAKE ONTARIO
MICHIGAN
Saginaw Bay
LAKE ERIE
Long Point Bay
OHIO
PENNSYLVANIA
NEW
WEST VIRGINIA
VIRGINIA
KENTUCKY
TENNESSEE
ALLEGHENY MOUNTAINS
APPALACHIAN MOUNTAINS
BLUE RIDGE
Shenandoah Mountains
Cumberland Mtn
Bruce Peninsula National Park
Georgian Bay Island National Park
Point Pelee National Park
Cuyahoga Valley National Recreation Area
Shenandoah National Park
Mt Rogers National Recreation Area
Toronto
Mississauga
Brampton
Hamilton
Burlington
Kitchener
London
Windsor
Detroit
Flint
Lansing
Saginaw
Toledo
Cleveland
Akron
Youngstown
Erie
Buffalo
Niagara Falls
Rochester
Pittsburgh
Columbus
Dayton
Cincinnati
Charleston
Huntington
Roanoke
Lynchburg
Richmond
Harrisburg
Washington D.C.
Arlington
Alexandria
Baltimore
Metres
Feet
6000
19686
5000
16404
4000
13124
3000
9843
2000
6562
1000
3281
500
1640
200
656
SEA
LEVEL
Lambert Conformal Conic Projection

1:3.5M

© Bartholomew

Km Miles
200 — 125
175 — 100
150 —
125 — 75
100 —
75 — 50
50 —
25 — 25
0 — 0

continuation at the same scale

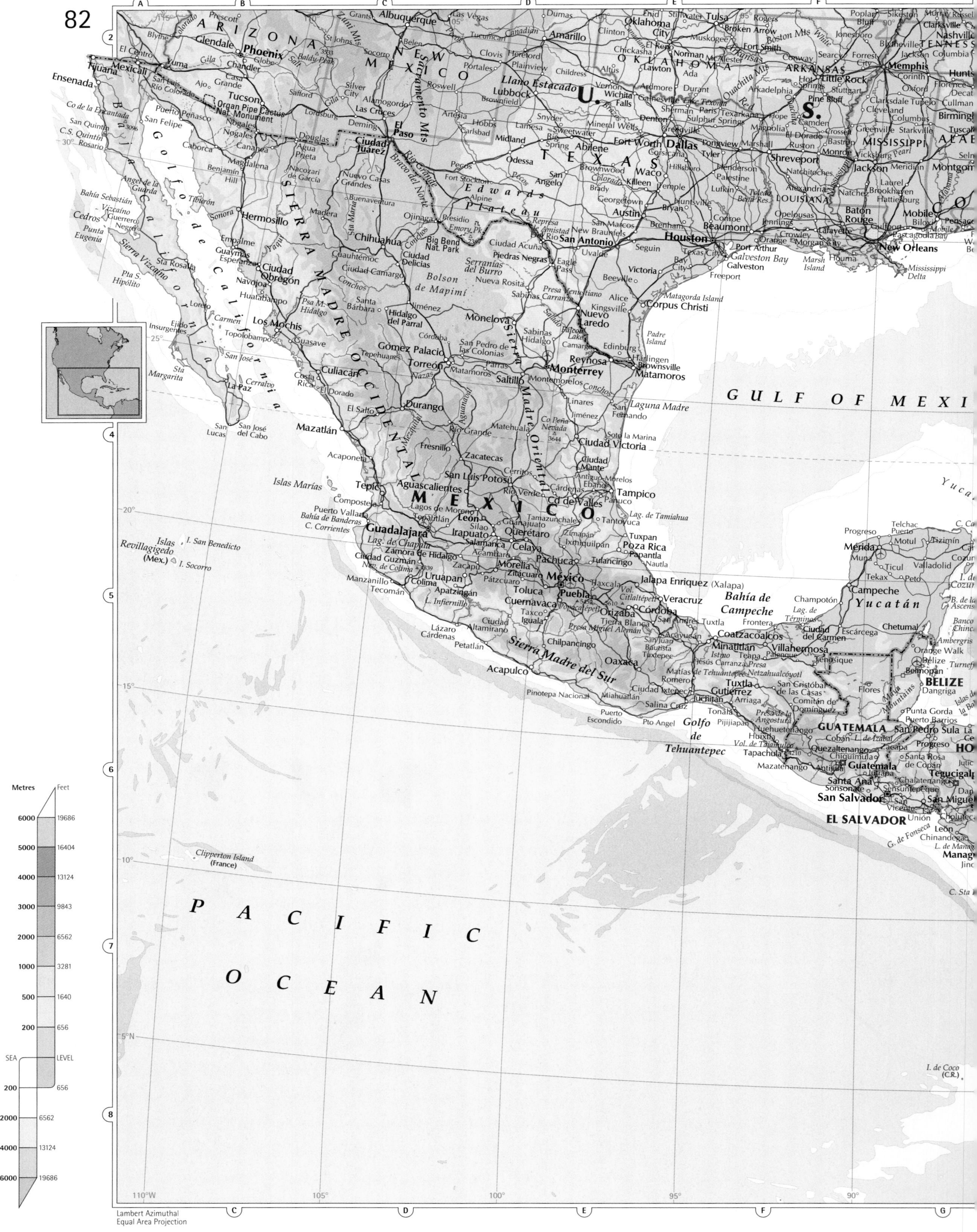

A B C D E F

ARIZONA NEW MEXICO OKLAHOMA ARKANSAS TENNESSEE

Phoenix Tucson Las Cruces El Paso U. S. Dallas Fort Worth MISSISSIPPI

Mexicali Ensenada TEXAS Austin Houston LOUISIANA New Orleans

SIERRA MADRE OCCIDENTAL Chihuahua Monterrey San Antonio Corpus Christi GULF OF MEXICO

Hermosillo Ciudad Juárez Saltillo Matamoros

Mazatlán Durango Zacatecas Tampico Yucatán

Guadalajara MEXICO San Luis Potosí Mérida Campeche

Puerto Vallarta León Querétaro Veracruz BELIZE

México Puebla Coatzacoalcos GUATEMALA

Acapulco Sierra Madre del Sur Oaxaca Tuxtla Gutiérrez San Salvador EL SALVADOR HONDURAS

PACIFIC OCEAN

Clipperton Island (France)

I. de Coco (C.R.)

Metres Feet
6000 19686
5000 16404
4000 13124
3000 9843
2000 6562
1000 3281
500 1640
200 656
SEA LEVEL
200 656
2000 6562
4000 13124
6000 19686

Lambert Azimuthal Equal Area Projection

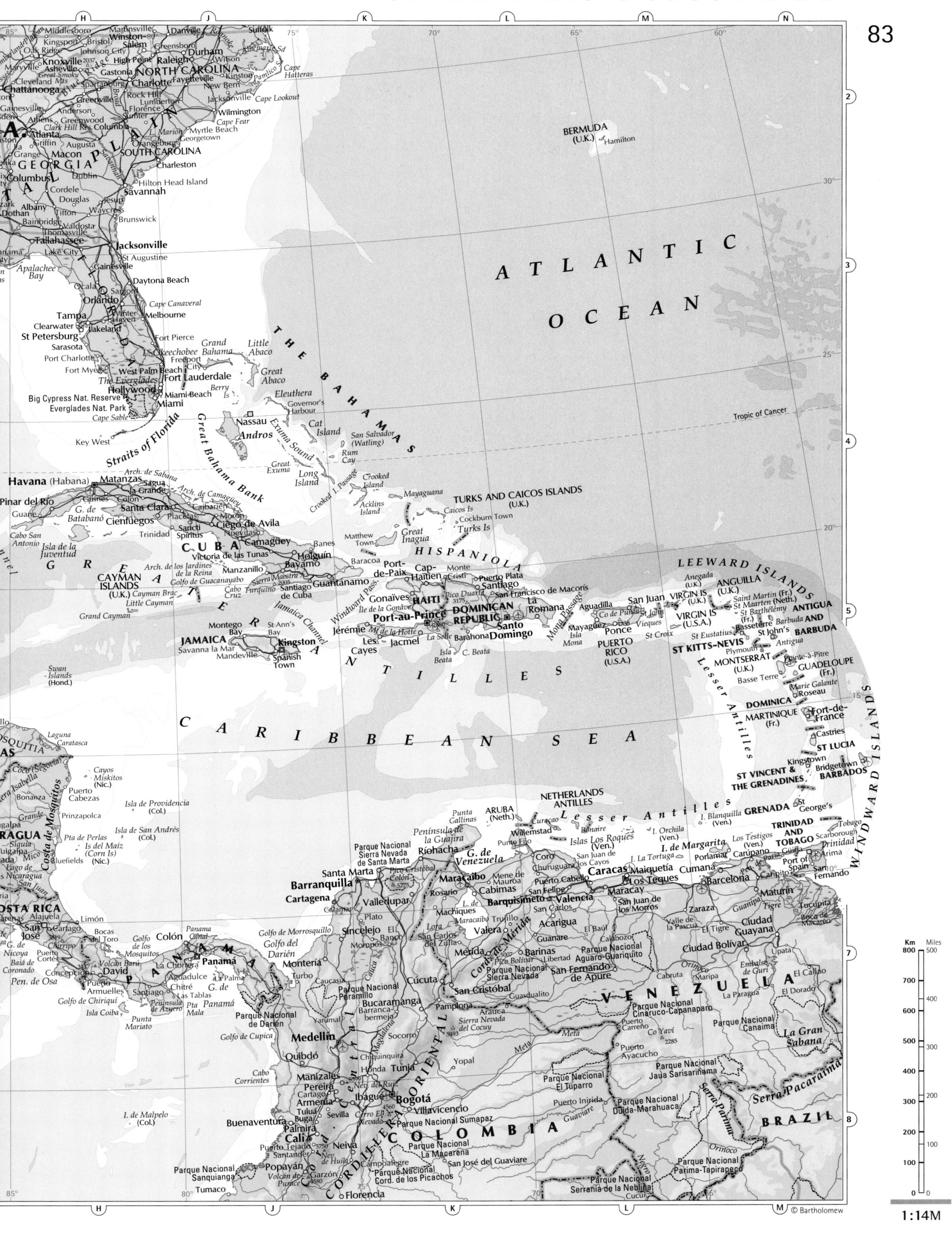

ATLANTIC OCEAN

CARIBBEAN SEA

NORTH CAROLINA
SOUTH CAROLINA
GEORGIA
PLAIN

Middlesboro Martinsville Danville Suffolk
Kingsport Bristol Winston-Salem Greensboro Durham Cape Hatteras
Knoxville High Point Raleigh Wilson Pamlico Sd
Asheville Salem Greenville New Bern
Gastonia Charlotte Spartanburg Burlington Fayetteville Kinston Lumberton Cape Lookout
Rock Hill Durham Wilmington
Greenwood Sumter Florence Georgetown
Columbia Orangeburg
Augusta Charleston
Macon Hilton Head Island
Savannah
Jesup Brunswick
Jacksonville Cape Canaveral
St Augustine
Gainesville Daytona Beach
Ocala Sanford Melbourne
Orlando Winter Haven Fort Pierce
Tampa Lakeland
Clearwater St Petersburg Sarasota
Port Charlotte Grand Bahama Little Abaco
Fort Myers West Palm Beach Fort Lauderdale Freeport Great Abaco
Big Cypress Nat. Reserve Hollywood Miami Beach Eleuthera Governor's Harbour
Everglades Nat. Park Miami Cat Island
Cape Sable Nassau Andros San Salvador (Watling)
Key West Exuma Sound Rum Cay

BERMUDA (U.K.) Hamilton

Tropic of Cancer

THE BAHAMAS

Great Bahama Bank

Straits of Florida

Havana (Habana) Matanzas
Pinar del Río Santa Clara Crooked Island
Guane Cienfuegos Placetas Trinidad Sancti Spíritus Ciego de Avila Crooked I. Passage
Isla de la Juventud CUBA Camagüey Banes Mayaguana
GREATER Victoria de las Tunas Holguín Matthew Town TURKS AND CAICOS ISLANDS (U.K.)
CAYMAN ISLANDS (U.K.) Manzanillo Bayamo Baracoa Great Inagua Caicos Is Cockburn Town Turks Is
Cayman Brac Santiago de Cuba Cabo Cruz Guantánamo Port-de-Paix HISPANIOLA
Little Cayman Grand Cayman Gonaïves HAITI Santiago Puerto Plata San Juan VIRGIN IS (U.K.) ANGUILLA (U.K.)
ANTILLES Port-au-Prince DOMINICAN REPUBLIC La Romana VIRGIN IS (U.S.A.) St Barthélemy (Fr.) ANTIGUA
JAMAICA Montego Bay Kingston Jérémie Jacmel Santo Domingo Ponce PUERTO RICO (U.S.A.) St Croix BARBUDA
Savanna la Mar Mandeville Spanish Town Les Cayes Barahona ST KITTS-NEVIS Basseterre St John's
C. Beata MONTSERRAT (U.K.) GUADELOUPE (Fr.)
LESSER Basse Terre Marie Galante Roseau
DOMINICA
MARTINIQUE (Fr.) Fort-de-France
Castries ST LUCIA
NETHERLANDS ANTILLES Kingstown ST VINCENT & THE GRENADINES BARBADOS Bridgetown
ARUBA (Neth.) Curaçao Bonaire Lesser Antilles GRENADA St George's
Punta Gallinas Willemstad Islas Los Roques (Ven.) I. Orchila (Ven.) I. Blanquilla (Ven.) TRINIDAD AND TOBAGO
Península de la Guajira Puerto Fijo Coro I. La Tortuga I. de Margarita (Ven.) Tobago
Parque Nacional Sierra Nevada de Santa Marta Riohacha Punto Fijo San Juan de los Cayos Porlamar Carúpano Scarborough Port of Spain
Santa Marta Maracaibo Mene de Mauroa Puerto Cabello Cumaná Arima San Fernando
Barranquilla Cabimas Caracas Maiquetía Barcelona Maturín
Cartagena Rosario San Felipe Valencia Maracay Los Teques Boca de Macareo

CUBA

C A R I B B E A N   S E A

G. de Venezuela

VENEZUELA

COLOMBIA

PANAMA

COSTA RICA

NICARAGUA

Swan Is. (Hond.)
Mosquitia Laguna Caratasca
Cayos Miskitos (Nic.)
Puerto Cabezas
Prinzapolca
Isla de Providencia (Col.)
Bonanza
Bluefields
Isla de San Andrés (Col.)
Is del Maíz (Corn Is) (Nic.)
Lago de Nicaragua
San Juan
Alajuela
San José Cartago Limón Bocas del Toro Colón Panamá
Chirripó David La Chorrera Panamá
Nicoya Aguadulce Chitré Las Tablas Pacific
Conceptión Santiago Península de Azuero
Golfo de Chiriquí Punta Mariato
I. de Coiba
I. de Malpelo (Col.)

Golfo de Morrosquillo Sincelejo El Montería Turbo
Golfo del Darién
Parque Nacional Paramillo
Parque Nacional de Darién
Golfo de Cupica
Cabo Corrientes
Quibdó
Medellín
Buenaventura
Cali
Popayán
Tumaco
Florencia

Barranquilla Valledupar San Carlos del Zulia Mérida Barinas
Cartagena Machiques San Cristóbal Aguaro-Guariquito El Baúl
Plato Banco San Carlos Acarigua Guanare El Tigre
Mompós Cúcuta Barquisimeto Valera San Fernando de Apure Ciudad Guayana
Barranca-bermeja Pamplona Arauca Trujillo Valle de la Pascua Ciudad Bolívar El Callao El Dorado
Socorro Bucaramanga Sierra Nevada del Cocuy Cabruta Puerto Carreño Embalse de Guri
Yarumal Yopal Puerto Ayacucho La Paragua
Honda Tunja Villavicencio Meta Puerto Inírida Duida-Marahuaca
Chiquinquirá Bogotá Parque Nacional El Tuparro Parque Nacional Jaua Sarisariñama La Gran Sabana
Manizales Pereira Armenia Ibagué Parque Nacional Sumapaz Guaviare
Buga Sevilla San José del Guaviare
Palmira Neiva Parque Nacional Serranía de la Neblina
Parque Nacional Sanquianga Garzón Parque Nacional Cord. de los Picachos Orinoco Parque Nacional Parima-Tapirapecó
Serra Pacaraima

BRAZIL

WINDWARD ISLANDS

LEEWARD ISLANDS

© Bartholomew

1:14M

Km	Miles
800	500
700	400
600	300
500	
400	200
300	
200	100
100	
0	0

G U L F   O F   M E X I C O

P A C I F I C   O C E A N

BAHÍA DE CAMPECHE

Golfo de Tehuantepec

Tropic of Cancer

MEXICO

GUATEMALA

SIERRA MADRE OCCIDENTAL

SIERRA MADRE ORIENTAL

SIERRA MADRE DEL SUR

COAHUILA

NUEVO LEÓN

TAMAULIPAS

DURANGO

ZACATECAS

SAN LUIS POTOSÍ

NAYARIT

JALISCO

GUANAJUATO

QUERÉTARO

HIDALGO

VERACRUZ

MICHOACÁN

COLIMA

MEXICO

MORELOS

PUEBLA

TLAXCALA

GUERRERO

OAXACA

CHIAPAS

TABASCO

CAMPECHE

YUCATÁN

SINALOA

AGUASCALIENTES

Laguna Madre

Metres / Feet

6000	19686
5000	16404
4000	13124
3000	9843
2000	6562
1000	3281
500	1640
200	656
SEA	LEVEL
200	656
2000	6562
4000	13124
6000	19686

Km / Miles

400	250
350	200
300	150
250	150
200	100
150	50
100	
50	0
0	

1:7M

Lambert Conformal Conic Projection

© Bartholomew

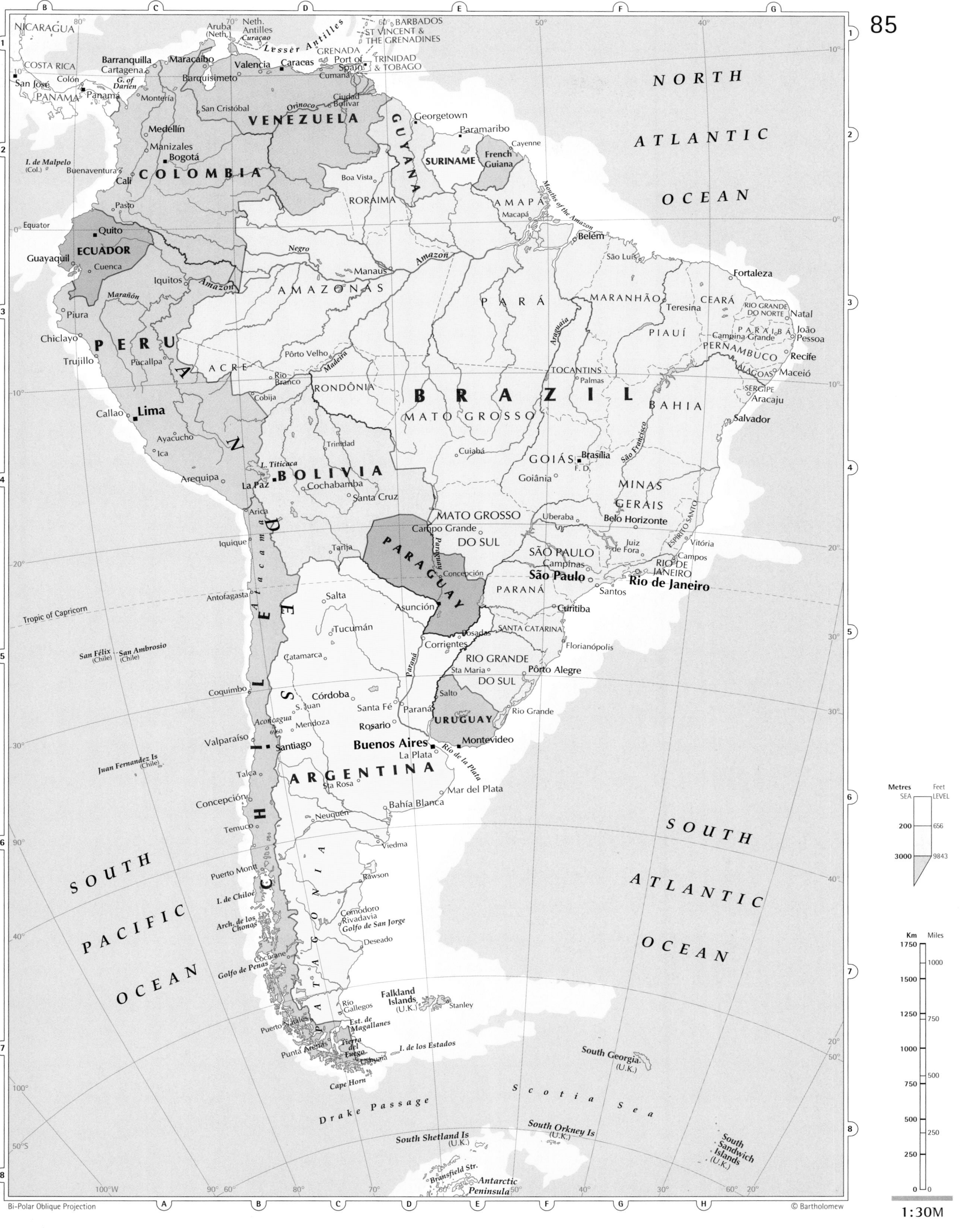
NORTH ATLANTIC OCEAN
SOUTH ATLANTIC OCEAN
SOUTH PACIFIC OCEAN
NICARAGUA
COSTA RICA
San José
Colón
PANAMA
Panamá
G. of Darien
Barranquilla
Cartagena
Maracaibo
Aruba (Neth.)
Neth. Antilles
Curaçao
Lesser Antilles
BARBADOS
ST VINCENT & THE GRENADINES
GRENADA
Port of Spain
TRINIDAD & TOBAGO
Valencia
Caracas
Cumaná
Barquisimeto
Montería
San Cristóbal
Orinoco
Ciudad Bolívar
VENEZUELA
GUYANA
Georgetown
Paramaribo
SURINAME
Cayenne
French Guiana
Medellín
Manizales
Bogotá
I. de Malpelo (Col.)
Buenaventura
Cali
COLOMBIA
Boa Vista
RORAIMA
AMAPÁ
Macapá
Mouths of the Amazon
Pasto
Equator
Quito
ECUADOR
Guayaquil
Cuenca
Negro
Amazon
Manaus
Belém
São Luís
Fortaleza
Iquitos
Marañón
AMAZONAS
PARÁ
MARANHÃO
CEARÁ
Teresina
RIO GRANDE DO NORTE
Natal
Piura
Chiclayo
PERU
PIAUÍ
Campina Grande
PARAÍBA
João Pessoa
PERNAMBUCO
Recife
ALAGOAS
Maceió
SERGIPE
Aracaju
Trujillo
Pucallpa
Pôrto Velho
Madeira
Araguaia
ACRE
Rio Branco
RONDÔNIA
TOCANTINS
Palmas
BRAZIL
BAHIA
Salvador
Cobija
MATO GROSSO
Callao
Lima
Ayacucho
Ica
Trinidad
Cuiabá
GOIÁS
Brasília
F.D.
São Francisco
Goiânia
L. Titicaca
BOLIVIA
La Paz
Cochabamba
Santa Cruz
Arequipa
MINAS GERAIS
Belo Horizonte
ESPÍRITO SANTO
Vitória
Arica
Uberaba
MATO GROSSO DO SUL
Campo Grande
PARAGUAY
Paraguay
Iquique
Tarija
SÃO PAULO
Campinas
São Paulo
Juiz de Fora
Campos
RIO DE JANEIRO
Rio de Janeiro
Santos
Concepción
PARANÁ
Antofagasta
Atacama
Salta
Asunción
Curitiba
Tropic of Capricorn
Tucumán
Posadas
SANTA CATARINA
Florianópolis
Corrientes
San Félix (Chile)
San Ambrosio (Chile)
Catamarca
RIO GRANDE DO SUL
Sta Maria
Pôrto Alegre
Coquimbo
Córdoba
S. Juan
Santa Fé
Paraná
Salto
URUGUAY
Rio Grande
Aconcagua
6960
Mendoza
Rosario
Valparaíso
Santiago
Buenos Aires
La Plata
Montevideo
Río de la Plata
Juan Fernandez Is (Chile)
Talca
ARGENTINA
Sta Rosa
Mar del Plata
Concepción
Bahía Blanca
Neuquén
Temuco
CHILE
Viedma
PATAGONIA
Puerto Montt
Rawson
I. de Chiloé
Arch. de los Chonos
Comodoro Rivadavia
Golfo de San Jorge
Deseado
Cochrane
Golfo de Penas
Rio Gallegos
Falkland Islands (U.K.)
Stanley
Puerto Natales
Est. de Magallanes
Tierra del Fuego
Punta Arenas
Ushuaia
I. de los Estados
Cape Horn
South Georgia (U.K.)
Scotia Sea
Drake Passage
South Orkney Is (U.K.)
South Shetland Is (U.K.)
South Sandwich Islands (U.K.)
Bransfield Str.
Antarctic Peninsula
Metres SEA
Feet LEVEL
200
656
3000
9843
Km
Miles
1750
1500
1250
1000
750
500
250
0
1:30M
Bi-Polar Oblique Projection
© Bartholomew

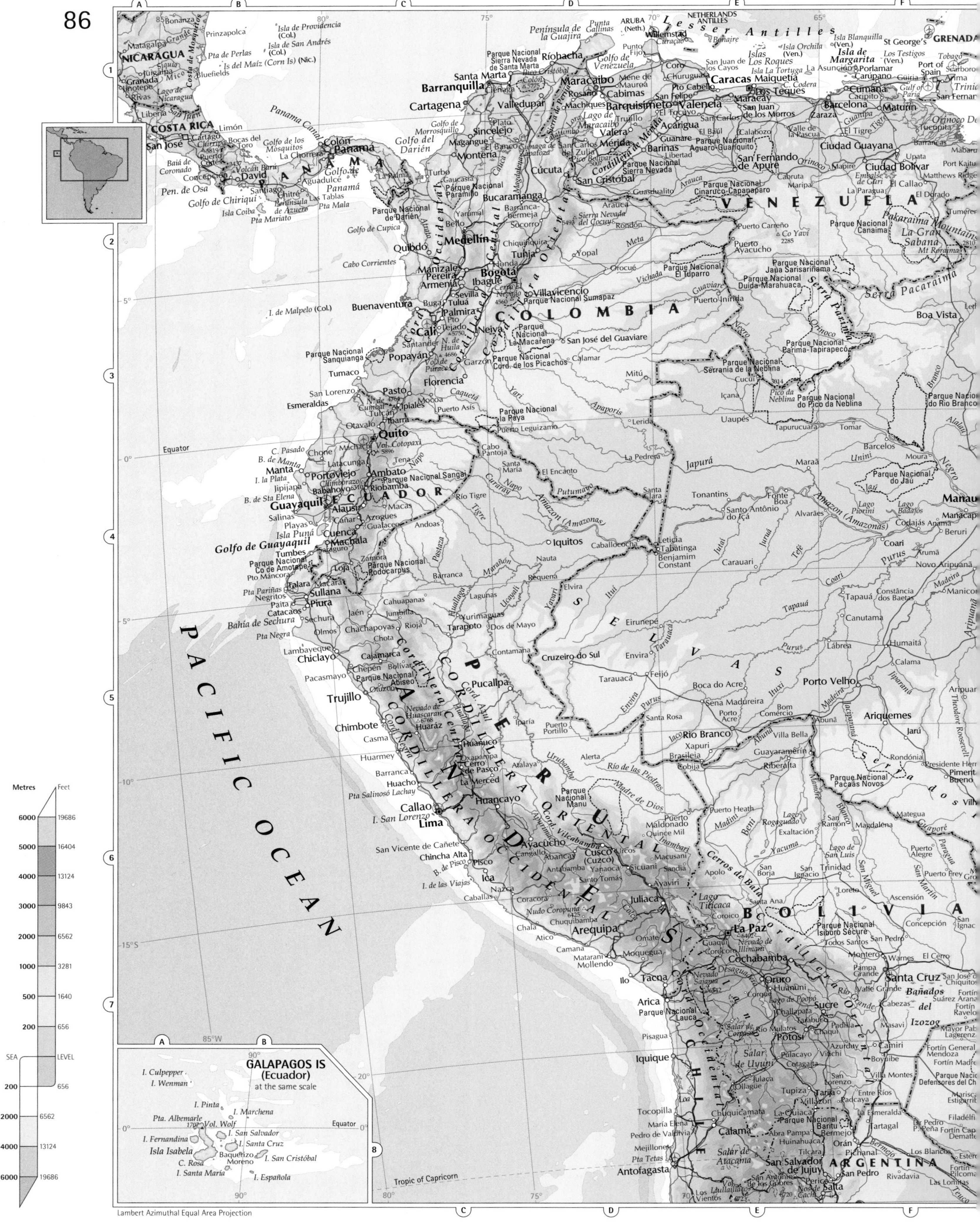

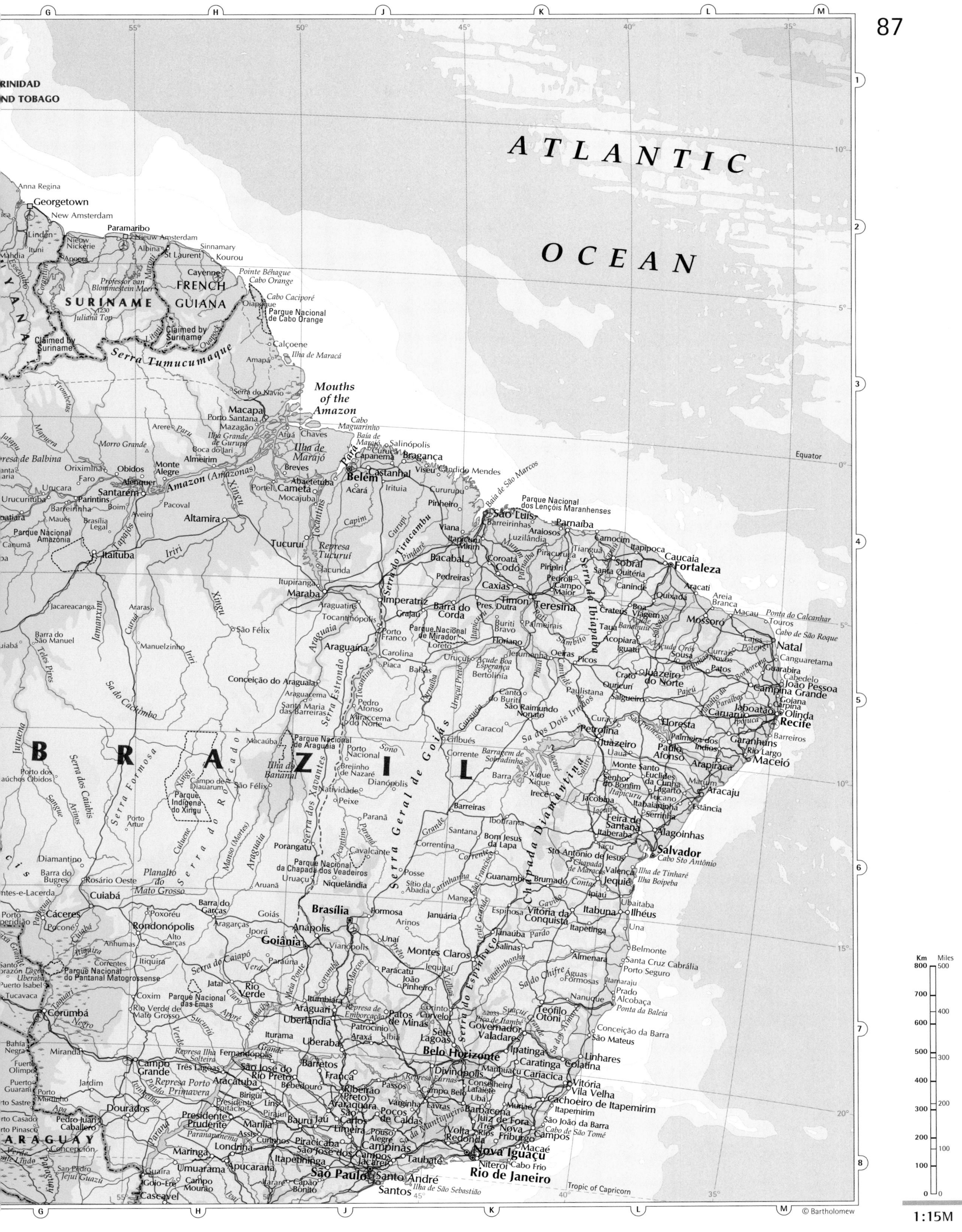

G   H   J   K   L   M

55°   50°   45°   40°   35°

**TRINIDAD
AND TOBAGO**

Anna Regina
□ Georgetown
New Amsterdam
Linden
Ituni
Mahdia
Apoera
Paramaribo □
Nieuw □ Nieuw Amsterdam
Nickerie   Albina   Sinnamary
St Laurent   Kourou
Professor van   Cayenne
Blommestein Meer   **FRENCH**
SURINAME **GUIANA**
Juliana Top
1230   Oiapoque   Pointe Béhague
Cabo Orange
Claimed by   Cabo Caciporé
Suriname   Oiapoque
Claimed by   Parque Nacional
Suriname   de Cabo Orange
Serra Tumucumaque   Calçoene
Amapá   Ilha de Maracá

ATLANTIC

OCEAN

Serra do Navio
Macapá   **Mouths**
Porto Santana   **of the**
Mazagão   **Amazon**
Ilha Grande   Cabo
de Gurupá   Maguarinho
Afuá   Chaves   Baía de
Ilha de   Marajó
Breves   **Marajó**   Salinópolis
Curuçá   Bragança
Almeirim   Pará   Curuçá   Apanema
Porto de   Abaetetuba   Salinópolis
Óbidos   Moju   **Belém**   Castanhal   Viseu   Candido Mendes
Santarém   Cametá   Acará   Irituia   Pinheiro
Alenquer   Boim   Mocajuba   Capim   Cururupu   Viana
Morro Grande   Oriximiná   Aveiro   Portel   Curuçá
Faro   Pacoval   Baía de São Marcos   Parque Nacional
Urucurituba   Parintins   Xingu   **São Luís**   dos Lençóis Maranhenses
Maués   Boa Vista   Altamira   Tocantins   Barreirinhas   Araioses
Brasília   Mirim   Luziânia   Parnaíba
Legal   Itupiranga   Bacabal   Coroatá   Piracuruca   Camocim
Parque Nacional   **Tucuruí**   Represa   Codó   Piripiri   Itapipoca   Caucaia
Amazônia   Tucuruí   Jacundá   Viana   Pedreiras   Tianguá   **Fortaleza**
Itaituba   Iriri   Maraba   Imperatriz   **Caxias**   Timon   Campo Maior   Sobral   Santa Quitéria   Canindé   Aracati
Jacareacanga   Araguatins   Barra do   Pres. Dutra   **Teresina**   Crateús   Quixadá   Areia
Corda   Buriti Bravo   Pedro II   Taua   Branca
Araras   Tocantinópolis   Grajaú   Parque Nacional   Floriano   Oeiras   Acopiara   Mossoró   Macau   Ponta do Calcanhar
Barra do   Xingu   de Mirador   Picos   Iguatú   Touros
São Manuel   São Félix   Carolina   Loreto   Jerumenha   Paulistana   Sousa   Lajes   Potengi   Cabo de São Roque
Manuelzinho   Araguaína   Uruçuí   Açude Boa   Canto   Currais   **Natal**
Teles Pires   Conceição do Araguaia   Balsas   Esperança   do Buriti   Ouricuri   Juazeiro   Patos   Canguaretama
Araguacema   Bertolínia   São Raimundo   do Norte   Jaboatão   Goiana
Santa Maria   Piaca   Nonato   Salgueiro   Campina   Carpina
das Barreiras   Pedro   Caracol   Petrolina   Floresta   Grande   Olinda
Macaúba   Afonso   Gilbués   Sa dos Dois Irmãos   Curaçá   **Recife**
Diamantino   Parque Nacional   Miracema   Juazeiro   Palmares   Garanhuns
de Araguaia   do Norte   Corrente   Barragem de   Paulo   Rio Largo   **Maceió**
Porto   Sobradinho   Afonso   Arapiraca
Nacional   Brejinho   Barra   Xique   Monte Santo   Euclides   Marituba
de Nazaré   Santo   Xique   da Cunha   **Aracaju**
Barra do   Dianópolis   Irecê   Senhor   Itabaiana   Estância
Bugres   Ilha do   Peixe   do Bonfim   Itapicuru   Serrinha
Bananal   Natividade   Barreiras   Jacobina   Itaberaba   Alagoinhas
Cáceres   Porto   Paranã   Santana   Feira de
Artur   Ibotirama   Bom Jesus   Santa Cruz   Santana   **Salvador**
Cuiabá   da Lapa   Sto Antônio de Jesus   Cabo Sto Antônio
Planalto   Parque Nacional   Correntina   Chapada   Valença   Ilha de Tinharé
do   da Chapada   Posse   Sítio da   Abadia   Guanambi   de Maracás   Jequié   Ilha Boipeba
Mato Grosso   dos Veadeiros   Carinhanha   Brumado   Ubaitaba
Poxoréu   Barra do   Niquelândia   Uruaçu   Manga   Ipiaú   Itabuna   **Ilhéus**
Barra do   Garças   Goiás   Formosa   **Brasília**   Espinosa   Vitória da
Rondonópolis   Iporá   **Anápolis**   Januária   Conquista   Itapetinga   Una
Alto   Januária   Janaúba   Belmonte
Goiânia   Unaí   Montes Claros   Salinas   Almenara   Santa Cruz Cabrália
Itumbiara   Vianópolis   Paracatu   Jequitaí   Itamaraju   Porto Seguro
Rio   Jataí   Paraúna   João   Salto   Águas   Prado   Ponta da Baleia
Verde   Pinheiro   Chifre   Formosas   Alcobaça
Araguari   Itumbiara   Patos   Curvelo   Rio de Itambé   Teófilo   Nanuque   Conceição da Barra
Uberlândia   de Minas   Araxá   Ibiá   Governador   Otôni   São Mateus
Ituiutaba   Uberaba   Sete   Valadares
Lagoas   **Belo Horizonte**   Ipatinga   Linhares
Campo   São José do   Barretos   França   Divinópolis   Caratinga   Caiacica   Colatina
Grande   Rio Preto   Ribeirão   Conselheiro   Vitória
Três Lagoas   Aracatuba   Preto   Lafaiete   Vila Velha
Dourados   Birigui   Bebedouro   Passos   Campo Belo   Lavras   Barbacena   Muriaé   Cachoeiro de Itapemirim
Presidente   Lins   Araraquara   Pocos   Juiz de Fora   Itapemirim
Prudente   Marília   Assis   Pirassununga   de Caldas   Três   Nova   Cabo de São Tomé
São   Rios   Friburgo
Maringá   Londrina   Bauru   Jaú   Carlos   Pouso   Volta   Macaé
Umuarama   Piracicaba   Limeira   Alegre   Redonda   **Rio de Janeiro**
Campo   Itapetininga   Campinas   Taubaté   **Nova Iguaçu**
Mourão   Jacareí   Niterói   Cabo Frio
Goio-Erê   Apucarana   **São Paulo**   Santo André
Cascavel   Capão Bonito   Santos   Ilha de São Sebastião   Tropic of Capricorn

BRAZIL

PARAGUAY

1
2
3
4
5
6
7
8

Equator

5°
0°
5°
10°
15°
20°

Km   Miles
800   500
700   400
600
500   300
400
300   200
200
100   100
0   0

© Bartholomew

1:15M

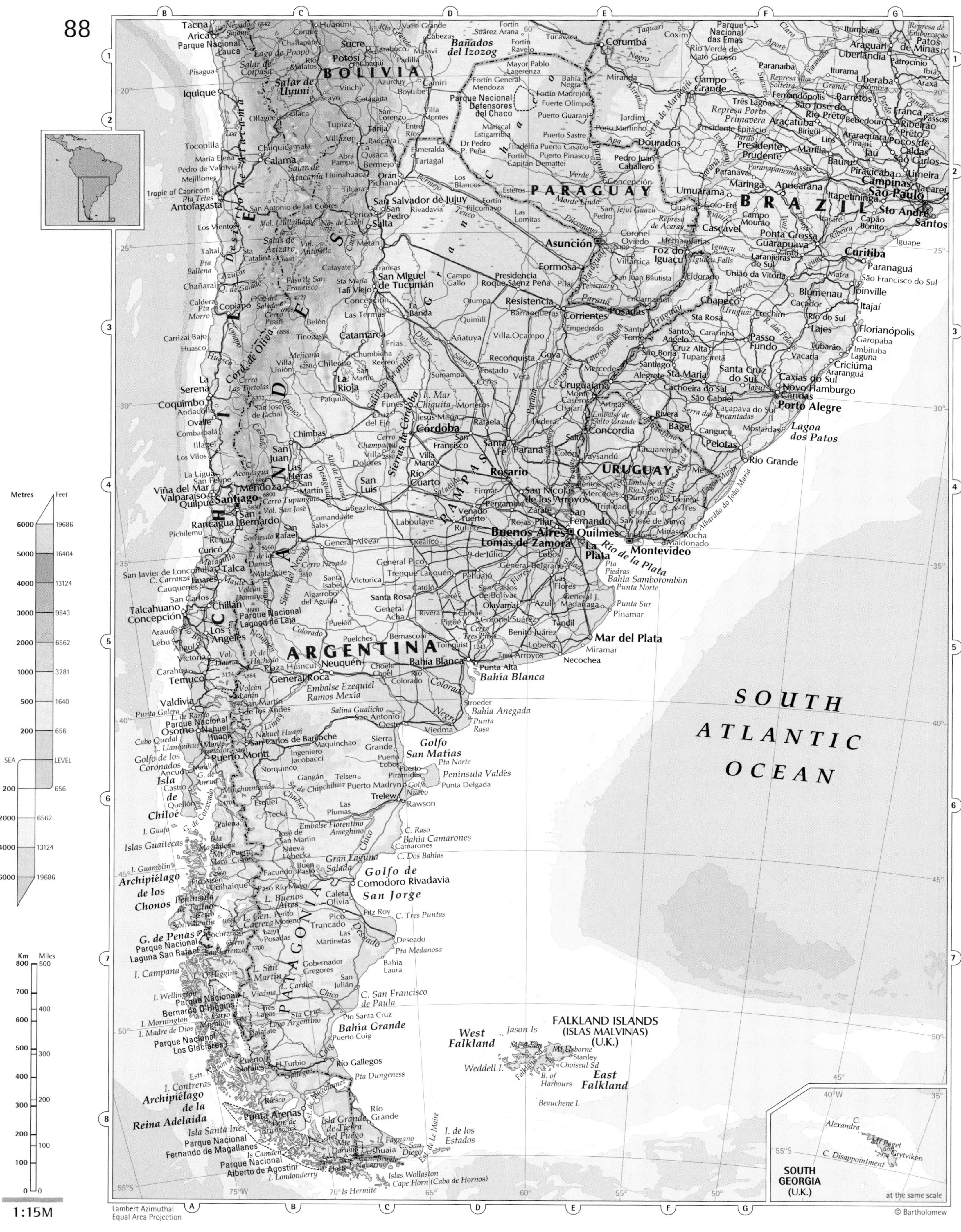

SOUTH ATLANTIC OCEAN

1:15M

Lambert Azimuthal
Equal Area Projection

© Bartholomew

CARIBBEAN SEA

Lesser Antilles

GRENADA

TRINIDAD AND TOBAGO

NETHERLANDS ANTILLES

ARUBA (Neth.)

Caracas

Maracaibo

Orinoco

V E N E Z U E L A

C O L O M B I A

Bogotá

Medellín

Cali

B R A Z I L

RORAIMA

A M A Z O N A S

PANAMA

Lambert Azimuthal Equal Area Projection

© Bartholomew

1:7.5M

Metres / Feet
6000 / 19686
5000 / 16404
4000 / 13124
3000 / 9843
2000 / 6562
1000 / 3281
500 / 1640
200 / 656
SEA LEVEL
200 / 656
2000 / 6562
4000 / 13124
6000 / 19686

Km / Miles
450
375 / 225
300 / 150
225 / 75
150
75
0 / 0

ATLANTIC

OCEAN

Tropic of Capricorn

Metres Feet

6000   19686

5000   16404

4000   13124

3000   9843

2000   6562

1000   3281

500   1640

200   656

SEA   LEVEL

200   656

2000   6562

4000   13124

6000   19686

Km Miles

450

375   225

300

225   150

150

75   75

0   0

1:7.5M

Lambert Azimuthal
Equal Area Projection

© Bartholomew

B R A Z I L

M I N A S   G E R A I S

B A H I A

G O I Á S

M A T O   G R O S S O

M A T O   G R O S S O   D O   S U L

S Ã O   P A U L O

P A R A N Á

PARAGUAY

DISTRITO

Salvador
Ilhéus
Itabuna
Vitória da Conquista
Teófilo Otóni
Governador Valadares
Belo Horizonte
Vitória
Vila Velha
Linhares
Campos
Macaé
Cabo Frio
Nova Friburgo
Rio de Janeiro
Nova Iguaçu
São Gonçalo
Volta Redonda
Juiz de Fora
Barbacena
São Paulo
São Bernardo do Campo
Santo André
Santos
Guarujá
São Vicente
Curitiba
Paranaguá
Brasília
Goiânia
Anápolis
Uberlândia
Uberaba
Ribeirão Preto
Franca
Barretos
Araraquara
São Carlos
Campinas
Jundiaí
Sorocaba
Bauru
Marília
Presidente Prudente
Londrina
Campo Grande
Dourados
Cuiabá
Rondonópolis
Montes Claros
Foz do Iguaçu
Cascavel
Toledo
Umuarama

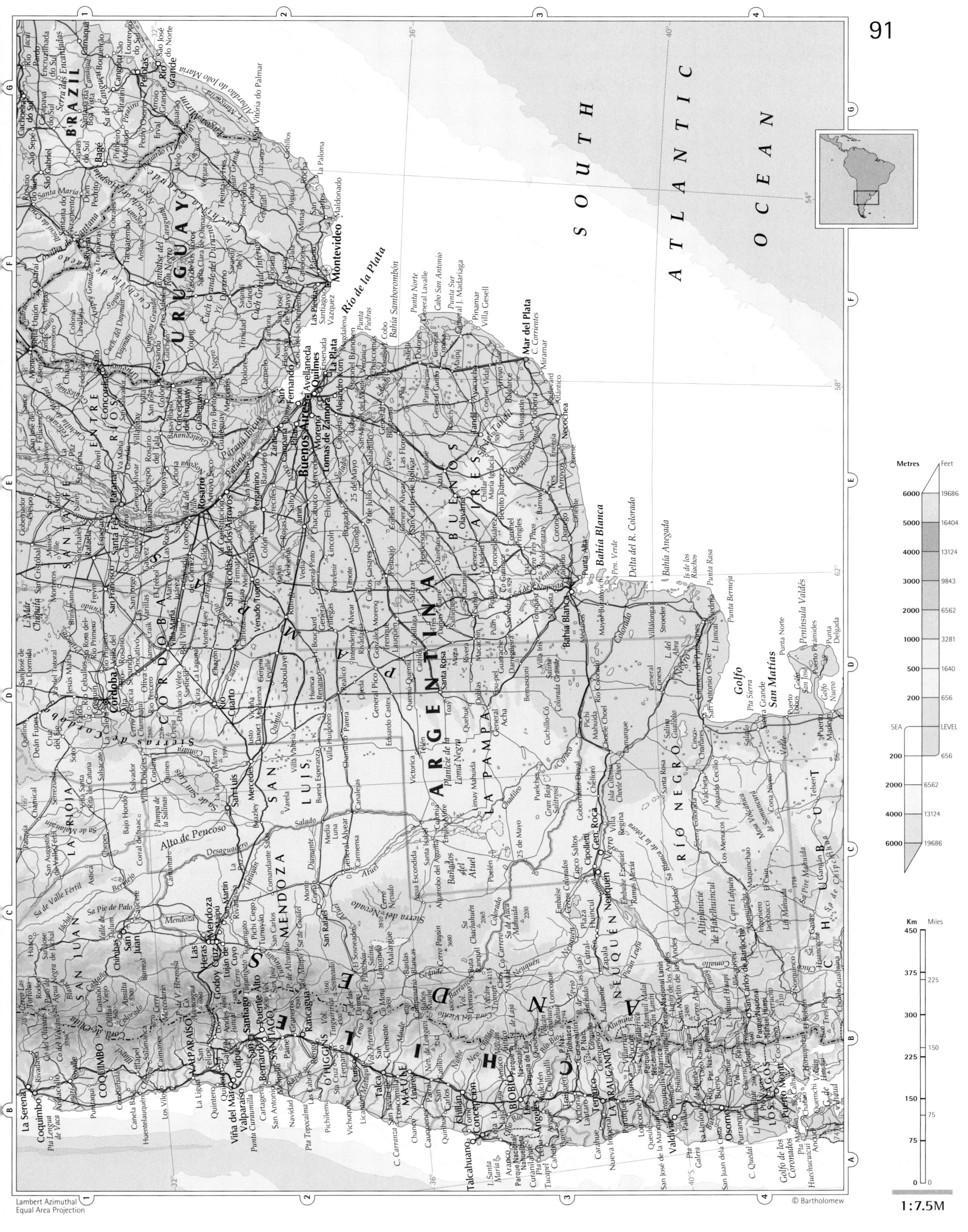

© Bartholomew

1:7.5M

Metres	Feet
6000	19686
5000	16404
4000	13124
3000	9843
2000	6562
1000	3281
500	1640
200	656
SEA	LEVEL
200	656
2000	6562
4000	13124
6000	19686

Km	Miles
450	
375	225
300	
225	150
150	75
75	
0	0

Antarctica

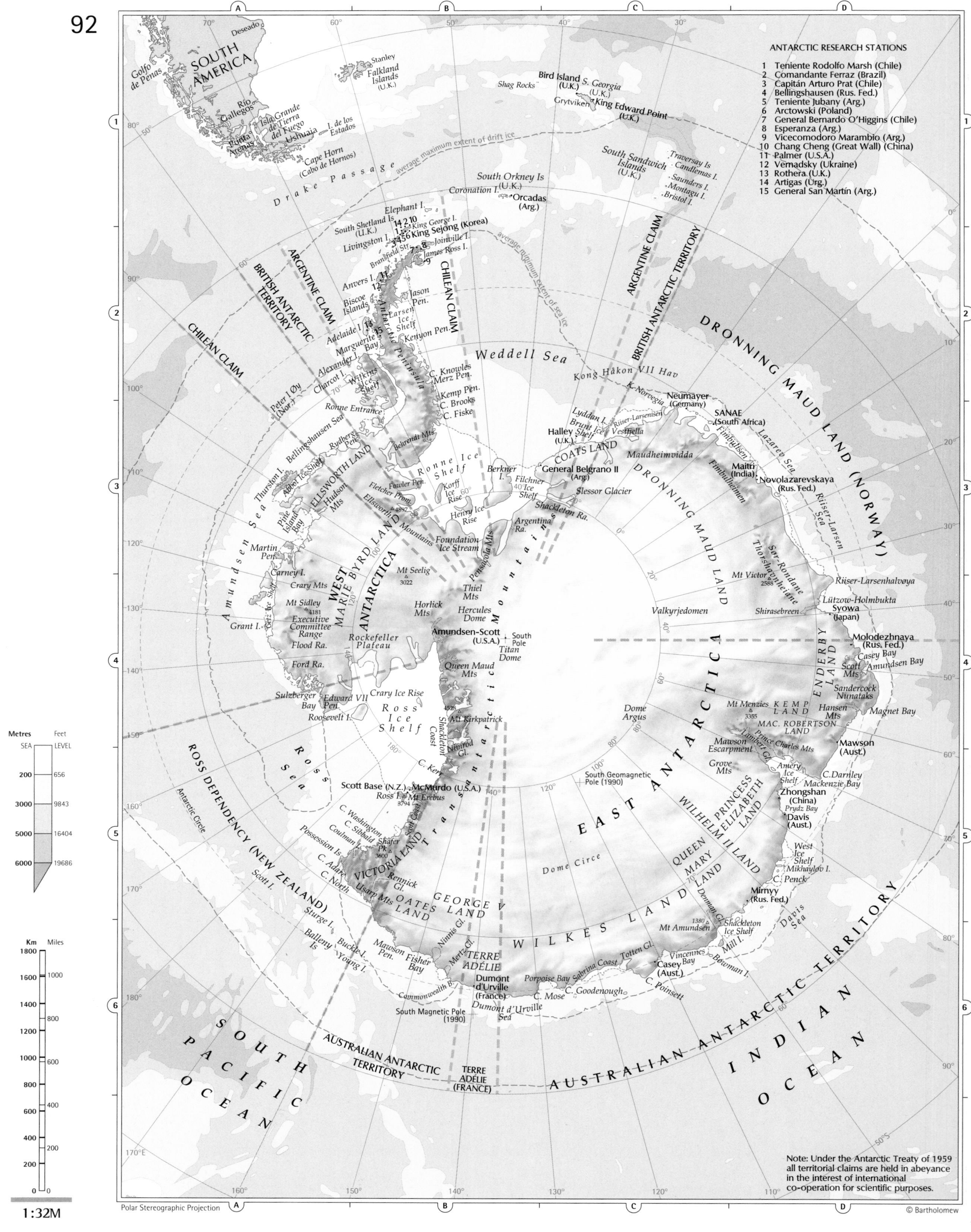

ANTARCTIC RESEARCH STATIONS

1 Teniente Rodolfo Marsh (Chile)
2 Comandante Ferraz (Brazil)
3 Capitán Arturo Prat (Chile)
4 Bellingshausen (Rus. Fed.)
5 Teniente Jubany (Arg.)
6 Arctowski (Poland)
7 General Bernardo O'Higgins (Chile)
8 Esperanza (Arg.)
9 Vicecomodoro Marambio (Arg.)
10 Chang Cheng (Great Wall) (China)
11 Palmer (U.S.A.)
12 Vernadsky (Ukraine)
13 Rothera (U.K.)
14 Artigas (Urg.)
15 General San Martín (Arg.)

Note: Under the Antarctic Treaty of 1959 all territorial claims are held in abeyance in the interest of international co-operation for scientific purposes.

Metres / Feet
SEA / LEVEL
200 / 656
3000 / 9843
5000 / 16404
6000 / 19686

Km / Miles
1800 / 1000
1600
1400 / 800
1200
1000 / 600
800 / 400
600
400 / 200
200
0 / 0

1:32M

Polar Stereographic Projection

© Bartholomew

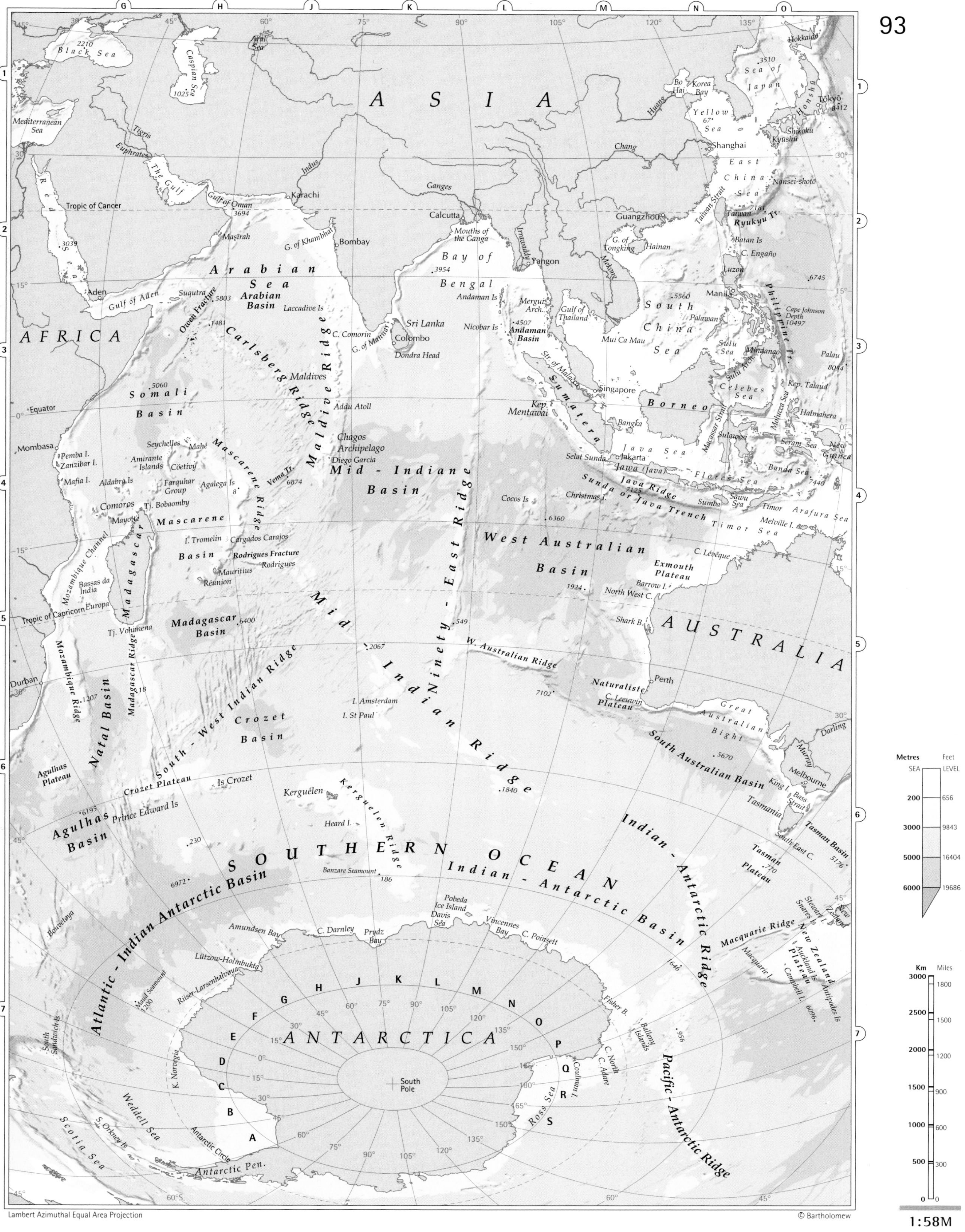

Map labels

ASIA

Black Sea · 2210 · Aral Sea · Sea of Japan · Hokkaidō · 3510 · Honshū
Mediterranean Sea · Caspian Sea · 1025 · Bo Hai · Korea Bay · Tokyo · 8412
Tigris · Euphrates · Shikoku · Kyūshū
Red Sea · The Gulf · Gulf of Oman · 3694 · Indus · Ganges · Huang · Yellow Sea · 67° · Chang · Shanghai · East China Sea · Nansei-shotō
Tropic of Cancer · · 3039 · Maşīrah · G. of Khambhat · Bombay · Calcutta · Mouths of the Ganga · G. of Tongking · Hainan · Guangzhou · Taiwan Strait · Taiwan · 7191 · Ryukyu Tr.
Aden · Gulf of Aden · Suqutra · 5803 · Owen Fracture · 1481 · Arabian Sea · Arabian Basin · Laccadive Is · Bay of · Bengal · 3954 · Andaman Is · Mergui Arch. · Gulf of Thailand · South China Sea · Manila · Batan Is · C. Engaño · Luzon · 6745
AFRICA · C. Comorin · G. of Mannar · Sri Lanka · Colombo · Dondra Head · Maldives · Nicobar Is · 4507 · Andaman Basin · Mui Ca Mau · Palawan · Mindanao · Palau · 8044
Somali Basin · 5060 · Maldive Ridge · Chagos Archipelago · Str. of Malacca · Sumatera · Singapore · Sulu Sea · Kep. Talaua
Equator · Mombasa · Pemba I. · Zanzibar I. · Seychelles · Mahé · Amirante Islands · Côetivy · Mascarene Ridge · Diego Garcia · Kep. Mentawai · Bangka · Borneo · Sulawesi · Celebes Sea · Halmahera
Mafia I. · Aldabra Is · Farquhar Group · Agalega Is · 8° · Vema Tr. · 6874 · Mid - Indian Basin · Jakarta · Java Sea · Seram Sea · New Guinea
Comoros · Tj. Bobaomby · Mayotte · Mascarene Basin · I. Tromelin · Cargados Carajos · Rodrigues Fracture · Rodrigues · Selat Sunda · Java (Jawa) · 125 · Flores Sea · Banda Sea · 7440
Mauritius · Réunion · West Australian Basin · Cocos Is · 6360 · Christmas I. · Sunda or Java Trench · Sumba · Sawu Spa · Timor · Arafura Sea
Tropic of Capricorn · Europa · Madagascar Ridge · Madagascar Basin · 6400 · 2067 · 549 · C. Lévêque · Exmouth Plateau · Barrow I. · 1924 · North West C. · Melville I. · Timor Sea
Durban · Natal Basin · 1207 · 18 · Crozet Basin · I. Amsterdam · I. St Paul · W. Australian Ridge · 7102 · Shark B. · **AUSTRALIA**
Mozambique Ridge · South - West Indian Ridge · Mid Indian Ridge · Ninety - East Ridge · Naturaliste Plateau · C. Leeuwin · Perth · Great Australian Bight · Darling
Agulhas Plateau · Crozet Plateau · Is Crozet · Kerguélen · Kerguelen Ridge · 1840 · 3670 · South Australian Basin · Murray · Melbourne
Agulhas Basin · 6195 · Prince Edward Is · Heard I. · King I. · Bass Str. · Tasmania · Tasman Basin · 5176
230 · **SOUTHERN OCEAN** · Indian - Antarctic Basin · South East C. · Tasman Plateau · 770
Atlantic - Indian Antarctic Basin · 6972 · Banzare Seamount · 186 · Indian - Antarctic Basin · Indian - Antarctic Ridge · Macquarie Ridge · New Zealand Plateau · Antipodes Is
Bouvetøya · Amundsen Bay · C. Darnley · Prydz Bay · Pobeda Ice Island · Davis Sea · Vincennes Bay · C. Poinsett · 1046 · Fisher B. · Macquarie I. · Stewart I. · Snares Is · Campbell I. · 6080
South Sandwich Is · Maud Seamount · 1200 · Lützow-Holmbukta · Rüser-Larsenhalvøya · K. Norvegia · **ANTARCTICA** · C. North · Coulman I. · C. Adare · Balleny Islands · 956 · New Zealand
South Orkney Is · A · South Pole · Ross Sea · Pacific - Antarctic Ridge
Scotia Sea · Weddell Sea · Antarctic Circle · Antarctic Pen.

Scale / legend

Metres	Feet
SEA	LEVEL
200	656
3000	9843
5000	16404
6000	19686

Km	Miles
3000	1800
2500	1500
2000	1200
1500	900
1000	600
500	300
0	0

Lambert Azimuthal Equal Area Projection

© Bartholomew

1:58M

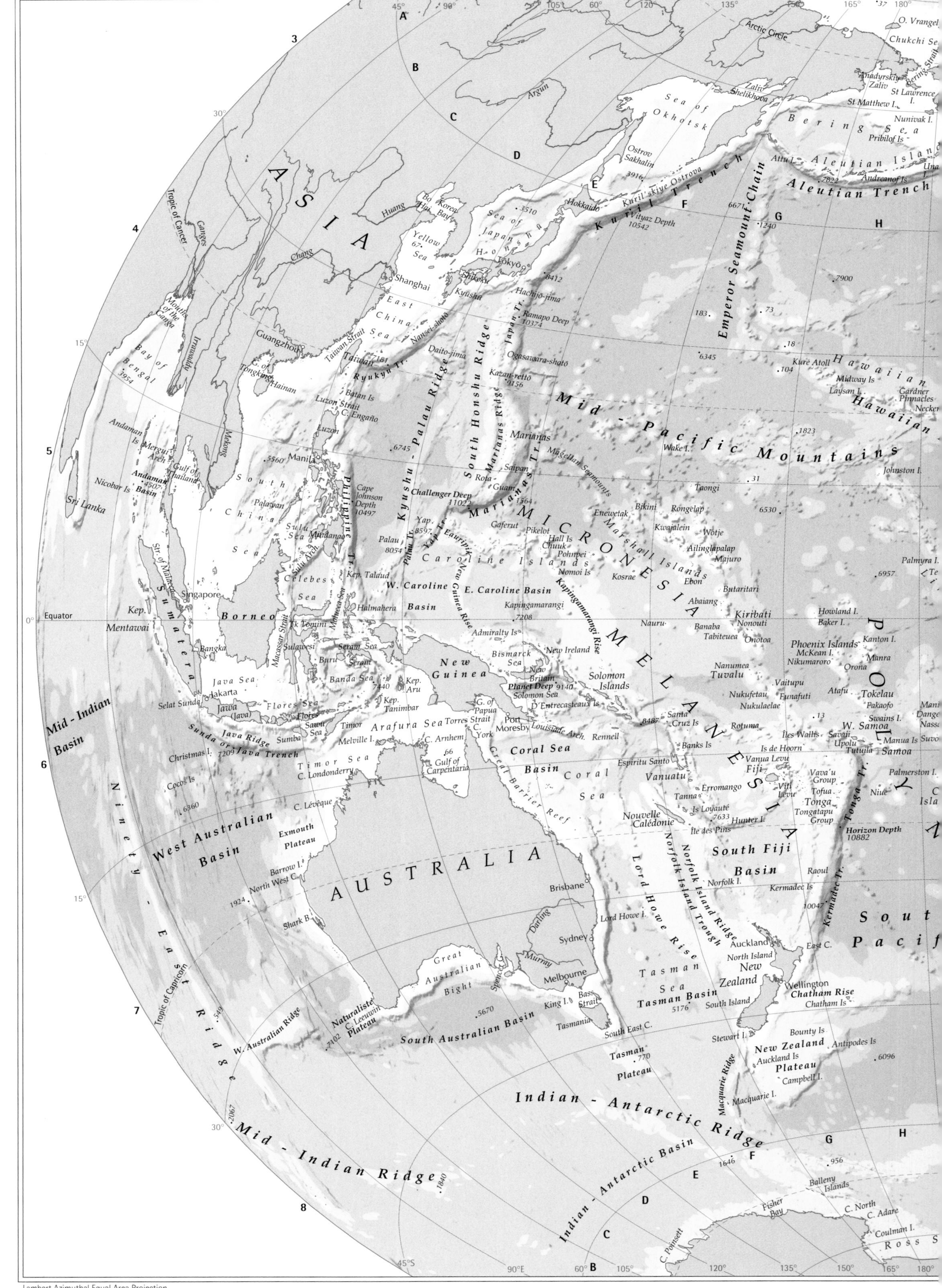

Lambert Azimuthal Equal Area Projection

Metres   Feet

SEA   LEVEL

200   656

3000   9843

5000   16404

6000   19686

NORTH AMERICA
SOUTH AMERICA
Hudson Bay
James Bay
Gulf of Alaska
Kodiak I.
Alexander Archipelago
Queen Charlotte Islands
Vancouver Island
Vancouver
Columbia
Mackenzie
Missouri
New York
C. Sable
Newfoundland
C. Hatteras
Bermuda
Bermuda Rise
North American Basin
Mid - Atlantic Ridge
Mendocino Seascarp
C. Mendocino
San Francisco
Los Angeles
Colorado
Erben Tablemount
Murray Seascarp
Guadalupe
Rio Grande
Mississippi
New Orleans
Gulf of Mexico
Str. of Florida
The Bahamas
Greater Antilles
Puerto Rico Tr.
Golfo de California
Yucatan Channel
Cayman Tr.
G. of Honduras
Bahía de Campeche
Molokai Fracture Zone
Maui
Hawaii
Is Revillagigedo
I. Socorro
I. Clarión
Clarion Fracture Zone
East Pacific Rise
G. de Tehuantepec
Tehuantepec Ridge
Middle America Trench
Venezuelan Basin
Caribbean Sea
Lesser Antilles
Colombian Basin
Caracas
Orinoco
Panamá
Guiana Basin
Clipperton Fracture Zone
Clipperton I.
I. de Coco
Cocos Ridge
I. de Malpelo
Kiritimati
Mouths of the Amazon
Amazon
Galapagos Is (Islas Galápagos)
Carnegie Ridge
G. de Guayaquil
Malden I.
Starbuck I.
Is Marquises
Nuku Hiva
Hiva Oa
Caroline I.
Flint I.
Tongareva
Is du Roi Georges
Îles de Désappointement
Is Tuamotu
Tahiti
Raiatea
Is de la Société
Rangiroa
Anaa
Hao
Hérébrétué
Îles Duc de Gloucester
Îles Maria
Mururoa
Groupe Actéon
Is Gambier
Tubuai
Raivavae
Is Tubuai
Rapa
Henderson I.
Pitcairn I.
Ducie I.
Lima
Peru - Chile Trench
Peru Basin
S.W. Peru or Nazca Ridge
Easter Island Fracture Zone
Easter I.
I. Sala y Gómez
San Félix
San Ambrosio
West Basin
Challenger Fracture Zone
Chile Basin
Is Juan Fernández
Robinson Crusoe
Santiago
Paraná
Rio de Janeiro
Buenos Aires
Río de la Plata
Golfo San Matías
Golfo de San Jorge
Argentine Basin
Falkland Islands
Cape Horn
Drake Passage
Scotia Sea
Scotia Ridge
Eltanin Fracture Zone
Pacific - Antarctic Ridge
South - East Pacific Basin
Peter I Øy
Amundsen Sea
Antarctic Circle

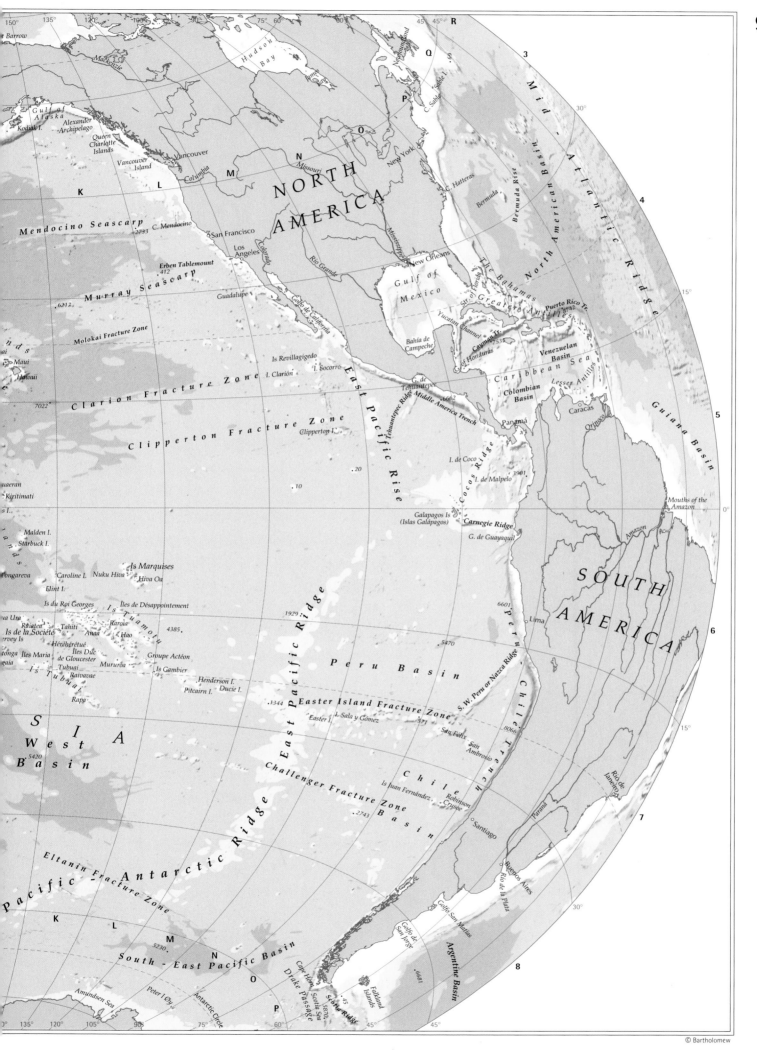

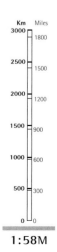

© Bartholomew

1:58M

ATLANTIC OCEAN

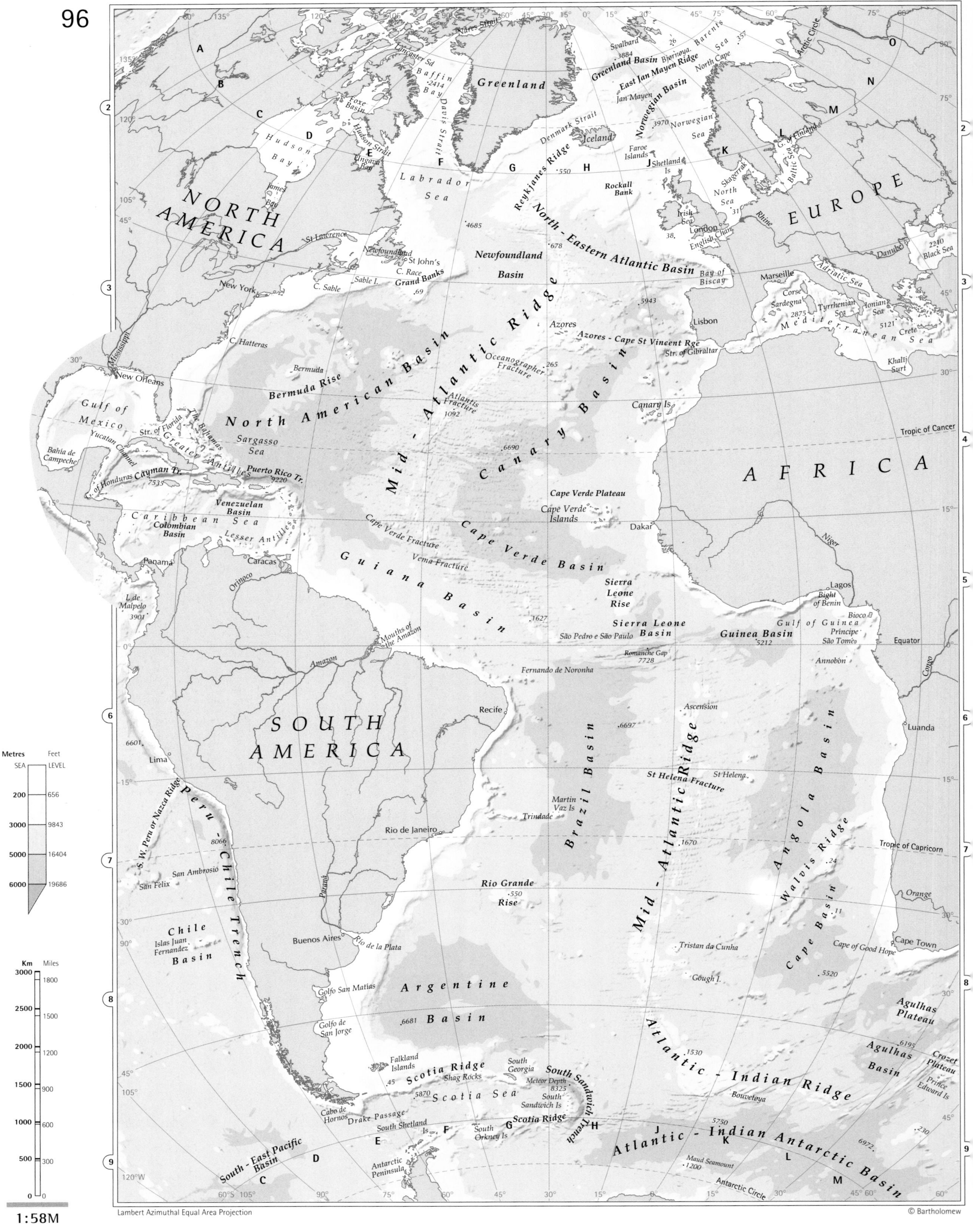

NORTH AMERICA

EUROPE

AFRICA

SOUTH AMERICA

Greenland

Greenland Basin
East Jan Mayen Basin
Jan Mayen
3884
Barents Sea
North Cape
357
Svalbard
26
Bjørnøya
O
N
M

Baffin Bay
2414
Davis Strait
Denmark Strait
Iceland
Norwegian Ridge
3970
Norwegian Sea
Faroe Islands
Shetland Is
K
L
G. of Finland
Baltic Sea

Lancaster Sd
Nares Strait
Foxe Basin
Hudson Strait
Ungava Bay
A
B
C
D
E
F
G
H
J

Hudson Bay
James Bay

Labrador Sea
Reykjanes Ridge
.550
Rockall Bank
North-Eastern Atlantic Ridge
North Sea
Skagerrak
Irish Sea
31
38

St Lawrence
Newfoundland
St John's
C. Race
Grand Banks
.69
Sable I.
C. Sable
New York
.4685
.678
Newfoundland Basin
Bay of Biscay
London
English Chan
Rhine
Marseille
Corse
Sardegna
2875
Tyrrhenian Sea
Ionian Sea
Adriatic Sea
Danube
2240
Black Sea

C. Hatteras
Bermuda
Bermuda Rise
North American Basin
Mid-Atlantic Ridge
.5943
Azores
Azores-Cape St Vincent Rge
Oceanographer Fracture
265
Atlantis Fracture
1092
Str. of Gibraltar
Lisbon
Mediterranean Sea
5121
Crete
Khalij Surt

Gulf of Mexico
New Orleans
Str. of Florida
The Bahamas
Sargasso Sea
Canary Basin
Canary Is
Tropic of Cancer

Bahia de Campeche
Yucatan Channel
G. of Honduras
Cayman Tr.
7535
Greater Antilles
Puerto Rico Tr.
9220
.6690
Cape Verde Plateau
Cape Verde Islands
Dakar

Venezuelan Basin
Caribbean Sea
Colombian Basin
Lesser Antilles
Guiana Basin
Cape Verde Fracture
Cape Verde Basin
Niger
Lagos
Bight of Benin
Bioco

Panama
Caracas
Orinoco
Vema Fracture
1627
Sierra Leone Rise
Sierra Leone Basin
São Pedro e São Paulo
Guinea Basin
.5212
Gulf of Guinea
Principe
São Tomé
Annobón
Equator
Congo

L. de Malpelo
3901
Mouths of the Amazon
Amazon
Romanche Gap
7728
Fernando de Noronha

Recife
.6697
Ascension
St Helena Fracture
St Helena
Luanda

6601
Lima
Brazil Basin
Mid-Atlantic Ridge
Angola Basin
Walvis Ridge

S.W. Peru or Nazca Ridge
Peru-Chile Trench
Martin Vaz Is
Trindade
1670
.24
Tropic of Capricorn

8066
San Ambrosio
San Felix
Rio de Janeiro
Rio Grande Rise
.550
Cape Basin
.11
Orange

Chile Basin
Islas Juan Fernandez
Buenos Aires
Rio de la Plata
Tristan da Cunha
Cape of Good Hope
Cape Town
.6195

Golfo San Matias
Argentine Basin
Gough I.
.5520
Agulhas Plateau

Golfo de San Jorge
.6681
.1530
Agulhas Basin
Crozet Plateau
Prince Edward Is

Falkland Islands
Scotia Ridge
.45
Shag Rocks
South Georgia
South Sandwich Is
South Sandwich Trench
Atlantic-Indian Ridge
Bouvetøya

Cabo de Hornos
Drake Passage
5870
Scotia Sea
Scotia Ridge
Meteor Depth 8325
5750
.6972
.230

South-East Pacific Basin
South Shetland Is
E
F
G
South Orkney Is
H
Atlantic-Indian Antarctic Basin
Maud Seamount
.1200
Antarctic Circle

120°W
C
D
Antarctic Peninsula
J
K
L
M

Scale

Metres	Feet
SEA LEVEL	LEVEL
200	656
3000	9843
5000	16404
6000	19686

Km	Miles
3000	1800
2500	1500
2000	1200
1500	900
1000	600
500	300
0	0

1:58M

Lambert Azimuthal Equal Area Projection

© Bartholomew

THE INDEX includes the names on the maps in the main map section of the ATLAS. The names are generally indexed to the largest scale map on which they appear, and can be located using the grid reference letters and numbers around the map frame. Names on insets have a symbol: □, followed by the inset number where more than one inset appears on the page.

Abbreviations used to describe features in the index are explained below.

Afgh. Afghanistan
AK Alaska
AL Alabama
Alg. Algeria
Alta Alberta
Ant. Antarctica
AR Arkansas
arch. archipelago
Arg. Argentina
Atl. Atlantic
Austr. Australia
AZ Arizona
Azer. Azerbaijan

b. bay
Bangl. Bangladesh
B.C. British Columbia
Bol. Bolivia
Bos.-Herz. Bosnia Herzegovina
Bulg. Bulgaria

c. cape
CA California
Can. Canada
C.A.R. Central African Republic
chan. channel
Co. County
CO Colorado
Col. Colombia
CT Connecticut

DC District of Colombia
DE Delaware
des. desert
div. division
Dom. Rep. Dominican Republic

Eng. England
escarp. escarpment
est. estuary
Eth. Ethiopia

Fin. Finland
FL Florida
Fr. Guiana French Guiana

g. gulf
GA Georgia
gl. glacier
Ger. Germany

h. hill, hills
hd headland
HI Hawaii

i. island
IA Iowa
ID Idaho
IL Illinois
in. inlet
IN Indiana
Indon. Indonesia
is islands
Isr. Israel

isth. isthmus

Kazak. Kazakstan
KS Kansas
KY Kentucky
Kyrg. Kyrgyzstan

l. lake, lakes
LA Louisiana
lag. lagoon
Lith. Lithuania
Lux. Luxembourg

MA Massachusetts
Madag. Madagascar
Man. Manitoba
Maur. Mauritania
MD Maryland
ME Maine
Mex. Mexico
MI Michigan
MN Minnesota
MO Missouri
Moz. Mozambique
MS Mississippi
mt mountain
MT Montana
mts mountains

N. North, Northern
nat. national
N.B. New Brunswick
NC North Carolina
ND North Dakota
NE Nebraska
Neth. Netherlands
Neth. Ant. Netherlands Antilles
Nfld Newfoundland
NH New Hampshire
Nic. Nicaragua
NJ New Jersey
NM New Mexico
N.S. Nova Scotia
N.S.W. New South Wales
NV Nevada
N.W.T. Northwest Territories
NY New York
N.Z. New Zealand

OH Ohio
OK Oklahoma
Ont. Ontario
OR Oregon

PA Pennsylvania
Pac. Pacific
Pak. Pakistan
Para. Paraguay
P.E.I. Prince Edward Island
pen. peninsula
Phil. Philippines
plat. plateau
P.N.G. Papua New Guinea
Pol. Poland
Port. Portugal
pt point

Qld. Queensland
Que. Quebec

r. river
reg. region
Rep. Republic
res. reserve
resr reservoir
rf reef
RI Rhode Island
Rus. Fed. Russian Federation

S. South
S.A. South Australia
Sask. Saskatchewan
S. Arabia Saudi Arabia
SC South Carolina
Scot. Scotland
SD South Dakota
Sing. Singapore
str. strait
Switz. Switzerland

Tajik. Tajikistan
Tanz. Tanzania
terr. territory
Thai. Thailand
TN Tennessee
Turk. Turkmenistan
TX Texas

U.A.E. United Arab Emirates
U.K. United Kingdom
Ukr. Ukraine
Uru. Uruguay
U.S.A. United States of America
UT Utah
Uzbek. Uzbekistan

v. valley
VA Virginia
Venez. Venezuela
Vic. Victoria
volc. volcano
VT Vermont

WA Washington
WV West Virginia
WY Wyoming

Y.T. Yukon Territory
Yugo. Yugoslavia

A

42 E4 **Aachen** Ger.
46 E6 **Aalen** Ger.
42 C4 **Aalst** Belgium
42 C4 **Aarschot** Belgium
26 A3 **Aba** China
56 D3 **Aba** Congo(Zaire)
54 C4 **Aba** Nigeria
18 B5 **Abā ad Dūd** S. Arabia
18 C4 **Abādān** Iran
18 D4 **Abādeh** Iran
54 B1 **Abadla** Alg.
90 D2 **Abaeté** *r.* Brazil
87 J4 **Abaetetuba** Brazil
26 E1 **Abag Qi** China
95 G5 **Abaiang** *i.* Pac. Oc.
73 E4 **Abajo Pk** *summit* U.S.A.
54 C4 **Abakaliki** Nigeria
24 B1 **Abakan** Rus. Fed.
24 A1 **Abakanskiy Khrebet** *mts* Rus. Fed.
51 E7 **Abana** Turkey
18 D4 **Āb Anbār** Iran
86 D6 **Abancay** Peru
18 D4 **Abarqū** Iran
28 J2 **Abashiri** Japan
28 J2 **Abashiri-wan** *b.* Japan
6 E3 **Abau** P.N.G.
56 D3 **Ābaya Hāyk'** *l.* Eth.
Ābay Wenz *r. see* **Blue Nile**
12 L4 **Abaza** Rus. Fed.
19 E3 **Abbāsābād** Iran
48 C4 **Abbasanta** *Sardinia* Italy
68 C2 **Abbaye, Pt** *pt* U.S.A.
56 E2 **Abbe, L.** *l.* Eth.
44 E1 **Abbeville** France
77 E6 **Abbeville** *LA* U.S.A.
79 D5 **Abbeville** *SC* U.S.A.
41 B5 **Abbeyfeale** Rep. of Ireland
40 E6 **Abbey Head** *hd* U.K.
41 D5 **Abbeyleix** Rep. of Ireland
38 D3 **Abbeytown** U.K.
36 Q4 **Abborrträsk** Sweden
92 A3 **Abbot Ice Shelf** *ice feature* Ant.
64 E5 **Abbotsford** Can.
68 B3 **Abbotsford** U.S.A.
73 F4 **Abbott** U.S.A.
22 C2 **Abbottabad** Pak.
17 H3 **'Abd al 'Azīz, J.** *h.* Syria
17 L5 **Abdanan** Iran
55 E3 **Abéché** Chad
19 E4 **Āb-e Garm** Iran
9 D4 **Abel Tasman National Park** N.Z.
54 B4 **Abengourou** Côte d'Ivoire
37 L9 **Åbenrå** Denmark
43 K6 **Abensberg** Ger.
54 C4 **Abeokuta** Nigeria
39 C5 **Aberaeron** U.K.
40 F3 **Aberchirder** U.K.
8 G2 **Abercrombie** *r.* Austr.
39 D6 **Aberdare** U.K.
39 C5 **Aberdaron** U.K.
8 H2 **Aberdeen** Austr.
65 H4 **Aberdeen** Can.
27 □ **Aberdeen** *H.K.* China
58 F6 **Aberdeen** S. Africa
40 F3 **Aberdeen** U.K.
81 E5 **Aberdeen** *MD* U.S.A.
77 F5 **Aberdeen** *MS* U.S.A.
76 D2 **Aberdeen** *SD* U.S.A.
72 B2 **Aberdeen** *WA* U.S.A.
65 J2 **Aberdeen Lake** *l.* Can.
39 C5 **Aberdyfi** U.K.
40 E4 **Aberfeldy** U.K.
38 F4 **Aberford** U.K.
40 D4 **Aberfoyle** U.K.
39 D6 **Abergavenny** U.K.
77 C5 **Abernathy** U.S.A.
39 C5 **Aberporth** U.K.
39 C5 **Abersoch** U.K.
39 C5 **Aberystwyth** U.K.
20 B6 **Abhā** S. Arabia
18 C2 **Abhar** Iran
18 C2 **Abhar** *r.* Iran
Abiad, Bahr el *r. see* **White Nile**
18 C3 **Ab-i Bazuft** *r.* Iran
89 A2 **Abibe, Serranía de** *mts* Col.
54 B4 **Abidjan** Côte d'Ivoire
19 H3 **Ab-i-Istada** *l.* Afgh.
56 D3 **Abijatta-Shalla National Park** Eth.
18 E3 **Ab-i-Kavir** *salt flat* Iran
76 D4 **Abilene** *KS* U.S.A.
77 D5 **Abilene** *TX* U.S.A.
39 F6 **Abingdon** U.K.
68 B5 **Abingdon** *IL* U.S.A.
80 C6 **Abingdon** *VA* U.S.A.
51 F6 **Abinsk** Rus. Fed.
19 G2 **Ab-i-Safed** *r.* Afgh.
86 C5 **Abiseo, Parque Nacional** *nat. park* Peru
65 H2 **Abitau Lake** *l.* Can.
66 D4 **Abitibi** *r.* Can.
66 E4 **Abitibi, Lake** *l.* Can.
54 B4 **Aboisso** Côte d'Ivoire
54 C4 **Abomey** Benin
22 C3 **Abonar** India
55 D4 **Abong Mbang** Cameroon
31 A4 **Aborlan** Phil.
55 D3 **Abou Déia** Chad
17 K1 **Abovyan** Armenia
40 F3 **Aboyne** U.K.
91 D4 **Abra, L. del** *l.* Arg.
45 B3 **Abrantes** Port.
88 C2 **Abra Pampa** Arg.
90 E2 **Abrolhos, Arquipélago dos** *is* Brazil
72 E2 **Absaroka Range** *mts* U.S.A.
43 H6 **Abtsgmünd** Ger.
18 C5 **Abū 'Alī** *i.* S. Arabia
18 D5 **Abual Jirab** *i.* U.A.E.
20 B6 **Abū 'Arīsh** S. Arabia
20 D5 **Abu Dhabi** U.A.E.
55 F3 **Abu Hamed** Sudan
54 C4 **Abuja** Nigeria
55 E3 **Abu Matariq** Sudan
18 D5 **Abū Mūsá** *i.* U.A.E.
86 E5 **Abunã** Brazil
86 E6 **Abunã** *r.* Bol.
20 A7 **Ābune Yosēf** *mt* Eth.
16 C6 **Abu Qīr, Khalīg** *b.* Egypt
15 F4 **Abu Road** India
55 F2 **Abu Simbel** Egypt
17 K6 **Abū Şukhayr** Iraq
9 C5 **Abut Head** *hd* N.Z.
31 C4 **Abuyog** Phil.
55 E3 **Abu Zabad** Sudan
Abū Zabī *see* **Abu Dhabi**
17 M6 **Abūzam** Iran
55 E3 **Abyad** Sudan
55 E4 **Abyei** Sudan
18 C2 **Ābyek** Iran
81 J2 **Acadia Nat. Park** U.S.A.
84 B2 **Acambaro** Mex.
84 E2 **Acancéh** Mex.
89 A2 **Acandí** Col.
45 B1 **A Cañiza** Spain
84 A2 **Acaponeta** Mex.
84 C3 **Acapulco** Mex.
87 J4 **Acará** Brazil
87 K4 **Acaraú** *r.* Brazil
90 A4 **Acaray** *r.* Para.
88 E3 **Acaray, Represa de** *resr* Para.
89 C2 **Acarigua** Venez.
84 C3 **Acatlan** Mex.
84 C3 **Acatzingo** Mex.
84 D3 **Acayucán** Mex.
54 B4 **Accra** Ghana
38 E4 **Accrington** U.K.
89 C3 **Achaguas** Venez.
22 D5 **Achalpur** India
21 B2 **Achampet** India
13 T3 **Achayvayam** Rus. Fed.
30 D1 **Acheng** China
42 A4 **Achicourt** France
41 B4 **Achill** Rep. of Ireland
41 A4 **Achill Island** *i.* Rep. of Ireland
40 C2 **Achiltibuie** U.K.
43 H1 **Achim** Ger.
24 B1 **Achinsk** Rus. Fed.
40 C3 **Achnasheen** U.K.
40 C3 **A'Chralaig** *mt* U.K.
51 F6 **Achuyevo** Rus. Fed.
16 B3 **Acıgöl** *l.* Turkey
16 B3 **Acıpayam** Turkey
48 F6 **Acireale** *Sicily* Italy
76 E3 **Ackley** U.S.A.
83 K4 **Acklins Island** *i.* Bahamas
39 J5 **Acle** U.K.
91 B2 **Aconcagua** *r.* Chile
87 L5 **Acopiara** Brazil
45 B1 **A Coruña** Spain
48 C2 **Acqui Terme** Italy
16 E5 **Acre** Israel
48 G5 **Acri** Italy
46 J7 **Ács** Hungary
5 O7 **Actéon, Groupe** *is* Pac. Oc.
80 B4 **Ada** *OH* U.S.A.
77 D5 **Ada** *OK* U.S.A.
45 D2 **Adaja** *r.* Spain
8 G4 **Adaminaby** Austr.
88 E8 **Adam, Mt** *h.* Falkland Is
81 G3 **Adams** *MA* U.S.A.
68 C4 **Adams** *WV* U.S.A.
21 B4 **Adam's Bridge** *rf* India/Sri Lanka
64 F4 **Adams L.** *l.* Can.
75 E2 **Adams McGill Reservoir** U.S.A.
64 C3 **Adams Mt.** *mt* U.S.A.
72 B2 **Adams, Mt** *mt* U.S.A.
74 B2 **Adams Peak** *mt* U.S.A.
21 C5 **Adam's Pk** Sri Lanka
'Adan *see* **Aden**
16 E3 **Adana** Turkey
41 C5 **Adare** Rep. of Ireland
92 A5 **Adare, C.** *c.* Ant.
75 E2 **Adaven** U.S.A.
20 C5 **Ad Dahnā'** *des.* S. Arabia
54 A2 **Ad Dakhla** Western Sahara
20 D4 **Ad Dammām** S. Arabia
18 B5 **Ad Dawādimī** S. Arabia
Ad Dawḩah *see* **Doha**
17 J4 **Ad Dawr** Iraq
18 B5 **Ad Dibdibah** *plain* S. Arabia
18 B6 **Ad Dilam** S. Arabia
20 C5 **Ad Dir'īyah** S. Arabia
56 D3 **Addis Ababa** Eth.
81 K2 **Addison** U.S.A.
17 K6 **Ad Dīwānīyah** Iraq
39 G6 **Addlestone** U.K.
10 J10 **Addu Atoll** *atoll* Maldives
17 J6 **Ad Duwayd** *well* S. Arabia
79 D6 **Adel** *GA* U.S.A.
76 E3 **Adel** *IA* U.S.A.
8 B3 **Adelaide** Austr.
79 E7 **Adelaide** Bahamas
59 G6 **Adelaide** S. Africa
92 B2 **Adelaide I** *i.* Ant.
6 D3 **Adelaide River** Austr.
74 D4 **Adelanto** U.S.A.
8 G3 **Adelong** Austr.
20 C7 **Aden** Yemen
42 E4 **Adenau** Ger.
43 J1 **Adendorf** Ger.
20 C7 **Aden, Gulf of** *g.* Somalia/Yemen
18 D5 **Adh Dhayd** U.A.E.
25 F7 **Adi** *i.* Indon.
56 D2 **Ādī Ārk'ay** Eth.
56 D2 **Ādīgrat** Eth.
22 D6 **Adilabad** India
17 J2 **Adilcevaz** Turkey
72 B3 **Adin** U.S.A.
55 D2 **Adīrī** Libya
81 F2 **Adirondack Mountains** U.S.A.
Ādīs Ābeba *see* **Addis Ababa**
56 D3 **Ādīs Alem** Eth.
56 D2 **Adi Ugri** Eritrea
16 G3 **Adıyaman** Turkey
47 N7 **Adjud** Romania
84 C2 **Adjuntas, Presa de las** *resr* Mex.
67 J3 **Adlavik Islands** *is* Can.
6 C3 **Admiralty Gulf** *b.* Austr.
63 K2 **Admiralty Inlet** *in.* Can.
64 C3 **Admiralty Island** *i.* U.S.A.
64 C3 **Admiralty Island Nat. Monument** *res.* U.S.A.
6 E2 **Admiralty Islands** *is* P.N.G.
21 B3 **Adoni** India
43 L4 **Adorf** Ger.
43 G3 **Adorf (Diemelsee)** Ger.
44 D5 **Adour** *r.* France
45 E4 **Adra** Spain
48 F6 **Adrano** *Sicily* Italy
54 B2 **Adrar** Alg.
54 A2 **Adrar** *mts* Alg.
54 C3 **Adrar des Ifôghas** *reg.* Mali
54 A2 **Adrar Maur**
19 F3 **Adraskand** *r.* Afgh.
55 E3 **Adré** Chad
69 E5 **Adrian** *MI* U.S.A.
77 C5 **Adrian** *TX* U.S.A.
48 E2 **Adriatic Sea** *sea* Europe
21 B4 **Adur** India
56 C3 **Adusa** Congo(Zaire)
56 D2 **Ādwa** Eth.
13 P3 **Adycha** *r.* Rus. Fed.
51 F6 **Adygeya, Respublika** *div.* Rus. Fed.
51 F6 **Adygeysk** Rus. Fed.
51 H6 **Adyk** Rus. Fed.
54 B4 **Adzopé** Côte d'Ivoire
49 L5 **Aegean Sea** *sea* Greece/Turkey
43 H2 **Aerzen** Ger.
45 B1 **A Estrada** Spain
56 D2 **Afabet** Eritrea
17 K3 **Afan** Iran
10 H6 **Afghanistan** *country* Asia
36 M5 **Åfjord** Norway
56 E3 **Afmadow** Somalia
62 C4 **Afognak I.** *i.* U.S.A.
45 C1 **A Fonsagrada** Spain
16 F3 **'Afrīn** *r.* Syria/Turkey
16 F2 **Afşin** Turkey
42 D2 **Afsluitdijk** *barrage* Neth.
72 E3 **Afton** U.S.A.
87 H4 **Afuá** Brazil
16 E5 **'Afula** Israel
16 C2 **Afyon** Turkey
43 L4 **Aga** Ger.
54 C3 **Agadez** Niger
54 B1 **Agadir** Morocco
15 F2 **Agadyr'** Kazak.
53 K7 **Agalega Islands** *is* Mauritius
23 G5 **Agartala** India
22 C6 **Agashi** India
69 F2 **Agate** Can.
49 M6 **Agathonisi** *i.* Greece
54 B4 **Agboville** Côte d'Ivoire
17 L1 **Ağcabädi** Azer.
17 L2 **Ağdam** Azer.
44 F5 **Agde** France
44 E4 **Agen** France
58 C4 **Aggeneys** S. Africa
42 F4 **Agger** *r.* Ger.
22 D1 **Aghil Pass** China
41 C3 **Aghla Mountain** *h.* Rep. of Ireland
49 L7 **Agia Vervara** Greece
16 G2 **Ağın** Turkey
49 K6 **Agios Dimitrios** Greece
49 L5 **Agios Efstratios** *i.* Greece
49 M5 **Agios Fokas, Akra** *pt* Greece
49 K5 **Agios Konstantinos** Greece
49 L7 **Agios Nikolaos** Greece
49 K4 **Agiou Orous, Kolpos** *b.* Greece
55 F3 **Agirwat Hills** *h.* Sudan
59 F3 **Agisanang** S. Africa
54 B4 **Agnibilékrou** Côte d'Ivoire
49 L2 **Agnita** Romania
26 A2 **Agong** China
22 D4 **Agra** India
51 H7 **Agrakhanskiy Poluostrov** *pen.* Rus. Fed.
45 F2 **Agreda** Spain
17 J2 **Ağrı** Turkey
49 K7 **Agria Gramvousa** *i.* Greece
48 E6 **Agrigento** *Sicily* Italy
49 J5 **Agrinio** Greece
91 B3 **Agrio** *r.* Arg.
48 F4 **Agropoli** Italy
17 K1 **Ağstafa** Azer.
17 M1 **Ağsu** Azer.
84 A2 **Agua Brava, L.** *lag.* Mex.
84 E3 **Aguada** Mex.
89 B3 **Aguadas** Col.
89 B3 **Agua de Dios** Col.
83 L5 **Aguadilla** Puerto Rico
91 D4 **Aguado Cecilio** Arg.
83 H7 **Aguadulce** Panama
91 C3 **Agua Escondida** Arg.
84 B1 **Aguanaval** *r.* Mex.
91 C1 **Agua Negra, Paso del** *pass* Arg./Chile
90 B3 **Aguapeí** *r.* Brazil
82 C2 **Agua Prieta** Mex.
90 A3 **Aguaray Guazú** *r.* Para.
89 D2 **Aguaro-Guariquito, Parque Nacional** *nat. park* Venez.
84 B2 **Aguascalientes** Mex.
84 B2 **Aguascalientes** *div.* Mex.
90 E2 **Águas Formosas** Brazil
90 C3 **Agudos** Brazil
75 F5 **Aguila** U.S.A.
45 D1 **Aguilar de Campóo** Spain
45 F4 **Águilas** Spain
31 B4 **Aguisan** Phil.
93 F7 **Agulhas Basin** *sea feature* Ind. Ocean
58 D7 **Agulhas, Cape** *c.* S. Africa
90 D3 **Agulhas Negras** *mt* Brazil
93 F6 **Agulhas Plateau** *sea feature* Ind. Ocean
33 E4 **Agung, G.** *volc.* Indon.
31 C4 **Agusan** *r.* Phil.
31 B4 **Agutaya** Phil.
18 B2 **Ahar** Iran
9 C5 **Ahaura** N.Z.
42 F2 **Ahaus** Ger.
9 F3 **Ahimanawa Ra.** *mts* N.Z.
9 D1 **Ahipara** N.Z.
9 D1 **Ahipara Bay** *b.* N.Z.
62 B4 **Ahklun Mts** *mts* U.S.A.
17 J2 **Ahlat** Turkey
43 F3 **Ahlen** Ger.
22 C5 **Ahmadabad** India
18 E4 **Ahmadī** Iran
21 A2 **Ahmadnagar** India
22 B3 **Ahmadpur East** Pak.
43 J4 **Ahorn** Ger.
18 C4 **Ahram** Iran
43 J1 **Ahrensburg** Ger.
17 J2 **Ahta D.** *mt* Turkey
36 T5 **Ähtäri** Fin.
37 U7 **Ahtme** Estonia
17 M6 **Āhū** Iran
84 B2 **Ahualulco** Mex.
44 F3 **Ahun** France
9 B6 **Ahuriri** *r.* N.Z.
18 C4 **Ahvāz** Iran
22 C5 **Ahwa** India
Ahwāz *see* **Ahvāz**
30 C3 **Ai** *r.* China
58 B3 **Ai-Ais** Namibia
26 D1 **Aibag Gol** *r.* China
18 D2 **Aidin** Turkm.
74 □1 **Aiea** U.S.A.
16 E4 **Aigialousa** Cyprus
49 K6 **Aigina** *i.* Greece
49 K5 **Aigio** Greece
44 H4 **Aigle de Chambeyron** *mt* France
91 F2 **Aiguá** Uru.
29 F5 **Aikawa** Japan
79 D5 **Aiken** U.S.A.
89 A2 **Ailigandi** Panama
95 G5 **Ailinglapalap** *i.* Pac. Oc.
42 A5 **Ailly-sur-Noye** France
69 G4 **Ailsa Craig** Can.
40 C5 **Ailsa Craig** *i.* U.K.
90 E2 **Aimorés, Sa dos** *h.* Brazil
54 C1 **Aïn Beïda** Alg.
54 B2 **'Aïn Ben Tili** Maur.
45 H4 **Aïn Defla** Alg.
45 H5 **Aïn el Hadjel** Alg.
54 B1 **Aïn Sefra** Alg.
67 H4 **Ainslie, Lake** *l.* Can.
76 D3 **Ainsworth** U.S.A.
Aintab *see* **Gaziantep**
45 H4 **Aïn Taya** Alg.
45 G5 **Aïn Tédélès** Alg.
89 B4 **Aipe** Col.
32 C5 **Air** *i.* Indon.
64 G4 **Airdrie** Can.
40 E5 **Airdrie** U.K.
42 D6 **Aire** *r.* France
44 D5 **Aire-sur-l'Adour** France
63 L3 **Air Force I.** *i.* Can.
26 D1 **Airgin Sum** China
54 C3 **Aïr, Massif de l'** *mts* Niger
65 H3 **Air Ronge** Can.
88 B7 **Aisén, Pto** Chile
26 F2 **Ai Shan** *h.* China
64 B2 **Aishihik** Can.
64 B2 **Aishihik Lake** *l.* Can.
44 G2 **Aisne** *r.* France
45 F3 **Aitana** *mt* Spain
6 E2 **Aitape** P.N.G.
76 E2 **Aitken** U.S.A.
5 L6 **Aitutaki** *i.* Pac. Oc.
47 L7 **Aiud** Romania
44 G5 **Aix-en-Provence** France
44 G4 **Aix-les-Bains** France
64 D3 **Aiyansh** Can.
23 F5 **Aiyar Res.** *resr* India
23 H5 **Aizawl** India
37 T8 **Aizkraukle** Latvia
37 R8 **Aizpute** Latvia
29 F6 **Aizu-wakamatsu** Japan
48 C4 **Ajaccio** *Corsica* France
89 B4 **Ajajú** *r.* Col.
84 C3 **Ajalpán** Mex.
21 A1 **Ajanta** India
Ajanta Range *h. see* **Sahyadriparvat Range**
36 O4 **Ajaureforsen** Sweden
9 D5 **Ajax, Mt** *mt* N.Z.
55 E1 **Ajdābiyā** Libya
a-Jiddét *gravel area see* **Jiddat al Ḩarāsīs**
28 G4 **Ajigasawa** Japan
16 E5 **'Ajlūn** Jordan
18 D5 **'Ajmān** U.A.E.
22 C4 **Ajmer** India
75 F5 **Ajo** U.S.A.
75 F5 **Ajo, Mt** *mt* U.S.A.
31 B4 **Ajuy** Phil.
28 H3 **Akabira** Japan
56 D4 **Akagera National Park** Rwanda
21 B2 **Akalkot** India
28 J3 **Akan National Park** Japan
16 D4 **Akanthou** Cyprus
9 D5 **Akaroa** N.Z.
9 D5 **Akaroa Har** *in.* N.Z.
23 H4 **Akas** *reg.* India
19 H3 **Akbar** Afgh.
23 E4 **Akbarpur** India
45 J4 **Akbou** Alg.
12 G4 **Akbulak** Rus. Fed.
16 F2 **Akçadağ** Turkey
17 G3 **Akçakale** Turkey
16 C1 **Akçakoca** Turkey
16 D3 **Akçali D.** *mt* Turkey
16 C3 **Ak D.** *mt* Turkey
17 H2 **Ak D.** *mts* Turkey
16 C3 **Akdağ** *mt* Turkey
16 E2 **Akdağmadeni** Turkey
37 Q7 **Åkersberga** Sweden
42 C2 **Akersloot** Neth.
56 C3 **Aketi** Congo(Zaire)
17 J1 **Akhalk'alak'i** Georgia
51 G7 **Akhalts'ikhe** Georgia
23 G5 **Akhaura** Bangl.
20 E5 **Akhḑar, Jabal** *mts* Oman
16 A2 **Akhisar** Turkey
16 F3 **Akhtarīn** Syria
51 H5 **Akhtubinsk** Rus. Fed.
17 J1 **Akhuryan** Armenia
29 C8 **Aki** Japan
66 D3 **Akimiski Island** *i.* Can.
16 E3 **Akıncı Burun** *pt* Turkey
16 G1 **Akıncılar** Turkey
28 G5 **Akita** Japan
54 A3 **Akjoujt** Maur.
36 P3 **Akkajaure** *l.* Sweden
28 J3 **Akkeshi** Japan
'Akko *see* **Acre**
16 E3 **Akkuş** Turkey
18 D1 **Akkyr, Gory** *h.* Turkm.
22 D4 **Aklera** India
37 R8 **Akmeņrags** *pt* Latvia
22 D1 **Akmeqit** China
14 F1 **Akmola** Kazak.
29 D7 **Akō** Japan
55 F4 **Akobo** Sudan
22 D5 **Akola** India
56 D2 **Akordat** Eritrea
16 D3 **Akören** Turkey
22 D5 **Akot** India
63 M3 **Akpatok Island** *i. Que.* Can.
67 G1 **Akpatok Island** *i.* Can.
36 B4 **Akranes** Iceland
51 C7 **Akrathos, Akra** *pt* Greece
37 J7 **Åkrehamne** Norway
19 G3 **Ak Robat Pass** Afgh.
72 G3 **Akron** *CO* U.S.A.
80 C4 **Akron** *OH* U.S.A.
80 C4 **Akron City Reservoir** U.S.A.
22 D2 **Aksai Chin** *terr.* China/India
16 E2 **Aksaray** Turkey
51 F6 **Aksay** Rus. Fed.
22 D2 **Aksayqin Hu** *l.* China/Jammu and Kashmir
16 C2 **Akşehir** Turkey
16 C2 **Akşehir Gölü** *l.* Turkey
16 C3 **Akseki** Turkey
18 D4 **Aks-e Rostam** *r.* Iran
14 E2 **Akshiganak** Kazak.
15 G2 **Aksu** China
16 C3 **Aksu** *r.* Turkey
56 D2 **Āksum** Eth.
23 F1 **Aktag** *mt* China
17 K2 **Aktas D.** *mt* Turkey
19 G2 **Aktash** Uzbek.
14 D2 **Aktau** Kazak.
15 F2 **Aktogay** Kazak.
47 O4 **Aktsyabrski** Belarus
14 D1 **Aktyubinsk** Kazak.
29 B8 **Akune** Japan
54 C4 **Akure** Nigeria
36 D4 **Akureyri** Iceland
23 G1 **Akxokesay** China
Akyab *see* **Sittwe**
16 G3 **Akziyaret** Turkey
37 L6 **Ål** Norway
18 C5 **Al 'Abā** S. Arabia
79 C5 **Alabama** *div.* U.S.A.
79 C6 **Alabama** *r.* U.S.A.
79 C5 **Alabaster** U.S.A.
31 B3 **Alabat** *i.* Phil.
17 K7 **Al 'Abṭīyah** *well* Iraq
16 E1 **Alaca** Turkey
16 F2 **Alacahan** Turkey
16 E1 **Alaçam** Turkey
16 B2 **Alaçam Dağları** *mts* Turkey
84 E2 **Alacrán, Arrecife** *atoll* Mex.
17 J2 **Ala Dag** *mt* Turkey
17 J2 **Ala Dağlar** *mts* Turkey
16 E3 **Ala Dağlar** *mts* Turkey
51 H7 **Alagir** Rus. Fed.
87 L6 **Alagoinhas** Brazil
45 F2 **Alagón** Spain
31 C5 **Alah** *r.* Phil.
36 S5 **Alahärmä** Fin.
17 L7 **Al Aḩmadī** Kuwait
19 H2 **Alai Range** *mts* Asia
36 S5 **Alajärvi** Fin.
83 H6 **Alajuela** Costa Rica
17 L2 **Alajujeh** Iran
22 D3 **Alaknanda** *r.* India
15 G2 **Alakol', Ozero** *l.* Kazak.
36 W3 **Alakurtti** Rus. Fed.
86 F4 **Alalaú** *r.* Brazil
17 J3 **Al 'Amādīyah** Iraq
18 B5 **Al'Amār** S. Arabia
17 L6 **Al 'Amārah** Iraq
23 H3 **Alamdo** China
17 K7 **Al Amghar** *waterhole* Iraq
31 A2 **Alaminos** Phil.
84 B1 **Alamítos, Sa de los** *mt* Mex.
75 E3 **Alamo** U.S.A.
75 F4 **Alamo Dam** *dam* U.S.A.
73 F5 **Alamogordo** U.S.A.
77 D6 **Alamo Heights** U.S.A.
73 E6 **Alamos** Mex.
70 E6 **Alamos** Mex.
73 F4 **Alamosa** U.S.A.
21 B3 **Alampur** India
36 O4 **Alanäs** Sweden
21 B2 **Aland** India
37 Q6 **Åland** *is* Fin.
43 K1 **Aland** *r.* Ger.
18 B2 **Aland** *r.* Iran
32 B5 **Alang Besar** *i.* Indon.
68 E3 **Alanson** U.S.A.
16 D3 **Alanya** Turkey
16 C1 **Alaplı** Turkey
Alappuzha *see* **Alleppey**
18 C6 **Al 'Aqūlah** *well* S. Arabia
45 E3 **Alarcón, Embalse de** *resr* Spain
20 C4 **Al Arţāwīyah** S. Arabia
33 E4 **Alas** Indon.
16 B2 **Alaşehir** Turkey
17 J6 **Al 'Ashūrīyah** *well* Iraq
62 D3 **Alaska** *div.* U.S.A.
62 D4 **Alaska, Gulf of** *g.* U.S.A.
64 E3 **Alaska Highway** Can./U.S.A.
62 B4 **Alaska Peninsula** U.S.A.
62 D3 **Alaska Range** *mts* U.S.A.
17 M2 **Älät** Azer.
19 F2 **Alat** Uzbek.
17 J6 **Al 'Athāmīn** *h.* Iraq
50 H4 **Alatyr'** Rus. Fed.
50 H4 **Alatyr'** *r.* Rus. Fed.
86 C4 **Alausí** Ecuador
17 K1 **Alaverdi** Armenia
36 T4 **Alavieska** Fin.
36 S5 **Alavus** Fin.
8 C3 **Alawoona** Austr.
17 L1 **Alazani** *r.* Azer./Georgia
17 K5 **Al 'Azīzīyah** Iraq
48 C2 **Alba** Italy
16 F3 **Al Bāb** Syria
45 F3 **Albacete** Spain

8 C3 Albacutya, L. l. Austr.
17 K6 Al Bādiyah al Janūbīyah h. Iraq
49 K1 Alba Iulia Romania
66 F3 Albanel, L. l. Can.
35 G4 Albania country Europe
6 B5 Albany Austr.
79 C6 Albany GA U.S.A.
68 E5 Albany IN U.S.A.
78 C4 Albany KY U.S.A.
81 G3 Albany NY U.S.A.
72 B2 Albany OR U.S.A.
66 C3 Albany r. Can.
91 G2 Albardão do João Maria coastal area Brazil
18 B5 Al Barrah S. Arabia
Al Başrah see Basra
17 K6 Al Baţḩa' marsh Iraq
17 L7 Al Bāţin, Wādī watercourse Asia
6 E3 Albatross Bay b. Austr.
55 E1 Al Bayḑā' Libya
86 □ Albemarle, Pta pt Galapagos Is Ecuador
79 E5 Albemarle Sd chan. U.S.A.
48 C2 Albenga Italy
45 D3 Alberche r. Spain
6 D4 Alberga watercourse Austr.
45 B2 Albergaria-a-Velha Port.
8 F2 Albert Austr.
44 F2 Albert France
80 E6 Alberta U.S.A.
64 F4 Alberta div. Can.
64 F4 Alberta, Mt mt Can.
58 D7 Albertinia S. Africa
42 D4 Albert Kanaal canal Belgium
8 B3 Albert, Lake l. Austr.
56 D3 Albert, Lake l. Congo(Zaire)/Uganda
76 E3 Albert Lea U.S.A.
56 D3 Albert Nile r. Sudan/Uganda
88 B8 Alberto de Agostini, Parque Nacional nat. park Chile
59 H3 Alberton S. Africa
44 H4 Albertville France
42 E6 Albestroff France
44 F5 Albi France
87 H2 Albina Suriname
74 A2 Albion CA U.S.A.
81 J2 Albion ME U.S.A.
68 E4 Albion MI U.S.A.
80 D3 Albion NY U.S.A.
45 E5 Alborán, Isla de i. Spain
37 L8 Ålborg Denmark
37 M8 Ålborg Bugt b. Denmark
64 F4 Albreda Can.
18 C5 Al Budayyi Bahrain
18 C6 Al Budū', Sabkhat salt pan S. Arabia
45 B4 Albufeira Port.
17 H4 Āl Bū Kamāl Syria
73 F5 Albuquerque U.S.A.
20 E5 Al Buraymī Oman
45 C3 Alburquerque Spain
8 F4 Albury Austr.
17 H4 Al Buşayrah Syria
16 G7 Al Busayţā' plain S. Arabia
17 L6 Al Buşayyah Iraq
18 B4 Al Bushūk well S. Arabia
45 B3 Alcácer do Sal Port.
45 E2 Alcalá de Henares Spain
45 E4 Alcalá la Real Spain
48 E6 Alcamo Sicily Italy
45 F2 Alcañiz Spain
45 C3 Alcántara Spain
45 E3 Alcaraz Spain
45 D4 Alcaudete Spain
45 E3 Alcázar de San Juan Spain
51 F5 Alchevs'k Ukr.
91 D2 Alcira Arg.
90 E2 Alcobaça Brazil
45 F2 Alcora Spain
91 E2 Alcorta Arg.
45 F3 Alcoy Spain
45 H3 Alcúdia Spain
57 E4 Aldabra Islands is Seychelles
17 K5 Al Daghghārah Iraq
84 C2 Aldama Mex.
13 O4 Aldan Rus. Fed.
13 P3 Aldan r. Rus. Fed.
39 J5 Aldeburgh U.K.
9 F2 Aldermen Is, The is N.Z.
44 D2 Alderney i. Channel Is U.K.
74 B4 Alder Peak summit U.S.A.
39 G6 Aldershot U.K.
80 C6 Alderson U.S.A.
18 D6 Al Dhafrah reg. U.A.E.
38 D3 Aldingham U.K.
39 F5 Aldridge U.K.
68 B5 Aledo U.S.A.
54 A3 Aleg Maur.
90 E3 Alegre Brazil
88 E3 Alegrete Brazil
91 E2 Alejandro Korn Arg.
50 E2 Alekhovshchina Rus. Fed.
50 F3 Aleksandrov Rus. Fed.
51 J5 Aleksandrov Gay Rus. Fed.
51 H6 Aleksandrovskoye Rus. Fed.
13 Q4 Aleksandrovsk-Sakhalinskiy Rus. Fed.
14 F1 Alekseyevka Kazak.
51 F5 Alekseyevka Belgorod. Obl. Rus. Fed.
51 F5 Alekseyevka Belgorod. Obl. Rus. Fed.
51 G5 Alekseyevskaya Rus. Fed.
50 F4 Aleksin Rus. Fed.
49 J3 Aleksinac Yugo.
84 C3 Alemán, Presa Miguel resr Mex.
56 B4 Alèmbé Gabon
16 E1 Alembeyli Turkey
90 D3 Além Paraíba Brazil
36 M5 Ålen Norway
44 E2 Alençon France
87 H4 Alenquer Brazil
74 □2 Alenuihaha Channel U.S.A.
16 F3 Aleppo Syria
86 D6 Alerta Peru
64 D4 Alert Bay Can.
44 G4 Alès France
47 L7 Aleşd Romania
48 C2 Alessandria Italy
36 K5 Ålesund Norway
60 A4 Aleutian Islands is U.S.A.
62 C4 Aleutian Range mts U.S.A.
95 H2 Aleutian Trench sea feature Pac. Oc.
13 R4 Alevina, Mys c. Rus. Fed.
Alevişik see Samandağı
81 K2 Alexander U.S.A.
64 B3 Alexander Archipelago is U.S.A.
58 B4 Alexander Bay S. Africa
58 B4 Alexander Bay b. Namibia/S. Africa
79 C5 Alexander City U.S.A.
92 A2 Alexander I. i. Ant.
8 E4 Alexandra Austr.
9 B6 Alexandra N.Z.
88 □ Alexandra, C. c. Atl. Ocean
49 K4 Alexandreia Greece
Alexandretta see İskenderun
81 F2 Alexandria Can.
55 E1 Alexandria Egypt
49 L3 Alexandria Romania
59 G6 Alexandria S. Africa
40 D5 Alexandria U.K.
68 E5 Alexandria IN U.S.A.
77 E6 Alexandria LA U.S.A.
76 E2 Alexandria MN U.S.A.
80 E5 Alexandria VA U.S.A.
81 F2 Alexandria Bay U.S.A.
8 B3 Alexandrina, L. l. Austr.
49 L4 Alexandroupoli Greece
68 B5 Alexis U.S.A.
67 J3 Alexis r. Can.
64 E4 Alexis Creek Can.
12 K4 Aleysk Rus. Fed.
42 F4 Alf Ger.
45 F1 Alfaro Spain
17 L7 Al Farwānīyah Kuwait
17 J4 Al Fatḩah Iraq
17 M7 Al Fāw Iraq
43 H3 Alfeld (Leine) Ger.
90 D3 Alfenas Brazil
17 M7 Al Fintās Kuwait
47 K7 Alföld plain Hungary
39 H4 Alford U.K.
81 F2 Alfred Can.
81 H3 Alfred U.S.A.
17 M7 Al Fuḩayḩīl Kuwait
Al-Fujayrah see Fujairah
18 B4 Al Fulayi watercourse S. Arabia
Al Furāt r. see Euphrates
37 J7 Algård Norway
91 C3 Algarrobo del Aguilla Arg.
45 B4 Algarve reg. Port.
50 G4 Algasovo Rus. Fed.
45 D4 Algeciras Spain
45 F3 Algemesí Spain
Alger see Algiers
69 E3 Alger U.S.A.
52 D3 Algeria country Africa
43 H2 Algermissen Ger.
17 K6 Al Ghammas Iraq
18 B5 Al Ghāţ S. Arabia
20 D6 Al Ghayḑah Yemen
48 C4 Alghero Sardinia Italy
54 C1 Algiers Alg.
59 F6 Algoa Bay b. S. Africa
68 D3 Algoma U.S.A.
76 E3 Algona U.S.A.
69 F4 Algonac U.S.A.
69 H3 Algonquin Park Can.
69 H3 Algonquin Provincial Park res. Can.
17 J7 Al Habakah well S. Arabia
18 B4 Al Ḩadaqah well S. Arabia
18 C5 Al Ḩadd Bahrain
18 A4 Al Hadhālīl plat. S. Arabia
17 J4 Al Ḩadīthah Iraq
17 J4 Al Ḩaḑr Iraq
16 F4 Al Ḩaffah Syria
18 B5 Al Ḩā'ir S. Arabia
19 E6 Al Hajar Oman
18 E5 Al Ḩajar al Gharbī mts Oman
17 G6 Al Hamad reg. Jordan/S. Arabia
55 D2 Al Ḩamādah al Ḩamrā' plat. Libya
45 F4 Alhama de Murcia Spain
17 J6 Al Hammām well Iraq
17 K7 Al Haniyah esc. Iraq
18 B6 Al Hariq S. Arabia
17 G6 Al Ḩarrah reg. S. Arabia
17 H3 Al Ḩasakah Syria
17 K5 Al Hāshimīyah Iraq
17 L5 Al Ḩayy Iraq
17 K5 Al Ḩillah Iraq
18 B6 Al Ḩillah S. Arabia
18 B6 Al Ḩilwah S. Arabia
18 C5 Al Ḩinnāh S. Arabia
54 B1 Al Hoceima Morocco
20 B7 Al Hudaydah Yemen
20 C4 Al Hufūf S. Arabia
18 D6 Al Ḩumrah reg. U.A.E.
18 C5 Al Ḩunayy S. Arabia
18 B6 Al Huwwah S. Arabia
18 D2 'Alīābād Iran
17 L4 'Alīābād Iran
19 E3 'Alīābād Iran
19 F4 'Alīābād Iran
49 M5 Aliağa Turkey
49 K4 Aliakmonas r. Greece
17 L5 'Alī al Gharbī Iraq
21 A2 Alībāg India
22 B4 Ali Bandar Pak.
17 M2 Āli Bayramlı Azer.
45 F3 Alicante Spain
59 G6 Alice S. Africa
77 D7 Alice U.S.A.
64 D3 Alice Arm Can.
6 D4 Alice Springs Austr.
79 F7 Alice Town Bahamas
31 B5 Alicia Phil.
22 D4 Aligarh India
18 C3 Alīgūdarz Iran
56 B4 Alima r. Congo
37 N8 Alingsås Sweden
16 B2 Aliova r. Turkey
22 B3 Alipur Pak.
23 G4 Alipur Duar India
80 C4 Aliquippa U.S.A.
56 E2 Ali Sabieh Djibouti
16 F6 'Al 'Īsāwīyah S. Arabia
17 K2 Alī Shah Iran
17 K5 Al Iskandarīyah Iraq
73 E6 Alisos r. Mex.
49 L5 Aliveri Greece
59 G5 Aliwal North S. Africa
64 G4 Alix Can.
55 E1 Al Jabal al Akhḑar mts Libya
17 K6 Al Jāfūrah des. S. Arabia
55 E2 Al Jaghbūb Libya
17 L7 Al Jahrah Kuwait
18 C5 Al Jamalīyah Qatar
18 C6 Al Jawb reg. S. Arabia
20 A4 Al Jawf S. Arabia
55 D1 Al Jawsh Libya
17 G3 Al Jazīrah reg. Iraq/Syria
18 C5 Al Jībān reg. S. Arabia
18 B6 Al Jifārah S. Arabia
17 J6 Al Jill well Iraq
18 B5 Al Jilh esc. S. Arabia
18 C5 Al Jishshah S. Arabia
16 E6 Al Jīzah Jordan
20 C4 Al Jubayl S. Arabia
18 B5 Al Jubaylah S. Arabia
18 B5 Al Jufayr S. Arabia
18 B5 Al Juray d S. Arabia
18 B5 Al Jurayfah S. Arabia
45 B4 Aljustrel Port.
20 E5 Al Khābūrah Oman
17 K5 Al Khāliş Iraq
20 E4 Al Khaşab Oman
18 A6 Al Khāşirah S. Arabia
18 D6 Al Khatam reg. U.A.E.
18 C5 Al Khawr Qatar
18 C5 Al Khīşah well S. Arabia
18 C5 Al Khobar S. Arabia
18 B5 Al Khuff reg. S. Arabia
55 E2 Al Khufrah Libya
55 D1 Al Khums Libya
17 K5 Al Kifl Iraq
18 C5 Al Kir'ānah Qatar
42 C2 Alkmaar Neth.
17 K5 Al Kūfah Iraq
17 L5 Al Kumayt Iraq
17 K5 Al Kūt Iraq
Al Kuwayt see Kuwait
17 H7 Al Labbah plain S. Arabia
Al Lādhiqīyah see Latakia
81 J1 Allagash ME U.S.A.
81 J1 Allagash r. ME U.S.A.
81 J1 Allagash Lake l. U.S.A.
23 E4 Allahabad India
16 F5 Al Lajā lava Syria
13 P3 Allakh-Yun' Rus. Fed.
59 G3 Allanridge S. Africa
59 H1 Alldays S. Africa
68 E4 Allegan U.S.A.
80 D4 Allegheny r. U.S.A.
80 C6 Allegheny Mountains U.S.A.
80 D4 Allegheny Reservoir U.S.A.
79 D5 Allendale U.S.A.
38 E3 Allendale Town U.K.
84 B1 Allende Mex.
43 G4 Allendorf (Lumda) Ger.
69 G3 Allenford Can.
41 C3 Allen, Lough l. Rep. of Ireland
81 F4 Allentown U.S.A.
21 B4 Alleppey India
43 J2 Aller r. Ger.
76 C3 Alliance NE U.S.A.
80 C4 Alliance OH U.S.A.
17 J6 Al Līfīyah well Iraq
37 O9 Allinge-Sandvig Denmark
69 H3 Alliston Can.
20 B5 Al Līth S. Arabia
40 E4 Alloa U.K.
21 C3 Allur India
21 C3 Alluru Kottapatnam India
17 J6 Al Lussuf well Iraq
67 F4 Alma Can.
68 E4 Alma MI U.S.A.
76 D3 Alma NE U.S.A.
75 H5 Alma NM U.S.A.
17 J6 Al Ma'ānīyah Iraq
45 B3 Almada Port.
17 K7 Al Ma'danīyāt well Iraq
45 D3 Almadén Spain
Al Madīnah see Medina
17 K5 Al Maḩmūdīyah Iraq
18 B5 Al Majma'ah S. Arabia
17 L1 Almalı Azer.
18 C5 Al Malsūnīyah reg. S. Arabia
18 C5 Al Manāmah Bahrain
74 B1 Almanor, Lake l. U.S.A.
45 F3 Almansa Spain
45 D2 Almanzor mt Spain
17 L6 Al Ma'qil Iraq
18 D6 Al Mariyyah U.A.E.
55 E1 Al Marj Libya
90 C1 Almas, Rio das r. Brazil
15 F2 Almaty Kazak.
Al Mawşil see Mosul
17 H4 Al Mayādīn Syria
18 B5 Al Mazāḩimīyah S. Arabia
45 E2 Almazán Spain
13 N3 Almaznyy Rus. Fed.
87 H4 Almeirim Brazil
45 B3 Almeirim Port.
42 E2 Almelo Neth.
90 E2 Almenara Brazil
45 C2 Almendra, Embalse de resr Spain
45 C3 Almendralejo Spain
42 D2 Almere Neth.
45 E4 Almería Spain
45 E4 Almería, Golfo de b. Spain
12 G4 Al'met'yevsk Rus. Fed.
37 O8 Älmhult Sweden
18 B5 Al Midhnab S. Arabia
45 D5 Almina, Pta pt Morocco
20 C4 Al Mish'āb S. Arabia
16 F5 Al Mismīyah Syria
45 B4 Almodôvar Port.
69 F4 Almont U.S.A.
69 J3 Almonte Can.
45 C4 Almonte Spain
20 C4 Al Mubarrez S. Arabia
16 E7 Al Mudawwara Jordan
18 C5 Al Muharraq Bahrain
20 C7 Al Mukallā Yemen
20 B7 Al Mukhā Yemen
45 E4 Almuñécar Spain
17 K5 Al Muqdādīyah Iraq
18 B5 Al Murabba S. Arabia
16 F1 Almus Turkey
18 B4 Al Musannāh ridge S. Arabia
17 K5 Al Musayyib Iraq
49 L7 Almyrou, Ormos b. Greece
74 □1 Alna Haina U.S.A.
38 F2 Alnwick U.K.
23 H5 Alon Myanmar
23 H3 Along India
49 K5 Alonnisos i. Greece
25 E7 Alor i. Indon.
25 E7 Alor, Kepulauan is Indon.
33 B1 Alor Setar Malaysia
Alost see Aalst
22 C5 Alot India
36 W4 Alozero Rus. Fed.
74 C4 Alpaugh U.S.A.
42 E3 Alpen Ger.
69 F3 Alpena U.S.A.
48 D1 Alpi Dolomitiche mts Italy
75 H5 Alpine AZ U.S.A.
77 C6 Alpine TX U.S.A.
72 E3 Alpine WY U.S.A.
34 F4 Alps mts Europe
20 C6 Al Qa'āmīyāt reg. S. Arabia
55 D1 Al Qaddāḩīyah Libya
16 F4 Al Qadmūs Syria
18 B5 Al Qā'īyah well S. Arabia
18 C6 Al Qalībah S. Arabia
17 H3 Al Qāmishlī Syria
18 B5 Al Qar'ah well S. Arabia
16 F4 Al Qaryatayn Syria
18 B5 Al Qaşab S. Arabia
20 C6 Al Qaţn Yemen
55 D2 Al Qaţrūn Libya
18 B4 Al Qayşūmah S. Arabia
16 E5 Al Qunayţirah Syria
20 B6 Al Qunfidhah S. Arabia
18 A5 Al Qurayn S. Arabia
17 L6 Al Qurnah Iraq
17 K6 Al Qusayr Iraq
18 B6 Al Qūşūrīyah S. Arabia
16 F5 Al Quţayfah Syria
18 A5 Al Quwārah S. Arabia
18 B5 Al Quwayīyah S. Arabia
44 H2 Alsace reg. France
39 E4 Alsager U.K.
17 J6 Al Samīt well Iraq
65 H4 Alsask Can.
43 H4 Alsfeld Ger.
43 K3 Alsleben (Saale) Ger.
38 E3 Alston U.K.
37 R8 Alsunga Latvia
36 S2 Alta Norway
36 S2 Altaelva r. Norway
91 D1 Alta Gracia Arg.
89 D2 Altagracia de Orituco Venez.
10 K5 Altai Mountains China/Mongolia
79 D6 Altamaha r. U.S.A.
87 H4 Altamira Brazil
9 B6 Alta, Mt mt N.Z.
48 G4 Altamura Italy
90 C1 Alta Paraiso de Goiás Brazil
84 A1 Altata Mex.
80 D6 Altavista U.S.A.
15 G2 Altay China
24 B2 Altay Mongolia
45 F3 Altea Spain
36 S1 Alteidet Norway
42 E4 Altenahr Ger.
42 F2 Altenberge Ger.
43 L4 Altenburg Ger.
42 F4 Altenkirchen (Westerwald) Ger.
23 H1 Altenqoke China
43 M1 Altentreptow Ger.
17 M1 Altıağaç Azer.
19 H3 Altimur Pass Afgh.
17 K4 Altin Köprü Iraq
49 M5 Altınoluk Turkey
16 C2 Altıntaş Turkey
86 E7 Altiplano plain Bol.
43 K2 Altmark reg. Ger.
43 J5 Altmühl r. Ger.
90 B2 Alto Araguaia Brazil
91 C2 Alto de Pencoso h. Arg.
89 B3 Alto de Tamar mt Col.
90 B2 Alto Garças Brazil
57 D5 Alto Molócuè Moz.
78 B4 Alton IL U.S.A.
77 F4 Alton MO U.S.A.
81 H3 Alton NH U.S.A.
76 D1 Altona Can.
80 D4 Altoona U.S.A.
90 B2 Alto Sucuriú Brazil
46 F6 Altötting Ger.
39 E4 Altrincham U.K.
43 L1 Alt Schwerin Ger.
24 A3 Altun Shan mts China
72 B3 Alturas U.S.A.
77 D5 Altus U.S.A.
16 G1 Alucra Turkey
37 U8 Alūksne Latvia
17 M5 Alūm Iran
80 B4 Alum Creek Lake l. U.S.A.
91 B3 Aluminé r. Arg.
91 B3 Aluminé, L. l. Arg.
51 E6 Alupka Ukr.
55 D1 Al 'Uqaylah Libya
18 C5 Al 'Uqayr S. Arabia
51 E6 Alushta Ukr.
17 K4 'Alut Iran
20 C4 Al 'Uthmānīyah S. Arabia
55 E2 Al 'Uwaynāt Libya
17 J6 Al 'Uwayqīlah S. Arabia
18 A5 Al 'Uyūn S. Arabia
17 L6 Al 'Uzayr Iraq
77 D4 Alva U.S.A.
84 D3 Alvarado Mex.
91 C2 Alvarado, P. de pass Chile
86 F4 Alvarães Brazil
37 M5 Alvdal Norway
37 O6 Älvdalen Sweden
37 O8 Alvesta Sweden
37 K6 Ålvik Norway
77 E6 Alvin U.S.A.
36 R4 Älvsbyn Sweden
14 B4 Al Wajh S. Arabia
18 C5 Al Wakrah Qatar
18 C5 Al Wannān S. Arabia
22 D4 Alwar India
18 B5 Al Warī'ah S. Arabia
21 B4 Alwaye India
17 H5 Al Widyān plat. Iraq/S. Arabia
18 B4 'Al Wusayţ well S. Arabia
26 A2 Alxa Youqi China
26 B2 Alxa Zuoqi China
6 D3 Alyangula Austr.
40 E4 Alyth U.K.
37 T9 Alytus Lith.
72 F2 Alzada U.S.A.
42 E5 Alzette r. Lux.
43 G5 Alzey Ger.
89 E3 Amacuro r. Guyana/Venez.
6 D4 Amadeus, Lake salt flat Austr.
63 L3 Amadjuak Lake l. Can.
75 G6 Amado U.S.A.
45 B3 Amadora Port.
29 A8 Amakusa-nada b. Japan
37 N7 Åmal Sweden
21 C2 Amalapuram India
24 D1 Amalat r. Rus. Fed.
89 B3 Amalfi Col.
58 F3 Amalia S. Africa
49 J6 Amaliada Greece
22 C5 Amalner India
25 F7 Amamapare Indon.
90 A3 Amambaí Brazil
90 A3 Amambaí r. Brazil
90 A3 Amambaí, Serra de h. Brazil/Para.
24 E4 Amami-guntō is Japan
24 E4 Amami-Ōshima i. Japan
14 E1 Amangel'dy Kazak.
48 G5 Amantea Italy
59 J5 Amanzimtoti S. Africa
87 H3 Amapá Brazil
45 C3 Amareleja Port.
74 D3 Amargosa Desert des. U.S.A.
74 D3 Amargosa Range mts U.S.A.
74 D3 Amargosa Valley U.S.A.
77 C5 Amarillo U.S.A.
48 F3 Amaro, Monte mt Italy
22 E4 Amarpatan India
16 E1 Amasya Turkey
84 D3 Amatán Mex.
84 A2 Amatlán de Cañas Mex.
42 D4 Amay Belgium
87 H4 Amazon r. S. America
89 D4 Amazonas div. Brazil
Amazonas r. see Amazon
87 G4 Amazônia, Parque Nacional nat. park Brazil
87 J3 Amazon, Mouths of the est. Brazil
22 C6 Ambad India
21 B2 Ambajogai India
22 D3 Ambala India
21 C5 Ambalangoda Sri Lanka
57 E6 Ambalavao Madag.
57 E5 Ambanja Madag.
18 E4 Ambar Iran
13 S3 Ambarchik Rus. Fed.
21 B4 Ambasamudram India
86 C4 Ambato Ecuador
57 E6 Ambato Boeny Madag.
57 E6 Ambato Finandrahana Madag.
57 E5 Ambatolampy Madag.
57 E5 Ambatomainty Madag.
57 E5 Ambatondrazaka Madag.
43 K5 Amberg Ger.
82 G5 Ambergris Cay i. Belize
44 G4 Ambérieu-en-Bugey France
69 G3 Amberley Can.
23 E5 Ambikapur India
57 E5 Ambilobe Madag.
64 C3 Ambition, Mt mt Can.
38 F2 Amble U.K.
38 E3 Ambleside U.K.
42 D4 Amblève r. Belgium
57 E6 Amboasary Madag.
57 E5 Ambohidratrimo Madag.
57 E6 Ambohimahasoa Madag.
25 E7 Ambon Indon.
25 E7 Ambon i. Indon.
57 E6 Ambositra Madag.
57 E6 Ambovombe Madag.
75 E4 Amboy CA U.S.A.
68 C5 Amboy IL U.S.A.
81 F3 Amboy Center U.S.A.
57 B4 Ambriz Angola
7 G3 Ambrym i. Vanuatu
21 B3 Ambur India
23 G2 Amdo China
84 A2 Ameca Mex.
42 D1 Ameland i. Neth.
80 E6 Amelia Court House U.S.A.
81 G4 Amenia U.S.A.
72 D3 American Falls U.S.A.
72 D3 American Falls Res. resr U.S.A.
75 G1 American Fork U.S.A.
5 K6 American Samoa terr. Pac. Oc.
79 C5 Americus U.S.A.
42 D2 Amersfoort Neth.
59 H3 Amersfoort S. Africa
39 G6 Amersham U.K.
65 L3 Amery Can.
92 D5 Amery Ice Shelf ice feature Ant.
76 E3 Ames U.S.A.
39 F6 Amesbury U.K.
81 H3 Amesbury U.S.A.
23 E4 Amethi India
49 K5 Amfissa Greece
13 P3 Amga Rus. Fed.
24 F2 Amgu Rus. Fed.
54 C2 Amguid Alg.
24 F1 Amgun' r. Rus. Fed.
67 H4 Amherst Can.
81 G3 Amherst MA U.S.A.
81 J2 Amherst ME U.S.A.
80 D6 Amherst VA U.S.A.
69 F4 Amherstburg Can.
48 D3 Amiata, Monte mt Italy
44 F2 Amiens France
17 H5 Amij, Wādī watercourse Iraq
21 A4 Amindivi Islands is India
29 D7 Amino Japan
58 C1 Aminuis Namibia
18 B3 Amīrābād Iran
Amirabad see Fūlād Maialleh
53 K6 Amirante Islands is Seychelles
19 F4 Amir Chah Pak.
65 J4 Amisk L. l. Can.
77 C6 Amistad Res. resr Mex./U.S.A.
22 D5 Amla Madhya Pradesh India
37 L7 Åmli Norway
39 C4 Amlwch U.K.
16 E6 'Ammān Jordan
39 D6 Ammanford U.K.
36 V4 Ämmänsaari Fin.
36 P4 Ammarnäs Sweden
43 F1 Ammerland reg. Ger.
43 J3 Ammern Ger.
46 E7 Ammersee l. Ger.
Ammochostos see Famagusta
30 D4 Amnyong-dan hd N. Korea
22 C5 Amod India
27 B6 Amo Jiang r. China
18 D2 Amol Iran
43 H5 Amorbach Ger.
49 L6 Amorgos i. Greece
66 E4 Amos Can.
Amoy see Xiamen
21 C5 Amparai India
90 C3 Amparo Brazil
46 E6 Amper r. Ger.
45 G2 Amposta Spain
22 D5 Amravati India
22 B5 Amreli India
22 B4 Amri Pak.
16 E4 'Amrit Syria
22 C3 Amritsar India
22 D3 Amroha India
36 Q4 Åmsele Sweden
42 C2 Amstelveen Neth.
42 C2 Amsterdam Neth.
59 J3 Amsterdam S. Africa
81 F3 Amsterdam U.S.A.
93 K6 Amsterdam, Île i. Ind. Ocean
46 G6 Amstetten Austria
55 E3 Am Timan Chad
19 F1 Amudar'ya r. Turkm./Uzbek.
63 J2 Amund Ringnes I. Can.
92 D4 Amundsen Bay b. Ant.
92 B4 Amundsen Gl. gl. Ant.
62 F2 Amundsen Gulf g. Can.
92 C5 Amundsen, Mt mt Ant.
92 B4 Amundsen-Scott U.S.A. Base Ant.
92 A3 Amundsen Sea sea Ant.
33 E3 Amuntai Indon.
Amur r. see Heilong Jiang
19 F4 Amursk Rus. Fed.
51 F6 Amvrosiyivka Ukr.
68 E1 Amyot Can.
23 H6 An Myanmar
25 E7 Anabanua Indon.
13 N2 Anabar r. Rus. Fed.
13 N2 Anabarskiy Zaliv b. Rus. Fed.
8 C2 Ana Branch r. Austr.
74 C4 Anacapa Is is U.S.A.
89 D2 Anaco Venez.
72 D2 Anaconda U.S.A.
72 B1 Anacortes U.S.A.
77 D5 Anadarko U.S.A.
16 F1 Anadolu Dağları mts Turkey
13 T3 Anadyr' Rus. Fed.
13 U3 Anadyrskiy Zaliv b. Rus. Fed.
49 L6 Anafi i. Greece
90 E1 Anagé Brazil
17 H4 'Ānah Iraq
74 D5 Anaheim U.S.A.
64 D4 Anahim Lake Can.
77 C7 Anáhuac Mex.
21 B4 Anaimalai Hills mts India
21 B4 Anai Mudi Pk mt India
21 C2 Anakapalle India
57 E5 Analalava Madag.
86 F4 Anamã Brazil
33 C2 Anambas, Kepulauan is Indon.
68 B4 Anamosa U.S.A.
16 D3 Anamur Turkey
16 D3 Anamur Burnu pt Turkey
29 D8 Anan Japan
22 C5 Anand India
23 F5 Anandapur India
23 F5 Anandpur r. India
21 B3 Anantapur India
22 C2 Anantnag Jammu and Kashmir
51 D6 Anan'yiv Ukr.
51 F6 Anapa Rus. Fed.
90 C2 Anápolis Brazil
18 D4 Anār Iran
18 D3 Anārak Iran
18 C3 Anarbar r. Iran
19 F3 Anardara Afgh.
16 D2 Anatolia reg. Turkey
7 G4 Anatom i. Vanuatu
88 D3 Añatuya Arg.
89 E4 Anauá r. Brazil
18 C2 Anbūh Iran
30 D4 Anbyon N. Korea
44 D3 Ancenis France
62 D3 Anchorage U.S.A.
69 F4 Anchor Bay b. U.S.A.
48 E3 Ancona Italy
88 B6 Ancud Chile
91 B4 Ancud, Golfo de g. Chile
91 B1 Andacollo Chile
23 F5 Andal India
36 K5 Åndalsnes Norway
45 D4 Andalucía div. Spain
77 G6 Andalusia U.S.A.
15 H6 Andaman and Nicobar Islands div. India
93 L3 Andaman Basin sea feature Ind. Ocean
15 H5 Andaman Islands Andaman and Nicobar Is
33 A1 Andaman Sea sea Asia
57 E5 Andapa Madag.
90 E1 Andaraí Brazil
36 P2 Andenes Norway
42 D4 Andenne Belgium
42 C4 Anderlecht Belgium
44 D4 Andernos-les-Bains France
62 D3 Anderson AK U.S.A.
68 E5 Anderson IN U.S.A.
77 E4 Anderson MO U.S.A.
79 D5 Anderson SC U.S.A.
62 F3 Anderson r. N.W.T. Can.
85 C3 Andes mts S. America
76 D3 Andes, Lake U.S.A.
36 P2 Andfjorden chan. Norway
21 B2 Andhra Pradesh div. India
57 E5 Andilamena Madag.
57 E5 Andilanatoby Madag.
18 C3 Andīmeshk Iran
16 F3 Andırın Turkey
51 H7 Andiyskoye Koysu r. Rus. Fed.
14 F2 Andizhan Uzbek.
19 G2 Andkhui r. Afgh.
19 G2 Andkhvoy Afgh.
57 E5 Andoany Madag.
86 C4 Andoas Peru
21 B2 Andol India
30 E5 Andong S. Korea
30 E5 Andong-ho l. S. Korea
34 F4 Andorra country Europe
45 G1 Andorra la Vella Andorra
39 F6 Andover U.K.
81 H2 Andover ME U.S.A.
80 C4 Andover OH U.S.A.
36 O2 Andøya i. Norway
90 B3 Andradina Brazil
50 E3 Andreapol' Rus. Fed.
38 C3 Andreas U.K.
56 C3 André Félix, Parc National de nat. park C.A.R.
90 D3 Andrelândia Brazil
77 C5 Andrews U.S.A.
48 G4 Andria Italy
57 E6 Androka Madag.
79 E7 Andros i. Bahamas
49 L6 Andros i. Greece
81 H2 Androscoggin r. U.S.A.
79 E7 Andros Town Bahamas
21 A4 Āndrott i. India
51 D5 Andrushivka Ukr.
36 Q2 Andselv Norway
45 D3 Andújar Spain
57 B5 Andulo Angola
54 C3 Anéfis Mali
83 M5 Anegada i. Virgin Is
91 D4 Anegada, Bahía b. Arg.
75 F5 Anegam U.S.A.
54 C4 Aného Togo
'Aneiza, Jabal h. see 'Unayzah, Jabal
75 H3 Aneth U.S.A.
45 G1 Aneto mt Spain
55 D3 Aney Niger
27 E5 Anfu China
57 E5 Angadoka, Lohatanjona hd Madag.
24 B1 Angara r. Rus. Fed.
24 C1 Angarsk Rus. Fed.
31 B3 Angat Phil.
37 O5 Ånge Sweden
82 B3 Angel de la Guarda i. Mex.
31 B3 Angeles Phil.
37 N8 Ängelholm Sweden
74 B2 Angels Camp U.S.A.
36 P4 Ångermanälven r. Sweden
44 D3 Angers France
65 K2 Angikuni Lake l. Can.
32 B2 Angkor Cambodia
39 C4 Anglesey i. U.K.
77 E6 Angleton U.S.A.
69 H2 Angliers Can.
Angmagssalik see Tasiilaq
32 □ Ang Mo Kio Sing.
56 C3 Ango Congo(Zaire)
57 D5 Angoche Moz.
19 E5 Angohrān Iran
91 B3 Angol Chile
68 E5 Angola U.S.A.
53 F7 Angola country Africa
96 K7 Angola Basin sea feature Atl. Ocean
84 D3 Angostura, Presa de la resr Mex.
44 E4 Angoulême France
12 J5 Angren Uzbek.
32 B2 Ang Thong Thai.
61 M8 Anguilla terr. Caribbean Sea
26 E1 Anguli Nur l. China
26 E2 Anguo China
90 A3 Anhanduí r. Brazil
37 M8 Anholt i. Denmark
27 D4 Anhua China
26 E3 Anhui div. China
90 A2 Anhumas Brazil
30 D5 Anhŭng S. Korea
90 C2 Anicuns Brazil
50 G3 Anikovo Rus. Fed.
75 H6 Animas U.S.A.
75 H6 Animas Peak summit U.S.A.
32 A2 Anin Myanmar
28 H1 Aniva Rus. Fed.
28 H1 Aniva, Mys c. Rus. Fed.
24 G2 Aniva, Zaliv b. Rus. Fed.
7 G3 Aniwa i. Vanuatu
42 B5 Anizy-le-Château France
37 U6 Anjalankoski Fin.
21 B4 Anjengo India
27 F4 Anji China
22 D5 Anji India
19 E3 Anjoman Iran
44 D3 Anjou reg. France
57 E5 Anjouan i. Comoros
57 E5 Anjozorobe Madag.
30 C4 Anjŭ N. Korea
57 E6 Ankaboa, Tanjona pt Madag.
26 C3 Ankang China
16 D2 Ankara Turkey
57 E6 Ankazoabo Madag.
57 E5 Ankazobe Madag.
32 D2 An Khê Vietnam
22 C5 Ankleshwar India
27 B5 Anlong China
32 C2 Ânlong Vêng Cambodia
26 D4 Anlu China
30 D5 Anmyŏn Do i. S. Korea
51 G5 Anna Rus. Fed.
54 C1 Annaba Alg.
43 M4 Annaberg-Buchholtz Ger.
16 F4 An Nabk Syria
20 B4 An Nafūd des. S. Arabia
38 A3 Annahilt U.K.
17 K6 An Najaf Iraq
80 E5 Anna, Lake l. U.S.A.
41 D3 Annalee r. Rep. of Ireland
41 F3 Annalong U.K.
40 E6 Annan Scot. U.K.
40 E6 Annan r. U.K.
40 E5 Annandale v. U.K.
80 E5 Annapolis U.S.A.
67 G5 Annapolis Royal Can.
23 E3 Annapurna mt Nepal
18 C5 An Naqīrah well S. Arabia
69 F4 Ann Arbor U.S.A.
87 G2 Anna Regina Guyana
17 L6 An Nāşirīyah Iraq
81 H3 Ann, Cape hd U.S.A.
44 H4 Annecy France
44 H3 Annemasse France
42 E1 Annen Neth.
64 C4 Annette I. i. U.S.A.
27 B5 Anning China
79 C5 Anniston U.S.A.
53 E6 Annobón i. Equatorial Guinea
44 G4 Annonay France
20 C4 An Nu'ayrīyah S. Arabia
17 K5 An Nu'mānīyah Iraq
76 E2 Anoka U.S.A.
57 E5 Anorontany, Tanjona hd Madag.
49 L7 Ano Viannos Greece
27 D6 Anpu China
27 C6 Anpu Gang b. China
27 E4 Anqing China
26 F2 Anqiu China
27 D5 Anren China
42 D4 Ans Belgium
26 C2 Ansai China
16 F4 Ansariye, J. el mts Syria
43 J5 Ansbach Ger.
30 B3 Anshan China
27 B5 Anshun China
91 C1 Ansilta mt Arg.
91 F1 Ansina Uru.
76 D3 Ansley U.S.A.
77 D5 Anson U.S.A.
54 C3 Ansongo Mali
66 D4 Ansonville Can.
80 C5 Ansted U.S.A.
22 D4 Anta India
86 D6 Antabamba Peru
16 F3 Antakya Turkey
57 F5 Antalaha Madag.
16 C3 Antalya Turkey
16 C3 Antalya Körfezi g. Turkey
57 E5 Antananarivo Madag.
92 B2 Antarctic Peninsula Ant.
40 C3 An Teallach mt U.K.
74 D2 Antelope Range mts U.S.A.
45 D4 Antequera Spain
73 F5 Anthony U.S.A.
54 B2 Anti Atlas mts Morocco
44 H5 Antibes France
67 H4 Anticosti, Île d' i. Can.
68 C3 Antigo U.S.A.
67 H4 Antigonish Can.
82 F6 Antigua Guatemala
83 M5 Antigua i. Antigua
61 M8 Antigua and Barbuda country Caribbean Sea
84 C2 Antiguo-Morelos Mex.
49 K7 Antikythira i. Greece
49 K7 Antikythiro, Steno chan. Greece
Anti Lebanon mts see Sharqi, Jebel esh
Antioch see Antakya
74 B3 Antioch CA U.S.A.
68 C4 Antioch IL U.S.A.
89 B3 Antioquia Col.
4 J9 Antipodes Islands is N.Z.
49 L5 Antipsara i. Greece
77 E5 Antlers U.S.A.
88 B2 Antofagasta Chile
88 C3 Antofalla, Vol. volc. Arg.
42 B4 Antoing Belgium
90 C4 Antonina Brazil
90 E1 Antônio r. Brazil
74 B3 Antonio r. U.S.A.
73 F4 Antonito U.S.A.
41 E3 Antrim U.K.
41 E2 Antrim Hills h. U.K.
57 E5 Antsalova Madag.
57 E5 Antsirabe Madag.
57 E5 Antsirañana Madag.
57 E5 Antsohihy Madag.
36 S3 Anttis Sweden
37 U6 Anttola Fin.
30 E1 Antu China
91 B3 Antuco Chile
91 B3 Antuco, Volcán volc. Chile
81 F2 Antwerp U.S.A.

42 C3 Antwerpen Belgium
28 C3 Anuchino Rus. Fed.
66 E2 Anuc, Lac l. Can.
23 F5 Anugul India
30 D6 Anŭi S. Korea
22 C3 Anupgarh India
21 C4 Anuradhapura Sri Lanka
18 D5 Anveh Iran
Anvers see Antwerpen
92 B2 Anvers I. i. Ant.
27 F5 Anxi Fujian China
24 B2 Anxi Gansu China
26 B4 An Xian China
27 D4 Anxiang China
26 E2 Anxin China
6 D5 Anxious Bay b. Austr.
26 E2 Anyang China
30 D5 Anyang S. Korea
49 L6 Anydro i. Greece
24 B3 A'nyêmaqên Shan mts China
27 E4 Anyi China
27 E5 Anyuan China
27 B4 Anyue China
13 S3 Anyuysk Rus. Fed.
89 B3 Anzá Col.
26 D2 Anze China
24 A1 Anzhero-Sudzhensk Rus. Fed.
56 C4 Anzi Congo(Zaire)
48 E4 Anzio Italy
7 G3 Aoba i. Vanuatu
32 A3 Ao Ban Don b. Thai.
26 F1 Aohan Qi China
28 G4 Aomori Japan
22 D3 Aonla India
Aoraki, Mt mt see Cook, Mt
9 D4 Aorere r. N.Z.
32 A3 Ao Sawi b. Thai.
48 B2 Aosta Italy
54 B2 Aoukâr reg. Mali/Maur.
87 G8 Apa r. Brazil
56 D3 Apac Uganda
75 H6 Apache U.S.A.
75 H5 Apache Creek U.S.A.
75 G5 Apache Junction U.S.A.
75 G6 Apache Peak summit U.S.A.
79 C6 Apalachee Bay b. U.S.A.
79 C6 Apalachicola U.S.A.
84 C3 Apan Mex.
89 C4 Apaporis r. Col.
17 K1 Aparan Armenia
90 B3 Aparecida do Tabuado Brazil
31 B2 Aparri Phil.
36 X3 Apatity Rus. Fed.
84 B3 Apatzingán Mex.
37 U8 Ape Latvia
42 D2 Apeldoorn Neth.
43 H2 Apelern Ger.
43 H1 Apensen Ger.
22 E3 Api mt Nepal
7 J3 Apia Western Samoa
9 E3 Apiti N.Z.
87 G2 Apoera Suriname
43 K3 Apolda Ger.
8 D5 Apollo Bay Austr.
86 E6 Apolo Bol.
31 C5 Apo, Mt volc. Phil.
79 D6 Apopka, L. l. U.S.A.
90 B2 Aporé Brazil
90 B2 Aporé r. Brazil
78 B2 Apostle Islands is U.S.A.
68 B2 Apostle Islands National Lakeshore res. U.S.A.
16 E4 Apostolos Andreas, Cape c. Cyprus
80 B6 Appalachia U.S.A.
80 C6 Appalachian Mountains U.S.A.
48 E3 Appennino Abruzzese mts Italy
48 D2 Appennino Tosco-Emiliano mts Italy
48 E3 Appennino Umbro-Marchigiano mts Italy
8 H3 Appin Austr.
42 E1 Appingedam Neth.
40 C3 Applecross U.K.
76 D2 Appleton MN U.S.A.
68 C3 Appleton WV U.S.A.
74 D4 Apple Valley U.S.A.
80 D6 Appomattox U.S.A.
48 E4 Aprilia Italy
51 F6 Apsheronsk Rus. Fed.
8 C4 Apsley Austr.
69 H3 Apsley Can.
44 G5 Apt France
90 B3 Apucarana Brazil
31 A4 Apurahuan Phil.
89 D3 Apure r. Venez.
86 D6 Apurimac r. Peru
16 E7 'Aqaba Jordan
14 B4 Aqaba, Gulf of g. Asia
18 D2 Aqbana Iran
19 G2 Āqchah Afgh.
18 B2 Aq Chai r. Iran
18 D3 Āqdā Iran
18 B2 Aqdoghmish r. Iran
17 K3 Āq Kān Dāgh, Kūh-e mt Iran
17 J3 'Aqrah Iraq
75 F4 Aquarius Mts mts U.S.A.
75 G3 Aquarius Plateau plat. U.S.A.
48 G4 Aquaviva delle Fonti Italy
90 A3 Aquidauana Brazil
90 A2 Aquidauana r. Brazil
84 B3 Aquila Mex.
89 D4 Aquio r. Col.
84 C2 Aquismón Mex.
44 D4 Aquitaine reg. France
23 F4 Ara India
19 G4 Arab Afgh.
79 C5 Arab U.S.A.
19 E3 'Arabābād Iran
55 E3 Arab, Bahr el watercourse Sudan
93 J3 Arabian Basin sea feature Ind. Ocean
10 H8 Arabian Sea sea Ind. Ocean
89 E3 Arabopó Venez.
89 E3 Arabopó r. Venez.
16 D1 Araç Turkey
89 E4 Araça r. Brazil
87 L6 Aracaju Brazil
89 D4 Aracamuni, Co summit Venez.
90 A4 Aracanguy, Mtes de h. Para.
87 L4 Aracati Brazil
90 E1 Aracatu Brazil
90 B3 Araçatuba Brazil
45 C4 Aracena Spain
90 E2 Aracruz Brazil
90 D2 Araçuaí Brazil
90 D2 Araçuaí r. Brazil
49 J1 Arad Romania
55 E3 Arada Chad
17 L6 Aradah Iraq
6 D2 Arafura Sea sea Austr./Indon.
90 B1 Aragarças Brazil
17 J1 Aragats Armenia
17 K1 Aragats Lerr mt Armenia
45 F2 Aragón div. Spain
45 F1 Aragón r. Spain
87 J5 Araguacema Brazil
89 D2 Aragua de Barcelona Venez.
87 J5 Araguaia r. Brazil
87 H6 Araguaia, Parque Nacional de nat. park Brazil
87 J5 Araguaína Brazil
90 C2 Araguari Brazil
90 C2 Araguari r. Brazil
87 J5 Araguatins Brazil
51 H7 Aragvi r. Georgia
29 F6 Arai Japan
87 K4 Araiosos Brazil
54 C2 Arak Alg.
18 C3 Arāk Iran
23 H5 Arakan Yoma mts Myanmar
21 B3 Arakkonam India
17 K2 Aralık Turkey
14 E2 Aral Sea l. Kazak./Uzbek.
14 E2 Aral'sk Kazak.
51 J5 Aralsor, Ozero l. Kazak.
18 B5 Aramah plat. S. Arabia
84 C1 Aramberri Mex.
22 D6 Aran r. India
45 E2 Aranda de Duero Spain
17 L4 Arandān Iran
49 J2 Aranđelovac Yugo.
21 B3 Arani India
41 C3 Aran Island i. Rep. of Ireland
41 B4 Aran Islands is Rep. of Ireland
45 E2 Aranjuez Spain
57 B6 Aranos Namibia
77 D7 Aransas Pass U.S.A.
90 B2 Arantes r. Brazil
7 H1 Aranuka i. Gilbert Is
29 B8 Arao Japan
54 B3 Araouane Mali
76 D3 Arapahoe U.S.A.
89 E4 Arapari r. Brazil
91 F1 Arapey Grande r. Uru.
87 L5 Arapiraca Brazil
49 L4 Arapis, Akra pt Greece
16 G2 Arapkir Turkey
90 B3 Arapongas Brazil
23 F4 A Rapti Doon r. Nepal
20 B3 'Ar'ar S. Arabia
88 G3 Araranguá Brazil
90 C3 Araraquara Brazil
87 H5 Araras Brazil
90 B4 Araras, Serra das mts Brazil
17 K2 Ararat Armenia
8 D4 Ararat Austr.
17 K2 Ararat, Mt mt Turkey
23 F4 Araria India
90 D3 Araruama, Lago de lag. Brazil
17 J6 'Ar'ar, W. watercourse Iraq/S. Arabia
17 J2 Aras Turkey
17 J1 Aras r. Turkey
90 E1 Arataca Brazil
89 C3 Arauca Col.
89 C3 Arauca r. Venez.
91 B3 Arauco Chile
89 C3 Arauquita Col.
89 C2 Araure Venez.
22 C4 Aravalli Range mts India
37 T7 Aravete Estonia
7 F2 Arawa P.N.G.
90 C2 Araxá Brazil
89 D2 Araya, Pen. de pen. Venez.
89 D2 Araya, Pta de pt Venez.
16 C2 Arayıt Dağı mt Turkey
17 M2 Araz r. Asia
17 K4 Arbat Iraq
50 J3 Arbazh Rus. Fed.
17 K3 Arbīl Iraq
37 O7 Arboga Sweden
65 J4 Arborfield Can.
40 F4 Arbroath U.K.
74 A2 Arbuckle U.S.A.
19 F4 Arbu Lut, Dasht-e des. Afgh.
44 D4 Arcachon France
79 D7 Arcadia U.S.A.
72 A3 Arcata U.S.A.
74 D2 Arc Dome summit U.S.A.
84 B3 Arcelia Mex.
50 G1 Archangel Rus. Fed.
6 E3 Archer r. Austr.
75 H2 Arches Nat. Park U.S.A.
18 E2 Archman Turkm.
17 M2 Ärçivan Azer.
72 D3 Arco U.S.A.
45 D4 Arcos de la Frontera Spain
63 K2 Arctic Bay Can.
3 □ Arctic Ocean ocean
62 C3 Arctic Plains U.S.A.
62 E3 Arctic Red r. Can.
92 B2 Arctowski Poland Base Ant.
18 C2 Ardabīl Iran
17 J1 Ardahan Turkey
18 D3 Ardakān Iran
18 C4 Ardal Iran
37 K6 Årdalstangen Norway
41 C3 Ardara Rep. of Ireland
49 L4 Ardas r. Bulg.
50 H4 Ardatov Mordov. Rus. Fed.
50 G4 Ardatov Nizheg. Rus. Fed.
69 G3 Ardbeg Can.
41 E4 Ardee Rep. of Ireland
8 A2 Arden, Mount h. Austr.
42 D5 Ardennes reg. Belgium
42 C5 Ardennes, Canal des canal France
18 D3 Ardestān Iran
41 F3 Ardglass U.K.
45 C3 Ardila r. Port.
84 B2 Ardilla, Cerro la mt Mex.
8 F3 Ardlethan Austr.
77 D5 Ardmore U.S.A.
40 B4 Ardnamurchan, Point of pt U.K.
40 C4 Ardrishaig U.K.
8 A3 Ardrossan Austr.
40 D5 Ardrossan U.K.
40 C3 Ardvasar U.K.
91 E2 Areco r. Arg.
87 L4 Areia Branca Brazil
42 E4 Aremberg h. Ger.
31 B4 Arena rf Phil.
74 A2 Arena, Pt pt U.S.A.
45 D2 Arenas de San Pedro Spain
37 L7 Arendal Norway
43 K2 Arendsee (Altmark) Ger.
39 D5 Arenig Fawr h. U.K.
49 K6 Areopoli Greece
86 D7 Arequipa Peru
87 H4 Arere Brazil
45 D2 Arévalo Spain
48 D3 Arezzo Italy
16 G6 'Arfajah well S. Arabia
26 D1 Argalant Mongolia
45 E2 Arganda Spain
31 B4 Argao Phil.
48 D2 Argenta Italy
44 D2 Argentan France
48 D3 Argentario, Monte h. Italy
48 B2 Argentera, Cima dell' mt Italy
42 F5 Argenthal Ger.
85 D6 Argentina country S. America
92 B3 Argentina Ra. mts Ant.
96 F8 Argentine Basin sea feature Atl. Ocean
88 B8 Argentino, Lago l. Arg.
49 L2 Argeș r. Romania
19 G4 Arghandab r. Afgh.
19 G4 Arghastan r. Afgh.
16 C2 Argıthanı Turkey
49 K6 Argolikos Kolpos b. Greece
49 K6 Argos Greece
49 J5 Argostoli Greece
45 F1 Arguís Spain
51 H7 Argun Rus. Fed.
24 E1 Argun' r. China/Rus. Fed.
74 D4 Argus Range mts U.S.A.
68 C4 Argyle U.S.A.
6 C3 Argyle, Lake l. Austr.
40 C4 Argyll reg. U.K.
37 M8 Århus Denmark
9 E3 Aria N.Z.
8 F3 Ariah Park Austr.
29 B8 Ariake-kai b. Japan
57 B6 Ariamsvlei Namibia
48 F4 Ariano Irpino Italy
89 B4 Ariari r. Col.
91 D2 Arias Arg.
15 F6 Ari Atoll Maldives
89 E2 Aribí r. Venez.
54 B3 Aribinda Burkina
88 B1 Arica Chile
40 C4 Arienas, Loch l. U.K.
16 F4 Arīḩā Syria
72 G4 Arikaree r. U.S.A.
89 E2 Arima Trinidad and Tobago
90 C1 Arinos Brazil
87 G6 Arinos r. Brazil
84 B3 Ario de Rosáles Mex.
89 C3 Ariporo r. Col.
86 F5 Aripuanã Brazil
86 F5 Aripuanã r. Brazil
86 F5 Ariquemes Brazil
90 B2 Ariranhá r. Brazil
58 B1 Aris Namibia
40 C4 Arisaig U.K.
40 C4 Arisaig, Sound of chan. U.K.
64 D4 Aristazabal I. i. Can.
75 G4 Arizona div. U.S.A.
70 D5 Arizpe Mex.
18 B5 'Arjah S. Arabia
36 P3 Arjeplog Sweden
89 B2 Arjona Col.
33 D4 Arjuna, G. volc. Indon.
51 G5 Arkadak Rus. Fed.
77 E5 Arkadelphia U.S.A.
40 C4 Arkaig, Loch l. U.K.
14 E1 Arkalyk Kazak.
77 E5 Arkansas div. U.S.A.
77 F5 Arkansas r. U.S.A.
77 D4 Arkansas City U.S.A.
23 G1 Arkatag Shan mts China
Arkhangel'sk see Archangel
50 G2 Arkhangel'skaya Oblast' div. Rus. Fed.
50 F4 Arkhangel'skoye Rus. Fed.
28 C3 Arkhipovka Rus. Fed.
41 E5 Arklow Rep. of Ireland
49 M6 Arkoi i. Greece
46 F3 Arkona, Kap hd Ger.
12 K2 Arkticheskogo Instituta, Ostrova is Rus. Fed.
81 F3 Arkville U.S.A.
44 G5 Arles France
59 G4 Arlington S. Africa
72 B2 Arlington OR U.S.A.
76 D2 Arlington SD U.S.A.
80 E5 Arlington VA U.S.A.
68 D4 Arlington Heights U.S.A.
54 C3 Arlit Niger
42 D5 Arlon Belgium
31 C5 Armadores i. Indon.
41 E3 Armagh U.K.
55 F2 Armant Egypt
51 G6 Armavir Rus. Fed.
89 B3 Armenia Col.
10 F5 Armenia country Asia
89 B3 Armero Col.
8 H1 Armidale Austr.
65 L2 Armit Lake l. Can.
22 E5 Armori India
64 B3 Armour, Mt mt Can./U.S.A.
41 E2 Armoy U.K.
64 F4 Armstrong B.C. Can.
66 C3 Armstrong Ont. Can.
28 E1 Armu r. Rus. Fed.
21 B2 Armur India
51 E6 Armyans'k Ukr.
16 D4 Arnaoutis, Cape c. Cyprus
67 F1 Arnaud r. Can.
37 M6 Årnes Norway
77 D4 Arnett U.S.A.
42 D3 Arnhem Neth.
6 D3 Arnhem Bay b. Austr.
6 D3 Arnhem, C. c. Austr.
6 D3 Arnhem Land reg. Austr.
48 D3 Arno r. Italy
39 F4 Arnold U.K.
68 D2 Arnold U.S.A.
69 H1 Arnoux, Lac l. Can.
69 J3 Arnprior Can.
43 G3 Arnsberg Ger.
43 J4 Arnstadt Ger.
69 H3 Arnstein Can.
43 H5 Arnstein Ger.
69 H1 Arntfield Can.
89 E3 Aro r. Venez.
57 B6 Aroab Namibia
43 H3 Arolsen Ger.
48 C2 Arona Italy
81 K1 Aroostook Can.
81 J1 Aroostook r. Can./U.S.A.
7 H2 Arorae i. Kiribati
31 B3 Aroroy Phil.
51 G7 Arpa r. Armenia/Turkey
17 J1 Arpaçay Turkey
19 G5 Arra r. Pak.
17 J5 Ar Ramādī Iraq
16 E7 Ar Ramlah Jordan
40 C5 Arran i. U.K.
17 G4 Ar Raqqah Syria
44 F1 Arras France
18 A5 Ar-Rass S. Arabia
16 F4 Ar Rastan Syria
17 J7 Ar Rawḑ well S. Arabia
18 C5 Ar Rayyān Qatar
89 C4 Arrecifal Col.
91 E2 Arrecifes Arg.
84 D3 Arriaga Chiapas Mex.
84 B2 Arriaga San Luis Potosí Mex.
91 E2 Arribeños Arg.
17 L6 Ar Rifā'ī Iraq
17 K6 Ar Rihāb salt flat Iraq
20 D5 Ar Rimāl reg. S. Arabia
75 H3 Arriola U.S.A.
Ar Riyāḑ see Riyadh
40 D4 Arrochar U.K.
91 G2 Arroio Grande Brazil
90 D1 Arrojado r. Brazil
68 B1 Arrow Lake l. Can.
41 C3 Arrow, Lough l. Rep. of Ireland
72 D3 Arrowrock Res. resr U.S.A.
9 C5 Arrowsmith, Mt mt N.Z.
74 B4 Arroyo Grande U.S.A.
91 F3 Arroyo Grande r. Arg.
91 E2 Arroyo Seco Arg.
84 C2 Arroyo Seco Mex.
18 B5 Ar Rubay'iyah S. Arabia
90 A1 Arruda Brazil
17 K6 Ar Rumaythah Iraq
16 G4 Ar Ruşāfah Syria
19 E6 Ar Rustāq Oman
17 H5 Ar Ruţba Iraq
18 B6 Ar Ruwayḑah S. Arabia
37 L8 Års Denmark
18 B2 Ars Iran
18 D4 Arsenajān Iran
28 C2 Arsen'yev Rus. Fed.
21 B3 Arsikere India
50 J3 Arsk Rus. Fed.
16 E3 Arslanköy Turkey
49 J5 Arta Greece
17 K2 Artashat Armenia
84 B3 Arteaga Mex.
28 C3 Artem Rus. Fed.
51 F5 Artemivs'k Ukr.
28 C3 Artemovskiy Rus. Fed.
44 E2 Artenay France
73 F5 Artesia U.S.A.
69 G4 Arthur Can.
80 C4 Arthur, Lake l. U.S.A.
6 F4 Arthur Pt pt Austr.
9 C5 Arthur's Pass N.Z.
9 C5 Arthur's Pass National Park N.Z.
79 F7 Arthur's Town Bahamas
91 F1 Artigas Uru.
92 B1 Artigas Uru. Base Ant.
17 J1 Art'ik Armenia
65 H2 Artillery Lake l. Can.
59 G2 Artisia Botswana
44 F1 Artois reg. France
42 A4 Artois, Collines d' h. France
17 J2 Artos D. mt Turkey
16 F1 Artova Turkey
51 D6 Artsyz Ukr.
15 F3 Artux China
17 H1 Artvin Turkey
56 D3 Arua Uganda
90 B1 Aruanã Brazil
61 L8 Aruba terr. Caribbean Sea
25 F7 Aru, Kepulauan is Indon.
86 F4 Arumã Brazil
23 F4 Arun r. Nepal
23 H3 Arunachal Pradesh div. India
39 G7 Arundel U.K.
56 D4 Arusha Tanz.
76 B4 Arvada U.S.A.
41 D4 Arvagh Rep. of Ireland
24 C2 Arvayheer Mongolia
22 D5 Arvi India
65 L2 Arviat Can.
67 F4 Arvida Can.
36 Q4 Arvidsjaur Sweden
37 N7 Arvika Sweden
74 C4 Arvin U.S.A.
18 B6 Arwā' S. Arabia
13 O2 Ary Rus. Fed.
50 G4 Arzamas Rus. Fed.
43 L4 Arzberg Ger.
45 F5 Arzew Alg.
51 H6 Arzgir Rus. Fed.
43 L4 Aš Czech Rep.
89 E3 Asa r. Venez.
54 C4 Asaba Nigeria
19 H3 Asadābād Afgh.
18 C3 Asadābād Iran
19 E3 Asadābād Iran
16 G3 Asad, Buḩayrat al resr Syria
32 A5 Asahan r. Indon.
28 H3 Asahi-dake volc. Japan
29 C7 Asahi-gawa r. Japan
28 H3 Asahikawa Japan
18 C2 Asālem Iran
30 D5 Asan Man b. S. Korea
23 F5 Asansol India
42 F4 Asbach Ger.
67 F4 Asbestos Can.
58 E4 Asbestos Mountains S. Africa
81 F4 Asbury Park U.S.A.
48 F4 Ascea Italy
86 F7 Ascensión Bol.
82 G5 Ascensión, B. de la b. Mex.
53 C6 Ascension Island i. Atl. Ocean
43 H5 Aschaffenburg Ger.
42 F3 Ascheberg Ger.
43 K3 Aschersleben Ger.
48 E3 Ascoli Piceno Italy
37 O8 Åseda Sweden
36 P4 Åsele Sweden
18 D4 Asemānjerd Iran
39 E6 Ashbourne U.K.
9 C5 Ashburton N.Z.
6 B4 Ashburton watercourse Austr.
68 D1 Ashburton Bay b. Can.
64 E4 Ashcroft Can.
16 E6 Ashdod Israel
77 E5 Ashdown U.S.A.
79 E5 Asheboro U.S.A.
79 D5 Asheville U.S.A.
39 H6 Ashford U.K.
75 F4 Ash Fork U.S.A.
19 E2 Ashgabat Turkm.
28 H3 Ashibetsu Japan
29 F6 Ashikaga Japan
38 F2 Ashington U.K.
50 J3 Ashit r. Rus. Fed.
29 C8 Ashizuri-misaki pt Japan
18 D4 Ashkazar Iran
77 D4 Ashland KS U.S.A.
80 B5 Ashland KY U.S.A.
81 J1 Ashland ME U.S.A.
72 F2 Ashland MT U.S.A.
81 H3 Ashland NH U.S.A.
80 B4 Ashland OH U.S.A.
72 B3 Ashland OR U.S.A.
80 E6 Ashland VA U.S.A.
68 B2 Ashland WV U.S.A.
76 D2 Ashley U.S.A.
50 C4 Ashmyany Belarus
75 H5 Ash Peak U.S.A.
16 E6 Ashqelon Israel
22 B4 Ashraf, Md. Pak.
17 J6 Ash Shabakah Iraq
17 H3 Ash Shaddādah Syria
17 H7 Ash Shaqīq well S. Arabia
18 B5 Ash Sha'rā' S. Arabia
17 J4 Ash Sharqāţ Iraq
17 L6 Ash Shaţrah Iraq
20 C7 Ash Shiḩr Yemen
17 K6 Ash Shināfīyah Iraq
18 E5 Ash Şhināş Oman
18 B4 Ash Shu'bah S. Arabia
18 B5 Ash Shumlūl S. Arabia
80 C4 Ashtabula U.S.A.
17 K1 Ashtarak Armenia
22 D5 Ashti India
21 A2 Ashti India
18 C3 Ashtiān Iran
58 D6 Ashton S. Africa
72 E2 Ashton U.S.A.
38 E4 Ashton-under-Lyne U.K.
63 M4 Ashuanipi Lake l. Can.
79 C5 Ashville U.S.A.
84 B2 Asientos Mex.
21 B2 Asifabad India
23 F6 Āsika India
16 F4 'Āşī, Nahr al r. Asia
48 C4 Asinara, Golfo dell' b. Sardinia Italy
12 K4 Asino Rus. Fed.
50 D4 Asipovichy Belarus
20 B5 'Asīr reg. S. Arabia
17 H2 Aşkale Turkey
37 M7 Asker Norway
37 O7 Askersund Sweden
37 M7 Askim Norway
24 B1 Askiz Rus. Fed.
17 L2 Aşlāndūz Iran
56 D2 Asmara Eritrea
37 O8 Åsnen l. Sweden
49 L3 Asneovgrad Bulg.
22 C4 Asop India
17 M3 Aspar Iran
38 D3 Aspatria U.K.
73 F4 Aspen U.S.A.
43 H6 Asperg Ger.
77 C5 Aspermont U.S.A.
9 B6 Aspiring, Mt mt N.Z.
65 H4 Asquith Can.
16 F4 As Sa'an Syria
56 E2 Assab Eritrea
18 C5 As Sabsab well S. Arabia
16 F3 As Safīrah Syria
18 C5 As Saji well S. Arabia
18 B5 As Salamiyah S. Arabia
17 K6 As Salmān Iraq
23 H4 Assam div. India
17 K6 As Samāwah Iraq
16 F5 Aş Şanamayn Syria
55 E2 As Sarīr reg. Libya
81 F5 Assateague I. i. U.S.A.
81 F6 Assateague Island National Seashore res. U.S.A.
42 E1 Assen Neth.
42 B3 Assenede Belgium
42 D4 Assesse Belgium
23 F5 Assia Hills h. India
55 D1 As Sidrah Libya
65 H5 Assiniboia Can.
65 K5 Assiniboine r. Can.
64 F4 Assiniboine, Mt mt Can.
90 B3 Assis Brazil
48 E3 Assisi Italy
43 G4 Aßlar Ger.
17 L7 Aş Şubayḩīyah Kuwait
18 B4 Aş Şufayrī well S. Arabia
17 G4 As Sukhnah Syria
17 K4 As Sulaymānīyah Iraq
20 C5 As Sulayyil S. Arabia
18 C5 Aş Şulb reg. S. Arabia
18 B5 Aş Şummān plat. S. Arabia
20 B5 As Sūq S. Arabia
17 H4 Aş Şuwār Syria
16 F5 As Suwaydā' Syria
19 E6 As Suwayq Oman
17 K5 Aş Şuwayrah Iraq
40 C2 Assynt, Loch l. U.K.
49 M7 Astakida i. Greece
Astalu Island i. see Astola Island
17 M3 Astaneh Iran
17 M2 Astara Azer.
Asterabad see Gorgān
48 C2 Asti Italy
74 A2 Asti U.S.A.
91 C1 Astica Arg.
19 F5 Astola Island i. Pak.
22 C2 Astor Jammu and Kashmir
22 C2 Astor r. Pak.
45 C1 Astorga Spain
72 B2 Astoria U.S.A.
37 N8 Åstorp Sweden
14 C2 Astrakhan' Rus. Fed.
Astrakhan' Bazar see Cälilabad
51 H6 Astrakhanskaya Oblast' div. Rus. Fed.
50 C4 Astravyets Belarus
92 D3 Astrid Ridge sea feature Ant.
45 C1 Asturias div. Spain
49 M6 Astypalaia i. Greece
88 E3 Asunción Para.
55 F2 Aswân Egypt
55 F2 Asyût Egypt
7 J4 Ata i. Tonga
89 D4 Atabapo r. Col./Venez.
88 C2 Atacama, Desierto de des. Chile
7 J2 Atafu i. Tokelau
54 C4 Atakpamé Togo
49 K5 Atalanti Greece
86 D6 Atalaya Peru
54 A2 Atâr Maur.
32 A1 Ataran r. Myanmar
75 H4 Atarque U.S.A.
74 B4 Atascadero U.S.A.
12 J5 Atasu Kazak.
25 E7 Atauro i. Indon.
55 F3 Atbara Sudan
55 F3 Atbara r. Sudan
14 E1 Atbasar Kazak.
77 F6 Atchafalaya Bay b. U.S.A.
76 E4 Atchison U.S.A.
84 A2 Atenguillo Mex.
48 E3 Aterno r. Italy
48 F3 Atessa Italy
42 B4 Ath Belgium
64 G4 Athabasca Can.
62 G4 Athabasca r. U.S.A.
65 G3 Athabasca, Lake l. Can.
41 E4 Athboy Rep. of Ireland
41 C4 Athenry Rep. of Ireland
69 K3 Athens Can.
49 K6 Athens Greece
79 C5 Athens AL U.S.A.
79 D5 Athens GA U.S.A.
80 B5 Athens OH U.S.A.
79 C5 Athens TN U.S.A.
77 E5 Athens TX U.S.A.
39 F5 Atherstone U.K.
42 A5 Athies France
Athina see Athens
41 C4 Athleague Rep. of Ireland
41 D4 Athlone Rep. of Ireland
21 A2 Athni India
9 B6 Athol N.Z.
81 G3 Athol U.S.A.
40 E4 Atholl, Forest of reg. U.K.
49 L4 Athos mt Greece
17 J4 Ath Tharthār, Wādī r. Iraq
41 E5 Athy Rep. of Ireland
55 D3 Ati Chad
86 D7 Atico Peru
65 J4 Atikameg L. l. Can.
66 B4 Atikokan Can.
67 H3 Atikonak L. l. Can.
31 B3 Atimonan Phil.
21 B4 Atirampattinam India
84 E4 Atitlán Guatemala
84 E4 Atitlán, Parque Nacional nat. park Guatemala
13 R3 Atka Rus. Fed.
51 H5 Atkarsk Rus. Fed.
18 B5 'Atk, W. al watercourse S. Arabia
84 C3 Atlacomulco Mex.
79 C5 Atlanta GA U.S.A.
68 C5 Atlanta IL U.S.A.
69 E3 Atlanta MI U.S.A.
16 D2 Atlantı Turkey
76 E3 Atlantic U.S.A.
81 F5 Atlantic City U.S.A.
96 J9 Atlantic-Indian Antarctic Basin sea feature Atl. Ocean
96 J9 Atlantic-Indian Ridge sea feature Ind. Ocean
58 C6 Atlantis S. Africa
96 G3 Atlantis Fracture sea feature Atl. Ocean
52 D3 Atlas Mountains Alg./Morocco
54 C1 Atlas Saharien mts Alg.
64 C3 Atlin Can.
64 C3 Atlin Lake l. Can.
64 C3 Atlin Prov. Park Can.
16 E5 'Atlit Israel
84 C3 Atlixco Mex.
21 B3 Atmakur India
21 B3 Atmakur India
77 G6 Atmore U.S.A.
77 D5 Atoka U.S.A.
84 B2 Atotonilco el Alto Mex.
32 C1 Atouat mt Laos
84 B3 Atoyac de Alvarez Mex.
23 G4 Atrai r. India
18 E2 Atrak r. Iran
89 A3 Atrato r. Col.
18 D2 Atrek r. Iran/Turkm.
81 F5 Atsion U.S.A.
20 B5 Aţ Ţā'if S. Arabia
79 C5 Attalla U.S.A.
32 C2 Attapu Laos
49 M6 Attavyros mt Greece
66 D3 Attawapiskat Can.
66 C3 Attawapiskat r. Can.
66 C3 Attawapiskat L. l. Can.
17 G7 Aţ Ţawīl mts S. Arabia
18 A4 At Taysīyah plat. S. Arabia
43 F3 Attendorn Ger.
46 F7 Attersee l. Austria
68 D5 Attica IN U.S.A.
80 B4 Attica OH U.S.A.
42 C5 Attigny France
81 H3 Attleboro U.S.A.
39 J5 Attleborough U.K.
16 F7 Aţ Ţubayq reg. S. Arabia
94 G2 Attu Island i. U.S.A.
18 B5 Aţ Ţulayḩī well S. Arabia
21 B4 Attur India
40 B2 a' Tuath, Loch b. U.K.
91 C2 Atuel r. Arg.
37 O7 Åtvidaberg Sweden
80 C4 Atwood Lake l. U.S.A.
14 D2 Atyrau Kazak.
43 J5 Aub Ger.
44 G5 Aubagne France
42 D5 Aubange Belgium
31 B2 Aubarede Point pt Phil.
44 G4 Aubenas France
42 D5 Auboué France
75 F4 Aubrey Cliffs cliff U.S.A.
62 F3 Aubry Lake l. Can.
8 B3 Auburn Austr.
69 G4 Auburn Can.
79 C5 Auburn AL U.S.A.
74 B2 Auburn CA U.S.A.
68 E5 Auburn IN U.S.A.
81 H2 Auburn ME U.S.A.
76 E3 Auburn NE U.S.A.
80 E3 Auburn NY U.S.A.
72 B2 Auburn WA U.S.A.
44 F4 Aubusson France
91 C3 Auca Mahuida, Sa de mt Arg.
44 E5 Auch France
40 E4 Auchterarder U.K.
9 E2 Auckland N.Z.
7 G7 Auckland Islands is N.Z.
81 H2 Audet Can.
39 J7 Audresselles France
42 A4 Audruicq France
43 L4 Aue Ger.
43 G2 Aue r. Ger.
43 L4 Auerbach Ger.
43 K5 Auerbach in der Oberpfalz Ger.
43 L4 Auersberg mt Ger.
41 D3 Augher U.K.
41 E3 Aughnacloy U.K.
41 E5 Aughrim Rep. of Ireland
58 D4 Augrabies S. Africa
58 D4 Augrabies Falls waterfall S. Africa
58 D4 Augrabies Falls National Park S. Africa
69 F3 Au Gres U.S.A.
46 E6 Augsburg Ger.
48 F6 Augusta Sicily Italy
79 D5 Augusta GA U.S.A.
77 D4 Augusta KS U.S.A.
81 J2 Augusta ME U.S.A.
68 B3 Augusta WV U.S.A.
89 B2 Augustin Cadazzi Col.
6 B4 Augustus, Mt mt Austr.
42 B4 Aulnoye-Aymeries France
39 J7 Ault France
57 B6 Auob r. Namibia
67 G2 Aupaluk Can.
32 C5 Aur i. Malaysia
37 S6 Aura Fin.
22 D4 Auraiya India
22 C6 Aurangābād India
42 F1 Aurich Ger.
90 B2 Aurilândia Brazil
44 F4 Aurillac France
33 D3 Aurkuning Indon.
31 B5 Aurora Phil.
72 F4 Aurora CO U.S.A.
68 C5 Aurora IL U.S.A.
81 J2 Aurora ME U.S.A.
77 E4 Aurora MO U.S.A.
57 B6 Aus Namibia
69 F3 Au Sable U.S.A.
69 E3 Au Sable r. U.S.A.
81 G2 Ausable r. U.S.A.
81 G2 Ausable Forks U.S.A.
68 D2 Au Sable Pt pt MI U.S.A.
69 F3 Au Sable Pt pt MI U.S.A.
40 F1 Auskerry i. U.K.
36 D4 Austari-Jökulsá r. Iceland
76 E3 Austin MN U.S.A.
74 D2 Austin NV U.S.A.
77 D6 Austin TX U.S.A.
4 D7 Australia country Oceania
92 B6 Australian Antarctic Territory reg. Ant.
8 G3 Australian Capital Territory div. Austr.
34 G4 Austria country Europe
36 O2 Austvågøy i. Norway
84 A3 Autlán Mex.
36 U3 Autti Fin.
44 G3 Autun France
44 F4 Auvergne reg. France
44 F3 Auxerre France
42 A4 Auxi-le-Château France
44 G3 Auxonne France
81 F3 Ava U.S.A.
44 F3 Avallon France
74 C5 Avalon U.S.A.
67 K4 Avalon Peninsula Can.
84 B1 Avalos Mex.
18 B2 Avān Iran
16 E2 Avanos Turkey
90 C3 Avaré Brazil
17 L2 Āvārsīn Iran
74 D4 Avawatz Mts mts U.S.A.
19 F3 Avaz Iran
87 G4 Aveiro Brazil
45 B2 Aveiro Port.
45 B2 Aveiro, Ria de est. Port.
17 M4 Āvej Iran
91 E2 Avellaneda Arg.
48 F4 Avellino Italy
74 B3 Avenal U.S.A.
8 E4 Avenel Austr.
42 C2 Avenhorn Neth.
48 F4 Aversa Italy
42 B4 Avesnes-sur-Helpe France
37 P6 Avesta Sweden
44 F4 Aveyron r. France
48 E3 Avezzano Italy
40 E3 Aviemore U.K.
48 F4 Avigliano Italy
44 G5 Avignon France
45 D2 Ávila Spain
45 D1 Avilés Spain
42 A4 Avion France
21 C5 Avissawella Sri Lanka
50 H2 Avnyugskiy Rus. Fed.
8 D4 Avoca Vic. Austr.
41 E5 Avoca Rep. of Ireland
76 E3 Avoca U.S.A.
8 D4 Avoca r. Vic. Austr.
48 F6 Avola Sicily Italy
68 B5 Avon U.S.A.
39 F5 Avon r. Eng. U.K.
39 F7 Avon r. Eng. U.K.
39 E6 Avon r. Eng. U.K.
75 F5 Avondale U.S.A.
39 E6 Avonmouth U.K.
79 D7 Avon Park U.S.A.
44 D2 Avranches France
42 A5 Avre r. France
7 G2 Avuavu Solomon Is
29 D7 Awaji-shima i. Japan
9 E3 Awakino N.Z.
18 C5 Awālī Bahrain
9 D1 Awanui N.Z.
9 B6 Awarua Pt pt N.Z.
56 E3 Āwash Eth.
56 D3 Āwash r. Eth.
28 F5 Awa-shima i. Japan
56 D3 Awash National Park Eth.
58 A2 Awasib Mts mts Namibia
9 D4 Awatere r. N.Z.
55 D2 Awbārī Libya
41 C5 Awbeg r. Rep. of Ireland
17 L6 'Awdah, Hawr al l. Iraq
56 E3 Aw Dheegle Somalia
55 E4 Aweil Sudan
40 C4 Awe, Loch l. U.K.
54 C4 Awka Nigeria
31 C6 Awu mt Indon.
8 E4 Axedale Austr.
63 J2 Axel Heiburg I. Can.
54 B4 Axim Ghana
39 E7 Axminster U.K.
42 C5 Ay France
29 D7 Ayabe Japan
91 E3 Ayacucho Arg.
86 D6 Ayacucho Peru
15 G2 Ayaguz Kazak.
24 A3 Ayakkum Hu l. China
45 C4 Ayamonte Spain
24 F1 Ayan Rus. Fed.
51 E7 Ayancık Turkey
30 C4 Ayang N. Korea
89 B2 Ayapel Col.
16 D1 Ayaş Turkey
86 D6 Ayaviri Peru
19 H2 Āybak Afgh.
51 F5 Aydar r. Ukr.
14 E2 Aydarkul', Ozero l. Uzbek.
16 A3 Aydın Turkey
16 A2 Aydın Dağları mts Turkey
32 □ Ayer Chawan, P. i. Sing.
32 □ Ayer Merbau, P. i. Sing.
6 D4 Ayers Rock h. Austr.
13 N3 Aykhal Rus. Fed.
50 J2 Aykino Rus. Fed.
9 D5 Aylesbury N.Z.
39 G6 Aylesbury U.K.
80 E6 Aylett U.S.A.
45 E2 Ayllón Spain
69 G4 Aylmer Can.
65 H2 Aylmer Lake l. Can.
18 C4 'Ayn al 'Abd well S. Arabia
19 H2 Ayní Tajik.
16 G3 'Ayn 'Īsá Syria
55 F4 Ayod Sudan
13 S3 Ayon, O. i. Rus. Fed.
54 B3 'Ayoûn el 'Atroûs Maur.
6 E3 Ayr Austr.
40 D5 Ayr U.K.
40 D5 Ayr r. U.K.
16 D3 Ayrancı Turkey
38 C3 Ayre, Point of pt Isle of Man
49 M3 Aytos Bulg.
32 B2 Ayutthaya Thai.
49 M5 Ayvacık Turkey
16 F2 Ayvalı Turkey
49 M5 Ayvalık Turkey
23 E4 Azamgarh India
54 B3 Azaouâd reg. Mali
54 C3 Azaouagh, Vallée de watercourse Mali/Niger
18 B2 Āzarān Iran

Azbine mts see
Aïr, Massif de l'
16 D1 Azdavay Turkey
10 F5 Azerbaijan country Asia
18 B2 Āzghān Iran
69 G2 Azilda Can.
81 H2 Aziscohos Lake l. U.S.A.
86 C4 Azogues Ecuador
12 F3 Azopol'ye Rus. Fed.
34 C5 Azores terr. Europe
96 H3 Azores - Cape St Vincent Ridge sea feature Atl. Ocean
51 F6 Azov Rus. Fed.
51 F6 Azov, Sea of sea Rus. Fed./Ukr.
54 B1 Azrou Morocco
73 F4 Aztec U.S.A.
45 D3 Azuaga Spain
88 B3 Azucar r. Chile
83 H7 Azuero, Península de pen. Panama
91 E3 Azul Arg.
84 E3 Azul r. Mex.
91 B4 Azul, Cerro mt Arg.
86 C5 Azul, Cordillera mts Peru
90 A1 Azul, Serra h. Brazil
29 G6 Azuma-san volc. Japan
86 F8 Azurduy Bol.
48 B6 Azzaba Alg.
16 F5 Az Zabadānī Syria
17 J6 Az Zafirī reg. Iraq
Az Zahrān see Dhahran
18 B5 Az Zilfī S. Arabia
17 L6 Az Zubayr Iraq

B

16 E5 Ba'abda Lebanon
16 F4 Ba'albek Lebanon
56 E3 Baardheere Somalia
49 M5 Baba Burnu pt Turkey
49 N2 Babadag Romania
17 M1 Babadağ mt Azer.
19 E2 Babadurmaz Turkm.
51 C7 Babaeski Turkey
86 C4 Babahoyo Ecuador
21 B1 Babai India
23 E3 Babai r. Nepal
26 B1 Babai Gaxun China
17 L2 Bābā Jān Iran
31 C5 Babak Phil.
19 H3 Bābā, Kūh-e mts Afgh.
20 B7 Bāb al Mandab str. Africa/Asia
25 E7 Babar i. Indon.
56 D4 Babati Tanz.
50 E3 Babayevo Rus. Fed.
51 H7 Babayurt Rus. Fed.
68 B2 Babbitt U.S.A.
70 F6 Babia r. Mex.
62 F4 Babine r. Can.
64 D4 Babine Lake l. Can.
25 F7 Babo Indon.
18 D2 Bābol Iran
58 C6 Baboon Point pt S. Africa
75 G6 Baboquivari Peak summit U.S.A.
56 B3 Baboua C.A.R.
50 D4 Babruysk Belarus
22 B4 Babuhri India
22 C2 Babusar Pass Pak.
31 A4 Babuyan Phil.
31 B2 Babuyan i. Phil.
27 F7 Babuyan Channel Phil.
31 B2 Babuyan Islands is Phil.
17 K5 Babylon Iraq
87 K4 Bacabal Brazil
16 C1 Bacakliyayla T. mt Turkey
25 E7 Bacan i. Indon.
31 B2 Bacarra Phil.
47 N7 Bacău Romania
8 E4 Bacchus Marsh Austr.
27 C6 Bac Giang Vietnam
75 F6 Bachiniva Mex.
15 F3 Bachu China
65 J1 Back r. Can.
49 H2 Bačka Palanka Yugo.
64 D2 Backbone Ranges mts Can.
36 P5 Backe Sweden
40 E4 Backwater Reservoir U.K.
27 B6 Bac Lac Vietnam
32 C3 Bac Liêu Vietnam
27 C6 Bac Ninh Vietnam
31 B4 Bacolod Phil.
31 B3 Baco, Mt mt Phil.
27 B6 Bac Quang Vietnam
66 F2 Bacqueville, Lac l. Can.
43 L6 Bad Abbach Ger.
21 A4 Badagara India
26 A1 Badain Jaran Shamo des. China
86 F4 Badajós, Lago l. Brazil
45 C3 Badajoz Spain
21 A3 Badami India
17 H6 Badanah S. Arabia
23 H4 Badarpur India
69 F4 Bad Axe U.S.A.
43 F5 Bad Bergzabern Ger.
43 G3 Bad Berleburg Ger.
43 J1 Bad Bevensen Ger.
43 K4 Bad Blankenburg Ger.
43 G4 Bad Camberg Ger.
67 H4 Baddeck Can.
19 G4 Baddo r. Pak.
43 H3 Bad Driburg Ger.
43 L3 Bad Düben Ger.
43 G5 Bad Dürkheim Ger.
43 L3 Bad Dürrenberg Ger.
16 C3 Bademli Geçidi pass Turkey
43 F4 Bad Ems Ger.
46 H6 Baden Austria
46 D7 Baden Switz.
46 D6 Baden-Baden Ger.
40 D4 Badenoch reg. U.K.
43 G5 Baden-Württemberg div. Ger.
43 G2 Bad Essen Ger.
67 J4 Badger Can.
43 J3 Bad Grund (Harz) Ger.
43 J3 Bad Harzburg Ger.
43 H4 Bad Hersfeld Ger.
46 F7 Bad Hofgastein Austria
43 G4 Bad Homburg vor der Höhe Ger.
48 D2 Badia Polesine Italy
22 B4 Badin Pak.
84 A1 Badiraguato Mex.
46 F7 Bad Ischl Austria
Bādiyat ash Shām des. see Syrian Desert
43 J4 Bad Kissingen Ger.
43 K3 Bad Kösen Ger.
43 F5 Bad Kreuznach Ger.
43 G4 Bad Laasphe Ger.
76 C2 Badlands reg. U.S.A.
76 C3 Badlands Nat. Park U.S.A.
43 J3 Bad Langensalza Ger.
43 J3 Bad Lauterberg im Harz Ger.
43 G3 Bad Lippspringe Ger.
43 F4 Bad Marienberg Ger.
43 H5 Bad Mergentheim Ger.
43 G4 Bad Nauheim Ger.
42 F4 Bad Neuenahr-Ahrweiler Ger.
43 J4 Bad Neustadt an der Saale Ger.
43 J1 Bad Oldesloe Ger.
26 D4 Badong China
32 C3 Ba Đông Vietnam
43 H3 Bad Pyrmont Ger.
17 K5 Badrah Iraq
46 F7 Bad Reichenhall Ger.
22 D3 Badrinath Peaks mts India
43 J3 Bad Sachsa Ger.
43 J2 Bad Salzdetfurth Ger.
43 G2 Bad Salzuflen Ger.
43 J4 Bad Salzungen Ger.
43 G4 Bad Schwalbach Ger.
43 J1 Bad Schwartau Ger.
46 E4 Bad Segeberg Ger.
6 E3 Badu I. i. Austr.
21 C5 Badulla Sri Lanka
43 G4 Bad Vilbel Ger.
43 K2 Bad Wilsnack Ger.
43 J5 Bad Windsheim Ger.
43 G1 Bad Zwischenahn Ger.
36 B3 Bæir Iceland
8 H2 Baerami Austr.
42 E4 Baesweiler Ger.
45 E4 Baeza Spain
54 D4 Bafang Cameroon
54 A3 Bafatá Guinea-Bissau
63 M2 Baffin Bay b. Can./Greenland
63 L2 Baffin Island i. Can.
54 D4 Bafia Cameroon
54 A3 Bafing, Parc National du nat. park Mali
54 A3 Bafoulabé Mali
54 D4 Bafoussam Cameroon
18 D4 Bāfq Iran
16 E1 Bafra Turkey
51 E7 Bafra Burnu pt Turkey
18 E4 Bāft Iran
56 C3 Bafwasende Congo(Zaire)
23 F4 Bagaha India
31 A5 Bagahak, Mt h. Malaysia
21 A2 Bagalkot India
56 D4 Bagamoyo Tanz.
33 B2 Bagan Datuk Malaysia
57 C5 Bagani Namibia
32 B4 Bagan Serai Malaysia
32 B5 Bagansiapiapi Indon.
75 F4 Bagdad U.S.A.
91 F1 Bagé Brazil
22 D3 Bageshwar India
72 F3 Baggs U.S.A.
39 C6 Baggy Point pt U.K.
22 C5 Bagh India
19 F2 Baghbaghū Iran
17 K5 Baghdād Iraq
18 C4 Bāgh-e Malek Iran
19 H2 Baghlān Afgh.
19 G3 Baghrān Afgh.
76 E2 Bagley U.S.A.
23 E3 Baglung Nepal
45 G1 Bagnères-de-Luchon France
44 G4 Bagnols-sur-Cèze France
23 F4 Bagnuiti r. Nepal
26 C2 Bag Nur l. China
Bago see Pegu
31 B4 Bago Phil.
47 K3 Bagrationovsk Rus. Fed.
31 C5 Baguio Phil.
31 B2 Baguio Phil.
22 D3 Bahadurgarh India
Bahāmabād see Rafsanjān
61 L7 Bahamas, The country Caribbean Sea
23 G4 Baharampur India
55 E2 Bahariya Oasis oasis Egypt
33 B2 Bahau Malaysia
22 C3 Bahawalnagar Pak.
22 B3 Bahawalpur Pak.
16 F3 Bahçe Turkey
26 C4 Ba He r. China
22 D3 Baheri India
56 D4 Bahi Tanz.
90 E1 Bahia div. Brazil
91 D3 Bahía Blanca Arg.
82 G5 Bahía, Islas de la is Honduras
88 C7 Bahía Laura Arg.
88 E2 Bahía Negra Para.
56 D2 Bahir Dar Eth.
18 C4 Bahmanyārī ye Pā'īn Iran
23 E4 Bahraich India
10 G7 Bahrain country Asia
18 C5 Bahrain, Gulf of g. Asia
17 M3 Bahrāmābād Iran
18 E4 Bahrāmjerd Iran
Bahr el Azraq r. see Blue Nile
19 F5 Bāhū Kālāt Iran
47 L7 Baia Mare Romania
18 D3 Baiazeh Iran
24 E2 Baicheng China
67 G4 Baie Comeau Can.
66 F3 Baie du Poste Can.
67 F4 Baie Saint Paul Can.
67 J4 Baie Verte Can.
26 E2 Baigou r. China
22 E5 Baihar India
26 D3 Baihe Shaanxi China
30 E2 Baihe China
17 J4 Baiji Iraq
24 C1 Baikal, Lake l. Rus. Fed.
49 K2 Băileşti Romania
49 K2 Băileştilor, Câmpia plain Romania
42 A4 Bailleul France
65 H2 Baillie r. Can.
41 E4 Baillieborough Rep. of Ireland
26 B3 Bailong Jiang r. China
24 C3 Baima China
39 G4 Bain r. U.K.
79 C6 Bainbridge GA U.S.A.
81 F3 Bainbridge NY U.S.A.
23 G3 Baingoin China
23 E2 Bairab Co l. China
23 F4 Bairagnia India
62 C3 Baird Mountains U.S.A.
4 J4 Bairiki i. Kiribati
26 F1 Bairing Qiao China
26 F1 Bairin Youqi China
26 F1 Bairin Zuoqi China
8 F4 Bairnsdale Austr.
16 F6 Bā'ir, Wādī watercourse Jordan
31 B4 Bais Phil.
27 C7 Baisha Hainan China
27 E5 Baisha Jiangxi China
26 C4 Baisha Sichuan China
30 D2 Baishan China
26 B3 Baishui Jiang r. China
27 B7 Bai Thương Vietnam
26 E1 Baitle r. China
30 A2 Baixingt China
26 B2 Baiyin China
55 F3 Baiyuda Desert des. Sudan
49 H1 Baja Hungary
82 A2 Baja California pen. Mex.
70 C6 Baja California Norte div. Mex.
70 D6 Baja California Sur div. Mex.
17 M3 Bajalān Iran
22 E3 Bajang Nepal
23 G5 Baj Baj India
19 E2 Bājgīrān Iran
89 A3 Bajo Baudó Col.
91 D1 Bajo Hondo Arg.
54 A3 Bakel Senegal
74 D4 Baker CA U.S.A.
72 F2 Baker MT U.S.A.
75 E2 Baker NV U.S.A.
72 C2 Baker OR U.S.A.
75 G4 Baker Butte summit U.S.A.
64 C3 Baker I. i. U.S.A.
7 J1 Baker Island i. Pac. Oc.
65 K2 Baker Lake Can.
65 K2 Baker Lake l. Can.
72 B1 Baker, Mt volc. U.S.A.
66 E2 Bakers Dozen Islands is Can.
74 C4 Bakersfield U.S.A.
32 C2 Bâ Kêv Cambodia
18 E2 Bakharden Turkm.
19 E2 Bakhardok Turkm.
19 F3 Bākharz mts Iran
22 B4 Bakhasar India
51 E6 Bakhchysaray Ukr.
51 E5 Bakhmach Ukr.
18 D4 Bakhtegan, Daryācheh-ye l. Iran
Bakı see Baku
16 B1 Bakırköy Turkey
56 D3 Bako Eth.
56 C3 Bakouma C.A.R.
56 B4 Bakoumba Gabon
51 G7 Baksan Rus. Fed.
17 M1 Baku Azer.
56 D3 Baku Congo(Zaire)
92 A4 Bakutis Coast coastal area Ant.
16 D2 Balâ Turkey
39 D5 Bala U.K.
31 A4 Balabac Phil.
31 A5 Balabac i. Phil.
33 E1 Balabac Strait str. Malaysia/Phil.
86 E6 Bala, Cerros de mts Bol.
17 K4 Balad Iraq
18 C2 Baladeh Iran
18 C4 Bālādeh Iran
18 C2 Baladeh Iran
22 E5 Balaghat India
21 A2 Balaghat Range h. India
19 E4 Bālā Ḥowz Iran
17 L1 Balakän Azer.
50 G3 Balakhna Rus. Fed.
8 B3 Balaklava Austr.
51 E6 Balaklava Ukr.
51 F5 Balakliya Ukr.
51 H4 Balakovo Rus. Fed.
33 E1 Balambangan i. Malaysia
19 F3 Bālā Morghāb Afgh.
22 B4 Bālān India
51 H5 Balanda r. Rus. Fed.
16 B3 Balan Dağı mt Turkey
31 B3 Balanga Phil.
23 E5 Balāngīr India
21 C5 Balangoda Sri Lanka
51 G5 Balashov Rus. Fed.
22 C5 Balasinor India
46 H7 Balaton l. Hungary
46 H7 Balatonboglár Hungary
46 H7 Balatonfüred Hungary
87 G4 Balbina, Represa de resr Brazil
41 E4 Balbriggan Rep. of Ireland
91 E3 Balcarce Arg.
49 N3 Balchik Bulg.
9 B7 Balclutha N.Z.
77 F5 Bald Knob U.S.A.
75 E3 Bald Mtn mt U.S.A.
65 K3 Baldock Lake l. Can.
69 H3 Baldwin Can.
79 D6 Baldwin FL U.S.A.
68 E4 Baldwin MI U.S.A.
68 A3 Baldwin WI U.S.A.
81 E3 Baldwinsville U.S.A.
75 H5 Baldy Peak mt U.S.A.
Baleares, Islas is see Balearic Islands
45 H3 Balearic Islands is Spain
33 D2 Baleh r. Malaysia
90 E2 Baleia, Ponta da pt Brazil
67 G2 Baleine, Rivière à la r. Can.
56 D3 Bale Mts National Park Eth.
31 B3 Baler Phil.
31 B3 Baler Bay b. Phil.
23 F5 Baleshwar India
37 K6 Balestrand Norway
9 B6 Balfour N.Z.
33 E4 Bali i. Indon.
33 A2 Balige Indon.
23 E5 Baliguda India
26 F1 Balihan China
16 A2 Balıkesir Turkey
33 E3 Balikpapan Indon.
31 A5 Balimbing Phil.
21 C2 Balimila Reservoir India
6 E2 Balimo P.N.G.
46 D6 Balingen Ger.
31 B2 Balintang Channel chan. Phil.
40 E3 Balintore U.K.
33 E4 Bali Sea g. Indon.
31 B5 Baliungan i. Phil.
19 H2 Baljuvon Tajik.
42 D2 Balk Neth.
49 K3 Balkan Mountains Bulg./Yugo.
19 G2 Balkh r. Afgh.
15 F2 Balkhash Kazak.
15 F2 Balkhash, Ozero l. Kazak.
51 H6 Balkuduk Kazak.
40 C4 Ballachulish U.K.
6 C5 Balladonia Austr.
8 G1 Balladoran Austr.
41 C4 Ballaghaderreen Rep. of Ireland
8 E4 Ballan Austr.
36 P2 Ballangen Norway
72 E2 Ballantine U.S.A.
40 D5 Ballantrae U.K.
8 D4 Ballarat Austr.
6 C4 Ballard, L. salt flat Austr.
22 D6 Ballarpur India
40 E3 Ballater U.K.
54 B3 Ballé Mali
88 B3 Ballena, Pta pt Chile
92 A6 Balleny Is is Ant.
23 F4 Ballia India
7 F4 Ballina Austr.
41 B3 Ballina Rep. of Ireland
41 C3 Ballinafad Rep. of Ireland
41 D4 Ballinalack Rep. of Ireland
41 D3 Ballinamore Rep. of Ireland
41 C4 Ballinasloe Rep. of Ireland
41 C4 Ballindine Rep. of Ireland
77 D6 Ballinger U.S.A.
40 E4 Ballinluig U.K.
41 B4 Ballinrobe Rep. of Ireland
81 G3 Ballston Spa U.S.A.
41 E3 Ballybay Rep. of Ireland
41 A6 Ballybrack Rep. of Ireland
41 B5 Ballybunnion Rep. of Ireland
41 E5 Ballycanew Rep. of Ireland
41 B3 Ballycastle Rep. of Ireland
41 E2 Ballycastle U.K.
41 F3 Ballyclare U.K.
41 A4 Ballyconneely Bay b. Rep. of Ireland
41 D3 Ballyconnell Rep. of Ireland
41 C4 Ballygar Rep. of Ireland
41 D3 Ballygawley U.K.
41 D2 Ballygorman Rep. of Ireland
41 C4 Ballyhaunis Rep. of Ireland
41 B5 Ballyheigue Rep. of Ireland
41 C5 Ballyhoura Mts h. Rep. of Ireland
41 D2 Ballykelly U.K.
41 D5 Ballylynan Rep. of Ireland
41 D5 Ballymacmague Rep. of Ireland
41 D4 Ballymahon Rep. of Ireland
41 E3 Ballymena U.K.
41 E2 Ballymoney U.K.
41 C3 Ballymote Rep. of Ireland
41 F3 Ballynahinch U.K.
41 C3 Ballyshannon Rep. of Ireland
41 E5 Ballyteige Bay b. Rep. of Ireland
41 B4 Ballyvaughan Rep. of Ireland
41 E3 Ballyward U.K.
40 A3 Balmartin U.K.
Balmer see Barmer
8 C4 Balmoral Austr.
77 C6 Balmorhea U.S.A.
19 G4 Balochistān div. Pak.
22 E5 Balod India
23 E5 Baloda Bazar India
6 E4 Balonne r. Austr.
22 C4 Balotra India
23 E4 Balrampur India
8 D3 Balranald Austr.
49 L2 Balş Romania
69 H2 Balsam Creek Can.
87 J5 Balsas Brazil
84 C3 Balsas Mex.
84 B3 Balsas r. Mex.
51 D6 Balta Ukr.
50 J3 Baltasi Rus. Fed.
40 □ Baltasound U.K.
22 D2 Baltero Gl. gl. Pak.
51 C6 Bălţi Moldova
12 C4 Baltic Sea g. Europe
16 C6 Balṭīm Egypt
59 H1 Baltimore S. Africa
80 E5 Baltimore U.S.A.
41 E5 Baltinglass Rep. of Ireland
22 C2 Baltistan reg. Jammu and Kashmir
47 J3 Baltiysk Rus. Fed.
19 E4 Baluch Ab well Iran
23 G4 Balurghat India
31 C5 Balut i. Phil.
43 F3 Balve Ger.
37 U8 Balvi Latvia
49 M5 Balya Turkey
14 D2 Balykshi Kazak.
19 E4 Bam Iran
19 E2 Bām Iran
27 C5 Bama China
6 E3 Bamaga Austr.
66 B3 Bamaji L. l. Can.
54 B3 Bamako Mali
54 B3 Bamba Mali
31 B2 Bambang Phil.
56 C3 Bambari C.A.R.
32 A5 Bambel Indon.
43 J5 Bamberg Ger.
79 D5 Bamberg U.S.A.
56 C3 Bambili Congo(Zaire)
59 G5 Bamboesberg mts S. Africa
56 C3 Bambouti C.A.R.
90 D3 Bambuí Brazil
17 M6 Bāmdezh Iran
54 D4 Bamenda Cameroon
18 E2 Bami Turkm.
19 G3 Bāmīān Afgh.
30 C2 Bamiancheng China
56 C3 Bamingui-Bangoran, Parc National de nat. park C.A.R.
19 F5 Bam Posht reg. Iran
19 F5 Bam Posht, Kūh-e mts Iran
39 D7 Bampton U.K.
19 F5 Bampūr Iran
19 E5 Bampūr watercourse Iran
19 F3 Bamrūd Iran
7 G2 Banaba i. Kiribati
87 L5 Banabuiu, Açude resr Brazil
91 C3 Bañados del Atuel marsh Arg.
86 F7 Bañados del Izozog swamp Bol.
41 D4 Banagher Rep. of Ireland
56 C3 Banalia Congo(Zaire)
59 K1 Banamana, Lagoa l. Moz.
54 B3 Banamba Mali
87 H6 Bananal, Ilha do i. Brazil
23 F6 Bānapur India
32 B2 Ban Aranyaprathet Thai.
22 D4 Banas r. India
16 B2 Banaz Turkey
32 B1 Ban Ban Laos
23 H3 Banbar China
32 B4 Ban Betong Thai.
41 E3 Banbridge U.K.
32 B2 Ban Bua Yai Thai.
39 F5 Banbury U.K.
31 A4 Bancalan i. Phil.
54 A2 Banc d'Arguin, Parc National du nat. park Maur.
32 A1 Ban Chiang Dao Thai.
40 F3 Banchory U.K.
82 G5 Banco Chinchorro is Mex.
31 A5 Bancoran i. Phil.
69 J3 Bancroft Can.
19 E3 Band Iran
56 C3 Banda Congo(Zaire)
22 E4 Banda India
33 A1 Banda Aceh Indon.
22 B2 Banda Daud Shah Pak.
32 A5 Bandahara, G. mt Indon.
29 F6 Bandai-Asahi National Park Japan
25 E7 Banda, Kepulauan is Indon.
19 F4 Bandān Iran
19 F4 Bandān Kūh mts Iran
Bandar see Machilipatnam
23 H5 Bandarban Bangl.
18 E5 Bandar-e 'Abbās Iran
18 C2 Bandar-e Anzalī Iran
18 C4 Bandar-e Deylam Iran
18 D5 Bandar-e Khoemir Iran
18 D5 Bandar-e Lengeh Iran
18 D5 Bandar-e Māqām Iran
18 C4 Bandar-e Ma'shur Iran
18 C4 Bandar-e Rīg Iran
Bandar-e Shāhpūr see Bandar Khomeynī
18 D2 Bandar-e Torkeman Iran
18 C4 Bandar Khomeynī Iran
22 D3 Bandarpunch mt India
33 D1 Bandar Seri Begawan Brunei
25 F7 Banda Sea Indon.
19 E5 Band Bonī Iran
18 D5 Band-e Chārak Iran
90 B1 Bandeirante Brazil
90 E3 Bandeiras, Pico de mt Brazil
59 H1 Bandelierkop S. Africa
18 D5 Band-e Moghūyeh Iran
84 A2 Banderas, Bahía de b. Mex.
18 D3 Band-e Sar Qom Iran
22 C4 Bandi r. Rajasthan India
22 E6 Bandia r. India
54 B3 Bandiagara Mali
19 G3 Band-i-Amir r. Afgh.
19 F3 Band-i-Baba mts Afgh.
16 A1 Bandırma Turkey
19 F3 Band-i-Turkestan mts Afgh.
41 C6 Bandon Rep. of Ireland
Ban Don see Surat Thani
41 C6 Bandon r. Rep. of Ireland
17 M2 Bändovan Burnu pt Azer.
17 M6 Band Qīr Iran
56 B4 Bandundu Congo(Zaire)
33 C4 Bandung Indon.
18 B3 Bāneh Iran
83 J4 Banes Cuba
64 F4 Banff Can.
40 F3 Banff U.K.
64 F4 Banff National Park Can.
54 B3 Banfora Burkina
56 C4 Banga Congo(Zaire)
31 C5 Banga Phil.
31 C5 Bangai Point pt Phil.
21 B3 Bangalore India
22 D4 Banganga r. India
23 G5 Bangaon India
31 B2 Bangar Phil.
56 C3 Bangassou C.A.R.
23 E2 Bangdag Co salt l. China
32 C1 Bangfai, Xée r. Laos
6 C2 Banggai Indon.
25 E7 Banggai, Kepulauan is Indon.
33 E1 Banggi i. Malaysia
55 E1 Banghāzī Libya
32 C1 Banghiang, Xé r. Laos
33 C3 Bangka i. Indon.
33 D4 Bangkalan Indon.
32 A5 Bangkaru i. Indon.
33 B3 Bangko Indon.
23 G3 Bangkog Co salt l. China
32 B2 Bangkok Thai.
32 B2 Bangkok, Bight of b. Thai.
10 K7 Bangladesh country Asia
54 B4 Bangolo Côte d'Ivoire
22 D2 Bangong Co l. China
41 F3 Bangor N. Ireland U.K.
39 C4 Bangor Wales U.K.
81 J2 Bangor ME U.S.A.
68 D4 Bangor MI U.S.A.
81 F4 Bangor PA U.S.A.
41 B3 Bangor Erris Rep. of Ireland
32 A3 Bang Saphan Yai Thai.
75 F3 Bangs, Mt mt U.S.A.
36 M4 Bangsund Norway
31 B2 Bangued Phil.
56 B3 Bangui C.A.R.
31 B2 Bangui Phil.
32 A5 Bangunpurba Indon.
57 C5 Bangweulu, Lake l. Zambia
32 B4 Ban Hat Yai Thai.
57 D6 Banhine, Parque Nacional de nat. park Moz.
32 B1 Ban Hin Heup Laos
32 A2 Ban Hua Hin Thai.
56 C3 Bani C.A.R.
31 A2 Bani Phil.
56 B3 Bania C.A.R.
18 D5 Banī Forūr, Jazīrah-ye i. Iran
22 C2 Banihal Pass and Tunnel Jammu and Kashmir
80 D6 Banister r. U.S.A.
55 D1 Banī Walīd Libya
18 C5 Banī Wuṭayfān well S. Arabia
16 E4 Bāniyās Syria
16 E5 Bāniyās Syria
48 G2 Banja Luka Bos.-Herz.
23 D3 Banjar India
33 D3 Banjarmasin Indon.
54 A3 Banjul The Gambia
17 M2 Bankä Azer.
23 F4 Banka India
32 A4 Ban Kantang Thai.
54 B3 Bankass Mali
32 A2 Ban Khao Yoi Thai.
32 C2 Ban Khemmarat Thai.
32 A3 Ban Khok Kloi Thai.
32 A1 Ban Khun Yuam Thai.
23 F5 Banki India
62 F2 Banks Island N.W.T. Can.
62 E4 Banks Island i. B.C. Can.
7 G3 Banks Islands is Vanuatu
72 C2 Banks L. l. U.S.A.
65 L2 Banks Lake l. Can.
9 D5 Banks Peninsula pen. N.Z.
32 A2 Ban Kui Nua Thai.
23 F5 Bankura India
32 A1 Ban Mae Sariang Thai.
32 A1 Ban Mae Sot Thai.
32 B1 Ban Mouang Laos
32 B2 Ban Muang Phon Thai.
41 E5 Bann r. Rep. of Ireland
41 E3 Bann r. U.K.
32 C1 Ban Na Kae Thai.
32 C1 Ban Nakham Laos
32 B1 Ban Na Noi Thai.
32 A3 Ban Na San Thai.
32 B4 Ban Na Thawi Thai.
68 C5 Banner U.S.A.
79 E7 Bannerman Town Bahamas
74 D5 Banning U.S.A.
91 B3 Baños Maule Chile
32 B1 Ban Pak-Leng Laos
32 B3 Ban Pak Phanang Thai.
32 B2 Ban Pak Thong Chai Thai.
32 C1 Ban Phaeng Thai.
32 B1 Ban Phai Thai.
32 B2 Ban Phanat Nikhom Thai.
32 C2 Ban Phon Laos
32 B1 Ban Phon Thong Thai.
32 A2 Banphot Phisai Thai.
32 A2 Ban Pong Thai.
32 B1 Ban Pua Thai.
32 A1 Ban Saraphi Thai.
32 B2 Ban Sattahip Thai.
32 A3 Ban Sawi Thai.
23 E4 Bansi India
32 A3 Ban Sichon Thai.
32 B2 Ban Si Racha Thai.
47 J6 Banská Bystrica Slovakia
32 A1 Ban Sut Ta Thai.
21 B2 Banswada India
22 C5 Banswara India
32 A3 Ban Takua Pa Thai.
31 B4 Bantayan i. Phil.
41 C5 Banteer Rep. of Ireland
32 A3 Ban Tha Chang Thai.
32 A1 Ban Tha Don Thai.
32 A3 Ban Thai Muang Thai.
32 A3 Ban Tha Kham Thai.
32 A1 Ban Tha Song Yang Thai.
32 B2 Ban Tha Tako Thai.
32 B2 Ban Tha Tum Thai.
32 C1 Ban Tha Uthen Thai.
32 A2 Ban Thung Luang Thai.
31 B3 Banton i. Phil.
32 C1 Ban Tôp Laos
41 B6 Bantry Rep. of Ireland
41 B6 Bantry Bay b. Rep. of Ireland
21 A3 Bantval India
32 B1 Ban Woen Laos
33 A2 Banyak, Pulau Pulau is Indon.
54 D4 Banyo Cameroon
45 H1 Banyoles Spain
33 D4 Banyuwangi Indon.
92 C6 Banzare Coast coastal area Ant.
93 J7 Banzare Seamount sea feature Ind. Ocean
43 K1 Banzkow Ger.
26 B3 Bao'an China
26 E2 Baoding China
26 D3 Baofeng China
26 C3 Baoji China
27 C4 Baojing China
26 D4 Baokang China
30 E1 Baolin China
30 B2 Baolizhen China
32 C3 Bao Lôc Vietnam
28 C1 Baoqing China
24 B4 Baoshan China
26 D1 Baotou China
27 B4 Baoxing China
26 F3 Baoying China
22 C4 Bap India
21 C3 Bapatla India
42 A4 Bapaume France
69 H3 Baptiste Lake l. Can.
23 H2 Baqên China
23 H3 Baqên China
17 K5 Ba'qūbah Iraq
86 □ Baquerizo Moreno Galapagos Is Ecuador
49 H3 Bar Yugo.
55 F3 Bara Sudan
56 E3 Baraawe Somalia
23 F4 Barabar Hills h. India
68 C4 Baraboo U.S.A.
68 B4 Baraboo r. U.S.A.
83 K4 Baracoa Cuba
91 E2 Baradero Arg.
8 G1 Baradine Austr.
8 G1 Baradine r. Austr.
68 C2 Baraga U.S.A.
23 E5 Baragarh India
89 C2 Baragua Venez.
83 K5 Barahona Dom. Rep.
23 H4 Barail Range mts India
23 H4 Barak r. India
56 D2 Baraka watercourse Eritrea/Sudan
45 E1 Barakaldo Spain
19 H3 Barakī Barak Afgh.
23 F5 Barākot India
22 D2 Bara Lacha Pass pass India
17 J5 Baḥr al Milḥ l. Iraq
65 K3 Baralzon Lake l. Can.
21 A2 Baramati India
22 D4 Baran India
22 B4 Baran r. Pak.
50 C4 Baranavichy Belarus
13 S3 Baranikha Rus. Fed.
51 C5 Baranivka Ukr.
19 F3 Bārān, Kūh-e mts Iran
89 B2 Baranoa Col.
64 B3 Baranof Island i. U.S.A.
90 A2 Barão de Melgaço Brazil
54 B3 Baraouéli Mali
42 D4 Baraque de Fraiture h. Belgium
25 E7 Barat Daya, Kepulauan is Indon.
8 B2 Baratta Austr.
22 D3 Baraut India
89 B4 Baraya Col.
90 D3 Barbacena Brazil
89 A4 Barbacoas Col.
61 N8 Barbados country Caribbean Sea
45 G1 Barbastro Spain
45 D4 Barbate de Franco Spain
74 □1 Barbers Pt pt U.S.A.
59 J2 Barberton S. Africa
80 C4 Barberton U.S.A.
44 D4 Barbezieux-St-Hilaire France
89 B3 Barbosa Col.
65 L2 Barbour Bay b. Can.
80 B6 Barbourville U.S.A.
31 B4 Barboza Phil.
83 M5 Barbuda i. Antigua
43 K3 Barby (Elbe) Ger.
6 E4 Barcaldine Austr.
45 H2 Barcelona Spain
89 D2 Barcelona Venez.
86 F4 Barcelos Brazil
43 J4 Barchfeld Ger.
54 B4 Barclayville Liberia
48 G2 Barcs Hungary
17 L1 Bärdä Azer.
36 E4 Bárðarbunga mt Iceland
91 C2 Bardas Blancas Arg.
23 F5 Barddhamān India
47 K6 Bardejov Slovakia
18 C5 Bardestān Iran
32 C2 Bar Đôn Vietnam
39 C5 Bardsey Island i. U.K.
78 C4 Bardstown U.S.A.
80 B5 Bardwell U.S.A.
22 D3 Bareilly India
12 C2 Barentsburg Svalbard
12 D2 Barentsøya i. Svalbard
12 F2 Barents Sea sea Arctic Ocean
56 D2 Barentu Eritrea
22 E3 Barga China
22 D5 Bargi India
40 D5 Bargrennan U.K.
43 J1 Bargteheide Ger.
23 G5 Barguna Bangl.
81 J2 Bar Harbor U.S.A.
48 G4 Bari Italy
32 C3 Ba Ria Vietnam
22 C3 Bari Doab lowland Pak.
23 E3 Barikot Nepal
89 E2 Barima r. Venez.
89 C2 Barinas Venez.
23 G5 Barisal Bangl.
33 B3 Barisan, Pegunungan mts Indon.
33 D3 Barito r. Indon.
86 F8 Baritu, Parque Nacional nat. park Arg.
19 E6 Barkā Oman
26 B4 Barkam China
18 C4 Barkan, Ra's-e pt Iran
37 U8 Barkava Latvia
64 E4 Barkerville Can.
78 C4 Barkley, L. l. U.S.A.
64 D5 Barkley Sd in. Can.
59 G5 Barkly East S. Africa
6 D3 Barkly Tableland reg. Austr.
58 F4 Barkly West S. Africa
24 B2 Barkol China
22 D3 Barkot India
18 E4 Barkūh Iran
47 N7 Bârlad Romania
44 G2 Bar-le-Duc France
6 B4 Barlee, L. salt flat Austr.
48 G4 Barletta Italy
8 F3 Barmedman Austr.
22 B4 Barmer India
8 C3 Barmera Austr.
39 C5 Barmouth U.K.
22 C3 Barnala India
38 F3 Barnard Castle U.K.
8 E1 Barnato Austr.
12 K4 Barnaul Rus. Fed.
81 F5 Barnegat U.S.A.
81 F5 Barnegat Bay b. U.S.A.
80 D4 Barnesboro U.S.A.
63 L2 Barnes Icecap ice cap Can.
42 D2 Barneveld Neth.
8 E2 Barneys Lake l. Austr.
75 G3 Barney Top mt U.S.A.
77 C6 Barnhart U.S.A.
38 F4 Barnsley U.K.
39 C6 Barnstaple U.K.
Barnstaple Bay b. see Bideford Bay
43 G2 Barnstorf Ger.
79 D5 Barnwell U.S.A.
Baroda see Vadodara
22 C1 Baroghil Pass Afgh.
23 H4 Barpathar India
23 G4 Barpeta India
68 D3 Barques, Pt Aux pt MI U.S.A.
69 F3 Barques, Pt Aux pt MI U.S.A.
89 C2 Barquisimeto Venez.
87 K6 Barra Brazil
40 A4 Barra i. U.K.
58 D7 Barracouta, Cape hd S. Africa
87 G6 Barra do Bugres Brazil
87 J5 Barra do Corda Brazil
90 B1 Barra do Garças Brazil
87 G5 Barra do São Manuel Brazil
86 C6 Barranca Lima Peru
86 C4 Barranca Loreto Peru
89 B3 Barranca-bermeja Col.
89 B2 Barrancas Col.
89 E2 Barrancas Venez.
91 B3 Barrancas r. Mendoza/Neuquén Arg.
88 E3 Barranqueras Arg.
89 B2 Barranquilla Col.
40 A3 Barra, Sound of chan. U.K.
81 G2 Barre U.S.A.
91 C1 Barreal Arg.
87 K6 Barreiras Brazil
87 G4 Barreirinha Brazil
87 K4 Barreirinhas Brazil
45 B3 Barreiro Port.
90 B1 Barreiro r. Brazil
87 L5 Barreiros Brazil
90 C3 Barretos Brazil
64 G4 Barrhead Can.
40 D5 Barrhead U.K.
69 H3 Barrie Can.
69 F3 Barrie I i. Can.
64 E4 Barrière Can.
8 C1 Barrier Range h. Austr.
65 J3 Barrington Lake l. Can.
8 H2 Barrington, Mt Austr.
68 B3 Barron U.S.A.
77 C7 Barroterán Mex.
91 E3 Barrow Arg.
62 C2 Barrow AK U.S.A.
41 E5 Barrow r. Rep. of Ireland
6 D4 Barrow Creek Austr.
6 B4 Barrow I. i. Austr.
38 D3 Barrow-in-Furness U.K.
62 C2 Barrow, Point c. U.S.A.
63 J2 Barrow Strait str. Can.
39 D6 Barry U.K.
58 D6 Barrydale S. Africa
69 J3 Barrys Bay Can.
22 C3 Barsalpur India
21 A2 Barsi India
22 D5 Barsi Takli India
43 H2 Barsinghausen Ger.
74 D4 Barstow U.S.A.
44 G2 Bar-sur-Aube France
46 F3 Barth Ger.
87 G2 Bartica Guyana
16 D1 Bartın Turkey
6 E3 Bartle Frere, Mt mt Austr.
75 G2 Bartles, Mt mt U.S.A.
71 G4 Bartlesville OK U.S.A.
76 D3 Bartlett NE U.S.A.
81 H2 Bartlett NH U.S.A.
64 F2 Bartlett Lake l. Can.
81 G2 Barton U.S.A.
38 G4 Barton-upon-Humber U.K.
47 K3 Bartoszyce Pol.
33 B2 Barumun r. Indon.
33 D4 Barung i. Indon.
32 A5 Barus Indon.
26 B1 Baruunsuu Mongolia
24 D2 Baruun Urt Mongolia
83 H7 Barú, Volcán volc. Panama
22 D5 Barwah India
22 C3 Barwala India
22 C5 Barwani India
6 E5 Barwon r. Austr.
50 D4 Barysaw Belarus
50 H4 Barysh Rus. Fed.
50 H4 Barysh r. Rus. Fed.
18 C3 Barzūk Iran
18 D5 Basaidu Iran
74 C2 Basalt U.S.A.
27 □ Basalt I. i. H.K. China
56 B3 Basankusu Congo(Zaire)
21 B2 Basar India

49 N2 Basarabi Romania
91 E2 Basavilbaso Arg.
31 B4 Basay Phil.
31 B1 Basco Phil.
46 C7 Basel Switz.
68 B1 Basewood Lake l. U.S.A.
19 E5 Bashākerd, Kūhhā-ye mts Iran
64 G4 Bashaw Can.
59 H6 Bashee r. S. Africa
19 H3 Bashgul r. Afgh.
50 G4 Bashmakovo Rus. Fed.
18 C4 Bāsht Iran
51 E6 Bashtanka Ukr.
22 D4 Basi India
23 F5 Basia India
31 B5 Basilan i. Phil.
31 B5 Basilan Strait chan. Phil.
39 H6 Basildon U.K.
72 E2 Basin U.S.A.
39 F6 Basingstoke U.K.
17 K4 Bāsīra r. Iraq
23 G5 Basirhat India
81 K2 Baskahegan Lake l. U.S.A.
17 K2 Başkale Turkey
69 K2 Baskatong, Réservoir resr Can.
51 H5 Baskunchak, Ozero l. Rus. Fed.
Basle see Basel
22 D5 Basoda India
56 C3 Basoko Congo(Zaire)
17 L6 Basra Iraq
48 D2 Bassano del Grappa Italy
54 C4 Bassar Togo
57 D6 Bassas da India i. Ind. Ocean
25 B5 Bassein Myanmar
38 D3 Bassenthwaite Lake l. U.K.
54 A3 Basse Santa Su The Gambia
83 M5 Basse Terre Guadeloupe
83 M5 Basseterre St Kitts-Nevis
76 D3 Bassett U.S.A.
75 G5 Bassett Peak summit U.S.A.
81 J2 Bass Harbor U.S.A.
54 B3 Bassikounou Maur.
54 C4 Bassila Benin
40 F4 Bass Rock i. U.K.
6 E5 Bass Strait str. Austr.
43 G2 Bassum Ger.
37 N8 Båstad Sweden
18 D5 Bastak Iran
18 B2 Bastānābād Iran
43 J4 Bastheim Ger.
23 E4 Basti India
48 C3 Bastia Corsica France
42 D4 Bastogne Belgium
77 F5 Bastrop LA U.S.A.
77 D6 Bastrop TX U.S.A.
19 G5 Basul r. Pak.
54 C4 Bata Equatorial Guinea
83 H4 Batabanó, Golfo de b. Cuba
31 B2 Batac Phil.
31 C3 Batag i. Phil.
13 P3 Batagay Rus. Fed.
22 B2 Batai Pass Pak.
22 C3 Batala India
45 B3 Batalha Port.
32 C5 Batam i. Indon.
13 O3 Batamay Rus. Fed.
31 B1 Batan i. Phil.
56 B3 Batangafo C.A.R.
31 B3 Batangas Phil.
33 B3 Batanghari r. Indon.
32 A5 Batangtoru Indon.
31 B1 Batan Islands is Phil.
90 C3 Batatais Brazil
68 C5 Batavia IL U.S.A.
80 D3 Batavia NY U.S.A.
51 F6 Bataysk Rus. Fed.
69 E2 Batchawana r. Can.
68 E2 Batchawana Bay Can.
66 D4 Batchawana Mtn h. Can.
6 D3 Batchelor Austr.
69 E2 Batchewana Can.
32 B2 Bătdâmbâng Cambodia
8 H3 Batemans B. b. Austr.
8 H3 Batemans Bay Austr.
77 F5 Batesville AR U.S.A.
77 F5 Batesville MS U.S.A.
50 D3 Batetskiy Rus. Fed.
67 G4 Bath N.B. Can.
69 J3 Bath Ont. Can.
39 E6 Bath U.K.
81 J3 Bath ME U.S.A.
80 E3 Bath NY U.S.A.
40 E5 Bathgate U.K.
22 C3 Bathinda India
8 G2 Bathurst Austr.
67 G4 Bathurst Can.
59 G6 Bathurst S. Africa
63 J2 Bathurst I. i. Can.
62 H3 Bathurst Inlet N.W.T. Can.
6 D3 Bathurst Island i. Austr.
8 G3 Bathurst, L. l. Austr.
18 D3 Bāṭlāq-e Gavkhūnī marsh Iran
38 F4 Batley U.K.
8 G3 Batlow Austr.
17 H3 Batman Turkey
54 C1 Batna Alg.
18 C6 Baṭn aṭ Ṭarfā' depression S. Arabia
77 F6 Baton Rouge U.S.A.
55 D4 Batouri Cameroon
90 B1 Batovi Brazil
16 E4 Batroûn Lebanon
36 V1 Båtsfjord Norway
21 C5 Batticaloa Sri Lanka
48 F4 Battipaglia Italy
65 G4 Battle r. Can.
68 E4 Battle Creek U.S.A.
65 H4 Battleford Can.
72 C3 Battle Mountain U.S.A.
22 C1 Battura Glacier gl. Jammu and Kashmir
32 B4 Batu Gajah Malaysia
31 C5 Batulaki Phil.
17 H1 Bat'umi Georgia
33 B2 Batu Pahat Malaysia
33 A3 Batu, Pulau Pulau is Indon.
32 B4 Batu Puteh, Gunung mt Malaysia
25 E7 Baubau Indon.
54 C3 Bauchi Nigeria
76 E1 Baudette U.S.A.
89 A3 Baudo, Serranía de mts Col.
44 D3 Baugé France
43 H5 Bauland reg. Ger.
67 K3 Bauld, C. hd Can.
44 H3 Baume-les-Dames France
22 C2 Baundal India
90 C3 Bauru Brazil
90 B2 Baús Brazil
42 E4 Bausendorf Ger.
37 T8 Bauska Latvia
46 G5 Bautzen Ger.
58 E6 Baviaanskloofberg mts S. Africa
70 E6 Bavispe r. Mex.
39 J5 Bawdeswell U.K.
33 D4 Bawean i. Indon.
42 F2 Bawinkel Ger.
55 E2 Bawiti Egypt
54 B3 Bawku Ghana
32 A1 Bawlake Myanmar
27 A4 Bawolung China
26 B3 Baxi China
26 E2 Ba Xian Hebei China
27 C4 Ba Xian Sichuan China
79 D6 Baxley U.S.A.
83 J4 Bayamo Cuba
22 D4 Bayana India
24 B3 Bayan Har Shan mts China
24 C2 Bayanhongor Mongolia
26 B1 Bayan Mod China
26 C1 Bayan Obo China
30 A1 Bayan Qagan China
18 D4 Bayāz Iran
31 C4 Baybay Phil.
17 H1 Bayburt Turkey
69 F4 Bay City MI U.S.A.
77 D6 Bay City TX U.S.A.
12 H3 Baydaratskaya Guba b. Rus. Fed.
56 E3 Baydhabo Somalia
43 L5 Bayerischer Wald mts Ger.
43 J5 Bayern div. Ger.
68 B2 Bayfield U.S.A.
49 M5 Bayındır Turkey
16 F6 Bāyir Jordan
Baykal, Ozero l. see Baikal, Lake
Baykal Range mts see Baykal'sky Khrebet
24 C1 Baykal'skiy Khrebet mts Rus. Fed.
17 H2 Baykan Turkey
31 B3 Bay, Laguna de lag. Phil.
12 G4 Baymak Rus. Fed.
18 D6 Baynūna'h reg. U.A.E.
31 B2 Bayombong Phil.
44 D5 Bayonne France
31 B4 Bayo Point pt Phil.
19 F2 Bayramaly Turkm.
49 M5 Bayramiç Turkey
43 K5 Bayreuth Ger.
77 F6 Bay St Louis U.S.A.
81 G4 Bay Shore U.S.A.
39 E5 Bayston Hill U.K.
19 G2 Baysun Uzbek.
19 G2 Baysuntau, Gory mts Uzbek.
77 E6 Baytown U.S.A.
9 F3 Bay View N.Z.
45 E4 Baza Spain
17 L1 Bazardyuzi, Gora mt Azer./Rus. Fed.
18 C2 Bāzār-e Māsāl Iran
17 K2 Bāzārgān Iran
51 H4 Bazarnyy Karabulak Rus. Fed.
57 D6 Bazaruto, Ilha do i. Moz.
19 G5 Bazdar Pak.
26 C4 Bazhong China
19 F5 Bazman Iran
19 F4 Bazmān, Kūh-e mt Iran
32 C3 Be r. Vietnam
76 C2 Beach U.S.A.
69 J3 Beachburg Can.
81 F5 Beach Haven U.S.A.
8 C4 Beachport Austr.
81 G4 Beachwood U.S.A.
39 H7 Beachy Head hd U.K.
81 G4 Beacon U.S.A.
59 G6 Beacon Bay S. Africa
27 □ Beacon Hill h. H.K. China
39 G6 Beaconsfield U.K.
88 C8 Beagle, Canal chan. Arg.
6 C3 Beagle Gulf b. Austr.
57 E5 Bealanana Madag.
39 E7 Beaminster U.K.
72 E3 Bear r. U.S.A.
65 N2 Bear Cove b. Can.
66 C4 Beardmore Can.
92 B4 Beardmore Gl. gl. Ant.
68 B5 Beardstown U.S.A.
66 D3 Bear Island i. Can.
12 C2 Bear Island i. Svalbard
72 E3 Bear L. l. U.S.A.
64 D3 Bear Lake Can.
22 D4 Bearma r. India
40 A4 Bearnaraigh i. U.K.
72 E1 Bear Paw Mtn mt U.S.A.
92 A3 Bear Pen. pen. Ant.
66 B3 Bearskin Lake Can.
74 B2 Bear Valley U.S.A.
22 C3 Beas r. India
22 C3 Beas Dam dam India
83 K5 Beata, Cabo c. Dom. Rep.
83 K5 Beata, I. i. Dom. Rep.
76 D3 Beatrice U.S.A.
64 E3 Beatton r. Can.
64 E3 Beatton River Can.
74 D3 Beatty U.S.A.
66 E4 Beattyville Can.
44 G5 Beaucaire France
88 E8 Beauchene I. i. Falkland Is
8 D4 Beaufort Austr.
33 E1 Beaufort Malaysia
79 D5 Beaufort U.S.A.
62 D2 Beaufort Sea Can./U.S.A.
58 E6 Beaufort West S. Africa
66 F4 Beauharnois Can.
40 D3 Beauly U.K.
40 D3 Beauly Firth est. U.K.
39 C4 Beaumaris U.K.
42 C4 Beaumont Belgium
9 B6 Beaumont N.Z.
77 F6 Beaumont MS U.S.A.
80 B5 Beaumont OH U.S.A.
77 E6 Beaumont TX U.S.A.
44 G3 Beaune France
44 D3 Beaupréau France
42 A4 Beauquesne France
42 C4 Beauraing Belgium
65 K4 Beausejour Can.
44 F2 Beauvais France
65 H3 Beauval Can.
42 A4 Beauval France
75 F2 Beaver U.S.A.
62 H4 Beaver r. Alta. Can.
64 D2 Beaver r. B.C./Y.T. Can.
66 C2 Beaver r. Ont. Can.
75 F2 Beaver r. U.S.A.
64 A2 Beaver Creek Can.
78 C4 Beaver Dam KY U.S.A.
68 C4 Beaver Dam WV U.S.A.
80 C4 Beaver Falls U.S.A.
72 D2 Beaverhead Mts mts U.S.A.
65 K4 Beaverhill L. l. Man. Can.
65 J2 Beaverhill L. l. N.W.T. Can.
68 E3 Beaver Island i. U.S.A.
77 E4 Beaver L. resr U.S.A.
64 F3 Beaverlodge Can.
80 D4 Beaver Run Reservoir U.S.A.
22 C4 Beawar India
91 C2 Beazley Arg.
90 C3 Bebedouro Brazil
39 D4 Bebington U.K.
43 H4 Bebra Ger.
66 F1 Bécard, Lac l. Can.
39 J5 Beccles U.K.
49 J2 Bečej Yugo.
45 C1 Becerreá Spain
54 B1 Béchar Alg.
43 J5 Bechhofen Ger.
80 C6 Beckley U.S.A.
43 G3 Beckum Ger.
43 L4 Bečov nad Teplou Czech Rep.
38 F3 Bedale U.K.
42 E4 Bedburg Ger.
81 J2 Beddington U.S.A.
56 D3 Bedelē Eth.
43 G1 Bederkesa Ger.
81 G2 Bedford Can.
59 J4 Bedford S. Africa
39 G5 Bedford U.K.
78 C4 Bedford IN U.S.A.
81 H3 Bedford MA U.S.A.
80 D4 Bedford PA U.S.A.
80 D6 Bedford VA U.S.A.
39 G5 Bedford Level lowland U.K.
8 F2 Bedgerebong Austr.
38 F2 Bedlington U.K.
32 □ Bedok Sing.
32 □ Bedok Res. resr Sing.
75 H2 Bedrock U.S.A.
42 E1 Bedum Neth.
39 F5 Bedworth U.K.
80 B5 Beech Fork Lake l. U.S.A.
68 C2 Beechwood U.S.A.
8 F4 Beechworth Austr.
8 H3 Beecroft Pen. pen. Austr.
43 L2 Beelitz Ger.
7 F4 Beenleigh Austr.
41 A5 Beenoskee h. Rep. of Ireland
42 B3 Beernem Belgium
16 E6 Beersheba Israel
Be'ér Sheva' see Beersheba
58 E6 Beervlei Dam dam S. Africa
43 L2 Beetzsee l. Ger.
77 D6 Beeville U.S.A.
56 C3 Befale Congo(Zaire)
57 E5 Befandriana Avaratra Madag.
8 G4 Bega Austr.
22 B3 Begari r. Pak.
45 H2 Begur, Cap de pt Spain
23 F4 Begusarai India
19 E3 Behābād Iran
81 H3 Béhague, Pointe pt Fr. Guiana
18 C4 Behbehān Iran
64 C3 Behm Canal in. U.S.A.
92 B3 Behrendt Mts mts Ant.
18 D2 Behshahr Iran
19 G3 Behsūd Afgh.
24 E2 Bei'an China
27 C4 Beibei China
26 B4 Beichuan China
27 C6 Beihai China
27 D6 Bei Jiang r. China
26 E2 Beijing China
26 E1 Beijing div. China
42 E2 Beilen Neth.
27 C7 Beili China
27 D6 Beiliu China
43 K5 Beilngries Ger.
40 C5 Beinn an Oir h. U.K.
40 D3 Beinn Dearg mt U.K.
30 A3 Beipiao China
57 D5 Beira Moz.
26 E3 Beiru r. China
16 E5 Beirut Lebanon
57 C6 Beitbridge Zimbabwe
40 D5 Beith U.K.
47 L7 Beiuș Romania
30 A3 Beizhen China
45 C3 Beja Port.
54 C1 Béja Tunisia
54 C1 Bejaïa Alg.
45 D2 Béjar Spain
19 E3 Bejestān Iran
22 B3 Beji r. Pak.
47 K7 Békés Hungary
47 K7 Békéscsaba Hungary
57 E6 Bekily Madag.
28 J3 Bekkai Japan
54 B4 Bekwai Ghana
23 E4 Bela India
19 G5 Bela Pak.
22 B3 Belab r. Pak.
59 H2 Bela-Bela S. Africa
55 D4 Bélabo Cameroon
49 J2 Bela Crkva Yugo.
81 E5 Bel Air U.S.A.
45 D3 Belalcázar Spain
43 L5 Bělá nad Radbuzou Czech Rep.
8 E2 Belaraboon Austr.
35 H3 Belarus country Europe
90 A3 Bela Vista Brazil
57 D6 Bela Vista Moz.
32 A5 Belawan Indon.
13 T3 Belaya r. Rus. Fed.
51 G6 Belaya Glina Rus. Fed.
51 G5 Belaya Kalitva Rus. Fed.
50 J3 Belaya Kholunitsa Rus. Fed.
47 J5 Bełchatów Pol.
80 B6 Belcher U.S.A.
63 K4 Belcher Islands is Can.
19 G3 Belchiragh Afgh.
16 F2 Belcik Turkey
41 D3 Belcoo U.K.
69 J1 Belcourt Can.
74 B1 Belden U.S.A.
56 E3 Beledweyne Somalia
18 D2 Belek Turkm.
87 J4 Belém Brazil
88 C3 Belén Arg.
16 F3 Belen Turkey
73 F5 Belen U.S.A.
7 G3 Bélep, Îles is New Caledonia
50 F4 Belev Rus. Fed.
9 D5 Belfast N.Z.
59 J2 Belfast S. Africa
41 F3 Belfast U.K.
81 J2 Belfast U.S.A.
41 F3 Belfast Lough in. U.K.
76 C2 Belfield U.S.A.
38 F2 Belford U.K.
44 H3 Belfort France
21 A3 Belgaum India
43 M3 Belgern Ger.
34 F3 Belgium country Europe
51 F5 Belgorod Rus. Fed.
51 F5 Belgorodskaya Oblast' div. Rus. Fed.
72 E2 Belgrade U.S.A.
49 J2 Belgrade Yugo.
54 D4 Beli Nigeria
48 E6 Belice r. Sicily Italy
50 G4 Belinskiy Rus. Fed.
33 C3 Belinyu Indon.
33 C3 Belitung i. Indon.
82 G5 Belize Belize
61 K8 Belize country Central America
28 E2 Belkina, Mys pt Rus. Fed.
13 P2 Bel'kovskiy, O. i. Rus. Fed.
8 G2 Bell r. Austr.
64 D4 Bella Bella Can.
44 E3 Bellac France
64 D4 Bella Coola Can.
77 E6 Bellaire U.S.A.
21 B3 Bellary India
91 F1 Bella Unión Uru.
80 B4 Bellefontaine U.S.A.
80 E4 Bellefonte U.S.A.
76 C2 Belle Fourche U.S.A.
76 C2 Belle Fourche r. U.S.A.
44 G3 Bellegarde-sur-Valserine France
79 D7 Belle Glade U.S.A.
44 C3 Belle-Île i. France
67 K3 Belle Isle i. Can.
63 N4 Belle Isle, Strait of Nfld Can.
67 J3 Belle Isle, Strait of str. Can.
75 G4 Bellemont U.S.A.
68 A5 Belle Plaine U.S.A.
69 H2 Belleterre Can.
69 J3 Belleville Can.
76 D4 Belleville U.S.A.
68 B4 Bellevue IA U.S.A.
72 D3 Bellevue ID U.S.A.
80 B4 Bellevue OH U.S.A.
72 B2 Bellevue WA U.S.A.
Bellin see Kangirsuk
38 E2 Bellingham U.K.
72 B1 Bellingham U.S.A.
92 B2 Bellingshausen Rus. Fed. Base Ant.
92 A3 Bellingshausen Sea sea Ant.
46 D7 Bellinzona Switz.
89 B3 Bello Col.
81 G3 Bellows Falls U.S.A.
22 B3 Bellpat Pak.
81 F5 Belltown U.S.A.
48 E1 Belluno Italy
21 B3 Belluru India
91 D2 Bell Ville Arg.
58 C6 Bellville S. Africa
43 G2 Belm Ger.
58 F4 Belmont S. Africa
40 □ Belmont U.K.
80 D3 Belmont U.S.A.
90 E1 Belmonte Brazil
82 G5 Belmopan Belize
41 B3 Belmullet Rep. of Ireland
42 B4 Belœil Belgium
81 G2 Beloeil Can.
24 E1 Belogorsk Rus. Fed.
57 E6 Beloha Madag.
90 D2 Belo Horizonte Brazil
76 D4 Beloit KS U.S.A.
68 C4 Beloit WV U.S.A.
50 E1 Belomorsk Rus. Fed.
23 G5 Belonia India
51 F6 Belorechensk Rus. Fed.
16 F3 Belören Turkey
12 G4 Beloretsk Rus. Fed.
Belorussia country see Belarus
57 E5 Belo Tsiribihina Madag.
50 F1 Beloye Rus. Fed.
Beloye More g. see White Sea
50 F2 Beloye, Ozero l. Rus. Fed.
50 F2 Belozersk Rus. Fed.
80 C5 Belpre U.S.A.
72 E1 Belt U.S.A.
74 D3 Belted Range mts U.S.A.
77 D6 Belton U.S.A.
21 A3 Belur India
31 A5 Beluran Malaysia
68 C4 Belvidere U.S.A.
50 H3 Belyshevo Rus. Fed.
50 E4 Belyy Rus. Fed.
12 J2 Belyy, O. i. Rus. Fed.
43 L2 Belzig Ger.
68 C6 Bement U.S.A.
76 E2 Bemidji U.S.A.
56 C4 Bena Dibele Congo(Zaire)
40 D4 Ben Alder mt U.K.
8 E4 Benalla Austr.
48 D6 Ben Arous Tunisia
45 D1 Benavente Spain
40 E3 Ben Avon mt U.K.
41 B4 Benbaun h. Rep. of Ireland
40 A3 Benbecula i. U.K.
41 C3 Benbulben h. Rep. of Ireland
41 E3 Benburb U.K.
40 C4 Ben Cruachan mt U.K.
72 B2 Bend U.S.A.
59 G5 Bendearg mt S. Africa
8 H1 Bendemeer Austr.
56 E3 Bender-Bayla Somalia
8 E4 Bendigo Austr.
8 G4 Bendoc Austr.
57 D5 Bene Moz.
81 J2 Benedicta U.S.A.
67 J3 Benedict, Mount h. Can.
57 E6 Benenitra Madag.
46 G6 Benešov Czech Rep.
42 E6 Bénestroff France
48 F4 Benevento Italy
26 F3 Beng r. China
10 K8 Bengal, Bay of sea Asia
56 C3 Bengamisa Congo(Zaire)
26 E3 Bengbu China
32 B5 Bengkalis Indon.
33 B3 Bengkulu Indon.
37 N7 Bengtsfors Sweden
57 B5 Benguela Angola
16 C6 Benha Egypt
40 B4 Ben Hiant h. U.K.
40 D2 Ben Hope mt U.K.
56 C3 Beni Congo(Zaire)
86 E6 Beni r. Bol.
54 B1 Beni-Abbès Alg.
45 F3 Benidorm Spain
54 B1 Beni Mellal Morocco
53 E5 Benin country Africa
54 C4 Benin, Bight of g. Africa
54 C4 Benin City Nigeria
54 B1 Beni-Saf Alg.
55 F2 Beni Suef Egypt
91 E3 Benito Juárez Arg.
31 B2 Benito Soliven Phil.
86 E4 Benjamim Constant Brazil
82 B2 Benjamín Hill Mex.
6 D2 Benjina Indon.
76 C3 Benkelman U.S.A.
40 D2 Ben Klibreck mt U.K.
40 D4 Ben Lawers mt U.K.
40 D4 Ben Lomond mt U.K.
40 D2 Ben Loyal h. U.K.
40 D4 Ben Lui mt U.K.
40 E3 Ben Macdui mt U.K.
40 B4 Ben More mt Scot. U.K.
40 B4 Ben More mt Scot. U.K.
40 D2 Ben More Assynt mt U.K.
9 C6 Benmore, L. l. N.Z.
13 Q2 Bennetta, O. i. Rus. Fed.
40 C4 Ben Nevis mt U.K.
81 G3 Bennington U.S.A.
59 H3 Benoni S. Africa
55 D4 Bénoué, Parc National de la nat. park Cameroon
43 G5 Bensheim Ger.
75 G6 Benson AZ U.S.A.
76 E2 Benson MN U.S.A.
19 E5 Bent Iran
33 B2 Benta Seberang Malaysia
80 D6 Bent Creek U.S.A.
25 E7 Benteng Indon.
6 D3 Bentinck I. i. Austr.
32 A3 Bentinck I. i. Myanmar
38 F4 Bentley U.K.
81 K2 Benton Can.
77 E5 Benton AR U.S.A.
74 C3 Benton CA U.S.A.
78 B4 Benton IL U.S.A.
68 D4 Benton Harbor U.S.A.
32 C3 Bên Tre Vietnam
32 B5 Bentung Malaysia
54 D4 Benue r. Nigeria
40 D4 Ben Vorlich mt U.K.
41 B4 Benwee h. Rep. of Ireland
41 B3 Benwee Head hd Rep. of Ireland
40 D3 Ben Wyvis mt U.K.
30 C3 Benxi Liaoning China
30 B3 Benxi Liaoning China
31 C5 Beo Indon.
Beograd see Belgrade
22 E5 Beohari India
54 B4 Béoumi Côte d'Ivoire
27 C5 Bepian Jiang r. China
29 B8 Beppu Japan
7 H3 Beqa i. Fiji
22 C4 Berach r. India
67 G2 Bérard, Lac l. Can.
22 D5 Berasia India
32 A5 Berastagi Indon.
49 H4 Berat Albania
33 E3 Beratus, Gunung mt Indon.
25 F7 Berau, Teluk b. Indon.
55 F3 Berber Sudan
56 E2 Berbera Somalia
56 B3 Berbérati C.A.R.
44 E1 Berck France
17 K1 Berd Armenia
13 O3 Berdigestyakh Rus. Fed.
24 A1 Berdsk Rus. Fed.
51 F6 Berdyans'k Ukr.
51 D5 Berdychiv Ukr.
80 A6 Berea U.S.A.
51 B5 Berehove Ukr.
6 E2 Bereina P.N.G.
65 K4 Berens r. Can.
65 K4 Berens River Can.
76 D3 Beresford U.S.A.
51 C5 Berezhany Ukr.
51 D6 Berezivka Ukr.
51 C5 Berezne Ukr.
50 G2 Bereznik Rus. Fed.
12 H3 Berezovo Rus. Fed.
43 K3 Berga Ger.
45 G1 Berga Spain
49 M5 Bergama Turkey
48 C2 Bergamo Italy
37 P6 Bergby Sweden
46 F3 Bergen Ger.
43 H2 Bergen Ger.
37 J6 Bergen Norway
42 C3 Bergen op Zoom Neth.
44 E4 Bergerac France
42 C6 Bergères-lès-Vertus France
42 E4 Bergheim Ger.
42 F4 Bergisches Land reg. Ger.
42 F4 Bergisch Gladbach Ger.
58 B1 Bergland Namibia
68 C2 Bergland U.S.A.
37 P6 Bergsjö Sweden
36 R4 Bergsviken Sweden
43 J5 Bergtheim Ger.
42 A4 Bergues France
42 E1 Bergum Neth.
59 H4 Bergville S. Africa
33 B3 Berhala, Selat chan. Indon.
13 S4 Beringa, O. i. Rus. Fed.
42 D3 Beringen Belgium
13 T3 Beringovskiy Rus. Fed.
13 T4 Bering Sea sea Pac. Oc.
62 B3 Bering Strait str. Rus. Fed./U.S.A.
18 E5 Berīzak Iran
36 M5 Berkåk Norway
42 E2 Berkel r. Neth.
74 A3 Berkeley U.S.A.
80 D5 Berkeley Springs U.S.A.
42 D2 Berkhout Neth.
92 B3 Berkner I. i. Ant.
49 K3 Berkovitsa Bulg.
39 F6 Berkshire Downs h. U.K.
42 C3 Berlare Belgium
36 V1 Berlevåg Norway
43 M2 Berlin Ger.
75 F5 Berlin MD U.S.A.
81 H2 Berlin NH U.S.A.
80 D5 Berlin PA U.S.A.
68 C4 Berlin WV U.S.A.
63 K2 Berlinguet Inlet in. Can.
80 C4 Berlin Lake l. U.S.A.
8 H4 Bermagui Austr.
91 D4 Bermeja, Pta pt Arg.
84 B1 Bermejillo Mex.
86 F8 Bermejo Bol.
91 C1 Bermejo r. San Juan Arg.
88 D2 Bermejo r. Chaco/Formosa Arg./Bol.
61 M6 Bermuda terr. Atl. Ocean
96 E3 Bermuda Rise sea feature Atl. Ocean
46 C7 Bern Switz.
73 F5 Bernalillo U.S.A.
88 A7 Bernardo O'Higgins, Parque Nacional nat. park Chile
91 D3 Bernasconi Arg.
43 K3 Bernburg (Saale) Ger.
43 G1 Berne Ger.
68 E5 Berne U.S.A.
46 C7 Berner Alpen mts Switz.
40 A3 Berneray i. U.K.
63 K2 Bernier Bay b. Can.
6 B4 Bernier I. i. Austr.
46 E7 Bernina Pass Switz.
42 F5 Bernkastel-Kues Ger.
57 E6 Beroroha Madag.
46 G6 Beroun Czech Rep.
46 F5 Berounka r. Czech Rep.
8 C3 Berri Austr.
40 E2 Berriedale U.K.
8 E3 Berrigan Austr.
8 H3 Berrima Austr.
45 H4 Berrouaghia Alg.
8 H3 Berry Austr.
44 E3 Berry reg. France
74 A2 Berryessa, Lake l. U.S.A.
79 E7 Berry Islands is Bahamas
58 B3 Berseba Namibia
43 F2 Bersenbrück Ger.
51 D5 Bershad' Ukr.
33 B1 Bertam Malaysia
87 K5 Bertolínia Brazil
55 D4 Bertoua Cameroon
41 B4 Bertraghboy Bay b. Rep. of Ireland
7 H2 Beru i. Kiribati
86 F4 Beruri Brazil
8 E5 Berwick Austr.
81 E4 Berwick U.S.A.
38 E2 Berwick-upon-Tweed U.K.
64 F3 Berwyn Can.
39 D5 Berwyn h. U.K.
51 E6 Beryslav Ukr.
57 E5 Besalampy Madag.
44 H3 Besançon France
19 G2 Beshir Turkm.
19 G2 Beshkent Uzbek.
18 D4 Besshneh Iran
17 H3 Beşiri Turkey
51 H7 Beslan Rus. Fed.
65 H3 Besnard Lake l. Can.
16 F3 Besni Turkey
41 E3 Bessbrook U.K.
79 C5 Bessemer AL U.S.A.
68 B2 Bessemer MI U.S.A.
57 E6 Betanty Madag.
45 B1 Betanzos Spain
55 D4 Bétaré Oya Cameroon
59 H3 Bethal S. Africa
58 B3 Bethanie Namibia
76 E3 Bethany MO U.S.A.
77 D5 Bethany OK U.S.A.
62 B3 Bethel AK U.S.A.
81 H2 Bethel ME U.S.A.
68 A6 Bethel MO U.S.A.
80 A5 Bethel OH U.S.A.
80 D4 Bethel Park U.S.A.
39 C4 Bethesda U.K.
80 E5 Bethesda MD U.S.A.
80 C4 Bethesda OH U.S.A.
58 F5 Bethesdaweg S. Africa
59 H4 Bethlehem S. Africa
81 F4 Bethlehem U.S.A.
16 E6 Bethlehem West Bank
59 F5 Bethulie S. Africa
42 A4 Béthune France
89 C2 Betijoque Venez.
57 E6 Betioky Madag.
14 F2 Betpak-Dala plain Kazak.
57 E6 Betroka Madag.
16 E5 Bet She'an Israel
67 G4 Betsiamites Can.
67 G4 Betsiamites r. Can.
57 E5 Betsiboka r. Madag.
68 D3 Betsie, Pt pt U.S.A.
68 E2 Betsy Lake l. U.S.A.
68 B5 Bettendorf U.S.A.
23 F4 Bettiah India
40 D2 Bettyhill U.K.
41 E4 Bettystown Rep. of Ireland
22 D5 Betul India
42 D3 Betuwe reg. Neth.
22 D4 Betwa r. India
39 D4 Betws-y-coed U.K.
43 F4 Betzdorf Ger.
8 D3 Beulah Austr.
68 D3 Beulah U.S.A.
39 H6 Beult r. U.K.
38 G4 Beverley U.K.
62 C4 Beverley, L. l. U.S.A.
81 H3 Beverly MA U.S.A.
80 C5 Beverly OH U.S.A.
74 C4 Beverly Hills U.S.A.
65 J2 Beverly Lake l. Can.
43 G1 Beverstedt Ger.
43 H3 Beverungen Ger.
42 C2 Beverwijk Neth.
42 F5 Bexbach Ger.
39 H7 Bexhill U.K.
18 B3 Beyānlū Iran
16 C3 Bey Dağları mts Turkey
16 B1 Beykoz Turkey
54 B4 Beyla Guinea
17 L2 Beyläqan Azer.
16 C1 Beypazarı Turkey
16 F2 Beypınarı Turkey
21 A4 Beypore India
Beyrouth see Beirut
16 C3 Beyşehir Turkey
16 C3 Beyşehir Gölü l. Turkey
51 F6 Beysug r. Rus. Fed.
17 J3 Beytüşşebap Turkey
18 E3 Bezameh Iran
50 J3 Bezbozhnik Rus. Fed.
50 D3 Bezhanitsy Rus. Fed.
50 F3 Bezhetsk Rus. Fed.
44 F5 Béziers France
Bezwada see Vijayawada
22 B4 Bhabhar India
23 E4 Bhabua India
22 B5 Bhadar r. India
23 F4 Bhadgaon Nepal
23 E4 Bhadohi India
22 C3 Bhadra India
21 C2 Bhadrachalam India
Bhadrachalam Road Sta. see Kottagudem
23 F5 Bhadrakh India
21 A3 Bhadra Reservoir India
21 A3 Bhadravati India
22 A3 Bhag Pak.
22 D2 Bhaga r. India
23 F4 Bhagalpur India
23 G5 Bhagirathi r. India
22 D5 Bhainsdehi India
23 G4 Bhairab Bazar Bangl.
23 E4 Bhairawa Nepal
21 B2 Bhalki India
24 B4 Bhamo Myanmar
21 C2 Bhamragarh India
22 D4 Bhander India
23 F6 Bhanjanagar India
22 C4 Bhanpura India
22 D5 Bhanrer Range h. India
22 D4 Bharatpur India
23 H4 Bhareli r. India
19 F5 Bhari r. Pak.
22 C5 Bharuch India
23 E5 Bhatapara India
21 A3 Bhatkal India
23 G5 Bhatpara India
21 B4 Bhavani India
21 B4 Bhavani r. India
22 C5 Bhavnagar India
22 C3 Bhawana Pak.
23 E6 Bhawanipatna India
59 J3 Bhekuzulu S. Africa
23 E3 Bheri r. Nepal
22 C4 Bhilwara India
21 B2 Bhima r. India
21 C2 Bhīmavaram India
22 D4 Bhind India
22 C4 Bhindar India
23 E4 Bhinga India
22 C4 Bhinmal India
22 D3 Bhiwani India
23 F4 Bhojpur Nepal
21 B2 Bhongir India
59 H5 Bhongweni S. Africa
22 D5 Bhopal India
21 C2 Bhopalpatnam India
21 A2 Bhor India
23 F5 Bhuban India
23 F5 Bhubaneshwar India
22 B5 Bhuj India
22 C5 Bhusawal India
10 K7 Bhutan country Asia
22 B4 Bhuttewala India
18 E5 Biābān mts Iran
22 C2 Biafo Gl. gl. Pak.
25 F7 Biak Indon.
25 F7 Biak i. Indon.
47 L4 Biała Podlaska Pol.
46 G4 Białogard Pol.
47 L4 Białystok Pol.
54 B4 Biankouma Côte d'Ivoire
30 B1 Bianzhao China
18 D2 Biārjmand Iran
44 D5 Biarritz France
18 B5 Bi'ār Tabrāk well S. Arabia
46 D7 Biasca Switz.
28 G3 Bibai Japan
57 B5 Bibala Angola
8 G4 Bibbenluke Austr.
48 D3 Bibbiena Italy
46 D6 Biberach an der Riß Ger.
23 G4 Bibiyana r. Bangl.
43 G5 Biblis Ger.
16 C2 Biçer Turkey
39 F6 Bicester U.K.
65 G4 Biche, Lac la l. Can.
51 G7 Bichvint'a Georgia
6 D3 Bickerton I. i. Austr.
39 D7 Bickleigh U.K.
75 G2 Bicknell U.S.A.
57 B5 Bicuari, Parque Nacional do nat. park Angola
54 C4 Bida Nigeria
31 A5 Bidadari, Tg pt Malaysia
18 D4 Bida Khabit Iran
21 B2 Bidar India
19 E6 Bidbid Oman
81 H3 Biddeford U.S.A.
42 D2 Biddinghuizen Neth.
40 C4 Bidean Nam Bian mt U.K.
39 C6 Bideford U.K.
39 C6 Bideford Bay b. U.K.
47 L4 Biebrza r. Pol.
43 G4 Biedenkopf Ger.
46 C7 Biel Switz.
46 H5 Bielawa Pol.
43 G2 Bielefeld Ger.
48 C2 Biella Italy
47 J6 Bielsko-Biała Pol.
47 L4 Bielsk Podlaski Pol.
43 J1 Bienenbüttel Ger.
32 C3 Biên Hoa Vietnam
Bienne see Biel
66 F2 Bienville, Lac l. Can.
42 C3 Biesbosch, Nationaal Park de nat. park Neth.
59 F3 Biesiesvlei S. Africa
43 H6 Bietigheim-Bissingen Ger.
42 D5 Bièvre Belgium
56 B4 Bifoun Gabon
67 J3 Big r. Can.
74 A2 Big r. U.S.A.
51 C7 Biga Turkey
16 B2 Bigadiç Turkey
49 M5 Biga Yarımadası pen. Turkey
68 D2 Big Bay U.S.A.
68 D3 Big Bay de Noc b. U.S.A.
74 D4 Big Bear Lake U.S.A.
72 E2 Big Belt Mts mts U.S.A.
59 J3 Big Bend Swaziland
77 C6 Big Bend Nat. Park U.S.A.
77 F5 Big Black r. U.S.A.
39 D7 Bigbury-on-Sea U.K.
79 D7 Big Cypress Nat. Preserve res. U.S.A.
68 C3 Big Eau Pleine Reservoir U.S.A.
65 L5 Big Falls U.S.A.
65 H4 Biggar Can.
40 E5 Biggar U.K.
64 B3 Bigger, Mt mt Can.
39 G5 Biggleswade U.K.
72 D2 Big Hole r. U.S.A.
72 F2 Bighorn r. U.S.A.
72 E2 Bighorn Canyon Nat. Recreation Area res. U.S.A.
72 F2 Bighorn Mountains U.S.A.
79 F7 Bight, The Bahamas
63 L3 Big Island i. N.W.T. Can.
64 F2 Big Island i. Can.
81 K2 Big Lake l. U.S.A.
54 A3 Bignona Senegal
80 D6 Big Otter r. U.S.A.
74 C3 Big Pine U.S.A.
68 E4 Big Rapids U.S.A.
68 C3 Big Rib r. U.S.A.
65 H4 Big River Can.
68 D3 Big Sable Pt pt U.S.A.
64 C2 Big Salmon r. Can.
65 K3 Big Sand Lake l. Can.
75 F4 Big Sandy r. U.S.A.
76 D2 Big Sioux r. U.S.A.
74 D2 Big Smokey Valley v. U.S.A.
77 C5 Big Spring U.S.A.
76 C3 Big Springs U.S.A.
80 B6 Big Stone Gap U.S.A.
74 B3 Big Sur U.S.A.
72 E2 Big Timber U.S.A.
66 C3 Big Trout Lake Can.
66 C3 Big Trout Lake l. Can.
75 G3 Big Water U.S.A.
69 H3 Bigwin Can.
48 F2 Bihać Bos.-Herz.
23 F4 Bihar div. India
23 F4 Bihar Sharif India
28 J3 Bihoro Japan
47 L7 Bihor, Vârful mt Romania
54 A3 Bijagós, Arquipélago dos is Guinea-Bissau
22 C4 Bijainagar India
21 A2 Bijapur India
18 B3 Bījār Iran
21 C2 Bijarpur India
49 H2 Bijeljina Bos.-Herz.
49 H3 Bijelo Polje Yugo.
27 B5 Bijie China
19 E5 Bijnābād Iran
23 G4 Bijni India
22 D3 Bijnor India
22 B3 Bijnot Pak.
22 C3 Bikaner India
24 F2 Bikin Rus. Fed.
28 D1 Bikin r. Rus. Fed.
4 H4 Bikini i. Marshall Is
56 B4 Bikoro Congo(Zaire)
26 B3 Bikou China
22 C4 Bilara India

85 E4 **Brazil** *country* S. America
96 H7 **Brazil Basin** *sea feature* Atl. Ocean
77 D5 **Brazos** *r.* U.S.A.
56 B4 **Brazzaville** Congo
49 H2 **Brčko** Bos.-Herz.
9 A6 **Breaksea Sd** *in.* N.Z.
9 E1 **Bream Bay** *b.* N.Z.
9 E1 **Bream Head** *hd* N.Z.
39 C6 **Brechfa** U.K.
40 F4 **Brechin** U.K.
42 C3 **Brecht** Belgium
76 D2 **Breckenridge** *MN* U.S.A.
77 D5 **Breckenridge** *TX* U.S.A.
46 H6 **Břeclav** Czech Rep.
39 D6 **Brecon** U.K.
39 D6 **Brecon Beacons** *h.* U.K.
39 D6 **Brecon Beacons National Park** U.K.
42 C3 **Breda** Neth.
58 D7 **Bredasdorp** S. Africa
8 G3 **Bredbo** Austr.
43 L2 **Breddin** Ger.
42 E3 **Bredevoort** Neth.
36 O3 **Bredviken** Norway
42 D3 **Bree** Belgium
80 D5 **Breezewood** U.S.A.
47 D6 **Bregenz** Austria
36 B4 **Breiðafjörður** *b.* Iceland
36 F4 **Breiðdalsvík** Iceland
43 G4 **Breidenbach** Ger.
46 C6 **Breisach am Rhein** Ger.
43 J1 **Breitenfelde** Ger.
43 J5 **Breitengüßbach** Ger.
36 S1 **Breivikbotn** Norway
87 J6 **Brejinho de Nazaré** Brazil
36 L5 **Brekstad** Norway
43 G1 **Bremen** Ger.
79 C5 **Bremen** *GA* U.S.A.
68 D5 **Bremen** *IN* U.S.A.
43 G1 **Bremerhaven** Ger.
72 B2 **Bremerton** U.S.A.
43 H1 **Bremervörde** Ger.
42 F4 **Bremm** Ger.
77 D6 **Brenham** U.S.A.
36 N4 **Brenna** Norway
46 E7 **Brenner Pass** Austria/Italy
69 H2 **Brent** Can.
48 D2 **Brenta** *r.* Italy
39 H6 **Brentwood** U.K.
74 B3 **Brentwood** *CA* U.S.A.
81 G4 **Brentwood** *NY* U.S.A.
48 D2 **Brescia** Italy
48 D1 **Bressanone** Italy
40 □ **Bressay** *i.* U.K.
44 D3 **Bressuire** France
51 B4 **Brest** Belarus
44 B2 **Brest** France
44 C2 **Bretagne** *reg.* France
42 A5 **Breteuil** France
77 F6 **Breton Sound** *b.* U.S.A.
9 E1 **Brett, Cape** *c.* N.Z.
43 G5 **Bretten** Ger.
39 E4 **Bretton** U.K.
79 D5 **Brevard** U.S.A.
87 H4 **Breves** Brazil
68 E2 **Brevort** U.S.A.
6 E4 **Brewarrina** Austr.
81 J2 **Brewer** U.S.A.
72 C1 **Brewster** U.S.A.
77 G6 **Brewton** U.S.A.
59 H3 **Breyten** S. Africa
Brezhnev *see* **Naberezhnyye Chelny**
47 J6 **Brezno** Slovakia
48 G2 **Brezovo Polje** *h.* Croatia
56 C3 **Bria** C.A.R.
44 H4 **Briançon** France
8 F3 **Bribbaree** Austr.
51 C5 **Briceni** Moldova
44 H4 **Bric Froid** *mt* France/Italy
41 C5 **Bride** *r.* Rep. of Ireland
75 G1 **Bridgeland** U.S.A.
39 D6 **Bridgend** U.K.
40 D4 **Bridge of Orchy** U.K.
74 C2 **Bridgeport** *CA* U.S.A.
81 G4 **Bridgeport** *CT* U.S.A.
76 C3 **Bridgeport** *NE* U.S.A.
72 E2 **Bridger** U.S.A.
72 F3 **Bridger Peak** *summit* U.S.A.
81 F5 **Bridgeton** U.S.A.
83 N6 **Bridgetown** Barbados
67 H5 **Bridgewater** Can.
81 K1 **Bridgewater** U.S.A.
8 C5 **Bridgewater, C.** *hd* Austr.
39 E5 **Bridgnorth** U.K.
81 H2 **Bridgton** U.S.A.
39 D6 **Bridgwater** U.K.
39 D6 **Bridgwater Bay** *b.* U.K.
38 G3 **Bridlington** U.K.
38 G3 **Bridlington Bay** *b.* U.K.
39 E7 **Bridport** U.K.
46 C7 **Brig** Switz.
38 G4 **Brigg** U.K.
72 D3 **Brigham City** U.S.A.
8 F4 **Bright** Austr.
39 J6 **Brightlingsea** U.K.
69 J3 **Brighton** Can.
9 C6 **Brighton** N.Z.
39 G7 **Brighton** U.K.
69 F4 **Brighton** U.S.A.
44 H5 **Brignoles** France
54 A3 **Brikama** The Gambia
43 G3 **Brilon** Ger.
48 G4 **Brindisi** Italy
91 D1 **Brinkmann** Arg.
8 B2 **Brinkworth** Austr.
67 H4 **Brion, Île** *i.* Can.
44 F4 **Brioude** France
67 F3 **Brisay** Can.
7 F4 **Brisbane** Austr.
81 K1 **Bristol** Can.
39 E6 **Bristol** U.K.
81 G4 **Bristol** *CT* U.S.A.
81 F4 **Bristol** *PA* U.S.A.
80 B6 **Bristol** *TN* U.S.A.
62 B4 **Bristol Bay** *b.* U.S.A.
39 C6 **Bristol Channel** *est.* U.K.
92 C1 **Bristol I.** *i.* Atl. Ocean
75 E4 **Bristol Lake** *l.* U.S.A.
75 E4 **Bristol Mts** *mts* U.S.A.
92 A2 **British Antarctic Territory** *reg.* Ant.
64 D3 **British Columbia** *div.* Can.
63 K1 **British Empire Range** *mts* Can.
10 J10 **British Ind. Ocean Territory** *terr.* Ind. Ocean
59 G2 **Brits** S. Africa
58 E5 **Britstown** S. Africa
Brittany *reg. see* **Bretagne**
44 E4 **Brive-la-Gaillarde** France
45 E1 **Briviesca** Spain
39 D7 **Brixham** U.K.
46 H6 **Brno** Czech Rep.
79 D5 **Broad** *r.* U.S.A.
81 F3 **Broadalbin** U.S.A.
66 E3 **Broadback** *r.* Can.
8 E4 **Broadford** Austr.
41 C5 **Broadford** Rep. of Ireland
40 C3 **Broadford** U.K.
40 E5 **Broad Law** *h.* U.K.
39 J6 **Broadstairs** U.K.
72 F2 **Broadus** U.S.A.
65 J4 **Broadview** Can.
76 C3 **Broadwater** U.S.A.
9 D1 **Broadwood** N.Z.
37 S8 **Broceni** Latvia
65 J3 **Brochet** Can.
65 J3 **Brochet, Lac** *l.* Can.
43 J3 **Brocken** *mt* Ger.
62 G2 **Brock I.** *i.* Can.
80 E3 **Brockport** U.S.A.
81 H3 **Brockton** U.S.A.
69 K3 **Brockville** Can.
69 F4 **Brockway** *MI* U.S.A.
80 D4 **Brockway** *PA* U.S.A.
63 K2 **Brodeur Peninsula** *pen.* Can.
68 C4 **Brodhead** U.S.A.
40 C5 **Brodick** U.K.
47 J4 **Brodnica** Pol.
51 C5 **Brody** Ukr.
77 E4 **Broken Arrow** U.S.A.
8 H2 **Broken B.** *b.* Austr.
76 D3 **Broken Bow** *NE* U.S.A.
77 E5 **Broken Bow** *OK* U.S.A.
8 C1 **Broken Hill** Austr.
43 J2 **Brome** Ger.
39 G6 **Bromley** U.K.
39 E5 **Bromsgrove** U.K.
37 L8 **Brønderslev** Denmark
59 H2 **Bronkhorstspruit** S. Africa
36 N4 **Brønnøysund** Norway
68 E5 **Bronson** U.S.A.
39 J5 **Brooke** U.K.
31 A4 **Brooke's Point** Phil.
68 C4 **Brookfield** U.S.A.
77 F6 **Brookhaven** U.S.A.
72 A3 **Brookings** *OR* U.S.A.
76 D2 **Brookings** *SD* U.S.A.
81 H3 **Brookline** U.S.A.
68 A5 **Brooklyn** *IA* U.S.A.
68 B5 **Brooklyn** *IL* U.S.A.
76 E2 **Brooklyn Center** U.S.A.
80 D6 **Brookneal** U.S.A.
65 G4 **Brooks** Can.
74 A2 **Brooks** *CA* U.S.A.
81 J2 **Brooks** *ME* U.S.A.
92 B3 **Brooks, C.** *c.* Ant.
62 D3 **Brooks Range** *mts* U.S.A.
79 D6 **Brooksville** U.S.A.
80 D4 **Brookville** U.S.A.
6 C3 **Broome** Austr.
40 C3 **Broom, Loch** *in.* U.K.
40 E2 **Brora** U.K.
37 O9 **Brösarp** Sweden
41 D4 **Brosna** *r.* Rep. of Ireland
72 B3 **Brothers** U.S.A.
27 □ **Brothers, The** *is* H.K. China
38 E3 **Brough** U.K.
40 E1 **Brough Head** *hd* U.K.
41 E3 **Broughshane** U.K.
8 B2 **Broughton** *r.* Austr.
63 M3 **Broughton Island** Can.
47 P5 **Brovary** Ukr.
37 L8 **Brovst** Denmark
77 C5 **Brownfield** U.S.A.
72 D1 **Browning** U.S.A.
8 B2 **Brown, Mt** *mt* Austr.
68 D6 **Brownsburg** U.S.A.
81 F5 **Browns Mills** U.S.A.
79 B5 **Brownsville** *TN* U.S.A.
77 D7 **Brownsville** *TX* U.S.A.
81 J2 **Brownville** U.S.A.
81 J2 **Brownville Junction** U.S.A.
77 D6 **Brownwood** U.S.A.
47 O4 **Brozha** Belarus
44 F1 **Bruay-en-Artois** France
68 C2 **Bruce Crossing** U.S.A.
66 D4 **Bruce Pen.** *pen.* Can.
69 G3 **Bruce Peninsula National Park** Can.
43 G5 **Bruchsal** Ger.
43 L2 **Brück** Ger.
46 G7 **Bruck an der Mur** Austria
39 E6 **Brue** *r.* U.K.
42 B3 **Bruges** Belgium
Brugge *see* **Bruges**
43 G5 **Brühl** *Baden-Württemberg* Ger.
42 E4 **Brühl** *Nordrhein-Westfalen* Ger.
75 G2 **Bruin Pt** *summit* U.S.A.
23 J3 **Bruint** India
58 C2 **Brukkaros** Namibia
68 B2 **Brule** U.S.A.
42 C5 **Brûly** Belgium
90 E1 **Brumado** Brazil
37 M6 **Brumunddal** Norway
43 K2 **Brunau** Ger.
72 D3 **Bruneau** U.S.A.
72 D3 **Bruneau** *r.* U.S.A.
11 N9 **Brunei** *country* Asia
36 O5 **Brunflo** Sweden
48 D1 **Brunico** Italy
9 C5 **Brunner, L.** *l.* N.Z.
65 H4 **Bruno** Can.
46 D4 **Brunsbüttel** Ger.
79 D6 **Brunswick** *GA* U.S.A.
81 J3 **Brunswick** *ME* U.S.A.
80 C4 **Brunswick** *OH* U.S.A.
88 B8 **Brunswick, Península de** *pen.* Chile
46 H6 **Bruntál** Czech Rep.
92 C3 **Brunt Ice Shelf** *ice feature* Ant.
59 J4 **Bruntville** S. Africa
6 E6 **Bruny I.** *i.* Austr.
72 G3 **Brush** U.S.A.
42 C4 **Brussels** Belgium
69 G4 **Brussels** Can.
68 D3 **Brussels** U.S.A.
47 O5 **Brusyliv** Ukr.
8 F4 **Bruthen** Austr.
Bruxelles *see* **Brussels**
80 A4 **Bryan** *OH* U.S.A.
77 D6 **Bryan** *TX* U.S.A.
92 A3 **Bryan Coast** *coastal area* Ant.
8 B2 **Bryan, Mt** *h.* Austr.
50 E4 **Bryansk** Rus. Fed.
50 E4 **Bryanskaya Oblast'** *div.* Rus. Fed.
51 H6 **Bryanskoye** Rus. Fed.
75 F3 **Bryce Canyon Nat. Park** U.S.A.
75 H5 **Bryce Mt** *mt* U.S.A.
37 J7 **Bryne** Norway
51 F6 **Bryukhovetskaya** Rus. Fed.
46 H5 **Brzeg** Pol.
7 F2 **Buala** Solomon Is
54 A3 **Buba** Guinea-Bissau
17 M7 **Būbīyān I.** *i.* Kuwait
31 B5 **Bubuan** *i.* Phil.
16 C3 **Bucak** Turkey
89 B3 **Bucaramanga** Col.
31 C4 **Bucas Grande** *i.* Phil.
8 G4 **Buchan** Austr.
54 A4 **Buchanan** Liberia
68 D5 **Buchanan** *MI* U.S.A.
80 D6 **Buchanan** *VA* U.S.A.
77 D6 **Buchanan, L.** *l.* U.S.A.
63 L2 **Buchan Gulf** *b.* Can.
67 J4 **Buchans** Can.
49 M2 **Bucharest** Romania
43 J1 **Büchen** Ger.
43 H5 **Buchen (Odenwald)** Ger.
43 L1 **Buchholz** Ger.
43 H1 **Bucholz in der Nordheide** Ger.
74 B4 **Buchon, Point** *pt* U.S.A.
47 M7 **Bucin, Pasul** *pass* Romania
8 E1 **Buckambool Mt** *h.* Austr.
43 H2 **Bückeburg** Ger.
43 H2 **Bücken** Ger.
75 F5 **Buckeye** U.S.A.
80 B5 **Buckeye Lake** *l.* U.S.A.
80 C5 **Buckhannon** U.S.A.
80 C5 **Buckhannon** *r.* U.S.A.
40 E4 **Buckhaven** U.K.
69 H3 **Buckhorn** Can.
75 H5 **Buckhorn** U.S.A.
69 H3 **Buckhorn Lake** *l.* Can.
80 B6 **Buckhorn Lake** *l.* U.S.A.
40 F3 **Buckie** U.K.
69 K3 **Buckingham** Can.
39 G5 **Buckingham** U.K.
80 D6 **Buckingham** U.S.A.
6 D3 **Buckingham Bay** *b.* Austr.
6 E4 **Buckland Tableland** *reg.* Austr.
92 A6 **Buckle I.** *i.* Ant.
75 F4 **Buckskin Mts** *mts* U.S.A.
74 B2 **Bucks Mt** *mt* U.S.A.
81 J2 **Bucksport** U.S.A.
43 L2 **Bückwitz** Ger.
București *see* **Bucharest**
80 B4 **Bucyrus** U.S.A.
47 P4 **Buda-Kashalyova** Belarus
47 J7 **Budapest** Hungary
22 D3 **Budaun** India
8 E1 **Budda** Austr.
92 C6 **Budd Coast** *coastal area* Ant.
40 F4 **Buddon Ness** *pt* U.K.
48 C4 **Buddusò** *Sardinia* Italy
39 C7 **Bude** U.K.
77 F6 **Bude** U.S.A.
51 H6 **Budennovsk** Rus. Fed.
43 H4 **Büdingen** Ger.
22 D5 **Budni** India
50 E3 **Budogoshch'** Rus. Fed.
23 H2 **Budongquan** China
48 C4 **Budoni** *Sardinia* Italy
54 C4 **Buea** Cameroon
74 B4 **Buellton** U.S.A.
91 D2 **Buena Esperanza** Arg.
89 A4 **Buenaventura** Col.
82 C3 **Buenaventura** Mex.
89 A4 **Buenaventure, B. de** *b.* Col.
73 F4 **Buena Vista** *CO* U.S.A.
80 D6 **Buena Vista** *VA* U.S.A.
45 E2 **Buendia, Embalse de** *resr* Spain
91 B4 **Bueno** *r.* Chile
91 E2 **Buenos Aires** Arg.
91 E3 **Buenos Aires** *div.* Arg.
88 B7 **Buenos Aires, L.** *l.* Arg./Chile
88 C7 **Buen Pasto** Arg.
80 D3 **Buffalo** *NY* U.S.A.
77 D4 **Buffalo** *OK* U.S.A.
76 C2 **Buffalo** *SD* U.S.A.
77 D6 **Buffalo** *TX* U.S.A.
68 B3 **Buffalo** *WI* U.S.A.
72 F2 **Buffalo** *WY* U.S.A.
64 G3 **Buffalo** *r.* Can.
68 B3 **Buffalo** *r.* U.S.A.
64 F3 **Buffalo Head Hills** *h.* Can.
64 F2 **Buffalo Lake** *l.* Can.
8 F4 **Buffalo, Mt** *mt* Austr.
65 H3 **Buffalo Narrows** Can.
58 B4 **Buffels** *watercourse* S. Africa
59 G1 **Buffels Drift** S. Africa
79 D5 **Buford** U.S.A.
49 L2 **Buftea** Romania
47 K4 **Bug** *r.* Pol.
89 A4 **Buga** Col.
89 A3 **Bugalagrande** Col.
8 G1 **Bugaldie** Austr.
18 D2 **Bugdayli** Turkm.
33 D4 **Bugel, Tanjung** *pt* Indon.
42 C3 **Buggenhout** Belgium
48 G2 **Bugojno** Bos.-Herz.
31 A4 **Bugsuk** *i.* Phil.
31 B2 **Buguey** Phil.
18 D4 **Būhābād** Iran
17 J5 **Buḩayrat ath Tharthār** *l.* Iraq
17 K4 **Buḩayrat Shārī** *l.* Iraq
57 D5 **Buhera** Zimbabwe
31 B3 **Buhi** Phil.
72 D3 **Buhl** *ID* U.S.A.
68 A2 **Buhl** *MN* U.S.A.
17 J3 **Bühtan** *r.* Turkey
47 N7 **Buhuşi** Romania
39 D5 **Builth Wells** U.K.
54 B4 **Bui National Park** Ghana
50 J4 **Buinsk** Rus. Fed.
17 L4 **Bu'in Soflā** Iran
24 D2 **Buir Nur** *l.* Mongolia
57 B6 **Buitepos** Namibia
49 J3 **Bujanovac** Yugo.
56 C4 **Bujumbura** Burundi
24 D1 **Bukachacha** Rus. Fed.
7 F2 **Buka I.** *i.* P.N.G.
18 D4 **Būkand** Iran
56 C4 **Bukavu** Congo(Zaire)
19 G2 **Bukhara** Uzbek.
31 C6 **Bukide** *i.* Indon.
32 □ **Bukit Batok** Sing.
32 B5 **Bukit Fraser** Malaysia
32 □ **Bukit Panjang** Sing.
32 □ **Bukit Timah** Sing.
33 B3 **Bukittinggi** Indon.
56 D4 **Bukoba** Tanz.
32 □ **Bukom, P.** *i.* Sing.
25 F7 **Bula** Indon.
50 J4 **Bula** *r.* Rus. Fed.
46 D7 **Bülach** Switz.
8 J2 **Bulahdelal** Austr.
31 B3 **Bulan** Phil.
16 G1 **Bulancak** Turkey
22 D3 **Bulandshahr** India
17 J2 **Bulanık** Turkey
57 C6 **Bulawayo** Zimbabwe
16 F3 **Bulbul** Syria
16 B2 **Buldan** Turkey
22 D5 **Buldana** India
59 J2 **Bulembu** Swaziland
26 B1 **Bulgan** Mongolia
24 C2 **Bulgan** Mongolia
35 H4 **Bulgaria** *country* Europe
9 D4 **Buller** *r.* N.Z.
8 F4 **Buller, Mt** *mt* Austr.
75 E4 **Bullhead City** U.S.A.
74 D4 **Bullion Mts** *mts* U.S.A.
58 B2 **Büllsport** Namibia
32 □ **Buloh, P.** *i.* Sing.
8 D4 **Buloke, Lake** *l.* Austr.
59 G4 **Bultfontein** S. Africa
31 C5 **Buluan** Phil.
6 C2 **Bulukumba** Indon.
13 O2 **Bulun** Rus. Fed.
56 B4 **Bulungu** *Bandundu* Congo(Zaire)
56 C4 **Bulungu** *Kasai-Occidental* Congo(Zaire)
19 G2 **Bulungur** Uzbek.
31 C3 **Bulusan** Phil.
56 C3 **Bumba** Congo(Zaire)
26 B1 **Bumbat Sum** China
75 F4 **Bumble Bee** U.S.A.
31 A5 **Bum-Bum** *i.* Malaysia
56 B4 **Buna** Congo(Zaire)
56 D3 **Buna** Kenya
56 D4 **Bunazi** Tanz.
41 C2 **Bunbeg** Rep. of Ireland
6 B5 **Bunbury** Austr.
41 E5 **Bunclody** Rep. of Ireland
41 D2 **Buncrana** Rep. of Ireland
56 D4 **Bunda** Tanz.
6 F4 **Bundaberg** Austr.
22 C4 **Bundi** India
41 C3 **Bundoran** Rep. of Ireland
23 F5 **Bundu** India
39 J5 **Bungay** U.K.
32 B2 **Bung Boraphet** *l.* Thai.
8 G3 **Bungendore** Austr.
92 C6 **Bunger Hills** *h.* Ant.
29 C8 **Bungo-suidō** *chan.* Japan
56 D3 **Bunia** Congo(Zaire)
56 C4 **Bunianga** Congo(Zaire)
8 D4 **Buninyong** Austr.
54 D3 **Buni-Yadi** Nigeria
22 C2 **Bunji** Jammu and Kashmir
75 E3 **Bunkerville** U.S.A.
77 E6 **Bunkie** U.S.A.
79 D6 **Bunnell** U.S.A.
16 E2 **Bünyan** Turkey
31 A6 **Bunyu** *i.* Indon.
18 C4 **Bu ol Kheyr** Iran
32 D2 **Buôn Hô** Vietnam
32 D2 **Buôn Mê Thuôt** Vietnam
13 P2 **Buorkhaya, Guba** *b.* Rus. Fed.
20 C4 **Buqayq** S. Arabia
56 D4 **Bura** Kenya
22 E3 **Burang** China
90 E2 **Buranhaém** *r.* Brazil
56 E3 **Burao** Somalia
31 C4 **Burauen** Phil.
20 B4 **Buraydah** S. Arabia
43 G4 **Burbach** Ger.
74 C4 **Burbank** U.S.A.
8 F2 **Burcher** Austr.
19 G2 **Burdalyk** Turkm.
16 C3 **Burdur** Turkey
56 D2 **Burē** Eth.
39 J5 **Bure** *r.* U.K.
36 R4 **Bureå** Sweden
24 F1 **Bureinskiy Khrebet** *mts* Rus. Fed.
16 D6 **Būr Fu'ad** Egypt
49 M3 **Burgas** Bulg.
79 E5 **Burgaw** U.S.A.
43 K2 **Burg bei Magdeburg** Ger.
43 J5 **Burgbernheim** Ger.
43 J2 **Burgdorf** Ger.
67 J4 **Burgeo** Can.
59 G5 **Burgersdorp** S. Africa
59 J2 **Burgersfort** S. Africa
39 G7 **Burgess Hill** U.K.
43 H4 **Burghaun** Ger.
46 F6 **Burghausen** Ger.
40 E3 **Burghead** U.K.
42 B3 **Burgh-Haamstede** Neth.
48 F6 **Burgio, Serra di** *h. Sicily* Italy
43 L5 **Burglengenfeld** Ger.
45 E1 **Burgos** Spain
43 L4 **Burgstädt** Ger.
37 Q8 **Burgsvik** Sweden
Burgundy *reg. see* **Bourgogne**
24 B3 **Burhan Budai Shan** *mts* China
49 M5 **Burhaniye** Turkey
22 D5 **Burhanpur** India
23 E5 **Burhar-Dhanpuri** India
23 F4 **Burhi Gandak** *r.* India
31 B3 **Burias** *i.* Phil.
23 H4 **Buri Dihing** *r.* India
23 E4 **Buri Gandak** *r.* Nepal
67 J4 **Burin Peninsula** *pen.* Can.
32 B2 **Buriram** Thai.
87 K5 **Buriti Bravo** Brazil
90 C1 **Buritis** Brazil
19 G4 **Burj** Pak.
92 A3 **Burke I.** *i.* Ant.
9 C6 **Burke Pass** N.Z.
6 D3 **Burketown** Austr.
52 D4 **Burkina** *country* Africa
69 H3 **Burk's Falls** Can.
72 D3 **Burley** U.S.A.
69 H4 **Burlington** Can.
76 C4 **Burlington** *CO* U.S.A.
68 B5 **Burlington** *IA* U.S.A.
68 D5 **Burlington** *IN* U.S.A.
81 J2 **Burlington** *ME* U.S.A.
81 G2 **Burlington** *VT* U.S.A.
68 C4 **Burlington** *WI* U.S.A.
Burma *country see* **Myanmar**
77 D6 **Burnet** U.S.A.
72 B3 **Burney** U.S.A.
81 J2 **Burnham** U.S.A.
6 E6 **Burnie** Austr.
38 G3 **Burniston** U.K.
38 E4 **Burnley** U.K.
72 C3 **Burns** U.S.A.
65 H1 **Burnside** *r.* Can.
62 F4 **Burns Lake** Can.
80 C5 **Burnsville Lake** *l.* U.S.A.
79 F7 **Burnt Ground** Bahamas
40 E4 **Burntisland** U.K.
67 H3 **Burnt Lake** *l.* Can.
65 K3 **Burntwood** *r.* Can.
65 J3 **Burnt Wood Lake** *l.* Can.
8 D3 **Buronga** Austr.
12 K5 **Burqin** China
16 G5 **Burqu'** Jordan
8 B2 **Burra** Austr.
40 □ **Burravoe** U.K.
40 F2 **Burray** *i.* U.K.
49 J4 **Burrel** Albania
8 G2 **Burrendong Reservoir** Austr.
8 H3 **Burrewarra Pt** *pt* Austr.
45 F3 **Burriana** Spain
8 G3 **Burrinjuck** Austr.
8 G3 **Burrinjuck Reservoir** Austr.
80 B5 **Burr Oak Reservoir** U.S.A.
82 D3 **Burro, Serranías del** *mts* Mex.
40 D6 **Burrow Head** *hd* U.K.
75 G2 **Burrville** U.S.A.
16 B1 **Bursa** Turkey
55 F2 **Bûr Safâga** Egypt
Bûr Sa'îd *see* **Port Said**
43 G5 **Bürstadt** Ger.
Bur Sudan *see* **Port Sudan**
8 C2 **Burta** Austr.
68 E3 **Burt Lake** *l.* U.S.A.
69 F4 **Burton** U.S.A.
66 E3 **Burton, Lac** *l.* Can.
41 C3 **Burtonport** Rep. of Ireland
39 F5 **Burton upon Trent** U.K.
36 R4 **Burträsk** Sweden
81 K1 **Burtts Corner** Can.
8 D2 **Burtundy** Austr.
25 E7 **Buru** *i.* Indon.
16 C6 **Burullus, Bahra el** *lag.* Egypt
53 G6 **Burundi** *country* Africa
56 C4 **Bururi** Burundi
64 B2 **Burwash Landing** Can.
40 F2 **Burwick** U.K.
51 E5 **Buryn'** Ukr.
39 H5 **Bury St Edmunds** U.K.
22 C2 **Burzil Pass** Jammu and Kashmir
56 C4 **Busanga** Congo(Zaire)
41 E2 **Bush** *r.* U.K.
18 C4 **Būshehr** Iran
23 E2 **Bushêngcaka** China
56 D4 **Bushenyi** Uganda
Bushire *see* **Būshehr**
41 E2 **Bushmills** U.K.
68 B5 **Bushnell** U.S.A.
56 C3 **Businga** Congo(Zaire)
32 □ **Busing, P.** *i.* Sing.
16 F5 **Buşrá ash Shām** Syria
6 B5 **Busselton** Austr.
42 D2 **Bussum** Neth.
77 C7 **Bustamante** Mex.
48 C2 **Busto Arsizio** Italy
31 A3 **Busuanga** Phil.
31 A3 **Busuanga** *i.* Phil.
56 C3 **Buta** Congo(Zaire)
32 A4 **Butang Group** *is* Thai.
91 C3 **Buta Ranquil** Arg.
56 C4 **Butare** Rwanda
95 G5 **Butaritari** *i.* Pac. Oc.
8 A2 **Bute** Austr.
40 C5 **Bute** *i.* U.K.
64 D4 **Butedale** Can.
64 D4 **Bute In.** *in.* Can.
40 C5 **Bute, Sound of** *chan.* U.K.
59 H4 **Butha Buthe** Lesotho
43 G1 **Butjadingen** *reg.* Ger.
68 E5 **Butler** *IN* U.S.A.
80 D4 **Butler** *PA* U.S.A.
41 D3 **Butlers Bridge** Rep. of Ireland
25 E7 **Buton** *i.* Indon.
43 L1 **Bützow** Ger.
72 D2 **Butte** U.S.A.
43 K3 **Buttelstedt** Ger.
74 B1 **Butte Meadows** U.S.A.
33 B1 **Butterworth** Malaysia
59 H6 **Butterworth** S. Africa
41 C5 **Buttevant** Rep. of Ireland
64 D5 **Buttle L.** *l.* Can.
40 B2 **Butt of Lewis** *hd* U.K.
63 J4 **Button Bay** *b.* Can.
74 C4 **Buttonwillow** U.S.A.
31 C4 **Butuan** Phil.
27 B5 **Butuo** China
51 G5 **Buturlinovka** Rus. Fed.
23 E4 **Butwal** Nepal
43 G4 **Butzbach** Ger.
56 E3 **Buulobarde** Somalia
56 E4 **Buur Gaabo** Somalia
56 E3 **Buurhabaka** Somalia
23 F4 **Buxar** India
43 H1 **Buxtehude** Ger.
39 F4 **Buxton** U.K.
50 G3 **Buy** Rus. Fed.
68 A1 **Buyck** U.S.A.
51 H7 **Buynaksk** Rus. Fed.
Büyük Ağrı *mt see* **Ararat, Mt**
16 A3 **Büyükmenderes** *r.* Turkey
30 B3 **Buyun Shan** *mt* China
42 C5 **Buzancy** France
49 M2 **Buzău** Romania
57 D5 **Búzi** Moz.
12 G4 **Buzuluk** Rus. Fed.
51 G5 **Buzuluk** *r.* Rus. Fed.
81 H4 **Buzzards Bay** *b.* U.S.A.
23 G4 **Byakar** Bhutan
49 L3 **Byala** Bulg.
49 K3 **Byala Slatina** Bulg.
47 O4 **Byalynichy** Belarus
62 H2 **Byam Martin I.** *i.* Can.
50 D4 **Byarezina** *r.* Belarus
50 C4 **Byaroza** Belarus
16 E4 **Byblos** Lebanon
46 J4 **Bydgoszcz** Pol.
50 D4 **Byerazino** Belarus
72 F4 **Byers** U.S.A.
47 O3 **Byeshankovichy** Belarus
37 K7 **Bygland** Norway
50 D4 **Bykhaw** Belarus
37 K7 **Bykle** Norway
63 L2 **Bylot Island** *i.* Can.
69 G3 **Byng Inlet** Can.
92 B5 **Byrd Gl.** *gl.* Ant.
37 K6 **Byrkjelo** Norway
68 C4 **Byron** *IL* U.S.A.
81 H2 **Byron** *ME* U.S.A.
7 F4 **Byron Bay** Austr.
13 M2 **Byrranga, Gory** *mts* Rus. Fed.
36 R4 **Byske** Sweden
13 P3 **Bytantay** *r.* Rus. Fed.
47 J5 **Bytom** Pol.
46 H3 **Bytów** Pol.
19 E2 **Byuzmeyin** Turkm.

C

88 E3 **Caacupé** Para.
90 A4 **Caaguazú, Cordillera de** *h.* Para.
90 A4 **Caaguazú** Para.
90 A3 **Caarapó** Brazil
90 A4 **Caazapá** Para.
86 C6 **Caballas** Peru
86 D4 **Caballococha** Peru
31 B3 **Cabanatuan** Phil.
67 G4 **Cabano** Can.
56 E2 **Cabdul Qaadir** Somalia
90 A1 **Cabeceira Rio Manso** Brazil
87 M5 **Cabedelo** Brazil
45 D3 **Cabeza del Buey** Spain
86 F7 **Cabezas** Bol.
91 E3 **Cabildo** Arg.
89 C2 **Cabimas** Venez.
56 B4 **Cabinda** Angola
56 B4 **Cabinda** *div.* Angola
72 C1 **Cabinet Mts** *mts* U.S.A.
89 B3 **Cable Way** *pass* Col.
90 D3 **Cabo Frio** Brazil
90 E3 **Cabo Frio, Ilha do** *i.* Brazil
66 E4 **Cabonga, Réservoir** *resr* Can.
77 E4 **Cabool** U.S.A.
7 F4 **Caboolture** Austr.
87 H3 **Cabo Orange, Parque Nacional de** *nat. park* Brazil
86 C4 **Cabo Pantoja** Peru
82 B2 **Caborca** Mex.
69 G3 **Cabot Head** *pt* Can.
67 J4 **Cabot Strait** *str.* Can.
90 D2 **Cabral, Serra do** *mts* Brazil
17 L2 **Cäbrayıl** Azer.
45 H3 **Cabrera** *i.* Spain
45 C1 **Cabrera, Sierra de la** *mts* Spain
45 F3 **Cabriel** *r.* Spain
89 D3 **Cabruta** Venez.
31 B2 **Cabugao** Phil.
88 F3 **Caçador** Brazil
84 C3 **Cacahuatepec** Mex.
49 J3 **Čačak** Yugo.
91 G1 **Caçapava do Sul** Brazil
80 D5 **Cacapon** *r.* U.S.A.
89 B3 **Cácares** Col.
48 C4 **Caccia, Capo** *pt Sardinia* Italy
87 G7 **Cáceres** Brazil
45 C3 **Cáceres** Spain
72 D3 **Cache Peak** *summit* U.S.A.
54 A3 **Cacheu** Guinea-Bissau
88 C3 **Cachi** *r.* Arg.
87 H5 **Cachimbo, Serra do** *h.* Brazil
89 B3 **Cáchira** Col.
90 E1 **Cachoeira** Brazil
90 B2 **Cachoeira Alta** Brazil
91 G1 **Cachoeira do Sul** Brazil
90 E3 **Cachoeiro de Itapemirim** Brazil
54 A3 **Cacine** Guinea-Bissau
87 H3 **Caciporé, Cabo** *pt* Brazil
57 B5 **Cacolo** Angola
56 B4 **Cacongo** Angola
74 D3 **Cactus Range** *mts* U.S.A.
90 B2 **Caçu** Brazil
90 D1 **Caculé** Brazil
47 J6 **Čadca** Slovakia
43 H1 **Cadenberge** Ger.
84 B1 **Cadereyta** Mex.
31 B3 **Cadig Mountains** Phil.
69 H1 **Cadillac** *Que.* Can.
65 H5 **Cadillac** *Sask.* Can.
68 E3 **Cadillac** U.S.A.
31 B4 **Cadiz** Phil.
45 C4 **Cádiz** Spain
45 C4 **Cádiz, Golfo de** *g.* Spain
75 E4 **Cadiz Lake** *l.* U.S.A.
44 D2 **Caen** France
39 C4 **Caernarfon** U.K.
39 C4 **Caernarfon Bay** *b.* U.K.
39 D6 **Caerphilly** U.K.
80 B5 **Caesar Creek Lake** *l.* U.S.A.
16 E5 **Caesarea** Israel
90 D1 **Caetité** Brazil
88 C3 **Cafayate** Arg.
31 B4 **Cagayan** *i.* Phil.
31 B2 **Cagayan** *r.* Phil.
31 C4 **Cagayan de Oro** Phil.
31 B4 **Cagayan Islands** *is* Phil.
48 E3 **Cagli** Italy
48 C5 **Cagliari** *Sardinia* Italy
48 C5 **Cagliari, Golfo di** *b. Sardinia* Italy
89 B4 **Caguán** *r.* Col.
41 B6 **Caha** *h.* Rep. of Ireland
79 C5 **Cahaba** *r.* U.S.A.
41 B6 **Caha Mts** *h.* Rep. of Ireland
41 A6 **Cahermore** Rep. of Ireland
41 D5 **Cahir** Rep. of Ireland
41 A6 **Cahirciveen** Rep. of Ireland
57 D5 **Cahora Bassa, Lago de** *resr* Moz.
41 E5 **Cahore Point** *pt* Rep. of Ireland
44 E4 **Cahors** France
86 C5 **Cahuapanas** Peru
51 D6 **Cahul** Moldova
57 D5 **Caia** Moz.
87 G6 **Caiabis, Serra dos** *h.* Brazil
57 C5 **Caianda** Angola
90 B2 **Caiapó** *r.* Brazil
90 B2 **Caiapônia** Brazil
90 B2 **Caiapó, Serra do** *mts* Brazil
83 J4 **Caibarién** Cuba
32 C3 **Cai Be** Vietnam
89 D3 **Caicara** Venez.
83 K4 **Caicos Is** *is* Turks and Caicos Is
91 B1 **Caimanes** Chile
31 A3 **Caiman Point** *pt* Phil.
45 F2 **Caimodorro** *mt* Spain
32 C3 **Cai Nước** Vietnam
40 E3 **Cairn Gorm** *mt* U.K.
40 E3 **Cairngorm Mountains** U.K.
40 C6 **Cairnryan** U.K.
6 E3 **Cairns** Austr.
40 E3 **Cairn Toul** *mt* U.K.
55 F1 **Cairo** Egypt
79 C6 **Cairo** U.S.A.
48 C2 **Cairo Montenotte** Italy
57 B5 **Caiundo** Angola
86 C5 **Cajamarca** Peru
31 B3 **Cajidiocan** Phil.
48 G1 **Čakovec** Croatia
16 B2 **Çal** Turkey
59 G5 **Cala** S. Africa
54 C4 **Calabar** Nigeria
69 J3 **Calabogie** Can.
89 D2 **Calabozo** Venez.
49 K3 **Calafat** Romania
88 B8 **Calafate** Arg.
31 B3 **Calagua Islands** *is* Phil.
45 F1 **Calahorra** Spain
57 B5 **Calai** Angola
44 E1 **Calais** France
81 K2 **Calais** U.S.A.
86 F5 **Calama** Brazil
88 C2 **Calama** Chile
89 B2 **Calamar** *Bolívar* Col.
89 B4 **Calamar** *Guaviare* Col.
31 A4 **Calamian Group** *is* Phil.
45 F2 **Calamocha** Spain
57 B4 **Calandula** Angola
55 E2 **Calanscio Sand Sea** *des.* Libya
31 B3 **Calapan** Phil.
49 M2 **Călărași** Romania
45 F2 **Calatayud** Spain
31 B3 **Calauag** Phil.
31 B3 **Calavite, Cape** *pt* Phil.
31 A3 **Calawit** *i.* Phil.
31 B2 **Calayan** *i.* Phil.
31 C3 **Calbayog** Phil.
43 K3 **Calbe (Saale)** Ger.
31 C4 **Calbiga** Phil.
91 B4 **Calbuco** Chile
87 L5 **Calcanhar, Ponta do** *pt* Brazil
77 E6 **Calcasieu L.** *l.* U.S.A.
87 H3 **Calçoene** Brazil
23 G5 **Calcutta** India
45 B3 **Caldas da Rainha** Port.
90 C2 **Caldas Novas** Brazil
43 H3 **Calden** Ger.
88 B3 **Caldera** Chile
17 J2 **Çaldıran** Turkey
72 C3 **Caldwell** U.S.A.
80 D3 **Caledon** Can.
58 C7 **Caledon** S. Africa
59 G5 **Caledon** *r.* Lesotho/S. Africa
69 H4 **Caledonia** Can.
68 B4 **Caledonia** U.S.A.
84 B2 **Calera** Mex.
88 C7 **Caleta Olivia** Arg.
75 E5 **Calexico** U.S.A.
38 C3 **Calf of Man** *i.* U.K.
64 G4 **Calgary** Can.
79 C5 **Calhoun** U.S.A.
89 A4 **Cali** Col.
31 C4 **Calicoan** *i.* Phil.
21 A4 **Calicut** India
74 C4 **Caliente** *CA* U.S.A.
75 E3 **Caliente** *NV* U.S.A.
74 B3 **California** *div.* U.S.A.
74 B3 **California Aqueduct** *canal* U.S.A.
82 B2 **California, Golfo de** *g.* Mex.
74 C4 **California Hot Springs** U.S.A.
17 M2 **Cälilabad** Azer.
73 D5 **Calipatria** U.S.A.
74 A2 **Calistoga** U.S.A.
58 D6 **Calitzdorp** S. Africa
84 E2 **Calkiní** Mex.
74 D2 **Callaghan, Mt** *mt* U.S.A.
79 D6 **Callahan** U.S.A.
41 D5 **Callan** Rep. of Ireland
69 H2 **Callander** Can.
40 D4 **Callander** U.K.
86 C6 **Callao** Peru
75 F2 **Callao** U.S.A.
84 C2 **Calles** Mex.
81 F4 **Callicoon** U.S.A.
39 C7 **Callington** U.K.
69 G2 **Callum** Can.
64 G4 **Calmar** Can.
68 B4 **Calmar** U.S.A.
75 E4 **Cal-Nev-Ari** U.S.A.
79 D7 **Caloosahatchee** *r.* U.S.A.
74 B2 **Calpine** U.S.A.
84 C3 **Calpulálpan** Mex.
48 F6 **Caltanissetta** *Sicily* Italy
68 C2 **Calumet** U.S.A.
57 B5 **Calunga** Angola
57 B5 **Caluquembe** Angola
31 B4 **Calusa** *i.* Phil.
56 F2 **Caluula** Somalia
75 G5 **Calva** U.S.A.
64 D4 **Calvert I.** *i.* Can.
48 C3 **Calvi** *Corsica* France
45 H3 **Calvià** Spain
84 B2 **Calvillo** Mex.
58 C5 **Calvinia** S. Africa
48 F4 **Calvo, Monte** *mt* Italy
39 H5 **Cam** *r.* U.K.
90 E1 **Camaçari** Brazil
74 B2 **Camache Reservoir** U.S.A.
84 B1 **Camacho** Mex.
57 B5 **Camacuio** Angola
57 B5 **Camacupa** Angola
89 D2 **Camaguán** Venez.
83 J4 **Camagüey** Cuba
83 J4 **Camagüey, Arch. de** *is* Cuba
33 B1 **Camah, Gunung** *mt* Malaysia
Çamalan *see* **Gülek**
86 D7 **Camana** Peru
57 C5 **Camanongue** Angola
90 B2 **Camapuã** Brazil
91 G1 **Camaquã** Brazil
91 G1 **Camaquã** *r.* Brazil
16 E3 **Çamardı** Turkey
84 C1 **Camargo** Mex.
84 A2 **Camaronero, L. del** *lag.* Mex.
88 C6 **Camarones** Arg.
88 C6 **Camarones, Bahía** *b.* Arg.
72 B2 **Camas** U.S.A.
32 C3 **Ca Mau** Vietnam
Cambay *see* **Khambhat**
Cambay, Gulf of *g. see* **Khambhat, Gulf of**
39 G6 **Camberley** U.K.
11 M8 **Cambodia** *country* Asia
39 B7 **Camborne** U.K.
44 F1 **Cambrai** France
74 B4 **Cambria** U.S.A.
39 D5 **Cambrian Mountains** *reg.* U.K.
69 G4 **Cambridge** Can.
9 E2 **Cambridge** N.Z.
39 H5 **Cambridge** U.K.
68 B5 **Cambridge** *IL* U.S.A.
81 H3 **Cambridge** *MA* U.S.A.
81 E5 **Cambridge** *MD* U.S.A.
76 E2 **Cambridge** *MN* U.S.A.
81 G3 **Cambridge** *NY* U.S.A.
80 C4 **Cambridge** *OH* U.S.A.
67 G2 **Cambrien, Lac** *l.* Can.
8 H3 **Camden** Austr.
79 C5 **Camden** *AL* U.S.A.
77 E5 **Camden** *AR* U.S.A.
81 J2 **Camden** *ME* U.S.A.
81 F5 **Camden** *NJ* U.S.A.
81 F3 **Camden** *NY* U.S.A.
79 D5 **Camden** *SC* U.S.A.
88 B8 **Camden, Isla** *i.* Chile
57 C5 **Cameia, Parque Nacional da** *nat. park* Angola
75 G4 **Cameron** *AZ* U.S.A.
77 E6 **Cameron** *LA* U.S.A.
76 E4 **Cameron** *MO* U.S.A.
77 D6 **Cameron** *TX* U.S.A.
68 B3 **Cameron** *WI* U.S.A.
32 B4 **Cameron Highlands** Malaysia
64 F3 **Cameron Hills** *h.* Can.
74 B2 **Cameron Park** U.S.A.
53 F5 **Cameroon** *country* Africa
54 C4 **Cameroun, Mt** *mt* Cameroon
87 J4 **Cametá** Brazil
31 B2 **Camiguin** *i.* Phil.
31 C4 **Camiguin** *i.* Phil.
31 B3 **Camiling** Phil.
79 C6 **Camilla** U.S.A.
86 F8 **Camiri** Bol.
87 K4 **Camocim** Brazil
6 D3 **Camooweal** Austr.
31 C4 **Camotes Sea** *g.* Phil.
91 E2 **Campana** Arg.
89 B4 **Campana, Co** *h.* Col.
88 A7 **Campana, I.** *i.* Chile
91 B2 **Campanario** *mt* Arg./Chile
64 D4 **Campania I.** *i.* Can.
58 E4 **Campbell** S. Africa

9 E4 Campbell, Cape *c.* N.Z.
4 H10 Campbell Island *i.* N.Z.
64 D4 Campbell River Can.
69 J3 Campbells Bay Can.
78 C4 Campbellsville U.S.A.
67 G4 Campbellton Can.
40 C5 Campbeltown U.K.
84 E3 Campeche Mex.
84 E3 Campeche *div.* Mex.
84 D3 Campeche, Bahía de *g.* Mex.
8 D5 Camperdown Austr.
49 L2 Câmpina Romania
87 L5 Campina Grande Brazil
90 C3 Campinas Brazil
90 C2 Campina Verde Brazil
54 C4 Campo Cameroon
89 B4 Campoalegre Col.
48 F4 Campobasso Italy
90 D3 Campo Belo Brazil
87 H6 Campo de Diauarum Brazil
90 C2 Campo Florido Brazil
88 D3 Campo Gallo Arg.
90 A3 Campo Grande Brazil
87 K4 Campo Maior Brazil
45 C3 Campo Maior Port.
90 B4 Campo Mourão Brazil
90 E3 Campos Brazil
90 C2 Campos Altos Brazil
90 D3 Campos do Jordão Brazil
90 B4 Campos Eré *reg.* Brazil
40 D4 Campsie Fells *h.* U.K.
80 B6 Campton *KY* U.S.A.
81 H3 Campton *NH* U.S.A.
49 L2 Câmpulung Romania
47 M7 Câmpulung Moldovenesc Romania
75 G4 Camp Verde U.S.A.
32 D3 Cam Ranh Vietnam
64 G4 Camrose Can.
39 B6 Camrose U.K.
65 G2 Camsell Lake *l.* Can.
65 H3 Camsell Portage Can.
51 C7 Çan Turkey
81 G3 Canaan U.S.A.
60 G4 Canada *country* N. America
91 E2 Cañada de Gómez Arg.
81 H2 Canada Falls Lake *l.* U.S.A.
77 C5 Canadian *r.* U.S.A.
89 E3 Canaima, Parque Nacional *nat. park* Venez.
81 F3 Canajoharie U.S.A.
51 C7 Çanakkale Turkey
Çanakkale Boğazı *str.* see Dardanelles
91 C2 Canalejas Arg.
80 E3 Canandaigua U.S.A.
80 E3 Canandaigua Lake *l.* U.S.A.
82 B2 Cananea Mex.
67 H2 Canatée, Lac *l.* Can.
90 C4 Cananéia Brazil
89 C4 Canapiare, Co *h.* Col.
86 C4 Cañar Ecuador
Canarias, Islas *is* see Canary Islands
96 G4 Canary Basin *sea feature* Atl. Ocean
34 D6 Canary Islands *div.* Spain
81 F3 Canastota U.S.A.
90 C2 Canastra, Serra da *mts* Brazil
84 A1 Canatlán Mex.
79 D6 Canaveral, Cape *c.* U.S.A.
45 E2 Cañaveras Spain
90 E1 Canavieiras Brazil
8 F1 Canbelego Austr.
8 G3 Canberra Austr.
72 B3 Canby *CA* U.S.A.
76 D2 Canby *MN* U.S.A.
82 G4 Cancún Mex.
73 F6 Candelaria *Chihuahua* Mex.
84 E3 Candelaria Mex.
45 D2 Candeleda Spain
8 G4 Candelo Austr.
87 J4 Cândido Mendes Brazil
16 D1 Çandır Turkey
65 H4 Candle Lake Can.
65 H4 Candle Lake *l.* Can.
92 C1 Candlemas I. *i.* Atl. Ocean
81 G4 Candlewood, Lake *l.* U.S.A.
76 D1 Cando U.S.A.
31 B2 Candon Phil.
91 B1 Canela Baja Chile
91 F2 Canelones Uru.
91 B3 Cañete Chile
45 F2 Cañete Spain
86 D6 Cangallo Peru
57 B5 Cangamba Angola
45 C1 Cangas del Narcea Spain
58 E6 Cango Caves *caves* S. Africa
87 L5 Canguaretama Brazil
91 G1 Canguçu Brazil
91 G1 Canguçu, Sa do *h.* Brazil
27 D6 Cangwu China
22 E2 Cangzhou China
67 G3 Caniapiscau Can.
67 G2 Caniapiscau *r.* Can.
63 L4 Caniapiscau, Lac *l.* Can.
67 G3 Caniapiscau, Rés. *resr* Can.
48 E6 Canicattì *Sicily* Italy
64 E4 Canim Lake Can.
64 E4 Canim Lake *l.* Can.
87 L4 Canindé Brazil
87 K5 Canindé *r.* Brazil
40 C2 Canisp *h.* U.K.
80 E3 Canisteo U.S.A.
80 E3 Canisteo *r.* U.S.A.
84 B2 Cañitas de Felipe Pescador Mex.
16 D1 Çankırı Turkey
31 B4 Canlaon Phil.
64 F4 Canmore Can.
40 B3 Canna *i.* U.K.
21 A4 Cannanore India
21 A4 Cannanore Islands *is* India
44 H5 Cannes France
39 E5 Cannock U.K.
8 G4 Cann River Austr.
89 E2 Caño Araguao *r.* Venez.
88 F3 Canoas Brazil
65 H3 Canoe L. *l.* Can.
90 B4 Canoinhas Brazil
89 E2 Caño Macareo *r.* Venez.
89 E2 Caño Manamo *r.* Venez.
89 E2 Caño Mariusa *r.* Venez.
73 F4 Canon City U.S.A.
8 C2 Canopus Austr.
65 J4 Canora Can.
8 G2 Canowindra Austr.
67 H4 Canso, C. *hd* Can.
45 D1 Cantábrica, Cordillera *mts* Spain
91 C2 Cantantal Arg.
89 D2 Cantaura Venez.
81 K2 Canterbury Can.
39 J6 Canterbury U.K.
9 C6 Canterbury Bight *b.* N.Z.
9 C5 Canterbury Plains *plain* N.Z.
32 C3 Cân Thơ Vietnam
31 C4 Cantilan Phil.
87 K5 Canto do Buriti Brazil
Canton see Guangzhou
68 B5 Canton *IL* U.S.A.
81 H2 Canton *ME* U.S.A.
68 B5 Canton *MO* U.S.A.
77 F5 Canton *MS* U.S.A.
81 F2 Canton *NY* U.S.A.
80 C4 Canton *OH* U.S.A.
80 E4 Canton *PA* U.S.A.
90 B4 Cantu *r.* Brazil
90 B4 Cantu, Serra do *h.* Brazil
91 E2 Cañuelas Arg.
87 G4 Canumã Brazil
86 F5 Canutama Brazil
9 D4 Canvastown N.Z.
39 H6 Canvey Island U.K.
77 C5 Canyon U.S.A.
72 C2 Canyon City U.S.A.
75 H3 Canyon de Chelly National Monument *res.* U.S.A.
72 D2 Canyon Ferry L. *l.* U.S.A.
75 H2 Canyonlands National Park U.S.A.
64 D2 Canyon Ranges *mts* Can.
72 B3 Canyonville U.S.A.
30 C3 Cao *r.* China
27 C6 Cao Băng Vietnam
32 D2 Cao Nguyên Đắc Lắc *plat.* Vietnam
30 C2 Caoshi China
26 E3 Cao Xian China
31 B5 Cap *i.* Phil.
89 D3 Capanaparo *r.* Venez.
87 J4 Capanema Brazil
90 B4 Capanema *r.* Brazil
90 C4 Capão Bonito Brazil
89 C3 Caparo *r.* Venez.
89 C4 Caparro, Co *h.* Brazil
31 B3 Capas Phil.
67 H4 Cap-aux-Meules Can.
67 F4 Cap-de-la-Madeleine Can.
6 E6 Cape Barren Island *i.* Austr.
96 K8 Cape Basin *sea feature* Atl. Ocean
67 H4 Cape Breton Highlands Nat. Park Can.
67 H4 Cape Breton Island *i.* Can.
67 J3 Cape Charles Can.
81 E6 Cape Charles U.S.A.
54 B4 Cape Coast Ghana
81 H4 Cape Cod Bay *b.* U.S.A.
81 J4 Cape Cod National Seashore *res.* U.S.A.
79 D7 Cape Coral U.S.A.
69 G3 Cape Croker Can.
63 L3 Cape Dorset Can.
79 E5 Cape Fear *r.* U.S.A.
77 F4 Cape Girardeau U.S.A.
94 D5 Cape Johnson Depth *depth* Pac. Oc.
90 D2 Capelinha Brazil
42 C3 Capelle aan de IJssel Neth.
81 F5 Cape May U.S.A.
81 F5 Cape May Court House U.S.A.
81 F5 Cape May Pt *pt* U.S.A.
57 B4 Capenda-Camulemba Angola
63 M5 Cape Sable *c.* Can.
67 J4 Cape St George Can.
67 H4 Cape Tormentine Can.
58 C6 Cape Town S. Africa
96 G5 Cape Verde Basin *sea feature* Atl. Ocean
96 F5 Cape Verde Fracture *sea feature* Atl. Ocean
96 H4 Cape Verde Plateau *sea feature* Atl. Ocean
81 E2 Cape Vincent U.S.A.
6 E3 Cape York Peninsula Austr.
83 K5 Cap-Haïtien Haiti
87 J4 Capim *r.* Brazil
92 B2 Capitán Arturo Prat *Chile Base* Ant.
90 A3 Capitán Bado Para.
73 F5 Capitan Peak *mt* U.S.A.
75 G2 Capitol Reef National Park U.S.A.
48 G3 Čapljina Bos.-Herz.
48 F5 Capo d'Orlando *Sicily* Italy
41 D5 Cappoquin Rep. of Ireland
48 C3 Capraia, Isola di *i.* Italy
6 F4 Capricorn Channel *chan.* Austr.
48 F4 Capri, Isola di *i.* Italy
57 C5 Caprivi Strip *reg.* Namibia
Cap St Jacques see Vung Tau
74 □2 Captain Cook U.S.A.
8 G3 Captain's Flat Austr.
80 C5 Captina *r.* U.S.A.
31 C3 Capul *i.* Phil.
86 C3 Caquetá *r.* Col.
89 B3 Cáqueza Col.
31 B3 Carabao *i.* Phil.
49 L2 Caracal Romania
89 E4 Caracarai Brazil
89 D2 Caracas Venez.
87 K5 Caracol Brazil
84 B3 Carácuaro Mex.
31 C5 Caraga Phil.
91 F2 Caraguatá *r.* Uru.
90 D3 Caraguatatuba Brazil
91 B3 Carahue Chile
90 E2 Caraí Brazil
90 D3 Carandaí Brazil
90 D3 Carangola Brazil
49 K2 Caransebeş Romania
67 H4 Caraquet Can.
89 B3 Carare *r.* Col.
83 H5 Caratasca, Laguna *lag.* Honduras
90 D2 Caratinga Brazil
86 E4 Carauari Brazil
Carauná *mt* see Grande, Serra
45 F3 Caravaca de la Cruz Spain
90 E2 Caravelas Brazil
88 F3 Carazinho Brazil
76 D1 Carberry Can.
48 C5 Carbonara, Capo *pt Sardinia* Italy
78 B4 Carbondale *IL* U.S.A.
81 F4 Carbondale *PA* U.S.A.
67 K4 Carbonear Can.
48 C5 Carbonia *Sardinia* Italy
90 D2 Carbonita Brazil
45 F3 Carcaixent Spain
31 B4 Carcar Phil.
91 E2 Carcarañá *r.* Arg.
44 F5 Carcassonne France
64 C2 Carcross Can.
6 B4 Cardabia Austr.
21 B4 Cardamon Hills *mts* India
84 C2 Cárdenas *San Luis Potosí* Mex.
84 D3 Cárdenas *Tabasco* Mex.
88 B7 Cardiel, L. *l.* Arg.
39 D6 Cardiff U.K.
39 C5 Cardigan U.K.
39 C5 Cardigan Bay *b.* U.K.
81 F2 Cardinal Can.
80 B4 Cardington U.S.A.
91 F2 Cardona Uru.
90 C4 Cardoso, Ilha do *i.* Brazil
9 B6 Cardrona N.Z.
64 G5 Cardston Can.
47 L7 Carei Romania
44 D2 Carentan France
80 B4 Carey U.S.A.
6 C4 Carey, L. *salt flat* Austr.
65 J2 Carey Lake *l.* Can.
93 J5 Cargados Carajos *is* Mauritius
44 C2 Carhaix-Plouguer France
91 D3 Carhué Arg.
90 E3 Cariacica Brazil
89 E2 Cariaco Venez.
61 L8 Caribbean Sea *sea* Atl. Ocean
64 E4 Cariboo Mts *mts* Can.
81 K1 Caribou U.S.A.
65 K3 Caribou *r. Man.* Can.
64 D2 Caribou *r. N.W.T.* Can.
68 E2 Caribou I. *i.* Can.
63 K4 Caribou Lake *l.* Can.
64 F3 Caribou Mountains Can.
31 C4 Carigara Phil.
42 D5 Carignan France
45 F2 Cariñena Spain
90 D1 Carinhanha Brazil
90 D1 Carinhanha *r.* Brazil
89 E2 Caripe Venez.
89 E2 Caripito Venez.
41 D3 Cark Mountain *h.* Rep. of Ireland
69 J3 Carleton Place Can.
59 G3 Carletonville S. Africa
72 C3 Carlin U.S.A.
41 E3 Carlingford Lough *in.* Rep. of Ireland/U.K.
38 E3 Carlisle U.K.
80 A5 Carlisle *KY* U.S.A.
80 E4 Carlisle *PA* U.S.A.
44 E5 Carlit, Pic *mt* France
91 E2 Carlos Casares Arg.
90 E2 Carlos Chagas Brazil
41 E5 Carlow Rep. of Ireland
40 B2 Carloway U.K.
74 D5 Carlsbad *CA* U.S.A.
73 F5 Carlsbad *NM* U.S.A.
77 C6 Carlsbad *TX* U.S.A.
73 F5 Carlsbad Caverns Nat. Park U.S.A.
93 J3 Carlsberg Ridge *sea feature* Ind. Ocean
92 B3 Carlson In. *in* Ant.
40 E5 Carluke U.K.
65 J5 Carlyle Can.
64 B2 Carmacks Can.
48 B2 Carmagnola Italy
65 K5 Carman Can.
39 C6 Carmarthen U.K.
39 C6 Carmarthen Bay *b.* U.K.
44 F4 Carmaux France
81 J2 Carmel U.S.A.
39 C4 Carmel Head *hd* U.K.
84 E3 Carmelita Guatemala
91 E2 Carmelo Uru.
89 B2 Carmen Col.
31 C4 Carmen Phil.
75 G6 Carmen U.S.A.
82 B3 Carmen *i.* Mex.
91 D4 Carmen de Patagones Arg.
84 E3 Carmen, Isla del *i.* Mex.
91 C2 Carmensa Arg.
78 B4 Carmi U.S.A.
74 B2 Carmichael U.S.A.
45 D4 Carmona Spain
44 C3 Carnac France
58 E5 Carnarvon S. Africa
41 D2 Carndonagh Rep. of Ireland
39 D4 Carnedd Llywelyn *mt* U.K.
6 C4 Carnegie, L. *salt flat* Austr.
95 O6 Carnegie Ridge *sea feature* Pac. Oc.
40 C3 Carn Eighe *mt* U.K.
68 D3 Carney U.S.A.
92 A3 Carney I. *i.* Ant.
38 E3 Carnforth U.K.
41 F3 Carnlough U.K.
40 E4 Carn nan Gabhar *mt* U.K.
56 B3 Carnot C.A.R.
6 D5 Carnot, C. *hd* Austr.
40 F4 Carnoustie U.K.
41 E5 Carnsore Point *pt* Rep. of Ireland
40 E5 Carnwath U.K.
65 H4 Carnwood Can.
69 F4 Caro U.S.A.
79 D7 Carol City U.S.A.
87 J5 Carolina Brazil
59 J3 Carolina S. Africa
5 M5 Caroline I. *i.* Kiribati
4 F4 Caroline Islands *is* Pac. Oc.
9 A6 Caroline Pk *summit* N.Z.
58 B4 Carolusberg S. Africa
89 E2 Caroní *r.* Venez.
89 C2 Carora Venez.
75 E3 Carp U.S.A.
47 L6 Carpathian Mountains Romania/Ukraine
6 D3 Carpentaria, Gulf of *g.* Austr.
44 G4 Carpentras France
48 D2 Carpi Italy
87 L5 Carpina Brazil
74 C4 Carpinteria U.S.A.
65 J5 Carpio U.S.A.
64 E4 Carp Lake Prov. Park *res.* Can.
81 H2 Carrabassett Valley U.S.A.
79 C6 Carrabelle U.S.A.
89 B2 Carraipía Col.
41 B4 Carra, Lough *l.* Rep. of Ireland
41 B6 Carran *h.* Rep. of Ireland
41 B6 Carrantuohill *mt* Rep. of Ireland
91 B2 Carranza, C. *pt* Chile
82 D3 Carranza, Presa V. *l.* Mex.
89 E3 Carrao *r.* Venez.
48 D2 Carrara Italy
8 E3 Carrathool Austr.
91 C3 Carrero, Co *mt* Arg.
89 E1 Carriacou *i.* Grenada
40 D5 Carrick *reg.* U.K.
41 F3 Carrickfergus U.K.
41 E4 Carrickmacross Rep. of Ireland
41 C4 Carrick-on-Shannon Rep. of Ireland
41 D5 Carrick-on-Suir Rep. of Ireland
8 B2 Carrieton Austr.
41 D4 Carrigallen Rep. of Ireland
41 C6 Carrigtwohill Rep. of Ireland
91 C4 Carri Lafquén, L. *l.* Arg.
76 D2 Carrington U.S.A.
88 B3 Carrizal Bajo Chile
75 H4 Carrizo *AZ* U.S.A.
75 G4 Carrizo *AZ* U.S.A.
74 D5 Carrizo Cr. *r.* U.S.A.
77 D6 Carrizo Springs U.S.A.
73 F5 Carrizozo U.S.A.
76 E3 Carroll U.S.A.
79 C5 Carrollton *GA* U.S.A.
78 C4 Carrollton *KY* U.S.A.
76 E4 Carrollton *MO* U.S.A.
80 C4 Carrollton *OH* U.S.A.
65 J4 Carrot *r.* Can.
65 J4 Carrot River Can.
38 B3 Carrowdore U.K.
41 B3 Carrowmore Lake *l.* Rep. of Ireland
81 F2 Carry Falls Reservoir U.S.A.
16 F1 Çarşamba Turkey
68 E4 Carson City *MI* U.S.A.
74 C2 Carson City *NV* U.S.A.
74 C2 Carson Lake *l.* U.S.A.
74 C2 Carson Sink *l.* U.S.A.
69 F4 Carsonville U.S.A.
91 B2 Cartagena Chile
89 B2 Cartagena Col.
45 F4 Cartagena Spain
89 B3 Cartago Col.
83 H7 Cartago Costa Rica
79 C5 Cartersville U.S.A.
68 B5 Carthage *IL* U.S.A.
77 E4 Carthage *MO* U.S.A.
81 F2 Carthage *NY* U.S.A.
77 E5 Carthage *TX* U.S.A.
69 G2 Cartier Can.
38 E3 Cartmel U.K.
67 J3 Cartwright Can.
87 L5 Caruarú Brazil
89 E2 Carúpano Venez.
74 D2 Carvers U.S.A.
42 A4 Carvin France
79 E5 Cary U.S.A.
54 B1 Casablanca Morocco
90 C3 Casa Branca Brazil
73 E6 Casa de Janos Mex.
75 G5 Casa Grande U.S.A.
75 G5 Casa Grande National Monument *res.* U.S.A.
48 C2 Casale Monferrato Italy
48 D2 Casalmaggiore Italy
89 C3 Casanare *r.* Col.
49 H4 Casarano Italy
68 B4 Cascade *IA* U.S.A.
72 D2 Cascade *ID* U.S.A.
72 E2 Cascade *MT* U.S.A.
9 B6 Cascade *r.* N.Z.
9 B6 Cascade Pt *pt* N.Z.
72 B3 Cascade Range *mts* U.S.A.
72 D2 Cascade Res. *resr* U.S.A.
45 B3 Cascais Port.
90 B4 Cascavel Brazil
81 J3 Casco Bay *b.* U.S.A.
48 F4 Caserta Italy
69 F4 Caseville U.S.A.
92 C6 Casey *Austr. Base* Ant.
92 D4 Casey Bay *b.* Ant.
41 D5 Cashel Rep. of Ireland
68 B4 Cashton U.S.A.
89 C2 Casigua *Falcón* Venez.
89 B2 Casigua *Zulia* Venez.
31 B2 Casiguran Phil.
91 E2 Casilda Arg.
7 F4 Casino Austr.
89 D4 Casiquiare, Canal *r.* Venez.
86 C5 Casma Peru
68 E4 Casnovia U.S.A.
74 A2 Caspar U.S.A.
45 F2 Caspe Spain
72 F3 Casper U.S.A.
Caspian Lowland *lowland* see Prikaspiyskaya Nizmennost'
10 F5 Caspian Sea *sea* Asia/Europe
80 D5 Cass U.S.A.
69 F4 Cass *r.* U.S.A.
80 D3 Cassadaga U.S.A.
57 C5 Cassai Angola
69 F4 Cass City U.S.A.
42 A4 Cassel France
81 F2 Casselman Can.
64 D3 Cassiar Can.
64 C3 Cassiar Mountains Can.
8 G2 Cassilis Austr.
48 E4 Cassino Italy
76 E2 Cass Lake U.S.A.
87 J4 Castanhal Brazil
91 C1 Castaño *r.* Arg.
77 C7 Castaños Mex.
91 C1 Castaño Viejo Arg.
48 D2 Castelfranco Veneto Italy
44 E4 Casteljaloux France
48 F4 Castellammare di Stabia Italy
91 F3 Castelli Arg.
45 F3 Castelló de la Plana Spain
45 C3 Castelo Branco Port.
45 C3 Castelo de Vide Port.
48 C4 Castelsardo *Sardinia* Italy
48 E6 Casteltermini *Sicily* Italy
48 E6 Castelvetrano *Sicily* Italy
8 C4 Casterton Austr.
67 G2 Castignon, Lac *l.* Can.
45 E3 Castilla - La Mancha *div.* Spain
45 D2 Castilla y León *div.* Spain
89 C2 Castilletes Col.
91 G2 Castillos Uru.
41 B4 Castlebar Rep. of Ireland
40 A4 Castlebay U.K.
41 E4 Castlebellingham Rep. of Ireland
41 E3 Castleblayney Rep. of Ireland
41 E3 Castlebridge Rep. of Ireland
38 E3 Castle Carrock U.K.
39 E6 Castle Cary U.K.
75 G2 Castle Dale U.S.A.
41 D3 Castlederg U.K.
41 E5 Castledermot Rep. of Ireland
75 E5 Castle Dome Mts *mts* U.S.A.
39 F5 Castle Donnington U.K.
40 E6 Castle Douglas U.K.
38 F4 Castleford U.K.
64 F5 Castlegar Can.
41 A5 Castlegregory Rep. of Ireland
41 B5 Castleisland Rep. of Ireland
8 E4 Castlemaine Austr.
41 B5 Castlemaine Rep. of Ireland
41 C6 Castlemartyr Rep. of Ireland
74 B4 Castle Mt *mt* U.S.A.
27 □ Castle Peak *h. H.K.* China
27 □ Castle Peak Bay *b. H.K.* China
9 F4 Castlepoint N.Z.
41 D4 Castlepollard Rep. of Ireland
41 C4 Castlerea Rep. of Ireland
8 G1 Castlereagh *r.* Austr.
73 F4 Castle Rock U.S.A.
68 B4 Castle Rock Lake *l.* U.S.A.
38 C3 Castletown Isle of Man
41 D5 Castletown Rep. of Ireland
65 G4 Castor Can.
44 F5 Castres France
42 C2 Castricum Neth.
83 M6 Castries St Lucia
90 C4 Castro Brazil
88 B6 Castro Chile
45 D4 Castro del Río Spain
45 E1 Castro-Urdiales Spain
45 B4 Castro Verde Port.
48 G5 Castrovillari Italy
74 B3 Castroville U.S.A.
9 A6 Caswell Sd *in.* N.Z.
17 H2 Çat Turkey
86 B5 Catacaos Peru
90 D3 Cataguases Brazil
77 E6 Catahoula L. *l.* U.S.A.
31 B3 Cataiñgan Phil.
17 J3 Çatak Turkey
90 C2 Catalão Brazil
45 G2 Cataluña *div.* Spain
88 C3 Catamarca Arg.
31 C3 Catanduanes *i.* Phil.
90 B4 Catanduvas Brazil
48 F6 Catania *Sicily* Italy
48 G5 Catanzaro Italy
77 D6 Catarina U.S.A.
31 C3 Catarman Phil.
45 F3 Catarroja Spain
89 B2 Catatumbo *r.* Venez.
31 C4 Catbalogan Phil.
79 E7 Cat Cays *is* Bahamas
31 C5 Cateel Phil.
31 C5 Cateel Bay *b.* Phil.
59 K3 Catembe Moz.
8 G4 Cathcart Austr.
59 G6 Cathcart S. Africa
59 H4 Cathedral Peak *mt* S. Africa
41 A6 Catherdaniel Rep. of Ireland
75 F2 Catherine, Mt *mt* U.S.A.
91 B3 Catillo Chile
79 E7 Cat Island *i.* Bahamas
66 B3 Cat L. *l.* Can.
82 G4 Catoche, C. *c.* Mex.
80 E5 Catonsville U.S.A.
84 B2 Catorce Mex.
91 D3 Catriló Arg.
89 E4 Catrimani Brazil
89 E4 Catrimani *r.* Brazil
81 G3 Catskill U.S.A.
81 F4 Catskill Mts *mts* U.S.A.
42 A4 Cats, Mont des *h.* France
59 K3 Catuane Moz.
89 E4 Cauamé *r.* Brazil
31 B4 Cauayan Phil.
67 H2 Caubvick, Mount *mt* Can.
89 B3 Cauca *r.* Col.
87 L4 Caucaia Brazil
89 B3 Caucasia Col.
35 K4 Caucasus *mts* Asia/Europe
91 C1 Caucete Arg.
81 J1 Caucomgomoc Lake *l.* U.S.A.
42 B4 Caudry France
31 C4 Cauit Point *pt* Phil.
91 B2 Cauquenes Chile
89 D3 Caura *r.* Venez.
67 G4 Causapscal Can.
44 G5 Cavaillon France
90 C1 Cavalcante Brazil
54 B4 Cavally *r.* Côte d'Ivoire
41 D4 Cavan Rep. of Ireland
77 F4 Cave City U.S.A.
90 E1 Caveira *r.* Brazil
8 D4 Cavendish Austr.
90 B4 Cavernoso, Serra do *mts* Brazil
80 B5 Cave Run Lake *l.* U.S.A.
31 B4 Cavili *rf* Phil.
31 B3 Cavite Phil.
40 E3 Cawdor U.K.
8 C2 Cawndilla Lake *l.* Austr.
39 J5 Cawston U.K.
87 K4 Caxias Brazil
88 F3 Caxias do Sul Brazil
57 B4 Caxito Angola
16 C2 Çay Turkey
79 D5 Cayce U.S.A.
16 D1 Çaycuma Turkey
17 H1 Çayeli Turkey
87 H3 Cayenne Fr. Guiana
16 E3 Çayhan Turkey
16 C1 Çayırhan Turkey
83 J5 Cayman Brac *i.* Cayman Is
61 K8 Cayman Islands *terr.* Caribbean Sea
96 D4 Cayman Trench *sea feature* Atl. Ocean
56 E3 Caynabo Somalia
69 H4 Cayuga Can.
80 E3 Cayuga Lake *l.* U.S.A.
81 F3 Cazenovia U.S.A.
57 C5 Cazombo Angola
91 F2 Cebollatí *r.* Uru.
31 B4 Cebu Phil.
31 B4 Cebu *i.* Phil.
68 C3 Cecil U.S.A.
48 D3 Cecina Italy
68 A4 Cedar *r. IA* U.S.A.
76 C2 Cedar *r. ND* U.S.A.
68 D4 Cedarburg U.S.A.
75 F3 Cedar City U.S.A.
77 D5 Cedar Creek Res. *resr* U.S.A.
68 A4 Cedar Falls U.S.A.
68 D4 Cedar Grove *WI* U.S.A.
80 C5 Cedar Grove *WV* U.S.A.
81 F6 Cedar I. *i.* U.S.A.
65 J4 Cedar L. *l.* Can.
68 D5 Cedar Lake *l.* U.S.A.
80 B4 Cedar Pt *pt* U.S.A.
68 B5 Cedar Rapids U.S.A.
75 G3 Cedar Ridge U.S.A.
81 F5 Cedar Run U.S.A.
69 F4 Cedar Springs Can.
68 E4 Cedar Springs U.S.A.
79 C5 Cedartown U.S.A.
59 H5 Cedarville S. Africa
68 E3 Cedarville U.S.A.
82 A3 Cedros *i.* Mex.
6 D5 Ceduna Austr.
56 E3 Ceeldheere Somalia
56 E2 Ceerigaabo Somalia
48 F5 Cefalù *Sicily* Italy
47 J7 Cegléd Hungary
27 B5 Ceheng China
16 E1 Çekerek Turkey
32 B4 Celah, Gunung *mt* Malaysia
84 B2 Celaya Mex.
41 E4 Celbridge Rep. of Ireland
Celebes *i.* see Sulawesi
33 E2 Celebes Sea *sea* Indon./Phil.
80 A4 Celina U.S.A.
48 F1 Celje Slovenia
43 J2 Celle Ger.
16 E1 Cemilbey Turkey
16 G2 Çemişgezek Turkey
25 F7 Cenderawasih, Teluk *b.* Indon.
27 C5 Cengong China
75 F5 Centennial Wash *r.* U.S.A.
77 E6 Center U.S.A.
81 G4 Centereach U.S.A.
79 C5 Center Point U.S.A.
80 B5 Centerville U.S.A.
59 G1 Central *div.* Botswana
53 F5 Central African Republic *country* Africa
19 G4 Central Brahui Range *mts* Pak.
68 B4 Central City *IA* U.S.A.
76 D3 Central City *NE* U.S.A.
89 A4 Central, Cordillera *mts* Col.
86 C5 Central, Cordillera *mts* Peru
31 B2 Central, Cordillera *mts* Phil.
27 □ Central District *H.K.* China
78 B4 Centralia *IL* U.S.A.
72 B2 Centralia *WA* U.S.A.
68 A2 Central Lakes U.S.A.
19 G5 Central Makran Range *mts* Pak.
72 B3 Central Point U.S.A.
6 E2 Central Ra. *mts* P.N.G.
79 C5 Centreville U.S.A.
27 D6 Cenxi China
Cephalonia *i.* see Kefallonia
89 D3 Cerbatana, Sa de la *mt* Venez.
75 E4 Cerbat Mts *mts* U.S.A.
65 G4 Cereal Can.
88 D3 Ceres Arg.
58 C6 Ceres S. Africa
89 B2 Cereté Col.
45 E2 Cerezo de Abajo Spain
48 F4 Cerignola Italy
16 D2 Çerikli Turkey
16 D1 Çerkeş Turkey
16 G3 Çermelik *r.* Syria
17 G2 Çermik Turkey
49 N2 Cernavodă Romania
84 C1 Cerralvo Mex.
82 C4 Cerralvo *i.* Mex.
49 H4 Cërrik Albania
84 B2 Cerritos Mex.
90 C4 Cerro Azul Brazil
84 C2 Cerro Azul Mex.
86 B4 Cerro de Amotape, Parque Nacional *nat. park* Peru
86 C6 Cerro de Pasco Peru
89 D3 Cerro Jáua, Meseta del *plat.* Venez.
89 C2 Cerrón, Co *mt* Venez.
84 A1 Cerro Prieto Mex.
91 C3 Cerros Colorados, Embalse *resr* Arg.
48 F4 Cervati, Monte *mt* Italy
48 C3 Cervione *Corsica* France
45 C1 Cervo Spain
89 B2 César *r.* Col.
48 E2 Cesena Italy
37 T8 Cēsis Latvia
46 G6 České Budějovice Czech Rep.
46 G6 Český Krumlov Czech Rep.
43 L5 Český Les *mts* Czech Rep./Ger.
49 M5 Çeşme Turkey
8 H2 Cessnock Austr.
49 H3 Cetinje Yugo.
48 F5 Cetraro Italy
45 D5 Ceuta Spain
44 F4 Cévennes *mts* France
16 E3 Ceyhan Turkey
16 E3 Ceyhan *r.* Turkey
17 H3 Ceylanpınar Turkey
19 F2 Chaacha Turkm.
42 A5 Chaalis, Abbaye de France
91 E2 Chacabuco Arg.
91 B4 Chacao Chile
91 C3 Chachahuén, Sa *mt* Arg.
86 C5 Chachapoyas Peru
50 D4 Chachersk Belarus
32 B2 Chachoengsao Thai.
22 B4 Chachro Pak.
64 C4 Chacon, C. *c.* U.S.A.
52 F4 Chad *country* Africa
15 H1 Chadan Rus. Fed.
59 G1 Chadibe Botswana
91 C3 Chadileo *r.* Arg.
55 D3 Chad, Lake *l.* Africa
76 C3 Chadron U.S.A.
32 A1 Chae Hom Thai.
30 C4 Chaeryŏng N. Korea
89 B4 Chafurray Col.
19 G4 Chagai Pak.
19 F4 Chagai Hills *mts* Afgh./Pak.
23 F2 Chagdo Kangri *reg.* China
19 G3 Chaghcharān Afgh.
44 G3 Chagny France
10 J10 Chagos Archipelago *is* British Ind. Ocean Terr.
50 J4 Chagra *r.* Rus. Fed.
89 D2 Chaguaramas Venez.
23 G3 Cha'gyüngoinba China
19 F4 Chahah Burjal Afgh.
19 E3 Chāh Ākhvor Iran
19 E3 Chahār Takāb Iran
18 D3 Chāh Badam Iran
19 F5 Chāh Bahār Iran
18 D4 Chāh-e Bāgh *well* Iran
18 E3 Chāh-e Kavīr *well* Iran
18 D3 Chāh-e Khorāsān *well* Iran
19 E3 Chāh-e Khoshāb Iran
19 E4 Chāh-e Malek Iran
18 D3 Chāh-e Mirzā *well* Iran
18 D3 Chāh-e Mūjān *well* Iran
18 D3 Chāh-e Nūklok Iran
18 D3 Chāh-e Nūklok *well* Iran
18 D4 Chāh-e Qeyşar *well* Iran
18 D3 Chāh-e Qobād *well* Iran
18 D4 Chāh-e Rāh Iran
19 E4 Chāh-e Raḥmān *well* Iran
18 D3 Chāh-e Shūr Iran
18 D3 Chāh-e Shur *well* Iran
18 D3 Chah Haji Abdulla *well* Iran
18 D4 Chāh Ḥaqq Iran
19 H2 Chah-i-Ab Afgh.
17 K4 Chah-i-Shurkh Iraq
18 D3 Chāh Pās *well* Iran
18 C4 Chāh Rūstā'ī Iran
19 F4 Chah Sandan Pak.
30 C2 Chai *r.* China
23 F5 Chāībāsa India
67 G3 Chaigneau, Lac *l.* Can.
32 B2 Chai Si *r.* Thai.
27 □ Chai Wan *H.K.* China
32 A3 Chaiya Thai.
32 B2 Chaiyaphum Thai.
91 F1 Chajarí Arg.
22 B3 Chakar *r.* Pak.
23 H5 Chakaria Bangl.
19 F4 Chakhānsūr Afgh.
23 E4 Chakia India
19 G5 Chakku Pak.
86 D7 Chala Peru
19 G3 Chalap Dalan *mts* Afgh.
82 G6 Chalatenango El Salvador
67 G4 Chaleur Bay *in.* Can.
27 D5 Chaling China
22 C5 Chalisgaon India
49 K5 Chalkida Greece
9 A7 Chalky Inlet *in.* N.Z.
44 D3 Challans France
86 E7 Challapata Bol.
94 E5 Challenger Deep *depth* Pac. Oc.
95 M8 Challenger Fracture Zone *sea feature* Pac. Oc.
72 D2 Challis U.S.A.
44 G2 Châlons-en-Champagne France
44 G3 Chalon-sur-Saône France
30 C2 Chaluhe China
18 C2 Chālūs Iran
43 L5 Cham Ger.
73 F4 Chama U.S.A.
57 D5 Chama Zambia
89 C2 Chama *r.* Venez.
91 D2 Chamaico Arg.
58 A3 Chamais Bay *b.* Namibia
19 G4 Chaman Pak.
22 D4 Chambal *r.* India
67 G3 Chambeaux, Lac *l.* Can.
65 H4 Chamberlain Can.
76 D3 Chamberlain U.S.A.
81 J1 Chamberlain Lake *l.* U.S.A.
75 H4 Chambers U.S.A.
80 E5 Chambersburg U.S.A.
44 G4 Chambéry France
57 D5 Chambeshi Zambia
48 C7 Chambi, Jebel *mt* Tunisia
44 G4 Chamechaude *mt* France
18 C3 Cham-e Ḩannā Iran
18 C3 Chameshk Iran
91 C1 Chamical Arg.
23 F4 Chamlang *mt* Nepal
32 B3 Châmnar Cambodia
66 F4 Chamouchouane *r.* Can.
23 E5 Champa India
64 B2 Champagne Can.
44 G2 Champagne *reg.* France
59 H4 Champagne Castle *mt* S. Africa
44 G3 Champagnole France
68 C5 Champaign U.S.A.
91 D1 Champaquí, Cerro *mt* Arg.
32 C2 Champasak Laos
23 H5 Champhai India
68 D2 Champion U.S.A.
81 G2 Champlain U.S.A.
81 G2 Champlain, L. *l.* Can./U.S.A.
84 E3 Champotón Mex.
21 B4 Chamrajnagar India
50 H4 Chamzinka Rus. Fed.
32 B4 Chana Thai.
88 B3 Chañaral Chile
89 E3 Chanaro, Co *mt* Venez.
91 B2 Chanco Chile
Chanda see Chandrapur
62 D3 Chandalar *r.* U.S.A.
23 E5 Chandarpur India
22 D3 Chandausi India
77 F6 Chandeleur Islands *is* U.S.A.
22 E5 Chandia India
22 D3 Chandigarh India
75 G5 Chandler U.S.A.
69 J3 Chandos Lake *l.* Can.
23 G5 Chandpur Bangl.
22 D3 Chandpur India
23 H5 Chandraghona Bangl.
22 D6 Chandrapur India
22 D5 Chandur India
57 D6 Changane *r.* Moz.
57 D5 Changara Moz.
30 E3 Changbai China
30 D3 Changbai Shan *mts* China/N. Korea
27 C7 Changcheng China
92 B1 Chang Cheng (Great Wall) *China Base* Ant.
30 C2 Changchun China
30 C1 Changchunling China
26 F2 Changdao China
27 D4 Changde China
30 D4 Changdo N. Korea
26 E3 Changfeng China
30 E5 Changgi Gap *pt* S. Korea
30 B4 Changhai China
30 D6 Changhang S. Korea
30 D5 Changhowan S. Korea
27 F5 Chang-hua Taiwan
32 D1 Changhua Jiang *r.* China
30 D6 Changhung S. Korea
32 □ Changi Sing.
27 C7 Changjiang China
Chang Jiang *r.* see Yangtze
Changjiang Kou *est.* see Yangtze, Mouth of the
30 D3 Changjin N. Korea
30 D3 Changjin Reservoir N. Korea
27 F5 Changle China
26 F2 Changli China
30 B1 Changling China
27 D5 Changning China
30 C4 Changnyŏn N. Korea
26 E1 Changping China
30 E5 Changp'yŏng S. Korea
30 C4 Changsan-got *pt* N. Korea
27 D4 Changsha China
27 F4 Changshan China
30 B4 Changshan Qundao *is* China
27 C4 Changshou China
27 D4 Changshoujie China
26 F4 Changshu China
27 C5 Changshun China
30 D6 Changsŏng S. Korea
27 E5 Changtai China
27 E5 Changting *Fujian* China
30 E1 Changting *Heilongjiang* China
30 C2 Changtu China
30 E6 Ch'angwŏn S. Korea
26 C3 Changwu China
30 A4 Changxing Dao *i.* China
27 D4 Changyang China
27 F2 Changyi China
30 C4 Changyŏn N. Korea
26 E3 Changyuan China
26 D2 Changzhi China
27 F4 Changzhou China
49 L7 Chania Greece
30 D3 Chanjin *r.* N. Korea
26 B3 Chankou China
21 B3 Channapatna India
74 C5 Channel Islands *is* U.S.A.
34 E4 Channel Islands *terr.* English Channel
74 B5 Channel Is Nat. Park U.S.A.
67 J4 Channel-Port-aux-Basques Can.
39 J6 Channel Tunnel *tunnel* France/U.K.
68 C2 Channing U.S.A.
45 C1 Chantada Spain

32 B2 Chanthaburi Thai.
44 F2 Chantilly France
77 E4 Chanute U.S.A.
12 J4 Chany, Ozero salt l. Rus. Fed.
26 E2 Chaobai Xinhe r. China
26 E4 Chao Hu l. China
32 B2 Chao Phraya r. Thai.
54 B1 Chaouèn Morocco
23 H2 Chaowula Shan mts China
26 E4 Chao Xian China
27 E6 Chaoyang Guangdong China
26 F1 Chaoyang Liaoning China
27 E6 Chaozhou China
90 E1 Chapada Diamantina, Parque Nacional nat. park Brazil
90 A1 Chapada dos Guimarães Brazil
90 C1 Chapada dos Veadeiros, Parque Nacional da nat. park Brazil
84 B2 Chapala Mex.
84 B2 Chapala, L. de l. Mex.
89 B4 Chaparral Col.
14 D1 Chapayev Kazak.
50 J4 Chapayevsk Rus. Fed.
88 F3 Chapecó Brazil
88 F3 Chapecó r. Brazil
39 F4 Chapel-en-le-Frith U.K.
79 E5 Chapel Hill U.S.A.
42 C4 Chapelle-lez-Herlaimont Belgium
39 F4 Chapeltown U.K.
68 D5 Chapin, Lake l. U.S.A.
69 F2 Chapleau Can.
50 F4 Chaplygin Rus. Fed.
51 E6 Chaplynka Ukr.
80 B6 Chapmanville U.S.A.
19 G3 Chapri Pass pass Afgh.
86 E7 Chaqui Bol.
22 D2 Char Jammu and Kashmir
84 B2 Charcas Mex.
23 H3 Char Chu r. China
92 A2 Charcot I. i. Ant.
65 G3 Chard Can.
39 E7 Chard U.K.
17 L3 Chārdagh Iran
17 L5 Chardāvol Iran
80 C4 Chardon U.S.A.
19 F2 Chardzhev Turkm.
44 E3 Charente r. France
19 H3 Chārīkār Afgh.
76 E3 Chariton r. U.S.A.
69 F3 Charity Is i. U.S.A.
12 G3 Charkayuvom Rus. Fed.
22 D4 Charkhari India
42 C4 Charleroi Belgium
71 L4 Charles, Cape pt VA U.S.A.
68 A4 Charles City U.S.A.
42 A5 Charles de Gaulle airport France
77 E6 Charles, Lake U.S.A.
9 C4 Charleston N.Z.
78 B4 Charleston IL U.S.A.
81 J2 Charleston ME U.S.A.
77 F4 Charleston MO U.S.A.
79 E5 Charleston SC U.S.A.
80 C5 Charleston WV U.S.A.
75 E3 Charleston Peak summit U.S.A.
41 C4 Charlestown Rep. of Ireland
81 G3 Charlestown NH U.S.A.
81 H4 Charlestown RI U.S.A.
80 E5 Charles Town U.S.A.
6 E4 Charleville Austr.
44 G2 Charleville-Mézières France
68 E3 Charlevoix U.S.A.
64 E3 Charlie Lake Can.
68 E4 Charlotte MI U.S.A.
79 D5 Charlotte NC U.S.A.
79 D7 Charlotte Harbor b. U.S.A.
80 D5 Charlottesville U.S.A.
67 H4 Charlottetown Can.
89 E2 Charlotteville Trinidad and Tobago
8 D4 Charlton Austr.
66 E3 Charlton I. i. Can.
50 F2 Charozero Rus. Fed.
22 B2 Charsadda Pak.
6 E4 Charters Towers Austr.
44 E2 Chartres France
91 E2 Chascomús Arg.
64 F4 Chase Can.
19 F2 Chashkent Turkm.
17 L4 Chashmeh Iran
18 E3 Chashmeh Nūrī Iran
18 D3 Chashmeh ye Palasi Iran
18 D3 Chashmeh ye Shotoran well Iran
50 D4 Chashniki Belarus
9 B7 Chaslands Mistake c. N.Z.
30 D3 Chasŏng N. Korea
18 D3 Chastab, Kūh-e mts Iran
44 D3 Châteaubriant France
44 E3 Château-du-Loir France
44 E2 Châteaudun France
81 F2 Chateaugay U.S.A.
81 G2 Châteauguay Can.
44 B2 Châteaulin France
44 F3 Châteauneuf-sur-Loire France
44 E3 Châteauroux France
42 E6 Château-Salins France
44 F2 Château-Thierry France
42 C4 Châtelet Belgium
44 E3 Châtellerault France
68 A4 Chatfield U.S.A.
67 G4 Chatham N.B. Can.
69 F4 Chatham Ont. Can.
39 H6 Chatham U.K.
81 H4 Chatham MA U.S.A.
81 G3 Chatham NY U.S.A.
80 D6 Chatham VA U.S.A.
7 J6 Chatham Islands is N.Z.
94 G8 Chatham Rise sea feature Pac. Oc.
64 C4 Chatham Sd chan. Can.
64 C3 Chatham Strait chan. U.S.A.
23 F4 Chatra India
69 G3 Chatsworth Can.
68 C5 Chatsworth U.S.A.
79 C5 Chattanooga U.S.A.
39 H5 Chatteris U.K.
32 B2 Chatturat Thai.
32 C3 Châu Đôc Vietnam
22 B4 Chauhtan India
23 H5 Chauk Myanmar
22 E4 Chauka r. India
44 G2 Chaumont France
32 A2 Chaungwabyin Myanmar
13 S3 Chaunskaya Guba b. Rus. Fed.
44 F2 Chauny France
23 F4 Chauparan India
80 D3 Chautauqua, Lake l. U.S.A.
21 C4 Chavakachcheri Sri Lanka
18 B3 Chavār Iran
87 J4 Chaves Brazil
45 C2 Chaves Port.
66 E2 Chavigny, Lac l. Can.
50 D4 Chavusy Belarus
22 A3 Chawal r. Pak.
27 B6 Chây r. Vietnam
Chāyul see Qayü
91 D2 Chazón Arg.
81 G2 Chazy U.S.A.
39 F5 Cheadle U.K.
80 D5 Cheat r. U.S.A.
46 F5 Cheb Czech Rep.
48 D7 Chebba Tunisia
50 H3 Cheboksary Rus. Fed.
68 E3 Cheboygan U.S.A.
51 H7 Chechen', Ostrov i. Rus. Fed.
51 H7 Chechenskaya Respublika div. Rus. Fed.
30 E5 Chech'ŏn S. Korea
77 E5 Checotah U.S.A.
30 A5 Chedao China
39 E6 Cheddar U.K.
65 G3 Cheecham Can.
92 B5 Cheetham, C. c. Ant.
62 B3 Chefornak AK U.S.A.
59 K1 Chefu Moz.
54 B2 Chegga Maur.
57 D5 Chegutu Zimbabwe
72 B2 Chehalis U.S.A.
19 H3 Chehardar Pass Afgh.
17 L5 Chehariz Iraq
18 E4 Chehell'āyeh Iran
30 D7 Cheju S. Korea
30 D7 Cheju-do i. S. Korea
30 D7 Cheju-haehyŏp chan. S. Korea
57 F4 Chekhov Rus. Fed.
72 B2 Chelan, L. l. U.S.A.
18 D2 Cheleken Turkm.
91 C3 Chelforó Arg.
45 G4 Chélif r. Alg.
14 D2 Chelkar Kazak.
47 L5 Chełm Pol.
39 H6 Chelmer r. U.K.
47 J4 Chełmno Pol.
39 H6 Chelmsford U.K.
81 H3 Chelmsford U.S.A.
39 E6 Cheltenham U.K.
45 F3 Chelva Spain
12 H4 Chelyabinsk Rus. Fed.
57 D5 Chemba Moz.
22 D2 Chem Co l. China
43 L4 Chemnitz Ger.
80 E3 Chemung r. U.S.A.
22 B3 Chenab r. Pak.
54 B2 Chenachane Alg.
81 F3 Chenango r. U.S.A.
72 C2 Cheney U.S.A.
77 D4 Cheney Res. resr U.S.A.
21 C3 Chengalpattu India
26 E2 Cheng'an China
27 D5 Chengbu China
26 E1 Chengde China
27 B4 Chengdu China
26 C3 Chenggu China
27 E6 Chenghai China
26 C4 Chengkou China
25 D5 Chengmai China
30 B4 Chengzitan China
26 F3 Cheniu Shan i. China
68 C5 Chenoa U.S.A.
27 D5 Chenxi China
27 D5 Chenzhou China
32 D2 Cheo Reo Vietnam
86 C5 Chepén Peru
91 C1 Chepes Arg.
39 E6 Chepstow U.K.
50 J3 Cheptsa r. Rus. Fed.
17 L5 Cheqad Kabūd Iran
68 B2 Chequamegon Bay b. U.S.A.
44 F3 Cher r. France
84 B3 Cherán Mex.
79 E5 Cheraw U.S.A.
44 D2 Cherbourg France
45 H4 Cherchell Alg.
50 J4 Cherdakly Rus. Fed.
24 C1 Cheremkhovo Rus. Fed.
28 D2 Cheremshany Rus. Fed.
50 F3 Cherepovets Rus. Fed.
50 H2 Cherevkovo Rus. Fed.
48 B7 Chéria Alg.
51 E6 Cherkasy Ukr.
51 G6 Cherkessk Rus. Fed.
21 C2 Cherla India
57 C5 Chermenze Angola
12 K2 Chernaya Rus. Fed.
50 J3 Chernaya Kholunitsa Rus. Fed.
28 C2 Chernigovka Rus. Fed.
51 D5 Chernihiv Ukr.
51 F6 Cherninivka Ukr.
51 C5 Chernivtsi Ukr.
24 B1 Chernogorsk Rus. Fed.
50 H3 Chernovskoye Rus. Fed.
51 D5 Chernyakhiv Ukr.
47 K3 Chernyakhovsk Rus. Fed.
51 F5 Chernyanka Rus. Fed.
13 N3 Chernyshevskiy Rus. Fed.
51 H6 Chernyye Zemli reg. Rus. Fed.
51 H5 Chernyy Yar Rus. Fed.
76 E3 Cherokee IA U.S.A.
77 D4 Cherokee OK U.S.A.
77 E4 Cherokees, Lake o' the l. U.S.A.
79 E7 Cherokee Sound Bahamas
91 B3 Cherquenco Chile
23 G4 Cherrapunji India
75 E2 Cherry Creek U.S.A.
75 E1 Cherry Creek Mts mts U.S.A.
81 K2 Cherryfield U.S.A.
7 G3 Cherry Island i. Solomon Is
69 J4 Cherry Valley Can.
81 F3 Cherry Valley U.S.A.
13 Q3 Cherskogo, Khrebet mts Rus. Fed.
51 G5 Chertkovo Rus. Fed.
50 J2 Cherva Rus. Fed.
49 L3 Cherven Bryag Bulg.
51 C5 Chervonohrad Ukr.
51 E5 Chervonozavods'ke Ukr.
50 D4 Chervyen' Belarus
39 F6 Cherwell r. U.K.
50 D4 Cherykaw Belarus
69 E4 Chesaning U.S.A.
81 E6 Chesapeake U.S.A.
81 E5 Chesapeake Bay b. U.S.A.
39 G6 Chesham U.K.
81 G3 Cheshire U.S.A.
39 E4 Cheshire Plain lowland U.K.
19 F2 Cheshme 2-y Turkm.
12 F3 Cheshskaya Guba b. Rus. Fed.
19 F3 Chesht-e Sharīf Afgh.
39 G6 Cheshunt U.K.
39 E4 Chester U.K.
74 B1 Chester CA U.S.A.
78 B4 Chester IL U.S.A.
72 E1 Chester MT U.S.A.
81 F5 Chester PA U.S.A.
79 D5 Chester SC U.S.A.
81 E5 Chester r. U.S.A.
39 F4 Chesterfield U.K.
7 F3 Chesterfield, Îles is New Caledonia
63 J3 Chesterfield Inlet N.W.T. Can.
65 L2 Chesterfield Inlet Can.
65 L2 Chesterfield Inlet in. Can.
38 F3 Chester-le-Street U.K.
81 E5 Chestertown MD U.S.A.
81 G3 Chestertown NY U.S.A.
81 F2 Chesterville Can.
80 D4 Chestnut Ridge ridge U.S.A.
81 J1 Chesuncook U.S.A.
81 J1 Chesuncook Lake l. U.S.A.
48 B6 Chetaïbi Alg.
67 H4 Chéticamp Can.
21 A4 Chetlat i. India
82 G5 Chetumal Mex.
64 E3 Chetwynd Can.
27 □ Cheung Chau H.K. China
27 □ Cheung Chau i. H.K. China
9 D5 Cheviot N.Z.
38 E2 Cheviot Hills h. U.K.
38 E2 Cheviot, The h. U.K.
72 C1 Chewelah U.S.A.
77 D5 Cheyenne OK U.S.A.
72 F3 Cheyenne WY U.S.A.
76 C3 Cheyenne r. U.S.A.
76 C4 Cheyenne Wells U.S.A.
64 E4 Chezacut Can.
22 C4 Chhapar India
23 F4 Chhapra India
22 D4 Chhatarpur India
22 B3 Chhatr Pak.
22 D5 Chhindwara India
22 C5 Chhota Udepur India
22 C4 Chhoti Sadri India
23 G4 Chhukha Bhutan
27 F6 Chia-i Taiwan
32 B1 Chiang Kham Thai.
32 B1 Chiang Khan Thai.
32 A1 Chiang Mai Thai.
84 D3 Chiapas div. Mex.
48 C2 Chiari Italy
84 C3 Chiautla Mex.
29 G7 Chiba Japan
57 B5 Chibia Angola
57 D6 Chiboma Moz.
66 F4 Chibougamau Can.
66 F4 Chibougamau L. l. Can.
66 F4 Chibougamau, Parc de res. Can.
29 E6 Chibu-Sangaku Nat. Park Japan
59 K2 Chibuto Moz.
23 G2 Chibuzhang Hu l. China
Chicacole see Srikakulam
68 D5 Chicago U.S.A.
68 D5 Chicago Heights U.S.A.
68 C5 Chicago Ship Canal canal U.S.A.
89 B3 Chicamocha r. Col.
89 E3 Chicanán r. Venez.
64 B3 Chichagof U.S.A.
64 B3 Chichagof Island i. U.S.A.
26 E1 Chicheng China
39 G7 Chichester U.K.
6 B4 Chichester Range mts Austr.
29 F7 Chichibu Japan
29 F7 Chichibu-Tama National Park Japan
80 E6 Chickahominy r. U.S.A.
79 C5 Chickamauga L. l. U.S.A.
77 D5 Chickasha U.S.A.
45 C4 Chiclana de la Frontera Spain
86 C5 Chiclayo Peru
74 B2 Chico U.S.A.
88 C6 Chico r. Chubut Arg.
91 B4 Chico r. Chubut/Río Negro Arg.
88 C7 Chico r. Santa Cruz Arg.
59 L2 Chicomo Moz.
84 D4 Chicomucelo Mex.
81 G3 Chicopee U.S.A.
31 B2 Chico Sapocoy, Mt mt Phil.
67 F4 Chicoutimi Can.
59 J1 Chicualacuala Moz.
21 B4 Chidambaram India
59 L2 Chidenguele Moz.
67 H1 Chidley, C. c. Can.
30 D6 Chido S. Korea
59 L2 Chiducuane Moz.
79 D6 Chiefland U.S.A.
46 F7 Chiemsee l. Ger.
42 D5 Chiers r. France
48 F3 Chieti Italy
84 C3 Chietla Mex.
26 F1 Chifeng China
90 E2 Chifre, Serra do mts Brazil
12 J5 Chiganak Kazak.
67 G4 Chignecto B. b. Can.
89 A3 Chigorodó Col.
57 D6 Chigubo Moz.
23 G3 Chigu Co l. China
82 C3 Chihuahua Mex.
27 D6 Chikan China
21 B3 Chik Ballapur India
50 D3 Chikhachevo Rus. Fed.
22 D5 Chikhali Kalan Parasia India
22 D5 Chikhli India
21 A3 Chikmagalur India
29 F6 Chikuma-gawa r. Japan
64 E4 Chilanko Forks Can.
84 C3 Chilapa Mex.
15 F3 Chilas Jammu and Kashmir
21 B5 Chilaw Sri Lanka
74 B2 Chilcoot U.S.A.
64 E4 Chilcotin r. Can.
77 C5 Childress U.S.A.
85 C7 Chile country S. America
95 O8 Chile Basin sea feature Pac. Oc.
88 C3 Chilecito Arg.
51 H6 Chilgir Rus. Fed.
23 F6 Chilika Lake l. India
57 C5 Chililabombwe Zambia
64 E4 Chilko r. Can.
64 E4 Chilko L. l. Can.
91 B3 Chillán Chile
91 B3 Chillán, Nevado mts Chile
91 E3 Chillar Arg.
76 E4 Chillicothe MO U.S.A.
80 B5 Chillicothe OH U.S.A.
68 C5 Chillicothe U.S.A.
22 C1 Chillinji Pak.
64 E5 Chilliwack Can.
18 D1 Chil'mamedkum, Peski des. Turkm.
88 B6 Chiloé, Isla de i. Chile
72 B3 Chiloquin U.S.A.
84 C3 Chilpancingo Mex.
8 F4 Chiltern Austr.
39 G6 Chiltern Hills h. U.K.
68 C3 Chilton U.S.A.
27 F5 Chi-lung Taiwan
22 D2 Chiling Pass pass India
57 D4 Chimala Tanz.
42 C4 Chimay Belgium
91 C1 Chimbas Arg.
86 C4 Chimborazo mt Ecuador
86 C5 Chimbote Peru
89 B2 Chimichaguá Col.
57 D5 Chimoio Moz.
84 C1 China Mex.
10 L6 China country Asia
89 B3 Chinácota Col.
84 E3 Chinajá Guatemala
74 D4 China Lake l. CA U.S.A.
81 J2 China Lake l. ME U.S.A.
82 G6 Chinandega Nic.
74 C5 China Pt pt U.S.A.
86 C6 Chincha Alta Peru
64 F3 Chinchaga r. Can.
81 F6 Chincoteague B. b. U.S.A.
57 D5 Chinde Moz.
30 D6 Chindo S. Korea
30 D6 Chin-do i. S. Korea
24 B3 Chindu China
23 H5 Chindwin r. Myanmar
22 C2 Chineni Jammu and Kashmir
89 B3 Chingaza, Parque Nacional nat. park Col.
30 C4 Chinghwa N. Korea
57 C5 Chingola Zambia
57 B5 Chinguar Angola
30 E6 Chinhae S. Korea
57 D5 Chinhoyi Zimbabwe
22 C3 Chiniot Pak.
30 E6 Chinju S. Korea
56 C3 Chinko r. C.A.R.
75 H3 Chinle U.S.A.
75 H3 Chinle Valley v. U.S.A.
75 H3 Chinle Wash r. U.S.A.
27 F5 Chinmen Taiwan
27 F5 Chinmen Tao i. Taiwan
21 B2 Chinnur India
29 F7 Chino Japan
44 E3 Chinon France
75 F4 Chino Valley U.S.A.
57 D5 Chinsali Zambia
21 B3 Chintamani India
48 E2 Chioggia Italy
49 M5 Chios Greece
49 L5 Chios i. Greece
57 D5 Chipata Zambia
91 C4 Chipchihua, Sa de mts Arg.
57 B5 Chipindo Angola
57 D6 Chipinge Zimbabwe
21 A2 Chiplun India
39 E6 Chippenham U.K.
68 B3 Chippewa r. U.S.A.
68 B3 Chippewa Falls U.S.A.
68 B3 Chippewa, Lake l. U.S.A.
39 F6 Chipping Norton U.K.
39 E6 Chipping Sodbury U.K.
81 K2 Chiputneticook Lakes l. U.S.A.
82 G6 Chiquimula Guatemala
89 B3 Chiquinquira Col.
51 G5 Chir r. Rus. Fed.
21 C3 Chirada India
21 A4 Chirakkal India
21 C3 Chirala India
19 G3 Chiras Afgh.
22 C3 Chirāwa India
57 D6 Chiredzi Zimbabwe
75 H5 Chiricahua National Monument res. U.S.A.
75 H6 Chiricahua Peak summit U.S.A.
89 B2 Chiriguaná Col.
62 C4 Chirikof I. i. U.S.A.
83 H7 Chiriquí, Golfo de b. Panama
39 D5 Chirk U.K.
40 F5 Chirnside U.K.
49 L3 Chirpan Bulg.
83 H7 Chirripo mt Costa Rica
57 C5 Chirundu Zambia
66 E3 Chisasibi Can.
84 E4 Chisec Guatemala
68 A2 Chisholm U.S.A.
22 C3 Chishtian Mandi Pak.
27 B4 Chishur China
51 D6 Chişinău Moldova
47 K7 Chişineu-Criş Romania
50 J4 Chistopol' Rus. Fed.
24 D1 Chita Rus. Fed.
57 B5 Chitado Angola
57 D5 Chitambo Zambia
56 C4 Chitato Angola
65 H4 Chitek Lake Can.
57 B5 Chitembo Angola
57 D4 Chitipa Malawi
57 C5 Chitokoloki Zambia
28 G3 Chitose Japan
21 B3 Chitradurga India
22 B2 Chitral Pak.
22 B2 Chitral r. Pak.
83 H7 Chitré Panama
23 G5 Chittagong Bangl.
23 F5 Chittaranjan India
22 C4 Chittaurgarh India
21 B3 Chittoor India
21 B4 Chittur India
57 D5 Chitungulu Zambia
57 D5 Chitungwiza Zimbabwe
57 C5 Chiume Angola
57 D5 Chivhu Zimbabwe
91 E2 Chivilcoy Arg.
27 D6 Chixi China
17 J3 Chiya-e Linik h. Iraq
29 D7 Chizu Japan
50 G3 Chkalovsk Rus. Fed.
28 C2 Chkalovskoye Rus. Fed.
30 D6 Ch'o i. S. Korea
32 □ Choa Chu Kang Sing.
32 □ Choa Chu Kang h. Sing.
32 C2 Chŏâm Khsant Cambodia
91 B1 Choapa r. Chile
57 C5 Chobe National Park Botswana
30 D5 Choch'iwŏn S. Korea
75 E5 Chocolate Mts mts U.S.A.
89 B3 Chocontá Col.
30 C4 Cho Do i. N. Korea
43 L4 Chodov Czech Rep.
91 D3 Choele Choel Arg.
22 C2 Chogo Lungma Gl. gl. Pak.
51 H6 Chograyskoye Vdkhr. resr Rus. Fed.
65 J4 Choiceland Can.
7 F2 Choiseul i. Solomon Is
88 E8 Choiseul Sound chan. Falkland Is
46 H4 Chojnice Pol.
28 G5 Chōkai-san volc. Japan
77 D6 Choke Canyon L. l. U.S.A.
56 D2 Ch'ok'ē Mts mts Eth.
23 F3 Choksum China
13 Q2 Chokurdakh Rus. Fed.
57 D6 Chókwé Moz.
44 D3 Cholet France
91 B4 Cholila Arg.
82 G6 Choluteca Honduras
57 C5 Choma Zambia
30 E5 Chŏmch'ŏn S. Korea
23 G4 Chomo Lhari mt Bhutan
32 A1 Chom Thong Thai.
46 F5 Chomutov Czech Rep.
13 M3 Chona r. Rus. Fed.
30 D5 Ch'ŏnan S. Korea
32 B2 Chon Buri Thai.
30 D3 Ch'ŏnch'ŏn N. Korea
86 B4 Chone Ecuador
27 F5 Chong'an China
30 C4 Chongchon r. N. Korea
30 E6 Chongdo S. Korea
30 E3 Ch'ŏngjin N. Korea
30 C4 Chŏngju N. Korea
30 D6 Chŏngju S. Korea
30 D5 Ch'ŏngju S. Korea
32 B2 Chŏng Kal Cambodia
30 D4 Chŏngp'yŏng N. Korea
27 C4 Chongqing China
27 E5 Chongren China
59 K2 Chonguene Moz.
57 C5 Chongwe Zambia
27 D4 Chongyang China
27 F5 Chongyang Xi r. China
27 E5 Chongyi China
27 C6 Chongzuo China
30 D6 Ch'ŏnju S. Korea
23 F3 Cho Oyu mt China
32 C3 Chơ Phươc Hai Vietnam
90 B4 Chopim r. Brazil
90 B4 Chopimzinho Brazil
81 F5 Choptank r. U.S.A.
22 B4 Chor Pak.
38 E4 Chorley U.K.
51 D5 Chornobyl' Ukr.
51 E6 Chornomors'ke Ukr.
51 C5 Chortkiv Ukr.
30 D4 Ch'ŏrwŏn S. Korea
30 C3 Ch'osan N. Korea
29 G7 Chōshi Japan
91 B3 Chos Malal Arg.
46 G4 Choszczno Pol.
86 C5 Chota Peru
72 D2 Choteau U.S.A.
22 B3 Choti Pak.
54 A2 Choûm Maur.
74 B3 Chowchilla U.S.A.
64 F4 Chown, Mt mt Can.
24 D2 Choybalsan Mongolia
24 C2 Choyr Mongolia
46 H6 Chřiby h. Czech Rep.
68 D6 Chrisman U.S.A.
59 J3 Chrissiesmeer S. Africa
9 D5 Christchurch N.Z.
39 F7 Christchurch U.K.
59 F3 Christiana S. Africa
63 M2 Christian, C. pt Can.
69 G3 Christian I. i. Can.
Christiansåb see Qasigiannguit
80 C6 Christiansburg U.S.A.
64 C3 Christian Sound chan. U.S.A.
65 G3 Christina r. Can.
7 G6 Christina, Mt mt N.Z.
Christmas Island i. see Kiritimati
25 C8 Christmas Island terr. Ind. Ocean
46 G6 Chrudim Czech Rep.
49 L7 Chrysi i. Greece
15 F2 Chu Kazak.
12 H5 Chu r. Kazak.
23 G5 Chuadanga Bangl.
59 K2 Chuali, L. l. Moz.
26 F4 Chuansha China
72 D3 Chubbuck U.S.A.
91 C4 Chubut div. Arg.
88 C6 Chubut r. Arg.
75 E5 Chuckwalla Mts mts U.S.A.
51 D5 Chudniv Ukr.
50 D3 Chudovo Rus. Fed.
Chudskoye Ozero l. see Peipus, Lake
62 C4 Chugach Mountains mts U.S.A.
29 C7 Chūgoku-sanchi mts Japan
28 C2 Chuguyevka Rus. Fed.
72 F3 Chugwater U.S.A.
51 F5 Chuhuyiv Ukr.
75 G5 Chuichu U.S.A.
24 F1 Chukchagirskoye, Ozero l. Rus. Fed.
13 V3 Chukchi Sea sea Rus. Fed./U.S.A.
50 G3 Chukhloma Rus. Fed.
13 U3 Chukotskiy Poluostrov pen. Rus. Fed.
50 H1 Chulasa Rus. Fed.
74 D5 Chula Vista U.S.A.
12 K4 Chulym Rus. Fed.
23 G4 Chumbi China
88 C3 Chumbicha Arg.
24 F1 Chumikan Rus. Fed.
32 B1 Chum Phae Thai.
32 A3 Chumphon Thai.
32 B2 Chum Saeng Thai.
13 L4 Chuna r. Rus. Fed.
27 F4 Chun'an China
30 D5 Ch'unch'ŏn S. Korea
30 D5 Ch'ungju S. Korea
Chungking see Chongqing
30 E6 Ch'ungmu S. Korea
30 C4 Chŭngsan N. Korea
19 H3 Chungur, Koh-i- h. Afgh.
30 F2 Chunhua China
23 F3 Chunit Tso salt l. China
13 M3 Chunya r. Rus. Fed.
32 C3 Chuŏr Phnum Dâmrei mts Cambodia
32 C2 Chuŏr Phnum Dângrêk mts Cambodia/Thai.
32 B2 Chuŏr Phnum Krâvanh mts Cambodia
26 A4 Chuosijia China
17 L3 Chūplū Iran
86 D7 Chuquibamba Peru
88 C2 Chuquicamata Chile
46 D7 Chur Switz.
13 P3 Churapcha Rus. Fed.
65 L3 Churchill Can.
65 K3 Churchill r. Man./Sask. Can.
67 H3 Churchill r. Nfld Can.
63 J4 Churchill r. Sask. Can.
65 L3 Churchill, Cape c. Can.
67 H3 Churchill Falls Can.
65 H3 Churchill Lake l. Can.
64 D3 Churchill Peak summit Can.
66 E2 Churchill Sound chan. Can.
76 D1 Churchs Ferry U.S.A.
80 D5 Churchville U.S.A.
23 F4 Churia Ghati Hills mts Nepal
50 H3 Churov Rus. Fed.
22 C3 Churu India
89 C2 Churuguara Venez.
22 D2 Chushul Jammu and Kashmir
75 H3 Chuska Mountains mts U.S.A.
67 F4 Chute-des-Passes Can.
69 J2 Chute-Rouge Can.
69 K2 Chute-St-Philippe Can.
27 F5 Chu-tung Taiwan
4 G4 Chuuk i. Micronesia
50 H4 Chuvashskaya Respublika div. Rus. Fed.
26 F3 Chu Xian China
27 A5 Chuxiong China
32 D2 Chư Yang Sin mt Vietnam
17 K4 Chwārtā Iraq
51 D6 Ciadâr-Lunga Moldova
33 C4 Ciamis Indon.
33 C4 Cianjur Indon.
90 B3 Cianorte Brazil
73 E6 Cibuta Mex.
48 F2 Čičarija mts Croatia
16 E2 Çiçekdağı Turkey
51 E7 Cide Turkey
47 K4 Ciechanów Pol.
83 J4 Ciego de Avila Cuba
89 B2 Ciénaga Col.
89 B2 Ciénaga de Zapatoza l. Col.
84 B1 Ciénega de Flores Mex.
73 E6 Cieneguita Mex.
83 H4 Cienfuegos Cuba
45 F3 Cieza Spain
45 E2 Cifuentes Spain
17 M2 Çigil Adası i. Azer.
45 E3 Cigüela r. Spain
16 D2 Cihanbeyli Turkey
84 A3 Cihuatlán Mex.
45 D3 Cijara, Embalse de resr Spain
33 C4 Cilacap Indon.
17 J1 Çıldır Turkey
17 J1 Çıldır Gölü l. Turkey
27 D4 Cili China
17 K3 Cilo D. mt Turkey
17 N1 Çiloy Adası i. Azer.
75 E4 Cima U.S.A.
73 F4 Cimarron U.S.A.
77 D4 Cimarron r. U.S.A.
42 D5 Cimetière d'Ossuaire France
51 D6 Cimişlia Moldova
48 D2 Cimone, Monte mt Italy
17 H3 Çınar Turkey
89 C3 Cinaruco r. Venez.
89 D3 Cinaruco-Capanaparo, Parque Nacional nat. park Venez.
45 G2 Cinca r. Spain
80 A5 Cincinnati U.S.A.
81 F3 Cincinnatus U.S.A.
91 D4 Cinco Chañares Arg.
91 C3 Cinco Saltos Arg.
39 E6 Cinderford U.K.
16 B3 Çine Turkey
42 D4 Ciney Belgium
84 D3 Cintalapa Mex.
44 J5 Cinto, Monte mt France
90 B3 Cinzas r. Brazil
91 C3 Cipolletti Arg.
62 D3 Circle AK U.S.A.
72 F2 Circle U.S.A.
80 B5 Circleville OH U.S.A.
75 F2 Circleville UT U.S.A.
33 C4 Cirebon Indon.
39 F6 Cirencester U.K.
48 B2 Ciriè Italy
48 G5 Cirò Marina Italy
67 H2 Cirque Mtn mt Can.
68 C6 Cisco IL U.S.A.
77 D5 Cisco TX U.S.A.
75 H2 Cisco UT U.S.A.
89 B3 Cisneros Col.
84 C3 Citlaltépetl, Vol. volc. Mex.
48 G3 Čitluk Bos.-Herz.
58 C6 Citrusdal S. Africa
48 E3 Città di Castello Italy
49 L2 Ciucaş, Vârful mt Romania
82 D3 Ciudad Acuña Mex.
84 B3 Ciudad Altamirano Mex.
89 E3 Ciudad Bolívar Venez.
82 C3 Ciudad Camargo Mex.
84 E4 Ciudad Cuauhtémoc Mex.
84 E3 Ciudad del Carmen Mex.
90 A4 Ciudad del Este Para.
82 C3 Ciudad Delicias Mex.
84 C2 Ciudad del Maíz Mex.
89 C2 Ciudad de Nutrias Venez.
84 C2 Ciudad de Valles Mex.
89 E2 Ciudad Guayana Venez.
84 B3 Ciudad Guzmán Mex.
84 B3 Ciudad Hidalgo Mex.
84 D3 Ciudad Ixtepec Mex.
82 C2 Ciudad Juárez Mex.
84 B1 Ciudad Lerdo Mex.
84 C2 Ciudad Madero Mex.
84 C2 Ciudad Mante Mex.
84 C3 Ciudad Mendoza Mex.
84 C1 Ciudad Mier Mex.
82 C3 Ciudad Obregón Mex.
89 E3 Ciudad Piar Venez.
45 E3 Ciudad Real Spain
84 C1 Ciudad Río Bravo Mex.
45 C2 Ciudad Rodrigo Spain
84 C2 Ciudad Victoria Mex.
45 H2 Ciutadella de Menorca Spain
16 F1 Çıva Burnu pt Turkey
16 B2 Çivan Dağ mt Turkey
48 E1 Cividale del Friuli Italy
48 E3 Civita Castellana Italy
48 E3 Civitanova Marche Italy
48 D3 Civitavecchia Italy
16 B2 Çivril Turkey
27 F4 Cixi China
26 E2 Ci Xian China
17 J3 Cizre Turkey
39 J6 Clacton-on-Sea U.K.
41 D3 Clady U.K.
65 G3 Claire, Lake l. Can.
72 B3 Clair Engle L. resr U.S.A.
80 D4 Clairton U.S.A.
44 F3 Clamecy France
74 D2 Clan Alpine Mts mts U.S.A.
41 E4 Clane Rep. of Ireland
79 C5 Clanton U.S.A.
58 C6 Clanwilliam S. Africa
41 D4 Clara Rep. of Ireland
32 A3 Clara I. i. Myanmar
8 D2 Clare N.S.W. Austr.
8 B2 Clare S.A. Austr.
68 E4 Clare U.S.A.
41 C4 Clare r. Rep. of Ireland
41 C5 Clarecastle Rep. of Ireland
41 A4 Clare Island i. Rep. of Ireland
81 G3 Claremont U.S.A.
77 E4 Claremore U.S.A.
41 C4 Claremorris Rep. of Ireland
9 D5 Clarence N.Z.
92 B1 Clarence I. i. Ant.
64 C3 Clarence Str. chan. U.S.A.
79 F7 Clarence Town Bahamas
77 C5 Clarendon U.S.A.
67 K4 Clarenville Can.
64 G5 Claresholm Can.
76 E3 Clarinda U.S.A.
80 C5 Clarington U.S.A.
80 D4 Clarion U.S.A.
80 D4 Clarion r. U.S.A.
95 L4 Clarion Fracture Zone sea feature Pac. Oc.
61 G8 Clarión, Isla i. Mex.
76 D2 Clark U.S.A.
59 H5 Clarkebury S. Africa
6 E6 Clarke I. i. Austr.
70 D2 Clark Fork r. MT U.S.A.
79 D5 Clark Hill Res. resr U.S.A.
75 E4 Clark Mt mt U.S.A.
69 G3 Clark, Pt pt Can.
80 C5 Clarksburg U.S.A.
77 F5 Clarksdale U.S.A.
81 F4 Clarks Summit U.S.A.
72 C2 Clarkston U.S.A.
77 E5 Clarksville AR U.S.A.
68 A4 Clarksville IA U.S.A.
79 C4 Clarksville TN U.S.A.
90 B1 Claro r. Goiás Brazil
90 B2 Claro r. Goiás Brazil
41 D5 Clashmore Rep. of Ireland
41 D3 Claudy U.K.
31 B2 Claveria Phil.
42 D4 Clavier Belgium
81 G2 Clayburg U.S.A.
76 D4 Clay Center U.S.A.
75 F3 Clayhole Wash r. U.S.A.
79 D5 Clayton GA U.S.A.
73 G4 Clayton NM U.S.A.
81 E2 Clayton NY U.S.A.
81 J1 Clayton Lake l. U.S.A.
80 C6 Claytor Lake l. U.S.A.
41 B6 Clear, Cape c. Rep. of Ireland
69 G4 Clear Creek Can.
75 G4 Clear Creek r. U.S.A.
62 D4 Cleare, C. c. U.S.A.
80 D4 Clearfield PA U.S.A.
72 E3 Clearfield UT U.S.A.
80 B4 Clear Fork Reservoir U.S.A.
64 F3 Clear Hills mts Can.
76 E3 Clear Lake IA U.S.A.
68 A3 Clear Lake WV U.S.A.
74 A2 Clear Lake l. CA U.S.A.
75 F2 Clear Lake l. UT U.S.A.
72 B3 Clear L. Res. resr U.S.A.
79 D7 Clearwater U.S.A.
64 F4 Clearwater r. Alta. Can.
65 H3 Clearwater r. Sask. Can.
27 □ Clear Water Bay b. H.K. China
72 D2 Clearwater Mountains U.S.A.
65 H3 Clearwater River Provincial Park res. Can.
77 D5 Cleburne U.S.A.
72 B2 Cle Elum U.S.A.
38 G4 Cleethorpes U.K.
32 □ Clementi Sing.
80 C5 Clendenin U.S.A.
80 C4 Clendening Lake l. U.S.A.
31 A4 Cleopatra Needle mt Phil.
69 H1 Cléricy Can.
6 E4 Clermont Austr.
42 A5 Clermont France
79 D6 Clermont U.S.A.
42 D5 Clermont-en-Argonne France
44 F4 Clermont-Ferrand France
42 E4 Clervaux Lux.
48 D1 Cles Italy
39 E6 Clevedon U.K.
77 F5 Cleveland MS U.S.A.
80 C4 Cleveland OH U.S.A.
79 C5 Cleveland TN U.S.A.
68 D2 Cleveland Cliffs Basin l. U.S.A.
38 F3 Cleveland Hills h. U.K.
64 G5 Cleveland, Mt mt U.S.A.
38 D4 Cleveleys U.K.
41 B4 Clew Bay b. Rep. of Ireland
79 D7 Clewiston U.S.A.
41 A4 Clifden Rep. of Ireland
75 H5 Cliff U.S.A.
41 C3 Cliffoney Rep. of Ireland
9 E4 Clifford Bay b. N.Z.
75 H5 Clifton U.S.A.
80 D6 Clifton Forge U.S.A.
80 B6 Clinch r. U.S.A.
80 B6 Clinch Mountain U.S.A.
64 E4 Clinton B.C. Can.
69 G4 Clinton Ont. Can.
81 G4 Clinton CT U.S.A.
68 B5 Clinton IA U.S.A.
68 C5 Clinton IL U.S.A.
81 H3 Clinton MA U.S.A.
81 J2 Clinton ME U.S.A.
76 E4 Clinton MO U.S.A.
77 F5 Clinton MS U.S.A.
79 E5 Clinton NC U.S.A.
77 D5 Clinton OK U.S.A.
65 H2 Clinton-Colden Lake l. Can.
68 C5 Clinton Lake l. U.S.A.
68 C3 Clintonville U.S.A.
75 G4 Clints Well U.S.A.
95 L5 Clipperton Fracture Zone sea feature Pac. Oc.
82 C6 Clipperton Island terr. Pac. Oc.
40 B3 Clisham h. U.K.
38 E4 Clitheroe U.K.
59 G4 Clocolan S. Africa
41 D4 Cloghan Rep. of Ireland
41 C6 Clonakilty Rep. of Ireland
41 C6 Clonakilty Bay b. Rep. of Ireland
41 C4 Clonbern Rep. of Ireland
6 E4 Cloncurry Austr.
41 D3 Clones Rep. of Ireland
41 D5 Clonmel Rep. of Ireland
41 D4 Clonygowan Rep. of Ireland
41 B5 Cloonbannin Rep. of Ireland
41 D4 Clooneagh Rep. of Ireland
43 G2 Cloppenburg Ger.
68 A2 Cloquet U.S.A.
72 F2 Cloud Peak summit U.S.A.
9 E4 Cloudy Bay b. N.Z.
27 □ Cloudy Hill h. H.K. China
69 K1 Clova Can.
74 A2 Cloverdale U.S.A.
77 C5 Clovis U.S.A.
69 J3 Cloyne Can.
40 C3 Cluanie, Loch l. U.K.
65 H3 Cluff Lake Can.
47 L7 Cluj-Napoca Romania
39 D5 Clun U.K.
8 D4 Clunes Austr.
44 H3 Cluses France
39 D4 Clwydian Range h. U.K.
64 G4 Clyde Can.
80 E3 Clyde NY U.S.A.
80 B4 Clyde OH U.S.A.
40 D5 Clyde r. U.K.
40 D5 Clydebank U.K.
40 D5 Clyde, Firth of est. U.K.

75 E2 Currant U.S.A.
8 E1 Curranyalpa Austr.
79 E7 Current Bahamas
6 E5 Currie Austr.
75 E1 Currie U.S.A.
8 H3 Currockbilly, Mt Austr.
6 F4 Curtis I. *i.* Austr.
87 H5 Curuá *r.* Brazil
87 J4 Curuçá Brazil
33 B3 Curup Indon.
87 K4 Cururupu Brazil
89 E3 Curutú, Cerro *mt* Venez.
90 D2 Curvelo Brazil
86 D6 Cusco Peru
41 E2 Cushendall U.K.
41 E2 Cushendun U.K.
77 D4 Cushing U.S.A.
89 C3 Cusiana *r.* Col.
79 C5 Cusseta U.S.A.
68 A1 Cusson U.S.A.
66 E1 Cusson, Pte *pt* Can.
72 F2 Custer *MT* U.S.A.
76 C3 Custer *SD* U.S.A.
89 A4 Cutanga, Pico de *mt* Col.
72 D1 Cut Bank U.S.A.
79 C6 Cuthbert U.S.A.
65 H4 Cut Knife Can.
81 K2 Cutler U.S.A.
79 D7 Cutler Ridge U.S.A.
91 C3 Cutral-Co Arg.
23 F5 Cuttack India
75 G5 Cutter U.S.A.
43 G1 Cuxhaven Ger.
80 C4 Cuyahoga Falls U.S.A.
80 C4 Cuyahoga Valley National Recreation Area *res.* U.S.A.
74 C4 Cuyama *r.* U.S.A.
31 B3 Cuyapo Phil.
31 B4 Cuyo Phil.
31 B4 Cuyo *i.* Phil.
31 B4 Cuyo East Pass. *chan.* Phil.
31 B4 Cuyo Islands *is* Phil.
31 B4 Cuyo West Pass. *chan.* Phil.
89 E3 Cuyuni *r.* Guyana
Cuzco *see* Cusco
39 D6 Cwmbran U.K.
56 C4 Cyangugu Rwanda
49 L6 Cyclades *is* Greece
80 A5 Cynthiana U.S.A.
65 G5 Cypress Hills *mts* Can.
10 E6 Cyprus *country* Asia
65 G4 Czar Can.
34 G4 Czech Republic *country* Europe
46 H4 Czersk Pol.
47 J5 Częstochowa Pol.

D

30 C1 Da'an China
16 F6 Dab'a Jordan
89 C2 Dabajuro Venez.
54 B4 Dabakala Côte d'Ivoire
26 A2 Daban Shan *mts* China
26 C3 Daba Shan *mts* China
89 A3 Dabeiba Col.
43 K1 Dabel Ger.
22 C5 Dabhoi India
21 A2 Dabhol India
26 E4 Dabie Shan *mts* China
22 D4 Daboh India
54 A3 Dabola Guinea
54 B4 Daboya Ghana
22 D4 Dabra India
47 J5 Dąbrowa Górnicza Pol.
27 E5 Dabu China
30 B1 Dabusu Pao *l.* China
Dacca *see* Dhaka
46 E6 Dachau Ger.
26 A2 Dachechang China
21 B2 Dachepalle India
69 J3 Dacre Can.
16 D1 Daday Turkey
79 D6 Dade City U.S.A.
22 C5 Dadra India
22 C5 Dadra and Nagar Haveli *div.* India
22 A4 Dadu Pak.
27 B4 Dadu He *r.* China
32 C3 Đa Dung *r.* Vietnam
31 B3 Daet Phil.
27 B5 Dafang China
26 F3 Dafeng China
30 D2 Dafengman China
23 H4 Dafla Hills *mts* India
54 A3 Dagana Senegal
26 B3 Dagcanglhamo China
51 H7 Dagestan, Respublika *div.* Rus. Fed.
26 F2 Dagu *r.* China
27 B5 Daguan China
27 □ D'Aguilar Peak *h.* *H.K.* China
31 B2 Dagupan Phil.
23 H1 Dagur China
23 G3 Dagzê China
23 F3 Dagzê Co *salt l.* China
22 C6 Dahanu India
26 D1 Dahei *r.* China
30 C2 Dahei Shan *mts* China
28 C1 Dahezhen China
24 D2 Da Hinggan Ling *mts* China
56 E2 Dahlak Archipelago *is* Eritrea
56 E2 Dahlak Marine National Park Eritrea
42 E4 Dahlem Ger.
43 J1 Dahlenburg Ger.
48 C7 Dahmani Tunisia
43 F5 Dahn Ger.
22 C5 Dāhod India
22 D2 Dahongliutan China/Jammu and Kashmir
43 J2 Dähre Ger.
17 J3 Dahūk Iraq
30 C3 Dahuofang Shuiku *resr* China
30 B3 Dahushan China
26 D1 Dai Hai *l.* China
33 B3 Daik Indon.
40 D5 Dailly U.K.
19 E3 Daim Iran
29 C6 Daimanji-san *h.* Japan
45 E3 Daimiel Spain
91 E3 Daireaux Arg.
68 A2 Dairyland U.S.A.
29 C7 Daisen *volc.* Japan
27 G4 Daishan China
27 F5 Daiyun Shan *mts* China
6 D4 Dajarra Austr.
26 A4 Dajin Chuan *r.* China
26 B2 Dajing China
23 H1 Da Juh China
54 A3 Dakar Senegal
23 G3 Dakelangsi China
23 G5 Dakhin Shahbaz-pur I. *i.* Bangl.
55 E2 Dakhla Oasis *oasis* Egypt
32 C2 Dak Kon Vietnam
50 D4 Dakol'ka *r.* Belarus
76 D3 Dakota City U.S.A.
49 J3 Đakovica Yugo.
49 H2 Đakovo Croatia
57 C5 Dala Angola
54 A3 Dalaba Guinea
26 D1 Dalad Qi China
26 E1 Dalai Nur *l.* China
18 C4 Dalaki, Rud-e *r.* Iran
26 D1 Dalamamiao China
16 B3 Dalaman Turkey
16 B3 Dalaman *r.* Turkey
24 C2 Dalandzadgad Mongolia
31 B4 Dalanganem Islands *is* Phil.
4 J4 Dalap-Uliga-Darrit Marshall Is
32 D3 Đa Lat Vietnam
26 B1 Dalay Mongolia
19 G4 Dalbandin Pak.
40 E6 Dalbeattie U.K.
6 F4 Dalby Austr.
38 C3 Dalby U.K.
37 J6 Dale *Hordaland* Norway
37 J6 Dale *Sogn og Fjordane* Norway
80 E5 Dale City U.S.A.
77 G4 Dale Hollow Lake *l.* U.S.A.
42 E2 Dalen Neth.
23 H6 Dalet Myanmar
23 H5 Daletme Myanmar
37 O6 Dalfors Sweden
19 E5 Dalgān Iran
8 G4 Dalgety Austr.
77 C4 Dalhart U.S.A.
67 G4 Dalhousie Can.
26 D3 Dali *Shaanxi* China
24 C4 Dali *Yunnan* China
30 A4 Dalian China
27 B4 Daliang Shan *mts* China
30 B2 Dalin China
26 F1 Daling *r.* China
30 D3 Dalizi China
40 E5 Dalkeith U.K.
23 F4 Dālkola India
81 F4 Dallas *PA* U.S.A.
77 D5 Dallas *TX* U.S.A.
68 B5 Dallas City U.S.A.
72 B2 Dalles, The U.S.A.
64 C4 Dall I. *i.* U.S.A.
18 D5 Dalmā *i.* U.A.E.
91 D2 Dalmacio Vélez Sarsfield Arg.
22 E4 Dalman India
48 G3 Dalmatia *reg.* Croatia
40 D5 Dalmellington U.K.
28 D2 Dal'negorsk Rus. Fed.
28 C2 Dal'nerechensk Rus. Fed.
54 B4 Daloa Côte d'Ivoire
27 C5 Dalou Shan *mts* China
18 B5 Dalqān *well* S. Arabia
40 D5 Dalry U.K.
40 D5 Dalrymple U.K.
6 E4 Dalrymple, L. *l.* Austr.
6 E4 Dalrymple, Mt *mt* Austr.
23 F4 Daltenganj India
69 E1 Dalton Can.
59 J4 Dalton S. Africa
79 C5 Dalton *GA* U.S.A.
81 G3 Dalton *MA* U.S.A.
38 D3 Dalton-in-Furness U.K.
69 E1 Dalton Mills Can.
41 C5 Dalua *r.* Rep. of Ireland
31 B2 Dalupiri *i.* Phil.
31 C3 Dalupiri *i.* Phil.
36 D4 Dalvík Iceland
6 D3 Daly *r.* Austr.
74 A3 Daly City U.S.A.
6 D3 Daly Waters Austr.
22 C5 Daman India
22 C5 Daman and Diu *div.* India
55 F1 Damanhûr Egypt
18 C3 Damaq Iran
26 E1 Damaqun Shan *mts* China
31 C6 Damar Indon.
25 E7 Damar *i.* Indon.
16 F5 Damascus Syria
91 B2 Damas, P. de las *pass* Arg./Chile
54 D3 Damaturu Nigeria
18 D3 Damavand Iran
21 C5 Dambulla Sri Lanka
18 D2 Damghan Iran
26 E2 Daming China
27 C6 Daming Shan *mt* China
23 H2 Damjong China
31 B5 Dammai *i.* Phil.
42 B3 Damme Belgium
43 G2 Damme Ger.
22 D5 Damoh India
54 B4 Damongo Ghana
6 E2 Dampier Strait *chan.* P.N.G.
25 F7 Dampir, Selat *chan.* Indon.
Damqoq Kanbab *r.* *see* Maquan He
23 H2 Dam Qu *r.* China
23 H3 Damroh India
42 E1 Damwoude Neth.
54 B4 Danané Côte d'Ivoire
32 D1 Đa Năng Vietnam
31 C4 Danao Phil.
26 A4 Danba China
81 G4 Danbury *CT* U.S.A.
81 H3 Danbury *NH* U.S.A.
81 G3 Danby U.S.A.
75 E4 Danby Lake *l.* U.S.A.
26 E3 Dancheng China
56 D3 Dande Eth.
21 A3 Dandeli India
8 E4 Dandenong Austr.
30 C3 Dandong China
39 E4 Dane *r.* U.K.
63 Q2 Daneborg Greenland
81 K2 Danforth U.S.A.
27 E6 Dangan Liedao *is* China
23 G3 Dangbe La *pass* China
28 B2 Dangbizhen Rus. Fed.
26 B3 Dangchang China
5 P5 Danger Islands *is* Pac. Oc.
58 C7 Danger Pt *pt* S. Africa
56 D2 Dangila Eth.
Dangla *mts* *see* Tanggula Shan
23 G3 Dangqên China
82 G5 Dangriga Belize
26 E3 Dangshan China
26 F4 Dangtu China
27 D4 Dangyang China
72 E3 Daniel U.S.A.
58 E4 Daniëlskuil S. Africa
50 G3 Danilov Rus. Fed.
51 H5 Danilovka Rus. Fed.
50 G3 Danilovskaya Vozvyshennost' *reg.* Rus. Fed.
26 D2 Daning China
17 M1 Dänizkänarı Azer.
26 D3 Danjiangkou Sk. *resr* China
18 E6 Dank Oman
22 D2 Dankhar India
50 F4 Dankov Rus. Fed.
27 B4 Danleng China
82 G6 Danlí Honduras
Dannebrogsø *i.* *see* Qillak
81 G2 Dannemora U.S.A.
43 K1 Dannenberg (Elbe) Ger.
43 M1 Dannenwalde Ger.
9 F4 Dannevirke N.Z.
59 J4 Dannhauser S. Africa
32 B1 Dan Sai Thai.
80 E3 Dansville U.S.A.
22 C4 Danta India
21 C2 Dantewara India
49 M3 Danube *r.* Europe
68 D5 Danville *IL* U.S.A.
68 D6 Danville *IN* U.S.A.
78 C4 Danville *KY* U.S.A.
69 J5 Danville *PA* U.S.A.
80 D6 Danville *VA* U.S.A.
27 C7 Dan Xian China
26 F4 Danyang China
27 C5 Danzhai China
31 B4 Dao Phil.
27 C6 Đao Bach Long Vi *i.* Vietnam
27 C6 Đao Cai Bâu *i.* Vietnam
27 C6 Đao Cat Ba *i.* Vietnam
32 B3 Đao Phu Quôc *i.* Vietnam
32 B3 Đao Thô Chư *i.* Vietnam
54 B4 Daoukro Côte d'Ivoire
32 B3 Đao Vây *i.* Vietnam
27 D5 Dao Xian China
27 C4 Daozhen China
31 C4 Dapa Phil.
54 C3 Dapaong Togo
23 J4 Daphabum *mt* India
31 B4 Dapiak, Mt *mt* Phil.
31 B4 Dapitan Phil.
15 H3 Da Qaidam China
24 E2 Daqing China
18 D3 Daqq-e Dombūn Iran
19 F3 Daqq-e-Tundi, Dasht-e *l.* Afgh.
26 D1 Daquing Shan *mts* China
17 K4 Dāqūq Iraq
27 G4 Daqu Shan *i.* China
16 F5 Dar'ā Syria
18 D4 Dārāb Iran
31 B3 Daraga Phil.
47 O4 Darahanava Belarus
54 D1 Daraj Libya
18 D4 Dārākūyeh Iran
31 C4 Daram *i.* Phil.
18 D3 Darang, Kūh-e *h.* Iran
13 N4 Darasun Rus. Fed.
18 E4 Darband Iran
23 F4 Darbhanga India
74 C2 Dardanelle U.S.A.
77 E5 Dardanelle, Lake *l.* U.S.A.
49 M4 Dardanelles *str.* Turkey
43 J3 Dardesheim Ger.
16 F2 Darende Turkey
56 D4 Dar es Salaam Tanz.
48 D2 Darfo Boario Terme Italy
22 B2 Dargai Pak.
19 F1 Dargan-Ata Turkm.
9 D1 Dargaville N.Z.
8 F4 Dargo Austr.
24 C2 Darhan Mongolia
26 D1 Darhan Muminggan Lianheqi China
79 D6 Darien U.S.A.
89 A2 Darién, Golfo del *g.* Col.
83 J7 Darién, Parque Nacional de *nat. park* Panama
89 A2 Darién, Serranía del *mts* Panama
23 G4 Dārjiling India
18 C4 Darkhazīneh Iran
24 B3 Darlag China
8 D2 Darling *r.* Austr.
6 E4 Darling Downs *reg.* Austr.
6 B5 Darling Range *h.* Austr.
38 F3 Darlington U.K.
68 B4 Darlington U.S.A.
8 F3 Darlington Point Austr.
46 H3 Darłowo Pol.
18 B5 Darmā S. Arabia
22 E3 Darma Pass China/India
21 B2 Darmaraopet India
18 E4 Dar Mazār Iran
43 G5 Darmstadt Ger.
22 C5 Darna *r.* India
55 E1 Darnah Libya
59 J4 Darnall S. Africa
8 D2 Darnick Austr.
62 F3 Darnley Bay *b.* Can.
92 D5 Darnley, C. *c.* Ant.
45 F2 Daroca Spain
50 G3 Darovka Rus. Fed.
50 H3 Darovskoy Rus. Fed.
91 D3 Darregueira Arg.
18 E3 Darreh Bīd Iran
19 E2 Darreh Gaz Iran
17 L4 Darreh Gozaru *r.* Iran
19 H3 Darreh-ye Shekārī *r.* Afgh.
21 B3 Darsi India
17 M6 Darsīyeh Iran
39 D7 Dart *r.* U.K.
39 H6 Dartford U.K.
8 C4 Dartmoor Austr.
39 C7 Dartmoor *reg.* U.K.
39 D7 Dartmoor National Park U.K.
67 H5 Dartmouth Can.
39 D7 Dartmouth U.K.
38 F4 Darton U.K.
41 C3 Darty Mts *h.* Rep. of Ireland
6 E2 Daru P.N.G.
54 A4 Daru Sierra Leone
23 G3 Darum Tso *l.* China
48 G2 Daruvar Croatia
19 E1 Darvaza Turkm.
18 C4 Darvīsla Iran
19 G4 Darwazgai Afgh.
38 E4 Darwen U.K.
19 G4 Darweshan Afgh.
6 D3 Darwin Austr.
88 C8 Darwin, Mte *mt* Chile
22 B3 Darya Khan Pak.
19 E4 Dārzīn Iran
18 D5 Dās *i.* U.A.E.
26 D4 Dashennongjia *mt* China
20 E1 Dashkhovuz Turkm.
18 E2 Dasht Iran
19 F5 Dasht *r.* Pak.
18 E4 Dasht Āb Iran
18 C4 Dasht-e Palang *r.* Iran
19 F5 Dashtiari Iran
19 H2 Dashtiobburdon Tajik.
26 C2 Dashuikeng China
26 B2 Dashuitou China
22 C3 Daska Pak.
17 L1 Daşkäsän Azer.
22 C1 Daspar *mt* Pak.
43 H3 Dassel Ger.
58 C6 Dassen Island *i.* S. Africa
17 L2 Dastakert Armenia
18 E3 Dastgardān Iran
30 F2 Da Suifen *r.* China
49 M6 Datça Turkey
28 G3 Date Japan
75 F5 Dateland U.S.A.
22 D4 Datia India
27 E5 Datian China
26 A2 Datong *Qinghai* China
26 D1 Datong *Shanxi* China
26 B2 Datong He *r.* China
26 A2 Datong Shan *mts* China
31 C5 Datu Piang Phil.
33 C2 Datu, Tanjung *c.* Indon./Malaysia
50 C3 Daugava *r.* Belarus/Latvia
37 U9 Daugavpils Latvia
19 G2 Daulatabad Afgh.
22 C6 Daulatabad India
Daulatabad *see* Malāyer
42 E4 Daun Ger.
21 A2 Daund India
32 A2 Daung Kyun *i.* Myanmar
65 J4 Dauphin Can.
44 G4 Dauphiné *reg.* France
77 F6 Dauphin I. *i.* U.S.A.
65 K4 Dauphin L. *l.* Can.
22 D4 Dausa India
40 E3 Dava U.K.
17 M1 Däväçi Azer.
21 A3 Davangere India
31 C5 Davao Phil.
31 C5 Davao Gulf *b.* Phil.
19 F5 Dāvar Panāh Iran
59 H3 Davel S. Africa
74 A3 Davenport *CA* U.S.A.
68 B5 Davenport *IA* U.S.A.
39 F5 Daventry U.K.
59 H3 Daveyton S. Africa
83 H7 David Panama
65 H4 Davidson Can.
65 J3 Davin Lake *l.* Can.
74 B2 Davis U.S.A.
92 D5 Davis *Austr. Base* Ant.
75 E4 Davis Dam U.S.A.
67 H2 Davis Inlet Can.
92 D5 Davis Sea *sea* Ant.
63 N3 Davis Strait *str.* Can./Greenland
46 D7 Davos Switz.
30 B3 Dawa China
26 A1 Dawan China
23 F3 Dawaxung China
26 B4 Dawe China
Dawei *see* Tavoy
26 E3 Dawen *r.* China
18 C5 Dawḩat Salwah *b.* Qatar/S. Arabia
32 A1 Dawna Range *mts* Myanmar/Thai.
20 D6 Dawqah Oman
62 E3 Dawson *Y.T.* Can.
79 C6 Dawson *GA* U.S.A.
76 D2 Dawson *ND* U.S.A.
65 J4 Dawson Bay *b.* Can.
64 E3 Dawson Creek Can.
65 L2 Dawson Inlet *in.* Can.
64 B2 Dawson Range *mts* Can.
26 E4 Dawu *Hubei* China
24 C3 Dawu *Sichuan* China
44 D5 Dax France
26 C4 Daxian China
27 C6 Daxin China
26 E2 Daxing China
27 A4 Daxue Shan *mts* China
30 B4 Dayang *r.* China
23 H4 Dayang *r.* India
27 D6 Dayao Shan *mts* China
27 E4 Daye China
27 B4 Dayi China
8 E4 Daylesford Austr.
74 D3 Daylight Pass U.S.A.
91 F1 Daymán *r.* Uru.
91 F1 Daymán, Cuchilla del *h.* Uru.
27 D4 Dayong China
17 H4 Dayr az Zawr Syria
80 A5 Dayton *OH* U.S.A.
79 C5 Dayton *TN* U.S.A.
72 C2 Dayton *WA* U.S.A.
79 D6 Daytona Beach U.S.A.
27 E5 Dayu China
27 D5 Dayu Ling *mts* China
26 F3 Da Yunhe *r.* China
72 C2 Dayville U.S.A.
27 D7 Dazhou Dao *i.* China
27 C4 Dazhu China
27 B4 Dazu China
58 F5 De Aar S. Africa
68 D2 Dead *r.* U.S.A.
79 F7 Deadman's Cay Bahamas
75 E4 Dead Mts *mts* U.S.A.
81 H2 Dead River *r.* U.S.A.
16 E6 Dead Sea *salt l.* Asia
39 J6 Deal U.K.
59 F4 Dealesville S. Africa
27 E4 De'an China
64 D4 Dean *r.* Can.
39 E6 Dean, Forest of *forest* U.K.
91 D1 Deán Funes Arg.
69 F4 Dearborn U.S.A.
64 D3 Dease *r.* Can.
64 C3 Dease Lake Can.
62 H3 Dease Strait *chan.* Can.
74 D3 Death Valley *v.* U.S.A.
74 D3 Death Valley Junction U.S.A.
74 D3 Death Valley National Monument *res.* U.S.A.
44 E2 Deauville France
33 D2 Debak Malaysia
27 C6 Debao China
49 J4 Debar Macedonia
65 H4 Debden Can.
39 J5 Debenham U.K.
75 H2 De Beque U.S.A.
81 J2 Deblois U.S.A.
56 D3 Debre Birhan Eth.
47 K7 Debrecen Hungary
56 D2 Debre Markos Eth.
56 D2 Debre Tabor Eth.
56 D3 Debre Zeyit Eth.
79 C5 Decatur *AL* U.S.A.
79 C5 Decatur *GA* U.S.A.
68 C6 Decatur *IL* U.S.A.
68 E5 Decatur *IN* U.S.A.
68 E4 Decatur *MI* U.S.A.
21 B2 Deccan *plat.* India
69 H2 Decelles, Réservoir *resr* Can.
46 G5 Děčín Czech Rep.
68 B4 Decorah U.S.A.
39 F6 Deddington U.K.
43 J2 Dedeleben Ger.
43 J2 Dedelstorf Ger.
42 E2 Dedemsvaart Neth.
90 C4 Dedo de Deus *mt* Brazil
58 C6 De Doorns S. Africa
17 L1 Dedoplis Tsqaro Georgia
54 B3 Dédougou Burkina
50 D3 Dedovichi Rus. Fed.
57 D5 Dedza Malawi
39 D4 Dee *est.* *Wales* U.K.
39 E4 Dee *r.* *Eng./Wales* U.K.
40 F3 Dee *r.* *Scot.* U.K.
41 C5 Deel *r.* Rep. of Ireland
41 D3 Deele *r.* Rep. of Ireland
27 □ Deep Bay *b.* *H.K.* China
80 D5 Deep Creek Lake *l.* U.S.A.
75 F2 Deep Creek Range *mts* U.S.A.
69 J2 Deep River Can.
81 G4 Deep River U.S.A.
65 K1 Deep Rose Lake *l.* Can.
74 D3 Deep Springs U.S.A.
80 B5 Deer Creek Lake *l.* U.S.A.
81 K2 Deer I. *i.* Can.
81 J2 Deer I. *i.* U.S.A.
81 J2 Deer Isle U.S.A.
66 B3 Deer L. *l.* Can.
67 J4 Deer Lake *Nfld* Can.
66 B3 Deer Lake *Ont.* Can.
72 D2 Deer Lodge U.S.A.
88 D2 Defensores del Chaco, Parque Nacional *nat. park* Para.
80 A4 Defiance U.S.A.
79 C6 De Funiak Springs U.S.A.
24 B3 Dêgê China
56 E3 Degeh Bur Eth.
23 G3 Dêgên China
43 L6 Deggendorf Ger.
22 C3 Degh *r.* Pak.
42 B3 De Haan Belgium
18 D4 Dehaj Iran
19 F4 Dehak Iran
19 F5 Dehak Iran
18 D4 Deh Bīd Iran
18 C4 Deh-Dasht Iran
18 C4 Deh-e Khalīfeh Iran
18 C3 Deheq Iran
18 C2 Dehgāh Iran
18 B3 Dehgolān Iran
21 B5 Dehiwala-Mount Lavinia Sri Lanka
18 D5 Dehkūyeh Iran
18 B3 Dehlonān Iran
22 D3 Dehra Dun India
23 F4 Dehri India
19 E4 Deh Salm Iran
18 E4 Deh Sard Iran
17 K4 Deh Sheykh Iran
19 F4 Deh Shū Afgh.
27 F5 Dehua China
30 C1 Dehui China
42 B4 Deinze Belgium
16 E5 Deir el Qamer Lebanon
Deir-ez-Zor *see* Dayr az Zawr
47 L7 Dej Romania
27 C4 Dejiang China
68 C5 De Kalb *IL* U.S.A.
77 E5 De Kalb *TX* U.S.A.
81 F2 De Kalb Junction U.S.A.
20 A6 Dekemhare Eritrea
56 C4 Dekese Congo(Zaire)
19 G2 Dekhkanabad Uzbek.
42 C1 De Koog Neth.
42 C2 De Kooy Neth.
74 C4 Delano U.S.A.
75 F2 Delano Peak *summit* U.S.A.
19 F3 Delārām Afgh.
59 F3 Delareyville S. Africa
65 H4 Delaronde Lake *l.* Can.
68 C5 Delavan *IL* U.S.A.
68 C4 Delavan *WV* U.S.A.
80 B4 Delaware U.S.A.
81 F5 Delaware *div.* U.S.A.
81 F4 Delaware *r.* U.S.A.
81 F5 Delaware Bay *b.* U.S.A.
80 B4 Delaware Lake *l.* U.S.A.
81 F4 Delaware Water Gap National Recreational Area *res.* U.S.A.
43 G3 Delbrück Ger.
8 G4 Delegate Austr.
46 C7 Delémont Switz.
42 C2 Delft Neth.
21 B4 Delft I. *i.* Sri Lanka
42 E1 Delfzijl Neth.
57 E5 Delgado, Cabo *pt* Moz.
69 G4 Delhi Can.
22 D3 Delhi India
73 F4 Delhi *CO* U.S.A.
81 F3 Delhi *NY* U.S.A.
17 J2 Deli *r.* Turkey
16 E2 Delice Turkey
16 E1 Delice *r.* Turkey
18 C3 Delījān Iran
64 E1 Déline Can.
24 B3 Delingha China
65 H4 Delisle Can.
43 L3 Delitzsch Ger.
43 H3 Delligsen Ger.
76 D3 Dell Rapids U.S.A.
45 H4 Dellys Alg.
74 D5 Del Mar U.S.A.
75 E3 Delmar L. *l.* U.S.A.
43 G1 Delmenhorst Ger.
13 R2 De-Longa, O-va *is* Rus. Fed.
62 B3 De Long Mts *mts* U.S.A.
65 J5 Deloraine Can.
68 D5 Delphi U.S.A.
80 A4 Delphos U.S.A.
58 F4 Delportshoop S. Africa
79 D7 Delray Beach U.S.A.
73 E6 Del Rio Mex.
77 C6 Del Rio U.S.A.
37 P6 Delsbo Sweden
75 H2 Delta *CO* U.S.A.
68 A5 Delta *IA* U.S.A.
75 F2 Delta *UT* U.S.A.
62 D3 Delta Junction U.S.A.
81 F3 Delta Reservoir *resr* U.S.A.
79 D6 Deltona U.S.A.
41 D4 Delvin Rep. of Ireland
49 J5 Delvinë Albania
45 E1 Demanda, Sierra de la *mts* Spain
56 C4 Demba Congo(Zaire)
56 D3 Dembī Dolo Eth.
50 D4 Demidov Rus. Fed.
73 F5 Deming U.S.A.
89 E4 Demini *r.* Brazil
16 B2 Demirci Turkey
49 M4 Demirköy Turkey
46 F4 Demmin Ger.
79 C5 Demopolis U.S.A.
68 D5 Demotte U.S.A.
33 B3 Dempo, G. *volc.* Indon.
22 D2 Dêmqog China/India
50 H2 Dem'yanovo Rus. Fed.
47 Q2 Demyansk Rus. Fed.
58 D5 De Naawte S. Africa
56 E2 Denakil *reg.* Eritrea
56 E3 Denan Eth.
65 J4 Denare Beach Can.
19 G2 Denau Uzbek.
69 J3 Denbigh Can.
39 D4 Denbigh U.K.
42 C1 Den Burg Neth.
32 B1 Den Chai Thai.
33 C3 Dendang Indon.
42 C3 Dendermonde Belgium
59 H1 Dendron S. Africa
26 C1 Dengkou China
23 H3 Dêngqên China
26 D3 Deng Xian China
Den Haag *see* The Hague
6 B4 Denham Austr.
42 E2 Den Ham Neth.
42 C2 Den Helder Neth.
45 G3 Denia Spain
8 E3 Deniliquin Austr.
72 C3 Denio U.S.A.
76 E3 Denison *IA* U.S.A.
77 D5 Denison *TX* U.S.A.
16 B3 Denizli Turkey
8 H2 Denman Austr.
92 C5 Denman Glacier *gl.* Ant.
6 B5 Denmark Austr.
34 F3 Denmark *country* Europe
34 C2 Denmark Strait *str.* Greenland/Iceland
75 H3 Dennehotso U.S.A.
81 H4 Dennis Port U.S.A.
40 E4 Denny U.K.
81 K2 Dennysville U.S.A.
33 E4 Denpasar Indon.
81 F5 Denton *MD* U.S.A.
77 D5 Denton *TX* U.S.A.
6 F2 D'Entrecasteaux Islands *is* P.N.G.
6 B5 d'Entrecasteaux, Pt *pt* Austr.
7 G3 d'Entrecasteaux, Récifs *rf* New Caledonia
72 F4 Denver U.S.A.
23 F4 Deo India
22 D3 Deoband India
23 F5 Deogarh India
23 E5 Deogarh *mt* India
23 F4 Deoghar India
22 D5 Deori India
23 E4 Deoria India
22 C2 Deosai, Plains of *plain* Pak.
23 E5 Deosil India
42 A3 De Panne Belgium
42 D3 De Peel *reg.* Neth.
68 C3 De Pere U.S.A.
81 F3 Deposit U.S.A.
69 J2 Depot-Forbes Can.
69 J2 Depot-Rowanton Can.
68 C5 Depue U.S.A.
13 P3 Deputatskiy Rus. Fed.
24 B4 Dêqên China
27 D6 Deqing *Guangdong* China
27 F4 Deqing *Zhejiang* China
27 F5 Deqiu China
77 E5 De Queen U.S.A.
22 B3 Dera Bugti Pak.
22 B3 Dera Ghazi Khan Pak.
22 B3 Dera Ismail Khan Pak.
22 B3 Derawar Fort Pak.
51 J7 Derbent Rus. Fed.
19 G2 Derbent Uzbek.
6 C3 Derby Austr.
39 F5 Derby U.K.
81 G4 Derby *CT* U.S.A.
77 D4 Derby *KS* U.S.A.
41 D3 Derg *r.* Rep. of Ireland/U.K.
51 J5 Dergachi Rus. Fed.
41 C5 Derg, Lough *l.* Rep. of Ireland
51 F5 Derhachi Ukr.
77 E6 De Ridder U.S.A.
17 H3 Derik Turkey
16 E2 Derinkuyu Turkey
51 F5 Derkul *r.* Rus. Fed./Ukr.
58 C1 Derm Namibia
41 D4 Derravaragh, Lough *l.* Rep. of Ireland
81 H3 Derry U.S.A.
41 E5 Derry *r.* Rep. of Ireland
41 C3 Derryveagh Mts *h.* Rep. of Ireland
26 A1 Derstei China
55 F3 Derudeb Sudan
58 E6 De Rust S. Africa
48 G2 Derventa Bos.-Herz.
6 E6 Derwent *r.* Austr.
38 G4 Derwent *r.* U.K.
40 G6 Derwent Reservoir *resr* U.K.
38 D3 Derwent Water *l.* U.K.
14 E1 Derzhavinsk Kazak.
91 C2 Desaguadero *r.* Arg.
86 E7 Desaguadero *r.* Bol.
5 N6 Désappointement, Îles du *is* Pac. Oc.
74 D2 Desatoya Mts *mts* U.S.A.
69 F2 Desbarats Can.
62 F3 Des Bois, Lac *l.* Can.
65 J3 Deschambault L. *l.* Can.
65 J4 Deschambault Lake Can.
72 B2 Deschutes *r.* U.S.A.
56 D2 Desē Eth.
88 C7 Deseado Arg.
88 C7 Deseado *r.* Arg.
69 J3 Deseronto Can.
22 B3 Desert Canal *canal* Pak.
75 E5 Desert Center U.S.A.
75 F1 Desert Peak *summit* U.S.A.
64 G3 Desmarais Can.
76 E3 Des Moines *IA* U.S.A.
73 G4 Des Moines *NM* U.S.A.
68 A5 Des Moines *r.* *IA* U.S.A.
51 D5 Desna Ukr.
50 E5 Desna *r.* Rus. Fed.
50 E4 Desnogorsk Rus. Fed.
31 C4 Desolation Point *pt* Phil.
68 D4 Des Plaines U.S.A.
53 K6 Desroches *i.* Seychelles
43 L3 Dessau Ger.
42 B3 Destelbergen Belgium
69 H1 Destor Can.
64 B2 Destruction Bay Can.
49 J2 Deta Romania
64 G2 Detah Can.
57 C5 Dete Zimbabwe
43 G3 Detmold Ger.
68 D3 Detour, Pt *pt* U.S.A.
69 F3 De Tour Village U.S.A.
69 F4 Detroit U.S.A.
76 E2 Detroit Lakes U.S.A.
8 G3 Deua Nat. Park Austr.
43 L3 Deuben Ger.
42 D3 Deurne Neth.
48 F1 Deutschlandsberg Austria
43 L3 Deutzen Ger.
69 H2 Deux-Rivières Can.
49 K2 Deva Romania
21 B2 Devarkonda India
16 E2 Develi Turkey
42 E2 Deventer Neth.
46 H6 Devět Skal *h.* Czech Rep.
22 B4 Devikot India
41 D5 Devils Bit Mountain *h.* Rep. of Ireland
39 D5 Devil's Bridge U.K.
74 C4 Devils Den U.S.A.
74 C2 Devils Gate *pass* U.S.A.
68 B2 Devils I. *i.* U.S.A.
76 D1 Devils Lake U.S.A.
74 C3 Devils Peak *summit* U.S.A.
74 C3 Devils Postpile National Monument *res.* U.S.A.
79 F7 Devil's Pt Bahamas
39 F6 Devizes U.K.
22 C4 Devli India
49 M3 Devnya Bulg.
64 G4 Devon Can.
39 G5 Devon *r.* U.K.
63 J2 Devon Island *i.* Can.
6 E6 Devonport Austr.
16 C1 Devrek Turkey
16 D1 Devrekâni Turkey
16 E1 Devrez *r.* Turkey
21 A2 Devrukh India
22 D5 Dewas India
33 A2 Dewa, Tanjung *pt* Indon.
59 G4 Dewetsdorp S. Africa
80 B6 Dewey Lake *l.* U.S.A.
77 F5 De Witt *AR* U.S.A.
68 B5 De Witt *IA* U.S.A.
38 F4 Dewsbury U.K.
27 E4 Dexing China
81 J2 Dexter *ME* U.S.A.
77 F4 Dexter *MO* U.S.A.
81 E2 Dexter *NY* U.S.A.
26 B4 Deyang China
18 E3 Deyhuk Iran
17 M3 Deylaman Iran
19 F2 Deynau Turkm.
6 D2 Deyong, Tg *pt* Indon.
18 C5 Deyyer Iran
17 M6 Dez *r.* Iran
18 C3 Dezfūl Iran
18 C4 Dez Gerd Iran
26 E2 Dezhou China
18 B5 Dhahlān, J. *h.* S. Arabia
20 D4 Dhahran S. Arabia
23 G5 Dhaka Bangl.
23 G5 Dhaleswari *r.* Bangl.
23 H4 Dhaleswari *r.* India
20 B7 Dhamār Yemen
23 F5 Dhāmara India
22 C5 Dhamnod India
23 E5 Dhamtari India
22 B3 Dhana Sar Pak.
23 F5 Dhanbad India
22 C5 Dhandhuka India
23 E3 Dhang Ra. *mts* Nepal
22 C5 Dhar India
23 F4 Dharan Bazar Nepal
21 B4 Dharapuram India
22 B5 Dhari India
21 B3 Dharmapuri India
21 B3 Dharmavaram India
22 D2 Dharmshala India
21 A3 Dhārwād India
22 D4 Dhasan *r.* India
23 E3 Dhaulagiri *mt* Nepal
22 D4 Dhaulpur India
22 C4 Dhebar L. *l.* India
23 H4 Dhekiajuli India
16 E6 Dhībān Jordan
23 H4 Dhing India
21 B3 Dhone India
22 B5 Dhoraji India
22 B5 Dhrangadhra India
22 C5 Dhule India
23 F4 Dhulian India
23 F4 Dhunche Nepal
22 D4 Dhund *r.* India
56 E3 Dhuusa Marreeb Somalia
49 L7 Dia *i.* Greece
74 B3 Diablo, Mt *mt* U.S.A.
74 B3 Diablo Range *mts* U.S.A.
91 E2 Diamante Arg.
91 C2 Diamante *r.* Arg.
90 D2 Diamantina Brazil
6 D4 Diamantina *watercourse* Austr.
87 K6 Diamantina, Chapada *plat.* Brazil
90 A1 Diamantino Brazil
74 □1 Diamond Head *hd* U.S.A.
75 E2 Diamond Peak *summit* U.S.A.
27 D6 Dianbai China
27 B5 Dian Chi *l.* China
27 C4 Dianjiang China
87 J6 Dianópolis Brazil
54 B4 Dianra Côte d'Ivoire
28 B2 Diaoling China
54 C3 Diapaga Burkina
19 E6 Đibab Oman
23 H4 Dibang *r.* India
56 C4 Dibaya Congo(Zaire)
58 E3 Dibeng S. Africa
66 F2 D'Iberville, Lac *l.* Can.
59 G1 Dibete Botswana
23 H4 Dibrugarh India
77 C5 Dickens U.S.A.
81 J1 Dickey U.S.A.
76 C2 Dickinson U.S.A.
79 C4 Dickson U.S.A.
81 F4 Dickson City U.S.A.
Dicle *r.* *see* Tigris
31 B2 Didicas *i.* Phil.
22 C4 Didwana India
49 M4 Didymoteicho Greece
44 G4 Die France
42 F4 Dieblich Ger.
54 B3 Diébougou Burkina
43 G5 Dieburg Ger.
65 H4 Diefenbaker, L. *l.* Can.
93 J4 Diego Garcia *i.* British Ind. Ocean Terr.
42 E5 Diekirch Lux.
54 B3 Diéma Mali
43 H3 Diemel *r.* Ger.
27 B6 Điện Biên Vietnam
32 C1 Diễn Châu Vietnam
32 D2 Diễn Khanh Vietnam
43 G2 Diepholz Ger.
44 E2 Dieppe France
26 C2 Di'er Nonchang Qu *r.* China
30 C1 Di'er Songhua Jiang *r.* China
42 D3 Diessen Neth.
42 D4 Diest Belgium
46 D7 Dietikon Switz.
43 G4 Diez Ger.
55 D3 Diffa Niger
21 D2 Digapahandi India
67 G5 Digby Can.
23 F5 Digha India
44 H4 Digne-les-Bains France
44 F3 Digoin France
31 C5 Digos Phil.
22 D5 Digras India
22 B4 Digri Pak.
25 F7 Digul *r.* Indon.

54 B4 Digya National Park Ghana
44 G3 Dijon France
56 E2 Dikhil Djibouti
49 M5 Dikili Turkey
42 A3 Diksmuide Belgium
12 K2 Dikson Rus. Fed.
55 D3 Dikwa Nigeria
56 D3 Dīla Eth.
19 E4 Dilaram Iran
6 C2 Dili Indon.
17 K1 Dilijan Armenia
32 D3 Di Linh Vietnam
43 G4 Dillenburg Ger.
77 D6 Dilley U.S.A.
46 E6 Dillingen an der Donau Ger.
42 E5 Dillingen (Saar) Ger.
62 C4 Dillingham U.S.A.
65 H3 Dillon Can.
72 D2 Dillon *MT* U.S.A.
79 E5 Dillon *SC* U.S.A.
57 C5 Dilolo Congo(Zaire)
42 D3 Dilsen Belgium
17 K5 Diltāwa Iraq
23 H4 Dimapur India
16 F5 Dimashq Syria
56 C4 Dimbelenge Congo(Zaire)
54 B4 Dimbokro Côte d'Ivoire
8 D4 Dimboola Austr.
49 L3 Dimitrovgrad Bulg.
50 J4 Dimitrovgrad Rus. Fed.
16 E6 Dīmona Israel
58 D2 Dimpho Pan *salt pan* Botswana
31 C4 Dinagat *i.* Phil.
23 G4 Dinajpur Bangl.
44 C2 Dinan France
22 C2 Dinanagar India
42 C4 Dinant Belgium
23 F4 Dinapur India
16 C2 Dinar Turkey
48 G2 Dinara *mts* Croatia
18 C4 Dīnār, Kūh-e *mt* Iran
55 F3 Dinder National Park Sudan
21 B4 Dindigul India
59 K1 Dindiza Moz.
22 E5 Dindori India
16 D3 Dinek Turkey
26 C2 Dingbian China
56 B4 Dinge Angola
43 J3 Dingelstädt Ger.
27 G4 Dinghai China
23 F4 Dingla Nepal
41 A5 Dingle Rep. of Ireland
41 A5 Dingle Bay *b.* Rep. of Ireland
27 E5 Dingnan China
31 B2 Dingras Phil.
26 E3 Dingtao China
54 A3 Dinguiraye Guinea
40 D3 Dingwall U.K.
26 B3 Dingxi China
26 E2 Ding Xian China
26 E2 Dingxing China
26 E3 Dingyuan China
26 F2 Dingzi Gang *harbour* China
27 C6 Dinh Lâp Vietnam
43 J5 Dinkelsbühl Ger.
75 G3 Dinnebito Wash *r.* U.S.A.
23 F3 Dinngyê China
59 G1 Dinokwe Botswana
65 L5 Dinorwic Lake U.S.A.
75 H1 Dinosaur U.S.A.
72 E3 Dinosaur Nat. Mon. *res.* U.S.A.
42 E3 Dinslaken Ger.
54 B3 Dioïla Mali
90 B4 Dionísio Cerqueira Brazil
54 A3 Diourbel Senegal
23 H4 Diphu India
22 B4 Diplo Pak.
31 B4 Dipolog Phil.
9 B6 Dipton N.Z.
16 F2 Dirckli Turkey
54 B3 Diré Mali
6 E3 Direction, C. *c.* Austr.
56 E3 Dirē Dawa Eth.
57 C5 Dirico Angola
6 B4 Dirk Hartog I. *i.* Austr.
6 E4 Dirranbandi Austr.
75 G2 Dirty Devil *r.* U.S.A.
22 C4 Dīsa India
88 □ Disappointment, C. *c.* Atl. Ocean
72 A2 Disappointment, C. *c.* U.S.A.
6 C4 Disappointment, L. *salt flat* Austr.
8 G4 Disaster B. *b.* Austr.
8 C5 Discovery Bay *b.* Austr.
27 □ Discovery Bay *b.* *H.K.* China
Disko *i. see* Qeqertarsuatsiaq
Disko Bugt *b. see* Qeqertarsuup Tunua
81 E6 Dismal Swamp *swamp* U.S.A.
42 A6 Disneyland Paris France
23 G4 Dispur India
39 J5 Diss U.K.
90 C1 Distrito Federal *div.* Brazil
16 C6 Disûq Egypt
31 B4 Dit *i.* Phil.
58 E4 Ditloung S. Africa
48 F6 Dittaino *r.* *Sicily* Italy
31 C4 Diuata Mountains *mts* Phil.
31 C4 Diuata Pt *pt* Phil.
18 B3 Dīvāndarreh Iran
50 G4 Diveyevo Rus. Fed.
31 B2 Divilacan Bay *b.* Phil.
90 D3 Divinópolis Brazil
51 G6 Divnoye Rus. Fed.
54 B4 Divo Côte d'Ivoire
16 G2 Divriği Turkey
19 G5 Diwana Pak.
81 H2 Dixfield U.S.A.
81 J2 Dixmont U.S.A.
74 B2 Dixon *CA* U.S.A.
68 C5 Dixon *IL* U.S.A.
64 C4 Dixon Entrance *chan.* Can./U.S.A.
64 F3 Dixonville Can.
81 H2 Dixville Can.
17 J2 Diyadin Turkey
17 K5 Diyālā *r.* Iraq
17 H3 Diyarbakır Turkey
22 B4 Diyodar India
Dizak *see* Dāvar Panāh
18 D3 Diz Chah Iran
55 D2 Djado Niger
55 D2 Djado, Plateau du *plat.* Niger
56 B4 Djambala Congo
54 C2 Djanet Alg.
54 C1 Djelfa Alg.
56 C3 Djéma C.A.R.
54 B3 Djenné Mali
54 B3 Djibo Burkina
56 E2 Djibouti Djibouti
52 J4 Djibouti *country* Africa
41 E4 Djouce Mountain *h.* Rep. of Ireland
54 C4 Djougou Benin
36 F4 Djúpivogur Iceland
37 O6 Djurås Sweden
17 K1 Dmanisi Georgia
13 Q2 Dmitriya Lapteva, Proliv *chan.* Rus. Fed.
28 C2 Dmitriyevka *Primorskiy Kray* Rus. Fed.
50 G4 Dmitriyevka *Tambov.* Rus. Fed.
51 E4 Dmitriyev-L'govskiy Rus. Fed.
50 F3 Dmitrov Rus. Fed.
47 P5 Dnieper *r.* Europe
47 N6 Dniester *r.* Ukr.
47 Q7 Dnipro *r.* Ukr.
51 E5 Dniprodzerzhyns'k Ukr.
51 E5 Dnipropetrovs'k Ukr.
51 E6 Dniprorudne Ukr.
50 D3 Dno Rus. Fed.
Dnyapro *r. see* Dnieper
55 D4 Doba Chad
23 G3 Doba China
69 G3 Dobbinton Can.
37 S8 Dobele Latvia
43 M3 Döbeln Ger.
25 F7 Doberai, Jazirah Indon.
91 D3 Doblas Arg.
25 F7 Dobo Indon.
49 H2 Doboj Bos.-Herz.
43 K4 Döbra-berg *h.* Ger.
49 M3 Dobrich Bulg.
51 G4 Dobrinka Rus. Fed.
51 D4 Dobrush Belarus
31 A5 Doc Can *rf* Phil.
90 E2 Doce *r.* Brazil
39 H5 Docking U.K.
84 B2 Doctor Arroyo Mex.
73 F6 Doctor B. Domínguez Mex.
21 B3 Dod Ballapur India
49 M6 Dodecanese *is* Greece
Dodekanisos *is see* Dodecanese
72 C2 Dodge U.S.A.
68 A3 Dodge Center U.S.A.
77 C4 Dodge City U.S.A.
68 B4 Dodgeville U.S.A.
39 C7 Dodman Point *pt* U.K.
56 D4 Dodoma Tanz.
42 E3 Doetinchem Neth.
25 E7 Dofa Indon.
23 G2 Dogai Coring *salt l.* China
16 F2 Doğanşehir Turkey
64 E4 Dog Creek Can.
23 G3 Dogên Co *l.* China
67 H2 Dog Island *i.* Can.
65 K4 Dog L. *l.* Can.
69 E1 Dog Lake *l.* Can.
29 C6 Dōgo *i.* Japan
54 C3 Dogondoutchi Niger
29 C7 Dōgo-yama *mt* Japan
17 K2 Doğubeyazıt Turkey
23 G3 Do'gyaling China
18 C5 Doha Qatar
Dohad *see* Dāhod
23 H5 Dohazar Bangl.
23 G3 Doilungdêqên China
32 A1 Doi Saket Thai.
87 K5 Dois Irmãos, Serra dos *h.* Brazil
49 K4 Dojran, Lake *l.* Greece/Macedonia
37 M6 Dokka Norway
42 E1 Dokkum Neth.
22 B4 Dokri Pak.
47 N3 Dokshytsy Belarus
51 F6 Dokuchayevs'k Ukr.
25 F7 Dolak, Pulau *i.* Indon.
67 F4 Dolbeau Can.
39 C5 Dolbenmaen U.K.
44 D2 Dol-de-Bretagne France
44 G3 Dole France
39 D5 Dolgellau U.K.
43 M1 Dolgen Ger.
81 G3 Dolgeville U.S.A.
51 F4 Dolgorukovo Rus. Fed.
51 F4 Dolgoye Rus. Fed.
48 C5 Dolianova *Sardinia* Italy
24 G2 Dolinsk Rus. Fed.
88 E2 Dolleman I. *i.* Ant.
43 K6 Dollnstein Ger.
56 E3 Dolo Odo Eth.
91 E3 Dolores Arg.
91 E2 Dolores Uru.
75 H2 Dolores *r.* U.S.A.
84 B2 Dolores Hidalgo Mex.
62 G3 Dolphin and Union Str. Can.
27 B7 Đô Lương Vietnam
51 B5 Dolyna Ukr.
16 B2 Domaniç Turkey
22 E2 Domar China
46 F6 Domažlice Czech Rep.
23 H2 Domba China
37 L5 Dombås Norway
46 J7 Dombóvár Hungary
92 C4 Dome Angus *ice feature* Ant.
92 C5 Dome Circle *ice feature* Ant.
64 E4 Dome Creek Can.
64 D2 Dome Pk *summit* Can.
75 E5 Dome Rock Mts *mts* U.S.A.
44 D2 Domfront France
61 M8 Dominica *country* Caribbean Sea
61 L8 Dominican Republic *country* Caribbean Sea
43 K1 Dömitz Ger.
32 C2 Dom Noi, L. *r.* Thai.
48 C1 Domodossola Italy
49 K5 Domokos Greece
91 F1 Dom Pedrito Brazil
33 E4 Dompu Indon.
91 B3 Domuyo, Volcán *volc.* Arg.
21 B2 Don *r.* India
51 G5 Don *r.* Rus. Fed.
40 F3 Don *r.* U.K.
41 F3 Donaghadee U.K.
41 E3 Donaghmore U.K.
8 D4 Donald Austr.
Donau *r.* Austria/Ger. *see* Danube
46 D7 Donaueschingen Ger.
46 E6 Donauwörth Ger.
45 D3 Don Benito Spain
38 F4 Doncaster U.K.
57 B4 Dondo Angola
57 D5 Dondo Moz.
31 B4 Dondonay *i.* Phil.
21 C5 Dondra Head *c.* Sri Lanka
41 C3 Donegal Rep. of Ireland
41 C3 Donegal Bay *g.* Rep. of Ireland
51 F6 Donets'k Ukr.
51 F5 Donets'kyy Kryazh *h.* Rus. Fed./Ukr.
27 D5 Dong'an China
6 B4 Dongara Austr.
22 E5 Dongargarh India
27 B5 Dongchuan China
23 F2 Dongco China
27 C7 Dongfang China
28 C1 Dongfanghong China
30 C2 Dongfeng China
33 E3 Donggala Indon.
30 C4 Donggou China
27 E5 Donggu China
27 D6 Dongguan China
32 C1 Đông Ha Vietnam
26 F3 Donghai China
27 D6 Donghai Dao *i.* China
26 C3 Dong He *r.* *Sichuan* China
26 A1 Dong He *watercourse* *Nei Monggol* China
32 C1 Đông Hôi Vietnam
30 E1 Dongjingcheng China
23 H3 Dongjug *Xizang* China
23 H3 Dongjug *Xizang* China
27 D5 Dongkou China
23 G4 Dongkya La *pass* India
27 C5 Donglan China
26 A2 Dongle China
30 C2 Dongliao *r.* China
30 B1 Dongminzhutun China
30 F2 Dongning China
57 B5 Dongo Angola
56 B3 Dongou Congo
32 B1 Dong Phraya Fai *mts* Thai.
32 B2 Dong Phraya Yen *esc.* Thai.
27 D6 Dongping *Guangdong* China
26 E3 Dongping *Shandong* China
23 G3 Dongqiao China
27 E6 Dongshan China
27 E6 Dongshan Dao *i.* China
26 D2 Dongsheng China
26 F3 Dongtai *Jiangsu* China
26 F3 Dongtai *r.* China
27 D4 Dongting Hu *l.* China
27 F5 Dongtou China
24 D2 Dong Ujimqin Qi China
27 E4 Dongxiang China
26 B3 Dongxiangzu China
27 F4 Dongyang China
26 F2 Dongying China
26 B2 Dongzhen China
27 E4 Dongzhi China
64 B2 Donjek *r.* Can.
42 E1 Donkerbroek Neth.
23 G5 Donmanick Islands *is* Bangl.
77 C7 Don Martín Mex.
67 F4 Donnacona Can.
64 F3 Donnelly Can.
9 D1 Donnellys Crossing N.Z.
74 B2 Donner Pass U.S.A.
Donostia-San Sebastián *see* San Sebastián
49 L6 Donoussa *i.* Greece
50 F4 Donskoy Rus. Fed.
51 G6 Donskoye Rus. Fed.
31 B3 Donsol Phil.
32 C2 Don, Xé *r.* Laos
41 A4 Dooagh Rep. of Ireland
41 B5 Doonbeg *r.* Rep. of Ireland
40 D5 Doon, Loch *l.* U.K.
42 D2 Doorn Neth.
68 D3 Door Peninsula *pen.* U.S.A.
42 D3 Doorwerth Neth.
56 E3 Dooxo Nugaaleed *v.* Somalia
19 F4 Dor *watercourse* Afgh.
77 C5 Dora U.S.A.
48 C2 Dora Baltea *r.* Italy
39 E7 Dorchester U.K.
57 B6 Dordabis Namibia
44 E4 Dordogne *r.* France
42 C3 Dordrecht Neth.
59 G5 Dordrecht S. Africa
58 C1 Doreenville Namibia
65 H4 Doré L. *l.* Can.
65 H4 Doré Lake Can.
48 C4 Dorgali *Sardinia* Italy
54 B3 Dori Burkina
19 G4 Dori *r.* Afgh.
58 C5 Doring *r.* S. Africa
39 G6 Dorking U.K.
42 E3 Dormagen Ger.
42 B5 Dormans France
26 C1 Dorngovĭ *div.* Mongolia
40 D3 Dornoch Firth *est.* U.K.
42 F1 Dornum Ger.
50 E4 Dorogobuzh Rus. Fed.
47 N7 Dorohoi Romania
24 B2 Döröö Nuur *l.* Mongolia
36 P4 Dorotea Sweden
6 B4 Dorre I. *i.* Austr.
72 B3 Dorris U.S.A.
54 D4 Dorsale Camerounaise *slope* Cameroon/Nigeria
69 H3 Dorset Can.
42 F3 Dortmund Ger.
80 B6 Dorton U.S.A.
16 F3 Dörtyol Turkey
43 G1 Dorum Ger.
56 C3 Doruma Congo(Zaire)
18 E3 Dorūneh Iran
81 G2 Dorval Can.
43 H2 Dörverden Ger.
88 C6 Dos Bahías, C. *pt* Arg.
75 H5 Dos Cabezas U.S.A.
86 C5 Dos de Mayo Peru
27 C6 Đo Son Vietnam
74 B3 Dos Palos U.S.A.
43 L2 Dosse *r.* Ger.
54 C3 Dosso Niger
79 C6 Dothan U.S.A.
44 F1 Douai France
54 C4 Douala Cameroon
44 B2 Douarnenez France
27 □ Double I. *i.* *H.K.* China
74 C4 Double Peak *summit* U.S.A.
44 H3 Doubs *r.* France
9 A6 Doubtful Sound *in.* N.Z.
9 D1 Doubtless Bay *b.* N.Z.
54 B3 Douentza Mali
38 C3 Douglas Isle of Man
58 E4 Douglas S. Africa
40 E5 Douglas *Scot.* U.K.
64 C3 Douglas *AK* U.S.A.
75 H6 Douglas *AZ* U.S.A.
79 D6 Douglas *GA* U.S.A.
72 F3 Douglas *WY* U.S.A.
64 D4 Douglas Chan. *chan.* Can.
75 H2 Douglas Creek *r.* U.S.A.
44 F1 Doullens France
40 D4 Doune U.K.
90 C2 Dourada, Cach. *waterfall* Brazil
90 B2 Dourada, Serra *h.* Brazil
90 C1 Dourada, Serra *mts* Brazil
90 A3 Dourados Brazil
90 A3 Dourados *r.* Brazil
90 B3 Dourados, Serra dos *h.* Brazil
45 C2 Douro *r.* Port.
42 D5 Douzy France
39 F4 Dove *r.* *Eng.* U.K.
39 J5 Dove *r.* *Eng.* U.K.
67 J3 Dove Brook Can.
75 H3 Dove Creek U.S.A.
39 J6 Dover U.K.
81 F5 Dover *DE* U.S.A.
81 H3 Dover *NH* U.S.A.
81 F4 Dover *NJ* U.S.A.
80 C4 Dover *OH* U.S.A.
81 J2 Dover-Foxcroft U.S.A.
39 J7 Dover, Strait of *str.* France/U.K.
17 L5 Doveyrīch *r.* Iran/Iraq
68 D5 Dowagiac U.S.A.
18 D4 Dow Chāhī Iran
19 E2 Dowgha'ī Iran
32 A5 Dowi, Tg *pt* Indon.
19 F3 Dowlatābād Afgh.
19 G2 Dowlatābād Afgh.
18 D4 Dowlatābād Iran
18 E4 Dowlatābād Iran
19 F2 Dowlatābād Iran
19 G3 Dowl at Yār Afgh.
74 B2 Downieville U.S.A.
41 F3 Downpatrick U.K.
81 F3 Downsville U.S.A.
18 C3 Dow Rūd Iran
17 L4 Dow Sar Iran
19 E4 Dowsārī Iran
19 H3 Dowshī Afgh.
74 B1 Doyle U.S.A.
81 F4 Doylestown U.S.A.
29 C6 Dōzen *is* Japan
69 J2 Dozois, Réservoir *resr* Can.
90 B3 Dracena Brazil
42 E1 Drachten Neth.
49 L2 Drăgănești-Olt Romania
49 L2 Drăgășani Romania
89 E2 Dragon's Mouths *str.* Trinidad/Venez.
37 S6 Dragsfjärd Fin.
44 H5 Draguignan France
51 C4 Drahichyn Belarus
75 F4 Drake *AZ* U.S.A.
65 J5 Drake *ND* U.S.A.
59 H5 Drakensberg *mts* Lesotho/S. Africa
59 J2 Drakensberg *mts* S. Africa
85 C8 Drake Passage *str.* Ant.
49 L4 Drama Greece
37 M7 Drammen Norway
37 L7 Drangedal Norway
19 G5 Dran juk *h.* Pak.
43 H3 Dransfeld Ger.
41 E3 Draperstown U.K.
22 C2 Dras Jammu and Kashmir
46 F7 Drau *r.* Austria
64 G4 Drayton Valley Can.
48 B6 Dréan Alg.
43 H4 Dreistelz-berge *h.* Ger.
46 F5 Dresden Ger.
50 D4 Dretun' Belarus
44 E2 Dreux France
37 N6 Drevsjø Norway
80 D4 Driftwood U.S.A.
41 B6 Drimoleague Rep. of Ireland
48 G3 Drniš Croatia
49 K2 Drobeta-Turnu Severin Romania
43 H1 Drochtersen Ger.
41 E4 Drogheda Rep. of Ireland
51 B5 Drohobych Ukr.
Droichead Átha *see* Drogheda
39 E5 Droitwich U.K.
23 G4 Drokung India
43 J2 Drömling *reg.* Ger.
41 D4 Dromod Rep. of Ireland
41 E3 Dromore *Co. Down* U.K.
41 D3 Dromore *Co. Tyrone* U.K.
39 F4 Dronfield U.K.
63 Q2 Dronning Louise Land *reg.* Greenland
92 C3 Dronning Maud Land *reg.* Ant.
42 D2 Dronten Neth.
22 B2 Drosh Pak.
51 F4 Droskovo Rus. Fed.
8 E5 Drouin Austr.
88 D2 Dr Pedro P. Peña Para.
64 G4 Drumheller Can.
72 D2 Drummond *MT* U.S.A.
68 B2 Drummond *WV* U.S.A.
69 F3 Drummond Island *i.* U.S.A.
67 F4 Drummondville Can.
40 D6 Drummore U.K.
40 D4 Drumochter Pass U.K.
37 T10 Druskininkai Lith.
13 Q3 Druzhina Rus. Fed.
49 L3 Dryanovo Bulg.
64 B3 Dry Bay *b.* U.S.A.
65 L5 Dryberry L. *l.* Can.
68 E2 Dryburg U.S.A.
66 B4 Dryden Can.
92 D5 Drygalski I. *i.* Ant.
92 B5 Drygalski Ice Tongue *ice feature* Ant.
74 D2 Dry Lake *l.* U.S.A.
40 D4 Drymen U.K.
6 C3 Drysdale *r.* Austr.
18 C3 Dūāb *r.* Iran
27 C6 Du'an China
81 F2 Duane U.S.A.
23 G4 Duars *reg.* India
14 B4 Dubā S. Arabia
20 E4 Dubai U.A.E.
65 J2 Dubawnt *r.* Can.
62 H3 Dubawnt Lake *l.* *N.W.T.* Can.
65 J2 Dubawnt Lake *l.* Can.
Dubayy *see* Dubai
14 B4 Dubbagh, J. ad *mt* S. Arabia
8 G2 Dubbo Austr.
68 D1 Dublin Can.
41 E4 Dublin Rep. of Ireland
79 D5 Dublin U.S.A.
50 F3 Dubna Rus. Fed.
51 C5 Dubno Ukr.
72 D2 Dubois *ID* U.S.A.
72 E3 Dubois *WY* U.S.A.
80 D4 Du Bois U.S.A.
51 H5 Dubovka Rus. Fed.
51 G6 Dubovskoye Rus. Fed.
17 M1 Dübrar P. *pass* Azer.
54 A4 Dubréka Guinea
49 H3 Dubrovnik Croatia
51 C5 Dubrovytsya Ukr.
50 D4 Dubrowna Belarus
68 B4 Dubuque U.S.A.
37 S9 Dubysa *r.* Lith.
5 N7 Duc de Gloucester, Îles *is* Pac. Oc.
27 E4 Duchang China
75 G1 Duchesne U.S.A.
75 G1 Duchesne *r.* U.S.A.
5 P7 Ducie Island *i.* Pac. Oc.
79 C5 Duck *r.* U.S.A.
65 J4 Duck Bay Can.
65 H4 Duck Lake Can.
68 E4 Duck Lake U.S.A.
75 E2 Duckwater U.S.A.
75 E2 Duckwater Peak *summit* U.S.A.
32 D2 Đưc Pho Vietnam
32 D3 Đưc Trong Vietnam
89 B4 Duda *r.* Col.
42 E5 Dudelange Lux.
43 J3 Duderstadt Ger.
23 E4 Dudhi India
23 G4 Dudhnai India
12 K3 Dudinka Rus. Fed.
39 E5 Dudley U.K.
22 D6 Dudna *r.* India
40 F3 Dudwick, Hill of *h.* U.K.
54 B4 Duékoué Côte d'Ivoire
45 C2 Duero *r.* Spain
69 H1 Dufault, Lac *l.* Can.
92 B4 Dufek Coast *coastal area* Ant.
42 C3 Duffel Belgium
66 E2 Dufferin, Cape *hd* Can.
80 B6 Duffield U.S.A.
7 G2 Duff Is *is* Solomon Is
40 E3 Dufftown U.K.
66 E1 Dufrost, Pte *pt* Can.
19 G2 Dugab Uzbek.
48 F3 Dugi Otok *i.* Croatia
26 C2 Dugui Qarag China
26 D3 Du He *r.* China
89 D4 Duida, Co *mt* Venez.
86 E3 Duida-Marahuaca, Parque Nacional *nat. park* Venez.
42 E3 Duisburg Ger.
89 B3 Duitama Col.
59 J1 Duiwelskloof S. Africa
17 K4 Dukān Dam *dam* Iraq
59 G5 Dukathole S. Africa
64 C4 Duke I. *i.* U.S.A.
18 C5 Dukhān Qatar
47 Q3 Dukhovshchina Rus. Fed.
22 B3 Duki Pak.
27 A5 Dukou China
37 U9 Dūkštas Lith.
24 B3 Dulan China
88 D3 Dulce *r.* Arg.
23 E2 Dulishi Hu *salt l.* China
59 J2 Dullstroom S. Africa
42 F3 Dülmen Ger.
49 M3 Dulovo Bulg.
68 A2 Duluth U.S.A.
68 A2 Duluth/Superior *airport* U.S.A.
39 D6 Dulverton U.K.
16 F5 Dūmā Syria
31 B4 Dumaguete Phil.
33 B2 Dumai Indon.
31 B4 Dumaran *i.* Phil.
77 F5 Dumas *AR* U.S.A.
77 C5 Dumas *TX* U.S.A.
16 F5 Dumayr Syria
18 B3 Dumbakh Iran
40 D5 Dumbarton U.K.
59 J3 Dumbe S. Africa
47 J6 Ďumbier *mt* Slovakia
22 D2 Dumchele Jammu and Kashmir
23 H4 Dum Duma India
40 E5 Dumfries U.K.
23 F4 Dumka India
43 G2 Dümmer *l.* Ger.
66 E4 Dumoine, L. *l.* Can.
92 B6 Dumont d'Urville *France base* Ant.
92 B6 Dumont d'Urville Sea *sea* Ant.
42 E4 Dümpelfeld Ger.
55 F1 Dumyāt Egypt
43 J3 Dün *ridge* Ger.
Duna *r.* Hungary *see* Danube
46 H7 Dunajská Streda Slovakia
47 J7 Dunakeszi Hungary
41 E4 Dunany Point *pt* Rep. of Ireland
Dunărea *r.* Romania *see* Danube
49 N2 Dunării, Delta *delta* Romania
47 J7 Dunaújváros Hungary
Dunav *r.* Yugo. *see* Danube
51 C5 Dunayivtsi Ukr.
9 C6 Dunback N.Z.
40 F4 Dunbar U.K.
40 E4 Dunblane U.K.
41 E4 Dunboyne Rep. of Ireland
64 E5 Duncan Can.
75 H5 Duncan *AZ* U.S.A.
77 D5 Duncan *OK* U.S.A.
66 D3 Duncan, Cape *c.* Can.
66 E3 Duncan, L. *l.* Can.
80 E4 Duncannon U.S.A.
40 E2 Duncansby Head *hd* U.K.
68 B5 Duncans Mills U.S.A.
41 E5 Duncormick Rep. of Ireland
37 S8 Dundaga Latvia
69 G3 Dundalk Can.
41 E3 Dundalk Rep. of Ireland
80 E5 Dundalk U.S.A.
41 E4 Dundalk Bay *b.* Rep. of Ireland
Dundas *see* Uummannaq
64 C4 Dundas I. *i.* Can.
Dun Dealgan *see* Dundalk
59 J4 Dundee S. Africa
40 F4 Dundee U.K.
69 F5 Dundee *MI* U.S.A.
80 E3 Dundee *NY* U.S.A.
41 F3 Dundonald U.K.
40 E6 Dundrennan U.K.
41 F3 Dundrum U.K.
41 F3 Dundrum Bay *b.* U.K.
23 E4 Dundwa Range *mts* India/Nepal
9 C6 Dunedin N.Z.
79 D6 Dunedin U.S.A.
8 G2 Dunedoo Austr.
66 F2 Dune, Lac *l.* Can.
40 E4 Dunfermline U.K.
41 E3 Dungannon U.K.
22 C5 Dungarpur India
41 D5 Dungarvan Rep. of Ireland
39 H7 Dungeness *hd* U.K.
88 C8 Dungeness, Pta *pt* Arg.
42 F4 Düngenheim Ger.
41 E3 Dungiven U.K.
41 C3 Dungloe Rep. of Ireland
8 H2 Dungog Austr.
56 C3 Dungu Congo(Zaire)
33 B2 Dungun Malaysia
55 F2 Dungunab Sudan
30 E2 Dunhua China
24 B2 Dunhuang China
8 D4 Dunkeld Austr.
40 E4 Dunkeld U.K.
Dunkerque *see* Dunkirk
39 D6 Dunkery Beacon *h.* U.K.
44 F1 Dunkirk France
80 D3 Dunkirk U.S.A.
54 B4 Dunkwa Ghana
41 E4 Dún Laoghaire Rep. of Ireland
41 E4 Dunlavin Rep. of Ireland
41 E4 Dunleer Rep. of Ireland
41 E2 Dunloy U.K.
41 B6 Dunmanus Bay *b.* Rep. of Ireland
41 B6 Dunmanway Rep. of Ireland
41 C4 Dunmore Rep. of Ireland
79 E7 Dunmore Town Bahamas
74 D3 Dunmovin U.S.A.
41 F3 Dunmurry U.K.
79 E5 Dunn U.S.A.
40 E2 Dunnet Bay *b.* U.K.
40 E2 Dunnet Head *hd* U.K.
74 B2 Dunnigan U.S.A.
76 C3 Dunning U.S.A.
69 H4 Dunnville Can.
8 D4 Dunolly Austr.
40 D5 Dunoon U.K.
40 F5 Duns U.K.
76 C1 Dunseith U.S.A.
72 B3 Dunsmuir U.S.A.
39 G6 Dunstable U.K.
9 B6 Dunstan Mts *mts* N.Z.
42 D5 Dun-sur-Meuse France
9 C6 Duntroon N.Z.
40 B3 Dunvegan, Loch *in.* U.K.
22 B3 Dunyapur Pak.
26 E1 Duolun China
27 D5 Dupang Ling *mts* China
69 H1 Duparquet, Lac *l.* Can.
76 C2 Dupree U.S.A.
78 B4 Du Quoin U.S.A.
6 C3 Durack *r.* Austr.
Dura Europos *see* Qal'at as Sālihīyah
16 E1 Durağan Turkey
44 G5 Durance *r.* France
69 F4 Durand *MI* U.S.A.
68 B3 Durand *WV* U.S.A.
84 A1 Durango Mex.
45 E1 Durango Spain
73 F4 Durango U.S.A.
84 A1 Durango *div.* Mex.
77 D5 Durant U.S.A.
91 F2 Durazno Uru.
91 F1 Durazno, Cuchilla Grande del *h.* Uru.
59 J4 Durban S. Africa
44 F5 Durban-Corbières France
58 C6 Durbanville S. Africa
80 D5 Durbin U.S.A.
42 D4 Durbuy Belgium
42 E4 Düren Ger.
22 E5 Durg India
23 F5 Durgapur India
69 G3 Durham Can.
38 F3 Durham U.K.
74 B2 Durham *CA* U.S.A.
79 E4 Durham *NC* U.S.A.
81 H3 Durham *NH* U.S.A.
51 D6 Durlești Moldova
43 G6 Durmersheim Ger.
49 H3 Durmitor *mt* Yugo.
40 D2 Durness U.K.
49 H4 Durrës Albania
39 F6 Durrington U.K.
41 A6 Dursey Island *i.* Rep. of Ireland
16 B2 Dursunbey Turkey
19 F3 Dūruh Iran
16 F5 Durūz, Jabal ad *mt* Syria
9 D4 D'Urville Island *i.* N.Z.
6 D2 d'Urville, Tanjung *pt* Indon.
19 G3 Durzab Afgh.
19 G4 Dushai Pak.
19 E2 Dushak Turkm.
27 C5 Dushan China
19 H2 Dushanbe Tajik.
51 H7 Dushet'i Georgia
9 A6 Dusky Sound *in.* N.Z.
42 E3 Düsseldorf Ger.
75 F1 Dutch Mt *mt* U.S.A.
58 E1 Dutlwe Botswana
54 C3 Dutse Nigeria
75 F2 Dutton, Mt *mt* U.S.A.
50 H3 Duvannoye Rus. Fed.
67 F2 Duvert, Lac *l.* Can.
27 C5 Duyun China
19 F5 Duzab Pak.
16 C1 Düzce Turkey
Duzdab *see* Zāhedān
50 D4 Dvina, Western *r.* Rus. Fed.
51 F5 Dvorichna Ukr.
28 B2 Dvoryanka Rus. Fed.
22 B5 Dwarka India
59 G2 Dwarsberg S. Africa
68 C5 Dwight U.S.A.
42 E2 Dwingelderveld, Nationaal Park *nat. park* Neth.
72 C2 Dworshak Res. *resr* U.S.A.
58 D6 Dwyka S. Africa
50 E4 Dyat'kovo Rus. Fed.
40 F3 Dyce U.K.
68 D5 Dyer *IN* U.S.A.
74 C3 Dyer *NV* U.S.A.
69 G3 Dyer Bay Can.
63 M3 Dyer, C. *c.* Can.
79 B4 Dyersburg U.S.A.
68 B4 Dyersville U.S.A.
39 D5 Dyfi *r.* U.K.
40 E3 Dyke U.K.
51 G7 Dykh Tau *mt* Georgia/Rus. Fed.
43 L5 Dyleň *h.* Czech Rep.
47 J4 Dylewska Góra *h.* Pol.
59 H5 Dyoki S. Africa
68 A4 Dysart U.S.A.
58 E6 Dysselsdorp S. Africa
24 D2 Dzamïn Üüd Mongolia
57 E5 Dzaoudzi *Mayotte* Africa
50 G3 Dzerzhinsk Rus. Fed.
47 N5 Dzerzhyns'k Ukr.
18 D1 Dzhanga Turkm.
51 E6 Dzhankoy Ukr.
51 H5 Dzhanybek Rus. Fed.
19 G2 Dzharkurgan Uzbek.
18 D2 Dzhebel Turkm.
14 E1 Dzhetygara Kazak.
14 E2 Dzhezkazgan Kazak.
13 R3 Dzhigudzhak Rus. Fed.
19 G1 Dzhizak Uzbek.
24 F1 Dzhugdzhur, Khrebet *mts* Rus. Fed.
Dzhul'fa *see* Culfa
19 G2 Dzhuma Uzbek.
15 F2 Dzhungarskiy Alatau, Khr. *mts* China/Kazak.
12 H5 Dzhusaly Kazak.
47 K4 Działdowo Pol.
84 E3 Dzibalchén Mex.
24 C2 Dzuunmod Mongolia
50 C4 Dzyaniskavichy Belarus
50 C4 Dzyarzhynsk Belarus
47 N4 Dzyatlavichy Belarus

E

66 C3 Eabamet L. *l.* Can.
75 H4 Eagar U.S.A.
73 F4 Eagle U.S.A.
67 J3 Eagle *r.* Can.
81 F3 Eagle Bay U.S.A.
65 H4 Eagle Cr. *r.* Can.
74 D4 Eagle Crags *summit* U.S.A.
65 L5 Eagle L. *l.* Can.
72 B3 Eagle L. *l.* *CA* U.S.A.
81 J1 Eagle Lake *ME* U.S.A.
81 J1 Eagle Lake *l.* *ME* U.S.A.
68 B2 Eagle Mtn *h.* U.S.A.
77 C6 Eagle Pass U.S.A.
62 D3 Eagle Plain *plain* Can.
68 C2 Eagle River *MI* U.S.A.
68 C3 Eagle River *WV* U.S.A.
64 F3 Eaglesham Can.
75 F5 Eagle Tail Mts *mts* U.S.A.
66 B3 Ear Falls Can.
74 C4 Earlimart U.S.A.
40 F5 Earlston U.K.
69 H2 Earlton Can.
40 E4 Earn *r.* U.K.
40 D4 Earn, L. *l.* U.K.
77 C5 Earth U.S.A.
38 H4 Easington U.K.
79 D5 Easley U.S.A.
92 C5 East Antarctica *reg.* Ant.
81 F4 East Ararat U.S.A.
80 D3 East Aurora U.S.A.
77 F6 East Bay *b.* U.S.A.
81 G2 East Berkshire U.S.A.
39 H7 Eastbourne U.K.
80 D4 East Branch Clarion River Reservoir U.S.A.
81 H4 East Brooklyn U.S.A.
9 G2 East Cape *c.* N.Z.
75 G2 East Carbon U.S.A.
94 E5 East Caroline Basin *sea feature* Pac. Oc.
68 D5 East Chicago U.S.A.
24 E3 East China Sea Asia
9 E2 East Coast Bays N.Z.
81 G2 East Corinth U.S.A.
39 H5 East Dereham U.K.
5 R7 Easter Island *i.* Pac. Oc.
95 M7 Easter Island Fracture Zone *sea feature* Pac. Oc.
59 G5 Eastern Cape *div.* S. Africa
55 F2 Eastern Desert *des.* Egypt
23 E6 Eastern Ghats *mts* India
22 B4 Eastern Nara *canal* Pak.
Eastern Transvaal *div. see* Mpumalanga
65 K4 Easterville Can.
88 E8 East Falkland *i.* Falkland Is
81 H4 East Falmouth U.S.A.
42 E1 East Frisian Islands *is* Ger.
74 D2 Eastgate U.S.A.
76 D2 East Grand Forks U.S.A.
39 G6 East Grinstead U.K.
81 G3 Easthampton U.S.A.
81 G4 East Hampton U.S.A.
80 D4 East Hickory U.S.A.
81 G3 East Jamaica U.S.A.
96 K1 East Jan Mayen Ridge *sea feature* Atl. Ocean
68 E3 East Jordan U.S.A.
40 D5 East Kilbride U.K.
68 D3 Eastlake U.S.A.
27 □ East Lamma Channel *H.K.* China
39 F7 Eastleigh U.K.
80 C4 East Liverpool U.S.A.
40 B3 East Loch Tarbert *b.* U.K.
59 G6 East London S. Africa
80 B5 East Lynn Lake *l.* U.S.A.
66 E3 Eastmain *Que.* Can.
66 F3 Eastmain *r.* *Que.* Can.
81 G2 Eastman Can.
79 D5 Eastman U.S.A.
81 J2 East Millinocket U.S.A.
68 B5 East Moline U.S.A.
68 C5 Easton *IL* U.S.A.
81 E5 Easton *MD* U.S.A.
81 F4 Easton *PA* U.S.A.
95 M8 East Pacific Ridge *sea feature* Pac. Oc.
95 N5 East Pacific Rise *sea feature* Pac. Oc.
74 A2 East Park Res. *resr* U.S.A.
79 C5 East Point U.S.A.
67 H4 East Point *pt* *P.E.I.* Can.
81 K2 Eastport *ME* U.S.A.
68 E3 Eastport *MI* U.S.A.
74 D1 East Range *mts* U.S.A.
East Retford *see* Retford
78 B4 East St Louis U.S.A.
13 R2 East Siberian Sea *sea* Rus. Fed.
11 O10 East Timor *reg.* Asia
23 F4 East Tons *r.* India
68 C4 East Troy U.S.A.
81 F6 Eastville U.S.A.
74 C2 East Walker *r.* U.S.A.
81 G3 East Wallingford U.S.A.
79 D5 Eatonton U.S.A.
68 B3 Eau Claire U.S.A.
68 B3 Eau Claire *r.* U.S.A.
66 F2 Eau Claire, Lac à l' *l.* Can.
25 G6 Eauripik Atoll Micronesia
94 E5 Eauripik - New Guinea Rise *sea feature* Pac. Oc.
84 C2 Ebano Mex.
39 D6 Ebbw Vale U.K.
54 D4 Ebebiyin Equatorial Guinea
58 B2 Ebenerde Namibia
80 D4 Ebensburg U.S.A.
16 C2 Eber Gölü *l.* Turkey
43 J3 Ebergötzen Ger.
46 F4 Eberswalde-Finow Ger.
69 F4 Eberts Can.
28 G3 Ebetsu Japan
27 B4 Ebian China
48 F4 Eboli Italy
54 D4 Ebolowa Cameroon
95 G5 Ebon *i.* Pac. Oc.
17 K3 Ebrāhim Ḩeşār Iran
45 G2 Ebro *r.* Spain
43 J1 Ebstorf Ger.
49 M4 Eceabat Turkey
31 B2 Echague Phil.
45 E1 Echarri-Aranaz Spain
54 C1 Ech Chélif Alg.
45 E1 Echegárate, Puerto *pass* Spain
27 E4 Echeng China
64 F1 Echo Bay *N.W.T.* Can.
69 E2 Echo Bay *Ont.* Can.
75 G3 Echo Cliffs *cliff* U.S.A.
66 B3 Echoing *r.* Can.
69 K2 Échouani, Lac *l.* Can.
42 D3 Echt Neth.
42 E5 Echternach Lux.
8 E4 Echuca Austr.
43 G4 Echzell Ger.
45 D4 Écija Spain
43 K5 Eckental Ger.
68 E2 Eckerman U.S.A.

46 D3 Eckernförde Ger.
63 L2 Eclipse Sound *chan.* Can.
85 C3 Ecuador *country* S. America
66 E2 Écueils, Pte aux *pt* Can.
56 E2 Ed Eritrea
37 M7 Ed Sweden
65 H4 Edam Can.
42 D2 Edam Neth.
40 F1 Eday *i.* U.K.
55 E3 Ed Da'ein Sudan
55 F3 Ed Damazin Sudan
55 F3 Ed Damer Sudan
55 F3 Ed Debba Sudan
55 F3 Ed Dueim Sudan
6 E6 Eddystone Pt *pt* Austr.
42 D2 Ede Neth.
54 D4 Edéa Cameroon
65 K2 Edehon Lake *l.* Can.
90 C2 Edéia Brazil
8 G4 Eden Austr.
77 D6 Eden *TX* U.S.A.
38 E3 Eden *r.* U.K.
59 F4 Edenburg S. Africa
9 B7 Edendale N.Z.
41 D4 Edenderry Rep. of Ireland
8 C4 Edenhope Austr.
79 E4 Edenton U.S.A.
59 G3 Edenville S. Africa
49 K4 Edessa Greece
43 F1 Edewecht Ger.
81 H4 Edgartown U.S.A.
76 D2 Edgeley U.S.A.
76 C3 Edgemont U.S.A.
68 C4 Edgerton U.S.A.
41 D4 Edgeworthstown Rep. of Ireland
68 A5 Edina U.S.A.
77 D7 Edinburg U.S.A.
40 E5 Edinburgh U.K.
51 C7 Edirne Turkey
64 F4 Edith Cavell, Mt *mt* Can.
72 B2 Edmonds U.S.A.
64 G4 Edmonton Can.
65 K5 Edmore U.S.A.
68 B4 Edmund U.S.A.
65 L4 Edmund L. *l.* Can.
67 G4 Edmundston Can.
77 D6 Edna U.S.A.
64 C3 Edna Bay U.S.A.
49 M5 Edremit Turkey
37 O6 Edsbyn Sweden
64 F4 Edson Can.
91 D2 Eduardo Castex Arg.
8 E3 Edward *r.* Austr.
68 C1 Edward I. *i.* Can.
56 C4 Edward, Lake *l.* Congo(Zaire)/Uganda
81 F2 Edwards U.S.A.
77 C6 Edwards Plateau *plat.* U.S.A.
78 B4 Edwardsville U.S.A.
92 D4 Edward VIII Ice Shelf *ice feature* Ant.
92 A4 Edward VII Pen. *pen.* Ant.
64 C3 Edziza Pk *mt* Can.
42 B3 Eeklo Belgium
74 A1 Eel *r.* U.S.A.
42 E1 Eemshaven *pt* Neth.
42 E1 Eenrum Neth.
58 D3 Eenzamheid Pan *salt pan* S. Africa
7 G3 Éfaté *i.* Vanuatu
78 B4 Effingham U.S.A.
16 D1 Eflâni Turkey
75 E2 Egan Range *mts* U.S.A.
69 J3 Eganville Can.
47 K7 Eger Hungary
37 K7 Egersund Norway
43 G3 Eggegebirge *h.* Ger.
43 K5 Eggolsheim Ger.
42 C4 Eghezée Belgium
36 F4 Egilsstaðir Iceland
16 C3 Eğirdir Turkey
16 C3 Eğirdir Gölü *l.* Turkey
44 F4 Égletons France
41 D2 Eglinton U.K.
62 F2 Eglinton I. *i.* Can.
42 C2 Egmond aan Zee Neth.
9 D3 Egmont, Cape *c.* N.Z.
9 E3 Egmont, Mt *volc.* N.Z.
9 E3 Egmont National Park N.Z.
16 B2 Eğriğöz Dağı *mts* Turkey
38 G3 Egton U.K.
90 D1 Éguas *r.* Brazil
13 V3 Egvekinot Rus. Fed.
52 G3 Egypt *country* Africa
46 D6 Ehingen (Donau) Ger.
43 J2 Ehra-Lessien Ger.
75 E5 Ehrenberg U.S.A.
43 J5 Eibelstadt Ger.
42 E2 Eibergen Neth.
43 H4 Eichenzell Ger.
43 K6 Eichstätt Ger.
37 K6 Eidfjord Norway
37 M6 Eidsvoll Norway
42 E4 Eifel *reg.* Ger.
40 B4 Eigg *i.* U.K.
21 A4 Eight Degree Chan. India/Maldives
92 A3 Eights Coast *coastal area* Ant.
6 C3 Eighty Mile Beach *beach* Austr.
8 E4 Eildon Austr.
8 F4 Eildon, Lake *l.* Austr.
40 C4 Eilean Shona *i.* U.K.
65 H2 Eileen Lake *l.* Can.
43 L3 Eilenburg Ger.
43 J2 Eimke Ger.
43 H3 Einbeck Ger.
42 D3 Eindhoven Neth.
46 D7 Einsiedeln Switz.
86 E5 Eirunepé Brazil
43 H3 Eisberg *h.* Ger.
57 C5 Eiseb *watercourse* Namibia
43 J4 Eisenach Ger.
43 K4 Eisenberg Ger.
46 G4 Eisenhüttenstadt Ger.
46 H7 Eisenstadt Austria
43 J4 Eisfeld Ger.
40 C3 Eishort, Loch *in.* U.K.
43 K3 Eisleben Lutherstadt Ger.
43 H4 Eiterfeld Ger.
Eivissa *see* Ibiza
Eivissa *i. see* Ibiza
45 F1 Ejea de los Caballeros Spain
57 E6 Ejeda Madag.
82 B3 Ejido Insurgentes Mex.
26 C2 Ejin Horo Qi China
26 A1 Ejin Qi China
17 K1 Ejmiatsin Armenia
84 C3 Ejutla Mex.
37 S7 Ekenäs Fin.
42 C3 Ekeren Belgium
9 E4 Eketahuna N.Z.
15 F1 Ekibastuz Kazak.
13 M3 Ekonda Rus. Fed.
37 N6 Ekshärad Sweden
37 O8 Eksjö Sweden
58 B4 Eksteenfontein S. Africa
56 C4 Ekuku Congo(Zaire)
66 D3 Ekwan *r.* Can.
66 D3 Ekwan Point *pt* Can.
49 K6 Elafonisou, Steno *chan.* Greece
16 B6 El 'Alamein Egypt
84 D3 El Almendro Mex.
16 B6 El 'Âmirîya Egypt
59 H2 Elands *r.* S. Africa
59 H2 Elandsdoorn S. Africa
48 B7 El Aouinet Alg.
16 B6 El 'Arab, Khalîg *b.* Egypt
16 D6 El 'Arîsh Egypt
49 K5 Elassona Greece
16 E7 Elat Israel
17 G2 Elazığ Turkey
48 D3 Elba, Isola d' *i.* Italy
24 F1 El'ban Rus. Fed.
89 B2 El Banco Col.
16 D6 El Bardawîl, Sabkhet *lag.* Egypt
49 J4 Elbasan Albania
16 E2 Elbaşı Turkey
89 C2 El Baúl Venez.
54 C1 El Bayadh Alg.
43 J1 Elbe *r.* Ger.
68 D3 Elberta *MI* U.S.A.
75 G2 Elberta *UT* U.S.A.
73 F4 Elbert, Mount *mt* U.S.A.
79 D5 Elberton U.S.A.
44 E2 Elbeuf France
16 F2 Elbistan Turkey
47 J3 Elbląg Pol.
91 B4 El Bolsón Arg.
79 E7 Elbow Cay *i.* Bahamas
51 G7 Elbrus *mt* Rus. Fed.
42 D2 Elburg Neth.
45 E2 El Burgo de Osma Spain
91 C4 El Cain Arg.
74 D5 El Cajon U.S.A.
89 E3 El Callao Venez.
77 D6 El Campo U.S.A.
75 E5 El Centro U.S.A.
86 F7 El Cerro Bol.
89 D2 El Chaparro Venez.
45 F3 Elche Spain
84 D3 El Chichón *volc.* Mex.
6 D3 Elcho I. *i.* Austr.
89 B3 El Cocuy Col.
45 F3 Elda Spain
43 K1 Elde *r.* Ger.
69 H2 Eldee Can.
74 D5 El Descanso Mex.
89 B2 El Difícil Col.
13 P3 El'dikan Rus. Fed.
89 A4 El Diviso Col.
75 E6 El Doctor Mex.
68 A5 Eldon *IA* U.S.A.
76 E4 Eldon *MO* U.S.A.
88 F3 Eldorado Arg.
84 A1 El Dorado Mex.
77 E5 El Dorado *AR* U.S.A.
77 D4 El Dorado *KS* U.S.A.
77 C6 Eldorado U.S.A.
89 E3 El Dorado Venez.
56 D3 Eldoret Kenya
72 E2 Electric Peak *summit* U.S.A.
54 B2 El Eglab *plat.* Alg.
45 E4 El Ejido Spain
50 F4 Elektrostal' Rus. Fed.
86 D4 El Encanto Col.
43 J3 Elend Ger.
73 F5 Elephant Butte Res. *resr* U.S.A.
92 B1 Elephant I. *i.* Ant.
23 H5 Elephant Point *pt* Bangl.
17 J2 Eleşkirt Turkey
54 C1 El Eulma Alg.
79 E7 Eleuthera *i.* Bahamas
48 C6 El Fahs Tunisia
55 F2 El Faiyûm Egypt
55 E3 El Fasher Sudan
43 H4 Elfershausen Ger.
70 E6 El Fuerte Mex.
55 E3 El Geneina Sudan
55 F3 El Geteina Sudan
40 E3 Elgin U.K.
68 C4 Elgin *IL* U.S.A.
76 C2 Elgin *ND* U.S.A.
75 E3 Elgin *NV* U.S.A.
75 G2 Elgin *UT* U.S.A.
13 Q3 El'ginskiy Rus. Fed.
55 F2 El Gîza Egypt
84 B2 El Gogorrón, Parque Nacional *nat. park* Mex.
54 C1 El Goléa Alg.
55 F4 Elgon, Mount *mt* Uganda
48 B6 El Hadjar Alg.
16 B6 El Hammâm Egypt
16 F6 El Hazim Jordan
54 A2 El Hierro *i.* Canary Is
84 C2 El Higo Mex.
54 C2 El Homr Alg.
40 F4 Elie U.K.
9 C5 Elie de Beaumont *mt* N.Z.
62 B3 Elim *AK* U.S.A.
67 H2 Eliot, Mount *mt* Can.
45 F1 Elizondo Spain
El Iskandarîya *see* Alexandria
51 H6 Elista Rus. Fed.
68 B4 Elizabeth *IL* U.S.A.
81 F4 Elizabeth *NJ* U.S.A.
80 C5 Elizabeth *WV* U.S.A.
79 E4 Elizabeth City U.S.A.
81 H4 Elizabeth Is *is* U.S.A.
79 D4 Elizabethton U.S.A.
78 C4 Elizabethtown *KY* U.S.A.
79 E5 Elizabethtown *NC* U.S.A.
81 G2 Elizabethtown *NY* U.S.A.
80 E4 Elizabethtown *PA* U.S.A.
54 B1 El Jadida Morocco
16 F6 El Jafr Jordan
84 A1 El Jaralito Mex.
48 D7 El Jem Tunisia
47 L4 Ełk Pol.
74 A2 Elk U.S.A.
64 G4 Elk *r.* Can.
80 C5 Elk *r.* U.S.A.
16 F4 El Kaa Lebanon
48 C6 El Kala Alg.
55 F3 El Kamlin Sudan
77 D5 Elk City U.S.A.
74 A2 Elk Creek U.S.A.
74 B2 Elk Grove U.S.A.
55 F2 El Khârga Egypt
68 E5 Elkhart U.S.A.
El Khartûm *see* Khartoum
54 B2 El Khnâchîch *esc.* Mali
68 C4 Elkhorn U.S.A.
76 D3 Elkhorn *r.* U.S.A.
49 M3 Elkhovo Bulg.
80 D5 Elkins U.S.A.
64 G4 Elk Island Nat. Park Can.
69 G2 Elk Lake Can.
68 E3 Elk Lake *l.* U.S.A.
80 E4 Elkland U.S.A.
64 F5 Elko Can.
72 D3 Elko U.S.A.
65 G4 Elk Point Can.
76 E2 Elk River U.S.A.
81 F5 Elkton *MD* U.S.A.
80 D5 Elkton *VA* U.S.A.
17 G4 El Kubar Syria
65 M2 Ell Bay *b.* Can.
63 H2 Ellef Ringnes I. *i.* Can.
22 C3 Ellenabad India
76 D2 Ellendale U.S.A.
75 G2 Ellen, Mt *mt* U.S.A.
72 B2 Ellensburg U.S.A.
81 F4 Ellenville U.S.A.
8 G4 Ellery, Mt *mt* Austr.
63 K2 Ellesmere Island *i.* Can.
9 D5 Ellesmere, Lake *l.* N.Z.
39 E4 Ellesmere Port U.K.
62 H3 Ellice *r.* Can.
80 D3 Ellicottville U.S.A.
84 C2 El Limón Mex.
43 J5 Ellingen Ger.
59 G5 Elliot S. Africa
59 H5 Elliotdale S. Africa
69 F2 Elliot Lake Can.
72 D2 Ellis U.S.A.
59 G1 Ellisras S. Africa
40 F3 Ellon U.K.
81 J2 Ellsworth *ME* U.S.A.
68 A3 Ellsworth *WI* U.S.A.
92 A3 Ellsworth Land *reg.* Ant.
92 B3 Ellsworth Mountains Ant.
43 J6 Ellwangen (Jagst) Ger.
16 B3 Elmalı Turkey
74 D6 El Maneadero Mex.
55 F1 El Mansûra Egypt
89 E3 El Manteco Venez.
54 C1 El Meghaïer Alg.
89 E3 El Miamo Venez.
16 E4 El Mîna Lebanon
55 F2 El Minya Egypt
68 E3 Elmira *MI* U.S.A.
80 E3 Elmira *NY* U.S.A.
75 F5 El Mirage U.S.A.
45 E4 El Moral Spain
8 E4 Elmore Austr.
91 D2 El Morro *mt* Arg.
54 B2 El Mreyyé *reg.* Maur.
43 H1 Elmshorn Ger.
55 E3 El Muglad Sudan
69 G3 Elmwood Can.
68 C5 Elmwood *IL* U.S.A.
68 A3 Elmwood *WI* U.S.A.
36 K5 Elnesvågen Norway
89 B3 El Nevado, Cerro *mt* Col.
31 A4 El Nido Phil.
55 F3 El Obeid Sudan
89 C3 Elorza Venez.
54 C1 El Oued Alg.
75 G5 Eloy U.S.A.
84 A1 El Palmito Mex.
89 E2 El Pao *Bolívar* Venez.
89 C2 El Pao *Cojedes* Venez.
68 C5 El Paso *IL* U.S.A.
73 F6 El Paso *TX* U.S.A.
40 C2 Elphin U.K.
74 C3 El Portal U.S.A.
45 H2 El Prat de Llobregat Spain
84 E4 El Progreso Guatemala
45 C4 El Puerto de Santa María Spain
El Qâhira *see* Cairo
16 D6 El Qantara Egypt
16 E7 El Quweira Jordan
77 D5 El Reno U.S.A.
84 B2 El Retorno Mex.
68 B4 Elroy U.S.A.
84 B2 El Rucio Mex.
64 B2 Elsa Can.
16 C7 El Saff Egypt
84 B1 El Salado Mex.
16 D6 El Sâlhîya Egypt
84 A2 El Salto Mex.
84 B1 El Salvador Mex.
31 C4 El Salvador Phil.
61 K8 El Salvador *country* Central America
89 C3 El Samán de Apure Venez.
69 F1 Elsas Can.
43 G2 Else *r.* Ger.
23 H2 Elsen Nur *l.* China
16 D7 El Shatt Egypt
89 D2 El Sombrero Venez.
91 C2 El Sosneado Arg.
El Suweis *see* Suez
84 C2 El Tajin Ruins Mex.
95 L9 Eltanin Fracture Zone *sea feature* Pac. Oc.
48 C6 El Tarf Alg.
45 C1 El Teleno *mt* Spain
84 C3 El Tepozteco, Parque Nacional *nat. park* Mex.
16 E7 El Thamad Egypt
89 D2 El Tigre Venez.
84 E3 El Tigre, Parque Nacional *nat. park* Guatemala
43 J5 Eltmann Ger.
89 C2 El Tocuyo Venez.
51 H5 El'ton Rus. Fed.
51 H5 El'ton, Ozero *l.* Rus. Fed.
72 C2 Eltopia U.S.A.
89 E2 El Toro Venez.
91 E2 El Trébol Arg.
89 C3 El Tuparro, Parque Nacional *nat. park* Col.
55 F2 El Tur Egypt
88 B8 El Turbio Chile
21 C2 Eluru India
37 U7 Elva Estonia
89 A3 El Valle Col.
40 E5 Elvanfoot U.K.
45 C3 Elvas Port.
37 M6 Elverum Norway
89 B3 El Viejo *mt* Col.
89 C2 El Vigía Venez.
86 D5 Elvira Brazil
56 E3 El Wak Kenya
68 E5 Elwood U.S.A.
43 J3 Elxleben Ger.
39 H5 Ely U.K.
68 B2 Ely *MN* U.S.A.
75 E2 Ely *NV* U.S.A.
80 B4 Elyria U.S.A.
43 G4 Elz Ger.
43 H2 Elze Ger.
7 G3 Émaé *i.* Vanuatu
18 D2 Emāmrūd Iran
19 H2 Emām Şaḩēb Afgh.
17 L5 Emāmzadeh Naşrod Dīn Iran
37 O8 Emån *r.* Sweden
90 B2 Emas, Parque Nacional das *nat. park* Brazil
14 D2 Emba Kazak.
59 H3 Embalenhle S. Africa
65 G3 Embarras Portage Can.
90 C2 Emborcação, Represa de *resr* Brazil
81 F2 Embrun Can.
56 D4 Embu Kenya
42 F1 Emden Ger.
27 B4 Emei China
27 B4 Emei Shan *mt* China
8 E4 Emerald *Vic.* Austr.
6 E4 Emerald Austr.
67 G3 Emeril Can.
65 K5 Emerson Can.
16 B2 Emet Turkey
59 J2 Emgwenya S. Africa
75 E3 Emigrant Valley *v.* U.S.A.
59 J2 Emijindini S. Africa
55 D3 Emi Koussi *mt* Chad
84 E3 Emiliano Zapata Mex.
49 M3 Eminska Planina *h.* Bulg.
16 C2 Emir D. *mt* Turkey
16 C2 Emirdağ Turkey
37 O8 Emmaboda Sweden
37 S7 Emmaste Estonia
42 D2 Emmeloord Neth.
42 F4 Emmelshausen Ger.
42 E2 Emmen Neth.
46 D7 Emmen Switz.
42 E3 Emmerich Ger.
21 B3 Emmiganuru India
77 C6 Emory Pk *summit* U.S.A.
82 B3 Empalme Mex.
59 J4 Empangeni S. Africa
88 E3 Empedrado Arg.
94 G3 Emperor Seamount Chain *sea feature* Pac. Oc.
48 D3 Empoli Italy
76 D4 Emporia *KS* U.S.A.
80 E6 Emporia *VA* U.S.A.
80 D4 Emporium U.S.A.
65 G4 Empress Can.
19 E3 'Emrānī Iran
42 F2 Ems *r.* Ger.
69 H3 Emsdale Can.
42 F2 Emsdetten Ger.
42 F1 Ems-Jade-Kanal *canal* Ger.
42 F2 Emsland *reg.* Ger.
59 H3 Emzinoni S. Africa
36 N5 Enafors Sweden
25 F7 Enarotali Indon.
29 E7 Ena-san *mt* Japan
82 A2 Encantada, Co de la *mt* Mex.
91 G1 Encantadas, Serra das *h.* Brazil
31 B3 Encanto, Cape *pt* Phil.
84 B2 Encarnación Mex.
88 E3 Encarnación Para.
77 D6 Encinal U.S.A.
74 D5 Encinitas U.S.A.
73 F5 Encino U.S.A.
8 B3 Encounter Bay *b.* Austr.
90 E1 Encruzilhada Brazil
91 G1 Encruzilhada do Sul Brazil
64 D4 Endako Can.
32 B5 Endau Malaysia
6 E3 Endeavour Strait *chan.* Austr.
25 E7 Endeh Indon.
92 D4 Enderby Land *reg.* Ant.
81 E3 Endicott U.S.A.
64 C3 Endicott Arm *in.* U.S.A.
62 C3 Endicott Mts *mts* U.S.A.
91 E3 Energía Arg.
51 E6 Enerhodar Ukr.
94 F5 Enewetak *i.* Pac. Oc.
48 D6 Enfidaville Tunisia
81 G3 Enfield U.S.A.
68 E2 Engadine U.S.A.
36 L5 Engan Norway
31 B2 Engaño, Cape *c.* Phil.
Engaños, Río de los *r. see* Yari
28 H2 Engaru Japan
59 G5 Engcobo S. Africa
51 H5 Engel's Rus. Fed.
42 C1 Engelschmangat *chan.* Neth.
33 B4 Enggano *i.* Indon.
42 C4 Enghien Belgium
34 E3 England *div.* U.K.
67 J3 Englee Can.
79 F5 Englehard U.S.A.
69 H2 Englehart Can.
39 D7 English Channel *str.* France/U.K.
51 G7 Enguri *r.* Georgia
59 J4 Enhlalakahle S. Africa
77 D4 Enid U.S.A.
28 G3 Eniwa Japan
42 D2 Enkhuizen Neth.
37 P7 Enköping Sweden
48 F6 Enna *Sicily* Italy
65 J2 Ennadai Lake *l.* Can.
55 E3 En Nahud Sudan
55 E3 Ennedi, Massif *mts* Chad
41 D4 Ennell, Lough *l.* Rep. of Ireland
76 C2 Enning U.S.A.
41 C5 Ennis Rep. of Ireland
72 E2 Ennis *MT* U.S.A.
77 D5 Ennis *TX* U.S.A.
41 E5 Enniscorthy Rep. of Ireland
41 D3 Enniskillen U.K.
41 B5 Ennistymon Rep. of Ireland
46 G7 Enns *r.* Austria
36 W5 Eno Fin.
75 F3 Enoch U.S.A.
36 S2 Enontekiö Fin.
27 D6 Enping China
31 B2 Enrile Phil.
42 D2 Ens Neth.
8 F4 Ensay Austr.
42 E2 Enschede Neth.
43 G3 Ense Ger.
91 F2 Ensenada Arg.
82 A2 Ensenada Mex.
27 C4 Enshi China
64 F2 Enterprise *N.W.T.* Can.
69 J3 Enterprise *Ont.* Can.
79 C6 Enterprise *AL* U.S.A.
72 C2 Enterprise *OR* U.S.A.
75 F3 Enterprise *UT* U.S.A.
64 F4 Entrance Can.
86 F8 Entre Ríos Bol.
91 E2 Entre Ríos *div.* Arg.
45 B3 Entroncamento Port.
54 C4 Enugu Nigeria
13 V3 Enurmino Rus. Fed.
86 D5 Envira Brazil
86 D5 Envira *r.* Brazil
9 C5 Enys, Mt *mt* N.Z.
29 F7 Enzan Japan
42 D2 Epe Neth.
42 B5 Épernay France
75 G2 Ephraim U.S.A.
81 E4 Ephrata *PA* U.S.A.
72 C2 Ephrata *WA* U.S.A.
7 G3 Épi *i.* Vanuatu
44 H2 Épinal France
16 D4 Episkopi Cyprus
48 E4 Epomeo, Monte *h.* Italy
39 H6 Epping U.K.
43 G4 Eppstein Ger.
39 G6 Epsom U.K.
91 D3 Epu-pel Arg.
18 D4 Eqlīd Iran
53 E5 Equatorial Guinea *country* Africa
89 E3 Equeipa Venez.
31 A4 Eran Phil.
31 A4 Eran Bay *b.* Phil.
16 F1 Erbaa Turkey
43 L5 Erbendorf Ger.
95 L3 Erben Tablemount *depth* Pac. Oc.
42 F5 Erbeskopf *h.* Ger.
17 J2 Erçek Turkey
17 J2 Erciş Turkey
16 E2 Erciyes Dağı *mt* Turkey
47 J7 Érd Hungary
23 H2 Erdaogou China
30 D2 Erdao Jiang *r.* China
16 A1 Erdek Turkey
16 E3 Erdemli Turkey
26 C1 Erdenetsogt Mongolia
55 E3 Erdi *reg.* Chad
51 H6 Erdniyevskiy Rus. Fed.
89 D3 Erebato *r.* Venez.
92 B5 Erebus, Mt *mt* Ant.
17 K6 Erech Iraq
88 F3 Erechim Brazil
24 D2 Ereentsav Mongolia
16 E3 Ereğli *Konya* Turkey
16 C1 Ereğli *Zonguldak* Turkey
48 F6 Erei, Monti *mts Sicily* Italy
26 D1 Erenhot China
18 E3 Eresk Iran
45 D2 Eresma *r.* Spain
49 K5 Eretria Greece
Erevan *see* Yerevan
43 K4 Erfurt Ger.
17 G2 Ergani Turkey
54 B2 'Erg Chech *sand dunes* Alg./Mali
55 D3 Erg du Djourab *sand dunes* Chad
54 D3 Erg du Ténéré *des.* Niger
26 C1 Ergel Mongolia
49 M4 Ergene *r.* Turkey
54 B2 Erg Iguidi *sand dunes* Alg./Maur.
37 T8 Ērgļi Latvia
28 A1 Ergu China
Ergun He *r. see* Argun'
30 C3 Erhulai China
40 D2 Eriboll, Loch *in.* U.K.
40 D4 Ericht, Loch *l.* U.K.
68 B5 Erie *IL* U.S.A.
77 E4 Erie *KS* U.S.A.
80 C3 Erie *PA* U.S.A.
69 G4 Erie, Lake *l.* Can./U.S.A.
28 H3 Erimo Japan
28 H4 Erimo-misaki *c.* Japan
40 A3 Eriskay *i.* U.K.
52 H4 Eritrea *country* Africa
16 E2 Erkilet Turkey
43 K5 Erlangen Ger.
6 D4 Erldunda Austr.
30 E2 Erlong Shan *mt* China
30 C2 Erlongshan Sk. *resr* China
42 D2 Ermelo Neth.
59 H3 Ermelo S. Africa
16 D3 Ermenek Turkey
49 L6 Ermoupoli Greece
21 B4 Ernakulam India
21 B4 Erode India
58 A1 Erongo *div.* Namibia
42 D3 Erp Neth.
54 B1 Er Rachidia Morocco
55 F3 Er Rahad Sudan
57 D5 Errego Moz.
48 D7 Er Remla Tunisia
41 C2 Errigal *h.* Rep. of Ireland
41 A3 Erris Head *hd* Rep. of Ireland
81 H2 Errol U.S.A.
7 G3 Erromango *i.* Vanuatu
49 J4 Ersekë Albania
76 D2 Erskine U.S.A.
36 R5 Ersmark Sweden
51 G5 Ertil' Rus. Fed.
8 B1 Erudina Austr.
17 J3 Eruh Turkey
91 G2 Erval Brazil
80 D5 Erwin U.S.A.
43 G3 Erwitte Ger.
43 K2 Erxleben *Sachsen-Anhalt* Ger.
43 K2 Erxleben *Sachsen-Anhalt* Ger.
43 L4 Erzgebirge *mts* Czech Rep./Ger.
16 F3 Erzin Turkey
17 G2 Erzincan Turkey
17 H2 Erzurum Turkey
28 G4 Esan-misaki *pt* Japan
28 G4 Esashi Japan
28 H2 Esashi Japan
37 L9 Esbjerg Denmark
75 G3 Escalante U.S.A.
75 G3 Escalante *r.* U.S.A.
75 F3 Escalante Desert *des.* U.S.A.
68 D3 Escanaba U.S.A.
84 E3 Escárcega Mex.
31 B2 Escarpada Point *pt* Phil.
45 F2 Escatrón Spain
42 B4 Escaut *r.* Belgium
42 D3 Esch Neth.
42 E2 Esche Ger.
43 J2 Eschede Ger.
42 D5 Esch-sur-Alzette Lux.
43 J3 Eschwege Ger.
42 E4 Eschweiler Ger.
74 D5 Escondido U.S.A.
84 A2 Escuinapa Mex.
84 E4 Escuintla Guatemala
84 D4 Escuintla Mex.
89 C3 Escutillas Col.
16 B3 Eşen Turkey
18 D2 Esenguly Turkm.
42 F1 Esens Ger.
18 C3 Eşfahan Iran
18 D4 Esfandāran Iran
18 C4 Esfarjan Iran
19 E3 Eshāqābād Iran
18 D5 Eshkanān Iran
59 J4 Eshowe S. Africa
16 E6 Esh Sharā *mts* Jordan
18 C3 Eshtehārd Iran
57 C6 Esigodini Zimbabwe
59 K4 Esikhawini S. Africa
38 D2 Esk *r.* U.K.
40 E5 Eskdalemuir U.K.
67 G3 Esker Can.
36 F4 Eskifjörður Iceland
37 P7 Eskilstuna Sweden
62 E3 Eskimo Lakes *l.* Can.
17 J3 Eski Mosul Iraq
16 D1 Eskipazar Turkey
16 C2 Eskişehir Turkey
45 D1 Esla *r.* Spain
18 B3 Eslamābād e Gharb Iran
16 B3 Esler D. *mt* Turkey
43 G3 Eslohe (Sauerland) Ger.
37 N9 Eslöv Sweden
16 B2 Eşme Turkey
86 C3 Esmeraldas Ecuador
68 E1 Esnagi Lake *l.* Can.
42 B4 Esnes France
19 F5 Espakeh Iran
44 F4 Espalion France
69 G2 Espanola Can.
73 F4 Espanola U.S.A.
86 □ Española, Isla *i. Galapagos Is* Ecuador
74 A2 Esparto U.S.A.
43 G2 Espelkamp Ger.
6 C5 Esperance Austr.
91 E1 Esperanza Arg.
82 C3 Esperanza Mex.
31 C4 Esperanza Phil.
92 B2 Esperanza *Arg. Base* Ant.
45 B3 Espichel, Cabo *hd* Port.
45 D1 Espigüete *mt* Spain
84 B1 Espinazo Mex.
90 D2 Espinhaço, Serra do *mts* Brazil
90 D1 Espinosa Brazil
90 E2 Espírito Santo *div.* Brazil
31 B2 Espiritu Phil.
70 D7 Espíritu Santo *i.* Mex.
7 G3 Espíritu Santo *i.* Vanuatu
37 T6 Espoo Fin.
45 F4 Espuña *mt* Spain
88 B6 Esquel Arg.
64 E5 Esquimalt Can.
31 C5 Essang Indon.
54 B1 Essaouira Morocco
54 A2 Es Semara Western Sahara
42 C3 Essen Belgium
42 F3 Essen Ger.
43 F2 Essen (Oldenburg) Ger.
87 G3 Essequibo *r.* Guyana
69 F4 Essex Can.
75 E4 Essex U.S.A.
81 G2 Essex Junction U.S.A.
69 F4 Essexville U.S.A.
13 R4 Esso Rus. Fed.
88 D8 Estados, I. de los *i.* Arg.
18 D4 Eşţahbānāt Iran
69 G2 Estaire Can.
87 L6 Estância Brazil
45 G1 Estats, Pic d' *mt* France/Spain
59 H4 Estcourt S. Africa
43 H1 Este *r.* Ger.
45 E1 Estella Spain
45 D4 Estepa Spain
45 D4 Estepona Spain
65 J4 Esterhazy Can.
74 B4 Estero Bay *b.* U.S.A.
88 D2 Esteros Para.
88 E3 Esteros del Iberá *marsh* Arg.
65 J5 Estevan Can.
76 E3 Estherville U.S.A.
67 H4 Est, Île de l' *i.* Can.
79 D5 Estill U.S.A.
81 J1 Est, Lac de l' *l.* Can.
35 H3 Estonia *country* Europe
42 A5 Estrées-St-Denis France
45 C2 Estrela, Serra da *mts* Port.
45 E3 Estrella *mt* Spain
45 C3 Estremoz Port.
87 J5 Estrondo, Serra *h.* Brazil
17 M4 Estūh Iran
22 D4 Etah India
42 D5 Étain France
44 F2 Étampes France
44 E1 Étaples France
22 D4 Etawah India
59 J3 eThandakukhanya S. Africa
58 E4 E'Thembini S. Africa
53 H5 Ethiopia *country* Africa
16 D2 Etimesğut Turkey
40 C4 Etive, Loch *in.* U.K.
48 F6 Etna, Monte *volc. Sicily* Italy
37 J7 Etne Norway
64 C3 Etolin I. *i.* U.S.A.
57 B5 Etosha National Park Namibia
57 B5 Etosha Pan *salt pan* Namibia
49 L3 Etropole Bulg.
21 B4 Ettaiyapuram India
42 E5 Ettelbruck Lux.
42 C3 Etten-Leur Neth.
43 G6 Ettlingen Ger.
40 E5 Ettrick Forest *reg.* U.K.
84 A2 Etzatlán Mex.
8 F2 Euabalong Austr.
Euboea *i. see* Evvoia
6 C5 Eucla Austr.
80 C4 Euclid U.S.A.
87 L6 Euclides da Cunha Brazil
8 G4 Eucumbene, L. *l.* Austr.
8 B3 Eudunda Austr.
79 C6 Eufaula U.S.A.
77 E5 Eufaula Lake *resr* U.S.A.
72 B2 Eugene U.S.A.
82 A3 Eugenia, Pta *c.* Mex.
8 G2 Eugowra Austr.
8 G1 Eumungerie Austr.
77 E6 Eunice U.S.A.
42 E4 Eupen Belgium
17 K6 Euphrates *r.* Asia
37 S6 Eura Fin.
44 E2 Eure *r.* France
72 A3 Eureka *CA* U.S.A.
72 D1 Eureka *MT* U.S.A.
75 E2 Eureka *NV* U.S.A.
8 C1 Eurinilla *r.* Austr.
8 C1 Euriowie Austr.
8 E4 Euroa Austr.
57 E6 Europa, Île *i.* Ind. Ocean
45 D4 Europa Point *pt* Gibraltar
42 C3 Europoort *reg.* Neth.
42 E4 Euskirchen Ger.
8 D3 Euston Austr.
64 D4 Eustuk Lake *l.* Can.
79 C5 Eutaw U.S.A.
43 L3 Eutzsch Ger.
59 H3 Evander S. Africa
64 F4 Evansburg Can.
92 B3 Evans Ice Stream *ice feature* Ant.
66 E3 Evans, L. *l.* Can.
73 F4 Evans, Mt *mt CO* U.S.A.
72 D2 Evans, Mt *mt MT* U.S.A.
63 K3 Evans Strait *chan.* Can.
68 D4 Evanston *IL* U.S.A.
72 E3 Evanston *WY* U.S.A.
69 F3 Evansville Can.
78 C4 Evansville *IN* U.S.A.
68 C4 Evansville *WI* U.S.A.
72 F3 Evansville *WY* U.S.A.
68 E4 Evart U.S.A.
59 G3 Evaton S. Africa
18 D5 Evaz Iran
68 A2 Eveleth U.S.A.
13 R3 Evensk Rus. Fed.
6 D4 Everard Range *h.* Austr.
42 D3 Everdingen Neth.
23 F4 Everest, Mt *mt* China
81 K1 Everett Can.
72 B1 Everett U.S.A.
42 B3 Evergem Belgium
79 D7 Everglades Nat. Park U.S.A.
79 D7 Everglades, The *swamp* U.S.A.
77 G6 Evergreen U.S.A.
39 F5 Evesham U.K.
39 F5 Evesham, Vale of *reg.* U.K.
36 S5 Evijärvi Fin.
54 D4 Evinayong Equatorial Guinea
37 K7 Evje Norway
45 C3 Évora Port.
24 F1 Evoron, Ozero *l.* Rus. Fed.
17 K2 Evowghlī Iran
44 E2 Évreux France
49 K6 Evrotas *r.* Greece
16 D4 Evrychou Cyprus
49 L5 Evvoia *i.* Greece
74 □1 Ewa Beach U.S.A.
56 D3 Ewaso Ngiro *r.* Kenya
40 C3 Ewe, Loch *in.* U.K.
92 B2 Ewing I. *i.* Ant.
86 E6 Exaltación Bol.
59 G4 Excelsior S. Africa
74 C2 Excelsior Mt *mt* U.S.A.
74 C2 Excelsior Mts *mts* U.S.A.
76 E4 Excelsior Springs U.S.A.
39 D6 Exe *r.* U.K.
92 A4 Executive Committee Range *mts* Ant.
8 H3 Exeter Austr.
69 G4 Exeter Can.
39 D7 Exeter U.K.
74 C3 Exeter *CA* U.S.A.
81 H3 Exeter *NH* U.S.A.
42 E2 Exloo Neth.
39 D7 Exminster U.K.
39 D6 Exmoor Forest *reg.* U.K.
39 D6 Exmoor National Park U.K.
81 F6 Exmore U.S.A.
39 D7 Exmouth U.K.
6 B4 Exmouth Gulf *b.* Austr.
8 G1 Exmouth, Mt *mt* Austr.
93 M5 Exmouth Plateau *sea feature* Ind. Ocean
45 D3 Extremadura *div.* Spain
79 E7 Exuma Sound *chan.* Bahamas
56 D4 Eyasi, Lake *salt l.* Tanz.
39 J5 Eye U.K.
40 F5 Eyemouth U.K.
40 B2 Eye Peninsula *pen.* U.K.
36 D5 Eyjafjallajökull *ice cap* Iceland
36 D3 Eyjafjörður *in.* Iceland
56 E3 Eyl Somalia
39 F6 Eynsham U.K.
6 D4 Eyre, Lake (North) *salt flat* Austr.
6 D4 Eyre, Lake (South) *salt flat* Austr.
9 B6 Eyre Mountains *mts* N.Z.
6 D5 Eyre Peninsula *pen.* Austr.
43 H2 Eystrup Ger.
36 □ Eysturoy *i.* Faroe Is
59 J4 Ezakheni S. Africa
59 H3 Ezenzeleni S. Africa
91 C3 Ezequiel Ramos Mexía, Embalse *resr* Arg.
50 J2 Ezhva Rus. Fed.
49 M5 Ezine Turkey
16 F1 Ezinepazar Turkey
17 L6 Ezra's Tomb Iraq

F

21 A5 Faadhippolhu Atoll Maldives
77 B6 Fabens U.S.A.
64 F2 Faber Lake *l.* Can.
32 □ Faber, Mt *h.* Sing.
37 M9 Fåborg Denmark
48 E3 Fabriano Italy
89 B3 Facatativá Col.
42 B4 Faches-Thumesnil France
54 D3 Fachi Niger
81 F4 Factoryville U.S.A.
88 B7 Facundo Arg.
54 C3 Fada-Ngourma Burkina
48 D2 Faenza Italy
Faeroes *terr. see* Faroe Islands
25 F7 Fafanlap Indon.
56 E3 Fafen Shet' *watercourse* Eth.
49 L2 Făgăraş Romania
37 L6 Fagernes Norway
37 O7 Fagersta Sweden
88 C8 Fagnano, L. *l.* Arg./Chile
42 C4 Fagne *reg.* Belgium
54 B3 Faguibine, Lac *l.* Mali
36 E5 Fagurhólsmýri Iceland
55 F4 Fagwir Sudan
19 E4 Fahraj Iran
62 D3 Fairbanks U.S.A.
80 B5 Fairborn U.S.A.
76 D3 Fairbury U.S.A.
80 E5 Fairfax U.S.A.
74 A2 Fairfield *CA* U.S.A.
68 B5 Fairfield *IA* U.S.A.
78 C4 Fairfield *OH* U.S.A.
77 D6 Fairfield *TX* U.S.A.
81 G3 Fair Haven U.S.A.
41 E2 Fair Head *hd* U.K.
31 A4 Fairie Queen *sand bank* Phil.
40 G1 Fair Isle *i.* U.K.
76 E3 Fairmont *MN* U.S.A.
80 C5 Fairmont *WV* U.S.A.
73 F4 Fairplay U.S.A.
68 D3 Fairport U.S.A.
80 C4 Fairport Harbor U.S.A.
64 F3 Fairview Can.
69 E3 Fairview *MI* U.S.A.
77 D4 Fairview *OK* U.S.A.
75 G2 Fairview *UT* U.S.A.
27 □ Fairview Park *H.K.* China
64 B3 Fairweather, Cape *c.* U.S.A.
64 B3 Fairweather, Mt *mt* Can./U.S.A.
25 G6 Fais *i.* Micronesia
22 C3 Faisalabad Pak.
42 C5 Faissault France
76 C2 Faith U.S.A.
40 □ Faither, The *pt* U.K.
23 E4 Faizabad India
7 J2 Fakaofo *i.* Tokelau
39 H5 Fakenham U.K.
36 O5 Fåker Sweden
25 F7 Fakfak Indon.

18 D4 Fakhrabad Iran
30 B2 Faku China
39 C7 Fal r. U.K.
54 A4 Falaba Sierra Leone
44 D2 Falaise France
23 G4 Falakata India
23 H5 Falam Myanmar
18 C3 Falavarjan Iran
77 D7 Falcon Lake l. Mex./U.S.A.
77 D7 Falfurrias U.S.A.
64 F3 Falher Can.
43 M3 Falkenberg Ger.
37 N8 Falkenberg Sweden
43 L1 Falkenhagen Ger.
43 L3 Falkenhain Ger.
43 M2 Falkensee Ger.
43 L5 Falkenstein Ger.
40 E5 Falkirk U.K.
40 E4 Falkland U.K.
85 D8 Falkland Islands terr. Atl. Ocean
88 D8 Falkland Sound chan. Falkland Is
37 N7 Falköping Sweden
74 D5 Fallbrook U.S.A.
43 H2 Fallingbostel Ger.
74 C2 Fallon U.S.A.
81 H4 Fall River U.S.A.
72 F3 Fall River Pass U.S.A.
76 E3 Falls City U.S.A.
39 B7 Falmouth U.K.
80 A5 Falmouth KY U.S.A.
81 H3 Falmouth ME U.S.A.
68 E3 Falmouth MI U.S.A.
58 C7 False Bay b. S. Africa
37 M9 Falster i. Denmark
47 N7 Fălticeni Romania
37 O6 Falun Sweden
16 D4 Famagusta Cyprus
42 E5 Fameck France
42 D4 Famenne v. Belgium
65 K4 Family L. l. Can.
26 F4 Fanchang China
41 E4 Fane r. Rep. of Ireland
32 A1 Fang Thai.
26 D3 Fangcheng China
27 C4 Fangdou Shan mts China
27 F6 Fang-liao Taiwan
26 E2 Fangshan Beijing China
26 D2 Fangshan Shanxi China
27 F6 Fangshan Taiwan
26 D3 Fang Xian China
28 A2 Fangzheng China
27 □ Fanling H.K. China
40 C3 Fannich, Loch l. U.K.
19 E5 Fannūj Iran
48 E3 Fano Italy
27 F5 Fanshan China
26 D2 Fanshi China
27 B6 Fan Si Pan mt Vietnam
19 F2 Farab Turkm.
56 C3 Faradje Congo(Zaire)
57 E6 Farafangana Madag.
55 E2 Farafra Oasis oasis Egypt
19 F3 Farāh Afgh.
19 F4 Farah Rūd r. Afgh.
89 A4 Farallones de Cali, Parque Nacional nat. park Col.
54 A3 Faranah Guinea
25 G6 Faraulep Atoll Micronesia
39 F7 Fareham U.K.
9 D4 Farewell, Cape c. N.Z.
9 D4 Farewell Spit spit N.Z.
37 N7 Färgelanda Sweden
76 D2 Fargo U.S.A.
76 E2 Faribault U.S.A.
67 F2 Faribault, Lac l. Can.
22 D3 Faridabad India
22 C3 Faridkot India
23 G5 Faridpur Bangl.
54 A3 Farim Guinea-Bissau
19 E3 Farīmān Iran
37 P8 Färjestaden Sweden
19 H2 Farkhor Tajik.
17 M4 Farmahin Iran
68 C5 Farmer City U.S.A.
66 D2 Farmer Island i. Can.
64 E3 Farmington Can.
68 B5 Farmington IA U.S.A.
68 B5 Farmington IL U.S.A.
81 H2 Farmington ME U.S.A.
81 H3 Farmington NH U.S.A.
75 H3 Farmington NM U.S.A.
72 E3 Farmington UT U.S.A.
64 D4 Far Mt. mt Can.
80 D6 Farmville U.S.A.
39 G6 Farnborough U.K.
38 F2 Farne Islands is U.K.
39 G6 Farnham U.K.
64 F4 Farnham, Mt mt Can.
87 G4 Faro Brazil
64 C2 Faro Can.
45 C4 Faro Port.
37 Q8 Fårö i. Sweden
34 E2 Faroe Islands terr. Atl. Ocean
37 Q8 Fårösund Sweden
53 K7 Farquhar Group is Seychelles
18 D4 Farrāshband Iran
80 C4 Farrell U.S.A.
69 K3 Farrellton Can.
19 E3 Farrokhī Iran
Farrukhabad see Fatehgarh
18 D3 Farsakh Iran
49 K5 Farsala Greece
19 F3 Fārsī Afgh.
72 E3 Farson U.S.A.
37 K7 Farsund Norway
Farvel, Kap c. see Uummannarsuaq
77 C5 Farwell U.S.A.
18 D4 Fasā Iran
48 G4 Fasano Italy
43 J2 Faßberg Ger.
80 E4 Fassett U.S.A.
51 D5 Fastiv Ukr.
22 D4 Fatehgarh India
22 E4 Fatehpur Rajasthan India
22 E4 Fatehpur Uttar Pradesh India
18 D4 Fathābād Iran
69 G3 Fathom Five National Marine Park Can.
54 A3 Fatick Senegal
44 H2 Faulquemont France
59 F4 Fauresmith S. Africa
36 O3 Fauske Norway
75 F1 Faust U.S.A.
48 E6 Favignana, Isola i. Sicily Italy
64 G4 Fawcett Can.
39 F7 Fawley U.K.
66 C3 Fawn r. Can.
36 B4 Faxaflói b. Iceland
36 P5 Faxälven r. Sweden
27 B5 Faxian Hu l. China
55 D3 Faya Chad
68 D3 Fayette U.S.A.
77 E4 Fayetteville AR U.S.A.
79 E5 Fayetteville NC U.S.A.
79 C5 Fayetteville TN U.S.A.
16 D6 Fāyid Egypt
17 M7 Faylakah i. Kuwait
54 C4 Fazao Malfakassa, Parc National de nat. park Togo
22 C3 Fazilka India
18 C5 Fazrān, J. h. S. Arabia
54 A2 Fdérik Maur.
41 B5 Feale r. Rep. of Ireland
79 E5 Fear, Cape c. U.S.A.
74 B2 Feather Falls U.S.A.
9 E4 Featherston N.Z.
8 F4 Featherton, Mt Austr.
44 E2 Fécamp France
91 F1 Federación Arg.
88 E4 Federal Arg.
46 E3 Fehmarn i. Ger.
43 L2 Fehrbellin Ger.
90 E3 Feia, Lagoa lag. Brazil
26 E4 Feidong China
26 F3 Feihuanghe Kou est. China
86 D5 Feijó Brazil
9 E4 Feilding N.Z.
87 L6 Feira de Santana Brazil
26 E4 Feixi China
16 E3 Feke Turkey
45 H3 Felanitx Spain
68 D3 Felch U.S.A.
43 M1 Feldberg Ger.
46 D7 Feldberg mt Ger.
46 D7 Feldkirch Austria
46 G7 Feldkirchen in Kärnten Austria
91 E1 Feliciano r. Arg.
90 D2 Felixlândia Brazil
39 J6 Felixstowe U.K.
48 D1 Feltre Italy
37 M5 Femunden l. Norway
37 N5 Femundsmarka Nasjonalpark nat. park Norway
26 D2 Fen r. China
48 D3 Fenaio, Punta del pt Italy
75 H4 Fence Lake U.S.A.
69 H3 Fenelon Falls Can.
49 L4 Fengari mt Greece
27 E4 Fengcheng Jiangxi China
30 C3 Fengcheng Liaoning China
27 C4 Fengdu China
27 C5 Fenggang China
30 D1 Fengguang China
27 F4 Fenghua China
27 C5 Fenghuang China
26 C4 Fengjie China
27 D6 Fengkai China
27 F6 Fenglin Taiwan
27 E6 Fengnan China
26 E1 Fengning China
26 E3 Fengqiu China
27 C5 Fengshan China
27 E6 Fengshun China
26 E3 Fengtai China
27 E4 Fengxin China
26 E3 Fengyang China
26 D1 Fengzhen China
23 G5 Feni Bangl.
7 F2 Feni Is is P.N.G.
44 F5 Fenille, Col de la pass France
68 B4 Fennimore U.S.A.
57 E5 Fenoarivo Atsinanana Madag.
39 G5 Fens, The reg. U.K.
69 F4 Fenton U.S.A.
26 D2 Fenxi China
26 D2 Fenyang China
27 E5 Fenyi China
51 E6 Feodosiya Ukr.
48 B6 Fer, Cap de hd Alg.
19 E3 Ferdows Iran
14 F2 Fergana Uzbek.
69 G4 Fergus Can.
76 D2 Fergus Falls U.S.A.
6 F2 Fergusson I. i. P.N.G.
48 C7 Fériana Tunisia
54 B4 Ferkessédougou Côte d'Ivoire
48 E3 Fermo Italy
67 G3 Fermont Can.
45 C2 Fermoselle Spain
41 C5 Fermoy Rep. of Ireland
79 D6 Fernandina Beach U.S.A.
86 □ Fernandina, Isla i. Galapagos Is Ecuador
88 B8 Fernando de Magallanes, Parque Nacional nat. park Chile
96 G6 Fernando de Noronha i. Atl. Ocean
90 B3 Fernandópolis Brazil
72 B1 Ferndale U.S.A.
39 F7 Ferndown U.K.
64 F5 Fernie Can.
74 C2 Fernley U.S.A.
81 F4 Fernridge U.S.A.
41 E5 Ferns Rep. of Ireland
72 C2 Fernwood U.S.A.
48 D2 Ferrara Italy
90 B3 Ferreiros Brazil
77 F6 Ferriday U.S.A.
48 C4 Ferro, Capo pt Sardinia Italy
45 B1 Ferrol Spain
75 G2 Ferron U.S.A.
42 D1 Ferwerd Neth.
54 B1 Fès Morocco
56 B4 Feshi Congo(Zaire)
65 K5 Fessenden U.S.A.
76 F4 Festus U.S.A.
40 □ Fethaland, Point of pt U.K.
41 D5 Fethard Rep. of Ireland
16 B3 Fethiye Turkey
40 □ Fetlar i. U.K.
40 F4 Fettercairn U.K.
43 K5 Feucht Ger.
43 J5 Feuchtwangen Ger.
67 F2 Feuilles, Rivière aux r. Can.
16 F3 Fevzipaşa Turkey
19 H2 Feyzābād Afgh.
19 E3 Feyzābād Iran
Fez see Fès
39 D5 Ffestiniog U.K.
57 E6 Fianarantsoa Madag.
56 D3 Fichē Eth.
43 L4 Fichtelgebirge reg. Ger.
59 G4 Ficksburg S. Africa
64 F4 Field B.C. Can.
69 G2 Field Ont. Can.
49 H4 Fier Albania
68 E3 Fife Lake U.S.A.
40 F4 Fife Ness pt U.K.
8 F2 Fifield Austr.
68 B3 Fifield U.S.A.
44 F4 Figeac France
45 B2 Figueira da Foz Port.
45 H1 Figueres Spain
54 B1 Figuig Morocco
4 J6 Fiji country Pac. Oc.
88 D2 Filadélfia Para.
92 B3 Filchner Ice Shelf ice feature Ant.
38 G3 Filey U.K.
49 J5 Filippiada Greece
37 O7 Filipstad Sweden
36 L5 Fillan Norway
74 C4 Fillmore CA U.S.A.
75 F2 Fillmore UT U.S.A.
92 C3 Fimbulheimen mts Ant.
92 C3 Fimbulisen ice feature Ant.
81 F2 Finch Can.
40 E3 Findhorn r. U.K.
17 H3 Findık Turkey
80 B4 Findlay U.S.A.
6 E6 Fingal Austr.
66 E5 Finger Lakes l. U.S.A.
57 D5 Fingoè Moz.
16 C3 Finike Turkey
16 C3 Finike Körfezi b. Turkey
Finisterre, Cape c. see Fisterra, Cabo
35 H2 Finland country Europe
37 S7 Finland, Gulf of g. Europe
64 D3 Finlay r. Can.
64 D3 Finlay, Mt mt Can.
8 E3 Finley Austr.
43 K3 Finne ridge Ger.
36 P2 Finnsnes Norway
37 O7 Finspång Sweden
41 D3 Fintona U.K.
41 C3 Fintown Rep. of Ireland
40 C3 Fionn Loch l. U.K.
40 B4 Fionnphort U.K.
9 A6 Fiordland National Park N.Z.
Fırat r. see Euphrates
74 B3 Firebaugh U.S.A.
65 J2 Firedrake Lake l. Can.
81 G4 Fire Island National Seashore res. U.S.A.
Firenze see Florence
17 K6 Firk, Sha'īb watercourse Iraq
91 E2 Firmat Arg.
44 G4 Firminy France
43 J6 Firngrund reg. Ger.
47 Q2 Firovo Rus. Fed.
22 B3 Firoza Pak.
22 D4 Firozabad India
19 G3 Firozkoh reg. Afgh.
22 C3 Firozpur India
81 H2 First Connecticut L. l. U.S.A.
18 D4 Fīrūzābād Iran
Firuzabad see Räsk
42 F5 Fischbach Ger.
57 B6 Fish r. Namibia
58 D5 Fish r. S. Africa
92 B6 Fisher Bay b. Ant.
81 F6 Fisherman I. i. U.S.A.
81 H4 Fishers I. i. U.S.A.
65 N2 Fisher Strait chan. Can.
39 C6 Fishguard U.K.
64 E2 Fish Lake l. Can.
68 A2 Fish Lake l. MN U.S.A.
75 G2 Fish Lake l. UT U.S.A.
27 □ Fish Ponds l. H.K. China
69 F4 Fish Pt pt U.S.A.
92 B3 Fiske, C. c. Ant.
Fiskenæsset see Qeqertarsuatsiaat
42 B5 Fismes France
45 B1 Fisterra Spain
45 B1 Fisterra, Cabo c. Spain
81 H3 Fitchburg U.S.A.
65 G3 Fitzgerald Can.
79 D6 Fitzgerald U.S.A.
88 C7 Fitz Roy Arg.
6 C3 Fitzroy Crossing Austr.
69 G3 Fitzwilliam I. i. Can.
41 D3 Fivemiletown U.K.
48 D2 Fivizzano Italy
56 C4 Fizi Congo(Zaire)
37 L6 Flå Norway
59 H5 Flagstaff S. Africa
75 G4 Flagstaff U.S.A.
81 H2 Flagstaff Lake l. U.S.A.
66 E2 Flaherty Island i. Can.
68 B3 Flambeau r. U.S.A.
38 G3 Flamborough Head hd U.K.
43 L2 Fläming h. Ger.
72 E3 Flaming Gorge Res. l. U.S.A.
58 D5 Flamingvlei salt pan S. Africa
42 A4 Flandre reg. France
40 A2 Flannan Isles is U.K.
36 O4 Flåsjön l. Sweden
68 E4 Flat r. U.S.A.
72 D2 Flathead L. l. U.S.A.
70 D2 Flathead Lake l. U.S.A.
9 E4 Flat Point pt N.Z.
72 A1 Flattery, C. c. U.S.A.
6 E3 Flattery, C. pt Austr.
43 K2 Fleetmark Ger.
38 D4 Fleetwood U.K.
81 F4 Fleetwood U.S.A.
37 K7 Flekkefjord Norway
80 E3 Fleming U.S.A.
80 B5 Flemingsburg U.S.A.
37 P7 Flen Sweden
46 D3 Flensburg Ger.
44 D2 Flers France
69 G3 Flesherton Can.
65 H2 Fletcher Lake l. Can.
69 F3 Fletcher Pond l. U.S.A.
92 B3 Fletcher Prom. hd Ant.
6 E3 Flinders r. Austr.
6 B5 Flinders Bay b. Austr.
6 E5 Flinders I. i. Austr.
8 A2 Flinders Ranges mts Austr.
8 B1 Flinders Ranges Nat. Park Austr.
65 J4 Flin Flon Can.
39 D4 Flint U.K.
69 F4 Flint U.S.A.
79 C6 Flint r. GA U.S.A.
69 F4 Flint r. MI U.S.A.
5 M6 Flint I. i. Kiribati
37 N6 Flisa Norway
38 E2 Flodden U.K.
43 M4 Flöha Ger.
43 M4 Flöha r. Ger.
92 A4 Flood Ra. mts Ant.
68 A2 Floodwood U.S.A.
78 B4 Flora U.S.A.
44 F4 Florac France
42 E5 Florange France
69 F4 Florence Can.
48 D3 Florence Italy
79 C5 Florence AL U.S.A.
75 G5 Florence AZ U.S.A.
76 D4 Florence KS U.S.A.
80 C5 Florence OH U.S.A.
72 A3 Florence OR U.S.A.
79 E5 Florence SC U.S.A.
75 G5 Florence Junction U.S.A.
81 K1 Florenceville Can.
89 B4 Florencia Col.
42 C4 Florennes Belgium
88 C6 Florentino Ameghino, Embalse resr Arg.
82 G5 Flores Guatemala
25 E7 Flores i. Indon.
91 E2 Flores r. Arg.
90 C1 Flores de Goiás Brazil
25 D7 Flores Sea Indon.
87 L5 Floresta Brazil
87 K5 Floriano Brazil
88 G3 Florianópolis Brazil
91 F2 Florida Uru.
79 D6 Florida div. U.S.A.
79 D7 Florida Bay b. U.S.A.
79 D7 Florida City U.S.A.
7 G2 Florida Is is Solomon Is
71 K7 Florida Keys is FL U.S.A.
83 H4 Florida, Straits of str. Bahamas/U.S.A.
49 J4 Florina Greece
37 J6 Florø Norway
67 H3 Flour Lake l. Can.
68 A4 Floyd IA U.S.A.
80 C6 Floyd VA U.S.A.
77 C5 Floydada U.S.A.
75 F4 Floyd, Mt mt U.S.A.
42 D2 Fluessen l. Neth.
80 C5 Fly U.S.A.
6 E2 Fly r. P.N.G.
49 H3 Foča Bos.-Herz.
40 E3 Fochabers U.K.
59 G3 Fochville S. Africa
49 M2 Focşani Romania
27 D6 Fogang China
48 F4 Foggia Italy
54 □ Fogo i. Cape Verde
67 K4 Fogo I. i. Can.
40 D2 Foinaven h. U.K.
44 E5 Foix France
36 O3 Folda chan. Norway
36 N4 Foldereid Norway
36 M4 Foldfjorden chan. Norway
49 L6 Folegandros i. Greece
69 F1 Foleyet Can.
48 E3 Foligno Italy
39 J6 Folkestone U.K.
39 G5 Folkingham U.K.
79 D6 Folkston U.S.A.
37 M5 Folldal Norway
48 D3 Follonica Italy
74 B2 Folsom Lake l. U.S.A.
51 G6 Fomin Rus. Fed.
50 J2 Fominskiy Rus. Fed.
65 H3 Fond-du-Lac Can.
68 C4 Fond du Lac U.S.A.
65 J3 Fond du Lac r. Can.
45 B2 Fondevila Spain
48 E4 Fondi Italy
7 H2 Fongafale Tuvalu
48 C4 Fonni Sardinia Italy
82 G6 Fonseca, G. de b. Central America
67 F3 Fontanges Can.
64 E3 Fontas Can.
64 E3 Fontas r. Can.
86 E4 Fonte Boa Brazil
44 D3 Fontenay-le-Comte France
36 F3 Fontur pt Iceland
69 H3 Foot's Bay Can.
26 C3 Foping China
8 G2 Forbes Austr.
72 C1 Forbes, Mt mt Can.
43 K5 Forchheim Ger.
67 G2 Ford r. Can.
68 D2 Ford r. U.S.A.
37 J6 Førde Norway
65 K2 Forde Lake l. Can.
39 H5 Fordham U.K.
39 F7 Fordingbridge U.K.
92 A4 Ford Ra. mts Ant.
77 E5 Fordyce U.S.A.
54 A4 Forécariah Guinea
39 F7 Foreland hd U.K.
39 D6 Foreland Point pt U.K.
64 D4 Foresight Mtn mt Can.
69 G4 Forest Can.
77 F5 Forest MS U.S.A.
80 B4 Forest OH U.S.A.
81 G3 Forest Dale U.S.A.
8 F3 Forest Hill Austr.
74 B2 Foresthill U.S.A.
68 A3 Forest Lake U.S.A.
79 C5 Forest Park U.S.A.
67 G4 Forestville Can.
40 F4 Forfar U.K.
72 A2 Forks U.S.A.
81 J2 Forks, The U.S.A.
80 E4 Forksville U.S.A.
48 E2 Forlì Italy
38 D4 Formby U.K.
45 G3 Formentera i. Spain
45 H3 Formentor, Cap de pt Spain
90 D3 Formiga Brazil
88 E3 Formosa Arg.
90 C1 Formosa Brazil
87 G6 Formosa, Serra h. Brazil
90 D1 Formoso r. Brazil
40 E3 Forres U.K.
8 D5 Forrest Vic. Austr.
68 C5 Forrest U.S.A.
77 F5 Forrest City U.S.A.
68 C4 Forreston U.S.A.
36 P5 Fors Sweden
6 E3 Forsayth Austr.
36 S3 Forsnäs Sweden
37 S6 Forssa Fin.
77 E4 Forsyth MO U.S.A.
72 F2 Forsyth MT U.S.A.
69 J1 Forsythe Can.
22 C3 Fort Abbas Pak.
66 D3 Fort Albany Can.
87 L4 Fortaleza Brazil
75 H5 Fort Apache U.S.A.
64 G4 Fort Assiniboine Can.
68 C4 Fort Atkinson U.S.A.
40 D3 Fort Augustus U.K.
59 G6 Fort Beaufort S. Africa
72 E2 Fort Benton U.S.A.
65 H3 Fort Black Can.
74 A2 Fort Bragg U.S.A.
Fort-Chimo see Kuujjuaq
65 G3 Fort Chipewyan Can.
77 D5 Fort Cobb Res. resr U.S.A.
72 F3 Fort Collins U.S.A.
69 J3 Fort-Coulonge Can.
81 F2 Fort Covington U.S.A.
77 C6 Fort Davis U.S.A.
83 M6 Fort-de-France Martinique
79 C5 Fort Deposit U.S.A.
76 E3 Fort Dodge U.S.A.
76 E1 Fort Frances U.S.A.
66 E3 Fort George Can.
62 F3 Fort Good Hope Can.
40 D4 Forth r. U.K.
40 F4 Forth, Firth of est. U.K.
75 E2 Fortification Range mts U.S.A.
88 D2 Fortín Capitán Demattei Para.
88 D2 Fortín General Mendoza Para.
88 E2 Fortín Madrejón Para.
88 D2 Fortín Pilcomayo Arg.
86 F7 Fortín Ravelo Bol.
86 F7 Fortín Suárez Arana Bol.
81 J1 Fort Kent U.S.A.
79 D7 Fort Lauderdale U.S.A.
64 E2 Fort Liard Can.
68 B3 Fort McCoy U.S.A.
65 G3 Fort Mackay Can.
64 G5 Fort Macleod Can.
65 G3 Fort McMurray Can.
62 E3 Fort McPherson Can.
68 B5 Fort Madison U.S.A.
72 G3 Fort Morgan U.S.A.
79 D7 Fort Myers U.S.A.
64 E3 Fort Nelson Can.
64 E3 Fort Nelson r. Can.
64 D2 Fort Norman Can.
79 C5 Fort Payne U.S.A.
72 F1 Fort Peck U.S.A.
72 F2 Fort Peck Res. resr U.S.A.
79 D7 Fort Pierce U.S.A.
76 C2 Fort Pierre U.S.A.
64 F2 Fort Providence Can.
65 J4 Fort Qu'Appelle Can.
64 G2 Fort Resolution Can.
9 B7 Fortrose N.Z.
40 D3 Fortrose U.K.
74 A2 Fort Ross U.S.A.
66 E3 Fort Rupert Can.
64 E4 Fort St James Can.
64 E3 Fort St John Can.
64 G4 Fort Saskatchewan Can.
77 E4 Fort Scott U.S.A.
66 C2 Fort Severn Can.
14 D2 Fort-Shevchenko Rus. Fed.
64 E2 Fort Simpson Can.
65 G2 Fort Smith Can.
77 E5 Fort Smith U.S.A.
77 C6 Fort Stockton U.S.A.
73 F5 Fort Sumner U.S.A.
72 A3 Fortuna U.S.A.
76 C1 Fortune U.S.A.
67 J4 Fortune B. b. Can.
64 F3 Fort Vermilion Can.
79 C6 Fort Walton Beach U.S.A.
68 E5 Fort Wayne U.S.A.
40 C4 Fort William U.K.
77 D5 Fort Worth U.S.A.
62 D3 Fort Yukon U.S.A.
18 D5 Forūr, Jazīreh-ye i. Iran
36 N4 Forvik Norway
27 D6 Foshan China
48 B2 Fossano Italy
8 F5 Foster Austr.
63 Q2 Foster B. b. Greenland
64 B3 Foster, Mt mt Can./U.S.A.
80 B4 Fostoria U.S.A.
39 G4 Fotherby U.K.
44 D2 Fougères France
40 □ Foula i. U.K.
39 H6 Foulness Point pt U.K.
21 C4 Foul Pt pt Sri Lanka
9 C4 Foulwind, Cape c. N.Z.
54 D4 Foumban Cameroon
92 B3 Foundation Ice Stream ice feature Ant.
54 A3 Foundiougne Senegal
68 A4 Fountain U.S.A.
44 G2 Fourches, Mont des h. France
74 D4 Four Corners U.S.A.
59 H4 Fouriesburg S. Africa
42 C4 Fourmies France
49 M6 Fournoi i. Greece
68 C2 Fourteen Mile Pt pt U.S.A.
54 A3 Fouta Djallon reg. Guinea
9 A7 Foveaux Strait str. N.Z.
79 E7 Fowl Cay i. Bahamas
73 F4 Fowler CO U.S.A.
68 D5 Fowler IN U.S.A.
68 E4 Fowler MI U.S.A.
92 B3 Fowler Pen. pen. Ant.
6 D5 Fowlers Bay Austr.
17 M3 Fowman Iran
65 L3 Fox r. Can.
68 C4 Fox r. U.S.A.
64 F4 Fox Creek Can.
38 C3 Foxdale U.K.
63 K3 Foxe Basin g. Can.
63 K3 Foxe Channel str. Can.
63 L3 Foxe Peninsula Can.
9 C5 Fox Glacier N.Z.
64 G3 Fox Lake Can.
68 C4 Fox Lake U.S.A.
9 E4 Foxton N.Z.
40 D3 Foyers U.K.
41 D3 Foyle r. Rep. of Ireland/U.K.
41 D2 Foyle, Lough b. Rep. of Ireland/U.K.
41 B5 Foynes Rep. of Ireland
57 B5 Foz do Cunene Angola
90 A4 Foz do Iguaçu Brazil
45 G2 Fraga Spain
92 D4 Framnes Mts mts Ant.
90 C3 Franca Brazil
7 G3 Français, Récif des rf New Caledonia
34 E4 France country Europe
8 C4 Frances Austr.
64 D2 Frances r. Can.
64 D2 Frances Lake Can.
64 D2 Frances Lake l. Can.
68 D5 Francesville U.S.A.
56 B4 Franceville Gabon
76 D3 Francis Case, Lake l. U.S.A.
84 B1 Francisco I. Madero Coahuila Mex.
84 A1 Francisco I. Madero Durango Mex.
90 D2 Francisco Sá Brazil
81 H2 Francis, Lake l. U.S.A.
57 C6 Francistown Botswana
64 D4 François Lake l. Can.
72 E3 Francs Peak summit U.S.A.
42 D1 Franeker Neth.
43 M4 Frankenberg Ger.
43 G3 Frankenberg (Eder) Ger.
69 F4 Frankenmuth U.S.A.
43 G5 Frankenthal (Pfalz) Ger.
43 K4 Frankenwald forest Ger.
59 H3 Frankfort S. Africa
68 D5 Frankfort IN U.S.A.
78 C4 Frankfort KY U.S.A.
68 D3 Frankfort MI U.S.A.
43 G4 Frankfurt am Main Ger.
46 G4 Frankfurt an der Oder Ger.
75 E1 Frankin Lake l. U.S.A.
43 K5 Fränkische Alb reg. Ger.
43 K5 Fränkische Schweiz reg. Ger.
72 E3 Franklin ID U.S.A.
78 C4 Franklin IN U.S.A.
77 F6 Franklin LA U.S.A.
81 H3 Franklin MA U.S.A.
79 D5 Franklin NC U.S.A.
81 H3 Franklin NH U.S.A.
81 F4 Franklin NJ U.S.A.
80 D4 Franklin PA U.S.A.
79 C5 Franklin TN U.S.A.
80 E6 Franklin VA U.S.A.
80 D5 Franklin WV U.S.A.
62 F3 Franklin Bay b. Can.
72 C1 Franklin D. Roosevelt Lake l. U.S.A.
92 B5 Franklin I. i. Ant.
64 E2 Franklin Mountains Can.
9 A6 Franklin Mts mts N.Z.
63 J2 Franklin Str. Can.
8 E5 Frankston Austr.
37 P5 Fränsta Sweden
68 E1 Franz Can.
9 C5 Franz Josef Glacier N.Z.
12 G2 Franz Josef Land is Rus. Fed.
48 C5 Frasca, Capo della pt Sardinia Italy
48 E4 Frascati Italy
64 E4 Fraser r. B.C. Can.
67 H2 Fraser r. Nfld Can.
58 D5 Fraserburg S. Africa
40 F3 Fraserburgh U.K.
66 D4 Fraserdale Can.
7 F4 Fraser Island i. Austr.
64 E4 Fraser Lake Can.
64 E4 Fraser Plateau plat. Can.
9 F3 Frasertown N.Z.
68 E2 Frater Can.
46 D7 Frauenfeld Switz.
91 E2 Fray Bentos Uru.
42 E4 Frechen Ger.
38 E4 Freckleton U.K.
68 E3 Frederic MI U.S.A.
68 A3 Frederic WV U.S.A.
37 L9 Fredericia Denmark
80 E5 Frederick MD U.S.A.
77 D5 Frederick OK U.S.A.
77 D6 Fredericksburg TX U.S.A.
80 E5 Fredericksburg VA U.S.A.
64 C3 Frederick Sound chan. U.S.A.
77 F4 Fredericktown U.S.A.
67 G4 Fredericton Can.
Frederikshåb see Paamiut
37 M8 Frederikshavn Denmark
37 N9 Frederiksværk Denmark
75 F3 Fredonia AZ U.S.A.
80 D3 Fredonia NY U.S.A.
36 Q4 Fredrika Sweden
37 M7 Fredrikstad Norway
81 F4 Freehold U.S.A.
81 F4 Freeland U.S.A.
74 C2 Freel Peak summit U.S.A.
76 D3 Freeman U.S.A.
68 D5 Freeman, Lake l. U.S.A.
68 C4 Freeport IL U.S.A.
81 H3 Freeport ME U.S.A.
81 G4 Freeport NY U.S.A.
77 E6 Freeport TX U.S.A.
79 E7 Freeport City Bahamas
77 D7 Freer U.S.A.
59 G4 Free State div. S. Africa
54 A4 Freetown Sierra Leone
45 C3 Fregenal de la Sierra Spain
44 C2 Fréhel, Cap pt France
46 C6 Freiburg im Breisgau Ger.
42 F5 Freisen Ger.
46 E6 Freising Ger.
46 G6 Freistadt Austria
44 H5 Fréjus France
6 B5 Fremantle Austr.
68 E4 Fremont MI U.S.A.
76 D3 Fremont NE U.S.A.
80 B4 Fremont OH U.S.A.
75 G2 Fremont r. U.S.A.
80 B6 Frenchburg U.S.A.
80 C4 French Creek r. U.S.A.
85 E2 French Guiana terr. S. America
8 E5 French I. i. Austr.
74 C2 Frenchman U.S.A.
65 H5 Frenchman r. Can./U.S.A.
74 B2 Frenchman L. l. CA U.S.A.
75 E3 Frenchman L. l. NV U.S.A.
41 C4 Frenchpark Rep. of Ireland
9 D4 French Pass N.Z.
5 N6 French Polynesia terr. Pac. Oc.
3 □ French Southern and Antarctic Lands terr. Southern Ocean
81 J1 Frenchville U.S.A.
42 F2 Freren Ger.
41 D5 Freshford Rep. of Ireland
75 G6 Fresnal Canyon U.S.A.
84 B2 Fresnillo Mex.
74 C3 Fresno U.S.A.
74 C3 Fresno r. U.S.A.
45 H3 Freu, Cap des pt Spain
43 F4 Freudenberg Ger.
46 D6 Freudenstadt Ger.
42 A4 Frévent France
43 L1 Freyenstein Ger.
44 H2 Freyming-Merlebach France
91 D1 Freyre Arg.
54 A3 Fria Guinea
74 C3 Friant U.S.A.
88 C3 Frias Arg.
46 C7 Fribourg Switz.
43 F1 Friedeburg Ger.
43 M1 Friedland Ger.
46 D7 Friedrichshafen Ger.
81 J3 Friendship U.S.A.
43 L2 Friesack Ger.
42 D1 Friese Wad tidal flats Neth.
43 F1 Friesoythe Ger.
39 J6 Frinton-on-Sea U.K.
77 D6 Frio r. U.S.A.
40 B4 Frisa, Loch l. U.K.
75 F2 Frisco Mt mt U.S.A.
43 H3 Fritzlar Ger.
63 M3 Frobisher Bay b. Can.
65 H3 Frobisher Lake l. Can.
36 L5 Frohavet b. Norway
43 L3 Frohburg Ger.
42 A5 Froissy France
51 G5 Frolovo Rus. Fed.
50 K2 Frolovskaya Rus. Fed.
39 E6 Frome U.K.
8 B1 Frome Downs Austr.
6 D5 Frome, Lake salt flat Austr.
43 F3 Fröndenberg Ger.
84 D3 Frontera Mex.
84 D3 Frontera, Pta pt Mex.
80 D5 Front Royal U.S.A.
48 E4 Frosinone Italy
80 D5 Frostburg U.S.A.
36 L5 Frøya i. Norway
42 A4 Fruges France
75 H2 Fruita U.S.A.
75 G1 Fruitland U.S.A.
46 C7 Frutigen Switz.
47 J6 Frýdek-Místek Czech Rep.
81 H2 Fryeburg U.S.A.
27 F5 Fu'an China
27 D5 Fuchuan China
27 F4 Fuchun Jiang r. China
40 A3 Fuday i. U.K.
27 E5 Fude China
27 F5 Fuding China
45 E2 Fuenlabrada Spain
45 D3 Fuente Obejuna Spain
88 E2 Fuerte Olimpo Para.
54 A2 Fuerteventura i. Canary Is
31 B2 Fuga i. Phil.
26 E3 Fugou China
26 D2 Fugu China
17 J4 Fuhaymī Iraq
20 E4 Fujairah U.A.E.
29 F7 Fuji Japan
27 E5 Fujian div. China
26 C4 Fu Jiang r. China
29 F7 Fuji-Hakone-Izu National Park Japan
28 B1 Fujin China
29 F7 Fujinomiya Japan
29 F7 Fuji-san volc. Japan
28 H3 Fukagawa Japan
29 D7 Fukuchiyama Japan
29 A8 Fukue Japan
29 A8 Fukue-jima i. Japan
29 E6 Fukui Japan
29 B8 Fukuoka Japan
29 G6 Fukushima Japan
29 B9 Fukuyama Japan
18 D2 Fūlād Maialleh Iran
43 H4 Fulda Ger.
43 H3 Fulda r. Ger.
39 G6 Fulham U.K.
26 E3 Fuliji China
27 C4 Fuling China
65 M2 Fullerton, Cape hd Can.
68 B5 Fulton IL U.S.A.
78 B4 Fulton KY U.S.A.
76 F4 Fulton MO U.S.A.
81 E3 Fulton NY U.S.A.
59 K2 Fumane Moz.
42 C5 Fumay France
29 F7 Funabashi Japan
7 H2 Funafuti i. Tuvalu
54 A1 Funchal Port.
89 B2 Fundación Col.
45 C2 Fundão Port.
67 G5 Fundy, Bay of g. Can.
67 G4 Fundy Nat. Park Can.
74 D3 Funeral Peak summit U.S.A.
57 D6 Funhalouro Moz.
26 F3 Funing Jiangsu China
27 B6 Funing Yunnan China
26 D3 Funiu Shan mts China
54 C3 Funtua Nigeria
40 □ Funzie U.K.
27 F5 Fuqing China
30 D2 Fur r. China
28 H3 Furano Japan
18 E5 Fūrgun, Kūh-e mt Iran
50 G3 Furmanov Rus. Fed.
28 D3 Furmanovo Rus. Fed.
74 D3 Furnace Creek U.S.A.
90 C3 Furnas, Represa resr Brazil
6 E6 Furneaux Group is Austr.
43 F2 Fürstenau Ger.
43 M1 Fürstenberg Ger.
46 G4 Fürstenwalde Ger.
43 J5 Fürth Ger.
43 L5 Furth im Wald Ger.
28 G3 Furubira Japan
28 G5 Furukawa Japan
63 K3 Fury and Hecla Strait str. Can.
89 B3 Fusagasugá Col.
27 C7 Fushan Hainan China
30 A5 Fushan Shandong China
30 B3 Fushun Liaoning China
30 B3 Fushun Liaoning China
27 B4 Fushun Sichuan China
30 B3 Fushuncheng China
30 D2 Fusong China
27 C6 Fusui China
29 B8 Futago-san volc. Japan
7 H3 Futuna i. Vanuatu
27 E5 Futun Xi r. China
26 C3 Fu Xian China
30 A2 Fuxin Liaoning China
30 A2 Fuxin Liaoning China
28 F5 Fuya Japan
26 E3 Fuyang Anhui China
27 F4 Fuyang Zhejiang China
26 E2 Fuyang r. China
24 E2 Fuyu Heilongjiang China
30 C1 Fuyu China
27 B5 Fuyuan China
27 F5 Fuzhou Fujian China
27 E5 Fuzhou Jiangxi China
30 A4 Fuzhou Wan b. China
17 L2 Füzuli Azer.
37 M9 Fyn i. Denmark
40 C5 Fyne, Loch in. U.K.
F.Y.R.O.M. country see Macedonia

G

48 C6 Gaâfour Tunisia
56 E3 Gaalkacyo Somalia
59 F2 Gabane Botswana
74 D2 Gabbs U.S.A.
74 C2 Gabbs Valley Range mts U.S.A.
57 B5 Gabela Angola
54 D1 Gabès Tunisia
55 D1 Gabès, Golfe de g. Tunisia
8 G4 Gabo I. i. Austr.
53 F6 Gabon country Africa
57 C6 Gaborone Botswana
19 E5 Gābrīk Iran
19 E5 Gābrīk watercourse Iran
49 L3 Gabrovo Bulg.
54 A3 Gabú Guinea-Bissau
18 C2 Gach Sār Iran
18 C4 Gach Sārān Iran
21 A3 Gadag India
36 O4 Gäddede Sweden
43 K1 Gadebusch Ger.
22 B5 Gadhra India
22 B4 Gadra Pak.
79 C5 Gadsden U.S.A.
21 B2 Gadwal India
36 S2 Gædnovuoppe Norway
39 D6 Gaer U.K.
49 L2 Găeşti Romania
48 E4 Gaeta Italy
48 E4 Gaeta, Golfo di g. Italy
4 F4 Gaferut i. Micronesia
79 D5 Gaffney U.S.A.
54 C1 Gafsa Tunisia
50 E4 Gagarin Rus. Fed.
50 H4 Gagino Rus. Fed.
54 B4 Gagnoa Côte d'Ivoire
67 G3 Gagnon Can.
51 G7 Gagra Georgia
17 L4 Gahvāreh Iran
58 C3 Gaiab watercourse Namibia
23 G4 Gaibandha Bangl.
43 H6 Gaildorf Ger.
44 E5 Gaillac France

79 D6 Gainesville FL U.S.A.
79 D5 Gainesville GA U.S.A.
77 D5 Gainesville TX U.S.A.
39 G4 Gainsborough U.K.
6 D5 Gairdner, Lake salt flat Austr.
40 B1 Gairloch U.K.
40 C3 Gair Loch in. U.K.
30 B3 Gai Xian China
21 C2 Gajapatinagaram India
19 G5 Gajar Pak.
58 E3 Gakarosa mt S. Africa
22 C1 Gakuch Jammu and Kashmir
23 G3 Gala China
19 G2 Galaasiya Uzbek.
16 C7 Galâla el Baharîya, G. el plat. Egypt
56 D4 Galana r. Kenya
40 F5 Galashiels U.K.
49 N2 Galați Romania
49 H4 Galatina Italy
80 C6 Galax U.S.A.
41 C5 Galbally Rep. of Ireland
37 L6 Galdhøpiggen summit Norway
84 B1 Galeana Mex.
18 D5 Galeh Dār Iran
68 B4 Galena U.S.A.
89 E2 Galeota Pt pt Trinidad and Tobago
89 E2 Galera Pt pt Trinidad and Tobago
84 C4 Galera, Pta pt Mex.
91 B4 Galera, Punta pt Chile
68 B5 Galesburg U.S.A.
58 F4 Galeshewe S. Africa
68 B3 Galesville U.S.A.
80 E4 Galeton U.S.A.
51 G7 Gali Georgia
50 G3 Galich Rus. Fed.
50 G2 Galichskaya Vozvyshennost' reg. Rus. Fed.
45 C1 Galicia div. Spain
16 E5 Galilee, Sea of l. Israel
80 B4 Galion U.S.A.
48 C6 Galite, Canal de la chan. Tunisia
75 G5 Galiuro Mts mts U.S.A.
55 F3 Gallabat Sudan
79 C4 Gallatin U.S.A.
72 E2 Gallatin r. U.S.A.
21 C5 Galle Sri Lanka
88 B8 Gallegos r. Arg.
89 C1 Gallinas, Pta pt Col.
48 H4 Gallipoli Italy
80 B5 Gallipolis U.S.A.
36 R3 Gällivare Sweden
36 O5 Gällö Sweden
81 E3 Gallo I. i. U.S.A.
75 H4 Gallo Mts mts U.S.A.
40 D6 Galloway, Mull of c. U.K.
75 H4 Gallup U.S.A.
19 G1 Gallyaaral Uzbek.
40 B4 Galmisdale U.K.
8 G3 Galong Austr.
21 C4 Galoya Sri Lanka
21 C5 Gal Oya r. Sri Lanka
40 D5 Galston U.K.
74 B2 Galt U.S.A.
54 A2 Galtat Zemmour Western Sahara
41 C5 Galtee Mountains h. Rep. of Ireland
41 C5 Galtymore h. Rep. of Ireland
19 E3 Galūgāh-e Āsīyeh Iran
68 B5 Galva U.S.A.
77 E6 Galveston U.S.A.
77 E6 Galveston Bay b. U.S.A.
91 E2 Galvez Arg.
22 E3 Galwa Nepal
41 B4 Galway Rep. of Ireland
41 B4 Galway Bay g. Rep. of Ireland
27 B6 Gâm r. Vietnam
39 J8 Gamaches France
59 J5 Gamalakhe S. Africa
89 B2 Gamarra Col.
23 G3 Gamba China
56 D3 Gambēla Eth.
56 D3 Gambela National Park Eth.
62 A3 Gambell U.S.A.
22 D4 Gambhir r. India
52 C4 Gambia, The country Africa
5 O7 Gambier, Îles is Pac. Oc.
67 K4 Gambo Can.
56 B4 Gamboma Congo
75 H4 Gamerco U.S.A.
37 P8 Gamleby Sweden
36 S4 Gammelstaden Sweden
58 C4 Gamoep S. Africa
28 B3 Gamova, Mys pt Rus. Fed.
21 C5 Gampola Sri Lanka
19 F4 Gamshadzai K. mts Iran
10 J10 Gan Maldives
26 A3 Gana China
75 H4 Ganado U.S.A.
69 J3 Gananoque Can.
18 C4 Ganāveh Iran
17 L1 Gäncä Azer.
27 C7 Gancheng China
Gand see Gent
33 E3 Gandadiwata, Bukit mt Indon.
23 G3 Gandaingoin China
56 C4 Gandajika Congo(Zaire)
23 E4 Gandak Dam dam Nepal
23 B3 Gandari Mountain mt Pak.
22 A3 Gandava Pak.
67 K4 Gander Can.
43 G1 Ganderkesee Ger.
45 G2 Gandesa Spain
22 C5 Gandevi India
22 B5 Gāndhīdhām India
22 C5 Gandhinagar India
22 C4 Gāndhi Sāgar resr India
22 C4 Gāndhi Sāgar Dam dam India
45 F3 Gandía Spain
19 F4 Gand-i-Zureh plain Afgh.
90 E1 Gandu Brazil
21 C5 Ganga r. Sri Lanka
91 C4 Gangán Arg.
22 C3 Ganganagar India
22 D4 Gangapur India
23 H5 Gangaw Myanmar
21 B3 Gangawati India
26 A2 Gangca China
22 E3 Gangdisê Shan mts China
44 F5 Ganges France
23 G5 Ganges, Mouths of the est. Bangl./India
22 D3 Gangoh India
22 D3 Gangotri mt India
23 G4 Gangtok India
26 B3 Gangu China
21 D2 Ganjam India
18 C4 Ganjgān Iran
27 E4 Gan Jiang r. China
27 B4 Ganluo China
8 F3 Ganmain Austr.
44 F3 Gannat France
72 E3 Gannett Peak summit U.S.A.
22 C5 Ganora India
26 C2 Ganquan China
58 C7 Gansbaai S. Africa
26 B3 Gansu div. China
26 E2 Gantang China
51 G7 Gant'iadi Georgia
27 E5 Gan Xian China
58 F3 Ganyesa S. Africa
26 F3 Ganyu China
27 E5 Ganzhou China
55 F4 Ganzi Sudan
54 B3 Gao Mali
27 E4 Gao'an China
26 E2 Gaocheng China
26 F4 Gaochun China
27 E4 Gaohebu China
26 B2 Gaolan China
26 F2 Gaomi China
27 D5 Gaomutang China
26 D3 Gaoping China
26 A2 Gaotai China
26 E2 Gaotang China
26 C2 Gaotouyao China
54 B3 Gaoua Burkina
54 A3 Gaoual Guinea
27 B4 Gao Xian China
26 E2 Gaoyang China
26 E2 Gaoyi China
26 F3 Gaoyou China
26 F3 Gaoyou Hu l. China
27 D6 Gaozhou China
44 H4 Gap France
31 B3 Gapan Phil.
45 F5 Gap Carbon hd Alg.
22 E2 Gar China
19 F4 Garagheh Iran
41 C4 Gara, Lough l. Rep. of Ireland
56 C3 Garamba r. Congo(Zaire)
56 C3 Garamba, Park National de la nat. park Congo(Zaire)
87 L5 Garanhuns Brazil
59 G2 Ga-Rankuwa S. Africa
56 D3 Garba Tula Kenya
74 A1 Garberville U.S.A.
18 C3 Garbosh, Kūh-e mt Iran
43 H2 Garbsen Ger.
90 C3 Garça Brazil
90 B1 Garças, Rio das r. Brazil
23 G2 Garco China
17 K1 Gardabani Georgia
48 D2 Garda, Lago di l. Italy
48 B6 Garde, Cap de hd Alg.
43 K2 Gardelegen Ger.
76 C4 Garden City U.S.A.
68 D3 Garden Corners U.S.A.
74 C5 Garden Grove U.S.A.
65 L4 Garden Hill Can.
68 E3 Garden I. i. U.S.A.
78 C2 Garden Pen. pen. U.S.A.
19 H3 Gardez Afgh.
81 J2 Gardiner ME U.S.A.
72 E2 Gardiner MT U.S.A.
81 G4 Gardiners I. i. U.S.A.
68 C5 Gardner U.S.A.
81 K2 Gardner Lake l. U.S.A.
5 L2 Gardner Pinnacles is HI U.S.A.
74 C2 Gardnerville U.S.A.
40 D4 Garelochhead U.K.
68 E2 Gargantua, Cape c. Can.
17 M6 Gargar Iran
37 R9 Gargždai Lith.
22 D5 Garhakota India
22 E5 Garhchiroli India
22 A3 Garhi Khairo Pak.
22 D4 Garhi Malehra India
64 E5 Garibaldi, Mt mt Can.
64 E5 Garibaldi Prov. Park nat. park Can.
59 F5 Gariep Dam resr S. Africa
58 B5 Garies S. Africa
48 E4 Garigliano r. Italy
56 D4 Garissa Kenya
37 T8 Garkalne Latvia
80 D4 Garland PA U.S.A.
77 D5 Garland TX U.S.A.
18 C2 Garmī Iran
46 E7 Garmisch-Partenkirchen Ger.
18 D3 Garmsar Iran
19 F4 Garmsel reg. Afgh.
76 E4 Garnett U.S.A.
8 D2 Garnpung Lake l. Austr.
23 G4 Gāro Hills h. India
44 D4 Garonne r. France
56 E3 Garoowe Somalia
88 G3 Garopaba Brazil
55 D4 Garoua Cameroon
91 D3 Garré Arg.
75 E2 Garrison U.S.A.
41 F2 Garron Point pt U.K.
19 G4 Garruk Pak.
65 J1 Garry Lake l. Can.
40 D4 Garry, Loch l. U.K.
40 B2 Garrynahine U.K.
56 E4 Garsen Kenya
39 D5 Garth U.K.
43 K1 Gartow Ger.
58 B3 Garub Namibia
33 C4 Garut Indon.
41 E3 Garvagh U.K.
40 D3 Garve U.K.
68 D5 Gary U.S.A.
22 E3 Garyarsa China
29 C7 Garyū-zan mt Japan
22 D2 Gar Zangbo r. China
24 B3 Garzê China
89 B4 Garzón Col.
44 D5 Gascogne reg. France
76 E4 Gasconade r. U.S.A.
44 C5 Gascony, Gulf of g. France/Spain
6 B4 Gascoyne r. Austr.
Gascuña, Golfo de g. see Gascony, Gulf of
22 D2 Gasherbrum mt China/Jammu and Kashmir
19 F5 Gasht Iran
54 D3 Gashua Nigeria
19 E3 Gask Iran
33 C3 Gaspar, Selat chan. Indon.
67 H4 Gaspé Can.
67 H4 Gaspé, C. c. Can.
67 G4 Gaspé, Péninsule de pen. Can.
67 G4 Gaspésie, Parc de la nat. park Can.
42 E2 Gasselte Neth.
79 D5 Gastonia U.S.A.
91 C4 Gastre Arg.
45 E4 Gata, Cabo de c. Spain
16 D4 Gata, Cape c. Cyprus
50 D3 Gatchina Rus. Fed.
80 B6 Gate City U.S.A.
40 D6 Gatehouse of Fleet U.K.
38 F3 Gateshead U.K.
77 D6 Gatesville U.S.A.
75 H2 Gateway U.S.A.
81 F4 Gateway National Recreational Area res. U.S.A.
69 K3 Gatineau Can.
69 K2 Gatineau r. Can.
18 D4 Gatrūyeh Iran
17 M5 Gatvand Iran
7 H3 Gau i. Fiji
65 K3 Gauer Lake l. Can.
36 M5 Gaula r. Norway
80 C5 Gauley Bridge U.S.A.
42 D5 Gaume reg. Belgium
23 F4 Gauri Sankar mt China
59 G3 Gauteng div. S. Africa
19 G3 Gauzan Afgh.
19 F5 Gavāter Iran
18 D5 Gāvbandī Iran
18 D5 Gāvbūs, Kūh-e mts Iran
49 L7 Gavdos i. Greece
18 B3 Gaveh r. Iran
90 E1 Gavião r. Brazil
17 L4 Gavīleh Iran
74 B4 Gaviota U.S.A.
18 E4 Gāv Koshī Iran
37 P6 Gävle Sweden
50 F3 Gavrilov-Yam Rus. Fed.
58 B3 Gawachab Namibia
8 B3 Gawler Austr.
26 A1 Gaxun Nur salt l. China
23 F4 Gaya India
54 C3 Gaya Niger
30 E2 Gaya r. China
68 E3 Gaylord U.S.A.
16 E6 Gaza Gaza
59 K1 Gaza div. Moz.
16 E6 Gaza terr. Asia
20 F1 Gaz-Achak Turkm.
18 D2 Gazandzhyk Turkm.
19 H3 Gazdarra Pass Afgh.
16 F3 Gaziantep Turkey
19 F3 Gazīk Iran
16 D3 Gazipaşa Turkey
19 F1 Gazli Uzbek.
19 E5 Gaz Māhū Iran
19 E4 Gaz Şāleḩ Iran
54 A4 Gbangbatok Sierra Leone
54 B4 Gbarnga Liberia
54 C4 Gboko Nigeria
47 J3 Gdańsk Pol.
47 J3 Gdańsk, Gulf of g. Pol./Rus. Fed.
50 C3 Gdov Rus. Fed.
47 J3 Gdynia Pol.
40 C1 Gealldruig Mhor i. U.K.
43 J3 Gebesee Ger.
55 F3 Gedaref Sudan
43 H4 Gedern Ger.
42 C5 Gedinne Belgium
16 B2 Gediz Turkey
16 A2 Gediz r. Turkey
39 H5 Gedney Drove End U.K.
37 M9 Gedser Denmark
42 D3 Geel Belgium
8 E5 Geelong Austr.
58 D4 Geel Vloer salt pan S. Africa
42 F2 Geeste Ger.
43 J1 Geesthacht Ger.
26 F4 Ge Hu l. China
54 D3 Geidam Nigeria
43 H5 Geiersberg h. Ger.
65 J3 Geikie r. Can.
42 E4 Geilenkirchen Ger.
37 L6 Geilo Norway
37 K5 Geiranger Norway
68 E6 Geist Reservoir U.S.A.
43 L3 Geithain Ger.
27 B6 Gejiu China
48 F6 Gela Sicily Italy
56 E3 Geladī Eth.
32 B4 Gelang, Tanjung pt Malaysia
42 E3 Geldern Ger.
51 F6 Gelendzhik Rus. Fed.
47 L3 Gelgaudiškis Lith.
51 C7 Gelibolu Turkey
16 C2 Gelincik Dağı mt Turkey
18 E3 Gelmord Iran
43 H4 Gelnhausen Ger.
42 F3 Gelsenkirchen Ger.
32 B5 Gemas Malaysia
31 C5 Gemeh Indon.
56 B3 Gemena Congo(Zaire)
16 F2 Gemerek Turkey
16 B1 Gemlik Turkey
48 E1 Gemona del Friuli Italy
57 C6 Gemsbok National Park Botswana
58 D3 Gemsbokplein well S. Africa
56 E3 Genalē Wenz r. Eth.
42 C4 Genappe Belgium
91 D3 General Acha Arg.
91 E3 General Alvear Buenos Aires Arg.
91 E1 General Alvear Entre Rios Arg.
91 C2 General Alvear Mendoza Arg.
91 E2 General Belgrano Arg.
92 B3 General Belgrano II Arg. Base Ant.
92 B2 General Bernardo O'Higgins Chile Base Ant.
84 C1 General Bravo Mex.
88 B7 General Carrera, L. l. Chile
84 B1 General Cepeda Mex.
91 F3 General Conesa Buenos Aires Arg.
91 D4 General Conesa Rio Negro Arg.
91 F3 General Guido Arg.
91 F3 General J. Madariaga Arg.
91 E3 General La Madrid Arg.
91 F3 General Lavalle Arg.
91 D2 General Levalle Arg.
31 C4 General Luna Phil.
31 C4 General MacArthur Phil.
91 D2 General Pico Arg.
91 E2 General Pinto Arg.
91 C3 General Roca Arg.
92 B2 General San Martin Arg. Base Ant.
31 C5 General Santos Phil.
84 C1 General Terán Mex.
84 B2 General Vicente Guerrero Mex.
91 D2 General Villegas Arg.
80 D3 Genesee r. U.S.A.
68 B5 Geneseo IL U.S.A.
80 E3 Geneseo NY U.S.A.
59 G3 Geneva S. Africa
Geneva see Genève
68 C5 Geneva IL U.S.A.
76 D3 Geneva NE U.S.A.
80 E3 Geneva NY U.S.A.
80 C4 Geneva OH U.S.A.
Geneva, Lake l. see Léman, Lac
68 C4 Geneva, Lake l. U.S.A.
46 C7 Genève Switz.
45 D4 Genil r. Spain
42 D4 Genk Belgium
42 D3 Gennep Neth.
8 G4 Genoa Austr.
48 C2 Genoa Italy
Genova see Genoa
48 C2 Genova, Golfo di g. Italy
42 B3 Gent Belgium
43 L2 Genthin Ger.
6 B5 Geographe Bay b. Austr.
58 E6 George S. Africa
67 G2 George r. Can.
8 G3 George, L. l. N.S.W. Austr.
8 B4 George, L. l. S.A. Austr.
79 D6 George, L. l. U.S.A.
81 G3 George, Lake l. U.S.A.
9 A6 George Sd in. N.Z.
8 B2 Georgetown S.A. Austr.
79 F7 George Town Bahamas
69 H4 Georgetown Can.
87 G2 Georgetown Guyana
32 B1 George Town Malaysia
54 A3 Georgetown The Gambia
81 F5 Georgetown DE U.S.A.
68 D6 Georgetown IL U.S.A.
78 C4 Georgetown KY U.S.A.
80 B5 Georgetown OH U.S.A.
79 E5 Georgetown SC U.S.A.
77 D6 Georgetown TX U.S.A.
92 B2 George VI Sd chan. Ant.
92 B5 George V Land reg. Ant.
77 D6 George West U.S.A.
10 F5 Georgia country Asia
79 D5 Georgia div. U.S.A.
69 G3 Georgian Bay l. Can.
69 H3 Georgian Bay Island National Park Can.
64 E5 Georgia, Strait of chan. Can.
6 D4 Georgina watercourse Austr.
15 G2 Georgiyevka Kazak.
51 G6 Georgiyevsk Rus. Fed.
50 H3 Georgiyevskoye Rus. Fed.
43 L4 Gera Ger.
42 B4 Geraardsbergen Belgium
87 J6 Geral de Goiás, Serra h. Brazil
9 C6 Geraldine N.Z.
90 C1 Geral do Paraná, Serra h. Brazil
6 B4 Geraldton Austr.
18 D5 Gerāsh Iran
17 H3 Gercüş Turkey
16 D1 Gerede Turkey
16 D1 Gerede r. Turkey
19 G4 Gereshk Afgh.
32 B4 Gerik Malaysia
19 E3 Gerīmenj Iran
76 C3 Gering U.S.A.
72 C3 Gerlach U.S.A.
64 E3 Germansen Landing Can.
80 E5 Germantown U.S.A.
34 F3 Germany country Europe
43 G5 Germersheim Ger.
59 H3 Germiston S. Africa
43 G5 Gernsheim Ger.
42 E4 Gerolstein Ger.
43 J5 Gerolzhofen Ger.
75 G5 Geronimo U.S.A.
8 H3 Gerringong Austr.
43 H4 Gersfeld Ger.
43 J4 Gerstungen Ger.
43 K2 Gerwisch Ger.
23 F2 Gêrzê China
51 E7 Gerze Turkey
42 F3 Gescher Ger.
18 D3 Getcheh, Kūh-e h. Iran
42 D4 Gete r. Belgium
80 E5 Gettysburg PA U.S.A.
76 D2 Gettysburg SD U.S.A.
80 E5 Gettysburg National Military Park res. U.S.A.
27 C5 Getu He r. China
92 A4 Getz Ice Shelf ice feature Ant.
33 A2 Geumapang r. Indon.
8 G2 Geurie Austr.
17 J2 Gevaş Turkey
49 K4 Gevgelija Macedonia
45 E1 Gexto Spain
Gey see Nikshahr
32 □ Geylang Sing.
59 F3 Geysdorp S. Africa
16 C1 Geyve Turkey
58 F2 Ghaap Plateau S. Africa
54 C1 Ghadāmis Libya
18 D2 Ghaem Shahr Iran
22 C3 Ghaggar, Dry Bed of watercourse Pak.
22 E4 Ghaghara r. India
23 F5 Ghaghra India
53 D5 Ghana country Africa
18 D5 Ghanādah, Rās pt U.A.E.
22 C4 Ghanliala India
57 C6 Ghanzi Botswana
58 E1 Ghanzi div. Botswana
16 E6 Gharandal Jordan
54 C1 Ghardaïa Alg.
19 H2 Gharm Tajik.
18 C5 Ghār, Ras al pt S. Arabia
55 D1 Gharyān Libya
54 D2 Ghāt Libya
22 B3 Ghauspur Pak.
55 D3 Ghazal, Bahr el watercourse Chad
54 B1 Ghazaouet Alg.
22 D3 Ghaziabad India
23 E4 Ghazipur India
22 A3 Ghazluna Pak.
19 H3 Ghaznī Afgh.
19 H3 Ghazni r. Afgh.
19 G3 Ghazoor Afgh.
Ghent see Gent
47 M7 Gheorgheni Romania
47 L7 Gherla Romania
48 C3 Ghisonaccia Corsica France
19 G3 Ghizao Afgh.
22 C1 Ghizar Pak.
21 A2 Ghod r. India
23 G4 Ghoraghat Bangl.
19 H3 Ghorband r. Afgh.
19 H3 Ghorband Pass Afgh.
22 B4 Ghotāru India
22 B4 Ghotki Pak.
18 D4 Ghōwrī Iran
23 F4 Ghuari r. India
17 J5 Ghudāf, Wādī al watercourse Iraq
19 J2 Ghŭdara Tajik.
22 D6 Ghugus India
22 B4 Ghulam Mohammed Barrage barrage Pak.
19 F3 Ghurian Afgh.
42 A3 Ghyvelde France
32 C3 Gia Đinh Vietnam
51 G6 Giaginskaya Rus. Fed.
49 K4 Giannitsa Greece
59 H4 Giant's Castle mt S. Africa
41 E2 Giant's Causeway U.K.
33 E4 Gianyar Indon.
32 C3 Gia Rai Vietnam
48 F6 Giarre Sicily Italy
48 B2 Giaveno Italy
58 B2 Gibeon Namibia
34 E5 Gibraltar terr. Europe
45 C5 Gibraltar, Strait of str. Morocco/Spain
68 C5 Gibson City U.S.A.
6 C4 Gibson Desert Austr.
24 B2 Gichgeniyn Nuruu mts Mongolia
21 B3 Giddalur India
16 D6 Giddi, G. el h. Egypt
56 D3 Gīdolē Eth.
44 F3 Gien France
43 G4 Gießen Ger.
43 J2 Gifhorn Ger.
64 F3 Gift Lake Can.
29 E7 Gifu Japan
89 B4 Gigante Col.
77 B7 Gigantes, Llanos de los plain Mex.
40 C5 Gigha i. U.K.
45 D1 Gijón Spain
75 F5 Gila r. U.S.A.
75 F5 Gila Bend U.S.A.
75 F5 Gila Bend Mts mts U.S.A.
75 E5 Gila Mts mts U.S.A.
17 K4 Gīlan Garb Iran
17 M1 Gilāzi Azer.
75 G5 Gilbert AZ U.S.A.
80 C6 Gilbert WV U.S.A.
6 E3 Gilbert r. Austr.
7 H2 Gilbert Islands is Kiribati
87 J5 Gilbués Brazil
18 E3 Gil Chashmeh Iran
72 E1 Gildford U.S.A.
55 E2 Gilf Kebir Plateau plat. Egypt
64 D4 Gilford I. i. Can.
8 G1 Gilgandra Austr.
56 D4 Gilgil Kenya
22 C2 Gilgit Jammu and Kashmir
22 C2 Gilgit r. Jammu and Kashmir
8 F2 Gilgunnia Austr.
64 D4 Gil Island i. Can.
65 L3 Gillam Can.
68 C3 Gillett U.S.A.
72 F2 Gillette U.S.A.
39 H6 Gillingham Eng. U.K.
39 E6 Gillingham Eng. U.K.
38 F3 Gilling West U.K.
92 D5 Gillock I. i. Ant.
68 D3 Gills Rock U.S.A.
68 D5 Gilman IL U.S.A.
68 B3 Gilman WV U.S.A.
66 E2 Gilmour Island i. Can.
74 B3 Gilroy U.S.A.
81 G3 Gilsum U.S.A.
55 E3 Gimbala, Jebel mt Sudan
56 D3 Gīmbī Eth.
65 K4 Gimli Can.
21 C5 Gin Ganga r. Sri Lanka
21 B3 Gingee India
56 E3 Gīnīr Eth.
48 G4 Ginosa Italy
48 G4 Gioia del Colle Italy
8 E5 Gippsland reg. Austr.
22 B4 Girab India
19 E5 Gīran Iran
19 E4 Gīrān Rīg mt Iran
80 C3 Girard U.S.A.
22 B3 Girdao Pak.
19 G5 Girdar Dhor r. Pak.
19 F4 Girdi Iran
16 G1 Giresun Turkey
22 B5 Gir Forest forest India
23 F4 Giridih India
8 F1 Girilambone Austr.
22 C5 Girna r. India
45 H2 Girona Spain
44 D4 Gironde est. France
8 F2 Girral Austr.
40 D5 Girvan U.K.
50 E2 Girvas Rus. Fed.
22 E4 Girwan India
9 G3 Gisborne N.Z.
64 E4 Giscome Can.
37 N8 Gislaved Sweden
19 G2 Gissar Range mts Tajik./Uzbek.
56 C4 Gitarama Rwanda
56 C4 Gitega Burundi
48 E3 Giulianova Italy
49 L3 Giurgiu Romania
49 L2 Giuvala, Pasul pass Romania
42 C4 Givet France
44 G4 Givors France
42 C6 Givry-en-Argonne France
59 J1 Giyani S. Africa
16 C7 Giza Pyramids Egypt
19 G1 Gizhduvan Uzbek.
13 S3 Gizhiga Rus. Fed.
49 J4 Gjirokastër Albania
63 J3 Gjoa Haven Can.
36 L5 Gjøra Norway
37 M6 Gjøvik Norway
67 J4 Glace Bay Can.
64 B3 Glacier B. b. U.S.A.
64 B3 Glacier Bay National Park and Preserve U.S.A.
64 F4 Glacier Nat. Park Can.
72 D1 Glacier Nat. Park U.S.A.
72 B1 Glacier Peak volc. U.S.A.
36 M4 Gladstad Norway
8 B2 Gladstone S.A. Austr.
6 F4 Gladstone Austr.
68 D3 Gladstone U.S.A.
68 E4 Gladwin U.S.A.
40 E4 Glamis U.K.
31 C5 Glan Phil.
42 F5 Glan r. Ger.
41 B5 Glanaruddery Mts h. Rep. of Ireland
43 G2 Glandorf Ger.
38 F2 Glanton U.K.
69 G4 Glanworth Can.
40 D5 Glasgow U.K.
78 C4 Glasgow KY U.S.A.
72 F1 Glasgow MT U.S.A.
80 D6 Glasgow VA U.S.A.
65 H4 Glaslyn Can.
74 C3 Glass Mt mt U.S.A.
39 E6 Glastonbury U.K.
43 L4 Glauchau Ger.
12 G4 Glazov Rus. Fed.
51 F4 Glazunovka Rus. Fed.
47 P3 Glazunovo Rus. Fed.
81 H2 Glen U.S.A.
40 C3 Glen Affric v. U.K.
69 G2 Glen Afton Can.
9 E2 Glen Afton N.Z.
62 D3 Glenallen U.S.A.
59 H1 Glen Alpine Dam dam S. Africa
41 C4 Glenamaddy Rep. of Ireland
68 E3 Glen Arbor U.S.A.
9 C6 Glenavy N.Z.
40 C3 Glen Cannich v. U.K.
73 E4 Glen Canyon gorge U.S.A.
75 G3 Glen Canyon National Recreation Area res. U.S.A.
40 E4 Glen Clova v. U.K.
8 C4 Glencoe Austr.
69 G4 Glencoe Can.
59 J4 Glencoe S. Africa
40 C4 Glen Coe v. U.K.
69 E2 Glendale Can.
75 F5 Glendale AZ U.S.A.
74 C4 Glendale CA U.S.A.
75 E3 Glendale NV U.S.A.
75 F3 Glendale UT U.S.A.
80 D4 Glendale Lake l. U.S.A.
8 H2 Glen Davis Austr.
72 F2 Glendive U.S.A.
65 G4 Glendon Can.
72 F3 Glendo Res. l. U.S.A.
8 C4 Glenelg r. Austr.
40 F4 Glen Esk v. U.K.
40 A5 Glengad Head hd Rep. of Ireland
40 C3 Glen Garry v. Scot. U.K.
40 D4 Glen Garry v. Scot. U.K.
41 D3 Glengavlen Rep. of Ireland
6 F4 Glen Innes Austr.
40 D6 Glenluce U.K.
40 D4 Glen Lyon v. U.K.
40 D3 Glen More v. U.K.
40 D3 Glen Moriston v. U.K.
40 C4 Glen Nevis v. U.K.
69 F3 Glennie U.S.A.
75 G6 Glenn, Mt mt U.S.A.
80 E6 Glenns U.S.A.
64 C3 Glenora Can.
81 F2 Glen Robertson Can.
40 E4 Glenrothes U.K.
81 G3 Glens Falls U.S.A.
40 E4 Glen Shee v. U.K.
40 C3 Glen Shiel v. U.K.
41 C3 Glenties Rep. of Ireland
41 D2 Glenveagh National Park Rep. of Ireland
80 C5 Glenville U.S.A.
77 E5 Glenwood AR U.S.A.
75 H5 Glenwood NM U.S.A.
73 F4 Glenwood Springs U.S.A.
68 B2 Glidden U.S.A.
43 J1 Glinde Ger.
47 J5 Gliwice Pol.
75 G5 Globe U.S.A.
46 H5 Głogów Pol.
36 N3 Glomfjord Norway
37 M5 Glomma r. Norway
57 E5 Glorieuses, Îles is Ind. Ocean
8 H1 Gloucester Austr.
39 E6 Gloucester U.K.
81 H3 Gloucester MA U.S.A.
80 E6 Gloucester VA U.S.A.
81 F3 Gloversville U.S.A.
43 L2 Glöwen Ger.
28 D1 Glubinnoye Rus. Fed.
51 G6 Glubokiy Rus. Fed.
15 G1 Glubokoye Kazak.
43 H1 Glückstadt Ger.
36 □ Gluggarnir h. Faroe Is
38 F4 Glusburn U.K.
51 H5 Gmelinka Rus. Fed.
46 G6 Gmünd Austria
46 F7 Gmunden Austria
37 P5 Gnarp Sweden
43 H1 Gnarrenburg Ger.
46 H4 Gniezno Pol.
49 J3 Gnjilane Yugo.
21 A3 Goa India
21 A3 Goa div. India
58 B3 Goageb Namibia
8 H4 Goalen Head hd Austr.
23 G4 Goalpara India
40 C5 Goat Fell h. U.K.
56 E3 Goba Eth.
57 B6 Gobabis Namibia
58 C3 Gobas Namibia
91 E1 Gobernador Crespo Arg.
91 C3 Gobernador Duval Arg.
88 B7 Gobernador Gregores Arg.
11 M5 Gobi des. Mongolia
29 D8 Gobō Japan
42 E3 Goch Ger.
57 B6 Gochas Namibia
32 C3 Go Công Vietnam
39 G6 Godalming U.K.
21 C2 Godavari r. India
21 C2 Godavari, Mouths of the river mouth India
67 G4 Godbout Can.
74 C3 Goddard, Mt mt U.S.A.
56 E3 Godere Eth.
69 G4 Goderich Can.
22 C5 Godhra India
91 C2 Godoy Cruz Arg.
65 L3 Gods r. Can.
65 L4 Gods Lake l. Can.
65 M2 Gods Mercy, Bay of b. Can.
Godwin Austen mt see K2
42 B3 Goedereede Neth.
66 E4 Goéland, Lac au l. Can.
67 H2 Goélands, Lac aux l. Can.
42 B3 Goes Neth.
69 E2 Goetzville U.S.A.
75 E4 Goffs U.S.A.
69 G2 Gogama Can.
68 C2 Gogebic, Lake l. U.S.A.
68 C2 Gogebic Range h. U.S.A.
Gogra r. see Ghaghara
22 D4 Gohad India
87 M5 Goiana Brazil
90 C2 Goiandira Brazil
90 C2 Goiânia Brazil
90 B1 Goiás Brazil
90 B2 Goiás div. Brazil
90 B4 Goio-Erê Brazil
22 C3 Gojra Pak.
21 A2 Gokak India
51 C7 Gökçeada i. Turkey
16 B2 Gökçedağ Turkey
23 G3 Gokhar La pass China
16 E1 Gökirmak r. Turkey
19 F5 Gokprosh Hills mts Pak.
16 F2 Göksun Turkey
16 E3 Göksu Nehri r. Turkey
57 C5 Gokwe Zimbabwe
37 L6 Gol Norway
22 E3 Gola India
23 H4 Golaghat India
16 F3 Gölbaşı Turkey
12 K2 Gol'chikha Rus. Fed.
16 B1 Gölcük Turkey
47 L3 Gołdap Pol.
43 L1 Goldberg Ger.
7 F4 Gold Coast Austr.
54 B4 Gold Coast coastal area Ghana
64 F4 Golden Can.
9 D4 Golden Bay b. N.Z.
43 J3 Goldene Aue reg. Ger.
74 A3 Golden Gate National Recreation Area res. U.S.A.
64 D5 Golden Hinde mt Can.
43 G2 Goldenstedt Ger.
41 C5 Golden Vale lowland Rep. of Ireland
74 D3 Goldfield U.S.A.
74 D3 Gold Point U.S.A.
79 E5 Goldsboro U.S.A.
77 D6 Goldthwaite U.S.A.
17 J1 Göle Turkey
19 F3 Golestān Afgh.
18 D4 Golestānak Iran
74 C4 Goleta U.S.A.
77 D6 Goliad U.S.A.
30 A1 Golin Baixing China
16 F1 Gölköy Turkey
43 L2 Golm Ger.
17 K3 Golmānkhānen Iran
24 B3 Golmud China
23 H1 Golmud He r. China
31 B3 Golo i. Phil.
28 J3 Golovnino Rus. Fed.
18 C3 Golpāyegān Iran
16 C1 Gölpazarı Turkey
40 E3 Golspie U.K.
19 F3 Gol Vardeh Iran
49 L4 Golyama Syutkya mt Bulg.
49 L4 Golyam Persenk mt Bulg.
43 L2 Golzow Ger.
56 C4 Goma Congo(Zaire)
23 G3 Gomang Co salt l. China
22 E4 Gomati r. India
32 □ Gombak, Bukit h. Sing.
54 D3 Gombe Nigeria
56 D4 Gombe r. Tanz.
55 D3 Gombi Nigeria
54 A2 Gomera, La i. Canary Is
84 B1 Gómez Palacio Mex.
84 C1 Gómez, Presa M. R. resr Mex.
18 D2 Gomīshān Iran
43 K2 Gommern Ger.
23 F2 Gomo Co salt l. China
19 E2 Gonābād Iran
Gonabad see Jūymand
83 K5 Gonaïves Haiti
59 J1 Gonarezhou National Park Zimbabwe
83 K5 Gonâve, Île de la i. Haiti
18 D2 Gonbad-e Kavus Iran
23 E4 Gonda India
22 B5 Gondal India
56 D2 Gonder Eth.
22 E5 Gondia India
16 A1 Gönen Turkey
27 D4 Gong'an China
27 D5 Gongcheng China
27 A4 Gongga Shan mt China
26 A2 Gonghe China
26 E1 Gonghui China
90 E1 Gongogi r. Brazil
54 D3 Gongola r. Nigeria
27 B5 Gongwang Shan mts China
26 D3 Gong Xian Henan China
27 B4 Gong Xian Sichuan China
59 H6 Gonubie S. Africa
84 C2 Gonzáles Mex.
74 B3 Gonzales CA U.S.A.
77 D6 Gonzales TX U.S.A.
91 D2 González Moreno Arg.
80 E6 Goochland U.S.A.
92 C6 Goodenough, C. c. Ant.
6 F2 Goodenough I. i. P.N.G.
69 H3 Gooderham Can.
68 E3 Good Harbor Bay b. U.S.A.
58 C7 Good Hope, Cape of c. S. Africa
72 D3 Gooding U.S.A.
76 C4 Goodland U.S.A.
38 G4 Goole U.K.
8 E3 Goolgowi Austr.
8 G2 Goolma Austr.
8 G2 Gooloogong Austr.
8 B3 Goolwa Austr.
6 F4 Goondiwindi Austr.
67 H3 Goose r. Can.
72 B3 Goose L. l. U.S.A.
21 B3 Gooty India
46 D6 Göppingen Ger.
23 E4 Gorakhpur India
49 H3 Goražde Bos.-Herz.
50 G3 Gorchukha Rus. Fed.
79 E7 Gorda Cay i. Bahamas
16 B2 Gördes Turkey
47 P4 Gordeyevka Rus. Fed.
40 F5 Gordon U.K.
6 E6 Gordon, L. l. Austr.
64 G2 Gordon Lake l. Can.
80 D5 Gordon Lake l. U.S.A.
80 D5 Gordonsville U.S.A.
55 D4 Goré Chad
56 D3 Gorē Eth.
9 B7 Gore N.Z.
69 F3 Gore Bay Can.
40 E5 Gorebridge U.K.
41 E5 Gorey Rep. of Ireland
19 E4 Gorg Iran
18 D2 Gorgān Iran
89 A4 Gorgona, I. i. Col.
81 H2 Gorham U.S.A.
51 H7 Gori Georgia
42 C3 Gorinchem Neth.
17 L2 Goris Armenia
48 E2 Gorizia Italy
Gor'kiy see Nizhniy Novgorod
51 H5 Gor'ko-Solenoye, Ozero l. Rus. Fed.
50 G3 Gor'kovskoye Vdkhr. resr Rus. Fed.
47 K6 Gorlice Pol.
46 G5 Görlitz Ger.
22 D4 Gormi India
49 L3 Gorna Oryakhovitsa Bulg.
49 J2 Gornji Milanovac Yugo.
48 G3 Gornji Vakuf Bos.-Herz.
24 A1 Gorno-Altaysk Rus. Fed.
28 G1 Gornozavodsk Rus. Fed.
12 K4 Gornyak Rus. Fed.
28 C2 Gornye Klyuchi Rus. Fed.
28 C2 Gornyy Primorskiy Kray Rus. Fed.
51 J5 Gornyy Saratov. Obl. Rus. Fed.
51 H5 Gornyy Balykley Rus. Fed.
50 G3 Gorodets Rus. Fed.
51 H5 Gorodishche Rus. Fed.
51 G6 Gorodovikovsk Rus. Fed.
6 E2 Goroka P.N.G.
8 C4 Goroke Austr.
50 G3 Gorokhovets Rus. Fed.
54 B3 Gorom Gorom Burkina
57 D5 Gorongosa Moz.

25 E6 Gorontalo Indon.
51 F5 Gorshechnoye Rus. Fed.
41 C4 Gort Rep. of Ireland
41 C2 Gortahork Rep. of Ireland
90 D1 Gorutuba r. Brazil
51 F6 Goryachiy Klyuch Rus. Fed.
43 L2 Görzke Ger.
46 G4 Gorzów Wielkopolski Pol.
8 H2 Gosford Austr.
38 F2 Gosforth U.K.
68 E5 Goshen IN U.S.A.
81 F4 Goshen NY U.S.A.
28 G4 Goshogawara Japan
43 J3 Goslar Ger.
48 F2 Gospić Croatia
39 F7 Gosport U.K.
49 J4 Gostivar Macedonia
Göteborg see Gothenburg
37 N7 Götene Sweden
43 J4 Gotha Ger.
37 M8 Gothenburg Sweden
76 C3 Gothenburg U.S.A.
37 Q8 Gotland i. Sweden
49 K4 Gotse Delchev Bulg.
37 Q7 Gotska Sandön i. Sweden
29 C7 Gōtsu Japan
43 H3 Göttingen Ger.
64 E4 Gott Peak summit Can.
Gottwaldow see Zlín
30 A3 Goubangzi China
42 C2 Gouda Neth.
54 A3 Goudiri Senegal
54 D3 Goudoumaria Niger
68 E1 Goudreau Can.
96 J8 Gough Island i. Atl. Ocean
66 F4 Gouin, Réservoir resr Can.
68 E2 Goulais River Can.
8 G3 Goulburn Austr.
8 H2 Goulburn r. N.S.W. Austr.
8 E4 Goulburn r. Vic. Austr.
6 D3 Goulburn Is is Austr.
68 E2 Gould City U.S.A.
92 B4 Gould Coast coastal area Ant.
54 B3 Goundam Mali
45 G4 Gouraya Alg.
54 D3 Gouré Niger
58 D7 Gourits r. S. Africa
54 B3 Gourma-Rharous Mali
44 E2 Gournay-en-Bray France
8 G4 Gourock Range mts Austr.
42 A5 Goussainville France
81 F2 Gouverneur U.S.A.
65 H5 Govenlock Can.
90 E2 Governador Valadares Brazil
31 C5 Governor Generoso Phil.
79 E7 Governor's Harbour Bahamas
24 B2 Govĭ Altayn Nuruu mts Mongolia
23 E4 Govind Ballash Pant Sāgar resr India
22 D3 Govind Sagar resr India
19 G2 Govurdak Turkm.
80 D3 Gowanda U.S.A.
19 G4 Gowārān Afgh.
18 D4 Gowd-e Aḥmad Iran
18 E3 Gowd-e Hasht Tekkeh waterhole Iran
18 D4 Gowd-e Mokh l. Iran
39 C6 Gower pen. U.K.
69 G2 Gowganda Can.
19 E4 Gowk Iran
41 D4 Gowna, Lough l. Rep. of Ireland
88 E3 Goya Arg.
17 L1 Göyçay Azer.
17 H2 Göynük Turkey
28 G5 Goyō-zan mt Japan
17 M2 Göytäpä Azer.
19 F3 Gözareh Afgh.
16 G2 Gözene Turkey
22 E2 Gozha Co salt l. China
48 F6 Gozo i. Malta
58 F6 Graaff-Reinet S. Africa
58 C6 Graafwater S. Africa
43 J4 Grabfeld plain Ger.
54 B4 Grabo Côte d'Ivoire
58 C7 Grabouw S. Africa
43 K1 Grabow Ger.
48 F2 Gračac Croatia
69 J2 Gracefield Can.
43 L3 Gräfenhainichen Ger.
43 K5 Grafenwöhr Ger.
7 F4 Grafton Austr.
76 D1 Grafton ND U.S.A.
68 D4 Grafton WV U.S.A.
80 C5 Grafton WV U.S.A.
75 E2 Grafton, Mt mt U.S.A.
77 D5 Graham U.S.A.
Graham Bell Island i. see Greem-Bell, Ostrov
63 J2 Graham I. i. Can.
64 C4 Graham Island i. Can.
81 J2 Graham Lake l. U.S.A.
92 B2 Graham Land reg. Ant.
75 H5 Graham, Mt mt U.S.A.
59 G6 Grahamstown S. Africa
41 E5 Graigue Rep. of Ireland
54 A4 Grain Coast coastal area Liberia
87 J5 Grajaú Brazil
40 B1 Gralisgeir i. U.K.
49 J4 Grámmos mt Greece
40 D4 Grampian Mountains U.K.
8 D4 Grampians mts Austr.
58 C5 Granaatboskolk S. Africa
89 B4 Granada Col.
83 G6 Granada Nic.
45 E4 Granada Spain
76 C4 Granada U.S.A.
41 D4 Granard Rep. of Ireland
91 C3 Gran Bajo Salitroso salt flat Arg.
66 F4 Granby Can.
54 A2 Gran Canaria i. Canary Is
88 D3 Gran Chaco reg. Arg./Para.
78 C3 Grand r. MI U.S.A.
76 E3 Grand r. MO U.S.A.
79 E7 Grand Bahama i. Bahamas
67 J4 Grand Bank Can.
96 F2 Grand Banks sea feature Atl. Ocean
54 B4 Grand-Bassam Côte d'Ivoire
67 G4 Grand Bay Can.
69 G4 Grand Bend Can.
41 D4 Grand Canal canal Rep. of Ireland
75 F3 Grand Canyon U.S.A.
75 F3 Grand Canyon gorge U.S.A.
75 F3 Grand Canyon Nat. Park U.S.A.
83 H5 Grand Cayman i. Cayman Is
65 G4 Grand Centre Can.
72 C2 Grand Coulee U.S.A.
91 C3 Grande r. Arg.
87 J6 Grande r. Bahia Brazil
90 B2 Grande r. São Paulo Brazil
88 C8 Grande, Bahía b. Arg.
64 F4 Grande Cache Can.
44 H4 Grande Casse, Pointe de la mt France
57 E5 Grande Comore i. Comoros
91 F1 Grande, Cuchilla h. Uru.
90 D3 Grande, Ilha i. Brazil
64 F3 Grande Prairie Can.
55 D3 Grand Erg de Bilma sand dunes Niger
54 B1 Grand Erg Occidental des. Alg.
54 C2 Grand Erg Oriental des. Alg.
67 H4 Grande-Rivière Can.
66 F3 Grande Rivière de la Baleine r. Can.
72 C2 Grande Ronde r. U.S.A.
89 E4 Grande, Serra mt Brazil
67 G4 Grand Falls N.B. Can.
67 J4 Grand Falls Nfld Can.
64 F5 Grand Forks Can.
76 D2 Grand Forks U.S.A.
81 F3 Grand Gorge U.S.A.
81 K2 Grand Harbour Can.
68 D4 Grand Haven U.S.A.
64 F2 Grandin, Lac l. Can.
76 D3 Grand Island U.S.A.
68 D2 Grand Island i. U.S.A.
77 F6 Grand Isle LA U.S.A.
81 J1 Grand Isle ME U.S.A.
75 H2 Grand Junction U.S.A.
54 B4 Grand-Lahou Côte d'Ivoire
67 G4 Grand Lake l. N.B. Can.
67 J4 Grand Lake l. Nfld Can.
67 H3 Grand Lake l. Nfld Can.
77 E6 Grand Lake l. LA U.S.A.
81 K2 Grand Lake l. ME U.S.A.
69 F3 Grand Lake l. MI U.S.A.
81 J1 Grand Lake Matagamon l. U.S.A.
80 A4 Grand Lake St Marys l. U.S.A.
81 J1 Grand Lake Seboeis l. U.S.A.
81 K2 Grand Lake Stream U.S.A.
68 E4 Grand Ledge U.S.A.
67 G5 Grand Manan I. i. Can.
68 E2 Grand Marais MI U.S.A.
68 B2 Grand Marais MN U.S.A.
67 F4 Grand-Mère Can.
45 B3 Grândola Port.
7 G3 Grand Passage chan. New Caledonia
68 C2 Grand Portage U.S.A.
65 K4 Grand Rapids Can.
68 E4 Grand Rapids MI U.S.A.
76 E2 Grand Rapids MN U.S.A.
7 G3 Grand Récif de Cook rf New Caledonia
7 G4 Grand Récif du Sud rf New Caledonia
72 E3 Grand Teton mt U.S.A.
72 E3 Grand Teton Nat. Park U.S.A.
68 E3 Grand Traverse Bay b. U.S.A.
67 G4 Grand Vallée Can.
72 C2 Grandview U.S.A.
75 F3 Grand Wash r. U.S.A.
75 E4 Grand Wash Cliffs cliff U.S.A.
91 B2 Graneros Chile
41 D6 Grange Rep. of Ireland
72 E3 Granger U.S.A.
37 O6 Grängesberg Sweden
72 C2 Grangeville U.S.A.
64 D3 Granisle Can.
76 E2 Granite Falls U.S.A.
67 J4 Granite Lake l. Can.
75 E4 Granite Mts mts U.S.A.
72 E2 Granite Peak summit MT U.S.A.
75 F1 Granite Peak summit UT U.S.A.
48 E6 Granitola, Capo c. Sicily Italy
88 C6 Gran Laguna Salada l. Arg.
37 O7 Gränna Sweden
48 B2 Gran Paradiso mt Italy
46 E7 Gran Pilastro mt Austria/Italy
43 L3 Granschütz Ger.
43 M1 Gransee Ger.
39 G5 Grantham U.K.
83 A4 Grant I. i. Ant.
74 D2 Grant, Mt mt NV U.S.A.
74 C2 Grant, Mt mt NV U.S.A.
40 E3 Grantown-on-Spey U.K.
75 E2 Grant Range mts U.S.A.
73 F5 Grants U.S.A.
72 B3 Grants Pass U.S.A.
44 D2 Granville France
68 C5 Granville IL U.S.A.
81 G3 Granville NY U.S.A.
65 J3 Granville Lake l. Can.
90 D2 Grão Mogol Brazil
74 C4 Grapevine U.S.A.
74 D3 Grapevine Mts mts U.S.A.
81 G3 Graphite U.S.A.
59 J2 Graskop S. Africa
65 G2 Gras, Lac de l. Can.
81 F2 Grass r. U.S.A.
44 H5 Grasse France
38 F3 Grassington U.K.
65 H5 Grasslands Nat. Park Can.
72 E2 Grassrange U.S.A.
65 J4 Grass River Prov. Park res. Can.
74 B2 Grass Valley U.S.A.
79 E7 Grassy Cr. r. Bahamas
37 N7 Grästorp Sweden
68 B4 Gratiot U.S.A.
45 G1 Graus Spain
65 J2 Gravel Hill Lake l. Can.
42 A4 Gravelines France
59 J1 Gravelotte S. Africa
69 H3 Gravenhurst Can.
39 H6 Gravesend U.K.
48 G4 Gravina in Puglia Italy
68 E3 Grawn U.S.A.
44 G3 Gray France
81 H3 Gray U.S.A.
68 E3 Grayling U.S.A.
39 H6 Grays U.K.
72 A2 Grays Harbor in. U.S.A.
72 E3 Grays L. l. U.S.A.
80 B5 Grayson U.S.A.
67 H1 Gray Strait chan. Can.
78 B4 Grayville U.S.A.
46 G7 Graz Austria
79 E7 Great Abaco i. Bahamas
6 C5 Great Australian Bight g. Austr.
39 H6 Great Baddow U.K.
83 J3 Great Bahama Bank sea feature Bahamas
9 E2 Great Barrier Island i. N.Z.
6 E3 Great Barrier Reef rf Austr.
81 G3 Great Barrington U.S.A.
73 C4 Great Basin basin U.S.A.
75 E2 Great Basin Nat. Park U.S.A.
81 F5 Great Bay b. U.S.A.
64 E1 Great Bear r. Can.
64 E1 Great Bear Lake l. Can.
76 D4 Great Bend U.S.A.
58 C6 Great Berg r. S. Africa
40 B2 Great Bernera i. U.K.
41 A5 Great Blasket I. i. Rep. of Ireland
38 D3 Great Clifton U.K.
40 D5 Great Cumbrae i. U.K.
8 F4 Great Dividing Range mts Austr.
38 G3 Great Driffield U.K.
69 F3 Great Duck I. i. Can.
81 F5 Great Egg Harbor in. U.S.A.
83 H4 Greater Antilles is Caribbean Sea
83 J4 Great Exuma i. Bahamas
72 E2 Great Falls U.S.A.
59 G6 Great Fish r. S. Africa
59 G6 Great Fish Point pt S. Africa
23 F4 Great Gandak r. India
79 E7 Great Guana Cay i. Bahamas
79 E7 Great Harbour Cay i. Bahamas
83 K4 Great Inagua i. Bahamas
58 D5 Great Karoo plat. S. Africa
59 H6 Great Kei r. S. Africa
6 E6 Great Lake l. Austr.
39 E5 Great Malvern U.K.
80 A5 Great Miami r. U.S.A.
55 F2 Great Oasis, The oasis Egypt
39 D4 Great Ormes Head hd U.K.
39 H5 Great Ouse r. U.K.
81 G4 Great Peconic Bay b. U.S.A.
81 H4 Great Pt pt U.S.A.
39 D5 Great Rhos h. U.K.
56 D4 Great Ruaha r. Tanz.
81 F3 Great Sacandaga L. l. U.S.A.
48 B2 Great St Bernard Pass Italy/Switz.
79 E7 Great Sale Cay i. Bahamas
72 D3 Great Salt Lake l. U.S.A.
72 D3 Great Salt Lake Desert U.S.A.
55 E2 Great Sand Sea des. Egypt/Libya
6 C4 Great Sandy Desert Austr.
7 H3 Great Sea Reef rf Fiji
62 G3 Great Slave Lake N.W.T. Can.
64 G2 Great Slave Lake l. Can.
79 D5 Great Smoky Mts mts U.S.A.
79 D5 Great Smoky Mts Nat. Park U.S.A.
64 E3 Great Snow Mtn mt Can.
81 G4 Great South Bay b. U.S.A.
39 H7 Greatstone-on-Sea U.K.
39 J6 Great Stour r. U.K.
39 C7 Great Torrington U.K.
6 C4 Great Victoria Desert Austr.
26 F1 Great Wall China
39 H6 Great Waltham U.K.
81 K2 Great Wass I. i. U.S.A.
38 F3 Great Whernside h. U.K.
39 J5 Great Yarmouth U.K.
17 J3 Great Zab r. Iraq
48 E4 Greco, Monte mt Italy
45 D2 Gredos, Sa de mts Spain
35 H5 Greece country Europe
72 F3 Greeley U.S.A.
63 K1 Greely Fiord in. Can.
12 H1 Greem-Bell, Ostrov i. Rus. Fed.
78 C4 Green r. KY U.S.A.
75 H2 Green r. UT/WY U.S.A.
69 H3 Greenbank Can.
68 C3 Green Bay U.S.A.
68 D3 Green Bay b. U.S.A.
8 H4 Green C. hd Austr.
41 E3 Greencastle U.K.
78 C4 Greencastle U.S.A.
79 E7 Green Cay i. Bahamas
79 D6 Green Cove Springs U.S.A.
68 A4 Greene IA U.S.A.
81 F3 Greene NY U.S.A.
79 D4 Greeneville U.S.A.
74 B3 Greenfield CA U.S.A.
68 E6 Greenfield IN U.S.A.
81 G3 Greenfield MA U.S.A.
80 B5 Greenfield OH U.S.A.
68 C4 Greenfield WI U.S.A.
31 A4 Green Island Bay b. Phil.
65 H4 Green Lake Can.
68 C4 Green Lake l. U.S.A.
60 N2 Greenland terr. Arctic Ocean
96 J1 Greenland Basin sea feature Arctic Ocean
34 E1 Greenland Sea sea Arctic Ocean
40 F5 Greenlaw U.K.
81 G2 Green Mountains U.S.A.
40 D5 Greenock U.K.
41 E3 Greenore Rep. of Ireland
81 G4 Greenport U.S.A.
73 E4 Green River UT U.S.A.
72 E3 Green River WY U.S.A.
79 E4 Greensboro U.S.A.
78 C4 Greensburg IN U.S.A.
77 D4 Greensburg KS U.S.A.
80 D4 Greensburg PA U.S.A.
40 C3 Greenstone Point pt U.K.
71 L5 Green Swamp swamp NC U.S.A.
80 B5 Greenup U.S.A.
81 F2 Green Valley Can.
75 G6 Green Valley U.S.A.
68 C5 Greenview U.S.A.
54 B4 Greenville Liberia
79 C6 Greenville AL U.S.A.
74 B1 Greenville CA U.S.A.
79 D6 Greenville FL U.S.A.
81 J2 Greenville ME U.S.A.
68 E4 Greenville MI U.S.A.
77 F5 Greenville MS U.S.A.
79 E5 Greenville NC U.S.A.
81 H3 Greenville NH U.S.A.
80 A4 Greenville OH U.S.A.
80 C4 Greenville PA U.S.A.
79 D5 Greenville SC U.S.A.
77 D5 Greenville TX U.S.A.
65 J4 Greenwater Provincial Park res. Can.
8 H3 Greenwell Point Austr.
81 G4 Greenwich CT U.S.A.
81 G3 Greenwich NY U.S.A.
75 G2 Greenwich UT U.S.A.
77 F5 Greenwood MS U.S.A.
79 D5 Greenwood SC U.S.A.
77 E5 Greers Ferry Lake l. U.S.A.
76 D3 Gregory U.S.A.
6 C4 Gregory Lake salt flat Austr.
6 E3 Gregory Range h. Austr.
46 F3 Greifswald Ger.
43 L4 Greiz Ger.
16 E4 Greko, Cape c. Cyprus
37 M8 Grenå Denmark
77 F5 Grenada U.S.A.
61 M8 Grenada country Caribbean Sea
44 E5 Grenade France
37 M8 Grenen spit Denmark
8 G2 Grenfell Austr.
65 J4 Grenfell Can.
44 G4 Grenoble France
89 E1 Grenville Grenada
6 E3 Grenville, C. hd Austr.
72 B2 Gresham U.S.A.
38 F3 Greta r. U.K.
40 E6 Gretna U.K.
77 F6 Gretna U.S.A.
43 J3 Greußen Ger.
42 B3 Grevelingen chan. Neth.
72 F2 Greven Ger.
49 J4 Grevena Greece
42 D3 Grevenbicht Neth.
42 E3 Grevenbroich Ger.
42 E5 Grevenmacher Lux.
46 E4 Grevesmühlen Ger.
9 C5 Grey r. N.Z.
72 E2 Greybull U.S.A.
64 B2 Grey Hunter Pk summit Can.
67 J3 Grey Is is Can.
9 C5 Greymouth N.Z.
6 E4 Grey Range h. Austr.
59 J4 Greytown S. Africa
42 C4 Grez-Doiceau Belgium
51 G5 Gribanovskiy Rus. Fed.
74 B2 Gridley CA U.S.A.
68 C5 Gridley IL U.S.A.
79 C5 Griffin U.S.A.
8 F3 Griffith Austr.
69 J3 Griffith Can.
62 F2 Griffiths Point pt Can.
43 L3 Grimma Ger.
46 F3 Grimmen Ger.
69 H4 Grimsby Can.
38 G4 Grimsby U.K.
36 E3 Grímsey i. Iceland
64 F3 Grimshaw Can.
36 E4 Grímsstaðir Iceland
37 L7 Grimstad Norway
36 B5 Grindavík Iceland
37 L9 Grindsted Denmark
49 N2 Grindul Chituc spit Romania
76 E3 Grinnell U.S.A.
59 H5 Griqualand East reg. S. Africa
58 E4 Griqualand West reg. S. Africa
58 E4 Griquatown S. Africa
63 K2 Grise Fiord Can.
33 B3 Grisik Indon.
39 J7 Gris Nez, Cap pt France
40 F2 Gritley U.K.
48 G2 Grmeč mts Bos.-Herz.
42 C3 Grobbendonk Belgium
59 H2 Groblersdal S. Africa
58 E4 Groblershoop S. Africa
28 B2 Grodekovo Rus. Fed.
Grodno see Hrodna
58 B5 Groen watercourse Northern Cape S. Africa
58 E5 Groen watercourse Northern Cape S. Africa
44 C3 Groix, Île de i. France
48 D6 Grombalia Tunisia
42 F2 Gronau (Westfalen) Ger.
36 N4 Grong Norway
42 E1 Groningen Neth.
42 E1 Groninger Wad tidal flats Neth.
75 E3 Groom L. l. U.S.A.
58 D3 Groot-Aar Pan salt pan S. Africa
58 E7 Groot Brakrivier S. Africa
59 H3 Grootdraaidam dam S. Africa
58 D4 Grootdrink S. Africa
6 D3 Groote Eylandt i. Austr.
57 B5 Grootfontein Namibia
58 C3 Groot Karas Berg plat. Namibia
59 J1 Groot Letaba r. S. Africa
59 G2 Groot Marico S. Africa
58 D6 Groot Swartberg mts S. Africa
58 D5 Grootvloer salt pan S. Africa
59 G6 Groot Winterberg mt S. Africa
68 E3 Gros Cap U.S.A.
67 J4 Gros Morne Nat. Pk Can.
43 J3 Großengottern Ger.
43 G2 Großenkneten Ger.
43 H4 Großenlüder Ger.
43 J4 Großer Beerberg h. Ger.
43 J4 Großer Gleichberg h. Ger.
46 G7 Grosser Speikkogel mt Austria
48 D3 Grosseto Italy
43 G5 Groß-Gerau Ger.
48 E1 Großglockner mt Austria
43 J2 Groß Oesingen Ger.
43 K3 Großrudestedt Ger.
43 M2 Groß Schönebeck Ger.
58 C1 Gross Ums Namibia
72 E3 Gros Ventre Range mts U.S.A.
67 J3 Groswater Bay b. Can.
81 E3 Groton U.S.A.
80 D5 Grottoes U.S.A.
64 F3 Grouard Can.
66 D4 Groundhog r. Can.
42 D1 Grouw Neth.
80 C4 Grove City U.S.A.
79 C6 Grove Hill U.S.A.
74 B3 Groveland U.S.A.
92 D5 Grove Mts mts Ant.
74 B4 Grover Beach U.S.A.
81 H2 Groveton U.S.A.
75 F5 Growler U.S.A.
75 F5 Growler Mts mts U.S.A.
51 H7 Groznyy Rus. Fed.
49 M3 Grudovo Bulg.
47 J4 Grudziądz Pol.
40 C3 Gruinard Bay b. U.K.
57 B6 Grünau Namibia
36 B4 Grundarfjörður Iceland
80 B6 Grundy U.S.A.
43 G5 Grünstadt Ger.
51 F4 Gryazi Rus. Fed.
50 G3 Gryazovets Rus. Fed.
46 G4 Gryfice Pol.
46 G4 Gryfino Pol.
46 G5 Gryfów Śląski Pol.
36 P2 Gryllefjord Norway
88 □ Grytviken Atl. Ocean
23 F5 Gua India
83 J4 Guacanayabo, Golfo de b. Cuba
89 D2 Guacara Venez.
89 C3 Guacharía r. Col.
45 D4 Guadajoz r. Spain
84 B2 Guadalajara Mex.
45 E2 Guadalajara Spain
45 F2 Guadalaviar r. Spain
7 G2 Guadalcanal i. Solomon Is
45 C4 Guadalete r. Spain
45 F2 Guadalope r. Spain
45 D4 Guadalquivir r. Spain
84 B1 Guadalupe Nuevo León Mex.
84 B2 Guadalupe Zacatecas Mex.
74 B4 Guadalupe U.S.A.
70 C6 Guadalupe i. Mex.
77 D6 Guadalupe r. U.S.A.
84 A1 Guadalupe Aguilera Mex.
77 B6 Guadalupe Mts Nat. Park U.S.A.
77 B6 Guadalupe Pk mt U.S.A.
45 D3 Guadalupe, Sierra de mts Spain
84 A1 Guadalupe Victoria Mex.
84 A1 Guadalupe y Calvo Mex.
45 D2 Guadarrama, Sierra de mts Spain
61 M8 Guadeloupe terr. Caribbean Sea
91 C2 Guadel, Sa de mts Arg.
45 C4 Guadiana r. Port./Spain
45 E4 Guadix Spain
88 B6 Guafo, I. i. Chile
89 D4 Guainía r. Col./Venez.
89 E3 Guaiquinima, Cerro mt Venez.
90 A4 Guaíra Brazil
88 B6 Guaitecas, Islas is Chile
89 C1 Guajira, Península de pen. Col.
86 C4 Gualaceo Ecuador
74 A2 Gualala U.S.A.
91 E2 Gualeguay Arg.
91 E2 Gualeguay r. Arg.
91 E2 Gualeguaychu Arg.
91 B4 Gualjaina Arg.
4 F3 Guam terr. Pac. Oc.
88 A6 Guamblin, I. i. Chile
91 D3 Guaminí Arg.
84 A1 Guamúchil Mex.
89 A4 Guamués r. Col.
32 B4 Gua Musang Malaysia
84 A1 Guanacevi Mex.
91 D3 Guanaco, Co h. Arg.
84 B2 Guanajuato Mex.
84 B2 Guanajuato div. Mex.
90 D1 Guanambi Brazil
89 D4 Guaname r. Venez.
89 C2 Guanare Venez.
89 C2 Guanare r. Venez.
89 C2 Guanarito Venez.
89 C2 Guanarito r. Venez.
89 D3 Guanay, Sierra mts Venez.
26 D2 Guandi Shan mt China
83 H4 Guane Cuba
27 C4 Guang'an China
27 D6 Guangdong div. China
27 F4 Guangfeng China
27 D6 Guanghai China
26 B4 Guanghan China
27 E5 Guangchang China
26 B3 Guanghe China
27 E4 Guangji China
26 E2 Guangling China
30 B4 Guanglu Dao i. China
27 B5 Guangnan China
27 D6 Guangning China
26 F2 Guangrao China
26 E4 Guangshan China
26 D4 Guangshui China
27 C6 Guangxi div. China
26 B3 Guangyuan China
27 E5 Guangze China
27 D6 Guangzhou China
90 D2 Guanhães Brazil
90 D2 Guanhães r. Brazil
89 E2 Guanipa r. Venez.
27 B5 Guanling China
26 C4 Guanmian Shan mts China
26 D3 Guanpo China
30 C3 Guanshui China
89 D2 Guanta Venez.
83 J4 Guantánamo Cuba
26 E1 Guanting Sk. resr China
26 B4 Guan Xian China
27 D5 Guanyang China
26 F3 Guanyun China
89 A4 Guapí Col.
86 F6 Guaporé r. Bol./Brazil
86 E7 Guaquí Bol.
90 D1 Guará r. Brazil
87 L5 Guarabira Brazil
90 E3 Guarapari Brazil
88 F3 Guarapuava Brazil
90 C4 Guaraqueçaba Brazil
90 C3 Guaratinguetá Brazil
90 C4 Guaratuba, Baía de b. Brazil
45 C2 Guarda Port.
90 C2 Guarda Mor Brazil
45 D1 Guardo Spain
89 D2 Guárico r. Venez.
89 C3 Guarrojo r. Col.
90 C4 Guarujá Brazil
89 D4 Guasacavi r. Col.
89 C4 Guasacavi, Cerro h. Col.
89 B2 Guasare r. Venez.
82 C3 Guasave Mex.
89 C3 Guasdualito Venez.
84 C2 Guasima Mex.
89 E3 Guasipati Venez.
90 B4 Guassú r. Brazil
82 F6 Guatemala Guatemala
61 J8 Guatemala country Central America
89 D2 Guatope, Parque Nacional nat. park Venez.
91 D3 Guatrache Arg.
89 C4 Guaviare r. Col.
90 C3 Guaxupé Brazil
89 B4 Guayabero r. Col.
89 D3 Guayapo r. Venez.
86 C4 Guayaquil Ecuador
86 B4 Guayaquil, Golfo de g. Ecuador
86 E6 Guayaramerín Bol.
82 B3 Guaymas Mex.
56 D2 Guba Eth.
21 B3 Gubbi India
48 E3 Gubbio Italy
51 F5 Gubkin Rus. Fed.
26 D3 Gucheng China
51 G7 Gudaut'a Georgia
37 M6 Gudbrandsdalen v. Norway
51 H7 Gudermes Rus. Fed.
21 C2 Gudivada India
21 B3 Gudiyattam India
30 E2 Gudong r. China
19 G5 Gudri r. Pak.
16 D1 Güdül Turkey
21 B3 Gudur Andhra Pradesh India
37 K6 Gudvangen Norway
54 A4 Guéckédou Guinea
69 J1 Guéguen, Lac l. Can.
89 B4 Guejar r. Col.
54 C1 Guelma Alg.
54 A2 Guelmine Morocco
69 G4 Guelph Can.
84 C2 Guémez Mex.
42 E5 Guénange France
89 D2 Güera r. Venez.
67 G2 Guérard, Lac l. Can.
44 E3 Guéret France
72 F3 Guernsey U.S.A.
44 C2 Guernsey i. Channel Is U.K.
84 B3 Guerrero div. Mex.
82 B3 Guerrero Negro Mex.
63 M4 Guers, Lac l. Can.
18 D3 Gügerd, Kūh-e mts Iran
96 F5 Guiana Basin sea feature Atl. Ocean
8 B4 Guichen B. b. Austr.
27 E4 Guichi China
91 F2 Guichón Uru.
26 A3 Guide China
55 D4 Guider Cameroon
27 C5 Guiding China
48 E4 Guidonia-Montecelio Italy
54 B4 Guiglo Côte d'Ivoire
42 B5 Guignicourt France
59 K2 Guija Moz.
27 D6 Gui Jiang r. China
27 F4 Guiji Shan mts China
39 G6 Guildford U.K.
81 J2 Guilford U.S.A.
27 D5 Guilin China
66 E2 Guillaume-Delisle, Lac l. Can.
45 B2 Guimarães Port.
31 B4 Guimaras Str. chan. Phil.
26 E3 Guimeng Ding mt China
26 A3 Guinan China
74 A2 Guinda U.S.A.
31 C4 Guindulman Phil.
52 C4 Guinea country Africa
96 J5 Guinea Basin sea feature Atl. Ocean
52 C4 Guinea-Bissau country Africa
53 D5 Guinea, Gulf of g. Africa
83 H4 Güines Cuba
44 C2 Guingamp France
44 B2 Guipavas France
27 D6 Guiping China
90 B2 Guiratinga Brazil
89 E2 Güiria Venez.
42 B5 Guiscard France
42 B5 Guise France
31 C4 Guiuan Phil.
27 E4 Guixi China
27 C6 Gui Xian China
27 C5 Guiyang Guizhou China
27 D5 Guiyang Hunan China
27 C5 Guizhou div. China
22 B5 Gujarat div. India
22 C2 Gujar Khan Pak.
22 C2 Gujranwala Pak.
22 C2 Gujrat Pak.
75 G5 Gu Komelik U.S.A.
51 F5 Gukovo Rus. Fed.
17 K3 Gūk Tappeh Iran
22 D2 Gulabgarh Jammu and Kashmir
26 B2 Gulang China
8 G1 Gulargambone Austr.
21 B2 Gulbarga India
37 U8 Gulbene Latvia
16 E3 Gülek Turkey
77 F6 Gulfport U.S.A.
18 C4 Gulf, The g. Asia
8 G2 Gulgong Austr.
24 E1 Gulian China
27 B5 Gulin China
19 G4 Gulistan Pak.
14 E2 Gulistan Uzbek.
43 K1 Gülitz Ger.
68 E3 Gull I. i. U.S.A.
65 H4 Gull Lake Can.
36 R3 Gullträsk Sweden
16 D3 Gülnar Turkey
19 F3 Gulran Afgh.
51 G7 Gulrip'shi Georgia
16 E2 Gülşehir Turkey
56 D3 Gulu Uganda
22 B3 Gumal r. Pak.
57 C5 Gumare Botswana
18 D2 Gumdag Turkm.
23 F5 Gumia India
23 F5 Gumla India
42 F3 Gummersbach Ger.
16 E1 Gümüşhacıköy Turkey
17 G1 Gümüşhane Turkey
22 D4 Guna India
8 E3 Gunbar Austr.
8 G3 Gundagai Austr.
43 H5 Gundelsheim Ger.
16 D3 Gündoğmuş Turkey
16 B2 Güney Turkey
56 B4 Gungu Congo(Zaire)
51 H7 Gunib Rus. Fed.
65 K4 Gunisao r. Can.
8 H1 Gunnedah Austr.
92 D3 Gunnerus Ridge sea feature Ant.
8 G3 Gunning Austr.
73 F4 Gunnison CO U.S.A.
75 G2 Gunnison UT U.S.A.
73 E4 Gunnison r. U.S.A.
21 B3 Guntakal India
43 J3 Güntersberge Ger.
79 C5 Guntersville U.S.A.
79 C5 Guntersville L. l. U.S.A.
21 C2 Guntur India
33 A2 Gunungsitoli Indon.
32 A5 Gunungtua Indon.
21 C2 Gunupur India
46 E6 Günzburg Ger.
43 J5 Gunzenhausen Ger.
26 E1 Guojiatun China
26 E3 Guoyang China
26 A2 Gurban Hudag China
26 D1 Gurban Obo China
19 F5 Gurdim Iran
16 B2 Güre Turkey
22 D3 Gurgaon India
87 K5 Gurgueia r. Brazil
22 B4 Gurha India
89 E3 Guri, Embalse de resr Venez.
90 C2 Gurinhatã Brazil
51 H7 Gurjaani Georgia
19 E4 Gur Khar Iran
17 J2 Gürpınar Turkey
23 G3 Guru China
57 D5 Guruè Moz.
16 F2 Gürün Turkey
87 J4 Gurupi r. Brazil
22 C4 Guru Sikhar mt India
50 B4 Gur'yevsk Rus. Fed.
54 C3 Gusau Nigeria
43 K2 Güsen Ger.
50 B4 Gusev Rus. Fed.
30 B4 Gushan China
75 H1 Gusher U.S.A.
19 F3 Gushgy Turkm.
26 E3 Gushi China
31 A5 Gusi Malaysia
13 M2 Gusikha Rus. Fed.
50 D4 Gusino Rus. Fed.
13 M4 Gusinoozersk Rus. Fed.
23 F5 Guskara India
50 G4 Gus'-Khrustal'nyy Rus. Fed.
48 C5 Guspini Sardinia Italy
64 B3 Gustavus U.S.A.
43 K3 Güsten Ger.
74 B3 Gustine U.S.A.
43 L1 Güstrow Ger.
23 H3 Gutang China
43 M2 Güterfelde Ger.
43 G3 Gütersloh Ger.
75 H5 Guthrie AZ U.S.A.
78 C4 Guthrie KY U.S.A.
77 D5 Guthrie OK U.S.A.
77 C5 Guthrie TX U.S.A.
27 E5 Gutian Fujian China
27 F5 Gutian Fujian China
42 E5 Gutland reg. Ger./Lux.
23 F3 Gutsuo China
68 B4 Guttenberg U.S.A.
57 D5 Gutu Zimbabwe
23 G4 Guwahati India
17 J3 Guwēr Iraq
43 H3 Guxhagen Ger.
85 E2 Guyana country S. America
26 D1 Guyang China
77 C4 Guymon U.S.A.
18 D4 Gūyom Iran
8 H1 Guyra Austr.
26 E1 Guyuan Hebei China
26 C3 Guyuan Ningxia China
19 G2 Guzar Uzbek.
27 C4 Guzhang China
26 E3 Guzhen China
47 K3 Gvardeysk Rus. Fed.
8 G1 Gwabegar Austr.
19 F5 Gwadar Pak.
19 F5 Gwadar West Bay b. Pak.
22 D4 Gwalior India
57 C6 Gwanda Zimbabwe
19 G4 Gwash Pak.
19 F5 Gwatar Bay b. Pak.
41 C3 Gweebarra Bay b. Rep. of Ireland
41 C2 Gweedore Rep. of Ireland
57 C5 Gweru Zimbabwe
68 D2 Gwinn U.S.A.
55 D3 Gwoza Nigeria
8 H1 Gwydir r. Austr.
23 H3 Gyaca China
26 B3 Gyagartang China
23 F3 Gyangrang China
23 G3 Gyangzê China
23 G3 Gyaring Co l. China
24 B3 Gyaring Hu l. China
49 L6 Gyaros i. Greece
23 H3 Gyarubtang China
12 J2 Gydanskiy Poluostrov pen. Rus. Fed.
23 H3 Gyimda China
23 F3 Gyirong Xizang China
23 F3 Gyirong Xizang China
23 H2 Gyiza China
63 O3 Gyldenløves Fjord in. Greenland
7 F4 Gympie Austr.
47 J7 Gyöngyös Hungary
46 H7 Győr Hungary
65 K4 Gypsumville Can.
67 G2 Gyrfalcon Is i. Can.
49 K6 Gytheio Greece
47 K7 Gyula Hungary
17 J1 Gyumri Armenia
18 E2 Gyzylarbat Turkm.

H

36 T5 Haapajärvi Fin.
36 T4 Haapavesi Fin.
37 S7 Haapsalu Estonia
42 C2 Haarlem Neth.
58 E6 Haarlem S. Africa
43 G3 Haarstrang ridge Ger.
9 B5 Haast N.Z.
19 G5 Hab r. Pak.
Habana see Havana
21 C4 Habarane Sri Lanka
56 D3 Habaswein Kenya
64 F3 Habay Can.
20 C7 Habbān Yemen
17 J5 Habbānīyah Iraq
17 J5 Ḥabbānīyah, Hawr al l. Iraq
19 G5 Hab Chauki Pak.
23 G4 Habiganj Bangl.
26 E1 Habirag China
23 G5 Habra India
89 B5 Hacha Col.
91 B3 Hachado, P. de pass Arg./Chile
29 F8 Hachijō-jima i. Japan
28 G4 Hachinohe Japan
29 F7 Hachiōji Japan
16 F2 Hacıbektaş Turkey
17 H2 Hacıömer Turkey
57 D6 Hacufera Moz.
18 C6 Hadabat al Budū plain S. Arabia
21 A3 Hadagalli India
40 F5 Haddington U.K.
54 D3 Hadejia Nigeria
16 E5 Hadera Israel
37 L9 Haderslev Denmark
20 C6 Ḥaḍhramaut reg. Yemen
16 D3 Hadım Turkey
39 H5 Hadleigh U.K.
62 H2 Hadley Bay b. Can.
30 D6 Hadong S. Korea
16 F6 Ḥadraj, Wādī watercourse S. Arabia
37 M8 Hadsund Denmark
51 E5 Hadyach Ukr.
91 F1 Haedo, Cuchilla de h. Uru.
30 C4 Haeju N. Korea
30 C5 Haeju-man b. N. Korea
30 D6 Haenam S. Korea
59 H1 Haenertsburg S. Africa
18 B4 Hafar al Bāṭin S. Arabia
65 H4 Hafford Can.
16 F2 Hafik Turkey
22 C2 Hafizabad Pak.
23 H4 Hāflong India
36 C4 Hafnarfjörður Iceland
18 C4 Haft Gel Iran
36 B4 Hafursfjörður b. Iceland
69 G2 Hagar Can.
21 B3 Hagari r. India
56 D2 Hagar Nish Plateau plat. Eritrea
42 C4 Hageland reg. Belgium
42 F3 Hagen Ger.
6 E2 Hagen, Mount mt P.N.G.
43 K1 Hagenow Ger.
80 E5 Hagerstown U.S.A.
44 D5 Hagetmau France

37 N6 Hagfors Sweden
29 B7 Hagi Japan
27 B6 Ha Giang Vietnam
39 E5 Hagley U.K.
41 B5 Hag's Head hd Rep. of Ireland
65 H4 Hague Can.
44 D2 Hague, Cap de la pt France
44 H2 Haguenau France
24 G4 Hahajima-rettō is Japan
56 D4 Hai Tanz.
26 E2 Hai r. China
26 F3 Hai'an China
58 B4 Haib watercourse Namibia
30 B3 Haicheng China
43 K5 Haidenaab r. Ger.
27 C6 Hai Dương Vietnam
16 E5 Haifa Israel
16 E5 Haifa, Bay of b. Israel
27 E6 Haifeng China
43 G4 Haiger Ger.
27 D6 Haikang China
27 D6 Haikou China
20 B4 Hā'il S. Arabia
24 D2 Hailar China
69 H2 Haileybury Can.
30 E1 Hailin China
30 C2 Hailong China
39 H7 Hailsham U.K.
36 T4 Hailuoto Fin.
26 F4 Haimen China
27 C7 Hainan div. China
27 D7 Hainan i. China
64 B3 Haines U.S.A.
64 B2 Haines Junction Can.
43 J3 Hainich ridge Ger.
43 M4 Hainichen Ger.
43 J3 Hainleite ridge Ger.
27 C6 Hai Phong Vietnam
26 A2 Hairag China
26 B1 Hairhan Namag China
27 F5 Haitan Dao i. China
61 L8 Haiti country Caribbean Sea
27 C7 Haitou China
75 G5 Haivana Nakya U.S.A.
74 D3 Haiwee Reservoir U.S.A.
26 E2 Haixing China
55 F3 Haiya Sudan
26 A2 Haiyan Qinghai China
27 F4 Haiyan Zhejiang China
30 A5 Haiyang China
30 B4 Haiyang Dao i. China
26 B2 Haiyuan China
26 F3 Haizhou Wan b. China
47 K7 Hajdúböszörmény Hungary
48 C7 Hajeb El Ayoun Tunisia
20 D7 Ḩajhir mt Yemen
28 F5 Hajiki-zaki pt Japan
23 F4 Hajipur India
18 D4 Ḩajjīābād Iran
18 E4 Ḩajjīābād Iran
20 E6 Ḩajmah Oman
23 H5 Haka Myanmar
74 □2 Hakalau U.S.A.
91 C4 Hakelhuincul, Altiplanicie de plat. Arg.
Hakha see Haka
17 J3 Hakkâri Turkey
36 R3 Hakkas Sweden
29 D7 Hakken-zan mt Japan
28 H2 Hako-dake mt Japan
28 G4 Hakodate Japan
58 B1 Hakos Mts mts Namibia
58 D3 Hakseen Pan salt pan S. Africa
29 E6 Hakui Japan
29 E6 Haku-san volc. Japan
29 E6 Haku-san National Park Japan
22 B4 Hala Pak.
Ḩalab see Aleppo
18 B6 Halabān S. Arabia
17 K4 Ḩalabja Iraq
30 C1 Halaha China
30 C1 Halahai China
55 F2 Halaib Sudan
20 E6 Ḩalāniyāt, Juzur al is Oman
74 □2 Halawa U.S.A.
16 F4 Halba Lebanon
24 B2 Halban Mongolia
43 K3 Halberstadt Ger.
31 B3 Halcon, Mt mt Phil.
36 □ Haldarsvik Faroe Is
37 M7 Halden Norway
43 K2 Haldensleben Ger.
23 G5 Haldi r. India
23 G5 Haldia India
23 G4 Haldibari India
22 D3 Haldwani India
69 F3 Hale U.S.A.
17 G4 Halebiye Syria
74 □1 Haleiwa U.S.A.
39 E5 Halesowen U.K.
39 J5 Halesworth U.K.
16 F3 Halfeti Turkey
9 B7 Halfmoon Bay N.Z.
41 C6 Halfway Rep. of Ireland
64 E3 Halfway r. Can.
42 C2 Halfweg Neth.
23 E4 Halia India
69 H3 Haliburton Can.
67 H5 Halifax Can.
38 F4 Halifax U.K.
80 D6 Halifax U.S.A.
40 E2 Halkirk U.K.
36 P5 Hälla Sweden
30 D7 Halla-san mt S. Korea
63 K3 Hall Beach Can.
42 C4 Halle Belgium
42 E3 Halle Neth.
37 O7 Hällefors Sweden
46 F7 Hallein Austria
43 K3 Halle-Neustadt Ger.
43 K3 Halle (Saale) Ger.
92 A5 Hallett, C. c. Ant.
92 C3 Halley U.K. Base Ant.
4 G4 Hall Islands is Micronesia
36 Q4 Hällnäs Sweden
76 D1 Hallock U.S.A.
63 M3 Hall Peninsula pen. Can.
37 O7 Hallsberg Sweden
6 C3 Halls Creek Austr.
69 H3 Halls Lake Can.
42 B4 Halluin France
36 O5 Hallviken Sweden
25 E6 Halmahera i. Indon.
37 N8 Halmstad Sweden
22 C5 Halol India
37 M8 Hals Denmark
36 T5 Halsua Fin.
42 F3 Haltern Ger.
38 E3 Haltwhistle U.K.
18 D5 Ḩālūl i. Qatar
42 F3 Halver Ger.
42 B5 Ham France
29 C7 Hamada Japan
54 B2 Ḩamāda El Ḩaricha des. Mali
18 C3 Hamadān Iran
54 B2 Hamada Tounassine des. Alg.
16 F4 Ḩamāh Syria
28 G3 Hamamasu Japan
29 E7 Hamamatsu Japan
37 M6 Hamar Norway
36 O2 Hamarøy Norway
28 H2 Hamatonbetsu Japan
21 C5 Hambantota Sri Lanka
43 G1 Hambergen Ger.
38 F3 Hambleton Hills h. U.K.
43 H1 Hamburg Ger.
59 G6 Hamburg S. Africa
77 F5 Hamburg AR U.S.A.
80 D3 Hamburg NY U.S.A.
81 F4 Hamburg PA U.S.A.
43 G1 Hamburgisches Wattenmeer, Nationalpark nat. park Ger.
81 G4 Hamden U.S.A.
37 T6 Hämeenlinna Fin.
43 H2 Hameln Ger.
6 B4 Hamersley Range mts Austr.
30 D4 Hamhŭng N. Korea
24 B2 Hami China
18 C4 Ḩamīd Iran
55 F2 Hamid Sudan
8 D4 Hamilton Austr.
83 M2 Hamilton Bermuda
69 H4 Hamilton Can.
9 E2 Hamilton N.Z.
40 D5 Hamilton U.K.
79 C5 Hamilton AL U.S.A.
68 B5 Hamilton IL U.S.A.
72 D2 Hamilton MT U.S.A.
81 F3 Hamilton NY U.S.A.
80 A5 Hamilton OH U.S.A.
74 A2 Hamilton City U.S.A.
74 B3 Hamilton, Mt mt CA U.S.A.
75 E2 Hamilton, Mt mt NV U.S.A.
37 U6 Hamina Fin.
22 D3 Hamirpur India
17 H6 Ḩāmir, W. watercourse S. Arabia
67 J3 Hamiton Inlet in. Can.
30 D4 Hamju N. Korea
8 B3 Hamley Bridge Austr.
68 D3 Hamlin Lake l. U.S.A.
43 F3 Hamm Ger.
54 B2 Hammada du Drâa plat. Alg.
17 J3 Hammam Ali Iraq
48 D6 Hammamet Tunisia
55 D1 Hammamet, Golfe de b. Tunisia
17 L6 Ḩammār, Hawr al l. Iraq
36 P5 Hammarstrand Sweden
43 H4 Hammelburg Ger.
36 O5 Hammerdal Sweden
36 S1 Hammerfest Norway
42 E3 Hamminkeln Ger.
8 B2 Hammond Austr.
68 D5 Hammond IN U.S.A.
77 F6 Hammond LA U.S.A.
72 F2 Hammond MT U.S.A.
69 E3 Hammond Bay b. U.S.A.
80 E3 Hammondsport U.S.A.
81 F5 Hammonton U.S.A.
42 D4 Hamoir Belgium
9 C6 Hampden N.Z.
39 F6 Hampshire Downs h. U.K.
67 G4 Hampton Can.
77 E5 Hampton AR U.S.A.
81 H3 Hampton NH U.S.A.
81 E6 Hampton VA U.S.A.
17 K4 Hamrīn, Jabal h. Iraq
32 C3 Ham Tân Vietnam
22 D2 Hamta Pass pass India
19 E5 Ḩāmūn-e Jaz Mūrīān salt marsh Iran
19 F4 Hāmūn Helmand salt flat Afgh./Iran
19 G4 Hamun-i-Lora l. Pak.
19 F4 Hāmūn Pu marsh Afgh.
17 J2 Hamur Turkey
74 □2 Hana U.S.A.
58 E1 Hanahai watercourse Botswana/Namibia
74 □2 Hanalei U.S.A.
28 G5 Hanamaki Japan
43 G4 Hanau Ger.
26 D3 Hancheng China
80 D5 Hancock MD U.S.A.
68 C2 Hancock MI U.S.A.
81 F4 Hancock NY U.S.A.
40 C2 Handa Island i. U.K.
26 E2 Handan China
56 D4 Handeni Tanz.
74 C3 Hanford U.S.A.
21 A3 Hangal India
24 B2 Hangayn Nuruu mts Mongolia
26 C1 Hanggin Houqi China
26 C2 Hanggin Qi China
42 D4 Han, Grotte de Belgium
26 E2 Hangu China
22 B2 Hangu Pak.
27 D5 Hanguang China
27 F4 Hangzhou China
27 F4 Hangzhou Wan b. China
17 H2 Hanı Turkey
18 C5 Ḩanīdh S. Arabia
26 B2 Hanjiaoshui China
43 J2 Hankensbüttel Ger.
58 F6 Hankey S. Africa
37 S7 Hanko Fin.
75 G2 Hanksville U.S.A.
22 D2 Hanle Jammu and Kashmir
9 D5 Hanmer Springs N.Z.
19 F4 Hanmi Mashkel salt flat Pak.
65 G4 Hanna Can.
66 D3 Hannah Bay b. Can.
68 B6 Hannibal U.S.A.
43 H2 Hannover Ger.
43 H3 Hannoversch Münden Ger.
42 D4 Hannut Belgium
37 O9 Hanöbukten b. Sweden
27 B6 Ha Nôi Vietnam
Hanoi see Ha Nôi
69 G3 Hanover Can.
58 F5 Hanover S. Africa
81 G3 Hanover NH U.S.A.
80 E5 Hanover PA U.S.A.
92 D4 Hansen Mts mts Ant.
27 D4 Hanshou China
26 E4 Han Shui r. China
22 D3 Hansi India
36 Q2 Hansnes Norway
80 B6 Hansonville U.S.A.
37 L8 Hanstholm Denmark
42 E6 Han-sur-Nied France
50 C4 Hantsavichy Belarus
22 C3 Hanumangarh India
8 F3 Hanwood Austr.
27 E4 Hanyang China
26 C3 Hanyin China
27 B4 Hanyuan China
26 C3 Hanzhong China
5 N6 Hao i. Pac. Oc.
23 G5 Hāora India
36 T4 Haparanda Sweden
23 H4 Hāpoli India
67 H3 Happy Valley-Goose Bay Can.
30 E3 Hapsu N. Korea
22 D3 Hapur India
21 C5 Haputale Sri Lanka
18 C5 Ḩaraḑ well S. Arabia
18 C5 Ḩaraḑh S. Arabia
50 D4 Haradok Belarus
29 G6 Haramachi Japan
22 C2 Haramukh mt India
22 C3 Harappa Road Pak.
57 D5 Harare Zimbabwe
24 C2 Har-Ayrag Mongolia
54 A4 Harbel Liberia
24 E2 Harbin China
69 F4 Harbor Beach U.S.A.
68 E3 Harbor Springs U.S.A.
67 J4 Harbour Breton Can.
88 E8 Harbours, B. of b. Falkland Is
75 F5 Harcuvar Mts mts U.S.A.
22 D5 Harda Khās India
37 K6 Hardangervidda plat. Norway
37 K6 Hardangervidda Nasjonalpark nat. park Norway
58 B2 Hardap div. Namibia
58 B2 Hardap Dam dam Namibia
42 E2 Hardenberg Neth.
33 E2 Harden, Bukit mt Indon.
42 D2 Harderwijk Neth.
58 C5 Hardeveld mts S. Africa
43 H5 Hardheim Ger.
72 F2 Hardin U.S.A.
59 H5 Harding S. Africa
65 G4 Hardisty Can.
64 F2 Hardisty Lake l. Can.
22 E4 Hardoi India
81 G2 Hardwick U.S.A.
77 F4 Hardy U.S.A.
68 E4 Hardy Reservoir resr U.S.A.
16 D6 Hareidîn, W. watercourse Egypt
42 B4 Harelbeke Belgium
42 E1 Haren Neth.
42 F2 Haren (Ems) Ger.
56 E3 Hārer Eth.
81 F4 Harford U.S.A.
56 E3 Hargeysa Somalia
47 M7 Harghita-Mădăraş, Vârful mt Romania
17 H2 Harhal D. mts Turkey
26 C2 Harhatan China
24 B3 Har Hu l. China
22 D3 Haridwar India
21 A3 Harihar India
9 C5 Harihari N.Z.
29 D7 Harima-nada b. Japan
23 G5 Haringhat r. Bangl.
42 C3 Haringvliet est. Neth.
19 G3 Hari Rūd r. Afgh./Iran
37 S6 Harjavalta Fin.
76 E3 Harlan IA U.S.A.
80 B6 Harlan KY U.S.A.
39 C5 Harlech U.K.
72 E1 Harlem U.S.A.
39 J5 Harleston U.K.
42 D1 Harlingen Neth.
77 D7 Harlingen U.S.A.
39 H6 Harlow U.K.
72 E2 Harlowtown U.S.A.
42 B5 Harly France
81 J2 Harmony ME U.S.A.
68 A4 Harmony MN U.S.A.
43 J1 Harmsdorf Ger.
22 A3 Harnai Pak.
42 A4 Harnes France
72 B3 Harney Basin basin U.S.A.
72 C3 Harney L. l. U.S.A.
37 P5 Härnösand Sweden
24 E2 Har Nur China
24 B2 Har Nuur l. Mongolia
40 □ Haroldswick U.K.
54 B4 Harper Liberia
74 D4 Harper Lake l. U.S.A.
80 E5 Harpers Ferry U.S.A.
67 H2 Harp Lake l. Can.
43 H1 Harpstedt Ger.
17 G2 Harput Turkey
26 F1 Harqin China
26 F1 Harqin Qi China
75 F5 Harquahala Mts mts U.S.A.
17 G3 Harran Turkey
16 F5 Harrat er Rujeila lava Jordan
66 E3 Harricanaw r. Can.
79 C5 Harriman U.S.A.
81 G3 Harriman Reservoir U.S.A.
81 F5 Harrington U.S.A.
67 J3 Harrington Harbour Can.
40 B3 Harris U.K.
78 B4 Harrisburg IL U.S.A.
80 E4 Harrisburg PA U.S.A.
59 H4 Harrismith S. Africa
77 E4 Harrison AR U.S.A.
68 E3 Harrison MI U.S.A.
62 C2 Harrison Bay b. U.S.A.
80 D5 Harrisonburg U.S.A.
67 J3 Harrison, Cape c. Can.
64 E5 Harrison L. l. Can.
76 E4 Harrisonville U.S.A.
40 A3 Harris, Sound of chan. U.K.
69 F3 Harrisville MI U.S.A.
81 F2 Harrisville NY U.S.A.
80 C5 Harrisville WV U.S.A.
38 F4 Harrogate U.K.
43 H1 Harsefeld Ger.
18 B3 Harsin Iran
16 G1 Harşit r. Turkey
49 M2 Hârşova Romania
36 P2 Harstad Norway
43 H2 Harsum Ger.
68 D4 Hart U.S.A.
30 B2 Hartao China
58 D4 Hartbees watercourse S. Africa
46 G7 Hartberg Austria
37 K6 Harteigan mt Norway
40 E5 Hart Fell h. U.K.
81 G4 Hartford CT U.S.A.
68 D4 Hartford MI U.S.A.
76 D3 Hartford SD U.S.A.
68 C4 Hartford WV U.S.A.
64 E3 Hart Highway Can.
67 G4 Hartland Can.
39 C7 Hartland U.K.
81 J2 Hartland U.S.A.
39 C6 Hartland Point pt U.K.
38 F3 Hartlepool U.K.
77 C5 Hartley U.S.A.
64 D4 Hartley Bay Can.
37 U6 Hartola Fin.
64 E4 Hart Ranges mts Can.
46 E6 Härtsfeld h. Ger.
58 F3 Hartswater S. Africa
79 D5 Hartwell Res. resr U.S.A.
24 B2 Har Us Nuur l. Mongolia
19 F3 Harut watercourse Afgh.
68 C4 Harvard U.S.A.
73 F4 Harvard, Mt mt U.S.A.
81 K2 Harvey Can.
68 D2 Harvey MI U.S.A.
76 C2 Harvey ND U.S.A.
39 J6 Harwich U.K.
22 C3 Haryana div. India
16 F6 Ḩaşāh, Wādī al watercourse Jordan
18 B2 Hasan Iran
22 C2 Hasan Abdal Pak.
16 E2 Hasan Dağı mts Turkey
17 H3 Hasankeyf Turkey
18 E5 Ḩasan Langī Iran
21 B2 Hasanparti India
16 E5 Hasbani r. Lebanon
16 E2 Hasbek Turkey
17 K6 Ḩasb, Sha'īb watercourse Iraq
23 E5 Hasdo r. India
43 F2 Hase r. Ger.
42 F2 Haselünne Ger.
43 J4 Hasenkopf h. Ger.
18 C3 Hashtgerd Iran
18 C2 Hashtpar Iran
77 D5 Haskell U.S.A.
39 G6 Haslemere U.K.
47 M7 Hăşmaşul Mare mt Romania
21 B3 Hassan India
17 K4 Hassan Iraq
75 F5 Hassayampa r. U.S.A.
43 J4 Haßberge reg. Ger.
42 D4 Hasselt Belgium
42 E2 Hasselt Neth.
54 C1 Hassi Messaoud Alg.
37 N8 Hässleholm Sweden
8 E5 Hastings Austr.
9 F3 Hastings N.Z.
39 H7 Hastings U.K.
68 E4 Hastings MI U.S.A.
68 A3 Hastings MN U.S.A.
76 D3 Hastings NE U.S.A.
Hatay see Antakya
75 F3 Hatch U.S.A.
79 E7 Hatchet Bay Bahamas
65 J3 Hatchet Lake l. Can.
79 B5 Hatchie r. U.S.A.
8 D2 Hatfield Austr.
38 G4 Hatfield U.K.
24 C1 Hatgal Mongolia
22 D4 Hathras India
23 F4 Hatia Nepal
32 C3 Ha Tiên Vietnam
32 C1 Ha Tĩnh Vietnam
8 D3 Hattah Austr.
79 F5 Hatteras, Cape c. U.S.A.
36 N4 Hattfjelldal Norway
23 E6 Hatti r. India
79 B6 Hattiesburg U.S.A.
42 F3 Hattingen Ger.
56 E3 Haud reg. Eth.
37 K7 Hauge Norway
37 J7 Haugesund Norway
9 E3 Hauhungaroa mt N.Z.
37 K7 Haukeligrend Norway
36 T4 Haukipudas Fin.
37 V5 Haukivesi l. Fin.
65 H3 Haultain r. Can.
9 E2 Hauraki Gulf g. N.Z.
9 A7 Hauroko, L. l. N.Z.
54 B1 Haut Atlas mts Morocco
67 G4 Hauterive Can.
81 J3 Haut, Isle au i. U.S.A.
54 B1 Hauts Plateaux plat. Alg.
74 □1 Hauula U.S.A.
83 H4 Havana Cuba
68 B5 Havana U.S.A.
39 G7 Havant U.K.
75 E4 Havasu Lake l. U.S.A.
43 L2 Havel r. Ger.
42 D4 Havelange Belgium
43 L2 Havelberg Ger.
43 L2 Havelländisches Luch marsh Ger.
69 J3 Havelock Can.
79 E5 Havelock U.S.A.
9 F3 Havelock North N.Z.
39 C6 Haverfordwest U.K.
81 H3 Haverhill U.S.A.
21 A3 Haveri India
42 D4 Haversin Belgium
42 F3 Havixbeck Ger.
46 G6 Havlíčkův Brod Czech Rep.
36 T1 Havøysund Norway
49 M5 Havran Turkey
72 E1 Havre U.S.A.
67 H4 Havre Aubert, Île du i. Can.
81 E5 Havre de Grace U.S.A.
67 H3 Havre-St-Pierre Can.
49 M4 Havsa Turkey
16 E1 Havza Turkey
74 □2 Hawaii i. U.S.A.
5 K2 Hawaiian Islands is Pac. Oc.
94 H4 Hawaiian Ridge sea feature Pac. Oc.
74 □2 Hawaii Volcanoes National Park U.S.A.
17 L7 Ḩawallī Kuwait
39 D4 Hawarden U.K.
9 B6 Hawea, L. l. N.Z.
9 E3 Hawera N.Z.
38 E3 Hawes U.K.
74 □2 Hawi U.S.A.
40 F5 Hawick U.K.
17 L6 Ḩawīzah, Hawr al l. Iraq
9 B6 Hawkdun Range mts N.Z.
9 F3 Hawke Bay b. N.Z.
67 J3 Hawke Island i. Can.
8 B1 Hawker Austr.
81 F2 Hawkesbury Can.
75 F3 Hawkins Peak summit U.S.A.
69 F3 Hawks U.S.A.
81 K2 Hawkshaw Can.
81 F4 Hawley U.S.A.
17 J5 Ḩawrān, Wādī watercourse Iraq
58 C7 Hawston S. Africa
74 C2 Hawthorne U.S.A.
30 C1 Haxat China
38 F3 Haxby U.K.
8 E3 Hay Austr.
64 F2 Hay r. Can.
68 B3 Hay r. U.S.A.
26 B1 Haya China
28 G5 Hayachine-san mt Japan
18 B2 Haydarābād Iran
75 G5 Hayden AZ U.S.A.
72 C2 Hayden ID U.S.A.
65 L3 Hayes r. Can.
63 M2 Hayes Halvø pen. Greenland
39 B7 Hayle U.K.
16 D2 Haymana Turkey
80 E5 Haymarket U.S.A.
63 J3 Haynes r. Can.
81 J2 Haynesville U.S.A.
39 D5 Hay-on-Wye U.K.
51 C7 Hayrabolu Turkey
64 F2 Hay River Can.
76 D4 Hays U.S.A.
51 D5 Haysyn Ukr.
74 A3 Hayward CA U.S.A.
68 B2 Hayward WV U.S.A.
39 G7 Haywards Heath U.K.
19 G3 Hazarajat reg. Afgh.
80 B6 Hazard U.S.A.
23 F5 Hazāribāg India
23 E5 Hazaribagh Range mts India
42 A4 Hazebrouck France
64 D3 Hazelton Can.
81 F4 Hazelton U.S.A.
62 G2 Hazen Strait chan. Can.
42 C2 Hazerswoude-Rijndijk Neth.
17 G6 Ḩazm al Jalāmid ridge S. Arabia
19 G2 Hazrat Sultan Afgh.
17 H2 Hazro Turkey
41 B4 Headford Rep. of Ireland
74 A2 Healdsburg U.S.A.
8 E4 Healesville Austr.
39 F4 Heanor U.K.
93 J7 Heard Island i. Ind. Ocean
77 D6 Hearne U.S.A.
66 D4 Hearst Can.
92 B2 Hearst I. i. Ant.
39 H7 Heathfield U.K.
81 E6 Heathsville U.S.A.
77 D7 Hebbronville U.S.A.
26 E2 Hebei div. China
77 E5 Heber Springs U.S.A.
26 E3 Hebi China
67 H2 Hebron Can.
68 D5 Hebron IN U.S.A.
76 D3 Hebron NE U.S.A.
81 G3 Hebron NY U.S.A.
16 E6 Hebron West Bank
67 H2 Hebron Fiord in. Can.
62 E4 Hecate Strait B.C. Can.
64 C4 Hecate Strait chan. Can.
84 E2 Hecelchakán Mex.
64 C3 Heceta I. i. U.S.A.
27 C5 Hechi China
27 C4 Hechuan China
37 N5 Hede Sweden
37 O6 Hedemora Sweden
27 D6 Hede Sk. resr China
72 C2 He Devil Mt. mt U.S.A.
68 A5 Hedrick U.S.A.
42 D2 Heeg Neth.
42 F2 Heek Ger.
42 C4 Heer Belgium
42 E2 Heerde Neth.
42 D2 Heerenveen Neth.
42 C2 Heerhugowaard Neth.
42 D4 Heerlen Neth.
Ḩefa see Haifa
26 E4 Hefei China
27 D4 Hefeng China
28 B1 Hegang China
29 E6 Hegura-jima i. Japan
43 K3 Heidberg h. Ger.
46 D3 Heide Ger.
57 B6 Heide Namibia
43 G5 Heidelberg Ger.
59 H3 Heidelberg Gauteng S. Africa
58 D7 Heidelberg Western Cape S. Africa
59 G3 Heilbron S. Africa
43 H5 Heilbronn Ger.
46 E3 Heiligenhafen Ger.
27 □ Hei Ling Chau i. H.K. China
30 E1 Heilongjiang div. China
24 E2 Heilong Jiang r. China/Rus. Fed.
43 J5 Heilsbronn Ger.
36 M5 Heimdal Norway
37 U6 Heinola Fin.
32 A2 Heinze Is is Myanmar
30 B3 Heishan China
42 C3 Heist-op-den-Berg Belgium
26 E2 Hejian China
27 B4 Hejiang China
27 D6 He Jiang r. China
26 D3 Hejin China
16 F2 Hekimhan Turkey
36 D5 Hekla volc. Iceland
26 B2 Hekou Gansu China
27 B6 Hekou Yunnan China
36 N5 Helagsfjället mt Sweden
26 B2 Helan Shan mts China
43 K3 Helbra Ger.
23 H4 Helem India
77 F5 Helena AR U.S.A.
72 E2 Helena MT U.S.A.
74 D3 Helen, Mt mt U.S.A.
40 D4 Helensburgh U.K.
16 E6 Ḩeleẕ Israel
46 C3 Helgoland i. Ger.
46 D3 Helgoländer Bucht b. Ger.
36 C5 Hella Iceland
36 P2 Helland Norway
18 C4 Helleh r. Iran
42 C3 Hellevoetsluis Neth.
36 R2 Helligskogen Norway
45 F3 Hellín Spain
72 C2 Hells Canyon gorge U.S.A.
19 F4 Helmand r. Afgh.
43 K4 Helmbrechts Ger.
43 J3 Helme r. Ger.
57 B6 Helmeringhausen Namibia
58 B6 Helmeringhausen S. Africa
42 D3 Helmond Neth.
40 E2 Helmsdale U.K.
40 E2 Helmsdale r. U.K.
43 K2 Helmstedt Ger.
30 E2 Helong China
75 G2 Helper U.S.A.
37 N8 Helsingborg Sweden
37 N8 Helsingør Denmark
37 T6 Helsinki Fin.
39 B7 Helston U.K.
38 D3 Helvellyn mt U.K.
41 D5 Helvick Head hd Rep. of Ireland
55 F2 Helwân Egypt
39 G6 Hemel Hempstead U.K.
74 D5 Hemet U.S.A.
80 E3 Hemlock Lake l. U.S.A.
43 H2 Hemmingen Ger.
81 G2 Hemmingford Can.
43 H1 Hemmoor Ger.
77 D6 Hempstead U.S.A.
39 J5 Hemsby U.K.
37 Q8 Hemse Sweden
26 A3 Henan Qinghai China
26 D3 Henan div. China
45 E2 Henares r. Spain
28 F4 Henashi-zaki pt Japan
16 C1 Hendek Turkey
91 E3 Henderson Arg.
78 C4 Henderson KY U.S.A.
79 E4 Henderson NC U.S.A.
75 E3 Henderson NV U.S.A.
81 E3 Henderson NY U.S.A.
77 E5 Henderson TX U.S.A.
5 P7 Henderson Island i. Pac. Oc.
79 D5 Hendersonville NC U.S.A.
79 C4 Hendersonville TN U.S.A.
18 C4 Hendījān Iran
39 G6 Hendon U.K.
18 D5 Hendorābī i. Iran
24 B4 Hengduan Shan mts China
42 E2 Hengelo Neth.
27 D5 Hengshan Hunan China
26 C2 Hengshan Shaanxi China
30 F1 Hengshan China
27 D5 Heng Shan mt Hunan China
26 D2 Heng Shan mt China
26 E2 Hengshui China
27 C6 Heng Xian China
27 D5 Hengyang Hunan China
51 E6 Heniches'k Ukr.
9 C6 Henley N.Z.
39 G6 Henley-on-Thames U.K.
81 F5 Henlopen, Cape pt U.S.A.
42 F4 Hennef (Sieg) Ger.
59 G3 Hennenman S. Africa
43 M2 Hennigsdorf Berlin Ger.
81 H3 Henniker U.S.A.
77 D5 Henrietta U.S.A.
66 D2 Henrietta Maria, Cape c. Can.
75 G3 Henrieville U.S.A.
68 C5 Henry U.S.A.
92 B3 Henry Ice Rise ice feature Ant.
63 M3 Henry Kater, C. hd Can.
75 G2 Henry Mts mts U.S.A.
69 G4 Hensall Can.
43 H1 Henstedt-Ulzburg Ger.
57 B6 Hentiesbaai Namibia
8 F3 Henty Austr.
25 B5 Henzada Myanmar
65 H4 Hepburn Can.
27 E5 Heping China
27 C6 Hepu China
26 D2 Hequ China
19 F3 Herāt Afgh.
44 F5 Hérault r. France
65 H4 Herbert Can.
43 G4 Herborn Ger.
43 H4 Herbstein Ger.
92 B4 Hercules Dome ice feature Ant.
42 F3 Herdecke Ger.
43 F4 Herdorf Ger.
39 E5 Hereford U.K.
77 C5 Hereford U.S.A.
5 N6 Héréhérétué i. Pac. Oc.
42 C4 Herent Belgium
43 G2 Herford Ger.
43 J4 Heringen (Werra) Ger.
76 D4 Herington U.S.A.
18 B2 Herīs Iran
46 D7 Herisau Switz.
92 B3 Heritage Ra. mts Ant.
81 F3 Herkimer U.S.A.
43 J3 Herleshausen Ger.
40 □ Herma Ness hd U.K.
43 J2 Hermannsburg Ger.
58 C7 Hermanus S. Africa
59 H5 Hermes, Cape pt S. Africa
8 F1 Hermidale Austr.
72 C2 Hermiston U.S.A.
88 C9 Hermite, Is i. Chile
6 E2 Hermit Is is P.N.G.
Hermon, Mount mt see Sheikh, Jebel esh
91 B2 Hermosa, P. de V. pass Chile
89 B4 Hermosas, Parque Nacional las nat. park Col.
82 B3 Hermosillo Mex.
88 F3 Hernandarias Para.
42 F3 Herne Ger.
39 J6 Herne Bay U.K.
37 L8 Herning Denmark
68 D1 Heron Bay Can.
84 B2 Herradura Mex.
45 D3 Herrera del Duque Spain
84 A1 Herreras Mex.
43 J5 Herrieden Ger.
80 E4 Hershey U.S.A.
39 G6 Hertford U.K.
59 F4 Hertzogville S. Africa
42 D4 Herve Belgium
7 F4 Hervey Bay b. Austr.
5 M6 Hervey Islands is Pac. Oc.
43 L2 Herzberg Brandenburg Ger.
43 M3 Herzberg Brandenburg Ger.
42 F2 Herzlake Ger.
43 J5 Herzogenaurach Ger.
43 L1 Herzsprung Ger.
17 M4 Ḩeşar Iran
42 C4 Hesbaye reg. Belgium
42 F1 Hesel Ger.
27 C6 Heshan China
26 C3 Heshui China
26 D2 Heshun China
74 D4 Hesperia U.S.A.
64 C2 Hess r. Can.
43 J5 Heßdorf Ger.
43 J5 Hesselberg h. Ger.
43 H4 Hessen div. Ger.
43 H3 Hessisch Lichtenau Ger.
27 B6 Het r. Laos
74 B3 Hetch Hetchy Aqueduct canal U.S.A.
42 D3 Heteren Neth.
76 C2 Hettinger U.S.A.
38 E3 Hetton U.K.
43 K3 Hettstedt Ger.
38 E3 Hexham U.K.
26 F4 He Xian Anhui China
27 D5 He Xian Guangxi China
26 B2 Hexibao China
26 E1 Hexigten Qi China
58 C6 Hex River Pass S. Africa
26 D3 Heyang China
18 D4 Ḩeydarābād Iran
19 F4 Ḩeydarābād Iran
38 E3 Heysham U.K.
27 E6 Heyuan China
8 C5 Heywood Austr.
38 E4 Heywood U.K.
68 C5 Heyworth U.S.A.
26 E3 Heze China
27 B5 Hezhang China
26 B3 Hezheng China
26 B3 Hezuozhen China
79 D7 Hialeah U.S.A.
76 E4 Hiawatha U.S.A.
68 A2 Hibbing U.S.A.
79 D5 Hickory U.S.A.
9 G2 Hicks Bay N.Z.
65 K2 Hicks L. l. Can.
80 A4 Hicksville U.S.A.
77 D5 Hico U.S.A.
28 H3 Hidaka-sanmyaku mts Japan
84 C2 Hidalgo div. Mex.
82 C3 Hidalgo del Parral Mex.
82 C3 Hidalgo, Psa M. resr Mex.
90 C2 Hidrolândia Brazil
29 C7 Higashi-Hiroshima Japan
28 G5 Higashine Japan
29 D7 Higashi-ōsaka Japan
29 A8 Higashi-suidō chan. Japan
81 F3 Higgins Bay U.S.A.
68 E3 Higgins Lake l. U.S.A.
High Atlas mts see Haut Atlas
72 B3 High Desert U.S.A.
68 C3 High Falls Reservoir U.S.A.
68 E3 High I. i. U.S.A.
27 □ High Island Res. H.K. China
68 D4 Highland Park U.S.A.
74 C2 Highland Peak summit CA U.S.A.
75 E3 Highland Peak summit NV U.S.A.
64 F3 High Level Can.
23 F5 High Level Canal canal India
79 E5 High Point U.S.A.
64 F3 High Prairie Can.
64 G4 High River Can.
79 E7 High Rock Bahamas
65 J3 Highrock Lake l. Can.
38 E3 High Seat h. U.K.
81 F4 Hightstown U.S.A.
39 G6 High Wycombe U.K.
89 D2 Higuerote Venez.
37 S7 Hiiumaa i. Estonia
20 A4 Hijaz reg. S. Arabia
75 E3 Hiko U.S.A.
29 E7 Hikone Japan
9 G2 Hikurangi mt N.Z.
75 F3 Hildale U.S.A.
43 J4 Hildburghausen Ger.
43 J4 Hilders Ger.
43 H2 Hildesheim Ger.
23 G4 Hili Bangl.
92 B5 Hillary Coast coastal area Ant.
76 D4 Hill City U.S.A.
75 H2 Hill Creek r. U.S.A.
42 C2 Hillegom Neth.
37 N9 Hillerød Denmark
76 D2 Hillsboro ND U.S.A.
81 H3 Hillsboro NH U.S.A.
80 B5 Hillsboro OH U.S.A.
77 D5 Hillsboro TX U.S.A.
68 B4 Hillsboro WV U.S.A.
80 C5 Hillsboro WV U.S.A.
68 E5 Hillsdale MI U.S.A.
81 G3 Hillsdale NY U.S.A.
80 E4 Hillsgrove U.S.A.
40 F4 Hillside U.K.
75 F4 Hillside U.S.A.
8 E2 Hillston Austr.
80 C6 Hillsville U.S.A.
8 H3 Hilltop Austr.
74 □2 Hilo U.S.A.
59 J4 Hilton S. Africa
80 E3 Hilton U.S.A.
69 F2 Hilton Beach Can.
79 D5 Hilton Head Island U.S.A.
17 G3 Hilvan Turkey
42 D2 Hilversum Neth.
22 D3 Himachal Pradesh div. India
10 J6 Himalaya mts Asia
23 F3 Himalchul mt Nepal
36 S4 Himanka Fin.
49 H4 Himarë Albania
22 C5 Himatnagar India
29 D7 Himeji Japan
28 G5 Himekami-dake mt Japan
59 H4 Himeville S. Africa
29 E6 Himi Japan
16 F4 Ḩimş Syria
16 F4 Ḩimş, Baḩrat resr Syria
31 C4 Hinatuan Phil.
6 E3 Hinchinbrook I. i. Austr.
39 F5 Hinckley U.K.
68 A2 Hinckley MN U.S.A.
75 F2 Hinckley UT U.S.A.
81 F3 Hinckley Reservoir U.S.A.
22 D3 Hindan r. India
22 D4 Hindaun India
38 G3 Hinderwell U.K.
17 K5 Hindīyah Barrage Iraq
38 E4 Hindley U.K.
80 B6 Hindman U.S.A.
8 C4 Hindmarsh, L. l. Austr.
23 F5 Hindola India
19 G3 Hindu Kush mts Afgh./Pak.
21 B3 Hindupur India
64 F3 Hines Creek Can.
79 D6 Hinesville U.S.A.
22 D5 Hinganghat India
19 G5 Hinglaj Pak.
19 G5 Hingol r. Pak.
22 D6 Hingoli India
17 H2 Hınıs Turkey
74 D4 Hinkley U.S.A.
36 O2 Hinnøya i. Norway
31 B4 Hinobaan Phil.
45 D3 Hinojosa del Duque Spain
29 C7 Hino-misaki pt Japan
81 G3 Hinsdale U.S.A.
42 F1 Hinte Ger.
64 F4 Hinton Can.
80 C6 Hinton U.S.A.
42 C2 Hippolytushoef Neth.
17 K2 Hirabit Dağ mt Turkey
29 A8 Hirado Japan
29 A8 Hirado-shima i. Japan
23 E5 Hirakud Reservoir India
28 H3 Hiroo Japan
28 G4 Hirosaki Japan
29 C7 Hiroshima Japan
43 K5 Hirschaid Ger.
43 K4 Hirschberg Ger.
46 E7 Hirschberg mt Ger.
44 G2 Hirson France
37 L8 Hirtshals Denmark
17 M3 Hisar Iran
19 G3 Hisar, Koh-i- mts Afgh.
16 D1 Hisarönü Turkey
16 E6 Hisban Jordan
19 H2 Hisor Tajik.
83 K4 Hispaniola i. Caribbean Sea
22 C3 Hissar India
23 F4 Hisua India
17 J5 Hīt Iraq
29 G6 Hitachi Japan
29 G6 Hitachi-ōta Japan
29 B8 Hitoyoshi Japan
36 L5 Hitra i. Norway
43 K1 Hitzacker Ger.
29 C7 Hiuchi-nada b. Japan
5 O5 Hiva Oa i. Pac. Oc.
64 E4 Hixon Can.
17 J2 Hizan Turkey
37 O7 Hjälmaren l. Sweden
65 H2 Hjalmar Lake l. Can.
37 L5 Hjerkinn Norway
37 O7 Hjo Sweden
37 M8 Hjørring Denmark
59 J4 Hlabisa S. Africa
23 F3 Hlako Kangri mt China

59 J3 Hlatikulu Swaziland
51 E5 Hlobyne Ukr.
59 G4 Hlohlowane S. Africa
59 H4 Hlotse Lesotho
59 K4 Hluhluwe S. Africa
51 E5 Hlukhiv Ukr.
47 O4 Hlusha Belarus
50 C4 Hlybokaye Belarus
54 C4 Ho Ghana
57 B6 Hoachanas Namibia
6 E6 Hobart Austr.
77 D5 Hobart U.S.A.
77 C5 Hobbs U.S.A.
92 A4 Hobbs Coast coastal area Ant.
79 D7 Hobe Sound U.S.A.
37 L8 Hobro Denmark
56 E3 Hobyo Somalia
43 H5 Höchberg Ger.
32 C3 Hô Chi Minh Vietnam
46 G7 Hochschwab mt Austria
43 G5 Hockenheim Ger.
80 B5 Hocking r. U.S.A.
22 D4 Hodal India
38 E4 Hodder r. U.K.
39 G6 Hoddesdon U.K.
Hodeida see Al Hudaydah
81 K1 Hodgdon U.S.A.
47 K7 Hódmezővásárhely Hungary
45 J5 Hodna, Chott el salt l. Alg.
30 D4 Hodo dan pt N. Korea
42 C3 Hoek van Holland Neth.
42 D4 Hoensbroek Neth.
30 E2 Hoeryŏng N. Korea
30 D4 Hoeyang N. Korea
43 K4 Hof Ger.
43 J4 Hofheim in Unterfranken Ger.
59 F5 Hofmeyr S. Africa
36 F4 Höfn Iceland
37 P6 Hofors Sweden
36 D4 Hofsjökull ice cap Iceland
29 B7 Hōfu Japan
37 N8 Höganäs Sweden
54 C2 Hoggar plat. Alg.
81 F6 Hog I. i. U.S.A.
37 P8 Högsby Sweden
43 H5 Hohenloher Ebene plain Ger.
43 L3 Hohenmölsen Ger.
43 L2 Hohennauen Ger.
43 K4 Hohenwarte-talsperre resr Ger.
43 H4 Hohe Rhön mts Ger.
46 F7 Hohe Tauern mts Austria
42 E4 Hohe Venn moorland Belgium
26 D1 Hohhot China
23 G2 Hoh Xil Hu salt l. China
23 G2 Hoh Xil Shan mts China
32 D2 Hôi An Vietnam
56 D3 Hoima Uganda
27 B6 Hôi Xuân Vietnam
23 H4 Hojai India
29 C8 Hōjo Japan
9 D1 Hokianga Harbour in. N.Z.
9 C5 Hokitika N.Z.
28 H3 Hokkaidō i. Japan
37 L7 Hokksund Norway
17 K1 Hoktemberyan Armenia
37 L6 Hol Norway
21 B3 Holalkere India
37 M9 Holbæk Denmark
39 H5 Holbeach U.K.
75 G4 Holbrook U.S.A.
68 B3 Holcombe Flowage resr U.S.A.
65 G4 Holden Can.
75 F2 Holden U.S.A.
77 D5 Holdenville U.S.A.
76 D3 Holdrege U.S.A.
21 B3 Hole Narsipur India
83 J4 Holguín Cuba
37 N6 Höljes Sweden
68 D4 Holland U.S.A.
80 D4 Hollidaysburg U.S.A.
64 C3 Hollis AK U.S.A.
77 D5 Hollis OK U.S.A.
74 B3 Hollister U.S.A.
69 F4 Holly U.S.A.
77 F5 Holly Springs U.S.A.
72 D7 Hollywood U.S.A.
36 N4 Holm Norway
62 G2 Holman Can.
36 T2 Holmestrand Finnmark Norway
37 M7 Holmestrand Vestfold Norway
36 R5 Holmön i. Sweden
63 M2 Holms Ø i. Greenland
36 R5 Holmsund Sweden
58 B3 Holoog Namibia
37 L8 Holstebro Denmark
79 D4 Holston r. U.S.A.
80 C6 Holston Lake l. U.S.A.
39 C7 Holsworthy U.K.
39 J5 Holt U.K.
68 E4 Holt U.S.A.
76 E4 Holton U.S.A.
42 D1 Holwerd Neth.
41 D5 Holycross Rep. of Ireland
39 C4 Holyhead U.K.
39 C4 Holyhead Bay b. U.K.
38 F2 Holy Island i. Eng. U.K.
39 C4 Holy Island i. Wales U.K.
81 G3 Holyoke U.S.A.
39 D4 Holywell U.K.
43 L3 Holzhausen Ger.
46 E7 Holzkirchen Ger.
43 H3 Holzminden Ger.
18 C3 Homāyunshahr Iran
43 H3 Homberg (Efze) Ger.
54 B3 Hombori Mali
42 F5 Homburg Ger.
63 M3 Home Bay b. Can.
42 D5 Homécourt France
77 E5 Homer U.S.A.
79 D6 Homerville U.S.A.
79 D7 Homestead U.S.A.
79 C5 Homewood U.S.A.
21 B2 Homnabad India
31 C4 Homonhon pt Phil.
Homs see Ḥimş
51 D4 Homyel' Belarus
21 A3 Honavar India
89 B3 Honda Col.
31 A4 Honda Bay b. Phil.
75 H4 Hon Dah U.S.A.
58 B5 Hondeklipbaai S. Africa
26 C1 Hondlon Ju China
77 D6 Hondo U.S.A.
42 E1 Hondsrug reg. Neth.
61 K8 Honduras country Central America
37 M6 Hønefoss Norway
81 F4 Honesdale U.S.A.
74 B1 Honey Lake l. U.S.A.
81 E3 Honeyoye Lake l. U.S.A.
44 E2 Honfleur France
26 E4 Hong'an China
30 D5 Hongch'ŏn S. Korea
27 C6 Hông Gai Vietnam
27 E6 Honghai Wan b. China
27 B6 Honghe China
26 E3 Hong He r. China
27 D4 Honghu China
27 C5 Hongjiang China
27 E6 Hong Kong China
27 E6 Hong Kong div. China
27 □ Hong Kong Island i. H.K. China
26 C2 Hongliu r. China
26 B2 Hongliuyuan China
32 C3 Hông Ngư Vietnam
27 C6 Hong or Red River, Mouths of the est. Vietnam
27 C7 Hongqizhen China
26 B2 Hongshansi China
30 D2 Hongshi China
27 D6 Hongshui He r. China
27 C6 Hông, Sông r. Vietnam
26 D2 Hongtong China
67 G4 Honguedo, Détroit d' chan. Can.
30 D3 Hongwŏn N. Korea
30 B1 Hongxing China
26 B3 Hongyuan China
26 F3 Hongze China
26 F3 Hongze Hu l. China
7 F2 Honiara Solomon Is
39 D7 Honiton U.K.
28 G5 Honjō Japan
37 S6 Honkajoki Fin.
32 C3 Hon Khoai i. Vietnam
32 D2 Hon Lơn i. Vietnam
32 C1 Hon Mê i. Vietnam
21 A3 Honnali India
36 T1 Honningsvåg Norway
74 □2 Honokaa U.S.A.
74 □1 Honolulu U.S.A.
32 C3 Hon Rai i. Vietnam
29 C7 Honshū i. Japan
72 B2 Hood, Mt volc. U.S.A.
6 B5 Hood Pt pt Austr.
42 E2 Hoogeveen Neth.
42 E1 Hoogezand-Sappemeer Neth.
77 C4 Hooker U.S.A.
41 E5 Hook Head hd Rep. of Ireland
Hook of Holland see Hoek van Holland
64 B3 Hoonah U.S.A.
62 B3 Hooper Bay AK U.S.A.
81 E5 Hooper I. i. U.S.A.
68 D5 Hoopeston U.S.A.
59 F3 Hoopstad S. Africa
37 N9 Höör Sweden
42 D2 Hoorn Neth.
81 G3 Hoosick U.S.A.
75 E3 Hoover Dam dam U.S.A.
80 B4 Hoover Memorial Reservoir U.S.A.
17 H1 Hopa Turkey
81 F4 Hop Bottom U.S.A.
64 E5 Hope B.C. Can.
77 E5 Hope AR U.S.A.
75 F5 Hope AZ U.S.A.
9 D5 Hope r. N.Z.
67 J2 Hopedale Can.
58 C6 Hopefield S. Africa
84 E3 Hopelchén Mex.
67 H3 Hope Mountains Can.
12 D2 Hopen i. Svalbard
62 B3 Hope, Point c. U.S.A.
9 D4 Hope Saddle pass N.Z.
67 G2 Hopes Advance, Baie b. Can.
8 D3 Hopetoun Austr.
58 F4 Hopetown S. Africa
80 E6 Hopewell U.S.A.
66 E2 Hopewell Islands is Can.
6 C4 Hopkins, L. salt flat Austr.
78 C4 Hopkinsville U.S.A.
74 A2 Hopland U.S.A.
72 B2 Hoquiam U.S.A.
26 A3 Hor China
17 L2 Horadiz Azer.
17 J1 Horasan Turkey
37 N9 Hörby Sweden
68 C4 Horeb, Mount U.S.A.
26 B1 Hörh Uul mts Mongolia
68 C4 Horicon U.S.A.
26 D1 Horinger China
94 H6 Horizon Depth depth Pac. Oc.
50 D4 Horki Belarus
92 B4 Horlick Mts mts Ant.
51 F5 Horlivka Ukr.
19 F4 Hormak Iran
18 E5 Hormoz i. Iran
18 E5 Hormuz, Strait of str. Iran/Oman
46 G6 Horn Austria
36 B3 Horn c. Iceland
64 F2 Horn r. Can.
36 P3 Hornavan l. Sweden
77 E6 Hornbeck U.S.A.
43 J2 Hornburg Ger.
88 C9 Horn, Cape c. Chile
39 G4 Horncastle U.K.
37 P6 Horndal Sweden
43 H1 Horneburg Ger.
36 Q5 Hörnefors Sweden
80 E3 Hornell U.S.A.
66 D4 Hornepayne Can.
79 B6 Horn I. i. U.S.A.
46 D6 Hornisgrinde mt Ger.
7 J3 Horn, Îles de is Wallis and Futuna Is
58 B1 Hornkranz Namibia
91 B4 Hornopiren, V. volc. Chile
84 B1 Hornos Mex.
Hornos, Cabo de c. see Horn, Cape
8 H2 Hornsby Austr.
38 G4 Hornsea U.K.
37 P6 Hornslandet pen. Sweden
47 M6 Horodenka Ukr.
51 D5 Horodnya Ukr.
51 C5 Horodok Khmel'nyts'kyy Ukr.
51 B5 Horodok L'viv Ukr.
28 H2 Horokanai Japan
47 M5 Horokhiv Ukr.
28 H3 Horoshiri-dake mt Japan
30 A2 Horqin Shadi reg. China
24 E2 Horqin Youyi Qianqi China
30 A1 Horqin Youyi Zhongqi China
30 B2 Horqin Zuoyi Houqi China
30 B1 Horqin Zuoyi Zhongqi China
39 C7 Horrabridge U.K.
23 G3 Horru China
64 E4 Horsefly Can.
80 E3 Horseheads U.S.A.
67 J3 Horse Is is Can.
41 C4 Horseleap Rep. of Ireland
37 L9 Horsens Denmark
72 C3 Horseshoe Bend U.S.A.
8 D4 Horsham Austr.
39 G6 Horsham U.K.
43 L5 Horšovský Týn Czech Rep.
43 H4 Horst h. Ger.
42 F2 Hörstel Ger.
37 M7 Horten Norway
62 F3 Horton r. Can.
69 F1 Horwood Lake l. Can.
47 N5 Horyn' r. Ukr.
23 H2 Ho Sai Hu l. China
56 D3 Hosa'ina Eth.
43 H4 Hösbach Ger.
21 B3 Hosdurga India
17 L4 Hoseynābād Iran
18 C4 Ḥoseynīyeh Iran
19 F5 Hoshab Pak.
22 D5 Hoshangabad India
22 C3 Hoshiarpur India
21 B3 Hospet India
41 C5 Hospital Rep. of Ireland
91 F1 Hospital, Cuchilla del h. Uru.
88 C9 Hoste, I. i. Chile
36 O5 Hotagen l. Sweden
15 G3 Hotan China
58 E3 Hotazel S. Africa
75 G4 Hotevilla U.S.A.
8 F4 Hotham, Mt mt Austr.
36 P4 Hoting Sweden
77 E5 Hot Springs AR U.S.A.
76 C3 Hot Springs SD U.S.A.
64 F1 Hottah Lake l. Can.
83 K5 Hotte, Massif de la mts Haiti
42 D4 Houffalize Belgium
32 □ Hougang Sing.
68 C2 Houghton U.S.A.
68 E3 Houghton Lake U.S.A.
68 E3 Houghton Lake l. U.S.A.
38 F3 Houghton le Spring U.K.
81 K1 Houlton U.S.A.
26 D3 Houma China
77 F6 Houma U.S.A.
40 C3 Hourn, Loch in. U.K.
81 G3 Housatonic U.S.A.
75 F2 House Range mts U.S.A.
64 D4 Houston Can.
77 F4 Houston MO U.S.A.
77 F5 Houston MS U.S.A.
77 E6 Houston TX U.S.A.
59 H1 Hout r. S. Africa
6 B4 Houtman Abrolhos is Austr.
40 E2 Houton U.K.
58 E5 Houwater S. Africa
24 B2 Hovd Mongolia
39 G7 Hove U.K.
39 J5 Hoveton U.K.
18 C4 Hoveyzeh Iran
37 O8 Hovmantorp Sweden
26 C1 Hövsgöl Mongolia
24 C1 Hövsgöl Nuur l. Mongolia
24 C2 Hövüün Mongolia
68 E4 Howard City U.S.A.
65 H2 Howard Lake l. Can.
38 G4 Howden U.K.
8 G4 Howe, C. hd Austr.
69 F4 Howell U.S.A.
76 C2 Howes U.S.A.
81 G2 Howick Can.
59 J4 Howick S. Africa
8 F4 Howitt, Mt mt Austr.
81 J2 Howland U.S.A.
7 J1 Howland Island i. Pac. Oc.
8 F3 Howlong Austr.
41 E4 Howth Rep. of Ireland
18 D3 Ḥowz-e Dūmatu Iran
18 E4 Ḥowz-e Panj Iran
43 H3 Höxter Ger.
40 E2 Hoy i. U.K.
43 H2 Hoya Ger.
37 K6 Hoyanger Norway
46 G5 Hoyerswerda Ger.
36 N4 Høylandet Norway
43 K3 Hoym Ger.
36 V5 Höytiäinen l. Fin.
17 G2 Hozat Turkey
46 G5 Hradec Králové Czech Rep.
43 M4 Hradiště h. Czech Rep.
49 H3 Hrasnica Bos.-Herz.
17 K1 Hrazdan Armenia
51 E5 Hrebinka Ukr.
50 B4 Hrodna Belarus
27 F6 Hsi-hsu-p'ing Hsü i. Taiwan
27 F5 Hsin-chu Taiwan
27 F5 Hsueh Shan mt Taiwan
27 E5 Hua'an China
89 D4 Huachamacari, Cerro mt Venez.
26 C2 Huachi China
86 C6 Huacho Peru
28 B1 Huachuan China
75 G6 Huachuca City U.S.A.
91 C1 Huaco Arg.
26 D1 Huade China
30 D2 Huadian China
26 E1 Huai'an Hebei China
26 F3 Huai'an Jiangsu China
26 E3 Huaibei China
26 E3 Huaibin China
30 C2 Huaide China
30 C2 Huaidezhen China
26 F3 Huai He r. China
27 C5 Huaihua China
27 D6 Huaiji China
26 E1 Huailai China
27 B7 Huai Luang r. Thai.
26 E3 Huainan China
27 E4 Huaining China
26 D2 Huairen China
26 F3 Huaiyang China
26 F3 Huaiyin China
26 E3 Huaiyuan Anhui China
27 C5 Huaiyuan Guangxi China
26 B3 Huajialing China
84 C3 Huajuápan de León Mex.
25 E7 Huaki Indon.
75 F4 Hualapai Peak summit U.S.A.
27 F5 Hua-lien Taiwan
86 C5 Huallaga r. Peru
26 B2 Hualong China
57 B5 Huambo Angola
28 B1 Huanan China
91 C4 Huancache, Sa mts Arg.
86 C6 Huancayo Peru
26 E2 Huangbizhuang Sk. resr China
26 A2 Huangcheng China
26 E3 Huangchuan China
27 E4 Huanggang China
Huang Hai sea see Yellow Sea
26 E2 Huang He r. China
26 F2 Huanghe Kou est. China
23 H2 Huanghetan China
26 E2 Huanghua China
26 C3 Huangling China
27 C7 Huangliu China
27 E4 Huangmei China
30 D2 Huangnihe China
27 E4 Huangpi China
27 C5 Huangping China
26 D1 Huangqi Hai l. China
27 F4 Huangshan China
27 F4 Huang Shan mt China
27 E4 Huangshi China
26 B2 Huang Shui r. China
26 C2 Huangtu Gaoyuan plat. China
26 F2 Huang Xian China
27 F4 Huangyan China
26 A2 Huangyuan China
27 C5 Huanjiang China
26 C2 Huan Jiang r. China
30 C3 Huanren China
26 F2 Huantai China
86 C5 Huanuco Peru
86 E7 Huanuni Bol.
26 C2 Huan Xian China
27 G5 Hua-p'ing Hsü i. Taiwan
86 C5 Huaráz Peru
86 C6 Huarmey Peru
27 D4 Huarong China
86 C5 Huascaran, Nevado de mt Peru
88 B3 Huasco Chile
88 B3 Huasco r. Chile
30 D2 Huashulinzi China
82 C3 Huatabampo Mex.
26 C3 Huating China
30 A3 Huatong China
84 C3 Huatusco Mex.
84 C2 Huauchinango Mex.
84 C3 Huautla Mex.
27 D6 Hua Xian Guangdong China
26 E3 Hua Xian Henan China
26 D4 Huayuan Hubei China
27 C4 Huayuan Hunan China
27 C4 Huayun China
27 D6 Huazhou China
69 F3 Hubbard Lake l. U.S.A.
64 B2 Hubbard, Mt mt Can./U.S.A.
67 G2 Hubbard, Pointe hd Can.
26 D4 Hubei div. China
21 A3 Hubli India
30 D3 Huch'ang N. Korea
42 E3 Hückelhoven Ger.
39 F4 Hucknall U.K.
38 F4 Huddersfield U.K.
80 B6 Huddy U.S.A.
37 P6 Hudiksvall Sweden
68 E5 Hudson MI U.S.A.
81 G3 Hudson NY U.S.A.
68 A3 Hudson WI U.S.A.
78 F3 Hudson r. U.S.A.
65 J4 Hudson Bay Sask. Can.
63 K4 Hudson Bay b. Can.
81 G3 Hudson Falls U.S.A.
63 Q2 Hudson Land reg. Greenland
92 A3 Hudson Mts mts Ant.
64 E3 Hudson's Hope Can.
63 L3 Hudson Strait str. Can.
32 C1 Huê Vietnam
91 A4 Huechucuicui, Pta pt Chile
82 F5 Huehuetenango Guatemala
84 A1 Huehueto, Cerro mt Mex.
84 C3 Huejotzingo Mex.
84 C2 Huejutla Mex.
45 C4 Huelva Spain
91 B1 Huentelauquén Chile
91 B4 Huequi, Volcán volc. Chile
45 F4 Huércal-Overa Spain
45 F1 Huesca Spain
45 E4 Huéscar Spain
84 B3 Huétamo Mex.
80 E4 Hughesville U.S.A.
23 F5 Hugli est. India
23 G5 Hugli-Chunchura India
77 E5 Hugo U.S.A.
77 C4 Hugoton U.S.A.
26 D2 Huguan China
58 F3 Huhudi S. Africa
27 F5 Hui'an China
26 C2 Hui'anbu China
9 F3 Huiarau Range mts N.Z.
58 B3 Huib-Hoch Plateau plat. Namibia
27 E5 Huichang China
30 D3 Huich'ŏn N. Korea
27 E6 Huidong Guangdong China
27 B5 Huidong Sichuan China
30 D2 Huifa r. China
42 C3 Huijbergen Neth.
26 E3 Huiji r. China
27 E6 Huilai China
89 B4 Huila, Nevado de mt Col.
27 B5 Huili China
84 D3 Huimanguillo Mex.
26 E2 Huimin China
88 C2 Huinahuaca Arg.
30 D2 Huinan China
91 D2 Huinca Renancó Arg.
26 B3 Huining China
27 C5 Huishui China
23 G2 Huiten Nur l. China
27 C5 Huitong China
37 S6 Huittinen Fin.
84 C3 Huitzuco Mex.
26 C3 Hui Xian Gansu China
26 D3 Hui Xian Henan China
84 D4 Huixtla Mex.
27 B5 Huize China
27 E6 Huizhou China
24 C2 Hujirt Mongolia
27 E4 Hukou China
58 D1 Hukuntsi Botswana
68 E2 Hulbert Lake l. U.S.A.
18 B3 Hulilan Iran
28 C2 Hulin China
69 K3 Hull Can.
37 O8 Hultsfred Sweden
30 A3 Huludao China
24 D2 Hulun Nur l. China
51 F6 Hulyaypole Ukr.
24 E1 Huma China
86 F5 Humaitá Brazil
58 F7 Humansdorp S. Africa
18 B5 Humayyān, J. h. S. Arabia
38 H4 Humber, Mouth of the est. U.K.
65 H4 Humboldt Can.
72 C3 Humboldt r. U.S.A.
72 A3 Humboldt Bay b. U.S.A.
74 C1 Humboldt Lake l. U.S.A.
74 C1 Humboldt Range mts U.S.A.
74 D2 Humboldt Salt Marsh marsh U.S.A.
19 E5 Hūmedān Iran
27 D6 Hu Men chan. China
47 K6 Humenné Slovakia
8 F3 Hume Reservoir resr Austr.
74 C3 Humphreys, Mt mt U.S.A.
75 G4 Humphreys Peak summit U.S.A.
30 B3 Hun r. China
36 C4 Húnaflói b. Iceland
27 D5 Hunan div. China
30 F2 Hunchun China
30 F2 Hunchun r. China
43 L3 Hundeluft Ger.
37 M9 Hundested Denmark
49 K2 Hunedoara Romania
43 H4 Hünfeld Ger.
34 G4 Hungary country Europe
6 E4 Hungerford Austr.
30 D4 Hŭngnam N. Korea
72 D1 Hungry Horse Res. resr U.S.A.
27 □ Hung Shui Kiu H.K. China
27 C6 Hưng Yên Vietnam
30 D3 Hunjiang China
30 C3 Hun Jiang r. China
58 B3 Huns Mountains Namibia
42 F5 Hunsrück reg. Ger.
39 H5 Hunstanton U.K.
21 B3 Hunsur India
75 H4 Hunt U.S.A.
43 G2 Hunte r. Ger.
81 F3 Hunter U.S.A.
8 H2 Hunter r. Austr.
64 D4 Hunter I. i. Can.
7 H4 Hunter I. i. New Caledonia
6 E6 Hunter Is is Austr.
23 H6 Hunter's Bay b. Myanmar
9 C6 Hunters Hills, The h. N.Z.
81 F2 Huntingdon Can.
39 G5 Huntingdon U.K.
80 E4 Huntingdon U.S.A.
68 E5 Huntington IN U.S.A.
75 G2 Huntington UT U.S.A.
80 B5 Huntington WV U.S.A.
74 D5 Huntington Beach U.S.A.
9 E2 Huntly N.Z.
40 F3 Huntly U.K.
69 H3 Huntsville Can.
79 C5 Huntsville AL U.S.A.
77 E6 Huntsville TX U.S.A.
26 D2 Hunyuan China
22 C1 Hunza Pak.
22 C2 Hunza r. Pak.
30 B1 Huolin r. China
26 E2 Huolu China
32 C1 Hương Khê Vietnam
32 C1 Hương Thuy Vietnam
6 E2 Huon Peninsula pen. P.N.G.
26 E3 Huoqiu China
26 E4 Huoshan China
26 E4 Huo Shan mt China
27 F6 Huo-shao Tao i. Taiwan
26 D2 Huo Xian China
18 E4 Ḥūr Iran
69 G3 Hurd, Cape hd Can.
26 C1 Hure Jadgai China
30 A2 Hure Qi China
55 F2 Hurghada Egypt
68 C1 Hurkett Can.
41 C5 Hurler's Cross Rep. of Ireland
68 B2 Hurley U.S.A.
76 D2 Huron U.S.A.
68 C2 Huron Bay b. U.S.A.
69 F3 Huron, Lake l. Can./U.S.A.
68 D2 Huron Mts h. U.S.A.
75 F3 Hurricane U.S.A.
39 F6 Hursley U.K.
39 H6 Hurst Green U.K.
9 D5 Hurunui r. N.Z.
36 E3 Húsavík Norðurland eystra Iceland
36 C4 Húsavík Vestfirðir Iceland
47 O7 Huşi Romania
37 O8 Huskvarna Sweden
62 C3 Huslia U.S.A.
37 J7 Husnes Norway
23 F4 Hussainabad India
46 D3 Husum Ger.
36 Q5 Husum Sweden
24 C2 Hutag Mongolia
76 D4 Hutchinson U.S.A.
75 G4 Hutch Mtn mt U.S.A.
32 A1 Huthi Myanmar
28 C2 Hutou China
65 N2 Hut Point pt Can.
80 D5 Huttonsville U.S.A.
26 D2 Hutuo r. China
16 G3 Hüvek Turkey
26 C3 Hu Xian China
26 F4 Huzhou China
26 A2 Huzhu China
36 E4 Hvannadalshnúkur mt Iceland
48 G3 Hvar i. Croatia
51 E6 Hvardiys'ke Ukr.
36 C4 Hveragerði Iceland
37 L8 Hvide Sande Denmark
36 C4 Hvíta r. Iceland
30 E3 Hwadae N. Korea
57 C5 Hwange Zimbabwe
57 C5 Hwange National Park Zimbabwe
30 C4 Hwangju N. Korea
57 D5 Hwedza Zimbabwe
81 H4 Hyannis MA U.S.A.
76 C3 Hyannis NE U.S.A.
24 B2 Hyargas Nuur l. Mongolia
64 C3 Hydaburg U.S.A.
9 C6 Hyde N.Z.
6 B5 Hyden Austr.
80 B6 Hyden U.S.A.
81 G4 Hyde Park U.S.A.
75 F5 Hyder U.S.A.
21 B2 Hyderabad India
22 B4 Hyderabad Pak.
44 H5 Hyères France
44 H5 Hyères, Îles d' is France
30 E3 Hyesan N. Korea
64 D2 Hyland r. Can.
37 J6 Hyllestad Norway
37 N8 Hyltebruk Sweden
8 C4 Hynam Austr.
29 D7 Hyōnosen mt Japan
36 V4 Hyrynsalmi Fin.
64 F3 Hythe Can.
39 J6 Hythe U.K.
29 B8 Hyūga Japan
37 T6 Hyvinkää Fin.

I

86 E6 Iaco r. Brazil
87 K6 Iaçu Brazil
57 E6 Iakora Madag.
49 M2 Ialomiţa r. Romania
49 M2 Ianca Romania
47 N7 Iaşi Romania
31 A3 Iba Phil.
54 C4 Ibadan Nigeria
89 B3 Ibagué Col.
75 F1 Ibapah U.S.A.
86 C3 Ibarra Ecuador
20 B7 Ibb Yemen
43 F2 Ibbenbüren Ger.
32 A4 Ibi Indon.
54 C4 Ibi Nigeria
90 C2 Ibiá Brazil
87 K4 Ibiapaba, Serra da h. Brazil
91 F1 Ibicuí da Cruz r. Brazil
90 E2 Ibiraçu Brazil
45 G3 Ibiza Spain
45 G3 Ibiza i. Balearic Is Spain
48 F6 Iblei, Monti mts Sicily Italy
18 B5 Ibn Buşayyiş well S. Arabia
87 K6 Ibotirama Brazil
20 E5 Ibrā' Oman
20 E5 Ibrī Oman
31 B1 Ibuhos i. Phil.
29 B9 Ibusuki Japan
86 C6 Ica Peru
89 D4 Içana Brazil
89 D4 Içana r. Brazil
75 E3 Iceberg Canyon U.S.A.
16 E3 İçel Turkey
34 C2 Iceland country Europe
21 A2 Ichalkaranji India
21 D2 Ichchapuram India
29 B8 Ichifusa-yama mt Japan
28 G5 Ichinoseki Japan
13 R4 Ichinskaya Sopka mt Rus. Fed.
51 E5 Ichnya Ukr.
30 D4 Ich'ŏn N. Korea
30 D5 Ich'ŏn S. Korea
42 B3 Ichtegem Belgium
43 J4 Ichtershausen Ger.
64 B3 Icy Pt pt U.S.A.
64 B3 Icy Strait chan. U.S.A.
77 E5 Idabel U.S.A.
72 D2 Idaho div. U.S.A.
72 D3 Idaho City U.S.A.
72 D3 Idaho Falls U.S.A.
42 F5 Idar-Oberstein Ger.
55 F2 Idfu Egypt
54 D2 Idhān Awbārī des. Libya
55 D2 Idhān Murzūq des. Libya
56 B4 Idiofa Congo(Zaire)
62 C3 Iditarod U.S.A.
36 S2 Idivuoma Sweden
16 C6 Idku Egypt
16 F4 Idlib Syria
37 N6 Idre Sweden
43 G4 Idstein Ger.
59 H6 Idutywa S. Africa
37 T8 Iecava Latvia
90 B3 Iepê Brazil
42 A4 Ieper Belgium
49 L7 Ierapetra Greece
57 D4 Ifakara Tanz.
57 E6 Ifanadiana Madag.
54 C4 Ife Nigeria
36 U1 Ifjord Norway
33 D2 Igan Malaysia
90 C3 Igarapava Brazil
12 K3 Igarka Rus. Fed.
22 C6 Igatpuri India
17 K2 Iğdır Turkey
37 P6 Iggesund Sweden
48 C5 Iglesias Sardinia Italy
63 K3 Igloolik Can.
66 B4 Ignace Can.
37 U9 Ignalina Lith.
51 C7 İğneada Turkey
49 N4 İğneada Burnu pt Turkey
47 Q3 Igorevskaya Rus. Fed.
49 J5 Igoumenitsa Greece
12 H3 Igrim Rus. Fed.
90 B4 Iguaçu r. Brazil
90 A4 Iguaçu Falls waterfall Arg./Brazil
90 E1 Iguaí Brazil
89 B4 Iguaje, Mesa de h. Col.
84 C3 Iguala Mex.
45 G2 Igualada Spain
90 C4 Iguape Brazil
90 D3 Iguarapé Brazil
90 A3 Iguatemi Brazil
90 A3 Iguatemi r. Brazil
87 L5 Iguatu Brazil
Iguazú, Cataratas do waterfall see Iguaçu Falls
56 A4 Iguéla Gabon
56 D4 Igunga Tanz.
57 E5 Iharaña Madag.
24 C2 Ihbulag Mongolia
57 E6 Ihosy Madag.
30 B2 Ih Tal China
29 F6 Iide-san mt Japan
36 U2 Iijärvi l. Fin.
36 T4 Iijoki r. Fin.
36 U5 Iisalmi Fin.
29 B8 Iizuka Japan
54 C4 Ijebu-Ode Nigeria
17 K1 Ijevan Armenia
42 C2 IJmuiden Neth.
42 D2 IJssel r. Neth.
42 D2 IJsselmeer l. Neth.
37 S6 Ikaalinen Fin.
59 G2 Ikageleng S. Africa
59 G3 Ikageng S. Africa
49 M6 Ikaria i. Greece
37 L8 Ikast Denmark
28 H3 Ikeda Japan
56 C4 Ikela Congo(Zaire)
49 K3 Ikhtiman Bulg.
58 F4 Ikhutseng S. Africa
29 A8 Iki i. Japan
51 H6 Iki-Burul Rus. Fed.
54 C4 Ikom Nigeria
57 E6 Ikongo Madag.
51 H6 Ikryanoye Rus. Fed.
56 D4 Ikungu Tanz.
31 B2 Ilagan Phil.
56 D3 Ilaisamis Kenya
18 B3 Īlām Iran
23 F4 Ilam Nepal
54 C4 Ilaro Nigeria
47 J4 Iława Pol.
65 H3 Île-à-la-Crosse Can.
65 H3 Île-à-la-Crosse, Lac l. Can.
56 C4 Ilebo Congo(Zaire)
56 D3 Ileret Kenya
50 G2 Ileza Rus. Fed.
65 K3 Ilford Can.
39 H6 Ilford U.K.
39 C6 Ilfracombe U.K.
16 D1 Ilgaz Turkey
16 D1 Ilgaz D. mts Turkey
16 C2 Ilgın Turkey
89 D5 Ilha Grande Brazil
90 D3 Ilha Grande, Baía da b. Brazil
90 B3 Ilha Grande, Represa resr Brazil
90 B3 Ilha Solteira, Represa resr Brazil
45 B2 Ílhavo Port.
90 E1 Ilhéus Brazil
54 □ Ilhéus Secos ou do Rombo i. Cape Verde
62 C4 Iliamna Lake l. U.S.A.
16 G2 İliç Turkey
31 C4 Iligan Phil.
31 C4 Iligan Bay b. Phil.
50 H2 Il'insko-Podomskoye Rus. Fed.
81 F3 Ilion U.S.A.
21 B3 Ilkal India
39 F5 Ilkeston U.K.
38 F4 Ilkley U.K.
31 B5 Illana Bay b. Phil.
91 B1 Illapel Chile
91 B1 Illapel r. Chile
46 E7 Iller r. Ger.
51 D6 Illichivs'k Ukr.
86 E7 Illimani, Nevado de mt Bol.
68 C5 Illinois div. U.S.A.
68 C5 Illinois r. U.S.A.
68 B5 Illinois and Mississippi Canal canal U.S.A.
51 D5 Illintsi Ukr.
54 C2 Illizi Alg.
43 K4 Ilm r. Ger.
36 S5 Ilmajoki Fin.
43 J4 Ilmenau Ger.
43 J1 Ilmenau r. Ger.
50 D3 Il'men', Ozero l. Rus. Fed.
39 E7 Ilminster U.K.
86 D7 Ilo Peru
31 A4 Iloc i. Phil.
31 B4 Iloilo Phil.
36 W5 Ilomantsi Fin.
54 C4 Ilorin Nigeria
51 F6 Ilovays'k Ukr.
51 G5 Ilovlya Rus. Fed.
51 H5 Ilovlya r. Rus. Fed.
43 J2 Ilsede Ger.
63 N3 Ilulissat Greenland
29 C7 Imabari Japan
29 F6 Imaichi Japan
17 K6 Imām al Ḥamzah Iraq
16 E3 İmamoğlu Turkey
17 K5 Imām Ḥamīd Iraq
28 D2 Iman r. Rus. Fed.
29 A8 Imari Japan
89 E3 Imataca, Serranía de mts Venez.
37 V6 Imatra Fin.
29 E7 Imazu Japan
88 G3 Imbituba Brazil
90 B4 Imbituva Brazil
50 G3 Imeni Babushkina Rus. Fed.
19 F2 Imeni Chapayeva Turkm.
56 E3 Īmī Eth.
17 M2 İmişli Azer.
30 D6 Imja-do i. S. Korea
30 D4 Imjin r. N. Korea
48 D2 Imola Italy
59 H4 Impendle S. Africa
87 J5 Imperatriz Brazil
48 C3 Imperia Italy
76 C3 Imperial U.S.A.
74 D5 Imperial Beach U.S.A.
75 E5 Imperial Valley v. U.S.A.
56 B3 Impfondo Congo
23 H4 Imphal India
49 L4 İmroz Turkey
16 F5 Imtān Syria
31 A4 Imuruan Bay b. Phil.
29 E7 Ina Japan
86 E6 Inambari r. Peru
54 C2 In Aménas Alg.
9 C4 Inangahua Junction N.Z.
25 F7 Inanwatan Indon.
36 U2 Inari Fin.
36 U2 Inarijärvi l. Fin.
36 T2 Inarijoki r. Fin./Norway
45 H3 Inca Spain
51 C7 İnce Burnu pt Turkey
51 E7 İnce Burnu pt Turkey
16 D3 İncekum Burnu pt Turkey
16 E2 İncesu Turkey
41 E5 Inch Rep. of Ireland
40 C2 Inchard, Loch b. U.K.
40 E4 Inchkeith i. U.K.
30 D5 Inch'ŏn S. Korea
59 K2 Incomati r. Moz.
40 B5 Indaal, Loch in. U.K.
90 D2 Indaiá r. Brazil
90 B2 Indaiá Grande r. Brazil
36 P5 Indalsälven r. Sweden
37 J6 Indalsto Norway
84 A1 Indé Mex.
74 C3 Independence CA U.S.A.
68 B4 Independence IA U.S.A.
77 E4 Independence KS U.S.A.
68 A2 Independence MN U.S.A.
76 E4 Independence MO U.S.A.
80 C6 Independence VA U.S.A.
68 B3 Independence WI U.S.A.
72 C3 Independence Mts U.S.A.
14 D2 Inderborskiy Kazak.
21 B2 Indi India
10 J7 India country Asia
68 D2 Indian r. U.S.A.
80 D4 Indiana U.S.A.
68 D5 Indiana div. U.S.A.
68 D5 Indiana Dunes National Lakeshore res. U.S.A.
93 M7 Indian-Antarctic Basin sea feature Ind. Ocean
93 O7 Indian-Antarctic Ridge sea feature Pac. Oc.
68 D6 Indianapolis U.S.A.
Indian Desert see Thar Desert
67 J3 Indian Harbour Can.
81 F3 Indian Lake NY U.S.A.
68 D3 Indian Lake l. MI U.S.A.
80 B4 Indian Lake l. OH U.S.A.
80 D4 Indian Lake l. PA U.S.A.
76 E3 Indianola IA U.S.A.
77 F5 Indianola MS U.S.A.
75 F2 Indian Peak summit U.S.A.
68 E3 Indian River U.S.A.
75 E3 Indian Springs U.S.A.
75 G4 Indian Wells U.S.A.
13 Q2 Indigirka r. Rus. Fed.
49 J2 Inđija Yugo.
64 F2 Indin Lake l. Can.
74 D5 Indio U.S.A.
7 G3 Indispensable Reefs rf Solomon Is
11 N10 Indonesia country Asia
22 C5 Indore India
33 C4 Indramayu, Tanjung pt Indon.
33 B3 Indrapura Indon.
21 C2 Indravati r. India
44 E3 Indre r. France
Indur see Nizamabad
22 B4 Indus r. Pak.
22 A5 Indus, Mouths of the est. Pak.
59 G5 Indwe S. Africa
51 E7 İnebolu Turkey
16 B1 İnegöl Turkey
80 B6 Inez U.S.A.
58 D7 Infanta, Cape hd S. Africa
84 B3 Infiernillo, L. l. Mex.
68 D3 Ingalls U.S.A.
65 J2 Ingalls Lake l. Can.

56 C4 Kashyukulu Congo(Zaire)
50 G4 Kasimov Rus. Fed.
78 B4 Kaskaskia r. U.S.A.
65 L3 Kaskattama r. Can.
37 R5 Kaskinen Fin.
56 C4 Kasongo Congo(Zaire)
56 B4 Kasongo-Lunda Congo(Zaire)
49 M7 Kasos i. Greece
49 M7 Kasou, Steno chan. Greece
51 H7 Kaspi Georgia
51 H7 Kaspiysk Rus. Fed.
Kaspiyskoye More sea see Caspian Sea
47 P3 Kasplya Rus. Fed.
55 F3 Kassala Sudan
49 K4 Kassandra pen. Greece
49 K4 Kassandras, Kolpos b. Greece
43 H3 Kassel Ger.
54 C1 Kasserine Tunisia
68 A3 Kasson U.S.A.
16 D1 Kastamonu Turkey
42 F4 Kastellaun Ger.
49 K7 Kastelli Greece
42 C3 Kasterlee Belgium
49 J4 Kastoria Greece
50 E4 Kastsyukovichy Belarus
29 E7 Kasugai Japan
56 D4 Kasulu Tanz.
29 D7 Kasumi Japan
29 G6 Kasumiga-ura l. Japan
51 J7 Kasumkent Rus. Fed.
57 D5 Kasungu Malawi
22 C3 Kasur Pak.
81 J2 Katahdin, Mt mt U.S.A.
22 D2 Kataklik Jammu and Kashmir
56 C4 Katako-Kombe Congo(Zaire)
22 D5 Katangi India
6 B5 Katanning Austr.
19 H3 Katawaz Afgh.
56 C4 Katea Congo(Zaire)
49 K4 Katerini Greece
64 C3 Kate's Needle mt Can./U.S.A.
57 D5 Katete Zambia
23 E5 Katghora India
24 B4 Katha Myanmar
6 D3 Katherine r. Austr.
22 B5 Kathiawar pen. India
16 D6 Kathīb el Henu sand dunes Egypt
21 C4 Kathiraveli Sri Lanka
59 H3 Kathlehong S. Africa
23 F4 Kathmandu Nepal
58 E3 Kathu S. Africa
22 C2 Kathua Jammu and Kashmir
54 B3 Kati Mali
23 F4 Katihar India
9 E2 Katikati N.Z.
59 G6 Kati-Kati S. Africa
57 C5 Katima Mulilo Namibia
54 B4 Katiola Côte d'Ivoire
58 D4 Katkop Hills reg. S. Africa
Katmandu see Kathmandu
49 J5 Kato Achaïa Greece
22 D5 Katol India
32 □ Katong Sing.
8 H2 Katoomba Austr.
47 J5 Katowice Pol.
23 G5 Katoya India
37 P7 Katrineholm Sweden
40 D4 Katrine, Loch l. U.K.
54 C3 Katsina Nigeria
54 C4 Katsina-Ala Nigeria
29 G6 Katsuta Japan
29 G7 Katsuura Japan
29 E6 Katsuyama Japan
67 G2 Kattaktoc, Cap hd Can.
19 G2 Kattakurgan Uzbek.
19 G3 Kattasang Hills mts Afgh.
37 M8 Kattegat str. Denmark/Sweden
22 B3 Katuri Pak.
42 C2 Katwijk aan Zee Neth.
43 H5 Katzenbuckel h. Ger.
74 □2 Kauai i. U.S.A.
74 □2 Kauai Channel U.S.A.
43 F4 Kaub Ger.
43 H3 Kaufungen Ger.
37 S5 Kauhajoki Fin.
36 S5 Kauhava Fin.
36 T3 Kaukonen Fin.
74 □2 Kaula i. U.S.A.
74 □2 Kaulakahi Channel U.S.A.
67 H2 Kaumajet Mts mts Can.
74 □2 Kaunakakai U.S.A.
37 S9 Kaunas Lith.
37 U8 Kaunata Latvia
54 C3 Kaura-Namoda Nigeria
27 □ Kau Sai Chau i. H.K. China
36 S5 Kaustinen Fin.
36 S2 Kautokeino Norway
32 A3 Kau-ye Kyun i. Myanmar
49 K4 Kavadarci Macedonia
16 F1 Kavak Turkey
49 L4 Kavala Greece
28 D2 Kavalerovo Rus. Fed.
21 C3 Kavali India
18 D4 Kavār Iran
21 A4 Kavaratti i. India
49 N3 Kavarna Bulg.
21 B4 Kāveri r. India
18 D4 Kavīr des. Iran
18 D3 Kavir salt flat Iran
18 D3 Kavir salt flat Iran
18 D3 Kavir, Dasht-e des. Iran
18 D3 Kavīr-e Hāj Ali Qoli salt l. Iran
19 E3 Kavīr-i-Namak salt flat Iran
29 F7 Kawagoe Japan
29 F7 Kawaguchi Japan
74 □2 Kawaihae U.S.A.
9 E1 Kawakawa N.Z.
57 C4 Kawambwa Zambia
66 E5 Kawartha Lakes l. Can.
29 F7 Kawasaki Japan
9 E2 Kawau I. i. N.Z.
67 G2 Kawawachikamach Can.
9 F3 Kawerau N.Z.
9 E3 Kawhia N.Z.
9 E3 Kawhia Harbour in. N.Z.
74 D3 Kawich Range mts U.S.A.
32 A1 Kawkareik Myanmar
32 A1 Kawludo Myanmar
18 E6 Kawr, J. mt Oman
32 A3 Kawthaung Myanmar
54 B3 Kaya Burkina
16 F2 Kayadibi Turkey
13 M2 Kayak Rus. Fed.
33 E2 Kayan r. Indon.
56 C4 Kayanaza Burundi
21 B4 Kayankulam India
72 F3 Kaycee U.S.A.
57 C4 Kayembe-Mukulu Congo(Zaire)
75 G3 Kayenta U.S.A.
54 A3 Kayes Mali
54 A4 Kayima Sierra Leone
15 F2 Kaynar Kazak.
16 F2 Kaynar Turkey
16 F3 Kaypak Turkey
51 H5 Kaysatskoye Rus. Fed.
16 E2 Kayseri Turkey
33 B3 Kayuagung Indon.
12 K3 Kayyerkan Rus. Fed.
13 P2 Kazach'ye Rus. Fed.
Kazakh see Qazax
14 F1 Kazakskiy Melkosopochnik reg. Kazak.
10 G5 Kazakstan country Asia
50 J4 Kazan' Rus. Fed.
65 K2 Kazan r. Can.
16 D3 Kazancı Turkey
50 J4 Kazanka r. Rus. Fed.
49 L3 Kazanlŭk Bulg.
24 G4 Kazan-rettō is Japan
51 G5 Kazanskaya Rus. Fed.
51 H7 Kazbek mt Georgia/Rus. Fed.
49 M5 Kaz Dağı mts Turkey
18 C4 Kāzerūn Iran
50 J2 Kazhim Rus. Fed.
19 F5 Kazhmak r. Pak.
47 K6 Kazincbarcika Hungary
19 F5 Kazmīr Iran
51 H7 Kazret'i Georgia
51 J5 Kaztalovka Kazak.
28 G4 Kazuno Japan
12 H3 Kazymskiy Mys Rus. Fed.
49 L6 Kea i. Greece
41 E3 Keady U.K.
74 □2 Kealakekua Bay b. U.S.A.
17 M4 K-e-Alvand mt Iran
75 G4 Keams Canyon U.S.A.
76 D3 Kearney U.S.A.
75 G5 Kearny U.S.A.
16 G2 Keban Turkey
16 G2 Keban Barajı resr Turkey
54 A3 Kébémèr Senegal
16 F4 Kebīr r. Lebanon/Syria
55 E3 Kebkabiya Sudan
36 Q3 Kebnekaise mt Sweden
40 B2 Kebock Head hd U.K.
56 E3 K'ebrī Dehar Eth.
33 C4 Kebumen Indon.
64 D3 Kechika r. Can.
16 C3 Keçiborlu Turkey
47 J7 Kecskemét Hungary
17 H1 K'eda Georgia
37 S9 Kėdainiai Lith.
17 L4 K-e Dalakhāni h. Iraq
22 D3 Kedar Kanta mt India
22 D3 Kedarnath Peak mt India
67 G4 Kedgwick Can.
33 D4 Kediri Indon.
54 A3 Kédougou Senegal
64 D2 Keele r. Can.
64 C2 Keele Pk summit Can.
73 C4 Keeler U.S.A.
31 A5 Keenapusan i. Phil.
81 G3 Keene U.S.A.
40 F4 Keen, Mount mt U.K.
8 H1 Keepit Reservoir Austr.
42 C3 Keerbergen Belgium
57 B6 Keetmanshoop Namibia
65 L6 Keewatin Can.
65 L5 Keewatin U.S.A.
49 J5 Kefallonia i. Greece
25 E7 Kefamenanu Indon.
36 B4 Keflavík Iceland
21 C5 Kegalla Sri Lanka
15 F2 Kegen Kazak.
67 G2 Keglo, Baie de b. Can.
51 H6 Kegul'ta Rus. Fed.
37 T7 Kehra Estonia
38 F4 Keighley U.K.
37 T7 Keila Estonia
58 D4 Keimoes S. Africa
36 U5 Keitele Fin.
36 T5 Keitele l. Fin.
8 C4 Keith Austr.
40 F3 Keith U.K.
64 E1 Keith Arm b. Can.
67 G5 Kejimkujik National Park Can.
74 □2 Kekaha U.S.A.
47 K7 Kékes mt Hungary
22 C4 Kekri India
15 F6 Kelai i. Maldives
26 D2 Kelan China
33 B2 Kelang Malaysia
32 B4 Kelantan r. Malaysia
42 E4 Kelberg Ger.
43 K6 Kelheim Ger.
48 D6 Kelibia Tunisia
19 G2 Kelif Turkm.
19 F2 Kelifskiy Uzboy marsh Turkm.
43 G4 Kelkheim (Taunus) Ger.
17 G1 Kelkit Turkey
16 F1 Kelkit r. Turkey
64 E2 Keller Lake l. Can.
80 B4 Kelleys I. i. U.S.A.
72 C2 Kellogg U.S.A.
36 V3 Kelloselkä Fin.
41 E4 Kells Rep. of Ireland
37 S9 Kelmė Lith.
42 E4 Kelmis Belgium
55 D4 Kelo Chad
64 F5 Kelowna Can.
64 D4 Kelsey Bay Can.
74 A2 Kelseyville U.S.A.
40 F5 Kelso U.K.
75 E4 Kelso CA U.S.A.
72 B2 Kelso WA U.S.A.
33 B2 Keluang Malaysia
65 J4 Kelvington Can.
50 E1 Kem' Rus. Fed.
50 E1 Kem' r. Rus. Fed.
17 G2 Kemah Turkey
16 G2 Kemaliye Turkey
49 M5 Kemalpaşa Turkey
64 D4 Kemano Can.
16 C3 Kemer Antalya Turkey
16 B3 Kemer Muğla Turkey
16 B3 Kemer Barajı resr Turkey
24 A1 Kemerovo Rus. Fed.
36 T4 Kemi Fin.
36 U3 Kemijärvi Fin.
36 U3 Kemijärvi l. Fin.
36 T3 Kemijoki r. Fin.
72 E3 Kemmerer U.S.A.
43 K5 Kemnath Ger.
40 F3 Kemnay U.K.
36 T4 Kempele Fin.
42 E3 Kempen Ger.
42 C3 Kempen reg. Belgium
77 D5 Kemp, L. l. U.S.A.
92 D4 Kemp Land reg. Ant.
92 B2 Kemp Pen. pen. Ant.
79 E7 Kemp's Bay Bahamas
46 E7 Kempten (Allgäu) Ger.
66 F4 Kempt, L. l. Can.
59 H3 Kempton Park S. Africa
69 K3 Kemptville Can.
33 D4 Kemujan i. Indon.
22 E4 Ken r. India
62 C3 Kenai U.S.A.
62 C4 Kenai Mts mts U.S.A.
19 F3 Kenar-e-Kapeh Afgh.
38 E3 Kendal U.K.
65 M2 Kendall, Cape hd Can.
68 E5 Kendallville U.S.A.
33 C4 Kendang, Gunung volc. Indon.
25 E7 Kendari Indon.
33 D3 Kendawangan Indon.
55 D3 Kendégué Chad
23 F5 Kendrāparha India
72 C2 Kendrick U.S.A.
75 G4 Kendrick Peak summit U.S.A.
8 G1 Kenebri Austr.
77 D6 Kenedy U.S.A.
54 A4 Kenema Sierra Leone
56 B4 Kenge Congo(Zaire)
25 B4 Kengtung Myanmar
58 D4 Kenhardt S. Africa
54 A3 Kéniéba Mali
54 B1 Kénitra Morocco
26 F2 Kenli China
41 B6 Kenmare Rep. of Ireland
76 C1 Kenmare U.S.A.
41 A6 Kenmare River in. Rep. of Ireland
42 E5 Kenn Ger.
73 G5 Kenna U.S.A.
81 J2 Kennebec r. U.S.A.
81 H3 Kennebunk U.S.A.
81 H3 Kennebunkport U.S.A.
77 F6 Kenner U.S.A.
39 F6 Kennet r. U.K.
77 F4 Kennett U.S.A.
72 C2 Kennewick U.S.A.
69 G1 Kenogami Lake Can.
69 G1 Kenogamissi Lake l. Can.
64 B2 Keno Hill Can.
65 L5 Kenora Can.
68 D4 Kenosha U.S.A.
50 F2 Kenozero, Ozero l. Rus. Fed.
81 G4 Kent CT U.S.A.
77 B6 Kent TX U.S.A.
72 B2 Kent WA U.S.A.
38 E3 Kent r. U.K.
59 H6 Kentani S. Africa
68 D5 Kentland U.S.A.
80 B4 Kenton U.S.A.
80 A6 Kentucky div. U.S.A.
71 K4 Kentucky r. KY U.S.A.
79 B4 Kentucky Lake l. U.S.A.
67 H4 Kentville Can.
77 F6 Kentwood LA U.S.A.
68 E4 Kentwood MI U.S.A.
53 H5 Kenya country Africa
Kenya, Mount mt see Kirinyaga
68 A3 Kenyon U.S.A.
92 B2 Kenyon Pen. pen. Ant.
74 □2 Keokea U.S.A.
68 B5 Keokuk U.S.A.
32 C1 Keo Neua, Col de pass Laos/Vietnam
68 B5 Keosauqua U.S.A.
6 F4 Keppel Bay b. Austr.
32 □ Keppel Harbour chan. Sing.
16 B2 Kepsut Turkey
19 E4 Kerāh Iran
21 A4 Kerala div. India
8 D3 Kerang Austr.
54 C4 Kéran, Parc National de la nat. park Togo
37 T6 Kerava Fin.
45 G4 Kerba Alg.
51 F6 Kerch Ukr.
6 E2 Kerema P.N.G.
64 F5 Keremeos Can.
51 E7 Kerempe Burun pt Turkey
56 D2 Keren Eritrea
18 E2 Kergeli Turkm.
93 J7 Kerguélen i. Ind. Ocean
93 J7 Kerguelen Ridge sea feature Ind. Ocean
56 D4 Kericho Kenya
9 D1 Kerikeri N.Z.
37 V6 Kerimäki Fin.
33 B3 Kerinci, G. volc. Indon.
23 E2 Keriya Shankou pass China
42 E3 Kerken Ger.
19 G2 Kerki Turkm.
19 G2 Kerkichi Turkm.
49 K4 Kerkinitis, Limni l. Greece
49 H5 Kerkyra Greece
Kerkyra i. see Corfu
55 F3 Kerma Sudan
5 K8 Kermadec Islands is N.Z.
94 H8 Kermadec Tr. sea feature Pac. Oc.
18 E4 Kermān Iran
74 B3 Kerman U.S.A.
19 E4 Kermān Desert des. Iran
18 B3 Kermānshāh Iran
18 D4 Kermānshāhān Iran
77 C6 Kermit U.S.A.
73 C5 Kern r. U.S.A.
67 G2 Kernertut, Cap pt Can.
74 C4 Kernville U.S.A.
50 K2 Keros Rus. Fed.
49 L6 Keros i. Greece
54 B4 Kérouané Guinea
42 E4 Kerpen Ger.
92 B5 Kerr, C. c. Ant.
65 H4 Kerrobert Can.
77 D6 Kerrville U.S.A.
41 B5 Kerry Head hd Rep. of Ireland
32 B4 Kerteh Malaysia
37 M9 Kerteminde Denmark
16 D4 Keryneia Cyprus
50 H3 Kerzhenets r. Rus. Fed.
66 D3 Kesagami Lake l. Can.
37 V6 Kesälahti Fin.
51 C7 Keşan Turkey
16 G1 Keşap Turkey
28 G5 Kesennuma Japan
19 H2 Keshem Afgh.
19 G2 Keshendeh-ye Bala Afgh.
22 B5 Keshod India
17 M5 Keshvar Iran
16 D2 Keskin Turkey
50 E2 Keskozero Rus. Fed.
42 E3 Kessel Neth.
59 H4 Kestell S. Africa
36 W4 Kesten'ga Rus. Fed.
36 U4 Kestilä Fin.
69 H3 Keswick Can.
38 D3 Keswick U.K.
46 H7 Keszthely Hungary
12 K4 Ket' r. Rus. Fed.
54 C4 Keta Ghana
32 □ Ketam, P. i. Sing.
33 D3 Ketapang Indon.
64 C3 Ketchikan U.S.A.
42 D2 Ketelmeer l. Neth.
19 G5 Keti Bandar Pak.
39 G5 Kettering U.K.
80 A5 Kettering U.S.A.
64 F5 Kettle r. Can.
68 A2 Kettle r. U.S.A.
80 E4 Kettle Creek r. U.S.A.
74 C3 Kettleman City U.S.A.
72 C1 Kettle River Ra. mts U.S.A.
80 E3 Keuka Lake l. U.S.A.
37 T5 Keuruu Fin.
68 C5 Kewanee U.S.A.
68 D3 Kewaunee U.S.A.
68 C2 Keweenaw Bay b. U.S.A.
68 C2 Keweenaw Peninsula U.S.A.
68 D2 Keweenaw Pt pt U.S.A.
89 E3 Keweigek Guyana
68 F3 Keyano Can.
69 G3 Key Harbour Can.
79 D7 Key Largo U.S.A.
41 C3 Key, Lough l. Rep. of Ireland
39 E6 Keynsham U.K.
80 D5 Keyser U.S.A.
80 D5 Keysers Ridge U.S.A.
75 G6 Keystone Peak summit U.S.A.
80 D6 Keysville U.S.A.
9 A6 Key, The N.Z.
17 M4 Keytū Iran
79 D7 Key West FL U.S.A.
68 B4 Key West IA U.S.A.
81 H3 Kezar Falls U.S.A.
57 C6 Kezi Zimbabwe
47 K6 Kežmarok Slovakia
58 D2 Kgalagadi div. Botswana
59 G2 Kgatleng div. Botswana
58 D1 Kgomofatshe Pan salt pan Botswana
58 F2 Kgoro Pan salt pan Botswana
59 G3 Kgotsong S. Africa
24 F2 Khabarovsk Rus. Fed.
Khabis see Shahdāb
17 H4 Khabur r. Syria
17 J7 Khadd, W. al watercourse S. Arabia
18 B6 Khafs Daghrah S. Arabia
22 E4 Khaga India
23 G5 Khagrachari Bangl.
22 B3 Khairgarh Pak.
22 B4 Khairpur Pak.
19 G2 Khaja du Koh h. Afgh.
22 D4 Khajurāho India
57 C6 Khakhea Botswana
19 G3 Khakīr Afgh.
19 G4 Khak-rēz Afgh.
19 G4 Khakriz reg. Afgh.
19 G2 Khalach Turkm.
18 C4 Khalafabād Iran
18 C3 Khalajestan reg. Iran
22 D2 Khalatse Jammu and Kashmir
22 A3 Khalifat mt Pak.
19 E3 Khalilabad Iran
18 C2 Khalkhāl Iran
23 F6 Khallikot India
50 D4 Khalopyenichy Belarus
24 C1 Khamar-Daban, Khrebet mts Rus. Fed.
22 C5 Khambhat India
22 B5 Khambhat, Gulf of g. India
22 D5 Khamgaon India
32 C1 Khamkkeut Laos
18 B5 Khamma well S. Arabia
21 C2 Khammam India
13 N3 Khamra Rus. Fed.
18 C3 Khamseh reg. Iran
19 H2 Khānābād Afgh.
17 J5 Khān al Baghdādī Iraq
17 K5 Khān al Maḩāwīl Iraq
17 K5 Khān al Mashāhidah Iraq
17 K5 Khān al Muşalla Iraq
21 A3 Khanapur India
18 B2 Khānaqāh Iran
17 K4 Khānaqīn Iraq
17 K2 Khanasur Pass Iran/Turkey
16 F6 Khān az Zabīb Jordan
22 C2 Khanbari Pass pass Jammu and Kashmir
8 G4 Khancoban Austr.
22 B2 Khand Pass Afgh./Pak.
22 D5 Khandwa India
13 P3 Khandyga Rus. Fed.
22 B3 Khanewal Pak.
32 D2 Khanh Dương Vietnam
22 D4 Khaniadhana India
18 D4 Khanīyak Iran
17 K5 Khān Jadwal Iraq
28 C2 Khanka, Lake l. China/Rus. Fed.
Khanka, Ozero l. see Khanka, Lake
22 C2 Khanki Weir barrage Pak.
22 D3 Khanna India
22 B3 Khanpur Pak.
17 K6 Khān Ruḩābah Iraq
16 F4 Khān Shaykhūn Syria
15 F2 Khantau Kazak.
12 L3 Khantayskoye, Ozero l. Rus. Fed.
12 H3 Khanty-Mansiysk Rus. Fed.
16 E6 Khān Yūnis Gaza
32 A3 Khao Chum Thong Thai.
22 D5 Khapa India
18 C3 Khar r. Iran
51 H6 Kharabali Rus. Fed.
23 F5 Kharagpur India
18 E2 Kharakī Iran
19 G4 Kharan Pak.
18 E5 Khārān r. Iran
18 D3 Kharānaq Iran
18 E5 Kharbin Pass Afgh.
22 C6 Khardi India
22 D2 Khardung La pass India
19 F3 Kharez Ilias Afgh.
17 L6 Kharfiyah Iraq
18 C4 Khārg Islands is Iran
22 C5 Khargon India
22 C4 Khari r. Rajasthan India
22 C2 Kharian Pak.
23 E5 Khariar India
18 C6 Kharit S. Arabia
51 F5 Kharkiv Ukr.
Khar'kov see Kharkiv
49 L4 Kharmanli Bulg.
50 G3 Kharovsk Rus. Fed.
23 E5 Kharsia India
55 F3 Khartoum Sudan
18 E2 Khasardag, Gora mt Turkm.
51 H7 Khasav'yurt Rus. Fed.
19 F4 Khash Afgh.
19 F4 Khāsh Iran
19 F4 Khash Desert des. Afgh.
18 C5 Khashm Bijrān h. S. Arabia
19 F4 Khash Rūd r. Afgh.
51 G7 Khashuri Georgia
23 G4 Khāsi Hills h. India
49 L4 Khaskovo Bulg.
13 M2 Khatanga Rus. Fed.
13 M2 Khatanga, Gulf of b. Rus. Fed.
16 D6 Khatmia Pass Egypt
13 T3 Khatyrka Rus. Fed.
18 C4 Khāvar Iran
22 B5 Khavda India
19 H3 Khawak Pass Afgh.
18 E5 Khawr Fakkan U.A.E.
32 A2 Khawsa Myanmar
59 F5 Khayamnandi S. Africa
58 C7 Khayelitsha S. Africa
17 J3 Khāzir r. Iraq
32 C1 Khê Bo Vietnam
21 A2 Khed India
22 C4 Khedbrahma India
19 E3 Khedrī Iran
22 E3 Khela India
45 H4 Khemis Miliana Alg.
54 C1 Khenchela Alg.
54 B1 Khenifra Morocco
18 D4 Kherāmeh Iran
22 D4 Kherli India
18 C4 Khersan r. Iran
51 E6 Kherson Ukr.
18 C4 Khesht Iran
13 L2 Kheta r. Rus. Fed.
18 D4 Kheyrābād Iran
18 D2 Khezerābād Iran
22 D4 Khilchipur India
16 F4 Khirbat Isrīyah Syria
17 J6 Khirr, Wādī al watercourse S. Arabia
22 D2 Khitai P. pass China/Jammu and Kashmir
18 B2 Khīyāv Iran
37 V6 Khiytola Rus. Fed.
51 C5 Khmel'nyts'kyy Ukr.
51 C5 Khmil'nyk Ukr.
18 B2 Khodā Āfarīn Iran
19 G2 Khodzhambass Turkm.
14 D2 Khodzheyli Uzbek.
58 D2 Khokhowe Pan salt pan Botswana
22 B4 Khokhropar Pak.
50 G1 Kholmogory Rus. Fed.
24 G2 Kholmsk Rus. Fed.
47 Q3 Kholm-Zhirkovskiy Rus. Fed.
17 M3 Khoman Iran
58 B1 Khomas div. Namibia
58 A1 Khomas Highland reg. Namibia
18 C3 Khomeyn Iran
17 M4 Khondāb Iran
51 G7 Khoni Georgia
18 D5 Khonj Iran
13 Q3 Khonuu Rus. Fed.
51 G5 Khoper r. Rus. Fed.
24 F2 Khor Rus. Fed.
24 F2 Khor r. Rus. Fed.
22 B4 Khora Pak.
23 F5 Khordha India
18 C5 Khor Duweihin b. S. Arabia/U.A.E.
24 C1 Khorinsk Rus. Fed.
57 B6 Khorixas Namibia
28 C2 Khorol Rus. Fed.
51 E5 Khorol Ukr.
17 L2 Khoroslū Dāgh h. Iran
18 C3 Khorramābād Iran
17 M3 Khorram Darreh Iran
18 C4 Khorramshahr Iran
19 H2 Khorugh Tajik.
19 E3 Khosf Iran
51 H6 Khosheutovo Rus. Fed.
18 C4 Khosravī Iran
18 C4 Khosrowabad Iran
17 K4 Khosrowvī Iran
18 D4 Khowrjān Iran
18 D3 Khowrnag, Kūh-e mt Iran
19 H3 Khowst Afgh.
24 E1 Khrebet Dzhagdy mts Rus. Fed.
23 H5 Khreum Myanmar
23 G4 Khri r. India
50 H2 Khristoforovo Rus. Fed.
13 Q2 Khroma r. Rus. Fed.
14 D1 Khromtau Kazak.
28 D2 Khrustalnyy Rus. Fed.
47 O6 Khrystynivka Ukr.
19 G5 Khude Hills mts Pak.
58 F1 Khudumelapye Botswana
18 B5 Khuff S. Arabia
19 F5 Khūh Lab, Ra's pt Iran
58 D3 Khuis Botswana
14 E2 Khŭjand Tajik.
32 C2 Khu Khan Thai.
19 G3 Khulm r. Afgh.
23 G5 Khulna Bangl.
17 J1 Khulo Georgia
59 G3 Khuma S. Africa
22 C2 Khunjerab Pass China/Jammu and Kashmir
18 C3 Khunsar Iran
23 F5 Khunti India
19 E3 Khūr Iran
22 D4 Khurai India
18 D5 Khūran chan. Iran
19 G3 Khurd, Koh-i- mt Afgh.
22 D3 Khurja India
19 F3 Khurmalik Afgh.
22 C2 Khushab Pak.
17 M3 Khūshāvar Iran
19 E4 Khushk Rud Iran
19 F3 Khuspas Afgh.
51 B5 Khust Ukr.
59 G3 Khutsong S. Africa
19 G5 Khuzdar Pak.
19 F3 Khvāf Iran
50 J4 Khvalynsk Rus. Fed.
18 D3 Khvor Iran
18 E3 Khvord Nārvan Iran
18 C4 Khvormūj Iran
17 L3 Khvosh Maqām Iran
18 B2 Khvoy Iran
50 E3 Khvoynaya Rus. Fed.
32 A2 Khwae Noi r. Thai.
19 F4 Khwaja Ali Afgh.
19 H2 Khwaja Muhammad Range mts Afgh.
22 B2 Khyber Pass Afgh./Pak.
8 H3 Kiama Austr.
31 C5 Kiamba Phil.
56 C4 Kiambi Congo(Zaire)
77 E5 Kiamichi r. U.S.A.
36 V4 Kiantajärvi l. Fin.
18 D2 Kīāseh Iran
22 D2 Kibar India
31 C5 Kibawe Phil.
56 D4 Kibaya Tanz.
57 D4 Kibiti Tanz.
56 C4 Kibombo Congo(Zaire)
56 D4 Kibondo Tanz.
49 J4 Kičevo Macedonia
50 H3 Kichmengskiy Gorodok Rus. Fed.
54 C3 Kidal Mali
39 E5 Kidderminster U.K.
56 D3 Kidepo Valley National Park Uganda
54 A3 Kidira Senegal
22 D2 Kidmang Jammu and Kashmir
9 F3 Kidnappers, Cape c. N.Z.
39 E4 Kidsgrove U.K.
46 E3 Kiel Ger.
68 C4 Kiel U.S.A.
47 K5 Kielce Pol.
38 E2 Kielder Water resr U.K.
46 E3 Kieler Bucht b. Ger.
57 C5 Kienge Congo(Zaire)
42 F3 Kierspe Ger.
51 D5 Kiev Ukr.
54 A3 Kiffa Maur.
49 K5 Kifisia Greece
17 K4 Kifrī Iraq
56 D4 Kigali Rwanda
17 H2 Kiğı Turkey
67 H2 Kiglapait Mts mts Can.
56 C4 Kigoma Tanz.
36 S3 Kihlanki Fin.
37 S5 Kihniö Fin.
36 T4 Kiiminki Fin.
29 D8 Kii-sanchi mts Japan
29 D8 Kii-suidō chan. Japan
49 J2 Kikinda Yugo.
19 F5 Kikki Pak.
50 H3 Kiknur Rus. Fed.
28 G4 Kikonai Japan
57 C4 Kikondja Congo(Zaire)
6 E2 Kikori P.N.G.
6 E2 Kikori r. P.N.G.
56 B4 Kikwit Congo(Zaire)
37 P6 Kilafors Sweden
21 B4 Kilakkarai India
22 D2 Kilar India
74 □2 Kilauea U.S.A.
74 □2 Kilauea Crater crater U.S.A.
40 C5 Kilbrannan Sound chan. U.K.
30 E3 Kilchu N. Korea
41 E4 Kilcoole Rep. of Ireland
41 D4 Kilcormac Rep. of Ireland
41 E4 Kildare Rep. of Ireland
36 X2 Kil'dinstroy Rus. Fed.
56 B4 Kilembe Congo(Zaire)
40 C5 Kilfinan U.K.
77 E5 Kilgore U.S.A.
38 E2 Kilham U.K.
56 D4 Kilifi Kenya
56 D4 Kilimanjaro mt Tanz.
7 F2 Kilinailau Is is P.N.G.
57 D4 Kilindoni Tanz.
37 T7 Kilingi-Nõmme Estonia
16 F3 Kilis Turkey
51 D6 Kiliya Ukr.
41 B5 Kilkee Rep. of Ireland
41 F3 Kilkeel U.K.
41 D5 Kilkenny Rep. of Ireland
39 C7 Kilkhampton U.K.
49 K4 Kilkis Greece
41 B3 Killala Rep. of Ireland
41 B3 Killala Bay b. Rep. of Ireland
41 C5 Killaloe Rep. of Ireland
69 J3 Killaloe Station Can.
65 G4 Killam Can.
69 G3 Killarney Can.
41 B5 Killarney Rep. of Ireland
69 G2 Killarney National Park Can.
41 B6 Killarney National Park Rep. of Ireland
41 B4 Killary Harbour b. Rep. of Ireland
77 D6 Killeen U.S.A.
41 D5 Killenaule Rep. of Ireland
41 C4 Killimor Rep. of Ireland
40 D4 Killin U.K.
41 F3 Killinchy U.K.
41 E5 Killinick Rep. of Ireland
67 H1 Killiniq Can.
67 H1 Killiniq Island i. Can.
41 B5 Killorglin Rep. of Ireland
41 E5 Killurin Rep. of Ireland
41 C3 Killybegs Rep. of Ireland
41 D2 Kilmacrenan Rep. of Ireland
41 B4 Kilmaine Rep. of Ireland
41 C5 Kilmallock Rep. of Ireland
40 B3 Kilmaluag U.K.
40 D5 Kilmarnock U.K.
40 C4 Kilmelford U.K.
50 J3 Kil'mez' Rus. Fed.
50 J3 Kil'mez' r. Rus. Fed.
41 C6 Kilmona Rep. of Ireland
8 E4 Kilmore Austr.
41 E5 Kilmore Quay Rep. of Ireland
56 D4 Kilosa Tanz.
36 R2 Kilpisjärvi Fin.
36 X2 Kilp"yavr Rus. Fed.
41 E3 Kilrea U.K.
41 B5 Kilrush Rep. of Ireland
40 D5 Kilsyth U.K.
21 A4 Kiltān i. India
41 C4 Kiltullagh Rep. of Ireland
57 C4 Kilwa Congo(Zaire)
57 D4 Kilwa Masoko Tanz.
40 D5 Kilwinning U.K.
57 D4 Kimambi Tanz.
56 B4 Kimba Congo
76 C3 Kimball U.S.A.
6 F2 Kimbe P.N.G.
64 F5 Kimberley Can.
58 F4 Kimberley S. Africa
6 C3 Kimberley Plateau plat. Austr.
9 E4 Kimbolton N.Z.
30 E3 Kimch'aek N. Korea
30 E5 Kimch'ŏn S. Korea
37 S6 Kimito Fin.
30 D6 Kimje S. Korea
49 L6 Kimolos i. Greece
50 F4 Kimovsk Rus. Fed.
56 B4 Kimpese Congo(Zaire)
29 F5 Kimpoku-san mt Japan
50 F3 Kimry Rus. Fed.
56 B4 Kimvula Congo(Zaire)
33 E1 Kinabalu, Gunung mt Malaysia
31 A5 Kinabatangan r. Malaysia
49 M6 Kinaros i. Greece
40 E2 Kinbrace U.K.
69 G3 Kincardine Can.
40 E4 Kincardine U.K.
8 D2 Kinchega National Park Austr.
64 D3 Kincolith Can.
57 C4 Kinda Congo(Zaire)
23 H5 Kindat Myanmar
77 E6 Kinder U.S.A.
39 F4 Kinder Scout h. U.K.
65 H4 Kindersley Can.
54 A3 Kindia Guinea
56 C4 Kindu Congo(Zaire)
50 G3 Kineshma Rus. Fed.
6 F4 Kingaroy Austr.
74 B3 King City U.S.A.
92 C1 King Edward Point U.K. Base Ant.
80 E3 King Ferry U.S.A.
81 H2 Kingfield U.S.A.
77 D5 Kingfisher U.S.A.
92 B1 King George I. i. Ant.
66 E2 King George Islands is Can.
64 D4 King I. i. Can.
50 D3 Kingisepp Rus. Fed.
6 E5 King Island i. Austr.
69 H1 King Kirkland Can.
92 D5 King Leopold and Queen Astrid Coast coastal area Ant.
6 C3 King Leopold Ranges h. Austr.
75 E4 Kingman AZ U.S.A.
77 D4 Kingman KS U.S.A.
81 J2 Kingman ME U.S.A.
64 D3 King Mtn mt Can.
92 A3 King Pen. pen. Ant.
41 D5 Kings r. Rep. of Ireland
74 C3 Kings r. U.S.A.
39 D7 Kingsbridge U.K.
74 C3 Kingsburg U.S.A.
81 J2 Kingsbury U.S.A.
74 C3 Kings Canyon National Park U.S.A.
8 A3 Kingscote Austr.
41 E4 Kingscourt Rep. of Ireland
92 B2 King Sejong Korea Base Ant.
68 C3 Kingsford U.S.A.
79 D6 Kingsland GA U.S.A.
68 E5 Kingsland IN U.S.A.
39 H5 King's Lynn U.K.
7 H2 Kingsmill Group is Kiribati
39 H6 Kingsnorth U.K.
6 C3 King Sound b. Austr.
72 E3 Kings Peak summit U.S.A.
80 B6 Kingsport U.S.A.
69 J3 Kingston Can.
83 J5 Kingston Jamaica
9 B6 Kingston N.Z.
68 B6 Kingston IL U.S.A.
81 F4 Kingston NY U.S.A.
75 E4 Kingston Peak summit U.S.A.
8 B4 Kingston South East Austr.
38 G4 Kingston upon Hull U.K.
83 M6 Kingstown St Vincent
77 D7 Kingsville U.S.A.
39 E6 Kingswood U.K.
39 D5 Kington U.K.
40 D3 Kingussie U.K.
63 J3 King William I. i. Can.
59 G6 King William's Town S. Africa
77 E6 Kingwood TX U.S.A.
80 D5 Kingwood WV U.S.A.
65 J4 Kinistino Can.
28 G5 Kinka-san i. Japan
9 B6 Kinloch N.Z.
40 E3 Kinloss U.K.
69 H3 Kinmount Can.
37 N8 Kinna Sweden
41 D4 Kinnegad Rep. of Ireland
21 C4 Kinniyai Sri Lanka
36 T5 Kinnula Fin.
65 J3 Kinoosao Can.
40 E4 Kinross U.K.
41 C6 Kinsale Rep. of Ireland
56 B4 Kinshasa Congo(Zaire)
76 D4 Kinsley U.S.A.
79 E5 Kinston U.S.A.
37 R9 Kintai Lith.
54 B4 Kintampo Ghana
40 F3 Kintore U.K.
40 C5 Kintyre pen. U.K.
40 C5 Kintyre, Mull of hd U.K.
64 F3 Kinuso Can.
55 F4 Kinyeti mt Sudan
43 H4 Kinzig r. Ger.
69 H2 Kiosk Can.
66 E4 Kipawa, Lac l. Can.
81 F6 Kiptopeke U.S.A.
57 C5 Kipushi Congo(Zaire)
7 G3 Kirakira Solomon Is
21 C2 Kirandul India
50 D4 Kirawsk Belarus
43 G2 Kirchdorf Ger.
43 G5 Kirchheim-Bolanden Ger.
24 C1 Kirensk Rus. Fed.
5 L5 Kiribati country Pac. Oc.
17 H1 Kırık Turkey
16 F3 Kırıkhan Turkey
16 D2 Kırıkkale Turkey
50 F3 Kirillov Rus. Fed.
56 D3 Kirinyaga mt Kenya
50 E3 Kirishi Rus. Fed.
29 B9 Kirishima-yama volc. Japan
5 M4 Kiritimati i. Kiribati
16 A2 Kırkağaç Turkey
18 B2 Kirk Bulāg D. mt Iran
39 E4 Kirkby U.K.
39 F4 Kirkby in Ashfield U.K.
38 E3 Kirkby Lonsdale U.K.
38 E3 Kirkby Stephen U.K.
40 E4 Kirkcaldy U.K.
40 C6 Kirkcolm U.K.
41 F3 Kirkcubbin U.K.
40 D6 Kirkcudbright U.K.
37 N6 Kirkenær Norway
36 W2 Kirkenes Norway
69 H3 Kirkfield Can.
40 D5 Kirkintilloch U.K.
37 T6 Kirkkonummi Fin.
75 F4 Kirkland U.S.A.
75 F4 Kirkland Junction U.S.A.
69 G1 Kirkland Lake Can.
51 C7 Kırklareli Turkey
38 C3 Kirk Michael U.K.
38 E3 Kirkoswald U.K.
76 E3 Kirksville U.S.A.
17 K4 Kirkūk Iraq
40 F2 Kirkwall U.K.
59 F6 Kirkwood S. Africa
74 B2 Kirkwood CA U.S.A.
76 F4 Kirkwood MO U.S.A.
16 C1 Kırmır r. Turkey
42 F5 Kirn Ger.
50 E4 Kirov Kaluzh. Obl. Rus. Fed.
Kirov see Vyatka
Kirovabad see Gäncä
50 J3 Kirovo-Chepetsk Rus. Fed.
51 E5 Kirovohrad Ukr.
17 M2 Kirovsk Azer.
50 D3 Kirovsk Leningrad. Rus. Fed.
36 X3 Kirovsk Murmansk. Rus. Fed.
19 F2 Kirovsk Turkm.
50 J3 Kirovskaya Oblast' div. Rus. Fed.
28 C2 Kirovskiy Rus. Fed.
92 B4 Kirpatrick, Mt mt Ant.
18 E2 Kirpili Turkm.
40 E4 Kirriemuir U.K.
50 K3 Kirs Rus. Fed.
50 G4 Kirsanov Rus. Fed.
16 E2 Kırşehir Turkey
19 G5 Kirthar Range mts Pak.
43 H4 Kirtorf Ger.
36 R3 Kiruna Sweden
56 C4 Kirundu Congo(Zaire)
50 H4 Kirya Rus. Fed.
29 F6 Kiryū Japan
37 O8 Kisa Sweden
56 C3 Kisangani Congo(Zaire)

56 B4 Kisantu Congo(Zaire)
33 A2 Kisaran Indon.
24 A1 Kiselevsk Rus. Fed.
23 F4 Kishanganj India
22 B4 Kishangarh Rajasthan India
22 C4 Kishangarh Rajasthan India
22 C2 Kishen Ganga r. India/Pak.
29 B9 Kishika-zaki pt Japan
Kishinev see Chişinău
29 D7 Kishiwada Japan
23 G4 Kishorganj Bangl.
22 C2 Kishtwar Jammu and Kashmir
54 C4 Kisi Nigeria
56 D4 Kisii Kenya
65 K4 Kiskittogisu L. l. Can.
47 J7 Kiskunfélegyháza Hungary
47 J7 Kiskunhalas Hungary
51 G7 Kislovodsk Rus. Fed.
56 E4 Kismaayo Somalia
56 C4 Kisoro Uganda
29 E7 Kiso-sanmyaku mts Japan
54 A4 Kissidougou Guinea
79 D6 Kissimmee U.S.A.
79 D7 Kissimmee, L. l. U.S.A.
65 J3 Kississing L. l. Can.
Kistna r. see Krishna
56 D4 Kisumu Kenya
54 B3 Kita Mali
19 G2 Kitab Uzbek.
29 G6 Kitaibaraki Japan
28 G5 Kitakami Japan
28 G5 Kitakami-gawa r. Japan
29 F6 Kitakata Japan
29 B8 Kita-Kyūshū Japan
56 D3 Kitale Kenya
13 Q5 Kitami Japan
73 G4 Kit Carson U.S.A.
69 G4 Kitchener Can.
36 W5 Kitee Fin.
56 D3 Kitgum Uganda
64 D4 Kitimat Can.
36 U3 Kitinen r. Fin.
56 B4 Kitona Congo(Zaire)
29 B8 Kitsuki Japan
80 D4 Kittanning U.S.A.
81 F4 Kittatinny Mts h. U.S.A.
81 H3 Kittery U.S.A.
36 T3 Kittilä Fin.
79 F4 Kitty Hawk U.S.A.
56 D4 Kitunda Tanz.
64 D3 Kitwanga Can.
57 C5 Kitwe Zambia
46 F7 Kitzbüheler Alpen mts Austria
43 J5 Kitzingen Ger.
43 L3 Kitzscher Ger.
36 U5 Kiuruvesi Fin.
36 T5 Kivijärvi Fin.
37 U7 Kiviõli Estonia
56 C4 Kivu, Lake l. Congo(Zaire)/Rwanda
28 C3 Kiyevka Rus. Fed.
49 N4 Kıyıköy Turkey
12 G4 Kizel Rus. Fed.
50 H2 Kizema Rus. Fed.
16 B3 Kızılca D. mt Turkey
16 D1 Kızılcahamam Turkey
16 G2 Kızıl D. mt Turkey
16 D1 Kızılırmak Turkey
16 D2 Kızılırmak r. Turkey
16 C3 Kızılkaya Turkey
16 D3 Kızılören Turkey
17 H3 Kızıltepe Turkey
51 H7 Kizil"yurt Rus. Fed.
51 H7 Kizlyar Rus. Fed.
18 D2 Kizyl-Atrek Turkm.
19 G2 Kizylayak Turkm.
36 U1 Kjøllefjord Norway
36 P2 Kjøpsvik Norway
46 G5 Kladno Czech Rep.
46 G7 Klagenfurt Austria
75 H4 Klagetoh U.S.A.
37 R9 Klaipėda Lith.
36 □ Klaksvík Faroe Is
72 B3 Klamath r. U.S.A.
72 B3 Klamath Falls U.S.A.
72 B3 Klamath Mts mts U.S.A.
37 N6 Klarälven r. Sweden
46 F6 Klatovy Czech Rep.
58 C5 Klawer S. Africa
64 C3 Klawock U.S.A.
42 E2 Klazienaveen Neth.
64 E4 Kleena Kleene Can.
58 D4 Kleinbegin S. Africa
58 C3 Klein Karas Namibia
58 D6 Klein Roggeveldberg mts S. Africa
58 B4 Kleinsee S. Africa
58 D6 Klein Swartberg mts S. Africa
64 D4 Klemtu Can.
59 G3 Klerksdorp S. Africa
50 E4 Kletnya Rus. Fed.
51 G5 Kletskiy Rus. Fed.
42 E3 Kleve Ger.
58 F6 Klienpoort S. Africa
50 D4 Klimavichy Belarus
51 E4 Klimovo Rus. Fed.
50 F4 Klimovsk Rus. Fed.
50 F3 Klin Rus. Fed.
64 D4 Klinaklini r. Can.
43 H5 Klingenberg am Main Ger.
43 L4 Klingenthal Ger.
43 L1 Klink Ger.
46 F5 Klínovec mt Czech Rep.
37 Q8 Klintehamn Sweden
51 J5 Klintsovka Rus. Fed.
50 E4 Klintsy Rus. Fed.
58 C5 Kliprand S. Africa
48 G2 Ključ Bos.-Herz.
46 H5 Kłodzko Pol.
64 C3 Klondike Gold Rush National History Park U.S.A.
42 E2 Kloosterhaar Neth.
46 H6 Klosterneuburg Austria
43 K2 Klötze (Altmark) Ger.
66 F1 Klotz, Lac l. Can.
64 A2 Kluane Game Sanctuary res. Can.
64 B2 Kluane Lake l. Can.
64 B2 Kluane National Park Can.
46 J5 Kluczbork Pol.
22 B4 Klupro Pak.
50 C4 Klyetsk Belarus
13 S4 Klyuchevskaya Sopka volc. Rus. Fed.
37 O6 Knåda Sweden
38 F3 Knaresborough U.K.
65 L3 Knee Lake l. Can.
43 J5 Knetzgau Ger.
68 B1 Knife Lake l. Can./U.S.A.
64 D4 Knight In. in. Can.
39 D5 Knighton U.K.
68 E6 Knightstown U.S.A.
48 G2 Knin Croatia
46 G7 Knittelfeld Austria
49 K3 Knjaževac Yugo.
41 C4 Knock Rep. of Ireland
41 B6 Knockaboy h. Rep. of Ireland
41 B5 Knockacummer h. Rep. of Ireland
41 C3 Knockalongy h. Rep. of Ireland
41 B5 Knockalough Rep. of Ireland
40 F3 Knock Hill h. U.K.
41 E2 Knocklayd h. U.K.
42 B3 Knokke-Heist Belgium
43 M1 Knorrendorf Ger.
39 F5 Knowle U.K.
92 B2 Knowles, C. c. Ant.
81 J1 Knowles Corner U.S.A.
81 G2 Knowlton Can.
68 D5 Knox U.S.A.
64 C4 Knox, C. c. Can.
92 C6 Knox Coast Ant.
74 A2 Knoxville CA U.S.A.
68 B5 Knoxville IL U.S.A.
79 D4 Knoxville TN U.S.A.
40 C3 Knoydart reg. U.K.
63 N1 Knud Rasmussen Land reg. Greenland
58 E7 Knysna S. Africa
29 B9 Kobayashi Japan
36 V2 Kobbfoss Norway
29 D7 Kōbe Japan
København see Copenhagen
54 B3 Kobenni Maur.
42 F4 Koblenz Ger.
50 J3 Kobra Rus. Fed.
25 F7 Kobroör i. Indon.
50 C4 Kobryn Belarus
51 G7 K'obulet'i Georgia
49 K4 Kočani Macedonia
16 B1 Kocasu r. Turkey
48 F2 Kočevje Slovenia
32 A3 Ko Chan i. Thai.
30 D6 Kŏch'ang S. Korea
30 D6 Koch'ang S. Korea
32 B2 Ko Chang i. Thai.
23 G4 Koch Bihār India
43 H5 Kocher r. Ger.
Kochi see Cochin
29 C8 Kōchi Japan
50 H4 Kochkurovo Rus. Fed.
51 H6 Kochubey Rus. Fed.
51 G6 Kochubeyevskoye Rus. Fed.
21 B4 Kodaikanal India
21 D2 Kodala India
62 C4 Kodiak U.S.A.
62 C4 Kodiak Island i. U.S.A.
59 G1 Kodibeleng Botswana
50 F2 Kodino Rus. Fed.
55 F4 Kodok Sudan
51 G7 Kodori r. Georgia
51 D5 Kodyma Ukr.
49 L4 Kodzhaele mt Bulg./Greece
58 D6 Koedoesberg mts S. Africa
58 D4 Koegrabie S. Africa
58 C5 Koekenaap S. Africa
23 E4 Koel r. India
42 D3 Koersel Belgium
57 B6 Koës Namibia
75 F5 Kofa Mts mts U.S.A.
58 F4 Koffiefontein S. Africa
54 B4 Koforidua Ghana
29 F7 Kōfu Japan
66 E2 Kogaluc r. Can.
66 E2 Kogaluc, Baie de b. Can.
67 H2 Kogaluk r. Can.
37 N9 Køge Denmark
19 G5 Kohan Pak.
22 B2 Kohat Pak.
37 T7 Kohila Estonia
23 H4 Kohima India
22 B3 Kohlu Pak.
19 F3 Kohsan Afgh.
37 U7 Kohtla-Järve Estonia
9 E2 Kohukohunui h. N.Z.
30 D6 Kohŭng S. Korea
29 F6 Koide Japan
64 A2 Koidern Can.
21 B3 Koilkuntla India
30 D3 Koindong N. Korea
17 K3 Koi Sanjaq Iraq
30 E6 Kŏje do i. S. Korea
28 F4 Ko-jima i. Japan
29 F8 Ko-jima i. Japan
32 A1 Kok r. Thai.
81 J2 Kokadjo U.S.A.
14 E3 Kokand Uzbek.
37 R7 Kökar Fin.
19 H2 Kokcha r. Afgh.
37 R6 Kokemäenjoki r. Fin.
58 C4 Kokerboom Namibia
47 O3 Kokhanava Belarus
50 G3 Kokhma Rus. Fed.
21 C4 Kokkilai Sri Lanka
36 S5 Kokkola Fin.
74 □1 Koko Hd hd U.S.A.
68 D5 Kokomo U.S.A.
58 E2 Kokong Botswana
59 G3 Kokosi S. Africa
15 G2 Kokpekty Kazak.
30 D4 Koksan N. Korea
50 H3 Koksharka Rus. Fed.
14 E1 Kokshetau Kazak.
67 G2 Koksoak r. Can.
59 H5 Kokstad S. Africa
32 B3 Ko Kut i. Thai.
36 X2 Kola Rus. Fed.
Kolab r. see Sābari
19 G5 Kolachi r. Pak.
22 C2 Kolahoi mt India
25 E7 Kolaka Indon.
32 A4 Ko Lanta Thai.
32 A4 Ko Lanta i. Thai.
12 E3 Kola Peninsula pen. Rus. Fed.
21 B3 Kolar Karnataka India
22 E6 Kolar Madhya Pradesh India
22 D4 Kolaras India
21 B3 Kolar Gold Fields India
36 S3 Kolari Fin.
22 C4 Kolayat India
50 F3 Kol'chugino Rus. Fed.
54 A3 Kolda Senegal
37 L9 Kolding Denmark
56 C3 Kole Haute-Zaïre Congo(Zaire)
56 C4 Kole Kasai-Oriental Congo(Zaire)
45 H4 Koléa Alg.
36 R4 Koler Sweden
12 F3 Kolguyev, O. i. Rus. Fed.
23 F5 Kolhan reg. India
21 A2 Kolhapur India
32 A4 Ko Libong i. Thai.
37 S7 Kõljala Estonia
37 S8 Kolkasrags pt Latvia
19 H2 Kolkhozobod Tajik.
Kollam see Quilon
21 B3 Kollegal India
21 C2 Kolleru L. l. India
42 E1 Kollum Neth.
Köln see Cologne
46 G3 Kołobrzeg Pol.
50 H3 Kologriv Rus. Fed.
54 B3 Kolokani Mali
7 F2 Kolombangara i. Solomon Is
50 F4 Kolomna Rus. Fed.
51 C5 Kolomyya Ukr.
54 B3 Kolondiéba Mali
6 C2 Kolonedale Indon.
58 D3 Kolonkwane Botswana
12 K4 Kolpashevo Rus. Fed.
51 F4 Kolpny Rus. Fed.
Kol'skiy Poluostrov pen. see Kola Peninsula
20 B7 Koluli Eritrea
21 A2 Kolvan India
36 M4 Kolvereid Norway
36 T1 Kolvik Norway
19 G5 Kolwa reg. Pak.
57 C5 Kolwezi Congo(Zaire)
13 R3 Kolyma r. Rus. Fed.
13 R3 Kolymskaya Nizmennost' lowland Rus. Fed.
13 R3 Kolymskiy, Khrebet mts Rus. Fed.
50 H4 Kolyshley Rus. Fed.
49 K3 Kom mt Bulg.
28 G3 Komaga-take volc. Japan
58 B4 Komaggas S. Africa
58 B4 Komaggas Mts mts S. Africa
13 S4 Komandorskiye Ostrova is Rus. Fed.
46 J7 Komárno Slovakia
59 J2 Komatipoort S. Africa
29 E6 Komatsu Japan
29 D7 Komatsushima Japan
56 C4 Kombe Congo(Zaire)
54 B3 Kombissiri Burkina
33 B3 Komering r. Indon.
59 G6 Komga S. Africa
51 D6 Kominternivs'ke Ukr.
50 J2 Komi, Respublika div. Rus. Fed.
48 G3 Komiža Croatia
49 H1 Komló Hungary
19 F2 Kommuna Turkm.
56 B4 Komono Congo
29 F6 Komoro Japan
49 L4 Komotini Greece
58 D6 Komsberg mts S. Africa
14 E1 Komsomolets Kazak.
13 L1 Komsomolets, O. i. Rus. Fed.
50 G3 Komsomol'sk Rus. Fed.
19 F2 Komsomol'sk Turkm.
51 E5 Komsomol's'k Ukr.
51 H6 Komsomol'skiy Kalmykiya Rus. Fed.
50 H4 Komsomol'skiy Mordov. Rus. Fed.
24 F1 Komsomol'sk-na-Amure Rus. Fed.
12 H3 Komsonol'skiy Rus. Fed.
17 J1 Kömürlü Turkey
75 F6 Kom Vo U.S.A.
50 F3 Konakovo Rus. Fed.
23 F5 Konar Res. resr India
22 D4 Konch India
23 E6 Kondagaon India
69 J2 Kondiaronk, Lac l. Can.
56 D4 Kondoa Tanz.
50 E2 Kondopoga Rus. Fed.
50 E4 Kondrovo Rus. Fed.
63 P3 Kong Christian IX Land reg. Greenland
60 P2 Kong Christian X Land reg. Greenland
63 O3 Kong Frederik VI Kyst reg. Greenland
60 Q2 Kong Frederik VIII Land reg. Greenland
92 C2 Kong Håkon VII Hav sea Ant.
30 D5 Kongju S. Korea
12 D2 Kong Karl's Land is Svalbard
33 E2 Kongkemul mt Indon.
56 C4 Kongolo Congo(Zaire)
63 Q2 Kong Oscar Fjord in. Greenland
54 B3 Kongoussi Burkina
37 L7 Kongsberg Norway
37 N6 Kongsvinger Norway
32 C2 Kông, T. r. Cambodia
56 D4 Kongwa Tanz.
63 Q2 Kong Wilhelm Land reg. Greenland
32 C2 Kong, Xé r. Laos
43 K4 Königsee Ger.
42 F4 Königswinter Ger.
46 J4 Konin Pol.
24 F1 Konin r. Rus. Fed.
49 G3 Konjic Bos.-Herz.
58 B3 Konkiep watercourse Namibia
54 B3 Konna Mali
43 K3 Könnern Ger.
36 U5 Konnevesi Fin.
50 G2 Konosha Rus. Fed.
29 F6 Kōnosu Japan
51 E5 Konotop Ukr.
32 D2 Kon Plong Vietnam
43 L5 Konstantinovy Lázně Czech Rep.
46 D7 Konstanz Ger.
54 C3 Kontagora Nigeria
36 V5 Kontiolahti Fin.
36 U4 Konttila Fin.
32 C2 Kon Tum Vietnam
32 D2 Kontum, Plateau du plat. Vietnam
16 D3 Konya Turkey
42 E5 Konz Ger.
74 □1 Koolau Range mts U.S.A.
8 E3 Koondrook Austr.
80 D5 Koon Lake l. U.S.A.
8 G3 Koorawatha Austr.
72 C2 Kooskia U.S.A.
64 F5 Kootenay r. Can./U.S.A.
64 F5 Kootenay L. l. Can.
64 F4 Kootenay Nat. Park Can.
58 D5 Kootjieskolk S. Africa
51 H6 Kopanovka Rus. Fed.
22 C6 Kopargaon India
36 E3 Kópasker Iceland
48 E2 Koper Slovenia
18 E2 Kopet Dag, Khrebet mts Turkm.
32 B3 Ko Phangan i. Thai.
32 A3 Ko Phra Thong i. Thai.
32 A4 Ko Phuket i. Thai.
37 P7 Köping Sweden
36 O5 Köpmanholmen Sweden
59 F2 Kopong Botswana
21 B3 Koppal India
37 M6 Koppang Norway
37 O7 Kopparberg Sweden
59 G3 Koppies S. Africa
58 D3 Koppieskraalpan salt pan S. Africa
48 G1 Koprivnica Croatia
16 C3 Köprü r. Turkey
18 D4 Kor watercourse Iran
50 G4 Korablino Rus. Fed.
19 G5 Korak Pak.
66 E1 Korak, Baie b. Can.
21 B2 Korangal India
19 G5 Korangi Pak.
21 C2 Koraput India
Korat see Nakhon Ratchasima
23 E5 Korba India
48 D6 Korba Tunisia
43 G3 Korbach Ger.
32 B4 Korbu, Gunung mt Malaysia
49 J4 Korçë Albania
48 G3 Korčula Croatia
48 G3 Korčula i. Croatia
48 G3 Korčulanski Kanal chan. Croatia
17 M4 Kord Khvord Iran
18 D2 Kord Küy Iran
19 F5 Kords reg. Iran
18 D4 Kord Sheykh Iran
30 B4 Korea Bay g. China/N. Korea
11 O5 Korea, North country Asia
11 O6 Korea, South country Asia
29 A7 Korea Strait str. Japan/S. Korea
21 A2 Koregaon India
51 F6 Korenovsk Rus. Fed.
51 C5 Korets' Ukr.
16 B1 Körfez Turkey
92 B3 Korff Ice Rise ice feature Ant.
36 N3 Korgen Norway
54 B4 Korhogo Côte d'Ivoire
22 B5 Kori Creek in. India
49 K5 Korinthiakos Kolpos chan. Greece
49 K6 Korinthos Greece
46 H7 Kőris-hegy mt Hungary
49 J3 Koritnik mt Albania
29 G6 Kōriyama Japan
16 C3 Korkuteli Turkey
16 D4 Kormakitis, Cape c. Cyprus
46 H7 Körmend Hungary
54 B4 Koro Côte d'Ivoire
54 B3 Koro Mali
7 H3 Koro i. Fiji
51 F5 Korocha Rus. Fed.
16 D1 Köroğlu Dağları mts Turkey
16 D1 Köroğlu Tepesi mt Turkey
56 D4 Korogwe Tanz.
8 D5 Koroit Austr.
8 D4 Korong Vale Austr.
49 K4 Koronia, L. l. Greece
7 H3 Koro Sea b. Fiji
51 D5 Korosten' Ukr.
51 D5 Korostyshiv Ukr.
55 D3 Koro Toro Chad
37 T5 Korpilahti Fin.
37 R6 Korpo Fin.
24 G2 Korsakov Rus. Fed.
50 J3 Korshik Rus. Fed.
36 R5 Korsnäs Fin.
37 M9 Korsør Denmark
51 D5 Korsun'-Shevchenkivs'kyy Ukr.
47 K3 Korsze Pol.
36 S5 Kortesjärvi Fin.
50 J2 Kortkeros Rus. Fed.
42 B4 Kortrijk Belgium
50 G3 Kortsovo Rus. Fed.
8 E5 Korumburra Austr.
54 D4 Korup, Parc National de nat. park Cameroon
36 U3 Korvala Fin.
22 D4 Korwai India
24 H1 Koryakskaya Sopka volc. Rus. Fed.
13 S3 Koryakskiy Khrebet mts Rus. Fed.
50 H2 Koryazhma Rus. Fed.
30 E6 Koryŏng S. Korea
51 E5 Koryukivka Ukr.
49 M6 Kos i. Greece
32 B3 Ko Samui i. Thai.
30 D4 Kosan N. Korea
46 H4 Kościan Pol.
77 F5 Kosciusko U.S.A.
64 C3 Kosciusko I. i. U.S.A.
8 G4 Kosciusko, Mt mt Austr.
8 G4 Kosciusko National Park Austr.
17 G1 Köse Turkey
16 F1 Köse Dağı mt Turkey
21 B2 Kosgi India
15 G2 Kosh-Agach Rus. Fed.
29 A9 Koshikijima-rettō is Japan
19 F3 Koshkak Iran
19 F3 Koshk-e-Kohneh Afgh.
68 C4 Koshkoning, Lake l. U.S.A.
18 D1 Koshoba Turkm.
19 G1 Koshrabad Uzbek.
22 D4 Kosi India
22 D3 Kosi r. India
59 K3 Kosi Bay b. S. Africa
47 K6 Košice Slovakia
21 B3 Kosigi India
36 R3 Koskullskule Sweden
50 J2 Koslan Rus. Fed.
30 E4 Kosŏng N. Korea
30 E3 Kosŏng-ni N. Korea
49 J3 Kosovo div. Yugo.
49 J3 Kosovska Mitrovica Yugo.
4 H4 Kosrae i. Micronesia
43 K5 Kösseine h. Ger.
54 B4 Kossou, Lac de l. Côte d'Ivoire
49 K3 Kostenets Bulg.
59 G2 Koster S. Africa
55 F3 Kosti Sudan
49 K3 Kostinbrod Bulg.
12 K3 Kostino Rus. Fed.
50 D1 Kostomuksha Rus. Fed.
51 C5 Kostopil' Ukr.
50 G3 Kostroma Rus. Fed.
50 G3 Kostroma r. Rus. Fed.
50 G3 Kostromskaya Oblast' div. Rus. Fed.
46 G4 Kostrzyn Pol.
51 F5 Kostyantynivka Ukr.
46 H3 Koszalin Pol.
46 H7 Kőszeg Hungary
23 E5 Kota Madhya Pradesh India
22 C4 Kota Rajasthan India
33 B4 Kotaagung Indon.
22 C4 Kota Barrage barrage India
33 D3 Kotabaru Indon.
33 E3 Kotabaru Indon.
33 B1 Kota Bharu Malaysia
33 B3 Kotabumi Indon.
22 C4 Kota Dam dam India
33 E1 Kota Kinabalu Malaysia
32 A3 Ko Tao i. Thai.
21 C2 Kotaparh India
32 B5 Kotapinang Indon.
22 C4 Kotari r. India
33 B2 Kota Tinggi Malaysia
50 J3 Kotel'nich Rus. Fed.
51 G6 Kotel'nikovo Rus. Fed.
13 P2 Kotel'nyy, O. i. Rus. Fed.
22 D3 Kotgarh India
43 K3 Köthen (Anhalt) Ger.
22 E4 Kothi India
37 U6 Kotka Fin.
22 C3 Kot Kapura India
50 H2 Kotlas Rus. Fed.
22 C2 Kotli Pak.
62 B3 Kotlik AK U.S.A.
36 D5 Kötlutangi pt Iceland
37 V7 Kotly Rus. Fed.
48 G2 Kotor Varoš Bos.-Herz.
54 B4 Kotouba Côte d'Ivoire
51 H5 Kotovo Rus. Fed.
51 G4 Kotovsk Rus. Fed.
51 D6 Kotovs'k Ukr.
22 C4 Kotra India
22 B4 Kotri Pak.
21 C2 Kotri r. India
22 A5 Kot Sarae Pak.
21 C2 Kottagudem India
21 B4 Kottarakara India
21 B4 Kottayam India
21 B5 Kotte Sri Lanka
21 B3 Kotturu India
18 D2 Koturdepe Turkm.
13 M2 Kotuy r. Rus. Fed.
62 B3 Kotzebue U.S.A.
62 B3 Kotzebue Sound b. U.S.A.
43 L5 Kötzting Ger.
54 A3 Koubia Guinea
54 B3 Koudougou Burkina
58 E6 Koueveldberg mts S. Africa
55 D3 Koufey Niger
49 M7 Koufonisi i. Greece
58 E6 Kougaberg mts S. Africa
16 D4 Kouklia Cyprus
56 B4 Koulamoutou Gabon
54 B3 Koulikoro Mali
7 G4 Koumac New Caledonia
54 A3 Koundâra Guinea
54 B3 Koupéla Burkina
87 H2 Kourou Fr. Guiana
54 B3 Kouroussa Guinea
55 D3 Kousséri Cameroon
54 B3 Koutiala Mali
37 U6 Kouvola Fin.
36 W3 Kovdor Rus. Fed.
36 W3 Kovdozero, Oz. l. Rus. Fed.
51 C5 Kovel' Ukr.
50 G3 Kovernino Rus. Fed.
21 B4 Kovilpatti India
50 G3 Kovrov Rus. Fed.
50 G4 Kovylkino Rus. Fed.
50 F2 Kovzhskoye, Ozero l. Rus. Fed.
9 C5 Kowhitirangi N.Z.
27 □ Kowloon Peninsula H.K. China
27 □ Kowloon Pk h. H.K. China
30 D4 Kowŏn N. Korea
29 B7 Kōyama-misaki pt Japan
32 A3 Ko Yao Yai i. Thai.
16 B3 Köyceğiz Turkey
50 J2 Koygorodok Rus. Fed.
21 A2 Koyna Res. resr India
50 H1 Koynas Rus. Fed.
62 C3 Koyukuk r. U.S.A.
16 F1 Koyulhisar Turkey
50 F3 Koza Rus. Fed.
29 A7 Kō-zaki pt Japan
16 E3 Kozan Turkey
49 J4 Kozani Greece
48 G2 Kozara mts Bos.-Herz.
51 D5 Kozelets' Ukr.
50 E4 Kozel'sk Rus. Fed.
Kozhikode see Calicut
16 C1 Kozlu Turkey
50 H3 Koz'modem'yansk Rus. Fed.
49 K4 Kožuf mts Greece/Macedonia
29 F7 Kōzu-shima i. Japan
51 D5 Kozyatyn Ukr.
54 C4 Kpalimé Togo
32 A3 Krabi Thai.
32 A3 Kra Buri Thai.
32 C2 Krâcheh Cambodia
36 P4 Kraddsele Sweden
37 L7 Kragerø Norway
42 D2 Kraggenburg Neth.
49 J2 Kragujevac Yugo.
43 G5 Kraichgau reg. Ger.
32 A3 Kra, Isthmus of isth. Thai.
33 C4 Krakatau i. Indon.
32 C2 Krâkôr Cambodia
47 J5 Kraków Pol.
43 L1 Krakower See l. Ger.
32 B2 Krâlănh Cambodia
89 C1 Kralendijk Neth. Ant.
51 F5 Kramators'k Ukr.
36 P5 Kramfors Sweden
42 C3 Krammer est. Neth.
49 K6 Kranidi Greece
48 F1 Kranj Slovenia
32 □ Kranji Res. resr Sing.
59 J4 Kranskop S. Africa
50 H2 Krasavino Rus. Fed.
12 G2 Krasino Rus. Fed.
28 B3 Kraskino Rus. Fed.
37 U9 Krāslava Latvia
43 L4 Kraslice Czech Rep.
47 P4 Krasnapollye Belarus
50 D4 Krasnaya Gora Rus. Fed.
51 H5 Krasnoarmeysk Rus. Fed.
51 F5 Krasnoarmeyskaya Rus. Fed.
51 F5 Krasnoarmiys'k Ukr.
50 H2 Krasnoborsk Rus. Fed.
51 F6 Krasnodar Rus. Fed.
51 F6 Krasnodarskiy Kray div. Rus. Fed.
51 F5 Krasnodon Ukr.
50 D3 Krasnogorodskoye Rus. Fed.
51 G6 Krasnogvardeyskoye Rus. Fed.
51 E5 Krasnohrad Ukr.
51 E6 Krasnohvardiys'ke Ukr.
47 R2 Krasnomayskiy Rus. Fed.
51 E6 Krasnoperekops'k Ukr.
28 D2 Krasnorechenskiy Rus. Fed.
37 V6 Krasnosel'skoye Rus. Fed.
50 G4 Krasnoslobodsk Rus. Fed.
18 D2 Krasnovodskiy Zaliv b. Turkm.
18 D1 Krasnovodskoye Plato plat. Turkm.
24 B1 Krasnoyarsk Rus. Fed.
47 P3 Krasnyy Rus. Fed.
50 H3 Krasnyye Baki Rus. Fed.
51 H6 Krasnyye Barrikady Rus. Fed.
50 F3 Krasnyy Kholm Rus. Fed.
51 H5 Krasnyy Kut Rus. Fed.
50 D3 Krasnyy Luch Rus. Fed.
51 F5 Krasnyy Lyman Ukr.
51 J6 Krasnyy Yar Astrak. Rus. Fed.
51 H5 Krasnyy Yar Volgograd. Rus. Fed.
51 C5 Krasyliv Ukr.
51 H7 Kraynovka Rus. Fed.
42 E3 Krefeld Ger.
51 E5 Kremenchuk Ukr.
51 E5 Kremenchuts'ka Vodoskhovshche resr Ukr.
51 G5 Kremenskaya Rus. Fed.
46 G6 Křemešník h. Czech Rep.
72 F3 Kremmling U.S.A.
46 G6 Krems an der Donau Austria
13 U3 Kresta, Zaliv b. Rus. Fed.
50 E3 Kresttsy Rus. Fed.
37 R9 Kretinga Lith.
42 E4 Kreuzau Ger.
43 F4 Kreuztal Ger.
47 N3 Kreva Belarus
54 C4 Kribi Cameroon
59 H3 Kriel S. Africa
49 J5 Krikellos Greece
28 H2 Kril'on, Mys c. Rus. Fed.
15 F5 Krishna r. India
21 B3 Krishnagiri India
21 C3 Krishna, Mouths of the river mouth India
23 G5 Krishnanagar India
21 B3 Krishnaraja Sagara l. India
37 K7 Kristiansand Norway
37 O8 Kristianstad Sweden
36 K5 Kristiansund Norway
37 O7 Kristinehamn Sweden
37 R5 Kristinestad Fin.
Kriti i. see Crete
Krivoy Rog see Kryvyy Rih
48 G1 Križevci Croatia
48 F2 Krk i. Croatia
36 O5 Krokom Sweden
36 L5 Krokstadøra Norway
36 O3 Krokstranda Norway
51 E5 Krolevets' Ukr.
43 K4 Kronach Ger.
32 B3 Krŏng Kaôh Kŏng Cambodia
36 S5 Kronoby Fin.
63 P3 Kronprins Frederik Bjerge mt Greenland
32 A2 Kronwa Myanmar
59 G3 Kroonstad S. Africa
51 G6 Kropotkin Rus. Fed.
43 L3 Kropstädt Ger.
47 K6 Krosno Pol.
46 H5 Krotoszyn Pol.
59 J2 Kruger National Park S. Africa
47 O3 Kruhlaye Belarus
33 B4 Krui Indon.
58 F7 Kruisfontein S. Africa
49 H4 Krujë Albania
49 L4 Krumovgrad Bulg.
Krungkao see Ayutthaya
Krung Thep see Bangkok
47 O3 Krupki Belarus
49 J3 Kruševac Yugo.
43 L4 Krušné Hory mts Czech Rep.
64 B3 Kruzof I. i. U.S.A.
50 D4 Krychaw Belarus
51 F6 Krymsk Rus. Fed.
49 L6 Krytiko Pelagos sea Greece
51 E6 Kryvyy Rih Ukr.
54 B2 Ksabi Alg.
54 C1 Ksar el Boukhari Alg.
54 B1 Ksar el Kebir Morocco
51 F5 Kshenskiy Rus. Fed.
48 D7 Ksour Essaf Tunisia
50 H3 Kstovo Rus. Fed.
32 A4 Kuah Malaysia
32 B4 Kuala Kangsar Malaysia
32 B4 Kuala Kerai Malaysia
32 B5 Kuala Kubu Baharu Malaysia
33 B2 Kuala Lipis Malaysia
33 B2 Kuala Lumpur Malaysia
32 B4 Kuala Nerang Malaysia
32 B5 Kuala Pilah Malaysia
32 B5 Kuala Rompin Malaysia
33 D3 Kualasampit Indon.
32 A4 Kualasimpang Indon.
33 B1 Kuala Terengganu Malaysia
31 A5 Kuamut Malaysia
30 C3 Kuandian China
27 F6 Kuanshan Taiwan
33 B2 Kuantan Malaysia
51 G6 Kuban' r. Rus. Fed.
17 J5 Kubaysah Iraq
50 F3 Kubenskoye, Ozero l. Rus. Fed.
50 H4 Kubnya r. Rus. Fed.
49 M3 Kubrat Bulg.
22 C4 Kuchāman India
22 C4 Kuchera India
33 D2 Kuching Malaysia
29 A10 Kuchino-shima i. Japan
Kucing see Kuching
49 H4 Kuçovë Albania
21 A3 Kudal India
33 E1 Kudat Malaysia
21 B3 Kudligi India
21 A3 Kudremukh mt India
33 D4 Kudus Indon.
46 F7 Kufstein Austria
50 H3 Kugesi Rus. Fed.
62 E3 Kugmallit Bay b. Can.
19 F5 Kūhak Iran
23 E3 Kuhanbokano mt China
43 L1 Kuhbier Ger.
18 E4 Kūhbonān Iran
18 B3 Kūhdasht Iran
17 L2 Kūhhaye Sabalan mts Iran
17 M3 Kūhīn Iran
36 V4 Kuhmo Fin.
37 T6 Kuhmoinen Fin.
18 D3 Kūhpāyeh Iran
18 E5 Kūh, Ra's-al pt Iran
43 L3 Kühren Ger.
58 B2 Kuis Namibia
58 A1 Kuiseb Pass Namibia
57 B5 Kuito Angola
64 C3 Kuiu Island i. U.S.A.
36 T4 Kuivaniemi Fin.
18 B5 Kū', J. al h. S. Arabia
23 F5 Kujang India
30 C4 Kujang-Dong N. Korea
28 G4 Kuji Japan
29 B8 Kujū-san volc. Japan
69 F1 Kukatush Can.
49 J3 Kukës Albania
50 J3 Kukmor Rus. Fed.
32 B5 Kukup Malaysia
18 D5 Kūl r. Iran
16 B2 Kula Turkey
23 G3 Kula Kangri mt Bhutan
14 D2 Kulandy Kazak.
19 E5 Kulaneh reg. Pak.
19 G4 Kulao r. Pak.
13 P2 Kular Rus. Fed.
31 B5 Kulassein i. Phil.
23 H4 Kulaura Bangl.
37 R8 Kuldīga Latvia
58 D1 Kule Botswana
50 G4 Kulebaki Rus. Fed.
32 C2 Kulen Cambodia
50 H2 Kulikovo Rus. Fed.
32 B4 Kulim Malaysia
19 J2 Kuli Sarez l. Tajik.
22 D3 Kullu India
43 K4 Kulmbach Ger.
19 H2 Kŭlob Tajik.
17 H2 Kulp Turkey
22 D4 Kulpahar India
81 F4 Kulpsville U.S.A.
14 D2 Kul'sary Kazak.
43 H5 Külsheim Ger.
16 D2 Kulu Turkey
16 C3 Kulübe Tepe mt Turkey
12 J4 Kulunda Rus. Fed.
12 J4 Kulundinskoye, Ozero salt l. Rus. Fed.
18 D4 Külvand Iran
8 D3 Kulwin Austr.
30 D5 Kŭm r. S. Korea
51 H6 Kuma r. Rus. Fed.
29 F6 Kumagaya Japan
28 F3 Kumaishi Japan
33 D3 Kumai, Teluk b. Indon.
29 B8 Kumamoto Japan
29 E8 Kumano Japan
49 J3 Kumanovo Macedonia
54 B4 Kumasi Ghana
Kumayri see Gyumri
54 C4 Kumba Cameroon
21 B4 Kumbakonam India
16 C2 Kumbet Turkey
58 E1 Kumchuru Botswana
18 D3 Kumel well Iran
12 G4 Kumertau Rus. Fed.
30 E4 Kumgang-san mt N. Korea
30 E6 Kŭmho r. S. Korea
30 D4 Kumhwa S. Korea
30 E5 Kumi S. Korea
37 O7 Kumla Sweden
43 M2 Kummersdorf-Alexanderdorf Ger.
54 D3 Kumo Nigeria
30 D6 Kŭmō-do i. S. Korea
32 B1 Kumphawapi Thai.
58 C4 Kums Namibia
21 A3 Kumta India
51 H7 Kumukh Rus. Fed.
19 H3 Kunar r. Afgh.
24 G2 Kunashir, Ostrov i. Rus. Fed.
23 E2 Kunchuk Tso salt l. China
37 U7 Kunda Estonia
23 E4 Kunda India
21 A3 Kundāpura India
22 B2 Kundar r. Afgh./Pak.
19 H2 Kunduz Afgh.
19 H2 Kunduz r. Afgh.
37 M8 Kungälv Sweden
15 F2 Kungei Alatau mts Kazak./Kyrg.
64 C4 Kunghit I. i. Can.
37 N8 Kungsbacka Sweden
37 M7 Kungshamn Sweden
56 B3 Kungu Congo(Zaire)
22 D6 Kuni r. India
29 B8 Kunimi-dake mt Japan
23 F5 Kunjabar India
23 G4 Kunlui r. India/Nepal
15 F3 Kunlun Shan mts China
23 H2 Kunlun Shankou pass China
27 B5 Kunming China
22 D4 Kuno r. India
30 D6 Kunsan S. Korea
26 F4 Kunshan China
6 C3 Kununurra Austr.
22 D4 Kunwari r. India
50 D3 Kun'ya Rus. Fed.
30 A5 Kunyu Shan h. China
43 H5 Künzelsau Ger.
43 K3 Künzels-Berg h. Ger.
27 F4 Kuocang Shan mts China
37 T6 Kuohijärvi l. Fin.
36 V3 Kuolayarvi Rus. Fed.
36 U5 Kuopio Fin.
36 S5 Kuortane Fin.
48 2 Kupa r. Croatia/Slovenia
25 E8 Kupang Indon.
37 T9 Kupiškis Lith.
64 C3 Kupreanof Island i. U.S.A.
51 F5 Kup"yans'k Ukr.
15 G2 Kuqa China
17 M2 Kür r. Azer.
17 K1 Kura r. Azer./Georgia
51 G7 Kura r. Georgia/Rus. Fed.
51 H7 Kurakh Rus. Fed.
29 C7 Kurashiki Japan
23 E5 Kurasia India
29 C7 Kurayoshi Japan
16 B1 Kurban Dağı mt Turkey
51 E5 Kurchatov Rus. Fed.
17 M1 Kürdämir Azer.
17 M2 Kür Dili pt Azer.
21 A2 Kurduvadi India
49 L4 Kŭrdzhali Bulg.
29 C7 Kure Japan
16 D1 Küre Turkey
5 K2 Kure Atoll atoll HI U.S.A.
37 S7 Kuressaare Estonia
12 H4 Kurgan Rus. Fed.
51 G6 Kurganinsk Rus. Fed.
19 H2 Kuri Afgh.
22 B4 Kuri India
Kuria Muria Islands is see Ḥalāniyāt, Juzur al
36 S5 Kurikka Fin.
28 G5 Kurikoma-yama volc. Japan
24 G2 Kuril Islands is Rus. Fed.
24 G2 Kuril'sk Japan
Kuril'skiye Ostrova is see Kuril Islands
94 F2 Kuril Trench sea feature Pac. Oc.
55 F3 Kurmuk Sudan
21 B3 Kurnool India
16 E6 Kurnub Israel
29 E6 Kurobe Japan
28 G4 Kuroishi Japan
29 G6 Kuroiso Japan
43 J4 Kurort Schmalkalden Ger.
29 A9 Kuro-shima i. Japan
50 F4 Kurovskoye Rus. Fed.
9 C6 Kurow N.Z.
22 B2 Kurram r. Afgh./Pak.
8 H2 Kurri Kurri Austr.
Kuršių Marios lag. see Courland Lagoon
51 F5 Kursk Rus. Fed.
51 H6 Kurskaya Rus. Fed.
51 F5 Kurskaya Oblast' div. Rus. Fed.
Kurskiy Zaliv lag. see Courland Lagoon
16 D1 Kurşunlu Turkey
17 H3 Kurtalan Turkey
23 G4 Kuru r. Bhutan
16 G2 Kuruçay Turkey
22 D3 Kurukshetra India
24 A2 Kuruktag mts China
58 E3 Kuruman S. Africa
58 D3 Kuruman watercourse S. Africa

29 B8 Kurume Japan
24 D1 Kurumkan Rus. Fed.
21 C5 Kurunegala Sri Lanka
55 F2 Kurūsh, Jebel reg. Sudan
49 M6 Kuşadası Turkey
49 M6 Kuşadası Körfezi b. Turkey
64 B2 Kusawa Lake l. Can.
42 F5 Kusel Ger.
16 A1 Kuş Gölü l. Turkey
51 F6 Kushchevskaya Rus. Fed.
29 B9 Kushikino Japan
29 D8 Kushimoto Japan
28 J3 Kushiro Japan
28 J3 Kushiro-Shitsugen National Park Japan
19 F3 Kushka r. Turkm.
17 M5 Kūshkak Iran
14 E1 Kushmurun Kazak.
21 B3 Kushtagi India
23 G5 Kushtia Bangl.
26 C2 Kushui r. China
62 C3 Kuskokwim r. U.S.A.
62 B4 Kuskokwim Bay b. U.S.A.
62 C3 Kuskokwim Mts U.S.A.
30 C4 Kusŏng N. Korea
28 J3 Kussharo-ko l. Japan
14 E1 Kustanay Kazak.
43 F1 Küstenkanal canal Ger.
18 C4 Kut Iran
17 M6 Kūt Abdollāh Iran
32 A5 Kutacane Indon.
16 B2 Kütahya Turkey
51 G7 K'ut'aisi Georgia
Kut-al-Imara see Al Kūt
51 H6 Kutan Rus. Fed.
28 G3 Kutchan Japan
17 M5 Kūt-e Gapu Iran
48 G2 Kutina Croatia
48 G2 Kutjevo Croatia
47 J4 Kutno Pol.
56 B4 Kutu Congo(Zaire)
23 G5 Kutubdia I. i. Bangl.
62 G2 Kuujjua r. Can.
67 G2 Kuujjuaq Can.
Kuujjuarapik see Poste-de-la-Baleine
18 D1 Kuuli-Mayak Turkm.
36 V4 Kuusamo Fin.
37 U6 Kuusankoski Fin.
57 B5 Kuvango Angola
50 E3 Kuvshinovo Rus. Fed.
17 L7 Kuwait Kuwait
10 F7 Kuwait country Asia
17 L7 Kuwait Jun b. Kuwait
29 E7 Kuwana Japan
50 G1 Kuya Rus. Fed.
12 J4 Kuybyshev Novosibirsk Rus. Fed.
Kuybyshev see Samara
50 J4 Kuybyshevskoye Vdkhr. resr Rus. Fed.
26 D2 Kuye r. China
15 G2 Kuytun China
49 N6 Kuyucak Turkey
37 V6 Kuznechnoye Rus. Fed.
50 H4 Kuznetsk Rus. Fed.
51 F1 Kuznetsovo Rus. Fed.
51 C5 Kuznetsovs'k Ukr.
36 R1 Kvænangen chan. Norway
36 Q2 Kvaløya i. Norway
36 S1 Kvalsund Norway
Kvareli see Qvareli
48 F2 Kvarnerić chan. Croatia
62 C4 Kvichak Bay b. U.S.A.
64 D3 Kwadacha Wilderness Prov. Park res. Can.
27 □ Kwai Tau Leng h. H.K. China
95 G5 Kwajalein i. Pac. Oc.
32 A5 Kwala Indon.
59 J4 KwaMashu S. Africa
59 H2 KwaMhlanga S. Africa
30 D5 Kwangch'ŏn S. Korea
30 D6 Kwangju S. Korea
56 B4 Kwango r. Congo(Zaire)
56 D4 Kwangwazi Tanz.
30 D6 Kwangyang S. Korea
59 F6 Kwanobuhle S. Africa
59 F6 KwaNojoli S. Africa
59 G6 Kwanonqubela S. Africa
58 F5 Kwanonzame S. Africa
59 G6 Kwatinidubu S. Africa
59 H3 KwaZamokhule S. Africa
58 F6 Kwazamukucinga S. Africa
58 F5 Kwazamuxolo S. Africa
59 H3 KwaZanele S. Africa
59 J4 Kwazulu-Natal div. S. Africa
57 C5 Kwekwe Zimbabwe
58 F1 Kweneng div. Botswana
56 B4 Kwenge r. Congo(Zaire)
59 G5 Kwezi-Naledi S. Africa
47 J4 Kwidzyn Pol.
62 B4 Kwigillingok AK U.S.A.
6 E2 Kwikila P.N.G.
56 B4 Kwilu r. Angola/Congo(Zaire)
25 F7 Kwoka mt Indon.
27 □ Kwun Tong H.K. China
55 D4 Kyabé Chad
8 E4 Kyabram Austr.
32 A1 Kya-in Seikkyi Myanmar
24 C1 Kyakhta Rus. Fed.
8 D3 Kyalite Austr.
6 D5 Kyancutta Austr.
50 F1 Kyanda Rus. Fed.
32 A1 Kyaukhnyat Myanmar
23 H6 Kyaukpyu Myanmar
23 H5 Kyauktaw Myanmar
37 S9 Kybartai Lith.
8 C4 Kybybolite Austr.
22 D2 Kyelang India
26 A2 Kyikug China
Kyiv see Kiev
Kyklades is see Cyclades
65 H4 Kyle Can.
40 C3 Kyle of Lochalsh U.K.
42 E5 Kyll r. Ger.
49 K6 Kyllini mt Greece
8 E4 Kyneton Austr.
56 D3 Kyoga, Lake l. Uganda
29 D7 Kyōga-misaki pt Japan
32 A1 Kyondo Myanmar
30 E6 Kyŏngju S. Korea
29 D7 Kyōto Japan
49 J6 Kyparissia Greece
49 J6 Kyparissiakos Kolpos b. Greece
12 H4 Kypshak, Ozero salt l. Kazak.
49 L5 Kyra Panagia i. Greece
10 J5 Kyrgyzstan country Asia
43 L2 Kyritz Ger.
36 L5 Kyrksæterøra Norway
12 G3 Kyrta Rus. Fed.
50 H1 Kyssa Rus. Fed.
13 P3 Kytalyktakh Rus. Fed.
49 K6 Kythira i. Greece
49 L6 Kythnos i. Greece
32 A2 Kyungyaung Myanmar
29 B8 Kyūshū i. Japan
94 D5 Kyushu - Palau Ridge sea feature Pac. Oc.
49 K3 Kyustendil Bulg.
8 F3 Kywong Austr.
51 D5 Kyyivs'ke Vdskh. resr Ukr.
36 T5 Kyyjärvi Fin.
24 B1 Kyzyl Rus. Fed.
14 E2 Kyzylkum Desert Uzbek.
15 H1 Kyzyl-Mazhalyk Rus. Fed.
14 E2 Kzyl-Orda Kazak.
14 F1 Kzyltu Kazak.

L

42 F4 Laacher See l. Ger.
37 T7 Laagri Estonia
36 U2 Laanila Fin.
91 B3 La Araucania div. Chile
56 E3 Laascaanood Somalia
56 E2 Laasgoray Somalia
89 E2 La Asunción Venez.
54 A2 Laâyoune Western Sahara
51 G6 Laba r. Rus. Fed.
77 C6 La Babia Mex.
88 D3 La Banda Arg.
72 E3 La Barge U.S.A.
7 H3 Labasa Fiji
44 C3 La Baule-Escoublac France
54 A3 Labé Guinea
66 F4 Labelle Can.
68 B5 La Belle U.S.A.
64 B2 Laberge, Lake l. Can.
31 A5 Labian, Tg pt Malaysia
64 E2 La Biche r. Can.
51 G6 Labinsk Rus. Fed.
83 B5 Labis Malaysia
31 B3 Labo Phil.
16 F4 Laboué Lebanon
44 D4 Labouheyre France
91 D2 Laboulaye Arg.
67 H3 Labrador Can.
67 G3 Labrador City Can.
63 N3 Labrador Sea Can./Greenland
86 F5 Lábrea Brazil
33 E1 Labuan Malaysia
33 C4 Labuhan Indon.
33 B2 Labuhanbilik Indon.
32 A5 Labuhanruku Indon.
31 A5 Labuk r. Malaysia
33 E1 Labuk, Telukan b. Malaysia
25 E7 Labuna Indon.
12 H3 Labytnangi Rus. Fed.
49 H4 Laç Albania
91 D1 La Calera Arg.
91 B2 La Calera Chile
84 E3 Lacandón, Parque Nacional nat. park Guatemala
44 F2 La Capelle France
91 B4 Lacar, L. l. Arg.
91 D2 La Carlota Arg.
45 E3 La Carolina Spain
49 M2 Lăcăuţi, Vârful mt Romania
81 J1 Lac-Baker Can.
14 F5 Laccadive Islands India
65 K4 Lac du Bonnet Can.
82 G5 La Ceiba Honduras
89 C2 La Ceiba Venez.
8 B4 Lacepede B. b. Austr.
81 E4 Laceyville U.S.A.
81 H1 Lac Frontière Can.
50 F2 Lacha, Ozero l. Rus. Fed.
43 J2 Lachendorf Ger.
69 F3 Lachine U.S.A.
8 E3 Lachlan r. Austr.
83 J7 La Chorrera Panama
66 F4 Lachute Can.
17 L2 Laçın Azer.
44 G5 La Ciotat France
84 A2 La Ciudad Mex.
80 D3 Lackawanna U.S.A.
65 G4 Lac La Biche Can.
64 E4 Lac La Hache Can.
64 F2 Lac la Martre Can.
65 H3 Lac La Ronge Provincial Park res. Can.
67 F4 Lac Mégantic Can.
81 G2 Lacolle Can.
73 E6 La Colorada Mex.
64 G4 Lacombe Can.
84 D3 La Concordia Mex.
48 C5 Laconi Sardinia Italy
81 H3 Laconia U.S.A.
69 J1 La Corne Can.
68 B4 La Crescent U.S.A.
68 B4 La Crosse U.S.A.
89 A4 La Cruz Col.
84 A2 La Cruz Sinaloa Mex.
84 C1 La Cruz Tamaulipas Mex.
76 E4 La Cygne U.S.A.
22 D2 Ladakh Range mts India
32 A4 Ladang i. Thai.
16 E1 Lâdik Turkey
58 D6 Ladismith S. Africa
19 F4 Lādīz Iran
22 C4 Ladnun India
89 B3 La Dorada Col.
Ladozhskoye Ozero l. see Lagoda, Lake
23 H4 Ladu mt India
50 E2 Ladva Rus. Fed.
50 E2 Ladva-Vetka Rus. Fed.
63 K2 Lady Ann Strait chan. Can.
40 E4 Ladybank U.K.
59 G4 Ladybrand S. Africa
69 G2 Lady Evelyn Lake l. Can.
59 G5 Lady Frere S. Africa
59 G5 Lady Grey S. Africa
64 E5 Ladysmith Can.
59 H4 Ladysmith S. Africa
68 B3 Ladysmith U.S.A.
6 E2 Lae P.N.G.
32 B2 Laem Ngop Thai.
32 B4 Laem Pho pt Thai.
37 K6 Lærdalsøyri Norway
86 F8 La Esmeralda Bol.
89 D4 La Esmeralda Venez.
37 M8 Læsø i. Denmark
30 D2 Lafa China
91 D1 La Falda Arg.
72 F4 Lafayette CO U.S.A.
68 D5 Lafayette IN U.S.A.
77 E6 Lafayette LA U.S.A.
79 C5 La Fayette U.S.A.
42 B5 La Fère France
42 B5 La-Ferté-Milon France
42 B6 La Ferté-sous-Jouarre France
18 C5 Laffān, Ra's pt Qatar
54 C4 Lafia Nigeria
44 D3 La Flèche France
80 A6 La Follette U.S.A.
69 H2 Laforce Can.
69 G2 Laforest Can.
67 F3 Laforge Can.
89 B2 La Fría Venez.
18 D5 Laft Iran
48 C6 La Galite i. Tunisia
51 H6 Lagan' Rus. Fed.
41 E3 Lagan r. U.K.
87 L6 Lagarto Brazil
43 G3 Lage Ger.
37 L7 Lågen r. Norway
40 C5 Lagg U.K.
40 D3 Laggan U.K.
40 D4 Laggan, Loch l. U.K.
54 C1 Laghouat Alg.
23 F2 Lagkor Co salt l. China
89 B2 La Gloria Col.
90 D2 Lagoa Santa Brazil
50 D2 Lagoda, Lake l. Rus. Fed.
17 L1 Lagodekhi Georgia
32 D5 Lagong i. Indon.
31 B3 Lagonoy Gulf b. Phil.
88 B7 Lago Posadas Arg.
91 B4 Lago Ranco Chile
54 C4 Lagos Nigeria
45 B4 Lagos Port.
84 B2 Lagos de Moreno Mex.
72 C2 La Grande U.S.A.
66 E3 La Grande r. Can.
66 E3 La Grande 2, Réservoir de resr Can.
66 E3 La Grande 3, Réservoir de resr Can.
66 F3 La Grande 4, Réservoir de resr Can.
6 C3 Lagrange Austr.
79 C5 La Grange GA U.S.A.
81 J2 La Grange ME U.S.A.
68 D5 La Grange MI U.S.A.
68 B5 La Grange MO U.S.A.
77 D6 La Grange TX U.S.A.
68 E5 Lagrange U.S.A.
89 E3 La Gran Sabana plat. Venez.
88 G3 Laguna Brazil
74 D5 Laguna Beach U.S.A.
91 B3 Laguna de Laja, Parque Nacional nat. park Chile
84 E4 Laguna Lachua, Parque Nacional nat. park Guatemala
74 D5 Laguna Mts mts U.S.A.
86 C5 Lagunas Peru
88 A7 Laguna San Rafael, Parque Nacional nat. park Chile
84 C3 Lagunas de Chacahua, Parque Nacional nat. park Mex.
89 C2 Lagunillas Venez.
33 E1 Lahad Datu Malaysia
31 A5 Lahad Datu, Telukan b. Malaysia
74 □2 Lahaina U.S.A.
17 M3 Lahījān Iran
33 B3 Lahat Indon.
32 A5 Lahewa Indon.
20 B7 Laḥij Yemen
18 C2 Lāhījān Iran
74 □1 Lahilahi Pt pt U.S.A.
43 F4 Lahn r. Ger.
42 F4 Lahnstein Ger.
37 N8 Laholm Sweden
74 C2 Lahontan Res. resr U.S.A.
22 C3 Lahore Pak.
89 E3 La Horqueta Venez.
22 B3 Lahri Pak.
37 T6 Lahti Fin.
84 A3 La Huerta Mex.
55 D4 Laï Chad
26 F3 Lai'an China
27 C6 Laibin China
18 E4 Laidāru Iran
74 □1 Laie U.S.A.
74 □1 Laie Pt pt U.S.A.
27 C4 Laifeng China
44 E2 L'Aigle France
36 S5 Laihia Fin.
23 H4 Laimakuri India
58 D6 Laingsburg S. Africa
36 S3 Lainioälven r. Sweden
40 D2 Lairg U.K.
31 C5 Lais Phil.
37 R6 Laitila Fin.
48 D1 Laives Italy
26 E2 Laiwu China
26 F2 Laiyang China
26 E2 Laiyuan China
26 F2 Laizhou Wan b. China
91 B3 Laja r. Chile
91 B3 Laja, Lago de l. Chile
6 D3 Lajamanu Austr.
87 L5 Lajes Rio Grande do Norte Brazil
88 F3 Lajes Santa Catarina Brazil
73 G4 La Junta U.S.A.
72 E2 Lake U.S.A.
7 J3 Lakeba i. Fiji
16 D6 Lake Bardawîl Reserve Egypt
8 D4 Lake Bolac Austr.
8 F2 Lake Cargelligo Austr.
72 B1 Lake Chelan Nat. Recreation Area res. U.S.A.
79 D6 Lake City FL U.S.A.
68 E3 Lake City MI U.S.A.
68 A3 Lake City MN U.S.A.
79 E5 Lake City SC U.S.A.
38 D3 Lake District Nat. Park U.K.
74 D5 Lake Elsinore U.S.A.
69 H3 Lakefield Can.
68 C4 Lake Geneva U.S.A.
63 M3 Lake Harbour Can.
75 E4 Lake Havasu City U.S.A.
74 C4 Lake Isabella U.S.A.
79 D6 Lakeland U.S.A.
68 C2 Lake Linden U.S.A.
64 F4 Lake Louise Can.
75 E4 Lake Mead National Recreation Area res. U.S.A.
81 J2 Lake Moxie U.S.A.
72 B2 Lake Oswego U.S.A.
9 B5 Lake Paringa N.Z.
81 G2 Lake Placid U.S.A.
74 A2 Lakeport U.S.A.
9 C6 Lake Pukaki N.Z.
66 D3 Lake River Can.
69 H3 Lake St Peter Can.
8 G4 Lakes Entrance Austr.
68 E2 Lake Superior National Park Can.
8 H3 Lake Tabourie Austr.
9 C6 Lake Tekapo N.Z.
66 E4 Lake Traverse Can.
72 B3 Lakeview U.S.A.
72 F4 Lakewood CO U.S.A.
81 F4 Lakewood NJ U.S.A.
80 C4 Lakewood OH U.S.A.
79 D7 Lake Worth U.S.A.
50 D2 Lakhdenpokh'ya Rus. Fed.
22 E4 Lakhimpur India
22 D5 Lakhnadon India
22 B5 Lakhpat India
49 K6 Lakonikos Kolpos b. Greece
54 B4 Lakota Côte d'Ivoire
36 U1 Laksefjorden chan. Norway
36 T1 Lakselv Norway
14 F5 Lakshadweep div. India
23 G5 Laksham Bangl.
21 B2 Lakshettipet India
23 G5 Lakshmikantapur India
31 B5 Lala Phil.
91 D2 La Laguna Arg.
91 B3 La Laja Chile
56 B3 Lalara Gabon
43 L1 Lalendorf Ger.
18 C3 Lālī Iran
84 E3 La Libertad Guatemala
91 B2 La Ligua Chile
30 D1 Lalin China
45 B1 Lalín Spain
30 C1 Lalin r. China
45 D4 La Línea de la Concepción Spain
22 D4 Lalitpur India
31 B2 Lal-Lo Phil.
65 H3 La Loche Can.
65 H3 La Loche, Lac l. Can.
42 C4 La Louvière Belgium
50 H2 Lal'sk Rus. Fed.
23 H5 Lama Bangl.
48 C4 La Maddalena Sardinia Italy
31 A5 Lamag Malaysia
32 A2 Lamaing Myanmar
La Manche str. see English Channel
76 C4 Lamar CO U.S.A.
77 E4 Lamar MO U.S.A.
18 D5 Lamard Iran
48 C5 La Marmora, Punta mt Sardinia Italy
91 D3 Lamarque Arg.
77 E6 La Marque U.S.A.
64 F2 La Martre, Lac l. Can.
56 B4 Lambaréné Gabon
86 C5 Lambayeque Peru
41 F4 Lambay Island i. Rep. of Ireland
92 D4 Lambert Gl. gl. Ant.
58 C6 Lambert's Bay S. Africa
22 C3 Lambi India
39 F6 Lambourn Downs h. U.K.
32 C2 Lam Chi r. Thai.
45 C2 Lamego Port.
67 H4 Lamèque, I. i. Can.
86 C6 La Merced Peru
8 C3 Lameroo Austr.
77 C5 Lamesa U.S.A.
74 D5 La Mesa U.S.A.
49 K5 Lamia Greece
73 E6 La Misa Mex.
74 D5 La Misión Mex.
31 B5 Lamitan Phil.
27 □ Lamma I. i. H.K. China
9 B6 Lammerlaw Ra. mts N.Z.
40 F5 Lammermuir Hills h. U.K.
37 O8 Lammhult Sweden
37 T6 Lammi Fin.
68 C5 La Moille U.S.A.
81 G2 Lamoille r. U.S.A.
68 B5 La Moine r. U.S.A.
31 B3 Lamon Bay b. Phil.
76 E3 Lamoni U.S.A.
72 F3 Lamont U.S.A.
77 B6 La Morita Mex.
69 H1 La Motte Can.
32 B1 Lam Pao Res. resr Thai.
77 D6 Lampasas U.S.A.
70 F6 Lampazos Mex.
48 E7 Lampedusa, Isola di i. Sicily Italy
39 C5 Lampeter U.K.
32 B2 Lam Plai Mat r. Thai.
50 F4 Lamskoye Rus. Fed.
27 □ Lam Tin H.K. China
56 E4 Lamu Kenya
23 H6 Lamu Myanmar
74 □2 Lanai i. U.S.A.
74 □2 Lanai City U.S.A.
31 C5 Lanao, Lake l. Phil.
69 J3 Lanark Can.
40 E5 Lanark U.K.
68 C4 Lanark U.S.A.
31 A5 Lanas Malaysia
32 A3 Lanbi Kyun i. Myanmar
Lancang Jiang r. see Mekong
81 F2 Lancaster Can.
38 E3 Lancaster U.K.
74 C4 Lancaster CA U.S.A.
68 A5 Lancaster MO U.S.A.
81 H2 Lancaster NH U.S.A.
80 B5 Lancaster OH U.S.A.
81 E4 Lancaster PA U.S.A.
79 D5 Lancaster SC U.S.A.
68 B4 Lancaster WV U.S.A.
38 E4 Lancaster Canal canal U.K.
63 K2 Lancaster Sound str. Can.
48 F3 Lanciano Italy
91 B3 Lanco Chile
26 F2 Lancun China
46 F6 Landau an der Isar Ger.
43 G5 Landau in der Pfalz Ger.
46 E7 Landeck Austria
72 E3 Lander U.S.A.
43 H2 Landesbergen Ger.
65 H4 Landis Can.
46 E6 Landsberg am Lech Ger.
39 B7 Land's End pt U.K.
46 F6 Landshut Ger.
37 N9 Landskrona Sweden
42 F5 Landstuhl Ger.
43 G1 Land Wursten reg. Ger.
41 D4 Lanesborough Rep. of Ireland
32 C3 La Nga r. Vietnam
22 E3 La'nga Co l. China
26 C3 Langao China
19 F3 Langar Iran
40 B2 Langavat, Loch l. U.K.
58 E4 Langberg mts S. Africa
76 D1 Langdon U.S.A.
58 C6 Langeberg mts S. Africa
37 M9 Langeland i. Denmark
37 T6 Längelmäki Fin.
37 T6 Längelmävesi l. Fin.
43 J3 Langelsheim Ger.
43 G1 Langen Ger.
43 H2 Langenhagen Ger.
43 F4 Langenhahn Ger.
43 F5 Langenlonsheim Ger.
46 C7 Langenthal Switz.
43 K2 Langenweddingen Ger.
42 F1 Langeoog Ger.
42 F1 Langeoog i. Ger.
37 L7 Langesund Norway
32 B5 Langgapayung Indon.
43 G4 Langgöns Ger.
65 H4 Langham Can.
36 C4 Langjökull ice cap Iceland
33 A2 Langka Indon.
33 A1 Langkawi i. Malaysia
32 A3 Lang Kha Toek, Khao mt Thai.
58 D4 Langklip S. Africa
31 A5 Langkon Malaysia
69 K1 Langlade Can.
68 C3 Langlade U.S.A.
44 F4 Langogne France
36 O2 Langøya i. Norway
23 F3 Langphu mt China
39 E6 Langport U.K.
27 F5 Langqi China
44 G3 Langres France
22 D1 Langru China
33 A2 Langsa Indon.
32 A4 Langsa, Teluk b. Indon.
36 P5 Långsele Sweden
26 C1 Langshan China
26 C1 Lang Shan mts China
27 C6 Lang Sơn Vietnam
38 G3 Langtoft U.K.
77 C6 Langtry U.S.A.
44 F5 Languedoc reg. France
36 R4 Långvattnet Sweden
43 H2 Langwedel Ger.
26 F4 Langxi China
26 C4 Langzhong China
69 H2 Laniel Can.
65 H4 Lanigan Can.
74 □1 Lanikai U.S.A.
91 B3 Lanín, Parque Nacional nat. park Arg.
91 B3 Lanín, Volcán volc. Arg.
26 E3 Lankao China
17 M2 Länkäran Azer.
44 C2 Lannion France
84 A2 La Noria Mex.
36 S3 Lansån Sweden
68 C2 L'Anse U.S.A.
68 B4 Lansing IA U.S.A.
68 E4 Lansing MI U.S.A.
64 C2 Lansing r. Can.
27 D6 Lantau I. i. H.K. China
27 □ Lantau Island i. H.K. China
27 □ Lantau Peak h. H.K. China
31 C4 Lanuza Bay b. Phil.
27 E4 Lanxi China
55 F4 Lanya Sudan
27 F6 Lan Yü i. Taiwan
54 A2 Lanzarote i. Canary Is
26 B2 Lanzhou China
30 B1 Lanzijing China
31 B2 Laoag Phil.
31 C3 Laoang Phil.
27 B6 Lao Cai Vietnam
26 F1 Laoha r. China
26 D3 Laohekou China
30 A4 Laohutun China
30 D3 Laoling China
30 D3 Lao Ling mts China
44 F2 Laon France
68 C3 Laona U.S.A.
11 M7 Laos country Asia
26 F2 Lao Shan mt China
30 E2 Laotougou China
30 C3 Laotuding Shan h. China
Laowohi pass see Khardung La
26 A1 Laoximiao China
30 E2 Laoye Ling mts China
90 C4 Lapa Brazil
31 B5 Lapac i. Phil.
83 J7 La Palma Panama
45 C4 La Palma del Condado Spain
91 F2 La Paloma Uru.
91 D3 La Pampa div. Arg.
74 B4 La Panza Range mts U.S.A.
89 E3 La Paragua Venez.
31 A5 Laparan i. Phil.
91 E1 La Paz Entre Rios Arg.
91 C2 La Paz Mendoza Arg.
86 E7 La Paz Bol.
82 B4 La Paz Mex.
68 D5 Lapaz U.S.A.
86 E4 La Pedrera Col.
69 F4 Lapeer U.S.A.
28 G2 La Pérouse Strait str. Japan/Rus. Fed.
84 C2 La Pesca Mex.
84 B2 La Piedad Mex.
89 E3 La Piña r. Venez.
72 B3 La Pine U.S.A.
31 C3 Lapinig Phil.
31 C4 Lapinin i. Phil.
36 U5 Lapinlahti Fin.
16 D4 Lapithos Cyprus
77 F6 Laplace U.S.A.
76 C2 La Plant U.S.A.
91 F2 La Plata Arg.
89 B4 La Plata Col.
50 G1 Lapominka Rus. Fed.
68 D5 La Porte U.S.A.
68 A4 La Porte City U.S.A.
36 S5 Lappajärvi Fin.
36 S5 Lappajärvi l. Fin.
37 V6 Lappeenranta Fin.
43 L5 Lappersdorf Ger.
36 S2 Lappland reg. Europe
81 G2 La Prairie Can.
77 D6 La Pryor U.S.A.
49 M4 Lâpseki Turkey
Laptevykh, More sea see Laptev Sea
13 N2 Laptev Sea sea Rus. Fed.
36 S5 Lapua Fin.
31 B4 Lapu-Lapu Phil.
88 C2 La Quiaca Arg.
48 E3 L'Aquila Italy
74 D5 La Quinta U.S.A.
18 D5 Lār Iran
54 B1 Larache Morocco
18 E5 Lārak i. Iran
72 F3 Laramie U.S.A.
72 F3 Laramie Mts mts U.S.A.
Laranda see Karaman
90 B4 Laranjeiras do Sul Brazil
90 B3 Laranjinha r. Brazil
25 E7 Larantuka Indon.
25 F7 Larat i. Indon.
45 H4 Larba Alg.
37 Q8 Lärbro Sweden
69 G2 Larchwood Can.
69 H1 Larder Lake Can.
45 E1 Laredo Spain
77 D7 Laredo U.S.A.
79 D7 Largo U.S.A.
40 D5 Largs U.K.
18 B2 Lārī Iran
48 D6 L'Ariana Tunisia
65 K5 Larimore U.S.A.
88 C3 La Rioja Arg.
91 C1 La Rioja div. Arg.
45 E1 La Rioja div. Spain
49 K5 Larisa Greece
18 E5 Laristan reg. Iran
22 B4 Larkana Pak.
46 C7 Larmont mt France/Switz.
16 D4 Larnaka Cyprus
41 F3 Larne U.K.
76 D4 Larned U.S.A.
40 C6 Larne Lough in U.K.
45 D1 La Robla Spain
42 D4 La Roche-en-Ardenne Belgium
44 D3 La Rochelle France
44 D3 La Roche-sur-Yon France
45 E3 La Roda Spain
83 L5 La Romana Dom. Rep.
65 H3 La Ronge Can.
84 B1 La Rosa Mex.
6 D3 Larrimah Austr.
92 B2 Larsen Ice Shelf ice feature Ant.
36 S5 Larsmo Fin.
37 M7 Larvik Norway
75 H2 La Sal Junction U.S.A.
81 G2 La Salle Can.
68 C5 La Salle U.S.A.
66 E4 La Sarre Can.
89 D2 Las Aves, Islas is Venez.
91 B2 Las Cabras Chile
67 J4 La Scie Can.
73 F5 Las Cruces U.S.A.
83 K5 La Selle mt Haiti
91 B1 La Serena Chile
77 C7 Las Esperanças Mex.
91 E3 Las Flores Arg.
19 F5 Lāshār r. Iran
65 H4 Lashburn Can.
91 C2 Las Heras Arg.
24 B4 Lashio Myanmar
19 G4 Lashkar Gāh Afgh.
91 B3 Las Lajas Arg.
89 D3 Las Lajitas Venez.
88 D2 Las Lomitas Arg.
45 C4 Las Marismas marsh Spain
88 C7 Las Martinetas Arg.
89 D2 Las Mercedes Venez.
84 A1 Las Nieves Mex.
74 D5 Las Palmas r. Mex.
54 A2 Las Palmas de Gran Canaria Canary Is
48 C2 La Spezia Italy
91 F2 Las Piedras Uru.
88 C6 Las Plumas Arg.
91 E2 Las Rosas Arg.
72 B3 Lassen Pk volc. U.S.A.
72 B3 Lassen Volcanic Nat. Park U.S.A.
92 B2 Lassiter Coast coastal area Ant.
83 H7 Las Tablas Panama
88 D3 Las Termas Arg.
65 H4 Last Mountain L. l. Can.
56 B4 Lastoursville Gabon
48 G3 Lastovo i. Croatia
89 D3 Las Trincheras Venez.
43 F2 Lastrup Ger.
73 F6 Las Varas Chihuahua Mex.
84 A2 Las Varas Mex.
91 D1 Las Varillas Arg.
73 F5 Las Vegas NM U.S.A.
75 E3 Las Vegas NV U.S.A.
45 D3 Las Villuercas mt Spain
67 J3 La Tabatière Can.
86 C4 Latacunga Ecuador
92 A2 Latady I. i. Ant.
89 B5 La Tagua Col.
16 E4 Latakia Syria
69 H2 Latchford Can.
23 F5 Latehar India
44 D4 La Teste France
42 F2 Lathen Ger.
40 E2 Latheron U.K.
48 E4 Latina Italy
91 D2 La Toma Arg.
89 D2 La Tortuga, Isla i. Venez.
80 D4 Latrobe U.S.A.
42 E2 Lattrop Neth.
69 H2 Latulipe Can.
66 F4 La Tuque Can.
21 B2 Latur India
35 H3 Latvia country Europe
88 C1 Lauca, Parque Nacional nat. park Chile
46 F5 Lauchhammer Ger.
40 F5 Lauder U.K.
43 H1 Lauenbrück Ger.
43 J1 Lauenburg (Elbe) Ger.
43 K5 Lauf an der Pegnitz Ger.
44 H3 Laufen Switz.
68 D2 Laughing Fish Pt pt U.S.A.
37 S7 Lauka Estonia
36 V1 Laukvik Norway
28 D2 Laulyu Rus. Fed.
32 A3 Laun Thai.
6 E6 Launceston Austr.
39 C7 Launceston U.K.
41 B5 Laune r. Rep. of Ireland
32 A2 Launglon Bok Is is Myanmar
91 B4 La Unión Chile
89 A4 La Unión Col.
82 G6 La Unión El Salvador
84 B3 La Unión Mex.
31 B3 Laur Phil.
8 B2 Laura S.A. Austr.
6 E3 Laura Austr.
89 D3 La Urbana Venez.
81 F5 Laurel DE U.S.A.
77 F6 Laurel MS U.S.A.
72 E2 Laurel MT U.S.A.
80 D4 Laurel Hill h. U.S.A.
80 A6 Laurel River Lake l. U.S.A.
40 F4 Laurencekirk U.K.
67 F4 Laurentides, Réserve faunique des res. Can.
48 F4 Lauria Italy
79 E5 Laurinburg U.S.A.
68 C2 Laurium U.S.A.
46 C7 Lausanne Switz.
33 E3 Laut i. Indon.
91 B3 Lautaro Chile
43 H4 Lautersbach (Hessen) Ger.
33 E3 Laut Kecil, Kepulauan is Indon.
7 H3 Lautoka Fiji
36 V5 Lauvuskylä Fin.
66 F4 Laval Can.
44 D2 Laval France
48 F1 Lavant r. Austria/Slovenia
88 B5 Lavapié, Pta pt Chile
18 C4 Lāvar Kabkān Iran
84 D3 La Venta Mex.
6 C4 Laverton Austr.
89 D2 La Victoria Venez.
69 G2 Lavigne Can.
72 E2 Lavina U.S.A.
90 D3 Lavras Brazil
91 G1 Lavras do Sul Brazil
59 J3 Lavumisa Swaziland
22 B2 Lawa Pak.
92 C6 Law Dome ice feature Ant.
32 B4 Lawit, Gunung mt Malaysia
17 J7 Lawqah waterhole S. Arabia
54 B3 Lawra Ghana
76 E4 Lawrence KS U.S.A.
81 H3 Lawrence MA U.S.A.
79 C5 Lawrenceburg U.S.A.
81 K2 Lawrence Station Can.
80 E6 Lawrenceville U.S.A.
77 D5 Lawton U.S.A.
14 B4 Lawz, J. al mt S. Arabia
37 O7 Laxå Sweden
58 E3 Laxey S. Africa
38 C3 Laxey U.K.
40 C2 Laxford, Loch in. U.K.
40 □ Laxo U.K.
8 D5 Layers Hill Austr.
17 K4 Laylān Iraq
5 K2 Laysan Island i. HI U.S.A.
74 A2 Laytonville U.S.A.
49 J2 Lazarevac Yugo.
92 D3 Lazarev Sea sea Ant.
51 F7 Lazarevskoye Rus. Fed.
73 D6 Lázaro Cárdenas Baja California Mex.
84 B3 Lázaro Cárdenas Mex.
84 A1 Lázaro Cárdenas, Presa resr Mex.
91 F2 Lazcano Uru.
37 S9 Lazdijai Lith.
18 D5 Lāzeh Iran
13 P3 Lazo Rus. Fed.
28 C3 Lazo Rus. Fed.
32 B2 Leach Cambodia
68 E2 Leach I. i. Can.
76 C2 Lead U.S.A.
65 H4 Leader Can.
8 G2 Leadville Austr.
73 F4 Leadville U.S.A.
77 F6 Leaf r. U.S.A.
65 J3 Leaf Rapids Can.
77 D6 Leakey U.S.A.
69 F4 Leamington Can.
75 F2 Leamington U.S.A.
39 F5 Leamington Spa, Royal U.K.
27 E5 Le'an China
41 B5 Leane, Lough l. Rep. of Ireland
41 B6 Leap Rep. of Ireland
65 H4 Leask Can.
39 G6 Leatherhead U.K.
76 E4 Leavenworth KS U.S.A.
72 B2 Leavenworth WA U.S.A.
74 C2 Leavitt Peak summit U.S.A.
42 E5 Lebach Ger.
31 C5 Lebak Phil.
68 D5 Lebanon IN U.S.A.
76 D4 Lebanon KS U.S.A.
77 E4 Lebanon MO U.S.A.
81 G3 Lebanon NH U.S.A.
81 F4 Lebanon NJ U.S.A.
80 A5 Lebanon OH U.S.A.
72 B2 Lebanon OR U.S.A.
81 E4 Lebanon PA U.S.A.
79 C4 Lebanon TN U.S.A.
10 E6 Lebanon country Asia
42 C4 Lebbeke Belgium
50 F4 Lebedyan' Rus. Fed.
51 E5 Lebedyn Ukr.
44 E3 Le Blanc France
46 H3 Lębork Pol.
59 H2 Lebowakgomo S. Africa
45 C4 Lebrija Spain
46 H3 Łebsko, Jezioro lag. Pol.
91 B3 Lebu Chile
42 B4 Le Cateau-Cambrésis France
42 B4 Le Catelet France
49 H4 Lecce Italy
48 C2 Lecco Italy
46 E7 Lech r. Austria/Ger.
49 J6 Lechaina Greece
27 D5 Lechang China
42 C5 Le Chesne France
46 E7 Lechtaler Alpen mts Austria
46 D3 Leck Ger.
44 G3 Le Creusot France
44 E5 Lectoure France
32 B5 Ledang, Gunung mt Malaysia
39 E5 Ledbury U.K.
45 D2 Ledesma Spain
40 D2 Ledmore U.K.
50 E1 Ledmozero Rus. Fed.
27 C7 Ledong China
26 B2 Ledu China
64 G4 Leduc Can.
81 G3 Lee U.S.A.
76 E2 Leech L. l. U.S.A.
38 F4 Leeds U.K.
81 H2 Leeds Junction U.S.A.
39 B7 Leedstown U.K.
42 E1 Leek Neth.
39 E4 Leek U.K.
42 D3 Leende Neth.
80 D4 Leeper U.S.A.
42 F1 Leer (Ostfriesland) Ger.
79 D6 Leesburg FL U.S.A.
80 E5 Leesburg VA U.S.A.
43 H2 Leese Ger.
77 E6 Leesville U.S.A.
80 C4 Leesville Lake l. U.S.A.
8 F3 Leeton Austr.
58 D6 Leeu-Gamka S. Africa
42 D1 Leeuwarden Neth.
6 B5 Leeuwin, C. c. Austr.
74 C3 Lee Vining U.S.A.
83 M5 Leeward Islands is Caribbean Sea
16 D4 Lefka Cyprus
49 J5 Lefkada Greece
49 J5 Lefkada i. Greece
16 D4 Lefkara Cyprus
49 J5 Lefkimmi Greece
Lefkosia see Nicosia
31 B3 Legaspi Phil.
42 F2 Legden Ger.
74 A2 Leggett U.S.A.
48 D2 Legnago Italy
46 H5 Legnica Pol.
22 D2 Leh Jammu and Kashmir
44 E2 Le Havre France
81 F4 Lehighton U.S.A.
36 V5 Lehmo Fin.
43 L2 Lehnin Ger.
43 J2 Lehre Ger.
43 H2 Lehrte Ger.
36 S5 Lehtimäki Fin.
58 D1 Lehututu Botswana
22 B3 Leiah Pak.
46 G7 Leibnitz Austria
39 F5 Leicester U.K.
6 D3 Leichhardt r. Austr.
42 C2 Leiden Neth.
9 E2 Leigh N.Z.
38 E4 Leigh U.K.
39 G6 Leighton Buzzard U.K.
43 G5 Leimen Ger.
43 H2 Leine r. Ger.
43 J3 Leinefelde Ger.
41 E5 Leinster, Mount h. Rep. of Ireland
49 M6 Leipsoi i. Greece
43 L3 Leipzig Ger.
36 O3 Leiranger Norway
45 B3 Leiria Port.

27 C5 Leishan China
27 D5 Lei Shui r. China
43 L3 Leisnig Ger.
78 C4 Leitchfield U.S.A.
89 B4 Leiva, Co mt Col.
41 E4 Leixlip Rep. of Ireland
27 D5 Leiyang China
27 C6 Leizhou Bandao pen. China
27 D6 Leizhou Wan b. China
36 M4 Leka Norway
56 B4 Lékana Congo
48 C6 Le Kef Tunisia
58 B4 Lekkersing S. Africa
56 B4 Lékoni Gabon
37 O6 Leksand Sweden
36 W5 Leksozero, Oz. l. Rus. Fed.
68 E3 Leland MI U.S.A.
77 F5 Leland MS U.S.A.
54 A3 Lélouma Guinea
42 D2 Lelystad Neth.
88 C9 Le Maire, Estrecho de chan. Arg.
44 H3 Léman, Lac l. France/Switz.
44 E2 Le Mans France
76 D3 Le Mars U.S.A.
42 F5 Lemberg France
43 G2 Lembruch Ger.
90 C3 Leme Brazil
42 E2 Lemele Neth.
31 B3 Lemery Phil.
Lemesos see Limassol
43 G2 Lemgo Ger.
37 U6 Lemi Fin.
63 M3 Lemieux Islands is Can.
36 T2 Lemmenjoen Kansallispuisto nat. park Fin.
42 D2 Lemmer Neth.
76 C2 Lemmon U.S.A.
75 G5 Lemmon, Mt mt U.S.A.
74 C3 Lemoore U.S.A.
23 H5 Lemro r. Myanmar
32 A3 Lem Tom Chob pt Thai.
48 G4 Le Murge reg. Italy
37 L8 Lemvig Denmark
68 C4 Lena U.S.A.
24 C1 Lena r. Rus. Fed.
23 E2 Lenchung Tso salt l. China
87 K4 Lençóis Maranhenses, Parque Nacional dos nat. park Brazil
19 E4 Lengbarūt Iran
43 F2 Lengerich Ger.
26 A2 Lenglong Ling mts China
27 D5 Lengshuijiang China
27 D5 Lengshuitan China
91 B1 Lengua de Vaca, Pta hd Chile
39 H6 Lenham U.K.
37 O8 Lenhovda Sweden
19 H2 Lenin Tajik.
51 H7 Lenina, Kanal canal Rus. Fed.
Leningrad see St Petersburg
51 F6 Leningradskaya Rus. Fed.
50 E3 Leningradskaya Oblast' div. Rus. Fed.
13 T3 Leningradskiy Rus. Fed.
28 D2 Lenino Rus. Fed.
14 E2 Leninsk Kazak.
51 H5 Leninsk Rus. Fed.
50 F4 Leninskiy Rus. Fed.
24 A1 Leninsk-Kuznetskiy Rus. Fed.
50 H3 Leninskoye Rus. Fed.
43 F3 Lenne r. Ger.
79 D5 Lenoir U.S.A.
81 G3 Lenox U.S.A.
44 F1 Lens France
13 N3 Lensk Rus. Fed.
51 G7 Lentekhi Georgia
46 H7 Lenti Hungary
48 F6 Lentini Sicily Italy
43 K1 Lenzen Ger.
54 B3 Léo Burkina
46 G7 Leoben Austria
39 E5 Leominster U.K.
81 H3 Leominster U.S.A.
84 B2 León Mex.
82 G6 León Nic.
45 D1 León Spain
89 A3 León r. Col.
57 B6 Leonardville Namibia
16 E4 Leonarisson Cyprus
8 E5 Leongatha Austr.
6 C4 Leonora Austr.
90 D3 Leopoldina Brazil
65 H4 Leoville Can.
59 G1 Lephalala r. S. Africa
57 C6 Lephepe Botswana
59 F5 Lephoi S. Africa
27 E4 Leping China
44 G4 Le Pont-de-Claix France
36 U5 Leppävirta Fin.
44 F4 Le-Puy-en-Velay France
42 B4 Le Quesnoy France
59 G1 Lerala Botswana
59 G4 Leratswana S. Africa
55 D4 Léré Chad
89 C5 Lerida Col.
Lérida see Lleida
17 M2 Lerik Azer.
45 E1 Lerma Spain
51 G6 Lermontov Rus. Fed.
28 D1 Lermontovka Rus. Fed.
49 M6 Leros i. Greece
68 C5 Le Roy U.S.A.
37 N8 Lerum Sweden
40 □ Lerwick U.K.
49 L5 Lesbos i. Greece
83 K5 Les Cayes Haiti
67 G4 Les Escoumins Can.
81 J1 Les Étroits Can.
45 G1 Le Seu d'Urgell Spain
27 B4 Leshan China
49 J3 Leskovac Yugo.
40 E4 Leslie U.K.
44 B2 Lesneven France
50 K3 Lesnoy Rus. Fed.
28 D1 Lesopil'noye Rus. Fed.
12 L4 Lesosibirsk Rus. Fed.
53 G8 Lesotho country Africa
28 C2 Lesozavodsk Rus. Fed.
44 D3 Les Sables-d'Olonne France
42 D4 Lesse r. Belgium
83 L6 Lesser Antilles is Caribbean Sea
Lesser Caucasus mts see Malyy Kavkaz
64 G3 Lesser Slave Lake l. Can.
64 G3 Lesser Slave Lake Provincial Park res. Can.
42 B4 Lessines Belgium
36 T5 Lestijärvi Fin.
36 T5 Lestijärvi l. Fin.
Lesvos i. see Lesbos
46 H5 Leszno Pol.
59 J1 Letaba S. Africa
39 G6 Letchworth U.K.
22 D4 Leteri India
23 H5 Letha Range mts Myanmar
64 G5 Lethbridge Can.
86 G3 Lethem Guyana
86 E4 Leticia Col.
25 E7 Leti, Kepulauan is Indon.
26 F2 Leting China
59 F2 Letlhakeng Botswana
39 J7 Le Touquet-Paris-Plage France
44 E1 Le Tréport France
59 J1 Letsitele S. Africa
32 A3 Letsok-aw Kyun i. Myanmar
59 F3 Letsopa S. Africa
41 D3 Letterkenny Rep. of Ireland
33 C2 Letung Indon.
43 K2 Letzlingen Ger.
40 F4 Leuchars U.K.
50 G1 Leunovo Rus. Fed.
75 G4 Leupp Corner U.S.A.
42 D2 Leusden Neth.
33 A2 Leuser, G. mt Indon.
43 J5 Leutershausen Ger.
42 C4 Leuven Belgium
49 K5 Levadeia Greece
75 G2 Levan U.S.A.
36 M5 Levanger Norway
48 C2 Levanto Italy
48 E5 Levanzo, Isola di i. Sicily Italy
51 H7 Levashi Rus. Fed.
77 C5 Levelland U.S.A.
38 G4 Leven Eng. U.K.
40 F4 Leven Scot. U.K.
40 C4 Leven, Loch in. U.K.
40 E4 Leven, Loch l. U.K.
6 C3 Lévêque, C. c. Austr.
68 E3 Levering U.S.A.
42 E3 Leverkusen Ger.
47 J6 Levice Slovakia
9 E4 Levin N.Z.
67 F4 Lévis Can.
49 M6 Levitha i. Greece
81 G4 Levittown NY U.S.A.
81 F4 Levittown PA U.S.A.
49 L3 Levski Bulg.
39 H7 Lewes U.K.
81 F5 Lewes U.S.A.
40 B2 Lewis i. U.K.
80 E4 Lewisburg PA U.S.A.
80 C6 Lewisburg WV U.S.A.
9 D5 Lewis Pass pass N.Z.
72 D1 Lewis Range mts U.S.A.
79 C5 Lewis Smith, L. l. U.S.A.
75 G6 Lewis Springs U.S.A.
72 C2 Lewiston ID U.S.A.
81 H2 Lewiston ME U.S.A.
68 B4 Lewiston MN U.S.A.
68 B5 Lewistown IL U.S.A.
72 E2 Lewistown MT U.S.A.
80 E4 Lewistown PA U.S.A.
77 E5 Lewisville U.S.A.
77 D5 Lewisville, Lake l. U.S.A.
68 C5 Lexington IL U.S.A.
78 C4 Lexington KY U.S.A.
76 E4 Lexington MO U.S.A.
79 D5 Lexington NC U.S.A.
76 D3 Lexington NE U.S.A.
79 B5 Lexington TN U.S.A.
80 D6 Lexington VA U.S.A.
80 E5 Lexington Park U.S.A.
59 J1 Leydsdorp S. Africa
27 C5 Leye China
17 L3 Leyla D. h. Iran
31 C4 Leyte i. Phil.
31 C4 Leyte Gulf g. Phil.
49 H4 Lezhë Albania
27 B4 Lezhi China
51 E5 L'gov Rus. Fed.
23 H3 Lhari China
23 G3 Lhasa China
23 G3 Lhasa He r. China
23 F3 Lhazê China
23 F3 Lhazhong China
33 A1 Lhokseumawe Indon.
32 A4 Lhoksukon Indon.
23 H3 Lhorong China
23 H3 Lhünzê China
23 G3 Lhünzhub China
27 E5 Liancheng China
42 A5 Liancourt France
Liancourt Rocks i. see Tok-tō
31 C4 Lianga Phil.
31 C4 Lianga Bay b. Phil.
27 E4 Liangaz Hu l. China
26 D1 Liangcheng China
26 C3 Liangdang China
26 B3 Lianghekou China
27 C4 Liangping China
27 B5 Liangwang Shan mts China
26 C2 Liangzhen China
27 D5 Lianhua China
27 E6 Lianhua Shan mts China
27 F5 Lianjiang Fujian China
27 D6 Lianjiang Guangdong China
27 D5 Liannan China
27 E5 Lianping China
27 D5 Lianshan China
26 F3 Lianshui China
32 B2 Liant, C. pt Thai.
27 D5 Lian Xian China
27 D5 Lianyuan China
26 F3 Lianyungang Jiangsu China
30 F1 Lianzhushan China
30 B2 Liao r. China
26 E2 Liaocheng China
30 B3 Liaodong Bandao pen. China
30 A3 Liaodong Wan b. China
30 B3 Liaohe Kou river mouth China
30 B3 Liaoning div. China
30 B3 Liaoyang China
30 C2 Liaoyuan China
30 B3 Liaozhong China
49 H5 Liapades Greece
22 B2 Liaqatabad Pak.
64 E2 Liard r. Can.
64 D3 Liard River Can.
19 G5 Liari Pak.
40 C3 Liathach mt U.K.
16 F4 Liban, Jebel mts Lebanon
89 B3 Libano Col.
72 D1 Libby U.S.A.
56 B3 Libenge Congo(Zaire)
77 C4 Liberal U.S.A.
46 G5 Liberec Czech Rep.
83 G6 Liberia Costa Rica
53 D5 Liberia country Africa
89 C2 Libertad Venez.
89 C2 Libertad Venez.
68 B6 Liberty IL U.S.A.
81 J2 Liberty ME U.S.A.
76 E4 Liberty MO U.S.A.
81 F4 Liberty NY U.S.A.
77 E6 Liberty TX U.S.A.
42 D5 Libin Belgium
31 B3 Libmanan Phil.
27 C5 Libo China
59 H5 Libode S. Africa
44 D4 Libourne France
56 A3 Libreville Gabon
31 C5 Libuganon r. Phil.
52 F3 Libya country Africa
52 G3 Libyan Desert. Egypt/Libya
55 E1 Libyan Plateau plat. Egypt
81 D2 Licantén Chile
48 E6 Licata Sicily Italy
17 H2 Lice Turkey
43 G4 Lich Ger.
39 F5 Lichfield U.K.
57 D5 Lichinga Moz.
43 K4 Lichte Ger.
43 G3 Lichtenau Ger.
59 G3 Lichtenburg S. Africa
43 K4 Lichtenfels Ger.
42 E3 Lichtenvoorde Neth.
27 C4 Lichuan Hubei China
27 E5 Lichuan Jiangxi China
80 B5 Licking r. U.S.A.
50 C4 Lida Belarus
74 D3 Lida U.S.A.
58 C2 Lidfontein Namibia
37 N7 Lidköping Sweden
36 O4 Lidsjöberg Sweden
43 H2 Liebenau Ger.
43 J2 Liebenburg Ger.
43 M2 Liebenwalde Ger.
6 D4 Liebig, Mt mt Austr.
34 F4 Liechtenstein country Europe
42 D4 Liège Belgium
36 W5 Lieksa Fin.
47 M2 Lielupe r. Latvia
37 T8 Lielvārde Latvia
36 P5 Lien Sweden
56 C3 Lienart Congo(Zaire)
46 F7 Lienz Austria
37 R8 Liepāja Latvia
42 C3 Lier Belgium
37 J7 Liervik Norway
42 D3 Lieshout Neth.
42 A4 Liévin France
69 K2 Lièvre r. Can.
46 G7 Liezen Austria
41 E4 Liffey r. Rep. of Ireland
41 D3 Lifford Rep. of Ireland
91 C4 Lifi Mahuida mt Arg.
7 G4 Lifou i. New Caledonia
31 B3 Ligao Phil.
37 T8 Līgatne Latvia
57 D5 Ligonha r. Moz.
68 E5 Ligonier U.S.A.
Ligure, Mar sea see Ligurian Sea
44 J5 Ligurian Sea sea France/Italy
6 F2 Lihir Group is P.N.G.
74 □2 Lihue U.S.A.
27 D5 Li Jiang r. China
26 F2 Lijin China
57 C5 Likasi Congo(Zaire)
64 E4 Likely Can.
50 E3 Likhoslavl' Rus. Fed.
33 C2 Liku Indon.
50 G3 Likurga Rus. Fed.
48 C3 L'Île-Rousse Corsica France
43 G1 Lilienthal Ger.
27 D5 Liling China
22 C2 Lilla Pak.
37 N7 Lilla Edet Sweden
42 C3 Lille Belgium
44 F1 Lille France
37 L9 Lille Bælt chan. Denmark
37 M6 Lillehammer Norway
42 A4 Lillers France
37 L7 Lillesand Norway
37 M7 Lillestrom Norway
68 E4 Lilley U.S.A.
36 O5 Lillholmsjö Sweden
64 E4 Lillooet Can.
64 E4 Lillooet r. Can.
23 H4 Lilong India
57 D5 Lilongwe Malawi
31 B4 Liloy Phil.
8 B2 Lilydale Austr.
86 C6 Lima Peru
72 D2 Lima MT U.S.A.
80 A4 Lima OH U.S.A.
18 E5 Līmah Oman
51 H6 Liman Rus. Fed.
91 B1 Limarí r. Chile
23 E2 Lima Ringma Tso salt l. China
16 D4 Limassol Cyprus
41 E2 Limavady U.K.
91 C3 Limay r. Arg.
91 C3 Limay Mahuida Arg.
37 T8 Limbaži Latvia
54 C4 Limbe Cameroon
33 E3 Limbungan Indon.
43 G4 Limburg an der Lahn Ger.
32 □ Lim Chu Kang Sing.
32 □ Lim Chu Kang h. Sing.
58 E4 Lime Acres S. Africa
90 C3 Limeira Brazil
41 C5 Limerick Rep. of Ireland
68 A4 Lime Springs U.S.A.
81 K1 Limestone U.S.A.
36 N4 Limingen Norway
36 N4 Limingen l. Norway
81 H3 Limington U.S.A.
36 T4 Liminka Fin.
49 L5 Limnos i. Greece
81 F2 Limoges Can.
44 E4 Limoges France
83 H6 Limón Costa Rica
73 G4 Limon U.S.A.
16 E3 Limonlu Turkey
44 E4 Limousin reg. France
44 F5 Limoux France
59 K1 Limpopo r. Africa
18 A4 Līnah S. Arabia
36 W2 Linakhamari Rus. Fed.
27 F4 Lin'an China
31 A4 Linapacan i. Phil.
31 A4 Linapacan Strait chan. Phil.
91 B2 Linares Chile
84 C1 Linares Mex.
45 E3 Linares Spain
24 C4 Lincang China
26 E2 Lincheng China
27 E5 Linchuan China
91 E2 Lincoln Arg.
39 G4 Lincoln U.K.
74 B2 Lincoln CA U.S.A.
68 C5 Lincoln IL U.S.A.
81 J2 Lincoln ME U.S.A.
69 F3 Lincoln MI U.S.A.
76 D3 Lincoln NE U.S.A.
81 H2 Lincoln NH U.S.A.
72 A2 Lincoln City U.S.A.
69 F4 Lincoln Park U.S.A.
60 M1 Lincoln Sea sea Can./Greenland
39 G4 Lincolnshire Wolds reg. U.K.
81 J2 Lincolnville U.S.A.
90 E1 Linda, Sa h. Brazil
43 L2 Lindau Ger.
46 D7 Lindau (Bodensee) Ger.
43 K3 Linden Ger.
87 G2 Linden Guyana
79 C5 Linden AL U.S.A.
79 C5 Linden TN U.S.A.
68 A2 Linden Grove U.S.A.
63 O3 Lindenow Fjord in. Greenland
43 F2 Lindern (Oldenburg) Ger.
37 K7 Lindesnes c. Norway
57 D4 Lindi Tanz.
56 C3 Lindi r. Congo(Zaire)
Lindisfarne i. see Holy Island
59 G3 Lindley S. Africa
49 N6 Lindos, Akra pt Greece
81 K1 Lindsay N.B. Can.
69 H3 Lindsay Ont. Can.
74 C3 Lindsay U.S.A.
5 L4 Line Islands is Pac. Oc.
26 D2 Linfen China
21 A3 Linganamakki Reservoir India
31 B2 Lingayen Phil.
31 B2 Lingayen Gulf b. Phil.
26 D3 Lingbao China
26 E3 Lingbi China
27 D5 Lingchuan Guangxi China
26 D3 Lingchuan Shanxi China
59 G6 Lingelethu S. Africa
59 F6 Lingelihle S. Africa
42 F2 Lingen (Ems) Ger.
33 B3 Lingga, Kepulauan is Indon.
31 C5 Lingig Phil.
72 F3 Lingle U.S.A.
56 C3 Lingomo Congo(Zaire)
26 E2 Lingqiu China
27 C6 Lingshan China
27 C7 Lingshui China
21 B2 Lingsugur India
26 C3 Lingtai China
27 C5 Lingtou China
54 A3 Linguère Senegal
27 D5 Lingui China
26 C2 Lingwu China
27 D5 Ling Xian China
26 F1 Lingyuan China
27 C5 Lingyun China
22 D2 Lingzi Thang Plains l. China/Jammu and Kashmir
27 F4 Linhai China
90 E2 Linhares Brazil
32 C1 Linh Cam Vietnam
26 C1 Linhe China
81 H1 Linière Can.
30 D3 Linjiang China
37 O7 Linköping Sweden
30 F1 Linkou China
27 D4 Linli China
40 E5 Linlithgow U.K.
26 D2 Linlü Shan mt China
40 C4 Linnhe, Loch in. U.K.
42 E4 Linnich Ger.
74 A1 Linn, Mt mt U.S.A.
26 E2 Linqing China
26 F2 Linqu China
26 E3 Linquan China
26 D3 Linru China
90 C3 Lins Brazil
26 F3 Linshu China
27 C4 Linshui China
26 B3 Lintan China
26 B3 Lintao China
76 C2 Linton U.S.A.
26 C3 Lintong China
26 F1 Linxi China
26 B3 Linxia China
26 D2 Lin Xian China
27 D4 Linxiang China
26 E2 Linyi Shandong China
26 F3 Linyi Shandong China
26 D3 Linyi Shanxi China
26 E3 Linying China
46 G6 Linz Austria
26 A2 Linze China
44 F5 Lion, Golfe du g. France
69 G3 Lion's Head Can.
81 F4 Lionville U.S.A.
56 B3 Liouesso Congo
31 B3 Lipa Phil.
48 F5 Lipari Italy
48 F5 Lipari, Isola i. Italy
48 F5 Lipari, Isole is Italy
51 F4 Lipetsk Rus. Fed.
51 F4 Lipetskaya Oblast' div. Rus. Fed.
50 F2 Lipin Bor Rus. Fed.
27 C5 Liping China
49 J1 Lipova Romania
28 B2 Lipovtsy Rus. Fed.
43 E3 Lippe r. Ger.
43 G3 Lippstadt Ger.
22 E3 Lipti Lekh pass Nepal
8 E5 Liptrap, C. hd Austr.
27 D5 Lipu China
56 D3 Lira Uganda
56 B4 Liranga Congo
31 C6 Lirung Indon.
56 C3 Lisala Congo(Zaire)
41 D3 Lisbellaw U.K.
Lisboa see Lisbon
45 B3 Lisbon Port.
68 C5 Lisbon IL U.S.A.
81 H2 Lisbon ME U.S.A.
76 D2 Lisbon ND U.S.A.
81 H2 Lisbon NH U.S.A.
80 C4 Lisbon OH U.S.A.
41 E3 Lisburn U.K.
41 B5 Liscannor Bay b. Rep. of Ireland
41 B4 Lisdoonvarna Rep. of Ireland
27 F5 Li-shan Taiwan
26 D2 Lishi China
30 C2 Lishu China
26 F4 Lishui Jiangsu China
27 F4 Lishui Zhejiang China
27 D4 Li Shui r. China
44 E2 Lisieux France
39 C7 Liskeard U.K.
51 F5 Liski Rus. Fed.
42 A5 L'Isle-Adam France
44 G5 L'Isle-sur-la-Sorgue France
41 D5 Lismore Rep. of Ireland
40 C4 Lismore i. U.K.
41 D3 Lisnarrick U.K.
41 D3 Lisnaskea U.K.
69 G4 Listowel Can.
41 B5 Listowel Rep. of Ireland
36 O5 Lit Sweden
27 C6 Litang Guangxi China
24 C3 Litang Sichuan China
87 H3 Litani r. Fr. Guiana/Suriname
16 E5 Līṭāni r. Lebanon
74 B1 Litchfield CA U.S.A.
78 B4 Litchfield IL U.S.A.
71 H2 Litchfield MN U.S.A.
44 D4 Lit-et-Mixe France
8 H2 Lithgow Austr.
35 H3 Lithuania country Europe
81 E4 Lititz U.S.A.
46 G5 Litoměřice Czech Rep.
79 E7 Little Abaco i. Bahamas
79 E7 Little Bahama Bank sand bank Bahamas
9 E2 Little Barrier i. N.Z.
68 D3 Little Bay de Noc b. U.S.A.
72 E2 Little Belt Mts mts U.S.A.
83 H5 Little Cayman i. Cayman Is
75 H4 Little Colorado r. U.S.A.
75 F3 Little Creek Peak summit U.S.A.
69 G3 Little Current Can.
66 C3 Little Current r. Can.
39 D7 Little Dart r. U.K.
8 C4 Little Desert Nat. Park Austr.
81 F5 Little Egg Harbor in. U.S.A.
79 F7 Little Exuma i. Bahamas
76 E2 Little Falls MN U.S.A.
81 F3 Little Falls NY U.S.A.
75 F3 Littlefield AZ U.S.A.
77 C5 Littlefield TX U.S.A.
76 E1 Little Fork U.S.A.
68 A1 Little Fork r. U.S.A.
23 F4 Little Gandak r. India
65 K4 Little Grand Rapids Can.
39 G7 Littlehampton U.K.
80 C5 Little Kanawha r. U.S.A.
58 C3 Little Karas Berg plat. Namibia
58 D6 Little Karoo plat. S. Africa
68 D2 Little Lake U.S.A.
67 H3 Little Mecatina r. Can.
80 A5 Little Miami r. U.S.A.
40 B3 Little Minch str. U.K.
76 C2 Little Missouri r. U.S.A.
39 H5 Little Ouse r. U.K.
68 D1 Little Pic r. Can.
22 B5 Little Rann marsh India
77 E5 Little Rock U.S.A.
68 D4 Little Sable Pt pt U.S.A.
79 F7 Little San Salvador i. Bahamas
64 F4 Little Smoky r. Can.
73 F4 Littleton CO U.S.A.
81 H2 Littleton NH U.S.A.
80 C5 Littleton WV U.S.A.
68 E3 Little Traverse Bay b. U.S.A.
17 J4 Little Zab r. Iraq
57 D5 Litunde Moz.
64 B3 Lituya Bay b. U.S.A.
30 B2 Liu r. China
26 C3 Liuba China
27 F6 Liuchiu Yü i. Taiwan
27 C5 Liuchong He r. China
30 B5 Liugong Dao i. China
26 F1 Liugu r. China
30 C2 Liuhe China
27 D4 Liujiachang China
27 C5 Liujiang China
26 B3 Liujiaxia Sk. resr China
26 C3 Liupan Shan mts China
27 B5 Liupanshui China
27 D4 Liuyang China
27 C5 Liuzhou China
28 C3 Livadiya Rus. Fed.
37 U8 Līvāni Latvia
74 B2 Live Oak CA U.S.A.
79 D6 Live Oak FL U.S.A.
6 C3 Liveringa Austr.
74 B3 Livermore U.S.A.
81 H2 Livermore Falls U.S.A.
77 B6 Livermore, Mt mt U.S.A.
8 H2 Liverpool Austr.
67 H5 Liverpool Can.
39 E4 Liverpool U.K.
39 D4 Liverpool Bay U.K.
62 E3 Liverpool Bay b. Can.
63 L2 Liverpool, C. c. Can.
8 H1 Liverpool Plains Austr.
8 H1 Liverpool Ra. mts Austr.
40 E5 Livingston U.K.
74 B3 Livingston CA U.S.A.
72 E2 Livingston MT U.S.A.
79 C4 Livingston TN U.S.A.
77 E6 Livingston TX U.S.A.
57 C5 Livingstone Zambia
92 B2 Livingston I. i. Ant.
77 E6 Livingston, L. l. U.S.A.
48 G3 Livno Bos.-Herz.
51 F4 Livny Rus. Fed.
36 U4 Livojoki r. Fin.
69 F4 Livonia U.S.A.
48 D3 Livorno Italy
90 E1 Livramento do Brumado Brazil
18 E5 Liwā Oman
57 D4 Liwale Tanz.
26 B3 Li Xian Gansu China
27 D4 Li Xian Hunan China
26 B4 Li Xian Sichuan China
26 E3 Lixin China
26 F4 Liyang China
39 B8 Lizard U.K.
39 B8 Lizard Point pt U.K.
42 B5 Lizy-sur-Ourcq France
48 F1 Ljubljana Slovenia
37 O8 Ljugarn Sweden
37 P5 Ljungan r. Sweden
37 P5 Ljungaverk Sweden
37 N8 Ljungby Sweden
37 P6 Ljusdal Sweden
37 O6 Ljusnan r. Sweden
37 P6 Ljusne Sweden
88 B5 Llaima, Volcán volc. Chile
39 C5 Llanbadarn Fawr U.K.
39 D5 Llanbister U.K.
39 D6 Llandeilo U.K.
39 C6 Llandissilio U.K.
39 D6 Llandovery U.K.
39 D5 Llandrindod Wells U.K.
39 D4 Llandudno U.K.
39 C5 Llandysul U.K.
39 C6 Llanegwad U.K.
39 C6 Llanelli U.K.
39 C4 Llanerchymedd U.K.
39 D5 Llanfair Caereinion U.K.
39 C4 Llangefni U.K.
39 D5 Llangollen U.K.
39 D5 Llangurig U.K.
39 C4 Llanllyfni U.K.
39 C5 Llannor U.K.
77 D6 Llano U.S.A.
77 D6 Llano r. U.S.A.
77 C5 Llano Estacado plain U.S.A.
89 C3 Llanos reg. Col./Venez.
91 B4 Llanquihue, L. l. Chile
39 C5 Llanrhystud U.K.
39 D6 Llantrisant U.K.
39 D5 Llanuwchllyn U.K.
39 D5 Llanwnog U.K.
39 D4 Llay U.K.
45 G2 Lleida Spain
45 C3 Llerena Spain
45 F3 Llíria Spain
45 E1 Llodio Spain
62 F4 Lloyd George, Mt Can.
65 H3 Lloyd Lake l. Can.
65 G4 Lloydminster Can.
45 H3 Llucmajor Spain
88 C2 Llullaillaco, Vol. volc. Chile
27 B6 Lô r. China/Vietnam
75 G2 Loa U.S.A.
88 C2 Loa r. Chile
50 J3 Loban' r. Rus. Fed.
45 D4 Lobatejo mt Spain
57 C6 Lobatse Botswana
43 K3 Löbejün Ger.
43 L3 Löbenberg h. Ger.
91 E3 Loberia Arg.
57 B5 Lobito Angola
91 E2 Lobos Arg.
43 L2 Loburg Ger.
40 D4 Lochaber reg. U.K.
40 C4 Lochaline U.K.
69 E1 Lochalsh Can.
40 A3 Lochboisdale U.K.
40 C3 Lochcarron U.K.
38 C1 Lochearnhead U.K.
42 E2 Lochem Neth.
44 E3 Loches France
40 E4 Lochgelly U.K.
40 C4 Lochgilphead U.K.
40 C2 Lochinver U.K.
40 A3 Lochmaddy U.K.
40 E4 Lochnagar mt U.K.
80 E5 Loch Raven Reservoir U.S.A.
40 D4 Lochy, Loch l. U.K.
40 E5 Lockerbie U.K.
8 F3 Lockhart Austr.
77 D6 Lockhart U.S.A.
80 E4 Lock Haven U.S.A.
80 D3 Lockport U.S.A.
32 C3 Lôc Ninh Vietnam
80 B5 Locust Grove U.S.A.
16 E6 Lod Israel
8 D3 Loddon r. Austr.
44 F5 Lodève France
50 E2 Lodeynoye Pole Rus. Fed.
72 F2 Lodge Grass U.S.A.
22 B3 Lodhran Pak.
48 C2 Lodi Italy
74 B2 Lodi CA U.S.A.
80 B4 Lodi OH U.S.A.
36 O2 Lødingen Norway
56 D3 Lodwar Kenya
47 J5 Łódź Pol.
19 H3 Loe Dakka Afgh.
58 C5 Loeriesfontein S. Africa
36 N2 Lofoten is Norway
51 G5 Log Rus. Fed.
73 G5 Logan NM U.S.A.
80 B5 Logan OH U.S.A.
72 E3 Logan UT U.S.A.
80 C6 Logan WV U.S.A.
64 D2 Logan Mountains mts Can.
64 A2 Logan, Mt mt Can.
62 D3 Logan, Mt mt Can.
68 D5 Logansport U.S.A.
48 F2 Logatec Slovenia
45 E1 Logroño Spain
23 H4 Logtak L. l. India
58 E4 Lohatlha S. Africa
43 H3 Lohfelden Ger.
36 T3 Lohiniva Fin.
37 S6 Lohjanjärvi l. Fin.
43 G2 Löhne Ger.
43 G2 Lohne (Oldenburg) Ger.
36 S4 Lohtaja Fin.
32 A1 Loikaw Myanmar
32 A1 Loi Lan mt Myanmar/Thai.
37 S6 Loimaa Fin.
44 E3 Loire r. France
86 C4 Loja Ecuador
45 D4 Loja Spain
33 E1 Lokan r. Malaysia
36 U3 Lokan tekojärvi l. Fin.
42 C3 Lokeren Belgium
58 D2 Lokgwabe Botswana
56 D3 Lokichar Kenya
56 D3 Lokichokio Kenya
37 L8 Løkken Denmark
36 L5 Løkken Norway
47 P2 Loknya Rus. Fed.
54 C4 Lokoja Nigeria
54 C4 Lokossa Benin
51 E4 Lokot' Rus. Fed.
37 T7 Loksa Estonia
63 M3 Loks Land i. Can.
54 B4 Lola Guinea
74 B2 Lola, Mt mt U.S.A.
37 M9 Lolland i. Denmark
56 D4 Lollondo Tanz.
72 D2 Lolo U.S.A.
58 E3 Lolwane S. Africa
49 K3 Lom Bulg.
37 L6 Lom Norway
56 C4 Lomami r. Congo(Zaire)
91 D3 Loma Negra, Planicie de la plain Arg.
19 G3 Lomar Pass pass Afgh.
84 C2 Lomas del Real Mex.
91 E2 Lomas de Zamora Arg.
33 E4 Lombok i. Indon.
33 E4 Lombok, Selat chan. Indon.
54 C4 Lomé Togo
56 C4 Lomela Congo(Zaire)
56 C4 Lomela r. Congo(Zaire)
42 A4 Lomme France
42 D3 Lommel Belgium
40 D4 Lomond, Loch l. U.K.
50 G1 Lomovoye Rus. Fed.
25 D7 Lompobattang, Gunung mt Indon.
74 B4 Lompoc U.S.A.
47 L4 Łomża Pol.
22 D6 Lonar India
91 B3 Loncoche Chile
91 B3 Loncopue Arg.
69 G4 London Can.
39 G6 London U.K.
80 A6 London KY U.S.A.
80 B5 London OH U.S.A.
41 D3 Londonderry U.K.
81 G3 Londonderry U.S.A.
6 C3 Londonderry, C. c. Austr.
88 B9 Londonderry, I. i. Chile
90 B3 Londrina Brazil
74 C3 Lone Pine U.S.A.
27 C6 Long'an China
13 T2 Longa, Proliv chan. Rus. Fed.
39 E6 Long Ashton U.K.
91 B3 Longavi, Nev. de mt Chile
79 E5 Long Bay b. U.S.A.
9 C6 Longbeach N.Z.
74 C5 Long Beach CA U.S.A.
81 G4 Long Beach NY U.S.A.
81 F4 Long Branch U.S.A.
68 A6 Long Branch Lake l. U.S.A.
27 B4 Longchang China
27 E5 Longchuan China
39 F5 Long Eaton U.K.
30 D1 Longfengshan Sk. resr China
41 D4 Longford Rep. of Ireland
27 E5 Longhai China
27 □ Long Harbour in. H.K. China
38 F2 Longhoughton U.K.
33 E3 Longiram Indon.
83 J4 Long Island i. Bahamas
66 E3 Long Island i. Can.
6 E2 Long Island i. P.N.G.
81 G4 Long Island i. U.S.A.
81 G4 Long Island Sound chan. U.S.A.
27 C5 Long Jiang r. China
23 H3 Longju China
26 F2 Longkou Wan b. China
66 C4 Longlac Can.
81 F3 Long Lake NY U.S.A.
66 C4 Long Lake l. Can.
81 J1 Long Lake l. ME U.S.A.
68 E3 Long Lake l. MI U.S.A.
69 F3 Long Lake l. MI U.S.A.
76 C2 Long Lake l. ND U.S.A.
81 F2 Long Lake l. NY U.S.A.
27 C5 Longli China
27 B5 Longlin China
40 D4 Long, Loch in. U.K.
39 H5 Long Melford U.K.
27 E6 Longmen China
26 B3 Longmen Shan mts China
72 F3 Longmont U.S.A.
27 E5 Longnan China
69 G4 Long Point pt Can.
9 B7 Long Point pt N.Z.
69 G4 Long Point Bay b. Can.
38 E3 Long Preston U.K.
27 F4 Longquan China
27 F4 Longquan Xi r. China
63 N5 Long Range Mountains Can.
67 J4 Long Range Mts h. Can.
6 E4 Longreach Austr.
26 B3 Longriba China
27 C4 Longshan China
27 D5 Longsheng China
72 F3 Longs Peak summit U.S.A.
39 J5 Long Stratton U.K.
27 D4 Longtian China
38 E2 Longtown U.K.
66 F4 Longueuil Can.
42 D5 Longuyon France
74 A2 Longvale U.S.A.
75 F3 Long Valley Junction U.S.A.
77 E5 Longview TX U.S.A.
72 B2 Longview WA U.S.A.
28 C2 Longwangmiao Rus. Fed.
26 B3 Longxi China
26 C3 Long Xian China
27 E5 Longxi Shan mt China
32 C3 Long Xuyên Vietnam
27 E5 Longyan China
26 E2 Longyao China
27 C6 Longzhou China
43 F2 Löningen Ger.
37 O8 Lönsboda Sweden
8 D4 Lonsdale, Lake l. Austr.
44 G3 Lons-le-Saunier France
90 B3 Lontra r. Brazil
31 B3 Looc Phil.
68 E4 Looking Glass r. U.S.A.
81 F4 Lookout U.S.A.
66 D2 Lookout, Cape c. Can.
79 E5 Lookout, Cape c. U.S.A.
74 C3 Lookout Mt mt U.S.A.
69 F3 Lookout, Pt pt U.S.A.
68 C1 Loon Can.
64 F3 Loon r. Can.
65 H4 Loon Lake Can.
81 J1 Loon Lake l. U.S.A.
41 B5 Loop Head hd Rep. of Ireland
22 E1 Lop China
24 G1 Lopatina, Gora mt Rus. Fed.
50 H4 Lopatino Rus. Fed.
32 B2 Lop Buri Thai.
31 B3 Lopez Phil.
81 E4 Lopez U.S.A.
24 B2 Lop Nur l. China
56 C3 Lopori r. Congo(Zaire)
36 R1 Lopphavet b. Norway
50 J2 Loptyuga Rus. Fed.
19 G4 Lora r. Afgh.
89 B2 Lora r. Venez.
45 D4 Lora del Río Spain
80 B4 Lorain U.S.A.
22 B3 Loralai Pak.
22 B3 Loralai r. Pak.
80 A4 Loramie, Lake l. U.S.A.
45 F4 Lorca Spain
43 F4 Lorch Ger.
31 A4 Lord Auckland sand bank Phil.
18 C4 Lordegān Iran
7 F5 Lord Howe Island i. Pac. Oc.
94 F8 Lord Howe Rise sea feature Pac. Oc.
75 H5 Lordsburg U.S.A.
43 F4 Loreley Ger.
90 D3 Lorena Brazil
25 F7 Lorentz r. Indon.
86 F7 Loreto Bol.
87 J5 Loreto Brazil
82 B3 Loreto Mex.
31 C4 Loreto Phil.
89 B2 Lorica Col.
44 C3 Lorient France
65 L1 Lorillard r. Can.
8 D5 Lorne Austr.
40 C4 Lorn, Firth of est. U.K.
23 H3 Loro r. China
44 G2 Lorraine reg. France
43 G5 Lorsch Ger.
43 F2 Lorup Ger.
22 C4 Losal India
73 F5 Los Alamos U.S.A.
91 B2 Los Andes Chile
91 B3 Los Angeles Chile
74 C5 Los Angeles CA U.S.A.
74 C4 Los Angeles Aqueduct canal U.S.A.
74 B3 Los Banos U.S.A.
88 D2 Los Blancos Arg.
88 B7 Los Chonos, Archipiélago de is Chile
74 D5 Los Coronados is Mex.
74 B3 Los Gatos U.S.A.
88 B8 Los Glacieres, Parque Nacional nat. park Arg.
42 E5 Losheim Ger.
48 F2 Lošinj i. Croatia
59 H2 Loskop Dam dam S. Africa
91 B4 Los Lagos div. Chile
73 F5 Los Lunas U.S.A.
84 C2 Los Mármoles, Parque Nacional nat. park Mex.
91 C4 Los Menucos Arg.
82 C3 Los Mochis Mex.
74 A1 Los Molinos U.S.A.
56 B3 Losombo Congo(Zaire)
84 B3 Los Reyes Mex.
89 D2 Los Roques, Islas is Venez.
42 E2 Losser Neth.
40 E3 Lossie r. U.K.
40 E3 Lossiemouth U.K.

56 C4 Mali Congo(Zaire)
54 A3 Mali Guinea
52 D4 Mali *country* Africa
26 C3 Malian *r.* China
22 E4 Malihabad India
19 F4 Malik Naro *mt* Pak.
32 A2 Mali Kyun *i.* Myanmar
25 E7 Malili Indon.
33 C4 Malimping Indon.
84 C3 Malinche, Parque Nacional La *nat. park* Mex.
56 E4 Malindi Kenya
41 D2 Malin Head *hd* Rep. of Ireland
41 C3 Malin More Rep. of Ireland
28 D2 Malinovka *r.* Rus. Fed.
27 B6 Malipo China
48 F2 Mali Raginac *mt* Croatia
31 C5 Malita Phil.
32 A3 Maliwun Myanmar
22 B5 Maliya India
17 L5 Malkaili Iran
22 D5 Malkapur India
51 C7 Malkara Turkey
47 N4 Mal'kavichy Belarus
49 M4 Malko Tŭrnovo Bulg.
8 G4 Mallacoota Austr.
8 G4 Mallacoota Inlet Austr.
40 C4 Mallaig U.K.
8 B3 Mallala Austr.
8 D3 Mallee Cliffs Nat. Park Austr.
65 K2 Mallery Lake *l.* Can.
45 H3 Mallorca *i.* Spain
41 C5 Mallow Rep. of Ireland
39 D5 Mallwyd U.K.
36 M4 Malm Norway
36 R3 Malmberget Sweden
42 E4 Malmédy Belgium
58 C6 Malmesbury S. Africa
39 E6 Malmesbury U.K.
37 N9 Malmö Sweden
50 J3 Malmyzh Rus. Fed.
7 G3 Malo *i.* Vanuatu
31 B3 Malolos Phil.
81 F2 Malone U.S.A.
27 B5 Malong China
57 C5 Malonga Congo(Zaire)
50 F2 Maloshuyka Rus. Fed.
37 J6 Måløy Norway
50 F4 Maloyaroslavets Rus. Fed.
86 B3 Malpelo, Isla de *i.* Col.
21 A3 Malprabha *r.* India
37 U8 Malta Latvia
72 F1 Malta U.S.A.
34 G5 Malta *country* Europe
48 F6 Malta Channel Italy/Malta
57 B6 Maltahöhe Namibia
39 F4 Maltby U.K.
39 H4 Maltby le Marsh U.K.
38 G3 Malton U.K.
25 E7 Maluku *is* Indon.
37 N6 Malung Sweden
59 H4 Maluti Mountains *mts* Lesotho
7 G2 Malu'u Solomon Is
21 A2 Malvan India
77 E5 Malvern U.S.A.
Malvinas, Islas *terr.* see Falkland Islands
51 D5 Malyn Ukr.
13 S3 Malyy Anyuy *r.* Rus. Fed.
18 D2 Malyy Balkhan, Khrebet *h.* Turkm.
51 H6 Malyye Derbety Rus. Fed.
51 G7 Malyy Kavkaz *mts* Asia
13 Q2 Malyy Lyakhovskiy, Ostrov *i.* Rus. Fed.
51 J5 Malyy Uzen' *r.* Kazak./Rus. Fed.
13 Q3 Mama *r.* Rus. Fed.
59 H3 Mamafubedu S. Africa
21 C3 Māmallapuram India
31 A5 Mambahenauhan *i.* Phil.
31 C4 Mambajao Phil.
56 C3 Mambasa Congo(Zaire)
56 B3 Mambéré *r.* C.A.R.
31 B3 Mamburao Phil.
59 H2 Mamelodi S. Africa
54 C4 Mamfé Cameroon
75 G5 Mammoth U.S.A.
78 C4 Mammoth Cave Nat. Park U.S.A.
74 C3 Mammoth Lakes U.S.A.
86 E6 Mamoré *r.* Bol./Brazil
54 A3 Mamou Guinea
57 E5 Mampikony Madag.
54 B4 Mampong Ghana
91 B3 Mamuil Malal, P. *pass* Arg./Chile
33 E3 Mamuju Indon.
58 D1 Mamuno Botswana
54 B4 Man Côte d'Ivoire
89 B3 Manacacias *r.* Col.
86 F4 Manacapuru Brazil
45 H3 Manacor Spain
25 E6 Manadao Indon.
82 G6 Managua Nic.
82 G6 Managua, L. de *l.* Nic.
57 E6 Manakara Madag.
9 D5 Manakau *mt* N.Z.
6 E2 Manam I. *i.* P.N.G.
74 □1 Manana *i.* U.S.A.
57 E6 Mananara *r.* Madag.
57 E5 Mananara Avaratra Madag.
57 E5 Mananara, Parc National de *nat. park* Madag.
8 D3 Manangatang Austr.
57 E6 Mananjary Madag.
21 B4 Mānantavādi India
89 D2 Manapire *r.* Venez.
9 A6 Manapouri, L. *l.* N.Z.
57 E5 Manarantsandry Madag.
23 G4 Manas *r.* Bhutan
22 D3 Mana Shankou *pass* India
24 A2 Manas Hu *l.* China
23 F3 Manaslu *mt* Nepal
80 E5 Manassas U.S.A.
25 E7 Manatuto Indon.
86 F4 Manaus Brazil
16 C3 Manavgat Turkey
9 E4 Manawatu *r.* N.Z.
31 C5 Manay Phil.
16 F3 Manbij Syria
39 H4 Manby U.K.
68 E3 Mancelona U.S.A.
39 E4 Manchester U.K.
74 A2 Manchester *CA* U.S.A.
81 G4 Manchester *CT* U.S.A.
68 B4 Manchester *IA* U.S.A.
80 B6 Manchester *KY* U.S.A.
69 E4 Manchester *MI* U.S.A.
81 H3 Manchester *NH* U.S.A.
80 B5 Manchester *OH* U.S.A.
79 C5 Manchester *TN* U.S.A.
81 G3 Manchester *VT* U.S.A.
22 A4 Manchhar L. *l.* Pak.
16 F2 Mancılık Turkey
75 H3 Mancos U.S.A.
75 H3 Mancos *r.* U.S.A.
19 F5 Mand Pak.
18 D4 Mand *r.* Iran
57 E6 Mandabe Madag.
33 B2 Mandah Indon.
32 □ Mandai Sing.
19 F3 Mandal Afgh.
22 C4 Mandal India
37 K7 Mandal Norway
25 G7 Mandala, Pk *mt* Indon.
25 B4 Mandalay Myanmar
24 C2 Mandalgovĭ Mongolia
17 K5 Mandalī Iraq
26 D1 Mandalt Sum China
76 C2 Mandan U.S.A.
31 B3 Mandaon Phil.
55 D4 Manda, Parc National de *nat. park* Chad
55 D3 Mandara Mountains Cameroon/Nigeria
48 C5 Mandas *Sardinia* Italy
56 E3 Mandera Kenya
75 F2 Manderfield U.S.A.
42 E4 Manderscheid Ger.
83 J5 Mandeville Jamaica
9 B6 Mandeville N.Z.
22 B4 Mandha India
54 B3 Mandiana Guinea
22 C3 Mandi Burewala Pak.
57 D5 Mandié Moz.
57 D5 Mandimba Moz.
59 J4 Mandini S. Africa
23 F5 Mandira Dam *dam* India
22 E5 Mandla India
57 E5 Mandritsara Madag.
22 C4 Mandsaur India
31 A6 Mandul *i.* Indon.
6 B5 Mandurah Austr.
48 G4 Manduria Italy
22 B5 Mandvi *Gujarat* India
22 C5 Mandvi *Gujarat* India
21 B3 Mandya India
21 B2 Maner *r.* India
48 D2 Manerbio Italy
47 M5 Manevychi Ukr.
48 F4 Manfredonia Italy
48 G4 Manfredonia, Golfo di *g.* Italy
90 D1 Manga Brazil
54 B3 Manga Burkina
56 B4 Mangai Congo(Zaire)
5 M7 Mangaia *i.* Pac. Oc.
9 E3 Mangakino N.Z.
21 C2 Mangalagiri India
23 H4 Mangaldai India
49 N3 Mangalia Romania
21 A3 Mangalore India
21 A2 Mangalvedha India
23 G4 Mangan India
22 C2 Mangapet India
31 C6 Mangarang Indon.
59 G4 Mangaung S. Africa
9 E3 Mangaweka N.Z.
23 G4 Mangde *r.* Bhutan
41 B6 Mangerton Mt *h.* Rep. of Ireland
33 C3 Manggar Indon.
24 B3 Mangnai China
57 D5 Mangochi Malawi
25 E7 Mangole *i.* Indon.
39 E6 Mangotsfield U.K.
22 B5 Māngral India
79 E7 Mangrove Cay Bahamas
45 C2 Mangualde Port.
22 B3 Manguchar Pak.
91 G2 Mangueira, L. *l.* Brazil
90 B4 Mangueirinha Brazil
55 D2 Manguéni, Plateau du *plat.* Niger
24 E1 Mangui China
31 C5 Mangupung *i.* Indon.
14 D2 Mangyshlak Kazak.
76 D4 Manhattan *KS* U.S.A.
74 D2 Manhattan *NV* U.S.A.
57 D6 Manhica Moz.
59 K3 Manhoca Moz.
90 D3 Manhuaçu Brazil
90 E2 Manhuaçu *r.* Brazil
89 B3 Mani Col.
57 E5 Mania *r.* Madag.
48 E1 Maniago Italy
86 F5 Manicoré Brazil
67 G3 Manicouagan Can.
67 G3 Manicouagan *r.* Can.
67 G3 Manicouagan, Réservoir Can.
18 C5 Manīfah S. Arabia
5 L6 Manihiki *i.* Pac. Oc.
Manikgarh see Rajura
22 E4 Manikpur India
31 B3 Manila Phil.
72 E3 Manila U.S.A.
8 G2 Manildra Austr.
8 H1 Manilla Austr.
Manipur see Imphal
23 H4 Manipur *div.* India
49 M5 Manisa Turkey
17 L5 Manisht Kūh *mt* Iran
38 C3 Man, Isle of *terr.* Europe
68 D3 Manistee U.S.A.
68 E3 Manistee *r.* U.S.A.
68 D3 Manistique U.S.A.
68 E2 Manistique Lake *l.* U.S.A.
66 B2 Manitoba *div.* Can.
65 K4 Manitoba, Lake *l.* Can.
65 H4 Manito L. *l.* Can.
65 K5 Manitou Can.
80 E3 Manitou Beach U.S.A.
66 B3 Manitou Falls Can.
68 D2 Manitou Island *i.* U.S.A.
78 C2 Manitou Islands *is* U.S.A.
69 G3 Manitou, Lake *l.* Can.
69 F3 Manitoulin I. *i.* Can.
69 G3 Manitowaning Can.
66 D4 Manitowik Lake *l.* Can.
68 D3 Manitowoc U.S.A.
69 K2 Maniwaki Can.
89 B3 Manizales Col.
57 E6 Manja Madag.
59 K2 Manjacaze Moz.
21 B4 Manjeri India
30 D3 Man Jiang *r.* China
17 M3 Manjil Iran
21 B2 Manjra *r.* India
76 E2 Mankato U.S.A.
59 J3 Mankayane Swaziland
54 B4 Mankono Côte d'Ivoire
21 C4 Mankulam Sri Lanka
8 H2 Manly Austr.
22 C5 Manmad India
33 B3 Manna Indon.
8 B2 Mannahill Austr.
21 B4 Mannar Sri Lanka
15 F6 Mannar, Gulf of India/Sri Lanka
21 B4 Mannar, Gulf of *g.* India/Sri Lanka
21 B3 Manneru *r.* India
43 G5 Mannheim Ger.
41 A4 Mannin Bay *b.* Rep. of Ireland
64 F3 Manning Can.
79 D5 Manning U.S.A.
39 J6 Manningtree U.K.
48 C4 Mannu, Capo *pt Sardinia* Italy
8 B3 Mannum Austr.
25 F7 Manokwari Indon.
56 C4 Manono Congo(Zaire)
32 A3 Manoron Myanmar
44 G5 Manosque France
63 L4 Manouane Lake *l.* Can.
30 D3 Manp'o N. Korea
7 J2 Manra *i.* Kiribati
45 G2 Manresa Spain
22 C3 Mānsa India
57 C5 Mansa Zambia
54 A3 Mansa Konko The Gambia
22 C2 Mansehra Pak.
63 L3 Mansel Island *i.* Can.
8 F4 Mansfield Austr.
39 F4 Mansfield U.K.
77 E5 Mansfield *LA* U.S.A.
80 B4 Mansfield *OH* U.S.A.
80 E4 Mansfield *PA* U.S.A.
87 H6 Manso *r.* Brazil
64 E3 Manson Creek Can.
17 M6 Manşūrī Iran
16 E3 Mansurlu Turkey
86 B4 Manta Ecuador
86 B4 Manta, B. de *b.* Ecuador
31 A4 Mantalingajan, Mount *mt* Phil.
30 E3 Mantapsan *mt* N. Korea
74 B3 Manteca U.S.A.
89 C3 Mantecal Venez.
43 L5 Mantel Ger.
79 F5 Manteo U.S.A.
44 E2 Mantes-la-Jolie France
21 B2 Manthani India
75 G2 Manti U.S.A.
90 D3 Mantiqueira, Serra da *mts* Brazil
68 E3 Manton U.S.A.
48 D2 Mantova Italy
37 T6 Mäntsälä Fin.
37 T5 Mänttä Fin.
Mantua see Mantova
50 H3 Manturovo Rus. Fed.
37 U6 Mäntyharju Fin.
36 U3 Mäntyjärvi Fin.
5 L6 Manua Islands *is* Pac. Oc.
75 H4 Manuelito U.S.A.
91 F2 Manuel J. Cobo Arg.
90 E1 Manuel Vitorino Brazil
87 H5 Manuelzinho Brazil
25 E7 Manui *i.* Indon.
19 E5 Manūjān Iran
31 B4 Manukan Phil.
9 E2 Manukau N.Z.
9 E2 Manukau Harbour *in.* N.Z.
31 A5 Manuk Manka *i.* Phil.
8 B2 Manunda *r.* Austr.
86 D6 Manu, Parque Nacional *nat. park* Peru
6 E2 Manus I. *i.* P.N.G.
21 B3 Manvi India
59 F2 Manyana Botswana
51 G6 Manych-Gudilo, Ozero *l.* Rus. Fed.
75 H3 Many Farms U.S.A.
56 D4 Manyoni Tanz.
16 D6 Manzala, Bahra el *l.* Egypt
45 E3 Manzanares Spain
83 J4 Manzanillo Cuba
84 A3 Manzanillo Mex.
18 C3 Manzariyeh Iran
24 D2 Manzhouli China
59 J3 Manzini Swaziland
55 D3 Mao Chad
Maó see Mahón
26 D4 Maocifan China
26 C2 Maojiachuan China
59 G3 Maokeng S. Africa
25 F7 Maoke, Pegunungan *mts* Indon.
30 B3 Maokui Shan *h.* China
30 B2 Maolin China
26 B2 Maomao Shan *mt* China
27 D6 Maoming China
27 □ Ma On Shan *h. H.K.* China
57 D6 Mapai Moz.
22 E3 Mapam Yumco *l.* China
59 F5 Maphodi S. Africa
84 B1 Mapimí Mex.
31 A5 Mapin *i.* Phil.
57 D6 Mapinhane Moz.
89 D3 Mapire Venez.
68 E4 Maple *r.* U.S.A.
65 H5 Maple Creek Can.
59 G4 Mapoteng Lesotho
87 G4 Mapuera *r.* Brazil
59 K2 Mapulanguene Moz.
57 D6 Maputo Moz.
59 K2 Maputo *div.* Moz.
59 K3 Maputo *r.* Moz.
59 G4 Maputsoe Lesotho
17 H6 Maqar an Na'am *well* Iraq
26 B3 Maqu China
23 E3 Maquan He *r.* China
56 B4 Maquela do Zombo Angola
91 C4 Maquinchao Arg.
91 C4 Maquinchao *r.* Arg.
68 B4 Maquoketa U.S.A.
68 B4 Maquoketa *r.* U.S.A.
19 G5 Mar *r.* Pak.
23 E5 Māra India
59 H1 Mara S. Africa
89 C2 Mara Venez.
65 H1 Mara *r.* Can.
86 E4 Maraã Brazil
87 J5 Marabá Brazil
89 C2 Maracaibo Venez.
89 C2 Maracaibo, Lago de *l.* Venez.
87 H3 Maracá, Ilha de *i.* Brazil
90 A3 Maracaju Brazil
90 A3 Maracajú, Serra de *h.* Brazil
90 E1 Maracás, Chapada de *reg.* Brazil
89 D2 Maracay Venez.
55 D2 Marādah Libya
54 C3 Maradi Niger
18 B2 Marāgheh Iran
90 E1 Maragogipe Brazil
31 B3 Maragondon Phil.
89 D4 Marahuaca, Co *mt* Venez.
87 J4 Marajó, Baía de *est.* Brazil
87 J3 Marajó, Ilha de *i.* Brazil
21 B3 Marakkanam India
56 D3 Maralal Kenya
22 C2 Marala Weir *barrage* Pak.
17 J1 Maralik Armenia
6 D5 Maralinga Austr.
7 G2 Maramasike *i.* Solomon Is
31 C5 Marampit *i.* Indon.
19 G4 Maran *mt* Pak.
17 K4 Marāna Iraq
75 G5 Marana U.S.A.
18 B2 Marand Iran
32 B4 Marang Malaysia
32 A3 Marang Myanmar
90 C1 Maranhão *r.* Brazil
86 D4 Marañón *r.* Peru
59 L2 Marão Moz.
45 C2 Marão *mt* Port.
89 D4 Marari *r.* Brazil
9 A6 Mararoa *r.* N.Z.
68 D1 Marathon Can.
79 D7 Marathon *FL* U.S.A.
77 C6 Marathon *TX* U.S.A.
90 E1 Maraú Brazil
33 D3 Marau Indon.
89 D4 Marauiá *r.* Brazil
31 C4 Marawi Phil.
17 M1 Märäzä Azer.
45 D4 Marbella Spain
6 B4 Marble Bar Austr.
75 G3 Marble Canyon U.S.A.
75 G3 Marble Canyon *gorge* U.S.A.
59 H2 Marble Hall S. Africa
81 H3 Marblehead U.S.A.
65 L2 Marble I. *i.* Can.
59 J5 Marburg S. Africa
43 G4 Marburg an der Lahn Ger.
80 E5 Marburg, Lake *l.* U.S.A.
46 H7 Marcali Hungary
39 H5 March U.K.
8 B2 Marchant Hill *h.* Austr.
42 D4 Marche-en-Famenne Belgium
45 D4 Marchena Spain
86 □ Marchena, Isla *i. Galapagos Is* Ecuador
91 D1 Mar Chiquita, L. *l.* Arg.
46 G6 Marchtrenk Austria
79 D7 Marco U.S.A.
42 B4 Marcoing France
66 E2 Marcopeet Islands *is* Can.
91 D2 Marcos Juárez Arg.
81 G2 Marcy, Mt *mt* U.S.A.
22 C2 Mardan Pak.
91 F3 Mar del Plata Arg.
17 H3 Mardin Turkey
7 G4 Maré *i.* New Caledonia
40 C3 Maree, Loch *l.* U.K.
68 A5 Marengo *IA* U.S.A.
68 C4 Marengo *IL* U.S.A.
48 E6 Marettimo, Isola *i. Sicily* Italy
50 E3 Marevo Rus. Fed.
77 B6 Marfa U.S.A.
23 F2 Margai Caka *salt l.* China
6 B5 Margaret River Austr.
89 E2 Margarita, Isla de *i.* Venez.
28 D3 Margaritovo Rus. Fed.
59 J5 Margate S. Africa
39 J6 Margate U.K.
19 F4 Margo, Dasht-i *des.* Afgh.
31 B5 Margosatubig Phil.
42 D4 Margraten Neth.
68 E3 Margrethe, Lake *l.* U.S.A.
64 E4 Marguerite Can.
92 B2 Marguerite Bay *b.* Ant.
23 G3 Margyang China
17 L5 Marhaj Khalīl Iraq
17 J3 Marhan D. *h.* Iraq
51 E6 Marhanets' Ukr.
88 C2 María Elena Chile
6 D3 Maria I. *i.* Austr.
91 E3 María Ignacia Arg.
95 J7 Maria, Îles *is* Pac. Oc.
94 E4 Marianas Ridge *sea feature* Pac. Oc.
94 E5 Marianas Tr. *sea feature* Pac. Oc.
23 H4 Mariani India
64 F2 Marian Lake *l.* Can.
77 F5 Marianna *AR* U.S.A.
79 C6 Marianna *FL* U.S.A.
46 F6 Mariánské Lázně Czech Rep.
84 A2 Marías, Islas *is* Mex.
83 H7 Mariato, Pta *pt* Panama
9 D1 Maria van Diemen, Cape *c.* N.Z.
48 F1 Maribor Slovenia
75 F5 Maricopa *AZ* U.S.A.
74 C4 Maricopa *CA* U.S.A.
75 F5 Maricopa Mts *mts* U.S.A.
55 E4 Maridi *watercourse* Sudan
92 A4 Marie Byrd Land *reg.* Ant.
83 M5 Marie Galante *i.* Guadeloupe
37 Q6 Mariehamn Fin.
90 B1 Mariembero *r.* Brazil
43 M4 Marienberg Ger.
42 F1 Marienhafe Ger.
57 B6 Mariental Namibia
37 N7 Mariestad Sweden
79 C5 Marietta *GA* U.S.A.
80 C5 Marietta *OH* U.S.A.
44 G5 Marignane France
24 G1 Marii, Mys *pt* Rus. Fed.
24 A1 Mariinsk Rus. Fed.
37 S9 Marijampolė Lith.
90 C3 Marília Brazil
77 C7 Marín Mex.
45 B1 Marín Spain
48 G5 Marina di Gioiosa Ionica Italy
50 D4 Mar"ina Horka Belarus
31 B3 Marinduque *i.* Phil.
68 D3 Marinette U.S.A.
90 B3 Maringá Brazil
45 B3 Marinha Grande Port.
78 B4 Marion *IL* U.S.A.
68 E5 Marion *IN* U.S.A.
81 K2 Marion *ME* U.S.A.
80 B4 Marion *OH* U.S.A.
79 E5 Marion *SC* U.S.A.
80 C6 Marion *VA* U.S.A.
79 D5 Marion, L. *l.* U.S.A.
89 D3 Maripa Venez.
74 C3 Mariposa U.S.A.
88 D2 Mariscal Estigarribia Para.
44 H4 Maritime Alps *mts* France/Italy
49 L3 Maritsa *r.* Bulg.
50 J3 Mari-Turek Rus. Fed.
51 F6 Mariupol' Ukr.
18 B3 Marīvān Iran
50 J3 Mariy El, Respublika *div.* Rus. Fed.
56 E3 Marka Somalia
17 K2 Mārkān Iran
21 B3 Markapur India
37 N8 Markaryd Sweden
69 G3 Markdale Can.
59 H1 Marken S. Africa
42 D2 Markermeer *l.* Neth.
39 G5 Market Deeping U.K.
39 E5 Market Drayton U.K.
39 G5 Market Harborough U.K.
41 E3 Markethill U.K.
38 G4 Market Weighton U.K.
13 N3 Markha *r.* Rus. Fed.
69 H4 Markham Can.
92 B4 Markham, Mt *mt* Ant.
51 F5 Markivka Ukr.
43 L3 Markkleeberg Ger.
43 H2 Marklohe Ger.
13 T3 Markovo Rus. Fed.
43 L3 Markranstädt Ger.
51 H5 Marks Rus. Fed.
43 H5 Marktheidenfeld Ger.
46 E7 Marktoberdorf Ger.
43 L4 Marktredwitz Ger.
68 B6 Mark Twain Lake *l.* U.S.A.
42 F3 Marl Ger.
81 H3 Marlborough U.S.A.
39 F6 Marlborough Downs *h.* U.K.
42 B5 Marle France
77 D6 Marlin U.S.A.
80 C5 Marlinton U.S.A.
8 G4 Marlo Austr.
44 E4 Marmande France
Marmara Denizi *g.* see Marmara, Sea of
16 B2 Marmara Gölü *l.* Turkey
16 B1 Marmara, Sea of *g.* Turkey
16 B3 Marmaris Turkey
76 C2 Marmarth U.S.A.
80 C5 Marmet U.S.A.
66 B4 Marmion L. *l.* Can.
48 D1 Marmolada *mt* Italy
44 F2 Marne-la-Vallée France
17 K1 Marneuli Georgia
43 K1 Marnitz Ger.
8 D4 Marnoo Austr.
57 E5 Maroantsetra Madag.
43 J4 Maroldsweisach Ger.
57 E5 Maromokotro *mt* Madag.
57 D5 Marondera Zimbabwe
87 H2 Maroni *r.* Fr. Guiana
5 N7 Marotiri *i.* Pac. Oc.
55 D3 Maroua Cameroon
57 E5 Marovoay Madag.
17 H4 Marqādah Syria
26 A3 Mar Qu *r.* China
59 G4 Marquard S. Africa
5 O5 Marquesas Islands *is* Pac. Oc.
79 D7 Marquesas Keys *is* U.S.A.
68 D2 Marquette U.S.A.
42 B4 Marquion France
8 D1 Marra Austr.
59 K2 Marracuene Moz.
54 B1 Marrakech Morocco
Marrakesh see Marrakech
59 L2 Marrangua, Lagoa *l.* Moz.
55 E3 Marra Plateau *plat.* Sudan
8 F3 Marrar Austr.
77 F6 Marrero U.S.A.
57 D5 Marromeu Moz.
57 D5 Marrupa Moz.
55 F2 Marsa Alam Egypt
55 D1 Marsa al Burayqah Libya
56 D3 Marsabit Kenya
48 E6 Marsala *Sicily* Italy
55 E1 Marsa Matrûh Egypt
43 G3 Marsberg Ger.
48 E3 Marsciano Italy
8 F2 Marsden Austr.
42 C2 Marsdiep *chan.* Neth.
44 G5 Marseille France
68 C5 Marseilles U.S.A.
90 D3 Mar, Serra do *mts* Brazil
36 O4 Marsfjället *mt* Sweden
65 H4 Marshall Can.
77 E5 Marshall *AR* U.S.A.
78 C4 Marshall *IL* U.S.A.
68 E4 Marshall *MI* U.S.A.
76 E2 Marshall *MN* U.S.A.
76 E4 Marshall *MO* U.S.A.
77 E5 Marshall *TX* U.S.A.
4 H3 Marshall Islands *country* Pac. Oc.
76 E3 Marshalltown U.S.A.
68 B3 Marshfield U.S.A.
79 E7 Marsh Harbour Bahamas
81 K1 Mars Hill U.S.A.
77 F6 Marsh Island *i.* U.S.A.
64 C2 Marsh Lake *l.* Can.
17 M3 Marshūn Iran
72 C3 Marsing U.S.A.
37 P7 Märsta Sweden
23 F4 Marsyangdi *r.* Nepal
32 A1 Martaban Myanmar
25 B5 Martaban, Gulf of Myanmar
33 D3 Martapura *Kalimantan* Indon.
33 B3 Martapura *Sumatera* Indon.
69 H2 Marten River Can.
65 H4 Martensville Can.
81 H4 Martha's Vineyard *i.* U.S.A.
46 C7 Martigny Switz.
47 J6 Martin Slovakia
76 C3 Martin *SD* U.S.A.
79 B4 Martin *TN* U.S.A.
84 C2 Martínez Mex.
84 A1 Martínez, E. Mex.
75 E5 Martinez Lake U.S.A.
61 M8 Martinique *terr.* Caribbean Sea
79 C5 Martin, L. *l.* U.S.A.
92 A3 Martin Pen. *pen.* Ant.
80 D4 Martinsburg *PA* U.S.A.
80 E5 Martinsburg *WV* U.S.A.
80 C4 Martins Ferry U.S.A.
80 D6 Martinsville U.S.A.
96 H7 Martin Vas, Is *is* Atl. Ocean
9 E4 Marton N.Z.
45 G2 Martorell Spain
45 E4 Martos Spain
14 D1 Martuk Kazak.
17 K1 Martuni Armenia
19 F3 Maruchak Afgh.
29 C7 Marugame Japan
9 D5 Maruia *r.* N.Z.
87 L6 Marum Brazil
51 G7 Marukhis Ugheltekhili *pass* Georgia/Rus. Fed.
8 G3 Marulan Austr.
18 D4 Marvast Iran
44 F4 Marvejols France
75 G2 Marvine, Mt *mt* U.S.A.
65 G4 Marwayne Can.
19 F2 Mary Turkm.
8 D4 Maryborough *Vic.* Austr.
7 F4 Maryborough Austr.
58 D3 Marydale S. Africa
50 J4 Mar'yevka Rus. Fed.
65 H2 Mary Frances Lake *l.* Can.
81 E5 Maryland *div.* U.S.A.
38 D3 Maryport U.K.
67 J3 Mary's Harbour Can.
67 K4 Marystown Can.
75 F2 Marysvale U.S.A.
67 G4 Marysville Can.
74 B2 Marysville *CA* U.S.A.
76 D4 Marysville *KS* U.S.A.
80 B4 Marysville *OH* U.S.A.
79 C5 Maryville U.S.A.
76 E3 Maryville U.S.A.
43 L2 Marzahna Ger.
18 D4 Masāhūn, Kūh-e *mt* Iran
56 D4 Masaka Uganda
59 G5 Masakhane S. Africa
17 M2 Masallı Azer.
6 C2 Masamba Indon.
30 E6 Masan S. Korea
81 J1 Masardis U.S.A.
57 D5 Masasi Tanz.
86 F7 Masavi Bol.
31 B3 Masbate Phil.
31 B4 Masbate *i.* Phil.
54 C1 Mascara Alg.
93 H4 Mascarene Basin *sea feature* Ind. Ocean
93 J4 Mascarene Ridge *sea feature* Ind. Ocean
81 G2 Mascouche Can.
59 G4 Maseru Lesotho
59 H4 Mashai Lesotho
27 C6 Mashan China
22 D2 Masherbrum *mt* Pak.
19 E2 Mashhad Iran
22 C4 Mashi *r.* India
17 L2 Mashīrān Iran
18 E4 Mashīz Iran
19 F5 Mashket *r.* Pak.
19 F4 Mashki Chah Pak.
19 F5 Māshkīd *r.* Iran
36 S2 Masi Norway
59 G5 Masibambane S. Africa
59 G4 Masilo S. Africa
56 D3 Masindi Uganda
31 A3 Masinloc Phil.
58 E5 Masinyusane S. Africa
20 E5 Maşīrah *i.* Oman
20 E6 Maşīrah, Gulf of *b.* Oman
17 K1 Masis Armenia
18 C4 Masjed Soleymān Iran
16 G3 Maskanah Syria
41 B4 Mask, Lough *l.* Rep. of Ireland
19 E5 Maskūtān Iran
19 G4 Maslti Pak.
57 F5 Masoala, Tanjona *c.* Madag.
68 E4 Mason *MI* U.S.A.
74 C2 Mason *NV* U.S.A.
77 D6 Mason *TX* U.S.A.
9 A7 Mason Bay *b.* N.Z.
76 E3 Mason City *IA* U.S.A.
68 C5 Mason City *IL* U.S.A.
80 D5 Masontown U.S.A.
Masqaţ see Muscat
48 D2 Massa Italy
81 G3 Massachusetts *div.* U.S.A.
81 H3 Massachusetts Bay *b.* U.S.A.
75 H1 Massadona U.S.A.
48 G4 Massafra Italy
55 D3 Massakory Chad
48 D3 Massa Marittimo Italy
57 D6 Massangena Moz.
57 B4 Massango Angola
56 D2 Massawa Eritrea
81 G2 Massawippi, Lac *l.* Can.
81 F2 Massena U.S.A.
64 C4 Masset Can.
69 F2 Massey Can.
44 F4 Massif Central *mts* France
80 C4 Massillon U.S.A.
54 B3 Massina Mali
57 D6 Massinga Moz.
57 D6 Massingir Moz.
59 K1 Massingir, Barragem de *resr* Moz.
59 K2 Massintonto *r.* Moz./S. Africa
92 D5 Massivet *mts* Ant.
69 K3 Masson Can.
92 D5 Masson I. *i.* Ant.
17 M1 Maştağa Azer.
19 H2 Mastchoh Tajik.
9 E4 Masterton N.Z.
49 M5 Masticho, Akra *pt* Greece
79 F7 Mastic Point Bahamas
22 C1 Mastuj Pak.
19 G4 Mastung Pak.
50 C4 Masty Belarus
29 B7 Masuda Japan
17 M3 Masuleh Iran
Masulipatam see Machilipatnam
57 D6 Masvingo Zimbabwe
16 F4 Maşyāf Syria
69 G2 Matachewan Can.
73 F6 Matachic Mex.
89 D4 Matacuni *r.* Venez.
56 B4 Matadi Congo(Zaire)
83 G6 Matagalpa Nic.
66 E4 Matagami Can.
66 E4 Matagami, Lac *l.* Can.
77 D6 Matagorda I. *i.* U.S.A.
32 C5 Matak *i.* Indon.
9 F2 Matakana Island *i.* N.Z.
57 B5 Matala Angola
21 C5 Matale Sri Lanka
54 A3 Matam Senegal
84 B1 Matamoros *Coahuila* Mex.
84 C1 Matamoros *Tamaulipas* Mex.
31 B5 Matanal Point *pt* Phil.
57 D4 Matandu *r.* Tanz.
67 G4 Matane Can.
22 B2 Matanui Pak.
83 H4 Matanzas Cuba
Matapan, Cape *pt* see Tainaro, Akra
67 G4 Matapédia *r.* Can.
91 B2 Mataquito *r.* Chile
21 C5 Matara Sri Lanka
33 E4 Mataram Indon.
86 D7 Matarani Peru
6 D3 Mataranka Austr.
45 H2 Mataró Spain
59 H5 Matatiele S. Africa
9 B7 Mataura N.Z.
9 B7 Mataura *r.* N.Z.
89 C3 Mataveni *r.* Col.
9 F3 Matawai N.Z.
86 F6 Mategua Bol.
84 B2 Matehuala Mex.
57 D5 Matemanga Tanz.
48 G4 Matera Italy
48 C6 Mateur Tunisia
66 D4 Matheson Can.
77 D6 Mathis U.S.A.
8 E3 Mathoura Austr.
22 D4 Mathura India
31 C5 Mati Phil.
23 G4 Matiali India
27 D5 Matianxu China
22 B4 Matiari Pak.
84 D3 Matías Romero Mex.
67 G3 Matimekosh Can.
69 F2 Matinenda Lake *l.* Can.
81 J3 Matinicus I. *i.* U.S.A.
23 G5 Matla *r.* India
59 G2 Matlabas S. Africa
59 G2 Matlabas *r.* S. Africa
22 B4 Matli Pak.
39 F4 Matlock U.K.
89 D3 Mato *r.* Venez.
89 D3 Mato, Co *mt* Venez.
86 G7 Mato Grosso Brazil
90 A1 Mato Grosso *div.* Brazil
90 A3 Mato Grosso do Sul *div.* Brazil
90 A1 Mato Grosso, Planalto do *plat.* Brazil
59 K2 Matola Moz.
45 B2 Matosinhos Port.
20 E5 Maţraḩ Oman
58 C6 Matroosberg *mt* S. Africa
29 C7 Matsue Japan
28 G4 Matsumae Japan
29 E6 Matsumoto Japan
29 E7 Matsusaka Japan
27 F5 Matsu Tao *i.* Taiwan
29 C8 Matsuyama Japan
66 D4 Mattagami *r.* Can.
69 H2 Mattawa Can.
81 J2 Mattawamkeag U.S.A.
46 C7 Matterhorn *mt* Italy/Switz.
72 D3 Matterhorn *mt* U.S.A.
89 E3 Matthews Ridge Guyana
83 K4 Matthew Town Bahamas
18 D6 Maţţī, Sabkhat *salt pan* S. Arabia
78 B4 Mattoon U.S.A.
Matturai see Matara
21 C5 Matugama Sri Lanka
7 H3 Matuku *i.* Fiji
Matun see Khowst
89 E2 Maturín Venez.
31 C5 Matutuang *i.* Indon.
59 G4 Matwabeng S. Africa
22 E4 Mau *Uttar Pradesh* India
23 E4 Mau *Uttar Pradesh* India
23 E4 Mau Aimma India
42 B4 Maubeuge France
44 E5 Maubourguet France
40 D5 Mauchline U.K.
92 C3 Maudheimvidda *mts* Ant.
93 E7 Maud Seamount *depth* Ind. Ocean
87 G4 Maués Brazil
23 E4 Mauganj India
74 □2 Maui *i.* U.S.A.
95 J7 Mauke *i.* Pac. Oc.
43 G6 Maulbronn Ger.
91 B2 Maule *div.* Chile
91 B2 Maule *r.* Chile
91 B4 Maullín Chile
41 B3 Maumakeogh *h.* Rep. of Ireland
80 B4 Maumee U.S.A.
80 B4 Maumee *r.* U.S.A.
69 F5 Maumee Bay *b.* U.S.A.
41 B4 Maumturk Mts *h.* Rep. of Ireland
57 C5 Maun Botswana
74 □2 Mauna Kea *volc.* U.S.A.
74 □2 Mauna Loa *volc.* U.S.A.
74 □1 Maunalua B. *b.* U.S.A.
59 G1 Maunatlala Botswana
9 E2 Maungaturoto N.Z.
23 H5 Maungdaw Myanmar
32 A2 Maungmagan Is *is* Myanmar
62 F3 Maunoir, Lac *l.* Can.
6 D4 Maurice, L. *salt flat* Austr.
42 D3 Maurik Neth.
52 C3 Mauritania *country* Africa
53 K7 Mauritius *country* Ind. Ocean
68 B4 Mauston U.S.A.
89 D4 Mavaca *r.* Venez.
57 C5 Mavinga Angola
59 G5 Mavuya S. Africa
22 D3 Mawana India
56 B4 Mawanga Congo(Zaire)
27 D4 Ma Wang Dui China
32 A3 Mawdaung Pass Myanmar/Thai.
9 G3 Mawhai Pt *pt* N.Z.
92 D4 Mawson *Austr. Base* Ant.
92 D5 Mawson Coast *coastal area* Ant.
92 D4 Mawson Escarpment *esc.* Ant.
92 B6 Mawson Pen. *pen.* Ant.
32 A3 Maw Taung *mt* Myanmar
76 C2 Max U.S.A.
84 E2 Maxcanú Mex.
48 C5 Maxia, Punta *mt Sardinia* Italy
68 D5 Maxinkuckee, Lake *l.* U.S.A.
36 S5 Maxmo Fin.
69 F2 Maxton U.S.A.
74 A2 Maxwell U.S.A.
33 C3 Maya *i.* Indon.
24 F1 Maya *r.* Rus. Fed.
83 K4 Mayaguana *i.* Bahamas
83 L5 Mayagüez Puerto Rico
54 C3 Mayahi Niger
19 H2 Mayakovskogo *mt* Tajik.
56 B4 Mayama Congo
18 D2 Mayamey Iran
82 G5 Maya Mountains *mts* Belize/Guatemala
26 B3 Mayan China
27 C5 Mayang China
28 F5 Maya-san *mt* Japan
40 D5 Maybole U.K.
17 K4 Maydān Iraq
19 H3 Maydā Shahr Afgh.
42 F4 Mayen Ger.
44 D2 Mayenne France
44 D2 Mayenne *r.* France
75 F4 Mayer U.S.A.
64 F4 Mayerthorpe Can.
9 C5 Mayfield N.Z.
78 B4 Mayfield U.S.A.
73 F5 Mayhill U.S.A.
30 E1 Mayi *r.* China
40 F4 May, Isle of *i.* U.K.
51 G6 Maykop Rus. Fed.
24 B4 Maymyo Myanmar
24 B1 Mayna Rus. Fed.
21 A2 Mayni India
69 J3 Maynooth Can.
64 B2 Mayo Can.
91 E2 Mayo, 25 de *Buenos Aires* Arg.
91 C3 Mayo, 25 de *La Pampa* Arg.
31 C5 Mayo Bay *b.* Phil.
56 B4 Mayoko Congo
64 B2 Mayo Lake *l.* Can.
31 B3 Mayon *volc.* Phil.
91 D3 Mayor Buratovich Arg.
9 F2 Mayor I. *i.* N.Z.
88 D1 Mayor Pablo Lagerenza Para.
53 J7 Mayotte *terr.* Africa
31 B2 Mayraira Point *pt* Phil.
24 E1 Mayskiy Rus. Fed.
80 B5 Maysville U.S.A.
56 B4 Mayumba Gabon
23 E3 Mayum La *pass* China
21 B4 Mayuram India

69 F4 Mayville MI U.S.A.
76 D2 Mayville ND U.S.A.
80 D3 Mayville NY U.S.A.
68 C4 Mayville WV U.S.A.
76 C3 Maywood U.S.A.
91 D3 Maza Arg.
50 F3 Maza Rus. Fed.
57 C5 Mazabuka Zambia
87 H4 Mazagão Brazil
44 F5 Mazamet France
22 D1 Mazar China
48 E6 Mazara del Vallo Sicily Italy
19 G2 Mazār-e Sharīf Afgh.
19 G3 Mazar, Koh-i- mt Afgh.
89 E3 Mazaruni r. Guyana
82 F6 Mazatenango Guatemala
84 A2 Mazatlán Mex.
75 G4 Mazatzal Peak summit U.S.A.
18 C3 Mazdaj Iran
37 S8 Mažeikiai Lith.
17 G2 Mazgirt Turkey
37 S8 Mazirbe Latvia
56 D4 Mazomora Tanz.
17 M3 Mazr'eh Iran
17 M5 Māzū Iran
57 C6 Mazunga Zimbabwe
51 D4 Mazyr Belarus
59 J3 Mbabane Swaziland
54 B4 Mbahiakro Côte d'Ivoire
56 B3 Mbaïki C.A.R.
57 D4 Mbala Zambia
56 D3 Mbale Uganda
54 D4 Mbalmayo Cameroon
56 B4 Mbandaka Congo(Zaire)
54 C4 Mbanga Cameroon
56 B4 M'banza Congo Angola
56 D4 Mbarara Uganda
56 C3 Mbari r. C.A.R.
59 K3 Mbaswana S. Africa
54 D4 Mbengwi Cameroon
57 D4 Mbeya Tanz.
57 D5 Mbinga Tanz.
57 D6 Mbizi Zimbabwe
56 B3 Mbomo Congo
54 D4 Mbouda Cameroon
54 A3 Mbour Senegal
54 A3 Mbout Maur.
57 D4 Mbozi Tanz.
56 C4 Mbuji-Mayi Congo(Zaire)
56 D4 Mbulu Tanz.
56 D4 Mbuyuni Tanz.
57 D4 Mchinga Tanz.
59 G6 Mdantsane S. Africa
48 B6 M'Daourouch Alg.
77 C4 Meade U.S.A.
75 E3 Mead, Lake l. U.S.A.
65 H4 Meadow Lake Can.
65 H4 Meadow Lake Provincial Park res. Can.
75 E3 Meadow Valley Wash r. U.S.A.
80 C4 Meadville U.S.A.
69 G3 Meaford Can.
28 J3 Meaken-dake volc. Japan
40 A2 Mealasta Island i. U.K.
45 B2 Mealhada Port.
40 D4 Meall a'Bhuiridh mt U.K.
67 J3 Mealy Mountains Can.
19 F2 Meana Turkm.
64 F3 Meander River Can.
31 C5 Meares i. Indon.
44 F2 Meaux France
56 B4 Mebridege r. Angola
20 A5 Mecca S. Arabia
81 H2 Mechanic Falls U.S.A.
80 B4 Mechanicsburg U.S.A.
68 B5 Mechanicsville U.S.A.
42 C3 Mechelen Belgium
42 D4 Mechelen Neth.
54 B1 Mecheria Alg.
42 E4 Mechernich Ger.
16 E1 Mecitözü Turkey
42 F4 Meckenheim Ger.
46 E3 Mecklenburger Bucht b. Ger.
43 K1 Mecklenburgische Seenplatte reg. Ger.
43 L1 Mecklenburg-Vorpommern div. Ger.
57 D5 Mecula Moz.
45 C2 Meda Port.
21 B2 Medak India
33 A2 Medan Indon.
91 D3 Médanos Arg.
88 C7 Medanosa, Pta pt Arg.
21 C4 Medawachchiya Sri Lanka
21 B2 Medchal India
81 K2 Meddybemps L. l. U.S.A.
45 H4 Médéa Alg.
43 G3 Medebach Ger.
89 B3 Medellín Col.
39 F4 Meden r. U.K.
54 D1 Medenine Tunisia
54 A3 Mederdra Maur.
72 B3 Medford OR U.S.A.
68 B3 Medford WV U.S.A.
81 F5 Medford Farms U.S.A.
49 N2 Medgidia Romania
17 L4 Medhīkhan Iran
68 B5 Media U.S.A.
91 C2 Media Luna Arg.
47 M7 Mediaș Romania
72 C2 Medical Lake U.S.A.
72 F3 Medicine Bow U.S.A.
72 F3 Medicine Bow Mts mts U.S.A.
72 F3 Medicine Bow Peak summit U.S.A.
65 G4 Medicine Hat Can.
77 D4 Medicine Lodge U.S.A.
90 E2 Medina Brazil
20 A5 Medina S. Arabia
80 D3 Medina NY U.S.A.
80 C4 Medina OH U.S.A.
45 E2 Medinaceli Spain
45 D2 Medina del Campo Spain
45 D2 Medina de Rioseco Spain
23 F5 Medinīpur India
34 F5 Mediterranean Sea sea Africa/Europe
48 B6 Medjerda, Monts de la mts Alg.
12 G4 Mednogorsk Rus. Fed.
94 G2 Mednyy, Ostrov i. Rus. Fed.
44 D4 Médoc reg. France
50 H3 Medvedevo Rus. Fed.
51 H5 Medveditsa r. Rus. Fed.
48 F2 Medvednica mts Croatia
13 S2 Medvezh'i, O-va is Rus. Fed.
24 F2 Medvezh'ya, Gora mt China/Rus. Fed.
50 E2 Medvezh'yegorsk Rus. Fed.
39 H6 Medway r. U.K.
6 B4 Meekatharra Austr.
75 H1 Meeker U.S.A.
74 B2 Meeks Bay U.S.A.
67 J4 Meelpaeg Res. resr Can.
43 L4 Meerane Ger.
42 E3 Meerlo Neth.
22 D3 Meerut India
72 E2 Meeteetse U.S.A.
56 D3 Mēga Eth.
33 B3 Mega i. Indon.
23 G4 Meghalaya div. India
23 F5 Meghāsani mt India
23 G5 Meghna r. Bangl.
17 L2 Meghri Armenia
16 B3 Megisti i. Greece
36 U1 Mehamn Norway
19 G5 Mehar Pak.
6 B4 Meharry, Mt mt Austr.
22 D5 Mehekar India
23 G5 Meherpur Bangl.
80 E6 Meherrin r. U.S.A.
5 N6 Méhétia i. Pac. Oc.
17 L2 Mehrābān Iran
17 L5 Mehrān Iraq
18 D5 Mehrān watercourse Iran
42 E4 Mehren Ger.
18 D4 Mehriz Iran
19 H3 Mehtar Lām Afgh.
90 C2 Meia Ponte r. Brazil
55 D4 Meiganga Cameroon
27 B4 Meigu China
27 E5 Mei Jiang r. China
42 D3 Meijnweg, Nationaal Park De nat. park Neth.
40 D5 Meikle Millyea h. U.K.
25 B4 Meiktila Myanmar
43 J2 Meine Ger.
43 J2 Meinersen Ger.
43 J4 Meiningen Ger.
58 E6 Meiringspoort pass S. Africa
27 B4 Meishan China
46 F5 Meißen Ger.
27 C5 Meitan China
26 C3 Mei Xian China
27 E5 Meizhou China
22 D4 Mej r. India
88 C3 Mejicana mt Arg.
88 B2 Mejillones Chile
56 D2 Mek'elē Eth.
54 A3 Mékhé Senegal
22 B3 Mekhtar Pak.
48 C7 Meknassy Tunisia
54 B1 Meknès Morocco
32 C2 Mekong r. Asia
24 B3 Mekong r. China
32 C3 Mekong, Mouths of the est. Vietnam
33 B2 Melaka Malaysia
94 G6 Melanesia is Pac. Oc.
31 A5 Melaut r. Malaysia
33 D3 Melawi r. Indon.
8 E4 Melbourne Austr.
79 D6 Melbourne U.S.A.
40 □ Melby U.K.
46 D3 Meldorf Ger.
69 F3 Meldrum Bay Can.
16 E2 Melendiz Dağı mt Turkey
50 G4 Melenki Rus. Fed.
67 F2 Mélèzes, Rivière aux r. Can.
55 D3 Mélfi Chad
48 F4 Melfi Italy
65 J4 Melfort Can.
36 M5 Melhus Norway
45 C1 Melide Spain
54 B1 Melilla Spain
91 E2 Melincué Arg.
33 E3 Melintang, Danau l. Indon.
91 B2 Melipilla Chile
42 B3 Meliskerke Neth.
65 J5 Melita Can.
51 E6 Melitopol' Ukr.
46 G6 Melk Austria
59 H1 Melkrivier S. Africa
39 E6 Melksham U.K.
36 T3 Mellakoski Fin.
36 Q5 Mellansel Sweden
43 G2 Melle Ger.
68 B2 Mellen U.S.A.
37 N7 Mellerud Sweden
43 J4 Mellrichstadt Ger.
43 G1 Mellum i. Ger.
59 J4 Melmoth S. Africa
91 F2 Melo Uru.
8 B2 Melrose Austr.
40 F5 Melrose U.K.
43 H3 Melsungen Ger.
31 A5 Melta, Mt mt Malaysia
39 G5 Melton Mowbray U.K.
44 F2 Melun France
65 J4 Melville Can.
63 M2 Melville Bugt b. Greenland
6 E3 Melville, C. c. Austr.
31 A5 Melville, C. c. Phil.
6 D3 Melville Island i. Austr.
62 G2 Melville Island i. Can.
67 J3 Melville, Lake l. Can.
63 K3 Melville Peninsula Can.
41 C3 Melvin, Lough l. Rep. of Ireland/U.K.
13 T3 Melyuveyem Rus. Fed.
23 E2 Mêmar Co salt l. China
25 F7 Memberamo r. Indon.
59 H3 Memel S. Africa
43 J5 Memmelsdorf Ger.
46 E7 Memmingen Ger.
42 C5 Mémorial Américain h. France
33 C2 Mempawah Indon.
16 C7 Memphis Egypt
68 A5 Memphis MO U.S.A.
79 B5 Memphis TN U.S.A.
77 C5 Memphis TX U.S.A.
81 G2 Memphrémagog, Lac l. Can.
28 H3 Memuro-dake mt Japan
51 E5 Mena Ukr.
77 E5 Mena U.S.A.
54 C3 Ménaka Mali
Mènam Khong r. see Mekong
77 D6 Menard U.S.A.
68 C3 Menasha U.S.A.
33 D3 Mendawai r. Indon.
44 F4 Mende France
17 M3 Mendejīn Iran
62 B4 Mendenhall, C. pt U.S.A.
64 C3 Mendenhall Glacier gl. U.S.A.
84 C1 Méndez Mex.
56 D3 Mendī Eth.
6 E2 Mendi P.N.G.
39 E6 Mendip Hills h. U.K.
74 A2 Mendocino U.S.A.
72 A3 Mendocino, C. c. U.S.A.
95 K3 Mendocino Seascarp sea feature Pac. Oc.
68 E4 Mendon U.S.A.
8 G1 Mendooran Austr.
74 B3 Mendota CA U.S.A.
68 C5 Mendota IL U.S.A.
68 C4 Mendota, Lake l. U.S.A.
91 C2 Mendoza Arg.
91 C2 Mendoza div. Arg.
91 C2 Mendoza r. Arg.
89 C2 Mene de Mauroa Venez.
89 C2 Mene Grande Venez.
49 M5 Menemen Turkey
26 E3 Mengcheng China
16 D1 Mengen Turkey
33 C3 Menggala Indon.
27 D5 Mengshan China
26 F3 Meng Shan mts China
26 E3 Mengyin China
27 B6 Mengzi China
67 G3 Menihek Can.
67 G3 Menihek Lakes l. Can.
8 D2 Menindee Austr.
8 D2 Menindee Lake l. Austr.
8 B3 Meningie Austr.
17 M4 Menjān Iran
13 O3 Menkere Rus. Fed.
44 F2 Mennecy France
68 D3 Menominee U.S.A.
68 D3 Menominee r. U.S.A.
68 C4 Menomonee Falls U.S.A.
68 B3 Menomonie U.S.A.
57 B5 Menongue Angola
45 J2 Menorca i. Spain
31 A6 Mensalong Indon.
33 A3 Mentawai, Kepulauan is Indon.
32 B5 Mentekab Malaysia
43 J3 Menteroda Ger.
75 H4 Mentmore U.S.A.
33 C3 Mentok Indon.
44 H5 Menton France
80 C4 Mentor U.S.A.
54 C1 Menzel Bourguiba Tunisia
48 D6 Menzel Temime Tunisia
6 C4 Menzies Austr.
92 D4 Menzies, Mt mt Ant.
42 E2 Meppel Neth.
42 F2 Meppen Ger.
59 K1 Mepuze Moz.
59 G4 Meqheleng S. Africa
50 G3 Mera r. Rus. Fed.
33 C4 Merak Indon.
36 M5 Meråker Norway
76 F4 Meramec r. U.S.A.
48 D1 Merano Italy
89 E3 Merari, Sa. mt Brazil
58 F1 Meratswe r. Botswana
33 E3 Meratus, Pegunungan mts Indon.
25 G7 Merauke Indon.
8 D3 Merbein Austr.
74 B3 Merced U.S.A.
91 B1 Mercedario, Cerro mt Arg.
91 E2 Mercedes Buenos Aires Arg.
88 E3 Mercedes Corrientes Arg.
91 D2 Mercedes San Luis Arg.
91 E2 Mercedes Uru.
80 A4 Mercer OH U.S.A.
68 B2 Mercer WV U.S.A.
64 F4 Mercoal Can.
9 E2 Mercury Islands is N.Z.
63 M3 Mercy, C. hd Can.
42 B4 Mere Belgium
39 E6 Mere U.K.
81 H3 Meredith U.S.A.
77 C5 Meredith, Lake l. U.S.A.
77 C5 Meredith Nat. Recreation Area, Lake res. U.S.A.
68 B6 Meredosia U.S.A.
51 F5 Merefa Ukr.
55 E3 Merga Oasis oasis Sudan
32 A2 Mergui Myanmar
32 A3 Mergui Archipelago is Myanmar
8 C3 Meribah Austr.
49 M4 Meriç r. Greece/Turkey
84 E2 Mérida Mex.
45 C3 Mérida Spain
89 C2 Mérida Venez.
89 C2 Mérida, Cordillera de mts Venez.
81 G4 Meriden U.S.A.
74 B2 Meridian CA U.S.A.
77 F5 Meridian MS U.S.A.
44 D4 Mérignac France
36 T4 Merijärvi Fin.
37 R6 Merikarvia Fin.
8 G4 Merimbula Austr.
8 C3 Meringur Austr.
8 C4 Merino Austr.
77 C5 Merkel U.S.A.
32 □ Merlimau, P. i. Sing.
55 F3 Merowe Sudan
6 B5 Merredin Austr.
40 D5 Merrick h. U.K.
69 K3 Merrickville Can.
68 C3 Merrill U.S.A.
68 D5 Merrillville U.S.A.
76 C3 Merriman U.S.A.
64 E4 Merritt Can.
79 D6 Merritt Island U.S.A.
8 H2 Merriwa Austr.
8 G1 Merrygoen Austr.
56 E2 Mersa Fatma Eritrea
42 E5 Mersch Lux.
43 K3 Merseburg (Saale) Ger.
39 E4 Mersey est. U.K.
Mersin see İçel
33 B2 Mersing Malaysia
37 S8 Mērsrags Latvia
22 C4 Merta India
39 D6 Merthyr Tydfil U.K.
56 D3 Merti Kenya
45 C4 Mértola Port.
92 B6 Mertz Gl. gl. Ant.
56 D4 Meru volc. Tanz.
19 F4 Merui Pak.
Merv see Mary
58 D6 Merweville S. Africa
16 E1 Merzifon Turkey
42 E5 Merzig Ger.
92 B2 Merz Pen. pen. Ant.
75 G5 Mesa U.S.A.
68 A2 Mesabi Range h. U.S.A.
48 G4 Mesagne Italy
49 L7 Mesara, Ormos b. Greece
75 H3 Mesa Verde Nat. Park U.S.A.
89 B4 Mesay r. Col.
43 G3 Meschede Ger.
36 P4 Meselefors Sweden
66 F3 Mesgouez L. l. Can.
50 J2 Meshchura Rus. Fed.
Meshed see Mashhad
19 E2 Meshkān Iran
51 G5 Meshkovskaya Rus. Fed.
68 E3 Mesick U.S.A.
49 K4 Mesimeri Greece
49 J5 Mesolongi Greece
17 J4 Mesopotamia reg. Iraq
75 E3 Mesquite NV U.S.A.
77 D5 Mesquite TX U.S.A.
75 E4 Mesquite Lake l. U.S.A.
57 D5 Messalo r. Moz.
48 F5 Messina Sicily Italy
59 J1 Messina S. Africa
48 F5 Messina, Stretta di str. Italy
69 J2 Messines Can.
49 K6 Messini Greece
49 K6 Messiniakos Kolpos b. Greece
63 Q2 Mesters Vig Greenland
43 K1 Mestlin Ger.
49 L5 Meston, Akra pt Greece
48 E2 Mestre Italy
16 F1 Mesudiye Turkey
89 C3 Meta r. Col./Venez.
69 G2 Metagama Can.
63 L3 Meta Incognita Pen. Can.
77 F6 Metairie U.S.A.
68 C5 Metamora U.S.A.
88 C3 Metán Arg.
96 H9 Meteor Depth depth Atl. Ocean
49 J6 Methoni Greece
81 H3 Methuen U.S.A.
40 E4 Methven U.K.
48 G3 Metković Croatia
64 C3 Metlakatla U.S.A.
57 D5 Metoro Moz.
33 C4 Metro Indon.
78 B4 Metropolis U.S.A.
42 C4 Mettet Belgium
43 F2 Mettingen Ger.
74 C4 Mettler U.S.A.
21 B4 Mettur India
56 D3 Metu Eth.
44 H2 Metz France
42 D4 Meuse r. Belgium/France
43 L3 Meuselwitz Ger.
39 C7 Mevagissey U.K.
26 B3 Mêwa China
77 D6 Mexia U.S.A.
82 A2 Mexicali Mex.
75 H3 Mexican Hat U.S.A.
73 F6 Mexicanos, L. de los l. Mex.
75 H3 Mexican Water U.S.A.
84 C3 México Mex.
81 H2 Mexico ME U.S.A.
76 F4 Mexico MO U.S.A.
81 E3 Mexico NY U.S.A.
61 H7 Mexico country Central America
84 C3 México div. Mex.
61 J7 Mexico, Gulf of g. Mex./U.S.A.
18 D3 Meybod Iran
43 L1 Meyenburg Ger.
19 G3 Meymaneh Afgh.
18 C3 Meymeh Iran
18 B3 Meymeh r. Iran
84 D3 Mezcalapa r. Mex.
49 K3 Mezdra Bulg.
12 F3 Mezen' Rus. Fed.
44 G4 Mézenc, Mont mt France
50 J2 Mezhdurechensk Rus. Fed.
24 A1 Mezhdurechensk Rus. Fed.
12 G2 Mezhdusharskiy, O. i. Rus. Fed.
47 K7 Mezőtúr Hungary
84 A2 Mezquital Mex.
84 A2 Mezquital r. Mex.
84 B2 Mezquitic Mex.
37 U8 Mežvidi Latvia
57 D5 Mfuwe Zambia
21 A2 Mhasvad India
59 J3 Mhlume Swaziland
22 C5 Mhow India
23 H5 Mi r. Myanmar
84 C3 Miahuatlán Mex.
45 D3 Miajadas Spain
75 G5 Miami AZ U.S.A.
79 D7 Miami FL U.S.A.
77 E4 Miami OK U.S.A.
79 D7 Miami Beach U.S.A.
18 C4 Mīān Āb Iran
19 F5 Mianaz Pak.
18 D3 Mīāndarreh Iran
18 B2 Miandowāb Iran
57 E5 Miandrivazo Madag.
18 B2 Mīāneh Iran
31 C5 Miangas i. Phil.
19 G5 Miani Hor b. Pak.
19 G3 Mianjoi Afgh.
27 B4 Mianning China
22 B2 Mianwali Pak.
26 C3 Mian Xian China
27 D4 Mianyang Hubei China
26 B4 Mianyang Sichuan China
26 B4 Mianzhu China
26 F2 Miao Dao i. China
26 F2 Miaodao Qundao is China
27 F5 Miaoli Taiwan
57 E5 Miarinarivo Madag.
12 H4 Miass Rus. Fed.
75 G5 Mica Mt mt U.S.A.
26 C3 Micang Shan mts China
47 K6 Michalovce Slovakia
65 H3 Michel Can.
43 K4 Michelau in Oberfranken Ger.
43 H5 Michelstadt Ger.
43 M2 Michendorf Ger.
68 C2 Michigamme Lake l. U.S.A.
68 C2 Michigamme Reservoir U.S.A.
68 D2 Michigan div. U.S.A.
68 D5 Michigan City U.S.A.
68 D4 Michigan, Lake l. U.S.A.
68 E2 Michipicoten Bay b. Can.
68 E2 Michipicoten I. i. Can.
68 E1 Michipicoten River Can.
84 B3 Michoacán div. Mex.
49 M3 Michurin Bulg.
50 G4 Michurinsk Rus. Fed.
83 H6 Mico r. Nic.
94 E5 Micronesia is Pac. Oc.
4 F4 Micronesia, Federated States of country Pac. Oc.
33 C2 Midai i. Indon.
96 F4 Mid-Atlantic Ridge sea feature Atl. Ocean
58 C6 Middelberg Pass S. Africa
42 B3 Middelburg Neth.
58 F5 Middelburg Eastern Cape S. Africa
59 H2 Middelburg Mpumalanga S. Africa
37 L9 Middelfart Denmark
42 C3 Middelharnis Neth.
58 D5 Middelpos S. Africa
59 G2 Middelwit S. Africa
72 C3 Middle Alkali Lake l. U.S.A.
94 N5 Middle America Trench sea feature Pac. Oc.
81 H4 Middleboro U.S.A.
80 E4 Middleburg U.S.A.
81 F3 Middleburgh U.S.A.
81 G2 Middlebury U.S.A.
9 C6 Middlemarch N.Z.
80 B6 Middlesboro U.S.A.
38 F3 Middlesbrough U.K.
74 A2 Middletown CA U.S.A.
81 G4 Middletown CT U.S.A.
81 F5 Middletown DE U.S.A.
81 F4 Middletown NY U.S.A.
80 A5 Middletown OH U.S.A.
68 E4 Middleville U.S.A.
39 G7 Midhurst U.K.
93 K4 Mid-Indian Basin sea feature Ind. Ocean
93 K6 Mid-Indian Ridge sea feature Ind. Ocean
69 H3 Midland Can.
69 E4 Midland MI U.S.A.
77 C5 Midland TX U.S.A.
41 C6 Midleton Rep. of Ireland
94 F4 Mid-Pacific Mountains sea feature Pac. Oc.
36 □ Miðvágur Faroe Is
Midway see Thamarīt
5 K2 Midway Islands is HI U.S.A.
72 F3 Midwest U.S.A.
77 D5 Midwest City U.S.A.
42 D2 Midwoud Neth.
17 H3 Midyat Turkey
40 □ Mid Yell U.K.
49 K3 Midzhur mt Bulg./Yugo.
37 U6 Miehikkälä Fin.
36 T3 Miekojärvi l. Fin.
47 K5 Mielec Pol.
57 D4 Miembwe Tanz.
36 U2 Mieraslompolo Fin.
47 M7 Miercurea-Ciuc Romania
45 D1 Mieres Spain
56 E3 Mī'ēso Eth.
43 K2 Mieste Ger.
80 E4 Mifflinburg U.S.A.
80 E4 Mifflintown U.S.A.
26 C3 Migang Shan mt China
59 F3 Migdol S. Africa
19 E4 Mīghān Iran
23 H3 Miging India
84 B1 Miguel Auza Mex.
16 C2 Mihaliççık Turkey
29 C7 Mihara Japan
29 F7 Mihara-yama volc. Japan
45 F2 Mijares r. Spain
42 C2 Mijdrecht Neth.
69 F3 Mikado U.S.A.
47 N4 Mikashevichy Belarus
50 F4 Mikhaylov Rus. Fed.
92 D5 Mikhaylov I. i. Ant.
28 C3 Mikhaylovka Primorskiy Kray Rus. Fed.
51 G5 Mikhaylovka Volgograd. Rus. Fed.
12 J4 Mikhaylovskiy Rus. Fed.
23 H4 Mikīr Hills mts India
37 U6 Mikkeli Fin.
37 U6 Mikkelin mlk Fin.
64 G3 Mikkwa r. Can.
56 D4 Mikumi Tanz.
50 J2 Mikun' Rus. Fed.
29 F6 Mikuni-sammyaku mts Japan
29 F8 Mikura-jima i. Japan
76 E2 Milaca U.S.A.
21 A5 Miladhunmadulu Atoll atoll Maldives
48 C2 Milan Italy
79 B5 Milan U.S.A.
8 B3 Milang Austr.
57 D5 Milange Moz.
Milano see Milan
16 A3 Milas Turkey
48 F5 Milazzo Sicily Italy
76 D2 Milbank U.S.A.
39 H5 Mildenhall U.K.
8 D3 Mildura Austr.
27 B5 Mile China
72 F2 Miles City U.S.A.
41 C5 Milestone Rep. of Ireland
48 F4 Miletto, Monte mt Italy
41 D2 Milford Rep. of Ireland
74 B1 Milford CA U.S.A.
81 G4 Milford CT U.S.A.
81 F5 Milford DE U.S.A.
68 D5 Milford IL U.S.A.
81 H3 Milford MA U.S.A.
81 J2 Milford ME U.S.A.
81 H3 Milford NH U.S.A.
81 F3 Milford NY U.S.A.
75 F2 Milford UT U.S.A.
39 B6 Milford Haven U.K.
9 A6 Milford Sound N.Z.
9 A6 Milford Sound in. N.Z.
45 H4 Miliana Alg.
62 G5 Milk r. Alta. Can.
72 F1 Milk r. Can./U.S.A.
13 R4 Mil'kovo Rus. Fed.
45 F2 Millárs r. Spain
44 F4 Millau France
74 B1 Mill Creek r. U.S.A.
79 D5 Milledgeville GA U.S.A.
68 C5 Milledgeville IL U.S.A.
76 E2 Mille Lacs L. l. U.S.A.
66 B4 Mille Lacs, Lac des l. Can.
76 D2 Miller U.S.A.
68 B3 Miller Dam Flowage resr U.S.A.
69 G3 Miller Lake Can.
51 G5 Millerovo Rus. Fed.
75 G6 Miller Peak summit U.S.A.
80 C4 Millersburg OH U.S.A.
80 E4 Millersburg PA U.S.A.
80 E6 Millers Tavern U.S.A.
74 C3 Millerton Lake l. U.S.A.
40 C5 Milleur Point pt U.K.
92 C6 Mill I. i. Ant.
8 C4 Millicent Austr.
69 F4 Millington MI U.S.A.
79 B5 Millington TN U.S.A.
81 J2 Millinocket U.S.A.
38 D3 Millom U.K.
40 D5 Millport U.K.
81 F5 Millsboro U.S.A.
64 F2 Mills Lake l. Can.
80 C5 Millstone U.S.A.
67 G4 Milltown Can.
41 B5 Milltown Malbay Rep. of Ireland
81 K1 Millville Can.
81 F5 Millville U.S.A.
81 J2 Milo U.S.A.
28 D3 Milogradovo Rus. Fed.
49 L6 Milos i. Greece
50 F4 Miloslavskoye Rus. Fed.
80 E4 Milroy U.S.A.
69 H4 Milton Can.
9 B7 Milton N.Z.
79 C6 Milton FL U.S.A.
68 A5 Milton IA U.S.A.
80 E4 Milton PA U.S.A.
81 G2 Milton VT U.S.A.
72 C2 Milton-Freewater U.S.A.
39 G5 Milton Keynes U.K.
80 C4 Milton, Lake l. U.S.A.
27 D4 Miluo China
68 D4 Milwaukee U.S.A.
51 G5 Milyutinskaya Rus. Fed.
44 D4 Mimizan France
56 B4 Mimongo Gabon
84 B1 Mina Mex.
74 C2 Mina U.S.A.
18 E5 Mīnāb Iran
25 E6 Minahassa, Semenanjung pen. Indon.
18 D5 Mina Jebel Ali U.A.E.
65 L4 Minaki Can.
29 B8 Minamata Japan
29 E7 Minami Alps National Park Japan
33 B2 Minas Indon.
91 F2 Minas Uru.
17 M7 Mīnā Sa'ūd Kuwait
67 H4 Minas Basin b. Can.
91 F1 Minas de Corrales Uru.
90 D2 Minas Gerais div. Brazil
90 D2 Minas Novas Brazil
84 D3 Minatitlán Mex.
23 H5 Minbu Myanmar
23 H5 Minbya Myanmar
88 B6 Minchinmávida volc. Chile
40 C2 Minch, The str. U.K.
48 D2 Mincio r. Italy
17 L2 Mincivan Azer.
31 C5 Mindanao i. Phil.
8 C3 Mindarie Austr.
54 □ Mindelo Cape Verde
69 H3 Minden Can.
43 G2 Minden Ger.
77 E5 Minden LA U.S.A.
74 C2 Minden NV U.S.A.
23 H6 Mindon Myanmar
8 D2 Mindona L. l. Austr.
31 B3 Mindoro i. Phil.
31 A3 Mindoro Strait str. Phil.
56 B4 Mindouli Congo
39 D6 Minehead U.K.
41 D6 Mine Head hd Rep. of Ireland
90 B2 Mineiros Brazil
77 E5 Mineola U.S.A.
74 B1 Mineral U.S.A.
74 C3 Mineral King U.S.A.
51 G6 Mineral'nyye Vody Rus. Fed.
68 B4 Mineral Point U.S.A.
77 D5 Mineral Wells U.S.A.
75 F2 Minersville U.S.A.
48 G4 Minervino Murge Italy
23 E1 Minfeng China
57 C5 Minga Congo(Zaire)
17 L1 Mingäçevir Azer.
17 L1 Mingäçevir Su Anbarı resr Azer.
67 H3 Mingan Can.
8 C2 Mingary Austr.
26 E3 Minggang China
45 F3 Minglanilla Spain
57 D5 Mingoyo Tanz.
27 B4 Ming-shan China
24 E2 Mingshui China
40 A4 Mingulay i. U.K.
27 E5 Mingxi China
26 B2 Minhe China
27 F5 Minhou China
21 A4 Minicoy i. India
6 B4 Minilya Austr.
67 H3 Minipi Lake l. Can.
65 J4 Minitonas Can.
27 F5 Min Jiang r. Fujian China
26 B4 Min Jiang r. Sichuan China
26 A2 Minle China
54 C4 Minna Nigeria
37 O5 Minne Sweden
76 E2 Minneapolis U.S.A.
65 K4 Minnedosa Can.
68 A2 Minnesota div. U.S.A.
71 G2 Minnesota r. MN U.S.A.
66 B4 Minnitaki L. l. Can.
45 B2 Miño r. Port./Spain
68 C3 Minocqua U.S.A.
68 B2 Minong U.S.A.
68 C5 Minonk U.S.A.
Minorca i. see Menorca
76 C1 Minot U.S.A.
26 B2 Minqin China
27 F5 Minqing China
26 B3 Min Shan mts China
23 H4 Minsin Myanmar
50 C4 Minsk Belarus
47 K4 Mińsk Mazowiecki Pol.
39 E5 Minsterley U.K.
22 C1 Mintaka Pass pass China/Jammu and Kashmir
67 G4 Minto Can.
62 G2 Minto Inlet in. Can.
66 F2 Minto, Lac l. Can.
73 F4 Minturn U.S.A.
16 C6 Minûf Egypt
24 B1 Minusinsk Rus. Fed.
23 J3 Minutang India
26 B3 Min Xian China
8 D4 Minyip Austr.
69 E3 Mio U.S.A.
66 E4 Miquelon Can.
67 J4 Miquelon i. N. America
89 A4 Mira r. Col.
19 F4 Mirabad Afgh.
81 F2 Mirabel Can.
90 D2 Mirabela Brazil
87 J5 Miracema do Norte Brazil
87 J5 Mirador, Parque Nacional de nat. park Brazil
89 B4 Miraflores Col.
90 D2 Miralta Brazil
91 F3 Miramar Arg.
84 E3 Miramar, L. l. Mex.
44 G5 Miramas France
67 G4 Miramichi r. Can.
49 L7 Mirampelou, Kolpos b. Greece
22 B2 Miram Shah Pak.
90 A3 Miranda Brazil
74 A1 Miranda U.S.A.
90 A3 Miranda r. Brazil
45 E1 Miranda de Ebro Spain
45 C2 Mirandela Port.
48 D2 Mirandola Italy
90 B3 Mirandópolis Brazil
17 H5 Mirā', Wādī al watercourse Iraq/S. Arabia
20 D6 Mirbāţ Oman
44 E5 Mirepoix France
33 D2 Miri Malaysia
19 F4 Miri mt Pak.
21 B2 Mirialguda India
91 G2 Mirim, Lagoa l. Brazil
19 F4 Mīrjāveh Iran
50 G2 Mirnyy Rus. Fed.
13 N3 Mirnyy Rus. Fed.
92 D5 Mirnyy Rus. Fed. Base Ant.
65 J3 Mirond L. l. Can.
43 L1 Mirow Ger.
22 C2 Mirpur Pak.
22 B4 Mirpur Batoro Pak.
22 B4 Mirpur Khas Pak.
22 A4 Mirpur Sakro Pak.
64 G4 Mirror Can.
27 □ Mirs Bay b. H.K. China
19 E5 Mīr Shahdād Iran
49 K6 Mirtoö Pelagos sea Greece
30 E6 Miryang S. Korea
19 F2 Mirzachirla Turkm.
23 E4 Mirzapur India
29 C8 Misaki Japan
28 G4 Misawa Japan
67 H4 Miscou I. i. Can.
22 C1 Misgar Pak.
28 B2 Mishan China
18 C5 Mishāsh al Hādī well S. Arabia
68 D5 Mishawaka U.S.A.
68 E1 Mishibishu Lake l. Can.
29 B7 Mi-shima i. Japan
23 H3 Mishmi Hills mts India
6 F3 Misima I. i. P.N.G.
83 H6 Miskitos, Cayos atolls Nic.
47 K6 Miskolc Hungary
25 F7 Misoöl i. Indon.
68 B2 Misquah Hills h. U.S.A.
55 D1 Mişrātah Libya
22 E4 Misrikh India
69 E1 Missanabie Can.
66 D3 Missinaibi r. Can.
69 F1 Missinaibi Lake l. Can.
65 J3 Missinipe Can.
76 C3 Mission SD U.S.A.
84 C1 Mission TX U.S.A.
64 E5 Mission City Can.
66 D3 Missisa L. l. Can.
69 F2 Mississagi r. Can.
69 H4 Mississauga Can.
68 E5 Mississinewa Lake l. U.S.A.
77 F5 Mississippi div. U.S.A.
69 J3 Mississippi r. Can.
77 F6 Mississippi r. U.S.A.
77 F6 Mississippi Delta delta U.S.A.
72 D2 Missoula U.S.A.
68 A6 Missouri div. U.S.A.
76 C2 Missouri r. U.S.A.
76 E3 Missouri Valley U.S.A.
63 L4 Mistassibi r. Can.
67 F4 Mistassini Can.
67 F4 Mistassini r. Can.
66 F3 Mistassini, L. l. Can.
67 H2 Mistastin Lake l. Can.
46 H6 Mistelbach Austria
64 C3 Misty Fjords National Monument res. U.S.A.
84 A2 Mita, Pta de hd Mex.
6 E4 Mitchell Austr.
69 G4 Mitchell Can.
76 D3 Mitchell U.S.A.
6 E3 Mitchell r. Qld. Austr.
8 F4 Mitchell r. Vic. Austr.
68 E3 Mitchell, Lake l. U.S.A.
79 D5 Mitchell, Mt mt U.S.A.
41 C5 Mitchelstown Rep. of Ireland
16 C6 Mît Ghamr Egypt
22 B3 Mithankot Pak.
22 B4 Mithi Pak.
22 B4 Mithrani Canal canal Pak.
49 M5 Mithymna Greece
64 C3 Mitkof I. i. U.S.A.
29 G6 Mito Japan
57 D4 Mitole Tanz.
9 E4 Mitre mt N.Z.
7 H3 Mitre Island i. Solomon Is
8 H3 Mittagong Austr.
8 F4 Mitta Mitta Austr.
43 G2 Mittellandkanal canal Ger.
43 L5 Mitterteich Ger.
43 L4 Mittweida Ger.
89 C4 Mitú Col.
89 C4 Mituas Col.
57 C5 Mitumba, Chaîne des mts Congo(Zaire)
56 C4 Mitumba, Monts mts Congo(Zaire)
56 B3 Mitzic Gabon
29 F7 Miura Japan
17 G4 Miyah, Wādī el watercourse Syria
29 F7 Miyake-jima i. Japan
28 G5 Miyako Japan
29 B9 Miyakonojō Japan
26 B4 Miyaluo China
22 B5 Miyāni India
29 B9 Miyazaki Japan
29 D7 Miyazu Japan
27 B5 Miyi China
29 C7 Miyoshi Japan
26 E1 Miyun China
26 E1 Miyun Sk. resr China
19 G3 Mīzāni Afgh.
56 D3 Mīzan Teferī Eth.
55 D1 Mizdah Libya
41 B6 Mizen Head hd Rep. of Ireland
51 B5 Mizhhir"ya Ukr.
26 D2 Mizhi China
23 H5 Mizoram div. India
28 G5 Mizusawa Japan
37 O7 Mjölby Sweden
56 D4 Mkata Tanz.
56 D4 Mkomazi Tanz.
57 C5 Mkushi Zambia
46 G5 Mladá Boleslav Czech Rep.
49 J2 Mladenovac Yugo.
47 K4 Mława Pol.
48 G3 Mljet i. Croatia
59 G5 Mlungisi S. Africa
47 M5 Mlyniv Ukr.
59 F2 Mmabatho S. Africa
59 G1 Mmamabula Botswana
59 F2 Mmathethe Botswana
37 J6 Mo Norway
75 H2 Moab U.S.A.
6 E3 Moa I. i. Austr.
7 H3 Moala i. Fiji
18 D3 Mo'alla Iran
59 K2 Moamba Moz.
75 E3 Moapa U.S.A.
41 D4 Moate Rep. of Ireland
56 C4 Moba Congo(Zaire)
29 G7 Mobara Japan
18 C3 Mobārakeh Iran
56 C3 Mobayi-Mbongo Congo(Zaire)
76 E4 Moberly U.S.A.
79 B6 Mobile AL U.S.A.
75 F5 Mobile AZ U.S.A.
79 B6 Mobile Bay b. U.S.A.
76 C2 Mobridge U.S.A.
Mobutu, Lake l. see Albert, Lake
87 J4 Mocajuba Brazil
57 E5 Moçambique Moz.
89 D2 Mocapra r. Venez.
27 B6 Môc Châu Vietnam
89 D2 Mochirma, Parque Nacional nat. park Venez.
57 C6 Mochudi Botswana
57 E5 Mocimboa da Praia Moz.
43 K2 Möckern Ger.
43 H5 Möckmühl Ger.
36 R4 Mockträsk Sweden
89 A4 Mocoa Col.

90 C3 **Mococa** Brazil
84 A1 **Mocorito** Mex.
84 B2 **Moctezuma** Mex.
57 D5 **Mocuba** Moz.
44 H4 **Modane** France
22 C5 **Modasa** India
58 F4 **Modder** *r.* S. Africa
48 D2 **Modena** Italy
75 F3 **Modena** U.S.A.
74 B3 **Modesto** U.S.A.
8 F5 **Moe** Austr.
39 D5 **Moel Sych** *h.* U.K.
37 M6 **Moely** Norway
36 Q2 **Moen** Norway
75 G3 **Moenkopi** U.S.A.
9 C6 **Moeraki Pt** *pt* N.Z.
42 E3 **Moers** Ger.
40 E5 **Moffat** U.K.
22 C3 **Moga** India
Mogadishu *see* **Muqdisho**
80 C4 **Mogadore Reservoir** *resr* U.S.A.
59 H1 **Mogalakwena** *r.* S. Africa
59 H2 **Moganyaka** S. Africa
43 L2 **Mögelin** Ger.
19 G2 **Moghiyon** Tajik.
90 C3 **Mogi-Mirim** Brazil
24 D1 **Mogocha** Rus. Fed.
48 C6 **Mogod** *mts* Tunisia
59 F2 **Mogoditshane** Botswana
24 B4 **Mogok** Myanmar
75 H5 **Mogollon Baldy** *mt* U.S.A.
75 H5 **Mogollon Mts** *mts* U.S.A.
75 G4 **Mogollon Rim** *plat.* U.S.A.
59 G2 **Mogwase** S. Africa
49 H2 **Mohács** Hungary
9 F3 **Mohaka** *r.* N.Z.
59 G5 **Mohale's Hoek** Lesotho
65 J5 **Mohall** U.S.A.
19 E3 **Mohammad** Iran
Moḥammadābād *see* **Darreh Gaz**
45 G5 **Mohammadia** Alg.
22 E3 **Mohan** *r.* India/Nepal
75 E4 **Mohave, L.** *l.* U.S.A.
75 F5 **Mohawk** U.S.A.
81 F3 **Mohawk** *r.* U.S.A.
75 F5 **Mohawk Mts** *mts* U.S.A.
57 E5 **Moheli** *i.* Comoros
41 D4 **Mohill** Rep. of Ireland
43 G3 **Möhne** *r.* Ger.
75 F4 **Mohon Peak** *summit* U.S.A.
57 D4 **Mohoro** Tanz.
77 C7 **Mohovano Ranch** Mex.
17 M5 **Moh Reza Shah Pahlavi** *resr* Iran
51 C5 **Mohyliv Podil's'kyy** Ukr.
37 K7 **Moi** Norway
59 G1 **Moijabana** Botswana
59 K2 **Moine** Moz.
47 N7 **Moinești** Romania
81 F2 **Moira** U.S.A.
36 O3 **Mo i Rana** Norway
23 H4 **Moirang** India
37 T7 **Mõisaküla** Estonia
91 E1 **Moisés Ville** Arg.
67 G3 **Moisie** Can.
67 G3 **Moisie** *r.* Can.
44 E4 **Moissac** France
74 C4 **Mojave** U.S.A.
74 D4 **Mojave** *r.* U.S.A.
74 D4 **Mojave Desert** *des.* U.S.A.
90 C3 **Moji das Cruzes** Brazil
90 C3 **Moji-Guaçu** *r.* Brazil
29 B8 **Mojikō** Japan
23 F4 **Mokāma** India
74 ☐1 **Mokapu Pen.** *pen.* U.S.A.
9 E3 **Mokau** N.Z.
9 E3 **Mokau** *r.* N.Z.
74 B2 **Mokelumne** *r.* U.S.A.
59 H4 **Mokhoabong Pass** Lesotho
59 H4 **Mokhotlong** Lesotho
48 D7 **Moknine** Tunisia
9 E1 **Mokohinau Is** *is* N.Z.
55 D3 **Mokolo** Cameroon
59 G2 **Mokolo** *r.* S. Africa
30 D6 **Mokp'o** S. Korea
50 G4 **Moksha** *r.* Rus. Fed.
50 H4 **Mokshan** Rus. Fed.
74 ☐1 **Mokuauia I.** *i.* U.S.A.
74 ☐1 **Mokulua Is** *is* U.S.A.
84 C2 **Molango** Mex.
45 F3 **Molatón** *mt* Spain
Moldavia *country see* **Moldova**
36 K5 **Molde** Norway
36 O3 **Moldjord** Norway
35 H4 **Moldova** *country* Europe
49 L2 **Moldoveanu, Vârful** *mt* Romania
39 D7 **Mole** *r.* U.K.
54 B4 **Mole National Park** Ghana
57 C6 **Molepolole** Botswana
37 T9 **Molėtai** Lith.
48 G4 **Molfetta** Italy
30 C2 **Molihong Shan** *h.* China
45 F2 **Molina de Aragón** Spain
68 B5 **Moline** U.S.A.
37 N7 **Molkom** Sweden
17 M4 **Mollā Bodāgh** Iran
23 H4 **Mol Len** *mt* India
43 M1 **Möllenbeck** Ger.
86 D7 **Mollendo** Peru
43 J1 **Mölln** Ger.
37 N8 **Mölnlycke** Sweden
50 F3 **Molochnoye** Rus. Fed.
36 X2 **Molochnyy** Rus. Fed.
92 D4 **Molodezhnaya** *Rus. Fed. Base* Ant.
50 E3 **Molodoy Tud** Rus. Fed.
74 ☐2 **Molokai** *i.* U.S.A.
95 K4 **Molokai Fracture Zone** *sea feature* Pac. Oc.
50 J3 **Moloma** *r.* Rus. Fed.
8 G2 **Molong** Austr.
58 F2 **Molopo** *watercourse* Botswana/S. Africa
55 D4 **Moloundou** Cameroon
65 K4 **Molson L.** *l.* Can.
Moluccas *is see* **Maluku**
25 E7 **Molucca Sea** *g.* Indon.
57 D5 **Moma** Moz.
8 D1 **Momba** Austr.
56 D4 **Mombasa** Kenya
23 H4 **Mombi New** India
90 B2 **Mombuca, Serra da** *h.* Brazil
51 C7 **Momchilgrad** Bulg.
68 D5 **Momence** U.S.A.
89 B2 **Mompós** Col.
37 N9 **Møn** *i.* Denmark
75 G2 **Mona** U.S.A.
40 A3 **Monach Islands** *is* U.K.
40 A3 **Monach, Sound of** *chan.* U.K.
34 F4 **Monaco** *country* Europe
40 D3 **Monadhliath Mountains** *mts* U.K.
41 E3 **Monaghan** Rep. of Ireland
77 C6 **Monahans** U.S.A.
83 L5 **Mona, I.** *i.* Puerto Rico
83 L5 **Mona Passage** *chan.* Dom. Rep./Puerto Rico
57 E5 **Monapo** Moz.
64 D4 **Monarch Mt.** *mt* Can.
73 F4 **Monarch Pass** U.S.A.
40 C3 **Monar, Loch** *l.* U.K.
64 F4 **Monashee Mts** *mts* Can.
48 D7 **Monastir** Tunisia
47 P3 **Monastyrshchina** Rus. Fed.
51 D5 **Monastyryshche** Ukr.
28 H2 **Monbetsu** Japan
28 H3 **Monbetsu** Japan
48 B2 **Moncalieri** Italy
45 F2 **Moncayo** *mt* Spain
36 X3 **Monchegorsk** Rus. Fed.
42 E3 **Mönchengladbach** Ger.
45 B4 **Monchique** Port.
79 E5 **Moncks Corner** U.S.A.
82 D3 **Monclova** Mex.
67 H4 **Moncton** Can.
45 C2 **Mondego** *r.* Port.
59 J3 **Mondlo** S. Africa
48 B2 **Mondovi** Italy
68 B3 **Mondovi** U.S.A.
48 E4 **Mondragone** Italy
49 K6 **Monemvasia** Greece
28 G1 **Moneron, Ostrov** *i.* Rus. Fed.
80 D4 **Monessen** U.S.A.
69 K1 **Monet** Can.
41 D5 **Moneygall** Rep. of Ireland
41 E3 **Moneymore** U.K.
48 E2 **Monfalcone** Italy
45 C1 **Monforte** Spain
56 C3 **Monga** Congo(Zaire)
27 C6 **Mông Cai** Vietnam
30 C4 **Monggŭmp'o-ri** N. Korea
32 A1 **Mong Mau** Myanmar
10 L5 **Mongolia** *country* Asia
22 C2 **Mongora** Pak.
57 C5 **Mongu** Zambia
81 J3 **Monhegan I.** *i.* U.S.A.
40 E5 **Moniaive** U.K.
74 D2 **Monitor Mt** *mt* U.S.A.
74 D2 **Monitor Range** *mts* U.S.A.
41 C4 **Monivea** Rep. of Ireland
69 G4 **Monkton** Can.
23 F3 **Mon La** *pass* China
39 E6 **Monmouth** U.K.
68 B5 **Monmouth** *IL* U.S.A.
81 H2 **Monmouth** *ME* U.S.A.
64 E4 **Monmouth Mt.** *mt* Can.
39 E6 **Monnow** *r.* U.K.
54 C3 **Mono** *r.* Togo
74 C3 **Mono Lake** *l.* U.S.A.
81 H4 **Monomoy Pt** *pt* U.S.A.
68 D5 **Monon** U.S.A.
68 B4 **Monona** U.S.A.
48 G4 **Monopoli** Italy
80 C5 **Monongahela** *r.* U.S.A.
45 F2 **Monreal del Campo** Spain
48 E5 **Monreale** *Sicily* Italy
77 E5 **Monroe** *LA* U.S.A.
69 F5 **Monroe** *MI* U.S.A.
79 D5 **Monroe** *NC* U.S.A.
81 F4 **Monroe** *NY* U.S.A.
75 F2 **Monroe** *UT* U.S.A.
68 C4 **Monroe** *WV* U.S.A.
68 B6 **Monroe City** U.S.A.
79 C6 **Monroeville** U.S.A.
54 A4 **Monrovia** Liberia
42 B4 **Mons** Belgium
42 E4 **Monschau** Ger.
48 D2 **Monselice** Italy
43 F4 **Montabaur** Ger.
57 E5 **Montagne d'Ambre, Parc National de la** *nat. park* Madag.
58 D6 **Montagu** S. Africa
68 D4 **Montague** U.S.A.
92 C1 **Montagu I.** *i.* Atl. Ocean
48 F5 **Montalto** *mt* Italy
48 G5 **Montalto Uffugo** Italy
49 K3 **Montana** Bulg.
72 E2 **Montana** *div.* U.S.A.
44 F3 **Montargis** France
44 E4 **Montauban** France
81 G4 **Montauk** U.S.A.
81 H4 **Montauk Pt** *pt* U.S.A.
44 G3 **Montbard** France
45 G2 **Montblanc** Spain
44 G4 **Montbrison** France
44 G3 **Montceau-les-Mines** France
42 C5 **Montcornet** France
44 D5 **Mont-de-Marsan** France
44 F2 **Montdidier** France
87 H4 **Monte Alegre** Brazil
90 C1 **Monte Alegre de Goiás** Brazil
90 D1 **Monte Azul** Brazil
66 E4 **Montebello** Can.
48 F6 **Montebello Ionico** Italy
48 E2 **Montebelluna** Italy
91 D2 **Monte Buey** Arg.
44 H5 **Monte Carlo** Monaco
91 F1 **Monte Caseros** Arg.
59 G1 **Monte Christo** S. Africa
91 C2 **Monte Comán** Arg.
83 K5 **Monte Cristi** Dom. Rep.
48 D3 **Montecristo, Isola di** *i.* Italy
83 J5 **Montego Bay** Jamaica
44 G4 **Montélimar** France
88 E2 **Monte Lindo** *r.* Para.
48 F4 **Montella** Italy
68 C4 **Montello** U.S.A.
84 C1 **Montemorelos** Mex.
45 B3 **Montemor-o-Novo** Port.
49 H3 **Montenegro** *div.* Yugo.
57 D5 **Montepuez** Moz.
48 D3 **Montepulciano** Italy
44 F2 **Montereau-faut-Yonne** France
74 B3 **Monterey** *CA* U.S.A.
80 D5 **Monterey** *VA* U.S.A.
74 B3 **Monterey Bay** *b.* U.S.A.
89 B2 **Montería** Col.
86 F7 **Montero** Bol.
84 B1 **Monterrey** Mex.
48 F4 **Montesano sulla Marcellana** Italy
87 L6 **Monte Santo** Brazil
90 D2 **Montes Claros** Brazil
48 F3 **Montesilvano** Italy
48 D3 **Montevarchi** Italy
91 F2 **Montevideo** Uru.
76 E2 **Montevideo** U.S.A.
73 F4 **Monte Vista** U.S.A.
68 A5 **Montezuma** U.S.A.
75 G4 **Montezuma Castle National Monument** *res.* U.S.A.
75 H3 **Montezuma Creek** U.S.A.
74 D3 **Montezuma Peak** *summit* U.S.A.
42 D3 **Montfort** Neth.
39 D5 **Montgomery** U.K.
79 C5 **Montgomery** U.S.A.
46 C7 **Monthey** Switz.
77 F5 **Monticello** *AR* U.S.A.
79 D6 **Monticello** *FL* U.S.A.
68 B4 **Monticello** *IA* U.S.A.
68 D5 **Monticello** *IN* U.S.A.
81 K1 **Monticello** *ME* U.S.A.
68 B5 **Monticello** *MO* U.S.A.
81 F4 **Monticello** *NY* U.S.A.
75 H3 **Monticello** *UT* U.S.A.
68 C4 **Monticello** *WV* U.S.A.
91 E1 **Montiel, Cuchilla de** *h.* Arg.
44 E4 **Montignac** France
42 C4 **Montignies-le-Tilleul** Belgium
42 E5 **Montigny-lès-Metz** France
45 D4 **Montilla** Spain
67 G4 **Mont Joli** Can.
69 K2 **Mont-Laurier** Can.
67 G4 **Mont Louis** Can.
44 F3 **Montluçon** France
67 F3 **Montmagny** Can.
42 D5 **Montmédy** France
42 B6 **Montmirail** France
68 D5 **Montmorenci** U.S.A.
67 F4 **Montmorency** Can.
44 E3 **Montmorillon** France
42 B6 **Montmort-Lucy** France
6 F4 **Monto** Austr.
72 E3 **Montpelier** *ID* U.S.A.
68 E5 **Montpelier** *IN* U.S.A.
80 A4 **Montpelier** *OH* U.S.A.
81 G2 **Montpelier** *VT* U.S.A.
44 F5 **Montpellier** France
66 F4 **Montréal** Can.
69 G2 **Montreal** *r.* Can.
69 F2 **Montreal** *r.* Can.
68 E2 **Montreal I.** *i.* Can.
65 H4 **Montreal L.** *l.* Can.
65 H4 **Montreal Lake** Can.
69 J3 **Montréal-Mirabel** Can.
68 E2 **Montreal River** Can.
46 C7 **Montreux** Switz.
40 F4 **Montrose** U.K.
73 F4 **Montrose** *CO* U.S.A.
69 F4 **Montrose** *MI* U.S.A.
81 F4 **Montrose** *PA* U.S.A.
58 D3 **Montrose** *well* S. Africa
61 M8 **Montserrat** *terr.* Caribbean Sea
67 G4 **Monts, Pte des** *pt* Can.
75 G3 **Monument Valley** *reg.* U.S.A.
24 B4 **Monywa** Myanmar
48 C2 **Monza** Italy
57 C5 **Monze** Zambia
45 G2 **Monzón** Spain
59 J4 **Mooi** *r.* S. Africa
58 B3 **Mooifontein** Namibia
59 J4 **Mooirivier** S. Africa
59 G1 **Mookane** Botswana
8 H1 **Moonbi Ra.** *mts* Austr.
8 A3 **Moonta** Austr.
72 F2 **Moorcroft** U.S.A.
80 D5 **Moorefield** U.S.A.
6 B4 **Moore, Lake** *salt flat* Austr.
79 E7 **Moores I.** *i.* Bahamas
81 K2 **Moores Mills** Can.
40 E5 **Moorfoot Hills** *h.* U.K.
76 D2 **Moorhead** U.S.A.
8 D2 **Moornanyah Lake** Austr.
8 C3 **Moorook** Austr.
8 E4 **Mooroopna** Austr.
58 C6 **Moorreesburg** S. Africa
66 D3 **Moose** *r.* Can.
66 D3 **Moose Factory** Can.
81 J2 **Moosehead Lake** *l.* U.S.A.
65 H4 **Moose Jaw** Can.
68 A2 **Moose Lake** U.S.A.
65 J4 **Moose Lake** *l.* Can.
81 H2 **Mooselookmeguntic Lake** *l.* U.S.A.
66 D3 **Moose River** Can.
65 J4 **Moosomin** Can.
66 D3 **Moosonee** Can.
8 D1 **Mootwingee** Austr.
59 H1 **Mopane** S. Africa
54 B3 **Mopti** Mali
19 G3 **Moqor** Afgh.
86 D7 **Moquegua** Peru
55 D3 **Mora** Cameroon
45 E3 **Mora** Spain
37 O6 **Mora** Sweden
91 B2 **Mora, Cerro** *mt* Arg./Chile
22 A3 **Morad** *r.* Pak.
22 D3 **Moradabad** India
57 E5 **Morafenobe** Madag.
21 B2 **Moram** India
57 E5 **Moramanga** Madag.
68 E3 **Moran** *MI* U.S.A.
72 E3 **Moran** *WY* U.S.A.
40 C4 **Morar, Loch** *l.* U.K.
21 B5 **Moratuwa** Sri Lanka
46 H6 **Morava** *r.* Austria/Slovakia
18 D2 **Moraveh Tappeh** Iran
81 E3 **Moravia** U.S.A.
40 E3 **Moray Firth** *est.* U.K.
42 F5 **Morbach** Ger.
48 C1 **Morbegno** Italy
22 B5 **Morbi** India
44 D4 **Morcenx** France
24 E1 **Mordaga** China
17 K3 **Mor Dağı** *mt* Turkey
65 K5 **Morden** Can.
8 E5 **Mordialloc** Austr.
50 H4 **Mordoviya, Respublika** *div.* Rus. Fed.
51 G4 **Mordovo** Rus. Fed.
76 C2 **Moreau** *r.* U.S.A.
38 E3 **Morecambe** U.K.
38 D3 **Morecambe Bay** *b.* U.K.
6 E4 **Moree** Austr.
6 E2 **Morehead** P.N.G.
80 B5 **Morehead** U.S.A.
79 E5 **Morehead City** U.S.A.
22 D4 **Morel** *r.* India
84 B3 **Morelia** Mex.
45 F2 **Morella** Spain
40 D2 **More, Loch** *l.* U.K.
84 E3 **Morelos** Mex.
84 C3 **Morelos** *div.* Mex.
22 D4 **Morena** India
45 D3 **Morena, Sierra** *mts* Spain
75 H5 **Morenci** *AZ* U.S.A.
69 E5 **Morenci** *MI* U.S.A.
49 L2 **Moreni** Romania
91 E2 **Moreno** Arg.
73 E6 **Moreno** Mex.
74 D5 **Moreno Valley** U.S.A.
64 C4 **Moresby Island** *i.* Can.
58 F1 **Moreswe Pan** *salt pan* Botswana
39 F6 **Moreton-in-Marsh** U.K.
42 A5 **Moreuil** France
16 D4 **Morfou** Cyprus
16 D4 **Morfou Bay** *b.* Cyprus
8 B3 **Morgan** Austr.
77 F6 **Morgan City** U.S.A.
74 B3 **Morgan Hill** U.S.A.
74 C3 **Morgan, Mt** *mt* U.S.A.
81 F4 **Morgantown** *PA* U.S.A.
80 D5 **Morgantown** *WV* U.S.A.
59 H3 **Morgenzon** S. Africa
46 C7 **Morges** Switz.
23 F4 **Morhar** *r.* India
28 G3 **Mori** Japan
75 E2 **Moriah, Mt** *mt* U.S.A.
73 F5 **Moriarty** U.S.A.
89 C4 **Morichal** Col.
89 E2 **Morichal Largo** *r.* Venez.
59 G4 **Morija** Lesotho
43 H3 **Moringen** Ger.
50 D3 **Morino** Rus. Fed.
28 G5 **Morioka** Japan
8 H2 **Morisset** Austr.
28 G5 **Moriyoshi-zan** *volc.* Japan
36 S3 **Morjärv** Sweden
19 F4 **Morjen** *r.* Pak.
50 J3 **Morki** Rus. Fed.
44 C2 **Morlaix** France
38 F4 **Morley** U.K.
75 G4 **Mormon Lake** *l.* U.S.A.
6 D3 **Mornington I.** *i.* Austr.
88 A7 **Mornington, I.** *i.* Chile
22 A4 **Moro** Pak.
6 E2 **Morobe** P.N.G.
68 D5 **Morocco** U.S.A.
52 D3 **Morocco** *country* Africa
56 D4 **Morogoro** Tanz.
31 B5 **Moro Gulf** *g.* Phil.
59 G4 **Morojaneng** S. Africa
58 E3 **Morokweng** S. Africa
84 B2 **Moroleón** Mex.
57 E6 **Morombe** Madag.
83 J4 **Morón** Cuba
24 C2 **Mörön** Mongolia
57 E6 **Morondava** Madag.
45 D4 **Morón de la Frontera** Spain
57 E5 **Moroni** Comoros
25 E6 **Morotai** *i.* Indon.
56 D3 **Moroto** Uganda
51 G5 **Morozovsk** Rus. Fed.
69 G4 **Morpeth** Can.
38 F2 **Morpeth** U.K.
90 C2 **Morrinhos** Brazil
65 K5 **Morris** Can.
68 C5 **Morris** *IL* U.S.A.
76 E2 **Morris** *MN* U.S.A.
81 F2 **Morrisburg** Can.
68 C5 **Morrison** U.S.A.
75 F5 **Morristown** *AZ* U.S.A.
81 F4 **Morristown** *NJ* U.S.A.
81 F2 **Morristown** *NY* U.S.A.
79 D4 **Morristown** *TN* U.S.A.
81 F4 **Morrisville** *PA* U.S.A.
81 G2 **Morrisville** *VT* U.S.A.
74 B4 **Morro Bay** U.S.A.
89 C2 **Morrocoy, Parque Nacional** *nat. park* Venez.
87 H4 **Morro Grande** *h.* Brazil
88 B3 **Morro, Pta** *pt* Chile
89 B2 **Morrosquillo, Golfo de** *b.* Col.
43 H3 **Morschen** Ger.
68 D5 **Morse Reservoir** *resr* U.S.A.
50 G4 **Morshansk** Rus. Fed.
50 E2 **Morskaya Masel'ga** Rus. Fed.
48 C7 **Morsott** Alg.
44 E2 **Mortagne-au-Perche** France
44 D3 **Mortagne-sur-Sèvre** France
39 C6 **Mortehoe** U.K.
91 E1 **Morteros** Arg.
Mortes *r. see* **Manso**
8 D5 **Mortlake** Austr.
Mortlock Is *is see* **Tauu**
39 G5 **Morton** U.K.
68 C5 **Morton** *IL* U.S.A.
72 B2 **Morton** *WA* U.S.A.
8 H3 **Morton Nat. Park** Austr.
8 F3 **Morundah** Austr.
59 G1 **Morupule** Botswana
8 H3 **Moruya** Austr.
40 C4 **Morvern** *reg.* U.K.
Morvi *see* **Morbi**
8 F5 **Morwell** Austr.
43 H5 **Mosbach** Ger.
39 F4 **Mosborough** U.K.
50 F4 **Moscow** Rus. Fed.
72 C2 **Moscow** U.S.A.
92 C6 **Moscow Univ. Ice Shelf** *ice feature* Ant.
92 B6 **Mose, C.** *c.* Ant.
42 F4 **Mosel** *r.* Ger.
58 E2 **Moselebe** *watercourse* Botswana
44 H2 **Moselle** *r.* France
43 K2 **Möser** Ger.
72 C2 **Moses Lake** U.S.A.
74 D1 **Moses, Mt** *mt* U.S.A.
9 C6 **Mosgiel** N.Z.
58 E3 **Moshaweng** *watercourse* S. Africa
56 D4 **Moshi** Tanz.
68 C3 **Mosinee** U.S.A.
36 N4 **Mosjøen** Norway
36 N3 **Moskenesøy** *i.* Norway
50 F4 **Moskovskaya Oblast'** *div.* Rus. Fed.
Moskva *see* **Moscow**
46 H7 **Mosonmagyaróvár** Hungary
89 A4 **Mosquera** Col.
73 F5 **Mosquero** U.S.A.
83 H5 **Mosquitia** *reg.* Honduras
90 E1 **Mosquito** *r.* Brazil
80 C4 **Mosquito Creek Lake** *l.* U.S.A.
83 H7 **Mosquitos, Golfo de los** *b.* Panama
65 J2 **Mosquitto Lake** *l.* Can.
37 M7 **Moss** Norway
40 F3 **Mossat** U.K.
9 B6 **Mossburn** N.Z.
58 E7 **Mossel Bay** S. Africa
58 E7 **Mossel Bay** *b.* S. Africa
56 B4 **Mossendjo** Congo
8 E2 **Mossgiel** Austr.
6 E3 **Mossman** Austr.
87 L5 **Mossoró** Brazil
8 H3 **Moss Vale** Austr.
46 F5 **Most** Czech Rep.
18 D3 **Moștafaabad** Iran
54 C1 **Mostaganem** Alg.
48 G3 **Mostar** Bos.-Herz.
88 F4 **Mostardas** Brazil
65 G3 **Mostoos Hills** *h.* Can.
51 G6 **Mostovskoy** Rus. Fed.
33 E2 **Mostyn** Malaysia
17 J3 **Mosul** Iraq
37 L7 **Møsvatnet** *l.* Norway
37 O7 **Motala** Sweden
89 C2 **Motatán** *r.* Venez.
59 K2 **Motaze** Moz.
59 H2 **Motetema** S. Africa
22 D4 **Moth** India
40 E5 **Motherwell** U.K.
23 F4 **Motihari** India
45 F3 **Motilla del Palancar** Spain
9 F2 **Motiti I.** *i.* N.Z.
30 B3 **Motlan Ling** *h.* China
58 E2 **Motokwe** Botswana
84 D4 **Motozintla** Mex.
45 E4 **Motril** Spain
49 K2 **Motru** Romania
82 G4 **Motul** Mex.
5 M6 **Motu One** *i.* Pac. Oc.
27 A5 **Mouding** China
54 A3 **Moudjéria** Maur.
49 L5 **Moudros** Greece
37 S6 **Mouhijärvi** Fin.
56 B4 **Mouila** Gabon
8 E3 **Moulamein** Austr.
56 B4 **Moulèngui Binza** Gabon
44 F3 **Moulins** France
32 A1 **Moulmein** Myanmar
79 D6 **Moultrie** U.S.A.
71 L5 **Moultrie, Lake** *l. SC* U.S.A.
78 B4 **Mound City** *IL* U.S.A.
76 E3 **Mound City** *MO* U.S.A.
55 D4 **Moundou** Chad
80 C5 **Moundsville** U.S.A.
22 C4 **Mount Abu** India
79 C5 **Mountain Brook** U.S.A.
80 C6 **Mountain City** U.S.A.
77 E4 **Mountain Grove** U.S.A.
77 E4 **Mountain Home** *AR* U.S.A.
72 D3 **Mountain Home** *ID* U.S.A.
59 F6 **Mountain Zebra National Park** S. Africa
80 C6 **Mount Airy** U.S.A.
9 B6 **Mount Aspiring National Park** N.Z.
59 H5 **Mount Ayliff** S. Africa
76 E3 **Mount Ayr** U.S.A.
8 B3 **Mount Barker** Austr.
8 F4 **Mount Beauty** Austr.
41 C4 **Mount Bellew** Rep. of Ireland
8 F4 **Mt Bogong Nat.Park** Austr.
8 F4 **Mount Buffalo National Park** Austr.
81 K1 **Mount Carleton Provincial Park** *res.* Can.
75 F3 **Mount Carmel Junction** U.S.A.
68 C4 **Mount Carroll** U.S.A.
9 C5 **Mount Cook** N.Z.
9 C5 **Mount Cook National Park** N.Z.
57 D5 **Mount Darwin** Zimbabwe
81 J2 **Mount Desert Island** *i.* U.S.A.
59 H5 **Mount Fletcher** S. Africa
69 G4 **Mount Forest** Can.
59 H5 **Mount Frere** S. Africa
8 C4 **Mount Gambier** Austr.
80 B4 **Mount Gilead** U.S.A.
6 E2 **Mount Hagen** P.N.G.
8 E2 **Mount Hope** *N.S.W.* Austr.
80 C6 **Mount Hope** U.S.A.
6 D4 **Mount Isa** Austr.
81 G4 **Mount Kisco** U.S.A.
8 B3 **Mount Lofty Range** *mts* Austr.
69 G2 **Mount MacDonald** Can.
6 B4 **Mount Magnet** Austr.
8 D2 **Mount Manara** Austr.
74 B1 **Mount Meadows Reservoir** U.S.A.
41 D4 **Mountmellick** Rep. of Ireland
59 G5 **Mount Moorosi** Lesotho
8 D1 **Mount Murchison** Austr.
68 B5 **Mount Pleasant** *IA* U.S.A.
68 E4 **Mount Pleasant** *MI* U.S.A.
78 C3 **Mount Pleasant** *MI* U.S.A.
80 D4 **Mount Pleasant** *PA* U.S.A.
79 E5 **Mount Pleasant** *SC* U.S.A.
77 E5 **Mount Pleasant** *TX* U.S.A.
75 G2 **Mount Pleasant** *UT* U.S.A.
68 C5 **Mount Pulaski** U.S.A.
72 B2 **Mount Rainier Nat. Park** U.S.A.
64 F4 **Mount Robson Prov. Park** *res.* Can.
80 C6 **Mount Rogers National Recreation Area** *res.* U.S.A.
39 B7 **Mount's Bay** *b.* U.K.
39 F5 **Mountsorrel** U.K.
68 B6 **Mount Sterling** *IL* U.S.A.
80 B5 **Mount Sterling** *KY* U.S.A.
80 D5 **Mount Storm** U.S.A.
80 E4 **Mount Union** U.S.A.
79 B6 **Mount Vernon** *AL* U.S.A.
68 B5 **Mount Vernon** *IA* U.S.A.
78 B4 **Mount Vernon** *IL* U.S.A.
80 A6 **Mount Vernon** *KY* U.S.A.
80 B4 **Mount Vernon** *OH* U.S.A.
72 B1 **Mount Vernon** *WA* U.S.A.
92 C3 **Mt. Victor** *mt* Ant.
6 E4 **Moura** Austr.
86 F4 **Moura** Brazil
55 E3 **Mourdi, Dépression du** *depression* Chad
41 D3 **Mourne** *r.* U.K.
41 E3 **Mourne Mountains** *h.* U.K.
42 B4 **Mouscron** Belgium
55 D3 **Moussoro** Chad
25 E6 **Moutong** Indon.
42 A5 **Mouy** France
54 C2 **Mouydir, Mts de** *plat.* Alg.
42 D5 **Mouzon** France
41 C4 **Moy** *r.* Rep. of Ireland
56 D3 **Moyale** Eth.
54 A4 **Moyamba** Sierra Leone
21 B4 **Moyar** *r.* India
54 B1 **Moyen Atlas** *mts* Morocco
59 G5 **Moyeni** Lesotho
41 E4 **Moyer** *h.* Rep. of Ireland
67 G2 **Moyne, Lac Le** *l.* Can.
15 F2 **Moyynty** Kazak.
53 H8 **Mozambique** *country* Africa
57 E5 **Mozambique Channel** *str.* Africa
93 G5 **Mozambique Ridge** *sea feature* Ind. Ocean
51 H7 **Mozdok** Rus. Fed.
19 F2 **Mozdūrān** Iran
50 F4 **Mozhaysk** Rus. Fed.
19 F3 **Mozhnābād** Iran
23 H5 **Mozo** Myanmar
56 C4 **Mpala** Congo(Zaire)
56 D4 **Mpanda** Tanz.
57 D5 **Mpika** Zambia
59 J4 **Mpolweni** S. Africa
57 D4 **Mporokoso** Zambia
59 H2 **Mpumalanga** *div.* S. Africa
59 H5 **Mqanduli** S. Africa
48 G2 **Mrkonjić-Grad** Bos.-Herz.
54 D1 **M'Saken** Tunisia
50 D3 **Mshinskaya** Rus. Fed.
45 J5 **M'Sila** Alg.
50 E3 **Msta** *r.* Rus. Fed.
50 D4 **Mstsislaw** Belarus
59 H4 **Mt-aux-Sources** *mt* Lesotho
50 F4 **Mtsensk** Rus. Fed.
59 K4 **Mtubatuba** S. Africa
59 J4 **Mtunzini** S. Africa
57 E5 **Mtwara** Tanz.
56 B4 **Muanda** Congo(Zaire)
32 B2 **Muang Chainat** Thai.
32 A1 **Muang Chiang Rai** Thai.
27 B6 **Muang Hiam** Laos
32 B1 **Muang Hôngsa** Laos
32 B1 **Muang Kalasin** Thai.
32 C1 **Muang Khammouan** Laos
32 C2 **Muang Không** Laos
32 C2 **Muang Khôngxédôn** Laos
32 B1 **Muang Khon Kaen** Thai.
27 B6 **Muang Khoua** Laos
32 A3 **Muang Kirirath** *r.* Thai.
32 A1 **Muang Lampang** Thai.
32 A1 **Muang Lamphun** Thai.
32 B1 **Muang Loei** Thai.
32 B1 **Muang Lom Sak** Thai.
32 A1 **Muang Long** Thai.
32 A3 **Muang Luang** *r.* Thai.
32 C2 **Muang Mai** Thai.
32 C1 **Muang Mok** Laos
32 C1 **Muang Nakhon Phanom** Thai.
32 B2 **Muang Nakhon Sawan** Thai.
32 B1 **Muang Nan** Thai.
27 B6 **Muang Ngoy** Laos
32 C1 **Muang Nong** Laos
27 A6 **Muang Ou Nua** Laos
32 B1 **Muang Pakxan** Laos
32 C1 **Muang Phalan** Laos
32 A1 **Muang Phan** Thai.
32 A1 **Muang Phayao** Thai.
32 B1 **Muang Phetchabun** Thai.
32 B1 **Muang Phiang** Laos
32 B1 **Muang Phichai** Thai.
32 B1 **Muang Phichit** Thai.
32 C1 **Muang Phin** Laos
32 B1 **Muang Phitsanulok** Thai.
32 B1 **Muang Phôn-Hông** Laos
32 B1 **Muang Phrae** Thai.
32 B1 **Muang Roi Et** Thai.
32 C1 **Muang Sakon Nakhon** Thai.
32 B2 **Muang Samut Prakan** Thai.
32 B1 **Muang Souy** Laos
32 B2 **Muang Uthai Thani** Thai.
27 B6 **Muang Va** Laos
32 B1 **Muang Vangviang** Laos
32 B1 **Muang Xaignabouri** Laos
27 B6 **Muang Xay** Laos
27 B6 **Muang Xon** Laos
32 C2 **Muang Yasothon** Thai.
33 B2 **Muar** Malaysia
32 B5 **Muar** *r.* Malaysia
33 B3 **Muarabungo** Indon.
33 B3 **Muaradua** Indon.
33 A3 **Muarasiberut** Indon.
33 A2 **Muarasipongi** Indon.
33 B3 **Muaratembesi** Indon.
23 E4 **Mubarakpur** India
19 G2 **Mubarek** Uzbek.
17 H7 **Mubarraz** *well* S. Arabia
56 D3 **Mubende** Uganda
55 D3 **Mubi** Nigeria
89 E4 **Mucajaí** *r.* Brazil
89 E4 **Mucajaí, Serra do** *mts* Brazil
42 F4 **Much** Ger.
57 D5 **Muchinga Escarpment** *esc.* Zambia
27 B4 **Muchuan** China
40 B4 **Muck** *i.* U.K.
40 ☐ **Muckle Roe** *i.* U.K.
89 C3 **Muco** *r.* Col.
57 C5 **Muconda** Angola
89 E4 **Mucucuaú** *r.* Brazil
16 E2 **Mucur** Turkey
90 E2 **Mucuri** Brazil
90 E2 **Mucuri** *r.* Brazil
57 C5 **Mucussueje** Angola
32 B4 **Muda** *r.* Malaysia
21 A3 **Mudabidri** India
30 E1 **Mudanjiang** China
30 E1 **Mudan Jiang** *r.* China
16 B1 **Mudanya** Turkey
17 L7 **Mudayrah** Kuwait
80 C5 **Muddlety** U.S.A.
36 R3 **Muddus Nationalpark** *nat. park* Sweden
75 G2 **Muddy Creek** *r.* U.S.A.
75 E3 **Muddy Peak** *summit* U.S.A.
19 E3 **Mūd-e-Dahanāb** Iran
43 F4 **Mudersbach** Ger.
8 G2 **Mudgee** Austr.
21 A2 **Mudhol** India
22 C3 **Mudki** India
74 D3 **Mud Lake** *l.* U.S.A.
32 A1 **Mudon** Myanmar
16 C1 **Mudurnu** Turkey
50 F2 **Mud'yuga** Rus. Fed.
57 D5 **Mueda** Moz.
84 D3 **Muerto, Mar** *l.* Mex.
50 H1 **Muftyuga** Rus. Fed.
57 C5 **Mufulira** Zambia
57 C5 **Mufumbwe** Zambia
27 E4 **Mufu Shan** *mts* China
81 K2 **Mugaguadavic Lake** *l.* Can.
17 M2 **Muğan Düzü** *lowland* Azer.
23 F2 **Mugarripug** China
Mughalbhin *see* **Jati**
23 E4 **Mughal Sarai** India
18 D3 **Mūghār** Iran
16 F7 **Mughayrā'** S. Arabia
19 H2 **Mughsu** *r.* Tajik.
16 B3 **Muğla** Turkey
23 H2 **Mug Qu** *r.* China
23 E3 **Mugu Karnali** *r.* Nepal
23 H2 **Mugxung** China
55 F2 **Muhammad Qol** Sudan
18 B5 **Muḥayriqah** S. Arabia
43 L3 **Mühlanger** Ger.
43 M3 **Mühlberg** Ger.
43 J3 **Mühlhausen (Thüringen)** Ger.
36 T4 **Muhos** Fin.
56 C4 **Muhulu** Congo(Zaire)
32 C3 **Mui Ca Mau** *c.* Vietnam
32 D3 **Mui Dinh** *hd* Vietnam
32 D2 **Mui Nây** *pt* Vietnam
41 E5 **Muine Bheag** Rep. of Ireland
40 D5 **Muirkirk** U.K.
40 B2 **Muirneag** *h.* U.K.
40 D3 **Muir of Ord** U.K.
74 A3 **Muir Woods National Monument** *res.* U.S.A.
57 D5 **Muite** Moz.
30 D6 **Muju** S. Korea
51 B5 **Mukacheve** Ukr.
33 D2 **Mukah** Malaysia
23 F3 **Mükangsar** China
32 C1 **Mukdahan** Thai.
6 B5 **Mukinbudin** Austr.
33 B3 **Mukomuko** Indon.
19 G2 **Mukry** Turkm.
22 C3 **Muktsar** India
65 K4 **Mukutawa** *r.* Can.
68 C4 **Mukwonago** U.S.A.
22 D5 **Mul** India
21 A2 **Mula** *r.* India
22 A3 **Mula** *r.* Pak.
28 A2 **Mulan** China
31 B3 **Mulanay** Phil.
57 D5 **Mulanje, Mt** *mt* Malawi
18 B5 **Mulayḥ** S. Arabia
77 E5 **Mulberry** U.S.A.
91 B3 **Mulchén** Chile
43 L3 **Mulde** *r.* Ger.
56 D4 **Muleba** Tanz.
75 H5 **Mule Creek** *NM* U.S.A.
72 F3 **Mule Creek** *WY* U.S.A.
77 C5 **Muleshoe** U.S.A.
45 E4 **Mulhacén** *mt* Spain
42 E3 **Mülheim an der Ruhr** Ger.
44 H3 **Mulhouse** France
27 A5 **Muli** China
30 F1 **Muling** China
30 F1 **Muling** China
30 G1 **Muling** *r.* China
40 C4 **Mull** *i.* U.K.
17 M3 **Mulla Ali** Iran
41 B5 **Mullaghareirk Mts** *h.* Rep. of Ireland
21 C4 **Mullaittivu** Sri Lanka
8 G1 **Mullaley** Austr.
8 F1 **Mullengudgery** Austr.
33 D2 **Muller, Pegunungan** *mts* Indon.
68 E3 **Mullett Lake** *l.* U.S.A.
6 B4 **Mullewa** Austr.
40 F1 **Mull Head** *hd* U.K.
81 F5 **Mullica** *r.* U.S.A.
41 D4 **Mullingar** Rep. of Ireland
8 G2 **Mullion Cr.** Austr.
40 B4 **Mull, Sound of** *chan.* U.K.
57 C5 **Mulobezi** Zambia
21 A2 **Mulshi L.** *l.* India
22 D5 **Multai** India
22 B3 **Multan** Pak.
37 T5 **Multia** Fin.
42 A6 **Multien** *reg.* France
19 F5 **Mūmān** Iran
Mumbai *see* **Bombay**
8 G2 **Mumbil** Austr.
57 C5 **Mumbwa** Zambia
19 H2 **Mū'minobod** Tajik.
51 H6 **Mumra** Rus. Fed.
84 E2 **Muna** Mex.
13 N3 **Muna** *r.* Rus. Fed.
36 C3 **Munaðarnes** Iceland
43 K4 **Münchberg** Ger.
46 E6 **München** Ger.
43 G4 **Münchhausen** Ger.
89 A4 **Munchique, Co** *mt* Col.
64 D3 **Muncho Lake** Can.
64 D3 **Muncho Lake Provincial Park** *res.* Can.
30 D4 **Munch'ŏn** N. Korea
68 E5 **Muncie** U.S.A.
80 E4 **Muncy** U.S.A.
21 B5 **Mundel L.** *l.* Sri Lanka
39 J5 **Mundesley** U.K.
39 H5 **Mundford** U.K.
6 C5 **Mundrabilla** Austr.
22 C4 **Mundwa** India
21 C2 **Muneru** *r.* India
22 D4 **Mungaoli** India
56 C3 **Mungbere** Congo(Zaire)
23 E5 **Mungeli** India
23 F4 **Munger** India
32 D5 **Munggresak, Tanjung** *pt* Indon.
6 E4 **Mungindi** Austr.
Munich *see* **München**
87 K4 **Munim** *r.* Brazil
68 D2 **Munising** U.S.A.
90 E3 **Muniz Freire** Brazil
37 M7 **Munkedal** Sweden
36 V2 **Munkelva** Norway
37 N7 **Munkfors** Sweden
43 J4 **Münnerstadt** Ger.
59 H1 **Munnik** S. Africa
30 D5 **Munsan** S. Korea
46 C7 **Münsingen** Switz.
43 G5 **Münster** *Hessen* Ger.
43 J2 **Münster** *Niedersachsen* Ger.
42 F3 **Münster** *Nordrhein-Westfalen* Ger.
42 F3 **Münsterland** *reg.* Ger.
67 F3 **Muntviel, Lac** *l.* Can.
36 V4 **Muojärvi** *l.* Fin.
32 C1 **Mương Lam** Vietnam
27 B6 **Mương Nhie** Vietnam
36 S3 **Muonio** Fin.
36 S2 **Muonioälven** *r.* Fin./Sweden
30 A5 **Muping** China
56 E3 **Muqdisho** Somalia
17 M1 **Müqtädir** Azer.
17 J2 **Muradiye** Turkey
28 F5 **Murakami** Japan
88 B7 **Murallón, Cerro** *mt* Chile
56 C4 **Muramvya** Burundi
56 D4 **Muranga** Kenya
32 ☐ **Mura Res.** *resr* Sing.
50 J3 **Murashi** Rus. Fed.
17 H2 **Murat** *r.* Turkey
16 B2 **Murat Dağı** *mts* Turkey
16 A1 **Muratlı** Turkey
28 G5 **Murayama** Japan
18 C3 **Murcheh Khvort** Iran
8 E4 **Murchison** Austr.
6 B4 **Murchison** *watercourse* Austr.
56 D3 **Murchison Falls National Park** Uganda
45 F4 **Murcia** Spain
45 F4 **Murcia** *div.* Spain
76 C3 **Murdo** U.S.A.
67 G4 **Murdochville** Can.
57 D5 **Murehwa** Zimbabwe
47 M7 **Mureș** *r.* Romania
44 E5 **Muret** France
79 E4 **Murfreesboro** *NC* U.S.A.
79 C5 **Murfreesboro** *TN* U.S.A.
19 F2 **Murgab** Turkm.
19 F2 **Murgab** *r.* Turkm.
19 G3 **Murghab** *r.* Afgh.
22 B3 **Murgha Kibzai** Pak.
15 F3 **Murghob** Tajik.
19 H3 **Murgh Pass** Afgh.
26 A2 **Muri** China
23 F5 **Muri** India
18 E2 **Mūrī** Iran
90 D3 **Muriaé** Brazil
57 C4 **Muriege** Angola
43 L1 **Müritz** *l.* Ger.
43 M1 **Müritz, Nationalpark** *nat. park* Ger.
43 L1 **Müritz Seenpark** *res.* Ger.
36 X2 **Murmansk** Rus. Fed.
36 W2 **Murmanskaya Oblast'** *div.* Rus. Fed.
48 C4 **Muro, Capo di** *pt Corsica* France
50 G4 **Murom** Rus. Fed.
28 G3 **Muroran** Japan
45 B1 **Muros** Spain
29 D8 **Muroto** Japan
29 D8 **Muroto-zaki** *pt* Japan

12 H3 Ob' *r.* Rus. Fed.
54 D4 Obala Cameroon
29 D7 Obama Japan
40 C4 Oban U.K.
28 G5 Obanazawa Japan
45 C1 O Barco Spain
66 F4 Obatogama L. *l.* Can.
64 F4 Obed Can.
9 B6 Obelisk *mt* N.Z.
43 H4 Oberaula Ger.
43 J3 Oberdorla Ger.
43 J3 Oberharz *nat. park* Ger.
42 E3 Oberhausen Ger.
76 C4 Oberlin *KS* U.S.A.
80 B4 Oberlin *OH* U.S.A.
43 F5 Obermoschel Ger.
8 G2 Oberon Austr.
43 L5 Oberpfälzer Wald *mts* Ger.
43 H4 Obersinn Ger.
43 H4 Oberthulba Ger.
43 G4 Obertshausen Ger.
43 H3 Oberwälder Land *reg.* Ger.
25 E7 Obi *i.* Indon.
87 G4 Óbidos Brazil
19 H2 Obigarm Tajik.
28 H3 Obihiro Japan
51 H6 Obil'noye Rus. Fed.
89 C2 Obispos Venez.
24 F2 Obluch'ye Rus. Fed.
50 F4 Obninsk Rus. Fed.
56 C3 Obo C.A.R.
26 A2 Obo China
56 E2 Obock Djibouti
56 C4 Obokote Congo(Zaire)
30 E3 Obŏk-tong N. Korea
56 B4 Obouya Congo
51 F5 Oboyan' Rus. Fed.
50 G2 Obozerskiy Rus. Fed.
23 E4 Obra India
23 E4 Obra Dam *dam* India
70 E6 Obregón, Presa *resr* Mex.
49 J2 Obrenovac Yugo.
16 D2 Obruk Turkey
12 J2 Obskaya Guba *chan.* Rus. Fed.
54 B4 Obuasi Ghana
51 D5 Obukhiv Ukr.
50 J2 Ob"yachevo Rus. Fed.
79 D6 Ocala U.S.A.
89 D4 Ocamo *r.* Venez.
84 B1 Ocampo Mex.
89 B2 Ocaña Col.
45 E3 Ocaña Spain
86 E7 Occidental, Cordillera *mts* Chile
89 A4 Occidental, Cordillera *mts* Col.
86 C6 Occidental, Cordillera *mts* Peru
64 B3 Ocean Cape *pt* U.S.A.
81 F5 Ocean City *MD* U.S.A.
81 F5 Ocean City *NJ* U.S.A.
64 D4 Ocean Falls Can.
96 G3 Oceanographer Fracture *sea feature* Atl. Ocean
74 D5 Oceanside U.S.A.
77 F6 Ocean Springs U.S.A.
51 D6 Ochakiv Ukr.
51 G7 Och'amch'ire Georgia
40 E4 Ochil Hills *h.* U.K.
22 C1 Ochili Pass Afgh.
43 J5 Ochsenfurt Ger.
42 F2 Ochtrup Ger.
37 P6 Ockelbo Sweden
84 D3 Ococingo Mex.
47 M7 Ocolaşul Mare, Vârful *mt* Romania
71 K5 Oconee *r. GA* U.S.A.
68 C4 Oconomowoc U.S.A.
68 D3 Oconto U.S.A.
74 D5 Ocotillo Wells U.S.A.
84 B2 Ocotlán Mex.
54 B4 Oda Ghana
29 C7 Ōda Japan
36 E4 Ódáðahraun *lava* Iceland
30 E3 Odaejin N. Korea
28 G4 Ōdate Japan
29 F7 Odawara Japan
37 K6 Odda Norway
65 K3 Odei *r.* Can.
68 C5 Odell U.S.A.
45 B4 Odemira Port.
16 A2 Ödemiş Turkey
59 G3 Odendaalsrus S. Africa
37 M9 Odense Denmark
43 G5 Odenwald *reg.* Ger.
43 J3 Oder *r.* Ger./Pol.
46 G3 Oderbucht *b.* Ger.
51 D6 Odesa Ukr.
37 O7 Ödeshog Sweden
77 C6 Odessa U.S.A.
45 C4 Odiel *r.* Spain
54 B4 Odienné Côte d'Ivoire
50 F4 Odintsovo Rus. Fed.
32 C3 Ŏdôngk Cambodia
46 J6 Odra *r.* Ger./Pol.
87 K5 Oeiras Brazil
76 C3 Oelrichs U.S.A.
43 L4 Oelsnitz Ger.
68 B4 Oelwein U.S.A.
42 D1 Oenkerk Neth.
17 H1 Of Turkey
48 G4 Ofanto *r.* Italy
43 G4 Offenbach am Main Ger.
42 F6 Offenburg Ger.
49 M6 Ofidoussa *i.* Greece
28 G5 Ōfunato Japan
28 F5 Oga Japan
56 E3 Ogadēn *reg.* Eth.
28 F5 Oga-hantō *pen.* Japan
29 E7 Ōgaki Japan
76 C3 Ogallala U.S.A.
24 G4 Ogasawara-shotō *is* Japan
69 H2 Ogascanane, Lac *l.* Can.
54 C4 Ogbomoso Nigeria
76 E3 Ogden *IA* U.S.A.
72 E3 Ogden *UT* U.S.A.
64 C3 Ogden, Mt *mt* Can.
81 F2 Ogdensburg U.S.A.
62 E3 Ogilvie *r.* Can.
62 E3 Ogilvie Mts *mts* Can.
18 D2 Oglanly Turkm.
79 C5 Oglethorpe, Mt *mt* U.S.A.
48 D1 Oglio *r.* Italy
54 C4 Ogoja Nigeria
66 C3 Ogoki *r.* Can.
66 C3 Ogoki Res. *resr* Can.
49 K3 Ogosta *r.* Bulg.
37 T8 Ogre Latvia
48 F2 Ogulin Croatia
18 D2 Ogurchinskiy, Ostrov *i.* Turkm.
17 L1 Oğuz Azer.
9 A6 Ohai N.Z.
9 E3 Ohakune N.Z.
28 G4 Ōhata Japan
9 B6 Ohau, L. *l.* N.Z.
91 B2 O'Higgins *div.* Chile
88 B7 O'Higgins, L. *l.* Chile
80 B4 Ohio *div.* U.S.A.
78 C4 Ohio *r.* U.S.A.
43 G4 Ohm *r.* Ger.
43 J4 Ohrdruf Ger.
43 L4 Ohře *r.* Czech Rep.
43 K2 Ohre *r.* Ger.
49 J4 Ohrid Macedonia
49 J4 Ohrid, Lake *l.* Albania/Macedonia
59 J2 Ohrigstad S. Africa
43 H5 Öhringen Ger.
9 E3 Ohura N.Z.
87 H3 Oiapoque Brazil
40 D3 Oich, Loch *l.* U.K.
23 H3 Oiga China
42 A4 Oignies France
80 D4 Oil City U.S.A.
74 C4 Oildale U.S.A.
44 F2 Oise *r.* France
42 B5 Oise à l'Aisne, Canal de l' *canal* France
29 B8 Ōita Japan
49 K5 Oiti *mt* Greece
74 C4 Ojai U.S.A.
91 D2 Ojeda Arg.
68 B3 Ojibwa U.S.A.
82 D3 Ojinaga Mex.
84 C3 Ojitlán Mex.
29 F6 Ojiya Japan
88 C3 Ojos del Salado *mt* Arg.
50 G4 Oka *r.* Rus. Fed.
57 B6 Okahandja Namibia
9 E3 Okahukura N.Z.
57 B6 Okakarara Namibia
67 H2 Okak Islands *is* Can.
64 F5 Okanagan Falls Can.
64 F4 Okanagan Lake *l.* Can.
64 F5 Okanogan U.S.A.
72 C1 Okanogan *r.* Can./U.S.A.
72 B1 Okanogan Range *mts* U.S.A.
56 C3 Okapi, Parc National de la *nat. park* Congo(Zaire)
22 C3 Okara Pak.
18 D2 Okarem Turkm.
57 B5 Okaukuejo Namibia
57 C5 Okavango *r.* Botswana/Namibia
57 C5 Okavango Delta *swamp* Botswana
29 F6 Okaya Japan
29 C7 Okayama Japan
29 E7 Okazaki Japan
79 D7 Okeechobee U.S.A.
79 D7 Okeechobee, L. *l.* U.S.A.
79 D6 Okefenokee Swamp *swamp* U.S.A.
39 C7 Okehampton U.K.
54 C4 Okene Nigeria
43 J2 Oker *r.* Ger.
22 B5 Okha India
24 G1 Okha Rus. Fed.
23 F4 Okhaldhunga Nepal
22 B5 Okha Rann *marsh* India
13 Q3 Okhota *r.* Rus. Fed.
13 Q4 Okhotsk Rus. Fed.
24 G2 Okhotsk, Sea of *g.* Rus. Fed.
51 E5 Okhtyrka Ukr.
24 E4 Okinawa *i.* Japan
29 B7 Okino-shima *i.* Japan
29 C6 Oki-shotō *is* Japan
77 D5 Oklahoma *div.* U.S.A.
77 D5 Oklahoma City U.S.A.
77 D5 Okmulgee U.S.A.
56 B4 Okondja Gabon
64 G4 Okotoks Can.
50 E4 Okovskiy Les *forest* Rus. Fed.
56 B4 Okoyo Congo
36 S1 Øksfjord Norway
50 F2 Oksovskiy Rus. Fed.
19 H2 Oktyabr' Tajik.
14 D2 Oktyabr'sk Kazak.
50 J4 Oktyabr'sk Rus. Fed.
50 G2 Oktyabr'skiy *Archangel.* Rus. Fed.
51 G6 Oktyabr'skiy *Volgograd.* Rus. Fed.
24 H1 Oktyabr'skiy Rus. Fed.
12 G4 Oktyabr'skiy Rus. Fed.
19 G2 Oktyabr'skiy Uzbek.
12 H3 Oktyabr'skoye Rus. Fed.
13 L2 Oktyabr'skoy Revolyutsii, Ostrov *i.* Rus. Fed.
50 E3 Okulovka Rus. Fed.
28 F3 Okushiri-tō *i.* Japan
58 E1 Okwa *watercourse* Botswana
36 B4 Ólafsvík Iceland
74 C3 Olancha U.S.A.
74 C3 Olancha Peak *summit* U.S.A.
37 P8 Öland *i.* Sweden
36 W3 Olanga Rus. Fed.
8 C2 Olary Austr.
8 C2 Olary *r.* Austr.
76 E4 Olathe U.S.A.
91 E3 Olavarría Arg.
46 H5 Oława Pol.
75 G5 Olberg U.S.A.
48 C4 Olbia *Sardinia* Italy
80 D3 Olcott U.S.A.
21 C2 Old Bastar India
41 D4 Oldcastle Rep. of Ireland
62 E3 Old Crow Can.
42 D1 Oldeboorn Neth.
43 G1 Oldenburg Ger.
46 E3 Oldenburg in Holstein Ger.
42 E2 Oldenzaal Neth.
36 R2 Olderdalen Norway
81 F3 Old Forge *NY* U.S.A.
81 F4 Old Forge *PA* U.S.A.
38 E4 Oldham U.K.
41 C6 Old Head of Kinsale *hd* Rep. of Ireland
64 G4 Oldman *r.* Can.
40 F3 Oldmeldrum U.K.
81 H3 Old Orchard Beach U.S.A.
67 K4 Old Perlican Can.
64 G4 Olds Can.
81 J2 Old Town U.S.A.
65 H4 Old Wives L. *l.* Can.
75 E4 Old Woman Mts *mts* U.S.A.
80 D3 Olean U.S.A.
47 L3 Olecko Pol.
13 O4 Olekma *r.* Rus. Fed.
13 O3 Olekminsk Rus. Fed.
51 E5 Oleksandriya Ukr.
50 H1 Olema Rus. Fed.
37 J7 Ølen Norway
36 X2 Olenegorsk Rus. Fed.
13 N3 Olenek Rus. Fed.
13 O2 Olenek *r.* Rus. Fed.
13 O2 Olenek B. *b.* Rus. Fed.
50 E3 Olenino Rus. Fed.
51 C5 Olevs'k Ukr.
28 D3 Ol'ga Rus. Fed.
45 C4 Olhão Port.
59 J1 Olifants S. Africa
58 C5 Olifants *r.* S. Africa
58 C2 Olifants *watercourse* Namibia
58 E3 Olifantshoek S. Africa
58 C6 Olifantsrivierberg *mts* S. Africa
91 F2 Olimar Grande *r.* Uru.
90 C3 Olímpia Brazil
84 C3 Olinalá Mex.
87 M5 Olinda Brazil
57 D5 Olinga Moz.
59 G2 Oliphants Drift Botswana
91 D2 Oliva Arg.
45 F3 Oliva Spain
88 C3 Oliva, Cordillera de *mts* Arg./Chile
91 C1 Olivares, Co del *mt* Chile
80 B5 Olive Hill U.S.A.
90 D3 Oliveira Brazil
45 C3 Olivenza Spain
76 E2 Olivia U.S.A.
50 G4 Ol'khi Rus. Fed.
88 C2 Ollagüe Chile
91 B1 Ollita, Cordillera de *mts* Arg./Chile
91 B1 Ollitas *mt* Arg.
86 C5 Olmos Peru
81 G3 Olmstedville U.S.A.
39 G5 Olney U.K.
78 C4 Olney U.S.A.
37 O8 Olofström Sweden
46 H6 Olomouc Czech Rep.
50 E2 Olonets Rus. Fed.
31 B3 Olongapo Phil.
44 D5 Oloron-Ste-Marie France
45 H1 Olot Spain
24 D1 Olovyannaya Rus. Fed.
22 C5 Olpad India
43 F3 Olpe Ger.
47 K4 Olsztyn Pol.
46 C7 Olten Switz.
49 M2 Olteniţa Romania
17 H1 Oltu Turkey
31 B5 Olutanga *i.* Phil.
72 B2 Olympia U.S.A.
72 A2 Olympic Nat. Park *WA* U.S.A.
72 B2 Olympic Nat. Park *WA* U.S.A.
Olympus *mt see* Troödos, Mount
49 K4 Olympus *mt* Greece
72 B2 Olympus, Mt *mt* U.S.A.
13 S3 Olyutorskiy Rus. Fed.
13 T4 Olyutorskiy, Mys *c.* Rus. Fed.
13 S4 Olyutorskiy Zaliv *b.* Rus. Fed.
23 E2 Oma China
28 G4 Ōma Japan
29 E6 Ōmachi Japan
29 F7 Omae-zaki *pt* Japan
41 D3 Omagh U.K.
76 E3 Omaha U.S.A.
58 C1 Omaheke *div.* Namibia
72 C1 Omak U.S.A.
10 G8 Oman *country* Asia
19 E5 Oman, Gulf of *g.* Asia
9 B6 Omarama N.Z.
57 B6 Omaruru Namibia
57 B5 Omatako *watercourse* Namibia
86 D7 Omate Peru
58 E2 Omaweneno Botswana
28 G4 Ōma-zaki *c.* Japan
56 A4 Omboué Gabon
48 D3 Ombrone *r.* Italy
23 F3 Ombu China
58 E5 Omdraaisvlei S. Africa
55 F3 Omdurman Sudan
48 C2 Omegna Italy
8 F4 Omeo Austr.
56 D2 Om Hājer Eritrea
18 C4 Omīdīyeh Iran
64 D3 Omineca Mountains Can.
58 C1 Omitara Namibia
29 F7 Ōmiya Japan
64 C3 Ommaney, Cape *hd* U.S.A.
42 E2 Ommen Neth.
26 B1 Ömnögovĭ *div.* Mongolia
13 R3 Omolon *r.* Rus. Fed.
56 D3 Omo National Park Eth.
28 G5 Omono-gawa *r.* Japan
12 J4 Omsk Rus. Fed.
13 R3 Omsukchan Rus. Fed.
28 H2 Ōmu Japan
29 A8 Ōmura Japan
49 L2 Omu, Vârful *mt* Romania
68 B4 Onalaska U.S.A.
81 F6 Onancock U.S.A.
66 D4 Onaping Lake *l.* Can.
69 E3 Onaway U.S.A.
32 A2 Onbingwin Myanmar
91 D1 Oncativo Arg.
38 C3 Onchan U.K.
57 B5 Oncócua Angola
57 B5 Ondangwa Namibia
58 B1 Ondekaremba Namibia
58 D5 Onderstedorings S. Africa
57 B5 Ondjiva Angola
54 C4 Ondo Nigeria
24 D2 Öndörhaan Mongolia
30 A1 Ondor Had China
26 B1 Ondor Mod China
26 D1 Ondor Sum China
50 E2 Ondozero Rus. Fed.
58 D1 One Botswana
50 F2 Onega Rus. Fed.
50 F2 Onega *r.* Rus. Fed.
50 E2 Onega, Lake *l.* Rus. Fed.
64 E4 100 Mile House Can.
81 F3 Oneida U.S.A.
81 F3 Oneida Lake *l.* U.S.A.
76 D3 O'Neill U.S.A.
24 H2 Onekotan, O. *i.* Rus. Fed.
81 F3 Oneonta U.S.A.
9 E2 Oneroa N.Z.
47 N7 Oneşti Romania
50 E1 Onezhskaya Guba *g.* Rus. Fed.
Onezhskoye Ozero *l. see* Onega, Lake
23 E5 Ong *r.* India
56 B4 Onga Gabon
9 F3 Ongaonga N.Z.
58 E4 Ongers *watercourse* S. Africa
30 C5 Ongjin N. Korea
26 F1 Ongniud Qi China
21 C3 Ongole India
51 G7 Oni Georgia
57 E6 Onilahy *r.* Madag.
54 C4 Onitsha Nigeria
58 B1 Onjati Mountain *mt* Namibia
29 E7 Ōno Japan
7 J4 Ono-i-Lau *i.* Fiji
29 C7 Onomichi Japan
7 H2 Onotoa *i.* Kiribati
64 G4 Onoway Can.
58 C4 Onseepkans S. Africa
6 B4 Onslow Austr.
79 E5 Onslow Bay *b.* U.S.A.
30 F2 Onsong N. Korea
42 F1 Onstwedde Neth.
29 E7 Ontake-san *volc.* Japan
72 C2 Ontario U.S.A.
66 B3 Ontario *div.* Can.
69 H4 Ontario, Lake *l.* Can./U.S.A.
68 C2 Ontonagon U.S.A.
7 F2 Ontong Java Atoll *atoll* Solomon Is
6 D4 Oodnadatta Austr.
77 E4 Oologah L. *resr* U.S.A.
42 B3 Oostburg Neth.
Oostende *see* Ostend
42 D2 Oostendorp Neth.
42 C3 Oosterhout Neth.
42 B3 Oosterschelde *est.* Neth.
42 E2 Oosterwolde Neth.
42 A4 Oostvleteren Belgium
42 D1 Oost-Vlieland Neth.
64 D4 Ootsa Lake Can.
64 D4 Ootsa Lake *l.* Can.
80 E5 Opal U.S.A.
56 C4 Opala Congo(Zaire)
50 J3 Oparino Rus. Fed.
66 B3 Opasquia Can.
66 B3 Opasquia Provincial Park *res.* Can.
66 F3 Opataca L. *l.* Can.
46 H6 Opava Czech Rep.
79 C5 Opelika U.S.A.
77 E6 Opelousas U.S.A.
72 F1 Opheim U.S.A.
69 F2 Ophir Can.
33 B2 Ophir, Gunung *volc.* Indon.
9 C6 Opihi *r.* N.Z.
66 E3 Opinaca *r.* Can.
66 E3 Opinaca, Réservoir *resr* Can.
66 D3 Opinnagau *r.* Can.
17 K5 Opis Iraq
67 G3 Opiscotéo L. *l.* Can.
42 C2 Opmeer Neth.
50 D3 Opochka Rus. Fed.
46 H5 Opole Pol.
45 B2 Oporto Port.
9 F3 Opotiki N.Z.
79 C6 Opp U.S.A.
36 L5 Oppdal Norway
9 D3 Opunake N.Z.
57 B5 Opuwo Namibia
68 B5 Oquawka U.S.A.
81 H2 Oquossoc U.S.A.
75 G5 Oracle U.S.A.
75 G5 Oracle Junction U.S.A.
47 K7 Oradea Romania
36 E4 Öræfajökull *gl.* Iceland
49 J3 Orahovac Yugo.
22 D4 Orai India
54 B1 Oran Alg.
88 D2 Orán Arg.
32 C2 O Rang Cambodia
30 E3 Orang N. Korea
8 G2 Orange Austr.
44 G4 Orange France
81 G3 Orange *MA* U.S.A.
77 E6 Orange *TX* U.S.A.
80 D5 Orange *VA* U.S.A.
57 B6 Orange *r.* Namibia/S. Africa
79 D5 Orangeburg U.S.A.
87 H3 Orange, Cabo *c.* Brazil
Orange Free State *div. see* Free State
69 G3 Orangeville Can.
75 G2 Orangeville U.S.A.
82 G5 Orange Walk Belize
31 B3 Orani Phil.
43 M2 Oranienburg Ger.
57 B6 Oranjemund Namibia
89 C1 Oranjestad Aruba
41 C4 Oranmore Rep. of Ireland
57 C6 Orapa Botswana
31 C3 Oras Phil.
49 K2 Orăştie Romania
36 S5 Oravais Fin.
49 J2 Oravita Romania
22 E2 Orba Co *l.* China
48 D3 Orbetello Italy
45 D1 Orbigo *r.* Spain
8 G4 Orbost Austr.
92 B1 Orcadas *Arg. Base* Ant.
75 H2 Orchard Mesa U.S.A.
89 D2 Orchila, Isla *i.* Venez.
74 B4 Orcutt U.S.A.
6 C3 Ord *r.* Austr.
73 D4 Orderville U.S.A.
45 B1 Ordes Spain
6 C3 Ord, Mt *h.* Austr.
74 D4 Ord Mt *mt* U.S.A.
16 F1 Ordu Turkey
17 L2 Ordubad Azer.
73 G4 Ordway U.S.A.
Ordzhonikidze *see* Vladikavkaz
51 E6 Ordzhonikidze Ukr.
74 C1 Oreana U.S.A.
37 O7 Örebro Sweden
68 C4 Oregon *IL* U.S.A.
80 B4 Oregon *OH* U.S.A.
68 C4 Oregon *WV* U.S.A.
72 B3 Oregon *div.* U.S.A.
72 B2 Oregon City U.S.A.
50 F4 Orekhovo-Zuyevo Rus. Fed.
50 F4 Orel Rus. Fed.
24 F1 Orel', Ozero *l.* Rus. Fed.
75 G1 Orem U.S.A.
16 M6 Ören Turkey
16 A2 Ören Turkey
12 G4 Orenburg Rus. Fed.
91 E3 Orense Arg.
9 A7 Orepuki N.Z.
37 N9 Øresund *str.* Denmark
9 B7 Oreti *r.* N.Z.
9 E2 Orewa N.Z.
42 D4 Oreye Belgium
49 K4 Orfanou, Kolpos *b.* Greece
39 J5 Orford U.K.
39 J5 Orford Ness *spit* U.K.
75 F5 Organ Pipe Cactus National Monument *res.* U.S.A.
19 H3 Orgūn Afgh.
16 B2 Orhaneli Turkey
16 B1 Orhangazi Turkey
50 J3 Orichi Rus. Fed.
81 K2 Orient U.S.A.
86 E7 Oriental, Cordillera *mts* Bol.
89 B3 Oriental, Cordillera *mts* Col.
86 D6 Oriental, Cordillera *mts* Peru
91 E3 Oriente Arg.
45 F3 Orihuela Spain
51 E6 Orikhiv Ukr.
69 H3 Orillia Can.
37 T6 Orimattila Fin.
89 E2 Orinoco *r.* Col./Venez.
89 E2 Orinoco Delta *delta* Venez.
23 F5 Orissa *div.* India
37 S7 Orissaare Estonia
48 C5 Oristano *Sardinia* Italy
37 T6 Orivesi Fin.
36 V5 Orivesi *l.* Fin.
87 G4 Oriximiná Brazil
84 C3 Orizaba Mex.
36 L5 Orkanger Norway
37 N8 Örkelljunga Sweden
36 L5 Orkla *r.* Norway
59 G3 Orkney S. Africa
40 E1 Orkney Islands *is* U.K.
77 C6 Orla U.S.A.
74 A2 Orland U.S.A.
90 C3 Orlândia Brazil
79 D6 Orlando U.S.A.
44 E3 Orléans France
81 J4 Orleans *MA* U.S.A.
81 G2 Orleans *VT* U.S.A.
50 J3 Orlov Rus. Fed.
50 F4 Orlovskaya Oblast' *div.* Rus. Fed.
51 G6 Orlovskiy Rus. Fed.
19 G5 Ormara Pak.
19 G5 Ormara, Ras *hd* Pak.
31 C4 Ormoc Phil.
79 D6 Ormond Beach U.S.A.
38 E4 Ormskirk U.K.
81 G2 Ormstown Can.
44 D2 Orne *r.* France
36 N3 Ørnes Norway
36 Q5 Örnsköldsvik Sweden
30 D4 Oro N. Korea
89 C3 Orocué Col.
54 B3 Orodara Burkina
72 C2 Orofino U.S.A.
73 F5 Orogrande U.S.A.
67 G4 Oromocto Can.
16 E6 Oron Israel
7 J2 Orona *i.* Kiribati
81 J2 Orono U.S.A.
40 B4 Oronsay *i.* U.K.
Orontes *r. see* 'Āṣī, Nahr al
24 E1 Oroqen Zizhiqi China
31 B4 Oroquieta Phil.
87 L5 Orós, Açude *resr* Brazil
48 C4 Orosei *Sardinia* Italy
48 C4 Orosei, Golfo di *b. Sardinia* Italy
47 K7 Orosháza Hungary
75 G5 Oro Valley U.S.A.
74 B2 Oroville *CA* U.S.A.
72 C1 Oroville *WA* U.S.A.
74 B2 Oroville, Lake *l.* U.S.A.
8 B2 Orroroo Austr.
37 O6 Orsa Sweden
50 D4 Orsha Belarus
12 G4 Orsk Rus. Fed.
37 K5 Ørsta Norway
45 C1 Ortegal, Cabo *c.* Spain
44 D5 Orthez France
45 C1 Ortigueira Spain
89 D2 Ortíz Venez.
48 D1 Ortles *mt* Italy
38 E3 Orton U.K.
48 F3 Ortona Italy
76 D2 Ortonville U.S.A.
13 O3 Orulgan, Khrebet *mts* Rus. Fed.
58 B1 Orumbo Namibia
18 B2 Orūmīyeh Iran
18 B2 Orūmīyeh, Daryācheh-ye *salt l.* Iran
86 E7 Oruro Bol.
42 D5 Orval, Abbaye d' Belgium
48 E3 Orvieto Italy
92 B3 Orville Coast *coastal area* Ant.
80 C4 Orwell *OH* U.S.A.
81 G3 Orwell *VT* U.S.A.
37 M5 Os Norway
68 A4 Osage U.S.A.
76 E4 Osage *r.* U.S.A.
29 D7 Ōsaka Japan
83 H7 Osa, Pen. de *pen.* Costa Rica
37 N8 Osby Sweden
77 F5 Osceola *AR* U.S.A.
76 E3 Osceola *IA* U.S.A.
43 M3 Oschatz Ger.
43 K2 Oschersleben (Bode) Ger.
48 C4 Oschiri *Sardinia* Italy
69 F3 Oscoda U.S.A.
50 F4 Osetr *r.* Rus. Fed.
29 A8 Ōse-zaki *pt* Japan
69 K3 Osgoode Can.
15 F2 Osh Kyrg.
57 B5 Oshakati Namibia
28 G3 Oshamanbe Japan
69 H4 Oshawa Can.
28 G5 Oshika-hantō *pen.* Japan
28 F4 Ō-shima *i.* Japan
29 F7 Ō-shima *i.* Japan
76 C3 Oshkosh *NE* U.S.A.
68 C3 Oshkosh *WV* U.S.A.
18 B2 Oshnovīyeh Iran
54 C4 Oshogbo Nigeria
17 M5 Oshtorān Kūh *mt* Iran
17 M5 Oshtorīnān Iran
56 B4 Oshwe Congo(Zaire)
49 H2 Osijek Croatia
48 E3 Osimo Italy
22 C4 Osiyān India
59 J3 Osizweni S. Africa
48 G2 Osječenica *mt* Bos.-Herz.
36 O5 Ösjön *l.* Sweden
76 E3 Oskaloosa U.S.A.
37 P8 Oskarshamn Sweden
69 K1 Oskélanéo Can.
51 F5 Oskol *r.* Rus. Fed.
37 M7 Oslo Norway
31 B4 Oslob Phil.
37 M7 Oslofjorden *chan.* Norway
21 B2 Osmānābād India
16 E1 Osmancık Turkey
16 B1 Osmaneli Turkey
16 F3 Osmaniye Turkey
37 V7 Os'mino Rus. Fed.
43 G2 Osnabrück Ger.
49 K3 Osogovske Planine *mts* Bulg./Macedonia
91 B4 Osorno Chile
45 D1 Osorno Spain
91 B4 Osorno, Vol. *volc.* Chile
64 F5 Osoyoos Can.
37 J6 Osøyri Norway
6 E3 Osprey Reef *rf* Coral Sea Is Terr.
42 D3 Oss Neth.
6 E6 Ossa, Mt *mt* Austr.
68 B3 Osseo U.S.A.
69 F3 Ossineke U.S.A.
81 H3 Ossipee Lake *l.* U.S.A.
43 K3 Oßmannstedt Ger.
67 H3 Ossokmanuan Lake *l.* Can.
50 E3 Ostashkov Rus. Fed.
43 F2 Ostbevern Ger.
43 H1 Oste *r.* Ger.
42 A3 Ostend Belgium
47 P5 Oster Ukr.
43 K2 Osterburg (Altmark) Ger.
37 O8 Österbymo Sweden
37 N6 Österdalälven *l.* Sweden
37 M5 Østerdalen *v.* Norway
43 K3 Osterfeld Ger.
43 G1 Osterholz-Scharmbeck Ger.
43 J3 Osterode am Harz Ger.
36 O5 Östersund Sweden
43 J3 Osterwieck Ger.
Ostfriesische Inseln *is see* East Frisian Islands
42 F1 Ostfriesland *reg.* Ger.
37 Q6 Östhammar Sweden
46 J6 Ostrava Czech Rep.
47 J4 Ostróda Pol.
51 F5 Ostrogozhsk Rus. Fed.
43 L4 Ostrov Czech Rep.
50 D3 Ostrov Rus. Fed.
47 K5 Ostrowiec Świętokrzyski Pol.
47 K4 Ostrów Mazowiecka Pol.
46 H5 Ostrów Wielkopolski Pol.
49 L3 Osŭm *r.* Bulg.
29 B9 Ōsumi-Kaikyō *chan.* Japan
29 B9 Ōsumi-shotō *is* Japan
45 D4 Osuna Spain
81 F2 Oswegatchie U.S.A.
68 C5 Oswego *IL* U.S.A.
80 E3 Oswego *NY* U.S.A.
81 E3 Oswego *r.* U.S.A.
39 D5 Oswestry U.K.
29 F6 Ōta Japan
9 C6 Otago Peninsula *pen.* N.Z.
9 E4 Otaki N.Z.
36 U4 Otanmäki Fin.
89 B4 Otare, Co *h.* Col.
28 G3 Otaru Japan
9 B7 Otatara N.Z.
86 C3 Otavalo Ecuador
57 B5 Otavi Namibia
29 G6 Ōtawara Japan
9 C6 Otematata N.Z.
37 U7 Otepää Estonia
72 C2 Othello U.S.A.
84 A1 Otinapa Mex.
9 C5 Otira N.Z.
81 E3 Otisco Lake *l.* U.S.A.
67 F3 Otish, Monts *mts* Can.
57 B6 Otjiwarongo Namibia
38 F4 Otley U.K.
26 C2 Otog Qi China
28 H2 Otoineppu Japan
9 E3 Otorohanga N.Z.
66 C3 Otoskwin *r.* Can.
49 H4 Otranto Italy
49 H4 Otranto, Strait of *str.* Albania/Italy
13 T3 Otrozhnyy Rus. Fed.
68 E4 Otsego U.S.A.
68 E3 Otsego Lake *l. MI* U.S.A.
81 F3 Otsego Lake *l. NY* U.S.A.
81 F3 Otselic U.S.A.
29 D7 Ōtsu Japan
37 L6 Otta Norway
69 K3 Ottawa Can.
68 C5 Ottawa *IL* U.S.A.
76 E4 Ottawa *KS* U.S.A.
80 A4 Ottawa *OH* U.S.A.
69 H2 Ottawa *r.* Can.
66 D2 Ottawa Islands *is* Can.
38 E2 Otterburn U.K.
75 G2 Otter Creek Reservoir U.S.A.
68 D1 Otter I. *i.* Can.
66 D3 Otter Rapids Can.
43 H1 Ottersberg Ger.
39 C7 Ottery *r.* U.K.
42 C4 Ottignies Belgium
63 K1 Otto Fjord *in.* Can.
68 A5 Ottumwa U.S.A.
42 F5 Ottweiler Ger.
54 C4 Otukpo Nigeria
88 D3 Otumpa Arg.
86 C5 Otuzco Peru
8 D5 Otway, C. *c.* Austr.
77 E5 Ouachita *r.* U.S.A.
77 E5 Ouachita, L. *l.* U.S.A.
77 E5 Ouachita Mts *mts* U.S.A.
56 C3 Ouadda C.A.R.
55 E3 Ouaddaï *reg.* Chad
54 B3 Ouagadougou Burkina
54 B3 Ouahigouya Burkina
54 B3 Oualâta Maur.
56 C3 Ouanda-Djailé C.A.R.
54 B2 Ouarâne *reg.* Maur.
54 C1 Ouargla Alg.
54 B1 Ouarzazate Morocco
58 F6 Oubergpas *pass* S. Africa
42 B4 Oudenaarde Belgium
42 F1 Oude Pekela Neth.
58 E6 Oudtshoorn S. Africa
42 C3 Oud-Turnhout Belgium
45 F5 Oued Tlélat Alg.
54 B1 Oued Zem Morocco
48 B6 Oued Zénati Alg.
44 B2 Ouessant, Île d' *i.* France
56 B3 Ouésso Congo
54 C4 Ouidah Benin
54 B1 Oujda Morocco
36 T4 Oulainen Fin.
45 G4 Ouled Farès Alg.
36 T4 Oulu Fin.
36 U4 Oulujärvi *l.* Fin.
36 U4 Oulujoki *r.* Fin.
36 T4 Oulunsalo Fin.
44 H4 Oulx Italy
55 E3 Oum-Chalouba Chad
54 B4 Oumé Côte d'Ivoire
55 D3 Oum-Hadjer Chad
36 T3 Ounasjoki *r.* Fin.
39 G5 Oundle U.K.
55 E3 Ounianga Kébir Chad
42 D4 Oupeye Belgium
42 E5 Our *r.* Lux.
73 F4 Ouray *CO* U.S.A.
75 H1 Ouray *UT* U.S.A.
45 C1 Ourense Spain
87 K5 Ouricuri Brazil
90 C3 Ourinhos Brazil
90 C1 Ouro *r.* Brazil
90 D3 Ouro Preto Brazil
42 D4 Ourthe *r.* Belgium
42 E5 Our, Vallée de l' *v.* Ger./Lux.
38 G4 Ouse *r. Eng.* U.K.
39 H7 Ouse *r. Eng.* U.K.
67 G3 Outardes *r.* Can.
58 E6 Outeniekpas *pass* S. Africa
40 A2 Outer Hebrides *is* U.K.
68 B2 Outer I. *i.* U.S.A.
74 C5 Outer Santa Barbara Channel *chan.* U.S.A.
57 B6 Outjo Namibia
62 H4 Outlook Can.
36 V5 Outokumpu Fin.
40 □ Out Skerries *is* U.K.
7 G4 Ouvéa *i.* New Caledonia
27 D5 Ouyang Hai Sk. *resr* China
8 D3 Ouyen Austr.
39 G5 Ouzel *r.* U.K.
48 C4 Ovace, Pte d' *mt Corsica* France
17 G2 Ovacık Turkey
48 C2 Ovada Italy
7 H3 Ovalau *i.* Fiji
91 B1 Ovalle Chile
45 B2 Ovar Port.
91 D2 Oveja *mt* Arg.
8 F4 Ovens *r.* Austr.
42 F4 Overath Ger.
36 S3 Överkalix Sweden
75 E3 Overton U.S.A.
36 S3 Övertorneå Sweden
37 P8 Överum Sweden
42 C2 Overveen Neth.
68 E4 Ovid U.S.A.
45 D1 Oviedo Spain
36 T2 Øvre Anarjåkka Nasjonalpark *nat. park* Norway
36 Q2 Øvre Dividal Nasjonalpark *nat. park* Norway
37 M6 Øvre Rendal Norway
51 D5 Ovruch Ukr.
9 B7 Owaka N.Z.
56 B4 Owando Congo
29 E7 Owase Japan
76 E2 Owatonna U.S.A.
19 F3 Owbeh Afgh.
81 E3 Owego U.S.A.
93 H3 Owen Fracture *sea feature* Ind. Ocean
41 B3 Owenmore *r.* Rep. of Ireland
9 D4 Owen River N.Z.
74 C3 Owens *r.* U.S.A.
78 C4 Owensboro U.S.A.
74 D3 Owens Lake *l.* U.S.A.
69 G3 Owen Sound Can.
69 G3 Owen Sound *in.* Can.
6 E2 Owen Stanley Range *mts* P.N.G.
54 C4 Owerri Nigeria
64 D4 Owikeno L. *l.* Can.
80 B5 Owingsville U.S.A.
81 J2 Owls Head U.S.A.
54 C4 Owo Nigeria
69 E4 Owosso U.S.A.
17 L4 Owrāmān, Kūh-e *mts* Iran/Iraq
72 C3 Owyhee U.S.A.
72 C3 Owyhee *r.* U.S.A.
72 C3 Owyhee Mts *mts* U.S.A.
86 C6 Oxapampa Peru
36 E3 Öxarfjörður *b.* Iceland
65 J5 Oxbow Can.
81 J1 Oxbow U.S.A.
37 P7 Oxelösund Sweden
9 D5 Oxford N.Z.
39 F6 Oxford U.K.
69 F4 Oxford *MI* U.S.A.
77 F5 Oxford *MS* U.S.A.
81 F3 Oxford *NY* U.S.A.
81 F5 Oxford *PA* U.S.A.
65 K4 Oxford House Can.
65 K4 Oxford L. *l.* Can.
8 E3 Oxley Austr.
8 H1 Oxleys Pk *mt* Austr.
74 C4 Oxnard U.S.A.
69 H3 Oxtongue Lake Can.
36 N3 Øya Norway
29 F6 Oyama Japan
87 H3 Oyapock *r.* Brazil/Fr. Guiana
56 B3 Oyem Gabon
40 D3 Oykel *r.* U.K.
54 C4 Oyo Nigeria
44 G3 Oyonnax France
23 H5 Oyster I. *i.* Myanmar
43 H1 Oyten Ger.
17 J2 Özalp Turkey
31 B4 Ozamiz Phil.
79 C6 Ozark *AL* U.S.A.
68 E2 Ozark *MI* U.S.A.
77 E4 Ozark Plateau *plat.* U.S.A.
76 E4 Ozarks, Lake of the *l.* U.S.A.
18 E3 Ozbagū Iran
51 G7 Ozerget'i Georgia
24 H1 Ozernovskiy Rus. Fed.
50 E4 Ozernyy Rus. Fed.
47 L3 Ozersk Rus. Fed.
50 F4 Ozery Rus. Fed.
13 Q3 Ozhogino Rus. Fed.
48 C4 Ozieri *Sardinia* Italy
77 C6 Ozona U.S.A.
29 B7 Ozuki Japan

P

63 O3 Paamiut Greenland
32 A1 Pa-an Myanmar
58 C6 Paarl S. Africa
58 D4 Paballelo S. Africa
30 E3 Pabal-ri N. Korea
40 A3 Pabbay *i. Scot.* U.K.
40 A4 Pabbay *i. Scot.* U.K.
47 J5 Pabianice Pol.
23 G4 Pabna Bangl.
37 T9 Pabradė Lith.
19 G5 Pab Range *mts* Pak.
86 F6 Pacaás Novos, Parque Nacional *nat. park* Brazil
89 E4 Pacaraima, Serra *mts* Brazil
86 C5 Pacasmayo Peru
73 E6 Pacheco *Chihuahua* Mex.
84 B1 Pacheco Mex.
50 H2 Pachikha Rus. Fed.
48 F6 Pachino *Sicily* Italy
21 B1 Pachmarhi India
22 D5 Pachore India
84 C2 Pachuca Mex.
74 B2 Pacific U.S.A.
95 L9 Pacific-Antarctic Ridge *sea feature* Pac. Oc.
29 F8 Pacific Ocean *ocean*
31 C4 Pacijan *i.* Phil.
33 D4 Pacitan Indon.
87 H4 Pacoval Brazil
90 D2 Pacuí *r.* Brazil
46 H5 Paczków Pol.
31 C5 Padada Phil.
89 D4 Padamo *r.* Venez.
33 B3 Padang Indon.
33 B3 Padangpanjang Indon.
33 A2 Padangsidimpuan Indon.
33 C3 Padangtikar *i.* Indon.
50 E2 Padany Rus. Fed.
17 M5 Padatha, Kūh-e *mt* Iran
89 D4 Padauiri *r.* Brazil
86 F8 Padcaya Bol.
64 F3 Paddle Prairie Can.
80 C5 Paden City U.S.A.
43 G3 Paderborn Ger.
49 K2 Padeşu, Vârful *mt* Romania
86 F7 Padilla Bol.
36 P3 Padjelanta Nationalpark *nat. park* Sweden
23 G5 Padma *r.* Bangl.
Padova *see* Padua
77 D7 Padre Island *i.* U.S.A.
48 C3 Padro, Monte *mt Corsica* France
39 C7 Padstow U.K.

49 K3 **Petrokhanski Prokhod** *pass* Bulg.
69 F4 **Petrolia** Can.
87 K5 **Petrolina** Brazil
51 G5 **Petropavlovka** Rus. Fed.
12 H4 **Petropavlovsk** Kazak.
24 H1 **Petropavlovsk-Kamchatskiy** Rus. Fed.
49 K2 **Petroşani** Romania
51 H4 **Petrovsk** Rus. Fed.
24 C1 **Petrovsk-Zabaykal'skiy** Rus. Fed.
51 H5 **Petrov Val** Rus. Fed.
50 E2 **Petrozavodsk** Rus. Fed.
59 F4 **Petrusburg** S. Africa
59 H3 **Petrus Steyn** S. Africa
58 F5 **Petrusville** S. Africa
42 C2 **Petten** Neth.
41 D3 **Pettigo** U.K.
12 H4 **Petukhovo** Rus. Fed.
32 A4 **Peureula** Indon.
13 T3 **Pevek** Rus. Fed.
46 H6 **Pezinok** Slovakia
43 F5 **Pfälzer Wald** *forest* Ger.
43 G6 **Pforzheim** Ger.
46 D7 **Pfullendorf** Ger.
43 G5 **Pfungstadt** Ger.
22 C3 **Phagwara** India
59 G4 **Phahameng** *Free State* S. Africa
59 H2 **Phahameng** *Northern Province* S. Africa
59 J1 **Phalaborwa** S. Africa
22 C4 **Phalodi** India
22 B4 **Phalsund** India
21 A2 **Phaltan** India
32 A3 **Phangnga** Thai.
32 D3 **Phan Rang** Vietnam
32 D3 **Phan Ri** Vietnam
32 D3 **Phan Thiêt** Vietnam
77 D7 **Pharr** U.S.A.
27 C6 **Phat Diêm** Vietnam
32 B4 **Phatthalung** Thai.
23 H4 **Phek** India
65 J3 **Phelps Lake** *l.* Can.
32 B1 **Phen** Thai.
79 C5 **Phenix City** U.S.A.
32 A2 **Phet Buri** Thai.
32 C2 **Phiafai** Laos
77 F5 **Philadelphia** *MS* U.S.A.
81 F2 **Philadelphia** *NY* U.S.A.
81 F5 **Philadelphia** *PA* U.S.A.
76 C2 **Philip** U.S.A.
42 C4 **Philippeville** Belgium
80 C5 **Philippi** U.S.A.
42 B3 **Philippine** Neth.
11 O8 **Philippines** *country* Asia
31 C2 **Philippine Sea** *sea* Phil.
94 D5 **Philippine Trench** *sea feature* Pac. Oc.
59 F5 **Philippolis** S. Africa
43 G5 **Philippsburg** Ger.
80 D4 **Philipsburg** U.S.A.
42 C3 **Philipsdam** *barrage* Neth.
62 D3 **Philip Smith Mts** U.S.A.
58 F5 **Philipstown** S. Africa
8 E5 **Phillip I.** *i.* Austr.
81 H2 **Phillips** *ME* U.S.A.
68 B3 **Phillips** *WV* U.S.A.
76 D4 **Phillipsburg** *KS* U.S.A.
81 F4 **Phillipsburg** *NJ* U.S.A.
63 J1 **Phillips Inlet** *in.* Can.
80 D4 **Phillipston** U.S.A.
81 G3 **Philmont** U.S.A.
65 G3 **Philomena** Can.
80 C6 **Philpott Reservoir** *resr* U.S.A.
32 B2 **Phimae** Thai.
32 C2 **Phimun Mangsahan** Thai.
59 G3 **Phiritona** S. Africa
Phnom Penh *see* **Phnum Penh**
32 C2 **Phnum Aôral** *mt* Cambodia
32 C3 **Phnum Penh** Cambodia
75 F5 **Phoenix** U.S.A.
7 J2 **Phoenix Islands** *is* Pac. Oc.
59 G3 **Phomolong** S. Africa
25 C4 **Phôngsali** Laos
27 B6 **Phong Thô** Vietnam
32 B1 **Phon Phisai** Thai.
32 B1 **Phou Bia** *mt* Laos
32 C1 **Phou Cô Pi** *mt* Laos/Vietnam
27 B6 **Phou Sam Sao** *mts* Laos/Vietnam
32 A1 **Phrao** Thai.
32 B2 **Phra Phutthabat** Thai.
27 B6 **Phuc Yên** Vietnam
32 D2 **Phu Hôi** Vietnam
32 A4 **Phuket** Thai.
22 C4 **Phulera** India
23 G5 **Phultala** Bangl.
27 B6 **Phu Ly** Vietnam
32 B2 **Phumĭ Bânhchok Kon** Cambodia
32 C3 **Phumĭ Chhuk** Cambodia
32 C2 **Phumĭ Kâmpóng Trâlach** Cambodia
32 B3 **Phumĭ Kaôh Kŏng** Cambodia
32 B2 **Phumĭ Kiliĕk** Cambodia
32 C2 **Phumĭ Mlu Prey** Cambodia
32 B2 **Phumĭ Moŭng** Cambodia
32 B2 **Phumĭ Prâmaôy** Cambodia
32 B2 **Phumĭ Sâmraông** Cambodia
32 B2 **Phumĭ Toêng** Cambodia
32 D2 **Phu My** Vietnam
32 D2 **Phu Nhon** Vietnam
32 C3 **Phuớc Long** Vietnam
32 C3 **Phu Quôc** Vietnam
59 H4 **Phuthaditjhaba** S. Africa
27 B6 **Phu Tho** Vietnam
32 B1 **Phu Wiang** Thai.
87 J5 **Piaca** Brazil
48 C2 **Piacenza** Italy
26 D2 **Pianguan** China
48 D3 **Pianosa, Isola** *i.* Italy
47 N7 **Piatra Neamţ** Romania
87 K5 **Piauí** *r.* Brazil
48 E1 **Piave** *r.* Italy
55 F4 **Pibor** *r.* Sudan
55 F4 **Pibor Post** Sudan
68 D1 **Pic** *r.* Can.
75 F4 **Pica** U.S.A.
75 G5 **Picacho** *AZ* U.S.A.
75 E5 **Picacho** *CA* U.S.A.
44 F2 **Picardie** *reg.* France
79 B6 **Picayune** U.S.A.
88 D2 **Pichanal** Arg.
91 C2 **Pichi Ciego** Arg.
91 B2 **Pichilemu** Chile
70 D7 **Pichilingue** Mex.
91 D3 **Pichi Mahuida** Arg.
22 D4 **Pichor** India
84 D3 **Pichucalco** Mex.
68 D1 **Pic, I.** *i.* Can.
38 G3 **Pickering** U.K.
38 G3 **Pickering, Vale of** *v.* U.K.
68 E2 **Pickford** U.S.A.
66 B3 **Pickle Lake** Can.
34 C5 **Pico** *i.* Port.
89 C2 **Pico Bolívar** *mt* Venez.
89 D4 **Pico da Neblina** *mt* Brazil
89 D4 **Pico da Neblina, Parque Nacional do** *nat. park* Brazil
84 C3 **Pico de Orizaba, Parque Nacional** *nat. park* Mex.
84 B3 **Pico de Tancítaro, Parque Nacional** *nat. park* Mex.
83 K5 **Pico Duarte** *mt* Dom. Rep.
89 E4 **Pico Redondo** *summit* Brazil
89 E4 **Pico Rondon** *summit* Brazil
87 K5 **Picos** Brazil
88 C7 **Pico Truncado** Arg.
68 D1 **Pic River** Can.
8 H3 **Picton** Austr.
69 J4 **Picton** Can.
67 H4 **Pictou** Can.
68 D2 **Pictured Rocks National Lakeshore** *res.* U.S.A.
91 C3 **Picún Leufú** *r.* Arg.
19 F5 **Pidarak** Pak.
21 C5 **Pidurutalagala** *mt* Sri Lanka
89 B3 **Piedecuesta** Col.
91 C1 **Pie de Palo, Sa** *mts* Arg.
79 C5 **Piedmont** U.S.A.
80 C4 **Piedmont Lake** *l.* U.S.A.
82 D3 **Piedras Negras** *Coahuila* Mex.
84 C3 **Piedras Negras** *Veracruz* Mex.
91 F2 **Piedras, Punta** *pt* Arg.
86 D6 **Piedras, Río de las** *r.* Peru
68 C1 **Pie Island** *i.* Can.
36 U5 **Pieksämäki** Fin.
36 U5 **Pielavesi** Fin.
36 V5 **Pielinen** *l.* Fin.
59 H2 **Pienaarsrivier** S. Africa
68 E5 **Pierceton** U.S.A.
74 A2 **Piercy** U.S.A.
49 K4 **Pieria** *mts* Greece
40 F1 **Pierowall** U.K.
76 C2 **Pierre** U.S.A.
44 G4 **Pierrelatte** France
59 J4 **Pietermaritzburg** S. Africa
59 H1 **Pietersburg** S. Africa
48 G5 **Pietra Spada, Passo di** *pass* Italy
59 J3 **Piet Retief** S. Africa
47 M7 **Pietrosa** *mt* Romania
69 F4 **Pigeon** U.S.A.
69 F5 **Pigeon Bay** *b.* Can.
80 D6 **Pigg** *r.* U.S.A.
77 F4 **Piggott** U.S.A.
59 J2 **Pigg's Peak** Swaziland
91 D3 **Pigüé** Arg.
84 C2 **Piguicas** *mt* Mex.
22 E4 **Pihani** India
26 E3 **Pi He** *r.* China
37 V6 **Pihlajavesi** *l.* Fin.
37 R6 **Pihlava** Fin.
36 T5 **Pihtipudas** Fin.
36 T4 **Piippola** Fin.
36 V4 **Piispajärvi** Fin.
84 D4 **Pijijiapan** Mex.
50 E3 **Pikalevo** Rus. Fed.
80 D3 **Pike** U.S.A.
69 G3 **Pike Bay** Can.
4 G4 **Pikelot** *i.* Micronesia
58 C6 **Piketberg** S. Africa
80 B6 **Pikeville** U.S.A.
30 B4 **Pikou** China
91 E3 **Pila** Arg.
46 H4 **Piła** Pol.
59 G2 **Pilanesberg National Park** S. Africa
91 E2 **Pilar** Arg.
88 E3 **Pilar** Para.
31 B5 **Pilas** *i.* Phil.
91 B4 **Pilcaniyeu** Arg.
88 E2 **Pilcomayo** *r.* Bol./Para.
31 B3 **Pili** Phil.
22 D3 **Pilibhit** India
27 □ **Pillar Pt** *pt H.K.* China
91 E2 **Pillo, Isla del** *i.* Arg.
90 C2 **Pilões, Serra dos** *mts* Brazil
74 D2 **Pilot Peak** *summit* U.S.A.
8 G4 **Pilot, The** *mt* Austr.
77 F6 **Pilottown** U.S.A.
37 R8 **Piltene** Latvia
86 F6 **Pimenta Bueno** Brazil
22 C5 **Pimpalner** India
22 D2 **Pin** *r.* India
75 F6 **Pinacate, Cerro del** *summit* Mex.
22 D4 **Pinahat** India
75 G5 **Pinaleno Mts** *mts* U.S.A.
31 B3 **Pinamalayan** Phil.
91 F3 **Pinamar** Arg.
33 B1 **Pinang** *i.* Malaysia
16 F2 **Pınarbaşı** Turkey
83 H4 **Pinar del Río** Cuba
51 C7 **Pınarhisar** Turkey
47 K5 **Pińczów** Pol.
22 D3 **Pindar** *r.* India
87 J4 **Pindaré** *r.* Brazil
22 C2 **Pindi Gheb** Pak.
49 J5 **Pindos** *mts* Greece
Pindu Pass *see* **Pêdo La**
Pindus Mts *mts see* **Pindos**
75 G4 **Pine** *AZ* U.S.A.
68 E4 **Pine** *r. MI* U.S.A.
68 E3 **Pine** *r. MI* U.S.A.
68 C3 **Pine** *r. WI* U.S.A.
77 E5 **Pine Bluff** U.S.A.
72 F3 **Pine Bluffs** U.S.A.
67 K4 **Pine, C.** *c.* Can.
68 A3 **Pine City** U.S.A.
6 D3 **Pine Creek** Austr.
80 E4 **Pine Creek** *r.* U.S.A.
74 B2 **Pinecrest** U.S.A.
74 C3 **Pinedale** *CA* U.S.A.
72 E3 **Pinedale** *WY* U.S.A.
65 K4 **Pine Falls** Can.
74 C3 **Pine Flat Lake** *l.* U.S.A.
50 G1 **Pinega** Rus. Fed.
50 G1 **Pinega** *r.* Rus. Fed.
81 E4 **Pine Grove** U.S.A.
79 D6 **Pine Hills** U.S.A.
65 H3 **Pinehouse** Can.
68 A3 **Pine Island** Can.
92 A3 **Pine Island Bay** *b.* Ant.
81 F3 **Pine Lake** U.S.A.
77 E6 **Pineland** U.S.A.
74 B4 **Pine Mt** *mt* U.S.A.
75 F4 **Pine Peak** *summit* U.S.A.
64 G2 **Pine Point** Can.
76 C3 **Pine Ridge** U.S.A.
74 C3 **Pineridge** U.S.A.
48 B2 **Pinerolo** Italy
77 E5 **Pines, Lake O' the** *l.* U.S.A.
59 J4 **Pinetown** S. Africa
80 B6 **Pineville** *KY* U.S.A.
77 E6 **Pineville** *LA* U.S.A.
80 C6 **Pineville** *WV* U.S.A.
26 B2 **Ping'an** China
27 B6 **Pingbian** China
26 F3 **Ping Dao** *i.* China
26 D2 **Pingding** China
26 D3 **Pingdingshan** China
26 F2 **Pingdu** China
30 C2 **Pinggang** China
27 C6 **Pingguo** China
27 E5 **Pinghe** China
27 D4 **Pingjiang** China
27 D5 **Pingle** China
26 C3 **Pingli** China
26 C3 **Pingliang** China
26 D2 **Pinglu** China
26 C2 **Pingluo** China
27 F5 **Pingnan** *Fujian* China
27 D6 **Pingnan** *Guangxi* China
26 F1 **Pingquan** China
26 E2 **Pingshan** China
27 D5 **Pingshi** China
27 F5 **Pingtan** China
27 C5 **Pingtang** China
27 F6 **P'ing-tung** Taiwan
26 B3 **Pingwu** China
27 C6 **Pingxiang** *Guangxi* China
27 D5 **Pingxiang** *Jiangxi* China
27 F5 **Pingyang** China
26 D2 **Pingyao** China
26 E3 **Pingyi** China
26 E2 **Pingyin** China
26 E3 **Pingyu** China
27 E5 **Pingyuan** China
27 B6 **Pingyuanjie** China
27 □ **Ping Yuen Ho** *r. H.K.* China
27 C5 **Pingzhai** China
87 J4 **Pinheiro** Brazil
91 G1 **Pinheiro Machado** Brazil
39 D7 **Pinhoe** U.K.
33 A2 **Pini** *i.* Indon.
64 E3 **Pink Mountain** Can.
9 D4 **Pinnacle** *mt* N.Z.
8 C3 **Pinnaroo** Austr.
43 H1 **Pinneberg** Ger.
74 C4 **Pinos, Mt** *mt* U.S.A.
84 C3 **Pinotepa Nacional** Mex.
7 G4 **Pins, Î. des** *i.* New Caledonia
51 C4 **Pinsk** Belarus
69 G4 **Pins, Pointe aux** *pt* Can.
86 □ **Pinta, Isla** *i. Galapagos Is* Ecuador
75 F5 **Pinta, Sierra** *summit* U.S.A.
75 F3 **Pintura** U.S.A.
75 E3 **Pioche** U.S.A.
57 C4 **Piodi** Congo(Zaire)
12 K1 **Pioner, O.** *i.* Rus. Fed.
47 K3 **Pionerskiy** Rus. Fed.
47 K5 **Pionki** Pol.
9 E3 **Piopio** N.Z.
86 F4 **Piorini, Lago** *l.* Brazil
47 J5 **Piotrków Trybunalski** Pol.
19 F5 **Pip** Iran
30 E2 **Pipa Dingzi** *mt* China
22 C4 **Pipar** India
22 D5 **Piparia** India
49 L5 **Piperi** *i.* Greece
74 D3 **Piper Peak** *summit* U.S.A.
75 F3 **Pipe Spring Nat. Mon.** *nat. park* U.S.A.
76 D3 **Pipestone** U.S.A.
66 B3 **Pipestone** *r.* Can.
9 E3 **Pipiriki** N.Z.
22 C3 **Pipli** India
67 F4 **Pipmuacan, Réservoir** *resr* Can.
23 E4 **Pipra Dam** *dam* India
80 A4 **Piqua** U.S.A.
90 A2 **Piquiri** *r. Mato Grosso do Sul* Brazil
90 B4 **Piquiri** *r. Paraná* Brazil
90 C2 **Piracanjuba** Brazil
90 C3 **Piracicaba** Brazil
90 D2 **Piracicaba** *r. Minas Gerais* Brazil
90 C3 **Piracicaba** *r. São Paulo* Brazil
90 C3 **Piraçununga** Brazil
87 K4 **Piracuruca** Brazil
Piraeus *see* **Peiraias**
90 C4 **Piraí do Sul** Brazil
90 C3 **Pirajuí** Brazil
22 C5 **Piram I.** *i.* India
90 B2 **Piranhas** Brazil
90 B2 **Piranhas** *r. Goiás* Brazil
87 L5 **Piranhas** *r. Paraíba/Rio Grande do Norte* Brazil
89 C4 **Piraparaná** *r.* Col.
90 B3 **Pirapó** *r.* Brazil
90 D2 **Pirapora** Brazil
91 G1 **Piratini** Brazil
91 G1 **Piratini** *r.* Brazil
22 D4 **Pirawa** India
91 C4 **Pire Mahuida, Sa** *mts* Arg.
90 C2 **Pires do Rio** Brazil
23 G4 **Pirganj** Bangl.
87 K4 **Piripiri** Brazil
89 C2 **Piritu** Venez.
90 A2 **Pirizal** Brazil
42 F5 **Pirmasens** Ger.
49 K3 **Pirot** Yugo.
22 C2 **Pir Panjal Pass** India
22 C2 **Pir Panjal Range** *mts* India/Pak.
89 A3 **Pirre, Co** *mt* Panama
17 M2 **Pirsaat** Azer.
17 M1 **Pirsaatçay** *r.* Azer.
25 F7 **Piru** Indon.
48 D3 **Pisa** Italy
88 B1 **Pisagua** Chile
9 B6 **Pisa, Mt** *mt* N.Z.
81 F4 **Piscataway** U.S.A.
86 C6 **Pisco** Peru
86 C6 **Pisco, B. de** *b.* Peru
81 F3 **Piseco Lake** *l.* U.S.A.
46 G6 **Písek** Czech Rep.
19 F5 **Pishīn** Iran
22 A3 **Pishin** Pak.
19 G4 **Pishin Lora** *r.* Pak.
88 C3 **Pissis, Cerro** *mt* Arg.
48 G4 **Pisticci** Italy
48 D3 **Pistoia** Italy
45 D1 **Pisuerga** *r.* Spain
72 B3 **Pit** *r.* U.S.A.
54 A3 **Pita** Guinea
67 G3 **Pitaga** Can.
84 E3 **Pital** Mex.
89 A4 **Pitalito** Col.
90 B4 **Pitanga** Brazil
90 D2 **Pitangui** Brazil
8 D3 **Pitarpunga L.** *l.* Austr.
5 P7 **Pitcairn Islands** *i. Pitcairn Is* Pac. Oc.
5 P7 **Pitcairn Islands** *terr.* Pac. Oc.
36 R4 **Piteå** Sweden
36 R4 **Piteälven** *r.* Sweden
51 H5 **Piterka** Rus. Fed.
49 L2 **Piteşti** Romania
21 C2 **Pithapuram** India
73 D6 **Pitiquito** Mex.
50 D2 **Pitkyaranta** Rus. Fed.
40 E4 **Pitlochry** U.K.
91 B3 **Pitrufquén** Chile
59 F2 **Pitsane Siding** Botswana
40 F4 **Pitscottie** U.K.
64 D4 **Pitt I.** *i.* Can.
7 J6 **Pitt Island** *i.* Pac. Oc.
77 E4 **Pittsburg** U.S.A.
80 D4 **Pittsburgh** U.S.A.
68 B6 **Pittsfield** *IL* U.S.A.
81 G3 **Pittsfield** *MA* U.S.A.
81 J2 **Pittsfield** *ME* U.S.A.
81 H3 **Pittsfield** *NH* U.S.A.
81 G3 **Pittsfield** *VT* U.S.A.
65 K2 **Pitz Lake** *l.* Can.
90 D3 **Piumhí** Brazil
86 B5 **Piura** Peru
74 C4 **Piute Peak** *summit* U.S.A.
23 E3 **Piuthan** Nepal
47 O6 **Pivdennyy Buh** *r.* Ukr.
48 F2 **Pivka** Slovenia
22 D1 **Pixa** China
84 E3 **Pixoyal** Mex.
46 E7 **Piz Buin** *mt* Austria/Switz.
50 H3 **Pizhma** Rus. Fed.
50 H3 **Pizhma** *r.* Rus. Fed.
67 K4 **Placentia** Can.
67 K4 **Placentia B.** *b.* Can.
31 B4 **Placer** Phil.
31 C4 **Placer** Phil.
74 B2 **Placerville** U.S.A.
83 J4 **Placetas** Cuba
81 H4 **Plainfield** *CT* U.S.A.
68 C5 **Plainfield** *IL* U.S.A.
68 C3 **Plainfield** *WI* U.S.A.
68 A3 **Plainview** *MN* U.S.A.
76 D3 **Plainview** *NE* U.S.A.
77 C5 **Plainview** *TX* U.S.A.
81 J1 **Plaisted** U.S.A.
13 T3 **Plamennyy** Rus. Fed.
64 G4 **Plamondon** Can.
33 E4 **Plampang** Indon.
43 L5 **Planá** Czech Rep.
74 B3 **Planada** U.S.A.
90 C1 **Planaltina** Brazil
91 B2 **Planchón, P. de** *pass* Arg.
89 B2 **Planeta Rica** Col.
94 F6 **Planet Deep** *depth* Pac. Oc.
76 D3 **Plankinton** U.S.A.
68 C5 **Plano** *IL* U.S.A.
77 D5 **Plano** *TX* U.S.A.
79 D7 **Plantation** U.S.A.
77 F6 **Plaquemine** U.S.A.
45 C2 **Plasencia** Spain
81 K1 **Plaster Rock** Can.
28 E2 **Plastun** Rus. Fed.
86 B4 **Plata, I. la** *i.* Ecuador
48 E6 **Platani** *r. Sicily* Italy
91 F2 **Plata, Río de la** *chan.* Arg./Uru.
59 H4 **Platberg** *mt* S. Africa
13 V4 **Platinum** U.S.A.
89 B2 **Plato** Col.
76 C3 **Platte** *r.* U.S.A.
68 B4 **Platteville** U.S.A.
43 L6 **Plattling** Ger.
81 G2 **Plattsburgh** U.S.A.
76 E3 **Plattsmouth** U.S.A.
43 L1 **Plau** Ger.
43 L4 **Plauen** Ger.
43 L1 **Plauer See** *l.* Ger.
50 F4 **Plavsk** Rus. Fed.
73 E6 **Playa Noriega, L.** *l.* Mex.
86 B4 **Playas** Ecuador
32 D2 **Plây Cu** Vietnam
65 K4 **Playgreen L.** *l.* Can.
84 A1 **Playón** Mex.
91 C3 **Plaza Huincul** Arg.
81 J4 **Pleasant Bay** *b.* U.S.A.
75 G1 **Pleasant Grove** U.S.A.
75 F5 **Pleasant, Lake** *l.* U.S.A.
75 H5 **Pleasanton** *NM* U.S.A.
77 D6 **Pleasanton** *TX* U.S.A.
9 C6 **Pleasant Point** N.Z.
75 H3 **Pleasant View** U.S.A.
81 F5 **Pleasantville** U.S.A.
78 C4 **Pleasure Ridge Park** U.S.A.
44 F4 **Pleaux** France
32 C2 **Plei Doch** Vietnam
43 J5 **Pleinfeld** Ger.
9 F2 **Plenty, Bay of** *b.* N.Z.
72 F1 **Plentywood** U.S.A.
50 G2 **Plesetsk** Rus. Fed.
67 F3 **Plétipi L.** *l.* Can.
43 F3 **Plettenberg** Ger.
58 E7 **Plettenberg Bay** S. Africa
49 L3 **Pleven** Bulg.
49 H3 **Pljevlja** Yugo.
47 J4 **Płock** Pol.
48 G3 **Pločno** *mt* Bos.-Herz.
50 D2 **Plodovoye** Rus. Fed.
44 C3 **Ploemeur** France
49 M2 **Ploieşti** Romania
65 H3 **Plonge, Lac la** *l.* Can.
47 P2 **Ploskosh'** Rus. Fed.
50 G3 **Ploskoye** Rus. Fed.
46 G4 **Płoty** Pol.
44 B2 **Ploudalmézeau** France
44 B2 **Plouzané** France
49 L3 **Plovdiv** Bulg.
68 C3 **Plover** U.S.A.
68 C3 **Plover** *r.* U.S.A.
27 □ **Plover Cove Res.** *resr H.K.* China
84 C4 **Pluma Hidalgo** Mex.
81 G4 **Plum I.** *i.* U.S.A.
72 C2 **Plummer** U.S.A.
37 R9 **Plungė** Lith.
47 N3 **Plyeshchanitsy** Belarus
32 A1 **Ply Huey Wati, Khao** *mt* Myanmar/Thai.
83 M5 **Plymouth** Montserrat
39 C7 **Plymouth** U.K.
74 B2 **Plymouth** *CA* U.S.A.
68 D5 **Plymouth** *IN* U.S.A.
81 H4 **Plymouth** *MA* U.S.A.
81 H3 **Plymouth** *NH* U.S.A.
78 F3 **Plymouth** *PA* U.S.A.
68 D4 **Plymouth** *WI* U.S.A.
81 H4 **Plymouth Bay** *b.* U.S.A.
39 D5 **Plynlimon** *h.* U.K.
46 F6 **Plzeň** Czech Rep.
54 B3 **Pô** Burkina
93 L8 **Pobeda Ice Island** *ice feature* Ant.
12 K5 **Pobedy, Pik** *mt* China/Kyrg.
77 F4 **Pocahontas** U.S.A.
80 C5 **Pocatalico** *r.* U.S.A.
72 D3 **Pocatello** U.S.A.
51 C5 **Pochayiv** Ukr.
50 E4 **Pochep** Rus. Fed.
50 H4 **Pochinki** Rus. Fed.
50 E4 **Pochinok** Rus. Fed.
41 B6 **Pocket, The** *h.* Rep. of Ireland
46 F6 **Pocking** Ger.
38 G4 **Pocklington** U.K.
90 E1 **Poções** Brazil
81 F5 **Pocomoke City** U.S.A.
81 F6 **Pocomoke Sound** *b.* U.S.A.
90 A2 **Poconé** Brazil
81 F4 **Pocono Mountains** *h.* U.S.A.
81 F4 **Pocono Summit** U.S.A.
90 C3 **Poços de Caldas** Brazil
50 D3 **Poddor'ye** Rus. Fed.
51 F5 **Podgorenskiy** Rus. Fed.
49 H3 **Podgorica** Yugo.
12 K4 **Podgornoye** Rus. Fed.
21 B3 **Podile** India
13 L3 **Podkamennaya** *r.* Rus. Fed.
86 C4 **Podocarpus, Parque Nacional** *nat. park* Ecuador
50 F4 **Podol'sk** Rus. Fed.
50 E2 **Podporozh'ye** Rus. Fed.
48 G1 **Podravina** *reg.* Hungary
49 J3 **Podujevo** Yugo.
50 H2 **Podvoloch'ye** Rus. Fed.
50 J2 **Podz'** Rus. Fed.
58 C4 **Pofadder** S. Africa
69 G2 **Pogamasing** Can.
51 E4 **Pogar** Rus. Fed.
48 D3 **Poggibonsi** Italy
49 J4 **Pogradec** Albania
90 A2 **Poguba** *r.* Brazil
30 E5 **P'ohang** S. Korea
4 G4 **Pohnpei** *i.* Micronesia
51 D5 **Pohrebyshche** Ukr.
22 D4 **Pohri** India
49 K3 **Poiana Mare** Romania
56 C4 **Poie** Congo(Zaire)
92 C6 **Poinsett, C.** *c.* Ant.
74 A2 **Point Arena** U.S.A.
69 K2 **Point-Comfort** Can.
83 M5 **Pointe-à-Pitre** Guadeloupe
69 G3 **Pointe au Baril Sta.** Can.
56 B4 **Pointe-Noire** Congo
62 B3 **Point Hope** U.S.A.
64 G1 **Point Lake** *l.* Can.
69 F5 **Point Pelee National Park** Can.
81 F4 **Point Pleasant** *NJ* U.S.A.
80 B5 **Point Pleasant** *WV* U.S.A.
69 K3 **Poisson Blanc, Lac du** *l.* Can.
44 E3 **Poitiers** France
27 □ **Poi Toi I.** *i. H.K.* China
44 D3 **Poitou** *reg.* France
90 E1 **Pojuca** Brazil
22 B4 **Pokaran** India
23 E3 **Pokhara** Nepal
56 C3 **Poko** Congo(Zaire)
22 A4 **Pokran** Pak.
28 C2 **Pokrovka** Rus. Fed.
28 B3 **Pokrovka** Rus. Fed.
13 O3 **Pokrovsk** Rus. Fed.
51 F6 **Pokrovskoye** Rus. Fed.
50 H2 **Pokshen'ga** *r.* Rus. Fed.
31 B3 **Pola** Phil.
75 G4 **Polacca** U.S.A.
75 G4 **Polacca Wash** *r.* U.S.A.
45 D1 **Pola de Lena** Spain
45 D1 **Pola de Siero** Spain
81 F3 **Poland** U.S.A.
34 G3 **Poland** *country* Europe
66 D3 **Polar Bear Provincial Park** *res.* Can.
16 D2 **Polatlı** Turkey
50 D4 **Polatsk** Belarus
47 N3 **Polatskaya Nizina** *lowland* Belarus
21 C2 **Polavaram** India
36 R3 **Polcirkeln** Sweden
50 H2 **Poldarsa** Rus. Fed.
18 B2 **Pol Dasht** Iran
19 F2 **Pole-Khatum** Iran
19 H3 **Pol-e-Khomrī** Afgh.
50 B4 **Polessk** Rus. Fed.
33 E3 **Polewali** Indon.
55 D4 **Poli** Cameroon
46 G4 **Police** Pol.
48 G4 **Policoro** Italy
44 G3 **Poligny** France
31 B3 **Polillo** *i.* Phil.
31 B3 **Polillo Islands** *is* Phil.
31 B3 **Polillo Strait** *chan.* Phil.
16 D4 **Polis** Cyprus
51 D5 **Polis'ke** Ukr.
46 H5 **Polkowice** Pol.
21 B4 **Pollachi** India
43 H3 **Polle** Ger.
45 H3 **Pollença** Spain
48 G5 **Pollino, Monte** *mt* Italy
36 U1 **Polmak** Norway
36 V4 **Polo** Fin.
68 C5 **Polo** U.S.A.
51 F6 **Polohy** Ukr.
50 J3 **Polom** Rus. Fed.
31 C5 **Polomoloc** Phil.
21 C5 **Polonnaruwa** Sri Lanka
51 C5 **Polonne** Ukr.
39 C7 **Polperro** U.K.
72 D2 **Polson** U.S.A.
50 G1 **Polta** *r.* Rus. Fed.
51 E5 **Poltava** Ukr.
28 B2 **Poltavka** Rus. Fed.
37 T7 **Põltsamaa** Estonia
37 U7 **Põlva** Estonia
36 V5 **Polvijärvi** Fin.
36 X2 **Polyarnyy** Rus. Fed.
13 T3 **Polyarnyy** Rus. Fed.
36 X3 **Polyarnyye Zori** Rus. Fed.
49 K4 **Polygyros** Greece
49 K4 **Polykastro** Greece
94 H6 **Polynesia** *is* Pac. Oc.
37 S6 **Pomarkku** Fin.
90 D3 **Pomba** *r.* Brazil
45 B3 **Pombal** Port.
90 B3 **Pombo** *r.* Brazil
59 J4 **Pomeroy** S. Africa
41 E3 **Pomeroy** U.K.
80 B5 **Pomeroy** U.S.A.
48 E4 **Pomezia** Italy
58 E2 **Pomfret** S. Africa
6 F2 **Pomio** P.N.G.
74 D4 **Pomona** U.S.A.
49 M3 **Pomorie** Bulg.
46 G3 **Pomorska, Zatoka** *b.* Pol.
50 E1 **Pomorskiy Bereg** *coastal area* Rus. Fed.
Pomo Tso *l. see* **Puma Yumco**
79 D7 **Pompano Beach** U.S.A.
90 D2 **Pompéu** Brazil
50 H3 **Ponazyrevo** Rus. Fed.
77 D4 **Ponca City** U.S.A.
83 L5 **Ponce** Puerto Rico
73 F4 **Poncha Springs** U.S.A.
66 E3 **Poncheville, Lac** *l.* Can.
21 B4 **Pondicherry** India
63 L2 **Pond Inlet** Can.
67 J3 **Ponds, Island of** *i.* Can.
45 C1 **Ponferrada** Spain
9 F4 **Pongaroa** N.Z.
55 E4 **Pongo** *watercourse* Sudan
59 J3 **Pongola** *r.* S. Africa
59 J3 **Pongolapoort Dam** *resr* S. Africa
47 P3 **Ponizov'ye** Rus. Fed.
21 B3 **Ponnaivar** *r.* India
21 A4 **Ponnani** India
23 H5 **Ponnyadaung Range** *mts* Myanmar
64 G4 **Ponoka** Can.
54 □ **Ponta do Sol** Cape Verde
90 B4 **Ponta Grossa** Brazil
90 C2 **Pontalina** Brazil
44 H2 **Pont-à-Mousson** France
90 A3 **Ponta Porã** Brazil
44 H3 **Pontarlier** France
77 F6 **Pontchartrain, L.** *l.* U.S.A.
42 C4 **Pont-de-Loup** Belgium
45 B3 **Ponte de Sôr** Port.
38 F4 **Pontefract** U.K.
38 F2 **Ponteland** U.K.
87 G7 **Pontes-e-Lacerda** Brazil
45 B1 **Pontevedra** Spain
68 C5 **Pontiac** *IL* U.S.A.
69 F4 **Pontiac** *MI* U.S.A.
33 C3 **Pontianak** Indon.
44 C2 **Pontivy** France
44 B3 **Pont-l'Abbé** France
44 F2 **Pontoise** France
65 K4 **Ponton** Can.
77 F5 **Pontotoc** U.S.A.
48 D2 **Pontremoli** Italy
42 A5 **Pont-Ste-Maxence** France
69 H3 **Pontypool** Can.
39 D6 **Pontypool** U.K.
39 D6 **Pontypridd** U.K.
48 E4 **Ponza, Isola di** *i.* Italy
48 E4 **Ponziane, Isole** *is* Italy
39 F7 **Poole** U.K.
Poona *see* **Pune**
8 D2 **Pooncarie** Austr.
8 E1 **Poopelloe, L.** *l.* Austr.
86 E7 **Poopó, Lago de** *l.* Bol.
9 E1 **Poor Knights Is** *is* N.Z.
54 B3 **Pô, Parc National de** *nat. park* Burkina
89 A4 **Popayán** Col.
42 A4 **Poperinge** Belgium
13 M2 **Popigay** *r.* Rus. Fed.
8 C2 **Popiltah** Austr.
8 C2 **Popilta L.** *l.* Austr.
72 F1 **Poplar** U.S.A.
65 K4 **Poplar** *r.* Can.
77 F4 **Poplar Bluff** U.S.A.
80 C6 **Poplar Camp** U.S.A.
77 F6 **Poplarville** U.S.A.
84 C3 **Popocatépetl** *volc.* Mex.
56 B4 **Popokabaka** Congo(Zaire)
49 M3 **Popovo** Bulg.
43 J3 **Poppenberg** *h.* Ger.
47 K6 **Poprad** Slovakia
19 G5 **Porali** *r.* Pak.
9 F4 **Porangahau** N.Z.
90 C1 **Porangatu** Brazil
22 B5 **Porbandar** India
89 B3 **Porce** *r.* Col.
64 C4 **Porcher I.** *i.* Can.
62 E3 **Porcupine** *r.* Can./U.S.A.
67 J3 **Porcupine, Cape** *c.* Can.
65 J4 **Porcupine Hills** *h.* Can.
68 C2 **Porcupine Mts** *mts* U.S.A.
65 J4 **Porcupine Plain** Can.
65 J4 **Porcupine Prov. Forest** *res.* Can.
89 C3 **Pore** Col.
48 E2 **Poreč** Croatia
50 H4 **Poretskoye** Rus. Fed.
37 R6 **Pori** Fin.
9 E4 **Porirua** N.Z.
50 D3 **Porkhov** Rus. Fed.
89 E2 **Porlamar** Venez.
44 C3 **Pornic** France
31 C4 **Poro** *i.* Phil.
24 G2 **Poronaysk** Rus. Fed.
49 K6 **Poros** Greece
50 E2 **Porosozero** Rus. Fed.
92 C6 **Porpoise Bay** *b.* Ant.
36 T1 **Porsangen** *chan.* Norway
37 L7 **Porsgrunn** Norway
16 C2 **Porsuk** *r.* Turkey
8 B3 **Port Adelaide** Austr.
41 E3 **Portadown** U.K.
41 F3 **Portaferry** U.K.
81 J1 **Portage** *ME* U.S.A.
68 E4 **Portage** *MI* U.S.A.
68 C4 **Portage** *WI* U.S.A.
65 K5 **Portage la Prairie** Can.
76 C1 **Portal** U.S.A.
64 E5 **Port Alberni** Can.
8 F5 **Port Albert** Austr.
45 C3 **Portalegre** Port.
77 C5 **Portales** U.S.A.
64 C3 **Port Alexander** U.S.A.
59 G6 **Port Alfred** S. Africa
64 D4 **Port Alice** Can.
80 D4 **Port Allegany** U.S.A.
77 F6 **Port Allen** U.S.A.
72 B1 **Port Angeles** U.S.A.
41 D4 **Portarlington** Rep. of Ireland
6 E6 **Port Arthur** Austr.
77 E6 **Port Arthur** U.S.A.
40 B5 **Port Askaig** U.K.
8 A2 **Port Augusta** Austr.
83 K5 **Port-au-Prince** Haiti
69 F3 **Port Austin** U.S.A.
67 J3 **Port aux Choix** Can.
41 F3 **Portavogie** U.K.
58 D7 **Port Beaufort** S. Africa
15 H5 **Port Blair** Andaman and Nicobar Is
69 H3 **Port Bolster** Can.
45 H1 **Portbou** Spain
69 G4 **Port Burwell** Can.
8 D5 **Port Campbell** Austr.
69 H3 **Port Carling** Can.
9 C6 **Port Chalmers** N.Z.
79 D7 **Port Charlotte** U.S.A.
81 G4 **Port Chester** U.S.A.
64 C4 **Port Clements** Can.
80 B4 **Port Clinton** U.S.A.
81 J3 **Port Clyde** U.S.A.
69 H4 **Port Colborne** Can.
64 E5 **Port Coquitlam** Can.
69 H4 **Port Credit** Can.
83 K5 **Port-de-Paix** Haiti
32 B5 **Port Dickson** Malaysia
80 C3 **Port Dover** Can.
68 D3 **Porte des Morts** *chan.* U.S.A.
64 C4 **Port Edward** Can.
59 J5 **Port Edward** S. Africa
68 C3 **Port Edwards** U.S.A.
90 D1 **Porteirinha** Brazil
87 H4 **Portel** Brazil
69 G3 **Port Elgin** Can.
59 F6 **Port Elizabeth** S. Africa
40 B5 **Port Ellen** U.K.
8 B3 **Port Elliot** Austr.
38 C3 **Port Erin** U.K.
65 H2 **Porter Lake** *l.* Can.
64 C3 **Porter Landing** Can.
58 C6 **Porterville** S. Africa
74 C3 **Porterville** U.S.A.
8 D5 **Port Fairy** Austr.
9 E2 **Port Fitzroy** N.Z.
Port Fuad *see* **Bûr Fu'ad**
56 A4 **Port-Gentil** Gabon
8 B2 **Port Germein** Austr.
77 F6 **Port Gibson** U.S.A.
40 D5 **Port Glasgow** U.K.
54 C4 **Port Harcourt** Nigeria
64 D4 **Port Hardy** Can.
Port Harrison *see* **Inukjuak**
67 H4 **Port Hawkesbury** Can.
39 D6 **Porthcawl** U.K.
6 B4 **Port Hedland** Austr.
81 G2 **Port Henry** U.S.A.
39 B7 **Porthleven** U.K.
39 C5 **Porthmadog** U.K.
69 H4 **Port Hope** Can.
67 J3 **Port Hope Simpson** Can.
69 F4 **Port Huron** U.S.A.
17 M2 **Port-İliç** Azer.
45 B4 **Portimão** Port.
27 □ **Port Island** *i. H.K.* China
8 H2 **Port Jackson** *in.* Austr.
81 G4 **Port Jefferson** U.S.A.
81 F4 **Port Jervis** U.S.A.
86 G2 **Port Kaituma** Guyana
8 H3 **Port Kembla** Austr.
8 G2 **Portland** *N.S.W.* Austr.
8 C5 **Portland** *Vic.* Austr.
68 E5 **Portland** *IN* U.S.A.
81 H3 **Portland** *ME* U.S.A.
72 B2 **Portland** *OR* U.S.A.
64 C3 **Portland Canal** *in.* Can.
9 F3 **Portland I.** *i.* N.Z.
39 E7 **Portland, Isle of** *pen.* U.K.
41 D4 **Portlaoise** Rep. of Ireland
77 D6 **Port Lavaca** U.S.A.
41 D5 **Portlaw** Rep. of Ireland
40 F3 **Portlethen** U.K.
6 D5 **Port Lincoln** Austr.
54 A4 **Port Loko** Sierra Leone
8 C5 **Port MacDonnell** Austr.
64 D4 **Port McNeill** Can.
7 F5 **Port Macquarie** Austr.
67 H2 **Port Manvers** *in.* Can.
67 H4 **Port-Menier** Can.
62 B4 **Port Moller** *b.* U.S.A.
72 B1 **Port Moody** Can.
6 E2 **Port Moresby** P.N.G.
40 B2 **Portnaguran** U.K.
40 B5 **Portnahaven** U.K.
79 F7 **Port Nelson** Bahamas
40 B2 **Port Nis** U.K.
58 B4 **Port Nolloth** S. Africa
Port-Nouveau-Québec *see* **Kangiqsualujjuaq**
Porto *see* **Oporto**
86 E5 **Porto Acre** Brazil
90 B3 **Porto Alegre** *Mato Grosso do Sul* Brazil
88 F4 **Porto Alegre** *Rio Grande do Sul* Brazil
87 G6 **Porto Artur** Brazil
87 G6 **Porto dos Gaúchos Óbidos** Brazil
87 G7 **Porto Esperidião** Brazil
48 D3 **Portoferraio** Italy
87 J5 **Porto Franco** Brazil
89 E2 **Port of Spain** Trinidad and Tobago
48 E2 **Portogruaro** Italy
54 □ **Porto Inglês** Cape Verde
90 A2 **Porto Jofre** Brazil
74 B2 **Portola** U.S.A.
48 D2 **Portomaggiore** Italy
87 G8 **Porto Murtinho** Brazil
87 J6 **Porto Nacional** Brazil
54 C4 **Porto-Novo** Benin
Porto Novo *see* **Parangipettai**
90 B3 **Porto Primavera, Represa** *resr* Brazil
72 A3 **Port Orford** U.S.A.
87 H4 **Porto Santana** Brazil
90 E2 **Porto Seguro** Brazil
48 E2 **Porto Tolle** Italy
48 C4 **Porto Torres** *Sardinia* Italy
48 C4 **Porto-Vecchio** *Corsica* France
86 F5 **Porto Velho** Brazil
86 B4 **Portoviejo** Ecuador
40 C6 **Portpatrick** U.K.
69 H3 **Port Perry** Can.
8 E5 **Port Phillip Bay** *b.* Austr.
8 B2 **Port Pirie** Austr.
39 B7 **Portreath** U.K.
40 B3 **Portree** U.K.
64 E5 **Port Renfrew** Can.
69 G4 **Port Rowan** Can.
80 E5 **Port Royal** U.S.A.
41 E2 **Portrush** U.K.
55 F1 **Port Said** Egypt
79 C6 **Port St Joe** U.S.A.
59 H5 **Port St Johns** S. Africa
38 C3 **Port St Mary** U.K.
41 D2 **Portsalon** Rep. of Ireland
69 F4 **Port Sanilac** U.S.A.
69 H3 **Port Severn** Can.
27 □ **Port Shelter** *b. H.K.* China
59 J5 **Port Shepstone** S. Africa
64 C4 **Port Simpson** Can.
39 F7 **Portsmouth** U.K.
81 H3 **Portsmouth** *NH* U.S.A.
80 B5 **Portsmouth** *OH* U.S.A.
81 E6 **Portsmouth** *VA* U.S.A.
40 F3 **Portsoy** U.K.
41 E2 **Portstewart** U.K.
55 F3 **Port Sudan** Sudan
79 B6 **Port Sulphur** U.S.A.
39 D6 **Port Talbot** U.K.
36 U2 **Porttipahdan tekojärvi** *l.* Fin.
34 E5 **Portugal** *country* Europe
89 C2 **Portuguesa** *r.* Venez.
41 C4 **Portumna** Rep. of Ireland
44 F5 **Port-Vendres** France
7 G3 **Port Vila** Vanuatu
36 X2 **Port Vladimir** Rus. Fed.
9 E2 **Port Waikato** N.Z.
8 B3 **Port Wakefield** Austr.
68 D4 **Port Washington** U.S.A.
40 D6 **Port William** U.K.
68 B2 **Port Wing** U.S.A.
91 D2 **Porvenir** Arg.
37 T6 **Porvoo** Fin.
45 D1 **Posada de Llanera** Spain
88 E3 **Posadas** Arg.
49 H2 **Posavina** *reg.* Bos.-Herz./Croatia
69 F3 **Posen** U.S.A.
17 L5 **Posht-é-Kūh** *mts* Iran
18 C2 **Posht Kūh** *h.* Iran
36 V3 **Posio** Fin.
25 E7 **Poso** Indon.
17 J1 **Posof** Turkey
30 D6 **Posŏng** S. Korea
90 C1 **Posse** Brazil
92 A5 **Possession Is** *is* Ant.
43 K4 **Pößneck** Ger.
77 C5 **Post** U.S.A.
66 E2 **Poste-de-la-Baleine** Can.

58 E4 Postmasburg S. Africa
67 J3 Postville Can.
68 B4 Postville U.S.A.
48 G3 Posušje Bos.-Herz.
28 B3 Pos'yet Rus. Fed.
59 G3 Potchefstroom S. Africa
77 E5 Poteau U.S.A.
87 L5 Potengi r. Brazil
48 F4 Potenza Italy
9 A7 Poteriteri, L. l. N.Z.
58 F5 Potfontein S. Africa
59 H2 Potgietersrus S. Africa
77 D6 Poth U.S.A.
66 F2 Potherie, Lac La l. Can.
51 G7 P'ot'i Georgia
87 K5 Poti r. Brazil
21 C2 Potikal India
54 D3 Potiskum Nigeria
72 D2 Pot Mt. mt U.S.A.
80 E5 Potomac r. U.S.A.
80 D5 Potomac South Branch r. U.S.A.
86 E7 Potosí Bol.
76 F4 Potosi U.S.A.
75 E4 Potosi Mt mt U.S.A.
31 B4 Pototan Phil.
43 M2 Potsdam Ger.
81 F2 Potsdam U.S.A.
39 E6 Potterne U.K.
39 G6 Potters Bar U.K.
81 F4 Pottstown U.S.A.
81 E4 Pottsville U.S.A.
21 C5 Pottuvil Sri Lanka
64 E3 Pouce Coupe Can.
67 K4 Pouch Cove Can.
81 G4 Poughkeepsie U.S.A.
81 G3 Poultney U.S.A.
38 E4 Poulton-le-Fylde U.K.
32 B1 Pou San mt Laos
90 D3 Pouso Alegre Brazil
32 B2 Poŭthĭsăt Cambodia
47 J6 Považská Bystrica Slovakia
50 E2 Povenets Rus. Fed.
9 F3 Poverty Bay b. N.Z.
49 H2 Povlen mt Yugo.
45 B2 Póvoa de Varzim Port.
51 G5 Povorino Rus. Fed.
28 C3 Povorotnyy, Mys hd Rus. Fed.
74 D5 Poway U.S.A.
72 F2 Powder r. U.S.A.
72 F3 Powder River U.S.A.
72 E2 Powell U.S.A.
80 B6 Powell r. U.S.A.
75 G3 Powell, Lake resr U.S.A.
74 C2 Powell Mt mt U.S.A.
79 E7 Powell Pt pt Bahamas
64 E5 Powell River Can.
68 D3 Powers U.S.A.
80 E6 Powhatan U.S.A.
90 A1 Poxoréu Brazil
27 E4 Poyang Hu l. China
32 □ Poyan Res. resr Sing.
68 C3 Poygan, Lake l. U.S.A.
16 E3 Pozantı Turkey
49 J2 Požarevac Yugo.
84 C2 Poza Rica Mex.
48 G2 Požega Croatia
49 J3 Požega Yugo.
28 D1 Pozharskoye Rus. Fed.
46 H4 Poznań Pol.
45 D3 Pozoblanco Spain
48 F4 Pozzuoli Italy
33 B3 Prabumulih Indon.
46 G6 Prachatice Czech Rep.
23 F6 Prachi r. India
32 B2 Prachin Buri Thai.
32 A3 Prachuap Khiri Khan Thai.
44 F5 Prades France
90 E2 Prado Brazil
46 G5 Prague Czech Rep.
Praha see Prague
54 □ Praia Cape Verde
59 K2 Praia do Bilene Moz.
90 A1 Praia Rica Brazil
68 E5 Prairie Creek Reservoir U.S.A.
77 C5 Prairie Dog Town Fork r. U.S.A.
68 B4 Prairie du Chien U.S.A.
32 B2 Prakhon Chai Thai.
32 B2 Pran r. Thai.
21 B2 Pranhita r. India
33 A2 Prapat Indon.
53 K6 Praslin i. Seychelles
49 M7 Prasonisi, Akra pt Greece
90 C2 Prata Brazil
90 C2 Prata r. Brazil
48 D3 Prato Italy
77 D4 Pratt U.S.A.
77 G5 Prattville U.S.A.
21 A2 Pravara r. India
47 K3 Pravdinsk Rus. Fed.
33 E4 Praya Indon.
32 C2 Preăh Vihear Cambodia
47 O3 Prechistoye Rus. Fed.
65 J4 Preeceville Can.
50 B4 Pregolya r. Rus. Fed.
37 U8 Preiļi Latvia
69 H1 Preissac, Lac l. Can.
32 C3 Prêk Tnaôt l. Cambodia
8 G1 Premer Austr.
44 F3 Prémery France
43 L2 Premnitz Ger.
68 B3 Prentice U.S.A.
46 F4 Prenzlau Ger.
28 C3 Preobrazheniye Rus. Fed.
46 H6 Přerov Czech Rep.
81 F2 Prescott Can.
75 F4 Prescott U.S.A.
75 F4 Prescott Valley U.S.A.
49 J3 Preševo Yugo.
76 C3 Presho U.S.A.
88 D3 Presidencia Roque Sáenz Peña Arg.
87 K5 Presidente Dutra Brazil
90 B3 Presidente Epitácio Brazil
86 F6 Presidente Hermes Brazil
90 B3 Presidente Prudente Brazil
90 B3 Presidente Venceslau Brazil
77 B6 Presidio U.S.A.
49 M3 Preslav Bulg.
47 K6 Prešov Slovakia
49 J4 Prespa, Lake l. Europe
81 K1 Presque Isle U.S.A.
68 D2 Presque Isle Pt pt U.S.A.
39 D5 Presteigne U.K.
38 E4 Preston U.K.
72 E3 Preston ID U.S.A.
68 A4 Preston MN U.S.A.
77 E4 Preston MO U.S.A.
75 E2 Preston NV U.S.A.
40 F5 Prestonpans U.K.
80 B6 Prestonsburg U.S.A.
40 D5 Prestwick U.K.
90 E1 Preto r. Bahia Brazil
90 C2 Preto r. Minas Gerais Brazil
59 H2 Pretoria S. Africa
80 E5 Prettyboy Lake l. U.S.A.
43 L3 Pretzsch Ger.
49 J5 Preveza Greece
32 C3 Prey Vêng Cambodia
13 V4 Pribilof Islands is U.S.A.
49 H3 Priboj Yugo.
67 G4 Price Can.
75 G2 Price U.S.A.
64 D4 Price I. i. Can.
79 B6 Prichard U.S.A.
37 R8 Priekule Latvia
37 T8 Priekuļi Latvia
37 S9 Prienai Lith.
58 E4 Prieska S. Africa
72 C1 Priest L. l. U.S.A.
72 C1 Priest River U.S.A.
47 J6 Prievidza Slovakia
43 L1 Prignitz reg. Ger.
48 G2 Prijedor Bos.-Herz.
49 H3 Prijepolje Yugo.
12 F5 Prikaspiyskaya Nizmennost' lowland Kazak./Rus. Fed.
49 J4 Prilep Macedonia
84 C2 Primavera Mex.
43 L5 Přimda Czech Rep.
91 D1 Primero r. Arg.
37 V6 Primorsk Rus. Fed.
28 C2 Primorskiy Kray div. Rus. Fed.
51 F6 Primorsko-Akhtarsk Rus. Fed.
65 H4 Primrose Lake l. Can.
65 H4 Prince Albert Can.
58 E6 Prince Albert S. Africa
92 B5 Prince Albert Mts mts Ant.
65 H4 Prince Albert National Park Can.
62 G2 Prince Albert Peninsula Can.
58 D6 Prince Albert Road S. Africa
62 G2 Prince Albert Sound chan. Can.
62 F2 Prince Alfred, C. c. Can.
63 L3 Prince Charles I. i. Can.
92 D4 Prince Charles Mts mts Ant.
67 H4 Prince Edward Island div. Can.
93 G7 Prince Edward Islands is Ind. Ocean
69 J4 Prince Edward Pt pt Can.
80 E5 Prince Frederick U.S.A.
64 E4 Prince George Can.
62 B3 Prince of Wales, Cape c. U.S.A.
63 J2 Prince of Wales I. N.W.T. Can.
6 E3 Prince of Wales I. i. Austr.
64 C3 Prince of Wales Island i. U.S.A.
62 G2 Prince of Wales Strait chan. Can.
62 F2 Prince Patrick I. i. Can.
63 J2 Prince Regent Inlet chan. Can.
64 C4 Prince Rupert Can.
65 K2 Princes Mary Lake l. Can.
81 F5 Princess Anne U.S.A.
92 D3 Princess Astrid Coast coastal area Ant.
6 E3 Princess Charlotte Bay b. Austr.
92 D5 Princess Elizabeth Land reg. Ant.
92 D3 Princess Ragnhild Coast coastal area Ant.
64 D4 Princess Royal I. i. Can.
64 E5 Princeton Can.
74 A2 Princeton CA U.S.A.
68 C5 Princeton IL U.S.A.
78 C4 Princeton IN U.S.A.
78 C4 Princeton KY U.S.A.
81 K2 Princeton ME U.S.A.
76 E3 Princeton MO U.S.A.
81 F4 Princeton NJ U.S.A.
68 C4 Princeton WV U.S.A.
80 C6 Princeton WV U.S.A.
81 K2 Prince William Can.
62 D3 Prince William Sound b. U.S.A.
54 C4 Príncipe i. Sao Tome and Principe
72 B2 Prineville U.S.A.
12 C2 Prins Karls Forland i. Svalbard
83 H6 Prinzapolca Nic.
50 D2 Priozersk Rus. Fed.
Pripet r. see Pryp"yat
36 W2 Prirechnyy Rus. Fed.
49 J3 Priština Yugo.
43 K1 Pritzier Ger.
43 L1 Pritzwalk Ger.
44 G4 Privas France
48 F2 Privlaka Croatia
50 G3 Privolzhsk Rus. Fed.
50 H4 Privolzhskaya Vozvyshennost' reg. Rus. Fed.
51 G6 Priyutnoye Rus. Fed.
49 J3 Prizren Yugo.
33 D4 Probolinggo Indon.
43 K4 Probstzella Ger.
39 C7 Probus U.K.
68 A2 Proctor MN U.S.A.
81 G3 Proctor VT U.S.A.
87 G3 Professor van Blommestein Meer resr Suriname
82 G5 Progreso Honduras
77 C7 Progreso Coahuila Mex.
84 C2 Progreso Hidalgo Mex.
84 E2 Progreso Yucatán Mex.
51 H7 Prokhladnyy Rus. Fed.
12 K4 Prokop'yevsk Rus. Fed.
49 J3 Prokuplje Yugo.
50 D3 Proletariy Rus. Fed.
51 G6 Proletarsk Rus. Fed.
90 A2 Promissão Brazil
62 F4 Prophet r. Can.
64 E3 Prophet River Can.
68 C5 Prophetstown U.S.A.
6 E4 Proserpine Austr.
81 F3 Prospect U.S.A.
31 C4 Prosperidad Phil.
58 D7 Protem S. Africa
68 A4 Protivin U.S.A.
49 M3 Provadiya Bulg.
Prøven see Kangersuatsiaq
44 H5 Provence reg. France
81 H4 Providence U.S.A.
69 F3 Providence Bay Can.
9 A7 Providence, Cape c. N.Z.
77 F5 Providence, Lake U.S.A.
86 B1 Providencia, Isla de i. Col.
62 A3 Provideniya Rus. Fed.
81 H3 Provincetown U.S.A.
75 G1 Provo U.S.A.
65 G4 Provost Can.
90 B4 Prudentópolis Brazil
62 D2 Prudhoe Bay U.S.A.
42 E4 Prüm Ger.
42 E4 Prüm r. Ger.
48 C3 Prunelli-di-Fiumorbo Corsica France
47 K4 Pruszków Pol.
51 D6 Prut r. Moldova/Romania
92 D5 Prydz Bay b. Ant.
51 E5 Pryluky Ukr.
51 F6 Prymors'k Ukr.
71 G4 Pryor OK U.S.A.
47 M5 Pryp"yat r. Ukr.
47 N4 Prypyats' r. Belarus
47 L6 Przemyśl Pol.
49 L5 Psara i. Greece
51 G6 Psebay Rus. Fed.
51 F6 Pshish r. Rus. Fed.
50 D3 Pskov Rus. Fed.
37 U7 Pskov, Lake l. Estonia/Rus. Fed.
50 D3 Pskovskaya Oblast' div. Rus. Fed.
49 J4 Ptolemaïda Greece
48 F1 Ptuj Slovenia
26 C3 Pu r. China
91 D3 Puán Arg.
27 B5 Pu'an China
30 D6 Puan S. Korea
27 C6 Pubei China
86 D5 Pucallpa Peru
27 F5 Pucheng Fujian China
26 C3 Pucheng Shaanxi China
50 G3 Puchezh Rus. Fed.
30 D5 Puch'ŏn S. Korea
31 B4 Pucio Pt pt Phil.
46 J3 Puck Pol.
68 C4 Puckaway Lake l. U.S.A.
91 B3 Pucón Chile
Pudai watercourse see Dor
18 D3 Pūdanū Iran
36 U4 Pudasjärvi Fin.
58 F3 Pudimoe S. Africa
50 F2 Pudozh Rus. Fed.
38 F4 Pudsey U.K.
Puduchcheri see Pondicherry
21 B4 Pudukkottai India
84 C3 Puebla Mex.
84 C3 Puebla div. Mex.
45 C1 Puebla de Sanabria Spain
73 F4 Pueblo U.S.A.
89 C2 Pueblo Nuevo Venez.
84 D3 Pueblo Viejo Mex.
91 D3 Puelches Arg.
91 C3 Puelén Arg.
91 B2 Puente Alto Chile
84 C3 Puente de Ixtla Mex.
45 D4 Puente-Genil Spain
89 C2 Puente Torres Venez.
86 F6 Puerto Alegre Bol.
84 C4 Puerto Angel Mex.
84 D4 Puerto Arista Mex.
83 H7 Puerto Armuelles Panama
89 A4 Puerto Asís Col.
89 D3 Puerto Ayacucho Venez.
82 G5 Puerto Barrios Guatemala
89 B3 Puerto Berrío Col.
89 C2 Puerto Cabello Venez.
83 H6 Puerto Cabezas Nic.
89 D3 Puerto Carreño Col.
88 E2 Puerto Casado Para.
88 B6 Puerto Cisnes Chile
88 C8 Puerto Coig Arg.
83 H7 Puerto Cortés Costa Rica
89 C2 Puerto Cumarebo Venez.
84 C4 Puerto Escondido Mex.
89 C1 Puerto Estrella Col.
86 F6 Puerto Frey Bol.
88 E2 Puerto Guarani Para.
86 E6 Puerto Heath Bol.
89 D4 Puerto Inírida Col.
87 G7 Puerto Isabel Bol.
89 D2 Puerto La Cruz Venez.
86 D4 Puerto Leguízamo Col.
45 D3 Puertollano Spain
91 D4 Puerto Lobos Arg.
89 B3 Puerto Lopéz Col.
84 D4 Puerto Madero Mex.
91 D4 Puerto Madryn Arg.
86 E6 Puerto Maldonado Peru
86 B4 Puerto Máncora Peru
90 A4 Puerto Mendes Para.
89 D3 Puerto Miranda Venez.
91 B4 Puerto Montt Chile
88 B8 Puerto Natáles Chile
89 C3 Puerto Nuevo Col.
89 A2 Puerto Obaldia Panama
89 E2 Puerto Ordaz Venez.
89 D3 Puerto Páez Venez.
88 E2 Puerto Pinasco Para.
91 D4 Puerto Pirámides Arg.
83 K5 Puerto Plata Dom. Rep.
86 D5 Puerto Portillo Peru
31 A4 Puerto Princesa Phil.
89 A2 Puerto Rey Col.
61 M8 Puerto Rico terr. Caribbean Sea
92 E4 Puerto Rico Trench sea feature Atl. Ocean
88 E2 Puerto Sastre Para.
89 A4 Puerto Tejado Col.
84 A2 Puerto Vallarta Mex.
91 B4 Puerto Varas Chile
51 J4 Pugachev Rus. Fed.
22 C3 Pugal India
27 B5 Puge China
18 D5 Pūhāl-e Khamīr, Kūh-e mts Iran
45 H3 Puig Major mt Spain
45 H1 Puigmal mt France/Spain
27 □ Pui O Wan b. H.K. China
27 F4 Pujiang China
30 D3 Pujŏn Reservoir resr N. Korea
30 E3 Pujonryong Sanmaek mts N. Korea
9 C6 Pukaki, Lake l. N.Z.
68 E1 Pukaskwa r. Can.
68 E1 Pukaskwa National Park Can.
65 J3 Pukatawagan Can.
30 C3 Pukchin N. Korea
30 E3 Pukch'ŏng N. Korea
9 E2 Pukekohe N.Z.
9 D5 Puketeraki Ra. mts N.Z.
9 F4 Puketoi Range h. N.Z.
9 C6 Pukeuri Junction N.Z.
47 P3 Pukhnovo Rus. Fed.
50 G2 Puksoozero Rus. Fed.
30 D3 Puksubaek-san mt N. Korea
48 E2 Pula Croatia
86 E8 Pulacayo Bol.
30 A4 Pulandian Wan b. China
31 C5 Pulangi r. Phil.
81 E3 Pulaski NY U.S.A.
79 C5 Pulaski TN U.S.A.
80 C6 Pulaski VA U.S.A.
68 C3 Pulaski WV U.S.A.
47 K5 Puławy Pol.
42 E3 Pulheim Ger.
21 C3 Pulicat L. b. India
21 B3 Pulivendla India
21 B4 Puliyangudi India
36 T4 Pulkkila Fin.
72 C2 Pullman U.S.A.
36 X2 Pulozero Rus. Fed.
22 E1 Pulu China
17 G2 Pülümür Turkey
31 C5 Pulutan Indon.
23 G3 Puma Yumco l. China
86 B4 Puná, Isla i. Ecuador
23 G4 Punakha Bhutan
22 C2 Punch Jammu and Kashmir
64 E4 Punchaw Can.
23 G3 Püncogling China
59 J1 Punda Maria S. Africa
22 D3 Pundri India
21 A2 Pune India
32 □ Punggol Sing.
30 E3 P'ungsan N. Korea
57 D5 Púngoè r. Moz.
56 C4 Punia Congo(Zaire)
91 B1 Punitaqui Chile
22 C3 Punjab div. India
22 B3 Punjab div. Pak.
22 D2 Punmah Gl. gl. China/Jammu and Kashmir
23 F4 Punpun r. India
91 D3 Punta Alta Arg.
88 B8 Punta Arenas Chile
48 C4 Punta Balestrieri mt Italy
83 L5 Punta, Cerro de mt Puerto Rico
91 D4 Punta Delgada Arg.
82 G5 Punta Gorda Belize
79 D7 Punta Gorda U.S.A.
91 D4 Punta Norte Arg.
83 H6 Puntarenas Costa Rica
89 C2 Punto Fijo Venez.
80 D4 Punxsutawney U.S.A.
36 U4 Puokio Fin.
36 U4 Puolanka Fin.
27 D4 Puqi China
18 E5 Pūr Iran
12 J3 Pur r. Rus. Fed.
89 A4 Puracé, Parque Nacional nat. park Col.
89 A4 Puracé, Volcán de volc. Col.
77 D5 Purcell U.S.A.
64 F4 Purcell Mts mts Can.
91 B3 Purén Chile
73 G4 Purgatoire r. U.S.A.
23 F6 Puri India
42 C2 Purmerend Neth.
21 B2 Purna India
22 D5 Purna r. Maharashtra India
22 D6 Purna r. Maharashtra India
21 B1 Purna r. India
23 G4 Purnabhaba r. India
23 F4 Pūrnia India
91 B4 Purranque Chile
84 B2 Puruandíro Mex.
23 F5 Puruliya India
86 F4 Purus r. Brazil
37 V6 Puruvesi l. Fin.
33 C4 Purwakarta Indon.
33 D4 Purwodadi Indon.
33 C4 Purwokerto Indon.
30 E2 Puryŏng N. Korea
22 D6 Pus r. India
22 D6 Pusad India
30 E6 Pusan S. Korea
81 J2 Pushaw Lake l. U.S.A.
50 H2 Pushemskiy Rus. Fed.
22 C4 Pushkar India
50 D3 Pushkin Rus. Fed.
51 H5 Pushkino Rus. Fed.
50 D3 Pushkinskiye Gory Rus. Fed.
19 F4 Push-i-Rud reg. Afgh.
47 O2 Pustoshka Rus. Fed.
47 L4 Puszcza Augustowska forest Pol.
46 G4 Puszcza Natecka forest Pol.
24 B4 Putao Myanmar
27 F5 Putian China
33 D3 Puting, Tanjung pt Indon.
84 C3 Putla Mex.
19 G4 Putla Khan Afgh.
43 L1 Putlitz Ger.
49 M2 Putna r. Romania
81 H4 Putnam U.S.A.
81 G3 Putney U.S.A.
23 H3 Putrang La pass China
58 D4 Putsonderwater S. Africa
21 B4 Puttalam Sri Lanka
21 B4 Puttalam Lagoon lag. Sri Lanka
42 E5 Puttelange-aux-Lacs France
42 D2 Putten Neth.
42 C3 Puttershoek Neth.
46 E3 Puttgarden Ger.
86 D4 Putumayo r. Col.
16 G2 Pütürge Turkey
33 D2 Putusibau Indon.
50 G4 Putyatino Rus. Fed.
51 E5 Putyvl' Ukr.
37 V6 Puumala Fin.
74 □2 Puuwai U.S.A.
66 E1 Puvurnituq Can.
72 B2 Puyallup U.S.A.
26 E3 Puyang China
91 B4 Puyehue Chile
91 B4 Puyehue, Parque Nacional nat. park Chile
44 F5 Puylaurens France
9 A7 Puysegur Pt pt N.Z.
57 C4 Pweto Congo(Zaire)
39 C5 Pwllheli U.K.
50 E2 Pyal'ma Rus. Fed.
50 H4 P'yana r. Rus. Fed.
22 B1 Pyandzh r. Afgh./Tajik.
36 W3 Pyaozero, Ozero l. Rus. Fed.
36 W4 Pyaozerskiy Rus. Fed.
12 K2 Pyasina r. Rus. Fed.
51 G6 Pyatigorsk Rus. Fed.
51 E5 P"yatykhatky Ukr.
25 B5 Pyè Myanmar
9 B7 Pye, Mt h. N.Z.
51 D4 Pyetrykaw Belarus
36 T4 Pyhäjoki Fin.
36 T4 Pyhäjoki r. Fin.
36 U4 Pyhäntä Fin.
36 T5 Pyhäsalmi Fin.
36 V5 Pyhäselkä l. Fin.
23 H5 Pyingaing Myanmar
39 D6 Pyle U.K.
12 K3 Pyl'karamo Rus. Fed.
49 J6 Pylos Greece
80 C4 Pymatuning Reservoir U.S.A.
30 C5 Pyŏksŏng N. Korea
30 C3 Pyŏktong N. Korea
30 D4 P'yŏnggang N. Korea
30 E5 P'yŏnghae S. Korea
30 C4 P'yŏngsan N. Korea
30 D5 P'yŏngt'aek S. Korea
30 C4 P'yŏngyang N. Korea
8 E4 Pyramid Hill Austr.
74 C1 Pyramid Lake l. U.S.A.
68 E3 Pyramid Pt pt U.S.A.
74 C2 Pyramid Range mts U.S.A.
34 E4 Pyrenees mts France/Spain
49 J6 Pyrgos Greece
51 E5 Pyryatyn Ukr.
46 G4 Pyrzyce Pol.
50 H3 Pyshchug Rus. Fed.
47 N2 Pytalovo Rus. Fed.
49 K5 Pyxaria mt Greece

Q

63 M2 Qaanaaq Greenland
18 D6 Qābil Oman
17 J6 Qabr Bandar Iraq
59 H5 Qacha's Nek Lesotho
17 K4 Qādir Karam Iraq
17 J4 Qadissiya Dam dam Iraq
26 C1 Qagan Ders China
26 C2 Qagan Nur China
26 D1 Qagan Nur China
30 C1 Qagan Nur l. Jilin China
26 E1 Qagan Nur l. Nei Monggol China
26 E1 Qagan Nur resr China
26 D1 Qagan Teg China
26 E1 Qagan Us China
23 H3 Qagbasêrag China
23 E2 Qagcaka China
63 O3 Qagssimiut Greenland
26 D1 Qahar Youyi Qianqi China
26 D1 Qahar Youyi Zhongqi China
24 B3 Qaidam Pendi basin China
19 G3 Qaisar Afgh.
19 G3 Qaisar, Koh-i- mt Afgh.
17 K3 Qalā Diza Iraq
19 H2 Qal'aikhum Tajik.
19 G3 Qala Shinia Takht Afgh.
19 G3 Qalāt Afgh.
18 D4 Qalat Iran
17 H4 Qal'at as Sālihīyah Syria
16 E6 Qal'at el Hasal Jordan
17 L6 Qal'at Sālih Iraq
17 L6 Qal'at Sukkar Iraq
19 F3 Qala Vali Afgh.
18 B2 Qal'eh D. mt Iran
19 F3 Qal 'eh-ye Now Afgh.
19 G4 Qal 'eh-ye Bost Afgh.
17 M5 Qal'eh-ye-Now Iran
17 K7 Qalīb Bāqūr well Iraq
16 C6 Qalyûb Egypt
59 G5 Qamata S. Africa
22 B4 Qambar Pak.
22 B3 Qamruddin Karez Pak.
18 C3 Qamṣar Iran
18 B2 Qandaranbashi mt Iran
26 E1 Qangdin Sum China
17 M2 Qaraçala Azer.
17 J4 Qarachōq, J. mts Iraq
17 K4 Qara D. r. Iraq
17 H7 Qārah S. Arabia
19 H3 Qarah Bāgh Afgh.
18 A5 Qa'rah, J. al h. S. Arabia
17 L3 Qaranqu r. Iran
56 E3 Qardho Somalia
17 L3 Qar'eh Aqāj Iran
17 L2 Qareh D. mts Iran
17 L3 Qareh Dāsh, Kūh-e mt Iran
18 B2 Qareh Sū r. Iran
17 L3 Qareh Urgān, Kūh-e mt Iran
23 H1 Qarhan China
19 G2 Qarqīn Afgh.
17 K6 Qaryat al Gharab Iraq
18 B5 Qaryat al Ulyā S. Arabia
18 E3 Qasamī Iran
19 F3 Qasa Murg mts Afgh.
18 C4 Qash Qai reg. Iran
63 N3 Qasigiannguit Greenland
17 J5 Qasr al Khubbāz Iraq
17 M7 Qaṣr aṣ Ṣabīyah Kuwait
16 F6 Qasr el Azraq Jordan
19 F5 Qaṣr-e-Qand Iran
18 B3 Qasr-e-Shirin Iran
17 L6 Qaṣr Shaqrah Iraq
16 F5 Qaṭanā Syria
10 G7 Qatar country Asia
16 F6 Qaṭrāna Jordan
16 C7 Qaṭrâni, Gebel esc. Egypt
55 E2 Qattâra Depression depression Egypt
17 L1 Qax Azer.
19 E3 Qāyen Iran
23 H3 Qayū China
17 J4 Qayyarah Iraq
17 L2 Qazangödağ mt Azer.
17 K1 Qazax Azer.
22 B4 Qazi Ahmad Pak.
17 M1 Qazımämmäd Azer.
18 C2 Qazvīn Iran
26 A1 Qeh China
55 F2 Qena Egypt
63 N3 Qeqertarsuatsiaat Greenland
63 N3 Qeqertarsuatsiaq i. Greenland
63 N3 Qeqertarsuup Tunua b. Greenland
18 B3 Qeshlag r. Iran
17 L4 Qeshlaq Iran
18 E5 Qeshm Iran
18 C2 Qeydār Iran
18 D5 Qeys i. Iran
18 C2 Qezel Owzan r. Iran
16 E6 Qeẓi'ot Israel
26 C3 Qian r. China
26 F2 Qian'an China
30 C1 Qian'an China
27 C5 Qiancheng China
26 F3 Qiang r. China
30 C1 Qian Gorlos China
27 D4 Qianjiang Hubei China
27 C4 Qianjiang Sichuan China
30 E1 Qianjin China
26 A4 Qianning China
30 B1 Qianqihao China
30 B3 Qian Shan mts China
27 C5 Qianxi China
26 C3 Qian Xian China
27 D5 Qianyang Hunan China
26 C3 Qianyang Shaanxi China
27 F4 Qianyang Zhejiang China
26 D2 Qiaocun China
27 B5 Qiaojia China
17 K2 Qīās Iran
18 B5 Qibā' S. Arabia
59 G4 Qibing S. Africa
27 D5 Qidong Hunan China
26 F4 Qidong Jiangsu China
23 H2 Qidukou China
15 G3 Qiemo China
26 E2 Qihe China
27 C4 Qijiang China
12 L5 Qijiaojing China
19 G4 Qila Abdullah Pak.
19 F5 Qila Ladgasht Pak.
26 E1 Qilaotu Shan mts China
19 F4 Qila Safed Pak.
22 B3 Qila Saifullah Pak.
24 B3 Qilian Shan mts China
63 P3 Qillak i. Greenland
23 G1 Qimantag mts China
27 E4 Qimen China
26 D3 Qin r. China
26 B3 Qin'an China
30 C2 Qing r. China
30 B3 Qingchengzi China
26 F2 Qingdao China
26 A2 Qinghai div. China
26 A2 Qinghai Hu salt l. China
24 B3 Qinghai Nanshan mts China
28 A1 Qinghe China
30 C3 Qinghecheng China
26 D2 Qingjian China
26 F3 Qingjiang Jiangsu China
27 E4 Qingjiang Jiangxi China
27 D4 Qing Jiang r. China
27 E5 Qingliu China
27 B5 Qinglong Guizhou China
26 F1 Qinglong Hebei China
26 F2 Qinglong r. China
27 C6 Qingping China
26 F4 Qingpu China
26 C3 Qingshui China
26 D2 Qingshuihe China
27 F4 Qingtian China
26 E2 Qing Xian China
26 D2 Qingxu China
27 E4 Qingyang Anhui China
26 C2 Qingyang Gansu China
27 D6 Qingyuan Guangdong China
27 F5 Qingyuan Zhejiang China
30 C2 Qingyuan China
27 C5 Qingzhen China
26 F2 Qinhuangdao China
26 C3 Qin Ling mts China
26 C2 Qintongxia China
26 D3 Qin Xian China
26 D3 Qinyang China
26 D2 Qinyuan China
27 C6 Qinzhou China
27 C6 Qinzhou Wan b. China
27 D7 Qionghai China
27 B4 Qionglai China
26 B4 Qionglai Shan mts China
27 D7 Qiongshan China
27 C6 Qiongzhou Haixia str. China
24 E2 Qiqihar China
17 M5 Qīr Iran
18 D4 Qīr Iran
22 E1 Qira China
16 E6 Qiryat Gat Israel
16 F6 Qitab ash Shāmah crater S. Arabia
28 B2 Qitaihe China
27 B5 Qiubei China
26 F2 Qixia China
26 E3 Qi Xian Henan China
26 D2 Qi Xian Shanxi China
28 C1 Qixing r. China
27 D5 Qiyang China
26 C2 Qiying China
27 D7 Qizhou Liedao i. China
17 M2 Qızılağac Körfäzi b. Azer.
Qogir Feng mt see K2
26 C1 Qog Qi China
18 B2 Qojūr Iran
18 C3 Qom Iran
23 H3 Qomdo China
18 C3 Qomisheh Iran
Qomolangma Feng mt see Everest, Mt
17 M1 Qonaqkänd Azer.
18 C3 Qonāq, Kūh-e h. Iran
23 G3 Qonggyai China
26 C1 Qongi China
16 F4 Qornet es Saouda mt Lebanon
18 B3 Qorveh Iran
18 E5 Qoṭbābād Iran
17 K2 Qoṭūr Iran
81 G3 Quabbin Reservoir U.S.A.
74 D4 Quail Mts mts U.S.A.
43 F2 Quakenbrück Ger.
81 F4 Quakertown U.S.A.
65 K2 Quamarirjung Lake l. Can.
8 D3 Quambatook Austr.
8 F1 Quambone Austr.
77 D5 Quanah U.S.A.
26 D3 Quanbao Shan mt China
32 D2 Quang Ngai Vietnam
32 C1 Quang Tri Vietnam
27 C6 Quang Yen Vietnam
27 E5 Quannan China
27 F5 Quanzhou Fujian China
27 D5 Quanzhou Guangxi China
65 J4 Qu'Appelle Can.
65 J4 Qu'Appelle r. Can.
91 F1 Quaraí Brazil
91 F1 Quaraí r. Brazil
27 □ Quarry Bay H.K. China
48 C5 Quartu Sant'Elena Sardinia Italy
74 D3 Quartzite Mt mt U.S.A.
75 E5 Quartzsite U.S.A.
64 D4 Quatsino Sound in. Can.
17 M1 Quba Azer.
19 E2 Quchan Iran
8 G3 Queanbeyan Austr.
67 F4 Québec Can.
63 L4 Quebec div. Can.
90 C2 Quebra Anzol r. Brazil
89 C2 Quebrada del Toro, Parque Nacional de la nat. park Venez.
91 B4 Quedal, C. hd Chile
43 K3 Quedlinburg Ger.
64 E4 Queen Bess, Mt mt Can.
64 C4 Queen Charlotte Can.
64 C4 Queen Charlotte Islands is Can.
64 D4 Queen Charlotte Sound chan. Can.
64 D4 Queen Charlotte Str. chan. Can.
63 H1 Queen Elizabeth Islands Can.
56 D3 Queen Elizabeth National Park nat. park Uganda
92 C5 Queen Mary Land reg. Ant.
62 H3 Queen Maud Gulf b. Can.
Queen Maud Land reg. see Dronning Maud Land
92 B4 Queen Maud Mts mts Ant.
6 E4 Queensland div. Austr.
6 E4 Queenstown Austr.
9 B6 Queenstown N.Z.
59 G5 Queenstown S. Africa
32 □ Queenstown Sing.
81 E5 Queenstown U.S.A.
72 A2 Queets U.S.A.
91 F2 Queguay Grande r. Uru.
91 D3 Quehué Arg.
87 H4 Queimada ou Serraria, Ilha i. Brazil
57 D5 Quelimane Moz.
88 B6 Quellón Chile
Quelpart Island i. see Cheju-do
75 H4 Quemado U.S.A.
91 B4 Quemchi Chile
91 D3 Quemú-Quemú Arg.
91 E3 Quequén Grande r. Arg.
90 B3 Querência do Norte Brazil
84 B2 Querétaro Mex.
84 C2 Querétaro div. Mex.
43 K3 Querfurt Ger.
26 E3 Queshan China
64 E4 Quesnel Can.
64 E4 Quesnel r. Can.
64 E4 Quesnel L. l. Can.
68 B1 Quetico Provincial Park res. Can.
22 A3 Quetta Pak.
91 B3 Queuco Chile
91 B3 Queule Chile
82 F6 Quezaltenango Guatemala
31 A4 Quezon Phil.
31 B3 Quezon City Phil.
26 E3 Qufu China
57 B5 Quibala Angola
57 B4 Quibaxe Angola
89 A3 Quibdó Col.
44 C3 Quiberon France
57 B4 Quicama, Parque Nacional do nat. park Angola
32 C1 Qui Châu Vietnam
75 F5 Quijotoa U.S.A.
91 D1 Quilino Arg.
44 F5 Quillan France
65 J4 Quill Lakes l. Can.
91 B2 Quillota Chile
91 E2 Quilmes Arg.
21 B4 Quilon India
6 E4 Quilpie Austr.
91 B2 Quilpué Chile
56 B4 Quimbele Angola
88 D3 Quimilí Arg.
44 B3 Quimper France
44 C3 Quimperlé France
86 D6 Quince Mil Peru
74 B2 Quincy CA U.S.A.
79 C6 Quincy FL U.S.A.
68 B6 Quincy IL U.S.A.
81 H3 Quincy MA U.S.A.
91 D2 Quines Arg.
32 D2 Qui Nhon Vietnam
75 E3 Quinn Canyon Range mts U.S.A.
45 E3 Quintanar de la Orden Spain
91 B2 Quintero Chile
45 F2 Quinto Spain
91 D2 Quinto r. Arg.
57 E5 Quionga Moz.
57 B5 Quipungo Angola
91 B3 Quirihue Chile
57 B5 Quirima Angola
8 H1 Quirindi Austr.
91 E2 Quiroga Arg.
57 D6 Quissico Moz.
57 B5 Quitapa Angola
90 B2 Quitéria r. Brazil
79 D6 Quitman GA U.S.A.
79 B5 Quitman MS U.S.A.
86 C4 Quito Ecuador
73 D6 Quitovac Mex.
75 F4 Quivero U.S.A.
87 L4 Quixadá Brazil
27 D5 Qujiang China
27 C4 Qu Jiang r. China
27 D6 Qujie China
27 B5 Qujing China
17 L7 Qulbān Layyah well Iraq
19 H2 Qullai Garmo mt Tajik.
23 H2 Qumar He r. China
23 H2 Qumarlêb China
23 H2 Qumarrabdün China
23 H2 Qumaryan China
59 H5 Qumbu S. Africa
59 G6 Qumrha S. Africa
18 B6 Qunayy well S. Arabia
65 L2 Quoich r. Can.
40 C3 Quoich, Loch l. U.K.
41 F3 Quoile r. U.K.
58 C7 Quoin Pt pt S. Africa
23 E2 Quong Muztag mt China
58 F1 Quoxo r. Botswana
17 L3 Qurābeh Iran
19 E6 Qurayat Oman
19 H2 Qŭrghonteppa Tajik.
Qurlurtuuq see Coppermine
67 G2 Qurlutu r. Can.
17 K2 Qūrū Gol pass Iran
17 M1 Qusar Azer.
55 F2 Quseir Egypt
18 B2 Qūshchī Iran
17 L2 Qūsheh D. mts Iran
18 C3 Qūtīābād Iran
26 B2 Quwu Shan mts China
26 C4 Qu Xian China
23 G3 Qüxü China
32 C1 Quynh Luu Vietnam
27 B6 Quynh Nhai Vietnam
69 J3 Quyon Can.
26 E2 Quzhou Hebei China
27 F4 Quzhou Zhejiang China
51 H7 Qvareli Georgia
Qyteti Stalin see Kuçovë

R

46 H7 Raab r. Austria
36 T4 Raahe Fin.
36 V5 Rääkkylä Fin.
42 E2 Raalte Neth.
36 T3 Raanujärvi Fin.
33 D4 Raas i. Indon.
40 B3 Raasay i. U.K.
40 B3 Raasay, Sound of chan. U.K.
56 F2 Raas Caseyr c. Somalia
33 E4 Raba Indon.
22 E2 Rabang China
48 F7 Rabat Malta
54 B1 Rabat Morocco
19 E3 Rabāt-e Kamah Iran
6 F2 Rabaul P.N.G.
64 D3 Rabbit r. Can.
20 A5 Rābigh S. Arabia
23 G5 Rabnabad Islands is Bangl.
51 D6 Râbniţa Moldova
18 E4 Rābor Iran
80 B5 Raccoon Creek r. U.S.A.
67 K4 Race, C. c. Can.
81 H3 Race Pt pt U.S.A.
16 E5 Rachaïya Lebanon
77 D7 Rachal U.S.A.
75 E3 Rachel U.S.A.
32 C3 Rach Gia Vietnam
46 J5 Racibórz Pol.
68 D4 Racine U.S.A.
69 F1 Racine Lake l. Can.
68 E2 Raco U.S.A.

47 M7 Rădăuţi Romania
78 C4 Radcliff U.S.A.
80 C6 Radford U.S.A.
22 B5 Radhanpur India
66 E3 Radisson Can.
64 F4 Radium Hot Springs Can.
49 L3 Radnevo Bulg.
47 K5 Radom Pol.
49 K3 Radomir Bulg.
55 E4 Radom National Park Sudan
47 J5 Radomsko Pol.
51 D5 Radomyshl' Ukr.
49 K4 Radoviš Macedonia
39 E6 Radstock U.K.
50 C4 Radun' Belarus
37 S9 Radviliškis Lith.
47 M5 Radyvyliv Ukr.
22 E4 Rae Bareli India
64 F2 Rae-Edzo Can.
64 F2 Rae Lakes Can.
9 E3 Raetihi N.Z.
91 E1 Rafaela Arg.
16 E6 Rafah Gaza
56 C3 Rafaï C.A.R.
20 B4 Rafhā S. Arabia
18 E4 Rafsanjān Iran
31 C5 Ragang, Mt volc. Phil.
31 B3 Ragay Gulf b. Phil.
43 L1 Rägelin Ger.
81 J3 Ragged I. i. U.S.A.
18 B4 Raghwah S. Arabia
43 L2 Ragösen Ger.
43 L3 Raguhn Ger.
48 F6 Ragusa Sicily Italy
26 A3 Ra'gyagoinba China
6 C2 Raha Indon.
50 D4 Rahachow Belarus
Rahaeng see Tak
43 G2 Rahden Ger.
17 J5 Raḥḥālīyah Iraq
21 A2 Rahimatpur India
22 B3 Rahimyar Khan Pak.
18 C3 Rāhjerd Iran
91 B3 Rahue mt Chile
21 A2 Rahuri India
19 F3 Rahzanak Afgh.
21 B2 Raichur India
23 G4 Raiganj India
23 E5 Raigarh India
75 E2 Railroad Valley v. U.S.A.
67 G3 Raimbault, Lac l. Can.
8 D3 Rainbow Austr.
75 G3 Rainbow Bridge Nat. Mon. res. U.S.A.
64 F3 Rainbow Lake Can.
80 C6 Rainelle U.S.A.
72 B2 Rainier, Mt volc. U.S.A.
23 B3 Raini N. r. Pak.
66 B4 Rainy r. U.S.A.
63 J5 Rainy Lake l. Can.
65 L5 Rainy River Can.
23 E5 Raipur Madhya Pradesh India
22 C4 Raipur Rajasthan India
37 S6 Raisio Fin.
42 B4 Raismes France
21 C2 Rajahmundry India
36 V2 Raja-Jooseppi Fin.
21 B3 Rajampet India
33 D2 Rajang r. Malaysia
21 B4 Rajapalaiyam India
21 A2 Rajapur India
22 C4 Rajasthan div. India
22 C3 Rajasthan Canal canal India
23 F4 Rajauli India
23 G5 Rajbari Bangl.
22 C3 Rajgarh Rajasthan India
22 D4 Rajgarh Rajasthan India
16 F6 Rajil, W. watercourse Jordan
23 E5 Rajim India
22 B5 Rajkot India
23 F4 Rajmahal India
23 F4 Rajmahal Hills h. India
22 E5 Raj Nandgaon India
22 D3 Rajpura India
23 G4 Rajshahi Bangl.
21 B2 Rajura India
23 F3 Raka China
5 L5 Rakahanga i. Pac. Oc.
9 C5 Rakaia r. N.Z.
22 C1 Rakaposhi mt Pak.
23 F3 Raka Zangbo r. China
51 C5 Rakhiv Ukr.
22 B3 Rakhni Pak.
19 G5 Rakhshan r. Pak.
51 E5 Rakitnoye Belgorod. Obl. Rus. Fed.
28 D2 Rakitnoye Primorskiy Kray Rus. Fed.
37 U7 Rakke Estonia
37 M7 Rakkestad Norway
22 B3 Rakni r. Pak.
37 U7 Rakvere Estonia
79 E5 Raleigh U.S.A.
4 H4 Ralik Chain is Marshall Is
68 D2 Ralph U.S.A.
64 E2 Ram r. Can.
67 H2 Ramah Can.
75 H4 Ramah U.S.A.
90 D1 Ramalho, Serra do h. Brazil
16 E6 Ramallah West Bank
21 B3 Ramanagaram India
21 B4 Ramanathapuram India
94 E3 Ramapo Deep depth Pac. Oc.
21 A3 Ramas, C. c. India
59 F2 Ramatlabama S. Africa
6 E2 Rambutyo I. i. P.N.G.
21 A3 Ramdurg India
39 C7 Rame Head hd U.K.
57 E5 Ramena Madag.
50 F3 Rameshki Rus. Fed.
21 B4 Rameswaram India
22 D4 Ramganga r. India
23 G5 Ramgarh Bangl.
23 F5 Ramgarh Bihar India
22 B4 Ramgarh Rajasthan India
18 C4 Rāmhormoz Iran
16 E7 Ram, Jebel mt Jordan
16 E6 Ramla Israel
Ramlat Rabyānah des. see Rebiana Sand Sea
Ramnad see Ramanathapuram
22 D3 Ramnagar India
49 M2 Râmnicu Sărat Romania
49 L2 Râmnicu Vâlcea Romania
74 D5 Ramona U.S.A.
69 G1 Ramore Can.
57 C6 Ramotswa Botswana
22 D3 Rampur India
22 C4 Rampura India
Rampur Boalia see Rajshahi
23 F4 Rampur Hat India
23 H6 Ramree I. i. Myanmar
36 P5 Ramsele Sweden
69 F2 Ramsey Can.
38 C3 Ramsey Isle of Man
39 G5 Ramsey Eng. U.K.
39 B6 Ramsey Island i. U.K.
69 F2 Ramsey Lake l. Can.
39 J6 Ramsgate U.K.
22 D5 Ramtek India
37 T9 Ramygala Lith.
89 C4 Rana, Co h. Col.
23 G5 Ranaghat India
22 C5 Ranapur India
33 E1 Ranau Malaysia
91 B2 Rancagua Chile
23 F5 Ranchi India
91 B4 Ranco, L. de l. Chile
8 F3 Rand Austr.
41 E3 Randalstown U.K.
48 F6 Randazzo Sicily Italy
37 M8 Randers Denmark
81 H3 Randolph MA U.S.A.
81 G3 Randolph VT U.S.A.
37 N5 Randsjö Sweden
36 S4 Råneå Sweden
9 C6 Ranfurly N.Z.
32 B4 Rangae Thai.
23 H5 Rangamati Bangl.
9 D1 Rangaunu Bay b. N.Z.
81 H2 Rangeley U.S.A.
81 H2 Rangeley Lake l. U.S.A.
75 H1 Rangely U.S.A.
69 F2 Ranger Lake Can.
9 D5 Rangiora N.Z.
5 N6 Rangiroa i. Pac. Oc.
9 F3 Rangitaiki r. N.Z.
9 C5 Rangitata r. N.Z.
9 E4 Rangitikei r. N.Z.
Rangoon see Yangon
23 G4 Rangpur Bangl.
21 A3 Ranibennur India
23 F5 Raniganj India
23 E5 Ranijula Peak mt India
22 B4 Ranipur Pak.
77 C6 Rankin U.S.A.
65 L2 Rankin Inlet Can.
65 L2 Rankin Inlet in. Can.
8 F2 Rankin's Springs Austr.
37 U7 Ranna Estonia
40 D4 Rannoch, L. l. U.K.
40 D4 Rannoch Moor moorland U.K.
22 B4 Rann of Kachchh marsh India
32 A3 Ranong Thai.
32 B4 Ranot Thai.
50 G4 Ranova r. Rus. Fed.
17 M5 Rānsa Iran
37 N6 Ransby Sweden
25 F7 Ransiki Indon.
37 V5 Rantasalmi Fin.
33 A2 Rantauprapat Indon.
68 C5 Rantoul U.S.A.
47 R2 Rantsevo Rus. Fed.
36 T4 Rantsila Fin.
36 U4 Ranua Fin.
17 K3 Rānya Iraq
28 C1 Raohe China
27 E6 Raoping China
5 K7 Raoul i. N.Z.
5 N7 Rapa i. Pac. Oc.
48 C2 Rapallo Italy
22 B5 Rapar India
19 E5 Rapch watercourse Iran
91 B2 Rapel r. Chile
63 M3 Raper, C. pt Can.
41 D3 Raphoe Rep. of Ireland
80 E5 Rapidan r. U.S.A.
8 B3 Rapid Bay Austr.
76 C2 Rapid City U.S.A.
69 H2 Rapide-Deux Can.
69 H2 Rapide-Sept Can.
68 D3 Rapid River U.S.A.
37 T7 Rapla Estonia
80 E5 Rappahannock r. U.S.A.
23 E4 Rapti r. India
22 B5 Rapur India
31 C3 Rapurapu i. Phil.
81 F2 Raquette r. U.S.A.
81 F3 Raquette Lake U.S.A.
81 F3 Raquette Lake l. U.S.A.
81 F4 Raritan Bay b. U.S.A.
5 M7 Rarotonga i. Pac. Oc.
31 A4 Rasa i. Phil.
20 E5 Ra's al Ḥadd pt Oman
18 D5 Ra's al Khaymah U.A.E.
91 D4 Rasa, Pta pt Arg.
56 D2 Ras Dashen mt Eth.
37 S9 Raseiniai Lith.
16 C6 Rashîd Egypt
19 G4 Rashid Qala Afgh.
18 D3 Rasht Iran
18 C2 Rasht Iran
21 B4 Rasipuram India
19 F5 Rāsk Iran
22 C1 Raskam mts China
19 G4 Raskoh mts Pak.
55 F2 Ras Muhammad c. Egypt
63 J3 Rasmussen Basin b. Can.
88 C6 Raso, C. pt Arg.
50 D4 Rasony Belarus
23 E4 Rasra India
48 D6 Rass Jebel Tunisia
50 G4 Rasskazovo Rus. Fed.
20 D4 Ras Tannūrah S. Arabia
43 G1 Rastede Ger.
43 K1 Rastow Ger.
18 D5 Rasūl watercourse Iran
4 J3 Ratak Chain is Marshall Is
37 O5 Rätan Sweden
59 H3 Ratanda S. Africa
22 C3 Ratangarh India
23 E5 Ratanpur India
37 O5 Rätansbyn Sweden
32 A2 Rat Buri Thai.
22 D4 Rath India
41 E4 Rathangan Rep. of Ireland
41 D5 Rathdowney Rep. of Ireland
41 E5 Rathdrum Rep. of Ireland
23 H5 Rathedaung Myanmar
43 L2 Rathenow Ger.
41 E3 Rathfriland U.K.
41 C5 Rathkeale Rep. of Ireland
41 E2 Rathlin Island i. U.K.
41 C5 Rathluirc Rep. of Ireland
42 E3 Ratingen Ger.
22 C3 Ratiya India
22 C5 Ratlam India
21 A2 Ratnagiri India
21 C5 Ratnapura Sri Lanka
51 C5 Ratne Ukr.
22 B4 Rato Dero Pak.
73 F4 Raton U.S.A.
40 G3 Rattray Head hd U.K.
37 O6 Rättvik Sweden
43 J1 Ratzeburg Ger.
64 C3 Ratz, Mt mt Can.
32 B5 Raub Malaysia
91 E3 Rauch Arg.
17 L7 Raudhatain Kuwait
43 K4 Rauenstein Ger.
36 F3 Raufarhöfn Iceland
9 G2 Raukumara mt N.Z.
9 F3 Raukumara Range mts N.Z.
37 R6 Rauma Fin.
23 F5 Raurkela India
28 J2 Rausu Japan
36 V5 Rautavaara Fin.
37 V6 Rautjärvi Fin.
48 E5 Ravalli U.S.A.
17 L4 Ravānsar Iran
18 E4 Rāvar Iran
42 C3 Ravels Belgium
81 G3 Ravena U.S.A.
38 D3 Ravenglass U.K.
48 E2 Ravenna Italy
46 D7 Ravensburg Ger.
80 C5 Ravenswood U.S.A.
22 C3 Ravi r. Pak.
19 F2 Ravnina Turkm.
19 F2 Ravnina Turkm.
17 H4 Rāwah Iraq
5 K5 Rawaki i. Kiribati
22 C2 Rawalpindi Pak.
17 K3 Rawāndiz Iraq
22 C3 Rawatsar India
46 H5 Rawicz Pol.
80 D5 Rawley Springs U.S.A.
72 F3 Rawlins U.S.A.
88 C6 Rawson Arg.
23 F4 Raxaul India
21 B3 Rayachoti India
21 B3 Rayadurg India
21 C2 Rāyagarha India
16 F5 Rayak Lebanon
67 J4 Ray, C. hd Can.
24 E2 Raychikhinsk Rus. Fed.
39 H6 Rayleigh U.K.
64 G5 Raymond Can.
81 H3 Raymond NH U.S.A.
72 B2 Raymond WA U.S.A.
8 H2 Raymond Terrace Austr.
77 D7 Raymondville U.S.A.
32 B2 Rayong Thai.
80 D4 Raystown Lake l. U.S.A.
18 C3 Razan Iran
17 M5 Rāzān Iran
Razdan see Hrazdan
28 B3 Razdol'noye Rus. Fed.
18 C3 Razeh Iran
49 M3 Razgrad Bulg.
49 N2 Razim, Lacul lag. Romania
49 K4 Razlog Bulg.
44 B2 Raz, Pte du pt France
39 G6 Reading U.K.
81 F4 Reading U.S.A.
68 B4 Readstown U.S.A.
59 G2 Reagile S. Africa
91 D2 Realicó Arg.
44 F5 Réalmont France
32 B2 Reăng Kesei Cambodia
84 B1 Reata Mex.
42 B6 Rebais France
55 E2 Rebiana Sand Sea des. Libya
50 D2 Reboly Rus. Fed.
28 G2 Rebun-tō i. Japan
6 C5 Recherche, Archipelago of the is Austr.
22 C3 Rechna Doab lowland Pak.
51 D4 Rechytsa Belarus
87 M5 Recife Brazil
59 F7 Recife, Cape c. S. Africa
42 F3 Recklinghausen Ger.
88 E3 Reconquista Arg.
88 C3 Recreo Arg.
65 K5 Red r. Can./U.S.A.
77 E6 Red r. U.S.A.
33 B4 Redang i. Malaysia
81 F4 Red Bank NJ U.S.A.
79 C5 Red Bank TN U.S.A.
67 J3 Red Bay Can.
74 A1 Red Bluff U.S.A.
75 F4 Red Butte summit U.S.A.
38 F3 Redcar U.K.
65 G4 Redcliff Can.
8 D3 Red Cliffs Austr.
76 D3 Red Cloud U.S.A.
64 G4 Red Deer Alta. Can.
65 G4 Red Deer r. Alta. Can.
65 J4 Red Deer r. Sask. Can.
65 J4 Red Deer L. l. Can.
81 F5 Redden U.S.A.
59 G4 Reddersburg S. Africa
72 B3 Redding U.S.A.
39 F5 Redditch U.K.
81 F3 Redfield NY U.S.A.
76 D2 Redfield SD U.S.A.
8 B2 Redhill Austr.
75 H4 Red Hill U.S.A.
77 D4 Red Hills h. U.S.A.
67 J4 Red Indian L. l. Can.
68 E5 Redkey U.S.A.
75 E4 Red L. U.S.A.
65 L4 Red L. l. Can.
65 L4 Red Lake Can.
76 E1 Red Lakes l. U.S.A.
72 E2 Red Lodge U.S.A.
72 B2 Redmond U.S.A.
76 E3 Red Oak U.S.A.
45 C3 Redondo Port.
68 C1 Red Rock Can.
81 E4 Red Rock U.S.A.
52 H3 Red Sea sea Africa/Asia
64 D3 Redstone r. Can.
64 D2 Redstone r. Can.
65 L4 Red Sucker L. l. Can.
64 G4 Redwater Can.
67 H3 Red Wine r. Can.
68 A3 Red Wing U.S.A.
74 A3 Redwood City U.S.A.
76 E2 Redwood Falls U.S.A.
72 B3 Redwood Nat. Park U.S.A.
74 A2 Redwood Valley U.S.A.
68 E4 Reed City U.S.A.
74 C3 Reedley U.S.A.
68 C4 Reedsburg U.S.A.
72 A3 Reedsport U.S.A.
81 E6 Reedville U.S.A.
92 B4 Reedy Gl. gl. Ant.
9 C5 Reefton N.Z.
41 D4 Ree, Lough l. Rep. of Ireland
42 E3 Rees Ger.
16 G2 Refahiye Turkey
77 D6 Refugio U.S.A.
46 F6 Regen Ger.
43 L5 Regen r. Ger.
43 L5 Regensburg Ger.
43 L5 Regenstauf Ger.
54 C2 Reggane Alg.
48 F5 Reggio di Calabria Italy
48 D2 Reggio nell'Emilia Italy
47 M7 Reghin Romania
65 J4 Regina Can.
19 G4 Registan reg. Afgh.
36 W4 Regozero Rus. Fed.
43 L4 Rehau Ger.
43 H2 Rehburg Ger.
22 D5 Rehli India
43 K1 Rehna Ger.
57 B6 Rehoboth Namibia
75 H4 Rehoboth U.S.A.
81 F5 Rehoboth Bay b. U.S.A.
81 F5 Rehoboth Beach U.S.A.
16 E6 Rehovot Israel
43 L3 Reibitz Ger.
43 L4 Reichenbach Ger.
43 F6 Reichshoffen France
79 E4 Reidsville U.S.A.
39 G6 Reigate U.K.
44 D3 Ré, Île de i. France
75 G5 Reiley Peak summit U.S.A.
44 G2 Reims France
88 B8 Reina Adelaida, Archipiélago de la is Chile
68 A4 Reinbeck U.S.A.
43 J1 Reinbek Ger.
65 J3 Reindeer r. Can.
65 K4 Reindeer I. i. Can.
65 J3 Reindeer Lake l. Can.
36 N3 Reine Norway
43 J1 Reinfeld (Holstein) Ger.
9 D1 Reinga, Cape c. N.Z.
45 D1 Reinosa Spain
42 E5 Reinsfeld Ger.
36 B4 Reipholsfjöll mt Iceland
36 R2 Reisaelva r. Norway
36 S2 Reisa Nasjonalpark nat. park Norway
36 T5 Reisjärvi Fin.
59 H3 Reitz S. Africa
58 F3 Reivilo S. Africa
89 D3 Rejunya Venez.
42 F3 Reken Ger.
65 H2 Reliance Can.
54 C1 Relizane Alg.
43 H1 Rellingen Ger.
42 F4 Remagen Ger.
8 B2 Remarkable, Mt Austr.
19 E5 Remeshk Iran
58 B1 Remhoogte Pass Namibia
46 C6 Remiremont France
22 D2 Remo Gl. gl. India
51 G6 Remontnoye Rus. Fed.
42 F3 Remscheid Ger.
68 E4 Remus U.S.A.
37 M6 Rena Norway
21 B2 Renapur India
78 B4 Rend L. l. U.S.A.
7 F2 Rendova i. Solomon Is
46 D3 Rendsburg Ger.
69 J3 Renfrew Can.
40 D5 Renfrew U.K.
91 B2 Rengo Chile
26 C3 Ren He r. China
26 E4 Renheji China
27 D5 Renhua China
27 C5 Renhuai China
51 D6 Reni Ukr.
Renland reg. see Tuttut Nunaat
8 C3 Renmark Austr.
7 G3 Rennell i. Solomon Is
43 G4 Rennerod Ger.
44 D2 Rennes France
92 B5 Rennick Gl. gl. Ant.
65 H2 Rennie Lake l. Can.
74 C2 Reno U.S.A.
48 D2 Reno r. Italy
80 E4 Renovo U.S.A.
26 E2 Renqiu China
27 B4 Renshou China
68 D5 Rensselaer IN U.S.A.
81 G3 Rensselaer NY U.S.A.
42 D2 Renswoude Neth.
72 B2 Renton U.S.A.
23 E4 Renukut India
9 D4 Renwick N.Z.
54 B3 Réo Burkina
25 E7 Reo Indon.
19 F2 Repetek Turkm.
72 C1 Republic U.S.A.
76 D3 Republican r. U.S.A.
63 K3 Repulse Bay Can.
86 D5 Requena Peru
45 F3 Requena Spain
16 F1 Reşadiye Turkey
17 J2 Reşadiye Turkey
90 B4 Reserva Brazil
18 C2 Reshteh-ye Alborz mts Iran
18 E2 Reshteh-ye Esfarayen mts Iran
88 E3 Resistencia Arg.
49 J2 Reşiţa Romania
63 J2 Resolute Can.
63 M3 Resolution Island i. N.W.T. Can.
9 A6 Resolution Island i. N.Z.
84 E4 Retalhuleu Guatemala
32 □ Retan Laut, P. i. Sing.
39 G4 Retford U.K.
44 G2 Rethel France
43 H2 Rethem (Aller) Ger.
49 L7 Rethymno Greece
28 C2 Rettikhovka Rus. Fed.
43 L2 Reuden Ger.
53 K8 Réunion terr. Ind. Ocean
45 G2 Reus Spain
43 L1 Reuterstadt Stavenhagen Ger.
46 D6 Reutlingen Ger.
74 D3 Reveille Peak summit U.S.A.
44 F5 Revel France
64 F4 Revelstoke Can.
64 C3 Revillagigedo I. i. U.S.A.
82 B5 Revillagigedo, Islas is Mex.
42 C5 Revin France
16 E6 Revivim Israel
22 E4 Rewa India
22 D3 Rewari India
72 E3 Rexburg U.S.A.
67 H4 Rexton Can.
74 C4 Reyes Peak summit U.S.A.
74 A2 Reyes, Point pt U.S.A.
16 F3 Reyhanlı Turkey
36 C4 Reykir Iceland
96 G2 Reykjanes Ridge sea feature Atl. Ocean
36 B5 Reykjanestá pt Iceland
36 C4 Reykjavík Iceland
84 C1 Reynosa Mex.
37 U8 Rēzekne Latvia
17 M3 Rezvanshahr Iran
16 F5 Rharaz, W. watercourse Syria
39 D5 Rhayader U.K.
43 G3 Rheda-Wiedenbrück Ger.
42 E3 Rhede Ger.
Rhein r. Ger./Switz. see Rhine
42 F2 Rheine Ger.
42 E4 Rheinisches Schiefergebirge h. Ger.
42 F5 Rheinland-Pfalz div. Ger.
43 L1 Rheinsberg Ger.
43 G6 Rheinstetten Ger.
Rhin r. France see Rhine
46 C5 Rhine r. Europe
81 G4 Rhinebeck U.S.A.
68 C3 Rhinelander U.S.A.
43 L2 Rhinkanal canal Ger.
43 L2 Rhinluch marsh Ger.
43 L2 Rhinow Ger.
48 C2 Rho Italy
81 H4 Rhode Island div. U.S.A.
49 N6 Rhodes Greece
49 N6 Rhodes i. Greece
72 D2 Rhodes Pk summit U.S.A.
39 D6 Rhondda U.K.
44 G4 Rhône r. France/Switz.
39 D4 Rhyl U.K.
90 E2 Riacho Brazil
90 D1 Riacho de Santana Brazil
91 D4 Riachos, Is de los i. Arg.
90 C1 Rialma Brazil
90 C1 Rianópolis Brazil
22 C2 Riasi Jammu and Kashmir
33 B2 Riau, Kepulauan is Indon.
45 C1 Ribadeo Spain
45 D1 Ribadesella Spain
90 B3 Ribas do Rio Pardo Brazil
57 D5 Ribáuè Moz.
38 E4 Ribble r. U.K.
37 L9 Ribe Denmark
42 A5 Ribécourt-Dreslincourt France
90 C4 Ribeira r. Brazil
90 C3 Ribeirão Preto Brazil
42 B5 Ribemont France
44 E4 Ribérac France
86 E6 Riberalta Bol.
46 F3 Ribnitz-Damgarten Ger.
46 G6 Říčany Czech Rep.
75 E4 Rice U.S.A.
68 B3 Rice Lake U.S.A.
69 F2 Rice Lake l. Can.
68 A4 Riceville IA U.S.A.
80 D4 Riceville PA U.S.A.
59 K4 Richards Bay S. Africa
77 D5 Richardson U.S.A.
65 G3 Richardson r. Can.
81 H2 Richardson Lakes l. U.S.A.
62 E3 Richardson Mts N.W.T. Can.
9 B6 Richardson Mts mts N.Z.
75 F2 Richfield U.S.A.
81 F3 Richfield Springs U.S.A.
81 E3 Richford NY U.S.A.
81 G2 Richford VT U.S.A.
70 C2 Richland WA U.S.A.
68 B5 Richland U.S.A.
68 B4 Richland Center U.S.A.
80 C6 Richlands U.S.A.
8 H2 Richmond N.S.W. Austr.
6 E4 Richmond Austr.
69 K3 Richmond Can.
9 D4 Richmond N.Z.
59 J4 Richmond Kwazulu-Natal S. Africa
58 E5 Richmond Northern Cape S. Africa
38 F3 Richmond U.K.
68 E6 Richmond IN U.S.A.
80 A6 Richmond KY U.S.A.
81 J2 Richmond ME U.S.A.
69 F4 Richmond MI U.S.A.
80 E6 Richmond VA U.S.A.
81 G2 Richmond VT U.S.A.
69 H4 Richmond Hill Can.
9 D4 Richmond, Mt mt N.Z.
58 B4 Richtersveld National Park S. Africa
80 B4 Richwood OH U.S.A.
80 C5 Richwood WV U.S.A.
69 K3 Rideau r. Can.
69 J3 Rideau Lakes l. Can.
74 D4 Ridgecrest U.S.A.
80 D4 Ridgway U.S.A.
65 J4 Riding Mountain Nat. Park Can.
46 D6 Riedlingen Ger.
42 D4 Riemst Belgium
43 M3 Riesa Ger.
88 B8 Riesco, Isla i. Chile
58 D5 Riet r. S. Africa
37 R9 Rietavas Lith.
58 E5 Rietbron S. Africa
58 D3 Rietfontein S. Africa
48 E3 Rieti Italy
73 F4 Rifle U.S.A.
36 E3 Rifstangi pt Iceland
23 H3 Riga India
37 T8 Riga Latvia
37 S8 Riga, Gulf of g. Estonia/Latvia
19 E4 Rigān Iran
Rigas Jūras Līcis g. see Riga, Gulf of
81 F2 Rigaud Can.
72 C2 Riggins U.S.A.
67 J3 Rigolet Can.
40 E5 Rigside U.K.
18 E3 Rīgū Iran
23 E4 Rihand r. India
23 E4 Rihand Dam dam India
Riia Laht g. see Riga, Gulf of
37 T6 Riihimäki Fin.
92 D4 Riiser-Larsenhalvøya pen. Ant.
92 C3 Riiser-Larsenisen ice feature Ant.
92 D3 Riiser-Larsen Sea sea Ant.
73 D5 Riito Mex.
48 F2 Rijeka Croatia
Rijn r. Neth. see Rhine
28 G5 Rikuzen-takata Japan
49 K3 Rila mts Bulg.
72 C3 Riley U.S.A.
44 G4 Rillieux-la-Pape France
47 K6 Rimavská Sobota Slovakia
64 G4 Rimbey Can.
48 E2 Rimini Italy
67 G4 Rimouski Can.
43 H5 Rimpar Ger.
40 D2 Rimsdale, Loch l. U.K.
23 G3 Rinbung China
84 B2 Rincón de Romos Mex.
22 E4 Rind r. India
36 L5 Rindal Norway
22 C4 Ringas India
23 G2 Ring Co salt l. China
42 E2 Ringe Ger.
37 M6 Ringebu Norway
37 L8 Ringkøbing Denmark
41 E2 Ringsend U.K.
37 M9 Ringsted Denmark
36 Q2 Ringvassøy i. Norway
39 F7 Ringwood U.K.
91 B3 Riñihue Chile
91 B3 Riñihue, L. l. Chile
33 E4 Rinjani, G. volc. Indon.
43 H2 Rinteln Ger.
68 C4 Rio U.S.A.
90 A2 Rio Alegre Brazil
86 C4 Riobamba Ecuador
75 H2 Rio Blanco U.S.A.
86 E6 Rio Branco Brazil
90 C4 Rio Branco do Sul Brazil
89 E4 Rio Branco, Parque Nacional do nat. park Brazil
90 A3 Rio Brilhante Brazil
91 B4 Río Bueno Chile
89 E2 Río Caribe Venez.
91 D1 Río Ceballos Arg.
90 C3 Rio Claro Brazil
89 E2 Rio Claro Trinidad and Tobago
91 D3 Río Colorado Arg.
91 D2 Río Cuarto Arg.
90 D3 Rio de Janeiro Brazil
90 D3 Rio de Janeiro div. Brazil
88 G3 Rio do Sul Brazil
88 C8 Río Gallegos Arg.
88 C8 Río Grande Arg.
91 G2 Rio Grande Brazil
84 B2 Río Grande Mex.
86 F7 Río Grande r. Bol.
82 C2 Rio Grande r. Mex./U.S.A.
77 D7 Rio Grande City U.S.A.
96 G7 Rio Grande Rise sea feature Atl. Ocean
89 B2 Ríohacha Col.
86 C5 Rioja Peru
87 L5 Rio Largo Brazil
44 F4 Riom France
86 E7 Río Mulatos Bol.
90 C4 Rio Negro Brazil
91 C4 Río Negro div. Arg.
91 F2 Río Negro, Embalse del resr Uru.
51 G7 Rioni r. Georgia
91 G1 Rio Pardo Brazil
90 D1 Rio Pardo de Minas Brazil
91 D1 Río Primero Arg.
73 F5 Rio Rancho U.S.A.
75 G6 Rio Rico U.S.A.
91 D1 Río Segundo Arg.
89 A3 Ríosucio Col.
91 D2 Río Tercero Arg.
86 C4 Río Tigre Ecuador
31 A4 Rio Tuba Phil.
90 B2 Rio Verde Brazil
84 C2 Río Verde Mex.
90 A2 Rio Verde de Mato Grosso Brazil
74 B2 Rio Vista U.S.A.
90 A2 Riozinho r. Brazil
47 P5 Ripky Ukr.
38 F3 Ripley Eng. U.K.
39 F4 Ripley Eng. U.K.
80 B5 Ripley OH U.S.A.
79 B5 Ripley TN U.S.A.
80 C5 Ripley WV U.S.A.
45 H1 Ripoll Spain
38 F3 Ripon U.K.
74 B3 Ripon CA U.S.A.
68 C4 Ripon WV U.S.A.
39 D6 Risca U.K.
18 C4 Rīshahr Iran
28 G2 Rishiri-tō i. Japan
16 E6 Rishon Le Ẕiyyon Israel
19 F5 Rish Pish Iran
37 L7 Risør Norway
36 L5 Rissa Norway
37 U6 Ristiina Fin.
36 V4 Ristijärvi Fin.
36 W2 Ristikent Rus. Fed.
58 F4 Ritchie S. Africa
36 P3 Ritsem Sweden
43 G1 Ritterhude Ger.
73 C4 Ritter, Mt mt U.S.A.
45 E2 Rituerto r. Spain
72 C2 Ritzville U.S.A.
91 C2 Rivadavia Mendoza Arg.
91 D2 Rivadavia Pampas Arg.
88 D2 Rivadavia Salta Arg.
91 B1 Rivadavia Chile
48 D2 Riva del Garda Italy
83 G6 Rivas Nic.
19 E3 Rīvash Iran
91 D3 Rivera Arg.
91 F1 Rivera Uru.
54 B4 River Cess Liberia
81 G4 Riverhead U.S.A.
8 E3 Riverina reg. Austr.
58 D7 Riversdale S. Africa
59 H5 Riverside S. Africa
74 D5 Riverside U.S.A.
8 B3 Riverton Austr.
65 K4 Riverton Can.
9 B7 Riverton N.Z.
72 E3 Riverton U.S.A.
67 H4 Riverview Can.
44 F5 Rivesaltes France
79 D7 Riviera Beach U.S.A.
81 J1 Rivière Bleue Can.
67 G4 Rivière-du-Loup Can.
51 C5 Rivne Ukr.
9 D4 Riwaka N.Z.
20 C5 Riyadh S. Arabia
26 A2 Riyue Shankou pass China
18 D3 Riza well Iran
17 H1 Rize Turkey
26 F3 Rizhao China
16 E4 Rizokarpason Cyprus
18 E4 Rīzū'īyeh Iran
37 L7 Rjukan Norway
37 K7 Rjuvbrokkene mt Norway
54 A3 Rkîz Maur.
22 D3 Rnyar r. India
37 M6 Roa Norway
39 G5 Roade U.K.
36 M4 Roan Norway
75 H2 Roan Cliffs cliff U.S.A.
44 G3 Roanne France
79 C5 Roanoke AL U.S.A.
68 C5 Roanoke IL U.S.A.
80 D6 Roanoke VA U.S.A.
78 E4 Roanoke r. VA U.S.A.
79 E4 Roanoke Rapids U.S.A.
75 H2 Roan Plateau plat. U.S.A.
41 B6 Roaringwater Bay b. Rep. of Ireland
36 R5 Röbäck Sweden
18 E4 Robāṭ Iran
19 F4 Robāt r. Afgh.
18 E3 Robāṭ-e Khān Iran
19 F4 Robat Thana Pak.
6 E6 Robbins I. i. Austr.
8 B4 Robe Austr.
41 B4 Robe r. Rep. of Ireland
43 L1 Röbel Ger.
8 C1 Robe, Mt h. Austr.
77 C6 Robert Lee U.S.A.
72 D3 Roberts U.S.A.
74 D2 Roberts Creek Mt mt U.S.A.
36 R4 Robertsfors Sweden
23 E4 Robertsganj India
77 E5 Robert S. Kerr Res. resr U.S.A.
58 C6 Robertson S. Africa
92 B2 Robertson I. i. Ant.
54 A4 Robertsport Liberia
8 B2 Robertstown Austr.
67 F4 Roberval Can.
63 M1 Robeson Channel chan. Can./Greenland
38 G3 Robin Hood's Bay U.K.
27 □ Robin's Nest h. H.K. China
78 C4 Robinson U.S.A.
95 O8 Robinson Crusoe i. Pac. Oc.
6 B4 Robinson Ranges h. Austr.
8 D3 Robinvale Austr.
75 G5 Robles Junction U.S.A.
75 G5 Robles Pass U.S.A.
65 J4 Roblin Can.
64 F4 Robson, Mt mt Can.
77 D7 Robstown U.S.A.
84 D3 Roca Partida, Pta hd Mex.
48 E6 Rocca Busambra mt Sicily Italy
91 F2 Rocha Uru.
38 E4 Rochdale U.K.
90 A2 Rochedo Brazil
42 D4 Rochefort Belgium
44 D4 Rochefort France
66 F2 Rochefort, Lac l. Can.
50 G2 Rochegda Rus. Fed.
68 C5 Rochelle U.S.A.
8 E4 Rochester Austr.
39 H6 Rochester U.K.
68 D5 Rochester IN U.S.A.
68 A3 Rochester MN U.S.A.
81 H3 Rochester NH U.S.A.
80 E3 Rochester NY U.S.A.
39 H6 Rochford U.K.
43 L3 Rochlitz Ger.
44 C2 Roc'h Trévezel h. France
64 D2 Rock r. Can.
68 B5 Rock r. U.S.A.
96 H2 Rockall Bank sea feature Atl. Ocean
92 B4 Rockefeller Plateau plat. Ant.
68 C4 Rockford U.S.A.
65 H5 Rockglen Can.
6 F4 Rockhampton Austr.
68 C1 Rock Harbor U.S.A.
79 D5 Rock Hill U.S.A.
6 B5 Rockingham Austr.
79 E5 Rockingham U.S.A.
81 G2 Rock Island Can.
68 B5 Rock Island U.S.A.
76 D1 Rocklake U.S.A.
81 F2 Rockland Can.
81 H3 Rockland MA U.S.A.
81 J2 Rockland ME U.S.A.
66 C2 Rockland MI U.S.A.
8 D4 Rocklands Reservoir Austr.
75 H3 Rock Point U.S.A.
81 H3 Rockport U.S.A.
76 D3 Rock Rapids U.S.A.
72 F2 Rock Springs MT U.S.A.
72 E3 Rock Springs WY U.S.A.
77 C6 Rocksprings U.S.A.
8 F3 Rock, The Austr.
80 D3 Rockton Can.
68 D6 Rockville IN U.S.A.
80 E5 Rockville MD U.S.A.
81 J2 Rockwood U.S.A.
73 G4 Rocky Ford U.S.A.
80 B5 Rocky Fork Lake l. U.S.A.
69 F2 Rocky Island Lake l. Can.
79 E5 Rocky Mount NC U.S.A.
80 D6 Rocky Mount VA U.S.A.
64 G4 Rocky Mountain House Can.
72 F3 Rocky Mountain Nat. Park U.S.A.
60 E4 Rocky Mountains Can./U.S.A.
64 F4 Rocky Mountains Forest Reserve res. Can.
42 B5 Rocourt-St-Martin France
42 C5 Rocroi France
37 L6 Rodberg Norway
37 M9 Rødbyhavn Denmark
67 J3 Roddickton Can.
40 B3 Rodel U.K.
42 E1 Roden Neth.
43 K4 Rödental Ger.
91 C1 Rodeo Arg.
84 A1 Rodeo Mex.
75 H6 Rodeo U.S.A.
44 F4 Rodez France
43 L5 Roding Ger.
19 G5 Rodkhan Pak.
50 G3 Rodniki Rus. Fed.
49 L4 Rodopi Planina mts Bulg./Greece
Rodos see Rhodes
Rodos i. see Rhodes
93 J5 Rodrigues i. Ind. Ocean
93 J5 Rodrigues Fracture sea feature Ind. Ocean
6 B4 Roebourne Austr.
6 C3 Roebuck Bay b. Austr.
59 H2 Roedtan S. Africa
42 D3 Roermond Neth.
42 B4 Roeselare Belgium
63 K3 Roes Welcome Sound chan. Can.
86 E6 Rogaguado, Lago l. Bol.
43 K2 Rogätz Ger.
77 E4 Rogers U.S.A.
69 F3 Rogers City U.S.A.
74 D4 Rogers Lake l. U.S.A.
72 D3 Rogerson U.S.A.
80 B6 Rogersville U.S.A.
66 E3 Roggan r. Can.
58 D6 Roggeveld plat. S. Africa
58 D6 Roggeveldberge esc. S. Africa
36 O3 Rognan Norway
72 A3 Rogue r. U.S.A.
74 A2 Rohnert Park U.S.A.
46 F6 Rohrbach in Oberösterreich Austria
42 F5 Rohrbach-lès-Bitche France
22 B4 Rohri Pak.
22 D3 Rohtak India
5 N6 Roi Georges, Îles du is Pac. Oc.
42 B5 Roisel France
37 S8 Roja Latvia
91 E2 Rojas Arg.
22 B3 Rojhan Pak.
84 C2 Rojo, C. c. Mex.
33 B2 Rokan r. Indon.
37 T9 Rokiškis Lith.
36 R4 Roknäs Sweden
51 C5 Rokytne Ukr.
23 G2 Rola Co salt l. China
90 B3 Rolândia Brazil
76 F4 Rolla U.S.A.
37 L6 Rollag Norway
9 D5 Rolleston N.Z.
69 H2 Rollet Can.
79 F7 Rolleville Bahamas
69 J2 Rolphton Can.
6 E4 Roma Austr.
Roma see Rome
59 G4 Roma Lesotho
37 Q8 Roma Sweden
25 E7 Roma i. Indon.
79 E5 Romain, Cape c. U.S.A.
67 H3 Romaine r. Can.
47 N7 Roman Romania

96 H6 Romanche Gap sea feature Atl. Ocean
16 D6 Românî Egypt
35 H4 Romania country Europe
51 G5 Romanovka Rus. Fed.
24 D1 Romanovka Rus. Fed.
44 G4 Romans-sur-Isère France
62 B3 Romanzof, Cape c. U.S.A.
44 H2 Rombas France
31 B3 Romblon Phil.
31 B3 Romblon i. Phil.
48 E4 Rome Italy
79 C5 Rome GA U.S.A.
81 J2 Rome ME U.S.A.
81 F3 Rome NY U.S.A.
69 F4 Romeo U.S.A.
39 H6 Romford U.K.
44 F2 Romilly-sur-Seine France
19 G2 Romitan Uzbek.
80 D5 Romney U.S.A.
39 H6 Romney Marsh reg. U.K.
51 E5 Romny Ukr.
37 L9 Rømø i. Denmark
44 E3 Romorantin-Lanthenay France
32 B5 Rompin r. Malaysia
39 F7 Romsey U.K.
21 A3 Ron India
32 C1 Ron Vietnam
40 C3 Rona i. Scot. U.K.
40 C1 Rona i. Scot. U.K.
40 □ Ronas Hill h. U.K.
7 F2 Roncador Reef rf Solomon Is
87 H6 Roncador, Serra do h. Brazil
45 D4 Ronda Spain
37 L6 Rondane Nasjonalpark nat. park Norway
89 C3 Rondón Col.
86 F6 Rondônia Brazil
90 A2 Rondonópolis Brazil
15 F3 Rondu Jammu and Kashmir
27 C5 Rong'an China
27 B4 Rongchang China
30 B5 Rongcheng China
30 B5 Rongcheng Wan b. China
23 G3 Rong Chu r. China
65 H3 Ronge, Lac la l. Can.
94 G5 Rongelap i. Pac. Oc.
27 C5 Rongjiang China
27 C6 Rong Jiang r. China
23 H5 Rongklang Range mts Myanmar
9 E4 Rongotea N.Z.
27 C5 Rongshui China
27 D6 Rong Xian Guangxi China
27 B4 Rong Xian Sichuan China
37 O9 Rønne Denmark
37 O8 Ronneby Sweden
92 B3 Ronne Entrance str. Ant.
92 B3 Ronne Ice Shelf ice feature Ant.
43 H2 Ronnenberg Ger.
42 B4 Ronse Belgium
42 E1 Roodeschool Neth.
42 D1 Roordahuizum Neth.
22 D3 Roorkee India
42 C3 Roosendaal Neth.
75 G5 Roosevelt AZ U.S.A.
75 G1 Roosevelt UT U.S.A.
75 G5 Roosevelt Dam dam U.S.A.
92 A4 Roosevelt I. i. Ant.
64 D3 Roosevelt, Mt mt Can.
64 E2 Root r. Can.
68 B4 Root r. U.S.A.
50 K2 Ropcha Rus. Fed.
44 D4 Roquefort France
89 E4 Roraima div. Brazil
86 F2 Roraima, Mt mt Guyana
36 M5 Røros Norway
36 M4 Rørvik Norway
47 P6 Ros' r. Ukr.
86 □ Rosa, C. pt Galapagos Is Ecuador
74 C4 Rosamond U.S.A.
74 C4 Rosamond Lake l. U.S.A.
91 E2 Rosario Arg.
82 A2 Rosario Baja California Mex.
77 C7 Rosario Coahuila Mex.
84 A2 Rosario Mex.
31 B2 Rosario Phil.
31 B3 Rosario Phil.
89 B2 Rosario Venez.
91 E2 Rosario del Tala Arg.
91 F1 Rosário do Sul Brazil
90 A1 Rosário Oeste Brazil
48 F5 Rosarno Italy
81 F4 Roscoe U.S.A.
44 C2 Roscoff France
41 C4 Roscommon Rep. of Ireland
68 E3 Roscommon U.S.A.
41 D5 Roscrea Rep. of Ireland
83 M5 Roseau Dominica
65 K5 Roseau U.S.A.
67 J4 Rose Blanche Can.
72 B3 Roseburg U.S.A.
69 E3 Rose City U.S.A.
38 G3 Rosedale Abbey U.K.
55 F3 Roseires Reservoir Sudan
74 C2 Rose, Mt mt U.S.A.
77 E6 Rosenberg U.S.A.
37 K7 Rosendal Norway
59 G4 Rosendal S. Africa
46 F7 Rosenheim Ger.
64 C4 Rose Pt pt Can.
79 F7 Roses Bahamas
48 F3 Roseto degli Abruzzi Italy
65 H4 Rosetown Can.
Rosetta see Rashîd
65 J4 Rose Valley Can.
74 B2 Roseville CA U.S.A.
68 B5 Roseville IL U.S.A.
50 D2 Roshchino Leningrad. Rus. Fed.
28 D2 Roshchino Primorskiy Kray Rus. Fed.
19 E3 Roshkhvār Iran
58 B3 Rosh Pinah Namibia
19 H2 Roshtqal'a Tajik.
48 D3 Rosignano Marittimo Italy
49 L2 Roșiori de Vede Romania
37 N9 Roskilde Denmark
50 E4 Roslavl' Rus. Fed.
36 X2 Roslyakovo Rus. Fed.
9 C5 Ross N.Z.
64 C2 Ross r. Can.
48 G5 Rossano Italy
41 C3 Rossan Point pt Rep. of Ireland
77 F5 Ross Barnett Res. l. U.S.A.
67 G3 Ross Bay Junction Can.
41 B6 Ross Carbery Rep. of Ireland
92 A5 Ross Dependency reg. Ant.
7 F3 Rossel Island i. P.N.G.
92 B4 Ross Ice Shelf ice feature Ant.
67 H5 Rossignol, L. l. Can.
92 B5 Ross Island i. Ant.
41 E5 Rosslare Rep. of Ireland
39 A5 Rosslare Harbour Rep. of Ireland
43 L3 Roßlau Ger.
69 J3 Rossmore Can.
9 E4 Ross, Mt mt N.Z.
54 A3 Rosso Maur.
48 C3 Rosso, Capo pt Corsica France
39 E6 Ross-on-Wye U.K.
51 F5 Rossosh' Rus. Fed.
68 D1 Rossport Can.
64 C2 Ross River Can.
92 A5 Ross Sea sea Ant.
43 J5 Roßtal Ger.
36 O4 Røssvatnet l. Norway
68 D5 Rossville U.S.A.
43 M3 Roßwein Ger.
64 D3 Rosswood Can.
17 K3 Röst Iraq
19 H2 Rostāq Afgh.
18 D5 Rostāq Iran
65 H4 Rosthern Can.
46 F3 Rostock Ger.
50 F3 Rostov Rus. Fed.
51 F6 Rostov-na-Donu Rus. Fed.
51 G6 Rostovskaya Oblast' div. Rus. Fed.
36 R4 Rosvik Sweden
79 C5 Roswell GA U.S.A.
73 F5 Roswell NM U.S.A.
25 G5 Rota i. N. Mariana Is
43 J5 Rot am See Ger.
25 E8 Rote i. Indon.
43 H1 Rotenburg (Wümme) Ger.
43 K4 Roter Main r. Ger.
43 K5 Roth Ger.
43 G4 Rothaargebirge reg. Ger.
38 F2 Rothbury U.K.
38 F2 Rothbury Forest forest U.K.
43 J5 Rothenburg ob der Tauber Ger.
39 G7 Rother r. U.K.
92 B2 Rothera U.K. Base Ant.
9 D5 Rotherham N.Z.
39 F4 Rotherham U.K.
40 E3 Rothes U.K.
40 C5 Rothesay U.K.
68 C3 Rothschild U.S.A.
92 B2 Rothschild I. i. Ant.
39 G5 Rothwell U.K.
Roti i. see Rote
8 E2 Roto Austr.
9 C5 Rotomanu N.Z.
48 C3 Rotondo, Monte mt Corsica France
9 D4 Rotoroa, L. l. N.Z.
9 F3 Rotorua N.Z.
9 F3 Rotorua, L. l. N.Z.
46 F6 Rott r. Ger.
43 K5 Röttenbach Ger.
43 J5 Rottendorf Ger.
46 G7 Rottenmann Austria
42 C3 Rotterdam Neth.
43 J3 Rottleberode Ger.
42 E1 Rottumeroog i. Neth.
42 E1 Rottumerplaat i. Neth.
46 D6 Rottweil Ger.
7 H3 Rotuma i. Fiji
36 O5 Rötviken Sweden
43 L5 Rötz Ger.
44 F1 Roubaix France
44 E2 Rouen France
9 B6 Rough Ridge ridge N.Z.
Roulers see Roeselare
67 F3 Roundeyed, Lac l. Can.
38 F3 Round Hill h. U.K.
74 D2 Round Mountain U.S.A.
75 H3 Round Rock U.S.A.
72 E2 Roundup U.S.A.
40 E1 Rousay i. U.K.
81 G2 Rouses Point U.S.A.
44 F5 Roussillon reg. France
Routh Bank sand bank see Seahorse Bank
59 G5 Rouxville S. Africa
69 H1 Rouyn Can.
36 T3 Rovaniemi Fin.
51 F5 Roven'ki Rus. Fed.
48 D2 Rovereto Italy
32 C2 Rôviĕng Tbong Cambodia
48 D2 Rovigo Italy
48 E2 Rovinj Croatia
51 H5 Rovnoye Rus. Fed.
18 C3 Row'ān Iran
31 B4 Roxas Phil.
31 B4 Roxas Phil.
31 A4 Roxas Phil.
31 B3 Roxas Phil.
31 B2 Roxas Phil.
79 E4 Roxboro U.S.A.
9 B6 Roxburgh N.Z.
73 F4 Roy U.S.A.
41 E4 Royal Canal canal Rep. of Ireland
68 C1 Royale, Isle i. U.S.A.
59 H4 Royal Natal National Park S. Africa
69 F4 Royal Oak U.S.A.
44 D4 Royan France
42 A5 Roye France
66 E2 Roy, Lac le l. Can.
39 G5 Royston U.K.
51 D6 Rozdil'na Ukr.
51 E6 Rozdol'ne Ukr.
51 F6 Rozivka Ukr.
18 C3 Rozveh Iran
51 G4 Rtishchevo Rus. Fed.
48 E2 Rt Kamenjak pt Croatia
39 D5 Ruabon U.K.
57 B5 Ruacana Namibia
56 D4 Ruaha National Park Tanz.
9 E3 Ruapehu, Mt volc. N.Z.
9 B7 Ruapuke I. i. N.Z.
9 F3 Ruahine Range mts N.Z.
9 G2 Ruatoria N.Z.
50 D4 Ruba Belarus
20 C6 Rub' al Khālī des. S. Arabia
28 H3 Rubeshibe Japan
40 C2 Rubha Coigeach pt U.K.
40 B3 Rubha Hunish pt U.K.
40 C3 Rubha Reidh pt U.K.
74 B2 Rubicon r. U.S.A.
51 F5 Rubizhne Ukr.
12 K4 Rubtsovsk Rus. Fed.
62 C3 Ruby U.S.A.
75 E1 Ruby Lake l. U.S.A.
75 E1 Ruby Mountains U.S.A.
27 D5 Rucheng China
80 D5 Ruckersville U.S.A.
18 E5 Rudan Iran
23 E4 Rudauli India
19 F4 Rudbar Afgh.
17 M3 Rūdbār Iran
18 E2 Rūd-e Kāl-Shūr r. Iran
19 E4 Rūd-i-Shur watercourse Iran
37 M9 Rudkøbing Denmark
24 F2 Rudnaya Pristan' Rus. Fed.
50 K3 Rudnichnyy Rus. Fed.
50 D4 Rudnya Rus. Fed.
14 E1 Rudnyy Kazak.
28 D2 Rudnyy Rus. Fed.
12 G1 Rudolfa, O. i. Rus. Fed.
43 K4 Rudolstadt Ger.
26 F3 Rudong China
18 C2 Rūdsar Iran
68 E2 Rudyard U.S.A.
57 D4 Rufiji r. Tanz.
91 D2 Rufino Arg.
54 A3 Rufisque Senegal
57 C5 Rufunsa Zambia
26 F3 Rugao China
39 F5 Rugby U.K.
76 C1 Rugby U.S.A.
39 F5 Rugeley U.K.
46 F3 Rügen i. Ger.
80 B4 Ruggles U.S.A.
43 J5 Rügland Ger.
18 B5 Ruḩayyat al Ḩamr'ā' waterhole S. Arabia
56 C4 Ruhengeri Rwanda
37 S8 Ruhnu i. Estonia
42 E4 Ruhr r. Ger.
27 F5 Rui'an China
73 F5 Ruidoso U.S.A.
27 E5 Ruijin China
65 N2 Ruin Point pt Can.
57 D4 Ruipa Tanz.
84 A2 Ruiz Mex.
89 B3 Ruiz, Nevado del volc. Col.
37 T8 Rūjiena Latvia
18 C5 Rukbah well S. Arabia
23 E3 Rukumkot Nepal
56 D4 Rukwa, Lake l. Tanz.
18 E5 Rūl Ḑadnah U.A.E.
18 E3 Rūm Iran
40 B4 Rum i. Scot. U.K.
49 H2 Ruma Yugo.
18 B5 Rumāh S. Arabia
55 E4 Rumbek Sudan
79 F7 Rum Cay i. Bahamas
81 H2 Rumford U.S.A.
44 G4 Rumilly France
6 D3 Rum Jungle Austr.
28 G3 Rumoi Japan
26 E3 Runan China
9 C5 Runanga N.Z.
9 F2 Runaway, Cape c. N.Z.
39 E4 Runcorn U.K.
57 B5 Rundu Namibia
36 Q5 Rundvik Sweden
27 F4 Runheji China
26 A3 Ru'nying China
37 V6 Ruokolahti Fin.
24 A3 Ruoqiang China
23 H4 Rupa India
91 B4 Rupanco, L. l. Chile
8 D4 Rupanyup Austr.
33 B2 Rupat i. Indon.
72 D3 Rupert U.S.A.
66 E3 Rupert r. Can.
66 E3 Rupert Bay b. Can.
92 A4 Ruppert Coast coastal area Ant.
57 D5 Rusape Zimbabwe
49 L3 Ruse Bulg.
30 A5 Rushan China
39 G5 Rushden U.K.
68 B4 Rushford U.S.A.
68 C4 Rush Lake l. U.S.A.
23 H3 Rushon India
19 H2 Rushon Tajik.
68 B5 Rushville IL U.S.A.
76 C3 Rushville NE U.S.A.
8 E4 Rushworth Austr.
77 E6 Rusk U.S.A.
79 D7 Ruskin U.S.A.
65 J4 Russell Man. Can.
81 F2 Russell Ont. Can.
9 E1 Russell N.Z.
76 D4 Russell U.S.A.
64 F2 Russell Lake l. Can.
63 J2 Russell I. i. Can.
7 F2 Russell Is is Solomon Is
79 C4 Russellville AL U.S.A.
77 E5 Russellville AR U.S.A.
78 C4 Russellville KY U.S.A.
43 G4 Rüsselsheim Ger.
10 E3 Russian Federation country Asia/Europe
28 C3 Russkiy, Ostrov i. Rus. Fed.
17 K1 Rust'avi Georgia
59 G2 Rustenburg S. Africa
77 E5 Ruston U.S.A.
25 E7 Ruteng Indon.
75 E2 Ruth U.S.A.
43 G3 Rüthen Ger.
69 H2 Rutherglen Can.
39 D4 Ruthin U.K.
50 H3 Rutka r. Rus. Fed.
81 G3 Rutland U.S.A.
39 G5 Rutland Water resr U.K.
65 G2 Rutledge Lake l. Can.
22 D2 Rutog China
69 G2 Rutter Can.
36 T4 Ruukki Fin.
18 E5 Rū'us al Jibāl pen. Oman
57 D5 Ruvuma r. Moz./Tanz.
16 F5 Ruwayshid, Wādī watercourse Jordan
18 D5 Ruweis U.A.E.
27 D5 Ruyuan China
14 E1 Ruzayevka Kazak.
50 H4 Ruzayevka Rus. Fed.
47 J6 Ružomberok Slovakia
53 G6 Rwanda country Africa
18 D2 Ryābād Iran
50 D2 Ryadovo Rus. Fed.
40 C5 Ryan, Loch b. U.K.
50 F4 Ryazan' Rus. Fed.
50 G4 Ryazanskaya Oblast' div. Rus. Fed.
50 G4 Ryazhsk Rus. Fed.
12 E2 Rybachiy, Poluostrov pen. Rus. Fed.
50 F3 Rybinsk Rus. Fed.
50 F3 Rybinskoye Vdkhr. resr Rus. Fed.
50 J4 Rybnaya Sloboda Rus. Fed.
47 J5 Rybnik Pol.
50 F4 Rybnoye Rus. Fed.
64 F3 Rycroft Can.
37 O8 Ryd Sweden
92 B3 Rydberg Pen. pen. Ant.
39 F7 Ryde U.K.
39 H7 Rye U.K.
38 G3 Rye r. U.K.
51 E5 Ryl'sk Rus. Fed.
8 G2 Rylstone Austr.
30 D5 Ryoju S. Korea
29 F5 Ryōtsu Japan
47 L5 Rzeszów Pol.
51 G4 Rzhaksa Rus. Fed.
50 E3 Rzhev Rus. Fed.

S

18 E3 Sa'ābād Iran
18 D4 Sa'ādatābād Iran
18 D4 Sa'ādatābād Iran
43 K6 Saal an der Donau Ger.
43 K3 Saale r. Ger.
43 K4 Saalfeld Ger.
42 E5 Saar r. Ger.
42 E5 Saarbrücken Ger.
37 S7 Saaremaa i. Estonia
36 T3 Saarenkylä Fin.
42 E5 Saargau reg. Ger.
36 T5 Saarijärvi Fin.
36 U3 Saari-Kämä Fin.
36 R2 Saarikoski Fin.
42 E5 Saarland div. Ger.
42 E5 Saarlouis Ger.
17 M2 Saatlı Azer.
91 D3 Saavedra Arg.
16 F5 Sab' Ābār Syria
49 H2 Šabac Yugo.
45 H2 Sabadell Spain
29 E7 Sabae Japan
33 E1 Sabah div. Malaysia
32 B5 Sabak Malaysia
33 E4 Sabalana, Kep. is Indon.
22 D4 Sabalgarh India
83 H4 Sabana, Arch. de is Cuba
89 B2 Sabanalarga Col.
16 D1 Şabanözü Turkey
90 D2 Sabará Brazil
21 C2 Sābari r. India
22 C5 Sabarmati r. India
48 E4 Sabaudia Italy
19 E3 Sabeh Iran
58 E5 Sabelo S. Africa
55 D2 Sabhā Libya
18 B6 Şabḩā' S. Arabia
22 D3 Sabi r. India
59 K2 Sabie Moz.
59 J2 Sabie S. Africa
59 K2 Sabie r. Moz./S. Africa
82 D3 Sabinas Mex.
82 D3 Sabinas Hidalgo Mex.
77 E6 Sabine L. l. U.S.A.
17 M1 Sabirabad Azer.
31 B3 Sablayan Phil.
79 D7 Sable, Cape c. U.S.A.
7 F3 Sable, Île de i. New Caledonia
63 N5 Sable Island i. N.S. Can.
69 F2 Sables, River aux r. Can.
92 C6 Sabrina Coast coastal area Ant.
31 B1 Sabtang i. Phil.
45 C2 Sabugal Port.
68 B4 Sabula U.S.A.
20 B6 Şabyā S. Arabia
Sabzawar see Shīndand
19 E2 Sabzevār Iran
49 N2 Sacalinul Mare, Insula i. Romania
49 L2 Săcele Romania
57 B5 Sachanga Angola
66 B3 Sachigo r. Can.
66 B3 Sachigo L. l. Can.
22 C5 Sachin India
30 E6 Sach'ŏn S. Korea
22 D2 Sach Pass India
43 L3 Sachsen div. Ger.
43 K3 Sachsen-Anhalt div. Ger.
43 H6 Sachsenheim Ger.
62 F2 Sachs Harbour Can.
81 E3 Sackets Harbor U.S.A.
43 G4 Sackpfeife h. Ger.
67 H4 Sackville Can.
81 H3 Saco ME U.S.A.
72 F1 Saco MT U.S.A.
31 B5 Sacol i. Phil.
74 B2 Sacramento U.S.A.
74 B2 Sacramento r. U.S.A.
73 F5 Sacramento Mts mts U.S.A.
72 B3 Sacramento Valley v. U.S.A.
59 G6 Sada S. Africa
45 F1 Sádaba Spain
18 C4 Sa'dabad Iran
16 F4 Şadad Syria
32 B4 Sadao Thai.
59 J2 Saddleback pass S. Africa
32 C3 Sa Đec Vietnam
23 H3 Sadêng China
19 E5 Sadīj watercourse Iran
22 B3 Sadiqabad Pak.
22 C1 Sad Istragh mt Afgh./Pak.
17 L5 Sa'dīyah, Hawr as l. Iraq
18 D5 Sa'diyyat i. U.A.E.
18 E2 Sad-Kharv Iran
45 B3 Sado r. Port.
29 F6 Sadoga-shima i. Japan
24 F3 Sado-Shima i. Japan
45 H3 Sa Dragonera i. Spain
37 M8 Sæby Denmark
Safad see Zefat
17 L6 Safayal Maqūf well Iraq
19 H2 Safed Khirs mts Afgh.
19 G3 Safed Koh mts Afgh.
37 N7 Säffle Sweden
75 H5 Safford U.S.A.
39 H5 Saffron Walden U.K.
16 E6 Safi Jordan
54 B1 Safi Morocco
18 C2 Safīd r. Iran
18 D3 Safid Ab Iran
19 F4 Safidabeh Iran
17 M5 Safid Dasht Iran
16 F4 Şāfītā Syria
36 X2 Safonovo Murmansk. Rus. Fed.
50 E4 Safonovo Smolensk. Rus. Fed.
12 F3 Safonovo Rus. Fed.
18 A5 Safrā' al Asyāḩ esc. S. Arabia
16 D1 Safranbolu Turkey
17 L6 Safwān Iraq
23 F3 Saga China
29 B8 Saga Japan
29 F7 Sagamihara Japan
29 F7 Sagami-nada g. Japan
29 F7 Sagami-wan b. Japan
89 B3 Sagamoso r. Col.
32 A2 Saganthit Kyun i. Myanmar
21 B2 Sagar Karnataka India
21 A3 Sagar Karnataka India
22 D5 Sagar Madhya Pradesh India
51 H7 Sagarejo Georgia
23 G5 Sagar I. i. India
13 O2 Sagastyr Rus. Fed.
18 D3 Saghand Iran
19 F3 Saghar Afgh.
21 B3 Sagileru r. India
69 F4 Saginaw U.S.A.
69 F4 Saginaw Bay b. U.S.A.
67 H2 Saglek Bay b. Can.
48 C3 Sagone, Golfe de b. Corsica France
45 B4 Sagres Port.
23 H5 Sagu Myanmar
73 F4 Saguache U.S.A.
83 H4 Sagua la Grande Cuba
75 G5 Saguaro National Monument res. U.S.A.
67 F4 Saguenay r. Can.
45 F3 Sagunto-Sagunt Spain
22 C5 Sagwara India
89 B2 Sahagún Col.
45 D1 Sahagún Spain
17 L3 Sahand, Kūh-e mt Iran
52 D3 Sahara des. Africa
Saharan Atlas mts see Atlas Saharien
22 D3 Saharanpur India
23 F4 Saharsa India
22 D3 Sahaswan India
18 C6 Sahba', W. as watercourse S. Arabia
22 C3 Sahiwal Pak.
19 E3 Sahlābād Iran
17 L4 Şahneh Iran
17 K6 Şaḩrā al Ḩijārah reg. Iraq
75 G6 Sahuarita U.S.A.
84 B2 Sahuayo Mex.
32 D2 Sa Huynh Vietnam
Sahyadri mts see Western Ghats
22 C5 Sahyadriparvat Range h. India
22 E4 Sai r. India
32 B4 Sai Buri Thai.
32 B4 Sai Buri r. Thai.
Saïda see Sidon
18 D4 Sa'īdābād Iran
32 B2 Sai Dao Tai, Khao mt Thai.
19 F5 Sa'īdī Iran
23 G4 Saidpur Bangl.
22 C2 Saidu Pak.
29 C6 Saigō Japan
Saigon see Hô Chi Minh
23 H5 Saiha India
26 A1 Saihan Toroi China
29 C8 Saijō Japan
29 B8 Saiki Japan
27 □ Sai Kung H.K. China
37 V6 Saimaa l. Fin.
16 F2 Saimbeyli Turkey
18 D4 Sā'īn Iran
84 B2 Sain Alto Mex.
19 F4 Saindak Pak.
18 B2 Sa'īndezh Iran
40 F5 St Abb's Head hd U.K.
39 B7 St Agnes U.K.
39 A8 St Agnes i. U.K.
67 J4 St Alban's Can.
39 G6 St Albans U.K.
81 G2 St Albans VT U.S.A.
80 C5 St Albans WV U.S.A.
39 E7 St Alban's Head hd U.K.
64 G4 St Albert Can.
42 B4 St-Amand-les-Eaux France
44 F3 St-Amand-Montrond France
44 G3 St-Amour France
81 K2 St Andrews Can.
40 F4 St Andrews U.K.
83 J5 St Ann's Bay Jamaica
41 F6 St Ann's Head hd U.K.
67 J3 St Anthony Can.
72 E3 St Anthony U.S.A.
8 D4 St Arnaud Austr.
9 D5 St Arnaud Range mts N.Z.
67 J3 St-Augustin Can.
42 F4 St Augustin Ger.
79 D6 St Augustine U.S.A.
39 C7 St Austell U.K.
44 E3 St-Avertin France
42 E5 St-Avold France
83 M5 St Barthélémy i. Guadeloupe
38 D3 St Bees U.K.
38 D3 St Bees Head hd U.K.
39 B6 St Bride's Bay b. U.K.
44 C2 St-Brieuc France
75 G5 St Carlos Lake l. U.S.A.
69 H4 St Catharines Can.
79 D6 St Catherines I. i. U.S.A.
39 F7 St Catherine's Point pt U.K.
44 E4 St-Céré France
81 G2 St-Césaire Can.
44 G4 St-Chamond France
72 E3 St Charles ID U.S.A.
80 E5 St Charles MD U.S.A.
68 A4 St Charles MN U.S.A.
76 F4 St Charles MO U.S.A.
69 F4 St Clair U.S.A.
69 F4 St Clair Shores U.S.A.
44 G3 St-Claude France
39 C6 St Clears U.K.
76 E2 St Cloud U.S.A.
83 M5 St Croix i. Virgin Is
67 G4 St Croix r. Can.
68 A2 St Croix r. U.S.A.
68 A3 St Croix Falls U.S.A.
75 G6 St David U.S.A.
41 F6 St David's U.K.
39 B6 St David's Head hd U.K.
42 A6 St-Denis France
44 H2 St-Dié France
44 G2 St-Dizier France
65 K5 Ste Anne Can.
67 F4 Ste-Anne-de-Beaupré Can.
81 J1 Ste-Anne-de-Madawaska Can.
69 K2 Sainte-Anne-du-Lac Can.
67 G3 Ste Anne, L. l. Can.
81 H1 Ste-Camille-de-Lellis Can.
44 G4 St-Égrève France
81 H1 Sainte-Justine Can.
81 J1 St-Éleuthère Can.
64 B2 St Elias Mountains Can.
67 G3 Ste Marguerite r. Can.
44 H5 Ste-Maxime France
44 D4 Saintes France
68 E2 Ste-Thérèse Can.
44 G4 St-Étienne France
81 F2 St Eugene Can.
81 G2 St-Eustache Can.
83 M5 St Eustatius i. Neth. Ant.
67 F4 St-Félicien Can.
41 F3 Saintfield U.K.
48 C3 St-Florent Corsica France
44 F3 St-Florent-sur-Cher France
56 C3 St. Floris, Parc National nat. park C.A.R.
76 C4 St Francis KS U.S.A.
81 J1 St Francis ME U.S.A.
81 J1 St-Francis r. Can./U.S.A.
77 F4 St Francis r. U.S.A.
67 K4 St Francis, C. c. Can.
81 J1 St Froid Lake l. U.S.A.
46 D7 St Gallen Switz.
44 E5 St-Gaudens France
81 H2 St-Gédéon Can.
6 E4 St George Austr.
81 K2 St George Can.
79 D5 St George SC U.S.A.
75 F3 St George UT U.S.A.
7 F2 St George, C. pt P.N.G.
79 C6 St George I. i. U.S.A.
72 A3 St George, Pt pt U.S.A.
67 F4 St Georges Can.
83 M6 St George's Grenada
67 J4 St George's B. b. Can.
6 F2 St George's Channel P.N.G.
39 A6 St George's Channel Rep. of Ireland/U.K.
39 C6 St Govan's Head hd U.K.
68 E3 St Helen U.S.A.
74 A2 St Helena U.S.A.
53 D7 St Helena terr. Atl. Ocean
58 C6 St Helena Bay S. Africa
58 C6 St Helena Bay b. S. Africa
96 J7 St Helena Fracture sea feature Atl. Ocean
39 E4 St Helens U.K.
72 B2 St Helens U.S.A.
72 B2 St Helens, Mt volc. U.S.A.
44 C2 St Helier Channel Is U.K.
42 D4 St-Hubert Belgium
66 F4 St-Hyacinthe Can.
68 E3 St Ignace U.S.A.
68 C1 St Ignace I. i. Can.
39 C6 St Ishmael U.K.
39 B7 St Ives Eng. U.K.
39 G5 St Ives Eng. U.K.
81 J1 St-Jacques Can.
68 E3 St James U.S.A.
64 C4 St James, Cape pt Can.
44 D4 St-Jean-d'Angély France
44 C3 St-Jean-de-Monts France
67 F4 St-Jean, Lac l. Can.
66 F4 St-Jean-sur-Richelieu Can.
66 F4 St-Jérôme Can.
72 C2 St Joe r. U.S.A.
67 G4 St John Can.
75 F1 St John U.S.A.
83 M5 St John i. Virgin Is
81 K2 St John r. Can./U.S.A.
83 M5 St John's Antigua
67 K4 St John's Can.
75 H4 St Johns AZ U.S.A.
68 E4 St Johns MI U.S.A.
79 D6 St Johns r. U.S.A.
81 H2 St Johnsbury U.S.A.
38 E3 St John's Chapel U.K.
67 F4 St Joseph Can.
68 D4 St Joseph MI U.S.A.
76 E4 St Joseph MO U.S.A.
68 E5 St Joseph r. U.S.A.
69 F2 St Joseph I. i. Can.
77 D7 St Joseph I. i. U.S.A.
66 B3 St Joseph, Lac l. Can.
66 F4 St Jovité Can.
44 E4 St-Junien France
39 B7 St Just U.K.
42 A5 St-Just-en-Chaussée France
39 B7 St Keverne U.K.
61 M8 St Kitts-Nevis country Caribbean Sea
42 B3 St-Laureins Belgium
87 H2 St Laurent Fr. Guiana
St-Laurent, Golfe du g. see St Lawrence, Gulf of
67 K4 St Lawrence Nfld Can.
67 G4 St Lawrence in. Que. Can.
67 H4 St Lawrence, Gulf of g. Can./U.S.A.
62 B3 St Lawrence I. i. AK U.S.A.
69 K3 St Lawrence Islands National Park Can.
81 F2 St Lawrence Seaway chan. Can./U.S.A.
67 G4 St-Léonard Can.
67 J3 St Lewis Can.
67 J3 Saint Lewis r. Can.
44 D2 St-Lô France
54 A3 St Louis Senegal
68 E4 St Louis MI U.S.A.
76 F4 St Louis MO U.S.A.
68 A2 St Louis r. U.S.A.
61 M8 St Lucia country Caribbean Sea
59 K4 St Lucia Estuary S. Africa
59 K3 St Lucia, Lake l. S. Africa
83 M5 St Maarten i. Neth. Ant.
40 □ St Magnus Bay b. U.K.
44 D3 St-Maixent-l'École France
44 C2 St-Malo France
44 C2 St-Malo, Golfe de g. France
59 G6 St Marks S. Africa
83 M5 Saint Martin i. Guadeloupe
58 B6 St Martin, Cape hd S. Africa
68 D3 St Martin I. i. U.S.A.
65 K4 St Martin, L. l. Can.
39 A8 St Martin's i. U.K.
23 H5 St Martin's I. i. Bangl.
8 B1 St Mary Pk mt Austr.
69 G4 St Mary's Can.
40 F2 St Mary's U.K.
80 A4 St Marys OH U.S.A.
80 D4 St Marys PA U.S.A.
80 C5 Saint Marys U.S.A.
39 A8 St Mary's i. U.K.
80 A4 St Marys r. U.S.A.
67 K4 St Mary's, C. hd Can.
62 A3 St Matthew I. i. AK U.S.A.
6 E2 St Matthias Group is P.N.G.
66 F4 St Maurice r. Can.
39 B7 St Mawes U.K.
44 D4 St-Médard-en-Jalles France
67 J3 St Michaels Bay b. Can.
46 D7 St Moritz Switz.
44 C3 St-Nazaire France
39 G5 St Neots U.K.
44 H2 St-Nicolas-de-Port France
42 C3 St-Niklaas Belgium
44 F1 St-Omer France
81 J1 St-Pamphile Can.
67 G4 St Pascal Can.
65 G4 St Paul Can.
68 A3 St Paul MN U.S.A.
76 D3 St Paul NE U.S.A.
80 B6 St Paul VA U.S.A.
93 K6 St Paul, Île i. Ind. Ocean
44 C2 St Peter Port Channel Is U.K.
50 D3 St Petersburg Rus. Fed.
79 D7 St Petersburg U.S.A.
67 J4 St-Pierre St Pierre and Miquelon N. America
44 G5 St-Pierre mt France
63 N5 St Pierre and Miquelon terr. N. America
44 D4 St-Pierre-d'Oléron France
66 F4 St-Pierre, Lac l. Can.
44 F3 St-Pierre-le-Moûtier France
42 A4 St-Pol-sur-Ternoise France
46 G6 St Pölten Austria
44 F3 St-Pourçain-sur-Sioule France
81 H1 Saint-Prosper Can.
44 F2 St-Quentin France
44 H5 St-Raphaël France
81 F2 St Regis r. U.S.A.
81 F2 St Regis Falls U.S.A.
81 G2 St-Rémi Can.
81 H2 St-Sébastien Can.
67 G4 St Siméon Can.
79 D6 St Simons I. i. U.S.A.
81 K2 St Stephen Can.
79 E5 St Stephen U.S.A.
81 H2 St-Théophile Can.
65 L4 St Theresa Point Can.
69 G4 St Thomas Can.
44 H5 St-Tropez France
42 D4 St-Truiden Belgium
65 K5 St Vincent U.S.A.
61 M8 St Vincent and the Grenadines country Caribbean Sea
St Vincent, Cape c. see São Vicente, Cabo de
8 A3 St. Vincent, Gulf Austr.
42 E4 St-Vith Belgium
65 H4 St Walburg Can.
42 F5 St Wendel Ger.
69 G4 St Williams Can.
44 E4 St-Yrieix-la-Perche France
22 E3 Saipal mt Nepal
25 G5 Saipan i. N. Mariana Is
23 H5 Saitlai Myanmar
36 T3 Saittanulkki h. Fin.
27 □ Sai Wan H.K. China
86 E7 Sajama, Nevado mt Bol.
18 B5 Sājir S. Arabia
58 D5 Sak watercourse S. Africa
29 D7 Sakai Japan
29 C7 Sakaide Japan
29 C7 Sakaiminato Japan
20 B3 Sakākah S. Arabia
19 G5 Saka Kalat Pak.
76 C2 Sakakawea, Lake l. U.S.A.
66 E3 Sakami Can.
66 F3 Sakami r. Can.
66 E3 Sakami, Lac l. Can.
49 M4 Sakar mts Bulg.
16 C1 Sakarya Turkey
16 C1 Sakarya r. Turkey
28 F5 Sakata Japan
30 C3 Sakchu N. Korea
32 B2 Sa Keo r. Thai.
54 C4 Sakété Benin
24 G2 Sakhalin i. Rus. Fed.
24 G1 Sakhalinskiy Zaliv b. Rus. Fed.
22 C3 Sakhi India
59 H3 Sakhile S. Africa
18 C2 Sakht-Sar Iran
17 L1 Şäki Azer.
37 S9 Šakiai Lith.
22 A3 Sakir mt Pak.
24 E4 Sakishima-guntō is Japan
22 B4 Sakrand Pak.
32 □ Sakra, P. i. Sing.
58 D5 Sakrivier S. Africa
29 B9 Sakura-jima volc. Japan
51 E6 Saky Ukr.
37 S6 Säkylä Fin.
54 □ Sal i. Cape Verde
51 G6 Sal r. Rus. Fed.
37 S8 Sala Latvia
37 P7 Sala Sweden
66 F4 Salaberry-de-Valleyfield Can.
37 T8 Salacgrīva Latvia
48 F4 Sala Consilina Italy
75 E5 Salada, Laguna salt l. Mex.
91 E2 Saladillo Buenos Aires Arg.
91 D2 Saladillo r. Córdoba Arg.
91 E2 Salado r. Buenos Aires Arg.
91 C2 Salado r. Mendoza/San Luis Arg.
91 D4 Salado r. Rio Negro Arg.
91 E1 Salado r. Santa Fé Arg.
82 E3 Salado r. Mex.
88 B3 Salado, Quebrada de r. Chile
54 B4 Salaga Ghana
58 F1 Salajwe Botswana
55 D3 Salal Chad
20 D6 Şalālah Oman
84 E4 Salamá Guatemala
91 B1 Salamanca Chile
84 B2 Salamanca Mex.
45 D2 Salamanca Spain
80 D3 Salamanca U.S.A.
59 K3 Salamanga Moz.
18 B3 Salamatabad Iran
89 B3 Salamina Col.
16 F4 Salamīyah Syria
68 E5 Salamonie r. U.S.A.
68 E5 Salamonie Lake l. U.S.A.
23 F5 Salandi r. India
37 R8 Salantai Lith.
88 C2 Salar de Arizaro salt flat Arg.
88 C2 Salar de Atacama salt flat Chile
45 C1 Salas Spain
37 T8 Salaspils Latvia
25 F7 Salawati i. Indon.
22 B5 Salaya India
25 E7 Salayar i. Indon.
5 R7 Sala y Gómez, Isla i. Chile
91 D3 Salazar Arg.
37 T9 Šalčininkai Lith.
39 D7 Salcombe U.K.
45 D1 Saldaña Spain
89 B4 Saldaña r. Col.
58 B6 Saldanha S. Africa
58 B6 Saldanha Bay b. S. Africa
91 E3 Saldungaray Arg.
37 S8 Saldus Latvia
8 F5 Sale Austr.
17 L5 Şāleḩābād Iran
18 C3 Sāleḩābād Iran
12 H3 Salekhard Rus. Fed.
21 B4 Salem India
81 H3 Salem MA U.S.A.
77 F4 Salem MO U.S.A.
78 F4 Salem NJ U.S.A.
81 G3 Salem NY U.S.A.
80 C4 Salem OH U.S.A.
72 B2 Salem OR U.S.A.
78 D4 Salem VA U.S.A.
40 C4 Salen U.K.
40 C4 Salen U.K.
48 F4 Salerno Italy
48 F4 Salerno, Golfo di g. Italy
39 E4 Salford U.K.
87 L5 Salgado r. Brazil
47 J6 Salgótarján Hungary
87 L5 Salgueiro Brazil
19 F4 Salian Afgh.
31 C6 Salibabu i. Indon.
70 E4 Salida CO U.S.A.
44 D5 Salies-de-Béarn France
16 B2 Salihli Turkey
50 C4 Salihorsk Belarus
57 D5 Salima Malawi

15 F2 Saryozek Kazak.
15 F2 Saryshagan Kazak.
15 F3 Sary-Tash Kyrg.
19 F2 Sary Yazikskoye Vdkhr. resr Turkm.
75 G6 Sasabe U.S.A.
23 F4 Sasaram India
29 A8 Sasebo Japan
65 H4 Saskatchewan div. Can.
65 J4 Saskatchewan r. Can.
65 H4 Saskatoon Can.
13 N2 Saskylakh Rus. Fed.
59 G3 Sasolburg S. Africa
50 G4 Sasovo Rus. Fed.
81 F5 Sassafras U.S.A.
54 B4 Sassandra Côte d'Ivoire
48 C4 Sassari Sardinia Italy
43 G3 Sassenberg Ger.
46 F3 Sassnitz Ger.
51 H6 Sasykoli Rus. Fed.
54 A3 Satadougou Mali
29 B9 Sata-misaki c. Japan
22 C5 Satana India
21 A2 Satara India
59 J2 Satara S. Africa
51 G4 Satinka Rus. Fed.
23 G5 Satkhira Bangl.
21 B2 Satmala Range h. India
22 E4 Satna India
22 C5 Satpura Range mts India
29 B9 Satsuma-hantō pen. Japan
43 J5 Satteldorf Ger.
22 D2 Satti Jammu and Kashmir
47 L7 Satu Mare Romania
32 B4 Satun Thai.
91 E1 Sauce Arg.
84 B1 Sauceda Mex.
75 F5 Sauceda Mts mts U.S.A.
37 K7 Sauda Norway
36 D4 Sauðárkrókur Iceland
10 F7 Saudi Arabia country Asia
43 F3 Sauerland reg. Ger.
68 D4 Saugatuck U.S.A.
81 G3 Saugerties U.S.A.
76 E2 Sauk Center U.S.A.
68 C4 Sauk City U.S.A.
44 G3 Saulieu France
69 E2 Sault Ste Marie Can.
68 E2 Sault Ste Marie U.S.A.
25 F7 Saumlakki Indon.
44 D3 Saumur France
92 A4 Saunders Coast coastal area Ant.
92 C1 Saunders I. i. Atl. Ocean
23 F4 Saura r. India
57 C4 Saurimo Angola
49 J2 Sava r. Europe
7 J3 Savaii i. Western Samoa
51 G5 Savala r. Rus. Fed.
54 C4 Savalou Benin
Savanat see Eşṭahbānāt
68 B4 Savanna U.S.A.
79 D6 Savannah GA U.S.A.
79 B5 Savannah TN U.S.A.
79 D5 Savannah r. U.S.A.
79 E7 Savannah Sound Bahamas
32 C1 Savannakhét Laos
83 J5 Savanna la Mar Jamaica
66 B3 Savant Lake Can.
21 A3 Savanur India
36 R5 Sävar Sweden
49 M5 Savaştepe Turkey
54 C4 Savè Benin
57 D6 Save r. Moz.
18 C3 Sāveh Iran
36 V5 Saviaho Fin.
12 F3 Savinskiy Rus. Fed.
44 H4 Savoie reg. France
48 C2 Savona Italy
37 V6 Savonlinna Fin.
36 V5 Savonranta Fin.
17 J1 Şavşat Turkey
37 O8 Sävsjö Sweden
36 V3 Savukoski Fin.
17 H3 Savur Turkey
22 D4 Sawai Madhopur India
32 A1 Sawankhalok Thai.
73 F4 Sawatch Mts mts U.S.A.
40 A6 Sawel Mt h. U.K.
68 B2 Sawtooth Mountains h. U.S.A.
25 E7 Sawu Sea g. Indon.
39 G4 Saxilby U.K.
39 J5 Saxmundham U.K.
36 O4 Saxnäs Sweden
24 B1 Sayano-Shushenskoye Vdkhr. resr Rus. Fed.
19 F2 Sayat Turkm.
84 E3 Sayaxché Guatemala
20 D6 Sayḥūt Yemen
51 H5 Saykhin Kazak.
56 E2 Sāylac Somalia
24 D2 Saynshand Mongolia
45 F1 Sayoa mt Spain
28 E2 Sayon Rus. Fed.
77 D5 Sayre OK U.S.A.
80 E4 Sayre PA U.S.A.
84 B3 Sayula Jalisco Mex.
84 D3 Sayula Veracruz Mex.
22 C2 Sazin Pak.
50 E3 Sazonovo Rus. Fed.
54 B2 Sbaa Alg.
54 C1 Sbeitla Tunisia
38 D3 Scafell Pike mt U.K.
40 B4 Scalasaig U.K.
48 F5 Scalea Italy
40 □ Scalloway U.K.
41 C5 Scalp h. Rep. of Ireland
40 C3 Scalpay i. Scot. U.K.
40 B3 Scalpay i. Scot. U.K.
40 A5 Scalp Mountain h. Rep. of Ireland
40 E2 Scapa Flow in. U.K.
40 C4 Scarba i. U.K.
69 H4 Scarborough Can.
89 E2 Scarborough Trinidad and Tobago
38 G3 Scarborough U.K.
31 A3 Scarborough Shoal sand bank Phil.
40 A2 Scarp i. U.K.
Scarpanto i. see Karpathos
43 J1 Schaale r. Ger.
43 J1 Schaalsee l. Ger.
42 C4 Schaerbeek Belgium
46 D7 Schaffhausen Switz.
43 K3 Schafstädt Ger.
42 C2 Schagen Neth.
42 C2 Schagerbrug Neth.
58 B3 Schakalskuppe Namibia
19 F4 Schao watercourse Afgh./Iran
46 F6 Schärding Austria
42 B3 Scharendijke Neth.
43 J5 Schebheim Ger.
43 H1 Scheeßel Ger.
67 G3 Schefferville Can.
42 C3 Schelde r. Belgium
75 E2 Schell Creek Range mts U.S.A.
43 J2 Schellerten Ger.
81 G3 Schenectady U.S.A.
43 H1 Schenefeld Ger.
42 C2 Schermerhorn Neth.
40 D4 Schiehallion mt U.K.
43 L6 Schierling Ger.
42 E1 Schiermonnikoog Neth.
42 E1 Schiermonnikoog i. Neth.
42 E1 Schiermonnikoog Nationaal Park nat. park Neth.
43 G1 Schiffdorf Ger.
43 K1 Schilde r. Ger.
42 D4 Schinnen Neth.
48 D2 Schio Italy
43 L3 Schkeuditz Ger.
42 E4 Schleiden Ger.
43 K4 Schleiz Ger.
46 D3 Schleswig Ger.
43 H1 Schleswig-Holstein div. Ger.
43 J4 Schleusingen Ger.
43 H4 Schlitz Ger.
43 G3 Schloß Holte-Stukenbrock Ger.
43 H4 Schlüchtern Ger.
43 J5 Schlüsselfeld Ger.
43 G3 Schmallenberg Ger.
43 L4 Schneeberg Ger.
43 K3 Schneidlingen Ger.
43 H1 Schneverdingen Ger.
81 G3 Schodack Center U.S.A.
68 C3 Schofield U.S.A.
74 □1 Schofield Barracks U.S.A.
43 L1 Schönebeck Ger.
43 K2 Schönebeck (Elbe) Ger.
43 J2 Schöningen Ger.
43 H5 Schöntal Ger.
81 J2 Schoodic Lake l. U.S.A.
68 E4 Schoolcraft U.S.A.
42 C3 Schoonhoven Neth.
43 F5 Schopfloch Ger.
43 J2 Schöppenstedt Ger.
43 F1 Schortens Ger.
6 E2 Schouten Islands is P.N.G.
68 D1 Schreiber Can.
81 G3 Schroon Lake l. U.S.A.
75 F5 Schuchuli U.S.A.
41 B6 Schull Rep. of Ireland
65 K2 Schultz Lake l. Can.
74 C2 Schurz U.S.A.
42 F2 Schüttorf Ger.
81 G3 Schuylerville U.S.A.
43 K5 Schwabach Ger.
43 H5 Schwäbisch Hall Ger.
46 E6 Schwabmünchen Ger.
43 G2 Schwaförden Ger.
43 H4 Schwalmstadt-Ziegenhain Ger.
43 L5 Schwandorf Ger.
33 D3 Schwaner, Pegunungan mts Indon.
43 G1 Schwanewede Ger.
43 H2 Schwarmstedt Ger.
43 M3 Schwarze Elster r. Ger.
43 J1 Schwarzenbek Ger.
43 L4 Schwarzenberg Ger.
42 E4 Schwarzer Mann h. Ger.
58 B2 Schwarzrand mts Namibia
46 E7 Schwaz Austria
46 G4 Schwedt Ger.
43 G5 Schwegenheim Ger.
42 E5 Schweich Ger.
43 J4 Schweinfurt Ger.
43 M3 Schweinitz Ger.
43 L1 Schweinrich Ger.
59 F3 Schweizer-Reneke S. Africa
42 F3 Schwelm Ger.
46 D6 Schwenningen Ger.
43 K1 Schwerin Ger.
43 K1 Schweriner See l. Ger.
43 G5 Schwetzingen Ger.
46 D7 Schwyz Switz.
48 E6 Sciacca Sicily Italy
39 A8 Scilly, Isles of is U.K.
80 B5 Scioto r. U.S.A.
75 F2 Scipio U.S.A.
72 F1 Scobey U.S.A.
39 J5 Scole U.K.
8 H2 Scone Austr.
63 Q2 Scoresby Land reg. Greenland
63 Q2 Scoresby Sund chan. Greenland
96 F9 Scotia Ridge sea feature Atl. Ocean
85 E8 Scotia Sea sea Atl. Ocean
69 G4 Scotland Can.
34 E3 Scotland div. U.K.
92 B5 Scott Base N.Z. Base Ant.
59 J5 Scottburgh S. Africa
64 D4 Scott, C. c. Can.
76 C4 Scott City U.S.A.
92 B5 Scott Coast coastal area Ant.
80 D4 Scottdale U.S.A.
92 B4 Scott Gl. gl. Ant.
63 L2 Scott Inlet in. Can.
92 A5 Scott Island i. Ant.
65 H3 Scott Lake l. Can.
92 D4 Scott Mts mts Ant.
76 C3 Scottsbluff U.S.A.
79 C5 Scottsboro U.S.A.
78 C4 Scottsburg U.S.A.
73 E5 Scottsdale U.S.A.
74 A3 Scotts Valley U.S.A.
68 D4 Scottville U.S.A.
74 D3 Scotty's Junction U.S.A.
40 C2 Scourie U.K.
40 □ Scousburgh U.K.
40 E2 Scrabster U.K.
81 F4 Scranton U.S.A.
40 B4 Scridain, Loch in. U.K.
38 G4 Scunthorpe U.K.
39 H7 Seaford U.K.
81 F5 Seaford U.S.A.
69 G4 Seaforth Can.
31 A4 Seahorse Bank sand bank Phil.
65 K3 Seal r. Can.
8 D3 Sea Lake Austr.
58 E7 Seal, Cape pt S. Africa
81 J3 Seal I. i. U.S.A.
67 H3 Seal Lake l. Can.
58 F7 Seal Point pt S. Africa
75 E3 Seaman Range mts U.S.A.
38 G3 Seamer U.K.
75 E4 Searchlight U.S.A.
77 F5 Searcy U.S.A.
74 D4 Searles Lake l. U.S.A.
68 E4 Sears U.S.A.
81 J2 Searsport U.S.A.
74 B3 Seaside CA U.S.A.
72 B2 Seaside OR U.S.A.
40 D3 Seaton Eng. U.K.
38 D3 Seaton U.K.
72 B2 Seattle U.S.A.
81 F5 Seaville U.S.A.
81 H3 Sebago Lake l. U.S.A.
82 B3 Sebastián Vizcaíno, Bahía b. Mex.
81 J2 Sebasticook r. U.S.A.
33 E2 Sebatik i. Indon.
16 C1 Seben Turkey
49 K2 Sebeş Romania
33 C4 Sebesi i. Indon.
69 F4 Sebewaing U.S.A.
50 D3 Sebezh Rus. Fed.
16 E3 Sebil Turkey
16 G1 Şebinkarahisar Turkey
81 J2 Seboeis Lake l. U.S.A.
81 J2 Seboomook U.S.A.
81 J2 Seboomook Lake l. U.S.A.
79 D7 Sebring U.S.A.
51 G5 Sebrovo Rus. Fed.
86 B5 Sechura Peru
86 B5 Sechura, Bahía de b. Peru
43 H5 Seckach Ger.
81 H2 Second Lake l. U.S.A.
9 A6 Secretary Island i. N.Z.
59 H3 Secunda S. Africa
21 B2 Secunderabad India
76 E4 Sedalia U.S.A.
21 B2 Sedam India
8 B3 Sedan Austr.
44 G2 Sedan France
9 E4 Seddon N.Z.
9 C4 Seddonville N.Z.
19 E3 Sedeh Iran
81 J2 Sedgwick U.S.A.
54 A3 Sédhiou Senegal
46 G6 Sedlčany Czech Rep.
16 E6 Sedom Israel
75 G4 Sedona U.S.A.
48 B6 Sédrata Alg.
37 S9 Šeduva Lith.
43 J1 Seedorf Ger.
41 D5 Seefin h. Rep. of Ireland
43 K2 Seehausen Ger.
43 K2 Seehausen (Altmark) Ger.
57 B6 Seeheim Namibia
43 G5 Seeheim-Jugenheim Ger.
58 E6 Seekoegat S. Africa
75 E5 Seeley U.S.A.
92 B3 Seelig, Mt mt Ant.
43 H2 Seelze Ger.
44 E2 Sées France
43 J3 Seesen Ger.
43 J1 Seevetal Ger.
54 A4 Sefadu Sierra Leone
59 G1 Sefare Botswana
49 M5 Seferihisar Turkey
59 G1 Sefophe Botswana
37 M6 Segalstad Norway
31 A5 Segama r. Malaysia
33 B2 Segamat Malaysia
43 L2 Segeletz Ger.
50 E2 Segezha Rus. Fed.
45 F3 Segorbe Spain
54 B3 Ségou Mali
89 B3 Segovia Col.
45 D2 Segovia Spain
Segovia r. see Coco
50 E2 Segozerskoye, Oz. resr Rus. Fed.
45 G1 Segre r. Spain
55 D2 Séguédine Niger
54 B4 Séguéla Côte d'Ivoire
77 D6 Seguin U.S.A.
91 D1 Segundo r. Arg.
45 F3 Segura r. Spain
57 C6 Sehithwa Botswana
59 H4 Sehlabathebe National Park Lesotho
22 D5 Sehore India
36 S1 Seiland i. Norway
77 D4 Seiling U.S.A.
36 S5 Seinäjoki Fin.
66 B4 Seine r. Can.
44 E2 Seine r. France
44 D2 Seine, Baie de b. France
44 F2 Seine, Val de v. France
47 L3 Sejny Pol.
33 B3 Sekayu Indon.
58 F2 Sekhutlane watercourse Botswana
58 E2 Sekoma Botswana
54 B4 Sekondi Ghana
19 F4 Sekūheh Iran
32 D5 Sekura Indon.
72 B2 Selah U.S.A.
25 F7 Selaru i. Indon.
33 D3 Selatan, Tanjung pt Indon.
32 □ Selat Johor chan. Malaysia/Sing.
32 □ Selat Jurong chan. Sing.
32 □ Selat Pandan chan. Sing.
62 B3 Selawik U.S.A.
43 L4 Selb Ger.
36 L5 Selbekken Norway
36 M5 Selbu Norway
38 F4 Selby U.K.
76 C2 Selby U.S.A.
57 C6 Selebi-Phikwe Botswana
24 F1 Selemdzhinsky Khr. mts Rus. Fed.
16 B2 Selendi Turkey
44 H2 Sélestat France
32 □ Seletar Sing.
32 □ Seletar, P. i. Sing.
32 □ Seletar Res. resr Sing.
15 F1 Seletyteniz, Ozero l. Kazak.
Seleucia Pieria see Samandağı
76 C2 Selfridge U.S.A.
50 J2 Selib Rus. Fed.
54 A3 Sélibabi Maur.
43 G4 Seligenstadt Ger.
50 E3 Seliger, Oz. l. Rus. Fed.
75 F4 Seligman U.S.A.
55 E2 Selîma Oasis oasis Sudan
69 J5 Selinsgrove U.S.A.
47 Q2 Selishche Rus. Fed.
51 H6 Selitrennoye Rus. Fed.
47 Q2 Selizharovo Rus. Fed.
37 L7 Seljord Norway
43 K3 Selke r. Ger.
65 K4 Selkirk Can.
40 F5 Selkirk U.K.
64 F4 Selkirk Mountains mts Can.
38 D3 Sellafield U.K.
75 G6 Sells U.S.A.
42 F3 Selm Ger.
79 C5 Selma AL U.S.A.
74 C3 Selma CA U.S.A.
79 B5 Selmer U.S.A.
19 F4 Selseleh-ye Pīr Shūrān mts Iran
39 G7 Selsey Bill hd U.K.
32 C4 Seluan i. Indon.
86 D5 Selvas reg. Brazil
65 J3 Selwyn Lake l. Can.
64 C2 Selwyn Mountains mts Can.
62 E3 Selwyn Mts Can.
6 D4 Selwyn Range h. Austr.
33 D4 Semarang Indon.
33 C2 Sematan Malaysia
33 E3 Semayang, Danau l. Indon.
31 A6 Sembakung r. Indon.
32 □ Sembawang Sing.
56 B3 Sembé Congo
17 K3 Şemdinli Turkey
33 D4 Semenanjung Blambangan pen. Indon.
51 E4 Semenivka Ukr.
50 H3 Semenov Rus. Fed.
51 G6 Semikarakorsk Rus. Fed.
51 F5 Semiluki Rus. Fed.
72 F3 Seminoe Res. resr U.S.A.
77 C5 Seminole U.S.A.
79 C6 Seminole, L. l. U.S.A.
15 G1 Semipalatinsk Kazak.
31 B3 Semirara i. Phil.
31 B4 Semirara Islands is Phil.
18 C4 Semīrom Iran
18 D3 Semnān Iran
42 D5 Semois r. Belgium
42 D5 Semois, Vallée de la v. Belgium/France
33 E2 Semporna Malaysia
33 D4 Sempu i. Indon.
31 A5 Senaja Malaysia
51 G7 Senaki Georgia
86 E5 Sena Madureira Brazil
21 C5 Senanayake Samudra l. Sri Lanka
57 C5 Senanga Zambia
29 B9 Sendai Japan
28 G5 Sendai Japan
23 H3 Sêndo China
32 B5 Senebui, Tanjung pt Indon.
75 G5 Seneca AZ U.S.A.
68 C5 Seneca IL U.S.A.
72 C2 Seneca OR U.S.A.
80 E3 Seneca Falls U.S.A.
80 E3 Seneca Lake l. U.S.A.
80 D5 Seneca Rocks U.S.A.
80 C5 Senecaville Lake l. U.S.A.
52 C4 Senegal country Africa
54 A3 Sénégal r. Maur./Senegal
59 G4 Senekal S. Africa
68 E2 Seney U.S.A.
46 G5 Senftenberg Ger.
22 D4 Sengar r. India
56 D4 Sengerema Tanz.
50 J4 Sengiley Rus. Fed.
87 K6 Senhor do Bonfim Brazil
48 E3 Senigallia Italy
48 F2 Senj Croatia
36 P2 Senja i. Norway
17 J1 Şenkaya Turkey
22 D2 Senku Jammu and Kashmir
58 E2 Senlac S. Africa
30 F2 Senlin Shan mt China
44 F2 Senlis France
32 C2 Senmonorom Cambodia
39 B7 Sennen U.K.
69 J1 Senneterre Can.
59 H5 Senqu r. Lesotho
44 F2 Sens France
42 B4 Sensée r. France
82 G6 Sensuntepeque El Salvador
49 J2 Senta Yugo.
22 D3 Senthal India
75 F5 Sentinel U.S.A.
64 E3 Sentinel Pk summit Can.
92 B3 Sentinel Ra. mts Ant.
32 □ Sentosa i. Sing.
17 H3 Şenyurt Turkey
22 D5 Seoni India
23 E5 Seorinarayan India
30 D5 Seoul S. Korea
9 D4 Separation Pt pt N.Z.
17 L4 Separ Shāhābād Iran
90 D3 Sepetiba, Baía de b. Brazil
18 C4 Sepīdān Iran
6 E2 Sepik r. P.N.G.
30 D4 Sep'o N. Korea
67 G3 Sept-Îles Can.
74 C3 Sequoia National Park U.S.A.
17 L3 Serā Iran
51 G5 Serafimovich Rus. Fed.
19 F2 Serakhs Turkm.
25 F7 Seram i. Indon.
25 F7 Seram Sea g. Indon.
33 C4 Serang Indon.
32 □ Serangoon Harbour chan. Sing.
32 D5 Serasan i. Indon.
33 C2 Serasan, Selat chan. Indon.
32 D5 Seraya i. Indon.
32 □ Seraya, P. i. Sing.
49 J3 Serbia div. Yugo.
Serbija div. see Serbia
Serdar see Kaypak
56 E2 Serdo Eth.
51 H4 Serdoba r. Rus. Fed.
51 H4 Serdobsk Rus. Fed.
50 D3 Seredka Rus. Fed.
16 D2 Şereflikoçhisar Turkey
33 B2 Seremban Malaysia
56 D4 Serengeti National Park Tanz.
57 D5 Serenje Zambia
50 H4 Sergach Rus. Fed.
28 C3 Sergeyevka Rus. Fed.
50 F3 Sergiyev Posad Rus. Fed.
33 D2 Seria Brunei
33 D2 Serian Malaysia
49 L6 Serifos i. Greece
67 G2 Sérigny, Lac l. Can.
16 C3 Serik Turkey
25 E7 Sermata, Kepulauan is Indon.
50 J3 Sernur Rus. Fed.
19 E2 Sernyy Zavod Turkm.
51 H6 Seroglazka Rus. Fed.
12 H4 Serov Rus. Fed.
57 C6 Serowe Botswana
45 C4 Serpa Port.
89 E2 Serpent's Mouth chan. Trinidad/Venez.
50 F4 Serpukhov Rus. Fed.
90 C3 Serra da Canastra, Parque Nacional da nat. park Brazil
89 D4 Serrania de la Neblina, Parque Nacional nat. park Venez.
90 B2 Serranópolis Brazil
42 B5 Serre r. France
49 K4 Serres Greece
91 D1 Serrezuela Arg.
87 L6 Serrinha Brazil
90 D2 Sêrro Brazil
91 B4 Serrucho mt Arg.
48 C6 Sers Tunisia
90 C3 Sertãozinho Brazil
50 D2 Sertolovo Rus. Fed.
32 A4 Seruai Indon.
33 D3 Seruyan r. Indon.
24 B3 Sêrxu China
33 E2 Sesayap Indon.
31 A6 Sesayap r. Indon.
66 B3 Seseganaga L. l. Can.
69 G1 Sesekinika Can.
57 B5 Sesfontein Namibia
59 H1 Seshego S. Africa
57 C5 Sesheke Zambia
48 E4 Sessa Aurunca Italy
48 C2 Sestri Levante Italy
50 D2 Sestroretsk Rus. Fed.
28 F3 Setana Japan
44 F5 Sète France
90 D2 Sete Lagoas Brazil
36 Q2 Setermoen Norway
37 K7 Setesdal v. Norway
23 F4 Seti r. Gandakhi Nepal
22 E3 Seti r. Seti Nepal
54 C1 Sétif Alg.
29 E7 Seto Japan
32 C2 Set, P. mt Laos
54 B1 Settat Morocco
38 E3 Settle U.K.
45 B3 Setúbal Port.
45 B3 Setúbal, Baía de b. Port.
68 E3 Seul Choix Pt pt U.S.A.
66 B3 Seul, Lac l. Can.
17 K1 Sevan Armenia
Sevana Lich l. see Sevan, Lake
17 K1 Sevan, Lake l. Armenia
51 E6 Sevastopol' Ukr.
67 H2 Seven Islands Bay b. Can.
39 H6 Sevenoaks U.K.
Seven Pagodas see Māmallapuram
44 F4 Sévérac-le-Château France
59 G3 Severn S. Africa
66 B3 Severn r. Can.
39 E6 Severn r. U.K.
50 G2 Severnaya Dvina r. Rus. Fed.
51 H7 Severnaya Osetiya, Respublika div. Rus. Fed.
13 M1 Severnaya Zemlya is Rus. Fed.
66 B3 Severn L. l. Can.
12 H3 Severnyy Rus. Fed.
24 D1 Severo Baykal'skoye Nagorye mts Rus. Fed.
50 F1 Severodvinsk Rus. Fed.
13 R4 Severo-Kuril'sk Rus. Fed.
36 X2 Severomorsk Rus. Fed.
12 L3 Severo-Yeniseyskiy Rus. Fed.
51 F6 Severskaya Rus. Fed.
73 D4 Sevier r. U.S.A.
75 G2 Sevier Bridge Reservoir U.S.A.
75 F2 Sevier Desert. U.S.A.
75 F2 Sevier Lake salt l. U.S.A.
89 B3 Sevilla Col.
Sevilla see Seville
45 D4 Seville Spain
49 L3 Sevlievo Bulg.
22 C3 Sewāni India
62 D3 Seward AK U.S.A.
76 D3 Seward U.S.A.
62 B3 Seward Peninsula AK U.S.A.
64 F3 Sexsmith Can.
70 E6 Sextín r. Mex.
19 F3 Seyah Band Koh mts Afgh.
17 K2 Seyah Cheshmeh Iran
12 J2 Seyakha Rus. Fed.
84 E3 Seybaplaya Mex.
53 K6 Seychelles country Ind. Ocean
19 F2 Seydi Turkm.
16 C3 Seydişehir Turkey
36 F4 Seyðisfjörður Iceland
18 B2 Seydvān Iran
Seyhan see Adana
16 E3 Seyhan r. Turkey
51 E5 Seym r. Rus. Fed.
13 R3 Seymchan Rus. Fed.
8 E4 Seymour Austr.
59 G6 Seymour S. Africa
78 C4 Seymour IN U.S.A.
77 D5 Seymour TX U.S.A.
19 H3 Seyyedābād Afgh.
44 F2 Sézanne France
49 L7 Sfakia Greece
49 L2 Sfântu Gheorghe Romania
54 D1 Sfax Tunisia
49 K4 Sfikia, Limni resr Greece
42 D2 's-Graveland Neth.
's-Gravenhage see The Hague
40 C4 Sgurr Dhomhnuill h. U.K.
40 C3 Sgurr Mor mt U.K.
26 E2 Sha r. China
26 C3 Shaanxi div. China
18 B2 Shabestar Iran
67 G3 Shabogamo Lake l. Can.
56 C4 Shabunda Congo(Zaire)
15 F3 Shache China
92 B4 Shackleton Coast coastal area Ant.
92 B4 Shackleton Gl. gl. Ant.
92 D6 Shackleton Ice Shelf ice feature Ant.
92 C3 Shackleton Ra. mts Ant.
22 A4 Shadadkot Pak.
18 C4 Shādegān Iran
22 A3 Shadikhak Pass Pak.
18 E4 Shādkām watercourse Iran
68 D5 Shafer, Lake l. U.S.A.
92 B5 Shafer Pk summit Ant.
74 C4 Shafter U.S.A.
39 E6 Shaftesbury U.K.
62 C3 Shageluk U.S.A.
9 C6 Shag Pt pt N.Z.
92 B2 Shag Rocks is Atl. Ocean
18 C2 Shāh r. Iran
21 B2 Shahabad Karnataka India
22 E4 Shahabad Uttar Pradesh India
22 C5 Shahada India
33 B2 Shah Alam Malaysia
21 A3 Shahapur India
22 A4 Shahbandar Pak.
19 G5 Shahbaz Kalat Pak.
23 G5 Shahbazpur chan. Bangl.
19 E4 Shahdāb Iran
22 E5 Shahdol India
19 G3 Shah Fuladi mt Afgh.
22 B4 Shahgarh India
17 K3 Shahīdān Iraq
17 K3 Shahi Pen. pen. Iran
19 G4 Shah Ismail Afgh.
22 D4 Shahjahanpur India
18 E2 Shāh Jehān, Kūh-e mts Iran
19 E4 Shāh Kūh mt Iran
18 D3 Shahmīrzād Iran
21 B2 Shahpur India
22 B3 Shahpur Pak.
22 E5 Shahpura Madhya Pradesh India
22 D4 Shahpura Rajasthan India
19 G3 Shahrak Afgh.
19 F3 Shahrakht Iran
18 D4 Shahr-e Bābāk Iran
18 C3 Shahr-e Kord Iran
Shahrezā see Qomishēh
18 C3 Shahr Rey Iran
19 H2 Shahrtuz Tajik.
18 D3 Shahrud Bustam reg. Iran
19 G4 Shaikh Husain mt Pak.
18 C5 Shaj'ah, J. h. S. Arabia
30 C3 Shajianzi China
17 L3 Shakar Bolāghi Iran
59 J4 Shakaville S. Africa
19 H2 Shakh Tajik.
19 H2 Shakhdara r. Tajik.
18 E3 Shākhen Iran
50 E3 Shakhovskaya Rus. Fed.
19 G2 Shakhrisabz Uzbek.
51 G6 Shakhty Rus. Fed.
50 H3 Shakhun'ya Rus. Fed.
76 E2 Shakopee U.S.A.
28 G3 Shakotan-hantō pen. Japan
28 G3 Shakotan-misaki c. Japan
50 G2 Shalakusha Rus. Fed.
24 B3 Shaluli Shan mts China
23 J3 Shaluni mt India
65 L3 Shamattawa Can.
27 □ Sham Chun h. H.K. China
18 E5 Shamīl Iran
18 D6 Shamis U.A.E.
80 E4 Shamokin U.S.A.
77 C5 Shamrock U.S.A.
57 D5 Shamva Zimbabwe
41 B6 Shanacrane Rep. of Ireland
19 F4 Shand Afgh.
19 F4 Shāndak Iran
26 A2 Shandan China
17 M3 Shānderman Iran
26 E1 Shandian r. China
19 E2 Shandiz Iran
74 B4 Shandon U.S.A.
30 A5 Shandong div. China
26 F2 Shandong Bandao pen. China
17 K5 Shandrūkh Iraq
22 C1 Shandur Pass pass Pak.
57 C5 Shangani r. Zimbabwe
26 E3 Shangcai China
27 C5 Shangchao China
26 E4 Shangcheng China
23 G3 Shang Chu r. China
27 D6 Shangchuan Dao i. China
26 D1 Shangdu China
27 E4 Shanggao China
26 F4 Shanghai China
26 F4 Shanghai div. China
27 E5 Shanghang China
26 E2 Shanghe China
30 C3 Shanghekou China
26 D3 Shangjin China
27 C6 Shanglin China
26 D3 Shangman China
26 E3 Shangqiu Henan China
26 E3 Shangqiu Henan China
27 E4 Shangrao Jiangxi China
27 E4 Shangrao Jiangxi China
26 E3 Shangshui China
27 C6 Shangsi China
27 E4 Shangtang China
26 D1 Shangyi China
27 E5 Shangyou China
27 F4 Shangyu China
30 D1 Shangzhi China
26 C3 Shangzhou China
30 D1 Shanhetun China
41 C5 Shannon est. Rep. of Ireland
41 C4 Shannon r. Rep. of Ireland
60 R2 Shannon Island i. Greenland
41 B5 Shannon, Mouth of the est. Rep. of Ireland
30 D2 Shansonggang China
23 G5 Shāntipur India
27 E6 Shantou China
27 E6 Shanwei China
26 D2 Shanxi div. China
26 E3 Shan Xian China
26 C3 Shanyang China
26 D2 Shanyin China
27 D5 Shaodong China
27 D5 Shaoguan China
27 E5 Shaowu China
27 F4 Shaoxing China
27 D5 Shaoyang Hunan China
27 D5 Shaoyang Hunan China
38 E3 Shap U.K.
27 D6 Shapa China
40 F1 Shapinsay i. U.K.
20 C4 Shaqrā' S. Arabia
17 J6 Sharaf well Iraq
22 B3 Sharan Jogizai Pak.
19 G2 Shargun Uzbek.
51 D5 Sharhorod Ukr.
28 J3 Shari-dake volc. Japan
20 E4 Sharjah U.A.E.
47 N3 Sharkawshchyna Belarus
6 B4 Shark Bay b. Austr.
18 D2 Sharlouk Turkm.
81 G4 Sharon CT U.S.A.
80 C4 Sharon PA U.S.A.
27 □ Sharp Peak h. H.K. China
16 E5 Sharqi, Jebel esh mts Lebanon/Syria
50 H3 Shar'ya Rus. Fed.
57 C6 Shashe r. Botswana/Zimbabwe
56 D3 Shashemenē Eth.
27 D4 Shashi China
72 B3 Shasta L. l. U.S.A.
72 B3 Shasta, Mt volc. U.S.A.
27 □ Sha Tin H.K. China
50 H4 Shatki Rus. Fed.
17 M7 Shatt al Arab r. Iran/Iraq
17 K6 Shatt al Hillah r. Iraq
18 C4 Shaţţ, Ra's osh pt Iran
50 F4 Shatura Rus. Fed.
16 E6 Shaubak Jordan
65 H5 Shaunavon Can.
80 D5 Shavers Fork r. U.S.A.
81 F4 Shawangunk Mts h. U.S.A.
68 C3 Shawano U.S.A.
68 C3 Shawano Lake l. U.S.A.
66 F4 Shawinigan Can.
16 F4 Shawmarīyah, Jebel ash mts Syria
77 D5 Shawnee U.S.A.
27 F5 Sha Xi r. China
27 E5 Sha Xian China
27 D4 Shayang China
6 C4 Shay Gap Austr.
17 L5 Shaykh Jūwī Iraq
17 L5 Shaykh Sa'd Iraq
18 D4 Shaytūr Iran
19 J2 Shazud Tajik.
50 F4 Shchekino Rus. Fed.
13 S3 Shcherbakovo Rus. Fed.
51 F5 Shchigry Rus. Fed.
51 D5 Shchors Ukr.
50 C4 Shchuchyn Belarus
51 F5 Shebekino Rus. Fed.
19 G2 Sheberghān Afgh.
68 D4 Sheboygan U.S.A.
54 D4 Shebshi Mountains Nigeria
67 H4 Shediac Can.
64 D3 Shedin Pk summit Can.
41 D4 Sheelin, Lough l. Rep. of Ireland
41 D2 Sheep Haven b. Rep. of Ireland
59 J3 Sheepmoor S. Africa
75 E3 Sheep Peak summit U.S.A.
39 H6 Sheerness U.K.
67 H5 Sheet Harbour Can.
9 D5 Sheffield N.Z.
39 F4 Sheffield U.K.
79 C5 Sheffield AL U.S.A.
68 C5 Sheffield IL U.S.A.
80 D4 Sheffield PA U.S.A.
77 C6 Sheffield TX U.S.A.
69 G3 Sheguiandah Can.
26 B4 Shehong China
16 E5 Sheikh, Jebel esh mt Lebanon/Syria
22 C3 Shekhupura Pak.
27 □ Shek Kwu Chau i. H.K. China
27 □ Shek Pik Reservoir H.K. China
50 F3 Sheksna Rus. Fed.
27 □ Shek Uk Shan h. H.K. China
19 F4 Shelag watercourse Afgh./Iran
13 T2 Shelagskiy, Mys pt Rus. Fed.
68 A6 Shelbina U.S.A.
67 G5 Shelburne N.S. Can.
69 G3 Shelburne Ont. Can.
81 G3 Shelburne Falls U.S.A.
68 D4 Shelby MI U.S.A.
72 E1 Shelby MT U.S.A.
79 D5 Shelby NC U.S.A.
80 B4 Shelby OH U.S.A.
78 C4 Shelbyville IN U.S.A.
68 A6 Shelbyville MO U.S.A.
79 C5 Shelbyville TN U.S.A.
75 H5 Sheldon AZ U.S.A.
68 D5 Sheldon IL U.S.A.
81 G2 Sheldon Springs U.S.A.
67 H3 Sheldrake Can.
13 R3 Shelikhova, Zaliv g. Rus. Fed.
62 C4 Shelikof Strait U.S.A.
65 H4 Shellbrook Can.
72 D3 Shelley U.S.A.
8 H3 Shellharbour Austr.
74 A1 Shell Mt mt U.S.A.
64 F4 Shelter Bay Can.
74 A1 Shelter Cove U.S.A.
27 □ Shelter I. i. H.K. China
81 G4 Shelter I. i. U.S.A.
9 B7 Shelter Pt pt N.Z.
76 E3 Shenandoah IA U.S.A.
81 E4 Shenandoah PA U.S.A.
80 D5 Shenandoah VA U.S.A.
80 D5 Shenandoah r. U.S.A.
80 D5 Shenandoah Mountains U.S.A.
80 D5 Shenandoah National Park U.S.A.
80 C4 Shenango River Lake l. U.S.A.
54 C4 Shendam Nigeria
28 C1 Shending Shan h. China
26 G4 Shengsi China
27 F4 Sheng Xian China
50 G2 Shenkursk Rus. Fed.
26 D2 Shenmu China
26 D4 Shennongjia China
26 E3 Shenqiu China
28 A1 Shenshu China
30 B3 Shenwo Sk. resr China
30 B3 Shenyang China
27 E6 Shenzhen China
51 C5 Shepetivka Ukr.
7 G3 Shepherd Is is Vanuatu
8 E4 Shepparton Austr.
39 H6 Sheppey, Isle of i. U.K.
19 G2 Sherabad Uzbek.
39 E7 Sherborne U.K.
67 H4 Sherbrooke N.S. Can.
67 F4 Sherbrooke Que. Can.
81 F3 Sherburne U.S.A.
41 E4 Shercock Rep. of Ireland
19 H3 Sher Dahan Pass Afgh.
55 F3 Shereiq Sudan
22 C4 Shergarh India
77 E5 Sheridan AR U.S.A.
72 F2 Sheridan WY U.S.A.
39 J5 Sheringham U.K.
77 D5 Sherman U.S.A.
81 J2 Sherman Mills U.S.A.
75 E1 Sherman Mtn mt U.S.A.
23 G4 Sherpur Bangl.
65 J3 Sherridon Can.
42 D3 's-Hertogenbosch Neth.
39 F4 Sherwood Forest reg. U.K.
64 C3 Sheslay Can.
12 A3 Shetland i. U.K.
14 D2 Shetpe Kazak.
27 □ Sheung Shui H.K. China
27 □ Sheung Sze Mun chan. H.K. China
21 B4 Shevaroy Hills mts India
27 F4 She Xian China
26 F3 Sheyang China
76 D2 Sheyenne U.S.A.
76 D2 Sheyenne r. U.S.A.
18 D5 Sheykh Sho'eyb i. Iran
40 B3 Shiant Islands is U.K.
24 H2 Shiashkotan, O. i. Rus. Fed.
69 E4 Shiawassee r. U.S.A.
20 C6 Shibām Yemen
19 H3 Shibar Pass pass Afgh.
29 F6 Shibata Japan
28 J3 Shibetsu Japan
28 H2 Shibetsu Japan
16 C6 Shibîn el Kôm Egypt
29 F6 Shibukawa Japan
27 E5 Shicheng China
30 B4 Shicheng Dao i. China
81 E4 Shickshinny U.S.A.
16 G6 Shidād al Mismā' h. S. Arabia
30 B5 Shidao China
30 B5 Shidao Wan b. China
40 C4 Shiel, Loch l. U.K.
26 B4 Shifang China
50 J4 Shigony Rus. Fed.
26 D1 Shiguaigou China
15 G2 Shihezi China
26 E2 Shijiazhuang China
19 F4 Shikar r. Pak.
21 A3 Shikarpur India
22 B4 Shikarpur Pak.
22 D4 Shikohabad India
29 C8 Shikoku i. Japan
29 C8 Shikoku-sanchi mts Japan
28 G3 Shikotsu-Tōya National Park Japan
38 F3 Shildon U.K.
50 H1 Shilega Rus. Fed.
23 G4 Shiliguri India
27 D4 Shilipu China
22 D2 Shilla mt India
41 E5 Shillelagh Rep. of Ireland

69 G1 Shillington Can.
23 G4 Shillong India
51 J5 Shil'naya Balka Kazak.
81 F5 Shiloh U.S.A.
26 D2 Shilou China
50 G4 Shilovo Rus. Fed.
29 B8 Shimabara Japan
29 F7 Shimada Japan
24 E1 Shimanovsk Rus. Fed.
27 D4 Shimen China
27 B4 Shimian China
29 F7 Shimizu Japan
22 D3 Shimla India
29 F7 Shimoda Japan
21 A3 Shimoga India
56 D4 Shimoni Kenya
29 B8 Shimonoseki Japan
22 C1 Shimshal Jammu and Kashmir
50 D3 Shimsk Rus. Fed.
27 C6 Shinan China
19 F3 Shīndand Afgh.
22 B3 Shinghar Pak.
22 C1 Shinghshal Pass Pak.
68 D2 Shingleton U.S.A.
27 □ Shing Mun Res. resr H.K. China
29 E8 Shingū Japan
59 J1 Shingwedzi S. Africa
59 J1 Shingwedzi r. S. Africa
39 E4 Shining Tor h. U.K.
69 G2 Shining Tree Can.
28 G5 Shinjō Japan
19 G4 Shīnkāy Afgh.
40 D2 Shin, Loch l. U.K.
29 E6 Shinminato Japan
81 J1 Shin Pond U.S.A.
56 D4 Shinyanga Tanz.
28 G5 Shiogama Japan
29 D8 Shiono-misaki c. Japan
29 G6 Shioya-zaki pt Japan
79 E7 Ship Chan Cay i. Bahamas
27 B6 Shiping China
22 D3 Shipki Pass China/India
38 F4 Shipley U.K.
67 H4 Shippegan Can.
80 E4 Shippensburg U.S.A.
75 H3 Shiprock U.S.A.
75 H3 Shiprock Peak summit U.S.A.
27 F4 Shipu China
27 C5 Shiqian China
26 C3 Shiquan China
22 E2 Shiquan He r. China
26 C3 Shiquan Sk. resr China
17 M2 Shīrābād Iran
29 G6 Shirakawa Japan
24 F3 Shirane-san mt Japan
29 F6 Shirane-san volc. Japan
92 D4 Shirasebreen ice feature Ant.
92 A4 Shirase Coast coastal area Ant.
18 D4 Shīrāz Iran
16 C6 Shirbîn Egypt
28 J2 Shiretoko-misaki c. Japan
19 G4 Shirinab r. Pak.
28 G4 Shiriya-zaki c. Japan
81 G4 Shirley U.S.A.
81 J2 Shirley Mills U.S.A.
29 E7 Shirotori Japan
22 C5 Shirpur India
19 E2 Shīrvān Iran
17 L5 Shīrvān Iran
27 D4 Shishou China
27 E4 Shitai China
27 F4 Shitang China
17 J5 Shithāthah Iraq
22 B4 Shiv India
78 C4 Shively U.S.A.
22 D4 Shivpuri India
75 F3 Shivwits Plateau plat. U.S.A.
19 H2 Shiwal l. Afgh.
27 C6 Shiwan Dashan mts China
27 E5 Shixing China
26 D3 Shiyan China
27 C4 Shizhu China
27 B5 Shizong China
28 G5 Shizugawa Japan
26 C2 Shizuishan China
29 F7 Shizuoka Japan
50 D4 Shklow Belarus
49 H3 Shkodër Albania
12 K1 Shmidta, Ostrov i. Rus. Fed.
29 C7 Shōbara Japan
28 G3 Shokanbetsu-dake mt Japan
50 J2 Shomvukva Rus. Fed.
22 D2 Shor India
21 B4 Shoranur India
19 G5 Shorap Pak.
19 G4 Shorawak reg. Afgh.
17 K3 Shor Gol Iran
22 C3 Shorkot Pak.
28 G2 Shosanbetsu Japan
74 D4 Shoshone CA U.S.A.
72 D3 Shoshone ID U.S.A.
72 E2 Shoshone r. U.S.A.
72 E2 Shoshone L. l. U.S.A.
73 C4 Shoshone Mts mts U.S.A.
59 G1 Shoshong Botswana
72 E3 Shoshoni U.S.A.
51 E5 Shostka Ukr.
26 F2 Shouguang China
27 F5 Shouning China
26 E3 Shou Xian China
26 D2 Shouyang China
26 C3 Shouyang Shan mt China
23 E3 Shovo Tso salt l. China
75 G4 Show Low U.S.A.
51 G6 Shpakovskoye Rus. Fed.
51 D5 Shpola Ukr.
77 E5 Shreveport U.S.A.
39 E5 Shrewsbury U.K.
21 A2 Shrigonda India
23 G5 Shrirampur India
26 F3 Shu r. China
17 L6 Shu'aiba Iraq
27 A5 Shuangbai China
30 D1 Shuangcheng China
26 C4 Shuanghechang China
30 B2 Shuangliao China
27 D5 Shuangpai China
30 A3 Shuangtaizihe Kou b. China
30 C2 Shuangyang China
28 B1 Shuangyashan China
14 D2 Shubarkuduk Kazak.
26 E4 Shucheng China
27 F5 Shuiji China
26 A2 Shuiquanzi China
22 B3 Shujaabad Pak.
18 C4 Shūl watercourse Iran
30 D1 Shulan China
26 E2 Shulu China
28 H2 Shumarinai-ko l. Japan
57 C5 Shumba Zimbabwe
49 M3 Shumen Bulg.
50 H4 Shumerlya Rus. Fed.
47 O3 Shumilina Belarus
75 G4 Shumway U.S.A.
50 E4 Shumyachi Rus. Fed.
27 E5 Shunchang China
27 D6 Shunde China
62 C3 Shungnak U.S.A.
26 E1 Shunyi China
27 C6 Shuolong China
26 D2 Shuo Xian China
20 C7 Shuqrah Yemen
19 F3 Shūr r. Iran
18 D4 Shūr r. Iran
18 D4 Shūr r. Iran
19 E3 Shūr watercourse Iran
18 D4 Shūr watercourse Iran
18 D5 Shūr watercourse Iran
18 E3 Shūrāb Iran
18 D3 Shūrāb Iran
18 C3 Shūr Āb Iran
18 E4 Shūr Āb watercourse Iran
19 G2 Shurchi Uzbek.
18 D3 Shureghestan Iran
19 E4 Shūr Gaz Iran
18 D4 Shūrjestān Iran
57 D5 Shurugwi Zimbabwe
17 K6 Shuruppak Iraq
19 F4 Shusf Iran
18 C3 Shūsh Iran
18 C3 Shushtar Iran
64 F4 Shuswap L. l. Can.
19 G3 Shutar Khun Pass Afgh.
50 G3 Shuya Rus. Fed.
26 F3 Shuyang China
18 D4 Shūzū Iran
32 A1 Shwegun Myanmar
14 E2 Shymkent Kazak.
22 D2 Shyok Jammu and Kashmir
22 D2 Shyok r. India
51 F5 Shypuvate Ukr.
51 E6 Shyroke Ukr.
25 F7 Sia Indon.
22 D2 Siachen Gl. gl. India
19 F5 Siahan Range mts Pak.
19 G3 Siah Koh mts Afgh.
18 D3 Siāh Kūh mts Iran
19 G4 Siah Sang Pas Afgh.
22 C2 Sialkot Pak.
32 C5 Siantan i. Indon.
89 D4 Siapa r. Venez.
19 F4 Sīāreh Iran
31 C4 Siargao i. Phil.
31 B5 Siasi Phil.
31 B5 Siasi i. Phil.
31 B4 Siaton Phil.
37 S9 Šiauliai Lith.
19 F5 Sib Iran
18 C3 Sībak Iran
59 J1 Sibasa S. Africa
31 B4 Sibay i. Phil.
59 K3 Sibayi, Lake l. S. Africa
92 B5 Sibbald, C. c. Ant.
48 F3 Šibenik Croatia
33 A3 Siberut i. Indon.
22 A3 Sibi Pak.
56 D3 Sibiloi National Park Kenya
28 C2 Sibirtsevo Rus. Fed.
56 B4 Sibiti Congo
49 L2 Sibiu Romania
33 A2 Sibolga Indon.
32 A5 Siborongborong Indon.
23 H4 Sibsagar India
33 D2 Sibu Malaysia
31 B5 Sibuco Phil.
31 B5 Sibuguey r. Phil.
31 B5 Sibuguey Bay b. Phil.
56 B3 Sibut C.A.R.
31 A5 Sibutu i. Phil.
31 A5 Sibutu Passage chan. Phil.
31 B3 Sibuyan i. Phil.
31 B3 Sibuyan Sea sea Phil.
31 B2 Sicapoo mt Phil.
27 B4 Sichuan div. China
27 B4 Sichuan Pendi basin China
44 G5 Sicié, Cap c. France
Sicilia i. see Sicily
48 E6 Sicilian Channel Italy/Tunisia
48 E6 Sicily i. Italy
86 D6 Sicuani Peru
28 D2 Sidatun Rus. Fed.
22 C5 Siddhapur India
21 B2 Siddipet India
49 M7 Sideros, Akra pt Greece
58 E6 Sidesaviwa S. Africa
45 H5 Sidi Aïssa Alg.
45 G4 Sidi Ali Alg.
54 B1 Sidi Bel Abbès Alg.
54 C1 Sidi Bouzid Tunisia
48 D7 Sidi El Hani, Sebkhet de salt pan Tunisia
54 A2 Sidi Ifni Morocco
54 B1 Sidi Kacem Morocco
32 A5 Sidikalang Indon.
40 E4 Sidlaw Hills h. U.K.
92 A4 Sidley, Mt mt Ant.
39 D7 Sidmouth U.K.
64 E5 Sidney Can.
72 F2 Sidney MT U.S.A.
76 C3 Sidney NE U.S.A.
81 F3 Sidney NY U.S.A.
80 A4 Sidney OH U.S.A.
79 D5 Sidney Lanier, L. l. U.S.A.
23 H5 Sidoktaya Myanmar
16 E5 Sidon Lebanon
50 G3 Sidorovo Rus. Fed.
90 A3 Sidrolândia Brazil
59 J3 Sidvokodvo Swaziland
44 F5 Sié, Col de pass France
47 L4 Siedlce Pol.
43 G4 Siegen Ger.
32 B2 Siĕmréab Cambodia
48 D3 Siena Italy
47 J5 Sieradz Pol.
77 B6 Sierra Blanca U.S.A.
91 C4 Sierra Colorada Arg.
75 F5 Sierra Estrella mts U.S.A.
91 D4 Sierra Grande Arg.
52 C5 Sierra Leone country Africa
96 H5 Sierra Leone Basin sea feature Atl. Ocean
96 H5 Sierra Leone Rise sea feature Atl. Ocean
74 C4 Sierra Madre Mts mts U.S.A.
74 B1 Sierra Nevada mts U.S.A.
89 B2 Sierra Nevada de Santa Marta, Parque Nacional nat. park Col.
89 C2 Sierra Nevada, Parque Nacional nat. park Venez.
91 D4 Sierra, Punta pt Arg.
74 B2 Sierraville U.S.A.
75 G6 Sierra Vista U.S.A.
46 C7 Sierre Switz.
36 T5 Sievi Fin.
27 C6 Sifang Ling mts China
49 L6 Sifnos i. Greece
45 F5 Sig Alg.
47 L7 Sighetu Marmaţiei Romania
47 M7 Sighişoara Romania
32 □ Siglap Sing.
33 A1 Sigli Indon.
36 D3 Siglufjörður Iceland
31 B4 Sigma Phil.
46 D6 Sigmaringen Ger.
42 E4 Signal de Botrange h. Belgium
75 E5 Signal Peak summit U.S.A.
92 B1 Signy U.K. Base Ant.
42 C5 Signy-l'Abbaye France
68 A5 Sigourney U.S.A.
49 L5 Sigri, Akra pt Greece
45 E2 Sigüenza Spain
54 B3 Siguiri Guinea
37 T8 Sigulda Latvia
32 B3 Sihanoukville Cambodia
26 F3 Sihong China
22 E5 Sihora India
27 D6 Sihui China
36 T4 Siikajoki Fin.
36 U5 Siilinjärvi Fin.
17 H3 Siirt Turkey
33 B3 Sijunjung Indon.
22 B5 Sika India
64 E3 Sikanni Chief Can.
64 E3 Sikanni Chief r. Can.
22 C4 Sikar India
19 H3 Sikaram mt Afgh.
54 B3 Sikasso Mali
77 F4 Sikeston U.S.A.
24 F2 Sikhote-Alin' mts Rus. Fed.
49 L6 Sikinos i. Greece
23 G4 Sikkim div. India
36 P4 Siksjö Sweden
33 E1 Sikuati Malaysia
45 C1 Sil r. Spain
31 C4 Silago Phil.
37 S9 Šilalė Lith.
82 D4 Silao Mex.
31 B4 Silay Phil.
43 H1 Silberberg h. Ger.
23 H4 Silchar India
16 B1 Şile Turkey
21 C2 Sileru r. India
22 E3 Silgarhi Nepal
48 C6 Siliana Tunisia
16 D3 Silifke Turkey
23 G3 Siling Co salt l. China
Silistat see Bozkır
49 M2 Silistra Bulg.
16 B1 Silivri Turkey
37 O6 Siljan l. Sweden
37 L8 Silkeborg Denmark
37 U7 Sillamäe Estonia
22 C5 Sillod India
59 J3 Silobela S. Africa
23 G3 Silong China
77 E6 Silsbee U.S.A.
36 U3 Siltaharju Fin.
19 F5 Sīlūp r. Iran
37 R9 Šilutė Lith.
17 H2 Silvan Turkey
22 C5 Silvassa India
68 B2 Silver Bay U.S.A.
73 E5 Silver City U.S.A.
68 C1 Silver Islet Can.
72 B3 Silver Lake U.S.A.
74 D4 Silver Lake l. CA U.S.A.
68 D2 Silver Lake l. MI U.S.A.
41 C5 Silvermine Mts h. Rep. of Ireland
74 D3 Silver Peak Range mts U.S.A.
80 E5 Silver Spring U.S.A.
74 C2 Silver Springs U.S.A.
8 C1 Silverton Austr.
39 D7 Silverton U.K.
69 F3 Silver Water Can.
84 E3 Silvituc Mex.
33 D2 Simanggang Malaysia
31 B3 Simara i. Phil.
69 H2 Simard, Lac l. Can.
17 L5 Sīmareh r. Iran
23 F4 Simaria India
16 B2 Simav Turkey
16 B2 Simav Dağları mts Turkey
56 C3 Simba Congo(Zaire)
Simbirsk see Ul'yanovsk
Simbor i. see Pānikoita
69 G4 Simcoe Can.
69 H3 Simcoe, Lake l. Can.
23 F5 Simdega India
56 D2 Simēn Mountains mts Eth.
33 A2 Simeuluë i. Indon.
51 E6 Simferopol' Ukr.
23 E3 Simikot Nepal
89 B3 Simití Col.
74 C4 Simi Valley U.S.A.
73 F4 Simla U.S.A.
47 L7 Şimleu Silvaniei Romania
42 E4 Simmerath Ger.
42 F5 Simmern (Hunsrück) Ger.
74 C4 Simmler U.S.A.
75 F4 Simmons U.S.A.
79 F7 Simms Bahamas
36 U3 Simojärvi l. Fin.
64 F4 Simonette r. Can.
65 J4 Simonhouse Can.
46 D7 Simplon Pass Switz.
6 D4 Simpson Desert Austr.
68 D1 Simpson I. i. Can.
74 D2 Simpson Park Mts mts U.S.A.
37 O9 Simrishamn Sweden
31 A5 Simunul i. Phil.
24 H2 Simushir, O. i. Rus. Fed.
21 A2 Sina r. India
33 A2 Sinabang Indon.
32 A5 Sinabung volc. Indon.
55 F2 Sinai reg. Egypt
42 C5 Sinai, Mont h. France
84 A1 Sinaloa div. Mex.
48 D3 Sinalunga Italy
27 C5 Sinan China
30 C4 Sinanju N. Korea
23 H5 Sinbyugyun Myanmar
16 F2 Sincan Turkey
89 B2 Sincé Col.
89 B2 Sincelejo Col.
79 D5 Sinclair, L. l. U.S.A.
64 E4 Sinclair Mills Can.
58 B2 Sinclair Mine Namibia
40 E2 Sinclair's Bay b. U.K.
22 D4 Sind r. India
31 B4 Sindañgan Phil.
33 C4 Sindangbarang Indon.
22 B4 Sindari India
46 D6 Sindelfingen Ger.
21 B2 Sindgi India
22 B4 Sindh div. Pak.
21 B3 Sindhnur India
16 B2 Sındırgı Turkey
22 D6 Sindkhed India
22 C5 Sindkheda India
30 C4 Sin-do i. China
50 J2 Sindor Rus. Fed.
23 F5 Sindri India
22 B3 Sind Sagar Doab lowland Pak.
50 J3 Sinegor'ye Rus. Fed.
49 M4 Sinekçi Turkey
45 B4 Sines Port.
45 B4 Sines, Cabo de pt Port.
36 T3 Sinettä Fin.
54 B4 Sinfra Côte d'Ivoire
55 F3 Singa Sudan
22 E3 Singahi India
30 D3 Sin'galp'a China
22 D2 Singa Pass pass India
32 B5 Singapore Sing.
11 M9 Singapore country Asia
32 B5 Singapore, Strait of chan. Indon./Sing.
33 E4 Singaraja Indon.
32 B2 Sing Buri Thai.
69 G3 Singhampton Can.
56 D4 Singida Tanz.
6 C2 Singkang Indon.
33 C2 Singkawang Indon.
32 A5 Singkil Indon.
8 H2 Singleton Austr.
Singora see Songkhla
30 D4 Sin'gye N. Korea
30 D3 Sinhŭng N. Korea
48 C4 Siniscola Sardinia Italy
48 G3 Sinj Croatia
6 C2 Sinjai Indon.
17 H3 Sinjār Iraq
17 H3 Sinjār, Jabal mt Iraq
17 K3 Sīnji Iran
55 F3 Sinkat Sudan
Sinkiang Uighur Aut. Region div. see Xinjiang Uygur Zizhiqu
30 C4 Sinmi i. N. Korea
43 G4 Sinn Ger.
87 H2 Sinnamary Fr. Guiana
Sinneh see Sanandaj
49 N2 Sinoie, Lacul lag. Romania
51 E7 Sinop Turkey
30 D3 Sinpa N. Korea
30 E3 Sinp'o N. Korea
30 E3 Sinp'ung-dong N. Korea
30 D4 Sinp'yŏng N. Korea
30 D4 Sinsang N. Korea
43 G5 Sinsheim Ger.
33 D2 Sintang Indon.
77 D6 Sinton U.S.A.
89 A2 Sinú r. Col.
30 C3 Sinŭiju N. Korea
42 F4 Sinzig Ger.
31 B5 Siocon Phil.
46 J7 Siófok Hungary
46 C7 Sion Switz.
41 D3 Sion Mills U.K.
76 D3 Sioux Center U.S.A.
76 D3 Sioux City U.S.A.
76 D3 Sioux Falls U.S.A.
66 B3 Sioux Lookout Can.
31 B4 Sipalay Phil.
30 C2 Siping China
65 K3 Sipiwesk Can.
65 K3 Sipiwesk L. l. Can.
92 B4 Siple Coast coastal area Ant.
92 A4 Siple, Mt mt Ant.
22 C5 Sipra r. India
79 C5 Sipsey r. U.S.A.
33 A3 Sipura i. Indon.
83 H6 Siquia r. Nic.
31 B4 Siquijor Phil.
31 B4 Siquijor i. Phil.
22 B5 Sir r. Pak.
21 B3 Sira India
37 K7 Sira r. Norway
18 D5 Şīr Abū Nu'āyr i. U.A.E.
Siracusa see Syracuse
64 E4 Sir Alexander, Mt mt Can.
17 G1 Şiran Turkey
19 G5 Siranda Lake l. Pak.
18 D5 Şīr Banī Yās i. U.A.E.
17 M3 Sīrdān Iran
6 D3 Sir Edward Pellew Group is Austr.
68 A3 Siren U.S.A.
19 F5 Sirgān Iran
32 B1 Siri Kit Dam dam Thai.
18 D4 Sīrīz Iran
64 D2 Sir James McBrien, Mt mt Can.
Sirjan see Sa'īdābād
18 D4 Sīrjan salt flat Iran
18 E5 Sirk Iran
22 E4 Sirmour India
17 J3 Şırnak Turkey
21 C2 Sironcha India
22 D4 Sironj India
21 B2 Sirpur India
74 C4 Sirretta Peak summit U.S.A.
18 D5 Sīrrī, Jazīreh-ye i. Iran
22 C3 Sirsa Haryana India
23 E4 Sirsa Uttar Pradesh India
64 F4 Sir Sanford, Mt mt Can.
21 A3 Sirsi Karnataka India
22 D3 Sirsi India
21 B2 Sirsilla India
55 D1 Sirte Libya
55 D1 Sirte, Gulf of g. Libya
21 A2 Sirur India
17 J2 Şirvan Turkey
37 T9 Širvintos Lith.
17 K4 Sīrwān r. Iraq
64 F4 Sir Wilfred Laurier, Mt mt Can.
48 G2 Sisak Croatia
32 C2 Sisaket Thai.
18 C4 Sīsakht Iran
84 E2 Sisal Mex.
58 E3 Sishen S. Africa
17 L2 Sisian Armenia
68 C2 Siskiwit Bay b. U.S.A.
32 B2 Sisŏphŏn Cambodia
74 B4 Sisquoc r. U.S.A.
76 D2 Sisseton U.S.A.
81 K1 Sisson Branch Reservoir Can.
19 F4 Sīstan reg. Iran
19 F4 Sīstan, Daryācheh-ye marsh Afgh.
22 C5 Sitamau India
31 A5 Sitangkai Phil.
22 E4 Sitapur India
49 M7 Siteia Greece
59 J3 Siteki Swaziland
49 K4 Sithonia pen. Greece
90 C1 Sítio da Abadia Brazil
90 D1 Sítio do Mato Brazil
64 B3 Sitka U.S.A.
22 B3 Sitpur Pak.
42 D4 Sittard Neth.
23 H4 Sittaung Myanmar
43 H1 Sittensen Ger.
39 H6 Sittingbourne U.K.
23 H5 Sittwe Myanmar
27 □ Siu A Chau i. H.K. China
23 F5 Siuri India
21 B4 Sivaganga India
21 B4 Sivakasi India
18 D4 Sivand Iran
16 F2 Sivas Turkey
16 B2 Sivaslı Turkey
17 G3 Siverek Turkey
17 G2 Sivrice Turkey
16 C2 Sivrihisar Turkey
59 H3 Sivukile S. Africa
55 E2 Siwa Egypt
22 D3 Siwalik Range mts India/Nepal
23 F4 Siwan India
22 C4 Siwana India
44 G5 Six-Fours-les-Plages France
26 E3 Si Xian China
68 E4 Six Lakes U.S.A.
41 D3 Sixmilecross U.K.
59 H2 Siyabuswa S. Africa
26 F3 Siyang China
17 M1 Siyäzän Azer.
26 C1 Siyitang China
18 D3 Sīyunī Iran
26 D1 Siziwang Qi China
Sjælland i. see Zealand
49 J3 Sjenica Yugo.
37 N9 Sjöbo Sweden
36 P2 Sjøvegan Norway
89 E2 S. Juan r. Venez.
51 E6 Skadovs'k Ukr.
36 E4 Skaftafell National Park Iceland
36 E5 Skaftárós est. Iceland
36 D3 Skagafjörður in. Iceland
37 M8 Skagen Denmark
37 L8 Skagerrak str. Denmark/Norway
72 B1 Skagit r. Can./U.S.A.
64 B3 Skagway U.S.A.
36 T1 Skaidi Norway
36 P2 Skaland Norway
36 O4 Skalmodal Sweden
37 L8 Skanderborg Denmark
81 E3 Skaneateles Lake l. U.S.A.
68 C2 Skanee U.S.A.
49 L5 Skantzoura i. Greece
37 N7 Skara Sweden
37 R7 Skärgårdshavet Nationalpark nat. park Fin.
37 M6 Skarnes Norway
47 K5 Skarżysko-Kamienna Pol.
36 R3 Skaulo Sweden
47 J6 Skawina Pol.
64 D3 Skeena r. Can.
64 D3 Skeena Mountains mts Can.
39 H4 Skegness U.K.
36 R4 Skellefteå Sweden
36 Q4 Skellefteälven r. Sweden
36 R4 Skelleftehamn Sweden
41 A6 Skellig Rocks is Rep. of Ireland
38 E4 Skelmersdale U.K.
41 E4 Skerries Rep. of Ireland
37 M7 Ski Norway
49 K5 Skiathos i. Greece
41 B6 Skibbereen Rep. of Ireland
36 R2 Skibotn Norway
38 D3 Skiddaw mt U.K.
37 L7 Skien Norway
47 K5 Skierniewice Pol.
54 C1 Skikda Alg.
38 G4 Skipsea U.K.
8 D4 Skipton Austr.
38 E4 Skipton U.K.
37 L8 Skive Denmark
36 E4 Skjálfandafljót r. Iceland
37 L9 Skjern Denmark
37 K6 Skjolden Norway
36 K5 Skodje Norway
36 T2 Skoganvarre Norway
41 F6 Skokholm Island i. U.K.
68 D4 Skokie U.S.A.
39 B6 Skomer Island i. U.K.
49 K5 Skopelos i. Greece
50 F4 Skopin Rus. Fed.
49 J4 Skopje Macedonia
51 F5 Skorodnoye Rus. Fed.
37 N7 Skövde Sweden
81 J2 Skowhegan U.S.A.
37 S8 Skrunda Latvia
64 B2 Skukum, Mt mt Can.
59 J2 Skukuza S. Africa
74 D3 Skull Peak summit U.S.A.
68 B5 Skunk r. U.S.A.
37 R8 Skuodas Lith.
37 N9 Skurup Sweden
37 P6 Skutskär Sweden
51 D5 Skvyra Ukr.
40 B3 Skye i. U.K.
49 L5 Skyros Greece
49 L5 Skyros i. Greece
92 B3 Skytrain Ice Rise ice feature Ant.
37 M9 Slagelse Denmark
36 Q4 Slagnäs Sweden
33 C4 Slamet, Gunung volc. Indon.
41 E4 Slane Rep. of Ireland
41 E5 Slaney r. Rep. of Ireland
50 D3 Slantsy Rus. Fed.
51 G5 Slashchevskaya Rus. Fed.
68 D1 Slate Is is Can.
48 G2 Slatina Croatia
49 L2 Slatina Romania
65 G2 Slave r. Can.
54 C4 Slave Coast coastal area Africa
64 G3 Slave Lake Can.
15 F1 Slavgorod Rus. Fed.
47 O2 Slavkovichi Rus. Fed.
49 H2 Slavonija reg. Croatia
49 H2 Slavonski Brod Croatia
51 C5 Slavuta Ukr.
51 D5 Slavutych Ukr.
28 B3 Slavyanka Rus. Fed.
51 F6 Slavyansk-na-Kubani Rus. Fed.
50 D4 Slawharad Belarus
46 H3 Sławno Pol.
39 G4 Sleaford U.K.
41 A5 Slea Head hd Rep. of Ireland
40 C3 Sleat pen. U.K.
40 C3 Sleat, Sound of chan. U.K.
66 E2 Sleeper Islands is Can.
68 D3 Sleeping Bear Dunes National Seashore res. U.S.A.
68 D3 Sleeping Bear Pt pt U.S.A.
51 H7 Sleptsovskaya Rus. Fed.
92 C3 Slessor Glacier gl. Ant.
77 F6 Slidell U.S.A.
41 A5 Slievanea h. Rep. of Ireland
41 D3 Slieve Anierin h. Rep. of Ireland
41 D5 Slieveardagh Hills h. Rep. of Ireland
41 C4 Slieve Aughty Mts h. Rep. of Ireland
41 D3 Slieve Beagh h. Rep. of Ireland/U.K.
41 C5 Slieve Bernagh h. Rep. of Ireland
41 D4 Slieve Bloom Mts h. Rep. of Ireland
41 B5 Slievecallan h. Rep. of Ireland
41 B3 Slieve Car h. Rep. of Ireland
41 F3 Slieve Donard h. U.K.
41 B4 Slieve Elva h. Rep. of Ireland
41 C3 Slieve Gamph h. Rep. of Ireland
41 C3 Slieve League h. Rep. of Ireland
41 B5 Slieve Mish Mts h. Rep. of Ireland
41 B5 Slieve Miskish Mts h. Rep. of Ireland
41 A3 Slieve More h. Rep. of Ireland
41 D4 Slieve na Calliagh h. Rep. of Ireland
41 D5 Slievenamon h. Rep. of Ireland
41 D2 Slieve Snaght mt Rep. of Ireland
40 B3 Sligachan U.K.
41 C3 Sligo Rep. of Ireland
41 C3 Sligo Bay b. Rep. of Ireland
37 Q8 Slite Sweden
49 M3 Sliven Bulg.
50 H2 Sloboda Rus. Fed.
50 J2 Slobodchikovo Rus. Fed.
49 M2 Slobozia Romania
64 F5 Slocan Can.
42 E1 Slochteren Neth.
50 C4 Slonim Belarus
42 C2 Slootdorp Neth.
42 D2 Sloten Neth.
42 D2 Slotermeer l. Neth.
7 F2 Slot, The chan. Solomon Is
39 G6 Slough U.K.
35 G4 Slovakia country Europe
34 G4 Slovenia country Europe
48 F1 Slovenj Gradec Slovenia
51 F5 Slov''yans'k Ukr.
46 H3 Słupsk Pol.
36 P4 Slussfors Sweden
50 C4 Slutsk Belarus
41 A4 Slyne Head hd Rep. of Ireland
13 M4 Slyudyanka Rus. Fed.
81 J3 Small Pt pt U.S.A.
67 H3 Smallwood Reservoir Can.
50 D4 Smalyavichy Belarus
47 N3 Smarhon' Belarus
58 E5 Smartt Syndicate Dam resr S. Africa
65 J4 Smeaton Can.
49 J2 Smederevo Yugo.
49 J2 Smederevska Palanka Yugo.
80 D4 Smethport U.S.A.
51 D5 Smila Ukr.
42 E2 Smilde Neth.
37 T8 Smiltene Latvia
64 G3 Smith Can.
74 C2 Smith U.S.A.
80 C6 Smith r. U.S.A.
62 C2 Smith Bay b. U.S.A.
64 D4 Smithers Can.
59 G5 Smithfield S. Africa
79 E5 Smithfield NC U.S.A.
72 E3 Smithfield UT U.S.A.
92 A3 Smith Glacier gl. Ant.
92 B2 Smith I. i. S. Shetland Is Ant.
81 E5 Smith I. i. MD U.S.A.
81 F6 Smith I. i. VA U.S.A.
80 D6 Smith Mountain Lake l. U.S.A.
64 D3 Smith River Can.
69 J3 Smiths Falls Can.
63 L2 Smith Sound str. Can./Greenland
74 C1 Smoke Creek Desert U.S.A.
64 F4 Smoky r. Can.
76 C4 Smoky r. U.S.A.
66 D3 Smoky Falls Can.
76 D4 Smoky Hills h. U.S.A.
64 G4 Smoky Lake Can.
36 K5 Smøla i. Norway
50 E4 Smolensk Rus. Fed.
50 E4 Smolenskaya Oblast' div. Rus. Fed.
49 L4 Smolyan Bulg.
28 C3 Smolyoninovo Rus. Fed.
66 D4 Smooth Rock Falls Can.
66 C3 Smoothrock L. l. Can.
65 H4 Smoothstone Lake l. Can.
36 T1 Smørfjord Norway
92 B3 Smyley I. i. Ant.
81 F5 Smyrna DE U.S.A.
79 C5 Smyrna GA U.S.A.
80 C4 Smyrna OH U.S.A.
81 J1 Smyrna Mills U.S.A.
38 C3 Snaefell h. U.K.
36 F4 Snæfell mt Iceland
64 A2 Snag Can.
72 D3 Snake r. U.S.A.
75 E2 Snake Range mts U.S.A.
72 D3 Snake River Plain plain U.S.A.
79 E7 Snap Pt pt Bahamas
64 G2 Snare Lake Can.
7 G6 Snares Is is N.Z.
36 N4 Snasa Norway
42 D1 Sneek Neth.
41 B6 Sneem Rep. of Ireland
58 F6 Sneeuberg mts S. Africa
67 H3 Snegamook Lake l. Can.
39 H5 Snettisham U.K.
12 K3 Snezhnogorsk Rus. Fed.
48 F2 Snežnik mt Slovenia
47 K4 Śniardwy, Jezioro l. Pol.
51 E6 Snihurivka Ukr.
40 B3 Snizort, Loch b. U.K.
72 B2 Snohomish U.S.A.
72 B2 Snoqualmie Pass U.S.A.
36 N3 Snøtinden mt Norway
65 J2 Snowbird Lake l. Can.
39 C4 Snowdon mt U.K.
39 D5 Snowdonia National Park U.K.
75 G4 Snowflake U.S.A.
81 F5 Snow Hill MD U.S.A.
79 E5 Snow Hill NC U.S.A.
65 J4 Snow Lake Can.
8 B2 Snowtown Austr.
72 D3 Snowville U.S.A.
8 G4 Snowy r. Austr.
8 G4 Snowy Mts mts Austr.
67 J3 Snug Harbour Nfld Can.
69 G3 Snug Harbour Ont. Can.
32 C2 Snuŏl Cambodia
77 D5 Snyder OK U.S.A.
77 C5 Snyder TX U.S.A.
57 E5 Soalala Madag.
57 E5 Soanierana-Ivongo Madag.
30 D6 Soan kundo i. S. Korea
89 B3 Soata Col.
40 B3 Soay i. U.K.
30 D6 Sobaek Sanmaek mts S. Korea
55 F4 Sobat r. Sudan
43 F5 Sobernheim Ger.
25 G7 Sobger r. Indon.
29 B8 Sobo-san mt Japan
87 K6 Sobradinho, Barragem de resr Brazil
87 K4 Sobral Brazil
So-chaoson-man g. see Korea Bay
51 F7 Sochi Rus. Fed.
30 D5 Sŏch'on S. Korea
5 M6 Society Islands is Pac. Oc.
90 C3 Socorro Brazil
89 B3 Socorro Col.
73 F5 Socorro U.S.A.
82 B5 Socorro, I. i. Mex.
20 D7 Socotra i. Yemen
32 C3 Soc Trăng Vietnam
45 E3 Socuéllamos Spain
74 D4 Soda Lake l. U.S.A.
36 U3 Sodankylä Fin.
22 D2 Soda Plains plain China/Jammu and Kashmir
72 E3 Soda Springs U.S.A.
37 P6 Söderhamn Sweden
37 P7 Söderköping Sweden
37 P7 Södertälje Sweden
55 E3 Sodiri Sudan
56 D3 Sodo Eth.
37 Q6 Södra Kvarken str. Fin./Sweden
59 H1 Soekmekaar S. Africa
42 D3 Soerendonk Neth.
43 G3 Soest Ger.
42 D2 Soest Neth.
8 G2 Sofala Austr.
49 K3 Sofia Bulg.
Sofiya see Sofia
36 W4 Sofporog Rus. Fed.
29 G10 Sōfu-gan i. Japan
89 B3 Sogamoso Col.
17 G1 Soğanlı Dağları mts Turkey
42 F2 Sögel Ger.
37 K7 Søgne Norway
37 J6 Sognefjorden in. Norway
31 C4 Sogod Phil.
26 A1 Sogo Nur l. China
50 H2 Sogra Rus. Fed.
26 A3 Sogruma China
16 C1 Söğüt Turkey
30 D7 Sŏgwip'o S. Korea
23 H3 Sog Xian China
55 F2 Sohâg Egypt
22 D5 Sohagpur India
39 H5 Soham U.K.
22 B2 Sohan r. Pak.
7 F2 Sohano P.N.G.
23 E5 Sohela India
22 D3 Sohna India
30 E3 Sŏho-ri N. Korea
30 C6 Sohŭksan i. S. Korea
42 C4 Soignes, Forêt de forest Belgium
42 C4 Soignies Belgium
36 T5 Soini Fin.
44 F2 Soissons France
22 C4 Sojat India
31 B4 Sojoton Point pt Phil.
51 C5 Sokal' Ukr.
30 E4 Sokch'o S. Korea
49 M6 Söke Turkey
51 G7 Sokhumi Georgia
54 C4 Sokodé Togo
27 □ Soko Islands is H.K. China
50 G3 Sokol Rus. Fed.
47 L4 Sokółka Pol.
54 B3 Sokolo Mali
43 L4 Sokolov Czech Rep.
28 C3 Sokolovka Rus. Fed.
47 L4 Sokołów Podlaski Pol.
54 C3 Sokoto Nigeria
54 C3 Sokoto r. Nigeria
51 C5 Sokyryany Ukr.
22 D3 Solan India
9 A7 Solander I. i. N.Z.
21 A2 Solāpur India
89 B2 Soledad Col.
74 B3 Soledad U.S.A.
89 E2 Soledad Venez.
84 C3 Soledad de Doblado Mex.
51 G6 Solenoye Rus. Fed.
39 F7 Solent, The str. U.K.
36 N3 Solfjellsjøen Norway
17 H2 Solhan Turkey
50 G3 Soligalich Rus. Fed.
39 F5 Solihull U.K.
12 G4 Solikamsk Rus. Fed.
12 G4 Sol'-Iletsk Rus. Fed.
42 F3 Solingen Ger.
58 A1 Solitaire Namibia
17 M1 Şollar Azer.
36 P5 Sollefteå Sweden
43 L3 Söllichau Ger.
43 H3 Solling h. Ger.
43 J3 Sollstedt Ger.
43 G4 Solms Ger.
50 F3 Solnechnogorsk Rus. Fed.
33 B3 Solok Indon.
84 E4 Sololá Guatemala
4 H5 Solomon Islands country Pac. Oc.
6 F2 Solomon Sea sea P.N.G./Solomon Is
68 B2 Solon Springs U.S.A.
25 E7 Solor, Kepulauan is Indon.
46 C7 Solothurn Switz.
50 E1 Solovetskiye Ostrova is Rus. Fed.
50 H3 Solovetskoye Rus. Fed.
48 G3 Šolta i. Croatia
18 C4 Soltānābād Iran
19 E3 Soltānābād Iran
19 E2 Soltānābād Iran
43 H2 Soltau Ger.
50 D3 Sol'tsy Rus. Fed.
81 E3 Solvay U.S.A.
37 O8 Sölvesborg Sweden
40 E6 Solway Firth est. U.K.
57 C5 Solwezi Zambia
29 G6 Sōma Japan
16 A2 Soma Turkey
42 B4 Somain France
53 J5 Somalia country Africa
93 H3 Somali Basin sea feature Ind. Ocean
57 C4 Sombo Angola
49 H2 Sombor Yugo.
84 B2 Sombrerete Mex.
22 C4 Somdari India
81 J2 Somerset Junction U.S.A.
37 S6 Somero Fin.
78 C4 Somerset KY U.S.A.
68 E4 Somerset MI U.S.A.
80 D5 Somerset PA U.S.A.
59 F6 Somerset East S. Africa
63 J2 Somerset Island i. Can.

81 G3 **Somerset Reservoir** U.S.A.
58 C7 **Somerset West** S. Africa
81 H3 **Somersworth** U.S.A.
77 D6 **Somerville Res.** *resr* U.S.A.
37 O7 **Sommen** *l.* Sweden
43 K3 **Sömmerda** Ger.
67 G3 **Sommet, Lac du** *l.* Can.
22 B5 **Somnath** India
68 C5 **Somonauk** U.S.A.
91 C4 **Somuncurá, Mesa Volcánica de** *plat.* Arg.
23 F4 **Son** *r.* India
23 F5 **Sonamukhi** India
23 G5 **Sonamura** India
23 E5 **Sonapur** India
22 D4 **Sonar** *r.* India
23 H4 **Sonari** India
30 C4 **Sŏnch'ŏn** N. Korea
50 E2 **Sondaly** Rus. Fed.
37 L9 **Sønderborg** Denmark
43 J3 **Sondershausen** Ger.
63 N3 **Søndre Strømfjord** *in.* Greenland
48 C1 **Sondrio** Italy
21 B2 **Sonepet** India
22 B5 **Songad** India
26 E4 **Songbu** China
32 D2 **Sông Cau** Vietnam
32 C1 **Sông Con** *r.* Vietnam
27 B6 **Sông Đa** *r.* Vietnam
32 D2 **Sông Đa Răng** *r.* Vietnam
57 D5 **Songea** Tanz.
30 D3 **Songgan** N. Korea
32 C3 **Sông Hâu Giang** *r.* Vietnam
30 D2 **Songhua Hu** *resr* China
30 C1 **Songhua Jiang** China
28 B1 **Songhua Jiang** *r.* China
26 F4 **Songjiang** China
30 D2 **Songjianghe** China
27 C4 **Songkan** China
32 B4 **Songkhla** Thai.
27 C6 **Sông Ky Cung** *r.* Vietnam
24 E2 **Songling** China
26 F1 **Song Ling** *mts* China
27 B6 **Sông Ma** *r.* Laos/Vietnam
30 D5 **Sŏngnam** S. Korea
32 C1 **Sông Ngan Sau** *r.* Vietnam
30 C4 **Songnim** N. Korea
56 B4 **Songo** Angola
57 D5 **Songo** Moz.
26 B3 **Songpan** China
32 C3 **Song Saigon** *r.* Vietnam
23 G4 **Songsak** India
30 D7 **Sŏngsan** S. Korea
26 D3 **Song Shan** *mt* China
30 D3 **Songshuzhen** China
27 C4 **Songtao** China
27 F5 **Songxi** China
26 D3 **Song Xian** China
27 D4 **Songzi** China
32 D2 **Sơn Ha** Vietnam
26 D1 **Sonid Youqi** China
26 D1 **Sonid Zuoqi** China
22 D3 **Sonipat** India
36 U5 **Sonkajärvi** Fin.
27 B6 **Sơn La** Vietnam
19 G5 **Sonmiani** Pak.
19 G5 **Sonmiani Bay** *b.* Pak.
43 K4 **Sonneberg** Ger.
90 D2 **Sono** *r. Minas Gerais* Brazil
87 J6 **Sono** *r. Tocantins* Brazil
75 G6 **Sonoita** U.S.A.
75 F6 **Sonoita** *r.* Mex.
74 B3 **Sonora** *CA* U.S.A.
77 C6 **Sonora** *TX* U.S.A.
70 D6 **Sonora** *div.* Mex.
82 B3 **Sonora** *r.* Mex.
75 F6 **Sonoyta** Mex.
18 B3 **Sonqor** Iran
89 B3 **Sonsón** Col.
82 G6 **Sonsonate** El Salvador
27 B6 **Sơn Tây** Vietnam
59 H5 **Sonwabile** S. Africa
91 F1 **Sopas** *r.* Uru.
13 S4 **Sopka Shiveluch** *mt* Rus. Fed.
55 E4 **Sopo** *watercourse* Sudan
49 L3 **Sopot** Bulg.
47 J3 **Sopot** Pol.
46 H7 **Sopron** Hungary
48 E4 **Sora** Italy
23 F6 **Sorada** India
37 P5 **Soråker** Sweden
30 E4 **Sŏraksan** *mt* S. Korea
66 F4 **Sorel** Can.
6 E6 **Sorell** Austr.
16 E2 **Sorgun** Turkey
45 E2 **Soria** Spain
12 C2 **Sørkappøya** *i.* Svalbard
18 D3 **Sorkheh** Iran
18 D3 **Sorkh, Kūh-e** *mts* Iran
36 N4 **Sørli** Norway
23 F5 **Soro** India
51 D5 **Soroca** Moldova
90 C3 **Sorocaba** Brazil
12 G4 **Sorochinsk** Rus. Fed.
25 G6 **Sorol** *i.* Micronesia
25 F7 **Sorong** Indon.
56 D3 **Soroti** Uganda
36 S1 **Sørøya** *i.* Norway
45 B3 **Sorraia** *r.* Port.
36 Q2 **Sorreisa** Norway
8 E5 **Sorrento** Austr.
57 B6 **Sorris Sorris** Namibia
92 D3 **Sør-Rondane** *mts* Ant.
36 P4 **Sorsele** Sweden
31 C3 **Sorsogon** Phil.
50 D2 **Sortavala** Rus. Fed.
36 O2 **Sortland** Norway
50 J2 **Sortopolovskaya** Rus. Fed.
50 J3 **Sorvizhi** Rus. Fed.
30 D5 **Sŏsan** S. Korea
59 H2 **Soshanguve** S. Africa
51 F4 **Sosna** *r.* Rus. Fed.
91 C2 **Sosneado** *mt* Arg.
50 K2 **Sosnogorsk** Rus. Fed.
50 H2 **Sosnovka** *Archangel.* Rus. Fed.
50 G4 **Sosnovka** *Tambov.* Rus. Fed.
12 F3 **Sosnovka** Rus. Fed.
36 X4 **Sosnovyy** Rus. Fed.
37 V7 **Sosnovyy Bor** Rus. Fed.
47 J5 **Sosnowiec** Pol.
51 F6 **Sosyka** *r.* Rus. Fed.
89 A4 **Sotara, Volcán** *volc.* Col.
36 V4 **Sotkamo** Fin.
91 D1 **Soto** Arg.
84 C2 **Soto la Marina** Mex.
56 B3 **Souanké** Congo
54 B4 **Soubré** Côte d'Ivoire
81 F4 **Souderton** U.S.A.
49 M4 **Soufli** Greece
44 E4 **Souillac** France
42 D5 **Souilly** France
54 C1 **Souk Ahras** Alg.
Sŏul *see* **Seoul**
44 D5 **Soulom** France
Soûr *see* **Tyre**
45 H4 **Sour el Ghozlane** Alg.
65 J5 **Souris** *Man.* Can.
67 H4 **Souris** *P.E.I.* Can.
65 J5 **Souris** *r.* Can./U.S.A.
87 L5 **Sousa** Brazil
54 D1 **Sousse** Tunisia
44 D5 **Soustons** France
20 C7 **South** *div.* Yemen
53 G9 **South Africa, Republic of** *country* Africa
69 G3 **Southampton** Can.
39 F7 **Southampton** U.K.
81 G4 **Southampton** U.S.A.
63 K3 **Southampton I.** Can.
65 M2 **Southampton Island** *i.* Can.
80 E6 **South Anna** *r.* U.S.A.
39 F4 **South Anston** U.K.
67 H2 **South Aulatsivik Island** *i.* Can.
6 D5 **South Australia** *div.* Austr.
93 N6 **South Australian Basin** *sea feature* Ind. Ocean
77 F5 **Southaven** U.S.A.
73 F5 **South Baldy** *mt* U.S.A.
38 F3 **South Bank** U.K.
80 B4 **South Bass I.** *i.* U.S.A.
65 N2 **South Bay** *b.* Can.
69 F3 **South Baymouth** Can.
68 D5 **South Bend** *IN* U.S.A.
72 B2 **South Bend** *WA* U.S.A.
79 E7 **South Bight** *chan.* Bahamas
80 D6 **South Boston** U.S.A.
9 D5 **Southbridge** N.Z.
81 G3 **Southbridge** U.S.A.
South Cape *c. see* **Ka Lae**
79 D5 **South Carolina** *div.* U.S.A.
81 J2 **South China** U.S.A.
33 C1 **South China Sea** *sea* Pac. Oc.
76 C2 **South Dakota** *div.* U.S.A.
81 G3 **South Deerfield** U.S.A.
39 G7 **South Downs** *h.* U.K.
59 F2 **South East** *div.* Botswana
8 F5 **South East Cape** *Vic.* Austr.
6 E6 **South East Cape** *c.* Austr.
95 N10 **South-East Pacific Basin** *sea feature* Pac. Oc.
65 J3 **Southend** Can.
40 C5 **Southend** U.K.
39 H6 **Southend-on-Sea** U.K.
68 A5 **South English** U.S.A.
9 C5 **Southern Alps** *mts* N.Z.
6 B5 **Southern Cross** Austr.
65 K3 **Southern Indian Lake** *l.* Can.
55 E4 **Southern National Park** Sudan
3 □ **Southern Ocean** *ocean*
79 E5 **Southern Pines** U.S.A.
92 C1 **Southern Thule I.** *i.* Atl. Ocean
40 D5 **Southern Uplands** *reg.* U.K.
40 F4 **South Esk** *r.* U.K.
68 B6 **South Fabius** *r.* U.S.A.
94 G7 **South Fiji Basin** *sea feature* Pac. Oc.
73 F4 **South Fork** U.S.A.
74 A2 **South Fork Eel** *r.* U.S.A.
74 C4 **South Fork Kern** *r.* U.S.A.
80 D5 **South Fork South Branch** *r.* U.S.A.
68 E3 **South Fox I.** *i.* U.S.A.
92 C5 **South Geomagnetic Pole** Ant.
85 G8 **South Georgia** *i.* Atl. Ocean
40 A3 **South Harris** *i.* U.K.
23 G5 **South Hatia I.** *i.* Bangl.
68 D4 **South Haven** U.S.A.
65 K2 **South Henik Lake** *l.* Can.
81 G2 **South Hero** U.S.A.
80 D6 **South Hill** U.S.A.
94 E4 **South Honshu Ridge** *sea feature* Pac. Oc.
65 K3 **South Indian Lake** Can.
81 G4 **Southington** U.S.A.
9 C6 **South Island** *i.* N.Z.
31 A4 **South Islet** *rf* Phil.
23 F5 **South Koel** *r.* India
74 B2 **South Lake Tahoe** U.S.A.
57 D5 **South Luangwa National Park** Zambia
92 B6 **South Magnetic Pole** Ant.
68 D3 **South Manitou I.** *i.* U.S.A.
79 D7 **South Miami** U.S.A.
39 H6 **Southminster** U.K.
65 J4 **South Moose L.** *l.* Can.
80 E5 **South Mts** *h.* U.S.A.
64 D2 **South Nahanni** *r.* Can.
40 □ **South Nesting Bay** *b.* U.K.
85 F9 **South Orkney Islands** *is* Ant.
81 H2 **South Paris** U.S.A.
72 G3 **South Platte** *r.* U.S.A.
92 B4 **South Pole** Ant.
69 G1 **South Porcupine** Can.
38 D4 **Southport** U.K.
81 H3 **South Portland** U.S.A.
69 H3 **South River** Can.
40 F2 **South Ronaldsay** *i.* U.K.
81 G3 **South Royalton** U.S.A.
59 J5 **South Sand Bluff** *pt* S. Africa
85 H8 **South Sandwich Islands** *terr.* Atl. Ocean
96 H9 **South Sandwich Trench** *sea feature* Atl. Ocean
65 H4 **South Saskatchewan** *r.* Can.
65 K3 **South Seal** *r.* Can.
85 E9 **South Shetland Islands** *is* Ant.
38 F2 **South Shields** U.K.
38 G4 **South Skirlaugh** U.K.
68 A5 **South Skunk** *r.* U.S.A.
9 E3 **South Taranaki Bight** *b.* N.Z.
75 G2 **South Tent** *summit* U.S.A.
23 E4 **South Tons** *r.* India
66 E3 **South Twin I.** *i.* Can.
38 E3 **South Tyne** *r.* U.K.
40 A3 **South Uist** *i.* U.K.
9 A7 **South West Cape** *c.* N.Z.
93 H6 **South-West Indian Ridge** *sea feature* Ind. Ocean
95 J8 **South-West Pacific Basin** *sea feature* Pa. Oc.
95 O7 **South-West Peru Ridge** *sea feature* Pac. Oc.
68 E5 **South Whitley** U.S.A.
81 H3 **South Windham** U.S.A.
39 J5 **Southwold** U.K.
59 H1 **Soutpansberg** *mts* S. Africa
48 G5 **Soverato** Italy
50 B4 **Sovetsk** *Kaliningrad.* Rus. Fed.
50 J3 **Sovetsk** *Kirovsk.* Rus. Fed.
24 G2 **Sovetskaya Gavan'** Rus. Fed.
50 D2 **Sovetskiy** *Leningrad.* Rus. Fed.
50 J3 **Sovetskiy** *Mariy El.* Rus. Fed.
12 H3 **Sovetskiy** Rus. Fed.
59 G3 **Soweto** S. Africa
18 E4 **Sowghān** Iran
84 D3 **Soyaló** Mex.
28 G2 **Sōya-misaki** *c.* Japan
30 D4 **Soyang-ho** *l.* S. Korea
47 P4 **Sozh** *r.* Belarus
49 M3 **Sozopol** Bulg.
42 D4 **Spa** Belgium
92 B3 **Spaatz I.** *i.* Ant.
34 E4 **Spain** *country* Europe
39 G5 **Spalding** U.K.
39 D6 **Span Head** *h.* U.K.
69 F2 **Spanish** Can.
69 G2 **Spanish** *r.* Can.
75 G1 **Spanish Fork** U.S.A.
83 J5 **Spanish Town** Jamaica
74 C2 **Sparks** U.S.A.
80 C6 **Sparta** *NC* U.S.A.
68 B4 **Sparta** *WV* U.S.A.
79 D5 **Spartanburg** U.S.A.
49 K6 **Sparti** Greece
48 G6 **Spartivento, Capo** *c.* Italy
64 F5 **Sparwood** Can.
50 E4 **Spas-Demensk** Rus. Fed.
50 E2 **Spasskaya Guba** Rus. Fed.
24 F2 **Spassk-Dal'niy** Rus. Fed.
49 K7 **Spatha, Akra** *pt* Greece
64 D3 **Spatsizi Plateau Wilderness Provincial Park** *res.* Can.
76 C2 **Spearfish** U.S.A.
77 C4 **Spearman** U.S.A.
81 F3 **Speculator** U.S.A.
76 E3 **Spencer** *IA* U.S.A.
72 D2 **Spencer** *ID* U.S.A.
80 C5 **Spencer** *WV* U.S.A.
64 B3 **Spencer, Cape** *c.* U.S.A.
6 D5 **Spencer Gulf** *est.* Austr.
64 E4 **Spences Bridge** Can.
38 F3 **Spennymoor** U.K.
41 D3 **Sperrin Mountains** *h.* U.K.
80 D5 **Sperryville** U.S.A.
43 H5 **Spessart** *reg.* Ger.
49 K6 **Spetses** *i.* Greece
40 E3 **Spey** *r.* U.K.
43 G5 **Speyer** Ger.
19 G4 **Spezand** Pak.
43 F1 **Spiekeroog** *i.* Ger.
46 C7 **Spiez** Switz.
42 E1 **Spijk** Neth.
42 C3 **Spijkenisse** Neth.
48 E1 **Spilimbergo** Italy
39 H4 **Spilsby** U.K.
19 G4 **Spīn Būldak** Afgh.
22 B3 **Spintangi** Pak.
64 F3 **Spirit River** Can.
68 C3 **Spirit River Flowage** *resr* U.S.A.
65 H4 **Spiritwood** Can.
19 G3 **Spirsang Pass** *pass* Afgh.
47 K6 **Spišská Nová Ves** Slovakia
17 K1 **Spitak** Armenia
22 D3 **Spiti** *r.* India
12 C2 **Spitsbergen** *i.* Svalbard
46 F7 **Spittal an der Drau** Austria
48 G3 **Split** Croatia
65 K3 **Split Lake** Can.
65 K3 **Split Lake** *l.* Can.
72 C2 **Spokane** U.S.A.
48 E3 **Spoleto** Italy
32 C2 **Spong** Cambodia
68 B3 **Spooner** U.S.A.
43 K1 **Spornitz** Ger.
72 F2 **Spotted Horse** U.S.A.
67 J3 **Spotted Island** Can.
69 F2 **Spragge** Can.
64 E4 **Spranger, Mt** *mt* Can.
72 C2 **Spray** U.S.A.
46 G5 **Spree** *r.* Ger.
42 D4 **Sprimont** Belgium
69 F3 **Spring Bay** Can.
58 B4 **Springbok** S. Africa
67 J4 **Springdale** Can.
77 E4 **Springdale** U.S.A.
43 H2 **Springe** Ger.
73 F4 **Springer** U.S.A.
75 H4 **Springerville** U.S.A.
77 C4 **Springfield** *CO* U.S.A.
68 C6 **Springfield** *IL* U.S.A.
81 G3 **Springfield** *MA* U.S.A.
81 J2 **Springfield** *ME* U.S.A.
76 E2 **Springfield** *MN* U.S.A.
77 E4 **Springfield** *MO* U.S.A.
80 B5 **Springfield** *OH* U.S.A.
77 C4 **Springfield** *OR* U.S.A.
81 G3 **Springfield** *VT* U.S.A.
80 D5 **Springfield** *WV* U.S.A.
68 C6 **Springfield, Lake** *l.* U.S.A.
59 F5 **Springfontein** S. Africa
68 B4 **Spring Green** U.S.A.
68 B4 **Spring Grove** U.S.A.
67 H4 **Springhill** Can.
79 D6 **Spring Hill** U.S.A.
68 D4 **Spring Lake** U.S.A.
75 E3 **Spring Mountains** *mts* U.S.A.
9 D5 **Springs Junction** N.Z.
68 A4 **Spring Valley** U.S.A.
80 D3 **Springville** *NY* U.S.A.
75 G1 **Springville** *UT* U.S.A.
39 J5 **Sprowston** U.K.
64 G4 **Spruce Grove** Can.
80 D5 **Spruce Knob-Seneca Rocks National Recreation Area** *res.* U.S.A.
72 D3 **Spruce Mt.** *mt* U.S.A.
38 H4 **Spurn Head** *c.* U.K.
64 E5 **Spuzzum** Can.
64 E5 **Squamish** Can.
81 H3 **Squam Lake** *l.* U.S.A.
81 J1 **Squapan Lake** *l.* U.S.A.
81 J1 **Square Lake** *l.* U.S.A.
48 G5 **Squillace, Golfo di** *g.* Italy
82 A2 **S. Quintín, C.** *pt* Mex.
32 B3 **Srê Âmbĕl** Cambodia
13 R4 **Srednekolymsk** Rus. Fed.
Sredinnyy Khrebet *mts* Rus. Fed.
49 K3 **Sredna Gora** *mts* Bulg.
13 R3 **Srednekolymsk** Rus. Fed.
12 E4 **Sredne-Russkaya Vozvyshennost'** *reg.* Rus. Fed.
13 M3 **Sredne-Sibirskoye Ploskogor'ye** *plat.* Rus. Fed.
36 W4 **Sredneye Kuyto, Oz.** *l.* Rus. Fed.
49 L3 **Srednogorie** Bulg.
32 C2 **Srêpok, T.** *r.* Cambodia
24 D1 **Sretensk** Rus. Fed.
21 C3 **Srharikota I.** *i.* India
21 D2 **Srikakulam** India
21 B3 **Sri Kālahasti** India
22 D3 **Sri Kanta** *mt* India
10 K9 **Sri Lanka** *country* Asia
22 D3 **Srinagar** India
22 C2 **Srinagar** Jammu and Kashmir
21 B4 **Srirangam** India
32 B1 **Sri Thep** Thai.
21 B4 **Srivaikuntam** India
21 A2 **Srivardhan** India
21 B4 **Srivilliputtur** India
21 C2 **Srungavarapukota** India
43 H1 **Stade** Ger.
42 B4 **Staden** Belgium
42 E2 **Stadskanaal** Neth.
43 H4 **Stadtallendorf** Ger.
43 H2 **Stadthagen** Ger.
43 K4 **Stadtilm** Ger.
42 E3 **Stadtlohn** Ger.
43 H3 **Stadtoldendorf** Ger.
43 K4 **Stadtroda** Ger.
40 B4 **Staffa** *i.* U.K.
43 K4 **Staffelberg** *h.* Ger.
43 J4 **Staffelstein** Ger.
39 E5 **Stafford** U.K.
80 E5 **Stafford** U.S.A.
37 T8 **Staicele** Latvia
39 G6 **Staines** U.K.
51 F5 **Stakhanov** Ukr.
39 E7 **Stalbridge** U.K.
39 J5 **Stalham** U.K.
Stalingrad *see* **Volgograd**
64 E3 **Stalin, Mt** *mt* Can.
47 L5 **Stalowa Wola** Pol.
49 L3 **Stamboliyski** Bulg.
39 G5 **Stamford** U.K.
81 G4 **Stamford** *CT* U.S.A.
81 F3 **Stamford** *NY* U.S.A.
Stampalia *i. see* **Astypalaia**
57 B6 **Stampriet** Namibia
36 N2 **Stamsund** Norway
76 E3 **Stanberry** U.S.A.
42 C3 **Standdaarbuiten** Neth.
59 H3 **Standerton** S. Africa
69 F4 **Standish** U.S.A.
78 C4 **Stanford** U.S.A.
59 J4 **Stanger** S. Africa
79 E7 **Staniard Ck** Bahamas
49 K3 **Stanke Dimitrov** Bulg.
43 M5 **Staňkov** Czech Rep.
81 K1 **Stanley** Can.
27 □ **Stanley** *H.K.* China
88 E8 **Stanley** Falkland Is
38 F3 **Stanley** U.K.
72 D2 **Stanley** *ID* U.S.A.
76 C1 **Stanley** *ND* U.S.A.
68 B3 **Stanley** *WV* U.S.A.
56 C3 **Stanley, Mount** *mt* Congo(Zaire)/Uganda
21 B4 **Stanley Reservoir** India
38 F2 **Stannington** U.K.
13 R3 **Stanovaya** Rus. Fed.
24 D1 **Stanovoye Nagor'ye** *mts* Rus. Fed.
24 E1 **Stanovoy Khrebet** *mts* Rus. Fed.
39 H5 **Stanton** U.K.
80 B6 **Stanton** *KY* U.S.A.
68 E4 **Stanton** *MI* U.S.A.
76 C3 **Stapleton** U.S.A.
47 K5 **Starachowice** Pol.
Stara Planina *see* **Balkan Mts**
50 H4 **Staraya Kulatka** Rus. Fed.
51 H5 **Staraya Poltavka** Rus. Fed.
50 D3 **Staraya Russa** Rus. Fed.
47 P2 **Staraya Toropa** Rus. Fed.
50 J4 **Staraya Tumba** Rus. Fed.
49 L3 **Stara Zagora** Bulg.
5 M5 **Starbuck I.** *i.* Kiribati
46 G4 **Stargard Szczeciński** Pol.
50 E3 **Staritsa** Rus. Fed.
79 D6 **Starke** U.S.A.
77 F5 **Starkville** U.S.A.
46 E7 **Starnberger See** *l.* Ger.
51 F5 **Starobil's'k** Ukr.
47 Q4 **Starodub** Rus. Fed.
47 J4 **Starogard Gdański** Pol.
51 C5 **Starokostyantyniv** Ukr.
51 F6 **Starominskaya** Rus. Fed.
51 F6 **Staroshcherbinovskaya** Rus. Fed.
74 C1 **Star Peak** *mt* U.S.A.
39 D7 **Start Point** *pt* U.K.
47 O4 **Staryya Darohi** Belarus
51 F5 **Staryy Oskol** Rus. Fed.
43 K3 **Staßfurt** Ger.
80 E4 **State College** U.S.A.
79 D5 **Statesboro** U.S.A.
79 D5 **Statesville** U.S.A.
43 M3 **Stauchitz** Ger.
43 G4 **Staufenberg** Ger.
80 D5 **Staunton** U.S.A.
37 J7 **Stavanger** Norway
39 F4 **Staveley** U.K.
51 G6 **Stavropol'** Rus. Fed.
51 G6 **Stavropol'skaya Vozvyshennost'** *reg.* Rus. Fed.
51 G6 **Stavropol'skiy Kray** *div.* Rus. Fed.
8 D4 **Stawell** Austr.
59 H4 **Steadville** S. Africa
74 C2 **Steamboat** U.S.A.
72 F3 **Steamboat Springs** U.S.A.
92 B2 **Steele I.** *i.* Ant.
80 E4 **Steelton** U.S.A.
42 E2 **Steenderen** Neth.
59 J2 **Steenkampsberge** *mts* S. Africa
64 F3 **Steen River** Can.
72 C3 **Steens Mt.** *mt* U.S.A.
63 N2 **Steenstrup Gletscher** *gl.* Greenland
42 A4 **Steenvoorde** France
42 E2 **Steenwijk** Neth.
92 D4 **Stefansson Bay** *b.* Ant.
62 H2 **Stefansson I.** *i.* Can.
43 J5 **Steigerwald** *forest* Ger.
43 K5 **Stein** Ger.
43 K4 **Steinach** Ger.
65 K5 **Steinbach** Can.
43 G2 **Steinfeld (Oldenburg)** Ger.
43 G2 **Steinfurt** Ger.
57 B6 **Steinhausen** Namibia
43 H3 **Steinheim** Ger.
43 H2 **Steinhuder Meer** *l.* Ger.
36 M4 **Steinkjer** Norway
58 B4 **Steinkopf** S. Africa
75 H5 **Steins** U.S.A.
36 M4 **Steinsdalen** Norway
58 F3 **Stella** S. Africa
58 C6 **Stellenbosch** S. Africa
48 C3 **Stello, Monte** *mt Corsica* France
42 D5 **Stenay** France
43 K2 **Stendal** Ger.
27 □ **Stenhouse, Mt** *h. H.K.* China
40 E4 **Stenhousemuir** U.K.
37 M7 **Stenungsund** Sweden
Stepanakert *see* **Xankändi**
51 H7 **Step'anavan** Armenia
65 K5 **Stephen** U.S.A.
8 C2 **Stephens** *r.* Austr.
9 D4 **Stephens, Cape** *c.* N.Z.
8 C1 **Stephens Creek** Austr.
68 D3 **Stephenson** U.S.A.
64 C3 **Stephens Passage** *chan.* U.S.A.
67 J4 **Stephenville** Can.
77 D5 **Stephenville** U.S.A.
51 H5 **Stepnoye** Rus. Fed.
59 H4 **Sterkfontein Dam** *resr* S. Africa
59 G5 **Sterkstroom** S. Africa
58 D5 **Sterling** S. Africa
72 G3 **Sterling** *CO* U.S.A.
68 C5 **Sterling** *IL* U.S.A.
76 C2 **Sterling** *ND* U.S.A.
75 G2 **Sterling** *UT* U.S.A.
77 C6 **Sterling City** U.S.A.
69 F4 **Sterling Hgts** U.S.A.
14 D1 **Sterlitamak** Rus. Fed.
43 K1 **Sternberg** Ger.
64 G4 **Stettler** Can.
68 D2 **Steuben** U.S.A.
80 C4 **Steubenville** U.S.A.
39 G6 **Stevenage** U.K.
65 K4 **Stevenson L.** *l.* Can.
68 C3 **Stevens Point** U.S.A.
62 D3 **Stevens Village** U.S.A.
64 D3 **Stewart** Can.
64 B2 **Stewart** *r.* Can.
64 B2 **Stewart Crossing** Can.
9 A7 **Stewart Island** *i.* N.Z.
7 G2 **Stewart Islands** *is* Solomon Is
63 K3 **Stewart Lake** *l.* Can.
40 D5 **Stewarton** U.K.
68 A4 **Stewartville** U.S.A.
59 F5 **Steynsburg** S. Africa
46 G6 **Steyr** Austria
58 F6 **Steytlerville** S. Africa
42 D1 **Stiens** Neth.
64 C3 **Stikine** *r.* Can./U.S.A.
64 C3 **Stikine Ranges** *mts* Can.
58 D7 **Stilbaai** S. Africa
68 A3 **Stillwater** *MN* U.S.A.
74 C2 **Stillwater** *NV* U.S.A.
77 D4 **Stillwater** *OK* U.S.A.
73 C4 **Stillwater Ra.** *mts* U.S.A.
39 G5 **Stilton** U.K.
49 K4 **Štip** Macedonia
8 B3 **Stirling** Austr.
40 E4 **Stirling** U.K.
74 B2 **Stirling City** U.S.A.
8 A2 **Stirling North** Austr.
36 M5 **Stjørdalshalsen** Norway
46 H6 **Stockerau** Austria
43 K4 **Stockheim** Ger.
37 Q7 **Stockholm** Sweden
81 J1 **Stockholm** U.S.A.
39 E4 **Stockport** U.K.
74 B3 **Stockton** *CA* U.S.A.
76 D4 **Stockton** *KS* U.S.A.
75 F1 **Stockton** *UT* U.S.A.
68 B2 **Stockton I.** *i.* U.S.A.
77 E4 **Stockton L.** *l.* U.S.A.
38 F3 **Stockton-on-Tees** U.K.
81 J2 **Stockton Springs** U.S.A.
37 P5 **Stöde** Sweden
32 B2 **Stœng Sângke** *r.* Cambodia
32 C2 **Stœng Sên** *r.* Cambodia
32 C2 **Stœng Trêng** Cambodia
40 C2 **Stoer, Point of** *pt* U.K.
39 E4 **Stoke-on-Trent** U.K.
38 F3 **Stokesley** U.K.
36 C5 **Stokkseyri** Iceland
36 N3 **Stokkvågen** Norway
36 O2 **Stokmarknes** Norway
49 G3 **Stolac** Bos.-Herz.
42 E4 **Stolberg (Rheinland)** Ger.
51 C5 **Stolin** Belarus
43 L4 **Stollberg** Ger.
43 H2 **Stolzenau** Ger.
39 E5 **Stone** U.K.
69 J2 **Stonecliffe** Can.
81 F5 **Stone Harbor** U.S.A.
40 F4 **Stonehaven** U.K.
64 E3 **Stone Mountain Prov. Park** *res.* Can.
75 H3 **Stoner** U.S.A.
81 F4 **Stone Ridge** U.S.A.
65 K4 **Stonewall** Can.
80 C5 **Stonewall Jackson Lake** *l.* U.S.A.
69 F4 **Stoney Point** Can.
81 J2 **Stonington** U.S.A.
74 A2 **Stonyford** U.S.A.
81 E3 **Stony Pt** *pt* U.S.A.
65 H3 **Stony Rapids** Can.
36 Q3 **Stora Inlevatten** *l.* Sweden
36 P3 **Stora Sjöfallets Nationalpark** *nat. park* Sweden
36 Q4 **Storavan** *l.* Sweden
37 M9 **Store Bælt** *chan.* Denmark
36 M5 **Støren** Norway
36 O3 **Storforshei** Norway
36 O3 **Storjord** Norway
62 H2 **Storkerson Peninsula** Can.
59 G5 **Stormberg** S. Africa
59 G5 **Stormberg** *mts* S. Africa
76 E3 **Storm Lake** U.S.A.
37 K6 **Stornosa** *mt* Norway
40 B2 **Stornoway** U.K.
50 K2 **Storozhevsk** Rus. Fed.
51 C5 **Storozhynets'** Ukr.
81 G4 **Storrs** U.S.A.
40 B3 **Storr, The** *h.* U.K.
36 P4 **Storseleby** Sweden
36 O5 **Storsjön** *l.* Sweden
37 L5 **Storskrymten** *mt* Norway
36 R2 **Storslett** Norway
42 D1 **Stortemelk** *chan.* Neth.
36 P4 **Storuman** Sweden
36 P4 **Storuman** *l.* Sweden
37 P6 **Storvik** Sweden
37 M8 **Storvorde** Denmark
37 P7 **Storvreta** Sweden
39 G5 **Stotfold** U.K.
68 C4 **Stoughton** U.S.A.
39 E7 **Stour** *r. Eng.* U.K.
39 F5 **Stour** *r. Eng.* U.K.
39 J6 **Stour** *r. Eng.* U.K.
39 H6 **Stour** *r. Eng.* U.K.
39 E5 **Stourbridge** U.K.
39 E5 **Stourport-on-Severn** U.K.
65 L4 **Stout L.** *l.* Can.
50 C4 **Stowbtsy** Belarus
81 F4 **Stowe** U.S.A.
39 H5 **Stowmarket** U.K.
71 H3 **St Peter** *MN* U.S.A.
41 D3 **Strabane** U.K.
41 D4 **Stradbally** Rep. of Ireland
39 J5 **Stradbroke** U.K.
48 C2 **Stradella** Italy
75 G3 **Straight Cliffs** *cliff* U.S.A.
46 F6 **Strakonice** Czech Rep.
46 F3 **Stralsund** Ger.
58 C7 **Strand** S. Africa
36 K5 **Stranda** Norway
79 E7 **Strangers Cay** *i.* Bahamas
41 F3 **Strangford** U.K.
41 F3 **Strangford Lough** *l.* U.K.
40 C6 **Stranraer** U.K.
44 H2 **Strasbourg** France
80 D5 **Strasburg** U.S.A.
8 F4 **Stratford** Austr.
69 G4 **Stratford** Can.
9 E3 **Stratford** N.Z.
77 C4 **Stratford** *TX* U.S.A.
68 B3 **Stratford** *WV* U.S.A.
39 F5 **Stratford-upon-Avon** U.K.
8 B3 **Strathalbyn** Austr.
40 D5 **Strathaven** U.K.
40 G3 **Strathbeg, Loch of** *l.* U.K.
40 D3 **Strathcarron** *v.* U.K.
64 D5 **Strathcona Prov. Park** *res.* Can.
40 D3 **Strathconon** *v.* U.K.
40 D3 **Strath Dearn** *v.* U.K.
40 D2 **Strath Fleet** *v.* U.K.
64 G4 **Strathmore** Can.
64 E4 **Strathnaver** Can.
40 D2 **Strathnaver** *v.* U.K.
40 E2 **Strath of Kildonan** *v.* U.K.
69 G4 **Strathroy** Can.
40 E3 **Strathspey** *v.* U.K.
40 E2 **Strathy** U.K.
40 D2 **Strathy Point** *pt* U.K.
39 C7 **Stratton** U.K.
81 H2 **Stratton** U.S.A.
43 L6 **Straubing** Ger.
36 B3 **Straumnes** *pt* Iceland
68 B4 **Strawberry Point** U.S.A.
75 G1 **Strawberry Reservoir** U.S.A.
6 D5 **Streaky Bay** Austr.
6 D5 **Streaky Bay** *b.* Austr.
68 C5 **Streator** U.S.A.
39 E6 **Street** U.K.
49 K2 **Strehaia** Romania
43 M3 **Strehla** Ger.
13 R3 **Strelka** Rus. Fed.
37 T8 **Strenči** Latvia
43 L5 **Stříbro** Czech Rep.
40 F3 **Strichen** U.K.
49 K4 **Strimonas** *r.* Greece
91 D4 **Stroeder** Arg.
41 C4 **Strokestown** Rep. of Ireland
40 E2 **Stroma, Island of** *i.* U.K.
48 F5 **Stromboli, Isola** *i.* Italy
40 E2 **Stromness** U.K.
76 D3 **Stromsburg** U.S.A.
37 M7 **Strömstad** Sweden
36 O5 **Strömsund** Sweden
80 C4 **Strongsville** U.S.A.
40 F1 **Stronsay** *i.* U.K.
8 H2 **Stroud** Austr.
39 E6 **Stroud** U.K.
8 H2 **Stroud Road** Austr.
81 F4 **Stroudsburg** U.S.A.
37 L8 **Struer** Denmark
49 J4 **Struga** Macedonia
50 D3 **Strugi-Krasnyye** Rus. Fed.
58 D7 **Struis Bay** S. Africa
43 J5 **Strullendorf** Ger.
49 K4 **Struma** *r.* Bulg.
39 B5 **Strumble Head** *hd* U.K.
49 K4 **Strumica** Macedonia
49 L3 **Stryama** *r.* Bulg.
58 E4 **Strydenburg** S. Africa
37 K6 **Stryn** Norway
51 B5 **Stryy** Ukr.
79 D7 **Stuart** *FL* U.S.A.
80 C6 **Stuart** *VA* U.S.A.
64 E4 **Stuart Lake** *l.* Can.
80 D5 **Stuarts Draft** U.S.A.
8 G2 **Stuart Town** Austr.
9 C6 **Studholme Junction** N.Z.
36 Q5 **Studsviken** Sweden
77 C6 **Study Butte** U.S.A.
65 L4 **Stull L.** *l.* Can.
32 C2 **Stung Chinit** *r.* Cambodia
50 F4 **Stupino** Rus. Fed.
92 A6 **Sturge I.** *i.* Ant.
68 D2 **Sturgeon** *r.* U.S.A.
68 D3 **Sturgeon Bay** *WV* U.S.A.
65 K4 **Sturgeon Bay** *b.* Can.
68 E3 **Sturgeon Bay** *b.* U.S.A.
68 D3 **Sturgeon Bay Canal** *chan.* U.S.A.
69 H2 **Sturgeon Falls** Can.
66 B3 **Sturgeon L.** *l.* Can.
78 C4 **Sturgis** *KY* U.S.A.
68 E5 **Sturgis** *MI* U.S.A.
76 C2 **Sturgis** *SD* U.S.A.
6 C3 **Sturt Creek** *r.* Austr.
6 E4 **Sturt Desert** *des.* Austr.
59 G6 **Stutterheim** S. Africa
46 D6 **Stuttgart** Ger.
77 F5 **Stuttgart** U.S.A.
36 B4 **Stykkishólmur** Iceland
47 M5 **Styr** *r.* Ukr.
90 D2 **Suaçuí Grande** *r.* Brazil
55 F3 **Suakin** Sudan
27 F5 **Su'ao** Taiwan
73 E6 **Suaqui Gde** Mex.
89 B3 **Suárez** *r.* Col.
47 M3 **Subačius** Lith.
23 H4 **Subansiri** *r.* India
23 F5 **Subarnarekha** *r.* India
17 G6 **Şubayḩah** S. Arabia
33 C2 **Subi Besar** *i.* Indon.
49 H1 **Subotica** Yugo.
47 N7 **Suceava** Romania
28 C3 **Suchan** *r.* Rus. Fed.
41 C4 **Suck** *r.* Rep. of Ireland
43 K1 **Suckow** Ger.
86 E7 **Sucre** Bol.
89 B2 **Sucre** Col.
89 C3 **Sucuaro** Col.
90 B2 **Sucuriú** *r.* Brazil
51 E6 **Sudak** Ukr.
52 G4 **Sudan** *country* Africa
50 G3 **Suday** Rus. Fed.
17 K6 **Sudayr** *watercourse* Iraq
69 G2 **Sudbury** Can.
39 H5 **Sudbury** U.K.
55 E4 **Sudd** *swamp* Sudan
43 K1 **Sude** *r.* Ger.
46 H5 **Sudety** *mts* Czech Rep./Pol.
81 F5 **Sudlersville** U.S.A.
50 G4 **Sudogda** Rus. Fed.
16 D7 **Sudr** Egypt
36 □ **Suðuroy** *i.* Faroe Is
55 E4 **Sue** *watercourse* Sudan
45 F3 **Sueca** Spain
55 F2 **Suez** Egypt
55 F1 **Suez Canal** *canal* Egypt
55 F2 **Suez, Gulf of** *g.* Egypt
80 E6 **Suffolk** U.S.A.
18 B2 **Sūfīān** Iran
68 C4 **Sugar** *r.* U.S.A.
81 H2 **Sugarloaf Mt.** *mt* U.S.A.
31 C4 **Sugbuhan Point** *pt* Phil.
33 E1 **Sugut** *r.* Malaysia
31 A5 **Sugut, Tg** *pt* Malaysia
26 B2 **Suhait** China
20 E5 **Şuḩār** Oman
24 C1 **Sühbaatar** Mongolia
43 J4 **Suhl** Ger.
43 J2 **Suhlendorf** Ger.
16 C2 **Şuhut** Turkey
22 B3 **Sui** Pak.
28 B1 **Suibin** China
27 F4 **Suichang** China
27 E5 **Suichuan** China
26 D2 **Suide** China
30 F1 **Suifenhe** China
22 B4 **Suigam** India
24 E2 **Suihua** China
27 B4 **Suijiang** China
27 D5 **Suining** *Hunan* China
26 E3 **Suining** *Jiangsu* China
27 B4 **Suining** *Sichuan* China
26 E3 **Suiping** China
42 C5 **Suippes** France
41 D5 **Suir** *r.* Rep. of Ireland
26 E3 **Suixi** China
26 E3 **Sui Xian** China
27 C5 **Suiyang** China
26 F1 **Suizhong** China
26 D4 **Suizhou** China
26 C1 **Suj** China
22 C4 **Sujangarh** India
22 D3 **Sujanpur** India
22 B4 **Sujawal** Pak.
33 C4 **Sukabumi** Indon.
33 C3 **Sukadana** Indon.
29 G6 **Sukagawa** Japan
31 A5 **Sukau** Malaysia
30 C4 **Sukchŏn** N. Korea
28 C1 **Sukhanovka** Rus. Fed.
50 E4 **Sukhinichi** Rus. Fed.
50 H2 **Sukhona** *r.* Rus. Fed.
32 A1 **Sukhothai** Thai.
50 E2 **Sukkozero** Rus. Fed.
22 B4 **Sukkur** Pak.
21 C2 **Sukma** India
22 C4 **Sukri** *r.* India
50 F3 **Sukromny** Rus. Fed.
29 C8 **Sukumo** Japan
37 J6 **Sula** *i.* Norway
22 B3 **Sulaiman Ranges** *mts* Pak.
51 H7 **Sulak** *r.* Rus. Fed.
25 F7 **Sula, Kepulauan** *is* Indon.
18 C4 **Sūlār** Iran
40 B1 **Sula Sgeir** *i.* U.K.
33 E3 **Sulawesi** *i.* Indon.
17 K4 **Sulaymān Beg** Iraq
18 C2 **Suledeh** Iran
40 D1 **Sule Skerry** *i.* U.K.
40 D1 **Sule Stack** *i.* U.K.
16 F3 **Süleymanlı** Turkey
54 A4 **Sulima** Sierra Leone
43 G2 **Sulingen** Ger.
36 P3 **Sulitjelma** Norway
37 V6 **Sulkava** Fin.
86 B4 **Sullana** Peru
76 F4 **Sullivan** U.S.A.
65 G4 **Sullivan L.** *l.* Can.
81 J1 **Sully** Can.
48 E3 **Sulmona** Italy
77 E6 **Sulphur** U.S.A.
77 E5 **Sulphur Springs** U.S.A.
69 F2 **Sultan** Can.
Sultanabad *see* **Arāk**
16 C2 **Sultan Dağları** *mts* Turkey
16 D2 **Sultanhanı** Turkey
19 F4 **Sultan, Koh-i-** *mts* Pak.
23 E4 **Sultanpur** India
31 B5 **Sulu Archipelago** *is* Phil.
19 H2 **Sülüktü** Kyrg.
16 F2 **Sulusaray** Turkey
31 A4 **Sulu Sea** *sea* Phil.
43 K5 **Sulzbach-Rosenberg** Ger.
92 A4 **Sulzberger Bay** *b.* Ant.
19 E6 **Sumāil** Oman
88 D3 **Sumampa** Arg.
89 B4 **Sumapaz, Parque Nacional** *nat. park* Col.
17 K5 **Sūmar** Iran
33 B3 **Sumatera** *i.* Indon.
Sumatra *i. see* **Sumatera**
46 F6 **Šumava** *mts* Czech Rep.
25 E7 **Sumba** *i.* Indon.
18 D2 **Sumbar** *r.* Turkm.
25 D7 **Sumba, Selat** *chan.* Indon.
33 E4 **Sumbawa** *i.* Indon.
33 E4 **Sumbawabesar** Indon.
57 D4 **Sumbawanga** Tanz.
57 B5 **Sumbe** Angola
40 □ **Sumburgh** U.K.
40 □ **Sumburgh Head** *hd* U.K.
22 D2 **Sumdo** China/Jammu and Kashmir
17 M3 **Sume'eh Sarā** Iran
33 D4 **Sumenep** Indon.
Sumgait *see* **Sumqayıt**
29 F9 **Sumisu-jima** *i.* Japan
17 J3 **Summēl** Iraq
66 C3 **Summer Beaver** Can.
67 K4 **Summerford** Can.
68 D3 **Summer I.** *i.* U.S.A.
40 C2 **Summer Isles** *is* U.K.
67 H4 **Summerside** Can.
80 C5 **Summersville** U.S.A.
80 C5 **Summersville Lake** *l.* U.S.A.
64 E4 **Summit Lake** Can.
68 E5 **Summit Lake** *l.* U.S.A.
74 D2 **Summit Mt** *mt* U.S.A.
22 D2 **Sumnal** China/India
9 D5 **Sumner** N.Z.
68 A4 **Sumner** U.S.A.
9 D5 **Sumner, L.** *l.* N.Z.
64 C3 **Sumner Strait** *chan.* U.S.A.
29 F6 **Sumon-dake** *mt* Japan
29 D7 **Sumoto** Japan
46 H6 **Šumperk** Czech Rep.
17 M1 **Sumqayıt** Azer.
17 M1 **Sumqayıt** *r.* Azer.
22 B4 **Sumrahu** Pak.
79 D5 **Sumter** U.S.A.
51 E5 **Sumy** Ukr.
72 D2 **Sun** *r.* U.S.A.
50 J3 **Suna** Rus. Fed.
28 G3 **Sunagawa** Japan
23 G4 **Sunamganj** Bangl.
30 C4 **Sunan** N. Korea
40 C4 **Sunart, Loch** *in.* U.K.
18 D6 **Şunaynah** Oman
17 K4 **Sunbula Kuh** *mts* Iran
72 E1 **Sunburst** U.S.A.
8 E4 **Sunbury** Austr.
80 B4 **Sunbury** *OH* U.S.A.
80 E4 **Sunbury** *PA* U.S.A.
91 E1 **Sunchales** Arg.
30 C4 **Sunch'ŏn** N. Korea
30 D6 **Sunch'ŏn** S. Korea
59 G2 **Sun City** S. Africa
81 H3 **Suncook** U.S.A.
72 F2 **Sundance** U.S.A.
23 F5 **Sundargarh** India
22 D3 **Sundarnagar** India
33 C4 **Sunda, Selat** *chan.* Indon.
93 M4 **Sunda Trench** *sea feature* Ind. Ocean
38 F3 **Sunderland** U.K.
43 G3 **Sundern (Sauerland)** Ger.
16 C2 **Sündiken Dağları** *mts* Turkey
69 H3 **Sundridge** Can.
37 P5 **Sundsvall** Sweden

17 J1 Tba Khozap'ini l. Georgia
51 H7 T'bilisi Georgia
51 G6 Tbilisskaya Rus. Fed.
56 B4 Tchibanga Gabon
55 D2 Tchigaï, Plateau du plat. Niger
55 D4 Tcholliré Cameroon
47 J3 Tczew Pol.
84 A2 Teacapán Mex.
9 A6 Te Anau N.Z.
9 A6 Te Anau, L. l. N.Z.
84 D3 Teapa Mex.
9 G2 Te Araroa N.Z.
9 E2 Te Aroha N.Z.
9 E3 Te Awamutu N.Z.
38 E3 Tebay U.K.
65 K2 Tebesjuak Lake l. Can.
54 C1 Tébessa Alg.
48 B7 Tébessa, Monts de mts Alg.
88 E3 Tebicuary r. Para.
33 A2 Tebingtinggi Indon.
33 B3 Tebingtinggi Indon.
48 C6 Tébourba Tunisia
48 C6 Téboursouk Tunisia
51 H7 Tebulos Mt'a mt Georgia/Rus. Fed.
54 B4 Techiman Ghana
88 B6 Tecka Arg.
42 F2 Tecklenburger Land reg. Ger.
84 C2 Tecolutla Mex.
84 B3 Tecomán Mex.
74 D4 Tecopa U.S.A.
84 B3 Técpan Mex.
47 N7 Tecuci Romania
69 F5 Tecumseh U.S.A.
19 F2 Tedzhen Turkm.
19 F2 Tedzhen r. Turkm.
19 F2 Tedzhenstroy Turkm.
75 H3 Teec Nos Pos U.S.A.
15 H1 Teeli Rus. Fed.
38 F3 Tees r. U.K.
38 E3 Teesdale reg. U.K.
31 A4 Teeth, The mt Phil.
86 E4 Tefé r. Brazil
16 B3 Tefenni Turkey
33 C4 Tegal Indon.
43 M2 Tegel airport Ger.
39 D5 Tegid, Llyn l. U.K.
82 G6 Tegucigalpa Honduras
55 D3 Teguidda-n-Tessoumt Niger
74 C4 Tehachapi U.S.A.
73 C5 Tehachapi Mts mts U.S.A.
74 C4 Tehachapi Pass U.S.A.
65 K2 Tehek Lake l. Can.
Teheran see Tehrān
54 B4 Téhini Côte d'Ivoire
18 C3 Tehrān Iran
22 D3 Tehri Uttar Pradesh India
Tehri see Tikamgarh
84 C3 Tehuacán Mex.
84 D4 Tehuantepec, Golfo de g. Mex.
84 D3 Tehuantepec, Istmo de isth. Mex.
95 N5 Tehuantepec Ridge sea feature Pac. Oc.
84 C3 Tehuitzingo Mex.
39 C5 Teifi r. U.K.
39 D7 Teign r. U.K.
39 D7 Teignmouth U.K.
Tejo r. see Tagus
74 C4 Tejon Pass U.S.A.
9 D1 Te Kao N.Z.
9 C5 Tekapo, L. l. N.Z.
23 F4 Tekari India
82 G4 Tekax Mex.
56 D2 Tekezē Wenz r. Eritrea/Eth.
22 E1 Tekiliktag mt China
16 A1 Tekirdağ Turkey
21 D2 Tekkali India
17 H2 Tekman Turkey
23 H5 Teknaf Bangl.
68 E4 Tekonsha U.S.A.
9 E3 Te Kuiti N.Z.
23 E5 Tel r. India
51 H7 T'elavi Georgia
16 E5 Tel Aviv-Yafo Israel
46 G6 Telč Czech Rep.
82 G4 Telchac Puerto Mex.
64 C3 Telegraph Creek Can.
44 G3 Télégraphe, Le h. France
90 B4 Telêmaco Borba Brazil
91 D3 Telén Arg.
33 E2 Telen r. Indon.
49 L2 Teleorman r. Romania
74 D3 Telescope Peak summit U.S.A.
87 G5 Teles Pires r. Brazil
39 E5 Telford U.K.
43 F3 Telgte Ger.
54 A3 Télimélé Guinea
17 J3 Tel Kotchek Syria
64 D4 Telkwa Can.
62 B3 Teller AK U.S.A.
21 A4 Tellicherry India
42 D4 Tellin Belgium
17 L6 Telloh Iraq
32 □ Telok Blangah Sing.
84 C3 Teloloapán Mex.
91 C4 Telsen Arg.
37 S9 Telšiai Lith.
43 M2 Teltow Ger.
33 B2 Teluk Anson Malaysia
33 A2 Telukdalam Indon.
69 H2 Temagami Can.
69 G2 Temagami Lake l. Can.
33 D4 Temanggung Indon.
59 H2 Temba S. Africa
33 C2 Tembelan, Kepulauan is Indon.
13 L3 Tembenchi r. Rus. Fed.
33 B3 Tembilahan Indon.
59 H3 Tembisa S. Africa
56 B4 Tembo Aluma Angola
39 E5 Teme r. U.K.
74 D5 Temecula U.S.A.
16 D2 Temelli Turkey
33 B2 Temerloh Malaysia
17 M5 Temīleh Iran
15 F1 Temirtau Kazak.
69 H2 Temiscaming Can.
69 H2 Témiscamingue, Lac l. Can.
67 G4 Témiscouata, L. l. Can.
36 T4 Temmes Fin.
50 G4 Temnikov Rus. Fed.
8 F3 Temora Austr.
75 G5 Tempe U.S.A.
43 M2 Tempelhof airport Ger.
48 C4 Tempio Pausania Sardinia Italy
68 E3 Temple MI U.S.A.
77 D6 Temple TX U.S.A.
39 C5 Temple Bar U.K.
41 D5 Templemore Rep. of Ireland
31 A4 Templer Bank sand bank Phil.
38 E3 Temple Sowerby U.K.
43 M1 Templin Ger.
84 C2 Tempoal Mex.
51 F6 Temryuk Rus. Fed.
91 B3 Temuco Chile
9 C6 Temuka N.Z.
86 C4 Tena Ecuador
74 D1 Tenabo, Mt mt U.S.A.
21 C2 Tenali India
84 C3 Tenancingo Mex.
32 A2 Tenasserim Myanmar
32 A2 Tenasserim r. Myanmar
39 E5 Tenbury Wells U.K.
39 C6 Tenby U.K.
69 F2 Tenby Bay Can.
56 E2 Tendaho Eth.
44 H4 Tende France
15 H6 Ten Degree Chan. Andaman and Nicobar Is
28 G5 Tendō Japan
17 J2 Tendürük Dağı mt Turkey
54 B3 Ténenkou Mali
54 D3 Ténéré reg. Niger
54 D2 Ténéré du Tafassâsset des. Niger
54 A2 Tenerife i. Canary Is
45 G4 Ténès Alg.
33 E4 Tengah, Kepulauan is Indon.
32 □ Tengeh Res. resr Sing.
26 B2 Tengger Shamo des. China
32 B4 Tenggul i. Malaysia
14 E1 Tengiz, Oz. l. Kazak.
27 C7 Tengqiao China
54 B3 Tengréla Côte d'Ivoire
27 D6 Teng Xian Guangxi China
26 E3 Teng Xian Shandong China
92 B2 Teniente Jubany Arg. Base Ant.
92 B2 Teniente Rodolfo Marsh Chile Base Ant.
57 C5 Tenke Congo(Zaire)
13 Q2 Tenkeli Rus. Fed.
54 B3 Tenkodogo Burkina
6 D3 Tennant Creek Austr.
80 B6 Tennessee div. U.S.A.
79 C5 Tennessee r. U.S.A.
73 F4 Tennessee Pass U.S.A.
36 P2 Tennevoll Norway
91 B2 Teno r. Chile
36 U2 Tenojoki r. Fin./Norway
84 E3 Tenosique Mex.
72 F2 Ten Sleep U.S.A.
6 C2 Tenteno Indon.
39 H6 Tenterden U.K.
79 D7 Ten Thousand Islands is U.S.A.
45 C3 Tentudia mt Spain
90 B3 Teodoro Sampaio Brazil
90 E2 Teófilo Otôni Brazil
84 D3 Teopisca Mex.
84 C3 Teotihuacán Mex.
73 E6 Tepache Mex.
9 D1 Te Paki N.Z.
84 B3 Tepalcatepec Mex.
84 B2 Tepatitlán Mex.
17 H3 Tepe Turkey
17 J3 Tepe Gawra Iraq
84 A1 Tepehuanes Mex.
84 C3 Tepeji Mex.
49 J4 Tepelenë Albania
84 C3 Tepelmemec Mex.
43 L5 Tepelská Vrchovina reg. Czech Rep.
89 E4 Tepequem, Serra mts Brazil
84 A2 Tepic Mex.
9 C5 Te Pirita N.Z.
46 F5 Teplice Czech Rep.
50 K2 Teplogorka Rus. Fed.
50 F4 Teploye Rus. Fed.
9 F2 Te Puke N.Z.
84 D3 Tequisistlán Mex.
84 C2 Tequisquiapán Mex.
45 H1 Ter r. Spain
5 L4 Teraina i. Kiribati
22 D2 Teram Kangri mt China/Jammu and Kashmir
48 E3 Teramo Italy
8 D5 Terang Austr.
42 F2 Ter Apel Neth.
22 B3 Teratani r. Pak.
51 F4 Terbuny Rus. Fed.
17 H2 Tercan Turkey
34 C5 Terceira i. Port.
47 M6 Terebovlya Ukr.
51 H7 Terek Rus. Fed.
51 H7 Terek r. Rus. Fed.
50 J4 Teren'ga Rus. Fed.
90 A3 Terenos Brazil
89 C2 Terepaima, Parque Nacional nat. park Venez.
50 H4 Tereshka r. Rus. Fed.
87 K5 Teresina Brazil
90 D3 Teresópolis Brazil
42 B5 Tergnier France
16 F1 Terme Turkey
19 G2 Termez Uzbek.
48 E6 Termini Imerese Sicily Italy
84 E3 Términos, Lag. de lag. Mex.
48 F4 Termoli Italy
39 E5 Tern r. U.K.
25 E6 Ternate Indon.
42 B3 Terneuzen Neth.
28 E2 Terney Rus. Fed.
48 E3 Terni Italy
51 C5 Ternopil' Ukr.
8 B2 Terowie Austr.
24 G2 Terpeniya, Mys c. Rus. Fed.
24 G2 Terpeniya, Zaliv g. Rus. Fed.
64 D4 Terrace Can.
68 D1 Terrace Bay Can.
58 E2 Terra Firma S. Africa
36 N4 Terråk Norway
48 C5 Terralba Sardinia Italy
67 K4 Terra Nova Nat. Pk Can.
92 B6 Terre Adélie reg. Ant.
77 F6 Terre Bonne Bay b. U.S.A.
78 C4 Terre Haute U.S.A.
67 K4 Terrenceville Can.
72 F2 Terry U.S.A.
51 G5 Tersa r. Rus. Fed.
42 D1 Terschelling i. Neth.
48 C5 Tertenia Sardinia Italy
45 F2 Teruel Spain
32 A4 Terutao i. Thai.
36 T3 Tervola Fin.
48 G2 Tešanj Bos.-Herz.
56 D2 Teseney Eritrea
50 G4 Tesha r. Rus. Fed.
62 C2 Teshekpuk Lake l. U.S.A.
28 J3 Teshikaga Japan
28 G2 Teshio Japan
28 H3 Teshio-dake mt Japan
28 G2 Teshio-gawa r. Japan
64 C2 Teslin Can.
64 C2 Teslin r. Can.
64 C2 Teslin Lake l. Can.
90 B1 Tesouras r. Brazil
90 B2 Tesouro Brazil
54 C3 Tessaoua Niger
39 F6 Test r. U.K.
48 C6 Testour Tunisia
88 B2 Tetas, Pta pt Chile
57 D5 Tete Moz.
9 F3 Te Teko N.Z.
47 P5 Teteriv r. Ukr.
43 L1 Teterow Ger.
47 O6 Tetiyiv Ukr.
38 G4 Tetney U.K.
72 E2 Teton r. U.S.A.
72 E3 Teton Ra. mts U.S.A.
54 B1 Tétouan Morocco
49 J3 Tetovo Macedonia
22 B5 Tetpur India
50 J4 Tetyushi Rus. Fed.
88 D2 Teuco r. Arg.
58 B1 Teufelsbach Namibia
43 G1 Teufels Moor reg. Ger.
28 G2 Teuri-tō i. Japan
43 G2 Teutoburger Wald h. Ger.
37 R5 Teuva Fin.
Teverya see Tiberias
40 F5 Teviot r. U.K.
40 F5 Teviotdale v. U.K.
9 A7 Te Waewae Bay b. N.Z.
59 G1 Tewane Botswana
7 F4 Tewantin Austr.
9 E4 Te Wharau N.Z.
39 E6 Tewkesbury U.K.
26 B3 Têwo China
64 E5 Texada I. i. Can.
77 E5 Texarkana U.S.A.
77 D6 Texas div. U.S.A.
77 E6 Texas City U.S.A.
84 C3 Texcoco Mex.
42 C1 Texel i. Neth.
77 C4 Texhoma U.S.A.
77 D5 Texoma, Lake l. U.S.A.
59 G4 Teyateyaneng Lesotho
50 G3 Teykovo Rus. Fed.
19 G3 Teyvareh Afgh.
50 G3 Teza r. Rus. Fed.
84 C2 Teziutlán Mex.
23 H4 Tezpur India
23 J4 Tezu India
65 K2 Tha-anne r. Can.
59 H4 Thabana-Ntlenyana mt Lesotho
59 G4 Thaba Nchu S. Africa
59 G4 Thaba Putsoa mt Lesotho
59 H4 Thaba-Tseka Lesotho
59 G2 Thabazimbi S. Africa
32 B1 Tha Bo Laos
59 G3 Thabong S. Africa
18 B5 Thādiq S. Arabia
32 A2 Thagyettaw Myanmar
27 C6 Thai Binh Vietnam
22 B3 Thai Desert des. Pak.
11 M8 Thailand country Asia
32 B3 Thailand, Gulf of g. Asia
27 B6 Thai Nguyên Vietnam
18 C5 Thaj S. Arabia
22 E5 Thakurtola India
43 J4 Thal Ger.
22 B2 Thal Pak.
48 C7 Thala Tunisia
32 A3 Thalang Thai.
Thalassery see Tellicherry
43 K3 Thale (Harz) Ger.
32 B4 Thale Luang lag. Thai.
32 B1 Tha Li Thai.
19 G4 Thalo Pak.
59 F2 Thamaga Botswana
20 D6 Thamarīt Oman
20 C7 Thamar, J. mt Yemen
39 G5 Thame r. U.K.
9 E2 Thames N.Z.
39 H6 Thames est. Eng. U.K.
39 G6 Thames r. Eng. U.K.
69 G4 Thamesville Can.
32 A2 Thanbyuzayat Myanmar
22 C5 Thandla India
22 B5 Thangadh India
32 D2 Thăng Binh Vietnam
32 C1 Thanh Hoa Vietnam
21 B4 Thanjavur India
32 B1 Tha Pla Thai.
32 A3 Thap Put Thai.
32 B3 Thap Sakae Thai.
22 B4 Tharad India
22 B4 Thar Desert des. India/Pak.
49 L4 Thasos i. Greece
75 H5 Thatcher U.S.A.
27 C6 Thât Khê Vietnam
25 B5 Thaton Myanmar
23 H4 Thaungdut Myanmar
32 A1 Thaungyin r. Myanmar/Thai.
25 B5 Thayetmyo Myanmar
75 F5 Theba U.S.A.
76 C3 Thedford U.S.A.
42 C2 The Hague Neth.
32 A3 Theinkun Myanmar
65 H2 Thekulthili Lake l. Can.
65 J2 Thelon r. Can.
65 J2 Thelon Game Sanctuary res. Can.
43 J4 Themar Ger.
58 F6 Thembalesizwe S. Africa
59 H3 Thembalihle S. Africa
45 H4 Thenia Alg.
45 H5 Theniet El Had Alg.
86 F5 Theodore Roosevelt r. Brazil
75 G5 Theodore Roosevelt Lake l. U.S.A.
76 C2 Theodore Roosevelt Nat. Park U.S.A.
42 A5 Thérain r. France
81 F2 Theresa U.S.A.
49 K4 Thermaïkos Kolpos g. Greece
74 B2 Thermalito U.S.A.
72 E3 Thermopolis U.S.A.
42 A4 Thérouanne France
62 F2 Thesiger Bay b. Can.
69 F2 Thessalon Can.
49 K4 Thessaloniki Greece
39 H5 Thet r. U.K.
39 H5 Thetford U.K.
67 F4 Thetford Mines Can.
32 C1 Theun r. Laos
59 G4 Theunissen S. Africa
77 F6 Thibodaux U.S.A.
65 K3 Thicket Portage Can.
76 D1 Thief River Falls U.S.A.
92 B4 Thiel Mts mts Ant.
44 F4 Thiers France
54 A3 Thiès Senegal
56 D4 Thika Kenya
21 A5 Thiladhunmathee Atoll atoll Maldives
23 G4 Thimphu Bhutan
44 H2 Thionville France
Thira i. see Santorini
49 L6 Thirasia i. Greece
38 F3 Thirsk U.K.
Thiruvananthapuram see Trivandrum
37 L8 Thisted Denmark
49 K5 Thiva Greece
65 K2 Thlewiaza r. Can.
65 H2 Thoa r. Can.
59 J1 Thohoyandou S. Africa
42 C3 Tholen Neth.
42 F5 Tholey Ger.
80 D5 Thomas U.S.A.
79 C5 Thomaston GA U.S.A.
81 J2 Thomaston ME U.S.A.
81 K2 Thomaston Corner Can.
41 D5 Thomastown Rep. of Ireland
79 D6 Thomasville U.S.A.
42 E4 Thommen Belgium
65 K3 Thompson Man. Can.
68 D3 Thompson MI U.S.A.
81 F4 Thompson PA U.S.A.
64 E4 Thompson r. Can.
76 E3 Thompson r. U.S.A.
72 D2 Thompson Falls U.S.A.
79 D5 Thomson U.S.A.
32 C1 Thôn Cư Lai Vietnam
46 C7 Thonon-les-Bains France
32 D3 Thôn Sơn Hai Vietnam
73 E5 Thoreau U.S.A.
42 D3 Thorn Neth.
38 F3 Thornaby-on-Tees U.K.
68 E4 Thornapple r. U.S.A.
39 E6 Thornbury U.K.
69 H2 Thorne Can.
38 G4 Thorne U.K.
74 C2 Thorne U.S.A.
64 C3 Thorne Bay U.S.A.
68 D5 Thorntown U.S.A.
68 B3 Thorp U.S.A.
92 D3 Thorshavnheiane mts Ant.
59 G4 Thota-ea-Moli Lesotho
44 D3 Thouars France
81 E2 Thousand Islands is Can.
75 G2 Thousand Lake Mt mt U.S.A.
74 C4 Thousand Oaks U.S.A.
49 L4 Thrakiko Pelagos sea Greece
72 E2 Three Forks U.S.A.
64 G4 Three Hills Can.
9 D1 Three Kings Is is N.Z.
68 C3 Three Lakes U.S.A.
68 D5 Three Oaks U.S.A.
32 A2 Three Pagodas Pass Myanmar/Thai.
54 B4 Three Points, Cape c. Ghana
68 E5 Three Rivers MI U.S.A.
77 D6 Three Rivers TX U.S.A.
72 B2 Three Sisters mt U.S.A.
Thrissur see Trichur
77 D5 Throckmorton U.S.A.
65 G2 Thubun Lakes l. Can.
32 C3 Thu Dâu Môt Vietnam
42 C4 Thuin Belgium
Thule see Qaanaaq
57 C6 Thuli Zimbabwe
46 C7 Thun Switz.
68 C1 Thunder Bay Can.
68 C1 Thunder Bay b. Can.
69 F3 Thunder Bay b. U.S.A.
43 H5 Thüngen Ger.
32 A3 Thung Song Thai.
32 A4 Thung Wa Thai.
43 J4 Thüringen div. Ger.
43 K3 Thüringer Becken reg. Ger.
43 J4 Thüringer Wald mts Ger.
41 D5 Thurles Rep. of Ireland
80 E5 Thurmont U.S.A.
46 F7 Thurn, Paß pass Austria
81 F2 Thurso Can.
40 E2 Thurso U.K.
40 E2 Thurso r. Scot. U.K.
92 A3 Thurston I. i. Ant.
43 H2 Thüster Berg h. Ger.
38 E3 Thwaite U.K.
92 A3 Thwaites Gl. gl. Ant.
37 L8 Thyborøn Denmark
26 A1 Tiancang China
26 F3 Tianchang China
27 C6 Tiandeng China
27 C6 Tiandong China
27 C5 Tian'e China
87 K4 Tianguá Brazil
26 E2 Tianjin China
26 E2 Tianjin div. China
24 B3 Tianjun China
27 C5 Tianlin China
27 D4 Tianmen China
27 F4 Tianmu Shan mts China
30 E2 Tianqiaoling China
27 B4 Tianquan China
30 C3 Tianshifu China
26 B3 Tianshui China
22 D2 Tianshuihai China/Jammu and Kashmir
27 F4 Tiantai China
26 E1 Tiantaiyong China
27 C6 Tianyang China
26 B2 Tianzhu Gansu China
27 C5 Tianzhu Guizhou China
54 C1 Tiaret Alg.
54 B4 Tiassalé Côte d'Ivoire
90 B4 Tibagi r. Brazil
17 J5 Tibal, Wādī watercourse Iraq
55 D4 Tibati Cameroon
48 E3 Tiber r. Italy
16 E5 Tiberias Israel
Tiberias, Lake l. see Galilee, Sea of
72 E1 Tiber Res. resr U.S.A.
55 D2 Tibesti mts Chad
Tibet Aut. Region div. see Xizang Zizhiqu
Tibet, Plateau of plat. see Xizang Gaoyuan
6 E4 Tibooburra Austr.
23 E3 Tibrikot Nepal
23 E3 Tibrikot Nepal
37 O7 Tibro Sweden
82 B3 Tiburón i. Mex.
31 B3 Ticao i. Phil.
39 H6 Ticehurst U.K.
69 J3 Tichborne Can.
54 B3 Tîchît Maur.
54 A2 Tichla Western Sahara
46 D7 Ticino r. Switz.
81 G3 Ticonderoga U.S.A.
82 G4 Ticul Mex.
37 N7 Tidaholm Sweden
23 H5 Tiddim Myanmar
54 C2 Tidikelt, Plaine du plain Alg.
54 A3 Tidjikja Maur.
42 D3 Tiel Neth.
28 A1 Tieli China
30 B1 Tieling China
22 D2 Tielongtan China/Jammu and Kashmir
42 B4 Tielt Belgium
54 B4 Tiémé Côte d'Ivoire
42 C4 Tienen Belgium
10 K5 Tien Shan mts China/Kyrg.
Tientsin see Tianjin
37 P6 Tierp Sweden
73 F4 Tierra Amarilla U.S.A.
84 C3 Tierra Blanca Mex.
84 C3 Tierra Colorada Mex.
88 C8 Tierra del Fuego, Isla Grande de i. Arg./Chile
45 D2 Tiétar r. Spain
45 D2 Tiétar, Valle de v. Spain
90 C3 Tietê Brazil
90 B3 Tietê r. Brazil
80 B4 Tiffin U.S.A.
Tiflis see T'bilisi
79 D6 Tifton U.S.A.
49 L3 Tigheciului, Dealurile h. Moldova
51 D6 Tighina Moldova
23 F5 Tigiria India
55 D4 Tignère Cameroon
67 H4 Tignish Can.
86 C4 Tigre r. Ecuador/Peru
89 E2 Tigre r. Venez.
17 L5 Tigris r. Iraq/Turkey
20 B6 Tihāmah reg. S. Arabia
16 D7 Tih, Gebel el plat. Egypt
82 A2 Tijuana Mex.
90 C2 Tijuco r. Brazil
22 D4 Tikamgarh India
51 G6 Tikhoretsk Rus. Fed.
50 E3 Tikhvin Rus. Fed.
50 E3 Tikhvinskaya Gryada ridge Rus. Fed.
9 F3 Tikokino N.Z.
7 G3 Tikopia i. Solomon Is
17 J4 Tikrīt Iraq
36 W3 Tiksheozero, Oz. l. Rus. Fed.
13 O2 Tiksi Rus. Fed.
23 E3 Tila r. Nepal
23 F4 Tilaiya Reservoir India
18 D2 Tīlavar Iran
42 D3 Tilburg Neth.
39 H6 Tilbury U.K.
88 C2 Tilcara Arg.
23 H5 Tilin Myanmar
54 C3 Tillabéri Niger
72 B2 Tillamook U.S.A.
40 E4 Tillicoultry U.K.
69 G4 Tillsonburg Can.
40 F3 Tillyfourie U.K.
49 M6 Tilos i. Greece
8 E1 Tilpa Austr.
51 F5 Tim Rus. Fed.
50 K1 Timanskiy Kryazh ridge Rus. Fed.
17 J2 Timar Turkey
9 C6 Timaru N.Z.
51 F6 Timashevsk Rus. Fed.
54 B3 Timbedgha Maur.
6 D3 Timber Creek Austr.
74 D3 Timber Mt mt U.S.A.
80 D5 Timberville U.S.A.
8 D5 Timboon Austr.
54 B3 Timétrine reg. Mali
54 C2 Timimoun Alg.
49 J2 Timișoara Romania
69 G1 Timmins Can.
50 F3 Timokhino Rus. Fed.
87 K5 Timon Brazil
25 E7 Timor i. Indon.
6 C3 Timor Sea sea Austr./Indon.
50 H3 Timoshino Rus. Fed.
91 D2 Timote Arg.
37 P5 Timrå Sweden
79 C5 Tims Ford L. l. U.S.A.
22 D5 Timurni Muafi India
89 C2 Tinaco Venez.
21 B3 Tindivanam India
54 B2 Tindouf Alg.
32 C5 Tinggi i. Malaysia
27 E5 Ting Jiang r. China
23 F3 Tingri China
37 O8 Tingsryd Sweden
37 B2 Tinguiririca, Vol. volc. Chile
36 L5 Tingvoll Norway
40 E1 Tingwall U.K.
90 E1 Tinharé, Ilha de i. Brazil
32 C1 Tinh Gia Vietnam
25 G5 Tinian i. N. Mariana Is
88 C3 Tinogasta Arg.
49 L6 Tinos i. Greece
42 B5 Tinqueux France
54 C2 Tinrhert, Plateau du plat. Alg.
23 H4 Tinsukia India
39 C7 Tintagel U.K.
8 C3 Tintinara Austr.
40 E5 Tinto h. U.K.
80 E4 Tioga r. U.S.A.
33 B2 Tioman i. Malaysia
69 F1 Tionaga Can.
80 D4 Tionesta Lake l. U.S.A.
81 E3 Tioughnioga r. U.S.A.
45 H4 Tipasa Alg.
68 D5 Tippecanoe r. U.S.A.
68 E5 Tippecanoe Lake l. U.S.A.
41 C5 Tipperary Rep. of Ireland
23 F4 Tiptala Bhanjyang pass Nepal
68 B5 Tipton IA U.S.A.
68 D5 Tipton IN U.S.A.
75 E4 Tipton, Mt mt U.S.A.
68 E1 Tip Top Hill h. Can.
39 H6 Tiptree U.K.
89 C4 Tiquié r. Brazil
87 J4 Tiracambu, Serra do h. Brazil
49 H4 Tirana Albania
Tiranë see Tirana
48 D1 Tirano Italy
51 D6 Tiraspol Moldova
58 B3 Tiraz Mts mts Namibia
16 A2 Tire Turkey
40 B4 Tiree i. U.K.
22 B1 Tirich Mir mt Pak.
22 B2 Tirna r. India
21 A3 Tirthahalli India
23 F5 Tirtol India
21 B4 Tiruchchendur India
21 B4 Tiruchchirāppalli India
21 B4 Tiruchengodu India
21 B4 Tirunelveli India
21 B3 Tirupati India
21 B3 Tiruppattur India
21 B4 Tiruppur India
21 B4 Tirutturaippundi India
21 B3 Tiruvannamalai India
21 B4 Tisaiyanvilai India
65 J4 Tisdale Can.
21 C5 Tissamaharama Sri Lanka
45 G5 Tissemsilt Alg.
23 G4 Tista r. India
92 B4 Titan Dome ice feature Ant.
13 O2 Tit-Ary Rus. Fed.
86 E7 Titicaca, Lago l. Bol./Peru
23 E5 Titlagarh India
48 G2 Titov Drvar Bos.-Herz.
69 E4 Tittabawassee r. U.S.A.
49 L2 Titu Romania
79 D6 Titusville FL U.S.A.
80 D4 Titusville PA U.S.A.
69 G3 Tiverton Can.
39 D7 Tiverton U.K.
48 E4 Tivoli Italy
84 C3 Tixtla Mex.
84 B2 Tizapán el Alto Mex.
45 H4 Tizi El Arba h. Alg.
82 G4 Tizimín Mex.
45 J4 Tizi Ouzou Alg.
89 D2 Tiznados r. Venez.
54 B2 Tiznit Morocco
84 B1 Tizoc Mex.
59 J2 Tjaneni Swaziland
36 Q4 Tjappsåive Sweden
42 D2 Tjeukemeer l. Neth.
37 K7 Tjorhom Norway
84 C3 Tlacolula Mex.
84 D3 Tlacotalpán Mex.
84 B1 Tlahualilo Mex.
84 C3 Tlalnepantla Mex.
84 C3 Tlapa Mex.
84 B2 Tlaquepaque Mex.
84 C3 Tlaxcala Mex.
84 C3 Tlaxcala div. Mex.
84 C3 Tlaxiaco Mex.
54 B1 Tlemcen Alg.
58 E4 Tlhakalatlou S. Africa
59 H4 Tlholong S. Africa
59 F2 Tlokweng Botswana
53 E4 Toad River Can.
57 E5 Toamasina Madag.
91 D3 Toay Arg.
29 E7 Toba Japan
32 A5 Toba, Danau l. Indon.
86 F1 Tobago i. Trinidad and Tobago
22 A3 Toba & Kakar Ranges mts Pak.
25 E6 Tobelo Indon.
69 G3 Tobermory Can.
40 B4 Tobermory U.K.
65 J4 Tobin L. l. Can.
74 D1 Tobin, Mt mt U.S.A.
81 K1 Tobique r. Can.
28 F5 Tobi-shima i. Japan
33 C3 Toboali Indon.
12 H4 Tobol r. Kazak./Rus. Fed.
32 D2 Tô Bong Vietnam
87 J5 Tocantinópolis Brazil
87 J4 Tocantins r. Brazil
90 C1 Tocantinzinha r. Brazil
79 D5 Toccoa U.S.A.
22 B2 Tochi r. Pak.
37 M7 Töcksfors Sweden
88 B2 Tocopilla Chile
8 E3 Tocumwal Austr.
89 C2 Tocuyo r. Venez.
48 E3 Todi Italy
46 D7 Todi mt Switz.
28 H5 Todoga-saki pt Japan
28 G4 Todohokke Japan
86 E7 Todos Santos Bol.
74 D6 Todos Santos, Bahía de b. Mex.
64 G4 Tofield Can.
64 D5 Tofino Can.
40 □ Toft U.K.
68 B2 Tofte U.S.A.
7 J3 Tofua i. Tonga
25 E7 Togian, Kepulauan is Indon.
68 A2 Togo U.S.A.
53 E5 Togo country Africa
26 D1 Togtoh China
75 H4 Tohatchi U.S.A.
36 T5 Toholampi Fin.
26 B1 Tohom China
37 S6 Toijala Fin.
29 B9 Toi-misaki pt Japan
37 U5 Toivakka Fin.
74 D2 Toiyabe Range mts U.S.A.
19 H2 Tojikobod Tajik.
62 D3 Tok U.S.A.
29 F6 Tōkamachi Japan
9 B7 Tokanui N.Z.
55 F3 Tokar Sudan
24 E4 Tokara-rettō is Japan
16 F1 Tokat Turkey
30 D5 Tŏkchŏktŏ i. S. Korea
30 D4 Tŏkch'ŏn N. Korea
5 K5 Tokelau terr. Pac. Oc.
15 F2 Tokmak Kyrg.
51 E6 Tokmak Ukr.
9 G3 Tokomaru Bay N.Z.
9 E3 Tokoroa N.Z.
59 H3 Tokoza S. Africa
12 K5 Toksun China
29 B6 Tok-tō i. Japan
29 D7 Tokushima Japan
29 B7 Tokuyama Japan
29 F7 Tōkyō Japan
29 F7 Tōkyō-wan b. Japan
19 G3 Tokzār Afgh.
9 G3 Tolaga Bay N.Z.
57 E6 Tôlañaro Madag.
84 C2 Toleant Mex.
90 B4 Toledo Brazil
45 D3 Toledo Spain
68 A5 Toledo IA U.S.A.
80 B4 Toledo OH U.S.A.
77 E6 Toledo Bend Reservoir U.S.A.
45 D3 Toledo, Montes de mts Spain
91 B3 Tolhuaca, Parque Nacional nat. park Chile
57 E6 Toliara Madag.
89 B3 Tolima, Nev. del volc. Col.
25 E6 Tolitoli Indon.
12 K3 Tol'ka Rus. Fed.
43 M1 Tollensesee l. Ger.
50 D3 Tolmachevo Rus. Fed.
48 E1 Tolmezzo Italy
27 □ Tolo Channel chan. H.K. China
27 □ Tolo Harbour b. H.K. China
45 E1 Tolosa Spain
30 D6 Tolsan-do i. S. Korea
69 F3 Tolsmaville Can.
40 B2 Tolsta Head hd U.K.
89 B2 Tolú Col.
84 C3 Toluca Mex.
70 B4 Tolumne r. CA U.S.A.
36 W3 Tolvand, Oz. l. Rus. Fed.
50 J4 Tol'yatti Rus. Fed.
68 B4 Tomah U.S.A.
68 C3 Tomahawk U.S.A.
28 G3 Tomakomai Japan
28 G2 Tomamae Japan
7 H3 Tomanivi mt Fiji
89 E5 Tomar Brazil
45 B3 Tomar Port.
16 E2 Tomarza Turkey
91 F1 Tomás Gomensoro Uru.
47 L5 Tomaszów Lubelski Pol.
47 K5 Tomaszów Mazowiecki Pol.
40 E3 Tomatin U.K.
84 A3 Tomatlán Mex.
79 B6 Tombigbee r. U.S.A.
56 B4 Tomboco Angola
90 D3 Tombos Brazil
54 B3 Tombouctou Mali
75 G6 Tombstone U.S.A.
57 B5 Tombua Angola
59 H1 Tom Burke S. Africa
91 B3 Tomé Chile
59 L1 Tome Moz.
37 N9 Tomelilla Sweden
45 E3 Tomelloso Spain
69 H2 Tomiko Can.
8 G2 Tomingley Austr.
54 B3 Tominian Mali
25 E7 Tomini, Teluk g. Indon.
40 E3 Tomintoul U.K.
48 G3 Tomislavgrad Bos.-Herz.
36 O3 Tømmerneset Norway
13 O4 Tommot Rus. Fed.
89 D4 Tomo Col.
89 C3 Tomo r. Col.
26 D1 Tomortei China
13 P3 Tompo Rus. Fed.
6 B4 Tom Price Austr.
24 A1 Tomsk Rus. Fed.
37 O8 Tomtabacken h. Sweden
13 Q3 Tomtor Rus. Fed.
28 H3 Tomuraushi-yama mt Japan
51 G6 Tomuzlovka r. Rus. Fed.
84 D3 Tonalá Mex.
75 G3 Tonalea U.S.A.
86 E4 Tonantins Brazil
72 C1 Tonasket U.S.A.
39 H6 Tonbridge U.K.
25 E6 Tondano Indon.
37 L9 Tønder Denmark
39 E6 Tone r. U.K.
5 K7 Tonga country Pac. Oc.
59 J4 Tongaat S. Africa
8 E4 Tongala Austr.
27 F5 Tong'an China
5 M5 Tongareva i. Pac. Oc.
9 E3 Tongariro National Park nat. park N.Z.
7 J4 Tongatapu Group is Tonga
94 H7 Tonga Tr. sea feature Pac. Oc.
26 D3 Tongbai China
26 D3 Tongbai Shan mts China
26 E4 Tongcheng Anhui China
27 D4 Tongcheng Hubei China
30 D4 T'ongch'ŏn N. Korea
26 C3 Tongchuan China
27 C5 Tongdao China
26 A3 Tongde China
30 D5 Tongduch'ŏn S. Korea
42 D4 Tongeren Belgium
27 E4 Tonggu China
27 D7 Tonggu Jiao pt China
30 E5 Tonghae S. Korea
27 B5 Tonghai China
28 A2 Tonghe China
30 C3 Tonghua Jilin China
30 C3 Tonghua Jilin China
26 C4 Tongjiang China
30 B2 Tongjiangkou China
30 D4 Tongjosŏn Man b. N. Korea
27 C6 Tongking, Gulf of g. China/Vietnam
27 C4 Tongliang China
30 B2 Tongliao China
26 E4 Tongling China
27 F4 Tonglu China
30 E6 Tongnae S. Korea
27 B4 Tongnan China
31 B5 Tongquil i. Phil.
27 C5 Tongren Guizhou China
26 A3 Tongren Qinghai China
23 G4 Tongsa r. Bhutan
27 E4 Tongshan China
23 H2 Tongtian He r. China
40 D2 Tongue U.K.
72 F2 Tongue r. U.S.A.
79 E7 Tongue of the Ocean chan. Bahamas
26 B3 Tongwei China
26 E2 Tong Xian China
26 B2 Tongxin China
26 E4 Tongyanghe China
30 B1 Tongyu China
30 B3 Tongyuanpu China
27 C4 Tongzi China
68 C5 Tonica U.S.A.
22 C4 Tonk India
18 C2 Tonkābon Iran
27 B6 Tonkin reg. Vietnam
50 H3 Tonkino Rus. Fed.
32 C3 Tônle Basăk r. Cambodia
32 C2 Tônle Repou r. Laos
32 B2 Tônlé Sab l. Cambodia
28 G5 Tōno Japan
74 D2 Tonopah U.S.A.
89 E2 Tonoro r. Venez.
37 M7 Tønsberg Norway
37 K7 Tonstad Norway
75 G5 Tonto National Monument res. U.S.A.
23 H5 Tonzang Myanmar
72 D3 Tooele U.S.A.
8 D3 Tooleybuc Austr.
8 G3 Tooma r. Austr.
8 F5 Toora Austr.
8 G1 Tooraweenah Austr.
58 F6 Toorberg mt S. Africa
6 F4 Toowoomba Austr.
75 G6 Topawa U.S.A.
74 C2 Topaz U.S.A.
76 E4 Topeka U.S.A.
84 A1 Topia Mex.
64 D4 Topley Landing Can.
43 L2 Töplitz Ger.
91 B2 Topocalma, Pta pt Chile
75 E4 Topock U.S.A.
46 J6 Topoľčany Slovakia
82 C3 Topolobampo Mex.
49 M3 Topolovgrad Bulg.
36 W4 Topozero, Oz. l. Rus. Fed.
72 B2 Toppenish U.S.A.
81 K2 Topsfield U.S.A.
75 F3 Toquerville U.S.A.
56 D3 Tor Eth.
49 M5 Torbalı Turkey
19 E3 Torbat-e-Heydarīyeh Iran
19 F3 Torbat-e Jām Iran
50 G4 Torbeyevo Rus. Fed.
68 E3 Torch Lake l. U.S.A.
45 D2 Tordesillas Spain
36 S4 Töre Sweden
45 H1 Torelló Spain
42 D2 Torenberg h. Neth.
43 L3 Torgau Ger.
51 H5 Torgun r. Rus. Fed.
42 B3 Torhout Belgium
Torino see Turin
29 G9 Tori-shima i. Japan
55 F4 Torit Sudan
90 B2 Torixoreu Brazil
17 L3 Torkamān Iran
50 G3 Tor'kovskoye Vdkhr. resr Rus. Fed.
45 D2 Tormes r. Spain
36 S3 Torneälven r. Fin./Sweden
36 Q2 Torneträsk Sweden
36 Q2 Torneträsk l. Sweden

67 H2 Torngat Mountains Can.
36 T4 Tornio Fin.
91 D3 Tornquist Arg.
45 D2 Toro Spain
24 F1 Torom r. Rus. Fed.
8 H2 Toronto Austr.
69 H4 Toronto Can.
50 D3 Toropets Rus. Fed.
81 B4 Toro, Pico del mt Mex.
74 D5 Toro Pk summit U.S.A.
56 D3 Tororo Uganda
16 D3 Toros Dağları mts Turkey
40 F3 Torphins U.K.
39 D7 Torquay U.K.
74 C5 Torrance U.S.A.
45 B3 Torrão Port.
45 C2 Torre mt Port.
45 C2 Torreblanca Spain
48 F4 Torre del Greco Italy
45 D1 Torrelavega Spain
45 D4 Torremolinos Spain
8 A1 Torrens, Lake Austr.
45 F3 Torrent Spain
84 B1 Torreón Mex.
7 G3 Torres Islands is Vanuatu
45 B3 Torres Novas Port.
6 E2 Torres Strait str. Austr.
45 B3 Torres Vedras Port.
45 G3 Torreta, Sa h. Spain
45 F4 Torrevieja Spain
75 G2 Torrey U.S.A.
39 C7 Torridge r. U.K.
40 C3 Torridon, Loch in. U.K.
45 D3 Torrijos Spain
81 G4 Torrington CT U.S.A.
72 F3 Torrington WY U.S.A.
45 H1 Torroella de Montgrí Spain
37 N6 Torsby Sweden
36 □ Tórshavn Faroe Is
91 C1 Tórtolas, Cerro Las mt Chile
48 C5 Tortolì Sardinia Italy
48 C2 Tortona Italy
45 G2 Tortosa Spain
17 H1 Tortum Turkey
18 D3 Torūd Iran
17 G1 Torul Turkey
47 J4 Toruń Pol.
41 C2 Tory Island i. Rep. of Ireland
41 C2 Tory Sound chan. Rep. of Ireland
50 E3 Torzhok Rus. Fed.
29 C8 Tosa Japan
29 C8 Tosashimizu Japan
36 N4 Tosbotn Norway
58 E2 Tosca S. Africa
48 C3 Toscano, Arcipelago is Italy
28 G4 Tōshima-yama mt Japan
50 D3 Tosno Rus. Fed.
88 D3 Tostado Arg.
43 H1 Tostedt Ger.
29 B8 Tosu Japan
16 E1 Tosya Turkey
50 G3 Tot'ma Rus. Fed.
84 C3 Totolapan Mex.
92 C6 Totten Glacier gl. Ant.
39 F7 Totton U.K.
29 D7 Tottori Japan
54 B4 Touba Côte d'Ivoire
54 A3 Touba Senegal
54 B1 Toubkal, Jbel mt Morocco
26 B2 Toudaohu China
54 B3 Tougan Burkina
54 C1 Touggourt Alg.
54 A3 Tougué Guinea
44 G2 Toul France
44 G5 Toulon France
44 E5 Toulouse France
54 B4 Toumodi Côte d'Ivoire
25 B5 Toungoo Myanmar
27 D5 Toupai China
32 B1 Tourakom Laos
42 B4 Tourcoing France
42 B4 Tournai Belgium
44 G4 Tournon-sur-Rhône France
44 G3 Tournus France
87 L5 Touros Brazil
44 E3 Tours France
58 D6 Touwsrivier S. Africa
43 L4 Toužim Czech Rep.
89 C2 Tovar Venez.
75 F5 Tovey r. U.K.
17 K1 Tovuz Azer.
28 G4 Towada Japan
28 G5 Towada-Hachimantai National Park Japan
28 G4 Towada-ko l. Japan
9 E1 Towai N.Z.
81 E4 Towanda U.S.A.
75 H3 Towaoc U.S.A.
39 G5 Towcester U.K.
41 C6 Tower Rep. of Ireland
68 A2 Tower U.S.A.
65 J5 Towner U.S.A.
74 D3 Townes Pass U.S.A.
72 E2 Townsend U.S.A.
8 G4 Townsend, Mt mt Austr.
6 E3 Townsville Austr.
25 E7 Towori, Teluk b. Indon.
80 E5 Towson U.S.A.
28 G3 Tōya-ko l. Japan
29 E6 Toyama Japan
29 E6 Toyama-wan b. Japan
29 E7 Toyohashi Japan
29 E7 Toyokawa Japan
29 D7 Toyonaka Japan
29 D7 Toyooka Japan
29 E7 Toyota Japan
54 C1 Tozeur Tunisia
51 G7 Tqibuli Georgia
51 G7 Tqvarch'eli Georgia
42 F5 Traben Ger.
16 E4 Trâblous Lebanon
49 K4 Trabotivište Macedonia
17 G1 Trabzon Turkey
81 K2 Tracy Can.
74 B3 Tracy CA U.S.A.
76 E2 Tracy MN U.S.A.
68 A4 Traer U.S.A.
45 C4 Trafalgar, Cabo pt Spain
91 B3 Traiguén Chile
64 G4 Trail Can.
37 T9 Trakai Lith.
50 J2 Trakt Rus. Fed.
41 B5 Tralee Rep. of Ireland
41 B5 Tralee Bay b. Rep. of Ireland
89 E3 Tramán Tepuí mt Venez.
41 D5 Tramore Rep. of Ireland
37 O7 Tranås Sweden
88 C3 Trancas Arg.
37 N8 Tranemo Sweden
40 F5 Tranent U.K.
32 A4 Trang Thai.
25 F7 Trangan i. Indon.
8 F2 Trangie Austr.
91 F1 Tranqueras Uru.
92 B5 Transantarctic Mountains Ant.
65 G4 Trans Canada Highway Can.
65 K5 Transcona Can.
48 E5 Trapani Sicily Italy
8 F5 Traralgon Austr.
48 E3 Trasimeno, Lago l. Italy
45 E3 Trasvase, Canal de canal Spain
32 B2 Trat Thai.
46 F7 Traunsee l. Austria
46 F7 Traunstein Ger.
8 D2 Travellers L. l. Austr.
92 C1 Traversay Is is Atl. Ocean
68 E3 Traverse City U.S.A.
9 D5 Travers, Mt mt N.Z.
32 C3 Tra Vinh Vietnam
77 D6 Travis, L. l. U.S.A.
48 G2 Travnik Bos.-Herz.
48 F1 Trbovlje Slovenia
7 F2 Treasury Is is Solomon Is
43 M2 Trebbin Ger.
46 G6 Třebíč Czech Rep.
49 H3 Trebinje Bos.-Herz.
47 K6 Trebišov Slovakia
48 F2 Trebnje Slovenia
43 G5 Trebur Ger.
43 J3 Treffurt Ger.
68 B3 Trego U.S.A.
40 D4 Treig, Loch l. U.K.
91 F2 Treinta-y-Tres Uru.
88 C6 Trelew Arg.
37 N9 Trelleborg Sweden
42 C4 Trélon France
39 C5 Tremadoc Bay b. U.K.
66 F4 Tremblant, Mt h. Can.
48 F3 Tremiti, Isole is Italy
72 D3 Tremonton U.S.A.
45 G1 Tremp Spain
68 B3 Trempealeau r. U.S.A.
39 B7 Trenance U.K.
46 J6 Trenčín Slovakia
43 H3 Trendelburg Ger.
91 D2 Trenque Lauquén Arg.
38 G4 Trent r. U.K.
48 D1 Trento Italy
69 J3 Trenton Can.
76 E3 Trenton MO U.S.A.
81 F4 Trenton NJ U.S.A.
67 K4 Trepassey Can.
91 F2 Tres Arboles Uru.
91 E3 Tres Arroyos Arg.
39 A8 Tresco i. U.K.
90 D3 Três Corações Brazil
89 B4 Tres Esquinas Col.
40 B4 Treshnish Isles is U.K.
90 B3 Três Lagoas Brazil
88 B7 Tres Lagos Arg.
91 D3 Tres Lomas Arg.
90 D2 Três Marias, Represa resr Brazil
84 D4 Tres Picos Mex.
91 B4 Tres Picos mt Arg.
91 E3 Tres Picos, Cerro mt Arg.
73 F4 Tres Piedras U.S.A.
90 D3 Três Pontas Brazil
88 C7 Tres Puntas, C. pt Arg.
90 D3 Três Rios Brazil
84 C3 Tres Valles Mex.
84 D3 Tres Zapotes Mex.
37 M6 Tretten Norway
43 J6 Treuchtlingen Ger.
43 L2 Treuenbrietzen Ger.
37 L7 Treungen Norway
48 C2 Treviglio Italy
48 E2 Treviso Italy
39 B7 Trevose Head hd U.K.
49 M6 Tria Nisia i. Greece
49 N6 Trianta Greece
22 B2 Tribal Areas div. Pak.
49 H5 Tricase Italy
21 B4 Trichur India
42 A5 Tricot France
8 E2 Trida Austr.
42 E5 Trier Ger.
48 E2 Trieste Italy
48 E1 Triglav mt Slovenia
49 J5 Trikala Greece
16 D4 Trikomon Cyprus
25 F7 Trikora, Pk mt Indon.
41 E4 Trim Rep. of Ireland
21 C4 Trincomalee Sri Lanka
90 C2 Trindade Brazil
96 G7 Trindade, Ilha da i. Atl. Ocean
86 F6 Trinidad Bol.
89 C3 Trinidad Col.
83 J4 Trinidad Cuba
91 F2 Trinidad Uru.
73 F4 Trinidad U.S.A.
86 F1 Trinidad i. Trinidad and Tobago
61 M8 Trinidad and Tobago country Caribbean Sea
67 K4 Trinity Bay b. Can.
62 C4 Trinity Islands is U.S.A.
74 C1 Trinity Range mts U.S.A.
79 C5 Trion U.S.A.
43 K1 Tripkau Ger.
49 K6 Tripoli Greece
Tripoli see Trâblous
55 D1 Tripoli Libya
21 B4 Tripunittura India
23 G5 Tripura div. India
53 C9 Tristan da Cunha i. Atl. Ocean
22 D3 Trisul mt India
23 F4 Trisul Dam dam Nepal
43 J1 Trittau Ger.
42 E5 Trittenheim Ger.
21 B4 Trivandrum India
48 F4 Trivento Italy
46 H6 Trnava Slovakia
6 F2 Trobriand Islands is P.N.G.
36 N4 Trofors Norway
48 G3 Trogir Croatia
48 F4 Troia Italy
42 F4 Troisdorf Ger.
42 D4 Trois-Ponts Belgium
67 F4 Trois-Rivières Can.
51 H6 Troitskoye Rus. Fed.
37 N7 Trollhättan Sweden
87 G3 Trombetas r. Brazil
53 K7 Tromelin, Île i. Ind. Ocean
91 B3 Tromen, Volcán volc. Arg.
59 F5 Trompsburg S. Africa
36 Q2 Tromsø Norway
74 D4 Trona U.S.A.
91 B4 Tronador, Monte mt Arg.
36 M5 Trondheim Norway
36 M5 Trondheimsfjorden chan. Norway
16 D4 Troodos Cyprus
16 D4 Troödos, Mount mt Cyprus
40 D5 Troon U.K.
90 D1 Tropeiros, Serra dos h. Brazil
75 F3 Tropic U.S.A.
40 D4 Trossachs, The reg. U.K.
41 E2 Trostan h. U.K.
40 F3 Troup Head hd U.K.
64 E2 Trout r. Can.
69 H3 Trout Creek Can.
75 F2 Trout Creek U.S.A.
66 B3 Trout L. l. Can.
64 G3 Trout Lake Alta. Can.
64 E2 Trout Lake N.W.T. Can.
68 E2 Trout Lake U.S.A.
64 E2 Trout Lake l. Can.
68 C2 Trout Lake l. U.S.A.
72 E2 Trout Peak summit U.S.A.
80 E4 Trout Run U.S.A.
39 E6 Trowbridge U.K.
79 C6 Troy AL U.S.A.
72 D2 Troy MT U.S.A.
81 G3 Troy NH U.S.A.
81 G3 Troy NY U.S.A.
80 A4 Troy OH U.S.A.
80 E4 Troy PA U.S.A.
49 L3 Troyan Bulg.
44 G2 Troyes France
74 D4 Troy Lake l. U.S.A.
75 E2 Troy Peak summit U.S.A.
49 J3 Trstenik Yugo.
51 E4 Trubchevsk Rus. Fed.
45 C1 Truchas Spain
50 E3 Trud Rus. Fed.
28 C3 Trudovoye Rus. Fed.
83 G5 Trujillo Honduras
86 C5 Trujillo Peru
45 D3 Trujillo Spain
89 C2 Trujillo Venez.
42 F5 Trulben Ger.
81 G4 Trumbull U.S.A.
75 F3 Trumbull, Mt mt U.S.A.
33 A2 Trumon Indon.
8 F2 Trundle Austr.
32 C2 Trưng Hiệp Vietnam
27 C6 Trung Khanh China
67 H4 Truro Can.
39 B7 Truro U.K.
41 C3 Truskmore h. Rep. of Ireland
64 E3 Trutch Can.
73 F5 Truth or Consequences U.S.A.
46 G5 Trutnov Czech Rep.
49 L7 Trypiti, Akra pt Greece
37 N6 Trysil Norway
46 G3 Trzebiatów Pol.
24 A2 Tsagaannuur Mongolia
51 H6 Tsagan Aman Rus. Fed.
51 H6 Tsagan-Nur Rus. Fed.
51 G7 Ts'ageri Georgia
17 K1 Tsalka Georgia
57 E5 Tsaratanana, Massif du mts Madag.
58 B2 Tsaris Mts mts Namibia
51 H5 Tsatsa Rus. Fed.
58 A3 Tsaukaib Namibia
56 D4 Tsavo National Park Kenya
51 G6 Tselina Rus. Fed.
57 B6 Tses Namibia
57 C6 Tsetseng Botswana
24 C2 Tsetserleg Mongolia
57 C6 Tshabong Botswana
57 C6 Tshane Botswana
51 F6 Tshchikskoye Vdkhr. resr Rus. Fed.
56 B4 Tshela Congo(Zaire)
56 C4 Tshibala Congo(Zaire)
56 C4 Tshikapa Congo(Zaire)
56 C4 Tshikapa r. Congo(Zaire)
59 G3 Tshing S. Africa
59 J1 Tshipise S. Africa
57 C4 Tshitanzu Congo(Zaire)
56 C4 Tshofa Congo(Zaire)
59 J2 Tshokwane S. Africa
56 C4 Tshuapa r. Congo(Zaire)
51 G6 Tsimlyansk Rus. Fed.
51 G6 Tsimlyanskoye Vdkhr. resr Rus. Fed.
58 E3 Tsineng S. Africa
Tsingtao see Qingdao
27 □ Tsing Yi i. H.K. China
57 E6 Tsiombe Madag.
57 E5 Tsiroanomandidy Madag.
58 E6 Tsitsikamma Forest and Coastal National Park S. Africa
64 D4 Tsitsutl Pk summit Can.
50 H4 Tsivil'sk Rus. Fed.
51 G7 Ts'khinvali Georgia
50 G4 Tsna r. Rus. Fed.
22 D2 Tsokr Chumo l. India
59 H5 Tsolo S. Africa
59 G6 Tsomo S. Africa
22 D2 Tso Morari L. l. India
51 G7 Tsqaltubo Georgia
29 E7 Tsu Japan
29 G6 Tsuchiura Japan
27 □ Tsuen Wan H.K. China
28 G4 Tsugarū-Kaikyō str. Japan
57 B5 Tsumeb Namibia
57 B6 Tsumis Park Namibia
57 C5 Tsumkwe Namibia
23 G4 Tsunthang India
29 E7 Tsuruga Japan
29 D8 Tsurugi-san mt Japan
28 F5 Tsuruoka Japan
29 A7 Tsushima i. Japan
Tsushima-kaikyō str. see Korea Strait
29 D7 Tsuyama Japan
58 D1 Tswaane Botswana
59 F4 Tswaraganang S. Africa
59 F3 Tswelelang S. Africa
47 M4 Tsyelyakhany Belarus
36 X2 Tsyp-Navolok Rus. Fed.
51 E6 Tsyurupyns'k Ukr.
25 F7 Tual Indon.
41 C4 Tuam Rep. of Ireland
9 D4 Tuamarina N.Z.
5 N6 Tuamotu Archipelago arch. Pac. Oc.
27 B6 Tuân Giao Vietnam
32 A5 Tuangku i. Indon.
51 F6 Tuapse Rus. Fed.
32 □ Tuas Sing.
9 A7 Tuatapere N.Z.
75 G3 Tuba City U.S.A.
33 D4 Tuban Indon.
88 G3 Tubarão Brazil
31 A4 Tubbataha Reefs rf Phil.
41 C3 Tubbercurry Rep. of Ireland
46 D6 Tübingen Ger.
54 A4 Tubmanburg Liberia
31 B4 Tubod Phil.
55 E1 Tubruq Libya
5 M7 Tubuai Islands is Pac. Oc.
87 L6 Tucano Brazil
91 B3 Tucapel, Pta pt Chile
87 G7 Tucavaca Bol.
43 L1 Tüchen Ger.
43 L2 Tuchheim Ger.
64 D2 Tuchitua Can.
81 F5 Tuckerton U.S.A.
75 G5 Tucson U.S.A.
75 G5 Tucson Mts mts U.S.A.
89 B2 Tucuco r. Venez.
73 G5 Tucumcari U.S.A.
89 E2 Tucupita Venez.
87 J4 Tucuruí Brazil
87 J4 Tucuruí, Represa resr Brazil
17 M5 Tū Dār Iran
45 F1 Tudela Spain
45 C2 Tuela r. Port.
27 □ Tuen Mun H.K. China
23 H4 Tuensang India
18 C5 Ţufayḩ S. Arabia
59 J4 Tugela r. S. Africa
31 C4 Tugnug Point pt Phil.
31 B2 Tuguegarao Phil.
13 P4 Tugur Rus. Fed.
26 F2 Tuhai r. China
32 A5 Tuhemberua Indon.
45 B1 Tui Spain
89 A2 Tuira r. Panama
25 E7 Tukangbesi, Kepulauan is Indon.
66 E2 Tukarak Island i. Can.
9 F3 Tukituki r. N.Z.
62 E3 Tuktoyaktuk Can.
37 S8 Tukums Latvia
84 C2 Tula Mex.
50 F4 Tula Rus. Fed.
23 H1 Tulagt Ar Gol r. China
84 C2 Tulancingo Mex.
74 C3 Tulare U.S.A.
74 C4 Tulare Lake Bed l. U.S.A.
73 F5 Tularosa U.S.A.
21 C2 Tulasi mt India
58 C6 Tulbagh S. Africa
86 C3 Tulcán Ecuador
49 N2 Tulcea Romania
51 D5 Tul'chyn Ukr.
74 C3 Tule r. U.S.A.
18 D3 Tuleh Iran
23 G4 Tule-la Pass pass Bhutan
65 J2 Tulemalu Lake l. Can.
77 C5 Tulia U.S.A.
16 E5 Tulkarm West Bank
41 C5 Tulla Rep. of Ireland
79 C5 Tullahoma U.S.A.
8 F2 Tullamore Austr.
41 D4 Tullamore Rep. of Ireland
44 E4 Tulle France
36 O5 Tulleråsen Sweden
8 F2 Tullibigeal Austr.
77 E6 Tullos U.S.A.
41 E5 Tullow Rep. of Ireland
6 E3 Tully Austr.
41 D3 Tully U.K.
81 E3 Tully U.S.A.
50 D2 Tulos Rus. Fed.
77 D4 Tulsa U.S.A.
50 F4 Tul'skaya Oblast' div. Rus. Fed.
89 A3 Tuluá Col.
62 B3 Tuluksak AK U.S.A.
91 C1 Tulum, Valle de v. Arg.
24 C1 Tulun Rus. Fed.
33 D4 Tulungagung Indon.
23 H4 Tulung La pass China
31 A4 Tuluran i. Phil.
89 A4 Tumaco Col.
59 G3 Tumahole S. Africa
51 J6 Tumak Rus. Fed.
37 P7 Tumba Sweden
56 B4 Tumba, Lac l. Congo(Zaire)
33 D3 Tumbangsamba Indon.
31 C5 Tumbao Phil.
86 B4 Tumbes Peru
64 E3 Tumbler Ridge Can.
26 D1 Tumd Youqi China
26 D1 Tumd Zuoqi China
30 E2 Tumen China
30 E2 Tumen Jiang r. China/N. Korea
26 B2 Tumenzi China
86 F2 Tumereng Guyana
31 A5 Tumindao i. Phil.
21 B3 Tumkur India
23 G3 Tum La pass China
40 E4 Tummel, Loch l. U.K.
24 G2 Tumnin r. Rus. Fed.
19 F5 Tump Pak.
32 B4 Tumpat Malaysia
54 B3 Tumu Ghana
87 G3 Tumucumaque, Serra h. Brazil
8 G3 Tumut Austr.
18 D5 Tunb al Kubrā i. Iran
39 H6 Tunbridge Wells, Royal U.K.
17 G2 Tunceli Turkey
27 D7 Tunchang China
22 D4 Tundla India
57 D5 Tunduru Tanz.
49 M3 Tundzha r. Bulg.
21 B3 Tungabhadra r. India
21 A3 Tungabhadra Reservoir India
23 H3 Tunga Pass pass China/India
31 B5 Tungawan Phil.
27 □ Tung Chung Wan b. H.K. China
36 D4 Tungnaá r. Iceland
64 D2 Tungsten Can.
50 E1 Tunguda Rus. Fed.
24 C1 Tunguska, Nizhnyaya r. Rus. Fed.
27 □ Tung Wan b. H.K. China
21 C2 Tuni India
54 D1 Tunis Tunisia
48 D6 Tunis, Golfe de g. Tunisia
52 E2 Tunisia country Africa
8 G3 Tuniut r. Austr.
89 B3 Tunja Col.
26 D2 Tunliu China
36 N4 Tunnsjøen l. Norway
39 J5 Tunstall U.K.
36 V3 Tuntsa Fin.
36 W3 Tuntsayoki r. Fin./Rus. Fed.
67 H2 Tunungayualok Island i. Can.
91 C2 Tunuyán Arg.
91 C2 Tunuyán r. Arg.
26 E3 Tuo He r. China
26 F2 Tuoji Dao i. China
32 C3 Tuŏl Khpos Cambodia
74 B3 Tuolumne U.S.A.
74 C3 Tuolumne Meadows U.S.A.
27 B5 Tuoniang Jiang r. China
23 H2 Tuotuo He r. China
23 H2 Tuotuoyan China
90 B3 Tupã Brazil
90 C2 Tupaciguara Brazil
17 L3 Tūp Āghāj Iran
88 F3 Tupanciretã Brazil
89 C3 Tuparro r. Col.
77 F5 Tupelo U.S.A.
86 E8 Tupiza Bol.
81 F2 Tupper Lake U.S.A.
81 F2 Tupper Lake l. U.S.A.
91 C2 Tupungato Arg.
91 C2 Tupungato, Cerro mt Arg./Chile
17 K7 Tuqayyid well Iraq
30 A1 Tuquan China
89 A4 Túquerres Col.
27 C7 Tuqu Wan b. China
23 G4 Tura India
13 M3 Tura Rus. Fed.
20 B5 Turabah S. Arabia
89 D3 Turagua, Serranía mt Venez.
9 E4 Turakina N.Z.
18 E3 Turan Iran
24 F1 Turana, Khrebet mts Rus. Fed.
9 E3 Turangi N.Z.
18 E2 Turan Lowland lowland Asia
16 G6 Turayf S. Arabia
18 C5 Turayf well S. Arabia
37 T7 Turba Estonia
89 B2 Turbaco Col.
19 F5 Turbat Pak.
89 A2 Turbo Col.
47 L7 Turda Romania
18 C3 Tūreh Iran
Turfan see Turpan
14 E2 Turgay Kazak.
49 M3 Tŭrgovishte Bulg.
16 C2 Turgut Turkey
16 A2 Turgutlu Turkey
16 F1 Turhal Turkey
37 T7 Türi Estonia
45 F3 Turia r. Spain
89 D2 Turiamo Venez.
48 B2 Turin Italy
28 B2 Turiy Rog Rus. Fed.
51 C5 Turiys'k Ukr.
56 D3 Turkana, Lake salt l. Eth./Kenya
49 M4 Türkeli Adası i. Turkey
14 E2 Turkestan Kazak.
19 G2 Turkestan Range mts Asia
10 E6 Turkey country Asia
68 B4 Turkey r. U.S.A.
51 G5 Turki Rus. Fed.
12 G6 Turkmenbashi Turkm.
16 C2 Türkmen Dağı mt Turkey
10 G6 Turkmenistan country Asia
19 F2 Turkmen-Kala Turkm.
18 D2 Turkmenskiy Zaliv b. Turkm.
16 F3 Türkoğlu Turkey
61 L7 Turks and Caicos Islands terr. Caribbean Sea
83 K4 Turks Islands is Turks and Caicos Is
37 S6 Turku Fin.
56 D3 Turkwel watercourse Kenya
74 B3 Turlock U.S.A.
74 B3 Turlock L. l. U.S.A.
9 F4 Turnagain, Cape c. N.Z.
40 D5 Turnberry U.K.
75 G5 Turnbull, Mt mt U.S.A.
82 G5 Turneffe Is is Belize
69 F3 Turner U.S.A.
42 C3 Turnhout Belgium
65 H3 Turnor Lake l. Can.
49 L3 Turnu Măgurele Romania
8 G2 Turon r. Austr.
50 G3 Turovets Rus. Fed.
24 A2 Turpan China
24 A2 Turpan Pendi China
83 J4 Turquino mt Cuba
40 F3 Turriff U.K.
17 K5 Tursāq Iraq
20 F1 Turtkul' Uzbek.
68 B2 Turtle Flambeau Flowage resr U.S.A.
65 H4 Turtleford Can.
68 A3 Turtle Lake U.S.A.
15 F2 Turugart Pass China/Kyrg.
90 B2 Turvo r. Goiás Brazil
90 C3 Turvo r. São Paulo Brazil
75 F4 Tusayan U.S.A.
79 C5 Tuscaloosa U.S.A.
80 C4 Tuscarawas r. U.S.A.
80 E4 Tuscarora Mts h. U.S.A.
68 C6 Tuscola IL U.S.A.
77 D5 Tuscola TX U.S.A.
18 E3 Tusharīk Iran
79 C5 Tuskegee U.S.A.
80 D4 Tussey Mts h. U.S.A.
19 E4 Tūtak Iran
17 J2 Tutak Turkey
50 F3 Tutayev Rus. Fed.
21 B4 Tuticorin India
76 D4 Tuttle Creek Res. resr U.S.A.
46 D7 Tuttlingen Ger.
63 Q2 Tuttut Nunaat reg. Greenland
7 J3 Tutuila i. Pac. Oc.
57 C6 Tutume Botswana
84 C3 Tututepec Mex.
30 D3 Tuun, Mt mt N. Korea
36 W5 Tuupovaara Fin.
36 V5 Tuusniemi Fin.
4 J5 Tuvalu country Pac. Oc.
18 B5 Tuwayq, Jabal h. S. Arabia
84 B3 Tuxpan Jalisco Mex.
84 C2 Tuxpan Veracruz Mex.
84 D3 Tuxtla Gutiérrez Mex.
89 D2 Tuy r. Venez.
32 C2 Tuy Đức Vietnam
27 B6 Tuyên Quang Vietnam
32 D2 Tuy Hoa Vietnam
18 C3 Tūysarkān Iran
16 D2 Tuz Gölü salt l. Turkey
75 F4 Tuzigoot National Monument res. U.S.A.
17 K4 Tuz Khurmātū Iraq
49 H2 Tuzla Bos.-Herz.
17 H2 Tuzla r. Turkey
Tuz, Lake salt l. see Tuz Gölü
51 F6 Tuzlov r. Rus. Fed.
37 L7 Tvedestrand Norway
50 E3 Tver' Rus. Fed.
50 E3 Tverskaya Oblast' div. Rus. Fed.
69 J3 Tweed Can.
40 F5 Tweed r. Eng./Scot. U.K.
64 D4 Tweedsmuir Prov. Park res. Can.
58 C6 Tweefontein S. Africa
58 C2 Twee Rivier Namibia
42 E2 Twente reg. Neth.
74 D4 Twentynine Palms U.S.A.
67 K4 Twillingate Can.
72 D2 Twin Bridges U.S.A.
77 C6 Twin Buttes Res. resr U.S.A.
67 H3 Twin Falls Can.
72 D3 Twin Falls U.S.A.
64 F3 Twin Lakes Can.
81 H2 Twin Mountain U.S.A.
80 C6 Twin Oaks U.S.A.
74 B2 Twin Peak summit U.S.A.
43 G2 Twistringen Ger.
8 G4 Twofold B. b. Austr.
75 G4 Two Guns U.S.A.
68 B2 Two Harbors U.S.A.
65 G4 Two Hills Can.
72 D1 Two Medicine r. U.S.A.
68 D3 Two Rivers U.S.A.
23 H5 Tyao r. India/Myanmar
36 M5 Tydal Norway
80 D5 Tygart Lake l. U.S.A.
80 D5 Tygart Valley v. U.S.A.
24 E1 Tygda Rus. Fed.
77 E5 Tyler U.S.A.
77 F6 Tylertown U.S.A.
24 E1 Tynda Rus. Fed.
64 A2 Tyndall Gl. gl. U.S.A.
40 F4 Tyne r. U.K.
38 F2 Tynemouth U.K.
37 M5 Tynset Norway
16 E5 Tyre Lebanon
65 H2 Tyrell Lake l. Can.
36 T4 Tyrnävä Fin.
49 K5 Tyrnavos Greece
80 D4 Tyrone U.S.A.
8 D3 Tyrrell r. Austr.
8 D3 Tyrrell, L. l. Austr.
48 D4 Tyrrhenian Sea sea France/Italy
13 Q3 Tyubelyakh Rus. Fed.
14 J2 Tyukalinsk Rus. Fed.
94 D4 Tyukyu Trench sea feature Pac. Oc.
12 H4 Tyumen' Rus. Fed.
13 N3 Tyung r. Rus. Fed.
39 C6 Tywi r. U.K.
39 C5 Tywyn U.K.
59 J1 Tzaneen S. Africa

U

57 C5 Uamanda Angola
89 E4 Uatatás r. Brazil
87 L5 Uauá Brazil
89 D5 Uaupés Brazil
89 C4 Uaupés r. Brazil
18 B4 U'aywij well S. Arabia
17 J7 U'aywij, W. watercourse S. Arabia
90 D3 Ubá Brazil
90 D2 Ubaí Brazil
90 E1 Ubaitaba Brazil
56 B3 Ubangi r. C.A.R./Congo(Zaire)
89 B3 Ubate Col.
17 J5 Ubayyid, Wādī al watercourse Iraq/S. Arabia
29 B8 Ube Japan
45 E3 Úbeda Spain
90 C2 Uberaba Brazil
87 G7 Uberaba, Lagoa l. Bol./Brazil
90 C2 Uberlândia Brazil
32 □ Ubin, Pulau i. Sing.
32 B1 Ubolratna Res. resr Thai.
59 K3 Ubombo S. Africa
32 C2 Ubon Ratchathani Thai.
43 G5 Ubstadt-Weiher Ger.
56 C4 Ubundu Congo(Zaire)
17 L1 Ucar Azer.
86 D5 Ucayali r. Peru
22 B3 Uch Pak.
19 F2 Uch-Adzhi Turkm.
18 C2 Üchān Iran
15 G2 Ucharal Kazak.
28 G3 Uchiura-wan b. Japan
43 G2 Uchte Ger.
43 K2 Uchte r. Ger.
24 F1 Uchur r. Rus. Fed.
39 H7 Uckfield U.K.
64 D5 Ucluelet Can.
75 H3 Ucolo U.S.A.
72 F2 Ucross U.S.A.
13 P4 Uda r. Rus. Fed.
51 H6 Udachnoye Rus. Fed.
13 N3 Udachnyy Rus. Fed.
21 B4 Udagamandalam India
22 C4 Udaipur Rajasthan India
23 G5 Udaipur Tripura India
23 E5 Udanti r. India/Myanmar
21 B3 Udayagiri India
37 M7 Uddevalla Sweden
40 D5 Uddingston U.K.
36 P4 Uddjaure l. Sweden
42 D3 Uden Neth.
21 B2 Udgir India
50 H2 Udimskiy Rus. Fed.
48 E1 Udine Italy
67 J2 Udjuktok Bay b. Can.
50 E3 Udomlya Rus. Fed.
32 B1 Udon Thani Thai.
24 F1 Udskaya Guba b. Rus. Fed.
21 B4 Udumalaippetai India
21 A3 Udupi India
24 F1 Udyl', Ozero l. Rus. Fed.
46 G4 Ueckermünde Ger.
29 F6 Ueda Japan
6 C2 Uekuli Indon.
56 C3 Uele r. Congo(Zaire)
62 B3 Uelen Rus. Fed.
43 J2 Uelzen Ger.
56 C3 Uere r. Congo(Zaire)
43 H1 Uetersen Ger.
43 H5 Uettingen Ger.
43 J2 Uetze Ger.
12 G4 Ufa Rus. Fed.
43 J5 Uffenheim Ger.
57 B6 Ugab watercourse Namibia
56 D4 Ugalla r. Tanz.
53 H5 Uganda country Africa
59 H5 Ugie S. Africa
24 G2 Uglegorsk Rus. Fed.
28 C3 Uglekamensk Rus. Fed.
50 F3 Uglich Rus. Fed.
48 F2 Ugljan i. Croatia
50 E3 Uglovka Rus. Fed.
28 C3 Uglovoye Rus. Fed.
13 Q3 Ugol'naya Zyryanka Rus. Fed.
13 T3 Ugol'nyye Kopi Rus. Fed.
50 E4 Ugra Rus. Fed.
46 H6 Uherské Hradiště Czech Rep.
80 C4 Uhrichsville U.S.A.
40 B3 Uig U.K.
56 B4 Uíge Angola
30 D5 Ŭijŏngbu S. Korea
30 C3 Ŭiju N. Korea
36 W5 Uimaharju Fin.
75 F3 Uinkaret Plateau plat. U.S.A.
72 E3 Uinta Mts mts UT U.S.A.
57 B6 Uis Mine Namibia
41 D4 Uisneach h. Rep. of Ireland
30 E5 Ŭisŏng S. Korea
59 F6 Uitenhage S. Africa
42 C2 Uithoorn Neth.
42 E1 Uithuizen Neth.
67 H2 Uivak, Cape hd Can.
29 D7 Uji Japan
29 A9 Uji-guntō is Japan
22 C5 Ujjain India
33 E4 Ujung Pandang Indon.
17 J5 Ukhaydir Iraq
23 H4 Ukhrul India
50 K2 Ukhta Rus. Fed.
50 K2 Ukhta r. Rus. Fed.
74 A2 Ukiah CA U.S.A.
72 C2 Ukiah OR U.S.A.
63 N2 Ukkusissat Greenland
37 T9 Ukmergė Lith.
35 H4 Ukraine country Europe
50 J2 Uktym Rus. Fed.
29 A8 Uku-jima i. Japan
58 D1 Ukwi Botswana
58 D1 Ukwi Pan salt pan Botswana
24 C2 Ulaanbaatar Mongolia
24 B2 Ulaangom Mongolia
8 G2 Ulan Austr.
Ulan Bator see Ulaanbaatar
26 C1 Ulan Buh Shamo des. China
51 H6 Ulan Erge Rus. Fed.
51 H6 Ulan-Khol Rus. Fed.
26 C1 Ulansuhai Nur l. China
26 A1 Ulan Tohoi China
24 C1 Ulan-Ude Rus. Fed.
23 G2 Ulan Ul Hu l. China
16 F2 Ulaş Turkey
7 G2 Ulawa I. i. Solomon Is
19 E4 Ulāy, Kūh-e h. Iran
30 E5 Ulchin S. Korea
37 L7 Ulefoss Norway
37 U7 Ülenurme Estonia
21 A2 Ulhasnagar India
24 B2 Uliastay Mongolia
42 C3 Ulicoten Neth.
36 X2 Ulita r. Rus. Fed.
25 F6 Ulithi i. Micronesia
8 H3 Ulladulla Austr.
40 C3 Ullapool U.K.
36 S5 Ullava Fin.
38 E3 Ullswater l. U.K.
30 F5 Ullŭng-do i. S. Korea
46 D6 Ulm Ger.
42 E4 Ulmen Ger.
37 N8 Ulricehamn Sweden
42 E1 Ulrum Neth.
30 E6 Ulsan S. Korea
36 L5 Ulsberg Norway
41 D3 Ulster Canal canal Rep. of Ireland/U.K.
8 D3 Ultima Austr.
16 B1 Uluabat Gölü l. Turkey
16 C2 Uluborlu Turkey
16 B1 Uludağ mt Turkey
32 B5 Ulu Kali, Gunung mt Malaysia
16 E3 Ulukışla Turkey
59 J4 Ulundi S. Africa
24 A2 Ulungur Hu l. China
32 □ Ulu Pandan Sing.
Uluru h. see Ayers Rock
16 D1 Ulus Turkey
40 B4 Ulva i. U.K.
42 C3 Ulvenhout Neth.
38 D3 Ulverston U.K.
37 O6 Ulvsjön Sweden
19 H1 Ul'yanovo Uzbek.
50 J4 Ul'yanovsk Rus. Fed.
50 H4 Ul'yanovskaya Oblast' div. Rus. Fed.
77 C4 Ulysses U.S.A.
84 E2 Umán Mex.
51 D5 Uman' Ukr.
19 G4 Umarao Pak.
22 E5 Umaria India
22 D6 Umarkhed India
23 E6 Umarkot India
22 B4 Umarkot Pak.
72 C2 Umatilla U.S.A.
12 E3 Umba Rus. Fed.
81 H2 Umbagog Lake l. U.S.A.
6 E2 Umboi i. P.N.G.
36 R5 Umeå Sweden
36 Q4 Umeälven r. Sweden
59 J4 Umfolozi r. S. Africa
17 L7 Umgharah Kuwait
59 J4 Umhlanga S. Africa
62 H3 Umingmaktok Can.
66 E2 Umiujaq Can.
59 J5 Umkomaas S. Africa
59 J4 Umlazi S. Africa
17 K6 Umma Iraq
18 D5 Umm al Qaywayn U.A.E.
18 C5 Umm Bāb Qatar
55 E3 Umm Keddada Sudan
17 L6 Umm Qasr Iraq
55 F3 Umm Ruwaba Sudan
55 E1 Umm Sa'ad Libya
18 C5 Umm Sa'id Qatar
72 A3 Umpqua r. U.S.A.
57 B5 Umpulo Angola
22 D5 Umred India
22 C5 Umreth India
59 H5 Umtata S. Africa
59 J5 Umtentweni S. Africa
54 C4 Umuahia Nigeria
90 B3 Umuarama Brazil
59 H5 Umzimkulu S. Africa
59 J5 Umzinto S. Africa
90 E1 Una Brazil
48 G2 Una r. Bos.-Herz./Croatia
16 F6 'Unāb, W. al watercourse Jordan
90 C2 Unaí Brazil
19 H3 Unai Pass pass Afgh.
62 B3 Unalakleet U.S.A.
40 C2 Unapool U.K.
89 D2 Unare r. Venez.
16 E6 'Unayzah Jordan
20 B4 'Unayzah S. Arabia
17 G5 'Unayzah, Jabal h. Iraq
73 E4 Uncompahgre Plateau plat. U.S.A.
59 H4 Underberg S. Africa
8 C3 Underbool Austr.
76 C2 Underwood U.S.A.
50 E4 Unecha Rus. Fed.
8 F2 Ungarie Austr.
67 G2 Ungava Bay b. Can.
66 F1 Ungava, Péninsule d' pen. Can.
30 F2 Unggi N. Korea
51 C6 Ungheni Moldova
19 E2 Unguz, Solonchakovyye Vpadiny salt flat Turkm.
50 J3 Uni Rus. Fed.
90 B4 União da Vitória Brazil
89 B4 Unilla r. Col.
86 F4 Unini r. Brazil
90 A4 Unión Para.
81 J2 Union ME U.S.A.
79 D5 Union SC U.S.A.
80 C6 Union WV U.S.A.
68 E5 Union City OH U.S.A.
80 D4 Union City PA U.S.A.
79 B4 Union City TN U.S.A.
58 E6 Uniondale S. Africa
75 F4 Union, Mt mt U.S.A.
79 C5 Union Springs U.S.A.
80 D5 Uniontown U.S.A.
69 F4 Unionville U.S.A.
72 E3 Unita Mts. mts U.S.A.
10 G7 United Arab Emirates country Asia
34 E3 United Kingdom country Europe

12 J2 Vise, O. i. Rus. Fed.
87 J4 Viseu Brazil
45 C2 Viseu Port.
21 C2 Vishakhapatnam India
37 U8 Viški Latvia
22 C5 Visnagar India
49 H3 Visoko Bos.-Herz.
48 B2 Viso, Monte mt Italy
46 C7 Visp Switz.
43 H2 Visselhövede Ger.
74 D5 Vista U.S.A.
90 A2 Vista Alegre Brazil
49 L4 Vistonida, Limni lag. Greece
89 C3 Vita r. Col.
23 B3 Vitakri Pak.
48 E3 Viterbo Italy
48 G2 Vitez Bos.-Herz.
86 E8 Vitichi Bol.
45 C2 Vitigudino Spain
7 H3 Viti Levu i. Fiji
24 D1 Vitim r. Rus. Fed.
24 D1 Vitimskoye Ploskogor'ye plat. Rus. Fed.
90 E3 Vitória Brazil
Vitoria see Vitoria-Gasteiz
90 E1 Vitória da Conquista Brazil
45 E1 Vitoria-Gasteiz Spain
44 D2 Vitré France
42 A4 Vitry-en-Artois France
44 G2 Vitry-le-François France
50 D4 Vitsyebsk Belarus
36 R3 Vittangi Sweden
48 F6 Vittoria Sicily Italy
48 E2 Vittorio Veneto Italy
94 F3 Vityaz Depth depth Pac. Oc.
45 C1 Viveiro Spain
59 H1 Vivo S. Africa
Vizagapatam see Vishakhapatnam
82 B3 Vizcaíno, Sierra mts Mex.
51 C7 Vize Turkey
21 C2 Vizianagaram India
50 J2 Vizinga Rus. Fed.
42 C3 Vlaardingen Neth.
47 L7 Vlădeasa, Vârful mt Romania
51 H7 Vladikavkaz Rus. Fed.
28 D3 Vladimir Primorskiy Kray Rus. Fed.
50 G3 Vladimir Vladimir. Obl. Rus. Fed.
28 C3 Vladimiro-Aleksandrovskoye Rus. Fed.
24 F2 Vladivostok Rus. Fed.
50 G4 Vlaimirskaya Oblast' div. Rus. Fed.
59 H2 Vlakte S. Africa
49 K3 Vlasotince Yugo.
58 D7 Vleesbaai b. S. Africa
42 C1 Vlieland i. Neth.
42 B3 Vlissingen Neth.
49 H4 Vlorë Albania
43 G2 Vlotho Ger.
46 G6 Vltava r. Czech Rep.
46 F6 Vöcklabruck Austria
50 F2 Vodlozero, Ozero l. Rus. Fed.
40 □ Voe U.K.
42 D4 Voerendaal Neth.
43 H4 Vogelsberg h. Ger.
48 C2 Voghera Italy
43 L4 Vogtland reg. Ger.
43 L5 Vohenstrauß Ger.
Vohimena, Cape c. see Vohimena, Tanjona
57 E6 Vohimena, Tanjona c. Madag.
43 G3 Vöhl Ger.
37 T7 Võhma Estonia
56 D4 Voi Kenya
54 B4 Voinjama Liberia
44 G4 Voiron France
37 L9 Vojens Denmark
49 H2 Vojvodina div. Yugo.
50 H3 Vokhma Rus. Fed.
50 D1 Voknavolok Rus. Fed.
72 F2 Volborg U.S.A.
91 B1 Volcán, Co del mt Chile
Volcano Bay b. see Uchiura-wan
Volcano Is is see Kazan-rettō
37 K5 Volda Norway
42 D2 Volendam Neth.
51 H6 Volga r. Rus. Fed.
68 B4 Volga r. U.S.A.
51 G6 Volgodonsk Rus. Fed.
12 F5 Volgograd Rus. Fed.
51 H5 Volgogradskaya Oblast' div. Rus. Fed.
46 G7 Völkermarkt Austria
50 E3 Volkhov Rus. Fed.
50 D3 Volkhov r. Rus. Fed.
42 E5 Völklingen Ger.
59 H3 Volksrust S. Africa
28 B3 Vol'no-Nadezhdinskoye Rus. Fed.
51 F6 Volnovakha Ukr.
13 L2 Volochanka Rus. Fed.
51 C5 Volochys'k Ukr.
51 F6 Volodars'ke Ukr.
51 J6 Volodarskiy Rus. Fed.
14 E1 Volodarskoye Kazak.
47 O5 Volodars'k-Volyns'kyy Ukr.
47 N5 Volodymyrets' Ukr.
51 C5 Volodymyr-Volyns'kyy Ukr.
50 F3 Vologda Rus. Fed.
50 G3 Vologodskaya Oblast' div. Rus. Fed.
51 F5 Volokonovka Rus. Fed.
49 K5 Volos Greece
50 D3 Volosovo Rus. Fed.
47 P2 Volot Rus. Fed.
51 F4 Volovo Rus. Fed.
51 H4 Vol'sk Rus. Fed.
54 B4 Volta, Lake resr Ghana
90 D3 Volta Redonda Brazil
48 F4 Volturno r. Italy
49 K4 Volvi, L. l. Greece
50 J4 Volzhsk Rus. Fed.
51 H5 Volzhskiy Rus. Fed.
57 E6 Vondrozo Madag.
50 G1 Vonga Rus. Fed.
36 F4 Vopnafjörður Iceland
36 F4 Vopnafjörður b. Iceland
58 B2 Vörå Fin.
47 M3 Voranava Belarus
50 J3 Vorchanka Rus. Fed.
50 E2 Vorenzha Rus. Fed.
12 H3 Vorkuta Rus. Fed.
37 S7 Vormsi i. Estonia
51 G5 Vorona r. Rus. Fed.
51 F5 Voronezh Rus. Fed.
51 F5 Voronezh r. Rus. Fed.
51 G5 Voronezhskaya Oblast' div. Rus. Fed.
50 G3 Voron'ye Rus. Fed.
Voroshilovgrad see Luhans'k
47 Q3 Vorot'kovo Rus. Fed.
51 E5 Vorskla r. Rus. Fed.
37 T7 Võrtsjärv l. Estonia
37 U8 Võru Estonia
19 H2 Vorukh Tajik.
58 E5 Vosburg S. Africa
19 H2 Vose Tajik.
44 H2 Vosges mts France
37 K6 Voss Norway
Vostochno-Sibirskoye More sea see East Siberian Sea
24 B1 Vostochnyy Sayan mts Rus. Fed.
28 D1 Vostok Rus. Fed.
92 C5 Vostok Rus. Fed. Base Ant.
5 M6 Vostok I. i. Kiribati
28 D2 Vostretsovo Rus. Fed.
12 G4 Votkinsk Rus. Fed.
90 C3 Votuporanga Brazil
42 C5 Vouziers France
44 E2 Voves France
50 J3 Voya r. Rus. Fed.
78 A1 Voyageurs Nat. Park nat. park U.S.A.
36 W4 Voynitsa Rus. Fed.
50 G2 Vozhega Rus. Fed.
50 F2 Vozhe, Ozero l. Rus. Fed.
51 D6 Voznesens'k Ukr.
28 C3 Vrangel' Rus. Fed.
13 V4 Vrangelya, O. i. U.S.A.
49 J3 Vranje Yugo.
49 M3 Vratnik pass Bulg.
49 K3 Vratsa Bulg.
49 H2 Vrbas Yugo.
48 G2 Vrbas r. Bos.-Herz.
59 H3 Vrede S. Africa
59 G3 Vredefort S. Africa
58 B6 Vredenburg S. Africa
58 C5 Vredendal S. Africa
42 C5 Vresse Belgium
21 B4 Vriddhachalam India
42 E1 Vries Neth.
37 O8 Vrigstad Sweden
49 J2 Vršac Yugo.
58 F3 Vryburg S. Africa
59 J3 Vryheid S. Africa
50 D2 Vsevolozhsk Rus. Fed.
49 J3 Vučitrn Yugo.
49 H2 Vukovar Croatia
12 G3 Vuktyl' Rus. Fed.
59 H3 Vukuzakhe S. Africa
48 F5 Vulcano, Isola i. Italy
75 F5 Vulture Mts mts U.S.A.
32 C3 Vung Tau Vietnam
37 U6 Vuohijärvi Fin.
36 U4 Vuolijoki Fin.
36 R3 Vuollerim Sweden
36 U3 Vuostimo Fin.
50 H4 Vurnary Rus. Fed.
57 D4 Vwawa Tanz.
22 C5 Vyara India
50 J3 Vyatka Rus. Fed.
50 J3 Vyatka r. Rus. Fed.
50 E4 Vyaz'ma Rus. Fed.
50 G3 Vyazniki Rus. Fed.
51 H5 Vyazovka Rus. Fed.
50 D2 Vyborg Rus. Fed.
50 J2 Vychegda r. Rus. Fed.
50 H2 Vychegodskiy Rus. Fed.
50 C4 Vyerkhnyadzvinsk Belarus
50 D4 Vyetryna Belarus
50 E2 Vygozero, Ozero l. Rus. Fed.
50 G4 Vyksa Rus. Fed.
51 D6 Vylkove Ukr.
47 L6 Vynohradiv Ukr.
50 E3 Vypolzovo Rus. Fed.
50 D3 Vyritsa Rus. Fed.
39 D5 Vyrnwy, Lake l. U.K.
51 F6 Vyselki Rus. Fed.
50 G4 Vysha Rus. Fed.
51 D5 Vyshhorod Ukr.
50 E3 Vyshnevolotskaya Gryada ridge Rus. Fed.
50 E3 Vyshniy-Volochek Rus. Fed.
46 H6 Vyškov Czech Rep.
51 D5 Vystupovychi Ukr.
50 F2 Vytegra Rus. Fed.

W

54 B3 Wa Ghana
42 D3 Waal r. Neth.
42 D3 Waalwijk Neth.
66 B3 Wabakimi L. l. Can.
64 G3 Wabasca Can.
64 G3 Wabasca r. Can.
68 E5 Wabash U.S.A.
68 E5 Wabash r. U.S.A.
68 A3 Wabasha U.S.A.
69 E1 Wabatongushi Lake l. Can.
56 E3 Wabē Gestro r. Eth.
56 E3 Wabē Shebelē Wenz r. Eth.
65 K4 Wabowden Can.
66 C2 Wabuk Pt pt Can.
67 G3 Wabush Can.
67 G3 Wabush L. l. Can.
74 C2 Wabuska U.S.A.
79 D6 Waccasassa Bay b. U.S.A.
43 H4 Wächtersbach Ger.
77 D6 Waco U.S.A.
19 G5 Wad Pak.
8 G4 Wadbilliga Nat. Park Austr.
55 D2 Waddān Libya
42 C1 Waddeneilanden is Neth.
42 C2 Waddenzee chan. Neth.
64 D4 Waddington, Mt mt Can.
42 C2 Waddinxveen Neth.
39 C7 Wadebridge U.K.
65 J4 Wadena Can.
76 E2 Wadena U.S.A.
42 E5 Wadern Ger.
21 A2 Wadgaon India
42 E5 Wadgassen Ger.
55 E3 Wadi el Milk watercourse Sudan
55 F2 Wadi Halfa Sudan
55 E3 Wadi Howar watercourse Sudan
55 F3 Wad Medani Sudan
74 C2 Wadsworth U.S.A.
30 B4 Wafangdian China
17 L7 Wafra Kuwait
43 G2 Wagenfeld Ger.
43 J2 Wagenhoff Ger.
63 K3 Wager Bay b. Can.
8 F3 Wagga Wagga Austr.
22 C2 Wah Pak.
74 □1 Wahiawa U.S.A.
43 H3 Wahlhausen Ger.
76 D3 Wahoo U.S.A.
76 D2 Wahpeton U.S.A.
75 F2 Wah Wah Mts mts U.S.A.
21 A2 Wai India
74 □1 Waialee U.S.A.
74 □1 Waialua U.S.A.
74 □1 Waialua Bay b. U.S.A.
74 □1 Waianae U.S.A.
74 □1 Waianae Ra. mts U.S.A.
9 D5 Waiau r. N.Z.
46 G7 Waidhofen an der Ybbs Austria
25 F7 Waigeo i. Indon.
9 E2 Waiharoa N.Z.
9 E2 Waiheke Island i. N.Z.
9 E2 Waihi N.Z.
9 E2 Waihou r. N.Z.
25 D7 Waikabubak Indon.
9 B6 Waikaia r. N.Z.
74 □1 Waikane U.S.A.
9 D5 Waikari N.Z.
9 E2 Waikato r. N.Z.
9 F2 Waikawa Pt pt N.Z.
8 B3 Waikerie Austr.
74 □1 Waikiki Beach beach U.S.A.
9 C6 Waikouaiti N.Z.
74 □2 Wailuku U.S.A.
9 D5 Waimakariri r. N.Z.
74 □1 Waimanalo U.S.A.
9 C4 Waimangaroa N.Z.
9 F3 Waimarama N.Z.
9 C6 Waimate N.Z.
74 □1 Waimea HI U.S.A.
74 □2 Waimea HI U.S.A.
22 D5 Wainganga r. India
25 E7 Waingapu Indon.
39 C7 Winhouse Corner U.K.
65 G4 Wainwright Can.
62 C2 Wainwright AK U.S.A.
9 E3 Waiouru N.Z.
9 E3 Waipa r. N.Z.
9 B7 Waipahi N.Z.
74 □1 Waipahu U.S.A.
9 F3 Waipaoa r. N.Z.
9 B7 Waipapa Pt pt N.Z.
9 D5 Waipara N.Z.
9 F3 Waipawa N.Z.
9 F3 Waipukurau N.Z.
9 F3 Wairakei N.Z.
9 E4 Wairarapa, L. l. N.Z.
9 D4 Wairau r. N.Z.
9 F3 Wairoa N.Z.
9 F3 Wairoa r. Hawke's Bay N.Z.
9 E1 Wairoa r. Northland N.Z.
9 F3 Waitahanui N.Z.
9 B6 Waitahuna N.Z.
9 E2 Waitakaruru N.Z.
9 C6 Waitaki r. N.Z.
9 E3 Waitara N.Z.
9 E2 Waitoa N.Z.
9 E2 Waiuku N.Z.
9 B7 Waiwera South N.Z.
27 F5 Waiyang China
29 E6 Wajima Japan
56 E3 Wajir Kenya
29 D7 Wakasa-wan b. Japan
9 B6 Wakatipu, Lake l. N.Z.
65 H4 Wakaw Can.
29 D7 Wakayama Japan
76 D4 Wa Keeney U.S.A.
69 K3 Wakefield Can.
9 D4 Wakefield N.Z.
38 F4 Wakefield U.K.
68 C2 Wakefield MI U.S.A.
81 H4 Wakefield RI U.S.A.
80 E6 Wakefield VA U.S.A.
Wakeham see Kangiqsujuaq
4 H3 Wake Island i. Pac. Oc.
28 G4 Wakinosawa Japan
28 G2 Wakkanai Japan
59 J3 Wakkerstroom S. Africa
8 E3 Wakool Austr.
8 D3 Wakool r. Austr.
67 G2 Wakuach, Lac l. Can.
46 H5 Wałbrzych Pol.
8 H1 Walcha Austr.
46 E7 Walchensee l. Ger.
42 C4 Walcourt Belgium
46 H4 Wałcz Pol.
81 F4 Walden Montgomery U.S.A.
46 F6 Waldkraiburg Ger.
39 C7 Waldon r. U.K.
80 E5 Waldorf U.S.A.
92 C6 Waldron, C. c. Ant.
34 E3 Wales div. U.K.
6 E5 Walgett Austr.
92 A3 Walgreen Coast coastal area Ant.
56 C4 Walikale Congo(Zaire)
68 B4 Walker IA U.S.A.
76 E2 Walker MN U.S.A.
74 C2 Walker r. U.S.A.
58 C7 Walker Bay b. S. Africa
79 E7 Walker Cay i. Bahamas
74 C2 Walker Lake l. U.S.A.
92 A3 Walker Mts mts Ant.
74 C4 Walker Pass pass U.S.A.
69 G3 Walkerton Can.
76 C2 Wall U.S.A.
72 C2 Wallace U.S.A.
69 F4 Wallaceburg Can.
8 A2 Wallaroo Austr.
39 D4 Wallasey U.K.
8 F3 Walla Walla Austr.
72 C2 Walla Walla U.S.A.
43 H5 Walldürn Ger.
58 B5 Wallekraal S. Africa
8 G3 Wallendbeen Austr.
81 F4 Wallenpaupack, Lake l. U.S.A.
39 F6 Wallingford U.K.
81 G4 Wallingford U.S.A.
5 K6 Wallis and Futuna terr. Pac. Oc.
7 J3 Wallis, Îles is Pac. Oc.
81 F6 Wallops I. i. U.S.A.
72 C2 Wallowa Mts mts U.S.A.
40 □ Walls U.K.
65 H2 Walmsley Lake l. Can.
38 D3 Walney, Isle of i. U.K.
68 C5 Walnut U.S.A.
75 G4 Walnut Canyon National Monument res. U.S.A.
77 F4 Walnut Ridge U.S.A.
23 J3 Walong India
39 F5 Walsall U.K.
73 F4 Walsenburg U.S.A.
43 H2 Walsrode Ger.
21 C2 Waltair India
79 D5 Walterboro U.S.A.
79 C6 Walter F. George Res. resr U.S.A.
69 J3 Waltham Can.
78 C4 Walton KY U.S.A.
81 F3 Walton NY U.S.A.
57 B6 Walvis Bay Namibia
96 K7 Walvis Ridge sea feature Atl. Ocean
56 C3 Wamba Congo(Zaire)
22 B2 Wana Pak.
9 B6 Wanaka N.Z.
9 B6 Wanaka, L. l. N.Z.
27 E5 Wan'an China
69 G2 Wanapitei Lake l. Can.
81 F4 Wanaque Reservoir U.S.A.
8 C3 Wanbi Austr.
9 C6 Wanbrow, Cape c. N.Z.
28 C2 Wanda Shan mts China
60 R1 Wandel Sea sea Greenland
43 J4 Wandersleben Ger.
43 M2 Wandlitz Ger.
30 D6 Wando S. Korea
9 E3 Wanganui N.Z.
9 E3 Wanganui r. N.Z.
8 F4 Wangaratta Austr.
26 C3 Wangcang China
27 D4 Wangcheng China
43 F1 Wangerooge Ger.
43 F1 Wangerooge i. Ger.
30 A3 Wanghai Shan h. China
27 E4 Wangjiang China
27 C5 Wangmo China
30 E2 Wangqing China
22 B5 Wankaner India
56 E3 Wanlaweyn Somalia
43 G1 Wanna Ger.
27 E4 Wannian China
27 D7 Wanning China
26 E1 Wanquan China
42 D3 Wanroij Neth.
27 D6 Wanshan Qundao is China
9 F4 Wanstead N.Z.
39 F6 Wantage U.K.
69 G2 Wanup Can.
27 C4 Wan Xian China
27 C4 Wanxian China
26 C3 Wanyuan China
27 E4 Wanzai China
42 D4 Wanze Belgium
80 A4 Wapakoneta U.S.A.
68 B5 Wapello U.S.A.
66 C3 Wapikopa L. l. Can.
64 F4 Wapiti r. Can.
77 F4 Wappapello, L. resr U.S.A.
68 A5 Wapsipinicon r. U.S.A.
26 B3 Waqên China
18 C6 Waqr well S. Arabia
22 A4 Warah Pak.
21 B2 Warangal India
8 E4 Waranga Reservoir Austr.
22 E5 Waraseoni India
8 F5 Waratah B. b. Austr.
43 H3 Warburg Ger.
6 C4 Warburton Austr.
6 D4 Warburton watercourse Austr.
65 G2 Warburton Bay l. Can.
59 H3 Warden S. Africa
43 G1 Wardenburg Ger.
22 D5 Wardha India
22 D6 Wardha r. India
9 A6 Ward, Mt mt Southland N.Z.
9 B5 Ward, Mt mt West Coast N.Z.
64 D3 Ware Can.
81 G3 Ware U.S.A.
39 E7 Wareham U.K.
81 H4 Wareham U.S.A.
42 D4 Waremme Belgium
43 L1 Waren Ger.
43 F3 Warendorf Ger.
43 K1 Warin Ger.
32 C2 Warin Chamrap Thai.
9 E2 Warkworth N.Z.
38 F2 Warkworth U.K.
42 A4 Warloy-Baillon France
65 H4 Warman Can.
58 C4 Warmbad Namibia
59 H2 Warmbad S. Africa
39 E6 Warminster U.K.
81 F4 Warminster U.S.A.
42 C2 Warmond Neth.
74 D2 Warm Springs NV U.S.A.
80 D5 Warm Springs VA U.S.A.
58 D6 Warmwaterberg mts S. Africa
81 H3 Warner U.S.A.
72 B3 Warner Mts mts U.S.A.
79 D5 Warner Robins U.S.A.
86 F7 Warnes Bol.
22 D5 Warora India
8 D4 Warracknabeal Austr.
8 H3 Warragamba Reservoir Austr.
8 E5 Warragul Austr.
6 E4 Warrego r. Austr.
8 F1 Warren Austr.
69 G2 Warren Can.
77 E5 Warren AR U.S.A.
69 F4 Warren MI U.S.A.
76 D1 Warren MN U.S.A.
80 C4 Warren OH U.S.A.
80 D4 Warren PA U.S.A.
80 C4 Warrendale U.S.A.
41 E3 Warrenpoint U.K.
76 E4 Warrensburg MO U.S.A.
81 G3 Warrensburg NY U.S.A.
58 F4 Warrenton S. Africa
80 E5 Warrenton U.S.A.
54 C4 Warri Nigeria
9 C6 Warrington N.Z.
39 E4 Warrington U.K.
79 C6 Warrington U.S.A.
8 D5 Warrnambool Austr.
76 E1 Warroad U.S.A.
8 G1 Warrumbungle Ra. mts Austr.
47 K4 Warsaw Pol.
68 E5 Warsaw IN U.S.A.
76 E4 Warsaw MO U.S.A.
80 D3 Warsaw NY U.S.A.
80 E6 Warsaw VA U.S.A.
43 G3 Warstein Ger.
Warszawa see Warsaw
46 G4 Warta r. Pol.
6 F4 Warwick Austr.
39 F5 Warwick U.K.
81 F4 Warwick NY U.S.A.
81 H4 Warwick RI U.S.A.
73 E4 Wasatch Range mts U.S.A.
59 J4 Wasbank S. Africa
74 C4 Wasco U.S.A.
76 E2 Waseca U.S.A.
19 F5 Washap Pak.
68 C5 Washburn IL U.S.A.
81 J1 Washburn ME U.S.A.
76 C2 Washburn ND U.S.A.
68 B2 Washburn WI U.S.A.
22 D5 Wāshim India
80 E5 Washington DC U.S.A.
79 D5 Washington GA U.S.A.
68 B5 Washington IA U.S.A.
68 C5 Washington IL U.S.A.
78 C4 Washington IN U.S.A.
76 F4 Washington MO U.S.A.
79 E5 Washington NC U.S.A.
81 F4 Washington NJ U.S.A.
80 C4 Washington PA U.S.A.
75 F3 Washington UT U.S.A.
72 B2 Washington div. U.S.A.
92 B5 Washington, C. c. Ant.
80 B5 Washington Court House U.S.A.
68 D3 Washington Island i. U.S.A.
63 M1 Washington Land reg. Greenland
81 H2 Washington, Mt mt U.S.A.
77 D5 Washita r. U.S.A.
39 H5 Wash, The b. U.K.
19 G5 Washuk Pak.
18 B5 Wasī' S. Arabia
17 L5 Wasit Iraq
66 E3 Waskaganish Can.
65 K3 Waskaiowaka Lake l. Can.
42 C2 Wassenaar Neth.
58 C3 Wasser Namibia
43 H4 Wasserkuppe h. Ger.
43 J5 Wassertrüdingen Ger.
74 C2 Wassuk Range mts U.S.A.
66 E4 Waswanipi, Lac l. Can.
25 E7 Watampone Indon.
81 G4 Waterbury CT U.S.A.
81 G2 Waterbury VT U.S.A.
65 H3 Waterbury Lake l. Can.
41 D5 Waterford Rep. of Ireland
80 D4 Waterford U.S.A.
41 E5 Waterford Harbour harbour Rep. of Ireland
41 C5 Watergrasshill Rep. of Ireland
42 C4 Waterloo Belgium
69 G4 Waterloo Can.
68 A4 Waterloo IA U.S.A.
81 H3 Waterloo ME U.S.A.
80 E3 Waterloo NY U.S.A.
68 C4 Waterloo WV U.S.A.
39 F7 Waterlooville U.K.
59 H1 Waterpoort S. Africa
68 C2 Watersmeet U.S.A.
64 G5 Waterton Lakes Nat. Park Can.
81 E3 Watertown NY U.S.A.
76 D2 Watertown SD U.S.A.
68 C4 Watertown WV U.S.A.
59 J2 Waterval-Boven S. Africa
8 B2 Watervale Austr.
81 J2 Waterville U.S.A.
65 G3 Waterways Can.
69 G4 Watford Can.
39 G6 Watford U.K.
76 C2 Watford City U.S.A.
65 J3 Wathaman r. Can.
43 J2 Wathlingen Ger.
80 E3 Watkins Glen U.S.A.
Watling i. see San Salvador
77 D5 Watonga U.S.A.
65 H4 Watrous Can.
56 C3 Watsa Congo(Zaire)
68 D5 Watseka U.S.A.
56 C4 Watsi Kengo Congo(Zaire)
65 J4 Watson Can.
64 D2 Watson Lake Can.
74 B3 Watsonville U.S.A.
40 E2 Watten U.K.
40 E2 Watten, Loch l. U.K.
65 J2 Watterson Lake l. Can.
64 F3 Watt, Mt h. Can.
39 H5 Watton U.K.
68 C2 Watton U.S.A.
6 D2 Watubela, Kepulauan is Indon.
6 E2 Wau P.N.G.
55 E4 Wau Sudan
68 D3 Waucedah U.S.A.
79 D7 Wauchula U.S.A.
68 D4 Waukegan U.S.A.
68 C4 Waukesha U.S.A.
68 B4 Waukon U.S.A.
68 C3 Waupaca U.S.A.
68 C4 Waupun U.S.A.
77 D5 Waurika U.S.A.
68 C3 Wausau U.S.A.
80 A4 Wauseon U.S.A.
68 C3 Wautoma U.S.A.
68 C4 Wauwatosa U.S.A.
39 J5 Waveney r. U.K.
68 A4 Waverly IA U.S.A.
80 B5 Waverly OH U.S.A.
79 C4 Waverly TN U.S.A.
80 E6 Waverly VA U.S.A.
42 C4 Wavre Belgium
68 E1 Wawa Can.
54 C4 Wawa Nigeria
68 E5 Wawasee, Lake l. U.S.A.
74 C3 Wawona U.S.A.
77 D5 Waxahachie U.S.A.
79 D6 Waycross U.S.A.
68 B5 Wayland KY U.S.A.
68 B6 Wayland MO U.S.A.
76 D3 Wayne U.S.A.
79 D5 Waynesboro GA U.S.A.
77 F6 Waynesboro MS U.S.A.
80 E5 Waynesboro PA U.S.A.
80 D5 Waynesboro VA U.S.A.
80 C5 Waynesburg U.S.A.
77 E4 Waynesville U.S.A.
77 D4 Waynoka U.S.A.
55 D3 Waza, Parc National de nat. park Cameroon
22 C2 Wazirabad Pak.
54 C3 W du Niger, Parcs Nationaux du nat. park Niger
66 B3 Weagamow L. l. Can.
39 H6 Weald, The reg. U.K.
38 E3 Wear r. U.K.
6 E3 Weary B. b. Austr.
77 D5 Weatherford U.S.A.
72 B3 Weaverville U.S.A.
69 G2 Webbwood Can.
66 C3 Webequie Can.
64 D3 Weber, Mt mt Can.
56 E3 Webi Shabeelle r. Somalia
81 H3 Webster MA U.S.A.
76 D2 Webster SD U.S.A.
68 A3 Webster WV U.S.A.
76 E3 Webster City U.S.A.
80 C5 Webster Springs U.S.A.
88 D8 Weddell I. i. Falkland Is
92 B2 Weddell Sea sea Ant.
8 D4 Wedderburn Austr.
43 H1 Wedel (Holstein) Ger.
72 B3 Weed U.S.A.
80 D4 Weedville U.S.A.
59 J4 Weenen S. Africa
42 F1 Weener Ger.
42 E2 Weerribben, Nationaal Park De nat. park Neth.
42 D3 Weert Neth.
8 F2 Weethalle Austr.
42 E3 Wegberg Ger.
47 K3 Węgorzewo Pol.
26 B2 Wei r. Henan China
26 D3 Wei r. Shaanxi China
26 E1 Weichang China
43 L4 Weida Ger.
43 K5 Weidenberg Ger.
43 L5 Weiden in der Oberpfalz Ger.
26 F2 Weifang China
30 B5 Weihai China
30 D2 Weihu Ling mts China
43 G4 Weilburg Ger.
43 K4 Weimar Ger.
26 C3 Weinan China
43 G5 Weinheim Ger.
27 B5 Weining China
43 H5 Weinsberg Ger.
6 E3 Weipa Austr.
65 L3 Weir River Can.
80 C4 Weirton U.S.A.
72 C2 Weiser U.S.A.
26 E3 Weishan China
26 E3 Weishan Hu l. China
26 E3 Weishi China
43 J5 Weißenburg in Bayern Ger.
43 K3 Weißenfels Ger.
79 C5 Weiss L. l. U.S.A.
58 C2 Weissrand Mts mts Namibia
43 G5 Weiterstadt Ger.
27 B5 Weixin China
26 B3 Weiyuan Gansu China
27 B4 Weiyuan Sichuan China
46 G7 Weiz Austria
27 C6 Weizhou Dao i. China
30 B3 Weizi China
46 J3 Wejherowo Pol.
65 K4 Wekusko Can.
65 K4 Wekusko Lake l. Can.
80 C6 Welch U.S.A.
81 H2 Weld U.S.A.
56 D2 Weldiya Eth.
74 C4 Weldon U.S.A.
56 D3 Welk'īt'ē Eth.
59 G3 Welkom S. Africa
69 H4 Welland Can.
39 G5 Welland r. U.K.
69 H4 Welland Canal canal Can.
21 C5 Wellawaya Sri Lanka
69 G4 Wellesley Can.
6 D3 Wellesley Is is Austr.
64 B2 Wellesley Lake l. Can.
81 H4 Wellfleet U.S.A.
42 D4 Wellin Belgium
39 G5 Wellingborough U.K.
8 G2 Wellington N.S.W. Austr.
8 B3 Wellington S.A. Austr.
9 E4 Wellington N.Z.
58 C6 Wellington S. Africa
39 D7 Wellington Eng. U.K.
39 E5 Wellington Eng. U.K.
72 F3 Wellington CO U.S.A.
77 D4 Wellington KS U.S.A.
74 C2 Wellington NV U.S.A.
80 B4 Wellington OH U.S.A.
77 C5 Wellington TX U.S.A.
75 G2 Wellington UT U.S.A.
88 A7 Wellington, I. i. Chile
8 F5 Wellington, L. l. Austr.
68 B5 Wellman U.S.A.
64 E4 Wells Can.
39 E6 Wells U.K.
72 D3 Wells NV U.S.A.
81 F3 Wells NY U.S.A.
80 E4 Wellsboro U.S.A.
9 E2 Wellsford N.Z.
64 E4 Wells Gray Prov. Park res. Can.
6 C4 Wells, L. salt flat Austr.
39 H5 Wells-next-the-Sea U.K.
80 B5 Wellston U.S.A.
80 E3 Wellsville U.S.A.
75 E5 Wellton U.S.A.
46 G6 Wels Austria
81 K2 Welshpool Can.
39 D5 Welshpool U.K.
43 M3 Welsickendorf Ger.
39 G6 Welwyn Garden City U.K.
43 H6 Welzheim Ger.
39 E5 Wem U.K.
59 H4 Wembesi S. Africa
64 F3 Wembley Can.
66 E3 Wemindji Can.
79 E7 Wemyss Bight Bahamas
26 F3 Wen r. China
72 B2 Wenatchee U.S.A.
27 D7 Wenchang China
27 F5 Wencheng China
54 B4 Wenchi Ghana
26 B4 Wenchuan China
43 K5 Wendelstein Ger.
43 F4 Wenden Ger.
75 F5 Wenden U.S.A.
30 B5 Wendeng China
56 D3 Wendo Eth.
72 D3 Wendover U.S.A.
69 F2 Wenebegon Lake l. Can.
27 C5 Weng'an China
27 E5 Wengyuan China
26 B4 Wenjiang China
27 F4 Wenling China
86 □ Wenman, Isla i. Galapagos Is Ecuador
68 C5 Wenona U.S.A.
27 B6 Wenshan China
39 H5 Wensum r. U.K.
43 J1 Wentorf bei Hamburg Ger.
8 C3 Wentworth Austr.
81 H3 Wentworth U.S.A.
26 B3 Wen Xian China
27 F5 Wenzhou China
43 L2 Wenzlow Ger.
59 G4 Wepener S. Africa
33 A1 We, Pulau i. Indon.
43 K2 Werben (Elbe) Ger.
58 E2 Werda Botswana
43 L4 Werdau Ger.
43 L2 Werder Ger.
43 F3 Werdohl Ger.
43 F3 Werl Ger.
43 L5 Wernberg-Köblitz Ger.
42 F3 Werne Ger.
64 C2 Wernecke Mountains Can.
43 J3 Wernigerode Ger.
43 H3 Werra r. Ger.
8 E4 Werribee Austr.
8 C3 Werrimull Austr.
8 H1 Werris Creek Austr.
43 H5 Wertheim Ger.
42 B4 Wervik Belgium
42 E3 Wesel Ger.
42 E3 Wesel-Datteln-Kanal canal Ger.
43 L1 Wesenberg Ger.
43 J2 Wesendorf Ger.
43 G1 Weser chan. Ger.
43 H2 Weser r. Ger.
43 G2 Wesergebirge h. Ger.
76 C4 Weskan U.S.A.
69 J3 Weslemkoon Lake l. Can.
81 K2 Wesley U.S.A.
67 K4 Wesleyville Can.
6 D3 Wessel, C. c. Austr.
6 D3 Wessel Is is Austr.
59 H3 Wesselton S. Africa
76 D2 Wessington Springs U.S.A.
68 C4 West Allis U.S.A.
92 A4 West Antarctica reg. Ant.
93 L5 West Australian Basin sea feature Ind. Ocean
93 L6 West Australian Ridge sea feature Ind. Ocean
22 B5 West Banas r. India
16 E5 West Bank terr. Asia
67 J3 West Bay Can.
77 F6 West Bay b. U.S.A.
68 C4 West Bend U.S.A.
23 F5 West Bengal div. India
69 E3 West Branch U.S.A.
80 D4 West Branch Susquehanna r. U.S.A.
39 F5 West Bromwich U.K.
81 H3 Westbrook U.S.A.
40 □ West Burra i. U.K.
39 E6 Westbury U.K.
8 F3 Westby Austr.
68 B4 Westby U.S.A.
94 E5 West Caroline Basin sea feature Pac. Oc.
81 F5 West Chester U.S.A.
81 G2 West Danville U.S.A.
69 F3 West Duck Island i. Can.
79 E7 West End Bahamas
74 D4 Westend U.S.A.
79 E7 West End Pt pt Bahamas
43 F4 Westerburg Ger.
42 F1 Westerholt Ger.
46 D3 Westerland Ger.
42 C3 Westerlo Belgium
81 H4 Westerly U.S.A.
65 H1 Western r. Can.
6 C4 Western Australia div. Austr.
58 D6 Western Cape div. S. Africa
55 E2 Western Desert des. Egypt
21 A2 Western Ghats mts India
8 E5 Western Port b. Austr.
52 C3 Western Sahara terr. Africa
5 K6 Western Samoa country Pac. Oc.
42 B3 Westerschelde est. Neth.
43 F1 Westerstede Ger.
43 F4 Westerwald reg. Ger.
88 D8 West Falkland i. Falkland Is
76 D2 West Fargo U.S.A.
68 D5 Westfield IN U.S.A.
81 G3 Westfield MA U.S.A.
81 K1 Westfield ME U.S.A.
80 D3 Westfield NY U.S.A.
42 E1 Westgat chan. Neth.
81 K2 West Grand Lake l. U.S.A.
43 J6 Westhausen Ger.
40 F3 Westhill U.K.
76 C1 Westhope U.S.A.
92 D5 West Ice Shelf ice feature Ant.
42 B3 Westkapelle Neth.
27 □ West Lamma Chan. H.K. China
80 B5 West Lancaster U.S.A.
9 B5 Westland National Park N.Z.
39 J5 Westleton U.K.
74 B3 Westley U.S.A.
80 B6 West Liberty KY U.S.A.
80 B4 West Liberty OH U.S.A.
40 E5 West Linton U.K.
40 B2 West Loch Roag b. U.K.
64 G4 Westlock Can.
69 G4 West Lorne Can.
42 C3 Westmalle Belgium
77 F5 West Memphis U.S.A.
80 E5 Westminster MD U.S.A.
79 D5 Westminster SC U.S.A.
80 C5 Weston U.S.A.
39 E6 Weston-super-Mare U.K.
81 F5 Westover U.S.A.
79 D7 West Palm Beach U.S.A.
77 F4 West Plains U.S.A.
77 F5 West Point MS U.S.A.
81 F4 West Point NY U.S.A.
69 J3 Westport Can.
9 C4 Westport N.Z.
41 B4 Westport Rep. of Ireland
74 A2 Westport U.S.A.
65 J4 Westray Can.
40 E1 Westray i. U.K.
69 G2 Westree Can.
42 F5 Westrich reg. Ger.
64 E4 West Road r. Can.
81 H2 West Stewartstown U.S.A.
42 D1 West-Terschelling Neth.
81 H4 West Tisbury U.S.A.
81 G2 West Topsham U.S.A.
81 G3 West Townshend U.S.A.
68 B4 West Union IA U.S.A.
80 B5 West Union OH U.S.A.
80 C5 West Union WV U.S.A.
68 D5 Westville U.S.A.
80 C5 West Virginia div. U.S.A.
74 C2 West Walker r. U.S.A.
74 B1 Westwood U.S.A.
8 F2 West Wyalong Austr.
72 E2 West Yellowstone U.S.A.
42 C2 Westzaan Neth.
25 E7 Wetar i. Indon.
64 G4 Wetaskiwin Can.
68 D2 Wetmore U.S.A.
43 G4 Wetter r. Ger.
43 K3 Wettin Ger.
43 G4 Wetzlar Ger.
6 E2 Wewak P.N.G.
41 E5 Wexford Rep. of Ireland
65 H4 Weyakwin Can.
68 C3 Weyauwega U.S.A.
39 G6 Weybridge U.K.
65 J5 Weyburn Can.
43 G2 Weyhe Ger.
39 E7 Weymouth U.K.
81 H3 Weymouth U.S.A.
42 E2 Wezep Neth.
9 F2 Whakatane N.Z.
9 F3 Whakatane r. N.Z.
32 A3 Whale B. b. Myanmar
64 B3 Whale B. b. U.S.A.
79 E7 Whale Cay i. Bahamas
65 L2 Whale Cove Can.
40 □ Whalsay i. U.K.
9 E2 Whangamata N.Z.
9 E3 Whangamomona N.Z.
9 E1 Whangarei N.Z.
66 E2 Whapmagoostui Can.
38 F4 Wharfe r. U.K.
69 F2 Wharncliffe Can.
65 J2 Wharton Lake l. Can.
68 A5 What Cheer U.S.A.
72 F3 Wheatland U.S.A.
68 C5 Wheaton U.S.A.
73 F4 Wheeler Peak summit NM U.S.A.
75 E2 Wheeler Peak summit NV U.S.A.
80 C4 Wheeling U.S.A.
91 E2 Wheelwright Arg.
38 E3 Whernside h. U.K.

39 J5 Yare r. U.K.
50 K2 Yarega Rus. Fed.
7 G2 Yaren Nauru
50 J2 Yarensk Rus. Fed.
89 B4 Yari r. Col.
29 E6 Yariga-take mt Japan
89 C2 Yaritagua Venez.
69 J3 Yarker Can.
22 C1 Yarkhun r. Pak.
67 G5 Yarmouth Can.
39 F7 Yarmouth U.K.
81 H4 Yarmouth Port U.S.A.
75 F4 Yarnell U.S.A.
50 F3 Yaroslavl' Rus. Fed.
50 F3 Yaroslavskaya Oblast' div. Rus. Fed.
28 C2 Yaroslavskiy Rus. Fed.
8 F5 Yarram Austr.
8 E4 Yarra Yarra r. Austr.
23 H3 Yartö Tra La pass China
50 E4 Yartsevo Rus. Fed.
12 K3 Yartsevo Rus. Fed.
89 B3 Yarumal Col.
23 F5 Yasai r. India
7 H3 Yasawa Group is Fiji
51 F6 Yasenskaya Rus. Fed.
51 G6 Yashalta Rus. Fed.
51 H6 Yashkul' Rus. Fed.
28 E2 Yasnaya Polyana Rus. Fed.
8 G3 Yass Austr.
8 G3 Yass r. Austr.
18 C4 Yāsūj Iran
16 B3 Yatağan Turkey
7 G4 Yaté New Caledonia
77 E4 Yates Center U.S.A.
65 K2 Yathkyed Lake l. Can.
29 F7 Yatsuga-take volc. Japan
29 B8 Yatsushiro Japan
39 E6 Yatton U.K.
27 Yau Tong H.K. China
86 D5 Yavari r. Brazil/Peru
22 D5 Yavatmāl India
17 H2 Yavi Turkey
89 D3 Yaví, Co mt Venez.
51 B5 Yavoriv Ukr.
29 C8 Yawatahama Japan
23 E1 Yawatongguz He r. China
23 H5 Yaw Ch. r. Myanmar
84 E3 Yaxchilan Guatemala
18 D4 Yazd Iran
19 F3 Yazdān Iran
18 D4 Yazd-e Khvāst Iran
16 G2 Yazıhan Turkey
77 F5 Yazoo r. U.S.A.
77 F5 Yazoo City U.S.A.
37 L9 Yding Skovhøj h. Denmark
49 K6 Ydra i. Greece
32 A2 Ye Myanmar
8 E4 Yea Austr.
39 D7 Yealmpton U.K.
15 F3 Yecheng China
79 D7 Yeehaw Junction U.S.A.
50 F4 Yefremov Rus. Fed.
17 K2 Yeghegnadzor Armenia
51 G6 Yegorlyk r. Rus. Fed.
51 G6 Yegorlykskaya Rus. Fed.
28 E2 Yegoreva, Mys pt Rus. Fed.
50 F4 Yegor'yevsk Rus. Fed.
55 F4 Yei Sudan
26 E4 Yejiaji China
12 H4 Yekaterinburg Rus. Fed.
51 G5 Yelan' Rus. Fed.
51 G5 Yelan' r. Rus. Fed.
19 F2 Yelbarsli Turkm.
51 F4 Yelets Rus. Fed.
54 A3 Yélimané Mali
40 Yell i. U.K.
21 C2 Yellandu India
21 A3 Yellapur India
68 B3 Yellow r. U.S.A.
80 D4 Yellow Creek U.S.A.
62 G3 Yellowknife Can.
8 F2 Yellow Mt h. Austr.
Yellow River r. see Huang He
30 B6 Yellow Sea sea Pac. Oc.
72 F2 Yellowstone r. U.S.A.
72 E2 Yellowstone L. l. U.S.A.
72 E2 Yellowstone Nat. Park U.S.A.
72 E2 Yellowtail Res. resr U.S.A.
40 Yell Sound chan. U.K.
19 F2 Yeloten Turkm.
51 D5 Yel'sk Belarus
63 K1 Yelverton Bay b. Can.
10 F8 Yemen country Asia
50 G2 Yemetsk Rus. Fed.
50 G2 Yemtsa Rus. Fed.
50 J2 Yemva Rus. Fed.
36 W3 Yena Rus. Fed.
51 F5 Yenakiyeve Ukr.
23 H5 Yenangyat Myanmar
23 H5 Yenangyaung Myanmar
23 H6 Yenanma Myanmar
27 B6 Yên Bai Vietnam
8 F3 Yenda Austr.
54 B4 Yendi Ghana
56 B4 Yénéganou Congo
17 L3 Yengejeh Iran
16 D1 Yeniçağa Turkey
16 E3 Yenice Turkey
49 M5 Yenice Turkey
16 D2 Yeniceoba Turkey
16 B1 Yenişehir Turkey
12 L4 Yenisey r. Rus. Fed.
12 L4 Yeniseysk Rus. Fed.
12 L4 Yeniseyskiy Kryazh ridge Rus. Fed.
12 J2 Yeniseyskiy Zaliv in. Rus. Fed.
27 B6 Yên Minh Vietnam
51 H6 Yenotayevka Rus. Fed.
22 C5 Yeola India
Yeotmal see Yavatmāl
8 G2 Yeoval Austr.
39 E7 Yeovil U.K.
Yeo Yeo r. see Bland
6 F4 Yeppoon Austr.
19 E2 Yerbent Turkm.
13 M3 Yerbogachen Rus. Fed.
17 K1 Yerevan Armenia
51 H6 Yergeni h. Rus. Fed.
74 C2 Yerington U.S.A.
16 E2 Yerköy Turkey
21 A2 Yerla r. India
15 F1 Yermentau Kazak.
84 A1 Yermo Mex.
74 D4 Yermo U.S.A.
51 J5 Yershov Rus. Fed.
50 G2 Yertsevo Rus. Fed.
Yerushalayim see Jerusalem
51 H5 Yeruslan r. Rus. Fed.
30 D5 Yesan S. Korea
14 E1 Yesil' Kazak.
16 E2 Yeşilhisar Turkey
16 F1 Yeşilırmak r. Turkey
16 B3 Yeşilova Turkey
51 G6 Yessentuki Rus. Fed.
13 M3 Yessey Rus. Fed.
39 C7 Yes Tor h. U.K.
24 B4 Yeu Myanmar
44 C3 Yeu, Île d' i. France
17 L1 Yevlax Azer.
51 E6 Yevpatoriya Ukr.
26 D3 Ye Xian Henan China
26 F2 Ye Xian Shandong China
51 F6 Yeya r. Rus. Fed.
23 E1 Yeyik China
51 F6 Yeysk Rus. Fed.
50 H1 Yezhuga r. Rus. Fed.
50 D4 Yezyaryshcha Belarus
26 D3 Yi r. Henan China
26 E3 Yi r. Shandong China
91 F2 Yí r. Uru.
27 B4 Yibin China
23 F2 Yibug Caka salt l. China
27 D4 Yichang Hubei China
27 D4 Yichang Hubei China
26 D4 Yicheng Hubei China
26 D3 Yicheng Shanxi China
26 D3 Yichuan China
24 E2 Yichun Heilongjiang China
27 E5 Yichun Jiangxi China
27 D4 Yidu Hubei China
26 F2 Yidu Shandong China
27 E4 Yifeng China
27 E5 Yihuang China
26 C3 Yijun China
28 A1 Yilan China
49 M4 Yıldız Dağları mts Turkey
16 F2 Yıldızeli Turkey
27 B5 Yiliang Yunnan China
27 B5 Yiliang Yunnan China
26 C4 Yilong China
27 B6 Yilong Hu l. China
27 B5 Yimen China
30 E1 Yimianpo China
26 F3 Yinan China
26 C2 Yinchuan China
30 C2 Yingchengzi China
27 D5 Yingde China
27 C7 Yinggehai China
26 E3 Ying He r. China
30 B3 Yingkou Liaoning China
30 B3 Yingkou Liaoning China
26 B2 Yingpanshui China
27 E4 Yingshan Hubei China
26 C4 Yingshan Sichuan China
26 E3 Yingshang China
27 E4 Yingtan China
26 D2 Ying Xian China
15 G2 Yining China
27 C5 Yinjiang China
30 C1 Yinma r. China
23 H5 Yinmabin Myanmar
26 C1 Yin Shan mts China
23 H3 Yi'ong Zangbo r. China
27 A5 Yipinglang China
56 D3 Yirga Alem Eth.
23 G2 Yirna Tso l. China
27 C5 Yishan China
26 F2 Yi Shan mt China
26 F3 Yishui China
32 Yishun Sing.
30 C2 Yitong China
30 C1 Yitong r. China
24 B2 Yiwu China
30 A3 Yiwulü Shan mts China
27 E4 Yi Xian Anhui China
30 A3 Yi Xian China
26 F4 Yixing China
27 D4 Yiyang Hunan China
27 E4 Yiyang Jiangxi China
27 D5 Yizhang China
37 S6 Yläne Fin.
36 S5 Ylihärmä Fin.
36 T4 Yli-Ii Fin.
36 T4 Yli-Kärppä Fin.
36 U4 Ylikiiminki Fin.
36 V3 Yli-kitka l. Fin.
36 S5 Ylistaro Fin.
36 S3 Ylitornio Fin.
36 T4 Ylivieska Fin.
37 S6 Ylöjärvi Fin.
77 D6 Yoakum U.S.A.
28 G3 Yobetsu-dake volc. Japan
33 D4 Yogyakarta Indon.
64 F4 Yoho Nat. Park Can.
55 D4 Yokadouma Cameroon
29 E7 Yokkaichi Japan
55 D4 Yoko Cameroon
29 F7 Yokohama Japan
29 F7 Yokosuka Japan
28 G5 Yokote Japan
28 G4 Yokotsu-dake mt Japan
55 D4 Yola Nigeria
84 C3 Yoloxochitl Mex.
54 B4 Yomou Guinea
30 D5 Yŏnan N. Korea
29 G6 Yonezawa Japan
8 B2 Yongala Austr.
30 D6 Yongam S. Korea
27 E5 Yong'an China
30 E3 Yŏng-an N. Korea
26 A2 Yongchang China
26 E3 Yongcheng China
30 E6 Yŏngch'ŏn S. Korea
27 F5 Yongchun China
26 B2 Yongdeng China
27 E5 Yongding China
26 E2 Yongding r. China
30 E5 Yŏngdŏk S. Korea
27 C5 Yongfu China
30 D6 Yŏnggwang S. Korea
23 H3 Yonggyap pass India
30 D4 Yŏnghŭng N. Korea
30 D4 Yŏnghŭng-man b. N. Korea
30 D2 Yongji China
27 F4 Yongjia China
26 B3 Yongjing China
30 E5 Yŏngju S. Korea
27 F4 Yongkang China
30 C3 Yongling China
26 E2 Yongnian China
27 C6 Yongning China
27 A5 Yongren China
30 D6 Yŏngsan r. S. Korea
30 D6 Yŏngsanp'o S. Korea
27 C4 Yongshun China
27 F5 Yongtai China
27 D5 Yongxin China
27 E5 Yongxing China
27 E4 Yongxiu China
27 D5 Yongzhou China
30 D3 Yŏnhwa, Mt mt N. Korea
81 G4 Yonkers U.S.A.
44 F2 Yonne r. France
89 B3 Yopal Col.
6 B5 York Austr.
38 F4 York U.K.
76 D3 York NE U.S.A.
80 E5 York PA U.S.A.
79 D5 York SC U.S.A.
6 E3 York, C. c. Austr.
8 A3 Yorke Peninsula Austr.
8 A3 Yorketown Austr.
63 M2 York, Kap c. Greenland
38 E3 Yorkshire Dales National Park U.K.
38 G4 Yorkshire Wolds reg. U.K.
65 J4 Yorkton Can.
80 E6 Yorktown U.S.A.
38 F3 York, Vale of v. U.K.
54 B3 Yorosso Mali
74 C3 Yosemite National Park U.S.A.
74 C3 Yosemite Village U.S.A.
29 C8 Yoshino-gawa r. Japan
29 D7 Yoshino-Kumano National Park Japan
50 H3 Yoshkar-Ola Rus. Fed.
30 D6 Yŏsu S. Korea
16 E7 Yotvata Israel
41 D6 Youghal Rep. of Ireland
80 D5 Youghiogheny River Lake l. U.S.A.
27 C6 You Jiang r. China
8 G3 Young Austr.
91 F2 Young Uru.
8 B3 Younghusband Pen. pen. Austr.
92 A6 Young I. i. Ant.
80 C4 Youngstown U.S.A.
27 D4 You Shui r. China
54 B3 Youvarou Mali
27 F5 Youxi China
27 D5 You Xian China
27 C4 Youyang China
28 B1 Youyi China
26 D2 Youyu China
19 H2 Yovon Tajik.
16 E2 Yozgat Turkey
90 A3 Ypané r. Para.
90 A3 Ypé-Jhú Para.
72 B3 Yreka U.S.A.
Yr Wyddfa mt see Snowdon
42 A4 Yser r. France
42 D3 Ysselsteyn Neth.
37 N9 Ystad Sweden
39 D5 Ystwyth r. U.K.
15 F2 Ysyk-Köl Kyrg.
15 F2 Ysyk-Köl l. Kyrg.
40 F3 Ythan r. U.K.
13 P3 Ytyk-Kyuyel Rus. Fed.
27 F6 Yüalin Taiwan
26 D4 Yuan'an China
27 C5 Yuanbao Shan mt China
27 D4 Yuanjiang Hunan China
27 A6 Yuanjiang Yunnan China
27 D4 Yuan Jiang r. Hunan China
27 B6 Yuan Jiang r. Yunnan China
27 F5 Yüanli Taiwan
27 D4 Yuanling China
27 A5 Yuanmou China
26 D2 Yuanping China
26 D3 Yuanqu China
27 B6 Yuanyang China
74 B2 Yuba r. U.S.A.
74 B2 Yuba City U.S.A.
28 G3 Yūbari Japan
84 E2 Yucatan div. Mex.
82 F5 Yucatán pen. Mex.
82 G4 Yucatan Channel str. Cuba/Mex.
75 E4 Yucca U.S.A.
74 D3 Yucca L. l. U.S.A.
74 D4 Yucca Valley U.S.A.
26 E2 Yucheng China
26 D2 Yuci China
13 P4 Yudoma r. Rus. Fed.
27 E5 Yudu China
27 C4 Yuechi China
6 D4 Yuendumu Austr.
27 Yuen Long H.K. China
27 F4 Yueqing China
27 E4 Yuexi Anhui China
27 B4 Yuexi Sichuan China
27 D4 Yueyang China
27 E4 Yugan China
35 H4 Yugoslavia country Europe
13 R3 Yugo-Tala Rus. Fed.
50 K2 Yugydtydor Rus. Fed.
27 F4 Yuhuan China
26 E2 Yuhuang Ding mt China
27 E4 Yujiang China
27 D6 Yu Jiang r. China
13 R3 Yukagirskoye Ploskogor'ye plat. Rus. Fed.
16 E2 Yukarısarıkaya Turkey
56 B4 Yuki Congo(Zaire)
62 C3 Yukon r. Can./U.S.A.
64 B2 Yukon Territory div. Can.
17 K3 Yüksekova Turkey
79 D6 Yulee U.S.A.
27 F6 Yüli Taiwan
27 D6 Yulin Guangxi China
27 C7 Yulin Hainan China
26 C2 Yulin Shaanxi China
75 E5 Yuma U.S.A.
75 E5 Yuma Desert des. U.S.A.
89 A4 Yumbo Col.
24 B3 Yumen China
16 E3 Yumurtalık Turkey
16 C2 Yunak Turkey
27 D6 Yunan China
26 E3 Yuncheng Shandong China
26 D3 Yuncheng Shanxi China
27 D6 Yunfu China
27 B5 Yun Gui Gaoyuan plat. China
27 F4 Yunhe China
27 D6 Yunkai Dashan mts China
26 D4 Yunmeng China
27 A5 Yunnan div. China
26 D4 Yun Shui r. China
8 B2 Yunta Austr.
27 D6 Yunwu Shan mts China
26 D3 Yunxi China
26 D3 Yun Xian China
27 E6 Yunxiao China
26 D3 Yunyang Henan China
26 C4 Yunyang Sichuan China
27 C5 Yuping China
26 E1 Yuqiao Sk. resr China
27 C5 Yuqing China
24 A1 Yurga Rus. Fed.
86 C5 Yurimaguas Peru
89 E3 Yuruán r. Venez.
89 E3 Yuruari r. Venez.
89 C2 Yurubi, Parque Nacional nat. park Venez.
22 E1 Yurungkax He r. China
50 J3 Yur'ya Rus. Fed.
50 G3 Yur'yevets Rus. Fed.
50 F3 Yur'yev-Pol'skiy Rus. Fed.
27 F4 Yushan China
27 F6 Yü Shan mt Taiwan
26 D2 Yushe China
50 E1 Yushkozero Rus. Fed.
30 D1 Yushu China
24 B3 Yushu China
13 M2 Yushut r. Rus. Fed.
51 H6 Yusta Rus. Fed.
17 H1 Yusufeli Turkey
26 E3 Yutai China
23 E1 Yutian China
26 C2 Yuwang China
27 B5 Yuxi China
26 E2 Yu Xian Hebei China
26 D3 Yu Xian Henan China
26 D2 Yu Xian Shanxi China
27 F4 Yuyao China
28 G5 Yuzawa Japan
50 G3 Yuzha Rus. Fed.
24 D1 Yuzhno Muyskiy Khrebet mts Rus. Fed.
24 G2 Yuzhno-Sakhalinsk Rus. Fed.
51 H6 Yuzhno-Sukhokumsk Rus. Fed.
51 D6 Yuzhnoukrayinsk Ukr.
28 H1 Yuzhnoye Rus. Fed.
51 G6 Yuzhnyy Rus. Fed.
26 B3 Yuzhong China
18 B3 Yūzīdar Iran
46 C7 Yverdon Switz.
44 E2 Yvetot France
32 A1 Ywathit Myanmar

Z

19 H2 Zaamin Uzbek.
42 C2 Zaandam Neth.
24 D2 Zabaykal'sk Rus. Fed.
18 B2 Zab-e Kuchek r. Iran
20 B7 Zabīd Yemen
19 F4 Zābol Iran
19 F5 Zābolī Iran
82 G5 Zacapa Guatemala
84 B3 Zacapu Mex.
84 B2 Zacatecas Mex.
84 B2 Zacatecas div. Mex.
84 C3 Zacatlán Mex.
49 J6 Zacharo Greece
48 F2 Zadar Croatia
32 A3 Zadetkale Kyun i. Myanmar
32 A3 Zadetkyi Kyun i. Myanmar
23 H2 Zadoi China
51 F4 Zadonsk Rus. Fed.
17 L4 Zafarābād Iran
49 M6 Zafora i. Greece
45 C3 Zafra Spain
55 F1 Zagazig Egypt
18 E3 Zaghdeh well Iran
17 M5 Zāgheh Iran
48 D6 Zaghouan Tunisia
48 F2 Zagreb Croatia
18 B3 Zagros, Kūhhā-ye mts Iran
Zagros Mountains mts see Zagros, Kūhhā-ye
23 G3 Za'gya Zangbo r. China
19 F4 Zāhedān Iran
19 H3 Zahidabad Afgh.
16 E5 Zahlé Lebanon
Zaire country see Congo
Zaïre r. see Congo
49 K3 Zaječar Yugo.
19 F2 Zakhmet Turkm.
17 J3 Zākhō Iraq
55 D3 Zakouma, Parc National de nat. park Chad
49 J6 Zakynthos Greece
Zakynthos i. see Zante
46 H7 Zalaegerszeg Hungary
46 H7 Zalai-domsag h. Hungary
45 D3 Zalamea de la Serena Spain
47 L7 Zalău Romania
50 F3 Zales'ye Rus. Fed.
55 E3 Zalingei Sudan
47 M6 Zalishchyky Ukr.
50 D3 Zaluch'ye Rus. Fed.
16 E2 Zamanti r. Turkey
31 B3 Zambales Mts mts Phil.
57 D5 Zambeze r. Moz.
57 C5 Zambezi Zambia
57 C5 Zambezi r. Africa
53 G7 Zambia country Africa
31 B5 Zamboanga Phil.
31 B5 Zamboanga Peninsula Phil.
86 C4 Zamora Ecuador
45 D2 Zamora Spain
84 B3 Zamora de Hidalgo Mex.
47 L5 Zamość Pol.
26 A3 Zamtang China
89 C2 Zamuro, Pta pt Venez.
89 E3 Zamuro, Sierra del mts Venez.
22 D3 Zanda China
59 L2 Zandamela Moz.
42 C3 Zandvliet Belgium
80 C5 Zanesville U.S.A.
22 D2 Zangla Jammu and Kashmir
18 C2 Zanjān Iran
17 L3 Zanjān r. Iran
49 J6 Zante i. Greece
56 D4 Zanzibar Tanz.
56 D4 Zanzibar I. i. Tanz.
27 D4 Zaoshi China
54 C2 Zaouatallaz Alg.
26 D3 Zaoyang China
24 B1 Zaozernyy Rus. Fed.
26 E3 Zaozhuang China
17 J3 Zap r. Turkey
50 E3 Zapadnaya Dvina Rus. Fed.
Zapadnaya Dvina r. see Dvina, Western
49 K4 Zapadni Rodopi mts Bulg.
12 K3 Zapadno-Sibirskaya Ravnina plain Rus. Fed.
36 Y2 Zapadnyy Kil'din Rus. Fed.
15 G1 Zapadnyy Sayan reg. Rus. Fed.
91 B3 Zapala Arg.
77 D7 Zapata U.S.A.
89 B3 Zapatoca Col.
36 W2 Zapolyarnyy Rus. Fed.
51 E6 Zaporizhzhya Ukr.
28 D2 Zapovednik mt Rus. Fed.
22 E2 Zapug China
17 L1 Zaqatala Azer.
23 H2 Zaqên China
23 H2 Za Qu r. China
16 F2 Zara Turkey
19 G2 Zarafshon, Qatorkŭhi mts Tajik.
89 B3 Zaragoza Col.
73 F6 Zaragoza Chihuahua Mex.
45 F2 Zaragoza Spain
18 E4 Zarand Iran
19 F4 Zaranj Afgh.
16 E6 Zararikh Reserve res. Egypt
37 U9 Zarasai Lith.
91 E2 Zárate Arg.
89 D2 Zaraza Venez.
19 H1 Zarbdar Uzbek.
17 L1 Zärdab Azer.
36 W3 Zarechensk Rus. Fed.
17 M4 Zāreh Iran
64 C3 Zarembo I. i. U.S.A.
22 A3 Zargun mt Pak.
54 C3 Zaria Nigeria
51 C5 Zarichne Ukr.
18 B2 Zarīneh r. Iran
19 F3 Zarmardan Afgh.
17 L5 Zarneh Iran
49 L2 Zărneşti Romania
16 F5 Zarqā' Jordan
18 D4 Zarqān Iran
18 D3 Zarrīn Iran
28 B3 Zarubino Rus. Fed.
46 G5 Żary Pol.
89 A3 Zarzal Col.
55 D1 Zarzis Tunisia
36 W3 Zasheyek Rus. Fed.
22 D2 Zaskar r. India
22 D2 Zaskar Mts mts India
50 C4 Zaslawye Belarus
59 G5 Zastron S. Africa
43 L2 Zauche reg. Ger.
18 D3 Zavareh Iran
49 H2 Zavidoviči Bos.-Herz.
24 E1 Zavitinsk Rus. Fed.
26 A2 Zawa China
47 J5 Zawiercie Pol.
15 G2 Zaysan, Ozero l. Kazak.
24 B4 Zayü China
46 G6 Žďár nad Sázavou Czech Rep.
51 C5 Zdolbuniv Ukr.
37 M9 Zealand i. Denmark
17 K3 Zēbār Iraq
26 E3 Zecheng China
42 B3 Zedelgem Belgium
42 B3 Zeebrugge Belgium
59 G2 Zeerust S. Africa
42 B3 Zeeuwsch-Vlaanderen reg. Neth.
16 E5 Zefat Israel
43 M2 Zehdenick Ger.
43 J4 Zeil am Main Ger.
42 D2 Zeist Neth.
43 L3 Zeitz Ger.
26 A3 Zêkog China
36 X3 Zelenoborskiy Rus. Fed.
50 J4 Zelenodol'sk Rus. Fed.
37 V6 Zelenogorsk Rus. Fed.
50 F3 Zelenograd Rus. Fed.
50 B4 Zelenogradsk Rus. Fed.
51 G6 Zelenokumsk Rus. Fed.
50 H3 Zelentsovo Rus. Fed.
46 F7 Zell am See Austria
43 H5 Zellingen Ger.
42 B3 Zelzate Belgium
26 A3 Zēmdasam China
50 G4 Zemetchino Rus. Fed.
56 C3 Zémio C.A.R.
12 F1 Zemlya Aleksandry i. Rus. Fed.
Zemlya Frantsa-Iosifa is see Franz Josef Land
12 F2 Zemlya Georga i. Rus. Fed.
12 H1 Zemlya Vil'cheka i. Rus. Fed.
45 G5 Zemmora Alg.
84 C3 Zempoala Pyramids Mex.
84 D3 Zempoaltepetl mt Mex.
27 D6 Zengcheng China
30 E2 Zengfeng Shan mt China
74 A1 Zenia U.S.A.
49 G2 Zenica Bos.-Herz.
39 B7 Zennor U.K.
74 C2 Zephyr Cove U.S.A.
43 L3 Zerbst Ger.
42 E5 Zerf Ger.
43 J1 Zernien Ger.
43 L2 Zernitz Ger.
51 G6 Zernograd Rus. Fed.
51 G7 Zestap'oni Georgia
23 G3 Zêtang China
43 F1 Zetel Ger.
43 K4 Zeulenroda Ger.
43 H1 Zeven Ger.
42 E3 Zevenaar Neth.
24 E1 Zeya Rus. Fed.
24 E1 Zeya r. Rus. Fed.
19 F5 Zeyarat-e Shamil Iran
18 D4 Zeydābād Iran
19 E2 Zēydar Iran
18 E4 Zeynalābād Iran
24 E1 Zeyskoye Vdkhr. resr Rus. Fed.
45 C3 Zêzere r. Port.
47 J5 Zgierz Pol.
50 C4 Zhabinka Belarus
14 E1 Zhaltyr Kazak.
14 F2 Zhambyl Kazak.
26 E2 Zhang r. China
26 E1 Zhangbei China
30 E1 Zhangguangcai Ling mts China
30 B2 Zhanggutai China
26 E1 Zhangjiakou China
26 B3 Zhangla China
27 E5 Zhangping China
27 E5 Zhangpu China
30 B2 Zhangqiangzhen China
26 E2 Zhangwei Xinhe r. China
30 B2 Zhangwu China
26 B3 Zhang Xian China
26 A2 Zhangye China
27 E5 Zhangzhou China
26 D2 Zhangzi China
30 B4 Zhangzi Dao i. China
26 F2 Zhanhua China
27 D6 Zhanjiang China
27 B5 Zhanyi China
27 E6 Zhao'an China
27 B4 Zhaojue China
27 D5 Zhaoping China
27 D6 Zhaoqing China
30 B2 Zhaosutai r. China
27 B5 Zhaotong China
26 E2 Zhao Xian China
30 C1 Zhaoyuan China
27 D6 Zhapo China
23 F3 Zhari Namco salt l. China
15 G2 Zharkent Kazak.
50 E4 Zharkovskiy Rus. Fed.
15 G2 Zharma Kazak.
51 D5 Zhashkiv Ukr.
26 C3 Zhashui China
23 F2 Zhaxi Co salt l. China
22 D2 Zhaxigang China
27 F4 Zhejiang div. China
12 H2 Zhelaniya, M. c. Rus. Fed.
51 E4 Zheleznogorsk Rus. Fed.
26 C3 Zhen'an China
26 C3 Zhenba China
27 C4 Zheng'an China
26 E2 Zhengding China
27 F5 Zhenghe China
26 E1 Zhenglan Qi China
26 C3 Zhengning China
26 E1 Zhengxiangbai Qi China
26 E3 Zhengyang China
26 D3 Zhengzhou China
27 F4 Zhenhai China
26 F3 Zhenjiang China
26 B3 Zhenjiangguan China
27 B5 Zhenning China
26 D3 Zhenping China
27 B5 Zhenxiong China
26 C3 Zhenyuan Gansu China
27 C5 Zhenyuan Guizhou China
51 G5 Zherdevka Rus. Fed.
27 F5 Zherong China
50 J2 Zheshart Rus. Fed.
27 D4 Zhexi Sk. resr China
14 E2 Zhezkazgan Kazak.
27 D4 Zhicheng China
26 C2 Zhidan China
23 H2 Zhidoi China
13 O3 Zhigansk Rus. Fed.
27 D6 Zhigong China
23 G3 Zhigung China
27 D4 Zhijiang Hubei China
27 C5 Zhijiang Hunan China
27 E6 Zhijin China
Zhi Qu r. see Tongtian He
51 H5 Zhirnovsk Rus. Fed.
51 H5 Zhitkur Rus. Fed.
17 L4 Zhīvār Iran
50 D4 Zhlobin Belarus
51 D5 Zhmerynka Ukr.
22 B3 Zhob Pak.
22 B3 Zhob r. Pak.
13 R2 Zhokhova, O. i. Rus. Fed.
23 F3 Zhongba China
24 B4 Zhongdian China
26 B4 Zhongjiang China
26 B2 Zhongning China
27 D6 Zhongshan Guangdong China
27 D5 Zhongshan Guangxi China
92 D5 Zhongshan China Base Ant.
26 D3 Zhongtiao Shan mts China
26 B2 Zhongwei China
27 C4 Zhong Xian China
27 E5 Zhongxin China
27 B5 Zhongyicur China
27 D7 Zhongyuan China
26 C4 Zhou He r. China
26 B2 Zhoujiajing China
26 E3 Zhoukou China
27 F5 Zhouning China
26 D1 Zhouzi China
51 E5 Zhovti Vody Ukr.
30 B4 Zhuanghe China
26 B3 Zhuanglang China
26 F3 Zhucheng China
26 B3 Zhugqu China
27 D6 Zhuhai China
27 F4 Zhuji China
50 E4 Zhukovka Rus. Fed.
26 E2 Zhulong r. China
26 E3 Zhumadian China
26 E1 Zhuolu China
26 E2 Zhuo Xian China
26 D2 Zhuozang r. China
26 D3 Zhushan China
26 C3 Zhuxi China
27 D5 Zhuzhou Hunan China
27 D5 Zhuzhou Hunan China
51 C5 Zhydachiv Ukr.
51 C4 Zhytkavichy Belarus
51 D5 Zhytomyr Ukr.
26 F2 Zi r. China
47 J6 Žiar nad Hronom Slovakia
17 J3 Zībār Iraq
26 F2 Zibo China
26 C2 Zichang China
6 D4 Ziel, Mt mt Austr.
46 G5 Zielona Góra Pol.
43 H3 Zierenberg Ger.
43 L2 Ziesar Ger.
16 C6 Zifta Egypt
17 M1 Zığ Azer.
23 H5 Zigaing Myanmar
27 B4 Zigong China
27 D4 Zigui China
54 A3 Ziguinchor Senegal
37 U8 Žīguri Latvia
84 B3 Zihuatanejo Mex.
27 B5 Zijin China
42 E2 Zijpenberg h. Neth.
16 E5 Zikhron Ya'aqov Israel
16 E1 Zile Turkey
47 J6 Žilina Slovakia
24 C1 Zima Rus. Fed.
84 C2 Zimapán Mex.
84 C3 Zimatlán Mex.
57 C5 Zimba Zambia
53 G7 Zimbabwe country Africa
18 B3 Zimkan r. Iran
54 A4 Zimmi Sierra Leone
49 L3 Zimnicea Romania
51 G6 Zimovniki Rus. Fed.
16 E4 Zimrin Syria
19 F3 Zindajan Afgh.
54 C3 Zinder Niger
54 B3 Ziniaré Burkina
26 B2 Zinihu China
75 F3 Zion Nat. Park U.S.A.
66 B3 Zionz L. l. Can.
89 B3 Zipaquirá Col.
23 H2 Ziqudukou China
43 J5 Zirndorf Ger.
23 H4 Ziro India
27 D4 Zi Shui r. China
46 H6 Zistersdorf Austria
84 B3 Zitácuaro Mex.
46 G5 Zittau Ger.
17 K3 Zīveh Iran
27 E5 Zixi China
27 D5 Zixing China
26 E2 Ziya r. China
26 C3 Ziyang Shaanxi China
27 B4 Ziyang Sichuan China
27 D5 Ziyuan China
27 C5 Ziyun China
27 B4 Zizhong China
46 H6 Zlín Czech Rep.
51 D4 Zlynka Rus. Fed.
51 F5 Zmiyiv Ukr.
50 E4 Znamenka Rus. Fed.
51 E5 Znam"yanka Ukr.
46 H6 Znojmo Czech Rep.
58 D6 Zoar S. Africa
17 L4 Zobeyrī Iran
42 C2 Zoetermeer Neth.
17 K4 Zōhāb Iran
26 B3 Zoigê China
22 C2 Zoji La pass India
59 G6 Zola S. Africa
42 D3 Zolder Belgium
51 E5 Zolochiv Kharkiv Ukr.
51 C5 Zolochiv L'viv Ukr.
51 E5 Zolotonosha Ukr.
51 F4 Zolotukhino Rus. Fed.
57 D5 Zomba Malawi
Zongga see Gyirong
56 B3 Zongo Congo(Zaire)
16 C1 Zonguldak Turkey
23 G3 Zongxoi China
27 E4 Zongyang China
48 C4 Zonza Corsica France
43 L3 Zörbig Ger.
54 B3 Zorgo Burkina
54 B4 Zorzor Liberia
42 B4 Zottegem Belgium
55 D2 Zouar Chad
54 A2 Zouérat Maur.
26 E2 Zouping China
27 D4 Zoushi China
26 E3 Zou Xian China
26 D2 Zouyun China
49 J2 Zrenjanin Yugo.
43 M4 Zschopau Ger.
43 L3 Zschornewitz Ger.
89 D2 Zuata r. Venez.
91 D3 Zubillaga Arg.
50 G4 Zubova Polyana Rus. Fed.
54 B4 Zuénoula Côte d'Ivoire
46 D7 Zug Switz.
51 G7 Zugdidi Georgia
46 D7 Zuger See l. Switz.
46 E7 Zugspitze mt Austria/Ger.
Zuider Zee l. see IJsselmeer
42 E1 Zuidhorn Neth.
42 C2 Zuid-Kennemerland Nationaal Park nat. park Neth.
45 D3 Zújar r. Spain
89 B2 Zulia r. Col.
42 E4 Zülpich Ger.
57 D5 Zumbo Moz.
68 A3 Zumbro r. U.S.A.
68 A3 Zumbrota U.S.A.
84 C3 Zumpango Mex.
54 C4 Zungeru Nigeria
26 F1 Zunhua China
75 H4 Zuni U.S.A.
75 H4 Zuni Mts mts U.S.A.
27 C5 Zunyi Guizhou China
27 C5 Zunyi Guizhou China
27 C6 Zuo Jiang r. China/Vietnam
26 D2 Zuoquan China
17 K2 Zūrābād Iran
17 L5 Zurbāṭīyah Iraq
46 D7 Zürich Switz.
19 H3 Zurmat reg. Afgh.
42 E2 Zutphen Neth.
59 F6 Zuurberg National Park S. Africa
55 D1 Zuwārah Libya
50 J3 Zuyevka Rus. Fed.
37 T8 Zvejniekciems Latvia
50 J4 Zvenigovo Rus. Fed.
51 D5 Zvenyhorodka Ukr.
57 D6 Zvishavane Zimbabwe
47 J6 Zvolen Slovakia
49 H2 Zvornik Bos.-Herz.
54 B4 Zwedru Liberia
42 E2 Zweeloo Neth.
42 F5 Zweibrücken Ger.
59 G6 Zwelitsha S. Africa
43 M3 Zwethau Ger.
46 G6 Zwettl Austria
43 L4 Zwickau Ger.
43 L3 Zwochau Ger.
42 E2 Zwolle Neth.
43 L4 Zwönitz Ger.
13 R3 Zyryanka Rus. Fed.

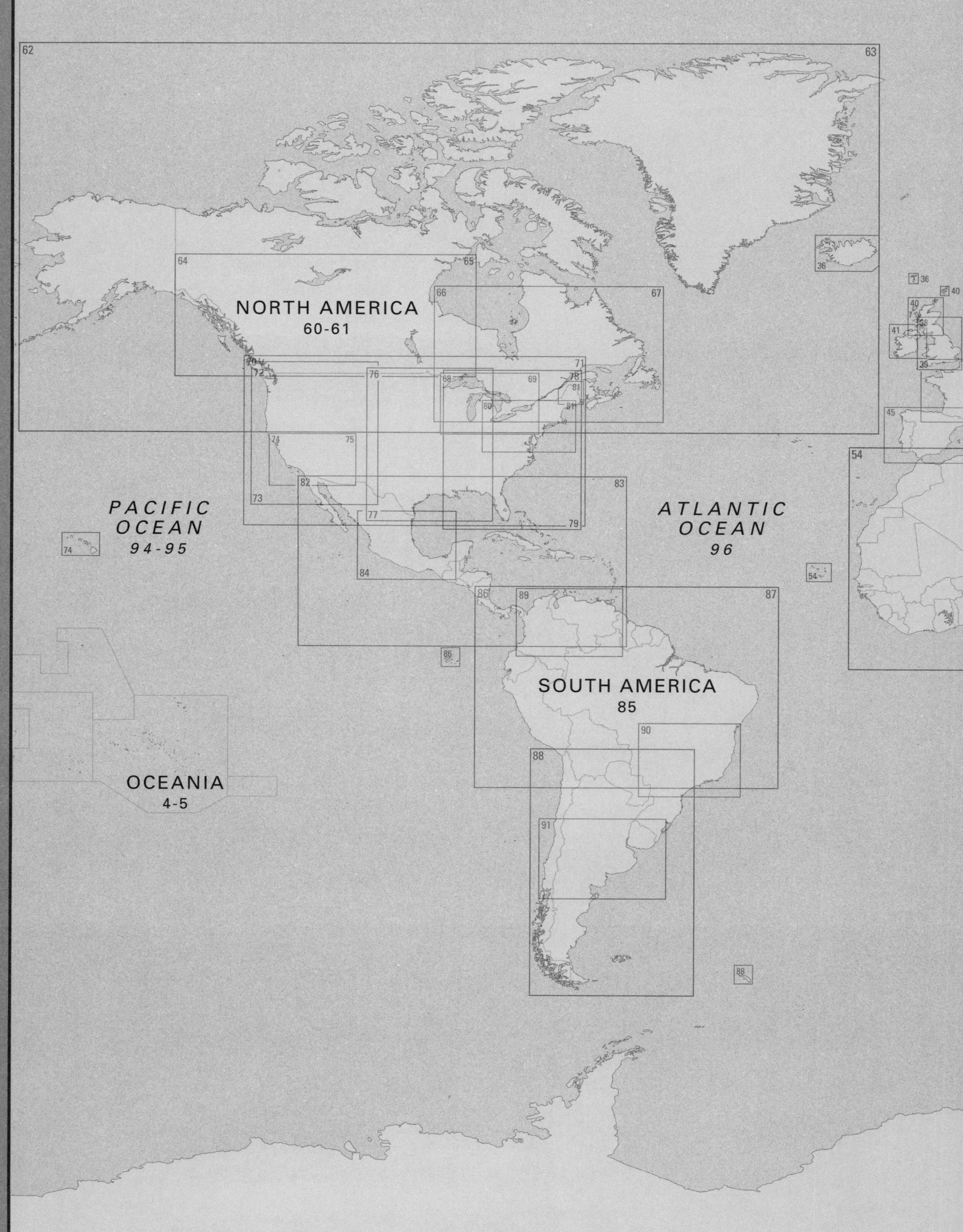

NORTH AMERICA
60-61

PACIFIC
OCEAN
94-95

ATLANTIC
OCEAN
96

OCEANIA
4-5

SOUTH AMERICA
85